Documentation for Derivatives

Documentation for Derivatives

Annotated Sample Agreements and Confirmations
for Swaps and Other Over-the-Counter Transactions

Fourth Edition

Volume I

Anthony C. Gooch
Cleary, Gottlieb, Steen & Hamilton
New York

Linda B. Klein
Dewey Ballantine LLP
New York

Published by Euromoney Books

Published by
Euromoney Books
Nestor House, Playhouse Yard,
London EC4V 5EX
United Kingdom
E-mail: books@euromoneyplc.com
www.euromoneybooks.com

Copyright © 2002, Anthony C. Gooch and Linda B. Klein
ISBN 1 85564 823 7

All rights reserved. No part of this book may be
reproduced in any form or by any means without
permission from both the publisher
and the copyright holders

No legal responsibility can be accepted by
Euromoney or the authors for the
information that appears in
this publication

Printed in Great Britain by Biddles Limited

CONTENTS

Volume I

About the Authors vii
Table of Abbreviations viii
Preface to the Fourth Edition xxv

General Introduction 1

Part 1: Legal Issues in Derivatives Documentation

Chapter 1. Power and Authority to Enter into Derivatives Transactions 31
Chapter 2. Statutes of Frauds and Parol Evidence Rules 39
Chapter 3. Commodities, Gaming and Bucket-Shop Laws 63
Chapter 4. Securities Laws 129
Chapter 5. Counterparty Relationships and Duties 177
Chapter 6. Damages and Close-Out Settlement 219
Chapter 7. Bankruptcy and Insolvency Concerns 268
Chapter 8. U.S. Withholding Tax Issues 350

Part 2: Sample Confirmations and Product Descriptions

Introduction to Part 2 369
Interest Rate Products
    Introductory Note 408
    Rate Swaps 421
    Sample Rate Swap Confirmation 427
    Caps and Floors 439
    Sample Rate Cap Confirmation 444
    Collars and Corridors 448
    Sample Rate Collar Confirmation 451
    Options on Swaps ("Swaptions") 455
    Sample Swaption Confirmation 464
    Forward Rate Agreements (FRAs) 476
    Sample FRA Confirmation 479
Currency Derivatives
    Introductory Note 484
    Currency Swaps 505
    Sample Cross-Currency Rate Swap Confirmation 508
    Forward Foreign Exchange Contracts 515
    Sample Confirmation for a Deliverable FX Transaction 518
    Currency Options 524
    Sample Confirmation for a Non-Deliverable Currency Option 531
Commodity Derivatives
    Introductory Note 543
    Sample Confirmation for a Cash-Settled Commodity Swap 574

Sample Confirmation for a Cash-Settled Commodity Price Floor	588
Sample Confirmation for a Cash-Settled Bullion Swap	594
Sample Confirmation for a Physically Settled Bullion Trade	601

Credit, Debt and Equity Derivatives

Introductory Note	605
Credit Default Swaps	639
Sample Confirmation for a Credit Default Swap	687
Equity Derivatives	717
Sample Confirmation for an Equity Index Swap	736

Weather Derivatives

Introductory Note	756
Sample Confirmation for an HDD Swap	765
Sample Confirmation for an ATDD Cap	779

Volume II

Part 3: Sample ISDA Multicurrency—Cross Border Master Agreement and Closing Documents

Introduction to Part 3	789
Sample Master Agreement	797
Schedule	899
Form of Guaranty	987
Form of Legal Opinion	997
Form of Closing Certificate	1001

Part 4: Sample ISDA Local Currency—Single Jurisdiction Master Agreement for Transactions with a U.S. Municipal Counterparty

Introduction to Part 4	1005
Sample Master Agreement	1014
Schedule	1036

Part 5: Credit Support

Introduction to Part 5	1057
Sample Documentation	
Credit Support Annex for Two-Way Credit Support	1142
Paragraph 13 for a One-Way Credit Support Annex	1260
Recouponing Provisions	1269
Provisions for a Securities-Linked Transaction	1272
Amendment to Adopt a Credit Support Annex	1276

Part 6: Cross-Product Master Agreements, Contract Bridges, Setoff and Other Approaches to Multiple Agreement Risk

Introduction to Part 6	1281
Sample Cross-Product Master Agreement	1311

Index 1359

ABOUT THE AUTHORS

Anthony C. Gooch is Of Counsel to Cleary, Gottlieb, Steen & Hamilton, based in the firm's New York office. He also serves as a member of the Board of Trustees of the International Institute of Rural Reconstruction, a not-for-profit organization that works to better the conditions of the rural poor and their communities in Asia, Africa and Latin America.

Mr. Gooch has worked on international financial and commercial transactions, including documentation for transactions of the kinds illustrated in this book, domestic and international loans, sovereign debt restructuring, international debt and equity issues, investment company offerings, asset securitizations, privatizations and cross-border mergers and acquisitions. Mr. Gooch grew up in Brazil, and his practice has included work for Brazilian private- and public-sector entities, as well as international investors, lenders and investment banks with interests in Brazil and other Latin American countries. He holds a B.A. degree from the University of the South, a diploma from the College of Europe and J.D. and M.C.J. degrees from New York University School of Law, where he was Articles Editor of the *Law Review*.

Linda B. Klein is a partner of Dewey Ballantine LLP, based in the firm's New York office. She works on a wide variety of domestic and international financial transactions. Her practice includes work on derivatives transactions of all kinds, as well as international loans and issues of debt and equity, particularly those involving Latin American borrowers and issuers, sovereign and private-sector debt restructuring, participation and assignment agreements and structured financings. She holds B.A. and M.A. degrees from Queens College and J.D. and Ph.D. degrees from Columbia University, where she taught Latin American literature from 1971 to 1976 and was Editor-in-Chief of the *Journal of Transnational Law* in 1978–1979.

Ms. Klein and Mr. Gooch are also the authors of Euromoney's book on *Documentation for Loans, Assignments and Participations*, now in its third edition, as well as numerous articles and contributions to collections of works on legal topics. They live in Redding, Connecticut.

TABLE OF ABBREVIATIONS

ADVANCED STRATEGIES — ADVANCED STRATEGIES IN FINANCIAL RISK MANAGEMENT (Robert J. Schwartz & Clifford W. Smith, Jr. eds., New York Institute of Finance 1993)

Annex A to the 1998 FX and Currency Option Definitions — ISDA, EMTA & THE FOREIGN EXCHANGE COMMITTEE, 1998 FX AND CURRENCY OPTION DEFINITIONS (1998), *available at* http://www.isda.org/publications/index.html

Annex to the 2000 ISDA Definitions — ISDA, ANNEX TO THE 2000 ISDA DEFINITIONS (JUNE 2000 VERSION), *available at* http://www.isda.org/publications/index.html[1]

Bank Products Legal Certainty Act — Legal Certainty for Bank Products Act of 2000, Pub. L. No. 106-554, Appendix E, tit. IV, 114 Stat. 2763, 2763A-457 (2000)

Bankruptcy Code — The United States Bankruptcy Code. The Bankruptcy Code is codified in 11 U.S.C. §§ 101–1330. The source for references to the Bankruptcy Code in this book is 11 U.S.C.A., including the 2002 cumulative annual pocket parts.

BIS — The Bank for International Settlements Web site: www.bis.org

BIS 2001 FX and Derivatives Market Survey — BIS, TRIENNIAL CENTRAL BANK SURVEY MARCH 2001: FOREIGN EXCHANGE AND DERIVATIVES MARKET ACTIVITY IN 2001 (2002), *available at* http://www.bis.org/publ/rpfx02t.pdf

---

[1] Some of the materials on the ISDA Web site can be downloaded without charge; others must be purchased. Certain materials on the site are available to ISDA members only.

Table of Abbreviations

CEA	The United States Commodities Exchange Act. The CEA is codified in 7 U.S.C. §§ 1–27f. The source for references to the CEA in this book is 7 U.S.C.A., including the 2002 cumulative pocket part.
CFMA	Commodity Futures Modernization Act of 2000, Pub. L. No. 106-554, Appendix E, 114 Stat. 2763 (2000)
COLLIER ON BANKRUPTCY	COLLIER ON BANKRUPTCY (Lawrence P. King ed.-in-chief, 15th ed. rev., LexisNexis 2002)
Commentary on the 2001 ISDA Amendments	ISDA, COMMENTARY ON THE FORM OF AMENDMENT TO ISDA MASTER AGREEMENTS (2001), *available at* http://www.isda.org/publications/index.html
COMMODITY-LINKED FINANCE	COMMODITY-LINKED FINANCE (J.P. Morgan & Co. Incorporated ed., Euromoney Publications 1992)
CPMA	CROSS-PRODUCT MASTER AGREEMENT (The Bond Market Association 2000), *available at* http://www.bondmarkets.com/agrees/cpmna.pdf
CPMA Guidance Notes	CROSS-PRODUCT MASTER AGREEMENT GUIDANCE NOTES (The Bond Market Association 2000), *available at* http://www.bondmarkets.com/agrees/cpmnanotes.pdf
CREDIT DERIVATIVES	CREDIT DERIVATIVES: TRADING & MANAGEMENT OF CREDIT & DEFAULT RISK 28, 73–76 (Satyajit Das ed., John Wiley & Sons (Asia) Pte Ltd 1998)
CREDIT DERIVATIVES: APPLICATIONS FOR RISK MANAGEMENT	CREDIT DERIVATIVES: APPLICATIONS FOR RISK MANAGEMENT (Euromoney Books 1998)
DERIVATIVES HANDBOOK	DERIVATIVES HANDBOOK: RISK MANAGEMENT AND CONTROL (Robert J. Schwartz and & Clifford W. Smith, Jr. eds., John Wiley & Sons, Inc. 1997)

DERIVATIVES RISK MANAGEMENT SERVICE	DERIVATIVES RISK MANAGEMENT SERVICE (G. Timothy Haight ed., A. S. Pratt & Sons 1996 & Supps. through 2001 Update No. 3)
DICTIONARY OF RISK MANAGEMENT	GARY L. GASTINEAU & MARK P. KRITZMAN, THE DICTIONARY OF FINANCIAL RISK MANAGEMENT (Frank J. Fabozzi Associates 1996)
DPG Voluntary Framework	DERIVATIVES POLICY GROUP, FRAMEWORK FOR VOLUNTARY OVERSIGHT (1995)
EMA form	BANKING FEDERATION OF THE EUROPEAN UNION, EUROPEAN SAVINGS BANKS GROUP & EUROPEAN ASSOCIATION OF COOPERATIVE BANKS, EUROPEAN MASTER AGREEMENT, *available at* http://www.fbe.be/ema.html, and *at* http://www.savingsbanks.com/esbg/Masteragreement/Masteragreement.htm
EMTA	EMTA (formerly Emerging Markets Traders Association) Web site: www.emta.com
End-Users' Guidelines	TREASURY MANAGEMENT ASSOCIATION, VOLUNTARY PRINCIPLES AND PRACTICES GUIDELINES FOR END-USERS OF DERIVATIVES (1995)
ERISA	The United States Employee Retirement Income Security Act. ERISA is codified at 29 U.S.C.A. §§ 1001–1461. The source for references to ERISA in this book is 29 U.S.C.A., including the 2002 cumulative annual pocket parts.
FASB	The U.S. Financial Accounting Standards Board

Table of Abbreviations

FDIA	The United States Federal Deposit Insurance Act. The FDIA is codified in 12 U.S.C. §§ 1811–1835a. The source for references to the FDIA in this book is 12 U.S.C.A., including the 2002 cumulative annual pocket parts.
FDIC	The United States Federal Deposit Insurance Commission
FDICIA	The United States Federal Deposit Insurance Corporation Improvement Act of 1991. FDICIA is codified to various sections of 12 U.S.C. The source for references to FDICIA in this book is 12 U.S.C.A., including the 2002 cumulative annual pocket parts. The text of FDICIA, as enacted, can be found in 3 FDIC, FEDERAL DEPOSIT INSURANCE CORPORATION: LAW, REGULATIONS, RELATED ACTS 8549 (2002).
FEOMA form	THE FOREIGN EXCHANGE COMMITTEE, in association with THE BRITISH BANKERS' ASSOCIATION, THE CANADIAN FOREIGN EXCHNAGE COMMITTEE & THE TOKYO FOREIGN EXCHANGE MARKET PRACTICES COMMITTEE, THE 1997 INTERNATIONAL FOREIGN EXCHANGE AND OPTIONS MASTER AGREEMENT (FEOMA) (1997), *available at* http://www.ny.frb.org/fmlg/feoma.pdf. A form of schedule for use with the FEOMA form is *available at* http://www.ny.frb.org/fmlg/feosch.doc.
FIRREA	The United States Financial Institutions Reform, Recovery and Enforcement Act of 1989. FIRREA is codified to 12 U.S.C. §§ 3331–52. The source for references to FIRREA in this book is 12 U.S.C.A., including the 2002 cumulative annual pocket part.

FSA London Code of Conduct	FINANCIAL SERVICES AUTHORITY, THE LONDON CODE OF CONDUCT: FOR PRINCIPALS AND BROKING FIRMS IN THE WHOLESALE MARKETS (1999), *available at* http://www.fsa.gov.uk
FX Collateral Annex	THE FOREIGN EXCHANGE COMMITTEE, THE 1999 COLLATERAL ANNEX TO FEOMA, ICOM OR IFEMA MASTER AGREEMENT (COLLATERAL ANNEX) (1999), *available at* http://www.ny.frb.org/fmlg/fxc000601.pdf
FX Collateral Annex Guide	THE FOREIGN EXCHANGE COMMITTEE, GUIDE TO THE FX COLLATERAL ANNEX TO THE FOREIGN EXCHANGE AND OPTIONS MASTER AGREEMENT (FEOMA), INTERNATIONAL FOREIGN EXCHANGE MASTER AGREEMENT (IFEMA), OR 1997 INTERNATIONAL CURRENCY OPTIONS MARKET (ICOM) MASTER AGREEMENT GUIDE, *available at* http://www.ny.frb.org/fmlg/ FEOMAUserGuide.pdf
GAO DERIVATIVES SALES PRACTICES REPORT	U.S. GENERAL ACCOUNTING OFFICE, OTC DERIVATIVES: ADDITIONAL OVERSIGHT COULD REDUCE COSTLY SALES PRACTICE DISPUTES (GAO/GGD-98-5)(October 1997), *available at* http://www.gao.gov
GFOA RECOMMENDED PRACTICE	Government Finance Officers Association, *Recommended Practice on Use of Derivatives by State and Local Governments* 2 (1994), *available at* http://www.gfoa.org/services/rp/cash.shtml#5

Table of Abbreviations xiii

GLBA	The Gramm-Leach-Bliley Act, Pub. L. No. 106-102, 113 Stat. 1338 (1999), as amended by Pub. L. No. 106-554, Appendix E, tit. III, 114 Stat. 2763A-449 (2000). The GLBA is codified to various sections of 12 U.S.C. and 15 U.S.C. The source for references to the GLBA in this book is 12 U.S.C.A. and 15 U.S.C.A., including the 2002 pocket parts. The text of the GLBA can be found in 3 FDIC, FEDERAL DEPOSIT INSURANCE CORPORATION: LAW, REGULATIONS, RELATED ACTS 8673.05 (2001).
Gooch & Klein, LOAN DOCUMENTATION	ANTHONY C. GOOCH & LINDA B. KLEIN, DOCUMENTATION FOR LOANS, ASSIGNMENTS AND PARTICIPATIONS (Euromoney Publications, 3d ed. 1996)
Gooch & Klein, *Review of Case Law I*	Anthony C. Gooch & Linda B. Klein, *A Review of International and U.S. Case Law Affecting Swaps and Related Derivative Products*, in ADVANCED STRATEGIES 387
Gooch & Klein, *Review of Case Law II*	Anthony C. Gooch & Linda B. Klein, *United States Case Law Involving Over-The-Counter Derivatives 1992–1996*, in DERIVATIVES HANDBOOK 57
HANDBOOK OF CREDIT DERIVATIVES	HANDBOOK OF CREDIT DERIVATIVES (Jack Clark Francis, Joyce A. Frost & J. Gregg Whittaker eds., McGraw Hill, 1999)
HANDBOOK OF RISK MANAGEMENT	THE HANDBOOK OF CURRENCY AND INTEREST RATE RISK MANAGEMENT (Robert J. Schwartz & Clifford W. Smith, Jr. eds., New York Institute of Finance 1990)

IBA	The United States International Banking Act, Pub. L. 95-369, 92 Stat. 607 (1978). The IBA is codified to various sections of 12 U.S.C. §§ 3101–11 various other sections of 12 U.S.C. The source for references to the IBA in this book is 12 U.S.C.A., including the 2002 pocket parts. The text of the IBA can be found in 3 FDIC, FEDERAL DEPOSIT INSURANCE CORPORATION: LAW, REGULATIONS, RELATED ACTS 8785 (2002).
IBMA	THE LONDON BULLION MARKET ASSOCIATION AND THE FOREIGN EXCHANGE COMMITTEE. 1994 INTERNATIONAL BULLION MASTER AGREEMENT TERMS
ICOM form	THE FOREIGN EXCHANGE COMMITTEE, in association with THE BRITISH BANKERS' ASSOCIATION, THE CANADIAN FOREIGN EXCHNAGE COMMITTEE & THE TOKYO FOREIGN EXCHANGE MARKET PRACTICES COMMITTEE, THE 1997 INTERNATIONAL CURRENCY OPTIONS MARKET (ICOM) MASTER AGREEMENT (1997), *available at* http://www.ny.frb.org/fmlg/(icom).pdf. A form of schedule for use with the ICOM form is *available at* http://www.ny.frb.org/fmlg/icomsch.doc.
ICOM Guide	THE FOREIGN EXCHANGE COMMITTEE, in association with THE BRITISH BANKERS' ASSOCIATION, THE CANADIAN FOREIGN EXCHNAGE COMMITTEE & THE TOKYO FOREIGN EXCHANGE MARKET PRACTICES COMMITTEE, GUIDE TO THE 1997 INTERNATIONAL CURRENCY OPTIONS MARKET (ICOM) MASTER AGREEMENT GUIDE, *available at* http://www.ny.frb.org/fmlg/icomgiu.pdf

Table of Abbreviations

IFEMA form	THE FOREIGN EXCHANGE COMMITTEE, in association with THE BRITISH BANKERS' ASSOCIATION, THE CANADIAN FOREIGN EXCHANGE COMMITTEE & THE TOKYO FOREIGN EXCHANGE MARKET PRACTICES COMMITTEE, THE 1997 INTERNATIONAL FOREIGN EXCHANGE MASTER AGREEMENT (IFEMA), *available at h*ttp://www.ny.frb.org/fmlg/ifema.pdf. A form of schedule for use with the IFEMA form is *available at* http://www.ny.frb.org/fmlg/ifemasch.doc.
IFEMA Guide	THE FOREIGN EXCHANGE COMMITTEE, in association with THE BRITISH BANKERS' ASSOCIATION, THE CANADIAN FOREIGN EXCHANGE COMMITTEE & THE TOKYO FOREIGN EXCHANGE MARKET PRACTICES COMMITTEE, THE 1997 INTERNATIONAL FOREIGN EXCHANGE MASTER AGREEMENT (IFEMA) GUIDE, *available at* http://www.ny.frb.org/fmlg/ifemagui.pdf
Investment Advisers Act	The United States Investment Advisers Act of 1940. The Investment Advisers Act is codified to 15 U.S.C. §§ 80b–1 to 80b–21. The source for references to the Investment Advisers Act in this book is 15 U.S.C.A., including the 2002 cumulative annual pocket part.
Investment Company Act	The United States Investment Company Act of 1940. The Investment Company Act is codified to 15 U.S.C. §§ 80a–1 to 80a–64. The source for references to the Investment Company Act in this book is 15 U.S.C.A., including the 2002 cumulative annual pocket part.
IRC	The United States Internal Revenue Code. The IRC is codified in 26 U.S.C. The source for references to the I.R.C. in this book is 26 U.S.C.A., including the 2002 cumulative annual pocket parts.
IRS	The United States Internal Revenue Service

ISDA	International Swaps and Derivatives Association, Inc. (formerly International Swap Dealers Association, Inc.) Web site: www.isda.org
ISDA CDS Confirmation Form	The form is supplied as an exhibit to the *1999 Credit Derivatives Definitions.*
ISDA Collateral Guidelines	ISDA, ISDA GUIDELINES FOR COLLATERAL PRACTITIONERS (1998), *available at* http://www.isda.org/press/pdf/colguide.pdf
ISDA Collateral Law Reform Report	ISDA, COLLATERAL ARRANGEMENTS IN THE EUROPEAN FINANCIAL MARKETS: THE NEED FOR NATIONAL LAW REFORM (2000), *available at* http://www.isda.org/press/pdf/eur_coll_law_reform.pdf
ISDA Collateral Survey 2000	ISDA, ISDA COLLATERAL SURVEY 2000 (2000), *available at* http://www.isda.org/docproj/index.html
ISDA Long-Form Credit Swap Confirmation	ISDA, Confirmation of OTC Credit Swap Transaction - Single Reference Entity - Non-Sovereign (1998), *available at* http://www.isda.org/publications/index.html
ISDA Margin Survey 2001	ISDA, ISDA MARGIN SURVEY 2001 (2001), *available at* http://www.isda.org/docproj/index.html
ISDA 2000 Operations Survey	ISDA 2000 OPERATIONS BENCHMARKING SURVEY: OVER-THE-COUNTER DERIVATIVES OPERATIONS ISSUES (2000), *available at* http://www.isda.org/publications/index.html
ISDA 2001 Operations Survey	ISDA 2001 OPERATIONS BENCHMARKING SURVEY: OVER-THE-COUNTER DERIVATIVES OPERATIONS ISSUES (2001), available at *http://www.isda.org/publications/index.html*

Table of Abbreviations

ISDA 2002 Operations Survey	ISDA 2002 OPERATIONS BENCHMARKING SURVEY: OVER-THE-COUNTER DERIVATIVES OPERATIONS ISSUES (2002), *available at* http://www.isda.org/publications/index.html
ISMA	International Securities Market Association Web site: www.isma.org
LBMA	London Bullion Market Association Web site: www.lbma.org.uk
MANAGEMENT OF CURRENCY RISK	MANAGEMENT OF CURRENCY RISK (Boris Antl ed., Euromoney Publications 1989)
MANAGEMENT OF RATE RISK	MANAGEMENT OF INTEREST RATE RISK (Boris Antl ed., Euromoney Publications 1988)
Margin Provisions	ISDA, ISDA 2001 MARGIN PROVISIONS (2001), as amended by ERRATUM TO PART 4 OF THE 2001 ISDA MARGIN PROVISIONS, both *available at* http://www.isda.org/publications/index.html
MCQUILLIN, MUNICIPAL CORPORATIONS	EUGENE MCQUILLIN, 10 THE LAW OF MUNICIPAL CORPORATIONS (3rd ed., vol. 10 rev. by Thomas Evans & Judith O'Gallagher, 1999 & 2001 Cumulative Supp.) & EUGENE MCQUILLIN, 10A THE LAW OF MUNICIPAL CORPORATIONS (3rd ed., vol. 10A rev. by Beth A. Jacobstahl & Mark S. Nelson, 1999& 2001 Cumulative Supp.)
NBA	The United States National Bank Act of 1864, as amended. The NBA is codified in numerous sections of 12 U.S.C. and other USCA titles. *See* the *Historical and Statutory Notes* following 12 U.S.C.A. § 38.
1987 ISDA Definitions	ISDA, 1987 INTEREST RATE AND CURRENCY EXCHANGE DEFINITIONS (1987), *available at* http://www.isda.org/publications/index.html

1991 ISDA Definitions	ISDA, 1991 ISDA DEFINITIONS (1991), *available at* http://www.isda.org/publications/index.html
1992 ISDA U.S. Municipal Counterparty Definitions	ISDA, 1992 ISDA U.S. MUNICIPAL COUNTERPARTY DEFINITIONS (1992), *available at* http://www.isda.org/publications/index.html
1993 ISDA Commodity Derivatives Definitions	ISDA, 1993 ISDA COMMODITY DERIVATIVES DEFINITIONS (1993), *available at* http://www.isda.org/publications/index.html
1993/2000 ISDA Commodity Derivatives Definitions	*The 1993 ISDA Commodity Derivatives Definitions*, as amended and supplemented by the *2000 Supplement to the 1993 ISDA Commodity Derivatives Definitions*, *available at* http://www.isda.org/publications/index.html
1994 ISDA Equity Option Definitions	ISDA, 1994 ISDA EQUITY OPTION DEFINITIONS (1995), *available at* http://www.isda.org/publications/index.html
1996 Equity Derivatives Definitions	ISDA, 1996 ISDA EQUITY DERIVATIVES DEFINITIONS (1996), *available at* http://www.isda.org/publications/index.html
1997 Government Bond Option Definitions	ISDA, 1997 ISDA GOVERNMENT BOND OPTION DEFINITIONS (1997), *available at* http://www.isda.org/publications/index.html
1997 ISDA Bullion Definitions	ISDA, 1997 ISDA BULLION DEFINITIONS (1997), *available at* http://www.isda.org/publications/index.html
1997 Short Form Bullion Definitions	ISDA, 1997 ISDA SHORT FORM BULLION DEFINITIONS (1997), *available at* http://www.isda.org/publications/index.html
1998 FX and Currency Option Definitions	ISDA, EMTA & THE FOREIGN EXCHANGE COMMITTEE, 1998 FX AND CURRENCY OPTION DEFINITIONS (1998), *available at* http://www.isda.org/publications/index.html

1998 Supplement to the 1991 ISDA Definitions	ISDA, 1998 SUPPLEMENT TO THE 1991, ISDA DEFINITIONS (1998), *available at* http://www.isda.org/publications/index.html
1999 Credit Derivatives Definitions	ISDA, 1999 ISDA CREDIT DERIVATIVES DEFINITIONS (1999), *available at* http://www.isda.org/publications/index.html
NYBL	The New York Banking Law. The source for references to the NYBL in this book is McKinney's, including the 2001–2002 Interim Pocket Part (§§229–599).
NYCPLR	The New York Civil Practice Law and Rules. The source for references to the NYCPLR in this book is McKinney's, including the 2002 Cumulative Supplementary Pamphlet Covering Years 1990 to 2001 (§§ 1–300) and the 2002 Cumulative pocket part (§§ 307–500).
NYGOL	The General Obligations Law of the State of New York. The source for references to NYGOL in this book is McKinney's, including the 2001–2002 Interim Pocket Parts.
NYUCC	The Uniform Commercial Code as in effect in the State of New York. The source for references to NYUCC in this book is McKinney's, including the 2001–2002 Interim Pocket Part (§§1–101 to 2–725) and the 2001–2002 Interim Supplementary Pamphlet (§§7–101 to End).
OCC	The United States Office of the Comptroller of the Currency Web site: http://www.occ.treas.gov/
OECD	The Organization for Economic Cooperation and Development
OTS	The Office of Thrift Supervision of the United States Department of the Treasury

PLI 1986	INTEREST RATE AND CURRENCY SWAPS 1986 (PLI Corp. L. & Practice Course Handbook Series No. 532, 1986)
PLI 1987	INTEREST RATE AND CURRENCY SWAPS 1987 (PLI Corp. L. & Practice Course Handbook Series No. 564, 1987)
PLI 1991 ADVANCED SWAPS	ADVANCED SWAPS AND DERIVATIVE FINANCIAL PRODUCTS (PLI Corp. L. & Practice Course Handbook Series No. 746, 1991)
PLI 1992	SWAPS AND OTHER DERIVATIVES IN 1992 (PLI Corp. L. & Practice Course Handbook Series No. 778, 1992)
PLI 1993	SWAPS AND OTHER DERIVATIVES IN 1993 (PLI Corp. L. & Practice Course Handbook Series No. B-815, 1993)
PLI 1998	SWAPS AND OTHER DERIVATIVES IN 1998 (PLI Corp. L. & Practice Course Handbook Series No. B-1086, 1998)
PLI 2000	SWAPS AND OTHER DERIVATIVES IN 2000 (PLI Corp. L. & Practice Course Handbook Series No. B–1215, 2000)
PLI 2001	SWAPS & OTHER DERIVATIVES IN 2001 (PLI Corp. L. & Practice Course Handbook Series No. B–1280, 2001)
Principles and Practices	FEDERAL RESERVE BANK OF NEW YORK ET AL., PRINCIPLES AND PRACTICES FOR WHOLESALE FINANCIAL MARKET TRANSACTIONS (August 1995)
PSA	Public Securities Association, now known as The Bond Market Association (TBMA) Web site: www.bondmarkets.com
Restructuring Supplement	ISDA, RESTRUCTURING SUPPLEMENT TO THE 1999 ISDA CREDIT DERIVATIVES DEFINITIONS (MAY 11, 2001), *available at* http://www.isda.org/publications/index.html, together with commentary

Table of Abbreviations

SEC	The United States Securities and Exchange Commission Web site: http://www.sec.gov/
Securities Act	The United States Securities Act of 1933. The Securities Act is codified to 15 U.S.C. §§ 77a–77aa. The source for references to the Securities Act in this book is 15 U.S.C.A., including the 2002 cumulative annual pocket part. Rules and Regulations under the Securities Act are codified to 17 C.F.R., and the references are to that source (2001).
SECURITIES & DERIVATIVES REGULATION	EDWARD F. GREENE, ALAN L. BELLER, EDWARD J. ROSEN, LESLIE N. SILVERMAN, DANIEL A. BRAVERMAN & SEBASTIAN R. SPERBER, U.S. REGULATION OF THE INTERNATIONAL SECURITIES AND DERIVATIVES MARKETS (6th ed. 2002)
Securities Exchange Act	The United States Securities Exchange Act of 1934. The Securities Exchange Act is codified in 15 U.S.C. §§ 78a–78mm. The source for references to the Securities Exchange Act in this book is 15 U.S.C.A., including the 2002 cumulative annual pocket part. Rules and Regulations under the Securities Exchange Act are codified to 17 C.F.R., and the references are to that source (2001).
SIA	Securities Industry Association Web site: www.sia.com
SIPA	The United States Securities Investor Protection Act of 1970, codified to 15 U.S.C. §§ 78aaa–78*lll*. The source for references to SIPA in this book is 15 U.S.C.A., including the 2002 pocket part.
SIPC	The United States Securities Investor Protection Corporation

Supplement Relating to Convertible, Exchangeable or Accreting Obligations	ISDA, SUPPLEMENT TO THE 1999 ISDA CREDIT DERIVATIVES DEFINITIONS RELATING TO CONVERTIBLE, EXCHANGEABLE OR ACCRETING OBLIGATIONS TO THE 1999 ISDA CREDIT DERIVATIVES DEFINITIONS (2001), *available at* http://www.isda.org/publications/index.html, together with commentary
Supplement Relating to Successor and Credit Events	ISDA, SUPPLEMENT RELATING TO SUCCESSOR AND CREDIT EVENTS TO THE 1999 ISDA CREDIT DERIVATIVES DEFINITIONS (2001), *available at* http://www.isda.org/publications/index.html, together with commentary
Swaps Code	ISDA, CODE OF STANDARD WORDING, ASSUMPTIONS AND PROVISIONS FOR SWAPS (1986 ed.), *available at* http://www.isda.org/publications/index.html
TBMA	The Bond Market Association, formerly known as PSA Web site: www.bondmarkets.com
Tortoriello, GUIDE TO BANK ACTIVITIES	ROBERT L. TORTORIELLO, GUIDE TO BANK UNDERWRITING, DEALING AND BROKERAGE ACTIVITIES (Glasser LegalWorks, 6th ed. 2001)
2000 ISDA Collateral Reform Report	ISDA, COLLATERAL ARRANGEMENTS IN THE EUROPEAN FINANCIAL MARKETS; THE NEED FOR NATIONAL LAW REFORM (2000)(referring to Country Reports available from ISDA that deal with the laws of the 15 Member States of the European Union), *available at* http://www.isda.org/publications/index.html
2000 ISDA Definitions	ISDA, 2000 ISDA DEFINITIONS (2000), *available at* http://www.isda.org/publications/index.html

Table of Abbreviations xxiii

2000 Supplement to the 1993 ISDA Commodity Derivatives Definitions	ISDA, 2000 SUPPLEMENT TO THE 1993 ISDA COMMODITY DERIVATIVES DEFINITIONS (2000), *available at* http://www.isda.org/publications/index.html
2001 CSA Amendments	The *2001 ISDA Credit Support Protocol* and the *2001 ISDA CSA Amendment Forms*, collectively
2001 ISDA Amendments	ISDA, *Form of Amendment to the ISDA Master Agreements* (October 2001), *available at* http://www.isda.org/publications/index.html
2001 ISDA Credit Support Protocol	ISDA, 2001 ISDA CREDIT SUPPORT PROTOCOL (2001), *available at* http://www.isda.org/publications/index.html
2001 ISDA CSA Amendment Forms	ISDA, AMENDMENT TO THE CREDIT SUPPORT ANNEX (ISDA AGREEMENTS SUBJECT TO NEW YORK LAW ONLY)(2001) and ISDA, AMENDMENT TO THE CREDIT SUPPORT ANNEX (ISDA AGREEMENTS SUBJECT TO ENGLISH LAW ONLY)(2001), *available at* http://www.isda.org/publications/index.html
TAX-EXEMPT DERIVATIVES	TAX-EXEMPT DERIVATIVES: A GUIDE TO LEGAL CONSIDERATIONS FOR LAWYERS, FINANCE PROFESSIONALS, AND MUNICIPAL ISSUERS (Steven D. Conlon & Vincent M. Aquilino, eds., American Bar Association, Section of Urban, State & Local Government Law 1994)
U.S.C.A.	UNITED STATES CODE ANNOTATED (West Publishing Co.)
User's Guide to the ISDA Credit Support Documents under English Law	ISDA, USER'S GUIDE TO THE ISDA CREDIT SUPPORT DOCUMENTS UNDER ENGLISH LAW (1999), *available at* http://www.isda.org/publications/index.html
User's Guide to the ISDA 1992 Master Agreements	ISDA, USER'S GUIDE TO THE 1992 ISDA MASTER AGREEMENTS (1993), *available at* http://www.isda.org/publications/index.html

User's Guide to the ISDA 1994 Credit Support Annex	ISDA, USER'S GUIDE TO THE 1994 ISDA CREDIT SUPPORT ANNEX (1994), *available at* http://www.isda.org/publications/index.html
User's Guide to the 1998 FX and Currency Option Definitions	ISDA, EMTA & THE FOREIGN EXCHANGE COMMITTEE, USER'S GUIDE TO THE 1998 FX AND CURRENCY OPTION DEFINITIONS (1999), *available at* http://www.isda.org/publications/index.html
User's Guide to the 2001 ISDA Margin Provisions	ISDA, USER'S GUIDE TO THE 2001 ISDA MARGIN PROVISIONS (2001), *available at* http://www.isda.org/publications/index.html
WEATHER RISK MANAGEMENT	ELEMENT RE CAPITAL PRODUCTS, INC., WEATHER RISK MANAGEMENT (Eric Banks ed. Palgrave 2002)
WEBB, DOCUMENTATION FOR HIGH YIELD DEBT	DAVID E. WEBB, DOCUMENTATION FOR HIGH YIELD DEBT (Euromoney Books 2001)

PREFACE TO THE FOURTH EDITION

This new edition of *Documentation for Derivatives* substantially updates and expands on the third edition (1993) and its two supplements, the *Credit Support Supplement* (1994) and the *Cross-Product Risk Management Supplement* (2000). Our aims remain to illustrate the kinds of documents that are most widely used for over-the-counter (OTC) derivatives, to explain the varying approaches most often found in the market and to analyze the main concerns raised by these documentation practices.

As a general matter, in this and the preceding editions we have sought to comment on documentation practices and related issues as we see them reflected not only in the standard agreements and terms published by industry groups and trade associations but also in the customized versions of those standard documents that market participants adopt to reflect their special concerns and institutional policies. Our commentary also reflects the lessons we have distilled from court decisions and documents filed in lawsuits relating to OTC derivatives, a topic we have explored in more detail elsewhere.[2]

We have formed the views expressed in this book as a result of our practice in the area, after taking into account the guidance notes or user's guides published by the associations or groups that have produced the standardized agreements and terms on which we comment as well as the ever-growing literature on the subject. They are our views and should not be attributed to others, including our respective law firms or their clients. We have advised, and our law firms regularly represent, a number of the entities involved in some of the cases described in this book and, in some cases, have acted as counsel or filed *amicus curiae* briefs in connection with those cases.

The views expressed in this book should not be thought of as legal advice. The book's sample agreements and confirmations are merely illustrations involving hypothetical parties and circumstances, and they should not be used for actual agreements or transactions. The documentation for a transaction must be carefully tailored to address the legal issues affecting the particular parties and the characteristics of the transaction. The documentation must take into account the law as it stands at the time of the transaction in the relevant jurisdictions and the institutional policies of the parties and the business goals they are seeking to serve by engaging in the transaction.

This book first appeared in 1987, as *Swap Agreement Documentation*, when it dealt only with interest rate and currency swaps. Participants in the market at the time used their own forms of agreement for those transactions, although many did so adopting terms published by ISDA (then known as the International Swap Dealers Association, Inc.) in the *Swaps Code*—the *Code of Standard Wording, Assumptions and Provisions for Swaps*. The standardization efforts of ISDA and other organizations over the years are

---

[2]*See* Gooch & Klein, *Review of Case Law I* and Gooch & Klein, *Review of Case Law II*. The Table of Abbreviations, *supra* p. viii, lists the abbreviated names that are used in this book to refer to various works and indicates the names of their publishers and, if applicable, where they can be found on the Internet.

discussed in detail in the General Introduction.[3] Later the same year ISDA published its first two master agreement forms, which we included, with ISDA's permission, together with our annotations, in the second edition of *Swap Agreement Documentation* (1988).

Changing the title to *Documentation for Derivatives*, we published a third edition in 1993, shortly after ISDA released its 1992 master agreement forms. With ISDA's permission, we included in that volume an annotated sample agreement prepared using the 1992 ISDA Master Agreement (Multicurrency—Cross Border) form and an annotated sample schedule reflecting the use of the Local Currency—Single Jurisdiction form, as well as annotated sample confirmations for many kinds of OTC derivatives.

Publication of the two supplements to the third edition was prompted by the release in 1994 of the first of ISDA's standard forms of Credit Support Annex and the release in 2000 of the Cross-Border Master Agreement form published by The Bond Market Association (TBMA) in cooperation with eight other organizations of market professionals.[4]

Since publication of the third edition, the documentation for derivatives—like the market itself—has become far more complex. New groups have formed to create or update standardized tools, and existing groups have expanded to include many more market participants, both professionals and end-users. This fourth edition reflects many of the new endeavors.

So, for example, the sample confirmations in Part 2 illustrate or discuss the use of many product-specific sets of definitions published by ISDA, either alone or in collaboration with other groups, as well as confirmation templates published by EMTA and the Weather Risk Management Association (WRMA). The sample documents and annotations in Parts 3, 4 and 5 deal with ISDA's 2001 amendments to its 1992 Master Agreements and its Credit Support Annex forms first published in the 1990s, the *2001 ISDA Margin Provisions*, various ongoing ISDA projects to update product-specific definition sets and to develop new master agreement forms and TBMA's continuing work on a new form of Cross-Product Master Agreement. This new edition also increases our earlier comparisons between the illustrated ISDA approaches and those reflected in the IFEMA, ICOM and FEOMA master agreement forms and the related credit support annex and adds fresh contrasts with the European Master Agreement (EMA) form published by the Banking Federation of the European Union, in cooperation with the European Savings Banks Group and the European Association of Cooperative Banks.

The reader will find that this new edition includes expanded treatment of the principal legal issues encountered by participants in the OTC derivatives markets. These subjects are addressed in the eight chapters of Part 1, which replace the topic notes that more briefly reviewed some of these subjects in the third edition. The subjects discussed are those that, in our experience, arise most frequently in the course of advising clients and preparing legal opinions, and in lawsuits relating to OTC derivatives. Many of the subjects discussed are also relevant for other kinds of contracts, but we concentrate on the

---

[3] *Infra* p. 18.

[4] *See infra* note 2078.

ways in which they relate to OTC derivatives, often with a focus on the substantial changes in these areas of New York and U.S. law that have occurred since 1993.

This edition also makes more extensive use of introductory notes, particularly to discuss issues that are common to multiple product types but are sometimes resolved in different ways in various product-specific documentation tools. We find that these comparisons bring into focus both fundamental product differences and, in some cases, the fact that changing market views and expectations are not immediately reflected in the standardized tools across all market segments.

We began by noting that our primary purpose, in this edition as before, has been to illustrate the most commonly found documentation practices, generally in the context of terms published as market standards. As discussed in the General Introduction, the derivatives market could not have grown as it has without the very considerable efforts devoted by countless individuals to the development of standard terms. The standard terms nonetheless require careful use and frequent reexamination. This is so for many reasons. First, the markets continue to evolve. In addition, compromises reached among those involved in the preparation of standard terms do not always prove successful in practice. Unfortunately, the need to revisit an established convention sometimes becomes apparent as a result of a dispute or as documentation backlogs mount because the published standard approach does not adequately serve the needs of the market. And then there is the fact that, if one size would have sufficed to fit all, the OTC market for customized derivatives would not have come to be what it is. For all these reasons, we have sought throughout this book to ask questions that will stimulate further analysis of the standardized terms and motivate practitioners to explore whether the standard that is offered truly reflects current practice, what changes to that practice are being considered by industry groups and, when the offered standard does not prove to be ideal, to weigh the cost of departing from it against the potential benefits to be derived from a new approach.

We wish to thank the International Swaps and Derivatives Association, Inc. and The Bond Market Association for permitting us to include some of their publications as the basis for the sample annotated documents included in this edition. We also wish to thank the many people, both colleagues and clients, who have helped and encouraged us over the years in our practice and writings in this field.

Anthony C. Gooch and Linda B. Klein
July 17, 2002

GENERAL INTRODUCTION

Documentation Challenges 1
   Customized OTC Derivatives and the Basic Challenges 1
   Customized vs. Standardized Derivatives 3
   Capturing the Derivatives Deal...5
   Placing the Deal in a Contractual Framework..6
      The Agreement Format 6
      The Credit-Sensitive Provisions...6
      Contract Enforceability..8
   Reflecting Accounting, Tax and Other Special Concerns...10
   Documenting Relationships and Responsibilities 16
Standardization of Terms for the Over-the-Counter Derivatives Market........................18
   The *Swaps Code*...18
   Master Agreement Forms and Definitions Booklets 19
   Collateral..21
   Cross-Product Risk Management..22
   The Current Situation..23
The Structure of This Book..24
Bibliographical Notes 26

This book is designed to deal with the documentation of OTC derivatives, such as swaps and similar products, and with the chief legal and practical concerns raised by that documentation. Throughout the book, our commentary focuses on issues that are peculiar to these products. We deal only incidentally with the host of other issues that the documentation for OTC derivatives transactions shares with the documentation for other kinds of transactions, including financings and cash market purchases and sales of the assets underlying derivatives products.

This General Introduction first identifies some of these special documentation challenges. The next section traces the history of industry efforts to streamline the process of negotiating and documenting OTC derivatives, through the establishment of a standard vocabulary and certain standard conventions for the business, the development of the master agreement format and the issuance of standard forms of confirmations and tools for documenting credit support arrangements, as well as other standard documents and provisions and recommended best practices. The third section explains the structure of this book, and the final section includes some bibliographical information.

DOCUMENTATION CHALLENGES

CUSTOMIZED OTC DERIVATIVES AND THE BASIC CHALLENGES

Many of the most commonly traded OTC derivatives are described in more detail in Part 2 of this book.[5] The descriptions and diagrams included there show how the prod-

---

[5] *Infra* p. 367. That Part consists of introductory notes on various product categories, together with product descriptions and sample confirmations. Brief descriptions of various kinds of derivatives transactions are included in DICTIONARY OF RISK MANAGEMENT. *See also* John D. Finnerty, *Structuring Derivative Instruments to Adjust Risk Exposure: The Arithmetic of Financial Instruments* (PricewaterhouseCoopers,

ucts are used to hedge or take on risks associated with assets, liabilities and other variables—often referred to as the "underlyings"—and to create "synthetic" assets and liabilities, products that capture single slices or combinations of risk that cannot be acquired independently, or that cannot be acquired as efficiently or cheaply through an actual purchase or sale of the underlying asset, rate or index in a cash market. These transactions are thought of as "derivatives" because their value at any time depends on (and, so, is derived from) the value of that "underlying" as measured in the relevant market, or the value the market places on protection against an uncertain outcome involving the underlying.

In many cases—and these are the majority—the value of the derivative turns on how the market assesses uncertainty about the future price of a physical asset, or the future price of, yield on or total return from, a financial asset. Or the uncertain outcome might be how an asset's price, yield or return will behave in comparison with that of another asset. In the most established segments of the markets, the underlying classes involved in these price, yield, total return and spread derivatives include interest rates on money market assets, such as LIBOR deposits and capital markets instruments (including bonds and stock), currencies, equity indices and physical commodities such as crude oil, natural gas and other energy products, and base and precious metals. For newer products, such as weather and credit derivatives, the uncertain outcome may be the number of days during a future period on which the temperature will rise above or fall below a specified level, or the number of inches of rain or snow that will fall, in a particular place, or whether a company or government will default on its borrowings, or become insolvent or declare a moratorium on its debt or reschedule it.

Generally speaking, these OTC derivatives are bundles of contractual rights and obligations embodied in the documents that set out their terms. The first challenge in documenting them is, simply, to get it right—to identify properly who will be required to pay or deliver what to whom, on what date or dates, in what circumstances. The second, related, challenge is to capture in legally enforceable agreements the more general terms that will apply in the parties' dealings. These general terms include the following, in particular.

- The procedures for normal scheduled payments or deliveries, including the conditions to these performance obligations

- collateral or other credit support for the parties' obligations

- compensation if payments or deliveries are late

- credit-sensitive terms that govern when there can be early close-out of a transaction (or all the parties' transactions)

- the payments to be made if close-out settlement should occur

- how the parties will memorialize and communicate about their subsequent dealings

---

undated). For an overview of the terminology used in connection with rate swaps and related products, *see* Schuyler K. Henderson & Linda B. Klein, *Glossary of Terms Used in Connection with Rate Swap, Currency Swap, Cap and Collar Agreements*, BUTTERWORTH'S J. INT'L BANK. & FIN. L., Supp. June 1987.

General Introduction 3

Further challenges involve ensuring that the documents reflect the transactions in a manner consistent with the parties' intent in light of any special tax, accounting, regulatory or other frameworks applicable to each of them. Another major challenge is to determine whether and how to reflect in the documentation the parties' understandings about the nature of their dealing relationship, and particularly the extent to which each of them assumes exclusive responsibility for certain matters, without reliance on the other.

CUSTOMIZED VS. STANDARDIZED DERIVATIVES

These challenges do not arise in the same way with standardized derivatives, such as traditional futures and options that are traded on exchanges,[6] or in standardized OTC derivatives that, increasingly, are available on other kinds of trading facilities. A somewhat simplified comparison of a traditional exchange-traded futures contract with a traditional OTC swap will serve to illustrate this.

By purchasing an exchange-traded futures contract, a buyer can effectively "lock in" the price at which it will be able to obtain a specified position in an underlying financial instrument or commodity for settlement on a specified date. The settlement dates and the amounts of the underlying instrument or commodity will be standard. The buyer's counterparty will be the clearing house for the exchange on which the futures contract is purchased. The applicable rules, including those relating to the amount of margin required of the buyer, will be based on the rules of the exchange. The increase or decline in the value of the contract will be realized or paid at the end of each day through adjustments to the buyer's margin account.[7] If the buyer decides to dispose of the futures contract, it may do so on the exchange, and at any time the buyer can effectively cancel its obligation to take delivery of the specified amount of the underlying instrument or commodity by entering into an offsetting sale of the same futures contract (in the absence of market disruptions that would prevent the sale). This offset mechanism and the liquidity that makes it possible depend on the standardized nature of the exchange-traded futures contracts.

The buyer in our example might choose instead to obtain the desired economic result through an OTC swap. In this case, the legal and documentation environment will be very different from the rigidly structured world of traditional exchange-traded products. In a conventional swap, the buyer would not assume an obligation to take delivery of the

---

[6]*See* U.S. CONGRESS, OFFICE OF TECHNOLOGY ASSESSMENT, ELECTRONIC BULLS AND BEARS: U.S. SECURITIES MARKETS AND INFORMATION TECHNOLOGY 196 (Sept. 1990) (glossary definition of "derivative product"). In addition to the traditional, fully standardized futures and options referred to here, there are also exchange-traded products that permit some customization of terms.

[7]All buyers and sellers of exchange-traded futures contracts are required to post margin. As the price of the underlying instrument or commodity rises or declines, the positive or negative impact on the value of the futures contract is either credited or debited to the owner's margin account. If the balance in the account after a debit is made is below the applicable "maintenance" level, the balance must be restored to the appropriate level. Margining with respect to exchange-traded options operates somewhat differently. *See, e.g.*, ELECTRONIC BULLS AND BEARS, *supra* note 6, at 101–04. In the United States, the margins levels for exchange members will be set by the exchange. The customers of the exchange members will, in turn, be required to post margin with the exchange members, in amounts that may be higher than what the members must post with the exchange's clearing house at the time.

underlying instrument or commodity.[8] Instead, it would agree to make payments to a counterparty calculated at a fixed price or at a fixed rate in exchange for receiving from the counterparty payments calculated at a market-based price or rate for the relevant instrument or commodity. Through the swap, the buyer can design a transaction involving the amounts, settlement dates and underlying instruments or commodities that it wishes without being constrained by the standardized terms of the exchange-traded products. The same can be true with physically settled OTC derivatives, which include forward contracts and options involving obligations to make and take delivery of currencies, debt and equity instruments and base and precious metals as well as energy products and other commodities.

With customized OTC derivatives, it may also be possible for the buyer in our example to negotiate credit support terms that do not involve cash margining or that require the delivery of cash or other collateral or support less frequently than would a transaction on an exchange. The critical terms relating to the close-out or transfer of its rights and obligations in connection with OTC derivatives will also be subject to negotiation, and the documentation will accommodate special features designed to meet the needs of both parties.[9]

Thus, in the usual OTC transaction, the buyer does not simply step into a predefined position in a highly structured situation. Instead, it executes an agreement customized to reflect the results of its negotiations with its counterparty. In the OTC transaction, the individualized agreement is the vehicle for setting forth the particular financial terms of the transaction as tailored to fit the needs of our hypothetical buyer, as well as the protections the parties have agreed are appropriate in light of the assessment that each of them makes of its credit exposure *vis-à-vis* the other party.

---

[8] In its traditional form, an OTC swap is a purely financial transaction and does not involve an obligation to deliver or take delivery of the instruments or commodities that are used as the basis for calculating the payments involved in the swap. Some futures contracts are also cash-settled by their nature. However, many futures provide for physical settlement, as do swaps of certain kinds, such as credit default swaps. In most circumstances this difference between traditional swaps and futures may be academic as a practical matter, since the obligation to make or take delivery involved in a futures contract can be discharged through the purchase or sale of an offsetting futures contract.

[9] It is a commonplace to observe that, because swaps, caps, floors and the like are individually negotiated, they can be specially tailored as a hedge for a specific liability or asset, with the maturity, amount and other details of the particular liability or asset exactly or very closely mirrored in the OTC derivative, whereas the futures and options available on exchanges are limited in their variety and involve standard terms that may or may not afford sufficient precision as a hedge. The comparison of the advantages and disadvantages of the OTC and exchange-traded alternatives for any particular situation is, however, quite complex. *See, e.g.*, Richard A. Hutchinson, *The mechanics of interest rate futures*, in MANAGEMENT OF RATE RISK 89; and Clifford W. Smith, Jr., Charles W. Smithson & Lee Macdonald Wakeman, *The Market for Interest Rate Swaps*, and George Handjinicolaou, *The Forward Foreign Exchange Market: An Alternative for Hedging Currency Risks*, in RISK MANAGEMENT, chs. 8 & 13. Even if an appropriate hedge can be created by putting together a bundle of exchange-traded derivative products, those positions will probably require active management, so the end-user may prefer to use an OTC transaction tailored to satisfy its needs that is provided by a market professional, since the end-user may not have the resources necessary to manage the exchange-traded components as required or may find that its resources can be better employed otherwise. The counterparty, as a professional participant in the derivatives market, will be in the business of managing a portfolio of exchange-traded and OTC derivatives and of combining them to design special products for end-users.

General Introduction 5

CAPTURING THE DERIVATIVES DEAL

The first of the documentation challenges mentioned above—getting the terms of the transaction right—is far from trivial, although it can be greatly simplified if the parties' agreement can be properly stated using published, standard terminology and conventions like those discussed and illustrated in this book. The use of these standardized documentation tools itself gives rise to challenges, however, because (1) the terminology and conventions can be quite complex and can involve ambiguity, (2) many important determinations are stated to be left to the Calculation Agent (often one of the parties) and (3) the forms often prescribe "default choices" that will be applied if the parties are silent on various questions.

Accordingly, documentation practitioners using the standardized tools must often engage in at least three critical tasks. First, they must identify matters in the standard provisions that could be clearer or that, though clear, may be inconsistent with the parties' business understanding. Second, they should seek to identify determinations that should involve both parties, rather than just the Calculation Agent[10] or, if a joint approach is not adopted, to work out any necessary additional contractual provisions for raising and resolving disputes about determinations made by the Calculation Agent. Third, the practitioners need to review any presumptions included in the standard provisions that will apply where the confirmation is silent, to determine with those making the business decisions whether the documents should override these presumptions. Even when the parties decide to adopt the standard presumptions, there may be cases in which they will decide to spell them out in the documentation, in the interests of clarity and certainty.

Whether or not the parties use standardized terminology and conventions, in preparing the documentation for derivatives—as in many other human endeavors—they must consider the possibilities of misunderstandings, unforeseen problems and, simply, mistakes.[11] These challenges have always existed in the traditional trading environment for

---

[10] Throughout this book, we identify some important determinations that are left to the Calculation Agent and point out the related concerns. There are special cases, some of which reflect accounting and tax analysis, in which end-users decidedly either do, or do not, wish to be involved in making certain determinations in order to achieve specific goals. Therefore, as with most other issues relating to derivatives documentation, practitioners must be alert to the possible need for exceptions from the norm.

[11] For example, lawsuits sometimes involve claims that the confirmation of a transaction misstates the parties' agreement or states it incompletely. *See generally* Chapter 2, *infra* p. 39. Lawsuits also arise because of unforeseen holidays. *See, e.g., Judge Awards French Bank $3.3 Million in Derivatives Action,* ANDREWS DERIVATIVE LITIG. REP., July 5, 1995, at 5. Not surprisingly, disputes most frequently relate to products that are relatively new at the time and are not covered by standardized formulations, or at least not by standard formulations that have been subjected to the tests of time and market crises. Thus, credit derivatives have recently been the subjects of a spate of disputes over issues ranging from basic matters such as the identity of the underlying credit risk—the Reference Entity—to more complex questions on whether an event—a Credit Event—triggering a payout has occurred and whether particular kinds of obligations can be tendered in physical settlement or used in cash settlement of these transactions. *See, e.g., Dealers Act to End Reference Confusion,* CREDITFLUX, Apr. 1, 2002, at 1, and *Reference Entity Case Settled, id.* at 4 (referring to disputes of the first kind following defaults under bonds of Railtrack PLC and Armstrong World Industries); *S.D.N.Y. Judge to Hear $20M Derivatives Suit Against JPMorgan Chase,* ANDREWS BANK AND LIABILITY REP., Apr. 18, 2002, at 9; *Korean Trusts Sue J.P. Morgan Chase Bank for $90 Million, id.,* May 2, 2002, at 7 (referring to disputes over whether an Argentine government exchange of existing bonds for new instruments constituted a Restructuring Credit Event); *A Non-Event? Conseco Loan Restructuring Confounds*

derivatives and, as market participants increasingly trade electronically, they will continue to exist, though perhaps in somewhat different forms.[12]

PLACING THE DEAL IN A CONTRACTUAL FRAMEWORK

THE AGREEMENT FORMAT

Looking beyond the individual transaction, a second, more general, documentation challenge arises when the parties use the master agreement format, which permits them to put into place a single agreement to govern their OTC derivatives transactions with each other at the outset of their relationship.[13] Each transaction is then memorialized in a short confirmation which supplements the master agreement. When the master agreement format is adopted, the parties will usually base their agreement on one of the standard forms that are widely used in the international markets or in the particular regional or product market in which the parties expect to be dealing, often accompanied by a related set of standard credit support terms. In some cases, however, the parties will use a proprietary form developed by a party that is a market professional.

The Introductions to Parts 3 and 4 of this book address important issues relating to how the pieces of these standard forms of contract—the master agreement terms, the confirmations of the transactions and the credit support documents—relate to each other and operate together. Those issues, as well as others involving the ways in which the derivatives documents work with related arrangements, such as contracts governing financings being hedged with the derivatives, are discussed throughout the book.

THE CREDIT-SENSITIVE PROVISIONS

Having selected an appropriate format and model for their agreement, the parties will customize the model, most often by negotiating the terms of a schedule to be attached to the master agreement. These negotiations are usually most challenging when the transactions the parties intend to engage in are complex or long-term. The degree of challenge will also depend on the nature, credit standing and prospects of the parties and any third party that may be offering support for a party's obligations. The parties' definitive schedule will, naturally, often represent a compromise between what each of the parties feels best satisfies its credit and other policies.

An interesting characteristic of the master agreement is that, even though it may be intended for use far into the future, it is negotiated in the context of the parties' relative bargaining power (usually a function of credit strength) at the outset of their dealing relationship. If substantial disparity exists at that time, some of the credit-related provisions will probably be drafted to apply in different ways to each of the parties, but many of the provisions will nonetheless apply in the same way to both of them. Within this framework of reciprocity, the challenge for each of the parties is to strike the right balance between

---

Credit Players, DERIVATIVES WEEK, Oct. 9, 2000, at 1 (referring to disputes over whether a corporate syndicated bank loan rescheduling constituted a Restructuring Credit Event).

[12]*See, e.g.,* Charles A. Fishkin, *Electronic Derivatives Markets and Operational Risk Analysis,* OPERATIONAL RISK, May 1 2000, available from http://www.watersinfo.com/news/RMO/index_home.asp.

[13]The history of the development of the master format and other industry standardization efforts are discussed *infra* p. 19. The benefits of the master agreement format are discussed *infra* p. 794.

the protections it would like to enjoy if the prospects of its counterparty, or the counterparty's source of credit support, deteriorate, on one hand, and the provisions with which the party itself will be comfortable if its own condition weakens, on the other hand. The discipline of reciprocity in the documentation of derivatives has great advantages in moving the parties towards agreement.

In some cases the normal tendency to apply more rigorous provisions to the party with the lesser credit standing may be reversed. This can be the case when the documentation is being put in place for a single transaction in which the weaker credit is discharging all of its obligations once and for all at the beginning of the transaction. This often arises in derivatives executed in connection with securitizations and other structured financings. In these instances, the principal challenge is often to overcome the natural bias—reflected in the institutional policies of the stronger credit—that normally lead it to object to restrictive provisions that apply only to it, or that are more onerous for it than for its counterparty.[14]

Other challenges also arise from the fact that the master agreement is being put into place for future use.[15] Some of the standard forms of master agreement most widely used in the market are designed to accommodate transactions of a great many different types. At the time the parties enter into the master agreement, it may be difficult for them to foresee all the types of transactions they may wish to enter into with each other. The task of the practitioner in this regard is to analyze the proposed master agreement terms in light of their potential consequences and to determine whether those terms make sense, given the possible consequences and any uncertainties about the nature of the parties' future dealings.

For example, a party might be asked to affirm that all the future transactions between the parties will fall within a specific legal category. Such affirmations are often sought in an effort to establish certain characterizations of the transactions for purposes of insolvency or tax laws. In these cases, each party should reflect on the accuracy of the contractual provision as applied to transactions of foreseeable types. It is good to keep in mind that issues about the proper characterization of a particular transaction, as well as other transaction-specific issues, can always be covered in the confirmation of that transaction.

If the parties agree to provisions in the master agreement that may not be accurate for particular categories of future transactions, they should put in place internal proce-

---

[14] As discussed *infra* note 644, derivatives related to securitizations and other structured financings often present other challenges to such policies because the objectives of the transaction—and the requirements of the rating agencies involved—require minimizing the circumstances in which the derivatives transaction can be closed out while the related financing is ongoing.

[15] Naturally, when a party negotiates a master agreement expecting changes that would affect it or a credit support provider for it (or its counterparty or its credit support provider, for that matter), or that would affect their proposed transactions, the standard master agreement terms should be appropriately modified to take the expected changes into account. ISDA's succession of standardized provisions for dealing with the introduction of the euro and the accession of various countries into the EMU are examples of terms often included in master agreements for this reason. The commentary in this book refers to various examples of other provisions adopted to deal with situations of expected changes, such as a party's reorganization into another type of legal entity, or the transfer of some or all of its derivatives activities from one entity in a corporate group, or from one office, to another.

dures designed to ensure that the master agreement will not be used for transactions that fall within those categories unless it is appropriately adapted. As a practical matter, it is often not realistic to think that procedures of this kind will operate exactly as they are designed, so it will be preferable to exclude the specialized provisions from the master and deal with the issue in confirmations.

CONTRACT ENFORCEABILITY

Another key part of the general documentation challenge is to produce documents that will create legal, valid, binding and enforceable obligations, subject, as nearly as possible, only to risks that each of the parties is willing to run if the other party or its credit support provider becomes insolvent.[16] The complexity of this aspect of the documentation exercise will, of course, vary depending on the characteristics of the parties and the legal regimes that are applicable to them in the jurisdictions in which they are organized and from which they are acting for purposes of their transactions with each other. As discussed in Chapter 1, legal issues relating to power and authority to enter into derivatives transactions can be complex and quite serious if the counterparty or its credit support provider is a regulated entity or a trust or other person with limited powers, or if there is a risk that the counterparty or provider of credit support will argue that whether or not it will be bound should be determined in accordance with the laws of its home jurisdiction, regardless of the law contractually chosen to govern the parties' agreement.[17]

When limitations on the power or authority of a prospective counterparty are at issue, a first step in responding to the challenge is usually to distinguish among (1) circumstances in which making a mistake can mean that a contract may be void or voidable, (2) cases in which the obligations of the counterparty may or may not be enforceable but the party itself may be subject to sanctions as a result of its dealings with that counterparty and (3) cases in which the counterparty's obligations will be enforceable but the counterparty may be subject to sanctions for having entered into unauthorized transactions. As discussed in Chapter 1 and in the Introduction to Part 4 of this book,[18] dealings with sovereigns and others in the public sector may fall into the first category. In some circumstances, dealings with pension plans can fall into the second.[19] Dealings with regulated

---

[16] Chapter 7, *infra* p. 268, discusses the issues that arise most frequently under insolvency and similar laws.

[17] *See infra* p. 31.

[18] *Infra* p. 1005.

[19] On issues that can arise if derivatives run afoul of restrictions applicable to pension plans subject to ERISA, *see* Jeffrey Brown, *Swaps With Pension Funds and Investment Companies*, *in* SWAPS AND OTHER DERIVATIVES IN 1994 (PLI Corp. L. & Practice Course Handbook Series No. 848, at 439, 1994); Gronislaw Grala, *Swaps Documentation with Erisa Plans*, *in* PENSION PLAN INVESTMENTS 1993: CONFRONTING TODAY'S LEGAL ISSUES (PLI Tax L. & Estate Planning Course Handbook Series Tax L. & Practice No. J4-3664, at 225, 1993); Richard Susko & Alan Wilmit, *Questions Most Frequently Asked by Traders Regarding Pension Funds, Investing in Derivatives, and Other OTC Instruments*, *in* PENSION PLAN INVESTMENTS: CONFRONTING TODAY'S ISSUES (PLI Tax L. & Estate Planning Course Handbook Series Tax L. & Practice No. J0-000O, at 171, 1998). Because of concerns relating to these restrictions, derivatives documents sometimes include representations like the one quoted below, which is set out in the schedules to the IFEMA, ICOM and FEOMA forms for elective use by the parties.

entities such as insurance companies often fall into the third.[20] As a result, part of this challenge for professional participants in the market is to ensure that they know who their counterparty is—a simple enough matter with counterparties acting as principal but more difficult in dealings with agents and brokers.[21]

Questions on choice of law can also be quite difficult, as has been shown by numerous disputes involving OTC derivatives, and these questions can arise regardless of whether the parties have—as they should—taken care to specify a governing law in their agreement[22] and—as they do in some cases of cross-border dealings—have also obtained local law opinions to the effect that the contractual choice of law is enforceable. Enforceability opinions usually speak only to the enforcement of the contractual provisions in the context of a claim of breach of contract. For reasons discussed in Chapter 7,[23] the opinion does not address issues that may arise if principles applicable in insolvency or similar proceedings displace those that might otherwise apply. Where security interests are concerned, the law chosen by the parties also may or may not be the same as the law that will apply to determine questions of perfection of those interests against third party claims and the effects of perfection, as is discussed in the Introduction to Part 5.[24] In addition, ques-

> [I]t is neither (i) an "employee benefit plan" as defined in Section 3(3) of the Employee Retirement Income Security Act of 1974 which is subject to Part 4 of Subtitle B of such Act; (ii) a "plan" as defined in Section 4975(e)(1) of the Internal Revenue Code of 1986; nor (ii) an entity the assets of which are deemed to be assets of any such "employee benefit plan" or "plan" by reason of the U.S. Department of Labor's plan asset regulation, 29 C.F.R. Section 2510.3–101.

Counsel should be consulted where ERISA issues may be involved and these representations cannot be made.

[20] Many of the special issues that can arise in dealings with regulated entities are beyond the scope of this book. On the use of derivatives by insurance companies in the United States, *see, e.g.,* M. Christina Amundson, *Insurers' Use of Derivatives: New York's Regulatory Framework,* 21 FUTURES & DERIVATIVES L. REP. 15 (Feb. 2002); Kevin Driscoll, *Replication (Synthetic Asset Transactions),* 9 J. OF DERIVATIVES 62 (Fall 2001); Michael P. Goldman & Michael J. Pinsel, *A Regulatory Overview of the Insurance Industry's Use of Over-the-Counter Derivatives,* DERIVATIVES, May-June 1998, at 202, *reprinted in* PLI 2000, at 555.

[21] Of course, certainty about the identity of the counterparty and other information relating to it (and perhaps its ownership) is also central to an assessment of credit risk and to efforts to comply with regulations relating to money laundering and suspicious funds transfers, as well as restrictions on dealings with persons from specified jurisdictions. Dealings through intermediaries with undisclosed principals may, therefore, be subject to close supervisory scrutiny for bank participants in the derivatives markets. *See, e.g.,* BOARD OF GOVERNORS OF THE FEDERAL RESERVE SYSTEM, TRADING AND CAPITAL-MARKETS ACTIVITIES MANUAL § 2020.1, at 11 (March 1999) (on dealing with unnamed counterparties and block trades with investment advisors). The Financial Markets Lawyers Group (FMLG) has published useful *Guidelines for Transactions Involving Intermediaries, available at* www.ny.frb.org/fmlg/document.html. (The FMLG, which is composed of legal representatives from commercial and investment banks active in the FX market, coordinates legal projects in connection with the Foreign Exchange Committee, *infra* note 58.) In creating documents for derivatives dealings with agents on behalf of their principals, some market professionals use as a starting point the terms published as Annex IV (Party Acting as Agent) to TBMA's form of master repurchase agreement. Whether those or different or additional provisions should be included must be examined in light of the particular circumstances.

[22] *See generally* Part 4(h) of the sample master agreement schedule in Part 3 and related annotations, *infra* p. 925.

[23] *Infra* p. 268.

[24] *Infra* p. 1057.

tions are sometimes raised about the application of the parties' contractual choice of law in connection with matters of power and authority[25] and the law governing claims that do not arise under contract law, such as tort claims involving fraud and negligence, claims of breach of fiduciary duty and claims that arise under statutes or otherwise involve public policy.[26]

REFLECTING ACCOUNTING, TAX AND OTHER SPECIAL CONCERNS

In documenting particular transactions, or particular types of transactions, or transactions with particular kinds of counterparties, there can be many other special challenges. Some of them arise because of statutes and regulatory regimes applicable to transactions, including derivatives, that are linked to securities or commodities.[27] Others come up under laws regulating financial transactions more generally. Still others may arise because of the particular goals that one of the parties is seeking to achieve through the transaction, often relating to how the transaction, or payments under the transaction, or payments under a larger structure that includes the transaction, will be treated for tax and accounting purposes or within regulatory frameworks, such as those applicable under capital adequacy regimes.

Tax. The general documentation issues relating to withholding taxes are discussed in Chapter 8.[28] The many other kinds of tax issues that may affect the ways derivatives transactions are documented and structured are beyond the scope of this book.[29] Those involved in the documentation process should work closely with tax counsel and other advisers whenever the achievement of specific tax goals is important.

Accounting. The accounting treatment of derivatives under generally accepted accounting principles in the United States (U.S. GAAP) has changed radically in recent years and is still in flux. Important changes in this regard are also taking place under International Accounting Standards.[30] Where U.S. GAAP is concerned, for most end-users

---

[25] *See infra* note 94 and accompanying text. *See also Indosuez Int'l Finance B.V. v. National Reserve Bank,* 2002 N.Y. LEXIS 1097 (N.Y. 2002), holding New York law applicable to questions of apparent authority to bind a Russian bank.

[26] *See* Gooch & Klein, *Review of Case Law II* at 82, for discussion of the ways in which some of these issues arose in the mid-1990s in cases involving leveraged derivatives (*P.T. Adimitra Rayapratama v. Bankers Trust Co.* and *Procter & Gamble Co. v. Bankers Trust Co.*). Similar issues surfaced in various ways in disputes involving non-deliverable forward and option transactions following the Russian financial crisis of 1998. *See, e.g., Parex Bank v. Russian Savings Bank,* 116 F. Supp. 2d 415 (S.D.N.Y. 2000) (analyzing the weight to be given to Russian law determinations that similar contracts might be unenforceable, in denying a motion to dismiss the suit as having been brought in an inconvenient forum).

[27] Issues of these kinds, and related documentation practices, are discussed in Chapter 3 (commodities), *infra* p. 63, and Chapter 4 (securities), *infra* p. 129.

[28] *Infra* p. 350.

[29] *See infra* note 1044, identifying some of those issues and reference resources.

[30] On accounting for financial instruments and financial derivatives, *see generally* COJE SCHMIDT, ACCOUNTING FOR DERIVATIVES: DEAL, ACCRUAL, REVOLUTION, RESULT (Euromoney Books 2002).

General Introduction

of derivatives the key changes in this area relate to Financial Accounting Statement 133 (FAS 133).[31] As stated in its opening Summary, FAS 133

> requires that an entity recognize all derivatives [including both freestanding derivatives and certain derivative instruments embedded in other contracts] as either assets or liabilities in the statement of financial position and measure those instruments at fair value. If certain conditions are met, a derivative may be specifically designated as (a) a hedge of the exposure to changes in the fair value of a recognized asset or liability or an unrecognized firm commitment, (b) a hedge of the exposure to variable cash flows of a forecasted transaction, or (c) a hedge of the foreign currency exposure of a net investment in a foreign operation, an unrecognized firm commitment, an available-for-sale security, or a foreign-currency-denominated forecasted transaction.[32]

The accounting for changes in the value of a derivative—gains and losses—under FAS 133 depends on the intended use of the derivative and effective designation of that use. Generally speaking, if a derivative is not appropriately designated as a hedging instrument, the gain or loss must be recognized in earnings in the period the change occurs, so changes in the values of derivatives can lead to volatility in reported earnings.[33] The same may be true to the extent a derivative designated as a hedge is not effective in achieving the expected results.[34] However, if the transaction is properly designated as a hedge, to the

---

[31] FASB, ACCOUNTING FOR CERTAIN DERIVATIVE INSTRUMENTS AND HEDGING ACTIVITIES (1998). FAS 138, issued in June 2000, amended FAS 133 and delayed the date on which its implementation would be required for most companies. Most companies were required to begin implementing FAS 133 in the first quarter of 2001. On May 1, 2002, the FASB issued an exposure draft of PROPOSED STATEMENT OF FINANCIAL ACCOUNTING STANDARDS that would further amend FAS 133 to reflect guidance issued by the FASB on implementation issues and decisions made as part of its Derivatives Implementation Group (DIG) process. Certain kinds of OTC derivatives are excluded from the coverage of the hedge accounting features of FAS 133 described here. See, e.g., Scott Edwards, Accounting and Tax Treatment, in WEATHER RISK MANAGEMENT 246, 248. On features of the proposed changes that are opposed by financial markets industry groups, see the letters to the FASB from ISDA and from the Joint Industry Working Group (JIWG) composed of ISDA, TMBA and the SIA, available at www.isda.org.

[32] FASB, ACCOUNTING FOR CERTAIN DERIVATIVE INSTRUMENTS AND HEDGING ACTIVITIES, at i.

[33] Naturally, the way in which investors and rating agencies perceive this volatility can be critical. See, e.g., MOODY'S INVESTORS SERVICE, FINANCIAL REPORTING OF DERIVATIVES & THE EFFECT ON U.S. CORPORATIONS: STILL EVOLVING, BUT UNLIKELY TO HAVE MAJOR CREDIT IMPLICATIONS 3 (Sept. 2001):

> Moody's believes that the overall effect of Statement 133 will be insignificant for the majority of the companies we rate, and that the direct rating impact of this standard is expected to be quite limited. *Moody's believes that the additional reported earnings volatility under Statement 133 is the most significant credit issue raised by the standard. However, Moody's expects that it will "look through"' this incremental financial reporting volatility if it is not reflective of additional economic volatility.*

[34] See Section 2 of Appendix A to FAS 133, on "Assessment of Hedge Effectiveness," a lengthy explanation, with examples, which begins (¶ 62) by explaining as follows:

> This Statement requires that an entity define at the time it designates a hedging relationship the method it will use to assess the hedge's effectiveness in achieving offsetting changes in fair value or offsetting cash flows attributable to the risk being hedged. It also requires that an entity use that defined method consistently throughout the hedge period (a) to assess at inception of the hedge and on an ongoing basis whether it expects the

extent it is effective as such for the designated purpose, changes in the fair value of the derivative will be reported together with, and offset by, the corresponding loss or gain on the hedged item, or reported with the cash flows being hedged, or as part of the cumulative translation adjustment for the relevant net investment in a foreign operation.[35]

FAS 133 itself created documentation requirements as a condition to hedge accounting treatment, as well as analytical issues that can sometimes be difficult.[36] Those involved in documenting the transactions may, as a result, become involved in the challenge of seeking to ensure that the contract terms are consistent with the accounting analysis and do not add complexity to that analysis. These concerns can become relevant to issues of compliance with applicable securities laws when entities are required to include their financial statements in the disclosure they make to investors.[37]

Securities Law Disclosures. Practitioners may also have concerns about the way in which certain kinds of transactions, and the resolution of key documentation issues—such as close-out rights and collateral requirements—will affect the disclosure required under applicable securities laws. For example, entities required to file reports with the SEC under the Securities Exchange Act may be required to take these matters into account in preparing required disclosure about the entity's use of derivatives or, more generally, the primary market risks to which the entity is exposed, how it manages its value at risk (VAR), "how derivatives alter the magnitude and even the direction of exposure relative to a 'pure play' on the basic risk in the industry" (*e.g.,* the risk of changes in the price of gold, for a gold mining company) and the entity's "vulnerability . . . to survive large swings in risk factors, given the rights of counterparties to demand settlement before volatility returns to 'normal' levels."[38]

Capital Adequacy. Documentation issues also arise with regard to the capital requirements applicable to many classes of participants in the derivatives markets, including

---

hedging relationship to be highly effective in achieving offset and (b) to measure the ineffective part of the hedge. If the entity identifies an improved method and wants to apply that method prospectively, it must discontinue the existing hedging relationship and designate the relationship anew using the improved method.

[35] FAS 133, at i.

[36] For an overview of FAS 133, *see* Arlette C. Wilson & Sharon N. Campbell, *Improved Accounting and Reporting for Derivative Instruments and Hedging Activities,* FUTURES & DERIVATIVES L. REP., Mar. 2002, at 1. On selected issues relating to FAS 133 from the perspective of the practitioner, *see* Ira Kawaller, *Impact of Accounting Rules on the Market for Swaps,* DERIVATIVES QUARTERLY (Spring 2001) and other pieces by the same author listed at www.kawaller.com/articles.htm.

[37] For example, in 2001 the SEC announced that, in its reviews of financial statements included in periodic filings required by the U.S. securities laws, the SEC staff would focus on compliance with all disclosure requirements of FAS 133. *See* SEC, Division of Corporation Finance, Current Accounting and Disclosure Issues (Aug. 31, 2001), at §§ II(D) & II(F).

[38] *Id.* These SEC disclosure requirements, which were imposed in 1997, are referred to *infra* p. 132. *See, e.g.,* Alan Blankley, Reinhold Lamb & Richard Schroeder, *Compliance with SEC Disclosure Requirements about Market Risk,* J. OF DERIVATIVES, Spring 2000, at 39. On aspects of standard market documents relating to vulnerability to close-out risk, *see* Christian Johnson, *Liquidity & the ISDA Master Agreement,* DERIVATIVES WEEK, Apr. 30, 2001, at 6 (Learning Curve column).

securities firms and some of their affiliates[39] and, perhaps with the greatest effect on the market, banks. The risk-weighted capital adequacy guidelines applicable to banks in many jurisdictions are local regulatory adaptations of the framework entitled *International Convergence of Capital Measurement and Capital Standards* (the "Basel Accord")[40] published in July 1988 by the Basel Committee on Banking Supervision, a committee of central banks and bank supervisors and regulators from the major industrialized countries, which is referred to as the Basel Committee because it usually meets at the Bank for International Settlements in Basel, Switzerland. The Basel Accord has since been amended on several occasions, and the Basel Committee has been involved since 1999 in a project[41] that is expected to result in the replacement of the Basel Accord by a framework referred to in its consultative documents as the New Basel Accord.[42]

Under the credit risk rules in the Basel Accord very simply and generally stated,[43] a bank must allocate a "risk-weight" to its assets and off-balance sheet positions (converted for the purpose to asset equivalents) and must meet a minimum capital requirement under which the ratio of its total capital to risk-weighted assets is at least 8%. This minimum regulatory capital requirement is intended to act as a cushion to absorb the loss the bank may incur if the counterparty defaults.[44] The risk weighting for a claim on a non-bank, private-sector corporate counterparty is generally 100%,[45] which translates to a

---

[39] On capital requirements applicable to full service securities brokers and dealers and affiliates of these entities that register with the SEC as derivatives dealers, *see infra* note 442. On derivatives as authorized investments of insurance companies under New York law, *see* Amundson, *Insurers' Use of Derivatives: New York's Regulatory Framework, supra* note 19, at 15.

[40] *Available at* http://www.bis.org/publ/bcbs04A.pdf.

[41] *See* SECRETARIAT OF THE BASEL COMMITTEE ON BANKING SUPERVISION, THE NEW BASEL CAPITAL ACCORD: AN EXPLANATORY NOTE (2001), available, along with the other published papers of the Basel Committee, at http:/www.bis.org. The announced objective is to finalize the New Basel Accord in the fourth quarter of 2003 and achieve implementation by local supervisory and regulatory agencies by year-end 2006. *See* Press Release, Bank for International Settlements, *Basel Committee Reaches Agreement on New Capital Accord Issues* (July 10, 2002), at 3, *available at* www.bis.org/press/p020710.htm (noting that some of the more than 100 countries that have implemented the Basel Accord have done so only fairly recently and may not implement the new framework until after 2006).

[42] BASEL COMMITTEE ON BANKING SUPERVISION, THE NEW BASEL CAPITAL ACCORD (2001), *available at* http://www.bis.org/publ/bcbsca03.pdf, sets forth a consultative draft of the New Basel Accord.

[43] The simplifications and generalizations in this description are many. It does not, for example, take into account the fact that applicable capital requirements are often calculated on a consolidated basis within a banking group, or the fact that short-term assets may be excluded. The description also does not address the ways in which the capital requirements may be satisfied, with capital treated in different tiers.

[44] Under the Basel Accord as it has been modified, some banks with significant trading activities must also measure and hold capital for exposure to market risk. This is an additional cushion to absorb risks associated with changes in the market value of an item resulting from broad market movements in interest rates, equity prices, foreign exchange rates and commodity prices (referred to as general market risk) as well as changes in market value of individual items in a trading portfolio due to factors other than broad market movements. Banks may be permitted to measure these risks using their own internal risk measurement models for calculating value at risk (VAR). *See, e.g., Risk Based Capital, Specific Risk*, OCC Bulletin 99–19 (Apr. 20, 1999).

[45] Some jurisdictions have reduced to 20% the risk weighting for claims on, or guaranteed by, qualifying securities firms. U.S. agencies that supervise banks and savings and loan institutions—the Board of Governors of the Federal Reserve System, the FDIC, the OCC and the OTS—adopted this reduction in a rule

capital charge of 8% for exposure on OTC derivatives, regardless of that counterparty's credit standing as reflected, say, in its credit ratings. The risk weighting for the same claim on a bank incorporated in a country that is a full member of the OECD would be only 20%, regardless of that counterparty's credit ratings, which translates to a capital charge of 1.6% (one-fifth of 8%), provided the OECD member country in which the bank is organized has not rescheduled its external sovereign debt in the preceding five years.[46]. A zero risk weighting and, therefore a zero capital charge, applies to cash and to claims on central governments and central banks, if they are denominated in national currency and funded in that currency, again, without regard to the country's debt ratings if the sovereign is a full member of the OECD and has not rescheduled its external debt in the preceding five years.[47]

This framework has affected the derivatives market and documentation practices in many ways. For example, bank use of credit risk mitigants, including collateral and credit derivatives, and their selection of types of collateral and counterparties for credit derivatives, may be motivated by the wish to obtain what is often referred to as regulatory capital relief in respect of the credit risk represented by outstanding derivatives and other positions. Stated, again, in simple terms, this means that, if local regulatory or supervisory authorities recognize the risk mitigant as effective, instead of calculating the amount of capital a bank must maintain in respect of derivatives positions by reference to the risk-weighting applicable to the counterparty, the bank may be able to perform the calculation by reference to the risk-weighting applicable to the entity obligated on the credit risk mitigant.

In these cases, those involved in the documentation must be sensitive to the ways in which regulatory capital requirements may have to be reflected in the terms of the documents under which the collateral is posted and the terms of other credit risk mitigants, such as credit derivatives, for capital relief to be available. In addition, as discussed in Chapter 7, in master agreements the practitioner must take into account the fact that banks subject to the Basel Accord will usually want to be sure that the agreement includes

---

that became effective July 1, 2002 (or, on a voluntary basis, earlier), treating as qualifying securities firms, (1) those incorporated in the United States, if the firms are registered with the SEC as broker-dealers and are in compliance with the SEC's net capital regulation, and (2) those incorporated in other member countries of the OECD, if the firms are demonstrably subject to supervisory and regulatory arrangements, including risk-based capital standards, comparable to those imposed on depository institutions under the Basel Accord. The capital requirements applicable to the institutions subject to supervision by these agencies are set out in the Capital Adequacy Guidelines for Bank Holding Companies: Risk-Based Measures, Regulation Y, 12 C.F.R. § 225, Appendix A, § 3(B); Capital Adequacy Guidelines for State Member Banks: Risk-Based Measure), 12 C.F.R. Appendix A to Part 208; Statement of Policy on Risk-Based Capital (for institutions supervised by the FDIC, including national banks), 12 C.F.R. § 325, Appendix A to Part 325; and Risk-based capital credit-risk weight categories (for thrifts subject to supervision by the OTS), 12 C.F.R. Part 567, § 567.6. The Final Rule, Risk-Based Capital Requirements on Securities Firms, as adopted by the four agencies, was published with a joint press release at www.federalreserve.gov/boarddocs/press/ boardacts/2002/20020409.

[46]*See* BASEL COMMITTEE ON BANKING SUPERVISION, AMENDMENT TO THE CAPITAL ACCORD OF JULY 1998 (Basel Committee Publication No. 12 (July 1994)).

[47]As indicated above, the actual capital requirements applicable to any particular bank, or to a banking group under a holding company umbrella, would be determined pursuant to applicable local law and regulation implementing the Basel Accord.

close-out netting and, sometimes other netting, arrangements that will enable them to calculate the capital they must maintain in respect of credit risk on their derivatives positions with a counterparty on a net basis.[48]

These challenges will continue under the proposed New Basel Accord, although it is designed to provide many banks with greater flexibility in the ways in which they measure the capital they must maintain to satisfy regulatory requirements in light of the risk mitigation techniques they use, giving far more regulatory recognition to the differing risk profiles of banks and rewarding more powerful and accurate risk measurement.[49] The following, excerpted from a Basel Committee comparison of the proposed New Basel Accord with the Basel Accord, summarizes the first of what are referred to as the three pillars of the new framework, introducing much of the related terminology[50]:

> The new Accord consists of three mutually reinforcing pillars, which together should contribute to safety and soundness in the financial system. ...
>
> The first pillar sets out minimum capital requirements. . . . It maintains . . . *the minimum capital requirement of 8% of capital to risk-weighted assets*. . . .
>
> The new framework proposes for the first time a measure for *operational risk*, while the *market risk* measure remains unchanged.
>
> For the measurement of credit risk, two principal options are being proposed. The first is the *standardised approach*, and the second the *internal rating based (IRB) approach*. . . . The use of IRB approach will be subject to approval by the supervisor, based on the standards established by the Committee. . . .
>
> The standardised approach is conceptually the same as the present Accord, but is more risk sensitive. . . . Under the new Accord, the risk weights are to be refined by reference to a rating provided by an external credit assessment institution (such as a rating agency) that meets strict standards. For example, for corporate lending, the existing Accord provides only one risk weight category of 100% but the new Accord will provide four categories (20%, 50%, 100% and 150%). . . .

---

[48] *See infra* p. 272.

[49] "The Basel Accord provided essentially only one option for measuring the appropriate capital of internationally active banks. . . . The new framework provides a spectrum of approaches from simple to advanced methodologies for the measurement of both credit risk and operational risk in determining capital levels. It provides a flexible structure in which banks, subject to supervisory review, will adopt approaches which best fit their level of sophistication and their risk profile. The framework also deliberately builds in rewards for stronger and more accurate risk measurement." SECRETARIAT OF THE BASEL COMMITTEE ON BANKING SUPERVISION, *supra* note 41, at 2.

[50] The three pillars are intended to operate in a mutually reinforcing manner. The first pillar relates to the measurement of the minimum capital requirement, the second, to supervisory review of the measurements and the third, through broadened disclosure, among other things, to safe and sound capital practices through market discipline. *Id.*

Under the IRB approach, banks will be allowed to use their internal estimates of borrower creditworthiness to assess credit risk in their portfolios, subject to strict methodological and disclosure standards. . . . [through] estimates [of] each borrower's creditworthiness, and the results are translated into estimates of a potential future loss amount, which form the basis of minimum capital requirements. The framework allows for both a foundation method and more advanced methodologies for corporate, sovereign and bank exposures. In the foundation methodology, banks estimate the probability of default associated with each borrower, and the supervisors will supply the other inputs. In the advanced methodology, a bank with a sufficiently developed internal capital allocation process will be permitted to supply other necessary inputs as well. Under both the foundation and the advanced IRB approaches, the range of risk weights will be far more diverse than those in the standardized approach, resulting in greater risk sensitivity.[51]

For the documentation practitioner, these changes to the Basel Accord will, at a minimum, increase the need for attention to provisions relating to credit ratings included in the documentation for OTC derivatives. These provisions are already widely used in connection with contractual grounds for close-out and the specification of eligible collateral and eligible providers of other risk mitigants, such as credit derivatives and financial guaranty insurance. As the New Basel Accord is implemented, existing formulations tied to ratings are likely to be refined, and the use of ratings-based provisions can be expected to grow.[52] The New Basel Accord will probably also require more careful consideration of provisions—which have already begun to appear with more frequency—under which a bank reserves the right to look to its counterparty for indemnification, or to close out transactions, as a result of changes in the regulatory requirements. For many of the most active bank participants in the derivatives market, there will be greater possibilities that these changes may be attributable to weaknesses in the bank's own capital-related risk management and measurement procedures and policies, and not solely to changes in the regulatory allocation of a risk weight to the counterparty or its credit support provider or to increased capital costs owing to a decline in ratings for one of those entities. In provisions of this kind, practitioners will also have to consider the importance of distinctions between regulatory treatment of different kinds of risk involved in capital requirements—credit risk, market risk and operational risk.

DOCUMENTING RELATIONSHIPS AND RESPONSIBILITIES

OTC derivatives documents and standardized documentation tools have, particularly since the mid-1990s, increasingly included provisions in which the parties describe

---

[51] *Id.* 2–4.

[52] U.S. bank supervisory agencies already permit the use of credit ratings in the risk weighting of assets for regulatory capital purposes to a limited extent, for certain securitization positions that are traded. *See* Final Rule, Risk-Based Capital Adequacy Guidelines; Capital Maintenance: Capital Treatment of Recourse, Direct Credit Substitutes and Residual Interests in Asset Securitizations, January 1, 2002, adopted jointly by the Federal Reserve Board, the FDIC, the OCC and the OTS, changing their respective regulatory capital standards as set out in 12 CFR Parts 208 and 225 (Federal Reserve Board), Part 325 (FDIC), Part 3 (OCC) and Part 567 (OTS).

the nature of their dealing relationship and the roles in which they are acting, and in which each of them goes on to confirm that it is taking, and will continue to take, responsibility for understanding the related risks, without reliance on the other party. Chapters 4 and 5 discuss these provisions in the context of disputes in which parties to OTC derivatives and providers of credit support for derivatives transactions have claimed damages and other relief, or have denied having contractual obligations, on the basis of claims that their counterparties or related entities or the beneficiaries of the credit support engaged in fraud or breached or were negligent in performing fiduciary or other special duties.

These disputes have typically arisen in connection with substantial losses by end-users of derivatives and have often been followed by regulatory enforcement proceedings and shareholder actions brought against both parties involved in the disputes—the end-user and its counterparty—and their officers and directors. Chapter 5 also addresses the need to analyze these widely used features of derivatives documentation (representations and disclaimers, waivers of defenses and the like) in the context of the theories underlying these enforcement and shareholder actions.

Those involved with derivatives documentation need to understand which situations these provisions cover and which ones they do not or may not cover. For example, when the standard ISDA representations on the subject were published years ago, there was general acknowledgment that they were not intended to provide defenses against actual fraud but, rather, to define matters in respect of which there should not exist grounds for a claim of fraud against a party merely as a result of its not having explained to the other party matters that the other party should be responsible for analyzing and understanding, either by itself or with the assistance of its own advisers.

Over time, there have been fewer disputes in which claims of this kind have been made, in part because of the healthy exercise of including in the documents clear statements about the parties' expectations in this respect. On the other hand, the courts have continued to be presented with lawsuits in which a party has alleged fraudulent concealment or affirmative misrepresentation regarding matters argued to be both material and beyond the scope of the diligence that the market's standard representations and disclaimers relating to reliance were intended to address.

The more recent cases have often involved claims that transactions documented as derivatives were actually disguised loans or formed parts of structures that effectively operated as loans.[53] Those involved with documentation for complex derivatives or structures that include derivatives are well aware that the characterization of these transactions, and of the larger structures, often raises difficult questions.[54] Derivatives practitioners must, therefore, continue to be attentive to the technical complexities and the serious im-

---

[53]This was so, for example, in the *Mahonia* case discussed *infra* p. 989, which was filed after Enron's collapse, and in actions brought by Sumitomo Corporation against The Chase Manhattan Bank and two JP Morgan entities seeking to hold them responsible for massive losses incurred by Sumitomo as a result of unauthorized commodity trading by one of its employees. The Sumitomo actions have reportedly been settled. *See Sumitomo Settles $1.2B Derivatives Dispute With Two N.Y. Banks*, ANDREWS BANK & LENDER LIABILITY LITIG. REP., May 30, 2002, at 11.

[54]*See, e.g.,* 2 SECURITIES & DERIVATIVES REGULATION § 13.02[2][*ii*] on questions that may arise regarding the characterization of collars and options that are deep in the money (such as options to purchase stock at a price per share substantially below its market value at the time the option is written).

plications they may have for tax, accounting, disclosure and other purposes. It may not be fruitful, however, to draw broad conclusions for documentation or other purposes from the narrow facts of these cases as pleaded.

STANDARDIZATION OF TERMS FOR THE OVER-THE-COUNTER DERIVATIVES MARKET

At the beginning of the OTC derivatives market, each transaction was often negotiated and executed between two end-users, usually with the assistance of an investment bank advisor. The individually negotiated transactions were documented through freestanding agreements signed at the same time the trade was executed. This process was laborious and expensive. Financial institutions soon saw that a different business model could be adopted that would permit the OTC derivatives market to grow at a fast clip and present significant profit potentials. The institutions began to stand between the end-users—to intermediate the transactions—and, soon, to "warehouse" or take positions without seeking to put the other side of the transaction in place simultaneously. In these cases the intermediary's risk needed to be hedged, often imperfectly, in some other way, usually in the cash markets (*e.g.*, by going long or short a U.S. government security to hedge a fixed-floating U.S. dollar swap). Each derivatives transaction continued to be documented in an individual agreement.

The pace of the market picked up enormously, and it became common to agree to the transactions on the telephone and leave the documentation for later, often much later. The documentation backlog grew at the major institutions. The absence of an agreed vocabulary for the market led to a fairly high frequency of misunderstandings about the deal that had been struck. There were even cases in which two parties hung up the telephone thinking they had the deal they wanted, only to find out later that each of them thought it was on the same side of the trade. Numerous disputes of varying degrees of seriousness also arose as a result of the absence of a commonly understood set of assumptions about the aspects of the deals that were not expressly addressed by the traders.

These problems—the documentation backlog and the absence of industry terminology and standards—led to a trend toward standardization in the mid-1980s in various geographic and product segments of the market. It should be noted that this was not "standardization" in the sense of reducing the market to a limited number of products with the same terms. Rather, the objective was to create a standard terminology and set of assumptions to facilitate the market's ability to produce an ever increasing number of deals, each tailored to the parties' individual needs for customized solutions, together with standard forms that would provide a framework for negotiations between any two given parties.[55]

THE *SWAPS CODE*

The 1980s saw a series of group efforts to overcome the described obstacles to the growth of the OTC derivatives markets. In the U.S. swaps market, a great deal was accomplished with the first edition of the *Code of Standard Wording, Assumptions and Pro-*

---

[55]*See generally* Barry Taylor-Brill, *OTC Derivatives: The Contractual Architecture of Private Regulation, in* PLI 2000, at 93.

visions for SWAPS, known as the "*Swaps Code*," which was published by ISDA in the spring of 1985. It was basically a vocabulary or compendium of terms reflecting many of the mechanisms widely used by major market players at the time in their U.S. dollar interest rate swap agreements. The terms included rates used to compute swap payments and conventions for netting and rounding, for the treatment of payments scheduled to be made on holidays, and for measuring loss of bargain upon early termination of a swap. In effect the *Swaps Code* attached a label (in some cases a catch word, in others a section number) to each of those terms so that the parties to a swap could use the labels as a shorthand method of stating the terms of their agreement with respect to each transaction. A revised edition published in 1986 built on that start by adding new terms to the vocabulary and in some cases by revising the terms included before.

MASTER AGREEMENT FORMS AND DEFINITIONS BOOKLETS

By this time, market participants and their counsel had begun to understand the potential of the master agreement format for the OTC derivatives market. The first efforts in this direction that we are aware of involved masters for groups of very similar transactions—say, all the fixed-floating U.S. dollar interest rate swaps between the same two parties. This format allowed each new deal to be added to an existing agreement through a supplement setting out the variables for the transaction. A market participant then took the lead with a "master multi-rate" form that made it possible to trade deals of a great many different types under the same master agreement.

In 1987, ISDA published a master agreement form for U.S. dollar interest rate swaps, to be used with the *Swaps Code*. That code was not designed for swaps involving currencies other than U.S. dollars, so a similar lexicon was needed to facilitate communication regarding currency swaps and swaps involving non-U.S. dollar rates. This need was met by the *1987 ISDA Definitions*, published as a companion to ISDA's Interest Rate and Currency Exchange Agreement form, released in the same year. These tools created a basis for a common language for dealing with swaps involving 15 currencies.

Market participants proceeded to adapt the terms published in the *Swaps Code* and the *1987 ISDA Definitions* for use in connection with OTC derivatives other than rate swaps, such as caps, floors, collars, options on swaps and commodity price and equity index derivatives. As might be expected, the variety of practices that developed in this sort of adaptation presented substantial obstacles to the execution and documentation of these transactions. To overcome them for caps, floors and collars, in 1989 ISDA published addenda, known as the "Cap Addenda," to its two standard master forms for swap agreements to accommodate those transactions. Addenda to deal with "swaptions," known as the "Option Addenda," followed in 1990. The standard terminology and some of the other terms incorporated in those addenda became part of the *1991 ISDA Definitions*, which also modified some of the terms of the *1987 ISDA Definitions*, to reflect changes in market practice, and added defined terms and rate options to deal with swaps involving additional currencies.

Contributions to the development of standardized terms also came from other sources, and particularly the efforts of the British Bankers' Association, whose Interest Rate Swap Working Party and Forward Rate Agreement Working Party (in association with the Foreign Exchange and Currency Deposit Brokers' Association) produced recommended terms and conditions for short-term London interbank interest rate and currency swaps and FRAs in 1985, referred to as the "BBAIRS terms"[56] and the "FRABBA terms.[57] Their approach differed from that of the *Swaps Code* and its progeny, in that the ISDA approaches offer a "menu" of terms among which the parties may choose, whereas the BBA terms have consisted of specific sets of selected terms recommended for transactions in the London interbank market.

Also important at this early stage were efforts to improve market practices and documentation in the currency option and FX markets, including the publication by the British Bankers' Association, the Foreign Exchange Committee[58] and others in 1992 of the ICOM form for use in documenting currency option transactions and, in 1993, of the IFEMA form for use in documenting spot and forward foreign exchange transactions.[59] Also in 1993, the Energy Risk Management Association (ERMA)[60] published a form of master agreement for energy price swaps, caps, floors and collars.

Further steps towards standardization came with the publication of the two 1992 ISDA master agreement forms annotated in this book and the various booklets of definitions published to facilitate the documentation of various kinds of OTC derivatives under agreements prepared using those forms.[61] Newer versions of the ICOM and IFEMA forms have been published, and there is now a third standard agreement used for currency options, FX forwards and spot transactions—the 1997 International Foreign Exchange and Options Master Agreement (FEOMA) form, published by the Foreign Exchange Committee in association with the British Bankers' Association and others.[62] In addition, the

---

[56] The British Bankers' Association London Interbank Interest Rate Swaps Recommended Terms and Conditions (1985).

[57] The British Bankers' Association London Interbank Forward Rate Agreements Recommended Terms and Conditions (1985).

[58] The Foreign Exchange Committee is an independent body operating under the sponsorship of the Federal Reserve Bank of New York to provide a forum for discussing matters of mutual concern in the foreign exchange market. The members, which are institutions selected by the New York Fed, include U.S. and foreign commercial and investment banks as well as FX brokers. *See also infra* note 1321. Further information regarding the Committee and its activities is available at www.ny.frb.org/fxc.

[59] The history of these efforts, including the participation of the Financial Markets Lawyers Group, in the publication of the documents known in the market as the LICOM Terms (1985) and the ICOM Terms (1989), as well as the original ICOM and IFEMA forms, is spelled out in more detail at *ICOM Guide* 1.

[60] ERMA's founders were mostly commodity users, producers and trading companies. The ERMA master agreement form was intended for use mainly in transactions involving members and their affiliates. In the 1990s, other groups began to produce master agreement forms for energy, electricity and other commodity transactions. ISDA and others have been working to bring physical trades and cash-settled derivatives in those products within a single framework. One such project involves the creation of standardized terms that could be included as an additional part of a schedule to an ISDA-based master agreement. *See infra* note 2092.

[61] ISDA's *1991 ISDA Definitions* were revised and supplemented in 1998 and then followed by the *2000 ISDA Definitions*. Specialized booklets of definitions for various product categories have been published and updated from time to time. These booklets, and the types of transactions they cover, are listed in the table *infra* p. 374.

[62] The Canadian Foreign Exchange Committee and The Tokyo Foreign Exchange Market Practices Committee.

General Introduction 21

Banking Federation of the European Union, in cooperation with the European Savings Banks Group and the European Association of Cooperative Banks, has published the European Master Agreement (EMA) form, with General Terms that are used together with product-specific terms set out in Annexes.[63] Country-specific master terms or special provisions have also been produced, or are being produced, in many jurisdictions. In October 2001 ISDA published the modifications to its agreement forms illustrated in Part 3 of this book, together with a form of amendment to facilitate their adoption, and began to create new master agreement forms.[64]

COLLATERAL

As discussed in the Introduction to Part 5,[65] collateralization of OTC derivatives, or margining, was initially something of a rarity in the market but has taken on ever-increasing importance. In 1994, ISDA published its Credit Support Annex (Bilateral Form) for use with master agreements governed by New York law. This was followed in 1995 by ISDA's Credit Support Annex and Credit Support Deed for use in bilateral arrangements under English law.[66]

The severe market stresses of 1997 and 1998 led to an acceleration of the efforts of senior collateral practitioners to document the state of collateral management practice, to analyze the lessons learned during the period of increased market volatility and to take a leadership role in improving market practice in the area. Collateral Working Groups, which were first formed by ISDA in 1996, began to consider improvements and streamlining in the documentation and practices in the area. In 1998, ISDA published the *ISDA Collateral Guidelines*, which were the work of the Collateral Working Groups, outside counsel and the ISDA Board of Directors. These guidelines include information about structuring, implementing and maintaining a collateralized relationship that can be of great interest to lawyers and documentation specialists. Reflecting similar efforts relating

---

[63] *See infra* p. 1285.

[64] In addition to these various documents, ISDA, the Foreign Exchange Committee, EMTA and other organizations have published recommendations on best practices, as well as standardized terms for use in bringing terms documented under one agreement into another framework. Referred to as bridges, these provisions are discussed in the Introduction to Part 6, *infra* p. 1298. ISDA has also published standardized terms for novation arrangements, *see infra* p. 911, standardized sets of representations on various matters, *see infra* p. 179, and other documentation tools.

[65] *Infra* p. 1057.

[66] The *User's Guide to the ISDA Credit Support Documents under English Law*, published by ISDA in 1999, compares the two forms. The discussion of ISDA's forms of credit support annexes in Part 5, *infra* p. 1086, and the annotations to the sample documents in Part 5, *infra* p. 1141, compare the English and New York law forms of annex and compare those forms with ISDA's *Margin Provisions*, published in 2001. In 1995 ISDA also published a credit support annex for use with security interests in collateral denominated in Japanese yen under Japanese law. That document has been described as combining provisions for a Japanese law pledge and provisions that create loan collateral in way that is comparable to the English law title transfer of collateral. A *User's Guide to the 1995 ISDA Credit Support Annex (Security Interest - Japanese Law)* is also available from ISDA. The Association Française des Banques has published an annex for title-transfer arrangements under French law, for use with the AFB's form of master agreement for OTC derivatives. The English law Credit Support Deed, the Japanese law Credit Support Annex and the AFB form are not discussed in detail in this book. All of the ISDA standard credit support documents and terms are available to ISDA members at www.isda.org.

to practice in the FX segment of the market, in 1999 the Foreign Exchange Committee published the *FX Collateral Annex* for use with the 1997 versions of the FEOMA, IFEMA and ICOM forms for FX spot, forward and option transactions.

A further result of the increased attention to credit risk mitigation was the *ISDA 1999 Collateral Review,* which set forth 22 recommendations on various aspects of collateral arrangements. Of particular interest from a legal and documentation perspective are the recommendations included under the headings (1) Dispute Resolution, (2) Shortening the Collateral Cycle to Reduced Exposures, (3) Initial Margin, (4) Legal and Documentation Issues and (5) Cross-Product Netting and Collateralization. In 2001, ISDA published the *Margin Provisions*, the *2001 ISDA Credit Support Protocol* and the *2001 ISDA CSA Amendment Forms*, which are discussed in the Introduction to Part 5, as frameworks for implementing some of these recommendations.

The efforts of the ISDA Collateral Working Groups are ongoing. An updated version of the collateral guidelines, dealing with further developments, is at the project stage. Topics of particular interest to these groups are the relative merits of collateral under pledge and title-transfer arrangements, cross-product or enterprise-wide collateralization, netting, the valuation of collateral and of transactions, margin cushions, and forms of documentation, including additional standardized tools for defining collateral asset classes and for the reconciliation of the transactions between two parties that are subject to collateral arrangements. Among practitioners in Europe, another focus of continuing interest is the Directive of the European Parliament and of the Council on financial collateral arrangements, which was adopted in May 2002.[67] Various ISDA groups propose to monitor implementation of the Directive by EU member states, and practitioners will no doubt be called on to reflect the implementation in credit support documents used with OTC derivatives.

CROSS-PRODUCT RISK MANAGEMENT

In recent years, participants in various sectors of the financial product markets have become increasingly concerned about the risks associated with the common practice of documenting different products under separate agreements, including contracts based on widely used master agreement forms published by various industry associations. In particular, a group of 12 major, internationally active commercial and investment backs formed as the Counterparty Risk Management Policy Group (CRMPG) "with the objective of promoting enhanced strong practices in counterparty credit and market risk management after the market disruptions of 1997 and 1998."[68] In 1999 the CRMPG published a report that, among other things, focused on inconsistencies among standardized documents used in various segments of the financial markets and recommended changes to introduce greater harmony, so as to reduce what the CRMPG characterized as documentation basis risk.[69] In light of the heightened concern about the issues highlighted in the

---

[67]The EU Financial Collateral Directive of the European Parliament and the Council, 2002/47/EC, June 6, 2002, is available at http://europa.eu.int/eur-lex/en/dat/2002/l_168/l_16820020627en00430050.pdf. An Explanatory Memorandum presented by the Commission, March 27, 2001, is available at http://www.europa.eu.int/eur-lex/en/com/pdf/2001/en_501PC0168.pdf.

[68]*See* Letter dated December 15, 2000, of the Global Documentation Steering Committee, *available at* http://www.ny.frb.org/globaldoc/gd_docs.html.

[69]*See infra* note 2075.

CRMPG report, TBMA, in coordination with eight other organizations of market professionals whose members include frequent users of these various contract forms, published a standard form of Cross-Product Master Agreement (CPMA) in February 2000.

Part 6 of this book includes an annotated sample agreement prepared using that form of the CPMA, as well as a discussion of the issues raised by the use of multiple contracts and ways in which those issues are being addressed in the market, including various approaches to setoff and alternative forms of contract bridges published by ISDA to bring transactions documented under separate agreements, or the close-out settlement obligations created under those agreements, under a master agreement prepared using an ISDA form. TBMA has been broadening its efforts in this area through a project to develop another master netting agreement that would address not only agreements between two parties but also agreements between either of them or its affiliates with the other party or it affiliates. In January 2002 the Global Documentation Steering Committee, which is continuing the work begun by the CRMPG, recommended that market participants consider master netting agreements like the CPMA in the management of the risks created by their financial market dealings.[70]

THE CURRENT SITUATION

The process of developing standardized terms and terminology for the OTC derivatives market has been carried quite far and has greatly enhanced the ability of the market to expand. More business can be done more quickly if less time is needed to clarify basics. In addition, the standardization process has taught the market much—the need to define the method for setting a rate or for calculating an early termination payment has resulted in greater precision and better understanding of the problems involved. However, some of the new tools to define the standardized language are themselves quite complex and, as a result, the people who actually execute the trades have not adopted all the terminology as their own. Moreover, the jargon used in the market does not remain static, and the continuing development of new products leads to a continuing need to further the standardization process, where terminology is concerned.

Where credit issues are concerned, there are natural limits to standardization. Because market participants operate subject to their own institutional policies and differing regulatory frameworks, in many cases some of them cannot agree to terms that others believe should be "standard." In fact, the differences of opinion often affect the most sensitive aspects of the documentation, since they arise as a result of institutional and credit-related concerns. Standardization of derivatives documentation will, therefore, never be complete, and the success of the efforts to work with standard forms should not be measured in terms of the number of printed master agreements that are executed without change. Indeed, as indicated in this book, the very structure of the master agreement forms widely used in the derivatives markets recognize this reality by permitting the parties to vary the printed terms through completions and additions on items of a schedule to be attached to the master agreement.

---

[70] Letter dated January 10, 2002, *available at* http://www.ny.frb.org/globaldoc/gd_docs.html.

THE STRUCTURE OF THIS BOOK

In this fourth edition, we have retained annotated sample agreements and confirmations as the basic format of the book. The annotations explain how various provisions of the documents operate together and address the legal and business issues underlying the provisions. We have also included much new textual material. As suggested in the Preface, the reader will find much of the new material in Part 1, which deals in eight chapters with a number of the broad legal and documentation issues faced by participants in the OTC derivatives market. As in the past, the sample confirmations are preceded by product descriptions, which seek to describe a typical transaction and how and why it might be used. We have also made more extensive use of introductory notes, particularly to discuss documentation issues that are common to a number of different products and bring into focus how conventions differ from one set of product-specific standard terms to another.

To give an example of these organizational features of the book, and of how they might affect its use, a lawyer or documentation specialist called upon to work on an equity swap for the first time would benefit from turning first to the introductory note on credit, debt and equity derivatives.[71] That note explores the special shared concerns presented by the three categories of products. With that background, the reader would then turn to the product description for equity swaps[72] and then to the sample confirmation for an equity swap,[73] with its detailed annotations.

The following is an overview of the six Parts of this book.

PART 1

This part contains eight chapters, dealing with (1) power and authority to enter into derivatives transactions, and their authorization, (2) legal issues relating to the formation of derivatives contracts, including statutes of frauds and parol evidence rules, (3) commodities regulation and state gaming and bucket-shop laws, including cases in which it has been argued that a derivatives agreement should not be enforced because it violated laws of these kinds, (4) questions relating to derivatives transactions that arise under the securities laws, (5) counterparty relationships and duties, including duties of principals acting at arm's length, duties of advisers, brokers and dealers and duties of disclosure in sales of securities and their possible applications to derivatives transactions, (6) damages and close-out settlement, (7) bankruptcy and insolvency concerns, and (8) U.S. withholding tax issues for OTC derivatives.

PART 2

This Part deals in detail with various OTC derivatives products. The Introduction explains much of the basic terminology defined in the various booklets of definitions published by ISDA to facilitate the documentation of OTC derivatives. It includes comparisons between these sets of definitions and between the ISDA definitions, on one hand, and standard terms used in other market standard forms, on the other. The Introduction to

---

[71] *Infra* p. 605.

[72] *Infra* p. 717.

[73] *Infra* p. 736.

General Introduction 25

Part 2 also deals with the use of a confirmation or similar document within the structure of a master agreement of the kinds illustrated and discussed in Parts 3 and 4, as well as the use of confirmations before a master agreement is in place.

The Introduction to Part 2 is followed by coverage of interest rate products—an introductory note and then product descriptions and sample confirmations for rate swaps, rate caps and floors, rate collars and corridors, forward rate agreements ("FRAs"), and options on swaps ("swaptions"). That section is followed by successive, similar, treatments of foreign exchange products; commodities products; credit derivatives and other products linked to debt and equity; and weather derivatives. In each case, in addition to the introductory notes, there are specific product descriptions followed by one or more annotated sample confirmations.

PART 3

The Introduction to Part 3[74] discusses the reasons why, over the years, many regular participants in the market, and certainly most professional market participants, have adopted the master agreement approach as the basic framework for their derivatives transactions, moving away from documenting each individual transaction in a separate agreement. The Introduction to Part 3 also describes the principal differences between ISDA's Multicurrency—Cross Border form of master agreement published in 1992, which is annotated in Part 3, and ISDA's Local Currency—Single Jurisdiction form of the same year, which is annotated in Part 4. The Introduction also describes the principal differences between the 1992 ISDA master agreement forms and their predecessors published by ISDA in 1987.

Part 3 then illustrates the use of ISDA's Multicurrency—Cross Border form, which is designed to accommodate transactions in any currency, or more than one currency, between parties from the same or different jurisdictions. The annotations to the sample master agreement in Part 3 also discuss some of the differences between the ISDA Multicurrency—Cross Border form and other standard documents used in the markets for particular types of derivatives—principally the FEOMA, ICOM and IFEMA forms and the EMA form.

ISDA's 1992 forms of ISDA master agreement offer a framework in which the provisions applicable to all transactions between the parties from time to time appear in the printed terms of the master agreement, as they are completed and supplemented or modified in the schedule attached by the parties to the printed terms. The annotated sample master agreement in Part 3 includes a sample of such a schedule, as well as forms of some closing documents that might be used with an agreement of that kind. Since the sample schedule assumes that the obligations of one of the parties to the master agreement will be guaranteed, the schedule also includes a supplemental form of guaranty.

PART 4

Part 4 illustrates the use of ISDA's second form of master agreement, which is identified on its cover as the "Local Currency—Single Jurisdiction" form. This form is designed to accommodate transactions in local currency between parties from the same

---

[74] *Infra* p. 794.

jurisdiction. That form, with ISDA's form of U.S. Municipal Counterparty Schedule, is used in Part 4 to provide an example of the documentation for derivatives transactions with U.S. municipalities and other public-sector counterparties. In addition to describing some of the special problems that can arise in this segment of the market, this Part comments on the *1992 ISDA U.S. Municipal Counterparty Definitions.*

PART 5

Part 5 deals with credit support for derivatives transactions. The Introduction to Part 5 discusses the principal approaches to managing credit risk that have prevailed in the market, including some of the basic questions that the parties typically consider in the context of these approaches to credit risk management. The discussion relates these issues to standard credit support documents that are widely used in the OTC derivatives market. It also focuses on the main documentation issues raised by collateralization arrangements under the bilateral credit support arrangements and describes in general terms how some of the issues are dealt with in the Credit Support Annex (Bilateral Form) published by ISDA in 1994 for use with master agreements governed by New York law and the form of Credit Support Annex published in 1995 for use in bilateral arrangements under English law involving credit support through transfers of title (the "Title Transfer CSA"). The fifth and final sections of the Introduction to Part 5 discuss the *Margin Provisions* and the *2001 CSA Amendments.* The Introduction is followed by an annotated sample Credit Support Annex using the first of those ISDA forms and illustrates, again with annotations, the *2001 CSA Amendments.* Part 5 concludes with a further sample document, which illustrates how the parties can modify the same form used for bilateral collateral arrangements for use in arrangements under which only one party will provide support.

PART 6

As noted above, participants in various sectors of the financial product markets have become increasingly concerned about the risks associated with the practice of documenting different products under separate agreements, including separate master agreements on forms published by various industry associations. Part 6 of this book discusses the issues raised by the use of multiple contracts and various ways in which those issues are being addressed in the market. It includes an annotated sample agreement prepared using the standard form of Cross-Product Master Agreement (CPMA) published by TBMA, in coordination with other organizations of market professionals whose members include frequent users of these various contract forms, in February 2000.

BIBLIOGRAPHICAL NOTES

The chapters in Part 1 and the sample documents and their introductory material include references to specialized literature about derivatives products and about some of the business and regulatory issues that they raise. Many of the reading selections cited appear in anthologies and in the published materials prepared for seminars on swaps and other derivatives. To avoid needless repetition of the titles of these collections and of other frequently cited works, references to them are made in abbreviated form, and the abbreviations are explained in a Table of Abbreviations.[75]

---

[75]*Supra* p. viii.

General Introduction 27

For an overview of the terminology used in connection with rate swaps and related products, *see* Schuyler K. Henderson & Linda B. Klein, *Glossary of Terms Used in Connection with Rate Swap, Currency Swap, Cap and Collar Agreements*.[76] Brief descriptions of various kinds of derivatives transactions are included in *Dictionary of Risk Management*.[77] For legal and documentation issues, the materials produced in connection with the programs on derivatives put on annually, or sometimes more frequently, by the Practising Law Institute (PLI), are particularly helpful. A useful loose-leaf is DERIVATIVES RISK MANAGEMENT SERVICE. There are numerous specialized periodicals, many of which are cited in the footnotes in the introductory material and product descriptions in this book. Specialized materials can also often be found by consulting electronic bibliographies on derivatives topics.[78]

We refer in this book to New York and U.S. law. There are studies of legal issues under the laws of other jurisdictions, including *The Law of Financial Derivatives in Canada*[79] and, as to French law, *Les Swaps*.[80] As noted above, in many jurisdictions bankers' associations have produced guidance on special local concerns relating to derivatives as well as recommended provisions for adapting standard market documents for use locally or separate master agreements reflecting those concerns and practices in local markets.

---

[76]BUTTERWORTH'S J. INT'L BANK. & FIN. L., Supp. June 1987.

[77]*See also* John D. Finnerty, *Structuring Derivative Instruments to Adjust Risk Exposure: The Arithmetic of Financial Instruments* (PricewaterhouseCoopers, undated).

[78]*See generally* Robert T. Daigler, *Derivatives on the Internet, in* DERIVATIVES RISK MANAGEMENT SERVICE 1D. *See also* http://www.swaplaw.com; http://ourworld.compuserve.com/homepages/jweinstein.

[79]MARGARET E. GROTTENTHALER & PHILIP J. HENDERSON, THE LAW OF FINANCIAL DERIVATIVES IN CANADA (Carswell 1999 & Supps. through 2002–Release 1). *See also*, as to derivatives litigation in Australia, Canada, the U.K. and the U.S., the sources referred to *infra* note 505.

[80]PIERRE-ANTOINE BOULAT & PIERRE-YVES CHABERT, LES SWAPS (1992).

Part 1

Legal Issues in Derivatives Documentation

CONTENTS OF PART 1

1. Power and Authority to Enter into Derivatives Transactions 31
2. Statutes of Frauds and Parol Evidence Rules 39
3. Commodities, Gaming and Bucket-Shop Laws 63
4. Securities Laws 129
5. Counterparty Relationships and Duties 177
6. Damages and Close-Out Settlement 219
7. Bankruptcy and Insolvency Concerns 268
8. U.S. Withholding Tax Issues 350

CHAPTER 1

POWER AND AUTHORITY TO ENTER INTO DERIVATIVES TRANSACTIONS

The enforceability of any contract of a legal entity is, theoretically, subject to challenge under the *ultra vires* doctrine, which permits the avoidance of contracts not within the powers of the entity. At least in the United States, however, the doctrine is no longer deemed to apply as such to transactions of private-sector companies,[81] so its practical application is now limited to transactions with public-sector entities and certain other entities with limited powers, such as trusts. Related concerns have been highlighted by lawsuits over the enforceability of derivatives transactions. These suits have involved both public- and private-sector entities and allegations that transactions should be voided because they violated policies applicable to public funds or were entered into without the required internal corporate authorizations or governmental approvals.

Counsel for derivatives market participants have been concerned with possible *ultra vires* problems in transactions with public-sector entities since the beginning of the market. These concerns arose, in particular, because the novelty of the transactions made it hard to find them included in the basic grants of powers to municipalities and other public-sector entities. Any belief that counsel's fears were overstated was dispelled by the decision of the House of Lords in *Hazell v. Hammersmith & Fulham London Borough Council*,[82] where it was held that numerous derivatives transactions of the Borough were *ultra vires*, that is, outside its powers, and, therefore, void as contractual obligations. The

---

[81] *See* Richard A. Spehr, *"Lack of Authority" Claims in Derivatives Litigation*, in DERIVATIVES RISK MANAGEMENT SERVICE 2B-1; Richard A. Spehr, *California Federal District Court Rejects Orange County's "Ultra Vires" Claim Seeking to Void Reverse Repurchase Agreements*, in DERIVATIVES RISK MANAGEMENT SERVICE 2K-1 For a discussion of these issues as they relate to U.S. municipalities, *see* David H. Wysoki, *Municipal Swaps and Other Derivatives*, in 15TH ANNUAL INSTITUTE ON MUNICIPAL FINANCE: HOW TO COMPLY WITH INCREASING MARKET REGULATION, LITIGATION AND ENFORCEMENT (PLI Corp. L. & Practice Course Handbook Series No. B-974, 1997); Daniel L. Johnson, William M. Libit & Elizabeth D. Swanson, *Municipal Law Considerations for Municipal Interest Rate Swaps: A Growing Trend in the Municipal Marketplace*, in TAX-EXEMPT DERIVATIVES 154; Thomas A. McGavin, Jr., *Interest Rate Swaps in the Municipal Markets*, in PLI 1992, at 267. An example of statutory abrogation of the *ultra vires* doctrine under state law is Section 124 of the Delaware Code: "No act of a corporation and no conveyance or transfer of real or personal property to or by a corporation shall be invalid by reason of the fact that the corporation was without capacity or power to do such act or to make or receive such conveyance or transfer . . . ." The provision goes on to state the cases in which such lack of capacity or power may be asserted in an action for loss or damages. Many participants in the derivatives market are organized as Delaware corporations.

[82] [1990] 2 W.L.R. 17, [1992] Q.B. 697 (Div'l Ct. 1989), *aff'd in part and rev'd in part*, [1990] 2 W.L.R. 1039, [1992] Q.B. 697 (C.A. 1990), *reinstated*, 2 A.C. 1, [1991] All E.R. 545, [1991] 2 W.L.R. 372 (H.L. 1991). For a detailed description of the *Hammersmith and Fulham* case, *see* Gooch & Klein, *Review of Case Law I*, at 387, 403–412. *See also* Andrew J.C. Clark, *Derivatives Litigation in the United Kingdom*, in DERIVATIVES HANDBOOK 178; Stephen Revell & John Jakeways, *Swaps: The Hammersmith Ruling*, BUTTERWORTHS J. INT'L BANK. & FIN. L. 291 (June 1991).

court reasoned that English local authorities are statutory corporations whose powers are limited to those expressly given to them and those required to take other steps calculated to facilitate, or conducive or incidental to, the discharge of any of their functions. On the basis of this reasoning, the court found that the transactions in question did not fall within the Borough's enumerated or incidental powers.

Lawsuits brought in U.S. courts since the *Hammersmith & Fulham* case serve as further reminders that end-users with limited powers may seek to reverse their losses on transactions that have proved unfavorable by arguing that the transactions were beyond their powers or not duly authorized. By way of example, *State of West Virginia v. Morgan Stanley & Co.*[83] related, among other things, to trading in government securities and reverse repurchase agreements between West Virginia (the "State") and Morgan Stanley and the sale by the State to Morgan Stanley of a put option.[84] In connection with these transactions, the State was investing tax revenues, federal funds and various service fees, as part of a trading and investment program that the State's Investment Division pursued over several years. After early successes, the program led to losses in the hundreds of millions of dollars. The State sought damages on various theories, two of which can be seen as ways of seeking to hold its counterparty responsible for the State's having entered into transactions beyond its powers. The first theory was that there had been a violation of a provision of state law (the "State investment policy") requiring that any investment made by the State be made "with the exercise of that degree of judgment and care, under circumstances then prevailing, which men of experience, prudence, discretion and intelligence exercise in the management of their own affairs, not for speculation but for investment, considering the probable safety of their capital as well as the probable income to be derived."[85] The second was that there had been actual and constructive fraud and negligence and civil conspiracy by the counterparty with staff of the State to commit unlawful acts by entering into the transactions in violation of the State investment policy.[86] The trial court awarded summary judgment to the State, but West Virginia's highest court reversed the judgment. The case was subsequently settled.[87]

The lessons to be learned from *West Virginia*, *Hammersmith & Fulham* and the other cases involving the use of derivatives by public-sector entities[88] are largely the same: where a counterparty with limited power may seek the protection of the doctrine of

---

[83]*State v. Morgan Stanley*, 1995 W. Va. LEXIS 94, No. Civ. 89-C-3700 (June 5, 1995). For a detailed discussion of the case, *see* Gooch & Klein, *Review of Case Law II*, at 65–68.

[84]Other entities named as defendants in this case and other similar cases were Chase Securities, Inc., Citibank, N.A., County NatWest Government Securities, Inc., County NatWest, Inc., Goldman, Sachs & Co., Greenwich Capital Markets, Inc., Merrill Lynch & Co. and Salomon Brothers, Inc. *See* Leslie Wayne, *Morgan Stanley Will Pay West Virginia $20 Million*, N.Y. TIMES, Aug. 15, 1996, at D2.

[85]*Id.* at *13 (quoting from W. Va. Code § 12-6-12 (1978)).

[86]The other theories for recovery included alleged violations by Morgan Stanley of the antifraud provisions of the West Virginia securities laws and the federal Securities Act and breach of an alleged fiduciary duty owed by Morgan Stanley, as a securities dealer, to the plaintiff.

[87]*See* Wayne, *supra* note 84; *WV and Morgan Stanley Settle Suit over Fund's Losses in Derivatives*, DERIVATIVES LITIGATION REP., Aug. 26, 1996, at 11.

[88]On other such cases, including those involving Orange County, California, *see* Gooch & Klein, *Review of Case Law II*, at 112.

ultra vires or of a statute like the one at issue in *West Virginia*, or may seek to avoid liability under a contract by arguing it was not duly authorized, the provider of a derivatives transaction to such a counterparty can be at risk of losing the benefit it bargained for and, in effect, of being treated as an insurer of favorable results for the counterparty. It is, therefore, critical to identify such counterparties and to undertake appropriate legal diligence about their power and authority before entering into a transaction with them.

Other lawsuits brought in the U.S. courts since *Hammersmith & Fulham* illustrate that appropriate diligence on questions of power and authority can be critical with counterparties other than municipalities and sovereign states. Indeed, failure by a professional market participant to engage in such diligence may be cited in support of actions by counterparties to avoid contractual liability under various theories. For example, the failure to conduct due diligence may be alleged to support a theory that a market participant should have known that transactions were illegal for the other party or not properly authorized, because diligence would have disclosed it. Also, the counterparty may allege that a professional market participant breached a duty to the counterparty by failing to ensure that transactions between them were authorized, and that the market participant aided and abetted a breach of fiduciary duty owed to the counterparty by its own employee who participated in the transactions without authority.

These concerns are illustrated by two cases that were brought before a federal district court in New York,[89] involving substantial dealings in FX derivatives and swaps over prolonged periods between a U.S. dealer and two Chinese entities. When the customers failed to post required collateral, the transactions were closed out, leaving substantial obligations of the customers to the dealer. The defenses raised by the customers included allegations that the individual who executed the alleged contracts was not authorized to do so and that the transactions were illegal under Chinese law. Like the *West Virginia* case, these actions should impress upon professional participants in the OTC derivatives market that issues involving the power and authority of a counterparty to engage in a transaction may be used by the counterparty not only as a means of seeking to avoid its obligations, under the doctrine of *ultra vires*, expressed in one form or another, but also as a means of seeking to hold the provider of the transactions responsible for misconduct of an employee or representative of the counterparty in entering into allegedly unauthorized transactions. Whereas the traditional approach, under the *ultra vires* defense,

---

[89] *Lehman Bros. Commercial Corp. v. China Int'l United Petroleum & Chemicals Co.*, [1995–1996 Transfer Binder] FED. SEC. L. REP. (CCH) ¶ 99,000 (S.D.N.Y. 1995) and *Lehman Bros. Commercial Corp. v. Minmetals Int'l Non-Ferrous Metals Trading Co.*, [1995–1996 Transfer Binder] FED. SEC. L. REP. (CCH) ¶ 99,001 (S.D.N.Y. 1995). In *China International*, the court dismissed two of the customer's counterclaims for failure to state a cause of action, and the case has since reportedly been settled. *See* Sara Webb, *Lehman Settles Derivatives Feud with China Firm*, ASIAN WALL ST. J., Sept. 10, 1996, at 1, *available at* 1996 WL-WSJA 10222455. In *Minmetals*, motions for summary judgment have been granted in part and denied in part. *Lehman Bros. Commercial Corp. v. Minmetals Int'l Non-Ferrous Metals Trading Co.*, No. 94 Civ. 8301 (JFK), 2000 WL 1702039 (S.D.N.Y. 2000); *Lehman Bros. Commercial Corp. v. Minmetals Int'l Non-Ferrous Metals Trading Co.*, No. 94 Civ. 8301 (JFK), 2001 WL 1646101 (S.D.N.Y. Dec. 21, 2001). A third action involving a Chinese counterparty and similar claims of lack of authorization was settled earlier. *See Sinochem (USA) Inc. v. Lehman Bros.*, No. 96-CIV-0062 (S.D.N.Y. Jan. 4, 1996). In cases involving defenses based on lack of authority of the person involved in the trades, where actual authority does not exist, the party seeking relief is likely to argue that apparent authority existed and that its contract should, therefore, be enforced. *See infra* note 94.

involves a risk of loss of bargain for the professional market participant, the second approach, illustrated in the cases referred to above, also involves a risk of damage to the business reputation and franchise of the market participant.

In some cases there may be uncertainty with respect to authority or limitations on derivatives activities of regulated entities, such as insurance companies, mutual funds and pension funds.[90] Where U.S. banks are concerned, most questions about authority to participate in the OTC derivatives markets have been favorably resolved, at least at the federal level and by New York State banking authorities.[91]

Legal opinions, though often dispensed with in transactions between dealers, should be required in connection with agreements with sovereign states, municipal counterparties and others where there is reason to be concerned about power and authority. The annotations to the sample master agreement in Part 4 and the introduction to that part refer to the sorts of legal opinions and representations and warranties that may be required in connection with a master agreement with a municipal counterparty.[92] The matters that should be addressed in such an opinion and in such representations will, however, vary from case to case and depend both on the factual circumstances and on the applicable law.

The substance of the opinions relating to the power of the entity to enter into the transactions and to the steps required for due authorization should, therefore, be probed by counsel to ensure that the special concerns that arise in the area have been given informed attention. Even though it does not seem that the controversies discussed above could have been avoided through mere changes in the agreements used to document the voided or

---

[90] Some of these uncertainties are described in Donald R. Crawshaw, *Legal and Regulatory Issues for Institutional Investors and Money Managers Investing in Derivative Products*, a paper prepared for presentation at an Institute for International Research program held on September 25, 1992 on Regulation of Derivative Products and included in the materials collected under the same title for distribution at the seminar. Where investment companies are concerned, some of the principal issues relate to how swaps and other derivatives will be treated for purposes of rules and restrictions on (1) the issuance of senior securities that may expose a fund's shareholders to significant risk of loss (*see* § 18(f) of the Investment Company Act), (2) custodial arrangements for assets of a fund and the application of those restrictions to collateral that a fund might provide to secure OTC derivative obligations (*see* § 17(f) of the Investment Company Act), (3) daily calculation of a fund's assets for purposes of § 22(c) of the Investment Company Act, and (4) illiquid investments by open-end funds, as well as appropriate treatment of swaps and related derivatives in determining whether a fund is meeting its stated policies and, generally, on disclosing fund activities involving derivatives. *See* the General Policy Statement of the SEC, Securities Trading Practices of Registered Investment Companies, 17 SEC DOCKET 319 (May 2, 1979). On derivatives as authorized investments of insurance companies in the U.S., *see* the sources cited *supra* note 19.

[91] *See generally* Tortoriello, GUIDE TO BANK ACTIVITIES, Pt. II. Guarantees may pose special power and authority questions. For example, if a bank is asked to provide a guaranty or similar support, the parties should inquire into the bank's power to issues guaranties in the particular circumstances, and the bank itself should analyze whether the provision raises questions under regulations that may limit its ability to issue guaranties or that require the bank to receive security from the affiliate or other party whose obligations it guarantees. If the party asked to execute a provision that could operate as a guaranty is an investment company, limited partnership or other entity whose assets should, under fiduciary principles, be applied only for the benefit of its own equity investors or pursuant to obligations incurred for their benefit, both the entity agreeing to the provision and the counterparty seeking its protection should carefully examine the propriety of the provision.

[92] *Infra* p. 1005.

challenged transactions, greater attention to the issues of power and authority at the documentation stage, and insistent reference to these issues from different angles in the documentation, might have reduced the risks involved. As illustrated in the sample agreement in Part 3,[93] standard practice in documentation for swaps and related derivatives (sometimes relaxed for transactions between established dealers) has always required that each party to an agreement deliver to the other evidence of the steps taken by the party to authorize its execution and delivery of the agreement and any confirmations thereunder, together with incumbency and specimen signature certificates for the persons signing the documentation on its behalf.

Legal opinions of the kind generally obtained in connection with derivatives contracts go to the due authorization, execution and delivery, and enforceability, of documents. These opinions can also be helpful in identifying special public policy issues that may be raised by the parties' contract. They do not, however, and generally cannot, address the possibility that the particular factual circumstances surrounding the parties' dealings may give rise to claims under all parts of the law of a given jurisdiction, such as tort claims and claims based on the application of equitable principles or statutory expressions of public policy.

The legal opinion will, of course, relate to the laws of the jurisdiction of the lawyer rendering the opinion and thus will not necessarily cover the laws of all jurisdictions that may have an interest in the resolution of a dispute arising under the agreement. As suggested by the cases discussed above, issues of power and authority to contract and issues of governmental or similar approval, are generally governed, for each party, by the law of its home jurisdiction.[94] In cases involving a party acting from an office outside its home jurisdiction, some questions of this kind may be resolved through application of the law of the jurisdiction where the office is situated.[95] For that reason, it is often appropriate to obtain an opinion on these issues from local counsel in a party's jurisdiction of organization and, in some cases, a separate opinion from counsel in the jurisdiction from which the party is acting in connection with the derivatives transactions.

In some situations, even if the counterparty's counsel has given a favorable legal opinion on power and authority, and even if the counterparty itself has made appropriate representations, the opinion and representations may not preclude a decision that the transaction is void or that the counterparty may avoid its obligations, although the likelihood of a challenge undoubtedly is reduced when appropriate diligence is done and documented on these critical issues. Indeed, a discussion of these concerns and of the contents of the legal opinion should be among the first things to happen in connection with derivatives transactions with a public-sector entity, because it may not be prudent to

---

[93] *Infra* p. 916.

[94] However, *Indosuez Int'l Finance B.V. v. National Reserve Bank*, 2002 N.Y. LEXIS 1097 (N.Y. 2002), held that New York law is applicable to apparent authority and ratification questions, in a case involving 14 confirmations of NDF transactions, ten of which included a choice of New York law while the others included a choice of English law, where NRB argued that whether or not the transactions were properly authorized should be determined under principles of Russian agency law.

[95] This statement, of course, assumes a party that is a legal entity rather than a natural person acting as principal. The issue of capacity to contract, for a natural person, is generally decided under the law of the jurisdiction where that person is domiciled.

enter into such transactions if counsel cannot furnish adequate assurance of the power and authority of the public-sector end-user to enter into transactions of the kind.

The issues of power and authority for some governments and public-sector entities have become simpler to analyze, if not totally resolved, as legislatures and other governmental bodies have taken actions to address swaps and similar transactions directly, particularly in the wake of the *Hammersmith and Fulham* judgment.[96] Where this has not yet happened, troublesome doubt may remain, because state, national and local governments and statutory corporations may have powers limited by the terms of their constitutions, enabling statutes, charters and the like, and swaps and other derivatives rarely fall neatly into the constitutional, statutory or other categories of stated powers and permitted or prohibited, or limited, activities. In many instances, public-sector entities also have the power to take such actions and enter into such contracts as may be necessary or incidental to the exercise of a power expressly granted to them, so long as the action or contract does not involve a power expressly prohibited. When a public-sector market participant relies on such incidental powers, at a minimum its counsel should be asked to opine that the relevant transaction is not expressly prohibited and does not fall within a limitation that the terms of the transaction may surpass,[97] and appropriate findings or determinations by the

---

[96]For example, some of U.S. states have adopted statutes expressly authorizing certain kinds of swap transactions, or swap transactions in connection with certain kinds of debt issuances, for their state and local governments or for specific public authorities (such as a metropolitan airport authority or state housing authority), as well as related credit support arrangements, generally provided that an appropriate governmental body makes certain required prior determinations and, in some cases provided that prior notice is given to a governmental authority or the public in the relevant municipality. In California, for example, swaps are authorized for any "State or local government" (defined to mean any "department, agency, board, commission, or authority of the state, or any city, city and county, county, public district, public corporation or other public entity"), "[i]n connection with, or incidental to, the issuance or carrying of bonds, or acquisition or carrying of any investment or program of investment," where the state or local government determines the transaction "to be necessary or appropriate to place the obligation or investment . . . on the interest rate, currency, cash-flow, or other basis desired by the state or local government," but only "after giving due consideration for the creditworthiness of the counterparties," and, in the case of a local government, only if its governing body

> first determines that the contract or arrangement or program of contracts is designed to reduce the amount or duration of payment, currency, rate, spread, or similar risk or result in a lower cost of borrowing when used in combination with the issuance of bonds or enhance the relationship between risk and return with respect to the investment or program of investment in connection with, or incident to, the contract or arrangement which is to be entered into.

Cal. Gov't Code. §§ 5921–22 (1995). On reported use of this authority, *see infra* note 1778. For other examples of state legislation on derivatives, *see* Johnson, *supra* note 81, at 159. *See also* Michael McDonald, *New York City Wants to Swap, and Big Savings Could Result*, THE BOND BUYER, June 7, 2002, p. 1 (discussing New York City's efforts to obtain expanded powers). ISDA has developed a Model Statute Authorizing Governmental Entities To Enter into Swap Transactions. *See* Lynn Stevens Hume, *Swap Dealers Group's Model Legislation Would Give Issuers Authority for Swaps*, BOND BUYER, Oct. 23, 1991, at 1.

On the situation in: Australia, *see* M. Pearce, *Hammersmith and Fulham, The consequences for Australian statutory corporations*, 6 AUSTRALIAN BANK. L. BULL. 61 (1991); Canada generally, *see* GROTTENTHALER, *supra* note 79; Quebec, *see* M.B. Barbeau, *Quebec clarifies public sector swap powers*, 11 INT'L FIN. L. REV. 10 (July 1992); France, *see* François Poudelet, *France Gets to Grips with Local Authority Swaps*, 11 INT'L FIN. L. REV. 25 (Dec. 1992) and *see* Boulat, *supra* note 80.

[97]For example, in many jurisdictions there may be a constitutional or statutory limitation on long-term obligations; however, there is often an exception for obligations payable only out of special funds or

governing body should be made and furnished to the provider of the derivatives transaction, to indicate that it was entered into incidental to, or to aid in the discharge of, an express power of the public-sector entity, and pursuant to all steps required to authorize actions taken pursuant to the express power or function.

Insofar as *ultra vires* doctrines and statutes with similar effect in the United States are concerned, only legislative change can bring the needed certainty to the market, particularly given the principle, often referred to as Dillon's rule, that the powers of a municipality should be narrowly construed.[98] If entities charged with a public trust are to be able to avail themselves of derivatives to manage their assets and liabilities, the rules on their power and authority to do so should be clear, so that their potential counterparties, acting as principals, and pricing transactions on the assumption that they are incurring only the risks that principals normally do, are not unexpectedly charged with the losses incurred by their public-sector counterparties as a result of the failed derivatives strategies pursued by them. It seems logical that the public sector should be held accountable for assessment and management of the risks that it undertakes, either through internal resources or through advisers paid to act as such. Financial markets do not operate efficiently when pricing does not accurately reflect risk.

If it is not clear that the power and authorization issues can be favorably disposed of, the potential provider of a derivative to a public-sector end-user should explore what the consequences could be if the transaction proves to be *ultra vires* for the end-user or is not properly authorized. The following are some of the questions that should be considered.

- Would the law entitle the end-user to deny its liability with respect to the transaction at any time?

- If so, what relief, if any, might the counterparty obtain—only recovery of payments made by it? Not even that, with any certainty?

- Under the applicable law, could the end-user be estopped from denying its liability in respect of an *ultra vires* or improperly authorized transaction in some circumstances? If so, what are they, and do they exist in connection with the proposed transaction?

- In each of these areas, is there a difference between transactions that are *ultra vires* and those that suffer from some irregularity in the authorization process?

---

revenue sources. Medium and long-term derivatives have often been entered into in reliance on this kind of exception as well as appropriate determinations relating to power to enter into the arrangements. Another commonly found limitation is a statutory or constitutional requirement that certain kinds of contracts be entered into by public-sector entities only pursuant to public bidding. As a result, in some instances public-sector entities have conducted auctions in which potential swap providers bid for all or a part of a hedging program; in others counsel has concluded that the limitations do not apply. *See* Ted Hampton, *Can the Municipal Market Handle Bidding for Swaps? Some Have Their Doubts*, BOND BUYER, Oct. 22, 1991, at 4A.

[98]*See* Johnson, *supra* note 81, at 158–59, setting out Dillon's rule (named for the author of a classic treatise on municipal corporations) and discussing its greater and lesser vitality in various U.S. states.

If satisfactory answers to all these and related questions cannot be obtained, the end-user should be asked to seek a change in the law relating to its powers or to correct any lapse in the authorization process before the transaction is consummated. If this is not possible, or if the end-user is unwilling to attempt it, then the market professional should carefully weigh the wisdom of entering into the transaction in light of the answers it has obtained about the consequences of entering into an *ultra vires* or improperly authorized transaction with that end-user.

CHAPTER 2

STATUTES OF FRAUDS AND PAROL EVIDENCE RULES

Introduction 39
Statute of Frauds Concerns 42
      New York Law..43
      U.S. Law on Agreements with Certain Depository Institutions 51
      Relief When a Statute of Frauds Is Not Satisfied..55
Parol Evidence Rules 56
      The NYUCC and Common Law Rules..56
      Application to Derivatives Disputes 56
      Confirmation Practices in Light of the Cases..59

INTRODUCTION

Most OTC derivatives transactions are agreed to over the telephone and later confirmed in writing, though there is continued progress in the market toward the introduction of various forms of electronic trading and toward automation of the confirmation process.[99] The nature of the market is such that it can operate only if the parties are irrevocably bound from the moment they reach agreement, regardless of how they do so. The market depends on intermediaries, the "dealers," to operate, and the intermediaries make their profit through spreads between the payments they make and receive on any given transaction, on one hand, and those they make or receive on the hedge for that transaction, on the other. In the early days of the swaps market, the hedge was often a match, or mirror image, of the transaction that was being hedged. In today's developed derivatives market, each dealer manages a complex "book" or portfolio of transactions and hedges. Today, as in the past, the hedge must go on the dealer's books substantially simultaneously with the transaction that is being hedged, as part of the institution's overall risk management. Otherwise, movements in the rates and prices involved in the transaction may make it impossible for the dealer to hedge it at a profit.

Market participants for swaps and related derivatives have always been aware of the dangers posed by conducting their business on the basis of agreements initially made orally and memorialized only afterwards.[100] The most obvious concerns include (1) the possibility of a real[101] or feigned misunderstanding on whether an agreement had been

---

    [99]*See* ISDA 2002 OPERATIONS SURVEY 13, 24–31. Similar surveys are available for 2000 and 2001 at http://www.isda.org/publications/index.html. These surveys also contain detailed information on such matters as error rates, the confirmation process and payment failures.

    [100]For a more extensive discussion of this subject, and particularly the case law in the area, *see* Gooch & Klein, *Review of Case Law I*, at 389–403 and Gooch & Klein, *Review of Case Law II*, at 59–63.

    [101]Dealers responding to the ISDA 2002 OPERATIONS SURVEY reported that 14% of their plain-vanilla rate and currency swaps have to be rebooked, "as a result of an error or a change in trade details." *Id.* at 13–14.

reached or, if reached, as to the precise terms of the transaction[102] and (2) the absence of a detailed agreement at the outset as to what would constitute a default on the transaction and what the parties' rights and remedies would be in case of default. Their legal advisers have also been concerned that the oral agreement might not be legally enforceable until it had been reduced to writing, under provisions known as "statutes of frauds." These concerns are discussed in the first section of this chapter.

A separate, but related, series of legal concerns may arise even after documentation for a transaction has been executed, if a party alleges that the documentation incorrectly reflects the parties' agreement on the transaction and seeks to introduce extrinsic, or "parol," evidence to prove its point. These concerns, as they relate to New York law and its application to OTC derivatives, are discussed in the second section of this chapter.

As a result of market concerns relating to unwritten contracts and parol evidence, there is a premium on speedy documentation of transactions after their terms have been agreed to orally and on ensuring that all the critical terms are correctly reflected in the documentation.[103] During the early years of the market, the parties usually documented their understanding with respect to each transaction in a separate contract. To avoid the waste involved in this practice, the master agreement came to be the general vehicle for documenting swaps (and, later, other OTC derivatives) between parties that expected to enter into more than one transaction with each other.[104] Once the master framework is in place to govern the overall relationship between the parties with respect to the kinds of transactions that are covered, the parties bring each new transaction under the master agreement through the mechanism agreed to in that agreement.

---

[102] Market participants have correctly expected that, if detected early, misunderstandings over the terms of the oral agreement can usually be resolved through amicable negotiations. They have also realized that litigation might occasionally be required to resolve a dispute over the terms agreed to, or a dispute as to whether agreement had ever been reached, particularly if the misunderstanding was discovered only after a significant movement of rates or prices in favor of one of the parties. One of the earliest lawsuits concerning swaps in fact involved a situation in which a party sought to treat two swaps as not having been agreed to because the full agreement contemplated by the parties had not been signed by the time the transactions became disadvantageous to that party because of movements in interest rates. For a detailed description of this action, *Homestead Sav. v. Life Sav. & Loan Ass'n*, see Gooch & Klein, *Review of Case Law I*, at 392–98.

[103] *See, e.g.*, OCC, Supplemental Guidance 99-2 (1999), *available at* http://www.occ.teas.gov/ftp/bulletin/99-2.txt: "Banks need to redouble efforts to clean up unconfirmed trades and unsigned master agreements." In various jurisdictions, regulatory authorities or industry groups have adopted guidelines for confirming OTC derivatives and other financial products. *See, e.g.*, *FSA London Code of Conduct*, para. 78 ("Oral agreements are considered binding" (at 23)) and paras. 88–99 (at 25–27), which reflect the FSA's belief that "all participants in the wholesale markets should have, or be aiming to have, in place the capability to dispatch confirmations so that they are received and can be checked within a few hours of when the deal was struck" (para. 91) at least when the product is not very complex, and the recommendation that "the issuer of the confirmation has in place procedures for chasing a response if one is not forthcoming within a few hours of the confirmation being sent" (para. 92). Similarly, the principle that the parties are bound from the time they reach agreement and best practices regarding the prompt sending of confirmations are set out in §§ 6.1 and 6.2 (at 9) of the *Principles and Practices* produced jointly by representatives of EMTA, the Foreign Exchange Committee, ISDA, The New York Clearing House Association, the PSA (now TBMA) and the SIA through coordination by the Federal Reserve Bank of New York.

[104] *See infra* p. 794 on other reasons why the master agreement has become the standard vehicle for documenting OTC derivatives. The 65 dealers responding to the ISDA 2002 OPERATIONS SURVEY reported that they have master agreements in place with over 92% of their OTC derivatives customers. *Id.* at 4.

Statutes of Frauds 41

This mechanism generally consists of a confirmation which, under the standard master agreement forms widely used in the market, is to be sent by telex, facsimile transmission, hand or mail delivery or electronic messaging promptly after the deal is struck and will form an integral part of and supplement to the master agreement.[105] If the master agreement is not in place when the parties enter into their first transaction, or if the parties intend to use a stand-alone agreement for their transaction and it has not been finalized, they will usually rely at first on a confirmation of the financial terms of their transaction, often adding reference to a few additional terms thought to be particularly important and expressing their intention to enter into a fuller agreement promptly but, in the meantime, to treat the confirmation as a binding contract. In transactions confirmed using ISDA standards, if the parties have not yet executed a master agreement but intend to do so, there is a widespread practice of their agreeing in the confirmation that, until they execute such an agreement, the parties will treat the confirmation as forming part of, and being subject to, a master agreement incorporating the terms of one of the ISDA master agreement forms.[106] Under the usual formulation on this subject, as published by ISDA, the parties also agree that all their other confirmations of transactions entered into before they execute a master agreement will form part of the same deemed master agreement, so long as the confirmations refer to the same ISDA form.[107]

The ISDA master agreement forms include an "integration" clause, through which the parties acknowledge that their master agreement (which is defined to include confirmations) "constitutes the entire agreement and understanding of the parties with respect to its subject matter and supersedes all oral communications and prior writings with respect thereto."[108] Practice in the foreign currency market as reflected in the FEOMA, ICOM and IFEMA forms for spot and forward foreign exchange agreements

---

[105]This is, for example, the rule under Section 9(e)(ii) of ISDA's 1992 Multicurrency—Cross Border form of master agreement, *infra* p. 872, and Section 8(e)(ii) of the Local Currency—Single Jurisdiction form, *infra* p. 1029.

[106]ISDA's standard formulations on this subject are included in footnotes to the forms of introductory language for confirmations published in exhibits to some booklets of ISDA definitions. For an example, see the Introduction to Part 2, *infra* p. 378, which discusses the formulation included in Exhibit I to the *2000 ISDA Definitions*. *See also infra* p. 1077, on concerns related to having required credit support in place at the time a transaction is entered into by the parties. In many jurisdictions, guaranties and grants of security interests (at least with respect to certain kinds of collateral) must be expressed in writing and, in some cases, sealed writings, subject to specialized statutes of frauds.

[107]If an applicable statute of frauds has been satisfied by the confirmation, the mere reference in the confirmation to the parties' intent to enter into a fuller agreement at a later date should not affect recognition of the confirmation as a binding contract as to the terms set forth in the confirmation, so long as the confirmation expresses the essential terms of the transaction. *See Conopco, Inc. v. Wathne Ltd.*, 593 N.Y.S.2d 787 (App. Div. 1993) (disregarding a deposition on a party's subjective intent that a letter agreement not be a binding agreement); and *Four Seasons Hotel Ltd. v. Vinnik*, 515 N.Y.S.2d 1, 6 (App. Div. 1987) ("A contract does not necessarily lack all effect merely because it expresses the idea that something is left to future agreement"). On the weight given to the parties' express statement of their intent as to whether a preliminary agreement is binding, *see Universal Co. Ltd. v. St. Paul Fire & Marine Ins. Co.*, 1999 WL 771357 (S.D.N.Y. 1999).

[108]In the 1992 master agreement forms, the text appears in Section 9(a) of the Multicurrency—Cross-Border form, as illustrated *infra* p. 870, and in Section 8(a) of the Local Currency—Single Jurisdiction form, as illustrated *infra* p. 1028. The rule that the agreement consists of the master agreement terms together with all confirmations is set forth in Section 1(c) of each of these forms. *See infra* pp. 799 & 1014.

and currency options, is different. Those forms provide that recordings of telephonic conversations between the parties may be submitted in evidence for the purpose of establishing any matters pertinent to the parties' agreement,[109] and this rule does not distinguish between the periods before and after a confirmation has memorialized the terms of a transaction. The discussion below refers to cases in which the courts have looked at these practices in determining whether a party should be permitted to look beyond an executed confirmation as evidence of a contract's terms.

STATUTE OF FRAUDS CONCERNS

Statutes of frauds generally provide that certain kinds of agreements will be unenforceable unless they are in writing and signed or subscribed by the party to be charged. Most jurisdictions have statutes of frauds applicable to at least some kinds of agreements (such as the sale of land), but the requirements of the statutes and the kinds of contracts to which they apply can differ widely from jurisdiction to jurisdiction. As suggested by the name,[110] the statutes are intended to protect against fraudulent claims based on alleged oral contracts supported by perjured testimony.[111] Although in the extreme case the statute may be satisfied only by a contract or deed executed under seal, in many cases far less than a full-blown contract is required.

These statutes have caused concern for parties to oral agreements within their purview. The principal concern relates to a party's inability to enforce its oral contract if the counterparty defaults or seeks to repudiate the contract before signing or subscribing a writing that will satisfy the applicable statute. These causes for concern have been removed by statute in New York for derivatives with many, but not all, counterparties. The amendments to the New York statutes did not, however, eliminate all concerns over statutes of frauds relating to derivatives governed by New York law and, as discussed below, the parties to derivatives may wish to tailor their documentation practices to ensure that they will be able to enjoy the benefits of the revised statutes.

There are several New York statutes of frauds rules that might theoretically be applicable to an OTC derivatives transaction, and another might be applicable under U.S. law to claims against the Federal Deposit Insurance Corporation (FDIC) as receiver or conservator for certain failed U.S. depository institutions.

---

[109] The rule is set out in Section 11.3 of the FEOMA form, Section 8.3 of the ICOM form and Section 11.3 of the IFEMA form.

[110] Rules with the effects of a statute of frauds are not necessarily expressly identified as such. For example, the FDIA includes certain writing and authorization requirements that must be satisfied to permit enforcement of a claim against the Federal Deposit Insurance Corporation when it is acting, *e.g.*, as receiver for a failed depository institution. These requirements and a "safe harbor" clarifying how they may be deemed satisfied in connection with swaps and other "qualified financial contracts" are discussed *infra* p. 51.

[111] As described by the New York Court of Appeals, quoting from *Williston on Contracts*, statutes of frauds were intended to guard against the peril of perjury and not "enacted to afford persons a means of evading just obligations" based on contracts 'fairly, and admittedly, made." *Morris Cohon & Co. v. Russell*, 23 N.Y.S.2d 569 (N.Y. 1969).

NEW YORK LAW

The Generally Applicable New York Statutes of Frauds. The New York statutes of frauds potentially applicable to OTC derivatives transactions are found in Sections 1–206 and 2–201 of the Uniform Commercial Code as in effect in the State of New York (the "NYUCC") and Section 5–701 of New York's General Obligations Law (the "NYGOL"). Whether or not these provisions would apply to a transaction depends on the particular circumstances of the case.[112]

Section 1–206 of the NYUCC applies to contracts for the sale of personal property, other than contracts for the sale of goods or securities, and it generally limits recovery under such contracts to $5,000 unless there is "some writing" that "indicates that a contract for sale has been made between the parties at a defined or stated price, reasonably identifies the subject matter, and is signed by the party against whom enforcement is sought or by his authorized agent."

Section 2–201 of the NYUCC applies to contracts for the sale of goods with a price of $500 or more and has been held to apply to spot and FX transactions in which foreign currencies are treated as "goods," rather than as a payment medium.[113] Subject to certain exceptions, Section 2–201 provides that such contracts for the sale of goods are not enforceable "unless there is some writing sufficient to indicate that a contract for sale has been made between the parties and signed by the party against whom enforcement is sought or by his authorized agent or broker."[114]

Section 5–701 of the NYGOL applies to other kinds of agreements that by their terms are not to be performed within one year from their making. Many derivatives with terms greater than one year and "delayed start" transactions with terms shorter than one year, but ending more than one year from their trade date, fall under this statute of frauds. Section 5–701 provides that any such agreement is void "unless it or some note or memorandum thereof be in writing, and subscribed by the party to be charged therewith, or by his lawful agent . . . ."[115]

---

[112]Where both the more general statute of frauds in NYGOL 5–701 and a more specific and less stringent statute of frauds provided in the NYUCC have been found applicable to the same transaction, the less stringent NYUCC provision has been held applicable. *Elevator Motors Corp. v. Leistritz AG*, 1992 WL 91904 (E.D.N.Y. 1992).

[113]NYUCC § 2–105(1) (which specifically excludes money in which the price is to be paid from the definition of "goods") and cmt. 1, which states that "[g]oods is intended to cover the sale of money when money is being treated as a commodity but not to include it when money is the medium of payment." Section 2–201 of the NYUCC was, for example, treated as applicable to FX forward transactions in *Intershoe, Inc. v. Bankers Trust Co.*, 77 N.Y.2d 517, 521, 571 N.E.2d 641, 644, 569 N.Y.S.2d 333, 336 (1991) ("[t]here seems to be no question that the UCC applies to foreign currency transactions . . ."), and *Saboundjian v. Bank Audi (USA)*, 556 N.Y.S.2d 258, 261 n.2 (App. Div. 1990).

[114]NYUCC § 2–201(1). This provision goes on to state that "[a] writing is not insufficient because it omits or incorrectly states a term agreed upon but the contract is not enforceable under this paragraph beyond the quantity of goods shown in such writing." *Id.* As summarized in the official comments, "[a]ll that is required is that the writing afford a basis for believing that the offered oral evidence rests on a real transaction." NYUCC § 2–201(1), cmt. 1. *See Iandoli v. Asiatic Petroleum Corp.*, 57 A.D.2d 815, 816 (1977) (citing that Official Comment as support for its holding), *appeal denied*, 42 N.Y.2d 1011 (1977).

[115]NYGOL § 5–701(a).

A fourth statute of frauds potentially applicable to some securities-linked derivatives was embodied until 1997 in Section 8–319 of the NYUCC, which applied to contracts for the purchase or sale of a security. In connection with a general revision to Article 8 of the NYUCC in that year, prior New York law was reversed through repeal of the statute of frauds in Section 8–319 and adoption of Section 8–113 to the effect that, subject to an exception for sales of stock or similar interests in a real estate cooperative, "a contract or modification of a contract for the sale or purchase of a security is enforceable whether or not there is a writing signed or record authenticated by a party against whom enforcement is sought, even if the contract or modification is not capable of performance within one year of its making."[116] Section 8–113 does not apply retroactively to render enforceable a contract for the purchase or sale of a security, or the modification of such a contract—including an OTC derivative that qualifies as such—if it was entered into before the 1997 amendment to the NYUCC came into effect.[117] Therefore, the statute of frauds in Section 8–319 could still, theoretically, apply to outstanding securities-linked derivatives and was, in fact, argued to apply in *Lehman Brothers Inc. v. Canadian Imperial Bank of Commerce*,[118] a case discussed in more detail below,[119] which involved a dispute over whether a payment was due from Lehman Brothers to CIBC under transactions characterized by the former as a repurchase agreement and separate sale of securities and by the latter as a "synthetic asset swap."[120]

Special Rules for Derivatives and Other Qualified Financial Contracts. Effective September 1994, the statutes of frauds in Section 5–701 of the NYGOL and Sections 1–206 and 2–201 of the NYUCC were amended as they apply to any "qualified financial contract." That term was defined to mean:

> an agreement as to which each party thereto is other than a natural person and which is:
>
> (a) for the purchase and sale of foreign exchange, foreign currency, bullion, coin or precious metals on a forward, spot, next-day value or other basis;
>
> (b) a contract (other than a contract for the purchase and sale of a commodity for future deliver[y] on, or subject to the rules of, a contract market or board of trade) for the purchase, sale or transfer of any commodity or any similar good, article, service, right, or interest which is presently or in the future becomes the subject of dealing in the forward contract trade, or any product or byproduct thereof, with a maturity date more than two days after the date the contract is entered into;
>
> (c) for the purchase and sale of currency, or interbank deposits denominated in United States dollars;

---

[116] NYUCC § 8–113.

[117] NYUCC § 8–601(b).

[118] No. 97 Civ. 8226 (WHP), 2000 WL 1425098 (S.D.N.Y. Sept. 27, 2000).

[119] *See infra* p. 58.

[120] 2000 WL 1425098 at *4.

(d) for a currency option, currency swap or cross-currency rate swap;

(e) for a commodity swap or a commodity option (other than an option contract traded on, or subject to the rules of, a contract market or board of trade);

(f) for a rate swap, basis swap, forward rate transaction, or an interest rate option;

(g) for a security-index swap or option or a security (or securities) price swap or option;

(h) an agreement which involves any other similar transaction relating to a price or index (including, without limitation, any transaction or agreement involving any combination of the foregoing, any cap, floor, collar or similar transaction with respect to a rate, commodity price, commodity index, security (or securities) price, security-index or other price index); and

(i) an option with respect to any of the foregoing.[121]

One of the key features of the amended statutes is that, so long as neither of the parties is a natural person, qualified financial contracts entered into orally or through electronic communication will not be subject to otherwise applicable writing requirements contained in the statutes if "the parties thereto, by means of a prior or subsequent written contract, have agreed to be bound by the terms of such qualified financial contract from the time they reach agreement (by telephone, by exchange of electronic messages, or otherwise) on those terms."[122] As a result, if a disputed oral qualified financial contract is covered by a master agreement that satisfies this requirement and neither of the parties is a natural person, defenses based on the New York statutes of frauds will no longer be available.

This requirement would be met by a master agreement on one of the 1992 ISDA master agreement forms, which provide[123] that "the parties intend that they are legally bound by the terms of each Transaction from the moment they agree on those terms (whether orally or otherwise)." A "Transaction" is any transaction between the parties that they intend to have governed by their master agreement. An important consideration, however, is the need to show a link between the oral agreement that is sought to be enforced and the agreement of the parties to be bound by oral agreements. If the parties' master agreement includes an understanding that the parties will be bound from the moment they conclude a deal, orally or otherwise, but there is not a clear link between trans-

---

[121] NYGOL § 5–701(b)(2). The method chosen in clause (h) to bring new products within the definition of "qualified financial contract" is somewhat less expansive than practitioners might like, inasmuch as it refers to other agreements and similar transactions "relating to a price or index." As a result, some practitioners use the term "index" in describing new products that do not involve a price as the underlying for the transaction. *See, e.g., infra* p. 765, in the sample confirmation for a weather index derivative.

[122] NYGOL § 5–701(b)(2); NYUCC §§ 1–206(3) & 2–201(4). The NYUCC provisions incorporate the definition of "qualified financial contract" by reference from the NYGOL provision.

[123] Section 9(e)(ii) of the Multicurrency—Cross Border form, *infra* p. 872, and Section 8(e)(ii) of the Local Currency—Single Jurisdiction form, *infra* p. 1029.

actions subsequently entered into and that master agreement until a confirmation exists, one of the parties might still argue that the above-described part of the amendments and the agreement to be bound in the master agreement do not foreclose a statute of frauds defense. As a result, the parties to master agreements governing their derivatives transactions may find it desirable to provide in their master agreements that all qualified financial contracts between the parties entered into after the date of the master agreement (as well as agreed previously existing transactions) will be subject to that agreement. Some, but not all, of the standardized master agreement forms used in the OTC derivatives market today include such terms,[124] but in some cases modifications of a master agreement may be prudent to ensure that the master agreement governs all intended future derivatives transactions between the parties.[125]

The second key feature of the amended statutes establishes the rule that, so long as neither of the parties is a natural person, qualified financial contracts entered into orally or through electronic communication will not be unenforceable for lack of a writing if "sufficient evidence to indicate that a contract has been made" exists.[126] This rule applies regardless of whether there is a prior or subsequent written contract under which the parties have agreed to be bound by agreements that are not in writing. The amendments contemplate a variety of ways in which a party may provide "sufficient evidence" that a contract has been made, including "the recording of a telephone call or the tangible written text produced by computer retrieval" of an electronic communication, so long as that evidence is admissible under New York law and is "sufficient to indicate that in such communication a contract was made between the parties."[127] In this regard, market participants should analyze the restrictions on admissibility that are most likely to apply in connection with the methods they use to confirm transactions.

A party will also be able, under the amended statutes, to provide sufficient evidence to prove that a contract exists if (1) it sends a confirmation in writing that is sufficient against the sender, (2) the confirmation is received by the counterparty against whom enforcement is sought not later than the fifth business day after the contract is made (or such other period as the parties may agree to in writing), and (3) by the third business day (or such other period as agreed) after the receipt by the counterparty of the confirmation, the sender does not receive a written objection to a material term of the

---

[124]This kind of linkage, requiring rebuttal of a presumption that the master agreement governs, is the approach taken, for example, in the 1997 ICOM and IFEMA and FEOMA forms of master agreement for transactions of the types covered by each of the forms (in Section 2.1 of each form). The matter is clearest in the forms' treatment of FX forward and spot transactions, which are identified as "FX Transactions." "FX Transaction" is defined (in Section 1) to cover all foreign currency forward and spot transactions in respect of which the parties have agreed "whether orally, electronically or in writing" on specified fundamental terms. The agreement to be bound from the time of oral agreement is somewhat less clear where currency options are concerned, since "Option" is simply defined to cover any currency option "which is or shall become subject to the Agreement." However, Section 2.3 makes clear that a writing memorializing an agreed Option's terms is not required for the Option to be binding, since it provides that "[t]he failure by a Party to issue a Confirmation shall not prejudice or invalidate the terms of" any Option.

[125]Part 5(b) of the schedule to the sample master agreement in Part 3 of this book, *infra* p. 928, illustrates how this may be done.

[126]NYGOL § 5–701(b)(1); NYUCC §§ 1–206(3) & 2–201(4).

[127]NYGOL § 5–701(b)(3)(a).

Statutes of Frauds 47

confirmation. For these purposes, the time of receipt of the confirmation or the objection is deemed to be the earlier of actual receipt by an individual responsible for the transaction and constructive receipt, which occurs at the time when actual receipt would have occurred had the addressee organization exercised reasonable diligence. "Business day" is defined as a day on which both parties are open and transacting business of the kind involved in the qualified financial contract.[128] This change affords substantial relief to the senders of confirmations, since the sender will no longer need to be concerned about satisfaction of one of the amended statutes of frauds merely because the recipient of the confirmation never responds, assuming neither party is a natural person, the confirmed transaction is otherwise eligible for treatment as a qualified financial contract for purposes of the amendments and the confirmation is sufficient as against the sender.

In light of these provisions, market participants should carefully review the procedures they follow for checking and replying to confirmations they receive. If parties find the period prescribed in this amendment to the New York Statutes of Frauds too long or too short, they may provide for a different period in their master agreement in a provision along the lines of the statutory exception. Some market participants have long used such contractual clauses, and since 1997 such clauses have been included in the FEOMA, ICOM and IFEMA forms of master agreements for FX forwards, spot transactions and currency options.[129]

Special Rules for Certain Foreign Currency Transactions between Merchants. Since qualified financial contracts involving natural persons are not covered by the 1994 amendments to the New York statutes of frauds discussed above, Sections 1–206 and 2–201 of the NYUCC and Section 5–701 of the NYGOL may, generally, apply to derivatives with natural persons.[130] However, if the relevant transaction is entered into between "merchants," a special set of rules may apply under Section 2–201(2) of the NYUCC, which applies to certain transactions for the sale of "goods" and has been treated as applicable to foreign exchange forward transactions and foreign currency options.[131] Since natural persons are relatively active in the foreign currency segment of the

---

[128] NYGOL § 5–701(b)(3)(b). The protection afforded to the senders of confirmations by this amendment is similar to that which already applied under Section 2–201(2) of the NYUCC to derivatives contracts involving foreign currencies if the contracts are between "merchants," as discussed below.

[129] The clause appears in the 1997 versions of the FEOMA (Section 11.15), ICOM (Section 8.15) and IFEMA (Section 11.15) forms.

[130] However, as noted, if a derivatives transaction qualifies as a contract for the purchase or sale of a security for purposes of Section 8–113 of the NYUCC and was entered into after that statute came into effect in 1997, the other New York statutes of frauds discussed in this chapter should not apply, even if a natural person is a party to the transaction.

[131] *See infra* p. 56. We are not aware of any court decision that extends the same treatment to currency swaps or other OTC derivatives involving foreign currency; however, if a currency swap were viewed as a series of spot and forward FX transactions, the treatment afforded to currency forwards under existing cases could easily be extended to currency swaps. It is not, however, clear that this will be the case, and at least one commentator has questioned whether the provisions of Article 2 of the Uniform Commercial Code have been correctly applied to FX forward transactions in *Intershoe* and other cases. *See* Cathy L. Scarborough, *Statute of Frauds' Issues and Foreign Exchange Transactions/Contracts, in* PLI 1992.

derivatives market, this special rule of Section 2–201(2) of the NYUCC can be of importance.[132]

Under subsection (2) of Section 2–201, the statute of frauds in subsection (1) is treated as satisfied if one of the "merchant" parties to a transaction sends the other a writing sufficient against the sender within a reasonable time and the recipient has reason to know of the contents but fails to respond with written notice of objection within ten days after receiving the writing. Therefore, to the extent NYUCC Section 2–201(2) is applicable to a transaction between merchants, it will not always be strictly necessary to obtain a signed confirmation from a counterparty, unless the parties' agreement suggests otherwise. Indeed, some market participants include in their master agreements contractual provisions that expressly overcome any suggestion elsewhere in the agreement that an exchange of confirmations is required for a binding transition.[133]

For purposes of this special NYUCC rule, a transaction will be "between merchants" if both parties are chargeable with the knowledge or skill of merchants in the transaction,[134] and "merchant," in this context, means "a person who deals in goods of the kind or otherwise by his occupation holds himself out as having knowledge or skill peculiar to the practices or goods involved in the transaction or to whom such knowledge or skill may be attributed by his employment of an agent or broker or other intermediary who by his occupation holds himself out as having such knowledge or skill."[135] In OTC derivatives, "between merchants" should include sophisticated market participants, whether or not they are professional market participants.[136]

What Kind of Writing May Be Required? Where a qualified financial contract is concerned, if a signed writing is still required to satisfy one of the NYGOL and NYUCC statutes of frauds discussed above, the 1994 amendments to the statutes supply expanded rules on what will be treated as a "writing" and a "signing." Under the amendments, "the tangible written text produced by telex, telefacsimile, computer retrieval or other process by which electronic signals are transmitted by telephone or otherwise shall constitute a writing and any symbol executed or adopted by a party with the present intention to

---

[132] The case most often cited in this regard is *Salomon Forex Inc v. Tauber*, 795 F. Supp. 768 (E.D. Va. 1992), *aff'd*, 8 F.3d 966 (4th Cir. 1993), which involved a wealthy surgeon who engaged regularly in FX forward, currency option and other derivatives transactions with the plaintiff and other major financial institutions. The action was brought to recover close to $26 million in damages, plus interest, after Dr. Tauber's failure to pay amounts due in respect of 68 Swiss franc and Australian dollar FX forward and option agreements. He filed a counterclaim challenging the validity of over 2700 OTC transactions with the dealer, including the 68 on which the claim was based. This aspect of the case is discussed further in Gooch & Klein, *Review of Case Law I*, at 396 n.24 & 401 n.38. For discussion of other aspects of the *Tauber* case, *see infra* p. 57 & notes 167, 226, & 232.

[133] *See infra* p. 372 for an example of such a provision. In the *Tauber* case, the confirmations of some of the relevant FX forward transactions sent by the dealer to the customer expressly recited as a contractual provision the substance of Section 2–201(2) of the Uniform Commercial Code.

[134] NYUCC § 2–104(3).

[135] NYUCC § 2–104(1).

[136] In the *Tauber* case, the court expressly found Dr. Tauber to be a merchant for purposes of § 2–201(2). *Salomon Forex v. Tauber*, Civ. No. 91-1415-A (E.D. Va.) (order of March 24, 1992). In so doing, the court cited *Armco, Inc. v. New Horizon Dev. Co. of Virginia*, 331 S.E.2d 456 (Va. 1985), to the effect that a merchant is "a business professional as opposed to a casual or inexperienced seller or buyer."

authenticate a writing shall constitute a signing."[137] This rule should be read together with the Electronic Signatures in Global and National Commerce Act, a federal statute that generally became effective in October 2000, with certain exceptions not relevant to derivatives products.[138] The Act provides that transactions in or affecting interstate or foreign commerce are not to be denied legal effect solely because the relevant contract or signature is in electronic form.[139]

The "note or memorandum" required by Section 5–701(a)(1) of the NYGOL can be assembled from more than one document.[140] All the "essential" terms must appear in the documents; that is, none of them may be supplied by testimonial evidence. What terms are "essential" will turn on the facts of the case.[141] Documents that are not subscribed may be considered together with documents that are subscribed, if the documents that are subscribed are sufficient to demonstrate the existence of the contractual relationship, and if the unsubscribed documents show, on their face, that they relate to the same transaction.[142] In the *CIBC* case referred to above, the court applied these rules in finding that Section 5–701 of the NYGOL, as amended to apply to qualified financial contracts, was satisfied by reading together a signed facsimile and electronic Bloomberg messages sent by the defendant to the plaintiff and a tape-recorded telephone call between representa-

---

[137] Under New York law as it existed prior to the amendments, it had been held that a telex could be a "writing" for statute of frauds purposes, and that a typed signature on a telex could be a "subscription" for those purposes. *See Interocean Shipping Co. v. National Shipping & Trading Corp.*, 523 F.2d 527, 537–38 (2d Cir. 1975); *Royal Air Maroc v. Servair, Inc.*, 603 F. Supp. 836, 841 (S.D.N.Y. 1985); *La Mar Hosiery Mills, Inc. v. Credit & Commodity Corp.*, 28 Misc. 2d 764, 768, 216 N.Y.S.2d 186, 190 (N.Y. City Court 1961) (typed signature on telegram sufficient). Generally, for the subscription rule to be satisfied, the writing was required to be subscribed at the end. *Steinberg v. Universal Machinenfabrik GMBH*, 264 N.Y.S.2d 757, 759–60 (App. Div. 1965), *aff'd*, 18 N.Y.2d 943, 223 N.E.2d 567, 277 N.Y.S.2d 142 (1966). *Compare Seidman v. Dean Witter & Co.*, 418 N.Y.S.2d 6 (App. Div. 1979) (stating that the purpose of the rule is to prevent fraudulent additions and refusing to apply it to a preliminary prospectus).

[138] Pub. L. 106-229, June 30, 2000, 114 Stat. 464, 15 U.S.C.A. §§ 7001–06, 7021, 7031 (cumulative annual pocket part 2001). A number of states (but not New York) have adopted statutes relating to electronic signatures that are based on the Uniform Electronic Transactions Act ("UETA"), *available at* http://www.law.upenn.edu/bll/ulc/fnact99/1990s/ueta99.htm. Generally speaking, the federal statute does not preempt state law that adopts UETA or otherwise establishes the principle of recognition of electronic signatures on a basis that does not favor any particular technology. *See Id.* § 102(a).

[139] *See generally* Sullivan & Cromwell, *Memorandum: Electronic Signatures in Global and National Commerce Act*, June 28, 2000, in PLI 2000, at 135.

[140] *See, e.g., Crabtree v. Elizabeth Arden Sales Corp.*, 305 N.Y. 48, 54–55, 110 N.E.2d 551, 553 (1953).

[141] *See Crabtree*, 305 N.Y. at 57, 110 N.E.2d at 555.

[142] The New York courts have shown greater willingness to admit unsubscribed documents if they have been prepared by the defendant rather than the plaintiff. In the *Crabtree* case, for example, the New York Court of Appeals held that the statute of frauds did not prohibit the use of unsigned documents to establish the existence of an enforceable contract where the documents had been prepared by the defendant. *See also Ideal Structures Corp. v. Levine Huntsville Dev. Corp.*, 396 F.2d 917, 928 (5th Cir. 1968) (applying New York law). The statute of frauds involved in the *Homestead* case referred to *supra* note 102 was quite similar to the cited provision of New York's General Obligations Law. *See* Gooch & Klein, *Review of Case Law I*, at 394–95.

tives of the parties. Accepting CIBC's proposition that, for purposes of weighing a statute of frauds defense, the parties' dealings with each other should be viewed as a form of rate swap and, therefore, a qualified financial contract, the court found that this evidence, taken together, satisfied the requirement of "sufficient evidence to indicate that a contract had been made," for purposes of Section 5–701(2) of the NYGOL.[143]

Guaranties and Other Special Cases. The foregoing refers only to the general statutes of frauds that may be applicable under New York law to conventional OTC derivatives. Special statutes of frauds may apply in some cases given the nature of the party against whom enforcement is sought. For example, as discussed below in this chapter, an agreement with a U.S. federally insured financial institution cannot serve as the basis for a claim against the FDIC in a receivership or conservatorship proceeding involving the financial institution unless certain writing and other requirements of the FDIA[144] are satisfied. Also, special statutes of frauds may apply to guaranties of obligations in connection with OTC derivative obligations.

The risk that this may be so has been demonstrated through various cases. In one, *Lehman Bros. Commercial Corp. v. Minmetals International Non-Ferrous Metals Trading Co.*,[145] a complaint seeking to enforce a guaranty was dismissed on the basis of a statute of frauds defense under a Delaware statute of frauds requiring obligations for the debt of another to be evidenced by a writing signed by the party to be bound, or some other person authorized in writing to bind that party. Such a defense was also raised before the New York courts in *Daiwa America Corp. v. Rowayton Capital Management, Inc.*,[146] on the basis of Section 5–701(a)(2) of the NYGOL, under which a "special promise to answer for the debt . . . of another person" is void unless "it or some note or memorandum thereof be in writing, and subscribed by the party to be charged therewith, or by his lawful agent . . . ."[147] The court rejected the defense in this case, finding that the contractual provisions were sufficiently clear in constituting a guaranty to satisfy the requirements of that statute of frauds.

When the protection of a guaranty is important, appropriate diligence should address compliance with any special statute of frauds applicable to guaranties, along with the other matters normally considered, such as the power of the relevant party to provide a guaranty, the due authorization of the relevant agreement in the manner required for guaranties by that party, the authority of each relevant individual to execute a guaranty and the regulatory or fiduciary implications, if any, of such a guaranty.[148]

---

[143]*Lehman Brothers Inc. v. Canadian Imperial Bank of Commerce*, No. 97 Civ. 8226 (WHP), 2000 WL 1425098 at *14 (S.D.N.Y. Sept. 27, 2000).

[144]*See infra* p. 51.

[145][1995–1996 Transfer Binder] FED. SEC. L. REP. (CCH) ¶ 98,841 (S.D.N.Y. 1995). For a detailed description of this action, *see* Gooch & Klein, *Review of Case Law II*, at 61 & 68–72. *See supra* note 89 regarding subsequent developments in the case.

[146]*Daiwa America Corp. v. Rowayton Capital Management, Inc.*, No. 118148/95 (N.Y. Sup. Ct. filed July 24, 1995). For a detailed description of this case, *see* Gooch & Klein, *Review of Case Law II*, at 61–63.

[147]NYGOL § 5–701(a)(2).

[148]*See supra* note 91 on power and authority issues.

Choice-of-Law Issues. In considering the risks associated with the effect of statutes of frauds on their derivatives activities, market participants should, of course, begin by analyzing which law may be applicable. For example, the liberal amendments to the New York statutes described above may not be applied in actions brought outside New York against defendants who were acting from an office outside New York when they agreed to the transaction. A New York court has, however, indicated that, if faced with a decision about whether to apply the special provisions on qualified financial contracts in the NYUCC and the NYGOL or a statute of frauds of another jurisdiction, applying New York's principles of conflict of laws, the court would choose to apply the New York statute, viewing its "concededly unique" nature as expressing a "strong interest" of New York in enforcing its special provision, in the absence of evidence that any other jurisdiction has a stronger interest.[149]

An opinion of local counsel in the jurisdiction of a counterparty or provider of credit support may afford protection with regard to the enforceability of a contract where a statute of frauds concern exists. In some circumstances, special care should be taken to obtain the opinion through a process involving diligence about the ways in which the contractual provisions may be characterized (*i.e.*, might a special statute of frauds apply if a provision is characterized as a guaranty?), as well as diligence about any special rules that may apply if enforcement of the contract is sought against a receiver or similar official appointed for the counterparty in connection with its insolvency or financial distress.

U.S. LAW ON AGREEMENTS WITH CERTAIN DEPOSITORY INSTITUTIONS

As indicated above, depending on the identity of the counterparty, in addition to a general statute of frauds determined to be applicable to a transaction (by virtue of the parties' contractual choice of law or a court's application of principles of conflict of laws), an extra layer of writing requirements may have to be satisfied, at least for purposes of enforcing the contract in circumstances involving the counterparty's insolvency. This is the case with contracts entered into with depository institutions for which the FDIC may be appointed as conservator or receiver pursuant to the FDIA.

Section 13(e) of the FDIA, as amended by FIRREA, provides that an agreement that "tends to diminish or defeat the interest" of the FDIC in "any asset" acquired by it, *inter alia*, as receiver of any insured depository institution will only be valid against the FDIC if the agreement:

(A)   is in writing,

(B)   was executed by the depository institution and any person claiming an adverse interest thereunder, including the obligor, contemporaneously with the acquisition of the asset by the depository institution,

(C)   was approved by the board of directors of the depository institution or its loan committee, which approval shall be reflected in the minutes of said board or committee, and

---

[149] *See AIG Trading Corp. v. Valero Gas Marketing, L.P.*, 679 N.Y.S.2d 587, 588 (App. Div. 1998) (*dictum*).

(D) has been, continuously, from the time of its execution, an official record of the depository institution.[150]

As is evident, these requirements (the severity of which has been attenuated through FDIC safe harbors described below) include both the kind of writing requirement that is normally associated with a statute of frauds and additional requirements related to authorization of contracts.

In the context of an OTC derivative, the "asset" is the derivatives transaction itself so, when derivatives transactions are governed by master agreements, the statute, by its terms, seems to require a written confirmation under the master agreement relating to the particular transaction which is executed by both parties contemporaneously with the parties' agreement on the transaction, as well as satisfaction of the requirements set forth in clauses (3) and (4) above. It is less clear from the face of the statute how its words should be read to apply to a claim based on a depository institution's grant to a derivatives counterparty of a security interest to secure the depository's obligations under the transactions governed by a master agreement. It would not seem logical to read the statute as requiring that the depository institution have acquired each relevant item of collateral before it enters into the transaction or master agreement. The logical reading, consistent with the purpose of the statute and other parts of the FDIA relating to qualified financial contracts, would require execution by the parties of a security agreement contemporaneously with the grant of the security interest.

This reading seems appropriate for a variety of reasons. First, the requirement for security is not always imposed at the time the master agreement or a particular transaction is executed. For example, the security arrangements might be entered into at a later date in connection with the parties' agreement to facilitate additional dealings with each other through security arrangements that will enable them to reduce the impact of their dealings under capital adequacy rules or in connection with a deterioration of the credit standing of either or both of the parties. Second, tying the execution of the writing to the time of the grant of the security interest is consistent with the provision of the FDIA which, as a general matter, limits the circumstances in which the FDIC may avoid a legally enforceable and perfected security interest to interests taken in contemplation of the depository institution's insolvency or with the intent to hinder, delay, or defraud the relevant depository institution or its creditors[151] and, with respect to qualified financial contracts (QFCs), a term that includes many OTC derivatives as well as other financial contracts, such as forward contracts, securities contracts and repurchase agreements, as those terms are defined

---

[150] FDIA § 13(e) Under a related provision, Section 11(d)(9)(A), any agreement that does not meet the requirements of Section 13(e) may not "form the basis of, or substantially comprise," a claim against the FDIC. Counterpart requirements apply under Section 11(n)(4)(I) to claims against "bridge banks" to which assets and liabilities of a failed depository institution may be transferred as part of the process of "resolution" contemplated in the FDIA. Similarly, Section 618–a(1)(e) of the NYBL limits claims against the New York banking superintendent as receiver for the New York business and property of a New York banking organization, including a New York branch or agency of a foreign bank, to cases in which the agreement under which the claim arises is reflected in the books, accounts or records of the banking organization or a party provides documentary evidence of such agreement." *See infra* p. 324.

[151] FDIA § 11(e)(11).

in the FDIA,[152] further limits that avoidance power to circumstances involving an intent to hinder, delay or defraud.[153]

Fortunately, the FDIC adopted a Statement of Policy on Qualified Financial Contracts (the "QFC Policy Statement")[154] and a Statement of Policy Regarding Treatment of Security Interests After Appointment of the FDIC as Conservator or Receiver (the "Security Interest Policy Statement")[155] clarifying the FDIC's intentions, *inter alia*, on application of the writing requirement aspects of Section 13(e) of the FDIA and creating "safe harbors" for bona fide transactions between depository institutions and nonaffiliated counterparties. The QFC Policy Statement applies to any QFC and provides a safe harbor in the sense that it states that any QFC and any ancillary agreement, "such as a master agreement or security arrangements," that complies with the following criteria will be deemed to satisfy the requirements of Section 13(e) of the FDIA:[156]

- The QFC is evidenced by a writing (including a confirmation) that either is sent by the depository institution to the counterparty or by the counterparty to the depository institution. In either case, the writing must be sent reasonably contemporaneously with the parties' agreement to enter into the specific QFC transaction. The writing need not be signed unless otherwise required by applicable noninsolvency law;

- The depository institution, by corporate action, was authorized under applicable noninsolvency law to enter into the QFC. A depository institution will be deemed to have taken such corporate action if the counterparty has relied in good faith either on a resolution (or extract thereof) provided by the institution's corporate secretary or assistant secretary or on a written representation (whether in a master agreement or otherwise) from an officer of the level of vice president or higher, as to the depository institution's authority; and

- The writing (or a copy thereof) evidencing the QFC and the evidence of authority must be maintained by the depository institution in its official books and records. However, the counterparty may, by appropriate evidence (including the production of copies maintained by the counterparty) establish the existence of the writing and the evidence of authority.

The QFC Policy Statement goes on to indicate that the Board of Directors of the FDIC intends that the FDIC apply these criteria and the requirements of the FDIA "in a manner

---

[152]*See infra* p. 278 for discussion of qualified financial contracts under the FDIA.

[153]FDIA § 11(e)(8)(C)(ii).

[154]This Statement of Policy was adopted by order of the Board of Directors of the FDIC on December 12, 1989 and is available at http://www.fdic.gov/regulations/laws/rules/5000-1100.html.

[155]58 Fed. Reg. 16,833 (Mar. 23, 1993), *available at* http://www.fdic.gov/regulations/laws/rules/5000-3500.html, as supplemented by an Addendum dated February 10, 1997, *available at* http://www.fdic.gov/regulations/laws/rules/5000-4300.html.

[156]The related requirements of §§ 11(d)(9) and 11(n)(4)(I) are also deemed satisfied. *See supra* note 150 on the way these requirements are related.

generally consistent with reasonable business trading practices in the QFC markets" and will look at "the totality of the circumstances surrounding such transactions including the counterparty's good faith attempt to comply with all reasonable trading practices and requirements, any noninsolvency law requirements and the requirements stated herein [in the QFC Policy Statement]."

The Security Interest Policy Statement adds to the QFC Policy Statement's safe harbor a clarification that the FDIC will not seek to avoid an otherwise legally enforceable and perfected security interest "solely because the security agreement granting or creating such security interest does not meet the 'contemporaneous' requirement" of the FDIA sections referred to above or "solely because the secured obligation or collateral subject to the security interest (a) was not acquired by the [depository] Institution contemporaneously with the approval and execution of the security agreement granting the security interest and/or (b) may change, increase, or be subject to substitution from time to time during the period that the security interest is enforceable and perfected."[157]

A very significant part of the day-to-day activity in the derivatives market involves financial institutions for which the FDIC may be appointed as receiver or conservator. As a result, notwithstanding the existence of the safe harbors described above, industry groups have for some time sought statutory change that would provide greater certainty about the issues raised by Section 13(e) of the FDIA.

Proposals in this regard have been included in successive bills to amend the FDIA and other federal laws relating to the treatment of OTC derivatives and other financial contracts in insolvency and similar proceedings in the U.S.[158] One of those reform initiatives, which is discussed at length in Chapter 7 of this book, is H.R. 3211, which was introduced to propose enactment of the Financial Contracts Bankruptcy Reform Act of 2001. That reform legislation would amend Section 13(e)(2) of the FDIA to provide as follows in relation to credit support arrangements involving qualified financial contracts:

> (2) EXEMPTIONS FROM CONTEMPORANEOUS EXECUTION REQUIREMENTS – An agreement to provide for the lawful collateralization of—
>
> . . .
>
> (D) one or more qualified financial contracts, as defined in section 11(e)(8)(D),
>
> shall not be deemed invalid pursuant to paragraph (1)(B) solely because such agreement was not executed contemporaneously with the acquisition of the collat-

---

[157] 58 Fed. Reg. 16,834. The Security Interest Policy Statement deals with grants of security interests other than in connection with QFCs and, in some respects, seems to impose requirements that go beyond those imposed by the FDIA and the QFC Policy Statement insofar as security interests supporting obligations under QFCs are concerned. Footnote 4 of the Security Interest Policy Statement expressly indicates, however, that nothing in the Security Interest Policy Statement should be interpreted as contradicting or impairing the policies expressed in the QFC Policy Statement. *Id.* at 16,833 n.4.

[158] *Infra* p. 313.

eral or because of pledges, delivery, or substitution of the collateral made in accordance with such agreement.[159]

RELIEF WHEN A STATUTE OF FRAUDS IS NOT SATISFIED

Where statutes of frauds and similar requirements apply, the consequences of failure to comply will normally be as set forth in the laws that establish those requirements. So, for example, if the special writing and authorization requirements described in the preceding part of this chapter are not satisfied, a party to a derivatives transaction with certain U.S. depository institutions may be unable to enforce the contract against the FDIC in receivership or conservatorship proceedings. Where one of the New York statutes of fraud discussed in this chapter applies, if the statute's requirements are not satisfied, a party to a derivatives transaction will find itself without the remedies for breach of contract described in Chapter 6 but will not necessarily be totally without relief if the counterparty defaults or repudiates the contract. Because statutes of fraud exist, as noted, to protect against fraudulent claims based on alleged oral contracts but are not meant to be used as "a means of evading just obligations,"[160] a body of judge-made law known as the doctrine of promissory estoppel has been developed to avoid injustice when an applicable statute of frauds is not satisfied. This doctrine is, however, reserved for "that limited class of cases where 'the circumstances are such as to render it unconscionable' to deny the promise upon which the [party] has relied."[161] When the doctrine is applied to bar a defense based on the statute of frauds, the party seeking relief generally will be required to show a clear and unambiguous promise made to it, its reasonable and foreseeable reliance on that promise and injury to it by reason of its reliance.[162]

---

[159]H.R. 3211 § 10. The proposed amendment extends the same relief to other arrangements involving collateral for certain deposits and extensions of credit. As discussed in Chapter 7, *infra* p. 313, other bankruptcy reform initiatives being considered in the U.S. congress include the same proposed substantive change.

[160]*See supra* note 111.

[161]*Chromalloy Amer. Corp. v. Universal Hous. Sys.*, 495 F. Supp. 544 (S.D.N.Y. 1980) (alteration in original) (quoting from *Philo Smith & Co. v. USLIFE Corp.* 554 F.2d 34 (2d Cir. 1977)), *aff'd* 697 F.2d 289 (2d Cir. 1982) (denying relief under the doctrine, *inter alia*, because the actions taken by the plaintiff, which could not satisfy the statute of frauds, were not "unequivocably referable" to the oral agreement on which its claim was based). *See also Merex A.G. v. Fairchild Weston Sys., Inc.*, 29 F.3d 821, 826 (2d Cir. 1994), *cert. denied*, 513 U.S. 1084 (1995), to the effect that "unconscionable" injury, for these purposes, is "injury beyond that which flows from the non-performance of the unenforceable agreement." Another theory under which a party might seek relief if its contract were not enforceable for failure to satisfy a statute of frauds is the doctrine of unjust enrichment, "a quasi-contractual theory for restitution that implies a contract in circumstances where one does not exist in fact." *Pickering v. American Express Travel Related Services Co., Inc.*, 1999 WL 1225246 (S.D.N.Y. 1999). Under this doctrine, relief is limited to the reasonable value of any benefits or services conferred on the other party. *See Grappo v. Alitalia Linee Aeree Italiane, S.p.A.*, 56 F.3d 427, 433 (2d Cir. 1995).

[162]*See, e.g., Esquire Radio & Elecs. Inc. v. Montgomery Ward & Co., Inc.*, 804 F.2d 787, 793 (2d Cir. 1986) (citing the criteria set forth in Section 90 of the *Restatement (Second) of Contracts* as generally the same as those applied under New York law). *See also Farash v. Sykes Datatronics, Inc.*, 59 N.Y.2d 500, 503, 452 N.E.2d 1245, 1246–47, 465 N.Y.S.2d 917, 918–19 (1983) and Jeffrey G. Steinberg, *Promissory estoppel as a Means of Defeating the Statute of Frauds*, 44 FORDHAM L. REV. 114 (1975).

PAROL EVIDENCE RULES

Even when there is written documentation of a transaction, such as a signed confirmation, one of the parties may assert that the documentation does not correctly reflect its understanding of what the parties agreed. In many such instances the relevant part of the confirmation is acknowledged by both parties to be a mistake and a substitute confirmation is executed. In others, the party that questions the accuracy of the writing may seek to present extrinsic evidence to prove its point. The cases discussed below involving derivatives illustrate the courts' approach to such situations. Two of the cases were decided applying the parol evidence rule in Section 2–202 of the NYUCC. The third applies the common-law parol evidence rules as pronounced by New York's courts in the context of particular cases.

THE NYUCC AND COMMON-LAW RULES

As noted, some foreign currency derivatives have been treated as falling within the purview of Article 2 of the NYUCC, which applies to sales of goods and to sales of foreign currency where the currency is treated as a commodity, as opposed to a medium of payment. The parol evidence rule applicable in these transactions is set forth in Section 2–202 of the NYUCC, which provides that, if a writing is "intended by the parties as a final expression of their agreement with respect to such terms as are included therein," it may not be contradicted by evidence of prior or contemporaneous oral agreements, though its contents may be explained or supplemented by a course of dealing, trade usage, course or performance and may, unless "intended also as a complete and exclusive statement of the terms of the agreement," be explained or supplemented by evidence of consistent additional terms.

The New York parol evidence rule applicable to derivatives transactions that do not fall within the reach of Article 2 of the NYUCC is generally the same. As stated by the courts, this common-law rule provides that, when the parties have reduced their agreement to writing, extrinsic evidence of prior or contemporaneous agreements may not be offered to contradict, vary or subtract from the terms of the writing.[163] However, where the writing does not appear to express the entire agreement of the parties, evidence that the writing which purports to be a contract is in fact not a contract at all, or to explain any ambiguities or omissions in the writing, is admissible.[164]

APPLICATION TO DERIVATIVES DISPUTES

Intershoe, Inc. v. Bankers Trust Co.[165] is perhaps the best known case applying the parol evidence rule of Article 2 of the NYUCC to an OTC derivatives transaction. The case involved an FX forward entered into over the telephone. The dealer sent a confirmation slip indicating that the transaction involved a sale of lire by the customer to the dealer. The customer signed and returned it. The customer later contended that the confirmation was wrong and that it had purchased, not sold, the lire. The only evidence of-

---

[163] *Aratari v. Chrysler Corp.*, 316 N.Y.S.2d 680 (App. Div. 1970).

[164] *See id.*

[165] 571 N.E.2d 641, 569 (N.Y. 1991). The case is discussed in more detail in Gooch & Klein, *Review of Case Law I*, at 398.

Statutes of Frauds 57

fered by Intershoe was an affidavit of its treasurer. There was, therefore, no dispute over satisfaction of the applicable statute of frauds; rather, the question was whether the relevant signed confirmation was subject to challenge through extrinsic evidence as an incorrect statement of the terms agreed. The customer argued that the confirmation should not be viewed as a final expression of the parties' agreement because it did not contain an express statement to that effect. New York State's highest court rejected that argument, saying that to accept it would be to "introduce a technical, formal requirement not contemplated by the [NYUCC] . . . and one that would frustrate the Code's purpose of facilitating sales transactions by easing the process of contract formation."[166]

The same NYUCC provision was applied in *Salomon Forex Inc v. Tauber*,[167] where Dr. Tauber contended, among other things, that the dealer had breached an express representation of "best pricing" made by one of its salespersons, by overcharging him for FX options and forwards. Citing *Intershoe*, the court found that this NYUCC parol evidence rule barred Dr. Tauber from introducing extrinsic evidence to support this contention, which was an attempt to add new or contradictory terms to contradict the final expression of the parties' agreements as embodied in the written confirmations of the transactions.

The derivatives market has taken comfort from the result in cases like *Intershoe*, because *Intershoe* stands for the proposition that, under the parol evidence rule in Section 2–202 of the NYUCC, the parties do not need to state in their trade confirmations that the confirmation is the complete and final expression of the financial terms of the relevant transaction. The *Intershoe* facts have, however, been distinguished in cases in which the courts have found reason to doubt whether trade confirmations constituted the final expression of the parties' agreement. These cases have been decided under the parol evidence rule applied in *Intershoe* and under New York's common-law parol evidence rule.

The parol evidence rule in Section 2–202 of the NYUCC was applied in *Compañía Sud-Americana de Vapores, S.A. v. IBJ Schroder Bank & Trust Co.*[168] In this case, a customer alleged that the trade confirmations of its FX transactions with IBJ Schroder related to a course of trading in which the bank had made, and breached, an oral promise to give the customer preferred client status in setting the applicable FX rates. In denying the bank's motion for summary judgment based on the trade confirmations, which included no reference to agreed preferred rates, the court concluded that, because of the long history of the parties' foreign exchange dealings with each other, a jury could find that the confirmations were not the complete and final expression of the parties' agreement because there was an "overarching" prior oral agreement governing the totality of the parties' relationship.[169]

---

[166] 571 N.E.2d at 644–45 (quoting from the dissent in the lower court, in the second part of the quoted text).

[167] 795 F. Supp. 768 (E.D. Va. 1992), *aff'd*, 8 F.3d 966 (4th Cir. 1993). Other aspects of this case are discussed *supra* note 132 and *infra* notes 226 & 232.

[168] 785 F. Supp. 411 (S.D.N.Y. 1992). For further discussion of this case, *see* Gooch & Klein, *Review of Case Law II*, at 63–64.

[169] 785 F. Supp. at 427–33. This case is discussed further at Gooch & Klein, *Review of Case Law II*, at 98–100. *See also Société Nationale d'Exploitation Industrielle des Tabacs et Allumettes v. Salomon Bros. Int'l Ltd.*, 702 N.Y.S.2d 258, 259 (App. Div. 2000), where the court held that evidence as to the general

More recently, a New York court distinguished *Intershoe* as involving a single, discrete transaction, and instead turned to the decision in *Sud-Americana de Vapores* for guidance in considering the parol evidence issue raised in a case involving multiple and apparently related transactions, *Lehman Brothers Inc. v. Canadian Imperial Bank of Commerce*.[170] The case was before the court on motions for summary judgment by both parties, both of which were denied.

In *CIBC*, Lehman sued to recover damages for alleged breach by CIBC of its obligations in connection with multiple transactions that the parties characterized in different ways. The transactions originated with four sales of U.S. Treasury securities by Lehman to CIBC. Each sale was then followed by two successive "repos"—(1) a first transaction in which CIBC sold the same securities back to Lehman but agreed to repurchase them at a later date and (2) yet another repo, in which Lehman then sold the same securities back to CIBC but agreed to repurchase them at a later date.[171]

Lehman contended that, giving effect to the documentation for each part of the transaction as written, CIBC paid it approximately $16.5 million less than was due. CIBC's position was that all the transactions should be taken together, as a single, three-legged "synthetic asset swap" designed to replicate a par interest rate swap, and that the agreed economics of the whole transaction were such that it did not owe the claimed amount.

The parol evidence issue arose out of Lehman's argument that CIBC should be precluded from seeking to prove a contract different from that reflected by certain documents in the case, consisting of (1) confirmations of the sale transactions mailed to CIBC, to which CIBC never objected, and (2) in the case of the repos, a Master Repurchase Agreement between CIBC and a Lehman entity. The confirmations of the initial sales recited: "You agree that the confirmation of the trade indicated on the face of this confirmation shall be deemed to be correct in all respects and constitutes conclusive proof of this contract unless written notice of any objection is given to us within five (5) days of the trade date."[172] The Master Repurchase Agreement, for its part, recited that it would apply to, and would be conclusive evidence of the terms agreed by the parties, in connection with simultaneous purchases and agreements to repurchase securities and financial instruments entered into by the parties from time to time.[173] CIBC asserted that the inte-

---

business terms governing the parties' contractual relationship was not precluded by the parol evidence rule, despite the presence of an integration clause in their master agreement, where the business term in question was not incompatible with the provisions of the master agreement.

[170] No. 97 Civ. 8226 (WHP), 2000 WL 1425098 (S.D.N.Y. Sept. 27, 2000).

[171] Under the first series, on or about the date of each tranche of the sale, CIBC sold the relevant Treasury notes to Lehman GSI, promising to repurchase them for stated principal plus interest at the fixed rate applicable under the notes. Under the second series, Lehman GSI entered into a simultaneous reverse transaction, selling them back to CIBC and agreeing to repurchase them for a different stated principal plus interest at LIBOR minus six or seven basis points. The stated principal in the second series included the par amount of the notes plus premium, but not the accrued interest, reflected in the sale price. These repo and reverse repo transactions were rolled over or renewed quarterly until the underlying Treasury notes matured. 2000 WL 1425098, at *2.

[172] *Id.*

[173] *Id.* at *1.

grated view of the three legs of the synthetic asset swap, which it urged on the court, would be seen by reading the confirmations in the context of the faxed term sheets, Bloomberg electronic messages and recorded telephone conversations.

The court held that "neither contractual scheme can be said as a matter of law to comprise the agreement of the parties with respect to the Subject Transaction and, therefore, neither party is entitled to summary judgment."[174] In determining whether the repo contract on which Lehman sought recovery was a complete and integrated expression of the parties' agreement, the court found *Sud-Americana de Vapores* closer to the facts as they appeared from the record than *Intershoe*, after pointing to statements by Lehman employees to the effect that the sale tranches and the repos were related and that an important term (the extendible nature of the repos) was not memorialized in the written confirmations. The court also gave weight to evidence from Lehman witnesses that, given the "non-standard or even 'unusual' nature" of the Repos," the terms of the parties' dealings were likely to be memorialized in term sheets, as opposed to written confirmations and, indeed, that Lehman's computer system had an "operational inability" to "synthesize the complete terms" of the multi-part transaction. Other evidence was to the effect that Lehman employees corroborated CIBC's view that the transactions were part of a single structure. Accordingly, the court concluded that the parties did not intend the Master Repurchase Agreement and sale confirmations to be the complete integration of all their mutual promises and, therefore, that parol evidence was admissible to prove the terms of the parties' agreement.[175]

CONFIRMATION PRACTICES IN LIGHT OF THE CASES

The existence of these disputes and of cases like *Intershoe*, which allegedly involved a mistake, have led market participants to consider whether their confirmation should include the kind of "merger" or "integration" clause that is contained in most formal swap agreements: an express statement something to the effect that the confirmation, together with the terms of the master agreement it supplements, where applicable, constitutes the entire agreement of the parties with respect to the terms of the transaction covered by the confirmation and, as to those terms, supersedes all prior agreements and contemporaneous oral agreements with respect to that transaction. *Intershoe* stands for the proposition that such a provision is not necessary under Section 2–202 of the NYUCC. However, as illustrated by the discussion above, *Intershoe* may not be viewed by the courts as persuasive in the facts of a particular case, and parties whose agreements are governed by the laws of other jurisdictions should consider whether the law governing their agreement may be different.[176]

---

[174]Lehman also contended that CIBC should be precluded from proving its position because of the statute of frauds in Section 5–701 of the NYGOL. The court disagreed, holding that the evidence constituted sufficient evidence of the existence of a qualified financial contract for purposes of the amended statute.

[175]*Id.* *14.

[176]*See* 9 WIGMORE, EVIDENCE IN TRIALS AT COMMON LAW § 2425 (Chadbourn rev. 1981), for a discussion of and citations to similar parol evidence rules in the United States.

The parties must weigh the potential benefit of the provision, and the element of finality it may lend to the debate,[177] against the desire in the market to keep the confirmation as brief as possible. Inclusion of such a provision may be attractive to entities that believe they themselves will make few mistakes and, in any event, would prefer to live with mistakes so as to avoid litigation if necessary. The inclusion of a "merger" clause in the confirmation may be particularly appropriate if a transaction is unusually complex. In such a case, the desire for brevity and economy might well give way to a desire for accuracy and completeness.

The cases seem to indicate that there is a greater possibility that a court will permit the introduction of extrinsic evidence to prove terms at odds with those set out in a confirmation or other writing if the parties have engaged in a long series of dealings with each other. The *CIBC* case,[178] in particular, points to risks that may arise when the parties engage in transactions that at least one of them believes are linked to others and should be interpreted in relation to them. When market participants use automated confirmation systems for their dealings with each other, they should have procedures in place for identifying cases in which automated confirmations should not be used, if, for example, the available fields for information will not accommodate necessary statements about the transaction, or as in the *CIBC* case, intended linkages between trades. In those cases, the confirmation should be generated manually, with due attention to documenting the special features or linkages.

In weighing the various considerations, professional market participants should consider the sorts of discussions that sales personnel tend to have with customers as they are shaping a transaction.[179] For example, sales personnel may discuss the way in which a transaction could be expected to operate in certain scenarios without clearly stating the assumptions implicit in their conclusions. The following guidance on this subject provided by the Federal Reserve Board of Governors for institutions it supervises is instructive in this regard:

> Institutions should establish policies governing the content of sale materials provided to their customers. Typically, these policies call for sales materials that accurately describe the terms of the proposed transaction and provide a fair representation of the risks involved. Policies may also identify the types of analysis to be provided to the customer and often specify that analyses include stress tests of the proposed instrument or transaction over a sufficiently broad range of possible outcomes to ade-

---

[177]There are well-established exceptions to the courts' willingness to allow general "merger" clauses to preclude extrinsic evidence, where the evidence is proposed, not to contradict the written agreement, but to attack its character as an agreement at all, on grounds such as fraud in the inducement of the contract. *Sabo v. Delman*, 3 N.Y.2d 155, 164 N.Y.S.2d 714 (1957).

[178]*Supra* note 170.

[179]*See, e.g.*, Gooch & Klein, *Review of Case Law II*, at 95–96 & 100–10, discussing the lower court decision in *Société Nationale d'Exploitation Industrielle des Tabacs et Allumettes v. Salomon Bros. Int'l Ltd.*, 1998 N.Y. Misc. LEXIS 219 (Sup. Ct. 1998), *aff'd*, 674 N.Y.S.2d 648 (App. Div. 1998) (dealer allegedly promised to "immunize" customer against loss on a swap) and *Procter & Gamble Co. v. Bankers Trust Co.*, 925 F. Supp. 1270 (S.D. Ohio 1996) (customer alleged that the dealer promised customer would have the right to lock in a favorable rate on a swap with reset features).

quately assess the risk. Some institutions use standardized disclosure statements and analyses to inform customers of the risks involved and suggest that the customer independently obtain advice about the tax, accounting, legal, and other aspects of a proposed transaction.[180]

Or sales personnel might tell the customer that the firm would unwind a transaction at the customer's request, intending no more than an informal expression of the general way in which the firm seeks to accommodate client requests, but the customer might believe, or at least contend that it believed, that it is being given an enforceable right to unwind the transaction. A statement in the confirmation that it (and the related master agreement, if there is one) represents the complete and final expression of the parties' agreement may be a desirable supplement to appropriate training of sales personnel about being clear with customers on when they are generalizing about economic matters or the firm's policies, and when they are agreeing to terms of the trade that are reflected in its pricing. Indeed, some market participants include in their master agreements acknowledgments of each party to the effect that it will not have a contractual right to unwind any transaction under the master agreement unless the confirmation of that transaction expressly provides otherwise.

The need for clear policies to be followed by personnel continues after the transaction has been agreed to, particularly on questions having to do with ongoing valuation of the transaction form the customer's point of view. On this subject, the Federal Reserve manual quoted above provides:

> Many customers request periodic valuations of their positions. Institutions that provide periodic valuations of customers' holdings should have internal policies and procedures governing the manner in which such quotations are derived and transmitted to the customer, including the nature and form of disclosure and any disclaimers. Price quotes can be either indicative, meant to give a general level of market prices for a transaction, or firm, which represent prices at which the institution is willing to execute a transaction. When providing a quote to a counterparty, institutions should be careful that the counterparty does not confuse indicative quotes for firm prices. Firms receiving dealer quotes should be aware that these values may not be the same as those used by the dealer for its internal purposes and may not represent other "market" or model-based valuations.[181]

Market participants that consider including special provisions in their confirmations on mistakes and on attempts to contradict the terms of a signed confirmation should bear in mind the distinction between clarifying the terms of a confirmation through extrinsic evidence and contradicting them. Because confirmations—even those prepared on standardized forms—are often completed with less than total precision in the use of technical terminology (such as the terms defined in the *2000 ISDA Definitions*), extrinsic evidence on the course of dealing or usage of trade, or evidence of consistent additional

---

[180] BOARD OF GOVERNORS OF THE FEDERAL RESERVE SYSTEM, *supra* note 21, § 2150.1, at 2 (Feb. 1998).

[181] BOARD OF GOVERNORS OF THE FEDERAL RESERVE SYSTEM, *supra* note 21, § 2150.1, at 2–3.

terms, may prove extremely useful to explain or clarify an ambiguity in a confirmation. If a market participant takes this view, it would want to avoid being precluded from using extrinsic evidence for clarification purposes, even if it chose to provide in the confirmation that extrinsic evidence could not be used to contradict a term in the confirmation.

Another documentation question for institutions that are particularly concerned about the high cost of mistakes or of challenge to their contracts in connection with complex transactions, is whether to include in their documentation a provision that expressly permits the contradiction of a signed confirmation through certain kinds of contemporaneous extrinsic evidence.[182] Market participants that electronically record their OTC derivatives trades should consider whether this kind of provision is desirable, as well as appropriate safeguards relating to the legality and integrity of recordings.[183]

---

[182]The original IFEMA form, published in 1993, included such a provision (in Section 8.3) for FX spot and forward transactions documented under those terms: "In the event of any dispute between the Parties as to the terms of an FX Transaction governed by these Terms . . . , the Parties may use electronic recordings as the preferred evidence of the terms of such FX Transaction, notwithstanding the existence of any writing to the contrary." The 1997 versions of the FEOMA, ICOM and IFEMA forms provide only that the parties may record telephone conversations and that the recordings are admissible in evidence in proceedings relating to the agreement.

[183]*See* Barry Taylor-Brill, *Negotiating and Opining on ISDA Masters*, *in* PLI 2000, at 71, 82.

CHAPTER 3

COMMODITIES, GAMING AND BUCKET-SHOP LAWS

Introduction 63
The Sources of Legal Uncertainty
    The Commodity Exchange Act 66
    Gaming Laws 71
    Bucket-Shop Laws 72
The Commodity Exchange Act
    History 73
        Pre-CFMA Statutory Exclusions 74
        CFTC Exemptions and Safe Harbors 78
        CFMA Exclusions 82
    Exemptions and Exclusions and Related Representations 83
        Eligible Swap Participant and Eligible Contract Participant Status 85
        Excluded Swap Transactions 91
        Covered Swap Agreements Offered by Banks 92
        Transactions in Exempt and Excluded Commodities 95
            Excluded Commodities and Exempt Commodities 95
            Trading Facilities 96
            The CEA Section 2(d) and 2(h) Exclusions 98
    Other CEA Exclusions and Exemptions
        Statutory Exclusions 101
        CFTC Exemptions 104
Preemptions of Gaming and Bucket-Shop Laws 112
Provisions on Contract Enforcement and CEA Interpretation 113

INTRODUCTION

Much of the legal risk associated with OTC derivatives in the United States has involved uncertainty created by the broad terms of the laws discussed in this chapter, which are

- the provisions in the federal Commodity Exchange Act (CEA) that deal with futures and options on commodities and securities;

- state statutes that prohibit unregulated gambling, or gaming; and

- state statutes that outlaw so-called bucket shops—operations involving sham transactions in commodities and securities.[184]

---

[184] They are called "bucket shops" because, for all practical purposes, the operator throws the customer's order in the waste basket—the "bucket." In *Gatewood v. North Carolina*, 203 U.S. 531, 536 (1906), the Supreme Court described a bucket shop as "an establishment, nominally for the transaction of a stock exchange business, or business of similar character, but really for the registration of bets, or wagers, usually for small accounts, on the rise or fall of the prices of stock, grain, oil, etc., there being no transfer or delivery of the stock or commodities nominally dealt in" (quoting from the Century Dictionary).

The prohibitions in these statutes have given rise to legal risk because a transaction that violates them may be illegal, and illegal contracts may be unenforceable.[185] In addition, the parties to contracts that run afoul of these laws may be subject to enforcement or similar proceedings.

Participants in the OTC derivatives market have always been aware of these risks, and they have structured their transactions and prepared the related documentation taking these laws into account. In the 1990s, the market's concerns about these risks were heightened by challenges to transactions of various kinds and by the institution of proceedings against professionals that were parties to them. In the *Tauber* case, for example, a wealthy doctor who frequently participated in the currency markets sought to avoid his obligations under currency options and FX forwards by arguing, among other things, that the transactions were illegal because they violated gaming and bucket-shop laws and prohibitions on off-exchange commodity options and futures in the CEA.[186] Other events that caused alarm included a U.S. court's finding that widely traded contracts in Brent blend crude oil were illegal under the CEA,[187] an enforcement proceeding before the Commodity Futures Trading Commission (CFTC) charging a market professional with violation of the antifraud rules applicable to commodity trading advisers (CTAs) by virtue of its dealings in leveraged swaps,[188] and a CFTC enforcement proceeding in which a condition to settlement was that a market professional inform its customers that their contracts in energy products were illegal off-exchange commodity futures and, therefore, void.[189]

This chapter first summarizes how state gaming and bucket-shop laws and the provisions of the CEA at issue in these and other legal proceedings have given rise to uncertainty for users of OTC derivatives. The remainder of the chapter discusses how much of the uncertainty has been eliminated through statutory exclusions and administrative exemptions from the CEA and through federal preemption of these state laws. The exclusions, exemptions and preemptions are reviewed in the context of contractual provisions—largely representations—often included in derivatives documentation by parties seeking to establish that their transactions fall outside the reach of the prohibitions in the CEA and these state gaming and bucket-shop laws.

The primary sources of the statutory exclusions, administrative exemptions, safe harbors and preemptive provisions are the following:

---

[185] *See* RESTATEMENT OF CONTRACTS (SECOND) § 178 (1981).

[186] *Salomon Forex v. Tauber*, 795 F. Supp. 768 (E.D. Va. 1992), *aff'd*, 8 F.3d 966 (4th Cir. 1993). The court rejected these arguments, as discussed *infra* notes 226, 232 & 242, in Gooch & Klein, *Review of Case Law I*, at 412–22, and in Gooch & Klein, *Review of Case Law II*, at 73–74. Other aspects of the *Tauber* case are discussed *supra* pp. 48 & 57.

[187] That finding was made in *Transnor (Bermuda) Ltd. v. BP North American Petroleum*, 738 F. Supp. 1472 (S.D.N.Y. 1990), discussed *infra* p. 77.

[188] *See* Gooch & Klein, *Review of Case Law II*, at 84 & 100–08, on the proceedings brought by the CFTC against Bankers Trust Company in connection with leveraged swaps with Procter & Gamble involving U.S. treasury instruments and deutsche mark swap rates. The CFTC did not, in fact, find that the swaps were futures or option contracts subject to the CEA or otherwise justify its conclusion on the applicability of these antifraud regulations. The proceedings were settled without admission of guilt on the part of Bankers Trust.

[189] *See infra* p. 77 on proceedings involving MG Refining & Marketing, Inc.

Statutory Exclusions and Preemptive Provisions:

- the CEA, which

    (1) from the outset has included a provision—commonly referred to as the "Forward Contract Exclusion"[190]—that takes many physically settled derivatives transactions out of the reach of the CEA and

    (2) has subsequently been amended to provide relief for other OTC derivatives, both cash and physically settled, under:

    (a) the Treasury Amendment—so called because it was enacted (in 1974) at the request of the U.S. Department of the Treasury,[191]

    (b) Title V of the Futures Trading Practices Act of 1992 (FTPA), which authorized exemptions for certain transactions between appropriate persons[192] and

    (c) the Commodity Futures Modernization Act of 2000 (CFMA)[193]

- The Legal Certainty for Bank Products Act of 2000 (the "Bank Products Legal Certainty Act"), which was enacted as Title IV of the CFMA[194]

CFTC Exemptions

- the Trade Option Exemption, adopted by the CFTC pursuant to the broad authorization given to it in Section 4c(b) of the CEA [195]

- the Exemption for Certain Swap Agreements (the "1993 Swap Agreement Exemption"), adopted by the CFTC pursuant to the FTPA,[196]

- the Exemption for Certain Contracts Involving Energy Products (the "Energy Contracts Exemption"), adopted by the CFTC pursuant to the FTPA,[197]

---

[190]CEA § 1a(19). *See infra* p. 76.

[191]Pub. L. No. 93-463, 88 Stat. 1389 (1974). *See infra* p. 74.

[192]Pub. L. No. 102-546, 106 Stat. 3590 (1992). *See infra* p. 79.

[193]Pub. L. No. 106-554, Appendix E, 114 Stat. 2763 (2000). *See infra* p. 82.

[194]*Id.* at 2673A-457. *See infra* p. 92.

[195]17 C.F.R. § 32.4(a) (2002). *See infra* p. 78. The CFTC has used its broad exemptive authority relating to commodity options under Section 4c(b) of the CEA to grant other exemptions that are not discussed in this chapter because they do not have any general effect on documentation in wide use in the OTC derivatives market. *See* 2 SECURITIES & DERIVATIVES REGULATION § 13.08[2][a]. *See also infra* note 252.

[196]17 C.F.R. §§ 35.1-35.2 (2002). *See infra* p. 79.

[197]58 Fed. Reg. 21,286, 1993 W.L. 120,137 (F.R.) (April 20, 1993). *See infra* p. 79.

CFTC Safe Harbors

- the 1989 Policy Statement Concerning Swap Transactions (the "Swap Policy Statement")[198]

- the 1990 Interpretative Letter on the Eligibility of "Collar Agreements" for Safe Harbor Treatment Under the CFTC's Policy Statement Concerning Swap Transactions (the "Collar Interpretation")[199]

This chapter deals only with the laws of the United States and the State of New York. Similar laws exist in many other jurisdictions, and they may give rise to uncertainties of the kinds described this chapter. Before engaging in OTC derivatives transactions, the parties should seek to determine whether such uncertainties exist in respect of the transactions they intend to enter into and whether special contract provisions of the kinds described below may be useful in averting challenges to the legality and enforceability of their transactions under the laws of the jurisdictions that may be involved.

Since the focus of this book is OTC derivatives, the preceding list does not refer to the statutory exclusions or CFTC exemptions, statutory interpretations and other actions relating to hybrid instruments, understood to be instruments that provide for payments that are indexed to commodity values, levels or rates.[200] This chapter does, however, include passing mention of these exclusions and CFTC actions.

THE SOURCES OF LEGAL UNCERTAINTY

THE COMMODITY EXCHANGE ACT

Background. The CEA has been one of the main sources of legal uncertainty for participants in the OTC derivatives markets in the United States.[201] A Presidential Working Group on Financial Markets set up in 1998 described the problem as follows:

> The CEA subjects contracts for the sale of a commodity for future delivery and options on such contracts to the exclusive jurisdiction of the CFTC. The CFTC also has jurisdiction over commodity option contracts, although the CEA does not unambiguously characterize the CFTC's jurisdiction over such instruments as exclusive. In addition, transactions in, or

---

[198] 54 Fed. Reg. 30,694, 1989 W.L. 278, 866 (F.R.) (July 21, 1989). *See infra* p. 78.

[199] CFTC-OETF Interpretative Letter No. 90-1, 1987–90 COMM. FUT. L. REP. (CCH) ¶ 24,583, at 36,516 (Jan. 18, 1990). *See infra* p. 79.

[200] The legal uncertainty that has existed in the past with respect to hybrids dates to 1987, when the CFTC announced its view that instruments with embedded features like those of commodity futures and options were within the reach of the CEA's trading restrictions applicable to futures and options and within the jurisdiction of the CFTC. *See* CFTC, Advance Notice of Proposed Rulemaking, 54 Fed. Reg. 47,022, 1987 W.L. 145,008 (F.R.) (Dec. 11, 1987).

[201] The principal and very broad stated basis for the application of the CEA to any transaction or person is a connection between the transaction, the underlying commodity or the person's relevant conduct with interstate commerce, which is defined in Section 1a(22) of the CEA to include commerce "(A) between any State, territory, or possession, or the District of Columbia, and any place outside thereof" or "(B) between points within the same State, territory, or possession, or the District of Columbia, but through any place outside thereof, or within any territory or possession, or the District of Columbia." 7 U.S.C.A. § 1a(22) (Supp. 2001).

in connection with, commodity futures contracts and commodity options contracts must be conducted in accordance with the CEA and regulations promulgated by the CFTC. In general, this means that, except as provided by certain administrative exemptions currently granted by the CFTC, transactions must be conducted on, or subject to the rules of, a contract market designated by the CFTC. The CEA defines "commodity" to include specific agricultural commodities and "all other goods and articles, . . . and all services, rights, and interests in which contracts for future delivery are presently or in the future dealt in."[202]

Essentially, the uncertainty has related to three facts: (1) the statute gives little guidance about the characteristics of covered futures and options,[203] (2) the CFTC has taken the expansive view that contracts and instruments that function economically like futures and options may be subject to its jurisdiction and the CEA[204] and, (3) even where exceptions have been carved out by the statute itself or by CFTC administrative action, subsequent interpretations by the CFTC and the courts have at times indicated that the exceptions may be narrower than they seemed or that they might be inapplicable if the parties traded or cleared their transactions on what might be viewed as an unauthorized exchange.[205]

The CFMA has now removed these uncertainties for many OTC derivatives transactions, provided they do not involve agricultural commodities.[206] The analysis is simplest when the transactions are individually negotiated,[207] are not executed on multilateral execution platforms treated under the CEA as trading facilities[208] and are between parties that

---

[202] REPORT OF THE PRESIDENT'S WORKING GROUP ON FINANCIAL MARKETS, OVER-THE-COUNTER DERIVATIVES MARKETS AND THE COMMODITY EXCHANGE ACT 6–7 (1999) (footnotes omitted) (textual omission in original).The working group was asked by Congress to develop a coherent policy with respect to derivatives transactions after various actions by the CFTC viewed by the derivatives market as suggesting that the agency would seek to regulate OTC derivatives. These matters and a temporary Congressional moratorium on the CFTC's rule-making authority at the time are summarized in a memorandum of law submitted on behalf of ISDA, the SIA and TBMA, as *amici curiae*, in *Cary Oil Co., Inc. v. MG Refining & Marketing, Inc.*, 99 Civ. 1725 (WM) (DFE), February 22, 2002 (S.D.N.Y.), in connection with further proceedings in the action referred to *infra* p. 872. The memorandum urged the court to hold that Section 25(a)(4) of the CEA, which is aimed at fostering legal certainty with respect to derivatives as described *infra* p. 113, applies to causes of action accruing on and after the date of enactment of the Futures Trading Act of 1982.

[203] *See infra* p. 76, discussing court decisions that seek to identify futures contracts by distinguishing them from cash sales of commodities for deferred delivery. *See also* 2 SECURITIES & DERIVATIVES REGULATION § 13.08[2][a].

[204] *See infra* p. 73.

[205] *See infra* notes 240 & 347 and accompanying text.

[206] The CFMA also removed the uncertainty that has existed, for similar reasons, in connection with hybrid instruments—those which provide for the delivery of a commodity or for payments that are indexed to commodity values, levels or rates. *See infra* note 368 and the source cited therein. For an interesting overview of the CFMA's changes from the perspective of a CFTC commissioner, *see* Thomas J. Erickson, *Regulatory Uncertainty Under the Commodity Futures Modernization Act of 2000*, FUTURES & DERIVATIVES L. REP., Apr. 2001, at 6.

[207] *See infra* p. 298.

[208] *See infra* p. 96.

qualify as "eligible contract participants."[209] These transactions are now clearly outside the jurisdiction of the CFTC and not vulnerable to attack on the basis that they run afoul of the CEA.[210] Analysis of the CEA issues is more complex if (1) the transaction involves an agricultural commodity, (2) either of the parties is not an eligible contract participant, (3) the transaction is executed on a trading facility or (4) the material economic terms of the transaction other than price and volume are not subject to individual negotiation, that is, the transaction is offered on a take-it-or-leave-it basis except as to those terms.

There are exclusions established by statute and exemptions adopted by the CFTC that may be available in some of these cases, but specified antifraud and antimanipulation provisions of the CEA may apply even though an exclusion or exemption affords relief from the CEA's trading restrictions on commodity futures and options.[211] Whether an exclusion or exemption applies, and the extent of its reach, may depend on the nature of the underlying commodity and on whether the parties have used a trading facility to execute the transaction. In this regard, as discussed below, the CEA draws distinctions between exempt electronic trading facilities[212] and all others and between exempt commodities—largely physically deliverable commodities with a finite supply—and excluded commodities—broad categories that include securities, interest and exchange rates and other financial, macroeconomic, economic and commercial indexes and variables that are not within the parties' control, as well as weather and other contingencies with potential economic impact.[213]

The sheer number of different CFMA exclusions and exemptions, and the distinctions among them, can be confusing, although one simple rule is that the parties' mere decision to mitigate credit risk by clearing their mutual transaction exposures will not affect whether a CEA exclusion is available for the relevant transactions.[214] In seeking to make sense of these CFMA distinctions and, more generally, to assess the potential impact of the CEA on their transactions, market participants may find the following to be useful generalizations.

Futures and Options. The exemptions and exclusions discussed below provide that the various CEA trading restrictions will not apply in certain situations, and that the CEA's antifraud and antimanipulation provisions may or may not apply, but they all leave unanswered the basic question of whether a swap, cap, floor or other OTC derivatives transaction that functions economically like a commodity futures contract or option is

---

[209] *See infra* p. 85.

[210] These transactions are removed from the reach of the CEA through two provisions enacted by the CFMA. One is an amendment to the CEA. *See infra* p. 91. The other is a provision in the Bank Products Legal Certainty Act that effectively operates like that CEA provision but applies only to transactions entered into or offered or provided by banks. *See infra* p. 92.

[211] *See, e.g.,* Charles R. Mills, *Antifraud Concepts Under the Commodity Futures Modernization Act of 2000,* FUTURES & DERIVATIVES L. REP., Feb. 2001, at 12.

[212] *See infra* p. 97.

[213] *See infra* p. 95.

[214] The clearing facilities they use for the purpose will, however, be subject to regulation under the CEA or another regulatory regime *See infra* pp. 97 & 286 and 2 SECURITIES & DERIVATIVES REGULATION § 13.09[6].

subject, as such, to the CEA. Therefore, although the simplest route to comfort on CEA issues is to find an exclusion or exemption that is plainly available given the nature of the underlying commodity, the identity of the parties and the way they are trading, the lack of a clearly applicable exclusion or exemption does not, in itself, mean that an OTC derivatives transaction will run afoul of the CEA. In fact, as discussed at the close of this chapter, one of the provisions added to the CEA by the CFMA provides that the exemptions and exclusions that are established for certain transactions, contracts and agreements should not be construed as implying or creating any presumption that those transactions, contracts or agreements are or would otherwise be subject to the CEA.[215]

Contract Enforcement Provisions. The CFMA enacted provisions that are described as "contract enforcement" provisions. As discussed below,[216] they foreclose challenges to the legality and enforceability of transactions solely on the basis that they fail to comply with the terms or conditions of the CEA or a CFTC regulation. The CFMA also amended the CEA to provide that the legality, validity, or enforceability of certain agreements, contracts and transactions entered into on electronic trading facilities will not be subject to challenge merely because that facility fails to satisfy exemptive criteria imposed by the CEA.[217] Furthermore, to prevent erosion of the legal certainty for derivatives users that is sought through the exemptions, exclusions and contract enforcement provisions described in this chapter, the CFMA also amended the statute to prohibit any construction of its terms that would narrow those protections, as noted in the preceding paragraph.

Retail Transactions and Transactions in Agricultural Commodities. While most of the CEA exclusions added by the CFMA are available only for transactions between eligible contract participants and none of those exclusions is available for transactions in agricultural commodities, one partial exclusion for some retail transactions in foreign currency was created by the CFMA. A pre-CFMA exclusion or exemption may also be available for other retail transactions and for transactions in agricultural commodities. The discussion below of the Treasury Amendment and the Forward Contract Exclusion deals with these subjects.[218]

Standard Terms and Trading Facilities. As indicated, the most liberal CEA exclusions are available for transactions in which the material economic terms (other than price and quantity) are subject to individual negotiation between eligible contract participants who are not dealing with each other on a trading facility. The underlying rationale for this favored treatment appears to be that these wholesale market participants, when engaged in direct, negotiated dealings with one another, should be able to protect their own interests without the benefit of special CEA rules or CFTC oversight. The tiering of the other exclusions, which are less liberal, is perhaps best understood by way of contrast with that presumption.

---

[215]*Infra* p. 113.

[216]*Infra* p. 113.

[217]CEA § 2(e)(3). These exemptive criteria apply to electronic trading facilities used in the execution and trading of transactions in exempt commodities. *See infra* p. 97.

[218]*See infra* p. 74.

That is, there is an implicit presumption of greater need for CFTC oversight—because of greater risk of price manipulation or lack of market transparency—if the material terms of the transactions other than price and quantity are offered on a take-it-or-leave-it basis or if the parties are dealing with each other at the remove implied, say, by dealings in a trading pit and through an intermediary. In this context, transactions in excluded commodities are treated more liberally than transactions in exempt commodities,[219] because the limited supply of exempt commodities is presumed to involve a greater risk of manipulative behavior. Where the law provides exclusions for transactions that are executed on electronic trading facilities, they are limited to cases in which the parties are acting on a principal-to-principal basis or are intermediaries subject to regulation.[220]

Commercial vs. Speculative Transactions. Some of the statutory exclusions and CFTC exemptions discussed below directly or implicitly draw a distinction between speculative and commercial transactions. Thus, the availability of an exclusion or exemption may turn on whether one or both of the parties is using the transaction to manage risk, is a commercial user of the underlying commodity or is otherwise engaged in a business that involves the underlying commodity or dealing in its associated risks other than pure price risk—the traditional attraction for speculators. Indeed, the related tests of commercial use in some cases look at whether the transaction itself involves a binding commitment to make or take actual delivery of the underlying commodity.

As discussed below, this distinction dates to the oldest exception from the CEA's trading restrictions, the Forward Contract Exclusion.[221] In that case, the apparent rationale for the exclusion and exemption was that intervention by the CFTC was not necessary to protect the public interest in the integrity of the commercial markets in contracts involving farmers, grain elevators and others engaged in actual sales of commodities—as

---

[219] *See infra* p. 95.

[220] *See infra* p. 97. In addition, where exempt commodities are concerned, there is a distinction between electronic trading facilities that limit access to certain eligible commercial entities and trading facilities that give access to others. *See infra* p. 99. The underlying presumptions described above are, however, perhaps most clearly manifested in the CEA's provisions on exempt boards of trade, as added by the CFMA. They make the CEA's general trading restrictions inapplicable to exempt boards of trade which, to qualify as such, must limit trading access to eligible contract participants and limit trading to futures, options and options on futures with an underlying commodity that has "(A) a nearly inexhaustible deliverable supply; (B) a deliverable supply that is sufficiently large, and a cash market sufficiently liquid, to render any contract traded on the commodity highly unlikely to be susceptible to the threat of manipulation; or (C) no cash market." CEA § 5d(b). However, the CEA's antifraud and antimanipulation provisions continue to apply to the parties who engage in commodity futures, options or options on futures on exempt boards of trade and, if the CFTC determines that an exempt board of trade is a significant source of price discovery for transactions in the cash market for a commodity, the CFTC may require the board of trade to disseminate, on a daily basis, trading volume, opening and closing price ranges, open interest, and other trading data as appropriate to the market. For reasons relating to agreement between the CFTC and the SEC regarding their respective jurisdictions, exempt boards of trade may not trade security futures or options or options on security futures. *Id.*

[221] *See infra* p. 76.

opposed to speculators.[222] This distinction has been carried forward in many of the other exclusions and exemptions discussed below.[223]

GAMING LAWS

In the United States, the regulation of gambling and gambling promoters is largely a matter of state law. In New York, the General Obligations Law provides that gambling contracts are unlawful and void.[224] The Penal Law provides that "[a] person engages in gambling when he stakes or risks something of value upon the outcome of a contest of chance or a future contingent event not under his control or influence, upon an agreement or understanding that he will receive something of value in the event of a certain outcome."[225] Because of the breadth of this definition—and of similar provisions in the gaming laws of other jurisdictions—there has long been concern over whether they might be cited by a party seeking to avoid liability under swaps and other OTC derivatives.

Agreements that seem to fall within the broad terms of gaming laws if they are read literally may nonetheless be enforceable if they are entered into for a business purpose. This is the case in New York, under judge-made exceptions to the state's gaming statute created for contracts between parties who have a legitimate interest in the outcome of future events, such as an insurable interest or an investment.[226] As a result, from the earliest days of the market, OTC derivatives documentation has often included representations regarding the business contexts of the transactions.

---

[222]*See* Armando T. Belly, *Introduction to Derivatives and the Role of the Commodity Exchange Act*, *in* ASSOCIATION OF THE BAR OF THE CITY OF NEW YORK, AN INTRODUCTION TO EXCHANGE TRADED DERIVATIVES & OVER-THE-COUNTER DERIVATIVES 2, 18–23 (2000), on the predecessor provisions in the Futures Trading Act (enacted in 1921) and the Grain Futures Act (enacted in 1922) and the continuing emphasis on commercial contracts for physical delivery when the Grain Futures Act was extensively amended and renamed the Commodity Exchange Act.

[223]*See infra* pp. 78–82 on the Swap Agreement Exemption, the Energy Contracts Exemption and the Swap Policy Statement. The commercial/speculative distinction is also carried forward in various exclusions enacted by the CFMA, which either give favorable treatment to transactions between eligible commercial entities (a subset of eligible contract participants) or in some cases give eligible contract participant status to a person because of the use the person is making of the relevant transaction or because the person ordinarily deals in the underlying commodity or its associated risks, other than mere price risk, in its business. *See infra* pp. 99 & 124.

[224]*See* NYGOL §§ 5–401 & 5–411.

[225]N.Y. Penal Law § 225.00(2) (McKinney 2000).

[226]*Liss v. Manuel*, 296 N.Y.S.2d 627, 631 (Civ. Ct. 1968); *see also O'Farrell v. Martin*, 292 N.Y. Supp. 581, 584 (City Ct. 1936) ("[A] gambling contract generally exists only between parties who have no interest in the subject-matter except as to the possible gain or loss resulting"). In *Salomon Forex Inc v. Tauber*, 795 F. Supp. 768 (E.D. Va. 1992), *aff'd*, 8 F.3d 966 (4th Cir. 1993), for example, an action was brought to recover close to $26 million in damages, plus interest, after Dr. Tauber's failure to pay amounts due in respect of 68 Swiss franc and Australian dollar FX forward and option agreements. He filed a counterclaim challenging the validity of over 2700 OTC transactions with the dealer, including the 68 on which the claim was based. Dr. Tauber characterized these dealings as speculative transactions that violated the gaming laws of New York and Virginia, and he sought to have them ruled void. The court found that the transactions fell within the judge-made exception for transactions with a valid business purpose. *Salomon Forex Inc v. Tauber*, Civ. No. 91-1415-A, Transcript of proceedings on March 24, 1992, at 60–61. For discussion of other aspects of the *Tauber* case, *see supra* pp. 48 & 57 and *infra* notes 232 & 245.

As discussed in more detail below, the antigaming provisions of state and local law in the U.S. have now been preempted by federal law for many OTC derivatives transactions.[227] When the parties think federal preemption is applicable, they—or at least one of them—may prefer to use a special representation expressly or implicitly referring to the federal preemption, rather than a representation to the effect that they are not entering into the transaction for speculative purposes, since speculative intent is not necessarily inconsistent with a business purpose. Indeed, speculation is at the heart of the business of many professional investors.

BUCKET-SHOP LAWS

Almost half the states in the United States have bucket-shop laws.[228] As noted in the Introduction to this chapter, these laws were adopted to protect the public against unscrupulous practices that involve taking orders for the purchase or sale of commodities or securities without actually effecting the transactions or arranging for delivery.[229] According to one study on the subject, violations of these laws are usually felonies, and contracts entered into in violation of these laws are generally void, regardless of whether they are entered into for speculative purposes or to hedge a business risk.[230]

The New York statute prohibits offering to make, or making, contracts for the purchase or sale of commodities or securities upon credit or margin, if the offer or the contract is made "not intending the actual bona fide receipt or delivery of any such securities or commodities, but intending a settlement of such contract based upon the difference in [the] . . . public market quotations of [prices made on any board of trade or exchange or market upon which such commodities or securities are dealt in] or such prices at which said securities or commodities are, or are asserted to be, bought or sold."[231] The statute sets forth other, similar offenses, all of which constitute felonies. The general view among derivatives practitioners is that the statute applies only to sham transactions, and

---

[227] *See infra* p. 112.

[228] Barry W. Taylor, *The Commodity Exchange Act and Other Bucket Shop Laws: The Future of Commodity Swaps without Preemption*, in SWAPS AND OTHER DERIVATIVES IN 1990, at 501, 517 & n.37 (PLI Corp. L. & Practice Course Handbook Series No. 689). Section 4b(a)(iii) of the CEA makes it unlawful . . . to bucket [an . . . order, or to fill such order by offset against the order or orders of any other person, or willfully and knowingly and without the prior consent of such person, to become the buyer in respect to any selling order of such person, or become the seller in respect to any buying order of such person." On the CFTC's view of conduct that may involve direct and indirect bucketing, *see, e.g.,* Press Release (No. 4667-02), CFTC (July 9, 2002), *available at* www.cftc.gov/opa/enf02/opa4667-02.htm (attaching the complaint in an administrative action, *In re Contrino* (CFTC docket no. 02-13)). Section 2(5) of the CFMA states that one purpose of the law is to clarify the CFTC's jurisdiction over "certain retail foreign exchange transactions and bucket shops that may not otherwise be regulated." 114 Stat. at 2763A-366.

[229] For discussion of state bucket-shop laws and the interplay between them and the Commodity Exchange Act, *see* Barry W. Taylor, *Swaps: Commodities Laws in Transition* and sources cited therein and Thomas A. Russo, David S. Mitchell & Andrew M. Shainberg, *Federal and State Regulation of Swap Transactions*, in PLI 1991 ADVANCED SWAPS, at 43 & 133, respectively, and Edwin W. Patterson, *Hedging and Wagering on Produce Exchanges*, 40 YALE L.J. 843 (1931).

[230] *See* Taylor, *supra* note 229, at 56–57. *See also* 1 PHILIP MCBRIDE JOHNSON & THOMAS LEE HAZEN, COMMODITIES REGULATION §§ 1.02[7], 2.02[1]–[3] (3d ed. 1999 & Supps. 2000 & 2001), on the approach to bucket shops in the CEA before the enactment of the CFMA.

[231] N.Y. GEN. BUS. § 351(3) (McKinney 1988).

not to bona fide commercial dealings, and this view has also been expressed by a federal circuit court in a case involving FX forwards and options, where one of the parties invoked New York's bucket-shop law in seeking to avoid its contractual obligations.[232]

THE COMMODITY EXCHANGE ACT

HISTORY

The present state of the law concerning the applicability of the CEA to OTC derivatives is best understood against the backdrop of events since the definition of "commodity" for purposes of the statute was expanded beyond tangible commodities to include financial "underlyings." The amendment was enacted in 1974, and controversy regarding the scope of the statute, and of the CFTC's jurisdiction, began at roughly the same time and has persisted ever since.

The CFTC has taken the position that whether a transaction constitutes an option or futures contract should be determined by assessing "the transaction as a whole with a critical eye toward its underlying purpose."[233] This position has in the past been the source of market concerns that the CEA's restrictions on trading in futures and options might be viewed as applicable to OTC derivatives because swaps, caps, floors and similar transactions may function economically like commodity futures and options.[234]

The principal sources of the CEA's restrictions on trading in futures and options are

- CEA § 4(a), on commodity futures contracts, which we refer to below as the "Futures Trading Restrictions," under which dealings in commodity futures that are subject to the CFTC's jurisdiction and do not benefit from an exclusion or exemption are unlawful unless they are (1) conducted on a board of trade that the CFTC has designated as a contract market for the relevant commodity, (2) conducted on and subject to the rules of a board of trade, exchange or market outside the U.S. or, (3) since the enactment of the CFMA, conducted on a derivatives transaction execution facility (DTEF), registered with the CFTC,[235]

---

[232]The trial court's decision in *Tauber* held that the New York and Virginia bucket-shop statutes are not applicable to off-exchange FX forward and option agreements. The opinion did not, unfortunately, explain the rationale for this conclusion. In affirming the lower court's decision on this matter, the appellate court noted the following in interpreting the New York statute's application to transactions settled by offsetting trades: "The New York statute does not ban legally enforceable trades settled by further transactions, but only sham transactions." 8 F.3d at 978. For further discussion of this aspect of the case, *see* Gooch & Klein, *Review of Case Law I*, at 420–21, and Gooch & Klein, *Review of Case Law II*, at 73–74. For discussion of other aspects of the *Tauber* case, *see supra* pp. 48 & 57, *supra* note 226 and *infra* note 242.

[233]Statutory Interpretation Concerning Certain Hybrid Instruments, 54 Fed. Reg. 1139 (Jan. 11, 1989) (footnote omitted).

[234]*See* 2 SECURITIES & DERIVATIVES REGULATION § 13.07[4] for discussion of the CFTC's positions on economic equivalence and possible regulation of the OTC derivatives market.

[235]Section 4(a) of the CEA provides that, unless exempted by the CFTC, "it shall be unlawful for any person to offer to enter into, to enter into, to execute, to confirm the execution of, or to conduct any of-

- CEA § 4c(b), on commodity options, which we refer to below as the "Options Trading Restrictions," under which dealings in commodity options that are subject to regulation by the CFTC and do not benefit from an exclusion or exemption are unlawful unless conducted in accordance with rules and regulations adopted by the CFTC, and

- CEA § 2(a)(1)(D)(ii), on security futures contracts and options on security futures contracts,[236] which we refer to below as the "Security Futures Restrictions" and which (together with other provisions of the CEA and the federal securities laws) has replaced the parts of the jurisdictional accord between the SEC and the SEC that formerly banned futures on individual stocks and narrow-based stock indexes and restricted trading in futures on broad-based securities indexes and is commonly referred to as the Shad-Johnson Accord.[237]

PRE-CFMA STATUTORY EXCLUSIONS

Until the CFTC adopted the 1993 Swap Agreement Exemption, two statutory exclusions from the CEA were the principal sources of legal comfort for participants in the OTC derivatives market when they analyzed the risk that their transactions might be challenged as illegal under the Futures Trading Restrictions and the Options Trading Restrictions. One is generally referred to as the Treasury Amendment, and the other as the Forward Contract Exclusion.

The Treasury Amendment. In the same act that broadened the definition of "commodity," Congress also amended the CEA to provide that "[n]othing in this Act shall be deemed to govern or in any way be applicable to transactions in foreign currency, security warrants, security rights, resales of installment loan contracts, repurchase options, government securities, or mortgages and mortgage purchase commitments, unless such transactions involve the sale thereof for future delivery conducted on a board of trade."[238]

---

fice or business anywhere in the United States, its territories or possessions, for the purpose of soliciting, or accepting any order for, or otherwise dealing in" commodity futures, unless the futures transactions are conducted on or subject to the rules of a foreign board of trade, exchange or market or on or subject to the rules of a board of trade designated by the CFTC as a contract market or a DTEF registered with the CFTC. Section 5a of the CEA deals with the registration of a DTEF with the CFTC. A board of trade designated by the CFTC as a contract market or a DTEF may also operate an electronic trading facility, so long as the operations are kept separate. CEA § 2(e)(2). Designated contract markets may also separately operate electronic trading facilities that are exempt from regulation under the CEA, provided they limit trading to derivatives covered by the exemptions and exclusions provided for in Sections 2(d)(2), 2(g) and 2(h)(3) of the CEA, which are described below in this chapter. *See infra* pp. 91 & 98. As indicated *supra* note 220, under Section 5d of the CEA, the Futures Trading Restrictions and the Options Trading Restrictions do not apply to exempt boards of trade.

[236] *See infra* p. 84.

[237] The name identifies the Chairmen of the SEC and the CFTC in 1982, when these agencies resolved their dispute over whether the 1974 amendments to the CEA discussed above in the report deprived the SEC of jurisdiction over futures involving a "security," as that term is used in the federal securities laws. *See infra* p. 79.

[238] 7 U.S.C.A. § 2 (1999).

Although the Treasury Amendment has traditionally been an important source of comfort for participants in the OTC currency derivatives market, over the years the reach of this apparently simple and broad exclusion became the subject of substantial debate. The principal questions involved the CFTC's view that the statutory exclusion was far narrower than it seemed on its face,[239] as well as questions over what might be treated as a "board of trade"[240] and, until a Supreme Court decision on the matter in 1997, over whether "transactions in foreign currency" included currency options.[241] These issues cast a shadow on reliance on the Treasury Amendment, at least for currency derivatives involving certain categories of counterparties. Doubts in this regard were heightened in the 1990s by the *Tauber* case, in which a wealthy individual sought to avoid his obligations under currency options and FX forwards by arguing, among other things, that they were void because they violated the Futures Trading Restrictions and the Options Trading Restrictions of the CEA.[242] Ultimately, the Treasury Amendment was modified by the CFMA to remove many of the lingering doubts and to provide that many retail transactions in foreign currency are subject to the CEA and to the jurisdiction of the CFTC.[243] Although other CFMA exclusions discussed below also apply to some transactions covered by the Treasury Amendment, it retains vitality as a potentially useful, supplemental

---

[239] In response to off-exchange foreign currency futures contracts offered to the general public, in 1985 the CFTC expressed its view on the reach of the Treasury Amendment in a Statutory Interpretation and Request for Comments on Trading in Foreign Currencies for Future Delivery, 50 Fed. Reg. 42,983, 1985 WL 140,374 (F.R.) (Oct. 23, 1985). *See* Gooch & Klein, *Review of Case Law II*, at 74–76, for discussion of several cases rejecting or upholding the CFTC's view (expressed at *42,984 of that Statutory Interpretation) that only transactions between banks and certain other "sophisticated and informed institutional participants" were within the Treasury Amendment's exclusion. *See also* 2 SECURITIES & DERIVATIVES REGULATION § 13.09[4] on the Treasury Amendment generally.

[240] Before it was amended in the CFMA, the term "board of trade" was defined in Section 1a(1) of the CEA to mean "any exchange or association, whether incorporated or unincorporated of persons who are engaged in the business of buying or selling any commodity or receiving the same for sale on consignment." The CFTC took the position that, given this definition, an "association of persons" entering into transactions with the general public could constitute a board of trade. The competing views on this subject taken by the CFTC (*see, e.g., In re Global Link Miami Corp*, 1998-99 COMM. FUT. L. REP. ¶ 27,669 (June 21, 1999)) and the U.S. Treasury Department, and the inconsistent results in cases addressing the issue, were among the reasons cited in support of change to the Treasury Amendment in REPORT OF THE PRESIDENT'S WORKING GROUP ON FINANCIAL MARKETS, *supra* note 202, at 24–26. The CFMA amended the definition of "board of trade" to include only organized exchanges and other trading facilities and enacted new detailed definitions of the terms "organized exchange" and "trading facility." *See* CEA §§ 1a(2), 1a(27) & 1a(33). *See infra* p. 101 for discussion of the Treasury Amendment's language as amended by the CFMA. On cases involving disagreements over the meaning of "board of trade" prior to the CFMA amendment of the term, *see* Gooch & Klein, *Review of Case Law II*, at 74–76.

[241] *See* Gooch & Klein, *Review of Case Law II*, at 75–76, and 2 SECURITIES & DERIVATIVES REGULATION § 13.09[4][a] for discussion of how some courts have treated this issue. In *Dunn v. CFTC*, 519 U.S. 465, 470 (1997), the Supreme Court ruled that the Treasury Amendment's reference to "transactions in" foreign currency extends to a foreign currency option and any other transaction "in which foreign currency is the fungible good whose fluctuating market price provides the motive for trading."

[242] *Salomon Forex v. Tauber*, 795 F. Supp. 768 (E.D. Va. 1992), *aff'd*, 8 F.3d 966 (4th Cir. 1993). In *Tauber* the court rejected the defendant's arguments. *See* Gooch & Klein, *Review of Case Law II*, at 73–74, on the claims in the *Tauber* case involving the CEA. Other claims, involving gaming and bucket shop laws, are discussed *supra* notes 226 & 232. Still other aspects of the case are discussed *supra* pp. 48 & 57.

[243] *See infra* p. 101.

exclusion because those other exclusions are only available for eligible contract participants, as discussed below.

The Forward Contract Exclusion. The other pre-CFMA statutory exclusion, which also predated the 1974 amendments, is known as the Forward Contract Exclusion. It states that the term "future delivery" does not include "any sale of any cash commodity for deferred payment or delivery"[244] and, therefore, excludes these sales—referred to as forward contracts—from the CEA's provisions on commodity futures. As a result, court decisions sometimes discuss the hallmark features of futures contracts through contrast with cash sales of commodities for deferred delivery. An often cited example is the following:

> A "futures contract" . . . is generally understood to be an executory, mutually binding agreement providing for the future delivery of a commodity on a date certain where the grade, quantity, and price at the time of delivery are fixed. To facilitate the development of a liquid market in these transactions, these contracts are standardized and transferable. Trading in futures seldom results in physical delivery of the subject commodity, since the obligations are often extinguished by offsetting transactions that produce a net profit or loss. The main purpose realized by entering into futures transactions is to transfer price risks from suppliers, processors and distributors (hedgers) to those more willing to take the risk (speculators). Since the prices of futures are contingent on the vagaries of both the production of the commodity and the economics of the marketplace, they are particularly susceptible to manipulation and excessive speculation.
>
> In contrast to the fungible quality of futures, cash forwards are generally individually negotiated sales of commodities between principals in which actual delivery of the commodity is anticipated, but is deferred for reasons of commercial convenience or necessity. These contracts are not readily transferable and therefore are usually entered into between parties able to make and receive physical delivery of the subject goods.[245]

Broad segments of the OTC derivatives market, including those involving currencies, metals and energy products, have long looked to the Forward Contract Exclusion for comfort that the legality of their transactions would not be challenged under the Futures Trading Restrictions. However, the reach of this exclusion too has been the subject of substantial debate and doubt. Also, the exclusion's focus on delivery has limited its usefulness to the derivatives market, as the transfer of risks relating to non-deliverable commodities has become a central part of the market.

Given the statutory focus on sales for deferred payment or delivery, court determinations regarding the availability of the Forward Contract Exclusion have centered mainly on (1) whether the parties were commercial participants in the market for the un-

---

[244] CEA § 1a(19).

[245] *Salomon Forex v. Tauber*, 8 F.3d 966, 971 (4th Cir. 1993) (footnote omitted). The court held that Dr. Tauber's FX forwards and currency options with Salomon Forex were not covered by the CEA because they were exempted by the Treasury Amendment.

derlying commodity, (2) whether they in fact had the ability to make and take delivery and (3) whether, at the time the parties contracted, there was a legitimate expectation, or intent, that they would make or take delivery or whether their intent, on the other hand, was purely speculative. The courts and the CFTC have thus been faced with difficult issues regarding exactly what should be treated as delivery for purposes of the Forward Contract Exclusion.[246]

The limitations of the Forward Contract Exclusion as a source of comfort for the derivatives market became acutely apparent in 1990, when a U.S. federal court held in the *Transnor* case that contracts in Brent blend crude oil were illegal commodity futures under the CEA.[247] The court found that the Forward Contract Exclusion was not available for the transactions because of the widespread practice in the market of settling the transactions through "book-outs," with cash settlement payments, rather than actual physical delivery.

After reports that the decision was affecting participation in the market by U.S. firms, the CFTC sought to calm market concerns by adopting a Statutory Interpretation Concerning Forward Transactions, noting that Congress had not addressed the reach of the Forward Contract Exclusion "in today's commercial environment."[248] The interpretation clarified that the ultimate settlement through book-out, or cash settlement, of an individually negotiated forward contract should not disqualify the transaction from the exclusion if the parties are commercial entities with the capacity to make or take delivery of the underlying commodity, routinely do so, have binding obligations under the contract to make and take delivery and do not have the right to transfer their respective contract positions without the counterparty's consent.[249]

The comfort that the market took from this statutory interpretation was, however, again cast in doubt by enforcement proceedings brought by the CFTC in 1995 against a U.S. affiliate of Metallgesellschaft.[250] At issue in the proceedings were Firm Fixed Price

---

[246] *See* Gooch & Klein, *Review of Case Law II*, at 77–82.

[247] *Transnor (Bermuda) Ltd. v. BP North American Petroleum*, 738 F. Supp. 1472 (S.D.N.Y. 1990). *See id.* at 78–79 for further discussion of the case.

[248] 55 Fed. Reg. 39,188, *39,191, 1990 W.L. 327,735 (F.R.) (Sept. 25, 1990).

[249] 2 SECURITIES & DERIVATIVES REGULATION § 13.08[3][a][ii][B] discusses this statutory interpretation, known as the "Brent Forward Interpretation," in greater detail and places it in the context of earlier views on the Forward Contract Exclusion expressed by the CFTC and the courts.

[250] *In re MG Refining & Marketing, Inc.*, 1995 CFTC LEXIS 190, CFTC Docket No. 95–14, 1995 WL 447455 *2, *6 (July 27, 1995). *See* Gooch & Klein, *Review of Case Law II*, at 79–82 and sources cited *infra* note 627. The role of MG Refining & Marketing (MGRM) and other members of the Metallgesellschaft group, including Deutsche Bank AG, a major shareholder of Metallgesellschaft, in proposing the offer of settlement that resulted in the issuance of the consent order was subsequently cited as the basis for claims for damages against them in a private action premised on breach of the duty of good faith and fair dealing inherent in the contracts—referred to as "flexies"—in seeking and agreeing to the CFTC order on various theories under which Deutsche Bank and other Deutsche Bank entities should be held responsible for MGRM's breach of the flexies and should, independently, be held responsible for tortiously interfering with plaintiffs' contracts with MGRM. *See Cary Oil Co., Inc. v. MG Refining & Marketing, Inc.*, 90 F. Supp. 2d 401 (S.D.N.Y. 2000) (denying the MG Group's motion to dismiss, or for summary judgment on, the claims against its members, dismissing some of the claims on consent of the parties, granting the Deutsche Bank defendants' motion to dismiss some of the claims and denying that motion in respect of other claims).

(45-Day) Agreements for the Sale of Petroleum Product with independent gasoline stations and heating oil distributors, which were recognized by the CFTC as commercial entities with the requisite capacity to make and take delivery. The contracts called for delivery at an agreed price on a date to be set by the purchaser with 45 days' notice, and they permitted deferral of delivery for up to ten years. They also gave the purchaser a cash-settlement option if the underlying product reached a specified price level. Given these features and the way the contracts were marketed, the CFTC found them to be illegal off-exchange futures because MG Refining and its customers never intended that the contracts would be settled by delivery and were using the contracts purely for speculation. Therefore, the CFTC required MG Refining & Marketing, as a condition to settlement of the proceedings, to inform the customers that the contracts were void.[251]

CFTC EXEMPTIONS AND SAFE HARBORS

Prior to the enactment of the FTPA in 1992, the CFTC had the authority to grant exemptions from the CEA's Option Trading Restrictions but not the Futures Trading Restrictions.

The Trade Option Exemption. Using its exemptive authority with respect to options, in 1976 the CFTC adopted the Trade Option Exemption.[252] Although often relied on in OTC derivatives transactions, the Trade Option Exemption, like the Forward Contract Exclusion, is of limited use, because for it to apply the party offering the option must have a reasonable basis for belief that the offeree is a "producer, processor or a commercial user of, or a merchant handling" the commodity that is the subject of the relevant option transaction, or the products or by-products of that commodity, and the offeree must also be entering into the transaction "solely for purposes related to its business as such."[253] Subject to these and related limitations discussed below, this exemption from the CEA continues to retain vitality and may be particularly useful where one of the parties to a transaction is ineligible for the benefits of other exemptions or the exclusions discussed below, which were provided by the CFMA.[254]

The Swap Policy Statement. The CFTC recognized as early as 1989 that legal uncertainty regarding the Options Trading Restrictions and the Futures Trading Restrictions was hindering development in the U.S. of the OTC derivatives market for swaps and similar transactions, given the CFTC's announced view that transactions that functioned economically like commodity options and futures could be regulated as such under the CEA. Lacking the power to grant an exemption from the Futures Trading Restrictions, however, the CFTC was limited in its ability to offer comfort. It therefore issued the Swap Policy Statement, stating that, in the absence of use of exchange-style clearing and mar-

---

[251] The consent order in these proceedings is available at 1995 WL 447455 (C.F.T.C.).

[252] 17 C.F.R. § 32.4(a) (2002). This exemptive authority, found in Section 4c(b) of the CEA, was also used by the CFTC to adopt the Hybrid Option Rules, Regulation of Hybrid Instruments, 54 Fed. Reg. 30,684, 1989 WL 278,779 (F.R.) (July 21, 1989), exempting certain hybrid instruments with features that function like commodity options from the CEA's restrictions on commodity option trading discussed in this chapter. *See infra* note 368.

[253] 17 C.F.R. § 32.4(a) (2002).

[254] *See infra* p. 109 for further discussion of the Trade Option Exemption and a sample representation alluding to the exemption.

gining, swap agreements with individually tailored terms, if entered into by each party in conjunction with a line of business and not marketed to the general public, are "not appropriately regulated" and "will not be subject to regulation as futures or commodity option transactions" under the CEA.[255] Under the Collar Interpretation[256] the CFTC subsequently extended the coverage of the Swap Policy Statement from swaps to certain collar transactions, but the statement itself remained, and remains today, a mere reflection of administrative policy, or safe harbor, as it is often called, rather than an actual exemption from the CEA. That critical fact and its various criteria for the transactions it covered have limited the usefulness of the Swap Policy Statement for the OTC derivatives market.[257] It nonetheless retains vitality and may be a source of limited comfort to market participants in connection with retail transactions and transactions involving agricultural commodities, areas in which the exclusions enacted by the CFMA are generally unavailable.

The Swap Agreement Exemption and the Energy Contracts Exemption. As indicated, through the FTPA, the U.S. Congress gave the CFTC authority to grant exemptions from the Futures Trading Restrictions.[258] The FTPA did not deal specifically with swap agreements or any other type of transaction. Rather, broadly speaking, it conferred jurisdiction on the CFTC to grant exemptions when it found them to be in the public interest, provided the exempted transactions would be entered into only by statutorily defined classes of "appropriate persons."[259] The FTPA did not, however, extend this new exemptive authority to the Security Futures Trading Restrictions as they were expressed at the time in the Shad-Johnson Accord.

An attempt to resolve jurisdictional disagreements between the SEC and CFTC through compromise (the Treasury Amendment having been inadequate to avert the disagreements[260]), the Shad-Johnson Accord had been incorporated into the CEA and other legislation in 1982 and 1983[261] and spelled out which financial instruments fell within

---

[255] 54 Fed. Reg. at *30,694 & *30,696 (July 21, 1989).

[256] *See supra* note 199.

[257] *See infra* p. 110.

[258] The authorization was granted through a new Section 4(c)(1) of the CEA.

[259] This limiting feature was added through Section 4(c)(2) of the CEA, which also conditions the granting of an exemption on the CFTC's concluding that the Futures Trading Restrictions of Section 4(a) of the CEA should not be applied and that the exempted agreement, contract or transaction will not have a material adverse effect on the ability of the CFTC or any CFTC-designated futures contract market to discharge its regulatory or self-regulatory duties under the CEA.

[260] *See* 2 SECURITIES & DERIVATIVES REGULATION § 13.07[2].

[261] In the CEA, the Accord was reflected in Section 2(a)(1)(B). *Board of Trade v. SEC*, 187 F.3d 713 (7th Cir. 1999), and *Chicago Mercantile Exchange v. SEC*, 883 F.2d 537 (7th Cir. 1989), provide some color on the background of the SEC-CFTC disagreements over jurisdiction and their linkage to each agency's support for its "clients"—the stock exchanges and futures exchanges—even after the Shad-Johnson Accord. The later case involved the SEC's conclusion that the Chicago Board of Trade should not be permitted to trade futures based on Dow Jones securities indexes because the indexes did not meet the criteria in Section 2(a)(ii)(III) of the CEA for a "broad-based" index reflecting a substantial segment of the market. On a petition for review, the court vacated the SEC's order. The earlier case involved a Chicago Mercantile Exchange challenge to the SEC's approval of applications from three stock exchanges to trade IPs, index participations. Finding that contracts were futures within the then exclusive jurisdiction of the CFTC, the court set the SEC's orders aside.

each agency's jurisdiction. As then enacted, the Shad-Johnson Accord banned both exchange-traded and off-exchange futures on most individual securities and narrowly based groups or indexes of securities. It permitted exchange trading of futures on broadly based groups and indexes of securities only if the SEC and the CFTC, in cooperation, found them to "be predominantly composed of the securities of unaffiliated issuers" and to be "a widely published measure of, and . . . reflect, the market for all publicly traded equity or debt securities or a substantial segment thereof," or to "be comparable to such measure."[262]

The FTPA expressly indicated that the new exemptive authority given to the CFTC could not be applied to security futures contracts subject to the Shad-Johnson Accord. As a result, although soon after the enactment of the FTPA the CFTC used that authority to adopt exemptions,[263] including the Swap Agreement Exemption and the Energy Contracts Exemption, thereby providing substantial relief to the OTC derivatives market generally, serious concerns over the applicability of the CEA to securities-based swaps and similar OTC derivatives remained. Those concerns were, as discussed below, largely removed by the exclusions enacted by the CFMA.[264]

From the perspective of legal certainty, the Swap Agreement Exemption and the Energy Contracts Exemption represented a significant improvement for the OTC derivatives market. Unlike the Swap Policy Statement and the Statutory Interpretation Concerning Forward Transactions, these CFTC exemptions actually provide that the Futures Trading Restrictions do not apply to qualifying transactions and, at the same time, make clear that the relevant exemption should not be viewed as meaning that the transactions would have been subject to the CEA in the absence of the exemption.[265] As discussed below, the FTPA also provided that the CEA would preempt all state and local gaming and

---

[262]Prior to the enactment of the CFMA, the ban on futures on individual securities and narrow-based indices of securities was set forth in Section 2(a)(1)(B)(v) of the CEA and was subject to exceptions only for certain securities treated as exempt under the federal securities laws. Section 2(a)(1)(B)(ii) of the CEA set out the quoted minimum requirements for broad-based indices or groups of securities that might be authorized subjects of exchange-traded futures contracts.

[263]The CFTC used the exemptive authority granted by the FTPA to adopt the Swap Agreement Exemption and the Energy Contracts Exemption discussed in this chapter, as well as the Hybrid Exemption, Regulation of Hybrid Instruments, 58 Fed. Reg. 5580, 1993 W.L. 10,462 (F.R.) (Jan. 22, 1993).

[264]In defining the term "security future," Section §1(a)(31) of the CEA makes clear that the term—and, therefore, the Security Futures Restrictions—does not include any agreement, contract, or transaction excluded from the CEA under the various exclusions discussed in this chapter.

[265]That is, whether those provisions have any application to a qualifying swap agreement is not a matter dealt with by the 1993 Swap Agreement Exemption. In issuing the exemption, the CFTC stated that the "issuance of this rule should not be construed as reflecting any determination that the swap agreements covered by [its] terms . . . are subject to the [Commodity Exchange] Act, as the Commission has not made and is not obligated to make any such determination." Exemption for Certain Swap Agreements, 58 Fed. Reg. 5587, *5588, 1993 W.L. 10,463 (F.R.) (Jan. 22, 1993). Section 2(i) of the CEA also provides a rule against reading the CEA, including its Section 4(c)(i)—under which the 1993 Swap Agreement Exemption applies—to give rise to any implication or presumption that the CEA would apply to any transaction but for an exemption or exclusion. The FTPA expressly authorized this approach, in response to market concerns. The aim was to forestall arguments that the mere grant of exemptive authority to the CFTC, or its exercise, implied a view that the CEA is applicable to OTC derivatives not covered by an exemption.

bucket-shop laws as applied to transactions covered by CFTC exemptions adopted pursuant to this FTPA grant of authority.[266]

On the other hand, the Swap Agreement Exemption and the Energy Contracts Exemption in various ways fell short of the degree of legal certainty needed for the further development of the OTC derivatives markets in the U.S. For example, the Swap Agreement Exemption provides no relief for transactions if they are "part of a fungible class of agreements that are standardized as to their material economic terms."[267] Many engaged in "plain vanilla" swaps of various kinds have been concerned by the possible implications of this criterion. Others have been concerned because, although the generic list of transaction classes covered by the exemption is quite broad and is written to extend to other similar agreements and transactions,[268] the Swap Agreement Exemption nonetheless involves some exercise in characterization of covered transactions. By way of comparison, many of the statutory exclusions enacted by the CFMA apply to any contract, transaction or agreement in a relevant commodity and otherwise qualifying for the exclusion, as discussed below.[269] In addition, the Swap Agreement Exemption is not available for a party to a transaction unless the creditworthiness of its counterparty, or another obligor, is a material consideration, or if the transaction is entered into on or through a multilateral transaction execution facility.[270] Like similar criteria in the Swap Policy Statement, these features of the Swap Agreement Exemption have proved troublesome as the market has evolved and sought to take advantage of electronic trading platforms and the potential risk-management benefits of clearing systems. A comparison of the requirements of the Swap Agreement Exemption with the broader relief available under exclusions enacted through the CFMA is included below.[271]

In addition, as administrative actions, the Swap Agreement Exemption and the Energy Contract Exemption are subject to change or withdrawal by the CFTC. Concerns over this possibility became widespread in the late 1990s. Several factors prompted these concerns, but they became especially acute in 1998, when the CFTC issued a Concept Release indicating that the agency believed it appropriate to review its regulatory approach to OTC derivatives.[272] Although the Concept Release indicated that the CFTC had "no preconceived result in mind" and was "open both to evidence in support of easing current restrictions and evidence indicating a need for additional safeguards,"[273] the mere discussion in the release of the CFTC's oversight of the OTC derivatives market and suggestion that the CFTC could require market participants to register with or report to the CFTC seemed to imply an assertion of jurisdiction where the market believed none should be presumed.

---

[266]*See infra* p. 112.

[267]*See infra* note 345.

[268]*See infra* note 344 and accompanying text.

[269]*See, e.g., infra* p. 91.

[270]*See infra* notes 346 & 347.

[271]*See infra* p. 85.

[272]CFTC, *Over-the-Counter Derivatives* (May 7, 1998), *available at* www.cftc.gov/mntn.htm.

[273]*Id.* at 1.

In response to alarm in the market and a joint request of the Department of the Treasury, the Federal Reserve Board and the SEC, the U.S. Congress enacted legislation that temporarily limited the CFTC's rulemaking authority with respect to swaps and hybrid instruments.[274] Thus, prior to enactment of the CFMA, the CFTC exemptions described above, together with the Swap Policy Statement, the Treasury Amendment and the Forward Contract Exclusion, were the main sources of comfort relied on by OTC derivatives market participants in connection with their CEA concerns.

CFMA EXCLUSIONS

In 1998, President Clinton set up a Working Group on Financial Markets, consisting of the Secretary of the Treasury and the Chairmen of the Board of Governors of the Federal Reserve System, the SEC and the CFTC, and the U.S. Congress asked the Working Group to develop policy and provide legislative recommendations with respect to OTC derivatives. The report of the President's Working Group, released in November 1999, became the blueprint for the amendments to the CEA and the federal securities and banking laws relating to OTC derivatives enacted in the CFMA.[275] The report presented its unanimous recommendations as appropriate to avoid the perpetuation of legal uncertainty in the OTC derivatives markets and to eliminate "unnecessary burdens and constraints on the development of these markets in the United States," as well as to

> remove legal impediments to the development of electronic trading systems, which have the potential to increase market liquidity and transparency, and appropriately regulated clearing systems, which can reduce systemic risk by allowing for the mutualization of risks among market participants.... [276]

The report considered these recommendations in the context of existing regulatory structures applicable to exchange-traded derivatives and statutes other than the CEA, made recommendations to eliminate legal uncertainty regarding hybrid instruments, addressed the conditions under which the trading of single-stock futures contracts might be permitted and recommended that the CFTC be given authority to provide appropriate relief for exchange-traded financial futures.

---

[274] This legislation, the Omnibus Consolidated and Emergency Supplemental Appropriations Act, Pub. L. No. 105–277, 112 Stat. 2681 (1998), provided that nothing in the 1998 CFTC Concept Release would "alter or affect the legal status of a qualifying hybrid instrument or swap agreement," and that the legislation itself should not "be construed as reflecting or implying a determination that a qualified hybrid instrument or swap agreement . . . is subject to the CEA." This legislation also prohibited the issuance by the CFTC of any rule, regulation, interpretation or policy statement that would restrict or regulate activity in specified hybrid instruments and qualifying swap agreements.

[275] The CFMA was enacted as part of the appropriations bill for the fiscal year ending September 30, 2001, Pub. L. No. 106-554, Appendix E, 114 Stat. 2763 (2000). The CFMA also introduced major changes to the CEA's approach to the regulation of contract markets for futures and options, to the role of the CFTC generally and to the treatment of hybrid instruments. On hybrids, see *supra* note 368 and the source cited therein.

[276] REPORT OF THE PRESIDENT'S WORKING GROUP ON FINANCIAL MARKETS, *supra* note 202, at 1–2.

The changes made by the CFMA in the law applicable to OTC derivatives are discussed in more detail in the following sections. They provide exclusions from the CEA's trading restrictions for most wholesale market transactions, including securities-based swaps and similar derivatives and, subject to specified conditions, transactions that are entered into on electronic trading facilities. Transactions involving agricultural commodities are not, however, covered by these exclusions.[277]

The CFMA also (1) provides a limited CEA exclusion for transactions in foreign currency between retail market participants, on one hand, and specified classes of regulated institutions, on the other,[278] (2) makes clear that this and the various wholesale market exclusions apply regardless of whether the parties manage the associated credit risk through permitted clearing systems and (3) provides various ancillary protections of legal certainty for participants in excluded transactions, through preemptions of state and local gaming and bucket-shop laws and provisions on contract enforcement.

EXEMPTIONS AND EXCLUSIONS AND RELATED REPRESENTATIONS

Under the CEA as amended in 1992 by the FTPA and in 2000 by the CFMA, the Futures Trading Restrictions, Options Trading Restrictions and Security Futures Trading Restrictions, and the CFTC's jurisdiction over futures and options, are subject to limitations, which include

- the express exemptions and exclusions described below for many OTC derivatives,[279]

- SEC jurisdiction over derivatives that have traditionally been identified as securities under the federal securities laws—such as puts and

---

[277] Under Section 5(e) of the CEA, to the extent that a designated contract market was authorized to trade futures contracts on specified agricultural commodities on the date of enactment of the CFMA, trading in futures on that commodity will be limited to that contract market. However, Section 5(e) also provides that, in order to promote responsible economic or financial innovation and fair competition, the CFTC may prescribe rules and regulations to provide for the offer and sale of contracts for future delivery on agricultural commodities, or options on those futures contracts, on a derivatives transaction execution facility.

[278] Section 105(c) of the CFMA, 114 Stat. 2763A-365 (2000), directed the Board of Governors of the Federal Reserve System, the Secretary of the Treasury, the CFTC and the SEC to conduct a study of issues involving the offering of swap agreements to retail participants in the market (persons who do not qualify as "eligible contract participants (ECPs)," *see infra* p. 85). The required topics were: (1) the potential uses of swap agreements by persons other than ECPs; (2) the extent to which financial institutions are willing to offer swap agreements to persons other than ECPs; (3) the appropriate regulatory structure to address customer protection issues that may arise in connection with the offer of swap agreements to persons other than ECPs; and (4) other relevant matters. The report on the study was submitted to the U.S. Senate on December 26, 2001. The report recommended that no legislative action be taken regarding swap agreements for persons other than ECPs, because (1) there appear to be sufficient instruments available to meet the needs of such persons, "including equity-linked notes, warrants, exchange-traded funds, mutual funds, exchange-traded options and, likely in 2002, exchange-traded security futures" and "there is currently a lack of interest among most major market participants in offering swaps to retail customers". *Joint Report on Retail Swaps* 5, 8 (2001), *available at* http://www.treas.gov/press/releases/docs/rss-final.pdf.

[279] Other exclusions for hybrid instruments, although not generally discussed below, are referred to *infra* note 368.

calls and physically settled forwards on one or more securities and baskets and indexes of securities,[280]

- joint SEC and CFTC jurisdiction over security futures (as defined in the CFMA) on individual securities and narrowly based security indexes, and over options on those futures—classes of transactions that were, as noted above, formerly prohibited,[281] and

- involvement of the Department of the Treasury, the Board of Governors of the Federal Reserve System and the SEC in matters concerning futures in commodities, securities and financial instruments under the jurisdiction of those other agencies.[282]

The following discussion covers the exemptions and exclusions most likely to be referred or alluded to in the documentation for OTC derivatives. In each case, we will examine the applicable terminology and requirements and the representations that the parties may use if they are seeking to establish that their transactions are entitled to the benefits of one or more of these exemptions or exclusions and the benefits of the related preemptive and contract enforcement provisions discussed later in this chapter.

Each of these CEA exemptions and exclusions has its own limitations. The broadest are discussed first, since they, naturally, are likely to be relevant for the greatest number of agreements and confirmations for derivatives. The limiting contours of the narrower exemptions and exclusions are quite varied. Some, for example, are available only for transactions in specified kinds of commodities, or only for options or forward contracts or only for transactions with specified classes of financial institutions. However, as users of OTC derivatives consider which of these exemptions and exclusions, and related representations, may be relevant to themselves and their derivatives activities, they should remember that many transactions may qualify for several of the exemptions or exclusions.

Moreover, the mere fact that a transaction does not satisfy all the requirements of any of the exemptions or exclusions does not necessarily mean that a transaction is subject to challenge as having been entered into in violation of the CEA's trading restrictions,

---

[280] Section 2(a)(1)(C)(i) of the CEA provides that nothing in the statute applies to those transactions, and that the CFTC shall have no jurisdiction to designate a board of trade as a contract market for any of those transactions. *See infra* p. 141 for discussion of U.S. statutory distinctions between securities and swaps agreements.

[281] *See* CEA § 2(a)(1)(D). The term "security future" is defined in Section 1a(31) of the CEA and in Securities Exchange Act § 3(a)(55)(A) to include those two products, and "narrow-based security index" is defined in Section 1a(25) of the CEA and Securities Exchange Act §3(a)(55)(B), as amended by the CFMA, largely by reference to the number of component securities in the index, the percentage of the index's weighting attributable to a single security or the five highest weighted component securities or, in some cases, the aggregate dollar value of average daily trading volume of component securities at the lowest end of the index's weighting. There are grandfathering and other special rules for security index futures listed before the enactment of the CFMA, for foreign securities index futures and other cases. Generally, the CFMA authorized trading in security futures beginning in late 2001 and provided that, after December 2004, the SEC and the CFTC, jointly, may permit trading in options on security futures. *See* CEA §§ 2(a)(1)(D)(i) & (iii).

[282] *See* CEA §§ 2(a)(1)(D) and 2(a)(8)(B).

since it could be protected by the contract enforcement provisions enacted by the CFMA, the Swap Policy Statement and rules in the CEA on its interpretation, as discussed in the last section of this chapter.[283]

ELIGIBLE SWAP PARTICIPANT AND ELIGIBLE CONTRACT PARTICIPANT STATUS

Prior to the enactment of the CFMA the broadest exemption from the CEA's trading restrictions available to the OTC derivatives market was the 1993 Swap Agreement Exemption, and its requirements have been reflected for many years in the representations included in derivatives documentation. By way of introduction to the exclusions and exemptions from CEA as amended by the CFMA, in this overview we compare the principal requirements of the 1993 Swap Agreement Exemption with those of the newer CFMA exclusions.[284] Since the threshold requirement, in the first case, is that each party be an eligible swap participant, and, in the second case, generally, that each party be an eligible contract participant,[285] we then compare the criteria applicable in the two cases and the evolution of the concepts that are reflected in the definitions of "eligible swap participant" and "eligible contract participant." Against this background, we then discuss various representations that market participants have used and are likely to continue to use to establish the applicability of the CEA exclusions and exemptions discussed below.

PRINCIPAL FEATURES OF CEA EXEMPTIONS AND EXCLUSIONS	
1993 Swap Agreement Exemption	*Exclusions added by the CFMA*
Transactions must be between eligible swap participants. In many but not all cases the classes of eligible swap participants are narrower than the related classes of eligible contract participants. *See* table, *infra* p. 115.	Transactions, generally, must be between eligible contract participants. Some exclusions are available only for transactions between or involving a narrower class of eligible contract participants, called "eligible commercial entities," or for transactions offered by banks, and a limited Treasury Amendment exclusion applies to retail foreign currency transactions with financial institutions.

---

[283] *Infra* p. 113.

[284] The table does not deal with the Treasury Amendment as amended by the CFMA or the Forward Contract Exclusion. *See infra* pp. 101 & 103 for discussion of those CEA exclusions.

[285] As discussed below, an exception to this general rule is provided by the Treasury Amendment as amended by the CFMA. It affords a partial exclusion from the CEA for OTC derivatives transactions in foreign currencies entered into by retail market participants—that is, persons who are not eligible contract participants—with counterparties, or proposed counterparties, who fall within specified classes of eligible contract participants that are subject to regulation by the CFTC, the SEC or a banking or insurance regulatory agency. *See infra* p. 101.

PRINCIPAL FEATURES OF CEA EXEMPTIONS AND EXCLUSIONS	
1993 Swap Agreement Exemption	*Exclusions added by the CFMA*
Not available for a transaction that is "part of a fungible class of agreements that are standardized as to their material economic terms," because of a requirement in the authorizing statute. See *infra* note 345.	The nonfungibility requirement does not apply, but some of the exemptions and exclusions require that the material terms (other than price and quantity) be subject to individual negotiation between the parties. See *infra* note 298.
Not available for transactions if they are traded on or through a multilateral transaction execution facility. See *infra* note 347.	Some of the exemptions and exclusions are available for transactions entered into or executed on an electronic trading facility.
Not available if the parties eliminate counterparty credit risk by substituting the credit of a clearinghouse for that of the counterparty.	Available notwithstanding the parties' use of authorized derivatives clearing organizations to mutualize or otherwise manage credit risk.
Applies regardless of the transaction's "underlying." It takes no position on its availability for securities-linked derivatives but expressly excludes any exemption from the Securities Trading Restrictions as they figured in the Shad-Johnson Accord before enactment of the CFMA.	Not available for a transaction in an agricultural commodity. Some apply only to transactions in "exempt" or "excluded" commodities. Those available for excluded commodities (CEA § 1a(33)(A)), and covered swap agreements offered by banks (Bank Products Legal Certainty Act § 407) and for excluded derivatives transactions (CEA §2(g)) include many securities-linked transactions.
Qualifying transactions and their parties are not exempt from CEA and CFTC antifraud and antimanipulation provisions and regulations.	Some excluded transactions and parties are totally outside CFTC regulation and the CEA (other than the preemptions of state and local gaming and bucket-shop laws and provisions related to clearing organizations or facilities through which transactions are executed, when applicable). Other provisions do not exempt the transactions and parties from antifraud and antimanipulation provisions of the CEA and related regulations.

Tables at the end of this chapter compare the criteria for various classes of eligible swap participants and eligible contract participants, which may vary depending on whether they are acting for their own account[286] or for the account of another.[287] As shown in the tables, many different criteria may be applicable in determining whether a party qualifies. They relate, among other things, to

- total assets

    (relevant for natural persons, broker-dealers and futures commission merchants (FCMs) who are natural persons, commodity pools, corporations, partnerships, proprietorships, organizations, trusts and other entities)

- net worth

    (relevant for some corporations, partnerships, proprietorships, organizations, trusts and other entities)

- the purpose for which the counterparty is entering into the transaction

    (relevant for some natural persons and corporations, partnerships, proprietorships, organizations, trusts and other entities)

- the investments it owns and invests on a discretionary basis

    (one of several qualifying characteristics for instrumentalities, agencies and departments of governments and multinational or supranational governmental entities under the CEA but not necessary under the 1993 Swap Agreement Exemption)

- its ability, directly or through separate contractual arrangements, to make or take delivery of the commodity underlying the relevant transaction in connection with its business

    (an alternative qualifying characteristic for instrumentalities, agencies and departments of governments and multinational or supranational governmental entities under the CEA but not necessary under the 1993 Swap Agreement Exemption)

- whether in connection with its business it incurs risks, in addition to price risk, related to the commodity underlying the transaction

    (a third possible qualifying characteristic for instrumentalities, agencies and departments of governments and multinational or supranational governmental entities under the CEA but not necessary under the 1993 Swap Agreement Exemption)

- whether in its business it is a dealer that regularly provides risk management or hedging services to, or engages in market-making activities with, eligible contract participants involving transactions to purchase or sell the relevant commodity or derivative agreements, contracts, or transactions in that commodity

---

[286] *See* table beginning *infra* p. 115.

[287] *See* table beginning *infra* p. 123.

(another qualifying characteristic for instrumentalities, agencies and departments of governments and multinational or supranational governmental entities under the CEA but not necessary under the 1993 Swap Agreement Exemption).

Evolution of the Concepts. When the CFTC received statutory authority to grant exemptions from the CEA's Futures Trading Restrictions in 1992, under Section 4(c)(1) of the CEA,[288] the authority was made available only for agreements, contracts and transactions that satisfy specified requirements, including the requirement that they be "entered into solely between appropriate persons."

"Appropriate person" is defined in Section 4(c)(3) of the CEA to include numerous classes of counterparties. Many of these classes are identified in the statute by reference to their status as regulated entities in the U.S. The statute also gives the CFTC power to determine that other classes of counterparties are "appropriate persons," "in light of their financial or other qualifications, or the applicability of appropriate regulatory protections."[289]

In issuing the 1993 Swap Agreement Exemption, the CFTC adopted the term "eligible swap participant" to avoid confusion with the statutory list of "appropriate persons," since the classes of eligible swap participants in some cases include classes of appropriate persons only subject to the additional conditions specified in the exemption. The CFTC's classes of eligible swap participants also go beyond the statutory list by adding persons organized outside the U.S. (referred to as "foreign") that are subject to regulation similar to that applicable to the classes of U.S. entities that qualify as eligible swap participants by virtue of their regulated status. The CFTC's category of eligible swap participants also includes natural persons "with total assets exceeding at least $10,000,000," whereas the statutory list of appropriate persons includes natural persons only if they qualify by virtue of a regulated status (as a securities broker-dealer, an FCM, a floor broker or a floor trader).

The classes of persons qualifying as eligible contract participants are in most, but not all, respects broader than the similar classes of appropriate persons and eligible swap participants.[290] For example, a natural person with total assets in excess of $5 million but less than $10 million will qualify as an eligible contract participant in connection with transactions entered into to manage specified assets, liabilities or risks, but not as an eligible swap participant. On the other hand, an instrumentality, agency or department of a government that qualifies as an appropriate person and an eligible swap participant will qualify as an eligible contract participant only if it also satisfies additional conditions.

In some cases, qualification of an entity as an eligible swap participant is predicated on its not having been formed solely for the purpose of qualifying. This requirement

---

[288]CEA § 4(c)(1).

[289]CEA § 4(c)(3)(K).

[290]Clause (A) of the definition identifies those who qualify as eligible contract participants when they are acting "for their own account." Clause (B) lists those who qualify when they are "acting as a broker or performing an equivalent agency function" on behalf of an eligible contract participant identified in clause (A) or a person who qualifies under clause (C) of the definition, which applies to persons determined by the CFTC to be eligible "in light of the financial or other qualification of the person." CEA § 1a(12).

does not apply to any class of eligible contract participant. Indeed, the definition of that term makes clear that if an entity—say a special purpose company, a trust or a commodity pool—qualifies under the statutory description for the relevant class of eligible contract participants, there is no "look through" required, or permitted, to determine whether the owners or investors who stand behind the entity, or for whose benefit it exists, qualify individually as eligible contract participants.

In the release accompanying the 1993 Swap Agreement Exemption, the CFTC stated that "it is sufficient that the parties have a reasonable basis to believe that the other party is an eligible swap participant" at the time the parties enter into the swap agreement, though this is not expressly provided in the exemption.[291] The CFTC further indicated that if a party "has a reasonable basis to believe its counterparty is also an eligible swap participant when it enters into a master agreement," that party may continue to rely on a representation to that effect made by the counterparty in a master agreement "absent information to the contrary."[292]

The operative exclusions of the CEA discussed below for transactions between eligible contract participants require that the parties actually qualify as eligible contract participants and not merely that each party have a reasonable belief that the other qualifies. The contract enforcement provisions of the CFMA discussed at the end of this chapter, however, make clear that an agreement, contract or transaction between eligible contract participants "or persons reasonably believed to be eligible contract persons" will not be void, voidable or unenforceable or otherwise subject to claims for rescission or recovery of payments made under it based solely on the failure of the agreement, contract or transaction to comply with the terms or conditions of an exemption or exclusion from a provision of the CEA or a CFTC regulation.[293]

Effects on Documentation. The documentation used in derivatives transactions with some connection to the United States has for some years included representations aimed at establishing that the parties are eligible swap participants and, in some cases, that their transactions otherwise qualify for the CEA exemption provided by the 1993 Swap Agreement Exemption. Since the enactment of the CFMA, similar representations have been included to refer to the parties' status as eligible contract participants and, in some cases, to other criteria applicable under the newer CFMA exclusions.

---

[291] 58 Fed. Reg. 5587, *5589, 1993 W.L. 10,463 (F.R.) (Jan. 22, 1993).

[292] *Id.* at 5589 n.19.

[293] *See infra* p. 113.

Examples of the general approach in representations relating to the parties' status are as follows.

| Party [A][B] is an "eligible swap participant," as that term is defined in the Exemption for Certain Swap Agreements adopted by the Commodity Futures Trading Commission, 17 C.F.R. § 35.1(b)(2). | Party [A][B] is an "eligible contract participant," as that term is defined in Section 1a(12) of the Commodity Exchange Act, as amended by the Commodity Futures Modernization Act of 2000. |

Such a representation is sometimes accompanied by another along the following lines:

[Party A] [Party B] is entering into [each] [the] transaction in connection with the conduct of its business or to manage the risk of an asset or liability owned or incurred in the conduct of its business or reasonably likely to be owned or incurred in the conduct of its business.

The latter representation is sometimes included because, as shown in the tables at the end of this chapter, if a corporation, partnership, proprietorship, organization, trust or other entity has net worth of at least $1 million but its assets do not exceed $10 million, its status as an eligible swap participant under the 1993 Swap Agreement Exemption, and as an eligible contract participant for purposes of the CEA, may turn on the relevant party's entering into a transaction, or the related agreement, for the risk-management purposes referred to in the representation.[294]

However, in many cases a party's purpose in entering into a transaction is not relevant to its status as an eligible swap participant or eligible contract participant. If an entity's assets exceed $10 million, the risk-management requirement is not a condition to eligible swap participant or eligible contract participant status and, as shown in the tables,[295] there are many categories of entities that may qualify as eligible swap participants without regard to any measure of assets or net worth.

Some market participants nonetheless retain use of the representation generally in their master agreements because the 1993 Swap Agreement Exemption and the CFMA exclusions from the CEA discussed below are not universally available to all OTC derivatives transactions and, even if the exemption or one of the exclusions may be available for purposes of U.S. federal law, concerns over the context in which a transaction is executed may exist under the local law applicable to a party.[296]

Finally, because a counterparty's status as an eligible swap participant or an eligible contract participant may depend on the capacity in which it is acting (that is, for its

---

[294] *See infra* p. 117. Under the 1993 Swap Agreement Exemption, a further requirement may be that the entity not have been formed solely for the specific purpose of constituting an eligible swap participant. *See* 17 C.F.R. § 35.1(b)(2)(vi) (2002).

[295] *Infra* p. 115.

[296] As discussed *supra* p. 78, the Swap Policy Statement safe harbor is available only for transactions entered into by each party in conjunction with a line of business. Therefore, in an OTC derivatives transaction with a retail market participant, for example, the representation could prove useful.

own account or otherwise), when the parties seek to rely on the 1993 Swap Agreement Exemption or on CFMA exclusions discussed below, their derivatives documents are likely, as a matter of form, to include a representation of each party to the effect that it is acting for its own account. If one of the parties is not acting for its own account, the documents may require details from that party about the capacity in which it is acting, again, as the basis for a reasonable belief that the party is an eligible contract participant.

The following description of the requirements of the CEA exclusions added by the CFMA and of the 1993 Swap Agreement Exemption and other CFTC exemptions and statutory exclusions sometimes relied upon by market participants also refers to the related representations that are sometimes included in the documentation for OTC derivatives.

EXCLUDED SWAP TRANSACTIONS

The broadest of the CEA exclusions added by the CFMA is found in Section 2(g) of the CEA,[297] on "excluded swap transactions." Any agreement, contract or transaction will qualify as an excluded swap transaction under Section 2(g) of the CEA if

- it is entered into between eligible contract participants,
- its material terms (other than price and quantity) are subject to individual negotiation by the parties,[298]
- it involves a commodity other than an agricultural commodity and
- it is not executed or traded on a trading facility.[299]

If a transaction is an excluded swap transaction under Section 2(g) of the CEA, it is excluded from all provisions of the CEA other than the beneficial preemptive provisions in Section 12(e)(2), which are discussed later in this chapter,[300] and, to the extent applicable, provisions relating to facilities on which the transaction is executed or cleared.[301] Under this exclusion there is no need to inquire whether an agreement, contract or transaction is or is not a commodity futures contract or option. However, as indicated, the transaction's material terms, other than price and quantity, must be subject to

---

[297]"Excluded swap transaction" is merely a section title, and not a defined term in the CEA.

[298]The report of the President's Working Group identifies individual negotiation of material terms and conditions as an important characteristic that distinguishes OTC derivatives from exchange-traded products, singling out "customization of these transactions to individual customer needs as to maturity, payment intervals, or other terms." REPORT OF THE PRESIDENT'S WORKING GROUP ON FINANCIAL MARKETS, *supra* note 202, at 5.

[299]As discussed *infra* p. 96, there are other exclusions for transactions in excluded commodities and exempt commodities that are entered into or executed on electronic trading facilities. The meaning of "trading facility" for these purposes is discussed below in connection with these additional exclusions.

[300]*See infra* p. 112.

[301]These provisions are Sections 5a, 5b and 5d of the CEA. Transactions eligible for treatment as excluded swap transactions may be executed on DTEFs that are registered with the CFTC and qualify as exempt boards of trade. If they are so executed, the provisions of Section 5a of the CEA apply, to the extent specified in Section 5a(g). *See supra* note 220 on exempt boards of trade, which, as indicated, may not trade security futures products. In addition, excluded swap transactions may be cleared through derivatives clearing organizations. Section 5b of the CEA would apply to the clearing of those transactions.

individual negotiation, rather than offered on a take-it-or-leave it basis. As discussed below, there are further CEA exclusions for transactions in excluded commodities and exempt commodities that do not include this requirement.

As market participants seek to establish that their transactions fall within the protections afforded by Section 2(g) of the CEA and thus also benefit from the related preemptions from state and local gaming and bucket-shop laws, the documents they use for their OTC derivatives will, as suggested above, require each party to state that it is an eligible contract participant, as that term is defined in Section 1a(12) of the CEA, and may also ask a party to show through further representations how it qualifies as an eligible contract participant.

The documents may also require each party to make a general representation along the following lines as to each transaction entered into by the parties:

> It is a transaction excluded from the Commodity Exchange Act under and to the extent provided in Section 2(g) of the Commodity Exchange Act.

Some market participants prefer to avoid including in their master agreements broad representations about transactions that have not yet been executed and, therefore, agree only to representations about their own status as a person entitled to the benefits of an exclusion or exemption, as an eligible contract participant, eligible swap participant or otherwise.

COVERED SWAP AGREEMENTS OFFERED BY BANKS

The Bank Products Legal Certainty Act includes an exclusion[302] from the CEA for OTC derivatives offered, entered into or provided by any "bank," as the term is defined in the Act.[303] The exclusion is largely coextensive with those available under the CEA for eligible contract participants. The Act's definition of "bank" includes U.S. depository institutions, branches and agencies of foreign banks in the United States, credit unions subject to regulation under the Federal Credit Union Act, trust companies, Edge Act corporations and agreement corporations as well as any subsidiary of any of these entities if the subsidiary is regulated as if it were part of the entity and is not a securities broker or dealer subject to regulation under the Securities Exchange Act or an FCM subject to regulation under the CEA.[304]

The broadest of the Bank Products Legal Certainty Act exclusions for bank transactions applies to any "covered swap agreement" offered, entered into or provided by a bank. There are paired sets of criteria applicable if the transactions (1) are not entered into or executed on a trading facility (whether electronic or not) or (2) are entered into or executed on an electronic trading facility.[305]

---

[302] Bank Products Legal Certainty Act § 407.

[303] Bank Products Legal Certainty Act § 402(a).

[304] *Id.* Except for the limitation on subsidiaries and the fact that institutions regulated by the Farm Credit Administration and financial holding companies regulated under the Bank Holding Company Act do not qualify as banks, the definition of "bank" is coextensive with the definition of "financial institution" in Section 1a(15) of the CEA.

[305] Bank Products Legal Certainty Act § 402(d).

Under this exclusion, covered swap agreements offered, entered into or provided by banks are totally removed from the reach of the CEA, except for the provisions that apply to transactions cleared through derivatives clearing organizations. As under the exclusion provided by Section 2(g) of the CEA on excluded swap transactions, there is no need to inquire whether a covered swap agreement is a commodity futures contract or a commodity option. The exclusion under Section 407 of the Bank Products Legal Certainty Act also provides that the CFTC may not exercise regulatory authority with respect to banks' covered swap agreements. The exclusion does not provide that the preemptive provisions in Section 12(e)(2) of the CEA apply to banks' covered swap agreements because, as discussed below, the Bank Products Legal Certainty Act provides a separate preemption from state gaming and bucket-shop laws for these agreements.[306]

An OTC derivatives transaction, including a credit or equity swap, will be a covered swap agreement for purposes of these Bank Products Legal Certainty Act exclusion and the related preemptive provision if it meets all of the following tests:[307]

- it is a "swap agreement," as that term is defined in Section 206(b) of the Gramm-Leach-Bliley Act (GLBA),[308]

- it is based on a commodity other than an agricultural commodity,

- it is between persons who qualify as eligible contract participants at the time it is entered into,[309] and

- the transaction either

    —is not entered into or executed on a trading facility or

    —is entered into or executed on an electronic trading facility and satisfies the following additional requirements:

    (1) it involves an excluded commodity[310]; and

    (2) the parties are either trading on a principal-to-principal basis for their own accounts or, as described in connection with the CEA exclusions for transactions in excluded commodities, are acting for an eligible contract participant as investment adviser, CTA or investment manager or fiduciary in respect of a discretionary account.

A "swap agreement" under Section 206(b) of the GLBA is defined as "any individually negotiated contract, agreement, warrant, note, or option that is based, in whole or in part,

---

[306]Bank Products Legal Certainty Act § 408(c). *See infra* p. 112.

[307]Bank Products Legal Certainty Act § 403(d).

[308]Section 402(d) of the Bank Products Legal Certainty Act expressly notes that a credit or equity swap may be a covered swap agreement.

[309]For purposes of this exclusion, the status of the bank's counterparty as an eligible contract participant relates to the definition of that term as embodied in Section 1a(12) of the CEA, as in effect on the date the CFMA was enacted.

[310]*See infra* p. 95.

on the value of, any interest in, or any quantitative measure of the occurrence of any event relating to, one or more commodities, securities, currencies, interest or other rates, or other assets" but not including any "identified banking product" of the kind defined in paragraphs (1) through (5) of Section 206(a) of the GLBA. Those paragraphs define traditional commercial banking products—deposit accounts, CDs, banker's acceptances, letters of credit and the like. As noted in the following discussion, there is another category of "identified banking products" consisting of "swap agreements" as defined for that purpose.

Reflecting the Bank Products Legal Certainty Act exclusion for covered swap agreements, in addition to representations regarding a party's status as an eligible contract participant, as discussed above, the derivatives documents used by entities that qualify as banks under the Act may include a special representation to the effect that each transaction, or the relevant transaction, is a covered swap agreement for purposes of Section 407 of the Act.

The other Bank Products Legal Certainty Act exclusions for OTC derivatives with banks are not likely to figure in derivatives documentation. This is because the terms of these exclusions are such that representations from the parties will not be particularly helpful. One of the exclusions is a grandfathering provision for "identified banking products," a term defined in Section 206 of the GLBA to include only individually negotiated swap agreements. These products are excluded from the CEA and from CFTC regulation if an appropriate banking agency certifies that the product has been commonly offered, entered into, or provided in the United States by any bank on or before December 5, 2000, under applicable banking law and the product was not prohibited by the CEA and regulated by the CFTC as a commodity futures contract or an option on such a contract or a commodity on or before that date.[311] A further exclusion applies to any identified banking product that was not commonly offered, entered into, or provided in the United States by any bank on or before December 5, 2000, under applicable banking law, but only if (1) the product has no payment indexed to the value, level, or rate of, and does not provide for the delivery of, any commodity or (2) the product or commodity is otherwise excluded from the CEA. That is, the second exclusion is coextensive with exclusions for nonbank OTC derivatives provided in or pursuant to the CEA.[312]

Participants in the market for OTC derivatives that qualify as "banks" for purposes of the Bank Products Legal Certainty Act exclusions described above should note that they do not need to specify whether they, in fact, are relying on one of these exclusions or, instead, on an exclusion provided by the CEA. Indeed, these banks will probably wish to avoid any such statement of election. In this regard, it should be noted, again, that the definition of "swap agreement" in Section 206(b) of the GLBA includes a requirement that the relevant agreement be individually negotiated. By way of contrast, while the exclusion provided in Section 2(g) of the CEA on excluded swap transactions includes the same requirement, as discussed above, the exclusions in Sections 2(d) and 2(h) of the

---

[311] Bank Products Legal Certainty Act § 403.

[312] Bank Products Legal Certainty Act § 404.

CEA discussed in the next section are available for otherwise qualifying transactions without regard to whether any of their terms are subject to individual negotiation.[313]

TRANSACTIONS IN EXEMPT AND EXCLUDED COMMODITIES

The remaining CEA exclusions added by the CFMA, like some of the Bank Products Legal Certainty Act exclusions described above, generally divide up their treatment of OTC derivatives on the basis of whether the underlying commodity is an excluded commodity or an exempt commodity and on whether the parties are engaging in their mutual dealings on or off a trading facility. These exclusions relating to transactions in excluded commodities (in Section 2(d) of the CEA) and exempt commodities (in Section 2(h) of the CEA) do not require that any of the material economic terms of the transaction be subject to individual negotiation between the parties.

Earlier[314] we described the presumptions implicit in these distinctions and how they seem linked to relative degrees of concern over the possible need for the application of the CEA's provisions and for oversight by the CFTC when a transaction's terms are offered on a take-it-or-leave it basis. As noted, the level of concern seems to turn on whether the parties are dealing directly with each on a principal-to-principal basis for their own accounts, or at some remove through intermediaries or on a multilateral trading facility, and on whether other factors (primarily the supply of the underlying commodity and the commercial nature of the parties' dealings in it) are such that the risk of fraud or manipulation, or the desire to protect the integrity of the market, justifies a higher level of government intervention under the CEA.

Excluded Commodities and Exempt Commodities

All commodities that are not agricultural commodities are either "excluded" commodities or "exempt" commodities. The CEA distinguishes between the two because of a perception that price manipulation is more likely to occur in the market for transactions in exempt commodities, which have a finite supply, than in the market for excluded commodities, which do not. The applicable exclusions for the two classes of commodities reflect this distinction.[315]

The term "excluded commodity" is broadly defined to cover

- interest rates, exchange rates, currencies, securities, security indexes, credit risk, measures of inflation and other macroeconomic indexes or measures;

- other economic and commercial indexes based on prices, rates, values or levels that are not within the control of a party;

---

[313] Therefore, the technical difference between the Bank Products Legal Certainty Act and CEA exclusions would not prevent a qualifying bank from relying on one of the CEA exclusions for transactions in excluded commodities or exempt commodities discussed in the following paragraphs if in any case there were concern about reliance on an exclusion under Section 407 of the Bank Products Legal Certainty Act.

[314] *Supra* p. 69.

[315] *See* table *infra* p. 101.

- weather and other contingencies associated with a financial or commercial consequence that are not within the control of the parties; and

- other rates, differentials, indexes and measures of economic or commercial risk, return or value based on commodities that have no cash market.[316]

If a commodity is not among these excluded commodities and is not an agricultural commodity, it is an "exempt commodity."[317] Energy products and metals, therefore, would be exempt commodities, as would bandwidth and chemicals.

Trading Facilities

For purposes of the CEA, and particularly the exclusions in the CEA and the Bank Products Legal Certainty Act that relate to transactions in excluded commodities and exempt commodities, "trading facility" implies multilateral, rather than bilateral, dealings and means

a person or group of persons that constitutes, maintains, or provides a physical or electronic facility or system in which multiple participants have the ability to execute or trade agreements, contracts, or transactions by accepting bids and offers made by other participants that are open to multiple participants in the facility or system[318]

but a facility on which bids, offers, and acceptances of bids and offers are not binding is not a trading facility.[319]

In this regard, it is also important to note the CEA provides that "[a] person or group of persons that would not otherwise constitute a trading facility shall not be considered to be a trading facility solely as a result of the submission to a derivatives clearing organization of transactions executed on or through the person or group of persons."[320] Under the CEA, "derivatives clearing organization" is defined to include "a clearinghouse, clearing association, clearing corporation, or similar entity, facility, system, or organization" that, with respect to an agreement, contract, or transaction does any of the following:

(i) enables each party to the agreement, contract, or transaction, to substitute, through novation, or otherwise, the credit of the derivatives clearing organization for the credit of the parties;

(ii) arranges or provides, on a multi-lateral basis, for the settlement or netting of obligations resulting from such agreements, contracts, or

---

[316] See CEA § 1a(13).

[317] See CEA § 1a(14).

[318] CEA § 1a(33)(A).

[319] CEA § 1a(33)(B)(iii). There is another exclusion from the definition of "trading facility" in this provision for U.S. government securities dealers and brokers, in their dealings as such. Id.

[320] CEA § 1a(33)(C).

transactions executed by participants in the derivatives clearing organization; or

(iii) otherwise provides clearing services or arrangements that mutualize or transfer among participants in the derivatives clearing organization the credit risk arising from such agreements, contracts, or transactions executed by the participants."[321]

In addition, the CEA exclusions added by the CFMA draw a basic distinction between traditional, trading pit, open outcry trading facilities, and multilateral trading facilities for electronic dealings between eligible contract participants. The CEA exclusions for transactions in exempt commodities and excluded commodities discussed below exist for transactions entered into or executed on an electronic trading facility, so long as the qualifying parties are either trading on a principal-to-principal basis for their own respective accounts or in other specified capacities in which they are subject to regulation (*e.g.*, as investment advisers or CTAs).

For this purpose,

"electronic trading facility" means a trading facility that "(A) operates by means of an electronic or telecommunications network" and "(B) maintains an automated audit trail of bids, offers, and the matching of orders or the execution of transactions on the facility," [322] but

a person or group of persons will not be treated as a trading facility solely by virtue of its or their constituting, maintaining or providing "an electronic facility or system that enables participants to negotiate the terms of and enter into bilateral transactions as a result of communications exchanged by the parties and not from interaction of multiple bids and multiple offers within a predetermined, nondiscretionary automated trade matching and execution algorithm."[323]

For example, if a party uses an electronic auction site to communicate to selected potential counterparties the terms of a transaction it would like to enter into and invite offers from them, and then enters into a transaction with one of the bidders through bilateral negotiations with a successful bidder, the parties would not be treated as having entered into or executed the transaction on a trading facility for purposes of the CEA exclusions discussed below or the Bank Products Legal Certainty Act exclusion discussed above. The result would be different if there had been an automatic match of the parties through a nondiscretionary execution algorithm.

---

[321] CEA § 1a(9). Section 5b of the CEA deals with derivatives clearing organizations that are required, or permitted voluntarily, to register with the CFTC and with the requirements and core principles applicable to those subject to CFTC oversight. Multilateral clearing organizations subject to regulation by U.S. bank supervisory agencies and clearing agencies subject to regulation by the SEC, for example, are not subject to CFTC oversight.

[322] CEA § 1a(10).

[323] CEA § 1a(33)(B)(i). Another exclusion from the definition of "trading facility" in this provision exists for U.S. government securities dealers and brokers, in their dealings as such. Section 1a(33)(B)(ii) of the CEA.

One final generalization may be useful for OTC derivatives market participants as they examine the potential impact of these exclusions on them and their transactions. For the reasons indicated above involving perceived differences in levels of risk of manipulative or fraudulent behavior—or stated otherwise, perceived differences in the need for government intervention in the form of CEA governance or CFTC oversight to protect against such behavior—some of these exclusions are total while others do not remove the parties or transactions from the reach of specified antifraud and antimanipulation provisions of the CEA or regulations adopted thereunder.[324] Market participants should, however, understand that this does not necessarily mean that these antifraud and antimanipulation provisions apply to their transactions. In fact, as already mentioned and discussed further at the close of this chapter, one of the provisions added to the CEA by the CFMA provides that the exemptions and exclusions discussed below relating to transactions, contracts and agreements should not be construed as implying or creating any presumption that those transactions, contracts or agreements are or would otherwise be subject to the CEA.[325]

The CEA Section 2(d) and 2(h) Exclusions

As indicated, in addition to the Bank Products Legal Certainty Act provisions described above relating to covered swap agreements in excluded and exempt commodities, there are two pairs of CEA exclusions (parallel to those in Section 407 of the Act) that relate to any agreement, contract or transaction in an excluded commodity (Section 2(d) of the CEA) or in an exempt commodity (Section 2(h) of the CEA). In each pair, one exclusion applies to an agreement, contract or transaction that is not entered into or traded on a trading facility and the other applies to an agreement, contract or transaction that is entered into or traded on an electronic trading facility.

For these exclusions to apply, as noted, none of the terms of the agreement, contract or transactions needs to be subject to individual negotiation. Both parties must, however, qualify as eligible contract participants at the time the relevant agreement, contract or transaction is executed. Moreover, if the transaction is executed or traded on an electronic trading facility, each of the parties either must be acting "on a principal-to-principal basis" for the party's own account or must be acting for an eligible contract participant in one of the following capacities:

- as an investment adviser subject to regulation under the Investment Advisers Act or, if a foreign person, performing a similar role or function and subject as such to foreign regulation;

---

[324] One such case is Section 4b of the CEA, which deals with fraudulent conduct in connection with "any order to make, or the making of, any contract of sale of any commodity for future delivery" if the futures contract is or may be used for "(A) hedging any transaction in interstate commerce in such commodity or the products or byproducts thereof, or (B) determining the price basis of any transaction in interstate commerce in such commodity, or (C) delivering any such commodity sold, shipped, or received in interstate commerce for the fulfillment thereof . . . ." Others are Section 4o of the CEA, which prohibits fraudulent conduct by CTAs, commodity pool operators and their respective associated persons, and Sections 6(c) and 6(d), which deal with CFTC authority relating to suspected fraud and commodity price manipulation. The regulations are those adopted by the CFTC on commodity options pursuant to Section 4c(b) of the CEA.

[325] *See infra* p. 113.

- as a CTA subject to regulation under the CEA or, if a foreign person, performing a similar role or function and subject as such to foreign regulation; or

- as an investment manager or fiduciary acting for a discretionary account of its eligible contract participant principal (that is, with authority from that principal to commit the principal to the relevant agreement, contract or transaction).[326]

As a result, if the parties enter into a document designed to express their general understanding with respect to transactions executed by them on an electronic trading facility, it is likely to include a representation on their status as eligible contract participants, like the one discussed above, perhaps modified along the following lines:

> [Party A][Party B] is an "eligible contract participant," as that term is defined in Section 1a(12) of the Commodity Exchange Act (the "CEA") and, in connection with each transaction between the parties entered into or executed on an electronic trading facility, as that term is defined in Section 1a(10) of the CEA, it is trading on a principal-to-principal basis for its own account.

If a party is not acting for its own account, it may be asked to make a representation regarding the capacity in which it is acting, and that representation will probably track the statutory language for one of the three permitted classes specified above.

In light of concerns over the potential for price manipulation in exempt commodities, with a finite supply, the applicable exclusion does not relieve the transactions or their parties from the antimanipulation or antifraud provisions of the CEA unless each of the parties qualifies as an eligible commercial entity.[327] Generally speaking, eligible commercial entities[328] are selected eligible contract participants whose participation in transactions in exempt commodities is, it seems, thought to require less government intervention to protect them, and the marketplace, against possible manipulative behavior. Included in these selected subsets are entities whose business in the relevant commodity regularly in-

---

[326] A person acting in this capacity may not be acting merely as a broker or in an equivalent agency function.

[327] In addition, under Section 5(h)(5) of the CEA, an electronic trading facility relying on exemption from regulation as a facility used to execute and trade transactions in exempt commodities between eligible commercial entities is subject to special rules. They require, *inter alia*, that the facility (1) notify the CFTC of various matters, including the commodity categories that the facility intends to list or otherwise make available for trading on the facility in reliance on the exemption, (2) make various certifications to the CFTC, (3) identify any derivatives clearing organization to which the facility transmits or intends to transmit transaction data for the purpose of facilitating the clearance and settlement of transactions conducted on the facility in reliance on the exemption, and (4) give the CFTC access to the facility's trading protocols and electronic access to the facility with respect to transactions conducted in reliance on the exemption or, in the alternative, provide reports regarding transactions executed on the facility in reliance on the exemption, from time to time upon request. Other requirements involve keeping certain records and providing information as requested by the CFTC, and permitting the CFTC to enforce the statute's requirements on limiting access to the facility to eligible commercial entities.

[328] "Eligible commercial entity" is defined in Section 1a(11) of the CEA. The table *infra* p. 124 lists the subsets of eligible contract participants that qualify as eligible commercial entities.

volves the assumption of risks beyond mere price risk. The definition also includes dealers that provide other eligible commercial entities and sophisticated and substantial investors with risk-management or hedging services relating to the commodity.

The common features of the exclusions for transactions in excluded commodities and exempt commodities, and the differences between them, are shown in the next table.

EXCLUDED AND EXEMPT COMMODITY PROVISIONS COMPARED		
Agreement, contract or transaction in	*Common Features*	*Differing Features*
Excluded commodity	The parties must qualify as eligible contract participants when the agreement, contract or transaction is executed. Identical extra requirements apply for transactions executed or traded on electronic trading facilities.	CEA inapplicable, except for § 12(e)(2)(B), preempting state and local gaming and bucket-shop laws and, if applicable, provisions on derivatives clearing organizations and exempt boards of trade registered as DTEFs
Exempt commodity		Same as above, except there is no exemption from provisions dealing with commodity price manipulation and, unless both parties are "eligible commercial entities," there is no exemption from CEA antifraud provisions or related CFTC regulations on commodity options, to the extent these antimanipulation and antifraud provisions and regulations are otherwise applicable

For energy products, the classes of eligible commercial entities are in many respects like the classes of appropriate persons entitled to rely on the CFTC's Energy Contracts Exemption discussed below. In providing that the CEA's antifraud and antimanipulation provisions will not apply to transactions in exempt commodities of these eligible commercial entities, the exclusion in Section 2(h) of the CEA continues the approach taken in the Energy Contracts Exemption. The Section 2(h) exclusion is, however, broader in various ways. Among other things, to qualify under the Energy Product Exemption, the material economic terms of a transaction must be subject to individual negotiation and the transactions must at the outset impose an obligation on the parties to make or take delivery and limit the right of cash settlement to cases involving the counterparty's consent except in limited circumstances.[329]

OTHER CEA EXCLUSIONS AND EXEMPTIONS

Statutory Exclusions

As discussed above, OTC derivatives market participants sometimes rely on the traditional, pre-CFMA exclusions from the CEA provided by the Treasury Amendment and the Forward Contract Exclusion. The Treasury Amendment has chiefly been important in connection with swaps, caps, floors and other products involving foreign currency, although it may also be useful for transactions involving securities warrants, securities rights, resales of installment loan contracts, repurchase options, government securities, or mortgages and mortgage purchase commitments.[330] The Forward Contract Exclusion, on the other hand, has mainly been important in physically settled derivatives involving commercial users of the underlying commodity, for the reasons outlined earlier.[331] The following is an overview of how reliance on these statutory exclusions may figure in the documentation for OTC derivatives.

The Treasury Amendment. Prior to the enactment of the CFMA, the market had not developed special representations relating to reliance on the CEA exclusion provided by the Treasury Amendment, given the breadth of the literal terms of the exclusion. As a result of the CFMA amendments, however, *retail* OTC derivatives in foreign currency are expressly made subject to the CEA and to the jurisdiction of the CFTC, if they are options on foreign currency or foreign currency futures contracts.[332]

A transaction will be treated as "retail" for this purpose if it is offered to, or entered into with, a person that is not an eligible contract participant, unless the counterparty, or the proposed counterparty, is one of the following:

- a financial institution,

- a securities broker or dealer registered with the SEC under the Securities Exchange Act,

- an FCM registered under the CEA,

- an associated person of one of these registered securities brokers or dealers or FCMs, if the broker, dealer or FCM makes and keeps rec-

---

[329] *See infra* p. 79.

[330] *See supra* p. 74 for discussion of the issues traditionally raised by the Treasury Amendment as it existed before enactment of the CFMA.

[331] *See supra* p. 76.

[332] FX options executed or traded on a national securities exchange registered under Section 6(a) of the Securities Exchange Act are expressly excluded from these retail provisions in Section 2(c)(2)(B)(i) of the CEA, just as they were excluded from the pre-CFMA text of the Treasury Amendment, even though transactions in foreign currency otherwise traded on a board of trade were previously within the reach of the CEA.

ords of the financial or securities activities of the associated person as required under the Securities Exchange Act or the CEA,

- an insurance company or regulated subsidiary or affiliate of an insurance company that qualifies as an eligible contract participant,
- a financial holding company subject to regulation under the Bank Holding Company, or
- an investment bank holding company subject to regulation under the Securities Exchange Act.

Listed entities that have previously relied on the Treasury Amendment in their OTC currency derivatives will not find it necessary to change their practices or their documentation relating to these transactions. The counterparty's status as an eligible contract participant will, however, be important to any participant that is not on this list under the Treasury Amendment, just as that status is relevant under the statutory exclusions discussed above in this chapter that were added by the CFMA.[333]

Subject to this rule for retail FX transactions, OTC derivatives in foreign currency are excluded by the Treasury Amendment from the provisions of the CEA other than the preemptive provisions discussed at the end of this chapter and, to the extent applicable, provisions regarding transactions that are cleared through derivatives clearing organizations or traded on exempt boards of trade that are DTEFs registered with the CFTC.[334]

The same exclusions apply under the Treasury Amendment to transactions in government securities, security warrants, security rights, resales of installment loan contracts, repurchase transactions in an excluded commodity and mortgages or mortgage purchase commitments,[335] subject to the following exceptions relating to the jurisdictional accord between the SEC and CFTC:

---

[333]CFTC Letter No. 02–05 of January 8, 2002, an interpretation of the Division of Trading and Markets of the CFTC, *available at* www.cftc.gov/tim/letters/02/letters/tm02-05.htm, brings into focus some of the issues that can be raised by these restrictions on FX dealings with retail customers in the context of electronic trading. The letter was written in reply to inquiries involving a trading platform for foreign currency trading over the Internet, using a software program licensed to licensees that marketed the platform as their own and received customer funds in their own names, although the licensee's agreement under the licensing agreement required it to transfer those customer funds to an account of the grantor of the license, which was a licensed FCM—one of the entities permitted under the Treasury Amendment to deal with retail customers after enactment of the CFMA. In Letter No. 02–05, the CFTC advised that, if the licensees wished to continue to have any role with the platform in connection with OTC FX futures or options transactions without themselves becoming registered as FCMs, they would have to cease acting as counterparties to their retail customers, cease receiving funds from customers in their own names, cease acting as conduits for funds due to customers from the grantor of the license, the registered FCM, and amend their customer agreements and their Web sites to reflect the role of the license grantor. Letter No. 02–05 also advised an FCM that it should immediately cease operating a platform that permitted direct trading between retail customers in FX futures or options transactions, even though the FCM guaranteed the integrity of the trades and allowed the trading customers to liquidate their positions as they wished with the registered FCM as their direct counterparty.

[334]To the extent they offer FX options and futures or options on FX futures, FCMs and some associated persons are also subject to the antifraud, antimanipulation and related provisions of the CEA enumerated in Section 2(c)(2)(C) of the CEA.

[335]CEA §§ 2(c)(1)(B)–(G).

Commodities, Gaming and Bucket-Shop Laws 103

- The Treasury Amendment exclusions do not apply to options on securities that are subject to the exclusive jurisdiction of the SEC, because the CEA's trading restrictions themselves do not apply to those options;

- the Security Futures Restrictions of the CEA apply (and the Treasury Amendment does not apply) to Security Futures Products, and

- the CEA's Options Trading Restrictions and Futures Trading Restrictions apply (with no Treasury Amendment relief) to commodity futures, commodity options and options on commodity futures that are executed or traded on an organized exchange that is within the CFTC's exclusive jurisdiction.[336]

"Organized exchange" is a term introduced in the CFMA for any trading facility that

(A) permits trading—

(i) by or on behalf of a person that is not an eligible contract participant; or

(ii) by persons other than on a principal-to-principal basis; or

(B) has adopted (directly or through another nongovernmental entity) rules that—

(i) govern the conduct of participants, other than rules that govern the submission of orders or execution of transactions on the trading facility; and

(ii) include disciplinary sanctions other than the exclusion of participants from trading.

The term was introduced to replace an earlier Treasury Amendment reference to transactions executed on a board of trade, which, as discussed above, had given rise to legal challenges involving the breadth of the pre-CFMA definition.[337]

The Forward Contract Exclusion. As discussed above, participants in the OTC derivatives market have traditionally relied on the Forward Contract Exclusion from the CEA for bilaterally negotiated OTC transactions when the underlying can be physically delivered, the parties have the ability to make and take delivery and they are committed to do so when they enter into their agreement.[338] For at least some OTC derivatives, the parties will continue to rely on the Forward Contract Exclusion because it does not require the parties to a transaction to fall within the classes of persons specified in the CFMA ex-

---

[336] CEA § 2(c)(2)(A).

[337] *See supra* note 240, sources cited therein and accompanying text. "Organized exchange" is defined in Section 1a(27) of the CEA.

[338] *See supra* p. 77 on the statutory interpretations of the Forward Contract Exclusion by the CFTC and on the uncertainty introduced by the CFTC's treatment of the forwards involved in its enforcement proceedings against MG Refining and Marketing. *See also* 2 SECURITIES & DERIVATIVES REGULATION § 13.08[3][a].

clusions or the CFTC exemptions for swap agreements and certain energy contracts discussed in this chapter (that is, specified classes of eligible swap participants, eligible contract participants or appropriate persons).

The contracts used to document commodity forwards between commercial parties sometimes include representations to the effect that the parties are entering into the transaction for purposes related to their respective businesses, and not for speculation.[339] Given CFTC and court interpretations of the Forward Contract Exclusion, these contracts are also structured to make clear that the parties are under binding obligations to make and take delivery of the underlying commodity. However, representations and other features aimed more broadly at addressing the requirements of the Forward Contract Exclusion, as it has been interpreted over time by the CFTC, are not widely used in OTC derivatives documentation for swaps and similar derivatives.

CFTC Exemptions

There are three exemptions from the CEA that are, with some regularity, referred or alluded to in OTC derivatives documentation. They are the 1993 Swap Agreement Exemption and the Energy Contracts Exemption—both adopted by the CFTC in 1993 pursuant to authority given to it in Section 4(c)(1) of the CEA by the FTPA—and the Trade Option Exemption.[340]

The 1993 Swap Agreement Exemption. In many, but not all, respects, the 1993 Swap Agreement Exemption is more limiting than the CEA exclusions added by the CFMA that are described in the preceding sections. The exemption nonetheless retains vitality and may be useful in some cases that would not be covered by those exclusions, such as transactions involving agricultural commodities and transactions involving some instrumentalities, agencies and departments of governments and multinational or supranational governmental entities.[341]

As a result, when the parties to OTC derivatives transactions seek to establish that their transactions should be treated as outside the Futures Trading Restrictions and the Options Trading Restrictions, as well as state gaming and bucket-shop laws, they may

---

[339] These representations negating speculative intent are mainly aimed at early court decisions holding that contracts that were offered to the general public were beyond the scope of the Forward Contract Exclusion because they were offered to persons not otherwise involved in commercial transactions in the underlying commodity. *See* 2 SECURITIES & DERIVATIVES REGULATION § 13.08[3][a][ii][A]. The linkage between the courts' focus on physical delivery and speculative intent can be seen, *e.g.,* in *CFTC v. Noble Metals,* 67 F.3d 766 (9th Cir. 1995), where the court found that sales of precious metals to the general public under a "Forward Delivery Program" were futures, rather than forwards excluded from the Futures Trading Restrictions under the Forward Contract Exclusion, because there never was a legitimate expectation that the defendant's customers would take delivery. The court reached this conclusion notwithstanding account information that specifically advised customers they would be required to make or take delivery, because the contract terms provided for up to three years' deferral of delivery and the defendants arranged for third-party agents to handle the deliveries, resulting in title transfer upon payment, but the same agents then sold the metal back to Noble.

[340] 17 C.F.R. § 32.4(a) (2002).

[341] This could be so because, although such an instrumentality, agency or department would qualify as an eligible swap participant, it might not qualify as an eligible contract participant in the same class, as listed in Section 1a(12)(vii) of the CEA. *See* table *infra* p. 118.

well continue to supplement the standard terms in their master agreement with a representation to the effect that each party is an "eligible swap participant," as that term is defined in the 1993 Swap Agreement Exemption[342] and, sometimes, with further representations in support of the party's status as such. These representations are included because an OTC derivatives agreement will not qualify for the exemption unless it is entered into between entities that are eligible swap participants at the time they enter into the agreement.

Also common is a representation that each transaction between the parties under a master agreement, or the specific transaction covered by a confirmation,

> is a "swap agreement" that satisfies the requirements set forth in the Exemption for Certain Swap Agreements adopted by the Commodity Futures Trading Commission, 17 C.F.R. § 35.2(b)–(d).[343]

For purposes of the 1993 Swap Agreement Exemption, "swap agreement" is defined to include most OTC swaps and related derivatives, such as caps, floors and collars, as well as FX forwards and swaps and similar agreements, combinations of these transactions and any master agreement for any of the listed types of derivatives, regardless of the nature of the underlying price, rate or index, as well as options to enter into these listed transactions.[344]

An agreement will satisfy the requirements referred to in the preceding representation, and thus qualify for the 1993 Swap Agreement Exemption, only if

- "the swap agreement is not part of a fungible class of agreements that are standardized as to their material economic terms,"[345]

- "the creditworthiness of any party having an actual or potential obligation under the swap agreement would be a material consideration in entering into or determining the terms of the swap agreement,"[346] and

---

[342] For an example of such a provision, *see supra* p. 90.

[343] As indicated above, some market participants are reluctant to make this sort of representation about future transactions in a master agreement prepared using a standard form, such as the ISDA form, that can be used to document transactions that may not be swap agreements.

[344] 17 C.F.R. § 35.1(b)(1) (2002). In defining "swap agreement," the 1993 Swap Agreement Exemption tracks the definition of the term as it existed in the Bankruptcy Code at the time. The Code definition has since been expanded to include spot FX transactions, Bankruptcy Code § 101(53B), but that discrepancy is irrelevant to cases like those described in this chapter, since conventional spot FX transactions are not commodity futures or options of the kinds that could be argued to be void under the CEA's Futures Trading Restrictions or Options Trading Restrictions.

[345] The nonfungibility requirement is prescribed by the authorizing statute, Section 4(c)(5)(B) of the CEA. In issuing the 1993 Swap Agreement Exemption, the CFTC indicated that this requirement was "designed to assure that the exemption does not encompass the establishment of a market in swap agreements, the terms of which are fixed and are not subject to negotiation, that functions essentially in the same manner as an exchange but for the bilateral execution of transactions." 58 Fed. Reg. at 5590. When this nonfungibility requirement is read in this light, it may in effect be no different from the requirement imposed by some of the CEA exclusions described above which require that the material terms of excluded transactions, other than price and quantity, be subject to individual negotiation.

[346] This requirement precludes reliance on the 1993 Swap Agreement Exemption for transactions in which credit risk is mutualized through use of a central clearinghouse as a counterparty. However, the ex-

- "[t]he swap agreement is not entered into and traded on or through a multilateral transaction execution facility."[347]

If a transaction qualifies as a swap agreement entered into between eligible swap participants, the 1993 Swap Agreement Exemption operates, under Section 4(c)(1) of the CEA, to exempt the transaction from most, but not all, regulation under the CEA and also exempts "any person or class of persons offering, entering into, rendering advice, or rendering other services with respect to" the agreement from the CEA, subject to two limitations.[348] First, the 1993 Swap Agreement Exemption does not exempt qualifying swap agreements or parties to them from the Security Futures Trading Restrictions and related requirements of the Shad-Johnson Accord as modified by the CFMA.[349] Second, the 1993 Swap Agreement Exemption does not provide an exemption from the antifraud and anti-

---

emption and the CFTC's description of the meaning of this requirement make clear that bilateral collateral or margin arrangements and bilateral netting are permitted, and that multilateral netting is also permitted "provided that the underlying gross obligations among the parties are not extinguished until all netted obligations are fully performed." 58 Fed. Reg. at 5591. The reference to netting in the exemption itself appears in a proviso. See 17 C.F.R. § 35.2 (2002). See CFTC, Order, 1988–99 Transfer Binder, COMM. FUT. L. REP. ¶ 27,764; CFTC, Order of Registration (October 29, 2001), COMM. FUT. L. REP. ¶ 28,660. In these Orders, the CFTC granted an application of The London Clearing House Limited (LCH) for an exemption from the exchange-trading requirements of the CEA for its SwapClear facility for clearing FRAs and swaps between dealers that met qualifications exceeding those applicable to appropriate persons under Section 4(c) of the CEA. The LCH represented that swaps eligible for clearing through SwapClear would, among other things, be limited to transactions that would qualify as swap agreements under the CFTC's 1993 Swap Agreement Exemption, that some of the material economic terms of the transactions would be subject to private negotiation, that LCH would not impose any requirement that the swap agreements have standardized contract specifications and the LCH would not provide a facility for arranging or executing swap agreements. The CFTC granted the exemptions using the same authority (given to it under the FTPA of 1992) that it used in adopting the Swap Agreement Exemption, making clear that in doing so it was not finding that the exempted swaps were in fact subject to the CEA. In doing so, however, it indicated that its action would not necessarily form the basis for a regulatory framework for other swaps clearing facilities, because the CFTC was largely deferring to the FSA, a foreign regulatory body with oversight over SwapClear in its home jurisdiction.

[347]These requirements are found in 17 C.F.R. § 35.2(b)–(d) (2002). The CFTC, in issuing the 1993 Swap Agreement Exemption, stated that a multilateral transaction execution facility "is a physical or electronic facility in which all market makers and other participants that are members simultaneously have the ability to execute transactions and bind both parties by accepting offers which are made by one member and open to all members of the facility." 58 Fed. Reg. at *5591. While the CFTC clarified that electronic trading systems are outside the Exemption, it stated that the limitation was not intended "to preclude participants from engaging in privately negotiated bilateral transactions, even where these participants use computer or other electronic facilities, such as 'broker screens,' to communicate simultaneously with other participants so long as they do not use such systems to enter orders to execute transactions." Id. (footnote omitted).

[348]17 C.F.R. § 35.2 (2002).

[349]As a result, although market participants have generally believed that privately negotiated securities-linked swaps and similar transactions should not be treated as futures contracts subject to the Security Futures Trading Restrictions, they have not counted on the 1993 Swap Agreement Exemption for comfort in their legal analysis of those transactions and have often sought to conduct their dealings so as to qualify for the safe harbor afforded by the Swap Policy Statement. If the parties to a swap based on a security or group or index of securities do not qualify as eligible contract participants for purposes of the CEA exemptions and exclusions introduced by the CFMA, they may look for comfort to the Swap Policy Statement and the contract enforcement provisions discussed infra p. 113.

manipulation provisions in Sections 4b and 4o of the CEA and regulations thereunder, if those provisions are applicable.

The Energy Contracts Exemption. The Energy Contracts Exemption applies to bilateral contracts for the future purchase and sale of crude oil, condensates, natural gas, natural gas liquids or their derivatives which are used primarily as an energy source, although the exemption's availability does not turn on whether the relevant commodity is ultimately used as an energy source.[350] The Energy Contracts Exemption removes these transactions from the reach of the Futures Trading Restrictions, provided several tests are satisfied.

First, the principal economic terms of the transaction must be subject to individual negotiation between parties who are acting as principal and each of whom,

> in connection with its business activities, incurs risks, in addition to price risk, related to the underlying physical commodities,
>
> has the demonstrable capacity or ability—broadly defined[351]—to make or take delivery under the terms of the contracts,
>
> is legally permitted and otherwise authorized to engage in such transactions,
>
> is not formed solely for the specific purpose of constituting an eligible entity pursuant to the exemption and
>
> falls within the following categories of appropriate persons contemplated in Section 4(c)(1) of the CEA:[352]
>
> > (1) banks or trust companies,
> >
> > (2) securities brokers or dealers subject to regulation under the Securities Exchange Act,
> >
> > (3) futures commissions merchants subject to regulation under the CEA,
> >
> > (4) corporations, partnerships, proprietorships, organizations, trusts or other business entities with a net worth exceeding U.S.$ 1 million or total assets exceeding U.S.$ 5 million (or whose obligations under the contract are guaranteed or otherwise supported by specified eligible providers of support), and

---

[350] Exemption for Certain Contracts Involving Energy Products, 58 Fed. Reg. 21,286, 21,289, 1993 W.L. 120,137 (F.R.) (Apr. 20, 1993).

[351] These requirements focus on capacity to bear the economic risks of ownership of the relevant commodity and acknowledge that capacity to take or make delivery includes bona fide contractual arrangements for delivery with and through other persons. Thus, "[p]assage of title and acceptance of the commodity constitutes performance under a *bona fide* contract regardless of whether the buyer lifts or otherwise takes delivery of the cargo or receives pipeline delivery, or as part of a subsequent separate contract, passes title to another intermediate purchaser in a 'chain', 'string' or 'circle' within a 'chain.'" *Id.* at 21,293.

[352] As it did in adopting the 1993 Swap Agreement Exemption, in adopting the Energy Contracts Exemption the CFTC stated that a reasonable belief that an entity falls within one of these categories will suffice. 58 Fed. Reg. at 21,294.

(5) governments, multinational and supranational governmental entities and their instrumentalities, agencies or departments.[353]

When the parties rely on this CEA exemption for transactions in qualifying energy products, the documents generally include representations from each party as to its status in one of the classes of qualifying appropriate persons, to enable the other party to form a reasonable belief that the applicable conditions are satisfied.[354] The documents may also include representations that track other conditions outlined above.

Second, each of the parties must have a binding obligation to make or take delivery of the underlying commodity, and neither party may have the right to transfer its position in the transaction or to effect a cash settlement of its obligations without the other's consent, except for cash settlement pursuant to a bona fide termination right arising in limited circumstances such as default. These requirements are, naturally, reflected in the parties' contract when they rely on the exemption[355] and do not, by way of contrast, apply under the 1993 Swap Agreement Exemption or the exclusions from the CEA described above relating to excluded swap transactions, transactions in exempt commodities, transactions in excluded commodities or covered swap agreements offered, entered into or provided by banks.

The Energy Contracts Exemption does not, however, require that the parties actually settle their forward contracts through physical delivery. It permits settlement through individually negotiated "book-out" or offset or netting arrangements providing for a cash payment, so long as the parties are initially bound to make and take physical delivery of the commodity and certain other requirements are met.[356]

In many ways, the Energy Contracts Exemption is like the CEA exclusion for transactions in exempt commodities. The principal differences are that: (1) unlike the Energy Contracts Exemption, the exclusion for transactions in exempt commodities does not "look through" an eligible contract participant to determine whether it is formed to qualify as such; (2) the statutory exclusion does not require that the material economic terms of the transaction be subject to individual negotiation, as does the Energy Contracts Exemption, nor does it impose any restrictions on terms relating to cash settlement or transfer of a party's position; (3) the classes of entities that qualify for the Energy Contracts Exemp-

---

[353] *Id.* at 21,294.

[354] Where asset or net worth conditions of a party are relevant, the counterparty often will also require financial statements and other information to support its belief as to satisfaction of these conditions, unless the information is otherwise available to it.

[355] The restriction on transfer without consent is consistent with general market practice. Under U.S. tax law there may be reasons why a total bar on transfer without consent may be undesirable. *See* Section 7 of the sample master agreement in Part 3, *infra* p. 867, and the related annotations.

[356] 58 Fed. Reg. at 21,294. The CFTC noted that "the terms 'book out' (crude oil) and 'book transfer' (other petroleum products) are cash market terms that generally refer to the cancellation or netting of physical delivery obligations between parties, the primary purpose of which is to prevent or minimize the uneconomic movement of the physical commodity." *Id.* at 21,293 n.25 The CFTC also sanctions other sorts of subsequent contract arrangements providing for settlement other than by physical delivery so long as the second contract "is incidental to a pre-existing, *bona fide* Energy Contract" and "one party cannot require its counterparty to agree in advance to the establishment of the second contract as a condition of acceptance of the initial Energy Contract." *Id.* at 21,293.

tion are in many cases narrower than the classes of eligible contract participants who qualify for the statutory exclusion for transactions in exempt commodities; and (4) the statutory exclusion applies to exempt commodities that are beyond the reach of the Energy Contracts Exemption.

The Energy Contracts Exemption (like the 1993 Swap Agreement Exemption) was made retroactive to October 23, 1974. Where applicable, it provides an exemption from the Futures Trading Restrictions but not from the Shad-Johnson Accord or from the antifraud or antimanipulation provisions of the CEA, "to the extent that these provisions prohibit manipulation of the market price of any commodity in interstate commerce or for future delivery on or subject to the rules of any contract market."[357] Although this language is opaque, it is understood to mean that the CFTC did not seek to reserve application of the CEA's antifraud and antimanipulation provisions to OTC derivatives that fall within the Energy Contracts Exemption.[358]

The Trade Option Exemption. References or allusions to the Trade Option Exemption are often found in the documentation for OTC derivatives with some classes of counterparties. For example, the documentation used by market professionals for commodity price caps, floors and collars with end-users sometimes includes a representation of the end-user to the following effect:

> it is a producer, processor, or a commercial user of, or a merchant handling, the commodity which is the subject of the transaction, or the products or by-products thereof, it is entering into the transaction solely for purposes related to its business as such, and not for speculation; and it is the offeree of the transaction.

This language tracks the Trade Option Exemption, which applies to a commodity option if the party offering the option has a reasonable basis to believe that the offeree satisfies the tests described in the representation. For this purpose, the offeree may be acting either as buyer or seller of the option.[359] The Trade Option Exemption does not, however, apply to options on agricultural commodities, which are the subject of a separate exemption.[360]

Notwithstanding the CEA exclusions for OTC derivatives added under the CFMA and the 1993 Swap Agreement Exemption, the Trade Option Exemption and related representations like the one set out above may continue to be useful to market participants in their dealings with some counterparties, since, like the Forward Contract Exclusion, the Trade Option Exemption does not require the producer, processor or commercial user of the relevant commodity, or its products or by-products, to satisfy the asset or net worth tests that corporations, partnerships and proprietorships, among others, must satisfy to qualify as eligible swap participants for purposes of the 1993 Swap Agreement Exemption or eligible contract participants for purposes of the CFMA provisions on excluded swap

---

[357] *Id.*

[358] The resulting controversy is manifest in the dissenting and concurring opinions of CFTC commissioners published with the release accompanying the exemption when it was issued. *Id.*

[359] *See* 2 SECURITIES & DERIVATIVES REGULATION § 13.10[4][a].

[360] *See id.* at § 13.10[4][b].

transactions, transactions in exempt commodities and covered swap agreements offered, entered into or provided by banks.

There are, however, obvious limitations on the usefulness of the Trade Option Exemption, since its availability turns on the offeree's status as a producer, processor or commercial user of the underlying commodity,[361] as well as the exemption's focus on why the party is entering into the transaction.[362]

THE SWAP POLICY STATEMENT

The various statutory exclusions and CFTC exemptions described above are in many respects far broader than the Swap Policy Statement, which was the CFTC's first formal position on how it would look at specified kinds of OTC derivatives within the context of the CEA's trading restrictions. Nonetheless, the Swap Policy Statement remains in effect and may be relied on by those who engage in transactions that might not be covered by the statutory exclusions and CFTC exemptions.

The Swap Policy Statement is a statement of policy, not a statutory interpretation. It does not afford any exclusion or exemption from the CEA. In fact, when it was adopted in 1989, the CFTC did not have authority to grant exemptions from the Futures Contract Trading Restrictions. Although it did have authority to grant exemptions from the Option Trading Restrictions, the statement only addresses CFTC policy with respect to transactions with economic features like those of futures contracts.[363]

This policy statement expresses the view of the CFTC that swap agreements with specified characteristics are "not appropriately regulated" and "will not be subject to regulation as futures or commodity option transactions" under the CEA. As indicated, in 1990 the CFTC issued the Collar Interpretation, which interpreted the Swap Policy Statement to be available for some collar transactions.[364]

A qualifying transaction under the Swap Policy Statement must be "an agreement between two parties to exchange a series of cash flows measured by different interest rates, exchange rates, or prices."[365] Therefore, the Swap Policy Statement appears to apply only to bilateral cash-settled transactions. There is, however, no restriction in this policy

---

[361] The CFTC has indicated that an entity must be involved commercially with a commodity on more than an occasional basis for it to qualify as a commercial user for purposes of the Trade Option Exemption. CFTC, Advance Notice of Proposed Rulemaking, 50 Fed. Reg. 10,786, 10,790, 1985 WL 86,090 (F.R.) (Mar. 18, 1985).

[362] See 2 SECURITIES & DERIVATIVES REGULATION § 13.10[4][a][I] n.571 on the possible limitations on the use of the Trade Option Exemption, for example, by entities involved in "cross-hedging" (hedging risk involving one commodity with options on another commodity with price correlation) and on the anomalies that arise from the exemption's focus on the offeree.

[363] See CFTC–OETF Interpretative Letter No. 90–1, Eligibility of "Collar Agreements" for Safe Harbor Treatment Under the CFTC's Policy Statement Concerning Swap Transactions, [1987–1990 Transfer Binder] COMM. FUT. L. REP. (CCH) ¶ 24,583 at 36,512 (CFTC OETF Jan. 18, 1990). The analysis of the collar transactions covered by this Interpretative Letter is somewhat opaque.

[364] See supra p. 79.

[365] Id. at 30,695.

statement on the type of "underlying" for a qualifying transaction, nor are there any criteria that eligible counterparties must meet.

The further requirements of a transaction that qualifies for the safe harbor provided by the Swap Policy Statement are as follows:

- the terms of the transaction must be tailored to reflect the business objectives of the parties, rather than standardized as are the terms of exchange-traded futures contracts,

- the transaction must be entered into by each party in connection with a line of its business, including financial intermediation, or the financing of a line of its business,

- the transaction may not be marketed to the public,

- neither party may have a right to terminate the transaction unilaterally (except in default circumstances), although early termination provisions may be negotiated at the outset,

- the counterparty credit risk involved in the transaction may not be eliminated through exchange-style margining or mutualization through a clearing organization, and restrictions on the use of other kinds of credit support are not clear.[366]

Several of these restrictions may affect a transaction's structure, but only one generally appears in the documents when the parties seek to establish their entitlement to rely on the Swap Policy Statement. This is the requirement relating to the purpose for which the parties are entering into the transaction. This requirement gave rise to the practice of requiring that each party represent more or less the following about itself:

It is entering into [each] [the] transaction in connection with a line of its business, including financial intermediation, or the financing of a line of its business.

Restrictions similar to this and other conditions applicable under the safe harbor created under the Swap Policy Statement have been preserved, albeit more narrowly, under the 1993 Swap Agreement Exemption, the Energy Contracts Exemption and some of CFMA exclusions discussed above. That is, the concepts of eligible swap participant, eligible contract participant and appropriate person used in many of the CEA exemptions and exclusions sometimes look at the purposes for which a person is engaging in the relevant transaction. In addition, while the Swap Policy Statement requires tailoring of the terms of a transaction, Section 2(g) of the CEA and Section 407 of the Bank Products Legal Certainty Act require only that the material economic terms (other than price and quantity) of a transaction be subject to individual negotiation by the parties for the transaction to qualify as an excluded swap transaction or a covered swap agreement. Moreover, the 1993 Swap Agreement Exemption limits the ways in which the parties may manage the credit risk associated with their transactions, and the Energy Contracts Exemption restricts provisions on termination.

---

[366]For discussion of this feature of the Swap Policy Statement, *see* 2 SECURITIES & DERIVATIVES REGULATION § 13.08[b][ii][C].

PREEMPTIONS OF GAMING AND BUCKET-SHOP LAWS

The Bank Products Legal Certainty Act and the CEA remove transactions excluded or exempted from the CEA through statutory exclusions and CFTC exemptions from the reach of state and local gaming and bucket-shop laws, except for antifraud provisions of general application. So, when the parties seek through representations like those illustrated above to establish that their transactions are eligible for these exemptions or exclusions, they are also seeking to obtain the benefit of these preemptions.

The preemptive provisions of the CEA and the Bank Products Legal Certainty Act, insofar they relate to OTC derivatives, provide as follows:

CEA § 12(e)(2):

> This Act shall supersede and preempt the application of any State or local law that prohibits or regulates gaming or the operation of bucket shops (other than antifraud provisions of general applicability) in the case of—
>
> ... (B) an agreement, contract, or transaction that is excluded from this Act under section 2(c), 2(d), 2(f), or 2(g) of this Act or title IV of the Commodity Futures Modernization Act of 2000, or exempted under section 2(h) or 4(c) of this Act (regardless of whether any such agreement, contract, or transaction is otherwise subject to this Act).[367]

Bank Products Legal Certainty Act § 408(c):

> This title shall supersede and preempt the application of any State or local law that prohibits or regulates gaming or the operation of bucket shops (other than antifraud provisions of general applicability) in the case of—
>
> ... or
>
> (2) a covered swap agreement.[368]

---

[367] Section 12(e)(2) of the CEA expands on an earlier preemptive provision added to Section 12 of the CEA by Title V of the Futures Trading Practices Act of 1992. Clause (A) applies to an electronic trading facility excluded from the CEA under Section 2(e).

[368] Clause (1) applies to certain hybrid instruments that provide for delivery of commodities or payments indexed to commodity values, levels or rates, to the extent excluded from the CEA as predominantly banking products under Section 405 of the Bank Products Legal Certainty Act. Section 2(f) of the CEA has parallel exclusions for hybrids that are predominantly securities. The predominance tests are easily applied and are satisfied if (1) the issuer receives full payment substantially contemporaneously with delivery; (2) the purchaser or holder is not required to make any payment in addition to the purchase price, whether as margin, settlement payment, or otherwise; (3) the issuer is not subject to mark-to-market margining requirements; and (4) the instrument is not marketed as a contract of sale of a commodity for future delivery (or option on such a contract). These margining requirements do not include an obligation of a secured debt instrument issuer to provide additional collateral to the purchaser. These exclusions render unnecessary the complex determinations required by earlier CFTC actions relating to hybrids: an exemption from the CEA (other than the provisions of the Shad-Johnson Accord) adopted by the CFTC in 1993 (*see* Regulation of Hybrid Instruments, 58 Fed. Reg. 5580, 1993 W.L. 10,462 (F.R.) (Jan. 22, 1993)), which applies to instruments with economic features similar to those of commodity futures or options, and the Hybrid Option Rules, Regulation of Hybrid Instruments (54 Fed. Reg. 30,684, 1989 WL 278,779 (F.R.) (July 21, 1989)),

PROVISIONS ON CONTRACT ENFORCEMENT AND CEA INTERPRETATION

Both the CEA and the Bank Products Legal Certainty Act include provisions described by their titles to involve "contract enforcement," which prohibit challenges to the legality and enforceability of transactions merely because they fail to comply with the terms or conditions of the CEA or a CFTC regulation. As they relate to OTC derivatives, these provisions in the CEA and the Legality Certainty Act state as follows:

CEA § 25(a)(4):

> No agreement, contract, or transaction between eligible contract participants or persons reasonably believed to be eligible contract participants . . . shall be void, voidable, or unenforceable, and no such party shall be entitled to rescind, or recover any payment made with respect to, such an agreement, contract, transaction, or instrument under this section or any other provision of Federal or State law, based solely on the failure of the agreement, contract, transaction, or instrument to comply with the terms or conditions of an exemption or exclusion from any provision of this Act or regulations of the Commission.

Bank Products Legal Certainty Act § 408(b):

> No covered swap agreement shall be void, voidable, or unenforceable, and no party to a covered swap agreement shall be entitled to rescind, or recover any payment made with respect to, a covered swap agreement under any provision of Federal or State law, based solely on the failure of the covered swap agreement to comply with the terms or conditions of an exemption or exclusion from any provision of the Commodity Exchange Act or any regulation of the Commodity Futures Trading Commission.

In addition, Section 2(e)(3) of the CEA provides that the legality, validity, or enforceability of an agreement, contract, or transaction involving an exempt commodity that is entered into on an electronic trading facility will not be subject to challenge merely because that facility fails to satisfy exemptive criteria imposed by the CEA.

Finally, to prevent erosion of the legal certainty for derivatives users that is sought through the exemptions, exclusions, preemptions and contract enforcement provisions described above, the CFMA also amended the CEA to prohibit any construction of its terms that would narrow those protections. Specifically, as amended by the CFMA, the CEA forbids construction of its terms as "implying or creating any presumption" either that the CEA applies to transactions that are not covered by its exclusions or exemptions or that transactions covered by those exclusions and exemptions would be subject to the

---

which provides an exemption only for hybrid instruments with economic features similar to those of commodity options. On hybrids under these earlier actions and a 1989 statutory interpretation relating to hybrids with *de minimis* features similar to those of commodity futures or options (Statutory Interpretation Concerning Certain Hybrid Instruments, 55 Fed. Reg. 13,582, 1990 W.L. 337,937 (F.R.) (Apr. 11, 1990)), *see* 2 SECURITIES & DERIVATIVES REGULATION §§ 13.08[3][c] & 13.09[5]. These actions followed a 1987 Advance Notice of Proposed Rulemaking, *supra* note 200, in which the CFTC announced its view that instruments with imbedded features like those of commodity futures and options were within the reach of the Futures Trading Restrictions and Option Trading Restrictions and the CFTC's jurisdiction.

CEA but for one of those exclusions or exemptions. A related provision forbids extension of the jurisdiction of the CFTC by way of implication. The provisions are set out as follows in Section 2(i) of the CEA:

> (1) No provision of this Act shall be construed as implying or creating any presumption that—
>
> (A) any agreement, contract, or transaction that is excluded from this Act under section 2(c), 2(d), 2(e), 2(f), or 2(g) of this Act or title IV of the Commodity Futures Modernization Act of 2000, or exempted under section 2(h) or 4(c) of this Act; or
>
> (B) any agreement, contract, or transaction, not otherwise subject to this Act, that is not so excluded or exempted,
>
> is or would otherwise be subject to this Act.
>
> (2) No provision of, or amendment made by, the [CFMA] . . . shall be construed as conferring jurisdiction on the Commission with respect to any such agreement, contract, or transaction, except as expressly provided in section 5a of this Act (to the extent provided in section 5a(g) of this Act), 5b of this Act, or 5d of this Act.[369]

The tables on the following pages summarize the requirements applicable to eligible swap participants, eligible contract participants and eligible commercial entities for purposes of the 1993 Swap Agreement Exemption and the CEA exclusions added by the CFMA which are described above in this chapter. The final table is an overview of those and the other CEA exclusions and exemptions discussed above. The discussion and tables do not take into account several, still inchoate, congressional proposals to modify the CEA's provisions as described, particularly in the area of energy contracts. Introduced in light of ongoing investigations into trading activities by Enron entities and other major market participants, these bills for the present do not have widespread support.

---

[369] This provision was added by Section 107 of the CFMA.

Commodities, Gaming and Bucket-Shop Laws

ELIGIBLE SWAP PARTICIPANT & ELIGIBLE CONTRACT PARTICIPANT COMPARED PARTY ACTING FOR ITS OWN ACCOUNT	
Eligible Swap Participants (1993 Swap Agreement Exemption)	*Eligible Contract Participants* (CEA § 1a(12)(A) & (C))
Financial Institutions	
No general category of "financial institution" is included. Separately included as eligible swap participants are any • bank, • trust company, • savings association, or • credit union.	Includes any • depository institution organized in the U.S., • agreement corporation or Edge Act corporation regulated pursuant to the Federal Reserve Act, • non-U.S. bank, • branch or agency in the U.S. of a non-U.S. bank, • trust company, • financial holding company subject to regulation under the Bank Holding Company Act of 1956, • institution regulated by the Farm Credit Administration, • federal or state credit union, or • subsidiary or affiliate of any of these entities if similarly regulated. (*See* Note 1 to Table)
Insurance Companies and Affiliates	
Insurance companies	Includes any • insurer regulated by any of the states of the United States, • non-U.S. insurer, if determined by the CFTC to be subject to regulation comparable to U.S. insurers, or • regulated subsidiary or affiliate of covered U.S. or foreign insurer.

Eligible Swap Participant & Eligible Contract Participant Compared
Party Acting for its Own Account

Eligible Swap Participants	*Eligible Contract Participants*
Investment Companies	
Includes any • investment company subject to regulation under the Investment Company Act, and • foreign person performing a similar role or function and subject as such to foreign regulation, provided the investment company or foreign person is not formed solely for the specific purpose of constituting an eligible swap participant.	Includes any • company registered as an investment company under the Investment Company Act, or • foreign person performing a similar role or function and subject as such to foreign regulation, regardless of whether each investor in the U.S. or foreign investment company is itself an eligible contract participant.
Commodity Pools	
Includes any • commodity pool formed and operated by a person subject to regulation under the CEA, or • a foreign person performing a similar role or function subject as such to foreign regulation, provided (1) the commodity pool or foreign person is not formed solely for the purpose of constituting an eligible swap participant and (2) it has total assets exceeding U.S.$ 5 million.	Includes any • commodity pool formed and operated by a person subject to regulation under the CEA, or • a foreign person performing a similar role or function subject as such to foreign regulation, provided the commodity pool or foreign person has total assets exceeding U.S.$ 5 million, regardless of whether each investor in the commodity pool or foreign person is itself an eligible contract participant.

Commodities, Gaming and Bucket-Shop Laws 117

ELIGIBLE SWAP PARTICIPANT & ELIGIBLE CONTRACT PARTICIPANT COMPARED **PARTY ACTING FOR ITS OWN ACCOUNT**	
Eligible Swap Participants	*Eligible Contract Participants*
Legal Entities Generally	
Includes any corporation, partnership, proprietorship, organization, trust or other entity if it is not formed solely for the purpose of constituting an eligible swap participant and if • it has total assets exceeding U.S.$ 10 million, or • its obligations are guaranteed or otherwise supported by a letter of credit or keepwell, support, or other agreement issued or entered into by a qualifying entity, or • it — (1) has a net worth exceeding U.S.$ 1 million, and (2) enters into the swap agreement in connection with the conduct of its business or to manage the risk associated with an asset or liability owned or incurred or reasonably likely to be owned or incurred by it in the conduct of its business. A credit support provider qualifies if it is an eligible swap participant that qualifies under: • this class by having total assets exceeding U.S.$ 10 million, or • any of the classes identified above in this Table or one of the classes described below relating to governments, multinational or supranational government entities and their instrumentalities, agencies and departments.	Includes any corporation, partnership, proprietorship, organization, trust or other entity if • it has total assets exceeding U.S.$ 10 million, or • its obligations are guaranteed or otherwise supported by a letter of credit or keepwell, support, or other agreement issued or entered into by a qualifying entity, or • it— (1) has a net worth exceeding U.S.$ 1 million, and (2) enters into an agreement, contract, or transaction in connection with the conduct of its business or to manage the risk associated with an asset or liability owned or incurred or reasonably likely to be owned or incurred by the entity in its business. A credit support provider qualifies if it is an eligible contract participant that qualifies under: • this class by having total assets exceeding U.S.$ 10 million, • any of the classes identified above or the class relating to governments, multinational or supranational government entities and their instrumentalities, agencies and departments, or • a future CFTC action for this purpose.

ELIGIBLE SWAP PARTICIPANT & ELIGIBLE CONTRACT PARTICIPANT COMPARED **PARTY ACTING FOR ITS OWN ACCOUNT**	
Eligible Swap Participants	*Eligible Contract Participants*
Governmental Entities	
Includes any • governmental entity (including the United States, a state, or a foreign government) or political subdivision thereof, • multinational or supranational government entity, or • instrumentality, agency, or department of any of the above.	Includes any • governmental entity (including the United States, a state, or a foreign government) or political subdivision thereof, • multinational or supranational government entity, or • instrumentality, agency, or department of any of the above, if (1) it (A) has a demonstrable ability, directly or through separate contractual arrangements, to make or take delivery of the commodity underlying the relevant transaction, or (B) incurs risks, in addition to price risk, related to the commodity, or (C) is a dealer that regularly provides risk management or hedging services to, or engages in market-making activities with, the foregoing entities involving transactions to purchase or sell the commodity or derivative agreements, contracts, or transactions in the commodity, (2) it owns and invests on a discretionary basis U.S.$25 million or more in investments, or (3) the other party to the relevant transaction is a regulated person in any of a number of listed classes and has offered the transaction to the governmental entity. (*See* Note 2 to Table.)

ELIGIBLE SWAP PARTICIPANT & ELIGIBLE CONTRACT PARTICIPANT COMPARED **PARTY ACTING FOR ITS OWN ACCOUNT**	
Eligible Swap Participants	*Eligible Contract Participants*
Employee Pension Plans	

Includes any
• employee benefit plan subject to the ERISA, or
• foreign person performing a similar role or function and subject as such to foreign regulation,
in each case if the plan satisfies one additional requirement:
(1) it has total assets exceeding $5,000,000, or
(2) the investment decisions of the plan are made by:
  (a) an investment adviser subject to regulation under the Investment Advisers Act,
  (b) a CTA subject to regulation under the CEA,
  (c) a bank,
  (d) a trust company, or
  (e) an insurance company treated as an eligible swap participant as described above.
	Includes any
	• employee benefit plan subject to the ERISA,
	• governmental employee benefit plan, or
	• foreign person performing a similar role or function and subject as such to foreign regulation,
	in each case if the plan satisfies one additional requirement:
	(1) it has total assets exceeding $5,000,000, or
	(2) the investment decisions of the plan are made by:
	  (a) an investment adviser subject to regulation under the Investment Advisers Act,
	  (b) a CTA subject to regulation under the CEA,
	  (c) a foreign person performing a role or function similar to that of an investment adviser or CTA and subject as such to foreign regulation,
	  (d) a financial institution, or
	  (e) an insurance company or affiliate that is an eligible contract participant.

Eligible Swap Participant & Eligible Contract Participant Compared **Party Acting for its Own Account**	
Eligible Swap Participants	*Eligible Contract Participants*
Broker-Dealers	
Includes any • legal entity that is a broker or dealer subject to regulation under the Securities Exchange Act, • legal entity that is a foreign person performing a similar role or function and subject as such to foreign regulation, or • natural person or proprietorship subject to such U.S. or foreign regulation as a broker or dealer, if the natural person or proprietorship also qualifies individually as an eligible swap participant under the tests applicable to the relevant class.	Includes any • legal entity that is a broker or dealer subject to regulation under the Securities Exchange Act, • legal entity that is a foreign person performing a similar role or function and subject as such to foreign regulation, • natural person or proprietorship subject to such U.S. or foreign regulation as a broker or dealer, if the natural person or proprietorship also qualifies individually as an eligible contract participant under the tests applicable to the relevant class, • associated person of a registered broker or dealer subject to regulation under the Securities Exchange Act, if the relevant registered broker or dealer makes and keeps records regarding the financial and securities activities of the associated person under that statute, • investment bank holding company subject to regulation under the Securities Exchange Act.

Commodities, Gaming and Bucket-Shop Laws

ELIGIBLE SWAP PARTICIPANT & ELIGIBLE CONTRACT PARTICIPANT COMPARED **PARTY ACTING FOR ITS OWN ACCOUNT**	
Eligible Swap Participants	*Eligible Contract Participants*
FCMs and Related Persons	
Includes any • legal entity that is a futures commission merchant subject to regulation under the CEA, • legal entity that is foreign person performing a similar role or function and subject as such to foreign regulation, • natural person or proprietorship subject to such U.S. or foreign regulation, if the FCM also qualifies individually as an eligible swap participant under the tests applicable to the relevant class.	Includes any • legal entity that is a futures commission merchant subject to regulation under the CEA, • legal entity that is foreign person performing a similar role or function and subject as such to foreign regulation, • natural person or proprietorship subject to such U.S. or foreign regulation, if the FCM also qualifies individually as an eligible contract participant under the tests applicable to the relevant class, or • floor broker or floor trader subject to regulation under the CEA, but only in connection with a transaction that takes place on or through the facilities of a registered entity or an exempt board of trade, or any affiliate thereof, on which the floor broker or floor trader regularly trades.

ELIGIBLE SWAP PARTICIPANT & ELIGIBLE CONTRACT PARTICIPANT COMPARED **PARTY ACTING FOR ITS OWN ACCOUNT**	
Eligible Swap Participants	*Eligible Contract Participants*
Natural Persons	
Includes only an individual who has total assets in an amount in excess of U.S.$ 10 million.	Includes any • individual who has total assets in an amount in excess of U.S.$ 10 million, or • individual who has total assets in excess of U.S.$5 million, if the individual also enters into the agreement, contract, or transaction in order to manage the risk associated with an asset owned or liability incurred, or reasonably likely to be owned or incurred, by the individual.
Others	
	Any other person the CFTC determines to be eligible in light of the financial or other qualifications of the person.
Notes to Table	
Note 1. The definition of "financial institution" is set out in CEA § 1a(15).	
Note 2. The relevant regulated counterparties are identified in CEA § 2(cc)(2)(I)–(VI), which is part of the Treasury Amendment as amended by the CFMA. They are (1) financial institutions, (2) securities brokers or dealers registered under the Securities Exchange Act, (3) futures commission merchants registered under the CEA, (4) associated persons of these registered brokers, dealers and FCMs, if the relevant broker or dealer or FCM makes and keeps specified related records, (5) insurance companies and regulated subsidiaries or affiliates of insurance companies that qualify as eligible contract participants, (6) financial holding companies subject to regulation under the Bank Holding Company Act, and (7) investment bank holding companies subject to regulation under the Securities Exchange Act.	

Commodities, Gaming and Bucket-Shop Laws

ELIGIBLE SWAP PARTICIPANT & ELIGIBLE CONTRACT PARTICIPANT COMPARED PARTY ACTING FOR ANOTHER	
Eligible Swap Participants (1993 Swap Agreement Exemption)	*Eligible Contract Participants* (CEA § 1a(12)(B))
The following, when acting on behalf of another eligible swap participant: • a bank, or • a trust company, and the following, subject to the qualifications listed in the preceding table for natural persons and proprietorships within these two categories: • a broker-dealer subject to regulation under the Securities Exchange Act, • a foreign person performing a similar role or function subject as such to foreign regulation.	**Brokers and Equivalent Agents; and Investment Managers for Discretionary Accounts.** Includes eligible contract participants within the following groups, when acting as authorized broker or performing an equivalent agency function on behalf of an eligible contract participant, or as investment manager or fiduciary for an eligible contract participant, • financial institutions • insurance companies and their regulated subsidiaries and affiliates • commodity pools • corporations, partnerships, proprietorships, organizations, trusts and other entities • securities broker-dealers and related persons • FCMs and related persons • CEA-regulated floor brokers and floor traders.
	Investment Advisers and CTAs. Includes any • Investment adviser subject to regulation under the Investment Advisers Act, • CTA subject to regulation under the CEA, or • foreign person performing similar roles or functions and subject as such to foreign regulation.

ELIGIBLE COMMERCIAL ENTITY	
Eligible Contract Participant Category (From preceding table)	*Additional Requirements* (CEA § 1a(11))
<ul><li>Financial institutions</li><li>Insurance companies and regulated affiliates</li><li>Corporations, partnerships, proprietorships, organizations, trusts and other entities</li><li>Governments, multinational and supranational governmental entities and their instrumentalities, agencies and departments</li><li>Securities broker-dealers and related persons</li><li>FCMs and related persons</li></ul>	In connection with its business and the contract, agreement or transaction, it meets (1) and (2) or (3): It (1) has a demonstrable ability, directly or through separate contractual arrangements, to make or take delivery of the underlying commodity, and (2) incurs risks, in addition to price risk, related to the commodity, or (3) is a dealer regularly providing risk management or hedging services to, or engaging in market-making activities with, the foregoing entities that involve purchases or sales of the commodity or such agreements, contracts, or transactions.
Any eligible contract participant other than a natural person or an instrumentality, department, or agency of a state or local governmental entity	It both: (1) Regularly enters into purchases or sales of the commodity or derivative agreements, contracts, or transactions in the commodity, and (2) is either<ul><li>part of a group under common control or management having aggregate total assets of at least $ 100 million and not an investment vehicle of the kind described below, or</li><li>a collective investment vehicle whose participants include persons that are not (i) qualified eligible persons, as defined in CFTC Rule 4.7(a), (ii) accredited investors, as defined in Regulation D under the Securities Act, or (iii) qualified purchasers, as defined in Investment Company Act § 2(a)(51)(A).</li></ul>

OVERVIEW OF CEA EXCLUSIONS AND EXEMPTIONS		
OTC Products and Underlyings	*Required Parties*	*Execution Mode or Context*
CEA § 2(g) (*supra* p. 91) and Bank Products Legal Certainty Act § 407 (*supra* p. 92)		
CEA: Any product if material terms (other than price and quantity) are subject to individual negotiation Bank Products Legal Certainty Act: Products must be "swap agreements" under GLBA § 206(b) Underlying: Agricultural commodities excluded	Eligible contract participants (*supra* p. 115). Bank Products Legal Certainty Act: A "bank" qualifying under § 402(a) must have offered, entered into or provided the transaction to the other eligible contract participant	Not on a trading facility (*supra* p. 96)
CEA §§ 2(d) & 2(h) (*supra* p. 98)		
Any product (without need for terms to be subject to negotiation) Underlying: Agricultural commodities excluded	Eligible contract participants Bank Products Legal Certainty Act: A "bank" qualifying under § 402(a) must have offered, entered into or provided the transaction to the other eligible contract participant If execution is on a qualifying electronic trading facility, exclusion from CEA antifraud and antimanipulation provisions differs depending on whether the parties are "eligible commercial entities"—a subset of eligible contract participants	Permitted for in excluded or exempt commodities, if (1) not executed or traded on a trading facility, or (2) executed or traded on electronic trading facility, but only if each eligible contract participant is (a) acting for its own account on a principal-to-principal basis or (b) a qualifying regulated entity (*supra* p.98) Exempt commodities on electronic trading facilities: exclusion from antifraud/antimanipulation provisions requires "eligible commercial entities" (*supra* p. 99)

OVERVIEW OF CEA EXCLUSIONS AND EXEMPTIONS		
OTC Products and Underlyings	*Required Parties*	*Execution Mode or Context*
Treasury Amendment (CEA § 2(c)) (*supra* p. 101)		
Any product subject to the CFTC's jurisdiction other than a commodity option, futures contract, or option on a futures contract, that is executed or traded on an organized exchange or a security futures product (Options on securities subject to SEC jurisdiction are excluded because not subject to the CEA) Underlying: foreign currency, securities warrants, securities rights, resales of installment loan contracts, repurchase options, government securities mortgages and mortgage purchase commitments	No party requirements except for foreign currency transactions For currency products, required parties are (1) eligible contract participants or (2) a person who is not an eligible contract person if dealing with a subset of regulated eligible contract participants (*supra* p. 101) Thus, the exclusion is not available for retail transactions in foreign currency, which are those involving a person who is not an eligible contract participant except as described in (2) above	*See* first column
Forward Contract Exclusion (CEA § 1a(19)) (*supra* p. 76)		
Options not covered Underlying must be deliverable physically	Interpreted to require parties that are able to make or take delivery	Sometimes interpreted to require parties to be acting with commercial, as opposed to speculative, intent
Trade Option Exemption (*supra* p. 78)		
Options only Underlying: Agricultural commodities excluded	Offeree must be producer, processor or commercial user of the underlying or a by-product	Offeree must be entering into option solely in connection with its business in one such capacity

OVERVIEW OF CEA EXCLUSIONS AND EXEMPTIONS		
OTC Products and Underlyings	*Required Parties*	*Execution Mode or Context*
Energy Contracts Exemption (*supra* p. 79)		
Bilateral contracts for purchase and sale of the underlying commodity, with material economic terms subject to individual negotiation— Contracts must at the outset impose a binding obligation to make or take delivery, not permit cash settlement without the counterparty's consent, except in limited circumstances (such as default), and restrict transfers without consent Underlying: only energy products	Five classes of legal persons (not natural persons) that qualify as appropriate persons, if they are not formed to take advantage of the exemption, have demonstrable ability and legal power and authority to make or take delivery under the contract's terms and, in connection with their business activities, incur risks in addition to price risk related to the underlying	Each party must be acting as principal
Swap Agreement Exemption (*supra* p. 79 (safe harbor))		
Swap agreements, if not part of a fungible class of agreements that are standardized as to their material economic terms Underlying: any commodity, subject to uncertainty about application to securities-linked transactions	Eligible swap participants (and, in some cases, not formed to qualify as such)	Transactions through multilateral transaction execution facilities excluded Parties must be acting as principal or, in some cases, for another eligible swap participant, and creditworthiness of an obligated party must be a material consideration

\multicolumn{3}{c}{**OVERVIEW OF CEA EXCLUSIONS AND EXEMPTIONS**}
OTC Products and Underlyings	*Required Parties*	*Execution Mode or Context*
\multicolumn{3}{c}{**Swap Policy Statement (*supra* p. 78 (safe harbor))**}
Options not covered and probably only cash-settled transactions covered. Contract terms must be tailored, not standardized, and, except in default, the right to terminate unilaterally must be negotiated at the outset. Underlying: any commodity		Each party must enter into the transaction in connection with a line of its business The transaction may not be marketed to the public Counterparty credit risk may not be eliminated through exchange-style margining or mutualization through a clearing organization

CHAPTER 4

SECURITIES LAWS

Introduction	129
Securities and Swap Agreements under U.S. Securities Laws	135
Securities	135
Swap Agreements	141
Security-Based Swap Agreements	145
Securities Law Concerns Reflected in the Documentation	149
Broker-Dealer Regulation	150
Securities Registration	159
Provisions on Fraud, Manipulation and Insider Trading	166

INTRODUCTION

If an OTC derivatives transaction is a security or may be settled through the delivery of a security or is otherwise linked to a security, the transaction may raise special concerns under laws applicable to the offer and sale of securities, the regulation of securities market professionals and the integrity of the public securities markets. This chapter is an overview of concerns of these kinds that arise under the two U.S. statutes that apply most broadly to these subjects, the Securities Act and the Securities Exchange Act,[370] and related rules and regulations adopted by the agency that administers them, the SEC. These concerns are reflected in provisions often found in the master agreements and transaction confirmations used by derivatives market professionals that are organized or operate in the United States, are affiliated with securities brokers or dealers regulated in the U.S. or are engaged in derivatives dealings with counterparties resident or organized in the United States.

The wide use of these provisions does not, of course, mean that they or the related U.S. legal concerns will necessarily be relevant in the particular dealings between two parties,[371] or that other special concerns may not arise under the securities laws of the

---

[370] The U.S. securities laws also include other statutes on narrower subjects, such as the Trust Indenture Act of 1939, the Investment Company Act and the Investment Advisers Act. *See* Section 3(a)(47) of the Securities Exchange Act, defining "securities laws."

[371] For example, market professionals organized and acting from outside the United States often provide in their master agreements and in their confirmations of securities-linked derivatives transactions that each of the parties is appointing a third party as its agent for specified purposes relating to the transactions. The agent in such a case is an affiliate of the market professional registered with the SEC under the Securities Exchange Act, while the party to the transaction itself is not. The approach is aimed at establishing that the market professional is not, by virtue of its participation in the transaction, engaged in unlawful securities dealings, because it is relying on an exemption from the Section 15(a)(1) broker-dealer registration requirements established in Rule 15a-6 under the Securities Exchange Act. Most of these exemptions turn on the involvement of a registered broker or dealer in manner specified in the Rule. For dealings of foreign brokers and dealers with certain supranational organizations, Rule 15a-6 provides a separate exemption that does not require that a registered broker or dealer participate in the transaction. Therefore, these kinds of standard

United States or other jurisdictions. Furthermore, not all the special issues that arise in connection with securities-linked derivatives arise under the securities laws. Chapter 3[372] deals with issues that arise under U.S. commodities regulation. In some jurisdictions, there may also be issues under antitrust laws or restrictions (constitutional or statutory) on ownership of companies that serve as public utilities or operate in a sector of the economy that has been totally or partially reserved to the state. If a derivatives transaction may result in a party's holding or otherwise controlling more than a specified threshold of the equity of such a company, or of debt convertible into, or exchangeable for, equity of such a company, the parties should explore the possible need for the approval of, or for reporting to, a governmental agency, and even the possibility that the transaction may be prohibited by law. Securities-linked derivatives may also give rise to special concerns under regulatory frameworks applicable to insurance companies and banks and their affiliates,[373] and they may raise highly technical issues under accounting rules,[374] tax laws[375] and restrictions on the use of credit to acquire or maintain a position in securities.[376]

A party may also be subject to contractual restrictions on disposing of securities that apply, or may be interpreted to apply, to positions in securities-linked derivatives. Typical examples are restrictions found in indentures or credit agreements and lock-up provisions—that is, covenants negotiated in connection with mergers and acquisitions or

---

provisions used by market professionals that relate to Rule 15a-6 are not necessary in transactions with these counterparties.

[372] *Supra* p. 63.

[373] For example, although the GLBA made substantial changes to U.S. law aimed at eliminating barriers to some securities activities for banks and bank affiliates, these liberalizing changes came with requirements that will make it necessary for U.S. banking organizations to engage in some securities activities through a registered broker or dealer. *See infra* note 462 and accompanying text. In addition, some equity derivatives used by many issuers in connection with stock buy-back programs raise special concerns for banking organizations under U.S. regulations involving capital adequacy requirements. *See* BOARD OF GOVERNORS OF THE FEDERAL RESERVE SYSTEM, DIVISION OF BANKING SUPERVISION AND REGULATION, THE USE OF FORWARD EQUITY TRANSACTIONS BY BANKING ORGANIZATIONS, SR 01–27 (Nov. 9, 2001), *available at* http://www.federalreserve.gov/boarddocs/SRLETTERS/2001/sr0127.htm.

[374] For example, issuers often use OTC equity derivatives to implement stock repurchase programs. The accounting rules applicable to these transactions are quite complex and dictate many of the features of the transactions by leading the issuer to insist, for example, that: (1) the issuer, and not its counterparty, must in all cases control decisions over whether the transaction will be settled other than through the physical delivery of the stock to the issuer, (2) the transaction include a ceiling on the number of shares that the issuer may be required to purchase, limiting that ceiling to authorized shares, and (3) in the event of the issuer's bankruptcy or insolvency, the counterparty's rights under the transaction must not be senior to the rights and claims available to the holders of the issuer's common stock. *See* FASB, *Accounting for Derivative Financial Instruments Indexed to, and Potentially Settled in, a Company's Own Stock* (EITF 00-19) (Jan. 17–18, 2001), *reprinted in* PLI 2001, at 719. *See also* Glen A. Rae, *Issuer Derivatives*, *in* PLI 2001, at 333, 345–46.

[375] *See* Erika W. Nijenhuis, *Taxation of Notional Principal Contracts*, in TAXATION OF FINANCIAL INSTRUMENTS, ch. 3 (Reuven S. Avi-Yonah, David B. Neman & Diane N. Ring eds. 1999); Richard G. Spears, *Tax Aspects of Equity Derivatives Used in Corporate Finance*, *in* DERIVATIVES RISK MANAGEMENT SERVICE 8B-1.

[376] In the United States, these restrictions are generally referred to as the margin regulations and are promulgated and administered by the Board of Governors of the Federal Reserve System. They restrict and require reporting of many kinds of transactions involving so-called purpose credit, which includes credit extended for the purpose of purchasing or carrying securities. *See infra* note 1471.

other transactions, under which a person agrees to continue to hold stock obtained in the transaction for a specified period and sometimes to dispose of the stock only in specified kinds of transactions and subject to rights of first refusal.

In some of these contexts, the outcome of the analysis of the issues may turn at least in part on whether the securities-linked derivatives transaction confers on a party some or all of the typical indicia of beneficial ownership or control of the related securities. As a result, derivatives linked to securities are often structured and documented to strike a fine balance with respect to such matters as voting rights, rights to receive dividends or other distributions and rights to direct a sale or other disposition of the related securities. Structural features of these kinds must, of course, be analyzed on a transaction-by-transaction basis.

Although this chapter focuses on securities law issues that are often reflected in derivatives documentation, the parties to securities-linked derivatives should not assume that all the relevant issues under applicable securities or similar laws will be reflected in the documentation. For example, under provisions of U.S. law aimed at stemming abuses from insider trading, the directors, officers and beneficial owners of more than 10% of the stock of a company with securities listed on a national securities exchange must generally report on their holdings and changes in their holdings in any class of the company's equity securities and may be required to turn over to the company the profits—often referred to as short-swing profits—obtained from some dealings in those securities. As discussed below, the rules that give rise to these reporting and disgorgement requirements are also applicable to an insider's OTC derivatives relating to these securities,[377] but the documentation of a derivatives transaction that could implicate these rules will not necessarily refer to the rules or related requirements.

Even though this chapter looks only at selected issues that often arise in connection with securities-linked derivatives, the U.S. securities laws may also give rise to concerns relating to derivatives usage more generally, at least in some circumstances or for some market participants. These concerns most often arise in connection with disclosure that issuers and others are required to make to prospective or existing investors.

Claims have, for example, been brought under the U.S. securities laws against the parties to interest rate and other OTC derivatives entered into in connection with securities offerings. Some of the fraud and other securities law claims in these cases have been based on allegations that the existence of the derivatives transaction between the issuer and its counterparty, and the interest of the counterparty under the transaction, were material matters that should have been but were not disclosed to investors in the securities, and related claims have been based on undisclosed conflicts of interest of a securities market professional involved in underwriting the securities because of its affiliation with the issuer's derivatives counterparty.[378]

---

[377] *See infra* p. 147 on these rules and *infra* p. 142 on security-based swap agreements.

[378] Allegations of these kinds were, for example, made in suits brought by Orange County California against Sallie Mae (the Student Loan Marketing Association) and Merrill Lynch & Co. and certain of its affiliates in connection with several issues of Sallie Mae callable notes purchased by the County and related but undisclosed interest rate swaps between Sallie Mae and a Merrill Lynch affiliate. The claims were based on various state and federal law fraud theories, including violation of Section 10(b) of the Securities Exchange Act and Rule 10b-5 thereunder. One of the claims involved failure to disclose that Orange County

Many participants in the markets must address their derivatives use in periodic (annual and quarterly) filings with the SEC. That is, subject to exceptions for registered investment companies and small business issuers, if an issuer has securities listed on a national securities exchange, it is required[379] to make considerable qualitative[380] and quantitative[381] disclosure about market risks that affect it, and these include market risks

---

would probably call the notes if the related swap were terminated. Other claims involved failures to disclose circumstances relating to the swaps that resulted in the setting of the note terms at levels that were unfavorable to investors so as to enable the Merrill Lynch swap counterparty to profit from the undisclosed swaps. Viewing the swaps and the notes together, Orange County also argued that Merrill Lynch's true underwriting compensation was not disclosed and was two to five times greater than what it would have been from underwriting Sallie Mae notes offered without a swap. The opportunity to profit from the swaps was also argued to have put Merrill Lynch in an undisclosed direct conflict of interest with its customers in recommending and selling the notes. For further description of these theories and the various kinds of relief sought by Orange County in these actions, *see* Gooch & Klein, *Review of Case Law II,* at 112. The claims were ultimately settled.

[379]The requirements are set forth under the heading "Quantitative and Qualitative Disclosures About Market Risk" in Item 305 of Regulation S-K under the Securities Act, the Securities Exchange Act and the Energy Policy and Conservation Act of 1975. Normally the information required by these reports, including estimates of exposure and loss given specified assumptions, as described in the following footnotes, will be generated by the registrant itself or by a provider of valuation services that is independent of the registrant's counterparty. In connection with highly tailored transactions, issuers required to make disclosure of this kind should consider whether they may need information from counterparties and, if so, whether they should be contractually obligated to supply it. There may also be other disclosure requirements relating to an issuer's material accounting policies regarding derivatives. Market participants should consult with their counsel and accountants about these matters.

[380]In the qualitative disclosure, the registrant must describe its primary market exposures as of the end of the latest fiscal year, how the exposures are managed (including objectives, general strategies and any instruments used to manage the exposures) and changes in the registrant's primary market risk exposures or how they are managed when compared with levels and approaches to risk management in effect during the most recently completed fiscal year, as well as what is known or expected to be in effect in future reporting periods. If interim period financial statements are included or required to be included in the relevant filing, there must also be discussion and analysis enabling the reader to assess the sources and effects of material changes in information that would be provided under Item 305 from the end of the preceding fiscal year to the date of the most recent interim balance sheet. Both the qualitative and the quantitative disclosure outlined in the next footnote must be presented separately for market risk sensitive instruments entered into for trading purposes and for purposes other than trading. The SEC requires registrants to identify the relevant primary market risk exposures by category—interest rate risk, foreign currency exchange rate risk, commodity price risk and other relevant market rate or price risks, such as equity price risk.

[381]The quantitative disclosure may be made in accordance with one of three alternative formats. The first involves tabular presentation of information related to market risk sensitive instruments, including fair values and contract terms sufficient to determine future cash flows from the instruments, categorized by expected maturity dates. The second involves disclosure of sensitivity analyses expressing the potential loss in future earnings, fair values or cash flows of market risk sensitive instruments resulting from one or more selected hypothetical changes in interest rates, exchange rates, commodity prices and other relevant market rates or prices over a selected period. The third alternative is value-at-risk disclosure expressing that potential loss, with a likelihood of occurrence, from changes in these kinds of variables. Under any of these alternatives, registrants are required to discuss material limitations that cause the information presented not to reflect fully the net market risk exposures of the registrant (such as summarized descriptions of positions or transactions omitted or features of included transactions that are not captured by the information). Registrants are required to present summarized risk information for the preceding fiscal year and to discuss the reasons for material quantitative changes in market risk exposures between the current and preceding fiscal years. In addition, if the registrant changes disclosure alternatives or key model characteristics, assumptions or parameters used in providing quantitative information and the effect of any such change is material, the regis-

inherent in derivative financial instruments, other financial instruments and derivative commodity instruments.[382] Moreover, if they seek for accounting purposes to treat derivatives as hedges, these issuers—registrants, as they are called by the SEC—may also have securities law concerns associated with complex accounting rules. SFAS No. 133, on "Accounting for Derivatives Instruments and Hedging Activities," imposes formal documentation requirements that must be met at the inception of a hedging relationship, and a registrant's failure to comply with these accounting requirements may become an issue under the U.S. securities laws, as the registrant's financial statements are included in its periodic filings with the SEC.[383]

Compliance with these securities law requirements relating to derivatives generally may also have an indirect impact on the contractual dealings of SEC registrants with their counterparties. This is so because in their derivatives documentation the parties often agree to deliver to each other specified financial information and represent as to its accuracy. An SEC registrant will often agree to deliver its periodic filings with the SEC, in satisfaction of these contractual obligations. Thus, through these contractual provisions, a material misrepresentation in the filings may become an event of default under the parties' contract.[384]

---

trant is required to explain the reasons for the change and either provide summarized comparable information under the new disclosure method for the preceding year or, in addition to providing disclosure for the current year under the new method, provide disclosures for that and the preceding fiscal year under the method used in the preceding year.

[382]The General Instructions to Paragraphs 305(a) and 305(b) of Regulation S-K explain that (1) "derivative financial instruments" has the meaning given to the term under GAAP and gives as an example paragraphs 5–7 of FASB Statement of Financial Accounting Standards No. 119 ("Disclosure about Derivative Financial Instruments and Fair Value of Financial Instruments"), including futures, forwards, swaps, options and other financial instruments with similar characteristics; (2) "other financial instruments" means all financial instruments, as defined by GAAP, for which fair value disclosures are required (citing as an example FASB Statement of Financial Accounting Standards No. 107 ("Disclosures about Fair Value of Financial Instruments"); and (3) "derivative commodity instruments" includes commodity futures, commodity forwards, commodity swaps, commodity options and other commodity instruments with similar characteristics that are permitted by contract or business custom to be settled in cash or with another financial instrument, to the extent such instruments are not "derivative financial instruments."

[383]In August 2001 the SEC indicated that "one significant focus of staff reviews [of filings by registrants] currently is to assure complete compliance with all the disclosure requirements of SFAS 133." Div. of Corp. Fin., SEC, *Current Accounting and Disclosure Issues* (Aug. 31, 2001) 19, *available at* www.sec.gov/divisions/corpfin/acctdisc.htm.

[384]*See* Annotation 4 to Section 3(d) of the sample master agreement in Part 3, *infra* p. 823, suggesting that parties consider whether the representation in that section, which relates to the accuracy and completeness of all information delivered by a party pursuant to a master agreement, should be modified for purposes of its application to financial statements, and *see* the sample formulation in Section 6 of the sample form of guaranty included in Part 3, *infra* p. 994. Modifications may be particularly appropriate in connection with information relating to market risks that SEC registrants are required to include in their periodic filings pursuant to Item 305 of Regulation S-K, as discussed *supra* note 379. Paragraph 305(d) of Regulation S-K makes clear that, "except for historical facts such as disclosure regarding the terms of particular contracts and the number of market risk sensitive instruments held during or at the end of a reporting period," for purposes of the antifraud provisions of the securities laws, disclosures provided pursuant to paragraphs (a)–(c) of Item 305 are considered "forward looking statements" for purposes of the safe harbors provided by Section 27A of the Securities Act and Section 21E of the Securities Exchange Act. To qualify for these safe harbors, the disclosure must be made by the issuer, a person acting on its behalf or an outside reviewer retained

This chapter, as indicated, looks at some of the ways in which the U.S. securities laws and related rules and regulations may have a more direct relation to OTC derivatives linked to securities and their users. It does so in two sections, the first of which provides the background by dealing with the distinction between securities and swap agreements for purposes of the Securities Act and the Securities Exchange Act and the further distinction under these laws between security-based swap agreements and nonsecurity-based swap agreements. The section ends with a review of the provisions of these statutes relating to fraud, manipulation and insider trading that, in December 2000, were made applicable to security-based swap agreements even though contemporaneous amendments made clear that security-based swap agreements are not securities.

Against this background, the second section of the chapter identifies issues under the Securities Act and the Securities Exchange Act commonly raised in connection with OTC derivatives linked to securities and illustrates how some of those issues may be reflected in the documentation for these transactions. In any particular case, the number and complexity of the issues can vary greatly depending on multiple factors. To impose some order on the possible combinations, the section presents the issues and related provisions of the law in the context of three questions:

1. Do the securities laws permit the parties to deal with each other and settle their transaction directly, or must a regulated intermediary be involved?

2. May the parties lawfully enter into the derivatives transaction, establish hedges through positions in the underlying securities and, if the transaction requires physical settlement, deliver the underlying securities, without registration or qualification of the transaction or the securities?

3. Are other duties or restrictions applicable in connection with the parties' dealings solely because the transaction involves a security, the issuer of an underlying security or someone with a special relationship to either?

When the answers to these and other questions relevant to a transaction indicate that a securities law concern may exist, participants in the OTC derivatives markets take particular care because the consequences of noncompliance with the securities laws may be severe. In private suits or administrative enforcement proceedings[385] the relief sought may, for example, include rescission of the transaction, the imposition of penalties or injunctions, damages claims and disgorgement of profits obtained from the transaction. In some cases violations of the securities laws are subject to criminal prosecution. In addition, in some cases, particularly in the area of fraud, the law may make it easier to establish a securities law claim than a common law claim based on the same conduct, because

---

by the issuer making a statement on behalf of the issuer or an underwriter, with respect to information provided by the issuer or information derived from information provided by the issuer.

[385] In some cases the same conduct may serve as the basis for both SEC enforcement action and private litigation. Civil liability is covered in 9 LOUIS LOSS & JOEL SELIGMAN, SECURITIES REGULATION, ch. 11 (3d ed. 1992 & Supp. 2002), and government litigation is covered in 10 *id.*, ch. 12 (3d ed. 1993 & Supp. 2002).

of the perceived public interest in maintaining public confidence in the integrity of the securities markets.[386]

SECURITIES AND SWAP AGREEMENTS UNDER U.S. SECURITIES LAWS

The documentation for OTC derivatives transactions often reflects concerns that may arise under the Securities Act and the Securities Exchange Act in three cases: when a transaction may be viewed as a security for purposes of these statutes, when it may involve settlement through the delivery of securities and when it may constitute a security-based swap agreement. In this regard, as discussed below in this section, the enactment of Title III of the CFMA, on Legal Certainty for Swap Agreements, made important changes to these and other U.S. securities laws by (1) introducing into them the concept of swap agreements, (2) providing that the many kinds of OTC derivatives that qualify as swap agreements for this purpose are not securities and (3) providing that a subset of swap agreements called security-based swap agreements are subject to specified provisions of the Securities Act and the Securities Exchange Act dealing with fraud, manipulation and insider trading.

SECURITIES

When courts in the United States are asked to decide U.S. securities law issues involving derivatives that are or may be viewed as securities or may be settled physically through the delivery of securities, they begin with the definition of the term "security" in the relevant statute. As amended by the CFMA in December 2000, Section 2(a)(1) of the Securities Act provides that, unless the context otherwise requires, the term "security" means:

> any note, stock, treasury stock, security future, bond, debenture, evidence of indebtedness, certificate of interest or participation in any profit-sharing agreement, collateral-trust certificate, preorganization certificate or subscription, transferable share, investment contract, voting-trust certificate, certificate of deposit for a security, fractional undivided interest in oil, gas, or other mineral rights, any put, call, straddle, option, or privilege on any security, certificate of deposit, or group or index of securities (including any interest therein or based on the value thereof), or any put, call, straddle, option, or privilege entered into on a national securities exchange relating to foreign currency, or, in general, any interest or instrument commonly known as a "security," or any certificate of interest or participation in, temporary or interim certificate for, receipt for, guarantee of, or warrant or right to subscribe to or purchase, any of the foregoing.[387]

The definition of "security" in Section 3(a)(10) of the Securities Exchange Act is largely the same and, as to matters of substance, viewed as encompassing the same instruments and contracts.[388]

---

[386] *See* 9 LOUIS LOSS & JOEL SELIGMAN, *supra* note 385, at 4184–85.

[387] Securities Act § 2(a)(1).

[388] The U.S. Supreme Court has given guidance to that effect. *See, e.g., Reves v. Ernst & Young,* 494 U.S. 56, 61 n.1 (1989).

Given these definitions, derivatives market participants have historically known that physically settled OTC forwards and options on securities and groups of securities are securities, as are options on indexes of securities and based on the value of security indexes. The express statutory references to puts, calls, straddles, options and privileges were added to the Securities Act and the Securities Exchange Act in 1982, in response to the evolution of the U.S. options markets.[389]

Security futures were added to these definitions of "security" in 2000, by the CFMA, as discussed in Chapter 3,[390] and are contracts of sale for future delivery "of a single security or of a narrow-based security index, including any interest therein or based on the value thereof," subject to limited exceptions.[391] The definition of "security future" in the Securities Act and the Securities Exchange Act makes clear, however, that an agreement, contract, or transaction that qualifies for one of the exclusions from the CEA discussed in Chapter 3[392]—including the security-based swap agreements discussed below—may not be treated as a security future.

Until the enactment of the CFMA, there was substantial uncertainty over whether OTC derivatives generally—and not merely those linked to securities—might be treated as securities for purposes of the U.S. securities laws. The uncertainty was only heightened if the existence or amount of a party's obligations under the derivatives transaction was based on the price, yield or level, or change in the price, yield or level of a security, a basket of securities or a securities index or a default or other credit-related trigger involving a security or its issuer. This was so because the SEC has taken the position in enforcement actions and otherwise that some such derivatives are securities,[393] and on the

---

[389] *See* 2 LOUIS LOSS & JOEL SELIGMAN, SECURITIES REGULATION 1135–1138.15 (3d ed. rev. 1999 & Supp. 2002), which also discusses the contexts in which the definitions had been interpreted as covering conventional stock options even before the 1982 amendments.

[390] *See supra* note 281 and accompanying text.

[391] In the Securities Exchange Act the definition appears in Section 3(a)(55). Section 2(a)(16) of the Securities Act adopts that definition for purposes of the Securities Act. There is an exception for securities that are exempt under Section 3(a)(12) of the Securities Exchange Act as in effect on the date of enactment of the Futures Trading Act of 1982, other than municipal securities as defined in Section 3(a)(29) of the Securities Exchange Act on that date.

[392] These are the exclusions in Sections 2(c), 2(d), 2(f) and 2(g) of the CEA and the exclusions enacted by the Bank Products Legal Certainty Act, as those exclusions came into effect on the date of the enactment of the CFMA. *See* Chapter 3, *supra* p. 63.

[393] The SEC took this position, for example, in enforcement proceedings related to transactions between Bankers Trust Co. and its affiliates with Gibson Greetings, Inc., which the SEC characterized as cash-settled put and call options constituting securities for purposes of the Securities Exchange Act. *See In re BT Securities Corp.*, Securities Act Release No. 7124, Exchange Act Release No. 35,136, Administrative Proceeding File No. 3-8579, [1994–1995 Transfer Binder] FED. SEC. L. REP. (CCH) ¶ 85,477, at 86,112–13 nn.6–7 (Dec. 22, 1994), and the discussion of these proceedings in Gooch & Klein, *Case Law II*, at 87. Although the courts rejected this SEC position in other litigation, the SEC continued to maintain it in subsequently settled proceedings. *See In re Gary S. Missner*, Securities Act Release No. 7304, Exchange Act Release No. 37301, Administrative Proceeding File No. 3–9025, [1994–95] Accounting and Auditing Enforcement Releases, FED. SEC. L. REP. (CCH) ¶ 74,306, 63,273 n.4 (June 11, 1996). The SEC's view that OTC derivatives linked to securities are, or at least may be, securities, and thus subject to the securities laws and its jurisdiction, was also the basis for its adoption of a set of regulations often referred to as "Broker-Dealer Lite," which permits qualifying "OTC derivatives dealers" to register with the SEC as such. These regulations provide for net capital and certain other requirements that are somewhat less burdensome than those

same theories parties to private litigation have brought claims seeking various kinds of relief for alleged violations by their counterparties of federal and state securities laws and regulations issued under those laws.

The most widely publicized private litigation and agency action involving claims like these were *Procter & Gamble Co. v. Bankers Trust Co.*[394] and enforcement proceedings brought by the SEC against an affiliate of Bankers Trust, BT Securities, in connection with a "Treasury-linked Swap" and a "Knock-out Call Option," which both P&G and the SEC characterized as securities. Under the first of the swaps, the linkage to securities consisted in a spread-setting feature pursuant to which Procter & Gamble would receive a fixed rate and pay a rate substantially below the commercial paper rate, provided the ratio between the yield on five-year Treasuries and the price of thirty-year Treasuries was within certain limits on a reset date but, through application of a formula, would pay a sharply higher rate if that ratio fell outside the agreed limits.[395] The second swap, similarly, involved payment obligations that depended on a spread-setting feature. Procter & Gamble was to receive a stream of payments provided a reference Deutsche Mark swap rate stayed within an agreed band during a look-back period but, pursuant to a formula, the payment stream would be eroded and Procter & Gamble could take on significant net payment obligations if the DEM swap rate moved outside the agreed band. The relevant yields, prices and rates moved adversely to Procter & Gamble, which ultimately commenced the lawsuit seeking rescission of the swaps, along with other relief.[396] Some of the claims were based on federal and state fraud and other securities law theories, which hinged on establishing that the swaps were securities.

One of Procter & Gamble's arguments in this regard was that the swaps involved options on securities, which, as seen above, are securities. The SEC had viewed the swaps in this way in its enforcement proceedings against BT Securities, which had been settled before the court was called on to decide the issue in this suit.[397] The court found that the swaps were not options on securities, noting that they did not contemplate any right to take possession of any security and rejecting the theory that transactions with embedded

---

applicable to full service registered brokers and dealers. Broker-Dealer Lite requires these derivatives dealers to limit their activities in specified ways and requires them to engage in certain activities through an affiliated registered broker-dealer. *See infra* pp. 152 & 153. The SEC, as *amicus curiae*—or friend of the court—also argued its position in *Caiola v. Citibank, N.A.*, a case discussed *infra* p. 138, where the federal court of appeals agreed, in relation to cash-settled options on common stock.

[394]*Procter & Gamble Co. v. Bankers Trust Co.*, 925 F. Supp. 1270 (S.D. Ohio 1996).

[395]Initially the P&G obligations were to be determined at the commercial paper rate minus 75 basis points, which was modified to CP minus 88 basis points when the parties pushed back the date at which the additional spread, if any, would be determined in accordance with a formula. *See* 925 F. Supp. at 1276.

[396]*See* Gooch & Klein, *Review of Case Law II*, at 100.

[397]*See supra* note 393. Under this theory, as stated by P&G, the first of the swaps was "a single security which can be decomposed into a plain vanilla swap with an embedded put option" on the reference notes and bonds, where the option was "a put on the 30-year bond price with an uncertain strike price" that depended on the level of the five-year Treasury yield at the agreed reset point. BT argued that, although both swaps contained terms that functioned as options, they were not options because they did not give either party the right to sell or buy anything and the only "option-like" feature was the spread calculation; any resemblance of the spread calculations to options on securities did not extend to the underlying swaps themselves, which had no option-like characteristics. *See* Gooch & Klein, *Review of Case Law II*, at 104.

option-like features should be treated as securities that Congress intended to regulate under the federal securities laws.[398] In so finding, the court expressly declined to follow the position on this issue that had been taken by the SEC in its settlement order in the enforcement proceedings against BT Securities.[399] After a lengthy analysis, the court also rejected other theories for finding that the swaps were securities—as notes, investment contracts or interests or instruments commonly known as a "security"—and, therefore, granted Bankers Trust summary judgment on P&G's securities law claims.[400]

From time to time after the *Procter & Gamble* decision and prior to the enactment of the CFMA, other courts were called on to consider whether OTC derivatives should be treated as securities for purposes of fraud claims under the federal securities laws. In several cases the courts adopted the *Procter & Gamble* court's analysis.[401] One such decision came shortly after the enactment of the CFMA, in a federal district court ruling in *Caiola v. Citibank, N.A.*,[402] which largely followed the *Procter & Gamble* court's analysis in findings that were later overturned at the appellate level.[403] Both decisions applied the law as in effect prior to the enactment of the CFMA.[404]

The *Caiola* case arose out of years of dealings between the plaintiff and Citibank, which involved both cash-settled, or synthetic, options on the common stock of Philip Morris and equity swaps like the one illustrated in Part 2 of this book[405] relating to the same securities. Mr. Caiola brought the action seeking damages, which he alleged he in-

---

[398] 925 F. Supp. at 1281.

[399] The findings in the orders in question, the court noted, by their own terms were solely for the purpose of the settlement, are not binding on any other person or in any other proceeding and were not binding on the *Procter & Gamble* court, in part because of the differences between the transactions involved. The court also observed, quoting the Supreme Court, that the "courts are the final authorities on the issues of statutory construction and are not obligated to stand aside and rubber-stamp their affirmance of administrative decisions that they deem inconsistent with a statutory mandate or that frustrate the congressional policy underlying a statute." *Id.*, quoting (approximately) from *SEC v. Sloan*, 436 U.S. 103 (1978) (citations omitted in original).

[400] The court's analysis is discussed at length in Gooch & Klein, *Review of Case Law II*, at 100. The court order was issued just before the parties settled the suit.

[401] An example is *Société Nationale d'Exploitation Industrielle des Tabacs et Allumettes v. Salomon Bros. Int'l Ltd.*, 702 N.Y.S.2d 258, 259 (App. Div. 2000).

[402] 137 F. Supp. 2d 362 (S.D.N.Y. 2001).

[403] No. 01-7545, 2002 U.S. App. LEXIS 13817 (2d Cir. June 27, 2002, amended July 17, 2002).

[404] Both the district court opinion, dismissing the federal securities law claims, and the appellate court decision reinstating those claims pointed to the change in the law and noted that, had the court been applying the Securities Exchange Act as amended by the CFMA, the court's decision would have been simpler because the transactions involved in the case would have been treated as security-based swap agreements which, as discussed below, are not securities but are subject to the antifraud provisions of the securities laws relied on by the plaintiff, Mr. Caiola. Neither court addressed the possible retroactive application of the CFMA to those transactions because the relevant issues were not properly raised. *Id.* The rationale for the lower court's statement about the appropriate treatment of the transactions under the CFMA has been criticized. *See* 2 SECURITIES & DERIVATIVES REGULATION § 13.05 at 13–62 (noting that the conclusion might have been correct as to some of the transactions but not for the reasons stated).

[405] *Infra* p. 736 (a sample confirmation for an equity-index swap). Equity swaps on a single stock are described in the discussion preceding the sample confirmation.

curred primarily for three reasons:[406] (1) Citibank declined to enter into further synthetic trading transactions with him (characterized in the complaint as a unilateral termination of its role as Mr. Caiola's counterparty), leading Mr. Caiola ultimately to ask Citibank to unwind his outstanding synthetic trading positions at a time that deprived him of the ability to benefit, as he had planned, from a rebound in the price of Philip Morris stock in relation to a hedge portfolio that he had established relying on assurances of a continuing trading relationship with Citibank; (2) contrary to earlier statements to Mr. Caiola and without his knowledge, Citibank changed the way in which it hedged the risks associated with its synthetic stock transactions with him to a "replication of Mr. Caiola's synthetic portfolio as a physical portfolio through the unauthorized purchases of real, physical securities and options corresponding to Mr. Caiola's synthetic positions, masked by false confirmations of synthetic transactions, all perpetrated in direct violation of the margin rules";[407] and (3) Citibank's undisclosed change in its hedging techniques led, in the course of its synthetic trading with Mr. Caiola, to market movements adverse to him[408] and, in connection with the unwind, to Citibank's calculation of the settlement amount taking into account the cancellation of its hedges, shifting to Mr. Caiola a "type of catastrophic risk on unwind" that he believed Citibank, not he, was to bear.[409]

Mr. Caiola's claims were dismissed by the district court, which found that the underlying transactions were not securities, largely relying on the *Procter & Gamble* analysis to conclude that the transactions were not investment contracts or instruments commonly known as securities and could not be treated as options because they did not confer on Mr. Caiola a right to receive the underlying securities.[410] The appellate court ordered the reinstatement of federal securities law claims that had been dismissed by the district court,[411] holding that "there is no textual basis for reading section 3(a)(10) [of the Securities Exchange Act] to define 'option' as including only transactions that give the holder the right to receive the underlying securities" and, therefore, that the cash-settled options

---

[406]This description is based on the Complaint, *Caiola v. Citibank, N.A.*, at 1, 51–52 & 56–58.

[407]Complaint, *Caiola v. Citibank, N.A.*, at 56. The federal margin rules are summarized *infra* p. 609.

[408]*Id.*

[409]*Id.* at 54. Specifically, Mr. Caiola alleged that, if Citibank had not refused to enter into three transactions proposed by him, as a result of the rebound in the price of the Philip Morris stock, he would have recovered approximately $43 million from the three transactions and, "had Mr. Caiola been permitted to continue to manage his positions consistent with his long established investment strategy, in accordance with the way he structured his existing positions, and consistent with the reasonable expectations created by Citibank's own words and deeds, he would have made the same sort of return he had made in prior years, making on average, approximately $15 million per year in 1996, 1997 and 1998, instead of the losses incurred from November 1998 through September 1999 of approximately $45 million." *Id.* at 58–59.

[410]137 F. Supp.2d 369–70. The district court also concluded that, even if the transactions had involved a purchase of securities by Mr. Caiola, his claims should be dismissed because his contractual disclaimer of reliance on Citibank foreclosed a claim of fraud under Section 10(b) of the Securities Exchange Act and Rule 10b-5 thereunder.

[411]No. 01-7545, 2002 U.S. App. LEXIS 13817 (2d Cir. June 27, 2002, amended July 17, 2002). In remanding the case to the district court for further proceedings involving these federal claims, the appellate court also reinstated the plaintiff's state-law claims, which had been dismissed for lack of jurisdiction when the district court concluded that there was no basis for the federal claims. The state-law claims were based on various theories, including fraud and breach of fiduciary duty.

on common stock involved in the case were securities.[412] Both decisions focused only on the cash-settled options in the case, and not on the parties' equity swap dealings.

The United States Supreme Court is the ultimate arbiter on the application of the U.S. securities laws, including the issue decided in *Caiola*. Neither the Supreme Court nor the federal courts of appeal have passed on the characterization for purposes of those laws of equity swaps and other cash-settled derivatives linked to securities, such as collars and similar combinations of cash-settled options linked to securities and credit default swaps on debt securities, such as bonds.[413]

The CFMA has largely (although not completely) eliminated the need to decide this issue in the context of some provisions of the federal securities laws relating to fraud, manipulation and insider trading because, as discussed below, claims relating to both securities and security-based swap agreements may exist under those provisions as they were amended by the CFMA. Whether a transaction should be treated as a security, on one hand, or a security-based swap agreement, on the other, may, however, still be critical to the OTC derivatives markets for other reasons. The chief reason why this is so is that, although the CFMA brought security-based swap agreements under antifraud, anti-manipulation and anti-insider trading provisions of the U.S. securities laws, in amending those laws the CFMA also made clear that security-based swap agreements should not be treated as securities for other purposes, including the regulation of securities brokers and dealers and investment advisers.

The distinction between securities and security-based swap agreements, therefore, continues to involve uncertainties in some cases, that is, primarily cases in which transactions could be argued to be options, or combinations of options, or to include imbedded options, relating to securities, rather than security-based swap agreements, which are not securities, as discussed below. Informative on the SEC's view in this regard is the *amicus curiae* brief that it submitted to the appellate court in *Caiola*. Citing the Supreme Court's guidance that "[i]n searching for the meaning and scope of the word 'security' * * * the

---

[412] 2002 U.S. App. LEXIS 13817, at *38. In reaching this conclusion, the court noted that the definition of "security" in the Securities Exchange Act expressly includes an option on a group or index of securities, making clear that cash-settled options are included. To read the definition as including those options but excluding options on a single stock unless they are physically settled would, the court indicated, produce "the odd consequence that Rule 10b-5 would cover options based on the value of two securities, but not options based on the value of a single security." In so holding, the court rejected Citibank's position in the lawsuit (which was supported by an *amicus curiae* brief of the SIA) that, when the U.S. Congress amended the definition of "security" to include the cited reference to an option on a group or index of securities, it did not intend to change existing law on single-security options, as to which the right to obtain physical delivery should be viewed as pivotal in the finding of a security subject to regulation under the federal securities laws. The *Caiola* court's decision was based solely on analysis of cash-settled options referred to in the pleadings and did not deal with the equity swaps between the parties. On the various arguments in this regard made by Caiola, Citibank, SEC and SIA, *see* Michael Sackheim & David M. Katz, *Synthetic Options: Evolving Legal Issues,* 21 FUTURES & DERIVATIVES L. REP. 1 (Dec. 2001) (written before the appellate court decision in the case).

[413] Some swaps linked to equity and debt securities and credit swaps, but not collars or credit default options, are expressly listed as swap agreements in the GLBA definition quoted *infra* p. 143. The list is, however, merely illustrative. If these transactions are swap agreements under that definition, they could be viewed as security-based swap agreements, and not as securities, for U.S. securities law purposes, as discussed *infra* p. 145. *See* 2 SECURITIES & DERIVATIVES REGULATION § 13.02[4][b] on issues relating to the analysis of credit default products as security-based swap agreements.

emphasis should be on economic reality,"[414] the SEC argued in that brief that cash-settlement and automatic-exercise features are economically insignificant attributes, and that the asymmetry of risks and benefits involved in an option is the key economic characteristic of this kind of security.[415]

It should also be noted that interpretations of the federal securities laws sometimes have ripple effects on the interpretation of state securities laws. It remains to be seen whether the *Caiola* decision will create new uncertainty under these state laws, where the characterization of cash-settled transactions has not yet been decided or cash settlement in the past has led to findings that OTC derivatives are not securities.[416]

SWAP AGREEMENTS

As noted, the distinction between securities and swap agreements for purposes of the U.S. securities laws was introduced through amendments enacted by Title III of the CFMA. The first of the amendments were effected through the addition of Section 2A of the Securities Act and Section 3A of the Securities Exchange Act. These provisions state that the definitions of "security" in Section 2(a)(1) of the Securities Act and Section 3(a)(10) of the Securities Exchange Act do not include any security-based swap agree-

---

[414] Brief of the SEC, *Amicus Curiae*, at 7, *Caiola v. Citibank, N.A.*, quoting from *United Hous. Found. Inc. v. Forman*, 421 U.S. 837, 848 (1975) (referred to incorrectly in the brief as *United States v. Forman*) (in turn quoting from *Tcherepnin v. Knight*, 389 U.S. 332, 336 (1967)).

[415] *Id.* at 7. That is, looking at an option from the perspective of the buyer, if the option expires worthless, the buyer's loss is limited to the premium it paid but the potential gain to the buyer is limited only by the difference between the option's strike price and the market value of the underlying used to calculate the payoff. Similarly, looking at an option from the perspective of the seller, its gain cannot exceed the premium received if the option expires worthless but the writer is exposed to potentially greater loss if the option is exercised.

[416] The distinction between conventional, physically settled options and other OTC derivatives with option-like features was pointed to as significant in a court decision finding FX transactions were not securities for purposes of New York's Martin Act (N.Y. Gen. Bus. Law § 352(1)), which grants the State's Attorney General the power to regulate fraud and deception in the sale of securities. *See Lehman Bros. Commercial Corp. v. Minmetals Int'l Non-Ferrous Metals Trading Co.*, No. 94 Civ. 8301 (JFK), 2001 WL 1646101, at *2 (S.D.N.Y. Dec. 21, 2001) (distinguishing the transactions from options inasmuch as they did not involve "the real possibility of foreign-currency positions changing hands" because at expiration of each position "'new positions were entered into that either rolled the trades further into the future or offset them with trades taking the opposite position'" (quoting from an affidavit presented on behalf of Lehman) and, in that context, concluding that the Martin Act's inclusion as "other securities" of "foreign currency orders, calls or options" does not apply to "a series of contracts that relate to foreign-currency prices, but, for all practical purposes, really do not anticipate an exchange of foreign currency positions"). In the course of the court's analysis, it also found that the FX transactions and the interest rate swaps involved in the case were not securities for purposes of the Martin Act as "other securities," under prior judicial rulings that the applicable test under the Martin Act is the same as the test established for "investment contracts" to constitute securities under the Securities Exchange Act by the U.S. Supreme Court in *SEC v. W.J. Howey Co.*, 328 U.S. 293, 298–99 (1946): "'a contract, transaction or scheme whereby a person [1] invests his money [2] in a common enterprise and [3] is led to expect profits solely from the efforts of the promoter or a third party.'" *Id.* (basing the analysis as to the swaps on the reasoning in *Procter & Gamble*) (numbering added in original). As to both the FX transactions and the interest rate swaps, the *Minmetals* court concluded that the commonality requirement of *Howey* was not met, because market movements, and not the entrepreneurial efforts of either party, would be the source of any gain on or value to be obtained from the FX transactions and swaps. *Id.*

ment or nonsecurity-based swap agreement, as those terms are defined in Sections 206B and 206C of the GLBA.[417]

For these purposes, a "security-based swap agreement" is a swap agreement (as defined in GLBA Section 206A) "of which a material term is based on the price, yield, value, or volatility of any security[418] or any group or index of securities, or any interest therein." All other swap agreements, as so defined, are nonsecurity-based swap agreements.

Under Section 206A(b) of the GLBA, the following are excluded from the definition of "swap agreement":

> (1) any put, call, straddle, option, or privilege on any security, certificate of deposit, or group or index of securities, including any interest therein or based on the value thereof;
>
> (2) any put, call, straddle, option, or privilege entered into on a national securities exchange registered pursuant to section 6(a) of the Securities Exchange Act relating to foreign currency;
>
> (3) any agreement, contract, or transaction providing for the purchase or sale of one or more securities on a fixed basis;
>
> (4) any agreement, contract, or transaction providing for the purchase or sale of one or more securities on a contingent basis, unless such agreement, contract, or transaction predicates such purchase or sale on the occurrence of a bona fide contingency that might reasonably be expected to affect or be affected by the creditworthiness of a party other than a party to the agreement, contract, or transaction;[419]
>
> (5) any note, bond, or evidence of indebtedness that is a security as defined in section 2(a)(1) of the Securities Act or section 3(a)(10) of the Securities Exchange Act; or
>
> (6) any agreement, contract, or transaction that is—
>
>> (A) based on a security; and
>>
>> (B) entered into directly or through an underwriter (as defined in section 2(a) of the Securities Act) by the issuer of such security for the purposes of raising capital, unless such agreement, contract, or transaction is entered into to manage a risk associated with capital raising.

---

[417] Sections 302 and 303 of the Bank Products Legal Certainty Act, respectively, added Section 2A to the Securities Act and Section 3A to the Securities Exchange Act.

[418] Section 206C(b) of the GLBA clarifies that the term "security" in this context is used with the meaning given to the term in Section 2(a)(1) of the Securities Act and Section 3(a)(10) of the Securities Exchange Act.

[419] Under the exception if a credit default swap provides for physical settlement, as described *infra* p. 643, through delivery of securities after, say, a default by the issuer of the security or the issuer's insolvency, the physical settlement term should not result in treatment of the transaction as a security if it otherwise qualifies as a swap agreement, as discussed in the following paragraphs.

Subject to these exclusions, any OTC derivatives transaction will qualify as a "swap agreement" under Section 206A(a) of the GLBA if three conditions are satisfied.

First, the parties must qualify, at the time they enter into the transaction, as eligible contract participants, as that term is defined in Section 1(a)(12) of the CEA. Second, the material economic terms of the transaction "(other than price and quantity)" must be "subject to individual negotiation." That is, they must not be offered on a take-it-or-leave it basis. Third, the transaction must:

> (1) be a put, call, cap, floor, collar, or similar option of any kind for the purchase or sale of, or based on the value of, one or more interest or other rates, currencies, commodities, indices, quantitative measures, or other financial or economic interests or property of any kind; or

> (2) provide for any purchase, sale, payment or delivery (other than a dividend on an equity security) that is dependent on the occurrence, non-occurrence, or the extent of the occurrence of an event or contingency associated with a potential financial, economic, or commercial consequence; or

> (3) provide on an executory basis for the exchange, on a fixed or contingent basis, of one or more payments based on the value or level of one or more interest or other rates, currencies, commodities, securities, instruments of indebtedness, indices, quantitative measures, or other financial or economic interests or property of any kind, or any interest therein or based on the value thereof, and that transfers, as between the parties to the transaction, in whole or in part, the financial risk associated with a future change in any such value or level without also conveying a current or future direct or indirect ownership interest in an asset (including any enterprise or investment pool) or liability that incorporates the financial risk so transferred, including any such agreement, contract, or transaction commonly known as an interest rate swap, including a rate floor, rate cap, rate collar, cross-currency rate swap, basis swap, currency swap, equity index swap, equity swap, debt index swap, debt swap, credit spread, credit default swap, credit swap, weather swap, or commodity swap; or

> (4) provide for the purchase or sale, on a fixed or contingent basis, of any commodity, currency, instrument, interest, right, service, good, article, or property of any kind; or

> (5) be any combination or permutation of, or option on, any agreement, contract, or transaction described in any of paragraphs (1) through (4).[420]

---

[420]*Id.* If a master agreement is used to document transactions that do and transactions that do not qualify as swap agreements under Section 206A(a) of the GLBA, the master agreement itself will be a swap agreement insofar as it relates to each of the transactions that qualifies as a swap agreement. GLBA § 206A(c). The second category would cover many credit derivatives. The first and third, appear to be broad enough to cover most other equity and debt-linked derivatives of the kinds discussed in this book although, as noted earlier, the SEC's broad view on what will constitute options that should be treated as securities may create some uncertainty in some cases.

The first two requirements for a swap agreement are discussed at some length in Chapter 3, which deals with the treatment of OTC derivatives under the CEA.[421] As discussed there, many exclusions from CEA regulation for these transactions turn on the parties' being eligible contract participants and some, further, turn on whether the terms of the transaction, other than price and quantity, are subject to individual negotiation. Some legal entities will not qualify as eligible contract participants unless their assets exceed U.S.$ 10 million, or their net worth exceeds U.S.$ 1 million and they are entering into the relevant transaction for specified risk-management purposes.[422] Also, natural persons will not qualify unless their total assets exceed U.S.$ 10 million or their total assets exceed U.S.$ 5 million and they are using the relevant transaction "to manage the risk associated with an asset owned or liability incurred, or reasonably likely to be owned or incurred," by the relevant person.[423]

As is apparent from the foregoing, not all swaps and similar OTC derivatives will qualify as swap agreements excluded from the definition of "security" in the Securities Act and the Securities Exchange Act. Participants in the derivatives markets should note, in this regard, however, that Title III of the CFMA includes a "savings provision" prohibiting the treatment of the various amendments to the securities laws relating to swap agreements summarized above as the basis for an inference that a swap or similar OTC derivative transaction is a security merely because it does not satisfy any of the criteria for swap agreements excluded from the definitions of "security" in the Securities Act and the Securities Exchange Act.[424]

As a result of the changes to the law introduced by the CFMA, there now exists in the U.S. securities laws the following curious anomaly. It largely reflects the fact that, where swap agreements are concerned, the CFMA embodies compromises aimed at eliminating some legal uncertainty relating to most, but not all, swap and similar transactions executed in the market at the time of its enactment. The anomaly is that conventional physically settled forward contracts and options on securities continue to be securities subject generally to the securities laws, including the rules and regulations involving securities brokers and dealers, but

- a swap, cap, floor, collar or similar transaction is not a security if it qualifies, as described above, as a nonsecurity-based swap agreement,

- a swap, cap, floor, collar or similar transaction is, as discussed below, subject to selected provisions of the U.S. securities laws relating to fraud, manipulation and insider trading even though it is not a security, if the transaction qualifies as a swap agreement under Section 206A of the GLBA but has any material term based on the price, yield, value,

---

[421] The term "swap agreement" is defined in defined in Section 206(b) of the Gramm-Leach-Bliley Act (GLBA). *See supra* note 308.

[422] *See supra* p. 117.

[423] *See supra* p. 122. Some regulated individuals may, however, qualify as eligible contract persons under other criteria.

[424] Section 304 of Title III of the CFMA provides that "[n]othing in this Act . . . shall be construed as a finding or implying that any swap agreement is or is not a security for any purpose under the securities laws."

Securities Laws 145

> or volatility of any security or any group or index of securities, or any interest therein, and
>
> - a swap, cap, floor, collar or similar transaction will, it appears, have to be analyzed *ad hoc,* under the facts and circumstances of the particular case, to determine whether it is or is not a security, if the transaction does not qualify as a swap agreement under Section 206A of the GLBA.

Moreover, as indicated in the preceding subsection, there is some uncertainty about the status of transactions that many in the derivatives market would view as security-based swap agreements but that the SEC might view as subject to treatment as options and, therefore, securities. Although one way or the other—as security-based swap agreements or as securities—these transactions would be subject to provisions of the securities laws prohibiting fraud, manipulation and insider trading, the appropriate characterization can be significant under other aspects of the securities laws. As noted above, perhaps the most important are the registration and other requirements applicable to securities brokers and dealers.

SECURITY-BASED SWAP AGREEMENTS

Listed below are the provisions of the Securities Act and the Securities Exchange Act dealing with fraud, manipulation and insider trading that were made applicable to security-based swap agreements through the enactment of the CFMA.[425]

- The antifraud provisions in Section 17(a) of the Securities Act

   These provisions make it unlawful for any person in the offer or sale of any securities or any security-based swap agreement to do any of the following, directly or indirectly:

   (1) to employ any device, scheme, or artifice to defraud, or

   (2) to obtain money or property by means of any untrue statement of a material fact or any omission to state a material fact necessary in order to make the statements made, in light of the circumstances under which they were made, not misleading; or

   (3) to engage in any transaction, practice, or course of business which operates or would operate as a fraud or deceit upon the purchaser.

- The antimanipulation provisions in paragraphs (2) through (5) of Section 9(a) of the Securities Exchange Act

---

[425] The list summarizes but does not necessarily quote the amended provisions, and the summaries omit references to the statutory linkage between the prohibited conduct and the use of so-called jurisdictional means, which include any means or instruments of transportation or communication in interstate commerce, the use of the U.S. mails and, in some cases, the use of a national securities exchange. References in the summarized statutory provisions to purchases and sales of security-based swap agreements are deemed to mean "the execution, termination (prior to its scheduled maturity date), assignment, exchange, or similar transfer or conveyance of, or extinguishing of rights or obligations under, a security-based swap agreement, as the context may require." Securities Act § 2A(b)(4); Securities Exchange Act § 3A(b)(4).

These provisions make the conduct specified below unlawful for any person, or the classes of persons specified, in connection with a security registered on a national securities exchange or a security-based swap agreement in respect of such a security:

(1) to effect (alone or with one or more other persons) a series of transactions creating actual or apparent active trading in the security, or raising or depressing the price of the security, and if the purpose of the transactions is to induce others to purchase or sell the security

(2) to induce the purchase or sale of the security or security-based swap agreement by the circulation or dissemination in the ordinary course of business of information to the effect that the price of any such security will or is likely to rise or fall because of market operations of any one or more persons conducted for the purpose of raising or depressing the price of such a security[426]

(3) to make, regarding any such security or security-based swap agreement, for the purpose of inducing the purchase or sale of the security or security-based swap agreement, any statement which was at the time and in the light of the circumstances under which it was made, false or misleading with respect to any material fact, and which the relevant person knew or had reasonable ground to believe was so false or misleading[427]

(5) to induce the purchase of any such security or security-based swap agreement by the circulation or dissemination of information to the effect that the price of any such security will or is likely to rise or fall because of the market operations of any one or more persons conducted for the purpose of raising or depressing the price of such security.[428]

- The antifraud provisions of Section 10(b) of the Securities Exchange Act

These provisions make it unlawful for any person to do any of the following, directly or indirectly: to use or employ, in connection with the purchase or sale of any security (whether or not registered on a national securities exchange) or any security-based swap agreement any manipulative or deceptive device or contrivance in contravention of

---

[426] This provision and the following one are applicable to a securities dealer or broker or any other person who is selling or offering for sale or purchasing or offering to purchase the relevant kind of security or a security-based swap agreement with respect to such a security.

[427] *See supra* note 426.

[428] This provision is applicable if the prohibited conduct is engaged in for consideration received directly or indirectly from a securities dealer or broker or another person selling or offering for sale or purchasing or offering to purchase the security or security-based swap agreement.

such rules and regulations as the SEC may prescribe as necessary or appropriate in the public interest or for the protection of investors.

- The antifraud provisions of Section 15(c)(1) of the Securities Exchange Act

    Paragraphs (A) through (C) of Section 15(c)(1) apply to securities brokers and dealers, municipal securities dealers and government securities dealers, respectively, and make it unlawful for these persons to effect any transaction in, or to induce or attempt to induce the purchase or sale of, the relevant kind of security, or any security-based swap agreement in respect of a relevant kind of security, by means of any manipulative, deceptive, or other fraudulent device or contrivance.[429]

- The anti-insider trading reporting and disgorgement provisions of Sections 16(a) and 16(b) of the Securities Exchange Act, often referred to as involving short-swing profits

    These provisions apply to the directors, officers and beneficial owners of more than 10% of the stock of a public company. Section 16(a) requires these insiders to report holdings and changes in holdings in any class of the equity securities of the relevant issuer, as well as security-based swap agreements in respect of those equity securities,[430] and Section 16(b) provides that the insider's profit realized from any purchase and sale, or any sale and purchase, of any nonexempted equity security of the issuer or a security-based swap agreement involving any such equity security within any period of less than six months will inure to the benefit of the issuer and be recoverable by it, unless the security or security-based swap agreement was acquired in good faith in connection with a debt previously contracted. The disgorgement provisions apply irrespective of the insider's intention but only apply if the relevant person is an insider at the time of both relevant transactions (the purchase and sale, or the sale and purchase).

- The antifraud provision of Section 20(d) of the Securities Exchange Act relating to trading while in possession of insider information

    Under this provision, if communicating, or purchasing or selling a security while in possession of material, nonpublic information would

---

[429] For securities brokers and dealers generally, the provision does not apply to commercial paper, bankers' acceptances, or commercial bills but does apply in connection with all other kinds of securities if the transaction is not effected on a national securities exchange of which the broker or dealer is a member. The provision also applies to any security-based swap agreement. For municipal securities dealers and government securities brokers and government securities dealers, the provisions apply only to municipal securities and security-based swap agreements relating to municipal securities, and to government securities and security-based swap agreements relating to government securities.

[430] The initial report must be filed shortly after the person becomes a beneficial owner, director, or officer. Subsequent reports must be filed after there has been a change in the person's ownership of the company's equity securities or if the person has purchased or sold a security-based swap agreement in respect of any such equity securities. Counsel should be consulted about the relevant periods.

violate, or result in liability to a purchaser or seller of the security under any provision of the Securities Exchange Act or any rule or regulation thereunder, the same conduct in connection with a purchase or sale of a put, call, straddle, option, privilege or security-based swap agreement with respect to that security, or with respect to a group or index of securities including that security, will also violate and result in comparable liability to any purchaser or seller of that security under the relevant statutory provision, rule, or regulation.

Thus, for example, if (1) Swap Party, while in possession of material nonpublic information about Company A, enters into a security-based swap agreement such as an equity swap related either to the stock of Company A or to an equity index including the stock of Company A, and (2) under all the same circumstances Swap Party's hypothetical purchase or sale of Company A stock would violate, say, Section 10(b) of the Securities Exchange Act and Rule 10b-5 thereunder or Section 20A under the Securities Exchange Act,[431] Swap Party's having entered into the swap will expose it to the same liability for violation of those provisions as it would be exposed to if it had engaged in the hypothetical purchase or sale.

Participants in the OTC derivatives markets should also bear in mind that violation of the listed provisions of the Securities Exchange Act can give rise to so-called controlling person liability for a person that directly or indirectly controls the person involved in the violation, pursuant to Section 20(a) of the Securities Exchange Act. Under that provision, the controlling person may be jointly and severally liable for the violation unless the controlling person has acted in good faith and did not directly or indirectly induce the act or acts constituting the securities law violation.

At the same time the listed provisions of the Securities Act and the Securities Exchange Act were amended to bring security-based swap agreements within their reach, the authority of the SEC with respect to security-based swap agreements was expressly limited by Section 2A(b) of the Securities Act and Section 3A(b) of the Securities Exchange Act. Under these provisions, the SEC is prohibited from registering, or requiring, recommending, or suggesting, the registration of any security-based swap agreement under the Securities Act or the Securities Exchange Act, and any registration statement under either of those statutes with respect to a security-based swap agreement will be void and without force or effect.[432] Furthermore, except as provided in Section 16(a) of the Securities Exchange Act (on reporting by insiders of their holdings, and

---

[431]Section 10(b) is described *supra* p. 146. Under Section 20A(a), any person who violates any provision of the Securities Exchange Act or the rules or regulations thereunder by purchasing or selling a security while in possession of material, nonpublic information will be liable to another person who, contemporaneously with that purchase, has sold securities of the same class, or who, contemporaneously with that sale, has purchased securities of the same class. There are limitations in Section 20A(b) on the liability that may be imposed in an action under Section 20A(a).

[432]Securities Act § 2A(b)(2); Securities Exchange Act § 3A(b)(2). In addition, if the SEC becomes aware that a registrant has filed a registration statement with respect to a security-based swap agreement, the SEC is required by the same provisions to give the registrant prompt notice of the circumstances.

changes in their holdings, of a public company's equity securities, as described above), the SEC is prohibited from promulgating, interpreting, or enforcing rules or issuing orders of general applicability under the Securities Act or the Securities Exchange Act in a manner that imposes or specifies reporting or recordkeeping requirements, procedures, or standards as prophylactic measures against fraud, manipulation, or insider trading with respect to any security-based swap agreement.[433]

As a result of a contemporaneous amendment to Section 10(b) of the Securities Exchange Act,[434] however, judicial precedents decided under Section 17(a) of the Securities Act and Sections 9, 15, 16, 20, and 21A[435] of the Securities Exchange Act, and judicial precedents decided under applicable rules promulgated by the SEC under those statutory provisions are applicable to security-based swap agreements to the same extent as they apply to securities, and rules promulgated under Section 10(b) of the Securities Exchange Act that prohibit fraud, manipulation, or insider trading (but not rules imposing or specifying reporting or record keeping requirements, procedures, or standards as prophylactic measures against fraud, manipulation, or insider trading), and judicial precedents decided under Section 10(b) of the Securities Exchange Act and rules promulgated thereunder that prohibit fraud, manipulation, or insider trading will apply to security-based swap agreements to the same extent as they apply to securities.

SECURITIES LAW CONCERNS REFLECTED IN THE DOCUMENTATION

The parties to derivatives linked to securities must, of course, consider the particular facts of their dealings to determine whether they may give rise to special concerns under regulatory frameworks addressing the offering of securities, securities market professionals and the integrity of the securities markets. Multiple factors, including the following, may be relevant to this analysis:

- the identities of the parties,

- the laws of the jurisdictions in which they are organized or from which they are operating for purposes of the transaction,

- the laws, and sometimes, the rules of a self-regulatory organization (SRO), applicable to a securities market professional (*e.g.,* a regulated broker or dealer) involved in the transaction as an agent for a party because of the transaction's securities linkage,

- the nature of the transaction itself and its linkage to a security—or, if that security is convertible to or exchangeable for another, the linkage to that other security,

---

[433] Securities Act § 2A(b)(3); Securities Exchange Act § 3A(b)(3).

[434] This amendment was effected through Section 303 of the Bank Products Legal Certainty Act.

[435] Section 21A(a)(1) of the Securities Exchange Act deals with civil penalties for violations of the provisions of the Act listed above as having been amended to apply to security-based swap agreements. Section 21A(a)(1) too was amended by the Bank Products Legal Certainty Act, to make it applicable to security-based swap agreements.

- the rules of an exchange or other organized market on which a relevant security is traded,

- the identity of the issuer of each relevant security,

- past, present or expected future relations between the issuer of a relevant security and one of the parties to the derivatives transaction (say, if a party is an affiliated company, an officer or a director or holds, has held or proposes to acquire a substantial interest in the issuer),

- the way in which a party may hedge against risks associated with the derivatives transaction and

- the way in which a party acquired a related cash position in an underlying security, if the party is entering into the derivatives transaction to transfer some or all of the risks associated with that cash market position.

There is no substitute for a step-by-step review of these and other potentially relevant factors in connection with each transaction. It is, however, often helpful to examine the factors in the context of a few questions framed to reflect key concerns addressed by the potentially applicable securities laws.

The discussion in this section is organized around questions of these kinds, the answers to which are often related to securities law provisions involving the registration of securities, the regulation of brokers and dealers, fraud and market manipulation and special restrictions or reporting requirements applicable to insiders and holders of substantial equity positions. The issues that may arise under the laws and regulations are complex and should be reviewed by market participants with the assistance of counsel. The discussion merely seeks to shed some light on the ways in which the issues sometimes arise in the context of securities-linked derivatives and, therefore, are reflected in derivatives documentation.[436]

BROKER-DEALER REGULATION

Background. In many jurisdictions those engaged locally or with local residents as brokers or dealers in securities or, more generally, investment products, must comply with registration or licensing and related requirements imposed by law with the objective of protecting investors from unscrupulous or predatory behavior. This objective is often reflected in rules aimed more particularly at ensuring that those who sell securities to the public meet appropriate standards relating, among other things, to training, maintenance of records, financial soundness and the safeguarding of customer property. Compliance with these requirements may be burdensome and costly but typically noncompliance can result in fines, injunctions and other relief sought by a local regulator and, sometimes, private actions for relief that may include rescission of transactions executed in violation of the registration or licensing requirements. As a result, the following question is often critical to one or both of the parties to a securities-linked derivatives transaction:

---

[436]The discussion below does not deal with special issues that may exist in connection with security futures.

Do the securities laws permit the parties to deal with each other and settle their derivatives transaction directly, or must a regulated intermediary be involved?

Under U.S. law (the Securities Exchange Act) a broadly drafted provision makes it unlawful for a broker or dealer to use the mails or any means or instrumentality of interstate commerce ("jurisdictional means") to effect any transaction in, or to induce or attempt to induce the purchase or sale of, any security, unless the broker or dealer is registered with the SEC or an applicable exemption (for the security or the broker or dealer) applies.[437] The definitions of the terms "broker" and "dealer" are also broad: the former applies in general to any person (whether or not a U.S. citizen or resident) who engages in the business of effecting transactions in securities for the account of others, and the latter in general to any person who engages in the business of buying and selling securities for his own account, through a broker or otherwise.

The following list identifies the sources of the broad prohibition and definitions in the Securities Exchange Act as well as exceptions and safe harbors in the statute or related rules that participants in the OTC derivatives markets sometimes rely on when they are not registered with the SEC as brokers or dealers and may enter into securities-linked derivatives that could trigger application of the broker-dealer registration requirements in the Securities Exchange Act:

Securities Exchange Act § 15(a)(1) (registration requirement)

Securities Exchange Act § 3(a)(4) (defining "broker" in clause (A) but subject to clause (B), pursuant to which a qualifying "bank"[438] will not be a broker solely because it engages in specified activities (there are 11 classes), including, transactions in "identified banking products" as defined in Section 206 of the GLBA to include (under subsection (a)(6)) any swap agreement, a term defined as shown above in Section 206A of the GLBA, although for purposes of these bank activity exceptions, equity swaps are not covered if "sold directly" to a person who is not a qualified investor (as defined in Section 3(a)(54) of the Securities Exchange Act))

Securities Exchange Act § 3(a)(5) (defining "dealer" in clause (A), in clause (B) clarifying that the term does not include a person that buys or sells securities for the person's own account, either individually or in a fiduciary capacity, but not as a part of a regular business, and, in clause (C), setting out an exception for banks that applies in connection with four categories of activities that, as described above, may be engaged in by banks without resulting in their treatment as brokers)

---

[437] There may also be separate, state-law registration requirements for brokers and dealers. The requirements discussed below are also separate from those that may be applicable under federal or state law to those found to be engaged in the business of giving investment advice.

[438] Under Section 3(a)(6) of the Securities Exchange Act, "bank" means (1) U.S. federally chartered banking institutions, (2) banks that are members of the Federal Reserve System and (3) other banking institutions that are doing business in the U.S. under state or federal law, are supervised and examined by state or federal bank supervisory authorities and are not operated for the purpose of evading regulation under the Securities Exchange Act, if a substantial portion of the bank's business consists of receiving deposits or exercising fiduciary powers similar to those permitted to national banks.

Rule 15a-1 under the Securities Exchange Act (which, together with related rules, is commonly referred to as "Broker-Dealer Lite" and permits qualifying affiliates of full service registered brokers and dealers to become registered with the SEC as "OTC derivative dealers,"[439] subjecting themselves to an alternative regulatory regime that: requires intermediation and in some cases "chaperoning" services to be rendered by an affiliated broker or dealer in connection with securities activities, limits the permitted securities activities of the OTC derivative dealer, imposes on it other special requirements (as to matters including the maintenance of a risk management control system, reporting and recordkeeping), and affords exemptions from or less burdensome alternatives to some rules applicable to full service brokers and dealers (such as the net capital and margin rules, as noted below) but also leaves in place other rules applicable to brokers and dealers generally)

Rule 15a-6 under the Securities Exchange Act (safe harbors from the broker-dealer registration requirements for foreign brokers and dealers in specified cases, including transactions in securities with or for persons that have not been solicited by the foreign broker or dealer, transactions with a bank acting in a broker or dealer capacity as permitted by U.S. law, transactions that occur outside the U.S. with any agency or branch of a U.S. person permanently located outside the U.S., transactions with U.S. citizens resident outside the U.S., if the transactions occur outside the U.S. and the foreign broker or dealer does not direct its selling efforts toward identifiable groups of U.S. citizens resident abroad, transactions with identified supranational and international organizations and their agencies, affiliates and pension funds, and, among the safe harbors most often relied on in the derivatives market, transactions with a broker or dealer registered with the SEC, whether it is acting as principal for its own account or as agent for others, and inducing or attempting to induce the purchase or sale of a security by a "U.S. institutional investor" or a "major U.S. institutional investor" provided that specified conditions are satisfied (including the execution of any resulting transaction through a broker or dealer registered with the SEC, the "chaperoning" of the foreign broker or dealer in permitted contacts with the investor in the U.S. by the registered broker or dealer and the registered broker or dealer's assumption of responsibility for:

(1) effecting the transactions conducted with the investor (but not the negotiation of their terms),

(2) issuing all required confirmations and statements to the investor,

(3) as between the foreign broker or dealer and the registered broker or dealer, extending or arranging for the extension of any credit to the investor in connection with the transactions,

---

[439]"OTC derivatives dealer" is defined in Rule 3b-12 under the Securities Exchange Act.

(4) maintaining required books and records relating to the transactions,

(5) complying with SEC net capital requirements with respect to the transactions and

(6) receiving, delivering and safeguarding funds and securities in connection with the transactions on behalf of the investor in compliance with SEC rules))

Impact on OTC Derivatives and Derivatives Documents. If OTC derivatives are securities or are settled through the delivery of securities, a market professional's participation in the transaction could trigger the broker-dealer registration requirements of the Securities Exchange Act, in the absence of an available exception, such as those identified in the preceding list. The SEC takes an expansive view of activities that may justify the application of the broker-dealer registration requirements of the Securities Exchange Act[440] and, as discussed earlier in this chapter, an expansive view of what derivatives may be viewed as securities. Since swap agreements are not securities, mere dealings in swap agreements, whether or not they are security-based swap agreements, should not trigger these registration requirements under the Securities Exchange Act. However, hedging of exposure under swap agreements through purchases and sales of securities may have to be done through a registered broker or dealer.

Traditionally, market professionals have sought, whenever possible, to use an entity other than an SEC-registered broker or dealer for their derivatives business for various reasons. Among the chief reasons is the competitive advantage effectively enjoyed by other market professionals if they can operate subject to lesser and less costly regulatory requirements. Often noted as prime examples in this regard are the differences between the risk-based capital requirements applicable to banks in connection with their derivatives activities and the heavier net capital rules applicable to brokers and dealers under the Securities Exchange Act.

As noted in the preceding list, qualifying affiliates of full service brokers or dealers registered with the SEC may voluntarily register as OTC derivative dealers so as to engage in some securities activities under a regime that is somewhat less burdensome than that applicable to other brokers and dealers. The Broker-Dealer Lite regime appears, however, to have attracted little use,[441] no doubt reflecting market perception that the relief afforded by this alternative regime remains insufficient, both in the abstract and when considered together with the limitations and special requirements imposed on OTC derivatives dealers.[442]

---

[440]*See, e.g.,* NORMAN S. POSER, BROKER-DEALER LAW AND REGULATION § 14.01[A] at 14-5 to 14-6 (3d ed. 2001).

[441]*See* THOMAS LEE HAZEN, LAW OF SECURITIES REGULATION § 14.5[3] & n.53, citing *So Far Only One Broker-Dealer Lite*, 33 SEC. REG. & L. REP. (BNA) 414 (March 19, 2001).

[442]Key areas of relief involve net capital and margin rules. Under the alternative net capital rules applicable to an OTC derivatives dealer pursuant to Rules 15c3-1(a)(5) and 15c3-1f under the Securities Exchange Act, the dealer [may calculate net worth including trading gains and unsecured receivables arising from transactions in "eligible OTC derivatives instruments" with any "permissible derivatives counterparty" and] may be authorized by the SEC to calculate capital charged for market and credit risk using a value-at-

For example, an OTC derivatives dealer must establish, document and maintain compliance with an internal risk management control system meeting certain requirements[443] and must limit its securities activities to the following four categories (or other activities designated by SEC order):[444] (i) dealer activities in "eligible OTC derivative instruments" that are securities; (ii) issuing and reacquiring securities that are issued by the dealer, including warrants on securities, hybrid securities and structured notes; (iii) "cash management securities activities,"[445] and (iv) "ancillary portfolio management securities activities."[446]

For this purpose, subject to specified exclusions, "eligible OTC derivative instruments" means any agreement, contract or transaction that

(1) Provides, in whole or in part, on a firm or contingent basis, for the purchase or sale of, or is based on the value of, or any interest in, one or more commodities, securities, currencies, interest or other rates, indices, quantitative measures, or other financial or economic interests or property of any kind; or

---

risk model, if the model has received SEC approval. However, an OTC derivatives dealer is subject to high minimum capital requirements (U.S.$ 100 million in tentative net capital and U.S. $20 million in net capital). Where the margin rules (*see infra* p. 609) are concerned, an OTC derivatives dealer is not subject to Regulation T of the Federal Reserve Board—as is a full service broker or dealer—but must comply with the margin rules in Regulation U. *See infra* note 1471 for a summary of these margin requirements.

Other parts of Broker-Dealer Lite exempt an OTC derivatives dealer from requirements (in Rules 15b9-2 and 36a1-2 under the Securities Exchange Act) under which brokers and dealers must be members of an SRO and subject to the Securities Investor Protection Act of 1970. The securities activities of OTC derivatives dealers must be subject to review by the designated examining authority for a broker or dealer affiliate (the NASD or the New York Stock Exchange). They also make the rules (Rules 8c-1 & 15c2-1 under the Securities Exchange Act) on hypothecation of securities carried by a broker or dealer for the account of a customer inapplicable to collateral delivered to an OTC derivatives dealer pursuant to a transaction in an eligible OTC derivative instrument, or pursuant to the OTC derivatives dealer's cash management securities activities or ancillary portfolio management securities activities, if the counterparty has received a "prominent written notice" from the OTC derivatives dealer of the kind discussed below. *See infra* note 455 and accompanying text.

[443] These requirements are set out in Rule 15c3-4 under the Securities Exchange Act. There are also special recordkeeping and reporting obligations for OTC derivatives dealers under Rules 17a-3(10) and 17a-12 under the Securities Exchange Act.

[444] The requirements are embodied in Rules 3b-12 and 15a-1(a) under the Securities Exchange Act, which also establish the requirement that the OTC derivatives dealer's securities activities consist primarily of those described in the first three listed categories.

[445] As defined in Rule 3b-14 under the Securities Exchange Act, these activities involve financing, cash management and the taking and disposing of collateral in connection with permitted securities activities and non-securities activities.

[446] Rule 3b-15 under the Securities Exchange Act defines these activities to include dealer activities conducted to reduce market or credit risk of the OTC derivatives dealer and incidental trading activities for portfolio management purposes, subject to specified conditions: they must be (1) limited to permitted transaction types (eligible OTC derivatives instruments, the issuance of securities by the dealer and others designated by SEC order), (2) within internally authorized risk exposure parameters included in the risk management control system maintained by the dealer in accordance with Rule 15c3-4 under the Securities Exchange Act, and (3) conducted by an associated person of the dealer that performs substantial duties for or on behalf of the dealer in connection with its dealer activities in eligible OTC derivative instruments.

(2) Involves any payment or delivery that is dependent on the occurrence or nonoccurrence of any event associated with a potential financial, economic, or commercial consequence; or

(3) Involves any combination or permutation of . . . [the foregoing].[447]

The specified exclusions include certain contracts for the purchase or sale of a security on a firm basis,[448] as well as any contract, agreement or transaction that "provides in whole or in part, on a firm or contingent basis, for the purchase or sale of, or is based on the value of, or any interest in, any security (or group or index of securities), if the material economic terms of the contract, agreement or transaction are not subject to individual negotiation[449] or the contract, agreement or transaction is listed or traded on or through a national securities exchange or related facility.

Furthermore, an OTC derivatives dealer must use a full service registered broker or dealer to execute its permitted securities activities and a registered broker or dealer must be involved in all communications and contacts (other than clerical and ministerial activities) of the OTC derivatives dealer with its counterparties, except that neither requirement applies to certain ancillary portfolio management securities activities in any "foreign security"[450] if the counterparty is acting as principal and is (i) a registered broker or dealer, (ii) a bank acting in a dealer capacity, as permitted by U.S. law, (iii) a foreign broker or dealer or (iv) an affiliate of the OTC derivatives dealer).[451] In most cases, the "chaperone" must be an affiliate of the OTC derivatives dealer.[452]

Because Broker-Dealer Lite has not attracted substantial use, the features of this alternative SEC regime have not given rise to widespread documentation practices. Market participants that register as OTC derivatives dealers can, however, be expected at a minimum to include in their documentation disclosures on certain matters relating to collateral posted by counterparties. This is so because, as indicated above, one of the benefits of Broker-Dealer Lite is that it exempts OTC derivatives dealers from rules relating to the hypothecation of customer securities, which are applicable to full service brokers and dealers.[453] For the OTC derivatives dealer to enjoy the benefit of the exemption in its

---

[447] Rule 3b-13 under the Securities Exchange Act.

[448] *See* Rule 3b-13(b)(1) under the Securities Exchange Act.

[449] Rule 3b-13(b)(2) provides in clause (i) that the relevant contract, agreement or transaction may not be listed or traded on or through a national securities exchange or registered national securities association or a facility or market of such an exchange or association and provides in clause (ii) that the contract, agreement or transaction must not be "one of a class of fungible instruments that are standardized as to their material economic terms," unless the SEC determines by order pursuant to Rule 15a-1(b)(2) that the class is within the scope of "eligible OTC derivatives instruments."

[450] These are securities of foreign issuers, provided the transaction does not take place on a national securities exchange or a market operated by such an exchange; depositary shares representing such securities, even if issued by U.S. banks, if initially offered and sold under Regulation S; and debt securities (including convertibles) of U.S. issuers initially offered and sold under Regulation S. Rule 15a-1(h) under the Securities Exchange Act.

[451] Rules 15a-1(c) and 15a-1(d) under the Securities Exchange Act.

[452] This requirement does not apply to issuing and reacquiring securities issued by the derivatives dealer.

[453] *See supra* note 442.

dealings with a counterparty, the counterparty must receive from the OTC derivatives dealer a "prominent written notice" alerting the counterparty to the fact that the dealer may repledge the collateral and that the counterparty will not have the benefit of certain protections it would otherwise enjoy.[454] A typical statement might read as follows:

> X hereby notifies the Counterparty as follows with respect to any collateral posted by the Counterparty in connection with this Agreement or the Security Agreement: (1) except as otherwise agreed in writing between X and the Counterparty, X may repledge or otherwise use any such collateral in its business; (2) in the event of X's failure, the Counterparty will probably be considered an unsecured creditor of X as to all such collateral, to the extent it or the equivalent has not previously been returned to the Counterparty or applied by X as permitted by this Agreement or the Security Agreement; (3) the Securities Investor Protection Act of 1970 (15 U.S.C.A. §§ 78aaa–78lll) does not protect the Counterparty with respect to any such collateral; and (4) such collateral will not be subject to the requirements of and customer protections afforded by the Securities and Exchange Commission customer protection rules and Rules 8c-1, 15c2-1, 15c3-2 and 15c3-3 under the Securities Exchange Act of 1934, as amended.

Those who deal with registered OTC derivatives dealers can also expect the dealer's customized documents to reflect the fact that, as summarized above, the OTC derivatives dealer will be required to use an affiliated, full service registered broker or dealer in the execution of permitted securities transactions with counterparties and in some communications and other contacts with the counterparty. As a result, master agreements, trade confirmations and other documents are likely to show the registered broker-dealer affiliate as signatory, as agent for the OTC derivatives dealer,[455] and the master agreement is also likely to include acknowledgments, like those set out in the following sample provisions, regarding the role, limited responsibilities and necessary involvement of that agent for the OTC derivatives dealer:

> X hereby notifies the Counterparty that X has appointed its affiliate, Y ["Affiliate"], to act as X's agent (in that capacity, the "Agent") in connection with Transactions under this Agreement. X hereby authorizes the Counterparty to assume, unless the Counterparty receives notice from X to the contrary, that all actions taken by the Agent on X's behalf in connection with this Agreement are actions that have been authorized by X and are being taken by the Agent pursuant to all necessary authorizations, approvals and other actions. The decision to enter into or otherwise act in connection with a Transaction directly or through the Agent shall lie solely with X, and X's representations herein regarding the legal, valid and binding nature of its obligations hereunder, and regarding the enforce-

---

[454] The statement is required for this purpose by Rule 8c-1(b)(1).

[455] One such formulation is "X, solely in its capacity as agent of Y and without responsibility in any other capacity."

ability of those obligations against X, apply equally to all Transactions, regardless of whether X is acting directly or through the Agent.[456]

The Counterparty confirms its understanding that, except as otherwise set forth in a writing executed by Affiliate,[457] all actions by Affiliate in connection with this Agreement are taken in its capacity as the Agent, Affiliate's sole function will be to act pursuant to instructions from X, Affiliate will have no responsibility or personal liability to the Counterparty to perform, or arising from any failure by X to perform, any obligation of X under this Agreement, and the Counterparty may not (and agrees that it will not) take any action against Affiliate or any of its property to enforce any of the Counterparty's rights or obtain any payment or other performance due from X in connection with this Agreement.

Notwithstanding anything to the contrary in this Agreement, except as otherwise requested by X, the Counterparty should direct any and all demands, notices and other communications to X relating to this Agreement exclusively to Affiliate, at its address specified in or pursuant to Section [ ].

Provisions like these, but somewhat more extensive, are also included in the customized agreements of many market participants that, as foreign brokers and dealers, engage in securities-linked OTC derivatives with counterparties in or otherwise connected with the United States in reliance on the safe harbors from the broker-dealer registration requirements discussed above based on Rule 15a-6 under the Securities Exchange Act. In some of these cases, the market professional, similarly, executes documents (including the master agreement and trade confirmations) through an affiliated broker or dealer registered with the SEC and includes in the master agreement special provisions relating to the broker-dealer's action, for specified purposes, as agent for each of the parties. Provisions of the following kind are commonly used:

The parties agree that Y, a broker-dealer registered with the U.S. Securities and Exchange Commission ("SEC"), will act as agent for each of the parties (in that capacity, the "Agent") in connection with each Transaction under this Agreement (each a "Security Transaction") that constitutes a security, as that term is defined in the Securities Exchange Act of 1934, as amended (the "Exchange Act"), to the extent necessary for the Transactions hereunder to be effected in accordance with Rule 15a-6 promulgated by the SEC pursuant to the Exchange Act.

---

[456]Market professionals have no particular motivation to include provisions like the sample paragraph in their own forms. The provisions are like those requested in master agreements between market professionals and counterparties—such as funds—that are acting through investment advisers or other agents.

[457]If the Affiliate named as the Agent is also a credit support provider or the parties' master agreement provides for setoff against claims or property of the named Affiliate, reference to a credit support document or to the relevant setoff provision may be appropriate.

Each of the parties confirms that, unless otherwise agreed in a writing executed by Y,[458] all actions by Y in connection with this Agreement are taken in its capacity as the Agent, Y's sole function will be to act pursuant to instructions from X and the Counterparty, Y will have no responsibility or personal liability to either party to perform, or arising from the nonperformance of, any obligation of either party under this Agreement, and neither party may (and each of them agrees that it will not) take any action against Y or any of its property to enforce any of that party's rights hereunder or obtain any payment or other performance due from the other party in connection with this Agreement.

As Agent, Y will (as and to the extent required by SEC regulations) in connection with each Security Transaction be responsible for: (a) effecting the Transaction (but not the negotiation of its terms); (b) issuing all required confirmations and statements to each of the parties, (c) maintaining books and records, and (d) receiving, delivering and safeguarding funds and securities treated as customer property for purposes of SEC regulations.[459]

Notwithstanding anything to the contrary elsewhere in this Agreement, except as otherwise agreed by the parties in writing, they will transmit to each other any and all demands, notices and other communications relating to Security Transactions under this Agreement exclusively through Y, at its address specified in or pursuant to Section [ ], in the manner there provided.

Provisions like those illustrated above have not traditionally been used in the OTC derivatives documents prepared by professional market participants that are banks, because in the past they have enjoyed a total exemption from the broker-dealer registration requirements of this statute.[460] The total exemption has, as indicated in the preceding list, been replaced by exceptions that are available to qualifying banks[461] only for transactions in identified banking products, as that term is defined in the GLBA, with the result that

---

[458]As observed in the preceding footnote, if the Agent is also a credit support provider or the master agreement provides for setoff against claims or property of the Agent, reference to a credit support document or to the relevant setoff provision may be appropriate.

[459]These provisions will often go on to refer to applicable law or regulation in the jurisdiction of the foreign broker or dealer acting as party to the OTC derivatives, especially when the relevant regulatory framework does not treat collateral or other property that may be received from or held for the counterparty as entitled to the benefits of local securities law rules involving customer property (such as rules requiring safe keeping and prohibiting the commingling of customer property with the property of a broker or dealer or use of customer property in the business of the broker or dealer).

[460]The exemption was included in the definitions of the terms "broker" and "dealer" in the Securities Exchange Act which, effective May 12, 2001, were replaced by the bank activity exceptions referred to above.

[461]The SEC has extended the bank activity exceptions to savings associations and savings banks, under Rule 15a-9 pursuant to the Securities Exchange Act.

some securities activities previously conducted in banks must be moved to a registered broker or dealer.[462]

The term "identified banking product" does not include OTC derivatives that constitute securities (such as conventional options on securities) but does include the kinds of securities-linked OTC derivatives identified above in this chapter as falling within the GLBA category of "swap agreements" when the parties qualify as eligible contract participants and the transactions have material terms (other than price and quantity) that are subject to individual negotiation.

As it applies to equity swaps, the bank activity exception from the broker-dealer registration requirement of the Securities Exchange Act appears to create something of an anomaly. The exception does not apply to an equity swap that is "sold directly to a person who is not a 'qualified investor,'" as that term is defined in Section 3(a)(54) of the Securities Exchange Act.[463] The anomaly exists because, under the amendments to the Securities Exchange Act described above, security-based swap agreements, including equity swaps, are not securities. The broker-dealer registration requirements apply only in connection with transactions in securities. An equity swap will qualify as a security-based swap agreement as long as the material terms of the swap, other than price and volume, are subject to individual negotiation and both parties are eligible contract participants. It would seem that the bank activity exception for equity swaps should be no narrower than the general exception from the definition of "security" for equity swaps. However, "qualified investor" includes an individual who does not satisfy any of the other tests (say, as a broker or dealer) only if the individual owns and invests at least U.S.$ 25 million, whereas an individual will be an eligible contract participant if he or she has assets of at least U.S.$10 million (or U.S.$5 million, if the individual also enters into the agreement, contract, or transaction in order to manage the risk associated with an asset owned or liability incurred, or reasonably likely to be owned or incurred, by the individual). As a result, in their documentation for securities-linked OTC derivatives, some banks may ask their counterparties to represent that they are qualified investors, as that term is defined in the Securities Exchange Act.[464]

SECURITIES REGISTRATION

Background. Many jurisdictions regulate the offer and sale of securities and other investment products. These laws and regulations often provide for registration of the secu-

---

[462] These requirements are commonly referred to as the GLBA "push-out" provisions. *See generally* TORTORIELLO, GUIDE TO BANK ACTIVITIES, at I-83, II-40.

[463] *See* TORTORIELLO, *supra* note 462, at II-18, to the effect that "banks should still be permitted to issue or originate such swaps as principal."

[464] The definition includes registered investment companies, investors excluded from the definition of investment company under Section 3(c)(7) of the Investment Company Act, banks, brokers, dealers, insurance companies, business development companies, SBICs, certain employee benefit plans, trusts whose purchases of securities are directed by any of the foregoing, market intermediaries exempt under the Investment Company Act, associated persons of broker-dealers other than natural persons, foreign governments, entities investing at least $25,000,000 ($10,000,000 for asset-backed securities and loan participations) on a discretionary basis, natural persons who own and invest at least $25,000,000 (or $10,000,000) on a discretionary basis, governments, and governmental subdivisions that own and invest at least $50,000,000 on a discretionary basis. *See* TORTORIELLO, *supra* note 462, at II-19 to II-20.

rities or the issuer with a local regulatory authority. They may permit offers and sales without registration if they are made in accordance with specified conditions, which may involve limitations on the size of the offering, the permitted classes of offerees and the ways in which the offering is conducted. These requirements differ substantially from jurisdiction to jurisdiction. As a result, a second threshold question for those engaged in securities-linked OTC derivatives is:

> May the parties lawfully enter into a securities-linked OTC derivatives transaction, establish hedges through positions in the underlying securities and, if the transaction requires physical settlement, deliver the underlying securities, without complying with potentially applicable registration or similar requirements?

Under U.S. law (the Securities Act) the security registration requirements apply generally to cases involving public offerings and sales, referred to as "distributions," unless the securities themselves or the offer and sale transaction are exempt from the registration requirements.[465] As described by the SEC, these requirements are designed to prevent "the creation of public markets in securities of issuers concerning which adequate current information is not available to the public."[466] The exceptions for the "exempt securities" and "exempt transactions" are embodied in the law—the Securities Act—and the SEC has elucidated some of the statutory provisions for exempt transactions and other cases in which the registration requirements will not be deemed to apply by rule and regulation. Some of these regulatory safe harbors are available for "primary market transactions" involving offers and sales by issuers and those acting on behalf of issuers. Others are available for "secondary market transactions" involving the resale of securities acquired directly or indirectly from the issuer or an affiliate of the issuer in a transaction or chain of transactions not involving a registered offering ("restricted securities"). The conditions to be met under the safe harbors in some cases turn on whether the resale and related offer is being made in respect of securities owned by an affiliate of the issuer ("control securities") and, for this purpose, "affiliate" is understood broadly to include any person that directly, or indirectly through one or more intermediaries, controls, or is controlled by, or is under common control with, the issuer.[467]

The following list identifies the sources of these Securities Act registration requirements and the related statutory exemptions and regulatory safe harbors that are most often referred or alluded to in or in connection with the documentation of OTC derivatives:

---

[465] There may also be registration or qualification requirements under state laws—often referred to as "blue sky" laws. Section 18 of the Securities Act provides a preemption from these requirements for any "covered security," which includes, among others, a security offered or sold to a "qualified purchaser," as that term is defined by SEC rule (Securities Act § 18(b)(3)). The SEC has proposed a rule that would define "qualified purchaser" for this purpose in the same way as "accredited investor" is defined in Rule 501(a) under the Securities Act. SEC, Release No. 33-8041 (RIN: 3235-AI25), *available at* www.sec.gov/rules/proposed/33-8041.htm. Rule 501(a) forms part of Regulation D under the Securities Act, which exempts from registration transactions "not involving any public offering" within the meaning of Section 4(2) of the Act. *See infra* pp. 161 & 163.

[466] Preliminary Note to Rule 144 under the Securities Act.

[467] The term is defined in Rule 144(a)(1) under the Securities Act.

Securities Act § 5 (the registration requirements)

Securities Act § 3(a) (identifying exempt securities)

Securities Act § 4 (identifying as exempted transactions, among others, (1) transactions by any person other than an issuer, an underwriter or a dealer; (2) transactions by an issuer not involving any public offering ("private placements"); (3) certain transactions by a dealer (including an underwriter no longer acting as an underwriter in respect of the security involved in the transaction); and (4) brokers' transactions executed upon customers' orders on an exchange or in the OTC market, but not the solicitation of such orders—all statutory exemptions that have been the subject of substantial judicial and SEC interpretation)

Regulation D under the Securities Act (Rules 501 through 508) (exempting from registration securities issued in small offerings and in other transactions that will be treated as private placements—for example, offers and sales to persons who qualify, or the issuer reasonably believes qualify, as "accredited investors" and offers and sales to limited numbers of other purchasers (often called "sophisticated investors") who alone or with a "purchaser representative" have (or are reasonably believed by the issuer to have) "knowledge and experience in financial and business matters" such that the purchaser "is capable of evaluating the merits and risks of the prospective investment"—if other conditions, including the filing with SEC of a notice of sale on Form D, the use of legends disclosing resale restrictions and, in some cases, information delivery requirements, are satisfied)

Regulation S under the Securities Act (providing that "offshore transactions" in securities may be made without registration by the issuer of the securities, a distributor or any of their respective affiliates or a person acting on behalf of any of them (Rule 903) or as a resale by any person outside these classes (Rule 904), where the offshore element may be satisfied in various ways, including offers and sales to or for the account of persons excluded from the definition of "U.S. person," but in all cases only if no "directed selling efforts" are made in the U.S. by specified persons and subject to other requirements (which include the use of legends and other disclosure on the existence of resale restrictions) that (1) are aimed at preventing abuse of Regulation S to circumvent the registration requirements of Section 5 of the Securities Act (in common parlance, to ensure that the securities "come to rest" offshore) and (2) involve conditions (including restrictions on hedging, in the case of equity securities of U.S. issuers) that differ, and are applicable during periods (the "distribution compliance period") that differ, depending on whether there is "substantial U.S. market interest," whether the security is equity or debt and other factors considered in assigning the security to one of three categories)

Rule 144 under the Securities Act (under which any person may sell restricted securities for that person's own account and a person may sell restricted securities for the account of an affiliate of the issuer, without being deemed to be engaged in a distribution, if an applicable "holding period" has lapsed and, subject to specified exceptions, adequate current public information with respect to the issuer is available, the resale complies with volume limitations and "manner of sale" requirements, and notice of the proposed sale on Form 144 is filed (by a person with a bona fide intention to sell the securities within a reasonable time after the filing) with the SEC (and, if the securities are admitted to trading on a national securities exchange, with the principal exchange on which the securities are admitted to trading), where:

(1) the holding period is counted from the later of (a) the date of acquisition of the securities from the issuer or an affiliate of the issuer and (b) any resale of the securities in reliance on the safe harbor, and the general rule provides for a holding period of one year, and various factors are considered in determining when the seller will be treated as having acquired the securities;

(2) transactions directly with a "market maker" (as defined in Section 3(a)(38) of the Securities Exchange Act) and brokers' transactions within the meaning of Section 4(4) of the Securities Act will satisfy the manner of sale requirements if the person selling the securities does not solicit or arrange for the solicitation of orders to buy the securities in anticipation of or in connection with the transaction or make any payment in connection with the offer or sale to any person other than the broker who executes the order to sell; and

(3) the volume limitations and information and manner of sale requirements cease to apply to restricted securities sold for the account of a person who is not an affiliate of the issuer at the time of sale and has not been an affiliate of the issuer during the preceding three months, if at least two years have elapsed since the later of the date the securities were acquired from the issuer or from an affiliate of the issuer)

Rule 144A under the Securities Act (for resales of some securities (1) if made to a "qualified institutional buyer" (QIB) or a person that the seller and any person acting on behalf of the seller reasonably believes is a QIB, (2) if reasonable steps are taken to ensure that the purchaser is aware that the seller may rely on Rule 144A, and (3) unless the issuer is an SEC reporting company, exempt from reporting pursuant to Rule 12g3-2(b) under the Exchange Act or a foreign government eligible to register securities under Schedule B of the Securities Act, if the holder and a prospective purchaser designated by the holder have the right to obtain from the issuer, upon request of the holder, and the prospective purchaser has received from the issuer, the seller or a person acting on behalf of either of them, reasonably current information about the nature of the issuer's business and the products and services it offers as well as the issuer's most recent balance sheet and profit and loss and retained earnings statements and similar financial statements for such part of the two preceding fiscal years as the issuer has been in operation)

Impact on OTC Derivatives and Derivatives Documents. In the absence of an available exemption, OTC derivatives that are securities are subject to the registration requirements of Section 5 of the Securities Act, as are transfers of a party's rights and obligations under these derivatives and transfers of restricted securities in the physical settlement of derivatives. In most cases the parties rely on the statutory exemption for private placements in Section 4(2) of the Securities Act in entering into or transferring their rights and obligations under derivatives that are securities, without complying with the literal terms of Regulation D. Nonetheless, as illustrated in the sample provisions set out below,[468] the parties to these derivatives sometimes also seek in their documentation to establish that some of the conditions of Regulation D are satisfied in their dealings, as indicia that the transaction is a private placement. For transfers of restricted securities in settlement of derivatives transactions, the parties often rely on Rule 144 under the Securities Act but may also rely on other safe harbors identified in the preceding list.

"Security-based swap agreements" and "nonsecurity-based swap agreements" are not subject to the registration requirements of Section 5 of the Securities Act. However, the SEC has long taken the position that the use of swaps and other OTC derivatives to transfer some or all of the market risk of restricted securities may be inconsistent with those registration requirements. For example, the offering restrictions of Rule 902(g)(1)(ii) under the Securities Act require a U.S. issuer of equity securities relying on Regulation S for an unregistered offshore offering to obtain an agreement in writing from each distributor not to engage in hedging transactions with respect to those securities prior to the expiration of the applicable distribution compliance period unless the hedging transactions themselves are in compliance with the Securities Act. The following is an excerpt from a 1997 Securities Act release in which the SEC summarized its concerns about hedging transactions and the registration requirements:

> [R]ecent years have evidenced the growth of a variety of hedging strategies in both the private and public securities markets associated with separating the bundle of rights that make up a security, including voting, price appreciation and dividend rights. Through the use of equity swaps and similar strategies, holders of restricted securities can retain legal title to their securities, but sell some or all of the rights associated with the securities in order to decrease or eliminate the risk that the market value of their investment will decline during a specific period of time. . . .
>
> . . . .
>
> Without risk, there is arguably no investment intent, suggesting that the holder is more of an underwriter than an investor. . . .
>
> [I]t is arguable that, in economic reality, a distribution occurs when a company sells unregistered restricted stock to an investor who, in turn,

---

[468] *See* the text accompanying note 472.

hedges the market risk through an equity swap with an investment bank, which then sells an equal number of securities to the market.[469]

In the context of these concerns, the SEC asked for comment on a number of possible regulatory approaches to the hedging of the market risk associated with the ownership of restricted securities, including whether a hedge should be considered a sale of the underlying security only if it results in a sale of securities of the same class to a third party and whether distinctions should be based on the nature or timing of the hedging transaction or the identity of the holder of the underlying security.[470]

The registration requirements of Section 5 of the Securities Act and the exemptions and safe harbors summarized in the preceding list figure in the documentation for OTC derivatives in many ways. The most frequently found provisions are representations, acknowledgments and covenants included in master agreements and transaction confirmations. As illustrated in the sample clauses set out below, some of the representations seek information about a party and are aimed at enabling the other party to justify reliance on a statutory exemption from the registration requirements or on one of the described safe harbors. Other representations or acknowledgments and covenants are more generally aimed at establishing that, unless the parties agree otherwise, in engaging in and settling their transactions, and if applicable in hedging its risks associated with the parties' transactions, each of them will be responsible for ensuring that its own actions will not violate applicable securities laws or receipt by the other party of securities that are subject to resale restrictions for any reason other than the transferee's own identity or relationship with the issuer or an affiliate of the issuer. The sample also illustrates that these special securities law provisions are often combined with representations on contractual restrictions that may affect a party's ability to engage in securities-linked derivatives.

Securities Law Provisions. If any Transaction entered into under this Agreement may be settled through the purchase or sale of a security (a "Security"), as that term is defined in the U.S. Securities Act of 1933, as amended (the "Securities Act"), or if the Transaction itself is a Security, each of the parties represents and agrees as follows, on the date of this Agreement and on the Trade Date of the Transaction, except to the extent that the Confirmation of the relevant Transaction expressly provides otherwise:

(a) Each of the parties will be entitled to rely on the other's representations set forth below in making the representations set forth below

---

[469] Revision of Rule 144, Rule 145 and Form 144, Securities Act Release No. 7391, [1997 Transfer Binder] Fed. Sec. L. Rep. (CCH) ¶ 85,908, at 89,270–71 (Feb. 20, 1997) (footnotes omitted).

[470] *See id.* at 89,271–72 (discussing (1) a possible distinction between swaps and short sales of restricted securities, on one hand, and other hedging transactions, on the other, since the former "most closely approximate a sale of the restricted securities," (2) a further possible distinction between an initial hedge and a subsequent "maintenance" hedge entered into as the value of the underlying securities fluctuates, since the latter, aimed at maintaining the same level of risk as initially envisioned "[p]resumably . . . [is an] adjustment [that] has less distributive aspects than the initial hedge" and (3) possible distinctions to permit some limited hedging by individuals who are affiliates of issuers because a significant portion of their net worth may be represented by restricted stock).

and in assuming that the parties may enter into the Transaction and, if applicable, may settle their obligations to each other under the Transaction through a purchase or sale of Securities as contemplated in the Confirmation of the Transaction, without the need to comply with the registration requirements of Section 5 of the Securities Act or any provision of the securities laws of any state of the United States of America or any other jurisdiction requiring the registration or qualification of securities or other investment products ("Registration Requirements").

(b) Its involvement in the Transaction does not, and the exercise of its rights and the performance of its obligations under the Transaction will not, violate any contractual or legal restriction applicable to it relating to the transfer of beneficial or record ownership of any Security.

(c) If the party settles any of its obligations under the Transaction through delivery of Securities, the party will ensure that at the time of the delivery, the Securities will not be subject to any contractual or legal restriction on transfer (whether as "restricted securities," as that term is defined in Rule 144(a)(3) under the Securities Act, or otherwise), other than any such restriction that arises solely as a result of the transferee's identity, its relationship with the issuer or an affiliate of the issuer of the Securities or the transferee's then existing holdings in other Securities.

(d) The party is not entering into any Transaction with a view to the distribution of any Security and acknowledges that Transactions hereunder will not be registered pursuant to the Registration Requirements. It understands that it may not and agrees that it will not offer, sell, pledge or otherwise transfer (1) its rights and obligations under a Transaction constituting a Security or (2) any Security received by it under a Transaction (whether as credit support or in full or partial settlement of the Transaction) except in compliance with all applicable Registration Requirements or pursuant to an available exemption from the relevant Registration Requirement. The party's agreement in the preceding sentence will not, however, limit any rights that it may have against the other party for breach of its obligations under paragraph (c) of this provision.

(e) The party acknowledges that the other party may enter into options on Securities and other Transactions that constitute Securities in reliance on the view that each such Transaction is exempt from all Registration Requirements, including the Registration Requirements of Section 5 of the Securities Act, by virtue of Section 4(2) of the Securities Act or otherwise. On the date of this Agreement, the party qualifies as an "accredited investor," as that term is defined in Rule 501(a) under the Securities Act,[471] and if it ceases to qualify as such hereafter, it will give the

---

[471] Among the accredited investors under Rule 501(a) are banks under Section 3(a)(2), insurance companies under Section 2(13) of the Securities Act, brokers and dealers registered under Section 15 of the Securities Exchange Act, investment companies registered under the Investment Company Act, employee benefit plans subject to ERISA, if acting through specified kinds of entities acting as fiduciaries, and natural persons if either of two tests is met: the person's individual net worth or joint net worth with the person's

other party notice to that effect before entering into any further Transaction that constitutes a Security. In addition, the party will not enter into any such Transaction unless it is satisfied (and by entering into each such Transaction, it will be deemed to confirm that it is satisfied) that it has been given the opportunity to ask questions of, and receive answers from, the other party concerning the terms and conditions of the Transaction, and to obtain any additional information that the other party possesses or can acquire without unreasonable efforts or expense, to the extent the information is material to its understanding of the Transaction, the other party and its business and all related risks.[472]

These sample provisions are, of course, drafted for insertion in a master agreement and, therefore, begin by assuming that there may be cases in which at least some of the provisions will not apply. In these cases, market practice is to include the parties' overriding agreement in the confirmation of the relevant transaction or another appropriate document. For example, in a transaction involving securities issued by one of the parties, that party might agree (either in the confirmation or separately) to seek to register the securities under Section 5 of the Securities Act, so that the counterparty may freely dispose of the securities, if they are delivered to the counterparty in settlement of the transaction.

The settlement features of transactions are sometimes structured so that they cannot come into play at a time when the underlying securities would be subject to resale restrictions. If the transaction's pricing terms are set assuming settlement with freely disposable securities and settlement may occur while the securities are subject to resale restrictions, the confirmation may provide for adjustment to reflect a discount at which restricted securities trade. Transactions may be structured so as to avoid running afoul of the manner of sale and resale volume limitations of Rule 144 under the Securities Act, if those restrictions are viewed as potentially applicable.[473]

PROVISIONS ON FRAUD, MANIPULATION AND INSIDER TRADING

Background. Prohibitions on deceptive, manipulative and otherwise abusive practices are generally at the heart of laws and regulations concerned with the offer, purchase and sale of securities and other investment products and the integrity of the related mar-

---

spouse exceeds U.S.$ 1 million at the time of the purchase of the security or the person had an individual income in excess of U.S.$ 200,000 in each of the two most recent years or joint income with the person's spouse in excess of U.S.$ 300,000 in each of those years and has a reasonable expectation of reaching the same income level in the current year.

[472] As indicated *supra* p. 163, although the parties to OTC derivatives linked to securities rarely rely on the safe harbor from the registration requirements of the Securities Act provided by Regulation D, they sometimes make, and ask their counterparties to make, representations like these to help establish that their transactions that constitute securities have the hallmarks of private placements.

[473] For example, if one of the parties to a transaction is an affiliate of the issuer of the underlying securities or holds restricted securities that remain subject to those volume limitations, the transaction may be structured so that the counterparty's hedging transactions, and the unwind of those hedges, will comply with those conditions and limitations, as a precaution against allegations that the transaction violates the registration requirements of the Securities Act because the counterparty is acting for the account of the affiliate of the issuer or the holder of the restricted securities.

kets. The typical targets are misrepresentation and the omission of material information by those with a duty of disclosure, trading on the basis of nonpublic information—as a presumed type of deceptive or manipulative behavior in at least some cases[474]—and practices aimed at creating a false impression of true market interest.[475] Often the frameworks dealing with these subjects combine broadly drafted prohibitions with provisions aimed at particular kinds of conduct, or conduct of specific classes of market participants—issuers, insiders (directors, officers, substantial shareholders and others with inside, nonpublic information about the issuer), market professionals, and those acting on behalf of these typical subjects. As a result, those who engage in securities-linked OTC derivatives sometimes seek to identify potential issues under these varied provisions by asking:

> Are there special duties, reporting requirements or restrictions applicable in connection with the parties' dealings solely because the transaction involves the issuer of an underlying security or someone with a special relationship to the issuer?

Both the Securities Act and the Securities Exchange Act and rules and regulations adopted thereunder include general and specific provisions aimed at fraud, market manipulation and trading by insiders or by others with inside information as well as some safe harbors, including those identified in the following list:

> **Securities Act § 12(2)** (providing a basis for fraud claims by purchasers against sellers in connection with an offer or sale of a security using a prospectus or oral communication "which includes an untrue statement of a material fact or omits to state a material fact necessary in order to make the statements, in the light of the circumstances under which they were made, not misleading (the purchaser not knowing of such untruth or omission)" provided that the person making the offer or sale cannot sustain the burden of proving that "he did not know, and in the exercise of reasonable care could not have known, of such untruth or omission")

---

[474] 7 LOUIS LOSS & JOEL SELIGMAN, SECURITIES REGULATION 3448–85 (3d ed. 1991 & Supp. 2002) describes the development of the treatment of trading on inside information under the common law theories (fraud and breach of fiduciary duty) and the securities laws in the U.S., and includes a review of the most common rationales for regulation, including the need to protect the investing public against informational disadvantages that it cannot hope to overcome if those with nonpublic information about the issuer of a security are permitted to trade on the information, and the related need to remove insiders' incentive to delay disclosure of material information.

[475] The proposed EU framework in this area, which (subject to specified exceptions) would apply to financial instruments, including derivative financial instruments, would, broadly define two classes of "market manipulation": "[t]ransactions or orders to trade, which give, or are likely to give, false or misleading signals as to the supply, demand or price of financial instruments, or which secure, by one or more persons acting in collaboration, the price of one or several financial instruments at an abnormal or artificial level, or which employ fictitious devices or any other form of deception or contrivance"; and "[d]issemination of information through the media, including the Internet, or by any other means, which gives, or is likely to give, false or misleading signals as to the supply, demand or price of financial instruments, including the dissemination of rumours and false or misleading news" (Article 1(2) of the Proposal for a Directive of the European Parliament and of the Council on insider dealing and market manipulation (market abuse) (COM(2001) 281 final), *available at* http://europa.eu.int/comm/internal_market/en/finances/mobil/com 281en.pdf). ISDA's comments on concerns raised by the scope of the proposed market abuse directive are available at http://www.isda.org/speeches/index.html.

Securities Act § 17(a) (an analog to Section 12(2) in administrative, injunctive and criminal proceedings)

Securities Exchange Act § 9 (involving manipulation of prices in connection with securities registered on a national securities exchange)[476]

Securities Exchange Act § 10(b)[477] and various rules thereunder, including Rule 10b-5 (broadly prohibiting fraud and deception in offers, sales or purchases in both primary- and secondary-market transactions, generally in cases involving false and misleading material statements but also in cases involving omissions of material information[478] (including nonpublic information); and, where market professionals are concerned, also involving various other kinds of conduct)[479]

Rule 10b5-1 under the Securities Exchange Act (providing that the manipulative and deceptive devices prohibited in Section 10(b) of the Securities Exchange Act include, among other things, the purchase or sale of a security of any issuer on the basis of material nonpublic information about that security or issuer in breach of a duty of trust or confidence that is owed directly, indirectly, or derivatively, to that issuer, to the shareholders of that issuer, or to any other person who is the source of the material nonpublic information;[480] but also creating two affirmative defenses for purchases and sales that are effected (1) pursuant to qualifying contracts, instructions or plans in effect before the person is aware of the information[481] and (2) for purchases and sales on behalf of legal entities made by

---

[476] *See supra* p. 145.

[477] *See supra* p. 146.

[478] *See* 7 LOUIS LOSS & JOEL SELIGMAN, *supra* note 474, at 3485.

[479] These include failure to disclose the capacity in which the professional is acting; mark-ups over or mark-downs under the market price of a security; undisclosed adverse interests and substantial positions or other biases that may be viewed as affecting buy or sell recommendations; recommendations that violate suitability rules imposed by an SRO; and churning (trading with improper intent through an account under a broker or dealer's control at a level that is excessive in light of the customer's investment objectives. *See* 8 LOUIS LOSS & JOEL SELIGMAN, SECURITIES REGULATION 3770–3992 (3d ed. 1991 & Supp. 2002). Theories of fraud based on excessive mark-ups without proper disclosure and on a broker or dealer's responsibility to recommend to a customer only securities that the broker or dealer has reasonable grounds to believe are suitable for the customer have been rejected by the courts applying New York law as bases for common-law fraud actions, including actions relating to OTC derivatives. *See Lehman Bros. Commercial Corp. v. Minmetals Int'l Non-Ferrous Metals Trading Co.,* No. 94 Civ. 8301 (JFK), 2001 WL 1646101 (S.D.N.Y. Dec. 21, 2001) and cases cited therein.

[480] Paragraph (b) of the rule provides that a purchase or sale of a security of an issuer is "on the basis of" material nonpublic information about that security or issuer if the person making the purchase or sale was aware of the material nonpublic information when the person made the purchase or sale.

[481] This first defense is available to a person who can demonstrate that, before becoming aware of the information, the person had (1) entered into a binding contract to purchase or sell the security, (2) instructed another person to purchase or sell the security for the instructing person's account, or (3) adopted a written plan for trading securities, in cases where the purchase or sale actually occurs pursuant to the contract, instruction or plan (entered into in good faith and not as part of a plan or scheme to evade the prohibitions of the rule). The plan must (1) specify the amount of securities to be purchased or sold and the price and date for the purchase or sale; or (2) provide a written formula or algorithm, or computer program, for

individuals with investment discretion who are unaware of the information because of "Chinese walls" and other policies and procedures adopted to ensure against trading on material nonpublic information by these individuals)[482]

Rule 10b-10 under the Securities Exchange Act (on prescribed disclosure in broker and dealer confirmations)[483]

Rule 10b-18 under the Securities Exchange Act (a limited exemption from the antimanipulation provisions of Section 9(a)(2) and the antifraud provisions of Rule 10b-5 available in connection with a qualifying "Rule 10b-18 purchase" of, or "Rule 10b-18 bid" for, common stock of an issuer by the issuer or an "affiliated purchaser of the issuer,"[484] subject to conditions relating to timing, price and (except for block purchases) volume as well as the use in all such purchases on any single day (other than those that are not solicited by or on behalf of the issuer or an affiliated purchaser) of only one broker or, if no broker is used, only one dealer)[485]

Section 13(d) of the Securities Exchange Act and related rules and regulations (on reporting of beneficial ownership of 5% or more of a class of equity securities registered pursuant to Section 12)

Securities Exchange Act § 15(c) (prohibitions on manipulative, deceptive or other fraudulent devices or contrivances by brokers and dealers, municipal securities dealers and government securities brokers and dealers in

---

determining the amount, price and trading date; or (3) provide that the person relying on this defense is not permitted to exercise any subsequent influence over how, when or whether to effect purchases or sales (and, in this case, any other person who does exercise such influence must not have been aware of the material nonpublic information when exercising the influence). *See* Rachel McTague, *Insider Trading: Periodic Trading Plans Free Insiders to Trade During Corporate Blackout Periods*, SEC. L. DAILY, Nov. 13, 2001, referring to these plans as "preset diversification programs (PDP)."

[482]The rule specifies (in paragraph (c)(2)(ii)) that the policies and procedures must be reasonable, must take into consideration the nature of the person's business and may include prohibitions on trading, or causing trading, on the basis of material nonpublic information, as well as policies and procedures that prevent individuals with investment discretion from becoming aware of such information.

[483]The rule is without prejudice to general antifraud provisions of the securities laws. It lists items of disclosure that a broker or dealer must include in a written notification given or sent to a customer before the completion of a securities transaction with or for the account of the customer or induced by the broker or dealer.

[484]The term includes a person acting in concert with the issuer for purpose of acquiring the issuer's securities as well as an affiliate which directly, or indirectly, controls the issuer's purchases of the issuer's securities, or whose purchases are controlled by the issuer or whose purchases are under common control with those of the issuer.

[485]The timing restrictions are subject to limited exceptions for purchases following the termination of a market-wide trading suspension but otherwise preclude reliance on the exemption in connection with trading at specified, key trading times (*e.g.*, the purchase of an exchange-traded security on a national securities exchange cannot be the opening transaction in the security on the relevant exchange or made during the last half hour before the scheduled close of trading on the exchange). Rule 10b-18(b)(2). The price restrictions are, generally speaking, ceilings set by independently determined market prices (*e.g.*, a bid or purchase on a national securities exchange cannot be made at a price higher than the current independent bid quotation or the last independent sale price on the exchange, whichever is higher). Rule 10b-18(b)(3).

effecting or inducing or attempting to induce a purchase or sale of specified securities and, in Section 15(c)(2)(A), specifically referring to the use of fictitious quotations)

Securities Exchange Act § 16 (providing in subsection (a) for the filing by "insiders" of reports of positions and position changes relating to a nonexempted equity security of a company with equity registered under Section 12 of the Act and, in subsection (b), in some cases permitting the company to recover from these insiders so-called short swing profits)[486]

Securities Exchange Act § 20(d) (extending liability for communicating, or purchasing or selling while in possession of material nonpublic information relating to a security to specified derivatives involving the security, as described above[487])

Regulation M under the Securities Exchange Act (generally aimed at manipulation of the market price of securities by persons with an interest in the outcome of public offerings and other "distributions"[488] (issuers, selling security holders, "distribution participants," "affiliated purchasers" and others); also providing exceptions and exemptions)[489]

Impact on OTC Derivatives and Derivatives Documents. As a general matter, these statutory provisions, rules and regulations may be applicable in connection with derivatives that are securities and in connection with the settlement of derivatives through the delivery of securities. In addition, as discussed above, the listed provisions on fraud, manipulation and insider trading in Sections 17 of the Securities Act and Sections 9(a)(2)–(5), 10(b), 16(a), 16(b) and 20(d) of the Securities Exchange Act apply to security-based swap agreements.

---

[486] *See supra* p. 147.

[487] *Supra* p. 147.

[488] For this purpose, "distribution" is broadly defined to include offerings of securities, whether or not subject to registration, if distinguished from ordinary trading transactions by the magnitude of the offering and the presence of special selling efforts and methods.

[489] The prohibitions apply to activities that include: (1) "stabilizing" (placing a bid or effecting a purchase "for the purpose of pegging, fixing, or maintaining the price of a security") except as permitted by Regulation M; (2) covering a short sale with offered securities purchased in a public offering from an underwriter or broker or dealer participating in an offering of securities for cash during specified periods preceding the pricing of the securities, subject to certain exceptions; and (3) bidding for, purchasing or attempting to induce bids and purchases of a "covered security" in connection with a distribution. The prohibitions relate to activities of "distribution participants" (that is, an underwriter, prospective underwriter, broker, dealer or other person who has agreed to participate or is participating in the distribution), the issuer, a selling security holder or any person (an "affiliated purchaser") acting, directly or indirectly, in connection with the acquisition or distribution of a security involved in the distribution, in concert with an issuer, selling security holder or distribution participant. The prohibitions apply to activities during the applicable "restricted period" involving a "covered security" (which includes both the "subject security" being distributed and any "reference security" into which a subject security may be converted, exchanged or which, under the terms of the subject security, may in whole or significant part determine the value of the subject security). The beginning and end points of the applicable restricted period depend on various factors, including whether the distribution involves a merger, acquisition or exchange offer and, in other cases, the level of worldwide average daily trading volume for the security during a specified period before the determination of the offering price or, for registered offerings, before the filing of the registration statement.

A person engaging in a securities-linked derivatives transaction with a counterparty whose identity or status subjects the counterparty to some of the provisions listed above may also have independent concerns over related market activities, such as putting on and unwinding hedges and acquiring or disposing of securities in connection with settlement of the relevant transaction. As indicated in the preceding list, for a market professional these concerns can, for example, arise under provisions such as Rule 10b-18 and Regulation M under the Securities Exchange Act, which apply to issuers and other identified persons as well as those who engage in specified transactions in securities in concert with an issuer or another of these identified persons and persons who directly, or indirectly, control, or are controlled by, or under common control with, the issuer or one of these persons in the prohibited conduct.

There are various ways in which derivatives documentation may reflect concerns raised by securities law provisions relating to fraud, manipulation and insider trading. The following paragraphs give some examples.[490]

Documents with Prescribed Contents. In some cases securities laws and regulations may prescribe disclosure of certain information. Rule 10b-10 under the Securities Exchange Act may lead a broker or dealer subject to the rule to include in a trade confirmation statements that a party unaware of the rule's requirements might find puzzling.[491] For example, if a broker or dealer is not a member of the Securities Investor Protection Corporation (SIPC), in some cases the transaction confirmation may so state to satisfy a requirement of Rule 10b-10. In order to comply with Rule 10b-10, a confirmation may also state that a broker or dealer is not acting as agent for the customer or any other person[492] and may state that notice of the date and time of a transaction will be furnished on written request.

Documentation Features Reflecting Safe Harbors. The parties to OTC derivatives linked to securities sometimes structure their dealings so that one or both of them may rely on a safe harbor from antifraud or antimanipulation provisions of the securities laws, including safe harbors described in the preceding list. When this occurs, the documentation will often reflect the conditions of the relevant safe harbor and may expressly refer to the parties' intent to comply with the conditions.

For example, one or both of the parties may be required to represent that, on the date the transaction is entered into, the party is not in possession of material nonpublic

---

[490] In referring to hypothetical transactions, the examples do not take into account the many and often complex tax, accounting and other considerations that may be relevant to one or both of the parties. Those issues are beyond the scope of this book.

[491] The requirement of the rule is that the prescribed information be disclosed to the customer at or before completion of a transaction, so the confirmation is not the exclusive vehicle for proving the information. In principal-to-principal dealings in OTC derivatives that are securities, some of the information prescribed by Rule 10b-10 may not be relevant. For example, in some cases the rule requires disclosure to the broker-dealer's customer of information about mark-ups and mark-downs and similar remuneration received on securities acquired by a broker for the customer or acquired by the customer from a dealer acting for its own account in a riskless principal transaction, in which the dealer, say, sells to the customer a security acquired contemporaneously from a third party.

[492] If the broker or dealer were acting as agent, the rule would require disclosure of the circumstances.

information relating to the issuer of the underlying security, and a party may also be deemed to repeat that representation in connection with settlement or unwind of the transaction. The documents may include provisions under which settlement or the exercise of an option that could lead to settlement will be prohibited or deferred if a party at the time is in possession of material nonpublic information. If a party might be expected to come into possession of material nonpublic information after the transaction's trade date, the parties may structure the transaction to fall within a safe harbor provided, as indicated in the preceding list, by Rule 10b5-1 under the Securities Exchange Act, so that the transaction can proceed to settlement notwithstanding the party's possession of such information. In these cases, the documents will probably be drafted, among other things, so that consummation of the transaction will occur without further exercise of discretion of any kind on the part of the party that might otherwise be subject to liability in connection with trading while in possession of material nonpublic information.

Similarly, if, as part of a stock repurchase program, an issuer enters into a transaction in respect of its own stock, say, as seller of a put option or as purchaser under a forward contract, various features of the transaction may be structured in light of the time, volume and manner of trading conditions applicable under Rule 10b-18 under the Securities Exchange Act. In these cases, the issuer may, for example, be required to agree that, until all obligations of the parties under the transaction have been settled, all purchases of the issuer's stock by or for the account of the issuer will be conducted only through the counterparty or a broker-dealer designated by it so that the counterparty can monitor compliance with the manner of sale requirements of the safe harbor in Rule 10b-18. Moreover, the provisions of the transaction relating to settlement may be spread over multiple days so as to ensure compliance with the volume limitations of the safe harbor, and the parties may agree that any settlement price set on any such day will be determined by reference to market data at a time permitted for a Rule 10b-18 purchase.[493]

In cases where the status of one of the parties, or its holdings of an underlying security, may give rise to a reporting obligation under the securities laws, it is not uncommon for the documents to include a representation and agreement of that party along the following lines:

> It has obtained any consent and made any report that it is required by law or contract to make to any governmental agency or third party before entering into the Transaction and has advised the other party of any such requirement. It will advise the other party of any future requirement that it obtain such a consent or make such a report as a result of its in-

---

[493] Features of this kind may also be reflected in the overall structure of the transaction, for example, if the forward price at which the issuer may acquire its shares will be determined in part by reference to the prices at which the issuer's stock can be acquired in the market by the counterparty. These structural features are, as noted above, intended for the benefit of both the issuer and its counterparty, if there is a risk that the counterparty's hedging activities, or the unwind of its hedging positions, may be attributed to the issuer or treated as effected in concert with or under the control of the issuer or might otherwise give rise to liability under the antifraud or antimanipulation provisions of the securities laws in a case where compliance with Rule 10b-18 might provide a safe harbor. The documents for these transactions sometimes provide that the counterparty will conduct its hedging activities and other purchases of stock of the issuer that are in any way related to the transaction in compliance with the conditions of Rule 10b-18, regardless of whether the rule is applicable.

volvement in the Transaction and the exercise of its rights and performance of its obligations under the Transaction and will obtain all such consents and make all such reports. If it fails to obtain any such consent or make any such report, it will not allege that such failure affects the legality or validity of the Transaction or the enforceability against it of its obligations under the Transaction.

Acknowledgments and Other Reflections of Antifraud Concerns. Other common features of derivatives documents that reflect securities law concerns included in the preceding list are representations, acknowledgments and exculpatory provisions aimed at forestalling at least some fraud claims. We have discussed and illustrated provisions of these kinds elsewhere in this book, in discussing the relationship between the parties to OTC derivatives and common-law fraud, negligence, breach of fiduciary or special duties and similar claims brought against professional market participants.[494] As discussed, these provisions—including several paragraphs of representations published by ISDA—usually involve each party's assumption of responsibility for obtaining such information as it considers relevant in connection with a transaction, its acknowledgment that it is not relying on the other party or its affiliates in entering into the transaction, its acknowledgment that any information given by the counterparty or its affiliates does not constitute advice or a recommendation, its representations regarding its own ability to understand and assume the risks involved in the transaction without reliance on the other party or its affiliates and an acknowledgment that the other party is acting not as a fiduciary, but rather as principal, all unless the parties agree otherwise in writing in connection with the transaction.

The emphasis on each party's independent duty of inquiry and nonreliance on its counterparty reflects the fact that, as discussed in connection with claims of fraud, misrepresentation and the like, one of the elements necessary to establish at least some fraud-based claims under the securities laws is the plaintiff's reliance on an alleged material false or misleading statement or omission of material information in circumstances where the reliance is justifiable.[495] A person's acknowledgment that it may not rely, and confirmation that it has not relied, on another may lead to a finding that this essential element has not been proved, at least when the parties' dealings are on a principal-to-principal basis and, where nondisclosure is concerned, the party alleging reliance has also acknowledged its ability to obtain, and to assess the risks relating to, relevant information independently or with the assistance of a third party and the relevant information would in fact have been discoverable through reasonable efforts of the party claiming reliance.[496] It is

---

[494] *See* Chapter 5, *supra* p. 177.

[495] *See, e.g., Press v. Chemical Inv. Servs. Corp.*, 166 F.3d 529, 534 (2d Cir. 1999) (to state a claim under Section 10(b) of the Securities Exchange Act and Rule 10b-5 thereunder, a plaintiff must allege that, in connection with the purchase or sale of a security, (1) the defendant made a material misrepresentation or omitted to disclose material information, (2) the defendant acted with the requisite state of mind or intent or reckless disregard for the facts —usually referred to as scienter; and (3) the plaintiff relied to its detriment on the defendant's fraudulent material statement or omission).

[496] In a dispute involving an OTC cash-settled option, the court stated that whether or not an alleged misrepresentation or failure of disclosure is material is to be determined on the basis of an objective standard, *Caiola v. Citibank, N.A.*, No. 01-7545, 2002 U.S. App. LEXIS 13817, at *43 (2d Cir. June 27, 2002, amended July 17, 2002), citing as authority *Basic Inc. v. Levinson*, 485 U.S. 224 (1988), as follows: "[T]o

important in this regard to note that the U.S. Supreme Court has indicated that, for silence to operate as a fraud actionable under Section 10(b) of the Securities Exchange Act in connection with the purchase or sale of securities, the liability must be premised on a duty to disclose arising from a relationship of trust and confidence between the parties to the transaction,[497] and it appears that this relationship must arise outside the securities laws.[498] Where affirmative material misrepresentations are alleged to have occurred, however, whether or not an independent duty to speak existed may be irrelevant, and the ability of the party charged with fraud to rely on a disclaimer of reliance by the other party will usually depend on whether the particular subject of the alleged misrepresentation was covered by the disclaimer.[499]

Professionals dealing in securities-linked derivatives often expand the representations and disclaimers in the documentation to include clauses modeled on documentation

---

fulfill the materiality requirement 'there must be a substantial likelihood that the disclosure of the omitted fact would have been viewed by the reasonable investor as having significantly altered the 'total mix' of information made available.' *Id.* at 231–32 (quoting *TSC Indus., Inc. v. Northway, Inc.*, 426 U.S. 438, 449 (1976))." The *Caiola* court went on to quote the following as further support in relation to both nondisclosure and affirmative misrepresentation: "'At the pleading stage, a plaintiff satisfies the materiality requirement of Rule 10b-5 by alleging a statement or omission that a reasonable investor would have considered significant in making investment decisions.' *Ganino v. Citizens Utils. Co.*, 228 F.3d 154, 161 (2d Cir. 2000)." Measured against these tests, the court found that Mr. Caiola had made allegations sufficient at the pleading stage to indicate that the alleged misrepresentations were material in the context of the parties' dealings.

[497] *Chiarella v. U.S.*, 445 U.S. 222, 227–28, 235 (1980) (stating that "there can be no fraud absent a duty to speak" and holding that "a duty to disclose under § 10(b) does not arise from the mere possession of nonpublic market information").

[498] *See, e.g., Grandon v. Merrill Lynch & Co.*, 147 F.3d 184, 189 (2d Cir. 1998); *Barker v. Henderson, Franklin, Starnes & Holt*, 797 F.2d 490, 497 (7th Cir. 1986).

[499] *Caiola v. Citibank, N.A.*, No. 01-7545, 2002 U.S. App. LEXIS 13817, at *48–*49 (2d Cir. June 27, 2002, amended July 17, 2002), where the court stated as follows, in connection with allegations of fraud based on misrepresentations about how Citibank would hedge its cash-settled stock options with Mr. Caiola and rejected Citibank's argument based on a contractual disclaimer of reliance and the lack of an independent duty on the part of Citibank to have made any disclosure about its hedging strategies: "Assuming Caiola can prove these allegations, the lack of an independent duty is not, under such circumstances, a defense to Rule 10b-5 liability because upon choosing to speak, one must speak truthfully about material issues. *See Rubin v. Schottenstein, Zox & Dunn*, 143 F.3d 263, 267–68 (6th Cir. 1998); *Ackerman v. Schwartz*, 947 F.2d 841, 848 (7th Cir. 1991); *Robbins v. Moore Med. Corp.*, 788 F. Supp. 179, 184 (S.D.N.Y. 1992). Once Citibank chose to discuss its hedging strategy, it had a duty to be both accurate and complete." The *Caiola* decision, *id.* at *47–*48, also reviewed as follows the subject of the broad disclaimer of reliance in documentation involved in that case as a potential bar to the plaintiff's claim of fraud under Rule 10b-5: "A disclaimer is generally enforceable only if it 'tracks the substance of the alleged misrepresentation . . . .' *Grumman Allied Indus., Inc. v. Rohr Indus., Inc.*, 748 F.2d 729, 735 (2d Cir. 1984). The disclaimer provisions contained in the Confirmation [of the cash-settled stock option] fall well short of tracking the particular misrepresentations alleged by Caiola. *See Mfrs. Hanover Trust Co. v. Yanakas*, 7 F.3d 310, 316 (2d Cir. 1993) (reciting rule that a valid disclaimer provision 'must contain explicit disclaimers of the particular representations that form the basis' of the fraud claim); *see also Harsco Corp. v. Segui*, 91 F.3d 337, 345–46 (2d Cir. 1996) (enforcing a contractual disclaimer containing specific representations). Caiola specifically alleges that Citibank offered false assurances that after the Travelers merger the parties' existing trading relationship would not change and that Citibank would continue to act as a delta hedging counterparty. The disclaimer in the Confirmation states only in general terms that neither party relies 'on any advice, statements or recommendation (whether written or oral) of the other party.' . . . This disclaimer is general, not specific, and says nothing about Citibank's commitment to delta hedging."

Securities Laws 175

used in private placement memoranda, in offering documents and in confirmations developed for use in connection with sales of securities. The following are examples of supplemental paragraphs sometimes included in derivatives transaction confirmations or in other documents that a counterparty may be asked to execute and deliver at or before the execution of a transaction:

> Having considered the risks involved in the Transaction and in light of its sophistication and experience with transactions of the same kind and transactions involving the same or similar risks and, if applicable, on the basis of advice that it has sought from third parties, the Counterparty has concluded that the Transaction is suitable and appropriate for it, given its commercial objectives and its existing authorizations and policies on investments and its use of derivatives linked to securities.
>
> Before entering into the Transaction, the Counterparty had access to all the information it considered relevant to its decision to enter into the Transaction, including its evaluation of the risks and potential benefits to it of the Transaction, and the Counterparty will be solely responsible for independently obtaining all the information necessary to permit it to assess, on an ongoing basis, whether to maintain or unwind its position in the Transaction.
>
> The Counterparty is aware that the Dealer may engage in other transactions involving securities underlying or otherwise related to the Transaction, in connection with its hedging activities or otherwise, and that the Dealer may have other dealings with the issuers of those securities. The Counterparty understands that the Dealer is acting as principal for its own account in connection with the Transaction and that the Dealer has no duty to disclose to Counterparty the existence or nature of any such other transactions or their possible effect, if any, on the interests of the Counterparty, and the Dealer has no obligation to account to the Counterparty in any way for any such transaction or its effects.

If options are or may be involved in the parties' transactions, the documents may, further, specifically refer to the counterparty's having received, read and understood an "options disclosure document" (or ODD) of the kind used to inform purchasers of standardized options about the general characteristics of those options and the rules of options trading. Brokers and dealers furnish this document to a customer before or at the time they approve the customer's account for options trading or accept the customer's order to trade options, pursuant to Rule 9b-1 under the Securities Exchange Act.[500] Such a document might contain acknowledgement from the customer that these OTC options are not exchange-traded and are not "standardized stock options" but involve similar and other specified risks.

---

[500]For this purpose, Rule 9b-1(a)(4) defines "standardized options" to include "options contracts trading on a national securities exchange, an automated quotations system of a registered securities association, or a foreign securities exchange which relate to options classes the terms of which are limited to specific expiration dates and exercise prices, or such other securities as the Commission may, by order, designate."

In credit derivatives transactions, further material along the following lines may be added:

> Each party acknowledges that is not entitled to rely, and irrevocably waives any claim that it may rely or has relied, on any representation of the other party relating to a Reference Obligation or a Reference Entity [other than the representations expressly made by that other party contained in this Confirmation]. Each party also acknowledges that any information about a Reference Entity or Reference Obligation delivered to it by the other party in connection with the Transaction contemplated in this Confirmation is not an assurance as to the future performance of any Reference Obligation or other Obligation that may be relevant to settlement under the Transaction, regardless of any reference in any such information to a credit rating assigned, or that any rating agency might (on the basis of any assumptions) assign, to any such Obligation or to the risk represented by Obligations under the Transaction.

Other representations relating to the parties' relationship, duties of disclosure and the like relating to credit derivatives and the obligations underlying them automatically apply when the parties make their transactions subject to the *1999 ISDA Credit Derivatives Definitions,* as discussed in Part 2 of this book.[501]

---

[501] *See* the further discussion of representations in credit, debt and equity derivatives, beginning *infra* p. 609 and in the description of credit derivatives beginning *infra* p. 639.

CHAPTER 5

COUNTERPARTY RELATIONSHIPS AND DUTIES

Introduction 177
Representations and Disclaimers 179
Industry and End-User Guidelines and Codes of Conduct 181
Disputes 190
    Court Analysis of the Parties' Relationship 191
    Contractual and Legal Sources of Duties 196
Responsibilities of Management 206
Sample Disclosure Statement 215

INTRODUCTION

The documentation for OTC derivatives frequently includes representations by the parties about the nature of their relationship. At a minimum, these provisions state that each party is acting as a principal for its own account; if a party is acting in some other capacity, its representation will identify the capacity in which it is acting.[502] In the United States, as discussed in Chapters 3 and 4, these representations are useful in many cases in establishing that the parties' transactions are excluded or exempt from most or all regulation under federal commodity and securities laws and state and local gaming and bucket-shop laws.[503] This is because many of the applicable exclusions and exemptions are available to qualifying persons only if they are acting as principals for their own account or for the account of other qualifying persons. The parties may also find these representations useful in analyzing whether they have enforceable rights of setoff and how their transactions may be treated in bankruptcy or similar proceedings affecting a counterparty.[504] In this chapter, we explore other reasons why the representations are widely used and why they are formulated not only to identify the nature of the parties' relationship but also to specify the matters as to which each party disclaims reliance on the other.

Market professionals began to include these representations and disclaimers as regular features of their derivatives documentation in the mid-1990s, after customers began to claim with increasing frequency that their contracts with market professionals should be rescinded, reformed or not enforced, or that they should be awarded damages, because of breach of a fiduciary or other special duty owed to them by the professionals,

---

[502] On the provisions used in some segments of the market when a party is acting as an agent, *see supra* note 21.

[503] These representations are discussed in some detail beginning *supra* p. 83.

[504] On the requirement of "mutuality" in connection with setoff, and how that requirement relates to the capacity in which a party is acting, *see infra* note 887. In the analysis of how transactions will be treated under applicable bankruptcy and similar laws, the identity of the true counterparty is always critical to identification of the laws likely to be applicable. On the treatment of setoff in relation to derivatives under U.S. bankruptcy and similar laws, *see* Chapter 7, *infra* p. 268.

or negligence or fraud by the professionals. As illustrated by cases referred to below,[505] in these claims the market professional is typically alleged to have abused the confidence of its customer, or to have fallen short of a duty of care owed to the customer, by inducing the customer (or its representative, acting beyond the scope of his or her authority) to violate company policy or even applicable law by engaging in unsuitable transactions[506] involving risks that the customer did not understand and relied on the market professional to avoid and explain—risks that, given its relative lack of sophistication or experience, the customer could not have discovered or properly assessed without information that the professional wrongfully withheld.[507]

Chapter 2 refers to some of these lawsuits in the context of statutes of frauds and parol evidence rules[508] and considers "merger" clauses, which provide that the parties' entire agreement on the relevant subject matter is reflected in the contract.[509] Statutes of frauds, parol evidence rules and general merger clauses do not, however, bar claims that a contract has been induced by fraud or that a party has breached a fiduciary duty or has been negligent in the performance of its duties.[510] The following sections of this chapter look at what various industry and end-user guidelines, and the courts, have said about principal-to-principal and fiduciary relationships and about fraud and negligence when

---

[505] The lawsuits described here, some of which are more fully described in Gooch & Klein, *Review of Case Law II*, were brought in the United States, mostly under New York and U.S. federal law. Similar cases in other jurisdictions are described in other chapters of DERIVATIVES HANDBOOK: Margaret E. Grottenthaler, *Derivatives Litigation in Canada* (at 135); Jamie Hutchinson, *Derivatives Litigation in Australia* (at 145); and Andrew J.C. Clark, *Derivatives Litigation in the United Kingdom* (at 178).

[506] On the legal theory of suitability-based claims under the antifraud provisions of the securities laws, *see* Committee on Securities Regulation, Association of the Bar of the City of New York, *Civil Liability of Dealers of Financial Instruments for "Suitability" Claims in the Institutional Market*, 53 THE RECORD 62 (1998) and the sources cited therein.

[507] In addition to causing concern to market professionals and their trade organizations, these lawsuits have worried regulators, supervisory agencies and legislative bodies, who have been concerned, among other things, with the damage that these disputes can do to the institutions involved and to the financial markets generally, and about whether the disputes are symptomatic of problems that should be addressed by regulation. On this subject generally, *see, e.g.,* Henry Hu, *Misunderstood Derivatives: The Causes of Informational Failure and the Promise of Regulatory Incrementalism*, 102 YALE L.J. 1457 (1993). The large and highly publicized losses incurred in 1994 by some users of OTC derivatives and other financial products, for example, led members of the U.S. Congress to ask the General Accounting Office to determine the prevalence of disputes. The resulting GAO DERIVATIVES SALES PRACTICES REPORT reflected some 1,800 responses to a survey sent to financial officers of randomly selected public- and private-sector entities.

[508] *See supra* p. 39. These and other cases are also discussed in other contexts in Chapter 1, *supra* p. 31, and Chapter 6, *infra* p. 219.

[509] *See supra* p. 59.

[510] For discussion of these subjects under New York law, *see, e.g., Bridgestone/Firestone, Inc. v. Recovery Credit Serv., Inc.*, 98 F.3d 13, 20 (2d Cir. 1996), *Fort Howard Paper Co. v. Witter*, 787 F.2d 784, 792–95 (2d Cir. 1986), and cases cited therein on actions based on fraudulent misrepresentation that is "collateral or extraneous to the contract" and actions for fraud that are not barred by statutes of fraud, and *see Danaan Realty Corp. v. Harris*, 157 N.E.2d 597, 598–600 (N.Y. 1959), and *Manufacturers Hanover Trust Co. v. Yanakas*, 7 F.3d 310 (2d Cir. 1993), and cases cited therein, on the distinction between general merger clauses and specific disclaimers of reliance in fraud actions. *But see infra* p. 201 regarding cases in which even a specific disclaimer will not bar justifiable reliance if the relevant information is peculiarly within the knowledge of the party charged with fraud.

those relationships exist. The chapter closes with a discussion of the interplay between the reliance element underlying many of these claims and the responsibilities that corporate directors and other fiduciaries owe to their firms, pension funds and other principals.

REPRESENTATIONS AND DISCLAIMERS

Market participants widely agree that, whatever the merits of any particular dispute, the ideal is to avoid disputes over the nature of the parties' relationship and the duties they owe each other. The professional and nonprofessional sides of the market do not, however, always agree about the presumptions that should apply regarding the nature of that relationship and the parties' duties when there is no express agreement on these subjects or the professional's conduct is argued to fall outside the express agreement.[511] The documentation used for OTC derivatives generally reflects the professionals' presumptions about these subjects and seeks acknowledgment that, unless the parties expressly agree otherwise, each party is acting as a principal for its own account and not as a fiduciary of the other party, and neither party will be entitled to rely on the other for advice.

The following "Representation Regarding Relationship Between Parties," which was published by ISDA in 1996, is commonly used as the basis for provisions on these and related subjects, often with variations of the kinds indicated in our footnotes to the standard ISDA paragraphs:[512]

[ ]. **Relationship Between Parties.**

Each party will be deemed to represent to the other on the date on which it enters into a Transaction that (absent a written agreement between the parties that expressly imposes affirmative obligations to the contrary for that Transaction):–

(a) *Non-Reliance.* It is acting for its own account, and it has made its own independent decisions to enter into that Transaction and as to whether that Transaction is appropriate or proper for it based upon its own judgment and upon advice from such advisers as it has deemed

---

[511] On determining whether a broker-dealer is acting as a fiduciary, it has been said that "[t]ypically there is no express meeting of the minds as to the nature of the relationship." 8 LOUIS LOSS & JOEL SELIGMAN, SECURITIES REGULATION 3830 (3d ed. 1991).

[512] The representation is designed for insertion into a master agreement schedule and, therefore, is always modified when used in the confirmation for a transaction. Additional, more specific representations about the parties' relationship and duties are often set out in a separate document that a market professional may ask a customer to sign at the inception of their relationship. This document is sometimes presented as general terms that will apply to dealings between the customer and all members of the professional's corporate group. It often addresses important matters in addition to generalities about the parties' relationship and should be carefully analyzed by the customer with its counsel for consistency with the terms that the customer understands will apply to particular transactions. For example, these terms may provide that all collateral posted by the customer with any member of the professional's corporate group, and all property of the customer held in an account with any group member, whether not delivered as collateral, will constitute security for the obligations owed by the customer to each of the group's members, may be liquidated to meet those obligations if there is a default by the customer under any of those obligations and may not be pledged by the customer to any third party without the professional's prior consent.

necessary.[513] It is not relying on any communication (written or oral) of the other party as investment advice or as a recommendation to enter into that Transaction;[514] it being understood that information and explanations related to the terms and conditions of a Transaction shall not be considered investment advice or a recommendation to enter into that Transaction. No communication (written or oral) received from the other party shall be deemed to be an assurance or guarantee as to the expected results of that Transaction.[515]

(b) *Assessment and Understanding*. It is capable of assessing the merits of and understanding (on its own behalf or through independent professional advice), and understands and accepts, the terms, conditions and risks of that Transaction. It is also capable of assuming and assumes, the risks of that Transaction.

(c) *Status of Parties*. The other party is not acting as a fiduciary for or an adviser to it in respect of that Transaction.[516]

Many of the subjects addressed in these representations, and others, are also addressed, often more broadly, in the documentation for particular kinds of transactions or for transactions—such as equity and credit derivatives[517]—and in credit support docu-

---

[513]This representation is sometimes broadened to state that the party has independently determined that each Transaction is consistent with, or permitted by, its corporate or other policies. When there are restrictions on how a party's funds may be used or held, the representation may be expanded to state that it has independently determined that it may, consistent with those restrictions, make the payments to be made by it and maintain the collateral or other credit support to be maintained by it as provided in the agreement and any related credit support document. Some market participants ask counterparties to represent that they have made their decision after negotiations conducted at arm's length and after determining independently that the Transaction's terms reflect those that would otherwise be available to it in the market or reflect general market conditions for similar transactions.

[514]This part is sometimes modified to provide that a party is not relying *at all* on any information given or representation made by the other party other than those set forth in the agreement, a confirmation or a related credit support document. See *infra* note 582 and accompanying text for discussion of why this difference may be critical. See also *infra* p. 870 for discussion of a proposal to add an acknowledgment to this effect to the proposed revised ISDA master agreement forms, in Section 9(a) (Entire Agreement). Another common addition is to the effect that the other party has not made promises relating to the unwind of the transaction. This additional language reflects, among other concerns, allegations that transactions were to be unwound only favorably, so as to immunize a party against loss. See *supra* note 179.

[515]This part is sometimes broadened to state that a party has not received from the other party or its agent any representation, guaranty or assurance as to the financial, tax, accounting, legal, regulatory or other benefits of the transaction. Similar statements, negating the advisory nature of the relationship, are generally included as legends on scenario analyses delivered by market professionals to end-users to illustrate how a transaction's terms would operate in stated market conditions or if stated changes in conditions occurred.

[516]Some add to this part an acknowledgment that the other party may be taking, and is free to take, positions in the market that may be adverse to, or have an adverse impact on, the Transaction's outcome for the party. See text accompanying note 553 on conflicts of interest in fiduciary relationships.

[517]For example, Section 9.1 of the *1999 Credit Derivatives Definitions* includes a representation of each of the Buyer and the Seller to a Credit Derivative Transaction to the effect that "(i) in connection with such Credit Derivative Transaction, neither the other party nor any of the other party's Affiliates has made any representation whatsoever with respect to the Reference Entity, any Reference Obligation, any Obligation or any Obligation Guarantor on which it is relying or is entitled to rely." See *infra* p. 656 on other sub-

ments.[518] When market professionals began to use these provisions, opponents voiced grave concerns that the provisions would shield unscrupulous behavior and argued against a standardized contractual acknowledgment that reflected the views of the professionals but not of many in the end-user community. According to a survey conducted by the General Accounting Office around that time, "about one-half of all end-users of plain vanilla or more complex OTC derivatives [surveyed] believed that a fiduciary relationship of some sort existed in some or all transactions between them and their dealer."[519]

The GAO survey, which did not define the term "fiduciary," was followed by interviews with selected respondents, most of whom explained that to them the fiduciary relationship "meant dealers had a duty to disclose adequate information about the products and their risks."[520] Many said that "dealers should be truthful and provide accurate information," and some "indicated that dealers should generally have the end-users' best interests in mind." The GAO's analysis indicated that "[o]fficials of state and local governments were more likely than those from most other organizations to report believing that a fiduciary relationship existed in some or all transactions involving OTC derivatives," while "entities whose primary function included operating or managing portfolios of financial assets—such as GSEs,[521] mutual funds, commodity pools, and money managers—were least likely to believe that a fiduciary relationship existed."[522] The survey indicated that about 60% of end-users "relied on dealers to provide investment advice from 'some' to a 'very great extent'" in transactions of varying degrees of complexity with those dealers.[523]

INDUSTRY AND END-USER GUIDELINES AND CODES OF CONDUCT

The division between market professionals and end-users has narrowed since the mid-1990s in part as a result of the attention that both groups, and regulators and supervisory agencies, have paid to defining the nature of the relationship of the parties to deriva-

---

jects covered by representations and agreements in Section 9.1 of these ISDA definitions and, therefore, made part of the parties' agreement when they incorporate the definitions by reference into their confirmations of credit derivatives. *See supra* p. 164 on securities law concerns that motivate market participants to seek broad representations or acknowledgments about the relationship between the parties and limitations on their ability to rely upon each other in derivatives linked to securities.

[518]*See infra* p. 989 for discussion of waivers often sought by the beneficiaries of guaranties, surety bonds and the like and ISDA's consideration of standardized formulations on these subjects, including an acknowledgment of nonreliance from the guarantor or surety.

[519]GAO DERIVATIVES SALES PRACTICES REPORT 5.

[520]*Id.* at 86.

[521]"GSE" is used here to mean a U.S. "government sponsored enterprise," such as Fannie Mae (the Federal National Mortgage Association) or Freddie Mac (the Federal Home Loan Mortgage Association).

[522]GAO DERIVATIVES SALES PRACTICES REPORT 86–87.

[523]*Id.* at 11. A table regarding this aspect of the survey appears in the report at 87–88. *See also* 8 LOUIS LOSS & JOEL SELIGMAN, SECURITIES REGULATION 3826–27 (3d ed. 1991), on the difficulties of distinguishing between "a broker-dealer firm that simply buys and sells securities as principal, rendering the incidental investment advice that is universal in the industry (except for discount brokers) and without which it could hardly operate" from the case of broker-dealers who "have by a course of conduct placed themselves in a position of trust and confidence as to their customers," quoting in the latter instance from *Arleen W. Hughes*, 27 SEC 629, 639 (1948), *aff'd sub nom. Hughes v. SEC*, 174 F.2d 969 (D.C. Cir. 1949).

tives transactions and to sales practices in the derivatives market. Some of those efforts are reflected in codes of conduct or voluntary principles and practices for end-users, for dealers or for participants in the wholesale financial markets generally.

Among these documents are:

- The *Framework for Voluntary Oversight* (the *"DPG Voluntary Framework"*) published in March 1995 by the Derivatives Policy Group, or "DPG," a group of representatives of six of the largest non-bank OTC derivatives dealers,[524] formed at the suggestion of the Chairman of the SEC to work with the CFTC and the SEC to design a voluntary oversight framework for the OTC derivatives activities of unregulated securities firm affiliates;

- The *Principles and Practices for Wholesale Financial Market Transactions* (the *"Principles and Practices"*) published in August 1995, prepared under the coordination of the Federal Reserve Bank of New York by representatives of associations of major participants, mostly professionals, in the OTC markets in the U.S.,[525] in an effort to "articulate a set of best practices" that participants in the wholesale financial markets "should aspire to achieve" in transactions in that market;[526] and

- The *Voluntary Principles and Practices Guidelines for End-Users of Derivatives* (the *"End-Users' Guidelines"*) published in October 1995, developed by the Government Relations Committee of the Treasury Management Association (now known as the Association of Financial Professionals) "to help treasury practitioners develop an appropriate framework of internal controls and disclosures specific to their organizations."[527]

The following table summarizes what these documents say about the nature of the parties' relationship and each party's responsibility for its decisions and reliance on its counterparty. The *End-Users' Guidelines* do not deal directly with the first subject.

---

[524] The firms are identified as CS First Boston, Goldman Sachs, Morgan Stanley, Merrill Lynch, Salomon Brothers and Lehman Brothers.

[525] *See supra* note 103. The published version was released after a comment period of approximately six weeks. The GAO DERIVATIVES SALES PRACTICES REPORT discusses (at 94–98) the reactions of some end-users to the DPG VOLUNTARY FRAMEWORK and the *Principles and Practices* and their objections to the process used to prepare the guidance in the latter.

[526] *Principles and Practices* 1.

[527] *End-Users' Guidelines* 1. *See also* THE FUTURES AND OPTIONS ASSOCIATION, MANAGING DERIVATIVES RISK: GUIDELINES FOR END-USERS OF DERIVATIVES (1995), as well as the sources cited *infra* note 630. FOA is a London-based trade association with an international membership that includes banks and other financial institutions, commodity houses, brokers, fund managers, exchanges and firms of lawyers and accountants.

DPG Voluntary Framework	***Principles and Practices***	***End-Users' Guidelines***
"OTC derivatives Transactions are predominantly arm's-length transactions" but if a professional and a nonprofessional have not stated their relationship in their documents and the professional "becomes aware that the . . . counterparty believes incorrectly that the professional . . . has assumed advisory or similar responsibilities . . ., the professional . . . should take steps to clarify the nature of the relationship." A professional should not "make representations . . . with a view to creating a misleading impression that [it] . . . will assume advisory or similar responsibilities toward its [nonprofessional] counterparty in connection with an OTC derivative transaction." (at 37)	If both parties regularly engage in transactions in the wholesale financial markets, each will assume that they are dealing with each other at arm's length, unless one tells the other in advance that it views their relationship differently and wishes to rely on the other for advice or recommendations.[528] However, a professional may want to have policies and procedures for cases in which a counterparty lacks the ability to understand and make independent decisions about a transaction or seems to have assumed incorrectly that it may rely on the professional for a recommendation or investment advice. A third example is a case in which the amount of the risk to the counterparty in the transaction seems to be "clearly disproportionate in relation to the size, nature and condition of the counterparty's business." (at 8)	"Independence of external advisors from counterparties is crucial." (at 7) "Before entering into a derivatives transaction, the user should ensure that he has the internal capability to value that transaction. If . . . [it] does not exist, the user should obtain the necessary information from an independent outside party, clearly stating the desired characteristics. . . . Users should not rely solely on valuations provided by the counterparty . . . While such valuations may be useful, they should be validated by an independent source." (at 9–10) "Before engaging in derivatives activities, the Board and senior management should ensure that the available resources and expertise are adequate and appropriate for the specific derivatives applications." (at 10) "Derivatives users must stay current on regulatory change, technological change, and change in the financial services environment . . . ." (at 10)

[528]*Principles and Practices* 5–6. A party that wishes to rely on its counterparty should first "(i) put its counterparty on notice in writing that it is relying on the counterparty, (ii) obtain the counterparty's agreement in writing to do business on that basis, and (iii) provide the counterparty with accurate information regarding its financial objectives and the size, nature and condition of its business sufficient to provide such recommendations or investment advice." However, "[c]ertain laws, rules or regulations expressly provide that, in some situations, an oral agreement or the facts and circumstances of a relationship alone may give

In the mid-1990s, when the *DPG Voluntary Framework* and the *Principles and Practices* were issued, the *London Code of Conduct*[529] supplied similar rules for professionals in the London wholesale markets for derivatives and other financial products. In fact, the presumption of a principal-to-principal relationship in the London market was influential in shaping that presumption in the *DPG Voluntary Framework* and the *Principles and Practices* in the OTC derivatives market in the U.S. The presumption was retained in subsequent rules or codes of conduct published by the Financial Services Authority,[530] which have been applicable only for professionals active in the relevant markets, although nonprofessionals have sometimes been expected to be aware of the professionals' presumptions.[531]

Although nonprofessional market participants do not necessarily subscribe to the presumptions about the parties' relationship set out in the *DPG Voluntary Framework* or the *Principles and Practices* or the similar presumptions in the wholesale markets for derivatives in London and elsewhere, provisions reflecting these presumptions, like the ISDA representation and disclaimers quoted above, are now widely used as a means of placing on each party the burden of explaining to the other exactly what it expects from

---

rise to an advisory or fiduciary relationship, in some cases even in the presence of a written agreement purporting to negate such a relationship." *Id.* at 6.

[529] Published by the Bank of England as Annex III to *The Regulation of the wholesale markets in sterling, foreign exchange and bullion* (July 1987).

[530] For example, *The London Code of Conduct: For principals and broking firms in the wholesale markets*, published in June 1999, maintained the described presumption (at 9) as follows:

> As a general rule, core principals [*i.e.*, banks, building societies and financial institutions authorized under the Financial Services Act] will assume that their counterparties have the capability to make independent decisions and to act accordingly; it is for each counterparty to decide if it needs to seek independent advice. If a non-core principal wishes to retain a core principal as its financial adviser it is strongly encouraged to do so in writing, setting forth the exact nature and extent of the reliance it will place upon the core principal. All principals should accept responsibility for entering into wholesale market transactions and any subsequent losses they might incur. They should assess for themselves the merits and risks of dealing in these markets. Non-core principals must recognise that it is possible for core principals to take proprietary positions which might be similar or opposite to their own.

The subsequent *FSA Handbook (available at* www.fsa.gov.uk) sets out principles of conduct, rules and guidance on their application that may differ depending on the nature of the parties' dealings and a counterparty's classification. *See, e.g., FSA Handbook, Market Conduct Sourcebook* (MAR), ch. 3: Inter-Professional Conduct (dealings between "market counterparties," which are presumed not to "need or expect the level of protection provided to *private customers or intermediate customers*" (§ 3.4.2) and may include certain end-users that opt to be treated as market counterparties); MAR 3 Anns 1G & 2G (tables on the scope of the code and listing other relevant Conduct of Business (COB) provisions); and MAR 3 Ann 3G (stating the FSA's understanding of "what is generally regarded as good market practice and conventions in certain areas")). Confirmations from a professional may, therefore, state how it is classifying the recipient.

[531] In part this is so because the Chartered Institute of Public Finance and Accountancy and the Association of Corporate Treasurers have over the years recommended the principles to their members as best practices.

their mutual dealings, so that each party can determine whether it wishes to participate in the relationship on those terms.[532]

Some would say that this so because dealers may refuse to trade with an end-user who is unwilling to have these standard provisions included in the parties' contract. A more complete view of the matter would focus on numerous factors, including the fact that most end-users now have a heightened understanding that they need to have the capability to assess the risks and merits of the derivatives they use, either internally or with the assistance of third parties, and the further fact that many more end-users have indeed developed that capability. For example, in 1999 the Treasury Management Association reported[533] that, of the 395 member organizations that responded to its survey of derivatives use and risk management practices, over 95% indicated that they had "the means, either internally or through independent third-party sources, to assess the appropriateness of potential derivatives transactions and determine their associated risks."[534] In fact, in the United States, given more recent changes in GAAP, potential derivatives users other than dealers may well find these transactions not to be attractive in many cases if the user is not

---

[532]Market professionals in regulated industries may insist on formalizing any counterparty relationship that is not on a principal-to-principal basis because of requirements or guidelines issued by their regulators. The following, for example, is included as guidance for examiners in reviewing the trading activities of financial institutions subject to Federal Reserve oversight:

> When an advisory relationship does not exist between a financial institution and its counterparty, the transaction is assumed to be conducted at "arms-length" and the counterparty is generally considered to be wholly responsible for the transactions it chooses to enter. At times, clients may not wish to make independent investment or hedging decisions and instead may wish to rely on a financial institution's recommendations and investment advice. . . . Financial institutions providing investment advice to clients . . . should formalize and set forth the boundaries of these relationships with their clients. Formal advisory relationships may entail significantly different legal and business obligations between an institution and its customers than less formal agency relationships. The authority, rights and responsibilities of both parties should be documented in a written agreement.

BOARD OF GOVERNORS OF THE FEDERAL RESERVE SYSTEM, *supra* note 21, § 2150.1, at 2 (Feb. 1998).

[533]TREASURY MANAGEMENT ASSOCIATION, 1999 SURVEY OF OTC DERIVATIVES USE AND RISK MANAGEMENT PRACTICES 3 (1999). The firms reflected "a diverse range of organizational activities," from the public and the private sectors, of which 48% indicated 12-month revenues greater than $500 million and 19% indicated 12-month revenues below $100 million. *Id.* at 2. "On an overall basis, 89% of the respondents were satisfied with the relationship they had with their OTC derivatives dealer" and "[o]nly 2% reported dissatisfaction, despite 5% reporting having a dispute with their dealer in the last three years." *Id.* at 3. The principal grounds for dissatisfaction were "quality of transaction documentation provided" and "provision of accurate mark-to-market pricing information." *Id.* at 13.

[534]Another report published in 1999 suggested that institutional investors that were not using derivatives, or were limiting their derivatives use, ascribed their decisions in this regard primarily to "increased investment risk" and "ability to meet objectives without them." "For the smaller institutions, the primary reasons for not using derivatives are the two already cited, followed by lack of knowledge and inability to control or monitor their use." Richard M. Levich, Gregory S. Hayt & Beth A. Ripston, *1998 Survey of Derivatives and Risk Management Practices by U.S. Institutional Investors*, October 1999, http://www.stern.nyu.edu/~rlevich/wp/Report-final.pdf, at 11. Even large institutional investors in many cases had not yet designated a risk manager or risk management committee and did not have written policies on derivatives use. *Id.* at 2. The survey is summarized in *Survey of Institutional Investors Finds Derivatives Phobia Alive and Well*, DERIVATIVES REPORT, May 2000.

able, internally or through third party services, to assess the transaction's effectiveness as a hedge.[535]

That is not to say that the dealers and end-users of derivatives necessarily agree on the nature of their dealing relationship in all cases. The same 1999 survey indicated that, "[o]n the question of whether a fiduciary relationship exists when an organization enters into an OTC derivatives contract with a dealer, 32% said 'yes-in some cases' while 17% said 'no' in either some or all cases" and 36% said "yes-in all cases."[536]

Against this background, it is worth noting several things that the ISDA standard representation set out above does and does not do:[537]

- It establishes a presumption that, when the parties enter into a transaction, each does so as a principal for its own account, and not in a fiduciary or advisory capacity.

- It does not preclude the possibility that one of the parties may in the future undertake special obligations that would not normally arise in a principal-to-principal relationship, but, in such a case, it calls for a written agreement to identify the special obligations that one of the parties may look to the other to perform.

- It does not pretend that the parties will always have equal expertise or equal access to information, nor does it pretend that market professionals never provide information to their customers in connection with proposed or actual transactions.[538] The representation does, however, seek to negate—in the absence of a written agreement to the contrary—a right of either party to rely on information provided by the other as (1) advice, (2) a recommendation to enter into a transaction, or (3) an assurance or guaranty as to the expected results of a transaction.[539] Moreover, by establishing the principal-to-principal nature of

---

[535] *See supra* p. 11.

[536] TREASURY MANAGEMENT ASSOCIATION, *supra* note 533, at 13.

[537] In this regard, it is instructive to compare the ISDA provision with the samples of supplemental paragraphs, *supra* p. 173, that market professionals often seek to include in the documentation for securities-linked derivatives.

[538] In this respect, the standard ISDA formulation differs from others sometimes used in the market, which propose that each party acknowledge, often contrary to fact, that the other has not made any representations or given any information in connection with any transaction.

[539] The references to "advice" and "recommendation" are chosen for the special meanings those terms may have for some market professionals. For example, if the OTC derivative constitutes a security, some market professionals may be prohibited, under sales practice requirements, from selling it without disclosing material information and assessing the suitability of the transaction for the customer. 5 LOUIS LOSS & JOEL SELIGMAN, SECURITIES REGULATION 2366–79, 2473 & 2652–2652.37 (3d ed. 2001) discusses the treatment of derivatives as securities under U.S. law. For interesting guidance on distinguishing between recommendations and other communications in this context, and the distinction between the requirements of the NASD's suitability rules and the "know-your-customer" obligations of NASD members, *see* NASD, *On line Suitability*, Notice to Members 01-12 (Apr. 2001), www.nasd.com/corpinfo/co_pub. html. GAO DERIVATIVES SALES PRACTICES REPORT 43 & 48 distinguishes between suitability rules and rules designed to protect market integrity and sales practice guidance. *Id.* at 50–53. For example, guidance from the OCC for

the parties' relationship, the ISDA representation also implies that each party should seek from third parties the information that it believes relevant to its independent decision to engage in a transaction.

- It does not presume that all transactions are appropriate for all parties or that the risks of transactions will always be plain. It does, however, seek to establish that each party is responsible for determining for itself whether a proposed transaction is appropriate for it, in the context of its goals and policies and applicable law.[540] It also seeks to place on each party the burden of understanding and evaluating those risks, with the help of third parties if necessary, by having each party represent that it is able to assess and assume them, and by having each party confirm that it in fact assumes those risks.

Basically, this ISDA standard provision, as noted, reflects the assumption that all market participants will, or should, understand the difference between principal-to-principal and advisory or other special relationships and should bargain for the relationship they are seeking to create.

Simply stated, this means that, when a professional engages in a transaction as principal, it does so seeking to further its own interests and to profit from the transaction. It prices the transaction accordingly, in light of its appetite for the market and credit risks involved in the transaction and the potential for competition from other professionals for the transaction. As a corollary, the professional assumes that its counterparty, too, will look out for its own interests in principal-to-principal dealings and will bargain for the best deal it believes it can obtain, after considering what is available elsewhere in the market and after taking advice from third parties, if it believes it needs advice. When these assumptions serve as the underpinnings for the parties' negotiations, the parties normally negotiate a transaction's financial and other key terms knowing that failure to perform the agreed obligations can give rise to a claim for damages, but not with the expectation that a party will be required to indemnify the other for loss simply because the other is disappointed with the results. Mindful that the market professional will be pursuing its own interests and profit, the end-user (or, for that matter, another market professional acting as

---

national banks, among others, indicates that they should not *recommend* transactions that they know, or have reason to know, would be inappropriate for counterparties, and that banks should understand the risks that counterparties are trying to manage or assume through the use of derivatives products. *See* OCC, RISK MANAGEMENT OF FINANCIAL DERIVATIVES: QUESTIONS AND ANSWERS RE: BC-277 (OCC Bulletin 94-31) (May 1994). *See also* BOARD OF GOVERNORS OF THE FEDERAL RESERVE SYSTEM, *supra* note 21, § 2150.1, at 2 (Feb. 1998); Conrad G. Bahlke & Junling Ma, *Derivatives: Suitability Issues for Banks and Bank Affiliates*, 12 REV. BANK. & FIN. SERVS. 187 (1996).

[540]*Cf.* GFOA RECOMMENDED PRACTICE ¶ 7: "Government entities should ... secure written acknowledgment from [a] broker or dealer that they have received, read, and understood the entity's debt and investment policies, including whether derivatives are currently authorized under the party's investment policy, and that the broker, dealer or investment manager has ascertained that the recommended product is suitable for the government entity."

counterparty) should, naturally, consider whether a principal-to-principal transaction is the best approach to achieving its objectives.[541]

In the other situation, when a market professional contracts to provide advisory services to a customer or to act as the customer's agent, it undertakes to act in the customer's interests for a fee. In this case, the parties normally agree on the fee through negotiations that expressly focus on the scope of the services to be provided and the consequences if the professional falls short in its performance. The parties are likely, for example, consciously to consider whether the fee should be given up, in whole or in part, if the customer does not achieve its stated goals and whether the customer should be made whole for defined types of loss caused by failure by the market professional to meet the agreed standard—as opposed, say, to loss that the customer incurs in connection with services provided by the professional in good faith and using the same care it applies in managing its own affairs or property.

In practice, the derivatives dealings between a dealer and a particular end-user are often multifaceted—the customer may have some principal-to-principal dealings with the market professional and, at the same time, have advisory or fiduciary or other special relationships with the same entity or another member of the same corporate group. Also, the nature of the dealings between a market professional and its customer may change over time. These realities are precisely why, when professionals and non-professionals deal with each other, they should seek at all times, and in all phases of their dealings as they evolve, to have a clear, written understanding about the nature of their relationship and about what the customer is entitled to expect from the market professional, in light of the bargains they make.

The *DPG Voluntary Framework* provides that "[a] professional intermediary should consider providing new nonprofessional counterparties with disclosure statements generally identifying the principal risks associated with OTC derivatives transactions and clarifying the nature of the relationship between the professional and its counterparty.[542] This practice has been widely adopted by the major dealers. We have included at the end of this chapter a sample generic disclosure document, consisting of a statement about the nature of the parties' relationship, with a general statement about the risks of OTC derivatives transactions attached.[543]

---

[541] For example, an end-user should consider the possibility that, as a financial intermediary, its professional counterparty can be expected to seek to protect its targeted profit by entering into, and later, exiting from, hedging transactions, and these related activities can, from the perspective of the end-user, adversely affect the value of its position in a transaction. *See supra* note 523 and the discussion of the *Caiola* case, *supra* p. 138. Other examples of inherent conflicts in the parties' respective interests are also evident in credit derivatives where, say, a lender may buy protection against loss from a borrower's default and then, by virtue of its own actions as lender, contribute to the circumstances—the Credit Event—that trigger the payout obligation of the other party to the credit derivative, as seller of protection. Section 9.1(b)(iii) of the *1999 Credit Derivatives Definitions* includes each party's agreement that these and similar circumstances may arise, so that neither has a claim (or defense) arising out of its extrinsic dealings, regardless of whether they have an adverse effect on the other party or its position in their transaction.

[542] DPG VOLUNTARY FRAMEWORK 37.

[543] *Infra* p. 215.

The debate over the general nature of the relationship between the derivatives dealer and its nonprofessional counterparties, and the possible need for regulation in this area, is ongoing but lately muted. Leaving aside cases of actionable fraud—discussed below—the heart of the matter for many is the proper allocation of a transaction's costs, as the following excerpts from the *GAO Derivatives Market Practices Report* concludes:

> As our survey and other information indicated, end-users believe they should be able to rely on the information that dealers provide. However, dealers and others told us that, if end-users want to rely on the information provided, then it would be considered investment advice and the dealers would have to increase transaction prices or arrange separate compensation to reflect the increased legal risk in providing such advice. . . .
>
> In January 1995 testimony before Congress, the Chairman of the Board of Governors of the Federal Reserve System also discussed how altering dealer responsibilities could create additional costs that are detrimental to the markets. The Chairman testified that dealers in financial institutions sometimes assume a role beyond that of a mere counterparty, such as when they provide advisory services. However, if dealers are required to ensure that an end-user's use of a product is appropriate, such requirements may serve as a means for end-users to shift a transaction's risk back to the dealer through legal actions. If such legal risks are exacerbated, dealers may begin charging a premium to cover uncertain future legal claims, and some dealers could move their activities overseas or withdraw from the market altogether. He said that such an outcome would present considerable costs to the economy because of the resulting interference in liquid and efficient markets. . . .
>
> [T]he Chairman stated that markets function most efficiently when both parties are free to enter transactions at their own discretion and are unhampered by the need to serve the interests of their counterparties. He emphasized that any consideration of regulation in this area should adhere to the principle that parties to financial transactions are responsible for their own decisions. However, he noted that misrepresentation and fraud could not be tolerated.[544]

Whether because they agree with this assessment of the conditions necessary for an efficient derivatives market or because they recognize that, ultimately, management may be held responsible for failure to assess and monitor the risks involved in derivatives use, as discussed further at the close of this chapter, those responsible for the development of best practices in most segments of the market have concluded that understanding the parties' relationship should be at the top of any list of guidelines for market participants.

---

[544]*GAO Derivatives Market Practices Report* 100–05 (footnote omitted), citing *Testimony by Alan Greenspan, Chairman, Board of Governors of the Federal Reserve System*, Committee on Banking, Housing and Urban Affairs, United States Senate (Washington, D.C., Jan. 5, 1995). For a thought-provoking piece on this debate in the contexts of the allocation of costs, public policy, principles of English law on fraud and misrepresentation and English regulatory rules, *see* Stephen R. Greene, *Suitability and the Emperor's new clothes*, 3 EUROPEAN FIN. SERV. L. 53 (Feb. 1996).

For example, the *Recommended Practice on Use of Derivatives by State and Local Governments* published in 1994 by the Government Finance Officers Association provides that: "Government entities should be aware if the broker or dealer with whom they are dealing is merely acting as an agent or intermediary in a derivative transaction or is taking a proprietary position. Any possible conflict of interest should be taken into consideration before entering into a transaction."[545]

In a set of standards published in 1998 to reflect the results of consultations among some 70 institutional investors, money managers, broker-dealers, regulators, academics, consultants, custodians and officers of financial exchanges,[546] Risk Standard 1 provides that: "Fiduciary responsibilities should be defined in writing and acknowledged in writing by the parties responsible."

The FOA guidelines for end-users emphasize that "[t]he account documentation or mandate to be entered into with each counterparty or broker should accurately reflect the relationship between the parties," specifying whether the parties "are dealing with each other at arm's length, and are relying on their own assessment of the risks and rewards when entering into any particular derivative transaction with each other" or whether "a counterparty or broker is acting in an advisory capacity and reliance is being placed on such advice."[547]

Although they do not establish presumptions about the parties' relationship, as do other similar pronouncements discussed above, all of these, and other similar sets of guidelines, seek to promote an approach to derivatives dealings aimed at avoiding disputes like those discussed below.

DISPUTES

There have been numerous lawsuits in which the courts have been asked to deal with issues involving the relationship between the parties to OTC derivatives and the duties that may arise because of these relationships. This section seeks to summarize some of the basic principles of New York law that the courts have applied or identified in a sampling of these cases as applicable to disputes relating to the parties' relationship and the duties that may arise out of that relationship.

These disputes generally involve claims for relief based on a multitude of theories, as listed below, beyond a simple breach of a contract's express terms.

- Violations of securities laws, commodity laws and other statutes[548]

---

[545] Recommended Practice 2.

[546] RISK STANDARDS WORKING GROUP, RISK STANDARDS FOR INSTITUTIONAL INVESTMENT MANAGERS AND INSTITUTIONAL INVESTORS 9 (1996), *available at* http://www.cmra.com/html/the_risk_standards.html.

[547] THE FUTURES AND OPTIONS ASSOCIATION, *supra* note 527, at ¶ 6.5.

[548] Many of the securities law, commodity law and other statutory theories expressed in the cases are discussed in Gooch & Klein, *Review of Case Law II*, at 73 & 104.

- Aiding and abetting a violation by the other party of laws applicable to it, or aiding and abetting an employee or agent of the other party in his or her violation of a duty owed to the complaining party[549]
- Breach of fiduciary duty
- Fraud
- Negligence and negligent misrepresentation
- Breach of an implied covenant of good faith and fair dealing

Typical commodities law and securities law claims are considered in Chapters 3[550] and 4.[551] The following summary refers to the ways in which the parties' relationship, and representations and disclaimers on that and related subjects, may have a bearing on claims based on the last four theories.

COURT ANALYSIS OF THE PARTIES' RELATIONSHIP

In many disputes between the parties to derivatives transactions, the nature of the parties' relationship is examined in connection with multiple allegations. The fundamental allegation is often that the customer thought the market professional was acting in a fiduciary capacity and was thus under an obligation to put the customer's interests first, but that the professional failed to do so, not disclosing to the customer that (or how, or how much) the professional was profiting from acting as principal.[552] Underlying these claims are principles of law to the effect that, in the absence of an agreement to the contrary, an agent or other fiduciary may be (1) required to act for the benefit of its principal, foregoing the fiduciary's own advantage if necessary, (2) required to account to the principal for

---

[549]*See id.* at 66. In a case involving leveraged derivatives, the court stated that the following elements are required to establish a claim of aiding and abetting a breach of fiduciary duty: (1) a fiduciary duty was breached, (2) the aider/abettor knew of that breach and (3) the aider/abettor substantially assisted in the achievement of the breach. *Lehman Bros. Commercial Corp. v. Minmetals Int'l Non-Ferrous Metals Trading Co.*, No. 94 Civ. 8301 (JFK), 2000 WL 1702039, at *28 (S.D.N.Y. Nov. 13, 2000) (citing *Samuel M. Feinberg Testamentary Trust v. Carter*, 652 F. Supp. 1066, 1082 (S.D.N.Y. 1987), in turn quoting from *ITT v. Cornfeld*, 619 F.2d 909, 922 (2d Cir. 1980)). In refusing to dispose of an aiding and abetting claim by summary judgment, the *Minmetals* court (1) noted that, although generally the second element requires actual knowledge of the primary violation, it may be satisfied by failure to investigate suspicious actions of a counterparty's agent, (2) found that there were enough "red flags" in *Minmetals* to enable a jury to find that failure to investigate should be treated as satisfying that element and (3) indicated that one of those red flags was failure by the counterparty's agent to execute the intended master agreement between the parties. *Id.* at *29. *See supra* note 103, on best practices for the confirmation process, including the need to "chase" missing confirmations. *See also Lehman Bros. Commercial Corp. v. Minmetals Int'l Non-Ferrous Metals Trading Co.*, No. 94 Civ. 8301 (JFK), 2001 WL 1646101 (S.D.N.Y. Dec. 21, 2001).

[550]*Supra* p. 63.

[551]*Supra* p. 129.

[552]Allegations of this kind were made in the cases discussed in Gooch & Klein, *Review of Case Law II*, at 68 & 95. For example, in *Société Nationale d'Exploitation Industrielle des Tabacs et Allumettes v. Salomon Bros. Int'l Ltd.*, 1998 N.Y. Misc. LEXIS 219 (Sup. Ct. 1998), *aff'd*, 674 N.Y.S.2d 648 (App. Div. 1998), commonly known as the *SEITA* case, the customer argued unsuccessfully that Salomon was acting as a broker and advisor and failed to disclose that it was also acting as principal to generate profits for itself at the customer's expense, in structures that greatly favored Salomon's interests over the customer's.

profits obtained in breach of this duty and (3) liable for unresolved conflicts of interest between itself, as fiduciary, and the principal.[553]

Questions about the nature of the parties' relationship also commonly arise in the context of claims that, because a market professional was acting as investment advisor or otherwise as a fiduciary vis-à-vis its customer, the professional had (and did not fulfill) duties of the following kinds, which were recited in a complaint relating to leveraged swaps: the duty to "determine all the material facts with respect to the business, financial capacity, investment objectives and risk parameters of [the customer] . . . in order to determine if the Swap Transactions were suitable for [the customer]" and the duty to determine if the person who purported to execute the transactions on behalf of the customer had authority to do so (which he or she allegedly did not), as well as the duties of investment brokers and advisors "to make full and fair disclosure of all material facts concerning the investments they recommend to their customers, including disclosure of the risks and benefits of the proposed transactions, of the profits the brokers or advisors are likely to make from the transactions, and of the suitability, or unsuitability of the investment for the customer."[554]

What impact do the parties' mutual representations and disclaimers have in the context of these and other claims based on the existence of a fiduciary or other special relationship? In theory, if a party acknowledges contractually that its counterparty is acting as principal, for its own account, and not as a fiduciary, there should be fewer misunderstandings, and therefore fewer lawsuits, at least over failure of the counterparty to disclose that it was acting in its own interests to profit from its transactions. The parties' characterization of their relationship may not, however, always prevent these disputes, or be dispositive, or so it seems from the court's decision in a case involving leveraged swaps, where the person who traded for the complaining party may not have understood the meaning of a principal-to-principal relationship and the court was required to treat that alleged misunderstanding as a matter of fact to be determined in further proceedings.[555]

When a representation about the parties' relationship is not dispositive, the courts may be called upon to determine whether the parties in fact acted as principals or whether their dealings were such that a fiduciary relationship may have existed. Applying New

---

[553]*See generally* RESTATEMENT (SECOND) OF AGENCY §§ 387–90 (1958). In *de Kwiatkowski v. Bear Stearns & Co.*, 126 F. Supp. 2d 672, 691 (S.D.N.Y. 2000), the court stated the following in the context of the duties owed by a broker to its customer: "[T]he broker is obligated to refrain from self-dealing and to disclose any conflicting or personal interest the broker may have in the transaction (*see Chasins v. Smith Barney & Co.*, 438 F.2d 1167, 1172 (2d Cir. 1971)) . . . ."

[554]These allegations were made in the complaint in *SEITA*, at 31–32.

[555]*See Lehman Bros. Commercial Corp. v. Minmetals Int'l Non-Ferrous Metals Trading Co.*, No. 94 Civ. 8301 (JFK), 2000 WL 1702039 (S.D.N.Y. Nov. 13, 2000), which presented a claim of breach of fiduciary duty. The parties had apparently acknowledged the principal-to-principal nature of their dealings in their confirmations. The court nonetheless found that, at least in the context of a motion for summary judgment (*see infra* note 556), this would not be dispositive, given the allegation that the person who purportedly traded on behalf of the complaining party was not a native English-speaker, was inexperienced with derivatives and did not understand the concepts of "principal" and "counterparty." *See also Lehman Bros. Commercial Corp. v. Minmetals Int'l Non-Ferrous Metals Trading Co.*, No. 94 Civ. 8301 (JFK), 2001 WL 1646101 (S.D.N.Y. Dec. 21, 2001).

York law, the courts have said that whether two parties have "a purely contractual relationship or some other connection" is a factual determination.[556] Mere conclusory allegations of the existence of a fiduciary relationship will not suffice to raise an issue of fact in "a conventional business relationship."[557] The courts have also repeatedly said that, "[i]f the parties find themselves or place themselves in the milieu of the 'workaday' mundane marketplace, and if they do not create their own relationship of higher trust, courts should not ordinarily transport them to the higher realm of relationship and fashion the stricter duty for them."[558]

Court decisions commonly refer to several facts as having a bearing on the existence of a fiduciary relationship. They include "the length of the relationship of the parties, their financial interdependence, and their sharing of confidential and proprietary information."[559] In cases involving derivatives, the courts have, however, declined to find fiduciary relationships merely because the complaining party has relied on the other party in connection with a longtime relationship and has given confidential information to the alleged fiduciary. Even when those allegations have been combined with allegations that the counterparty promised that the transactions would be tailored to the complaining party's needs and that the counterparty would monitor the transactions and look out for the complaining party's interests, in the absence of other special circumstances those facts, without more, have not led to a finding of a fiduciary relationship.[560]

---

[556]*See Salomon Bros. Inc. v. Huitong Int'l Trust & Investment Corp.*, 1996 WL 675795 (S.D.N.Y. 1996) *2, referring to *Minpeco, S.A. v. ContiCommodity Servs., Inc.*, 552 F. Supp. 327, 331 (S.D.N.Y. 1982) and other cases. Because the question is factual, claims based on alleged failures to act in accordance with fiduciary duties are usually not disposed of on motions to dismiss for failure to state a cause of action, because the court must view the claim in the light most favorable to the party that opposes the motion, must accept as true the well-pleaded facts stated by that party and must draw all reasonable inferences in favor of that party. *See, e.g., Zinermon v. Burch*, 494 U.S. 113, 118 (1990); *Scheuer v. Rhodes*, 416 U.S. 232, 237 (1974); and *Haines v. Kerner*, 404 U.S. 519 520–21 (1972). Applying these rules, a court may grant such a motion only if it appears beyond doubt that the party opposing the motion can prove no set of facts in support of its claim that would entitle it to relief. *Conley v. Gibson*, 355 U.S. 41, 45–46 (1957). Similar standards apply to motions for summary judgment, which may be granted only if there is no genuine issue as to any material fact and the moving party is entitled to a judgment as a matter of law. *See, e.g., Minmetals*, 2000 WL 1702039, at *10, discussing these rules in a case involving leveraged swaps.

[557]*Compañía Sud-Americana de Vapores v. IBJ Schroder Bank & Trust Co.*, 785 F. Supp. 411, 426 (S.D.N.Y. 1992). The court went on to say "New York law is quite clear . . . that 'a conventional business relationship, without more, does not become a fiduciary relationship by mere allegation'" (quoting from *Oursler v. Women's Interart Center, Inc.*, 566 N.Y.S.2d 295 (App. Div. 1991) and citing *National Westminster Bank, U.S.A. v. Ross*, 130 B.R. 656, 679 (Bankr. S.D.N.Y. 1991), which, in turn, cites *Beneficial Commercial Corp. v. Murray Glick Datsun*, 601 F. Supp. 770, 772 (S.D.N.Y. 1985)).

[558]*SEITA*, 1998 N.Y. Misc. LEXIS 219, at *4 (quoting from *Northeast Gen. Corp. v. Wellington Adv., Inc.*, 604 N.Y.S.2d 1 (1993)).

[559]*Id.* at *3, quoting from *ADT Operations, Inc. v. Chase Manhattan Bank, N.A.*, 662 N.Y.S.2d 190 (Sup. Ct. 1997).

[560]This combination of facts, or allegations, was present, for example, in *Procter & Gamble Co. v. Bankers Trust Co.*, 925 F. Supp. 1270 (S.D. Ohio 1996), where the court dismissed claims based on an alleged fiduciary duty. Thereafter, in *SEITA*, the trial court found that the plaintiff had not "made a showing, sufficient for the purpose of opposing summary judgment, that its relationship with [the defendant] was more extraordinary than that alleged in Procter & Gamble or the similar New York cases that have rejected claims of fiduciary duty." 1998 N.Y. Misc. LEXIS 219, at *4. The highly leveraged and complex swaps involved in *Procter & Gamble* are described in Gooch & Klein, *Review of Case Law II*, at 100–10. *See also* the discus-

What, then, is the required level of dependence and reliance for a finding of a fiduciary relationship where the relationship is not established by contract? In one of the disputes involving OTC derivatives, the court said:

> An informal fiduciary relationship may arise where "one party places special trust and confidence in another such that the first party becomes dependent upon the second party." However, such a relationship has generally not been found absent a showing of dramatically unequal bargaining power and fraudulent inducement, or a state of complete domination of one party by the other.[561]

Affirming dismissal of a claim of breach of fiduciary duty, the appellate court in that case further noted, "in this regard, that the requisite high degree of dominance and reliance must have existed prior to the transaction giving rise to the alleged wrong, and not as a result of it."[562] The cases suggest that, where there is a lack of evidence of this kind of domination and there is evidence that the parties negotiated the terms of their transactions and the complaining party exercised its independent judgment in deciding to go forward, the fact that one party has superior knowledge about derivatives will not suffice to justify a finding that a fiduciary relationship existed.[563]

The general rule recited by the courts in these cases is that, "where parties deal at arm's length in a commercial transaction, no relation of confidence or trust sufficient to find the existence of a fiduciary relationship will arise absent extraordinary circumstances."[564] The courts will look at the particular allegations in each case to determine whether they believe that extraordinary circumstances, in this sense, may be found to exist by a trier of fact. In a case involving leveraged derivatives between a market professional and its customer, one court has recently suggested that, although "the courts have held that a financial products dealer . . . normally does not undertake a fiduciary duty when it acts as a principal in transactions with an institutional counterparty in which no trading discretion is conferred," extraordinary circumstances sufficient to find the existence of a fiduciary duty might be found where the customer's representative was

---

sion in that article of the allegations in the *Sud-Americana de Vapores* case, *id.* at 98, and the discussion of *Bankers Trust Int'l Plc v. PT Dharmala Sakti Sejahtera* in Clark, *supra* note 82, at 200. In *PT Dharmala*, the court, applying English law, similarly declined to find the existence of a fiduciary duty in a case involving three complex transactions.

[561] *SEITA*, 1998 N.Y. Misc. LEXIS 219, at *4 (citations omitted), quoting from p. *Chimento Co. v. Banco Popular de Puerto Rico*, 617 N.Y.S.2d 158, 162 (App. Div. 1994).

[562] *SEITA*, 674 N.Y.S.2d 648, 649 (App. Div. 1998) (citation omitted), affirming the motion court's dismissal of the fiduciary duty claim.

[563] *See* discussion of these factors in the lower court decision in *SEITA*, 1998 N.Y. Misc. LEXIS 219, at *7, where the court quotes from *Procter & Gamble Co. v. Bankers Trust Co.*, 925 F. Supp. 1270 (S.D. Ohio 1996). In *Procter & Gamble*, the court found, on the facts before it, that the parties "were in a business relationship. They were counterparties. Even through . . . BT had superior knowledge in the swaps transactions, that does not convert their business relationship into one in which fiduciary duties are imposed." *Id.* at 1289.

[564] *SEITA*, 1998 N.Y. Misc. LEXIS 219, at *3 (quoting from *Compañía Sud-Americana de Vapores v. IBJ Schroder Bank & Trust Co.*, aff'd, 674 N.Y.S.2d 648 (App. Div. 1998), in turn quoting from *National Westminster Bank, U.S.A. v. Ross*, 130 B.R. 656, 679 (Bankr. S.D.N.Y. 1991)).

viewed by the professional's own employees as inexperienced with similar transactions and relatively unsophisticated and as trading on their "own ideas" in a very "strong relationship."[565]

If one of the parties is alleged to have been acting both as principal and as broker or advisor in handling an account for the other party—as has occurred in several disputes—the courts' analysis may begin differently, if there is a legal presumption of a fiduciary relationship between the parties.[566] This fact partly explains the practice described above of having derivatives documents provide that the parties are acting as principals, and not as fiduciaries, and that neither party may rely on any information given to it by the other party as investment advice.

In the end, however, the analysis of a claim of breach of fiduciary duty owed by a broker or advisor to its customer is just as fact-dependent as such a claim is where there is no brokerage or advisory relationship. In explaining why this is so, one court has stated:

> The wrong in a breach of fiduciary action is the failure to perform the particular duty imposed by the relation, thus constituting an offense to the relationship itself . . . . [T]he particular scope of duties corresponding to the fiduciary relationship are susceptible to being limited to predetermined tasks fixed by agreement, course of dealings or legal rules . . . .[567]

---

[565]*See Lehman Bros. Commercial Corp. v. Minmetals Int'l Non-Ferrous Metals Trading Co.*, No. 94 Civ. 8301 (JFK), 2000 WL 1702039, at *26–*28 (S.D.N.Y. Nov. 13, 2000), denying Lehman's motion for summary judgment after finding that, "[b]ased on the record before this Court, the relationship between Lehman and Non-Ferrous may not have been the garden-variety principal-to-principal arm's-length relationship that Lehman claims it was" and that, "[t]ogether, all of [the] . . . circumstances create a question of fact about the true nature of the relationship . . . ." As mentioned above, *supra* note 555, the person purportedly acting for *Minmetals* also stated that no one ever explained to him the meaning of the concepts of "counterparty" or "principal" and that Lehman created the impression that *Minmetals* and Lehman were on the "same team" by representing that Lehman would "look out" for his positions. *See also Lehman Bros. Commercial Corp. v. Minmetals Int'l Non-Ferrous Metals Trading Co.*, No. 94 Civ. 8301 (JFK), 2001 WL 1646101 (S.D.N.Y. Dec. 21, 2001).

[566]*See, e.g., Conway v. Icahn & Co.*, 16 F.3d 504, 510 (2d Cir. 1994): "[T]he relationship between a stockbroker and its customer is that of principal and agent and is fiduciary in nature, according to New York law." *But cf. Bissell v. Merrill Lynch & Co*, 937 F. Supp. 237, 246 (S.D.N.Y. 1996), discussing cases to the effect that "the mere existence of a broker-customer relationship is not proof of its fiduciary character" (quoting from *Rush v. Oppenheimer & Co.*, 681 F. Supp. 1045, 1055 (S.D.N.Y. 1988), in turn quoting from *Fey v. Walston & Co.*, 493 F.2d 1036, 1049 (7th Cir. 1974)) and to the effect that, in the absence of discretionary trading authority, a broker does not owe a general fiduciary duty to a client. This line of cases was distinguished in *de Kwiatkowski v. Bear Stearns & Co.*, 126 F. Supp. 2d 672, 693 (S.D.N.Y. 2000). In handling the breach of fiduciary duty claims in *SEITA*, the trial court was able to determine from the contracts that the defendant was acting as a principal and not as a broker, but it did not initially grant the motion to dismiss in full because of allegations that the defendant was acting as the plaintiff's investment advisor. Ultimately the court found that the plaintiff had failed to show the existence of "any agreement for investment advisory services" and that the defendant's faxes alleged to constitute investment advice were, "at worst ... mere salesmanship" or "in the words of the complaint, 'aggressive [ ] promoting.'" *SEITA*, 1998 N.Y. Misc. LEXIS 219, at *6. *See also* Clark, *supra* note 82, at 196, quoting from *Bankers Trust Int'l Plc v. PT Dharmala Sakti Sejahtera* on when a representation by a party should be considered a misrepresentation.

[567]*De Kwiatkowski*, 126 F. Supp. 2d at 693. Here a customer sued over losses incurred by it on numerous FX positions, claiming both breach of fiduciary duty and negligence by Bear Stearns, which acted both as principal and as broker in its handling of the customer's account. The jury did not find Bear Stearns liable for breach of fiduciary duty but did find it liable for the broader claim of negligence. The court's

Therefore, even assuming that information provided by one party to the other constitutes investment advice, at least where the parties are also dealing on a principal-to-principal basis, the provider of the advice may not be held liable for the recipient's loss on the derivatives transactions if the parties' contract circumscribed the advisor's responsibility or the recipient of the advice has "exercised its independent judgment in deciding to go forward."[568]

CONTRACTUAL AND LEGAL SOURCES OF DUTIES

Under New York law, the decision as to whether there was a fiduciary or other special relationship between the parties to derivatives transactions may have important consequences, which may be summarized as follows:

- When the parties merely act in a principal-to-principal relationship in business dealings, their duty to each other is to perform their express contractual obligations, and exercise their contractual rights, reasonably and in good faith,[569] and generally the law will imply no additional duties or higher standard of care. Therefore, in purely principal-to-principal dealings a party may have a claim for breach of contract but it will generally not have a separate claim for negligence in the performance of a contract.[570] For the same reason, when (as is often the case) one of the parties seeks to hold the other liable for fraud through nondisclosure, in the absence of an express contractual duty of disclosure or special circumstances the claim is likely to be rejected when the parties are dealing on a principal-to-principal basis.[571]

---

analysis quoted above was provided as background for its denial of Bear Stearns' motions for a new trial and for judgment as a matter of law, notwithstanding the jury's verdict. *See infra* notes 605–606 and accompanying text. For discussion of other cases involving FX transactions between customers and their brokers acting as principals, *see* Gooch & Klein, *Review of Case Law II*, at 97–100, discussing *Sud-Americana de Vapores* and *Bank Brussels Lambert S.A. v. Intermetals Corp.*, 779 F. Supp. 741 (S.D.N.Y. 1991). In those cases, breach of fiduciary duty and negligence claims against the market professional were rejected.

[568]*SEITA*, 1998 N.Y. Misc. LEXIS 219, at *7.

[569]*See* NYUCC § 1–203; *Wigand v. Bachman-Bette Brewing Co.*, 222 N.Y. 272, 118 N.E. 618 (1918).

[570]*See, e.g., Procter & Gamble*, 925 F. Supp. at 1292, ruling that "[w]here the parties' relationship is contractual, and the duty of good faith and fair dealing is implied in the contract, a negligence claim is redundant." *See also Autotech Leasing Assocs., L.P. v. Prudential Securities, Inc.*, N.Y.L.J., Oct. 19, 1995, at 28 (N.Y. Sup. Ct.), granting motions to dismiss causes of action for alleged breaches of an implied covenant of good faith a fair dealing, and fraudulent misrepresentations, because they were redundant when combined with a claim for breach of contract. For discussion of the situation under English law, and citations to cases, *see* Clark, *supra* note 82, at 192–93. *See also id.* at 194 on the impact of the doctrine of contributory negligence on this question, under English law.

[571]The *FSA Handbook Market Conduct* sourcebook, ch. 3, on Inter-Professional Conduct (MAR 3 §§ 3.4.2, 3.4.6 & 3.4.7) contains guidance to the effect that, in dealings between "market counterparties," which are presumed not to need or expect the level of protection provided to "private customers" or "intermediate customers," absent a "formal advisory arrangement," silence will not breach Conduct of Business (COB) Principle 7 that a firm communicate information to its clients in a way that is not misleading unless the silence, "in the circumstances . . . results in a *communication* made by a firm being misleading."

- When a fiduciary relationship exists, however, the law may impose duties on the fiduciary that lie beyond the scope of the parties' contract, such as the duty, noted above, to place the principal's interests first, unless the parties have circumscribed those duties in their contract. Also, a fiduciary may, by operation of law and for reasons of public policy, be required to exercise reasonable care and professional skill in the performance of its duties, although "[t]he manner and degree in which [it] . . . may properly fulfill these responsibilities in any given case may vary, depending to some extent upon the business sophistication of the client and the nature of the relationship between the parties."[572] When the law imputes these duties because of the parties' relationship, a party may be entitled to relief of various kinds (including rescission or damages) for breach of fiduciary duty or negligence, where appropriate, and not be limited to damages for loss of its contractual bargain.

In the typical case in which a party to an OTC derivatives transaction claims that the parties' relationship gave rise to duties beyond those provided for by the parties' contract, that party claims that the counterparty misrepresented the facts about the risks involved in the transactions or about how the transactions might operate, or failed to provide information relevant to an assessment of those risks, or provided the information only selectively.[573] The following discussion shows how New York courts have analyzed cases of this kind to determine whether a claim for relief may exist when the parties are dealing on a principal-to-principal basis, on one hand, or in a fiduciary or other special relationship, on the other.[574] As will be readily apparent, the court's analysis of each case is fact-specific, although the facts are viewed within the context of fairly well settled legal principles.

Implied Duties in Principal-to-Principal Relationships. In some cases, the complaint of failure of disclosure is framed as an action for breach of a covenant or the duty of good faith and fair dealing that is implied as a matter of New York law in every contract.[575] The New York courts have generally limited this implied duty of good faith and fair dealing to the performance of the parties' obligations as actually provided for in their

---

[572]*De Kwiatkowski*, 126 F. Supp. 2d at 691, referring specifically to the relationship between a securities broker and its customer, after drawing heavily on cases involving the duties of brokers in purchases and sales of securities and noting that "[f]or the purposes of assessing the broker's role and ascribing attendant legal duties, each transaction is considered separately." *Id.* at 690.

[573]*See* Gooch & Klein, *Review of Case Law II*, at 91–100, for discussion of various cases involving these claims.

[574]This discussion does not address cases dealing with claims of fraud and the like in the relationship between a guarantor or surety and the beneficiary of its guaranty or surety obligations. On this subject, *see infra* p. 989.

[575]This was, for example, the case in *SEITA*, where the court indicated that the claim was based solely on the allegation that the defendant failed to disclose the risks and benefits of the swap transactions. Finding that the plaintiff was aware of these risks when it executed the agreements, the court dismissed these claims. *Société Nationale d'Exploitation Industrielle des Tabacs et Allumettes v. Salomon Bros. Int'l Ltd.*, 1998 N.Y. Misc. LEXIS 219 (Sup. Ct. 1998), *aff'd*, 674 N.Y.S.2d 648 (App. Div. 1998).

contract, and have observed that the duty is not a license to the courts to modify the parties' bargain by imposing additional obligations or restricting the exercise of rights that are expressly provided for.[576] If viewed within these established limitations, this implied duty should not be treated as giving rise to duties of disclosure and delivery of information that are not provided for in the parties' contract when the parties are acting purely on a principal-to-principal basis.[577] If one of them does expect its counterparty to supply specific kinds of information in connection with a transaction, it should, therefore, ensure that the counterparty is expressly obligated to do so.[578]

More often, a party's complaint about nondisclosure or misrepresentation is framed as a common-law claim of fraud and raised as an affirmative defense in a suit by the other party for breach of contract. The theory may, for example, be that the contract was void and should be rescinded because it was induced by fraud. When a party raises this kind of affirmative defense or otherwise claims fraud in the course of the parties' dealings, the trier of fact will look for clear and convincing evidence of (1) fraud by a party with an intent to deceive, (2) the other party's actual and justifiable reliance on the fraud and (3) a resulting loss by that party.[579] Although each of these elements will raise

---

[576]*See, e.g., Banco Español de Credito v. Security Pac. Nat'l Bank*, 763 F. Supp. 36, 44 (S.D.N.Y. 1991), *aff'd*, 973 F.2d 51 (2d Cir. 1992). "'[T]he implied covenant of good faith and fair dealing does not provide a court *carte blanche* to rewrite the parties' agreement. Thus, a court cannot imply a covenant inconsistent with terms expressly set forth in the contract. . . . Nor can a court imply a covenant to supply additional terms for which the parties did not bargain."(citations omitted in original) (quoting from *Hartford Fire Ins. Co. v. Federated Dept. Stores, Inc.*, 723 F. Supp. 976, 991 (S.D.N.Y. 1989). "The implied covenant of good faith does not 'operate to create new contractual rights.'" *Id.*, quoting from *Don King Productions, Inc. v. Douglas*, 742 F. Supp. 741, 767 (S.D.N.Y. 1990). Much of the case law on this implied duty has dealt with disputes between sophisticated buyers and sellers of assets, including loan participations. *See* the annotations to Section 6.2(b) in the annotated sample participation agreement in GOOCH & KLEIN, LOAN DOCUMENTATION 290–91 for discussion of some of these cases.

[577]It should, however, be noted that, in what we view as overly expansive interpretations of both this implied duty under New York law and of the ISDA master agreement forms' covenant on delivery of documents, one court has stated that, at least in the case before it, a professional market participant may have been required by the implied covenant of good faith and fair dealing to provide its counterparty with information not specified in the contract, both before trading and over the term of a transaction. *See* Gooch & Klein, *Review of Case Law II*, at 102–04, discussing *dictum* in *Procter & Gamble*, where the Ohio federal district court indicated its belief that the defendant should have provided the plaintiff with information regarding correlations between yields and prices of U.S. Treasury bonds relevant to the outcome of the price reset feature of a leveraged swap as well as sensitivity tables and spreadsheets regarding volatility and documents relating to the yield curve.

[578]Under the framework provided by the ISDA master agreement forms, the parties may easily do this in the confirmation. As illustrated in the sample agreement in Part 3, *infra* p. 825, Section 4(a)(ii) of the 1992 ISDA forms sets out the covenant of each party to deliver to the other not only the documents provided for in the schedule to the master agreement but also the documents provided for in transaction confirmations. When a party agrees to supply information on an ongoing basis, it should ensure that any agreed limitations as to how the information may be used, or viewed, are also recorded.

[579]*See, e.g., Banque Arabe et Internationale D'Investissement v. Maryland Nat'l Bank*, 57 F.3d 146, 153 (2d Cir. 1995). If the fraud is alleged to consist of a failure to disclose rather than a misrepresentation, an additional required element is proof that the defendant had a duty to disclose the relevant material information. *Id.* On the standard of clear and convincing evidence in fraud actions, *see, e.g., Schlaifer Nance & Co. v. Estate of Warhol*, 119 F.3d 91, 98 (2d Cir. 1997). On concepts of loss causation and the measurement of damages in cases of fraud, *see Primavera Familienstifung v. Askin*, Nos. 95 Civ. 8905 (RWS) *et al.*, 2001 WL 96190, at 49–52 (S.D.N.Y. Feb. 5, 2001) and cases discussed therein.

Counterparty Relationships and Duties 199

questions of fact, the nature of the parties' relationship and the terms of their contract are generally most critical to the question of justifiable reliance.[580] Under New York law, this question may be treated differently depending on a variety of factors.

One of these factors is whether the parties agreed that neither was to rely on the other in reaching its decision to enter into the contract, or as to the particular matter relevant to the claim of fraud. If so, that agreement may suffice to foreclose a claim of reliance as to the specific matter referred to in the disclaimer, but not others.[581] As illustrated above, ISDA's standard formulation on this subject includes a disclaimer by each party of reliance on its counterparty as to the risks of each transaction and a transaction's expected outcome, and disclaimers like these have in fact been found to foreclose a party's claims of reliance on its counterparty about the risks of their transactions.[582]

In a case where a contractual disclaimer of reliance is found not to be sufficient, the courts will usually look at a number of additional factors in dealing with a party's claim that it has relied to its detriment on the other party's fraud. These factors would include whether the alleged fraud involved affirmative misrepresentation (actual fraud), on one hand, or fraud by omission (fraudulent concealment), on the other.[583] The courts will also examine whether the information alleged not to have been disclosed, or to have been affirmatively misrepresented, was easily accessible to the party claiming reliance or peculiarly within the other party's knowledge. In all cases, the general background for the analysis appears to be that "sophisticated businessmen [have] a duty to exercise ordinary diligence and conduct an independent appraisal of the risk they [are] assuming"[584] and, "[w]here sophisticated businessmen engaged in major transactions enjoy access to critical information but fail to take advantage of that access, New York courts are particularly disinclined to entertain claims of justifiable reliance."[585] The courts distinguish between

---

[580] *See, e.g., Gouldsbury v. Dan's Supreme Supermarket, Inc.*, 546 N.Y.S.2d 379, 381 (N.Y. App. Div. 1989).

[581] *Danaan Realty Corp. v. Harris*, 157 N.E.2d 597 (N.Y. 1959), is often cited for the proposition that, a party's contractual disclaimer of reliance on the other party as to a matter bars a claim that it was fraudulently induced to enter into the contract by reliance on a representation as to that specific matter. *See also Manufacturers Hanover Trust Co. v. Yanakas*, 7 F.3d 310, 315–17. (2d Cir. 1993) (distinguishing *Danann* on the ground that the disclaimer before it was not sufficiently specific for the *Danann* rule to apply). *See also* Clark, *supra* note 82, at 197–99 on disclaimer clauses under English law and particularly the effect on this question of the Unfair Contract Terms Act 1977.

[582] *See, e.g.*, the various decisions in the *SEITA* case, rejecting the plaintiff's contention that liability for fraud and negligence should be imposed on the defendant for failure to disclose, selective disclosure and the partial withholding of information relevant to assessing the risks presented by the swaps involved in that case. *Société Nationale d'Exploitation Industrielle des Tabacs et Allumettes v. Salomon Bros. Int'l Ltd.*, 1998 N.Y. Misc. LEXIS 219 (Sup. Ct. 1998), *aff'd*, 674 N.Y.S.2d 648 (App. Div. 1998).

[583] Actual fraud and fraudulent concealment or nondisclosure have been recognized as "different causes of action" and as demanding "different elements of proof under New York law." *See Lazard Freres & Co. v. Protective Life Ins. Co.*, 108 F.3d 1531, 1542 (2d Cir.), quoting from *Congress Fin. Corp. v. John Morrell & Co.*, 790 F. Supp. 459, 469 (S.D.N.Y. 1992), in declining to look to cases involving issues of nondisclosure in an action involving alleged affirmative misrepresentation.

[584] *Primavera*, 2001 WL 96190, at 43 (quoting from *Abrahami v. UPC Construction Co.*, 234 (N.Y. App. Div. 1996) (citations omitted)).

[585] *Grumman Allied Indus. v. Rohr Indus.*, 748 F.2d 729, 737 n.13 (2d Cir. 1984). This and similar statements in other cases are often cited by the courts and, in derivatives disputes have, for example, been

this standard and a less stringent test for ordinary persons who, it is said, may rely on representations made to them unless "under the circumstances, the facts should be apparent to one of [complainant's] knowledge and intelligence from a cursory glance" or the person "has discovered something which should serve as a warning that he is being deceived, [in which case] he is required to make an investigation of his own."[586]

Where actual fraud or affirmative misrepresentation is alleged, a general principle often enunciated by the courts is as follows:

> [W]here . . . a party has been put on notice of the existence of material facts which have not been documented and he nevertheless proceeds with a transaction without securing the available documentation or inserting appropriate language in the agreement for his protection, he may truly be said to have willingly assumed the business risk that the facts may not be as represented. Succinctly put, a party will not be heard to complain that he has been defrauded when it is his own evident lack of due care which is responsible for his predicament.[587]

In cases involving alleged fraudulent concealment, or nondisclosure, the approach generally taken by the courts has been described as follows:

> [W]hen misrepresentations concern matters that are not peculiarly within [the maker's] . . . knowledge, New York courts have rejected claims of justifiable reliance because:
>
>> [if plaintiff] has the means of knowing, by the exercise of ordinary intelligence, the truth, or the real quality of the subject of the representation, he must make use of those means, or he will not be heard to complain that he was induced to enter into the transaction by misrepresentations.[588]

In lawsuits involving derivatives, this principle has been variously stated by the courts in dismissing claims of fraud based, for example, on failure to disclose the risks involved in the relevant transactions and the fact that the rates involved in the transactions were far less favorable than those available from others in the market, notwithstanding disparity in the relative sophistication of the parties or their experience with the particular kinds of transactions.[589] That is, the mere fact that one of the parties has superior market knowl-

---

cited in *Compañía Sud-Americana de Vapores v. IBJ Schroder Bank & Trust Co.*, 785 F. Supp. 411, 419 (S.D.N.Y. 1992).

[586]*Primavera*, 2001 WL 96190, at 43 (quoting from *Twenty First Century L.P.I. v. LaBianca*, 19 F. Supp. 2d 35, 40 (E.D.N.Y. 1998)) (alterations in original).

[587]*Rodas v. Manitaras*, 552 N.Y.S.2d 618, 620 (App. Div. 1990). *See Lazard Freres & Co. v. Protective Life Ins. Co.*, 108 F.3d 1531, 1543 (2d Cir.), for discussion of the *Rodas* case in the context of a claim of fraud in the inducement by a "substantial and sophisticated player in the bank debt market."

[588]*Sud-Americana de Vapores*, 785 F. Supp. at 419 (quoting from *Mallis v. Bankers Trust Co.*, 615 F.2d 68, 80–81 (2d Cir. 1980), and citing *Grumman Allied Indus. v. Rohr Indus.*, 748 F.2d 729, 737 n.13 (2d Cir. 1984) (citations omitted in original)).

[589]*See, e.g.*, the discussion of *Sud-Americana de Vapores* and *Intermetals* in Gooch & Klein, *Review of Case Law II*, at 97–100. *See also* the *SEITA* decisions referred to *supra* note 582. *But see Lehman Bros. Commercial Corp. v. Minmetals Int'l Non-Ferrous Metals Trading Co.*, No. 94 Civ. 8301 (JFK), 2000 WL

edge or experience is not enough to prove that material information is peculiarly within the possession of that party.[590]

It has been said, on the other hand, that even the most specific disclaimer of reliance by a party, accompanied by the party's full acknowledgment of its own duty to engage in an independent investigation of all facts, may not foreclose that party from claiming that it has justifiably relied on a person it claims committed fraud, if material facts were peculiarly within that other person's knowledge.[591] Furthermore,

> the inquiry as to whether the defendant has peculiar knowledge of the facts at issue, of course, goes to the reasonableness of the plaintiff's reliance—if the plaintiff has the means of learning the facts *and* disclaims reliance on the defendant's representations, there simply is no reason to relieve it of the consequences of both its failure to protect itself and its bargain to absolve the defendant of responsibility. On the other hand, if the plaintiff has conducted the appropriate due diligence and reasonably believed that it has corroborated the defendant's representations, then a different result may be warranted.[592]

Useful insight on when information may be found to be peculiarly within the possession of a party may be found in cases involving alleged fraud relating to the valuation of complex investments.

In cases in which investors claimed that they justifiably relied on what they were told by a fund manager, the courts have said that reasonable investors must do their own diligence regarding the valuation of their investments[593] and that, even when matters of

---

1702039, at *30 (S.D.N.Y. Nov. 13, 2000), indicating that whether a party is too sophisticated to be entitled to rely on the other party was a question of fact to be determined by a jury and, therefore, denying summary judgment on the general fraud claims involved in the case. *See also Lehman Bros. Commercial Corp. v. Minmetals Int'l Non-Ferrous Metals Trading Co.*, No. 94 Civ. 8301 (JFK), 2001 WL 1646101 (S.D.N.Y. Dec. 21, 2001).

[590]*Banque Arabe Internationale D'Investissement v. Maryland Nat'l Bank*, 57 F.3d 146, 156 (2d Cir. 1995), illustrates how the courts might analyze the facts in such a case, seeking to determine not only whether the particular information involved was peculiarly within the knowledge of one of the parties but also whether that party knew that the other party was relying on it for disclosure of the information and whether the party claiming reliance had in fact "cared to ask" for the information. In *SEITA*, the plaintiff's claims of breach of a duty of disclosure about the transaction's risks were based, among other things, on disparity of the parties' knowledge about the risks. On appeal, the plaintiff contended that "it was unable itself to acquire the information needed independently to assess the risks and benefits of the transactions at issue," but the court found that this claim was "without support in the record." *Société Nationale d'Exploitation Industrielle des Tabacs et Allumettes v. Salomon Bros. Int'l Ltd.*, 702 N.Y.S.2d 258, 259 (App. Div. 2000).

[591]*See Tahini Investments, Ltd. v. Bobrowsky*, 470 N.Y.S.2d 431, 433 (App. Div. 1984).

[592]*Dimon Inc. v. Folium, Inc.*, 48 F. Supp. 2d 359, 368 (S.D.N.Y. 1999) (citation omitted).

[593]*See, e.g., Granite Partners, L.P. v. Bear Stearns & Co.*, 58 F. Supp. 2d 228, 260 (S.D.N.Y. 1999): "[N]o reasonable investor could rely solely on month-end valuations or portfolio analyses made after purchase without conducting some independent due diligence . . . ." This rule and the general principle stated in the *Rodas* case, *supra* note 587, may be relevant, say, in connection with derivatives valuations sought in many contexts, both before transactions are executed and during a transaction's term, when a counterparty is considering a "tear up" of the transaction, in connection with calls for collateral, and otherwise. When market professionals provide these valuations to their counterparties, they generally do so in documents that state

valuation are extremely complex, sophisticated investors cannot take the position that they have no duty to obtain independent advice, if the advice could indeed have generated the necessary information.[594] On the other hand, if the investors have received representations that valuations will be performed in a particular way and then, in an alleged fraud, the valuations are performed otherwise, there may be a genuine issue of material fact as to whether reliance on the representations by the investors was justifiable, regardless of their sophistication, if neither they nor independent advisers could be expected in the circumstances to have discovered how the valuations in fact were made or how the actual method of valuation was affecting their investment and associated risks.[595] As a general matter, these and cases involving concealment of information, or information discoverable only with substantial difficulty, are among the kinds of situations in which facts may be found to be peculiarly within the knowledge and control of a party charged with fraud. As one court has put it, "[i]n general, the more sophisticated the [party claiming to have been defrauded] . . . , the less accessible must be the information to be considered within [the other party's] . . . peculiar knowledge."[596]

Thus, absent special circumstances pointing to justifiable reliance on its counterparty, both ordinary persons and sophisticated persons in business may be expected to do their own diligence about matters that they should be expected to see as concerns and matters that are drawn to their attention, although the threshold at which an ordinary person has a duty of independent diligence appears higher than that applicable to those who are in business and sophisticated. Exactly where the burden of independent inquiry enters and who will be treated as sophisticated will depend on the nature of the alleged fraud and

---

that the valuations are purely indicative, do not necessarily reflect the actual price at which a transaction might be executed or unwound, the value at which the market professional does or might record the transaction on its own books for risk management or other purposes or the value that another market participant might ascribe to the transaction. The valuation documents may also state important assumptions on which the valuations are based.

[594] *Primavera*, 2001 WL 96190, at 47 (citing *Granite Partners* and *Stuart Silver Assocs., Inc. v. Baco Dev. Corp.*, 665 N.Y.S.2d 415 (App. Div. 1997), as examples, for the proposition that reliance is not justifiable where the plaintiffs could have obtained needed information "by consulting the legal and financial advisors," quoting from *Stuart Silver*, 415 N.Y.S.2d at 418).

[595] *See Primavera*, 2001 WL 96190, at 46, finding such a genuine issue of material fact about the plaintiffs' justifiable reliance on alleged misrepresentations, where the manager of a hedge fund was said to have represented that the fund's investments would be valued, generally, on the basis of "marks" obtained from independent brokers but in many cases used valuations negotiated with the brokers to levels that distorted reports of performance to the plaintiff investors. The court noted that, although the investors were given the opportunity to inquire about valuations and obtain information from the fund's auditors, the alleged concealment was such that this access to information "would hardly have helped," and it was "unrealistic to suggest that the Investors could have discovered the truth from the auditing firm." *Id.*

[596] *Dimon Inc. v. Folium, Inc.*, 48 F. Supp. 2d 359, 369 n.55 (S.D.N.Y. 1999), describing various cases. In *Dimon*, the court noted that the plaintiff had complete access to relevant books and records and that both sides were represented by able counsel who "carefully crafted" the detailed agreement in which plaintiff's disclaimer of reliance appeared. Therefore, the court noted that the plaintiff could reasonably be viewed as having bargained away some of the protection it might otherwise have had, through its disclaimer. Nonetheless, because data relevant to the subsequently discovered accounting irregularity at the base of the alleged fraud were virtually inaccessible without special access codes and because material facts were otherwise well concealed, the court found that a trier of fact might find the truth must be regarded as having been within the peculiar knowledge of the defendant. *Id.* at 369–72.

the facts of each case. The court decisions indicate that a complainant does not need to have experience with the particular kind of transaction or matter involved in the dispute to be viewed as having the degree of knowledge and awareness of risk requisite to give rise to some duty of independent inquiry higher than that due from an ordinary person.[597]

As noted above, a court or jury may be called on to weigh these issues of sophistication and the duty of independent inquiry if the parties' contract itself does not include a sufficient disclaimer to bar all claims of justifiable reliance. In this regard, general "cautionary language," say, about the risks of derivatives, may not suffice to protect parties charged with fraud in connection with specific "material misrepresentations or omissions [which they] . . . knew . . . were false when made."[598] The standard ISDA representation does not by its terms seek to protect a party against situations like this. Rather, the ISDA representation requires each party to acknowledge that it does not look on representations made or information given by the other party "as investment advice or as a recommendation to enter into" a transaction or as "an assurance or guarantee as to the expected results" of a transaction.

The difference between this kind of acknowledgment and a disclaimer of all reliance on representations made outside the parties' written agreement can be important.[599] As indicated by the description above of the debate over the use of disclaimers and representations in the OTC derivatives market, neither end-users nor the supervisory agencies that oversee many market professionals would be likely to countenance a shift in practice towards attempts to shield actual fraud by contract. On the other hand, when this debate is viewed in the context of market efficiency and pricing that reflects what the parties have bargained for, these supervisory agencies and many end-users believe it is fair for market professionals to seek, through representations like the 1996 ISDA standard representations discussed above, to require a customer to bargain expressly for the right to receive information and advice relating to a transaction, if the customer believes it lacks access to that information independently and requires advice. Generally, critical information and

---

[597] See *Primavera*, 2001 WL 96190, at 45, where the court noted that experience with the particular kind of investment or transaction is not necessary ("the Investors overstate their case when they contend that they can be considered sophisticated only if they were knowledgeable with respect to CMOs").

[598] *In re Prudential Sec. Inc. Limited Partnerships Lit.*, 930 F. Supp. 68, 72 (S.D.N.Y. 1996), a case involving the standard of reasonable reliance applicable in U.S. securities laws claims, rather than the standard of justifiable reliance applicable in claims of fraud under New York common law. *See Primavera*, 2001 WL 96190, at 43 & n.40, comparing the two standards and citing *Prudential* in connection with claims of aiding and abetting common law fraud.

[599] For discussion of the difference, *see Primavera*, 2001 WL 96190, at 44, where the court looked at the issue of justifiable reliance by investors in a hedge fund in the context of a private placement memorandum stating—as PPMs typically do—that the investors would conduct their own independent investigation of the risks involved in the investment and would have the opportunity to ask whatever questions they deemed appropriate. The court concluded that the PPM did not preclude the claimants' establishing at trial that they were justified in relying on misrepresentations made orally, since it expressly contemplated that responses would be made to the investors' questions, and those responses would necessarily be given outside the PPM. The court concluded that reliance on the alleged oral misrepresentations was "not unjustifiable per se," although an investor would not necessarily be entitled "to take whatever was told to her at face value" since that "would neither be 'independent' nor an investigation."

advice of this kind is usually best obtained from a third party, who can provide these fiduciary services in the customer's interest without the conflict that may be created by participation in the transaction as a principal. Of course, although this may be true as a general matter; there may always be difficult cases in which information argued to be material to the assessment of risk is allegedly withheld with intent to deceive so that the bargaining process could not function properly.[600]

Implied Duties in Fiduciary and Other Special Relationships. Although the existence of a fiduciary relationship may, as indicated above,[601] give rise to special duties owed by the fiduciary, the mere fact that a party is found to be a fiduciary vis-à-vis its counterparty will not necessarily change the outcome of a dispute over the duties owed to the counterparty. This is so because, as noted earlier, the particular scope of duties corresponding to a fiduciary relationship may be limited "to predetermined tasks fixed by agreement, course of dealings or legal rules."[602] Contractual disclaimers of reliance may, therefore, operate as effectively in a fiduciary-to-principal relationship as they do in a principal-to-principal relationship to allocate responsibilities and burdens, including those related to diligence and access to information. In addition, in the absence of a contractual disclaimer of reliance, a party found to have acted, say, both as principal and as advisor to its counterparty, or both as principal and as broker in respect of the account maintained by the counterparty for the relevant transactions, may nonetheless be found to have limited duties if the counterparty has "exercised its independent judgment in deciding to go forward,"[603] notwithstanding the advice, or if the account is nondiscretionary and the services provided by the broker are within the bounds ordinarily associated with nondiscretionary accounts.[604]

---

[600] *See infra* p. 989 for discussion of the *Mahonia* case, in which allegations of this kind were made by property casualty insurance companies that had issued surety bonds supporting obligations of Enron entities under transactions described in the related papers as forward contracts involving the purchase and sale of crude oil and natural gas.

[601] *See supra* note 553 and accompanying text.

[602] *De Kwiatkowski v. Bear Stearns & Co.*, 126 F. Supp. 2d 672, 693 (S.D.N.Y. 2000). *See supra* note 567.

[603] *SEITA*, 1998 N.Y. Misc. LEXIS 219, at *7 (finding that this was the case in Société Nationale's dealings with Salomon), *aff'd*, 674 N.Y.S.2d 648 (App. Div. 1998). The fact that the plaintiff made his own decisions may have been a factor in the jury's rejection of the claim of breach of fiduciary duty in the *de Kwiatkowski* case. On the other hand, the jury in that case found for the plaintiff on its negligence claim, in the context summarized in note 606. 126 F. Supp. 2d at 677.

[604] *See also* Gooch & Klein, *Review of Case Law II*, at 91–93 & 97–98, discussing two cases involving brokers and alleged nondisclosure to the principal of matters relating to interest rate swaps and FX trading: *BankAtlantic v. Blythe Eastman Paine Webber Inc.*, 127 F.R.D. 224 (S.D. Fla. 1989), *aff'd* 12 F.3d 1045 (11th Cir. 1994), where the court refused to set aside a jury decision in favor of the defendant broker in an action for breach of fiduciary duty in which the plaintiff claimed it had not understood the risks created by interest rate swaps involving an allegedly inappropriate counterparty; and *Bank Brussels Lambert, S.A. v. Intermetals Corp.*, 779 F. Supp. 741, 746–47 (S.D.N.Y. 1991), where the court rejected claims based on breach of fiduciary duty involving alleged failures of disclosure regarding the risks of foreign currency trading, which had begun with hedging and evolved into speculative transactions, noting that the customer's representatives were experienced businessmen who may not have had any experience with that kind of trading before they began with the defendant but were aware of the risk of fluctuations in foreign currency and indeed indicated that knowledge by entering into early hedging transactions.

The law of negligence may nonetheless impose a duty of care that arises out of "policy considerations unrelated to any contractual obligations binding particular parties"[605] where transactions are effected in the context of a brokerage relationship. In a case involving a nondiscretionary account, this duty has been said to consist of an obligation to perform obligations with "the degree of care expected of a reasonable or prudent . . . [person in the same kind of relationship] acting under the same circumstances."[606] Where this duty of care has been found to exist, it appears that the parameters of due care may be defined in various ways, including reference to custom and practice in the industry in handling the particular matters complained of and the policies and customary practices of the party charged with negligence.[607]

This legally imposed duty of care and the potential for negligence liability do not, by way of contrast, exist where the parties are merely acting as principals and a fiduciary or other special relationship does not exist. In those cases, as noted earlier, the parties' duties under New York law are to perform their obligations and exercise their rights in accordance with the terms of their contract, in good faith, and consistent with principles of fair dealing.[608] As illustrated by the ISDA representations and disclaimers discussed

---

[605] *De Kwiatkowski*, 126 F. Supp. 2d at 694.

[606] *Id.* at 688, describing the charge to the jury, where the jury found the defendant, as a broker, liable for negligence. The alleged shortcomings included initially placing the customer's unusually large FX position in the futures market—where its size could attract attention and make the customer vulnerable to predatory market activity by others; failing to seek assistance from the defendant's own foreign currency experts; failing to comply with industry practices and internal guidelines by not performing appropriate analysis of the risk involved in the customer's position as market conditions and the status of his account changed; neglecting to supervise and monitor the handling of the accounts; failing to provide the customer with the defendant's negative forecasts after having supplied him with earlier bullish reports; offering "assurances that may have been overly optimistic or unrealistic in the circumstances" relied on by the customer in maintaining his positions longer than may have been prudent; and charging excessive markups and commissions. *Id.* at 708–17. *See* Hutchinson, *supra* note 505, for discussion of a case in which an Australian court addressed a broker's duty of care relating to close-out of a customer's futures account.

[607] *See supra* notes 575 & 576 and accompanying text; *de Kwiatkowski*, 126 F. Supp. 2d at 711–12. For discussion of this duty of care under English law, "whenever a person assumes responsibility to perform professional or quasi-professional services for another and that other relies on the performance of those services" and in connection with contracts for advisory services, *see* Clark, *supra* note 82, at 183–84.

[608] *See supra* note 570 and accompanying text. The situation of corporate counterparties under English law has been summarized as follows in Clark, *supra* note 82, at 191:

> If a corporate plaintiff were to claim in a derivatives transaction that a duty of care had arisen, in reliance on the bank-customer line of cases, the plaintiff would have to demonstrate that it is entitled to the same sort of protections under English law as have been given to unsophisticated individuals and that derivatives fall into the same category of transactions as the less complex types of transactions seen in the cases referred to above. At one end of the scale, it is obvious that as a matter of English law a bank or other financial institution is not under a duty of care to advise its counterparty of the wisdom of entering into a derivatives transaction where the counterparty is of very considerable, or even equivalent, financial sophistication and does not rely on the institution for financial advice. At the other end of the scale, it is conceivable that an institution might enter into a derivatives transaction with a financially unsophisticated counterparty which, by virtue for example of a course of dealing, has come to rely on the institution for financial advice. In such a circumstance, the institution may well find itself under a duty to advise the counterparty as to the potential implications of the transaction, particularly where the

above, derivatives documentation does not generally seek to address the issues raised by claims of negligence because the customary representations and disclaimers presume that the parties are acting purely in a principal-to-principal relationship and, therefore, that neither owes to the other any special duty that could give rise to a negligence claim.

RESPONSIBILITIES OF MANAGEMENT

The representations and disclaimers discussed above, and disputes between parties to derivatives transactions over their relationships and duties, should be analyzed within a broader framework of principles of corporate governance and risk management. This has been driven home for the parties to the disputes, and for the market generally, by proceedings instituted by third parties against those involved in the disputes and by some of the legislative changes that were prompted by the disputes and the losses that brought them before the courts.[609]

Some of these proceedings involving market professionals were brought by supervisory or regulatory agencies, which imposed sanctions of various kinds on the institutions and their directors, officers and employees for noncompliance with requirements in several areas, including insufficient supervision of those directly involved in the practices complained of by customers.[610] Where end-users were concerned, some of the proceed-

---

counterparty is unsophisticated and the institution has aggressively marketed the transaction to the counterparty.

[609] According to GAO DERIVATIVES SALES PRACTICES REPORT 40, from January 1994 through September 1996, 14 states enacted laws intended to address these concerns. FLA. STAT. ch. 218.415 § 5 (1995) provides an example of the focus on improved risk management capabilities as a precondition for use of derivatives by local governments: "[i]nvestments in derivative products must be specifically authorized in the investment plan and may be considered only if the unit of local government's chief financial officer has developed sufficient understanding of the derivative products and has the expertise to manage them." *See also* State of Wisconsin, Legislative Audit Bureau, *An Evaluation of Investment Practices of the State of Wisconsin Investment Board*, Report 95-16, Appendix III (July 1995). The report was prompted by disclosure of a $95 million loss from 12 derivative "investments," including leveraged swaps involving exposure to movements in, *e.g.*, Italian lira and Spanish peseta interbank interest rates and the spread between the rates paid on certain Mexican government bonds and U.S. Treasury bonds. Responsibility for the investments and transactions lay with the State's Investment Board. Recognizing the ultimate responsibility of senior management for oversight of the Investment Board's activities and policies, the Audit Bureau Report identified a lack of effective management oversight and called, among other things, for important organizational changes and improvements in reporting to management, as well as improvements in the information provided to the Trustees of the Investment Board.

[610] For example, the Federal Reserve Bank of New York and the New York State Banking Department investigated the leveraged derivatives business of Bankers Trust in connection with losses incurred by Gibson Greetings, Inc. and other clients. The action culminated in a Written Agreement with the Federal Reserve Bank (Docket Nos. 94-082-WA/RB-BC, 94-082 WA/RB-SM, 94-082-WA/RB-HCS (Dec. 4, 1994), where Bankers Trust agreed to enhance the management and supervision of its leveraged derivatives business and to supply specific kinds of information to customers. The CFTC and the SEC brought related proceedings against BT Securities, alleging fraudulent conduct, which were settled without admission or denial of guilt. *See BT Sec. Corp.*, 1994 WL 711224 (CFTC Dec. 22, 1994), and *BT Sec. Corp.*, Securities Act Release No. 7,124, Exchange Act Release No. 35,136 (Dec. 22, 1994) [1994–1995 Transfer Binder] FED. SEC. L. REP. (CCH) ¶ 85,477, at 86,109. These proceedings and the CFTC/SEC jurisdictional theories are discussed in Gooch & Klein, *Review of Case Law II*, at 86–87. One result was that the Bankers Trust group was required to engage independent consultants to review such matters as compliance policies and procedures related to the marketing, offer, sale, purchase, amendment, termination or valuation of privately negotiated OTC derivative products. The public report is the Executive Summary and

ings were brought by regulatory agencies and some were brought by investors, in connection with allegedly faulty accounting practices and disclosure dealing with the related derivatives, in violation of requirements applicable to public companies under U.S. securities laws.[611] Associated with these proceedings were financial costs that are reported to have been very substantial and, in some cases, damage to the firm's reputation and business franchise.[612]

When companies have been involved in regulatory or supervisory proceedings like these, and in disputes with their counterparties and others over transactions, those proceedings have often been followed by lawsuits brought by shareholders against company directors and officers for alleged breach of the fiduciary duties owed by them to their company, and for waste of corporate assets.[613] In the United States, these claims are largely based on state law, which differs from state to state but, generally speaking, imposes on a company's directors a duty of care that requires them to act in good faith, in the honest belief that the action is in the best interest of the company, and with such care as an ordinarily prudent person in a like position would use in similar circumstances. Insofar as they involve this duty of care, the applicable principles of state law are often referred to as embodying a "business judgment rule" because they are interpreted by the courts in the light of a presumption that directors are entitled to be protected in the exercise of informed business judgment in the discharge of their duties. Generally speaking, if "a court has determined that the application of the business judgment rule is appropriate, it will not substitute its own view for those of the board or hold a director liable if it finds that he or she has made an honest mistake of judgment.[614] When shareholders believe, however, that the directors have breached their fiduciary duty, they may in some cases bring actions on behalf of the corporation, after first requesting that the board of directors bring the action unless the circumstances are such that this request should be excused, say because it would probably be futile given the board's involvement in the matter.

Recommendations of the Report on the OTC Derivatives Business of Bankers Trust During 1991–1994, dated June 30, 1996. *See also supra* p. 77 on CFTC proceedings against U.S. affiliates of Metallgesellschaft, AG.

[611] Proceedings were, for example, brought against Gibson Greetings, its chief financial officer and its treasurer by the SEC. Gibson Greetings, Inc., Exchange Act Release No. 36357, 7 FED. SEC. L. REP. (CCH) ¶ 74,245, at 63,126 (Oct. 11, 1995), Accounting and Auditing Enforcement Release No. 730. These proceedings were settled without admission or denial of the alleged violations, which included failure of Gibson Greetings to include in reports filed with the SEC information about OTC derivatives that was necessary to make the information filed not misleading; failure to maintain books and records that accurately and fairly reflected in reasonable detail the company's transactions (among other things, through failure to record the value of the relevant derivatives positions on a mark-to-market basis as required in light of the SEC's characterization of the positions as speculative); and failure to establish appropriate internal controls.

[612] *See* GAO DERIVATIVES SALES PRACTICES REPORT 78–82, which also discusses the additional funding costs incurred by parties when their derivatives losses, dispute settlement costs, regulatory fines and the like led to ratings downgrades.

[613] These are referred to as "derivative" actions not because they relate to derivatives transactions but because the shareholders' standing to bring the action derives from the corporation's claim against its directors or officers. *See, e.g., BRS Assocs., L.P. v. Dansker*, 246 B.R. 755, 771–72 (S.D.N.Y. 2000). Similar duties of care may arise under laws applicable to professional fiduciaries in their management of the assets of their principals.

[614] Robert C. Myers & Robert B. Stobaugh, Lewis v. Beall, *A Landmark Case in the Board's Duty of Oversight*, DIRECTOR'S MONTHLY 1, 2 (June 2001).

It is useful to put disclaimers of reliance on a counterparty in the context of these shareholder lawsuits against directors, since the theory behind the suits is that the directors should be held responsible for a company's derivatives losses because the directors cannot abdicate their responsibility for using due care in setting policy on derivatives use, in selecting qualified people to implement the policy and in supervising—or establishing an appropriate supervisory framework for—their activities. One such action was, for example, brought in the wake of a company's substantial losses from complex leveraged swaps that were admitted by management to have been inconsistent with company policy.[615] Another was brought in the wake of losses attributed to management's failure to ensure that the company's assets were appropriately hedged with simple and conventional transactions.[616] In each case the plaintiff alleged that the directors breached their duty of care by failing to attain sufficient knowledge and experience regarding the relevant transactions and by failing to supervise those directly involved with the transactions.[617] In an example from Australia, a court's analysis of the respective levels of responsibility of executive and nonexecutive, or independent, members of a company's board for negligence in connection with a company's losses on derivatives is reported to have "substantially

---

[615] A shareholder derivative action was brought against Procter & Gamble and certain of its directors and officers shortly after the company issued a press release announcing an after-tax charge of $102 million to close out two interest rate swaps described in the release as "leveraged swaps ... based on highly complex formulas ... [and] inconsistent with the company's policy." Complaint at 8, *Drage v. Procter & Gamble*, No. A9401998 (C.P., Hamilton County, Ohio, April 1994). The plaintiffs sought relief for corporate waste resulting from the swaps, an order that the Board of Directors and Audit Committee ensure that the company's investment policies be prudent and properly followed and an order that bonus compensation to the individual defendants based on increased earnings due to the speculative practices complained of be returned or not awarded by the company. *Id.* at 7. The case was dismissed because the plaintiff did not first demand that the directors bring the suit or plead with particularity why such a demand should be excused in the circumstances. *See* Memorandum of Decision entered January 19, 1996. Judgment was entered dismissing the action on February 27, 1996.

[616] *See Brane v. Roth*, 590 N.E.2d 587 (Ind. Ct. App. 1992), brought against the directors of a grain elevator cooperative for losses allegedly suffered because of the directors' failure to protect the cooperative's position by hedging in the grain market. The directors had authorized the cooperative's manager to engage in hedging after three years of declining profits and a substantial loss and a recommendation to hedge from the cooperative's accountant. However, only $20,050 in hedging contracts were entered into, although the cooperative had $7.3 million in grain sales. A second accounting firm later concluded that the primary cause of the cooperative's main loss was the failure to hedge. Damages plus interest were awarded, based on a finding that the directors breached their statutory duty of care because the directors (1) retained a manager inexperienced in hedging; (2) failed to maintain reasonable supervision over the manager and (3) failed to attain knowledge of the basic fundamentals of hedging sufficient to enable them to direct the hedging activities and supervise the manager properly.

[617] The complaint in *Drage v. Procter & Gamble* asserted (at 5–6), for example, that the level of risk involved in the leveraged swaps was "grossly unsafe and excessive ... , particularly for P&G in light of the Individual Defendants and management's utter and complete ignorance and inexperience in the field, their failure to keep informed, their failure to supervise ... ." The complaint also alleged that the defendants had a heightened fiduciary duty to ensure that the company's investment policies and practices were prudent and that it was not engaging in "dangerous high risk investments such as derivative leveraged interest rate swaps" (*id.* at 7) because the individual defendants had signed a periodic filing describing the company's use of swaps as aimed at minimizing exposure and reducing risk.

changed the way many companies and their directors in Australia deal with derivatives."[618]

Of particular interest is the fact that, in one of these actions, the directors sought unsuccessfully to defend themselves by reference to a common feature of corporate laws relating to directors' fiduciary duties, under which a director is authorized to rely on information, reports, and opinions of the corporation's officers and employees, if the director reasonably believes them to be reliable and competent, and on public accountants, as to matters that are reasonably believed by the director to be within the accountants' professional competence. The court found in that case that the directors could not claim the benefit of the statutory provision because they had failed to develop the understanding necessary to make an informed decision about whether their reliance on the chosen manager was prudent, and to direct and supervise his activities. As described by the court in that case, directors have a duty to inform themselves of all material information readily available to make their decisions, and the business judgment rule does not protect them if they have abdicated their functions or, absent a conscious decision, have failed to act.[619]

Similar issues of responsibility and its delegation are raised for fiduciaries in other, noncorporate contexts. Examples are fiduciaries for employee pension and other benefit plans subject to ERISA.[620] The fiduciaries for these plans may consider the use of derivatives in connection with investment of the plan's assets, to diversify and otherwise manage the investments and their associated risks.[621] There are quite complex rules under which a fiduciary may not, absent an applicable exemption, cause an ERISA plan to engage in any transaction that the fiduciary knows or should know to be prohibited by ERISA, and an ERISA plan's fiduciary must always act consistent with a duty of loyalty like that owed by corporate directors, and in accordance with the plan's specific documents to the extent they are consistent with ERISA.[622] The broader, overarching duty of a plan fiduciary, however, is to discharge its duties in accordance with a general standard

---

[618]Hutchinson, *supra* note 505, at 154. *See id.* at 147–58 for an interesting discussion of this unreported case, *AWA Ltd v. Koval and Others*, which involved unauthorized, speculative FX trading by an employee, the related action brought against the company's auditors and their defense based on the contributory negligence imputed to the company because of the negligence of its senior management and an executive director.

[619]*See Brane v. Roth*, 590 N.E.2d at 592, citing *Aronson v. Lewis*, 473 A.2d 805, 812 (Del. 1984). On the other hand, in Delaware, where many major U.S. corporations are organized, the law in this area is that "only a substantial or systematic failure of the board to exercise oversight—such as an utter failure to attempt to assure a reasonable information and reporting system exists—will establish the lack of good faith that is a necessary condition to liability." *In re Caremark Int'l, Inc., Derivative Litigation*, 698 A.2d 959 (Del. Ch. 1996), quoted and discussed in Myers & Stobaugh, *supra* note 614, at 2.

[620]ERISA applies to many kinds of nongovernmental pension and other plans maintained by employers for their employees, and by employee organizations representing employees, in the United States or engaged in commerce involving the U.S.

[621]In fact, in addition to the need to consider diversification, ERISA imposes on the fiduciary the specific duty to diversify the plan's investments to minimize the risk of substantial losses, unless it is clearly prudent not to do so under the circumstances that prevail at the time of investment. *See* ERISA § 404(a)(1)(B).

[622]The duties are to act solely in the interests of the plan's beneficiaries and participants and to defray the reasonable expenses of administering the plan, under ERISA §§ 404(a)(1)(A)(i) & (ii).

which in many ways resembles the standard discussed above to which corporate directors are held under state law.

In essence, this standard, which is sometimes referred to as the prudent person rule, requires the exercise of the degree of care, skill and diligence that a prudent person would, in the prevailing circumstances, use acting in a similar capacity, conducting a similar enterprise with similar aims.[623] The standard applies under ERISA to those who exercise discretion in the administration of an ERISA plan, who have authority or control over the plan's assets or who render investment advice for a fee with respect to plan assets, since generally speaking these are the persons identified as fiduciaries for purposes of ERISA.[624]

In March 1996 the Department of Labor, which is charged with overseeing the management of ERISA plans, released a letter specifically addressing how this prudent person standard applies to securities with embedded derivatives, while recognizing that "derivatives may be a useful tool for managing a variety of risks and for broadening investment alternatives in a plan's portfolio."[625] The letter indicated that "[i]nvestments in derivatives are subject to the fiduciary responsibility rules in the same manner as are any other plan investments" but that "investment in certain derivatives, such as structured notes and collateralized mortgage obligations, may require a higher degree of sophistication and understanding on the part of plan fiduciaries than other investments" because, among other characteristics, securities with embedded derivatives "may include extreme price volatility, a high degree of leverage, limited testing by markets, and difficulty in determining the market value of the derivative due to illiquid market conditions."[626]

As a result, the DOL set out the following as guidelines for ERISA plan fiduciaries in connection with investments in securities with embedded derivatives, although the guidelines are generally thought to represent DOL views on derivatives use by ERISA plans more broadly:

> As with any investment made by a plan, plan fiduciaries with the authority for investing in derivatives are responsible for securing sufficient information to understand the investment prior to making the investment. For example, plan fiduciaries should secure from dealers and other sellers of derivatives, among other things, sufficient information to allow an independent analysis of the credit risk and market risk being undertaken by the plan in making the investment in the particular derivative. The market risks presented by the derivatives purchased by the plan should be understood and evaluated in terms of the effects that they will

---

[623] As set forth in Section 404(a)(1) of ERISA, this standard applies when the participant or beneficiary of the plan does not directly control assets through specified individual accounts and, naturally, is supplemented by the requirement that the fiduciary act in accordance with the particular documents and instruments governing the plan, to the extent they are consistent with ERISA.

[624] *See* ERISA § 3(21).

[625] Letter from Olena Berg, Assistant Secretary for Pension and Welfare Benefits, U.S. Dept. of Labor, to Eugene A. Ludwig, Comptroller of the Currency (Mar. 21, 1996), at 2, *http://*www.dol.gov/dol/pwba/public/programs/ori/advisory96/driv4ltr.htm.

[626] *Id.*

have on the relevant segments of the plan's portfolio as well as the portfolio's overall risk.

Plan fiduciaries have a duty to determine the appropriate methodology used to evaluate market risk and the information which must be collected to do so. Among other things, this would include, where appropriate, stress simulation models showing the projected performance of the derivatives and of the plan's portfolio under various market conditions. Stress simulations are particularly important because assumptions which may be valid for normal markets may not be valid in abnormal markets, resulting in significant losses. To the extent that there may be little pricing information available with respect to some derivatives, reliable price comparisons may be necessary. After entering into an investment, a plan fiduciary should be able to obtain timely information from the derivatives dealer regarding the plan's credit exposure and the current market value of its derivatives positions, and, where appropriate, should obtain such information from third parties to determine the current market value of the plan's derivatives positions, with a frequency that is appropriate to the nature and extent of these positions.

. . .

As part of its evaluation of the investment, a fiduciary must analyze the operational risks being undertaken in making the investment. Among other things, the fiduciary should determine whether it possesses the requisite expertise, knowledge, and information to understand and analyze the nature of the risks and potential returns involved in a particular derivative investment. In particular, the fiduciary must determine whether the plan has adequate information and risk management systems in place given the nature, size and complexity of the plan's derivatives activity, and whether the plan fiduciary has personnel who are competent to manage these systems. If the investments are made by outside investment managers hired by the plan fiduciary, that fiduciary should consider whether the investment managers have such personnel and controls and whether the plan fiduciary has personnel who are competent to monitor the derivatives activities of the investment managers.

. . .

Also, as with any other investment, plan fiduciaries have a duty to properly monitor their investments in derivatives to determine whether they are still appropriately fulfilling their role in the portfolio. The frequency and degree of the monitoring will, of course, depend on the nature of such investments and their role in the plan's portfolio.[627]

Since release of the DOL letter setting out these guidelines, there have been numerous complaints against ERISA plan fiduciaries involving investments with embedded derivatives. In some the fiduciary has been found to have breached its duty under ERISA's prudent person standard, or has settled charges of such a breach brought by the DOL, as a

---

[627]*Id.* at 2–3.

result of the fiduciary's reliance on the seller's description of the instruments, alleged failure to conduct an independent investigation and lack of sufficient understanding of the investments and their risks.[628]

The court decisions have, however, also shown that, where appropriate research by the fiduciary or its delegate has been done, the derivative-like investment has been made pursuant to applicable investment guidelines for a permitted purpose and sensible risk management procedures have been put in place by a knowledgeable principal fiduciary or an investment manager hired by the principal fiduciary, a claim of breach of fiduciary duty may fail, under ERISA's prudent person rule, notwithstanding a substantial loss to the ERISA plan.[629] Like the business judgment rule applicable under state law to corporate directors, ERISA's prudent person rule does not apply the clarity lent by hindsight to second-guess decisions that were prudently made in light of circumstances at the time.

We have quoted at length from the DOL guidelines because they highlight themes that resound in the many sets of risk-management principles and practices that have been published by derivatives professionals and end-users alike. In all cases, great emphasis is placed on the importance of the ability to assess, value and monitor derivatives within the context of express policy on derivatives use, both before a transaction is executed and on an ongoing basis, independently or with the aid of a third party, and without relying on a counterparty.

For corporate and other end-users generally, an early example is found in the *End-Users' Guidelines*, which provide that the role of directors and senior management where derivatives are concerned is to inform itself sufficiently about derivatives to play an effective decision-making role and choose competent advisors to assist it in doing so. More specifically, senior management should be involved with a company's derivatives activities in:

- developing a formal risk management policy appropriate for the enterprise in light of the risks involved in its business or activities and addressing the parameters for the use of derivatives in the management of those risks;

- developing and implementing procedures designed to ensure that the policy is being pursued;

- monitoring compliance with the policy and procedures, through company personnel or external advisors with the necessary training and expertise, independent from those involved in the activities subject to the policy;

---

[628]*See* A. J. Alex Gelinas & Emily Sanderson, *Employee Benefit Plan Investments in Derivatives: Selected ERISA Issues*, DERIVATIVES REPORT, Oct. 2000, at 7, 8–9, discussing *Gilbert v. EMG Advisors Inc.*, No. 97-17256, 1999 U.S. App Lexis 4719 (9th Cir. March 17, 1999) and referring to DOL proceedings that have been settled.

[629]*See id.* at 9, on *Laborers Nat'l Pension Fund v. Northern Trust Quantitative Advisors, Inc.*, 173 F.3d 313 (5th Cir. 1999), *cert. denied*, 528 U.S. 967 (1999).

- ensuring that the financial accounts and books and records of the enterprise are being maintained in a way that properly reflects the use of derivatives, as well as the other activities of the enterprise, in accordance with applicable accounting principles; and

- producing and reviewing periodic reports about the foregoing and, in light of the contents of the reports and changes in circumstances involving the enterprise and the environment in which it operates, reassessing and, where appropriate, modifying the policies and procedures already in place.

This list consciously built on *Derivatives: Practices and Principles*, a report published in July 1993 by the Global Derivatives Study Group of the Group of Thirty, whose members are prominent individuals from the financial area, including commercial and investment bankers, regulators and academicians from many parts of the world. Far more detailed guidance, and sample policies and procedures, have been published by and for end-users[630] and by the governmental agencies that supervise or regulate some professional market participants.[631]

Since the publication of these guidelines, for many in the U.S. markets far more detailed attention to risk management and the use of derivatives has become a necessity because disclosure on these subjects is mandated by U.S. securities regulation and because U.S. GAAP conditions hedge accounting treatment for many derivatives on close analysis and documentation of the risks being managed and the effectiveness of the transaction as a hedge for the designated purpose.[632] Since the collapse of Enron in 2001 and

---

[630] In March 1998 the Treasury Management Association published a more detailed set of *Principles and Practices for The Oversight & Management of Financial Risk*, which it prepared in conjunction with Ernst & Young LLP. It includes general principles as well as policy and control guidelines, and a board-level checklist for risk management, among other useful features. Similar practical features are included in *Managing Derivatives Risk: guidelines for end-users of derivatives*, supra note 527, and in Coopers & Lybrand, *Generally Accepted Risk Principles* (1996), prepared in consultation with a review panel that included representatives from the derivatives industry, the Bank of England, the CFTC, the SEC, the SFA and the SIB. Illustrative Policy Examples and an Illustrative Control Procedures Reference Tool are among the useful supplements and appendices to the more general guidance in Committee of Sponsoring Organizations of the Treadway Commission ("COSO"), *Internal Control Issues in Derivatives Usage* (1996). COSO's members are the American Accounting Association, the American Institute of Certified Public Accountants, the Financial Executives Institute, the Institute of Internal Auditors and the Institute of Management Accountants. Interesting and useful tools for understanding how the controls that a company puts in place may be viewed by its auditors are found in Robert F. Dombrowski, *The Independent Auditor's Role in Reviewing Internal Controls for Derivative Activities*, in DERIVATIVES RISK MANAGEMENT SERVICE 9C-1.

[631] *See, e.g.*, INTERNATIONAL ORGANIZATION OF SECURITIES COMMISSIONS, RISK MANAGEMENT AND CONTROL GUIDANCE FOR SECURITIES FIRMS AND THEIR SUPERVISORS (May 1998). The guidance published by U.S. bank supervisory agencies includes the handbook published by the OCC on *Risk Management of Financial Derivatives* (Jan. 1997) and on *Internal Control* (Jan. 2001). *See also* BOARD OF GOVERNORS OF THE FEDERAL RESERVE SYSTEM, COMMERCIAL BANK EXAMINATION MANUAL § 2020.1 (on bank end-user activities) and § 2030.1 (on bank dealer activities) and BOARD OF GOVERNORS OF THE FEDERAL RESERVE SYSTEM, *supra* note 21, § 2000.1 (Feb. 1998) (an *Overview of Risk Management in Trading Activities*).

[632] *See supra* pp. 132 (SEC disclosure requirements) & 11 (FAS 133). The securities law issues for management will be substantially heightened by proposed requirements regarding certification of financial disclosure and more severe penalties for violations under bills that the U.S. congress has been considering in

the subsequent revelations about its dealings, central concerns in this area have been financial reporting and management oversight of off-balance sheet vehicles and of the use of derivatives in structures that may be viewed, but are not reported, as financings.[633] As legislators, regulatory authorities, investors and counterparties scrutinize these and other matters relating to corporate governance with a more critical eye, both end-users and professionals in the derivatives markets are revisiting their risk management policies and practices. As they do so, defining the parties' dealing relationships and their understanding about what each may expect from the other should, we believe, continue to figure prominently in the overall picture and in policies and practices relating to documentation.

Although the parties will often include representations and disclaimers like those discussed in this chapter in their master agreements, they should consciously consider the subjects of the representations and disclaimers in the context of their ongoing dealings. If their initial understanding, as reflected in the master agreement, changes, the documentation should reflect the change, and the way in which it will do so should be agreed before the relevant transaction is concluded. Counsel, often brought into an ongoing relationship for the first time when more complex transactions are being considered, should help clients focus on the possible need for a separate agreement on the parties' relationships and duties for the complex transactions.

The trade confirmation may not be the best place to record special agreements on the nature of the parties' relationship or a party's special obligations. Although the parties to OTC derivatives sometimes prepare and review draft confirmations before they engage in transactions, this practice is not the norm. In the absence of an exchange of draft confirmations, the confirmation is not likely to be a suitable vehicle for opening discussion about the parties' relationship, because after the transaction has been executed at an agreed price (whether expressed as a premium or as one of the rates applied in the transaction), it would be too late for one of the parties, in its reply to a confirmation of the agreed financial terms, to assert for the first time that it believes itself entitled to rely on its counterparty as an advisor in connection with the transaction. In any event, the parties should bear in mind that, if their expectations about their dealings are set out in many documents, and are different for individual cases, there is particular need for clarity about how the separate documents relate to each other. When confirmations are included in the mix, there is a somewhat greater risk that an important piece may be overlooked by those who may need to assess the full picture. It may be appropriate to create a central mechanism for identifying exceptions to the general rules in the parties' dealings.

---

light of Enron's collapse and investigations in 2001 and 2002 into faulty financial reporting by other major companies.

[633] *See infra* p. 989 for discussion of the *Mahonia* case, in which allegations of this kind were made. Many of the ongoing legal proceedings and investigations involving Enron management, directors and auditors, and market professionals who engaged in some of the derivatives, raise a variety of issues (including violation of antifraud provisions) under various U.S. laws, rather than the subjects discussed here.

SAMPLE DISCLOSURE STATEMENT

NATURE OF DEALER-CUSTOMER RELATIONSHIP

Ladies and Gentlemen,

We are pleased to provide you with this statement regarding our understanding of the nature of our relationship with your organization in the context of financial derivatives transactions and the attached general disclosure statement regarding Risks Associated with OTC Derivatives Transactions.

Please circulate copies of this statement and its attachment to all persons within your organization who will have responsibility for dealing with us in connection with the negotiation and execution of derivatives transactions. We also ask that you establish procedures so that new personnel receive copies and are given an opportunity to clarify any doubts they may have about this statement.

This statement was developed for our new and established derivatives customers in response to suggestions that OTC derivative dealers consider taking steps to ensure that market participants using OTC derivatives understand the nature of their relationships with dealers and their risk exposures before they enter into OTC derivatives transactions.

The attached general statement of Risks Associated with OTC Derivatives Transactions identifies, in general terms, some of the principal risks associated with individually negotiated OTC derivatives transactions. It does not purport to identify the nature of the specific market or other risks that may be associated with any particular transaction or category of transactions.

Before you enter into an OTC derivatives transaction with us, you should ensure that you fully understand the terms of the transaction, the relevant risk factors, the nature and extent of your risk of loss and the nature of your contractual relationship with us. You should also be sure that the transaction is appropriate for you in light of the experience of your personnel and independent advisors, your objectives and financial resources, and the other relevant circumstances. It is also important that you have the operational resources in place to monitor the associated risks and contractual obligations over the term of the transaction. If you are acting as a financial adviser or agent, you should evaluate these considerations in light of the circumstances of your principal or client and make sure that the transaction is within the scope of your authority.

If you believe you need assistance in evaluating and understanding the terms or risks of a particular OTC derivatives transaction, you should consult appropriate independent advisers before entering into the transaction.

We are not acting as your financial adviser or fiduciary. You should not regard transaction proposals, suggestions or other written or oral communications from us as recommendations or advice from us or as expressing our view as to whether a particular transaction is appropriate for you or meets your financial objectives.

Unless we have expressly agreed otherwise in writing, we are acting in the capacity of an arm's-length contractual counterparty to you in connection with every OTC derivatives transaction between us. In simple terms, this means that we are entering into these transactions in the expectation that they will be profitable for us.

Both in hedging the risks we take in our transactions with you, and otherwise, we and our affiliates may from time to time take proprietary positions and/or make a market in instruments of the same kind as our OTC derivatives transactions with you or of kinds that are economically related to them. Our proprietary activities, including hedging transactions related to the initiation or termination of an OTC derivatives transaction with you, may have an adverse effect on the market price, rate, index or other market factors underlying one or more of our OTC derivatives transactions with you and, consequently, on the value of the transactions to you.

We may have investment banking or other business relationships with the issuers of securities, financial instruments, or other interests underlying OTC derivatives transactions we enter into with you. We may have access to information provided to us by issuers that we do not disclose to you.

It is important to us that you understand our position regarding the nature of our relationship with you in connection with our derivatives dealings, which may be different from other relationships, past, present or future, that may we or our affiliates may have with you.

GENERAL STATEMENT OF RISKS

ASSOCIATED WITH OTC DERIVATIVES TRANSACTIONS

OTC derivatives transactions involve significant risks. The risks for you of a particular transaction necessarily depend on the terms of the transaction and on your circumstances. Generally speaking, all OTC derivatives transactions involve some combination of market risk, credit risk, funding risk and operational risk.

Market risk is the risk that the value to you of a transaction will be adversely affected by such factors as:

- fluctuations in the level of one or more market prices, rates or indexes,
- changes in volatility levels of market prices, rates or indexes,
- variances in the correlations or other relationship between various market factors, and
- the level of liquidity, or illiquidity, in the market for the relevant transaction or related markets.

Credit risk is the risk that a counterparty will fail to perform its obligations to you when due.

Funding risk is the risk that you or your counterparty will not have adequate cash available to fund current obligations, which might occur because of mismatches in cash flows due from or to your counterparties in OTC derivatives transactions or related hedging, trading, collateral or other transactions, or delays in payment.

Operational risk is the risk that you will incur losses because of inadequacies in your internal systems or your controls for monitoring and quantifying the risks and contractual obligations associated with OTC derivatives and related transactions, for recording and valuing the transactions or for detecting human error, or from systems failure or management failure.

Special risks. There may be other significant risks that you should consider based on the terms of a specific transaction. Highly customized OTC derivatives transactions, in particular, may present heightened liquidity risk and introduce other significant risk factors of a complex character. Highly leveraged transactions may experience substantial gains or losses in value as a result of relatively small changes in the value or level of an underlying or related market factor. Unusual or extreme changes in market factors may affect the value of a transaction and the risks associated with it in ways that are not taken into account in most available systems for modeling transaction risk.

Pricing. Because the price and other terms on which you may enter into or terminate an OTC derivatives transaction are individually negotiated, these may not represent the best price or terms available to you from other sources.

While market makers and dealers generally quote prices or terms for entering into or terminating OTC derivatives transactions and provide indicative or midmarket quotations with respect to the value of outstanding transactions, they are generally not contractually obligated to do so. In addition, it may not be possible to obtain indicative or midmarket quotations for an OTC derivatives transaction from a market maker or dealer that is not a party to the transaction. Consequently, it may also be difficult for you to establish an independent value for an outstanding OTC derivatives transaction. You should not regard your counterparty's provision of a valuation or indicative price at your request as an offer to enter into or terminate the relevant transaction at that value or price, unless the value or price is identified by the counterparty as firm or binding.

Please note that valuations performed in connection with requirements for posting collateral or other credit support in connection with a transaction do not necessarily reflect the value of the transaction for any other purpose.

Amendments and Termination. When you evaluate the risks associated with a transaction, you should also keep in mind that an OTC derivatives transaction may be modified or terminated only by mutual consent of the original parties, which will be subject to agreement on individually negotiated terms. Accordingly, it may not be possible for you to modify, terminate or offset your obligations or your exposure to the risks associated with a transaction before its scheduled termination date.

You should refrain from entering into any transaction unless you have fully understood the terms and risks of the transaction, including the extent of your potential risk of loss, and are willing to run that risk. If changes in the value of a transaction or portfolio of transactions may have an important effect on your financial condition under the accounting principles applicable to you, you should consider how any proposed transaction will be reflected in your financial statements and in the reports you make to your shareholders and others, and how it may affect your ability to comply with financial covenants contained in your credit agreements.

This brief statement does not purport to disclose all the risks and other material considerations associated with OTC derivatives transactions. You should not construe this general disclosure statement as business, legal, tax or accounting advice or as modifying applicable law. You should consult your own business, legal, tax and accounting advisers with respect to proposed OTC derivatives transactions and verify that each transaction is consistent with your policies and objectives.

CHAPTER 6

DAMAGES AND CLOSE-OUT SETTLEMENT

Introduction	219
Concepts of Loss and Gain on Derivatives Transactions	220
Who Is Required to Pay Whom on Close-Out?	225
The Fault/No-Fault Distinction	225
The Shift Away from the Fault/No-Fault Distinction	230
How Much Must Be Paid?	235
Introduction to Quantifying Loss and Gain	235
The Fault/No-Fault Distinction as Applied to Quantification	246
Overview of Legal Principles Affecting Quantification of Damages	249
Legal Principles on Liquidated Damages	249
Legal Principles on Recoverable Actual Damages	251
Damages Must Proximately Result From Breach	253
Damages Must Be the Natural and Probable or Foreseeable Consequence of Breach	255
Damages Must Be Reasonably Certain	257
Avoidable Damages May Not Be Recoverable	258
Actual Cover Is Not Required, but Cost of Cover May Limit Recovery	265
Reliance-Interest or Loss-of-Bargain Damages	266

INTRODUCTION

It is a characteristic of derivatives transactions that, at any time, the bundle of rights and obligations of one of the parties to the transaction is likely to have value to that party, in which case the transaction is said to be "in-the-money" (an asset) to that party. If a transaction is in-the-money to one of the parties, it will be "out-of-the-money" (a liability) to the other party, in approximately the same amount.[634] Claims for damages on breach by a party of its obligations and, more generally, other settlement payments in connection with a transaction's close-out, are rooted in these concepts, as discussed in more detail in the first section of this chapter.

If a derivatives transaction that is in-the-money to a party is terminated, liquidated, cancelled or otherwise closed out[635] prior to its stated maturity because of a default by the other party, the in-the-money party will have a claim against the defaulting party for damages. More difficult questions arise, however, when termination comes about because of a default by the in-the-money party itself, or because of events beyond the control of either party. The second section of this chapter deals with these questions, as to who must pay whom (if at all) on close-out.

---

[634] We say "approximately" because the existence of a bid-asked spread in the market may mean that there is something of a difference in the absolute values of the asset and the liability, as discussed *infra* p. 224.

[635] As in Chapter 7, *supra* p. 268, on bankruptcy and insolvency concerns, we will refer to early termination, liquidation and cancellation of transactions generically as "close-out."

Derivatives documentation often contains detailed provisions about the quantification of any payments that are to be made when a transaction is closed out before maturity.[636] These questions are covered in the third section of this chapter, which also reviews legal principles that may limit the enforceability of the documentation.[637]

CONCEPTS OF LOSS AND GAIN ON DERIVATIVES TRANSACTIONS

The value of a derivatives transaction to each of the parties moves with changes in the price or level of the underlying asset, rate, index or other economic variable to which the derivative relates. This is easy to see, for example, in the case of an option to buy stock—a "call" option. The option takes on value to the holder (and becomes a greater liability of the writer of the option) as the price of the stock rises above the strike price. This proposition, though less intuitive as applied to more complex derivatives transactions, is equally true for them: at any time, the bundle of rights and obligations of one of the parties will have a positive value (except when the transaction is precisely "at-the-market," in which case the value to both parties will be zero or very close to it). The aggregate value of all the rights and obligations of the other party will be negative, in an approximately equal amount. Generally speaking, if a derivatives transaction is closed out early, the party for whom the transaction is out of the money will be required to pay compensation, often referred to as "breakage," to the other party.[638]

The view of OTC derivatives as assets or liabilities—as in-the-money or out-of-the-money—is fundamental not only to the calculation of damages and other close-out settlement amounts but also to many of the legal, regulatory and business frameworks within which the parties to derivatives operate. It is, for example, behind the idea that the fair value of derivatives transactions should, in most cases, be reported in the parties' financial statements under U.S. GAAP[639] and the requirement that the potential loss from derivatives should be disclosed by issuers to the holders of their securities.[640] It is also at the root of the way in which market participants commonly agree to post collateral or other credit support for their future, contingent obligations under their transactions,[641] and it is behind the rule that capital adequacy levels for banks should be determined taking into account both current and potential exposure to loss on account of derivatives.[642] As

---

[636] The annotations to the sample agreements in Part 3, *infra* p. 787, analyze in greater detail some of the specific approaches to the calculation of the close-out settlement payment discussed in this chapter.

[637] *See infra* p. 249. Chapter 7, *infra* p. 268, discusses the additional impact that insolvency and similar laws may have on the enforceability of the parties' chosen approach to close-out settlement.

[638] In some cases, the parties may have bargained for a different approach. *See, e.g., infra* note 1508 on "flat settlement" of credit derivatives.

[639] *See supra* p. 11.

[640] *See supra* p. 132.

[641] Part 5, *infra* p. 1057, discusses the interplay between the quantification aspects of close-out settlement provisions and the standard ISDA approaches to credit support for OTC derivatives obligations.

[642] The Basel Committee explains this approach in paragraph 43 of the Basel Accord (at 13), which forms part of a brief statement of how the Basel Accord determines bank regulatory capital requirements for off-balance sheet items by using a conversion factor to determine a credit risk equivalent for them:

> Special treatment is needed for [these] items . . . because banks are not exposed to credit risk for the full face value of their contracts, but only to the cost of replacing the

Damages and Close-Out Settlement 221

discussed in Chapter 7, this view of a transaction's value may also be expressed in laws that affect whether provisions on close-out settlement will be enforceable in insolvency or similar proceedings for a party.[643] Therefore, as they negotiate the close-out settlement provisions of their contracts, the parties should consider the impact that their choices may have in these and other important contexts, such as one party's use of the value of its position under a transaction as security for obligations owed by it to third parties.[644]

In many derivatives transactions, one party pays a one-time premium at the beginning of the transaction, and all the remaining obligations are those of the other party. This is usually the case, for example, with options, caps, floors and swaptions. In those cases, the value of the derivatives position from the point of view of the "buyer" will almost always be positive, to a greater or lesser extent.[645] Conversely, the seller's position will usually be a liability. The value of the option at the time it is written is equal to the

---

cash flow if a counterparty defaults. Most members of the Committee accept that the correct method of assessing the credit risk on these items is to calculate the current replacement cost by marking to market and to add a factor to represent potential exposure during the remaining life of the contract.

The discussion refers to an alternative method, under which "conversion factors are based on the nominal principal sum underlying each contract according to its type and maturity." The two methods are described in Annex 3 to the Basel Accord, which discusses these concepts further and clarifies that the analysis described above would not be applied in respect of off-balance-sheet obligations that require exposure to loss of principal (such as the exchanges of currency amounts at the maturity of a conventional currency swap). The Basel Committee's views on what is referred to as the "add on" for potential future exposure has been refined over time. An interesting discussion of the subject is included in its July 1994 report, *The Treatment of the Credit Risk Associated with Certain Off-Balance-Sheet Items* (which set out amendments to Annex 3 as well as amendments to Annex 1 on the recognition of the effects of bilateral netting of exposures for capital adequacy purposes in certain cases. *See infra* note 684. Further amendments were adopted in April 1995 and are described in the Basel Committee's report entitled *Treatment of Potential Exposure for Off-Balance-Sheet Items,* which, among other things, expanded recognition for capital adequacy purposes of mark-to-market approaches under which a contract's market value is reset to zero through settlement of exposures following specified payment dates. In these cases, for purposes of calculating the add on, it may be possible to treat the contract's residual maturity as equal to the time until the next reset date. Positions that are subject to multilateral netting systems may be treated differently. *See* BASEL COMMITTEE ON BANKING SUPERVISION, INTERPRETATION OF THE CAPITAL ACCORD FOR THE MULTILATERAL NETTING OF FORWARD VALUE FOREIGN EXCHANGE TRANSACTIONS (Apr. 1996). The Basel Committee's publications are *available* at www.bis.org.

[643] *See infra* p. 271.

[644] When securitization structures involve derivatives, this is often done. That is, the trusts and other special purpose vehicles that issue notes and certificates in these asset-backed structures generally assign their rights under the derivatives to the trustee, as security for the benefit of the investors, among others. As a result, in analyzing the nonpayment and other default risks being assumed by the investors, rating agencies look, among other things, at the credit standing of the derivatives provider, the circumstances in which close-out of the derivatives transaction may occur, the way in which any related close-out settlement payment will be calculated and which of the parties may be required to make a payment. *See, e.g.*, STANDARD & POOR'S, GLOBAL SYNTHETIC SECURITIES CRITERIA 43, *available at* http://www.standardpoor.com/Resource Center/RatingsCriteria/Structured Finance/index.html. (on "Swap Agreement Criteria"). In addition, when one of the terms of a credit agreement is a requirement that the borrower hedge its loan obligations with OTC derivatives, the borrower's rights to receive payments, including any close-out settlement payment, under the derivatives is often part of the security package for the lenders.

[645] *See* CAL JOHNSON, AN INTRODUCTION TO OPTIONS 6 n.9 & 7 (Salomon Brothers 1987), on the value of deep into- and out-of-the-money options.

premium. Regardless of whether the option is executed on an exchange or over the counter, the agreed premium reflects the value of the rights being obtained by the buyer at that moment, in the market's then-prevailing conditions.

For example, suppose a seller writes a "put" option that grants the buyer the right to require the writer of the option to buy 10,000 shares of XYZ stock for $5 per share 14 months later. In setting the premium, the option seller will have considered, in addition to market conditions, the relationship of the current market price of the underlying stock to the strike price (that is, the amount by which the stock price must rise or fall before the expiration date 14 months later for the option buyer to benefit from exercising the option), the time to expiration, its cost of funds and the known data about price volatility for the stock, that is, the tendency of the price of the stock to vary over time.[646]

After an option or similar instrument (such as an OTC cap or floor) is written, the value of the instrument changes as the pricing factors change, and (in most cases) as the time between the valuation date and the exercise date grows shorter. In effect, the changes in the option's value, from this perspective, reflect changes in the market's view of the chances that the option will not be exercisable by the time it expires.[647] Therefore, if the option is closed out unexercised before it expires, the market's view of the value of the option at the time of close-out should be reflected in the premium that would be charged for the option rights for the unexpired portion of the option's terms.

In transactions of other types, no payment takes place at the outset. This is the case with futures and with swaps and forwards when they are executed "at-the-market," meaning that the aggregate scheduled payment obligations of the parties are, loosely speaking, seen to be of equal value at the moment when the parties strike their bargain, or "price" the transaction.[648] As time passes and market conditions change, however, the transaction will normally become an asset to one of the parties and a liability to the other, so, if the transaction is closed out before the end of its term, one of the parties will incur a

---

[646] The pricing of options is a complex subject about which much has been, and continues to be, written, as dealers and financial engineers improve their understanding of the interplay of these and other factors. The number of factors increases with the complexity of the option. Dealers consider their option pricing models to be proprietary. Landmark published works on the subject are Fischer Black and Myron S. Scholes, *The Pricing of Options and Corporate Liabilities*, JOURNAL OF POLITICAL ECONOMY 637 (May-June 1973), setting forth the famous Black-Scholes option pricing formula, and Robert C. Merton, *Theory of rational option pricing*, BELL JOURNAL OF ECONOMICS AND MANAGEMENT SCIENCE 141 (Spring 1973). *See also* JOHN C. HULL, OPTIONS, FUTURES, & OTHER DERIVATIVES, ch. 11 (4th ed. 2000) ("The Black-Scholes Model").

[647] From the perspective of the buyer of the option, however, the premium that it paid will naturally offset any payoff it receives if it is ultimately entitled to exercise the option (and, therefore, reduce its profit).

[648] *See* HULL, *supra* note 646, at 59. How that price is determined depends, naturally, among other things, on the current, or "cash" or "spot" market price or rate for the derivative's "underlying" (*e.g.*, in the case of an FX forward, the market rate for a spot foreign exchange transaction involving the relevant currencies), the term of the derivative and the points over that term when one of the parties will be required to tender performance at the agreed forward price or rate, the nature of the performance due from the other party in exchange and, where relevant, the yield curve, forward yield curve or carrying charges reflecting expectations of future rates applicable in calculating one of the parties' performance or the cost of financing a position in the "underlying" until its delivery is scheduled to be due at the agreed price or rate. *Id.*

Damages and Close-Out Settlement　　223

loss and the other will experience a roughly equal gain.[649] The process by which the parties determine the degree of the shift is generally referred to as "marking to market."[650]

In contrast, if the parties agree to execute a swap or forward transaction at an "off-market" rate or price,[651] one or the other will in some way (up front, at the end or otherwise) be required to pay the other the value of the difference between the off-market rate or price and the rate or price applicable at the time to an at-the-market transaction.[652]

The mark-to-market process for a swap operates on the principles used in pricing an off-market swap. For example, suppose that, at a given time, an at-the-market three-year dollar fixed/LIBOR rate swap with semiannual payments would be priced at a fixed rate of 3.00%. If so, as shown in the following table, at that time an outstanding U.S. dollar fixed/LIBOR swap with a remaining term of three years, and with the same remaining scheduled semiannual payment dates, would be in-the-money (an asset) to the fixed-rate payer if it was paying at the rate of 2.75%. On the other hand, it would be out-of-the-money (a liability) to the fixed-rate payer if it was paying at the rate of 3.25%. Conversely, the 2.75% transaction would be out-of-the-money (a liability) to the floating-rate payer, but the 3.25% transaction would be in-the-money (an asset) to that party, in an amount approximately equal and opposite to its value to the fixed-rate payer.

Current Market Fixed Rate	Transaction Fixed Rate	Fixed Rate Payer	Floating Rate Payer
3.00%	2.75%	In-the-money	Out-of-the-money
3.00%	3.25%	Out-of-the-money	In-the-money

---

[649]*See* ISDA COLLATERAL GUIDELINES 4 on the mark-to-market (MTM) exposure profile of an interest rate swap: "Two factors influence MTM exposure: the number of payments remaining and the potential movement of random variables on the underlying. The MTM exposure will begin to decrease as the number of payments remaining decreases. This is called the amortization effect. The replacement cost is the amount one party would lose if the other party were to default."

[650]In some cases, the process may be referred to as "marking to model" when the shift in value of a transaction is measured by reference to a pricing or other valuation model, say, because a market for the relevant transaction does not exist. *See, e.g.*, DICTIONARY OF RISK MANAGEMENT 180, defining "Mark to Market" as meaning "[t]o value a position or portfolio at current market prices," and commenting on "Mark to Model" as follows: "To price a position or portfolio at prices determined by using a financial model to interpolate between or among the market prices readily available. A mark to model is less reliable than a mark to market, because it depends on the realism of the assumptions in the model and may attribute a degree of liquidity to the instruments being priced that may not be present. With many complex financial instruments, where no ready market is available, a mark to model is the only practical valuation technique." *Id.*

[651]Say a fixed/LIBOR U.S. dollar rate swap with matching payment dates and a fixed rate of 3.00% when the market fixed rate for the swap would be 3.25%. Off-market transactions may have special tax consequences. *See supra* p. 361. *See also* BOARD OF GOVERNORS OF THE FEDERAL RESERVE SYSTEM, *supra* note 21, § 2050.1, at 4 (Feb. 1998) (on the special risks of transactions involving off-market rates).

[652]Referring to the example in the preceding footnote, this would be a front-end payment equal to the present value of a stream of payments made over the term, on the scheduled payment dates, calculated at 0.25% on the notional amount applicable for each period's scheduled swap payment (with each payment discounted back from its scheduled payment date to present value on the first day of the term of the swap).

Exchange-traded options, futures and similar instruments are valued with reference to the prices at which the instruments trade on the exchange. In the OTC market, valuation is based on the prices at which dealers are offering to trade at the relevant time, and the valuation process is complicated by a "bid-asked spread" that exists in the derivatives market, as it does in markets for securities and other financial products. This spread can be thought of as the difference between the bid and the offered price of a new transaction, reflecting supply and demand conditions at the time. The spread represents the profit that a dealer will make if it succeeds in doing a transaction at one end of the spread and hedging it at the other end. As a result of the existence of the spread, the actual cost to one party of replacing a transaction that is being closed out may not be exactly equal to the theoretical gain to the other party from being relieved of its obligations under that transaction as they were originally scheduled to fall due after the close-out. Therefore, depending on the purposes for which a transaction is being valued, the parties may have conflicting views as to the point on the bid-asked spread at which the valuation should be done.[653]

Derivatives dealings on an exchange between a buyer and a seller are, for the most party, anonymous.[654] As a result, exchange trading uses margining and daily settlements on account of changes in value to minimize the risk of default. These requirements occur at two levels. Brokers require their customers to provide and maintain margin accounts to protect the brokers against the risk of default by the customers as the market moves against them. The exchanges, in turn, require all trading to be done through members of the exchange, require all members to maintain margin accounts and require those accounts to be charged or credited daily as the transaction values change.[655] Through this typical structure, in what is sometimes loosely called the guaranty of all trades by the exchange, the exchange or its clearing house acts as the intermediary, that is, as the counterparty in all trades so that every exchange member has mutual rights and obligations only vis-à-vis the exchange or its clearing house.

In OTC derivatives, on the other hand, the parties have not traditionally used exchange-style mutualization and margining to manage counterparty credit risk.[656] There-

---

[653]On the effect of the bid-asked spread on quantification of damages, *see infra* p. 246. On the way in which the bid-asked spread figures in the cash settlement of swaptions and similar transactions, *see infra* p. 461.

[654]There are exceptions, for example, in connection with arrangements under which buyers and sellers are permitted to initiate and liquidate or tender delivery under futures positions through what are referred to as EFPs and EFSs—exchanges of futures positions for equal but opposite physical positions in the underlying commodity or equal but opposite exposure positions in OTC derivatives—and ADPs, nonstandard "alternate delivery procedures." *See, e.g.*, NEW YORK MERCANTILE EXCHANGE, HENRY HUB NATURAL GAS, *available at* www.nymex.com/markets/ cont_all.cfm, and MIDDLE EAST CRUDE OIL FUTURES AND OPTIONS CONTRACT SPECIFICATIONS, *available at* http://208.206.41.61/sourmarker/mescspec.htm.

[655]*See* HULL, *supra* note 646, at 26–27. The acceptable forms of margin may include, in addition to cash, specified securities or qualifying letters of credit. Examples of these requirements, as imposed by the Chicago Mercantile Exchange, can be seen in Chapter 8 of its rules (on Clearing House and Performance Bonds), *available at* 222.cmerulebook.com.

[656]Until recently, the use of clearing organizations to manage counterparty risk in OTC derivatives in the U.S. markets has involved substantial legal risk. This legal risk was, however, removed through the CFMA, as discussed *supra* p 96.

Damages and Close-Out Settlement

fore, the credit standing of the parties may be relevant to a transaction's valuation, when value is thought of as the amount each would pay (or charge) to enter into a replacement transaction. This is naturally so because the value today of a right to receive, say, a three-year stream of swap payments from a party with a "AAA" credit rating, reflecting the low likelihood it will default during the term of the swap, should in theory be higher than the value of the right to receive the same payments over the same period from a party with credit ratings several grades lower.

Other factors affecting the party at the time (such as the recent passage of a law or regulation affecting that party's ability to perform) may have a substantial impact on the economics of obtaining a replacement transaction. Factors such as these may also have a bearing on the extent to which there is a gap between the absolute amounts of the positive and negative values to the respective parties.

The following two sections discuss, against this conceptual background, the two fundamental questions that arise in connection with derivatives damages and close-out settlement payments: "Who is required to make a payment?" and "How much must be paid?"

WHO IS REQUIRED TO PAY WHOM ON CLOSE-OUT?

THE FAULT/NO-FAULT DISTINCTION

In the documentation for many kinds of OTC derivatives, a distinction has traditionally been drawn between close-out arising in connection with Events of Default and close-out in connection with "no-fault" events (Termination Events, in ISDA terminology)—a mixed bag of changes in circumstances that are beyond the control of the affected party or are treated as no-fault events because the parties wish to distinguish them from Events of Default.[657] This distinction can have a bearing on the subject of this section—which party (if any) has to make a payment—and on quantification questions, as discussed in the following section.[658]

The ISDA master agreement Events of Default and Termination Events are discussed in detail in the annotations to the sample documents in Part 3.[659] The Events of Default are as follows:

- Failure to Pay or Deliver
- Breach of Agreement
- Credit Support Default
- Misrepresentation
- Default under Specified Transaction

---

[657] An important reason for the distinction is that treatment of one of these events as an Event of Default can have serious consequences (*e.g.*, could give rise to close-out) under agreements between the party that is affected by the event and third parties.

[658] *Infra* p. 246.

[659] *See infra* p. 828 (Events of Default) and *infra* p. 840 (Termination Events).

- Cross Default (if specified in the relevant Schedule)
- Bankruptcy
- Merger Without Assumption[660]

The ISDA Termination Events are as follows:

- Illegality
- Tax Event
- Tax Event Upon Merger
- Credit Event Upon Merger
- Additional Termination Events (if the parties have specified them)
- Impossibility (if the parties adopt the optional provision included in the *User's Guide to the 1992 ISDA Master Agreements*)
- Force Majeure Event (if the parties adopt Attachment 9 to the *Form of Amendment to ISDA Master Agreements* published by ISDA in October 2001)[661]

The characterizations of various events as fault or no-fault grounds for close-out have not been uniform in all segments of the market for financial products or even within the OTC derivatives market. There have, in particular, been wide variations in the practices regarding force majeure events and impossibility or impracticability of performance. The FEOMA, ICOM and IFEMA forms have consistently included force majeure and acts of state among their no-fault events.[662] ISDA's first approach, on the other hand, was to treat Illegality as a no-fault event but to treat failures of performance due to other types of force majeure events on a "fault" basis,[663] although the parties were invited, where appropriate, to choose to do otherwise, and the *User's Guide to the 1992 ISDA Master Agreements* included an optional provision on impossibility that the parties could use for the purpose.[664] The ISDA forms did not expressly seek to preclude judicial application of

---

[660] The ISDA standard credit support documents include other Events of Default.

[661] *See infra* p. 247.

[662] Revised force majeure provisions, available at http://www.ny.frb.org/fxc/fmagagree.pdf, for use with those forms were published most recently in December 1999. *See also* Foreign Exchange Committee, *User's Guide: Revised Force Majeure Provisions* (December 1999), *available at* http://www.ny.frb.org/fxc/fmagguide.pdf.

[663] This is the case in ISDA's master agreement forms. Various product-specific sets of ISDA definitions make provision, however, for performance that cannot be tendered when due because, say, of market or settlement system disruptions.

[664] *See infra* p. 907. This approach was taken in 1992 because the focus then was on master agreement forms for a market in which transactions were largely cash-settled. It was thought that those engaged in physically settled transactions would, when appropriate, craft their own force majeure clauses or use the *User's Guide* provision on impossibility as a starting point, and it was also thought that the standard Illegality provision would deal adequately with exchange controls and other changes in law that might interfere with timely performance of payment obligations. Given the fungibility of money, it seemed relatively unlikely that other kinds of force majeure events would render payment impossible or impracticable on any scale that the market would find significant. Market experience with natural disasters, civil disturbances and

common-law doctrines of impracticability or frustration of contract,[665] and some market participants have reportedly operated on the assumption that those doctrines would be applicable to their ISDA-based agreements.[666]

There have also been other differences in the fault/no-fault characterization of events. For example, an event that would be treated as a no-fault Credit Event Upon Merger under ISDA documentation and as a Change of Circumstances known as a Credit Event upon Restructuring under the General Provisions of the European Master Agreement (EMA) form, might be treated as an Event of Default under the FEOMA, ICOM and IFEMA forms. Moreover, while the illegality, force majeure and similar provisions of these five forms all treat some payment and delivery failures as no-fault events, all payment and delivery failures are referred to as Events of Default under the PSA/ISMA Global Master Repurchase Agreement and TBMA's Master Repurchase Agreement.[667]

The fault/no-fault distinction may have various kinds of consequences of lesser or greater importance. For example, under the ISDA master agreement forms, if a party's delay in making a payment is treated as an Event of Default, the overdue payment will accrue interest at the Default Rate, but if the same delay is treated as a no-fault Termination Event, any interest that the Affected Party may be required to pay will accrue at the Non-default Rate.[668] In addition, if the overdue payment is attributable to an Event of Default, under Section 2(a)(iii) of the ISDA master agreement forms the payee will be entitled to withhold any performance that would otherwise be due from it pending cure of the payment failure, regardless of whether the payee has designated an Early Termination

---

the like led to increased pressure to include special treatment for force majeure cases in the standard forms. As a result (and also to deal with problems that have arisen under the Illegality provision, as further discussed *infra* at p. 977), ISDA has prepared the Force Majeure Event provisions available through Attachment 9 to the *2001 ISDA Amendments* published by ISDA in October 2001.

[665] *See generally* RESTATEMENT (SECOND) OF CONTRACTS, ch. 11 (1981) ("Impracticability of Performance and Frustration of Purpose").

[666] *See User's Guide to the ISDA 1992 Master Agreements* 64. If the parties are seeking to limit the application of such doctrines beyond what is expressly provided in their agreement, they should make that clear in the agreement. *See, e.g.*, RESTATEMENT (SECOND) OF CONTRACTS §§ 261 (dealing with supervening impracticability), 265 (frustration of contact) & 266 (existing impracticability or frustration) (1981), all of which are stated to apply "unless the language or circumstances indicate the contrary."

[667] Differences of this kind among the forms give rise to risks for parties that use multiple forms of agreement for their financial transactions with each other. See the Introduction to Part 6, *infra* p. 1281, and the annotations to the sample Cross-Product Master Agreement in this book, *infra* p. 1311.

[668] Default Rate interest is provided for in Section 2(e) of the 1992 forms and as part of a close-out settlement, in Section 6(e), through the definition of the term "Unpaid Amount." Non-default Rate interest is provided for only in connection with a close-out settlement, through Section 6(e) and the same definition. *See infra* pp. 814, 860 & 896. *See also* Annotation 2 to Section 5(c) of the sample master agreement in Part 3, *infra* p. 847, and Section 6(b)(v), added by the *2001 ISDA Amendments, infra* p. 981, on provisions pursuant to which the parties may agree to defer their mutual obligations until resolution of an Illegality, subject to having to pay interest on the payments that have been deferred. The distinction between a fault and a no-fault interest rate does not exist under the FEOMA, ICOM and IFEMA forms. *See infra* p. 245 on the provisions in these forms pursuant to which the close-out settlement calculations are adjusted for interest, at a single rate, on amounts that were scheduled to be paid before close-out. These forms do not provide for interest on overdue amounts except in the context of close-out or a close-out settlement payment that is not made when due.

Date, but the payee will not have the same right if the payment has not been made because of an Illegality, unless the parties have modified that provision (for example, by adopting Attachment 1 to the *2001 ISDA Master Agreement Amendment Form*).[669] The fault/no-fault distinction may also have an impact on the parties' rights under their credit support documents.[670]

Historically, the greatest importance of the fault/no-fault distinction has lain in how a party will be treated in connection with a close-out settlement payment. Not surprisingly, there has always been general agreement in all parts of the OTC derivatives market that, if a transaction is terminated because of the occurrence of an Event of Default at a time when it is in-the-money to the nondefaulting party, the defaulting party should pay damages to compensate the nondefaulting party for the loss, including the loss of bargain, that it suffers as a result of the termination—the loss of an asset.

This approach to damages is wholly consistent with the practice in financings and other kinds of financial transactions. The bank loan and institutional private placement financing markets provide ready examples. If the issuer of a five-year fixed-rate note defaults during year two, the note's acceleration clause will of course call for repayment of principal along with interest accrued through the accelerated repayment date. Moreover, the note's "make-whole" clause will typically require the issuer to indemnify the note's holder against loss if the interest rate on the note is higher, at the time of acceleration, than the return on an agreed type of hypothetical substitute investment. Commercial bank lenders have traditionally obtained similar protection, and indemnification against loss on unwinding their funding deposits, through the "broken funding" clauses in their Eurodollar, LIBOR-based, loan agreements.[671]

These models from the world of financing have not traditionally required an investor to make a payment to a defaulting issuer when market conditions are such at the time of acceleration that the investor could make a better rate of return on a new investment than the coupon on the accelerated note. Similarly, lenders have not normally agreed to pay over to defaulting borrowers any added profit they might make by relending the amounts prepaid to them when a loan is accelerated.

Many of those involved in the early days of the market for interest rate and currency swaps and related derivatives initially viewed the new derivatives products in the light of their experience with financings. As a result, they favored adoption of a similar, unilateral approach to damages payments for loss of bargain in the documentation for the derivatives. Accordingly, for many years the majority view in the swaps market was that, if a transaction was closed out because of the occurrence of an Event of Default and was

---

[669] *See infra* p. 803 for further discussion of this topic. It appears that the fault/no-fault distinction leads to the same disparity of result for the payee under the FEOMA, ICOM and IFEMA forms unless the parties have agreed that the payee is entitled to make reasonable requests for adequate assurances of the other party's ability to perform and, on the basis of such a request, is permitted to suspend its obligation to perform pending receipt of adequate assurances. *See infra* p. 912.

[670] *See, e.g., infra* p. 1151, on the conditions precedent to a party's obligation to post or return credit support under Paragraph 4(a) of ISDA's NY CSA published for use in connection with agreements governed by New York law.

[671] On broken-funding clauses and make-whole clauses, *see* GOOCH & KLEIN, LOAN DOCUMENTATION 90–91 & 383–86.

Damages and Close-Out Settlement 229

out-of-the-money to the nondefaulting party at the time of close-out, the gain enjoyed by that party as a result of being relieved of its obligations under the transaction was not required to be paid over to the defaulting party or shared with that party.

In ISDA documentation, this older majority approach was known as "Limited Two-Way Payments" in the *Swaps Code* and the 1987 master agreement forms and (with certain changes) as the "First Method" in the 1992 forms. Under the 1987 forms (but not the 1992 forms) this approach applied automatically unless the parties specified otherwise.[672] Critics of this approach often refer to provisions that adopt it as "walkaway clauses" because the nondefaulting party is entitled, at least in some cases, to walk away from close-out with a gain that it isn't required to account for, despite the fact that close-out has extinguished valuable rights of the defaulting party.[673]

The main features of the First Method may be simply stated as follows, using ISDA terminology:[674]

1. If a single Transaction between the parties is terminated as a result of the occurrence of an Event of Default at a time when the Transaction is in-the-money to the Non-defaulting Party, the Defaulting Party is required to pay damages to the Non-defaulting Party to compensate it for its loss resulting from the termination of the Transaction. This post-termination value element represents the net value at the time of all the regular Transaction payments or deliveries scheduled to be made after the Early Termination Date.

2. If a single Transaction between the parties is terminated as a result of the occurrence of an Event of Default and the Transaction is in-the-money to the Defaulting Party, the Non-defaulting Party will not be obligated to pay the corresponding post-termination value over to the Defaulting Party.

3. If multiple Transactions between the parties are terminated as a result of the occurrence of an Event of Default, the post-termination value of the Transactions that are in-the-money to the Defaulting Party is credited against the post-termination value of the Transactions that are in-the-money to the Non-defaulting Party. If the resulting net amount is in favor of the Non-defaulting Party, the Defaulting Party will be required to make a payment in that amount. No payment will, however, be due if the net amount is in favor of the Defaulting Party.

---

[672]This approach changed in the 1992 ISDA master agreement forms, and the rule adopted in 1992 continues to apply under the amendments to Section 6 of those forms provided for in the Replacement Value approach. *See infra* p. 972.

[673]As discussed in Chapter 6, walkaway clauses are not enforceable against receivers for certain financial institutions under New York law. *See infra* p. 233. Reform proposals now pending in the U.S. congress would provide that walkaway clauses in qualified financial contracts will not be enforceable against any entity subject to proceedings under the FDIA. *See infra* p. 337. On the treatment of walkaway clauses under the Basel Accord, *see infra* note 684.

[674]For simplicity's sake, this description assumes that all of the parties' mutual obligations on account of the period ending on the Early Termination Date have been fully performed.

Under the ISDA master agreement forms, Unpaid Amounts (that is, amounts that became due, or that were originally scheduled to be due, on or before the Early Termination Date) that are owed to a Defaulting Party are generally taken into account to reduce any Settlement Amount that would otherwise be owed by that party. However, under Limited Two-Way Payments (First Method), no cash payment would be due from the Non-defaulting Party to the Defaulting Party in respect of Unpaid Amounts if the balance were in the latter's favor.

For example, suppose Big Bank has a swap with Shaky Counterparty under a Master Agreement on a 1992 ISDA form that contains an election to apply the First Method and that the swap is in-the-money to Shaky Counterparty at all relevant times, with a payment of $1 million due to be made by Big Bank on October 16, 2002. Further, suppose that creditors of Shaky Counterparty initiate bankruptcy proceedings against it on October 14. If these proceedings are not dismissed, discharged, stayed or restrained, on October 16, Big Bank is entitled to withhold its payment, on the basis of Section 2(a)(iii) of the Master Agreement. If the proceedings still have not been dismissed, discharged, stayed or restrained when 30 days have passed after the filing,[675] Big Bank is entitled to designate an Early Termination Date under the Master Agreement. Because the parties elected to use the First Method approach, Big Bank is not required to make any payment to Shaky Counterparty, either in respect of the $1 million or in respect of the in-the-money value of the swap to Shaky Counterparty at the time of early termination. The enforceability of this aspect of the First Method should be studied in the light of any applicable law or public policy against forfeitures or unconscionable contracts.[676] The Second Method protects the right of the Non-defaulting Party to receive the $1 million (as well as a measure of the swap's value at close out).

THE SHIFT AWAY FROM THE FAULT/NO-FAULT DISTINCTION

The years have seen a shift to the view that the nondefaulting party should not be allowed to reap a windfall from a default and should, therefore, be required to pay over some measure of the gain realized by it as the result of an early termination. Originally known in ISDA terminology as the "Two-Way Payments" "approach to close-out settlement, this view is identified in the 1992 ISDA master agreement forms as the Second Method.[677] Various factors hastened this shift in practice. Some are largely of historical interest today; others involved regulatory action or changes in law that continue to be critical to practice regarding close-out settlement payments.

The early controversy over settlement payments to defaulting parties was, at least in part, fueled by the contrast with market practice in cases involving no-fault close-out.

---

[675] On this period, *see* Section 5(a)(vii) of the sample agreement in Part 3, *infra* p. 837.

[676] A common law rule against forfeitures exists under New York law. *See City of Rye v. Public Service Mutual Ins. Co.*, 315 N.E.2d 458, 459 (N.Y. 1974). *See infra* p. 249 on the related New York law principle applicable to liquidated damages clauses. Under New York law, as in many other legal systems, although the parties generally have freedom of contract, the courts may be permitted to treat as void, or to limit the application of, a contract, or a contract provision, determined by the court, as a matter of law, to have been unconscionable at the time it was made, subject to a party's ability to demonstrate the commercial setting, purpose and effect of the contract or provision. *See, e.g.*, NYUCC § 2–302.

[677] *See* the annotation to Section 6(e) in the sample master agreement in Part 3, *infra* p. 860.

Damages and Close-Out Settlement 231

In those cases, the consistent rule has been to require the party seen as gaining from close-out to share the gain, in whole or in part, with the other party. That is, under both the First Method and the Second Method (and their predecessors in pre-1992 ISDA terminology), if close-out of a transaction is brought about because of a Termination Event, whichever party stands to gain from close-out is required to share that gain with the other party, regardless of which party is affected by the Termination Event.

Market participants also contrasted Limited Two-Way Payments (First Method)—which might allow the nondefaulting party to walk away with a gain—with the willingness of the dealers, frequently avowed to their customers, to "tear up" a derivatives transaction in return for a payment reflecting the transaction's market value at any time.[678] A growing number of people asked: If the value of a transaction could be preserved for a party on Day 1 through negotiated close-out, why does that party get nothing if it defaults on Day 2?

Yet another contrast was noted, between the OTC derivatives market and the market for many exchange-traded derivatives, where member firms are required to settle daily on the basis of the changes in value of the instruments.[679]

The defaulting party's possible loss of an in-the-money transaction, without receiving any compensation, seemed particularly unfair in situations where the defaulting party had fully performed its payment obligations at the outset of the transaction's term by paying a premium or similar amount. As market professionals increasingly began to offer caps, floors and swaptions under the same master agreement forms they were using for swaps, which applied the Limited Two-Way Payments (First Method) approach, well-advised purchasers of these products were extremely reluctant to agree to have that approach apply to these prepaid transactions. As a result, in 1989 and 1990 ISDA published addenda that could be used with its 1987 master agreement forms so that the Limited Two-Way Payments (First Method) approach would not be applied to a party that had paid in full for caps, floors and swaptions so long as it did not have any remaining obligations under other transactions.[680]

In addition, while using the ISDA Limited Two-Way Payments (First Method) approach in their agreements for some OTC derivatives, the same parties were following the equivalent of a Two-Way Payments (Second Method) approach in their agreements for other financial products, and even for other kinds of derivatives. For example, beginning with their earliest published versions, the ICOM and IFEMA forms used for FX forwards and spot transactions and for currency options required the party that stood to benefit from close-out to pay the benefit to the other party in both fault and no-fault situations,

---

[678] The "tear-up" price would be quoted from the professional's side of the bid-asked spread. On this aspect of quantification of a transaction's value, *see infra* p. 246.

[679] *See supra* note 655 and sources cited therein.

[680] There were also other approaches in the market to the handling of these fully paid transactions. For example, the master agreement might provide that all the fully paid transactions should be valued together and that their net value should then be compared with the net value of executory transactions to determine whether any amount would be payable to a Defaulting Party. On this subject and the ISDA Cap Addenda and Option Addenda, *see User's Guide to the ISDA 1992 Master Agreements* 5–7.

and the same was true under the master agreements then most widely used in the repo markets.[681]

Professional market participants focused on these differences more intensely as they became increasingly interested in the benefits that might be derived from being able to net their exposures to loss vis-à-vis a counterparty across transactions and products. This interest in netting finds strong support in the bank supervisory community, because of the healthy impact that netting can have for the financial system at large (the "reduction of systemic risk") and for banks individually. Bank supervisory agencies have been opposed to the Limited Two-Way Payments (First Method) approach because of the negative effects that it can have on financial institutions and, especially, failed financial institutions involved in receivership, conservatorship and similar proceedings.[682] As a result, the use of a walkaway clause can result in a bank's inability to obtain the benefits of netting for purposes of applicable capital adequacy requirements.[683] This is so because the Basel Committee on Banking Supervision has adopted the view that netting arrangements with walkaway clauses introduce an undesirable element of instability and uncertainty into netting arrangements and, therefore, are inconsistent with the level of certainty that should obtain before netting can be given effect in calculating the appropriate level of capital in respect of counterparty credit risk.[684]

---

[681] Since the mid-1980s, the Master Repurchase Agreement widely used in the U.S. market for repos of U.S. government securities has provided that the net value, if any, to a defaulting party of the repo positions closed out early in connection with an event of default would be preserved. This reflects Section 559 of the Bankruptcy Code, under which the contractual right of a "repo participant" to "cause the liquidation of a repurchase agreement" (as defined) in connection with the insolvency of a debtor in a Bankruptcy Code case or related circumstances is linked to a requirement that the debtor's estate be treated as including the net value, if any, to the debtor of the securities underlying the liquidated repo. This approach continues to be reflected in the equivalent provisions of the Master Repurchase Agreement published by TBMA (Paragraph 11 of the September 1996 Version) prepared for use in the now broader U.S. domestic repo market. A similar approach is followed in the Global Master Repurchase Agreement published by TBMA and ISMA (Paragraph 10(b) of the 2000 Version) prepared for use in documenting repos or reverse repos and buy/sell backs of securities other than equities, U.S. Treasury instruments and so-called Net Paying Securities. *See Supplemental Guidance Notes, The Master Repurchase Agreement (1996 Version) and PSA/ISMA Global Master Repurchase Agreement (1995 Version)* § 4 (1997), *available at* http://www.bondmarkets.com/agrees/master_repo_supp_gn.pdf. *See also Guidance Notes for Use with the TBMA/ISMA Global Master Repurchase Agreement (2000 Version)* 14–15 (2000), *available at* http://www.bondmarkets.com/agrees/gmra_guidance_notes.pdf.

[682] *See* Ernest T. Patrikis, *Bank Regulatory Issues Relating to Swaps, in* PLI 1992, at 295, 315, where the author voiced concern over the extent to which the "walkaway" aspect of the Limited Two-Way Payments approach "might materially adversely affect the financial condition of an already weakened bank."

[683] *See supra* p. 13 on bank capital adequacy requirements.

[684] These conclusions were first suggested in an issues paper on netting prepared for the Basel Committee. *See The supervisory treatment of netting under the 1988 Basle Accord on Capital Standards: an issues paper* ¶ 13 (April 21, 1992). As subsequently adopted by the Basel Committee, it was formally included in the Basel Accord through an amendment published as Annex 1 to Basel Committee Publication No. 12, *The Treatment of the Credit Risk Associated with Certain Off-Balance Sheet Items* (July 1994), *available at* www.bis.org/cgi-bin/print.cgi, which states that "[c]ontracts containing walkaway clauses will not be eligible for netting for the purpose of calculating capital requirements pursuant to this Accord. A walkaway clause is a provision which permits a non-defaulting counterparty to make only limited payments, or no payment at all, to the estate of a defaulter, even if the defaulter is a net creditor" (*id.* at 2). The same concept was incorporated into Annex 3 of the Basel Accord through the amendments adopted in April 1995

Damages and Close-Out Settlement 233

Moreover, this approach would not be enforceable under the New York Banking Law in the receivership of a bank conducted pursuant to the rules of that statute, including some state-licensed branches and agencies of banks organized outside the United States.[685] Proposed changes to U.S. law would also render the approach unenforceable against a receiver or conservator for many other major participants in the OTC derivatives market, including the branches and agencies in the U.S. of banks organized abroad.[686]

The Bankruptcy Code does not address walkaway clauses in its special provisions, described in Chapter 7, relating to the close-out of swap agreements—broadly defined to include OTC derivatives generally. In the absence of a special provision in the Bankruptcy Code on the subject, whether a walkaway provision will be enforceable against a debtor in proceedings under that statute will turn on whether the provision is enforceable under applicable law governing the relevant contract. To our knowledge the Limited Two-Way Payments (First Method) approach has not been held unenforceable by any court in the United States applying the law of the State of New York (or, for that matter, the law of any other state).[687]

---

through the report entitled *Treatment of Potential Exposure for Off-Balance Sheet Items* (Basel Committee Publications No. 18). Whether or not this aspect of the Capital Accord will be applicable to a particular financial institution will depend on how local bank supervisory or regulatory authorities have translated the Basel Accord's capital requirements into law or regulation.

The Basel Accord sets additional requirements for the recognition of bilateral netting arrangements for capital adequacy purposes, including satisfaction of the national supervisor that the bank has "(1) a netting contract with the counterparty which creates a single legal obligation, covering all included transactions, such that the bank would have either a claim to receive or obligation to pay only the net sum of the positive and negative mark-to-market values of included individual transactions in the event a counterparty fails to perform due to any of the following: default, bankruptcy, liquidation or similar circumstances; (2) written and reasoned legal opinions that, in the event of a legal challenge, the relevant courts and administrative authorities would find the bank's exposure to be such a net amount" under the laws of various relevant jurisdictions and (3) "procedures in place to ensure that the legal characteristics of netting arrangements are kept under review in the light of possible changes in relevant law." BASEL ACCORD, as amended in Annex 1 to *The Treatment of the Credit Risk Associated with Certain Off-Balance Sheet Items* 1–2.

[685] NYBL § 618–a(2)(b).

[686] On the proposed amendment to the FDIA, *see infra* p. 337. *See also infra* p. 338 on the applicability of the FDIA's rule on the unenforceability of walkaway clauses under proposed changes to the provisions of FDICIA relating to certain netting contracts.

[687] Although there have been numerous defaults under agreements that adopted this approach, several of which involved insolvent entities, there are very few U.S. court decisions on Limited-Two-Way Payments (First Method). One of them is *Drexel Burnham Lambert Products Corp. v. Midland Bank PLC*, 92 Civ. 3098 (MP), which was disposed of by summary judgment. The action arose out of the early termination of a swap in connection with bankruptcy proceedings involving Drexel Burnham Lambert Group, Inc., which had guaranteed the swap obligations of the plaintiff ("Drexel Products"). The defendant ("Midland") invoked the Limited Two-Way Payments clause of the swap agreement and took the position that all payment obligations had automatically terminated as a result of the commencement of those proceedings. Drexel Products sought to recover the alleged value of the swap, arguing that the Limited Two-Way Payments clause was a penalty provision contrary to public policy. The court found the clause to be a valid liquidated damages provision and held that Drexel Products, a sophisticated financial institution, was foreclosed from challenging the validity of a contractual provision negotiated and drafted by its affiliate. (For discussion of the legal principles on liquidated damages provisions, *see infra* p. 249.) Although the defendant

Given the broad market movement away from the Limited Two-Way Payments (First Method) approach, it is now somewhat unusual for a court to be asked to pass on the enforceability of the approach. Even when the approach was more commonly used, there was a paucity of court actions, and a greater paucity of court decisions on the approach. The preference of the solvent parties for reaching negotiated settlements perhaps reflected doubts about whether Limited Two-Way Payments (First Method) would really be enforced as written. The accepted market wisdom, however, was that the clause should nonetheless be used, because the solvent counterparty would probably be able to negotiate a more favorable settlement in these cases if armed with the *in terrorem* effect of the clause. Although, of course, no negotiated settlement can be expected to be as favorable to the solvent party as avoiding all payment obligations in respect of the terminated transactions, the risks and costs of potentially prolonged litigation provide an incentive for that party to settle.

From the point of view of the insolvent party, termination and cash settlement is often attractive, since the *raison d'être* for the derivatives transaction has often disappeared by the point its insolvency proceedings begin, because the characteristics of the assets or liabilities that were hedged with the derivatives have radically changed as a result of the insolvency. The insolvent party or its representative may also be motivated to settle because cashing in (at least partially) on the valuable transactions offers a ready source of funds, whereas an attempt to recover their full value through a court challenge to the Limited Two-Way Payments (First Method) provision can involve significant cost and delay, and the outcome of such challenges may be unpredictable.[688]

---

initially took action to appeal, the parties subsequently settled their dispute. Some of the papers filed in the case and the Court's Findings of Fact and Conclusions of Law are reproduced *in* PLI 1993, at 105–65.

In litigation elsewhere an approach reported to be similar to Limited Two-Way Payments has also withstood legal challenge. *See, e.g., French Swap Case Upholds Termination Clause*, DERIVATIVES WEEK, Apr. 12, 1993, at 3, involving a dispute between Société Econecom Financière and Commerzbank, which involved an agreement prepared using the Association Française de Banque's standard documentation for swaps. According to the report, the relevant walkaway provision was invoked by Commerzbank when Econecom was unable to make a payment due under a currency swap at a time when the swap was in-the-money to Econecom. The court upheld Commerzbank's right to terminate the swap and rejected Econecom's claim for payment of the amount Commerzbank gained by terminating the swap.

More recently, in the *Peregrine* case discussed beginning *infra* p. 263, England's High Court of Justice indicated in *dictum* that the walkaway aspect of the First Method "reflects the position under English law following the repudiation of a contract: accrued liabilities are unaffected and the defaulter must compensate the non-defaulter for the loss of any unperformed obligations but he is not entitled to receive anything himself in respect of the lost bargain." *Peregrine Fixed Income Ltd v. Robinson Department Store Public Company Limited*, [2000] Lloyd's L.R. 309, at ¶23 (Q.B.). *See also* Schuyler K. Henderson, *English Cases Dealing with Settlement Provisions of the ISDA Master Agreement*, 15 BUTTERWORTHS J. INT'L BANK. & FINANCIAL L. 190, 194–96 (Summer 2000), discussing *Nuova Safim SpA v Sakura Bank Ltd.*, a case highlighting the impact of determining whether close-out is based on a fault or no-fault ground for termination when the Limited Two-Payments (First Method) approach applies. The enforceability of that approach was not, however, before the court.

[688]There are numerous reports of out-of-court settlements of disputes in connection with agreements that adopted Limited Two-Way Payments (First Method) or similar approaches. *See, e.g.*, Gooch & Klein, *Review of Case Law I*, at 433–37 (on the settlement in 1992 of *DFC New Zealand v. Security Pacific Australia* and *Atlantic Computer Systems v. Hill Samuel Bank Limited*); *Swappers Win in DC and NZ*, RISK 5 (Oct. 1992) (on the settlement of another of the court actions described in Gooch & Klein, *Review of Case Law I*);

Damages and Close-Out Settlement 235

It can now safely be said that the view that the nondefaulting party should be required to pay over some measure of the gain realized by it as the result of a close-out—the Two-Way Payments (Second Method) approach—reflects market practice. The quantification of the amount to be shared, including in particular the impact of the bid-asked spread on valuation for this purpose, is discussed in the following section.[689]

HOW MUCH MUST BE PAID?

INTRODUCTION TO QUANTIFYING LOSS AND GAIN

Inclusion of Loss of Bargain. In the early days of the market for interest rate and currency swaps, many drafters of the relevant documentation chose to rely on general indemnification provisions in their contracts, mainly to make a clear statement of the parties' intent that loss of bargain should be included as an element of damages. Given the novelty of these financial products at the time, it was generally felt that the contract should expressly provide that, upon early termination, the settlement payment mechanism should take account not only of the payments that had already accrued or fallen due but also the net value to each of the parties of the remaining future payment obligations through the scheduled end of the transaction.

Early drafting approaches thus left it to the party claiming damages to quantify its claim to the satisfaction of the trier of fact, to show why the amount claimed was in fact the amount necessary to put the party in as good a position as it would have been in if the transaction had not been closed out. This came to be reflected in ISDA documentation and terminology as the Loss, or Indemnification, approach. These are the terms that ISDA has used over the years for the general indemnification approach to quantifying a party's loss of bargain (or gain) resulting from the close-out of an OTC derivative. The term "Indemnification" was used in the *Swaps Code*. It was replaced by "Loss" in the master agreement forms published by ISDA in 1987. As slightly modified in ISDA's 1992 forms, Loss is defined to include "any loss of bargain, cost of funding or, at the election of such party but without duplication, loss or cost incurred as a result of its terminating, liquidating, obtaining or reestablishing any hedge or related trading position (or any gain resulting from any of them)."[690] The Loss approach permits, but does not require, a party to determine its Loss "by reference to quotations of relevant rates or prices from one or more leading dealers in the relevant markets." Loss might relate to "this Agreement or one or more Terminated Transactions."

The proposition that loss of bargain is an important element of derivatives close-out settlements is intuitive to people who work in the market and is now generally understood and accepted. The concept is not, however, universally understood today. A recent example that illustrates the sorts of difficulties that can arise in this connection is *First*

Drexel Settles One Of Its Swap-Related Law Suits, SWAPS MONITOR, Jan. 14, 1991, p. 5; Margaret E. Grottenthaler, *Derivatives Litigation in Canada*, in DERIVATIVES HANDBOOK 143, on the settlement, in the context of Canadian insolvency proceedings, of a dispute between Confederation Treasury Services Limited and CCG Equipment Limited.

[689]*See infra* p. 246.

[690]On the differences between the Loss approaches in the 1987 and 1992 ISDA master agreement forms, *see User's Guide to the ISDA 1992 Master Agreements* 25–26.

National Bank of Chicago v. Ackerley Communications, Inc.[691] The parties, a bank and its borrower, entered into a five-year fixed/floating interest rate swap transaction documented on an ISDA 1987 standard form. The transaction included an imbedded swaption—a right of the bank to extend the transaction for two additional years. The bank attempted to exercise this option, but the borrower took the position that notice of exercise had not been properly given and withheld further performance under the agreement. The court found in favor of the borrower on the issue of whether notice had been properly given. The court went on, however, to say, in what appears to be *dictum* but maybe an alternative holding, that the bank had failed to show that it had been damaged by the borrower's failure to perform.

Under the terms of the swap transaction, the borrower was to make payments at a fixed rate of 8.8% per year on a notional amount of $15 million. The bank was to make payments at a floating rate on the same notional amount. For the first calculation period, the floating rate was 9.4375% per year, so the first net payment was due from the bank to the borrower. Over time, however, interest rates in the market fell, so the transaction took on value to the bank, and successive net payments were due from the borrower to the bank. It appears that the agreement was in-the-money to the bank at the time of its attempted exercise of the option to extend the swap. The court nonetheless found that the bank had failed to show that it had suffered any damages as a result of the borrower's cessation of performance. The court characterized the bank's case as "purely theoretical," saying that the claim of loss failed because the bank did not "point to any countervailing swaps to the one in question . . . ." Since there appeared to be no such swaps, the court said, "[t]he bank had assumed all the risk and, of course, in assuming all the risk the bank took all the profit." There is some suggestion in the opinion that the bank might have fared better on this issue if it had described its claim as one for "loss of profits" rather than one for "damages."

Several features of ISDA's Loss definition should be noted in comparing this general indemnification approach with other approaches to quantifying close-out settlement and in considering the enforceability of the Loss approach under the applicable legal principles[692]:

- Loss can be computed for one transaction in isolation or for a portfolio of transactions.

- The definition of Loss permits the party making the determination to include its expected profit in the calculation.

- It is somewhat unclear whether the definition takes into account the credit standing of the parties. One fair reading could be that the credit standing of both of the parties would be taken into account.[693] For ex-

---

[691]No. 94 Civ. 7539 (KTD), 2001 WL 15693 (S.D.N.Y. Jan. 8, 2001).

[692]Loss and the other ISDA approaches to the quantification of a close-out settlement discussed below assume that, where necessary, the settlement amount as calculated will be translated to a single Termination Currency, so that settlement in respect of all transactions being closed out can be effected on a net basis. *See* Section 6(e) and related annotations in the sample master agreement in Part 3, *infra* p. 860.

[693]*But see*, as to Loss and the credit standing of the parties, the discussion of the *Peregrine* case, *infra* p. 264.

ample, if the party making the determination was an inferior credit, it could take its own standing into account in figuring out what a replacement transaction would be worth to it. If, however, the counterparty was also an inferior credit, arguably that fact should be taken into account in the same way, which would tend to diminish the value of the transaction or portfolio being replaced.

- The definition allows the party making the determination to take into account its losses or gains on other transactions, with entities other than the counterparty, that were designed to hedge, or were "related to" the transaction or portfolio being valued. This suggests that, if the party making the valuation would have paid out more on its hedge over the remaining life of the transaction than it would have received on the transaction, it is entitled to recover an amount that would make it entirely whole, without regard to the combined prospective loss on the transaction being valued and the hedge combined.

- The definition allows the party making the determination to include its "cost of funding."[694]

The following examples illustrate various ways in which looking to gain or loss on other transactions may affect the determination of Loss.

Example 1. Dealer Inc. and Counterparty A enter into a fixed-floating swap (Swap A) under an ISDA-based master agreement providing for Loss as the measure of damages, with Dealer paying 3-month LIBOR on a Notional Amount of $100 million and Counterparty A paying a fixed rate of 3% on the same amount. Dealer turns around and hedges the transaction by entering into a fixed-floating swap (Swap B) with Counterparty B with Dealer paying a fixed rate of 2.9% on a Notional Amount of $100 million and Counterparty B paying 3-month LIBOR on the same amount. An Event of Default occurs with respect to Counterparty A. The relevant market rates have fallen since the transaction was entered into, with the result that Swap A is in-the-money to Dealer to the extent of $1,000,000 (in the sense that this is the amount dealers furnishing quotations would charge Dealer to do a deal with it at the time of valuation that had the same economic characteristics as the remaining obligations under Swap A). Dealer negotiates a termination of Swap B, which is out-of-the-money to Dealer to the ex-

---

[694]It may seem strange to refer to "cost of funding" in the context of a derivatives transaction, which (unlike a loan, for example) is not usually "funded." The possible effects of this reference can be examined in the context of Example 2 in the text. Suppose that Counterparty B in the example was unwilling to agree to terminate Swap B and there was no opportunity in the market for Dealer Inc. to neutralize Swap B by entering into a new transaction. Dealer might obtain funds to pay Counterparty A by borrowing the necessary amount in the loan market. In that case, Dealer could take into account the cost of the borrowing in determining how much it would have to pay. The *Peregrine* case discussed *infra* p. 263 might have been decided differently if the court had taken cost of funding into account. The definition of Loss does not explicitly state that this cost should be taken into account without duplication of any cost already taken into account in some other way. A court called upon to interpret this aspect of the Loss definition might well read the "without duplication" concept into the definition. The recently developed ISDA Replacement Value approach expressly indicates that duplication is to be avoided in taking into account the various possible components of loss, costs and expenses contemplated in the definition. *See infra* p. 974.

tent of $975,000, and pays that amount to Counterparty B. Counterparty A must pay $1,000,000 to Dealer, so Dealer nets $25,000, its remaining profit on the combination of Swap A and Swap B.

Example 2. Same as Example 1, except that the relevant market rates have risen at the time of the Event of Default, so Swap A is out-of-the-money to Dealer to the extent of $975,000. Dealer negotiates a termination of Swap B, which is in-the-money to Dealer to the extent of $1,000,000, and receives that amount from Counterparty B.[695] Dealer must pay $975,000 to Counterparty A, so Dealer nets $25,000, its remaining profit on the combination of Swap A and Swap B.

Example 3. Dealer Inc. and Counterparty A enter into a fixed-floating swap (Swap A) under an ISDA-based master (providing for Loss as the measure of damages), with Dealer paying 3-month LIBOR on a Notional Amount of $100 million and Counterparty A paying a fixed rate of 3% on the same amount. Dealer fails to enter into a timely hedge, the market moves against it, and it hedges against further loss by entering into a fixed-floating swap (Swap B) under an ISDA-based master agreement with Counterparty B, with Dealer paying a fixed rate of 3.1% on a Notional Amount of $100 million and Counterparty B paying 3-month LIBOR on the same amount. Rates continue to rise. An Event of Default occurs with respect to Counterparty A. At the time of termination, Swap A is out-of-the-money to Dealer to the extent of $975,000. Dealer negotiates a termination of Swap B, which is in-the-money to Dealer to the extent of $950,000, and receives a payment of that amount from Counterparty B. Dealer must pay only $950,000 to Counterparty A, because (assuming the ISDA clause is given effect as it is written) Dealer may reduce what it pays out on Swap A so that it does not exceed what it receives on Swap B. Dealer's anticipated loss on the remainder of the transaction—produced by its own failure to hedge wisely—is eliminated.

Example 4. Same as Example 3, except that the relevant market rates have fallen at the time of the Event of Default, so Swap A is in-the-money to Dealer to the extent of $1,000,000. Dealer negotiates a termination of Swap B, which is out-of-the-money to Dealer to the extent of $1,025,000, and pays that amount to Counterparty B. Counterparty A must pay $1,025,000 to Dealer, because Dealer may increase its claim to reflect the full amount it had to pay out on the untimely hedge. Here again (on the same assumption), Dealer's anticipated loss on the remainder of the transaction is eliminated.

---

[695] One may ask why Counterparty B would agree to the termination, since the result is that it has to make a payment to Dealer Inc. In practice, the willingness of a party in this position to agree to a negotiated settlement may depend in large measure on the party's motivation for entering into the transaction in the first place. For example, a counterparty that is another dealer may be quite willing to terminate if it can turn around and remove or neutralize its own hedge and thus accelerate its remaining profit on the transaction. On the other hand, an end-user counterparty that had entered into Swap B to hedge a particular risk may not be willing to negotiate a termination. If Dealer cannot negotiate a termination of its hedge, it may be able to neutralize it by entering into a new off-market transaction, in which case the ISDA Loss definition would permit it to take into account how much it realized on the new transaction, as compared with what it had to pay out on Swap A.

Liquidated Damages. Other drafters of interest and currency swap documentation, who were uneasy about leaving a question as complicated as valuing swap damages to a trier of fact,[696] sought to bring greater certainty to the question by including in their agreements elaborate liquidated damages provisions. The best example is the ISDA Formula approach.

As offered in the *Swaps Code* (but not later ISDA standard forms), Formula contemplated a mathematical approach to quantifying the relevant party's loss of bargain, or gain. It did this by comparing the discounted present value of the scheduled post-termination fixed-rate payments in the swap with the discounted present value of the payment streams on hypothetical alternative borrowings and investments (subject to adjustment for the portion of the first post-termination payment described above that had already accrued). Formula is a method for valuing individual transactions, and the issue of whether a portfolio of transactions may have a value different from the sum of its parts does not arise under this method.

The operation of ISDA's Formula approach may be briefly summarized as follows, in the context of a simple fixed/floating interest rate swap (using defined terms from the *Swaps Code*):

- On early termination, a Formula Settlement Amount is calculated for each party, and the difference between the two amounts is the amount to be paid by the appropriate party if a payment is to be made.

- Each party's Formula Settlement Amount consists of the sum of its Current Calculation Period Adjustment and its Cost of Termination.

- The Current Calculation Period Adjustment is an element designed to avoid having to estimate of damages for the portion of the current Calculation Period that has already elapsed on the Early Termination Date.

- The Cost of Termination element of the formula in an estimate of damages for the unelapsed portion of the current Calculation Period and all subsequent scheduled Calculation Periods. It is calculated with reference to (i) the present value of the Fixed Rate Payor's remaining scheduled payments (to the extent not covered by the Current Calculation Period Adjustment) and (ii) the present value of streams of payments on hypothetical alternative borrowings and investments.

- The hypothetical replacement for the payment obligations of the Fixed Rate Payor is a series of interest payments it would be obligated to make on a fixed rate borrowing in an amount equal to the swap No-

---

[696] This same uneasiness has led some market participants to include in their master agreements a waiver of the right to a jury trial in respect of any dispute between the parties relating to the agreement. *See infra* p. 945. *See also User's Guide to the ISDA 1992 Master Agreements* 34 n.34. For discussion of derivatives cases in which there were jury trials, *see, e.g., supra* notes 567, 589 & 603. For cases in which a court acted as the finder of fact in derivatives cases, *see, e.g., supra* p. 235 & *infra* p. 265. The use of arbitration provisions in agreements relating to derivative transactions has been very limited to date, but it seems likely that in the future there will be increased reliance on arbitration to value derivatives transactions, particularly the more esoteric ones, in the event of early termination.

tional Amount with a term beginning on the Early Termination Date and ending on the originally scheduled Termination Date of the swap. The Fixed Rate Payor's loss of bargain (if any) is calculated by comparing the present value of this interest payment stream at the Early Termination Date with the present value at the same date of the Fixed Amounts that it would have had to make but for the termination. The present values are to be computed by discounting the payments at a rate equal to the rate for U.S. Treasury securities with a maturity equal to the remaining life of the transaction.[697]

- The hypothetical replacement for the post-termination obligations of a Floating Rate Payor is a stream of interest payments it would receive on an investment in U.S. government securities in an amount equal to the Notional Amount made by it on the Early Termination Date and scheduled to mature on the swap Termination Date. The substitute stream is discounted to its present value at the Early Termination Date. The Floating Rate Payor's loss of bargain (if any) is calculated by comparing the present value of this interest payment stream at the Early Termination Date with the present value at the same date of the post-termination Fixed Amounts that it would have received but for the termination.

This *Swaps Code* approach to Formula permits certain fine tuning through the use of spreads above and below certain of these substitute borrowing and investment rates, to take account of disparities in the relative creditworthiness of the parties to a transaction and the nature of the fault or no-fault ground for early termination.

As we have written elsewhere,[698] the Formula approach and other early attempts to liquidate damages in connection with early termination of swaps were at best flawed as tools for estimating loss of bargain and at worst could have operated to produce results that would subject the formula to challenge as a penalty under the legal principles relating to liquidated damages that are discussed in more detail below.[699] As a result, market participants have largely abandoned these approaches in favor of general indemnification clauses or of various alternatives that call for quantifying damages by reference to what the market would charge or pay to enter into replacement transactions, as discussed in the following subsection.

Market-Based Valuation. As liquidity in the swaps market increased, many drafters turned towards a newly introduced market-based approach, which was intended to permit a party to calculate loss of bargain, or gain, using a theoretical cost of "cover" in

---

[697] The *Swaps Code* set forth detailed rules for making the calculation, including provisions for interpolating between the rates on two Treasury securities, one maturing before and one maturing after the scheduled end date of the transaction.

[698] *See* Gooch & Klein, *Damages provisions in swap agreements*, 3 INT'L FIN. L. REV. 36, 38–39 (Oct. 1984), for analysis of these issues and examples of circumstances in which the Formula approach and earlier attempts at liquidating damages in connection with swaps could produce strikingly unequal amounts as the respective loss and gain of the two parties to a transaction.

[699] *See infra* p. 249.

Damages and Close-Out Settlement 241

the market—through an agreed mechanism for measuring the cost of a replacement transaction.[700] As discussed below, there is some uncertainty as to whether these clauses are properly viewed as liquidated damages provisions or (as we believe) as agreed methods for quantifying actual damages.[701]

This new approach came to be reflected in ISDA documentation and terminology as the Agreement Value and Market Quotation approaches.

"Agreement Value" was the term used in the *Swaps Code*. It was replaced by the term "Market Quotation" in ISDA's 1987 master agreement forms. Both approaches measure a party's loss of bargain (or gain) from close-out of a transaction or portfolio of transactions by looking at an average of firm quotations obtained by the Determining Party[702] from Reference Market-makers, for what they would pay (or charge) to enter into a Replacement Transaction (or portfolio of Replacement Transactions) with the Determining Party that would "have the effect of preserving for such party the economic equivalent" of the payments and deliveries that are scheduled to have due dates after the Early Termination Date.[703]

Under this approach, in the simplest example, the provider of the quotation would be giving a price for agreeing to undertake payment or delivery obligations identical to those that the Determining Party had bargained for in the Terminated Transaction, to the extent they are not scheduled to be determined or due until after the Early Termination Date.[704] Each of the ISDA formulations of this approach over the years has called for discarding the high and low quotations if three or more quotations are obtained, for using the remaining quotation if exactly three are obtained, for averaging the remaining quotations if more than three are obtained, and for falling back to Loss if fewer than three are obtained.

The *Swaps Code* and ISDA's 1987 forms contemplated that market quotations would be obtained separately for each Terminated Transaction. An innovation in the 1992 forms permitted the Determining Party to obtain quotations for "one or more Terminated Transactions," and the *User's Guide to the 1992 ISDA Master Agreements* makes clear that the intention was that "a quotation may now be obtained for an entire portfolio of

---

[700] *See* Gooch & Klein, *supra* note 698.

[701] *Infra* p. 250.

[702] The newer ISDA Replacement Value approach refers to the party making the determination as the "Determining Party"—a term that we will use in the following discussion in connection with Market Quotation and Loss as well, even though it is not part of the earlier ISDA terminology. On the effects of looking at the transaction from the perspective of one party or the other, *see infra* p. 246.

[703] The 1992 ISDA master agreement forms are slightly different from their ISDA predecessors in that they expressly provide that the party determining Market Quotation may seek quotations on a Transaction-by-Transaction basis, for all the Transactions as a whole or for smaller groups of Transactions. *See* the definition of "Market Quotation" in Section 14 of the sample master agreement included in Part 3, *infra* p. 888. The Reference Market-maker is to be asked to give its quotation "taking into account any existing Credit Support Document" for the obligations of the Determining Party. *Id.*

[704] *See* the annotations to the definitions of "Reference Market-maker" and "Market Quotation" and to Section 6(e) of the sample master agreement in Part 3, *infra* pp. 888, 891 & 860, for further discussion of how the mechanism works. In the EMA form (Section 7(1) of the General Provisions), a similar approach is used for the calculation of a "Transaction Value" for any transaction or group of transactions.

Terminated Transactions, a group of Terminated Transactions or one Terminated Transaction."[705] The flexibility afforded by this innovation was presumably designed to make it possible for the Determining Party to obtain quotations in circumstances where it would be difficult or commercially undesirable to value the Terminated Transactions one by one. In availing themselves of this flexibility, Determining Parties should be aware of the limitations that may apply under the principle of minimization of damages discussed below.[706]

Each of these ISDA approaches has defined the possible candidates for Reference Market-makers as "dealers of the highest credit standing which satisfy all the criteria that . . . [the Determining Party] applies generally at the time in deciding whether to offer or to make an extension of credit."[707]

These approaches seem to have these characteristics in common with Loss:

- They permit the party making the determination to include its expected profit in the calculation.

- The approaches appear to take into account the credit standing of the Determining Party.

Agreement Value and Market Quotation appear to differ from Loss in the following ways (in addition to the basic difference in the approach to valuation):

- The credit standing of the party other than the Determining Party is not taken into account—the Determining Party is expressly permitted to include in damages any cost associated with upgrading the credit of its counterparty to that of a dealer of the highest credit standing.

- These approaches do not take into account any "cost of funding."

- These approaches do not allow the Determining Party to consider its losses or gains on other transactions, with entities other than the counterparty, that were designed to hedge, or were "related to," the transaction or portfolio being valued.[708]

In ISDA's 1987 forms, Market Quotation was the quantification method to be used, with Loss being used as a fallback for determining loss of bargain in cases where it could not be valued through Market Quotation. The 1992 forms represented something of a retreat from the assumption that a single approach would suit in all cases. They introduced the idea that the parties would pick a "Payment Measure" for their master agreement (subject to departures for individual transactions), and that the Payment Measure might be either Loss or Market Quotation. If the parties' agreement on a Payment Meas-

---

[705] At 24.

[706] See infra p. 258.

[707] Under the 1992 ISDA master agreement forms, the Determining Party is directed, to the extent practicable, to choose Reference Market-makers that have offices in the same city.

[708] The differences between the Market Quotation and Loss Payment Measures as embodied in the 1987 and 1992 ISDA forms are summarized in the *User's Guide to the ISDA 1992 Master Agreements* 24–28 and discussed in the annotations to the sample agreement in Part 3, *infra* pp. 810, 888 & 890.

ure is silent, under the 1992 forms, the parties will be deemed to have agreed that Market Quotation will apply. As in the 1987 forms, if the parties to an agreement based on a 1992 ISDA form chose, or are deemed to have chosen, Market Quotation but the Market Quotation cannot be determined for a Transaction, Loss will be applied as the Payment Measure. Under both sets of master agreements a determination of Market Quotation for a Transaction will be treated as impossible if the party seeking to make the determination is unable to obtain at least three qualifying quotations for a Replacement Transaction, as described below.[709] In addition, under a feature added to ISDA's master agreement forms in 1992, even if Market Quotation for a Transaction has been determined pursuant to the parties' choice or deemed choice, if the Market Quotation "would not (in the reasonable belief of the party making the determination) produce a commercially reasonable result," Loss will be applied.[710]

ISDA's shift away from the emphasis on market quotations as the basic method for quantifying damages was explained in the *User's Guide* in terms of the existence in the market of products for which it may be impossible to obtain Market Quotations. Cited as examples are "products in a thinly-traded market or products for which quotations are given on a future value basis" and products for which Loss may be a more appropriate measure of damages, such as "Transactions that settle by physical delivery."[711]

Replacement Value. More recently, ISDA has supported the development of a new single formulation for quantifying damages, the "Replacement Value" approach.[712] Under the Replacement Value approach, Market Quotation and Loss are supplanted by a single concept of Replacement Value, and the parties' master agreement ceases to contemplate any choice of Payment Measures for purposes of the close-out settlement payment calculation. The new provision is framed as a general indemnification clause and permits a party to calculate loss of bargain, or gain, on the basis of quotations for actual cover in the market, but it also authorizes the use of indicative quotations for hypothetical cover and model-based calculations of loss of bargain, or gain. The following is a summary of the ways in which Replacement Value differs from Loss and Market Quotation:

- Like Loss but unlike Market Quotation, Replacement Value permits the use of third-party quotations for replacement transactions but does not specify how many quotations should be sought or how they should

---

[709] *See infra* p. 250. As indicated earlier, the 1992 ISDA master agreement forms expressly permit a party to seek to determine Market Quotation for a single Transaction, a group of Transactions or all Transactions that are subject to close-out at the time. There is no rule, however, about whether a party would, say, be entitled to fall back to Loss in relation to a Transaction if it initially sought unsuccessfully to determine Market Quotation for a group of Transactions including that particular Transaction but did not, when unsuccessful with that approach, seek to determine Market Quotation separately for that Transaction. Of course, if the Market Quotation and Loss approaches always produced the same, or quite similar, results, this theoretical question would be moot. On issues relating to the potentially different results that can be reached under the two Payment Measures, *see infra* p. 263.

[710] The quoted language is included in clause (b) of the definition of "Settlement Amount." *See infra* p. 893. The inclusion of this language gives added force to the view that the Market Quotation methodology is not a liquidated damages provision. *See infra* p. 250.

[711] *User's Guide to the ISDA 1992 Master Agreements* 23.

[712] The "Replacement Value" approach is embodied in Attachment 8 to the *2001 ISDA Amendments*, *infra* p. 974.

be used, nor does it seek to identify in any way the characteristics that the providers of quotations should have.

- Replacement Value substantially broadens the types of information that a Determining Party, or its agent, may use in calculating loss of bargain or gain to include indicative (and not just firm) quotations as well as information generated internally by the Determining Party or its agent or by third parties, and this information may be historical.[713]

- Replacement Value permits the application of pricing or other valuation models to this information.

- Replacement Value expressly authorizes the Determining Party or its agent to take into account, or to require third parties supplying information to take into account, "the current creditworthiness and documentation and other credit policies of the Determining Party, the size of the Terminated Transaction or Terminated Transactions, market liquidity and other factors relevant under then prevailing circumstances"—matters many assumed would be taken into account under Loss and Market Quotation but which are expressly addressed in light of restrictive court readings of these approaches.[714]

FX Transactions and Currency Options. Even though the ISDA approaches described above can be used with transactions documented using ISDA forms regardless of the nature of the transactions, other approaches to the quantification of damages for loss of bargain (or gain) have continuously been in wide use in the market for currency options and FX forwards (as well as spot FX transactions). The following summarizes these approaches—which we view as agreed methods for determining actual damages[715]— as they apply in the event of close-out on the grounds of an event of default under the FEOMA form published in 1997. The same approaches are taken in the 1997 versions of the ICOM form, for currency options, and the IFEMA form, for FX forwards and spot transactions.[716]

---

[713]Although the Determining Party or its agent is to seek to determine Replacement Values for all Terminated Transactions as of the Early Termination Date, if it "would not be commercially reasonable" for it to do so, the Determining Party or its agent may determine Replacement Values either "as of the latest date or dates before or the earliest date or dates after the Early Termination Date." The first of these possibilities is new and would permit the use of historical data.

[714]*See infra* p. 265. The Loss approach does not list any of these factors. Market Quotation specifies only that the quotation for a Replacement Transaction sought from each Reference Market-maker should be given "taking into account any existing Credit Support Document" with respect to the obligations of the party seeking the quotation. These credit-related factors are, however, to be disregarded in a close-out settlement in connection with Illegality or a Force Majeure Event under a new ISDA approach to these events. *See infra* p. 984.

[715]*See infra* p. 250 for a discussion of the difference between liquidated damages provisions and agreements as to procedures for quantifying actual damages and for the reasons why the distinction matters.

[716]*See infra* note 724 for discussion of some of the ways in which the approaches taken in the earlier editions of the ICOM and IFEMA forms were modified to produce the 1997 variants described above.

Under agreements prepared using the FEOMA form, the nondefaulting party is entitled, to the extent permitted by applicable law, to close out foreign exchange transactions and currency options that are covered by the agreement and to include settlement amounts calculated for those transactions in the net settlement.[717] If both currency options and FX forwards or spot transactions are included in the close-out, the amounts separately calculated as described below for these products are netted to produce a single settlement obligation, after translation, if necessary, to the Base Currency of the nondefaulting party.[718]

In the FEOMA form, "Currency Obligation" is the term used for any obligation of a party under an FX Transaction, a concept that includes any transaction between two parties for the purchase by one party of an agreed amount in one currency against the sale by it to the other of an agreed amount in another currency. If FX Transactions are closed out on a Close-Out Date that precedes the Value Date on which a Currency Obligation thereunder was scheduled to be due, the nondefaulting party is required to calculate, as of the "Close-Out Date or as soon thereafter as reasonably practicable," a Close-Out Amount for each of the Currency Obligations represented by those transactions and for each of the Currency Obligations represented by the FX Transactions with Value Dates that coincide with or precede the Close-Out Date.[719] In each case, the Close-Out Amount is the equivalent in the Base Currency of the nondefaulting party of the Currency Obligation increased (in the case of Currency Obligations with Value Dates preceding the Close-Out Date) by interest at overnight LIBOR in the relevant currency from and including the relevant Value Date to but excluding the Close-Out Date.

The nondefaulting party determines its net loss of bargain, called the "Closing Loss," or gain, called the "Closing Gain," on all these Currency Obligations by comparing the sum of the Close-Out Amounts that would have been payable by and to it but for the close-out, after discounting to their respective present values on the Close-Out Date the Close-Out Amounts for all Currency Obligations with Value Dates scheduled to occur after the Close-Out Date. The discounting is to be done, to the extent permitted by applicable law, at LIBOR for the injured party's Base Currency, or "at such other rate as may be prescribed by applicable law."[720]

---

[717]*See* Section 8.3 of the FEOMA form.

[718]This Base Currency, like the Termination Currency under the ISDA approaches, is specified by the parties in schedules to their agreements, although, as discussed *infra* p. 1341, some market participants reserve the right, as nondefaulting parties, to select the relevant currency at the time of close-out. Translation to the Base Currency for the various purposes described below is done at the "Spot Price" at which the nondefaulting party, at the time of the determination, could enter into a contract in the foreign exchange market to buy the nondefaulting party's Base Currency in exchange for the other relevant currency. If such a Spot Price is not available, the nondefaulting party is entitled to effect the translation using any commercially reasonable method. Although the form uses the term "conversion," we use the term "translation" because an actual conversion is not required. The ISDA forms do not include this kind of detail on translation to the Termination Currency.

[719]This statement is a simplification of the actual procedure.

[720]For this purpose, "LIBOR" is determined by the injured party at the time, by reference to "the average rate at which deposits in the Currency for the relevant amount and time period are offered by major banks in the London interbank as of 11:00 a.m. (London time) on such date, or, if major banks do not offer deposits in such Currency in the London interbank market on such date, the average rate at which deposits in

Under the FEOMA form, if currency options are being closed out,[721] the nondefaulting party determines a "settlement amount" (which is not a defined term) for them. If the options are unexercised, the basic component of this settlement amount is the current market premium, in the case of an option purchased by that party, or the unpaid premium, in the case of an option sold by that party. This amount is discounted to present value from the scheduled Premium Payment Date to the Close-Out Date if the premium is not yet due at the time of close-out, and increased by interest from and including the Premium Payment Date to but excluding the Close-Out Date if the premium is overdue. The prescribed discount rate is LIBOR for the relevant currency and period, and the prescribed interest rate is overnight LIBOR in the relevant currency. If the options have been exercised and are to be settled at their In-the-Money Amounts under the agreement's normally applicable provisions on option settlement,[722] the applicable In-the-Money Amount is the basic component of the close-out settlement amount. If the due date for that settlement has passed, it is increased by interest from and including the due date and to but excluding the Close-Out Date, at overnight LIBOR in the relevant currency. To these amounts, the non-defaulting party is permitted to add, without duplication, "its additional losses, costs and expenses" in connection with the terminated option, "for the loss of its bargain, its cost of funding, or the loss incurred as a result of terminating, liquidating, obtaining or reestablishing a delta hedge or related trading position" with respect to the option.

Many market participants now combine use of (1) a market-based approach for products with liquid markets, (2) a general indemnification approach for new or highly tailored products and (3) the product-specific approaches described above for FX forwards and currency options. Parties who adopt this composite approach seek to preserve the benefits of the precision and relative simplicity of product-specific approaches in forms like the FEOMA form while also gaining the advantage of certainty provided by Market Quotation, for cases in which they are confident that quotations will be forthcoming and reflective of market conditions, and reserving the right to calculate their loss or gain otherwise, in connection with products for which the market is illiquid.

THE FAULT/NO-FAULT DISTINCTION AS APPLIED TO QUANTIFICATION

Under the 1987 and 1992 ISDA master agreement forms, a fault/no-fault distinction exists in the quantification area. If early termination follows from an Event of Default, the Settlement Amount determination is calculated from the perspective of (and made by) the Non-defaulting Party. If it follows from a "Termination Event" affecting only one party (the "Affected Party"), the amount to be paid is calculated from the perspective of the other party (the "Non-Affected Party"). If early termination follows from a Termination Event involving two Affected Parties, each of the parties makes its own Set-

---

the Currency for the relevant amount and time period are offered by major banks in the relevant foreign exchange market at such time on such date as may be determined by the Party making the determination."

[721] *See infra* p. 946 for discussion of the right of a seller of a currency option to treat it as void, under Section 3.2(ii) of the FEOMA form, if the buyer has failed to pay the premium, and to exclude these voided options from the close-out settlement calculation.

[722] *See infra* p. 528 for discussion of "In-the-Money Amounts" under the FEOMA and ICOM forms.

Damages and Close-Out Settlement 247

tlement Amount determination and the close-out settlement payment is the average[723] of the absolute values of the two.[724]

ISDA has recently developed an alternative approach to the calculations prescribed by Section 6(e) as they apply to close-out on the grounds of Illegality and Force Majeure Events.[725] Under this approach, if early termination occurs because of Illegality or a Force Majeure Event, the close-out settlement payment for the Terminated Transactions will always be calculated at the middle of the market, even if there is only one Affected Party.[726]

In the net close-out settlement process, positive Loss, Market Quotation or Replacement Value numbers reflect Terminated Transactions that, at the time and as valued in the agreed manner, are in-the-money to the party making the determination, and negative Loss, Market Quotation or Replacement Value numbers will reflect Terminated Transactions that are out-of-the-money to that party.[727]

Leaving aside the new ISDA approach described above for cases involving Illegality or Force Majeure, the mechanics of the 1987/1992 ISDA close-out calculations upon termination because of the occurrence of a Termination Event are illustrated by the following examples:

---

[723] In the ISDA forms, this is conceptualized as half the difference between the two amounts. If, for example, the amounts were -100 and +90, half the difference would be 95. *See User's Guide to the ISDA 1992 Master Agreements* 28.

[724] The FEOMA, ICOM and IFEMA forms, as modified to incorporate amendments published in December 1999, provide for similar results. The amendments are available at http://www.ny.frb.org/fxc/fmagagree.pdf. Under the 1997 versions of those forms, however, the result would be different if close-out occurred in connection with force majeure, act of state, illegality or impossibility and both parties were affected by the circumstances. In those cases, under the 1997 form provisions, the party that gives the close-out notice is the party entitled to make the close-out settlement calculation. These forms state close-out calculation mechanisms as if the calculations were always to be made by a nondefaulting party. Therefore, the operative provisions on close-out in connection with these no-fault events provide that the party making the calculation will do so "as if it were the Non-Defaulting Party." *See* Section 9.1 of the sample FEOMA form.

[725] The new ISDA Illegality and Force Majeure approach is embodied in Attachment 9 to the *2001 ISDA Amendments, infra* p. 976.

[726] In addition, under this approach, the Reference Market-makers are to be asked to provide their midmarket quotations for Replacement Transactions assuming that the party requesting the quotations "is a dealer in the relevant market of the highest credit standing which satisfies all the credit criteria which such Reference Market-makers apply generally at the time in deciding whether to offer to make an extension of credit, and no account will be taken of any existing Credit Support Document." *Id.*, Paragraph (m). These new assumptions are aimed at eliciting quotations that will reflect the theoretical market value of a hypothetical Replacement Transaction, stripping away credit considerations and the special factors that would probably affect the quotations a Reference Market-maker would supply to an Affected Party in an Illegality or Force Majeure Event.

[727] Under the approaches to close-out settlement in the FEOMA, ICOM and IFEMA, the terms "Closing Gain" and "Closing Loss" are used to refer to the unadjusted liquidation values calculated for closed out "Currency Obligations" arising from FX spot and forward transactions, or from the result of netting these obligations, and the undefined term "settlement amount" is used to refer to the unadjusted positive or negative liquidation value of each closed out currency option. *See infra* p. 951 for a sample provision modeled on that approach.

Example 1. A Termination Event (say, the imposition of a new withholding tax) occurs under an ISDA-based master agreement between Dealer Inc. and South American Oil Co., which affects only the latter. There is only one Affected Transaction outstanding under the agreement, which is a fixed-floating swap with South American (the Affected Party) paying a fixed rate of 3.25% on a Notional Amount of $100 million and Dealer paying 3-month LIBOR on the same amount. The relevant market rates have fallen since the transaction was entered into, with the result that it is in-the-money to Dealer to the extent of $1,000,000 (in the sense that dealers furnishing quotations would, at the time of valuation, charge Dealer this amount to do a deal with it that would have the same economic characteristics as the remaining obligations under the swap being valued). The same transaction, viewed from the perspective of South American, might be a liability of only $925,000, because that is the amount dealers furnishing quotations would pay South American to do a deal with it having the same characteristics. The close-out payment would be $1,000,000, to be paid by South American to Dealer.[728] Economically, the provisions have operated to preserve for Dealer (and accelerate) the profit it would have made if the deal had proceeded as scheduled.

Example 2. Same as Example 1, except that the relevant rates have gone up between the time the transaction was entered into and the time of early termination. In this case, the Affected Transaction would be out-of-the-money to Dealer, in the sense that dealers furnishing quotations would pay Dealer to do a deal with it having the same characteristics. Viewed from the perspective of South American, the same Transaction would be an asset because dealers furnishing quotations would charge South American to do a deal with the same characteristics. If the dollar values were $975,000 (a liability) to Dealer and $1,050,000 (an asset) to South American, the close-out payment would be $975,000, this time to be paid to South American. As in Example 1, the economics operate to preserve for Dealer the profit it would have made if the deal had proceeded as scheduled.

Example 3. Same as Example 1, except that both parties are Affected Parties (say, because of the expiration of a favorable tax treaty between the parties' countries). The dollar values based on replacement cost quotations are $1,000,000 (an asset) to Dealer and $925,000 (a liability) to South American. The calculation mechanics where there are two Affected Parties are designed to find the termination value of the Affected Transaction at the middle of the market, splitting the value of the bid-asked spread between the parties. The close-out payment would be $962,500, to be paid to Dealer. Here, unlike Examples 1 and 2, Dealer receives only approximately half the profit it would have made if the deal had proceeded as scheduled.

---

[728] These approaches are described, with examples, in the *User's Guide to the ISDA 1992 Master Agreements* 26–28.

OVERVIEW OF LEGAL PRINCIPLES AFFECTING QUANTIFICATION OF DAMAGES

As discussed above, derivatives documentation (1) sometimes merely restates contract law by providing that the nondefaulting party will be entitled to damages including its loss of the benefit of the bargain, (2) sometimes seeks to remove the need for the injured party to prove actual damages by providing for liquidated damages and (3) sometimes seeks to provide for actual damages but add to that basic statement some guidance for the finder of fact as to how damages should be quantified.

From the point of view of enforceability, a question of great importance not only for the parties but also for any lawyer called upon to issue an enforceability opinion on the documentation, it is very important to be precise as to which of the three kinds of clause is involved.[729]

LEGAL PRINCIPLES ON LIQUIDATED DAMAGES

Under New York law, the parties to a contract may provide for liquidated damages, if (1) at the time the parties enter into their contract, the actual amount of damages that would be caused by breach is impossible or difficult to determine precisely and (2) the liquidated amount bears a reasonable proportion to the probable loss, in light of circumstances existing at the time the contract is signed. Enforceability turns on whether the provision agreed to by the parties was truly designed to liquidate damages, that is, to produce an estimate of damages that would compensate for probable loss in the event of future default, or whether, instead, the provision was designed to penalize and, through its *in terrorem* effect, induce performance or discourage default.[730]

If the amount stipulated by the parties to be recoverable as liquidated damages, or the formula to be used by them to liquidate damages, produces a result that bears no ascertainable relationship to that probable loss or is plainly or grossly disproportionate to it,

---

[729] The following discussion draws on principles of New York state contract law generally. Article 2 of the NYUCC has its own provisions on damages relating to breach and anticipatory repudiation for cases involving contracts for the sale of goods. *See infra* note 743. Some provisions of Article 2 of the NYUCC have in the past been found to apply to OTC derivatives on foreign currency. *See supra* p. 56.

[730] In fact, the focus on whether the clause is designed to produce a reasonable estimate of what actual damages would be or, rather, a disproportionate result, is aimed at disqualifying as penalties clauses that are included because of their *in terrorem* effect. *See Boyle v. Petrie Stores Corp.*, 518 N.Y.S.2d 854, 861 (Sup. Ct. 1985; supp. dec. 1987) (*dictum*), and Charles J. Goetz & Robert E. Scott, *Liquidated Damages, Penalties and the Just Compensation Principle: Some Notes on an Enforcement Model and a Theory of Efficient Breach*, 77 COLUM. L. REV. 554, 555 (1977) ("attempts to secure performance through *in terrorem* clauses are currently declared unenforceable even where the evidence shows a voluntary, fairly bargained exchange"). The Goetz & Scott article includes further discussion of this aspect of the law of liquidated damages (at p. 561) and case citations. This aspect of the law of liquidated damages is, perhaps, the one that makes the Limited Two-Way Payments (First Method) approach to early termination settlement most vulnerable to attack. *See* NYUCC § 2–718, cmt. 1, discussing situations in which a liquidated damages clause might be treated as unconscionable and voided if it fixed damages at an unreasonably small amount. However, *see* the *Midland* case discussed *supra* note 687, where the *in terrorem* effect of the clause was not discussed by the court.

the provision may be unenforceable as a penalty.[731] A mere difference between the stipulated amount of damages, or the result obtained from applying the agreed formula, on one hand, and the injured party's actual damages ascertained at the time of the default, on the other, should not result in characterization of a liquidated damages provision as a penalty.

Some market participants may view Market Quotation[732] as a method of determining liquidated damages. This view may be reflected in Section 6(e)(iv) of the ISDA master agreement forms published in 1987 and 1992, which provides as follows:

> (iv) *Pre-Estimate*. The parties agree that if Market Quotation applies an amount recoverable under this Section 6(e) is a reasonable pre-estimate of loss and not a penalty. Such amount is payable for the loss of bargain and the loss of protection against future risks and except as otherwise provided in this Agreement neither party will be entitled to recover any additional damages as a consequence of such losses.

The same provision, but without reference to the Market Quotation approach, is retained in ISDA's new Replacement Value approach to Section 6 of the 1992 ISDA forms and is included in the FEOMA form (Section 8.4), suggesting that some may also view the Replacement Value and FEOMA's close-out calculations as means of liquidating damages.

For various reasons, we believe that Market Quotation, Replacement Value and the various FEOMA methods of addressing loss of bargain and gain should be seen as agreed methods for determining actual damages and not liquidated damages provisions.

First, as indicated above, New York contract law permits the parties to agree to liquidated damages only if, at the time they contract, it appears that it will be impossible or difficult to determine precisely the actual damages that may be caused by breach in the future. Although this uncertainty about actual damages may, in fact, exist when parties adopt the Market Quotation approach, the approach itself is premised on the existence of conditions, at the time of breach, that would make it possible to ascertain actual damages. That is, Market Quotation uses actual, quotations for the cost of cover in the market through Replacement Transactions. Similarly, Replacement Value assumes that the calulation will be based on the Determining Party's actual cost of cover in the market or other approaches to determining actual damages, and FEOMA assumes use of a current market premium, for currency options, and cover in the spot market, for FX forwards.

Second, under New York law, when the parties are permitted to estimate damages through a liquidation provision because actual damages may be impossible or difficult to ascertain, they are also required to apply their agreed liquidation approach as the exclusive means of determining damages. An injured party is not permitted to seek its actual damages, even if they later become ascertainable.[733] However, Market Quotation is not an

---

[731] *See* Gooch & Klein, *supra* note 698, at 38 (Oct. 1984), for further discussion and n.5 in particular for case citations. *See* J. Trevor Brown, *Non-Tax Issues in Cross-Border Transactions*, *in* PLI 1987, at 573, 587, on similar English legal principles.

[732] Unless otherwise specified, the following discussion of the Market Quotation approach also applies to its predecessor in ISDA terminology, Agreement Value.

[733] *Dalston Constr. Corp. v. Wallace*, 214 N.Y.S.2d 191, 193 (Dist. Ct. 1960); *J.R. Stevenson Corp. v. County of Westchester*, 493 N.Y.S.2d 819 (App. Div. 1985).

exclusive method for determining loss of bargain or gain. When the parties agree to Market Quotation in an ISDA-based agreement, they also agree that Market Quotation will be supplanted by actual damages (Loss) if quotations are not obtained from at least three Reference Market-makers or, under the 1992 ISDA master agreement forms, if the party seeking to determine Market Quotation reasonably determines that Market Quotation will not produce a commercially reasonable result. Similarly, Replacement Value is not an exclusive agreed approach for estimating gain or loss. Rather, as noted, it is a list of various methods for calculating gain or loss, and it expressly contemplates that the methods may be used either as alternatives or in combination, so long as the combination does not result in duplication.

Accordingly, we believe the enforceability of these provisions should be measured not by the standards applicable to liquidated damages clauses, but by the provisions relating to quantification of actual damage, as discussed below.[734]

LEGAL PRINCIPLES ON RECOVERABLE ACTUAL DAMAGES

Clauses such as those used to implement ISDA's Agreement Value, Loss, Market Quotation and Replacement Value approaches seek to give the trier of fact varying degrees of guidance as to how actual damages (particularly loss of bargain) should be quantified. While New York contract law leaves the parties with substantial freedom to order their affairs, it does not leave them entirely free to do so in the area of quantifying damages for breach of contract. In deciding whether and to what extent it will follow the parties' guidance on this subject (or direct a jury to follow it), a court will determine whether or not the quantification rules established by the parties are permissible under the applicable legal principles. As a practical matter, judges can be expected to give considerable weight to the expressed desires of the parties, particularly since they relate to such highly technical matters and, when prepared on standard forms, reflect established practice in the relevant market.

---

[734] A Canadian court concluded for similar reasons that Market Quotation should not be treated as involving liquidated damages:

> Calculation of the amount of a claim by means of a formula itself is not sufficient to constitute the claim a liquidated one—whether the formula emerges from a 'termination methodology' which is standard in the industry, or from the contract in question between the parties, as it is said to do here. . . . [T]he gathering of a number of quotations according to some methodology for purposes of developing a sum payable depends upon the underlying opinion of the experts which is, in turn, based upon their assessment of any number of diverse factors at play in the bond option or swap agreement markets. It is not enough that at the end of the exercise a sum has been arrived at through the calculation. Where the ingredients of the formula depend upon the circumstances of the case and are fixed by opinion or assessment—as they are here—the characteristics of a liquidated amount are not present.

Margaret E. Grottenthaler, *Derivatives Litigation in Canada*, in DERIVATIVES HANDBOOK 141, quoting from a decision in Ontario proceedings in the insolvency of Confederation Life Insurance Company. In that case, the court denied an application of Citibank Canada for an order permitting setoff of a deposit obligation against a claim under a guaranty of obligations under bond options and swaps because the claim "was one sounding in damages; it was not a debt claim and it was not liquidated" but "the only serious basis for asserting set-off was . . . the set-off [of] mutual liquidated debts." *Id.* at 140.

The basic principles of New York contract law relating to damages for breach of contract recognize the right of an injured party to claim damages calculated to protect either of two basic interests:

1. its interest in having the benefit of its bargain—which is protected through damages (including appropriate proved lost profits) that will put it in as good a position as it would have been in if the contract had been performed; or

2. its interest in being made whole for loss caused by its reliance on the contract's existence—which is protected through damages that will put it in as a good a position as it would have been in if the contract had not been made.[735]

It should be noted that these theories are alternatives; the injured party is not allowed to compute its loss of bargain and then add its losses incurred in reliance on the existence of the agreement.[736]

When an injured party seeks to recover actual damages for its loss of bargain—the first theory set forth above—the principles of New York contract law discussed below allow for compensatory damages, but only if the loss claimed (1) is proximately caused by the breach, (2) can be proved or estimated with reasonable certainty, (3) arises out of the relevant transaction as the natural consequence of breach in the ordinary course or was reasonably foreseeable by the party in breach as a probable result of breach at the time the contract was made and (4) generally, could not have been avoided by reasonable action by the injured party. Subsections one through four below discuss these principles in detail, with a particular focus on how these principles of New York contract law may operate to limit recovery of damages computed in accordance with the Market Quotation, Loss, Replacement Value and FEOMA close-out settlement approaches.

Since the second theory of damages does not include lost profits, it will generally produce a lower number than damages for loss of bargain. As a result, it will ordinarily be sought only if the injured party would have suffered a loss on the transaction if it had proceeded to completion or is unable to provide sufficient proof of damages for its loss of bargain. In these cases, the injured party could seek damages based on its losses and costs incurred in reliance on the contract's existence (including those incurred in preparation for performance or in performance). However, these reliance damages must be reduced by any loss that the injured party would have suffered if the contract had been performed, as

---

[735] These damages are not the only possible remedies available to an injured party in the event of breach of contract, but they are the focus of the following discussion, since it addresses standard approaches to the calculation of close-out settlement payments. The Restatement of the Law of Contracts recognizes a third type of interest that may be protected, "restitution interest," which is the injured party's "interest in having returned to him any benefit that he has conferred on the other party." RESTATEMENT (SECOND) OF CONTRACTS § 344(c) (1981). The official comment to the section notes that, while this interest could produce damages equal in amount to those computed under one of the other theories, "it is ordinarily smaller because it includes neither the injured party's lost profit nor that part of his expenditures in reliance that resulted in no benefit to the other party." *Id.* at cmt. a.

[736] *See, e.g.*, RESTATEMENT (SECOND) OF CONTRACTS § 349 (1981), describing damages based on reliance interest an "an alternative" to expectation damages.

proved by the defaulting party with reasonable certainty. The final subsection below discusses the principles applicable to this theory of recovery.

DAMAGES MUST PROXIMATELY RESULT FROM BREACH

To be recoverable under general principles of New York contract law, an injured party's damages for breach of contract must be proximately caused by the other party's wrong.[737] Derivatives are generally executed to seek protection against risks associated with changes in rates, prices and other variables, or to trade those risks. As time passes and market conditions change, the net value to each party of the other party's promised performance will (as discussed in the first section of this chapter) normally increase for one party and become negative for the other. Accordingly, the market operates on the assumption that close-out of a transaction before the end of its scheduled term will give rise to gain to one party and loss to the other. Implicit in the Market Quotation, Loss, Replacement Value and the FEOMA approaches to gain and loss is the assumption that, when close-out occurs on account of breach before a transaction has been fully performed, the claim of the injured party, calculated applying the agreed approach, will always be proximately caused by close-out and, therefore, by the underlying breach that led to the close-out. As a result, the principle that damages must be proximately caused by breach should not generally prove problematic in connection with most OTC derivatives. However, as indicated by the earlier discussion of the *Ackerley Communications* case,[738] even today there seems to be some danger that a court unfamiliar with the ways of the derivatives market may not understand this fundamental market assumption.

Each of the market approaches under consideration places time constraints on the injured party's determination of its claim, so as to reduce the possibility that unreasonable delay will result in inflated claims for damages owing to changes or intervening events that are not reasonably associated with the close-out and underlying breach.[739] Loss is to be determined as of the Early Termination Date or, "if that is not reasonably practicable, as of the earliest date thereafter as is reasonably practicable," and Market Quotation is to be determined on the basis of quotations for Replacement Transactions, which Reference Market-makers are to be asked to provide "to the extent reasonably practicable as of the same day and time (without regard to different time zones) on or as soon as reasonably practicable after the relevant Early Termination Date."[740] Under the FEOMA method, the injured party is required to make its close-out settlement payment calculation as of the

---

[737] *See Lloyd v. Town of Wheatfield*, 492 N.E.2d 396 (N.Y. 1986).

[738] *See supra* note 691.

[739] *See infra* p. 261 for discussion of these constraints in connection with the principle on minimization of damages.

[740] *See* Annotation 4 to the definition of "Market Quotation" in the 1992 ISDA master agreement form included in Part 3, *infra* p. 890, regarding a slight difference from the 1987 ISDA master agreement formulations. *See also User's Guide to the ISDA 1992 Master Agreements* 24–25. Under the definition of "Market Quotation" in both sets of ISDA master agreement forms, the day and time as of which quotations are to be obtained are to be selected in good faith by the party obligated to make the determination, and if both parties are obligated to make the determination, they are to consult with each other.

Close-Out Date or a time as soon as reasonably practicable thereafter if determination as of the Close-Out Date is not commercially reasonable.[741]

Under the Replacement Value approach, Replacement Values for all Terminated Transactions are to be determined "as of the Early Termination Date, or, if that would not be commercially reasonable, as of the latest date or dates before or the earliest date or dates after the Early Termination Date as would be commercially reasonable under then prevailing circumstances." This new methodology thus opens the possibility of permitting valuation as of a moment before breach and early termination, using pre-breach data as the basis for determining loss or gain on early termination. This innovation raises issues as to whether quantification on the basis of pre-breach data provides a proper measure of damages, as discussed below.[742] It may also be viewed as raising proximate cause issues—if recoverable damages should be limited to those proximately caused by breach, is it legally permissible to use pre-breach, historical data as the basis for quantifying a claim?[743]

Adoption of this new feature of the Replacement Value approach largely reflects the difficulties that market participants have had in times of market stress. In such circumstances, the exchange rates or firm quotations for actual replacement transactions ordinarily used in close-out calculations have not always been available, and indicative quotations have sometimes been scarce or thought to be unreliable. In some cases this has been so because the necessary underlying information itself has been viewed as unreliable.[744] The challenge that the defaulting party could be expected to advance is that some intervening event between the time of breach/close-out and the time as of which the relevant data prevailed in the market, and not the breach itself, was the cause of all or part of the damages. The injured party should be prepared to demonstrate why it was not commercially reasonable to determine Replacement Value as of the Early Termination Date, and in the proper circumstances it might reasonably argue that it should not be required to show that its damages resulted solely from the underlying breach and related close-out to the exclusion of all other factors, but only that the breach (or close-out) contributed in a substantial measure to the claimed damages. It seems that, if there is a controversy as to

---

[741] In addition, under Section 6(a) of the ISDA forms, the Early Termination Date itself may not be more than 20 days after the notice of early termination is given and, if the notice is given in connection with an Event of Default, the Event of Default must be continuing. The FEOMA form (Section 8.1) similarly requires an Event of Default to be continuing for the right to close out to exist, although it does not place any particular outside limit on the Close-Out Date. Under the Market Quotation approach, the injured party is to request that the Reference Market-makers provide their quotations for Replacement Transactions to the extent practicable as of the same day and time.

[742] *See infra* p. 261.

[743] In this regard, it should be noted that Section 2–723(2) of the NYUCC, on the proof of market price in connection with anticipatory repudiation of a contract for the sale of goods, expressly authorizes evidence of market price within a reasonable time before or after the repudiation, if evidence of price prevailing at the time the aggrieved party learns of the repudiation is not readily available—although the party in breach must be given notice that this kind of evidence will be used, to prevent unfair surprise.

[744] For example, in 1998 Russia froze trading in some of its treasury securities and took action that was widely viewed as manipulating the rate of exchange of rubles for other currencies. In these circumstances, many market participants believed that the valuation of OTC derivatives involving these treasury securities and the ruble should, as a matter of commercial reasonableness, have been based on historical data adjusted to take account of market polls.

Damages and Close-Out Settlement 255

whether all or part of the claimed damages are not recoverable because they may be attributable to an intervening cause, the defaulting party would have the burden of proof on the question.[745]

Nonetheless, participants in the derivatives markets should be sensitive to the risk of challenge to claims for losses, costs and expenses included in calculating a close-out settlement, if they arguably are not proximately caused by the underlying ground for close-out or, under the various approaches described above, by the liquidation of hedging or related transactions.

The decisions of England's courts in *Australia and New Zealand Banking Group Ltd v. Société Générale*[746] are of interest in this regard. This case involved close-out in connection with no-fault Additional Termination Events included by the parties in the confirmations of complex Russian ruble/U.S. dollar non-deliverable forward transactions. The confirmations were agreed to pursuant to an ISDA-based master agreement between the parties that adopted the Loss approach. Close-out was triggered in 1998 in connection with Russia's declaration of a moratorium on certain kinds of payments by Russian banks, at a time when the transactions were in-the-money to ANZ. It appears that the parties conceded that the amounts of ANZ's actual loss and SG's actual gain on close-out were equal (though SG sought unsuccessfully to reverse its position on this point in its appeal). However, SG had hedged its position in each of the transactions with its Russian subsidiary and, in calculating the settlement amount to be paid to ANZ, it deducted its loss on those hedges. In the litigation, ANZ disputed the deductions, and both the trial court and the Court of Appeal agreed with ANZ that loss on the hedge was primarily a result of the banking moratorium declared by Russia and possibly a result of the ensuing inability of the Russian subsidiary of SG to make payment under the hedge transaction but, in any event, not the result of termination or liquidation of the hedging contracts. Although, as noted, these transactions were particularly complex, similar issues may arise whenever a party seeks to look to dealings outside the closed-out transaction in calculating its loss of bargain or gain. The principles of New York contract law addressed in the following point are also relevant in this context.

DAMAGES MUST BE THE NATURAL AND PROBABLE OR FORESEEABLE CONSEQUENCE OF BREACH

Both the Loss and Replacement Value approaches list various kinds of losses or gains and costs and expenses that a Determining Party may take into account in calculating its claim, so long as a combination of the various theories of recovery does not result in duplication. These include amounts associated with hedges and related trading positions. In dealing with closed-out currency options, the FEOMA approach similarly permits reference to hedges and related trading positions. In using these approaches, parties should take into account a basic distinction drawn by the courts in determining whether damages for breach of contract are recoverable under New York law. The courts distinguish between "general" damages, which flow directly from the immediate transaction as the natural and probable consequence of breach, and "special" or "consequential" dam-

---

[745] *Haven Assocs. v. Donro Realty Corp.*, 503 N.Y.S.2d 826, 830 (App. Div. 1986).

[746] [1999] 2 All E.R. (Comm) 624 (Q.B.), *aff'd*, [2000] 1 All E.R. (Comm) 682 (C.A.).

ages, which do not arise from the parties' own transaction.[747] Subject to other principles of law that might limit recovery, an injured party will ordinarily be entitled to its general damages, including lost profits, that flow from the parties' own transaction. It will, however, be entitled to recover special or consequential damages only if they were foreseeable and within the contemplation of the parties at the time the contract was made.[748]

In light of this distinction, if one of the parties to a transaction wishes to be permitted to look to dealings with third parties in formulating a claim for damages for loss of bargain in case of breach, it may wish, in confirming the transaction, to supplement the standard ISDA and FEOMA language on close-out settlement calculation with a specific acknowledgment from the other party that it is aware of the special circumstances that may be taken into account in calculating a damages claim,[749] even though the parties' negotiations prior to the making of the contract may also furnish evidence that the party in breach was aware of special circumstances at the time of contracting.[750]

The application of these principles to more straightforward close-out situations would be as follows. Suppose that Big Bank has entered into a fixed-floating swap transaction with Weak Credit under which Big Bank is paying 3-month LIBOR on a Notional Amount of $100 million and Weak Credit is paying a fixed rate on the same amount. Big Bank hedges the transaction with another fixed-floating swap, in which it is the Fixed Rate Payer, at a rate somewhat lower than the rate it is receiving from Weak Credit. Market rates rise sharply. Weak Credit's business deteriorates and it becomes insolvent, which results in close-out of the swap. Big Bank values its gain on the termination at $1 million on the basis of market quotations. Big Bank accordingly owes $1 million. This is so regardless of what happens to the hedge, unless the parties have agreed otherwise. Suppose, for example, that Big Bank is able to negotiate a favorable termination of its hedge and

---

[747]The discussion of the difference in the case law is sometimes confusing. For examples of analysis that draws the distinction fairly well, however, see *American List Corp. v. U.S. News & World Report, Inc.*, 549 N.E.2d 1161, 1164 (N.Y. 1989), and *437 Madison Avenue Ass'n v. A.T. Kearney, Inc.*, 488 N.Y.S.2d 950, 951 (App. Div. 1985).

[748]See *American List Corp. v. U.S. News & World Report, Inc.*, 549 N.E.2d 1161, 1164 (N.Y. 1989) and cases cited therein, and *Charles E.S. McLeod, Inc. v R.B. Hamilton Moving & Storage*, 453 N.Y.S.2d 251, 253 (App. Div. 1982).

[749]It appears that precisely this sort of special explanation was wanting in the documentation for the NDFs in the *ANZ* case. *See* discussion by the Court of Appeal, in *dictum*, of issues in this regard that Société Générale did not raise at the trial court level and requested leave, unsuccessfully, to raise on a retrial. [2000] 1 All E.R. (Comm) at 692. *See also* Schuyler K. Henderson, *English Cases Dealing with Settlement Provisions of the ISDA Master Agreement*, 15 BUTTERWORTHS J. INT'L BANK. & FINANCIAL L. 190, 191–94 (June 2000).

[750]See RESTATEMENT (SECOND) OF CONTRACTS § 351, cmt. b (1981). The following may be relevant if the parties have chosen English law to govern their agreement: "[A] defaulting party will not be liable to indemnify the other against loss suffered by the latter from a transaction in which the latter participated and which is unknown to the defaulting party. On the other hand, if the related operation is known to the defaulting party, the latter must make good the loss suffered by the other in relation to the linked transaction. . . . [This rule] explains the existence of the clause which is often met in swap contracts according to which each party recognizes that the other is or may be party to another transaction linked to the swap, and that the loss which may result by reason of the linked transaction will, in case of default, be reimbursed by the defaulting party." J. Trevor Brown, *English Law and Swaps*, in HANDBOOK OF RISK MANAGEMENT 35–23 to 35–24.

receive a cash payment of $1,050,000 from the counterparty. Market practice and standard documentation does not require that Big Bank account to Weak Credit for the $50,000 difference, which represents the present value of Big Bank's remaining profit on the transaction combined with the hedge. Suppose, however, that the counterparty on the hedge defaults at the same time as Weak Credit, with the result that Big Bank recovers only $300,000 on the hedge. This was essentially the situation presented in the *ANZ* case discussed in the preceding section,[751] where the English courts held that standard documentation would not permit Big Bank to set off its loss on the hedge against what it must pay Weak Credit, absent express agreement to the contrary.[752]

In highly tailored transactions, especially in the emerging markets, it is often the case that a market professional will be able to provide a derivatives transaction only by taking on special risks associated with one or more hedge or related positions. In these cases, the parties usually acknowledge quite expressly that these special risks are being passed on to the customer for which the transaction is being tailored. The ANZ case and the principles of New York contract law discussed above indicate the wisdom of including these clear acknowledgments.

DAMAGES MUST BE REASONABLY CERTAIN

In claims for loss of bargain occasioned by breach, damages for loss of profits, or gains prevented, as a result of the breach are often an important part of the claim. Under New York law, these damages must be reasonably certain to be recoverable, although the courts recognize that "[p]rediction of future profit is inevitably speculative to some degree" and "'nothing like precise mathematical accuracy can be obtained in the calculation of the amount of damages.'"[753] Therefore, the injured party is merely required to adduce "such evidence . . . as would enable a businessman to make a prediction with reasonably accuracy."[754] The ISDA Market Quotation, Loss and Replacement Value approaches and the FEOMA methods of calculating loss of bargain or gain all comport with these general guidelines.

---

[751] *Supra* p. 255.

[752] The court on appeal stated that "it is inherently unlikely that a party in ANZ's position entering into a futures contract with SG would agree to share the risk of the simple collapse in value of a hedge arranged by its counterparty." *Australia & New Zealand Banking Group Ltd v. Société Générale*, [2000] 1 All E.R. (Comm) at 689.

[753] *Haven Assocs. v. Donro Realty Corp.*, 503 N.Y.S.2d 826, 830 (App. Div. 1986), quoting from *Borne Chem. Co. v. Dictrow*, 445 N.Y.S.2d 406, 413 (1981). The rule stated in RESTATEMENT (SECOND) OF CONTRACTS § 348(3) (1981) is, in this regard, particularly relevant to most OTC derivatives: "If a breach is of a promise conditioned on a fortuitous event and it is uncertain whether the event would have occurred had there been no breach, the injured party may recover damages based on the value of the conditional right at the time of breach." Comment *d* reflects as follows on this rule: "It would be unfair to the party in breach to award damages on the assumption that the event would have occurred, but equally unfair to the injured party to deny recovery of damages on the ground of uncertainty. The injured party has . . . [u]nder the rule stated in Subsection (3) . . . the alternative remedy of damages based on the value of his conditional contract right at the time of breach, or what may be described as the value of his 'chance of winning.' The value of that right must itself be proved with reasonable certainty, as it may be if there is a market for such rights or if there is a suitable basis for determining the probability of the occurrence of the event."

[754] *Id.*, quoting from *Stanley Trading Co. Inc. v. Bensdorp, Inc.*, 102 N.Y.S.2d 887, 891 (App. Div. 1951).

It will, of course, be easier to demonstrate the certainty of the damage calculations to the satisfaction of a trier of fact when the injured party bases its Replacement Value claim on the cost of cover. In this context, cost of cover might be shown through quotations for replacement transactions or otherwise calculated to equal a present value of the difference between the agreed performance and the same performance at current rates or prices. The trier of fact could be expected to approach with greater skepticism a claim for Replacement Value determined by applying pricing or other valuation models to information generated internally by the injured party, or by its agent or a third party.[755]

It should be noted in this connection that the law does not treat the injured party's claim for lost profits as speculative merely because there are doubts about whether the injured party itself would have been able to perform if the contract had not been closed out. In fact, when a defaulting party has argued that the present value to the injured party of its lost bargain should be heavily discounted to reflect the risk that the injured party might have been unable to perform if it had not been relieved of its duty to perform by the breach, the court has rejected the theory, finding that this factor may not properly be considered where damages are sought by reason of anticipatory breach of the contract.[756]

AVOIDABLE DAMAGES MAY NOT BE RECOVERABLE

Under principles of New York law relating to claims for damages for breach of contract, the injured party generally has a duty to seek to minimize, or mitigate, its damages.[757] To state the rule in another way, if the injured party could reasonably have

---

[755]In the event of a challenge, the court's view on a model-based calculation may be affected by numerous factors, including the nondefaulting party's ability at the time to determine its damages on the basis of actual cost of cover in the market, how any such available cost of cover compares with the model-based claim and whether the internally generated information or model-based approach used by the nondefaulting party differed from the information or model-based approach used by it originally in pricing the transaction. RESTATEMENT (SECOND) OF CONTRACTS § 352, cmt. a (1981) notes that "increasing receptiveness on the part of courts to proof by sophisticated economic and financial data and by expert opinion has made it easier to meet the requirement of certainty." Comment *b* (p. 146) goes on to state that "damages may be established with reasonably certainty with the aid of expert testimony, economic and financial data, market surveys and analyses, business records of similar enterprises, and the like."

[756]*See American List Corp. v. U.S. News & World Report, Inc.*, 549 N.E.2d 1161, 1165 (N.Y. 1989), remanding the case to the trial court for a recalculation of damages. The trial court permitted the application of a high discount factor to payments that would have been due to the injured party after wrongful cancellation of the contract. Under the common law doctrine of anticipatory breach (said by the court to be "inapplicable to contracts for the payment of money only"), a wrongful repudiation relieves the nonrepudiating party of its obligation of future performance and gives rise to an immediate claim for total breach of the contract. Damages for the total breach are the present value of the lost bargain less costs reasonably saved by the nonrepudiating party as a result of being relieved of its obligations of future performance. Similarly, in the ISDA, FEOMA and other standard contracts used in the OTC derivatives market, when the nondefaulting party gives notice of close-out in connection with an event of default, the notice operates to terminate the obligations of both parties to tender performance scheduled to be due after the close-out, and the close-out settlement payment is intended to capture the present value of that performance owing to the nondefaulting party, less the present value of the counter performance it had agreed to supply.

[757]*See Hamilton v. McPherson*, 28 N.Y. 72 (1863). In some cases this duty is referred to as involving "mitigation," rather than "minimization" of damages. In RESTATEMENT (SECOND) OF CONTRACTS § 350 (1981), the underlying principle is referred to as "Avoidability as a Limitation on Damages," and the general principle is that "damages are not recoverable for loss that the injured party could have avoided without undue risk, burden or humiliation." As an exception to this general rule, the injured party is not, however, pre-

Damages and Close-Out Settlement 259

avoided some of the damages that it has claimed, without either disregarding its own interests or giving them less weight than those of the defaulting party, the injured party may not be permitted to recover those avoidable damages.[758] This principle may come into play in various ways in connection with the Market Quotation, Loss and Replacement Value approaches to determining loss or gain.

Market Quotation. First, at least theoretically, the identity of the Reference Market-makers may affect the amounts of the quotations received. Suppose, for example, that there is one transaction outstanding under an ISDA-based master agreement that has adopted the Market Quotation approach and that the transaction is in-the-money to the nondefaulting party at the time of a default. The agreement requires the nondefaulting party to go into the market and seek to obtain quotations from Reference Market-makers, defined as:

> four leading dealers in the relevant market selected by the party determining a Market Quotation in good faith (a) from among dealers of the highest credit standing which satisfy all the criteria that such party applies generally at the time in deciding whether to offer or to make an extension of credit and (b) to the extent practicable, from among such dealers having an office in the same city.

The party making the determination is to ask the Reference Market-makers for quotations on the following basis:

> Each quotation will be for an amount, if any, that would be paid to such party (expressed as a negative number) or by such party (expressed as a positive number) in consideration of an agreement between such party (taking into account any existing Credit Support Document with respect to the obligations of such party) and the quoting Reference Market-maker to enter into a transaction (the "Replacement Transaction") that would have the effect of preserving for such party the economic equivalent of any payment or delivery (whether the underlying obligation was absolute or contingent and assuming the satisfaction of each applicable condition precedent) by the parties under Section 2(a)(i) in respect of such Terminated Transaction or group of Terminated Transactions that would, but for

---

cluded from recovery to the extent that it has made "reasonable but unsuccessful efforts to avoid loss." In practice, the burden is on the party in breach to prove that the injured party's claim includes damages that were reasonably avoidable. *Jenkins v. Etlinger*, 432 N.E.2d 589, 591 (N.Y. 1982). *See, e.g., Air et Chaleur, S.A. v. Janeway*, 575 F.2d 489 (2d Cir. 1985), an action for damages for breach of a put option on restricted stock brought by the stockholders who held onto the stock after the defendant repudiated the put, where the court affirmed the trial court's holding that merely producing posted price quotations for the stock did not satisfy the defendant's burden of proving failure to mitigate by the plaintiffs.

[758]For a full discussion of the principle under which an injured party may be precluded from recovering damages for losses incurred without due regard for the duty to minimize, *see* Charles J. Goetz & Robert E. Scott, *The Mitigation Principle: Toward a General Theory of Contractual Obligation*, 69 VIRGINIA L. REV. 967 (1983) and sources cited therein. For discussion of the subject as it relates to swaps, *see* Gooch & Klein, *supra* note 698731, at 38 n.7 & 40. Under New York law, the requirement to minimize damages applies only if the contract in question was executory at the time of breach. *Spohn v. Fine*, 479 N.Y.S.2d 139 (Yates County Ct. 1984), cites *Becar v. Flues*, 64 N.Y. 518 (1876), to support a holding that an agreement to lease is not an executory contract giving rise to the duty to mitigate.

the occurrence of the relevant Early Termination Date, have been required after that date.

So, in our example, the nondefaulting party is required to ask each of the Reference Market-makers to quote the up-front fee it would charge to enter into a transaction with the nondefaulting party that would replace the transaction that is being lost because of the default.[759]

It could be argued that the duty to minimize damages imposes an obligation on the nondefaulting party to make a reasonable effort to get quotations from market participants that are likely to provide low quotations. In our example, the nondefaulting party might be able to find cheaper Replacement Transaction quotations by going to dealers of lesser credit standing. However, in our view, when parties agree, as they do in adopting Market Quotation, that an injured party may seek quotations from market participants of the highest credit standing, and from dealers that meet its other criteria for acceptable counterparties, this should be effective to eliminate the possibility that a claim based on quotations obtained as agreed would be reduced for failure of the injured party to seek to minimize damages simply because the resulting quotations may be somewhat higher than those it might have obtained from market-makers of a lesser credit standing.[760] A totally separate question, however, is whether adopting this approach makes commercial sense for any particular parties, in light of the transactions they intend to engage in.[761]

Second, the Market Quotation approach calls for obtaining various quotations, disregarding the highest and the lowest and averaging the middle quotations, or if only one remains, using that quotation. It could be argued that, under the principle of minimization of damages, recovery should be limited to the lowest quotation obtained. The averaging aspect of this ISDA approach to Market Quotation has not to our knowledge been subjected to scrutiny by a court applying New York law.[762] In practice, it may never be, since

---

[759] It is interesting to compare these mechanics with those for calculating Cash Settlement Amounts in transactions that are to be settled in cash and those for determining the amount of collateral to be posted in collateralized transactions, where similar issues arise. *See infra* pp. 459 (cash settlement) & 1082 (collateral).

[760] *See* RESTATEMENT (SECOND) OF CONTRACTS § 350(1) (1981). It should be noted, though, that courts applying New York law sometimes state the proposition that an injured party is not entitled to be put in a better position than it would have been in if the contract had been performed. *See*, e.g, *Madison Fund, Inc. v. The Charter Company*, 427 F. Supp. 597, 608 (S.D.N.Y. 1977) (*dictum*).

[761] For example, if the credit standing of one of the parties is an important factor in the initial pricing of the transaction, the parties (or one of them) might negotiate to have the measure of loss of bargain, or gain, on close-out of the transaction drafted in such a way that it would reflect the cost of a Replacement Transaction quoted between parties whose relative credit standings are equivalent to those of the parties at the inception of the transaction (after taking credit support into account).

[762] The agreement involved in case of *Drexel Lambert Products Corp. v. Midland Bank Plc, supra* note 687, seems to have included an agreement value provision based on the standard ISDA approach, which can result in averaging; however, in that case the court was asked to determine whether the provision was unenforceable as a penalty because of its Limited Two-Way Payments approach, that is, because it did not require the Non-defaulting Party to turn over to the Defaulting Party the value of the terminated swap. The averaging feature of the ISDA approach was not relevant in that case. In *Drexel Burnham Lambert Products Corp. v. MCorp.*, No. 88C-NO-80 (Super. Del. Feb. 23, 1989), *motion for reargument denied*, 1991 Del. Super. LEXIS 298 (Aug. 13, 1991), the court upheld a market quotation approach against a challenge that the damages claimed were not shown to have been the plaintiff's actual cost of cover. However, in analyzing the provision, the court noted that it defined "Agreement Value" as an amount equal to the lowest flat fee that

the cost of a court challenge is likely to far exceed the difference between the two quotations obtained by a Non-defaulting Party under the Market Quotation approach after having disregarded the highest and lowest of three or four obtained from Reference Market-makers.

Third, the duty to minimize damages may have some bearing on the time as of which an injured party may determine its damages.[763] Under the Market Quotation approach, the party seeking quotations for a Replacement Transaction, or its agent, is required to request that the Reference Market-makers provide quotations as of the same day and time, to the extent reasonably practicable, and the day and time as of which the quotations are to be provided must be chosen in good faith and must be on the Early Termination Date or a day as soon as reasonably practicable thereafter.[764] Also, under Section 6(a) of those forms, the Early Termination Date itself may not be more than 20 days after the notice of early termination is given and, if the notice is given in connection with an Event of Default, the Event of Default must be continuing. These constraints are intended to ensure that a claim for damages based on the approach will be consonant with the principle of minimization of damages, and to protect Defaulting Parties against claims for damages that might be inflated by unreasonable delay by a Non-defaulting Party or by its seeking to obtain quotations for various Terminated Transactions selectively, at times when the quotations will most favor the Non-defaulting Party.[765]

---

the nondefaulting party would have to pay for a replacement swap. *Id.* at 4. *See* Linda B. Klein, *Court Decision Regarding Automatic Termination and Agreement Value Provisions in a Swap Agreement*, 8 INT'L FIN. L. REV. 42 (Apr. 1989). Therefore, *MCorp* does not stand for approval of the averaging feature of Market Quotation.

[763]*See infra* p. 339 on a proposed bankruptcy law revision that would provide that, if certain kinds of financial contracts are liquidated, terminated or accelerated or rejected in a Debtor's Bankruptcy Code case, damages will generally be measured as of the earlier of (1) the date of the rejection or (2) the date of the liquidation, termination, or acceleration.

[764]The *Swaps Code* provided that quotations should be requested as of 11:00 a.m. on the Early Termination Date or, in the case of Immediate Early Termination in connection with insolvency and similar events, on a day after the Early Termination Date, since the nondefaulting party might learn of the Early Termination Date after its occurrence. The 1987 ISDA master agreement forms were somewhat more flexible than the code, in that the 11:00 a.m. time requirement was replaced with a requirement that the time be determined in good faith by the Determining Party or by agreement if there were more than one Determining Party.

[765]In *MCorp*, the court pointed to these constraints as elements of the approach designed to ensure its fairness. *See* the discussion of the case in Gooch & Klein, *Review of Case Law I*, at 428–30. *See also Air et Chaleur, S.A. v. Janeway*, 757 F.2d 489, 494 (2d Cir. 1985), discussing and upholding the trial court's finding that, when the holders of restricted stock and option rights to "put" it to the defendant learned that the defendant was repudiating the option, under the mitigation doctrine as expressed in New York contract law, the plaintiffs were not at liberty to hold the stock until the agreed tender date but, rather, were obligated to take reasonable action to minimize their damages. *See also Simon v. Electrospace Corp.*, 28 N.Y.2d 136, 145–46, 269 N.E.2d 21, 26, 320 N.Y.S.2d 225, 233 (1971), discussing damages for breach of contract to deliver stock under a related principle, under which the plaintiff was said to be free to seek cover by purchasing the stock in the market within "a reasonable time limit" after the breach, but that his cause of action could not "be converted into carrying a market 'call' or 'warrant' to acquire the stock on demand if the price rose above its value."

Fourth, these principles may be important in cases where more than one Terminated Transaction is being valued in accordance with the Market Quotation methodology. Under the 1992 ISDA forms, the Determining Party must decide whether to obtain Market Quotations for the entire portfolio of Terminated Transactions or separate sets of quotations for different groups of Terminated Transactions or individual Terminated Transactions.[766] As noted above, the flexibility afforded by this 1992 innovation will presumably be required to be exercised in such a way as to minimize any damages payable by the other party.

Loss, Replacement Value and the FEOMA Approach. The Loss, Replacement Value and FEOMA approaches may raise similar and additional issues under the doctrine of avoidable damages. Suppose, for example, that close-out occurs at a time when the market is rapidly getting worse, from the point of view of the defaulting party. Like Market Quotation, Loss and Replacement Value permit an injured party to make its close-out settlement calculation as of a time soon after the Early Termination Date, if determination as of the Early Termination Date is not "reasonably practicable" (Loss) or "commercially reasonable" (Replacement Value). The FEOMA form does the same. If not abused, this feature should operate consistently with the doctrine's aim of excluding from an injured party's recovery damages that it can reasonably avoid. Nondefaulting parties should be aware, however, that if the reasonableness of their actions is questioned, it will be because the defaulting party is looking at the claim with the benefit of hindsight. A nondefaulting party should, therefore, always consider whether the approach it proposes to take produces, or arguably produces, a result more favorable to it than valuation on the Early Termination Date and, then, should consider whether taking the proposed approach, in the circumstances, may be regarded as suspect.

Replacement Value. The feature of the Replacement Value approach that permits an injured party to use pre-breach data as the basis for determining its loss or gain on early termination, if determination as of the relevant Early Termination Date would not be commercially reasonable, should be viewed in the same light as the foregoing timing questions. New York contract law views as a question of fact whether action to mitigate damages is reasonable in a particular case.[767] Therefore, use of historical information as the basis for a Replacement Value determination would, if challenged as inconsistent with the duty to minimize damages, have to be analyzed in the context of the facts of the particular case. In this regard, it should be noted that the party in breach bears the burden of proving that an injured party could have lessened its damages.[768]

The doctrine of avoidable damages developed in the context of relatively simple claims for loss in connection with breach, where generally little attention is paid to the injured party's savings as a result of the breach—that is, as a result of being relieved of its

---

[766] *See supra* p. 241.

[767] *Losei Realty Corp. v. City of New York*, 254 N.Y. 41, 47 (1930).

[768] *See Air et Chaleur, S.A. v. Janeway*, 757 F.2d 489, 494, finding that the defendant in that case, which had repudiated its obligations under stock put options, as discussed *supra* note 757, had failed to meet that burden by merely adducing evidence of bid and asked prices for the stock in an over-the-counter market without presenting any evidence that plaintiffs could have sold their restricted stock in the market. *See also supra* note 743, regarding proof of market conditions using prices prevailing before a nondefaulting party learns of anticipatory repudiation of a contract by its counterparty, under the NYUCC.

Damages and Close-Out Settlement 263

obligation to continue to perform after the breach. The quantification of those savings, or the gain to a nondefaulting party on close-out of a transaction that is out-of-the-money to it, may, however, occupy a very central place under the standard agreements used in the derivatives market. This is so because, as discussed above, those agreements generally require the injured party to calculate its loss of bargain, or gain, in respect of all closed-out transactions on a net basis, thereby reducing its loss determined in respect of transactions that are in-the-money to it by its gain in respect of transactions that are out-of-the-money to it. As a result, disputes over an injured party's valuation of its gain, under the doctrine of minimization of damages or otherwise, could potentially be quite complex.

Some of the complexity that could surround disputes as to derivatives close-out settlement can be seen in an English case, *Peregrine Fixed Income Ltd (In Liquidation) v. Robinson Department Store Public Co.*,[769] where the court was asked to analyze an ISDA-based master agreement that provided for close-out settlement under the Market Quotation and Second Method approaches. The transaction involved in *Peregrine* was an unusual one, styled by the parties as a swap. It terminated automatically when Peregrine sought the appointment of a provisional liquidator for itself. At the time, all remaining obligations, a series of 25 annual payments of U.S.$ 6.85 million each, were owed to Peregrine. Robinson, the nondefaulting party, determined a Settlement Amount on the basis of quotations from three Reference Market-makers, by throwing out the highest and lowest (U.S.$ 25,500,000 and U.S.$ 750,000) and determining Market Quotation to be the remaining quotation (U.S.$ 9,694,901).

When Robinson obtained the quotations for Replacement Transactions, it too was in financial distress.[770] The wide disparity among the quotations apparently reflected the differing views of the Reference Market-makers about how to take Robinson's credit standing into account (that is, what discount to apply) in offering a front-end payment for the right to receive U.S.$ 171.25 million from Robinson over 25 years. The provisional liquidator for Peregrine, the defaulting party, challenged the use of the Market Quotation approach in these circumstances, submitting that it grossly undervalued Robinson's gain from early termination of the transaction. Peregrine's position was that Robinson could not reasonably conclude that Market Quotation produced a commercially reasonable result in the circumstances and, therefore, that the Settlement Amount payable by Robinson to Peregrine should be determined under the fallback Loss approach. The court, applying English law, agreed.

The court interpreted the interplay between the Market Quotation and Loss approaches and reached conclusions that some market participants found surprising. First, it was found that Market Quotation and Loss should yield roughly similar results, since both approaches purport to find loss of bargain and since, under the Market Quotation approach, Loss must be applied if Market Quotation cannot be determined or the nondefaulting party reasonably determines that Market Quotation would not produce a commercially reasonable result. Second, the court determined that, at least in the unusual facts of the case, the nondefaulting party's poor credit standing could not properly be

---

[769] [2000] Lloyd's L.R. 304 (Q.B.).

[770] At the time of the lawsuit, Robinson was involved in a restructuring of its debts under court supervision.

taken into account in determining how much it had gained from early termination. The termination of the transaction in fact relieved Robinson of an obligation to pay U.S.$ 171.25 million (with a present value, in accordance with "conventional discounting methods" of U.S.$ 87.3 million), and the court found no precedent in the law on the calculation of loss of bargain that supported reducing the nominal amount of such an obligation. The court noted in this connection that the definition of Loss does not expressly authorize consideration of the determining party's credit standing, whereas the definition of Market Quotation implicitly does, by providing that the quotations given by Reference Market-makers are to take into account existing credit support. Finally, the court concluded that a reasonable person in Robinson's position could not have concluded that Market Quotation would produce a commercially reasonable result in the circumstances; given the widely divergent quotations obtained from Reference Market-makers and the great disparity between the Market Quotation determined using those quotations and what Loss would have been if determined in accordance with the court's construction of the term.[771]

The *Peregrine* decision does not purport to state a rule that a nondefaulting party must calculate its close-out gain on out-of-the-money transactions in a manner designed to maximize the amount payable to the defaulting party. In fact, the *Peregrine* court pointedly rejected the argument that a nondefaulting party need do more than determine its loss or gain reasonably. The decision does, however, stand for the proposition that, under the ISDA concept of Loss, gain should not be calculated taking into account the nondefaulting party's credit standing. This result may have seemed especially appealing to the court in the *Peregrine* case because the economics of the transaction, although it was called a swap, seemed to resemble those of a loan. If the transaction had been documented as a loan on standard loan documentation, the insolvency of Peregrine, which would have been the lender, would not have resulted in accelerating Robinson's payment obligations.[772] The result may also have seemed appealing as the converse of a rule that an injured party's credit standing should not reduce its claim for damages for loss of bargain on a contract on the theory that it might not have been able to perform if it had not been relieved of its duty to do so by virtue of a contract's breach.[773]

However, if applied beyond the facts of the case, the *Peregrine* approach to calculation of Loss exposes a nondefaulting party to undue risk. If the nondefaulting party's credit standing actually affects what someone would pay to step into the shoes of the defaulting party in a replacement transaction but the nondefaulting party must disregard that effect in calculating its gain on a transaction, it is, by virtue of the other party's default, placed in the position of having to pay to the defaulting party an amount with a value in excess of what the defaulting party is losing by virtue of early termination. If the law is that recovery of damages on breach should leave an injured party in no worse position than it would have been in if the contract had been performed, the result surely should not be different if, instead of claiming damages, an injured party is calculating the benefit

---

[771] For further discussion of the *Peregrine* decision, including aspects of the court's analysis that are not mentioned above, *see* Henderson, *supra* note 687, at 197–99.

[772] *See* Annotation 2 to the proviso in Section 6(a) of the sample master agreement in Part 3, *infra* p. 850, for a discussion of various other problems that can arise from using Automatic Early Termination.

[773] *See supra* p. 258 for discussion of this rule under New York law applicable to executory contracts that have been wrongfully repudiated.

from close-out of the contract after breach that it will pay to the defaulting party, or credit to account in a net close-out settlement calculation.[774]

It would have been rather easy for the *Peregrine* court to have reached a different result, by giving effect to the language in the definition of "Loss" that permits the inclusion of "cost of funding" as an element of the value of the transaction being valued. It appears that the court used an average rate of around 6% per year in finding the present value of Robinson's obligations, surely a rate well below what Robinson would have had to pay in the market to obtain the funds to pay Peregrine early. The court could have (i) used Robinson's projected cost of funds as the discount rate and (ii) reduced the value of Robinson's gain from terminating the transaction by the difference between its projected cost of funds and the discount applied to its obligations to find their present value. With either approach, the Loss and Market Quotation valuations might well have produced similar numbers.

In part as a reaction to the *Peregrine* result, ISDA's new approach has defined Replacement Value, as noted above, in a way that makes clear that, in connection with the determination of Replacement Value, a "Determining Party (or its agent) may take into account, or may require third parties to supply . . . information to take into account, the current creditworthiness . . . of the Determining Party," as well as such other factors as the Determining Party's documentation and credit policies, the size of the Terminated Transaction or Terminated Transactions, market liquidity and other factors relevant under then prevailing circumstances." Those who continue to use the ISDA Loss approach may wish to incorporate similar language into their agreements.

ACTUAL COVER IS NOT REQUIRED, BUT COST OF COVER MAY LIMIT RECOVERY

Under principles of New York law applicable to the calculation of actual damages for breach of contract, a nondefaulting party is not required to obtain cover in order to base its damages claim on the cost of cover, although if it does obtain cover, its claim for damages based on cost of cover may be limited to its actual cost.[775] When parties calculate claims applying the Loss or Replacement Value approach, they should take this rule into account. The Market Quotation approach is consistent with these principles in that it permits a party to determine Market Quotation on the basis of quotations for Replacement Transactions without actually requiring that the party enter into a Replacement Transaction.

---

[774]By definition, where the law is that damages for loss of bargain should put the injured party in the position it would have been in if the contract had been performed, through cost of cover or otherwise, the *Peregrine* interpretation of Loss should not apply to the calculation of the nondefaulting party's positive loss of bargain on an in-the-money transaction where it has remaining obligations, because in any such case doubts about its ability to perform are likely to affect its cost of cover.

[775]"The injured party is limited to damages based on his actual loss caused by the breach. If he makes an especially favorable substitute transaction, so that he sustains a smaller loss than might have been expected, his damages are reduced by the loss avoided as a result of that transaction. . . . If he arranges a substitute transaction that he would not have been expected to do under the rules on avoidability . . . , his damages are similarly limited by the loss so avoided." RESTATEMENT (SECOND) OF CONTRACTS § 347, cmt. e (1981).

In the early days of the swap market, this aspect of the Market Quotation approach was upheld in *Drexel Burnham Lambert Products Corp. v. MCorp.*[776] In that case, the defendant challenged a swap agreement's Agreement Value measure on the theory that the damages provision was unenforceable as a penalty because it established damages on the basis of quotations but there was no proof that the Non-defaulting Party had actually covered its position after the swap terminated. The court rejected the argument, describing the agreement value approach embodied in the agreement as a market-based measure of the actual loss of the Non-defaulting Party.[777] Because there was no showing that the plaintiff had actually obtained a Replacement Transaction, the result does not necessarily mean that a party will be entitled to base a claim for damages on Market Quotation determined as contemplated in the ISDA master agreement forms if the party actually obtains a Replacement Transaction at a lower cost.[778]

As a practical matter, a market participant faced with a default situation should be aware of the advantages of actually covering the position, and doing so at a time as close as possible to breach and close-out.[779] Actually covering has the advantage of working to eliminate the charge that a damages claim is "purely theoretical," as occurred in the *Ackerley Communications* case discussed above.[780]

RELIANCE-INTEREST OR LOSS-OF-BARGAIN DAMAGES

Finally, as described above, the FEOMA approach to close-out settlement for currency options and the ISDA Loss and Replacement Value approaches all list a variety of ways in which an injured party may calculate its loss of bargain, or gain. In each case, the formulation makes clear that a combination of the alternatives may not result in duplica-

---

[776] No. 88C-NO-80 (Super. Del. Feb. 23, 1989), *motion for reargument denied*, 1991 Del. Super. LEXIS 298 (Aug. 13, 1991).

[777] For further discussion of the case, *see supra* note 762, and Gooch & Klein, *Review of Case Law I*, at 428.

[778] As a result, counsel asked to render a New York law enforceability opinion under on an ISDA-based master agreement where the parties have selected (or are deemed to have selected) Market Quotation as an applicable Payment Measure, may decide to express no opinion on Section 6(e) in any case in which it produces a claim in excess of actual damages. This kind of qualification is also useful to address the averaging feature of the Market Quotation approach, as discussed above in the context of principles of New York law regarding a nondefaulting party's duty to seek to minimize its damages.

[779] Discussing English law, Clark, *supra* note 82, at 193, has written:

> Where a counterparty faces losses on a transaction, it may decide to mitigate its losses by closing out the transaction. Should the market subsequently move in such a way as to reduce the losses which would have been suffered had the transaction not been closed out, it may not be open to the defendant to argue that the counterparty should not, in hindsight, have taken the steps which it did. This is especially the case if the counterparty takes the steps in mitigation after having taken advice. (citation omitted).

[780] *Supra* p. 235. *See also infra* p. 338 on a provision of the NYBL that provides that the liability of the New York banking superintendent, when acting as receiver for a branch or agency of a foreign bank, is limited to "actual direct compensatory damages . . . determined as of the date the superintendent took possession of the banking organization," and that compensatory damages, for this purpose, are deemed to include "normal and reasonable costs of cover or other reasonable measures of damages utilized among participants in the market for qualified financial contract claims, calculated as of the date of the . . . termination of such qualified financial contract in accordance with its terms."

tion. Although the statement seems obvious in a purely quantitative sense, it should also be taken into account in light of the principle that an injured party may seek damages *either* to compensate for its loss of bargain, so that it is left in a position that is as good as it would have been in if the contract had been performed, *or* to compensate for the expenses and losses that it has incurred in preparation for performance, or in performing under a contract, so that it is left in as good a position as it would have been in if it had never entered into the contract.

The second alternative, as noted, is rarely attractive, since it does not compensate for lost profit on a transaction, but if lost profits are difficult to prove, it should enable an injured party to claim costs associated with unwinding a hedge—one of the elements expressly mentioned in the Loss, Replacement Value and FEOMA approaches. As discussed above, if an injured party believes that it will not be made whole in connection with close-out of a transaction unless it is permitted to consider both loss on the transaction (loss of bargain) and loss or expenses relating to dealings with third parties, it should consider principles limiting recovery of special, or consequential, damages to those that are foreseeable at the time of contract. In these cases, a counterparty's acknowledgment of the special circumstances may be desirable.

CHAPTER 7

BANKRUPTCY AND INSOLVENCY CONCERNS

Introduction	268
Basic Terminology and Issues	270
Special Insolvency Treatment of OTC Derivatives	
Contract Categories	278
Protected Persons	282
Identifying the Applicable Insolvency Law	288
Bankruptcy Code	288
Federal Deposit Insurance Act	291
New York Banking Law	293
Bankruptcy Code	
Issues	294
Financial Contract Exceptions	303
Federal Deposit Insurance Act	
Issues	310
Exceptions for Qualified Financial Contracts	312
Other Federal Banking Laws	319
New York Banking Law	322
Issues	322
Exceptions for Qualified Financial Contracts	324
Netting Contracts	328
Claims for Damages and Walkaway Clauses	337
Schedule of Bankruptcy Code Definitions	340

INTRODUCTION

A critical concern for participants in the OTC derivatives market is whether the terms agreed on with a counterparty will be enforceable if the counterparty encounters financial difficulties. This chapter looks at this concern in the context of the provisions customarily found in OTC derivatives documents that treat as grounds for closing out agreements a variety of events that are indicators of a party's need for relief from its creditors' claims. These events, which we refer to as "Insolvency Events," often include not only the institution of bankruptcy, insolvency, reorganization or similar proceedings and the appointment of a trustee, receiver, liquidator, administrator, conservator or similar official for the counterparty or its property,[781] but also the counterparty's admission of inability to pay debts as they come due and actions by creditors to enforce rights against the counterparty's assets.[782]

---

[781] For discussion of this topic in the context of lawsuits involving insolvencies of parties to OTC derivatives transactions, *see* Gooch & Klein, *Review of Case Law I*, at 423–37, and Margaret E. Grottenthaler, *Derivatives Litigation in Canada, in* DERIVATIVES HANDBOOK 135.

[782] These Insolvency Events may also be made applicable to third parties, such as guarantors, that extend credit support for a party's obligations ("Credit Support Providers," in ISDA terminology). They may also be extended to other third parties ("Specified Entities") in cases in which the financial distress of the third party may be a sign of impending difficulty for a party or its Credit Support Provider, for example, when the party or its Credit Support Provider may be liable for the obligations of the Specified Entity. *See*

Bankruptcy and Insolvency Concerns 269

The chapter first identifies the basic enforceability issues most often analyzed in the light of insolvency and similar laws in connection with OTC derivatives and other financial products and introduces some of the terminology used in analyzing these issues. As will be seen from that discussion, the concerns that arise in the OTC derivatives context go well beyond the simple question whether the counterparty (or its credit supporter provider) will have the financial means to perform its obligations and raise highly technical issues involving close-out netting and setoff rights and the enforceability of collateral arrangements.

The second section of the chapter provides an overview of the cases in which insolvency or similar proceedings may be conducted in the United States under laws with broad potential for application to many participants in the OTC derivatives markets: the Bankruptcy Code, the FDIA, the National Bank Act (the "NBA"), the International Banking Act of 1970 (the "IBA") and the NYBL.[783]

As discussed in the third section, some, but not all, of these laws include special provisions on derivatives and other financial products designed to address issues of the kind discussed in this chapter. These special provisions may vary from statute to statute, and they may not be available for all categories of counterparties. They may also differ depending on the type of financial contracts involved and the identity of the creditor.

Separate sections of the chapter then look at these issues in the specific contexts of the Bankruptcy Code, the FDIA, the NBA and the IBA and the NYBL. The final sections address issues relating to netting contracts, damages and so-called walkaway clauses—provisions under which an amount that would otherwise be payable to a party under a contract is forfeited because it is a defaulting party—both in the context of these laws and in the context of the netting contract provisions of FDICIA.

In dealing with the subjects outlined above, we also describe proposed changes to the Bankruptcy Code, the FDIA and FDICIA, which have been considered in various forms by successive sessions of the U.S. congress since the 1990s and are still pending. The description in this chapter is based on H.R. 3211, a bill introduced in the U.S. House of Representatives on November 1, 2001, to enact the Financial Contracts Bankruptcy Reform Act of 2001.[784]

---

infra p. 900 on the treatment of bank affiliates as Specified Entities when U.S. law may impose such liability. *See also infra* p. 831 for the relevant event of default, called "Bankruptcy," in Section 5(a)(vii) of the 1992 ISDA Master Agreements, and *see infra* p. 965 on changes to that Event of Default under the *2001 ISDA Amendments*.

[783] It is entirely possible that laws other than those dealing with insolvency and similar proceedings may have an important impact on contractual rights in the context of a counterparty's insolvency. For example, the corporation laws of many states include provisions pursuant to which an obligation of a corporation to purchase its own stock may not be enforceable if incurred while the corporation's capital is impaired. The identification of possibly relevant laws of this kind is critical, since a creditor's claims in insolvency and similar proceedings are likely to be allowed only if, or to the extent, they are enforceable under noninsolvency law. This chapter looks only at insolvency and similar laws.

[784] The provisions on financial contracts included in H.R. 3211 were extracted from Title IX of separate bills—H.R. 333 and S. 420—adopted earlier in 2001 by the House and the Senate to enact the Bankruptcy Abuse Prevention and Consumer Protection Act of 2001, after progress towards the drafting of a compromise became stalled for reasons unrelated to the financial contract provisions of those earlier bills. As this book goes to press, congressional efforts in 2002 to reach a compromise on broader bankruptcy reform

This introductory section began with the observation that the issues discussed below arise under laws that may affect the parties' bargained-for rights when Insolvency Events occur. After reviewing with counsel the various circumstances that could give rise to insolvency or similar proceedings for a particular counterparty, market participants should then examine the Insolvency Events included in proposed contracts to see if they are adequate.[785] If important rights will, or may be, lost, or their exercise may be delayed, because of the commencement of insolvency or similar proceedings for the counterparty or its credit support provider, the parties may decide to expand the grounds for close-out of transactions.

Ultimately, participants in the markets for OTC derivatives and other financial products must generally transact with their counterparties, and require related credit support, with an awareness that the entity representing the "credit" behind the dealings (be it the counterparty or a credit support provider) may become the subject of insolvency or similar proceedings with little or no advance warning. Given this awareness, the party's analysis of the laws that might govern these proceedings should lead to a reasonably reliable ability to assess whether, or how much, those laws may interfere with management of the risk of loss from those dealings.

BASIC TERMINOLOGY AND ISSUES

In the following discussion, we use the term "Insolvency Laws" to refer generically to laws aimed at affording relief to persons who are insolvent, financially distressed or otherwise eligible for relief from claims of creditors or subject to insolvency or similar proceedings, as well as laws that may otherwise provide for an entity's liquidation or winding up. "Proceedings" is used to refer to any kind of action for relief or action taken for a person's liquidation or winding up under an Insolvency Law. "Debtor" is the term used to refer to the subject of Proceedings. "Estate" is used to refer to the Debtor's property involved in the Proceedings. "Insolvency Representative" is used to refer to a trustee, receiver, liquidator, administrator, conservator or other official appointed for the Debtor or the Estate in the Proceedings.

---

legislation that would again incorporate the provisions extracted to create H.R. 3211 have not succeeded, so our discussion describes the financial contract provisions as they were included in that separate bill.

[785] An informed decision on the drafting of the close-out provisions will depend on an understanding of the events and circumstances that may serve as the basis for the commencement of insolvency or similar proceedings for the relevant counterparty or its credit support provider. For example, if a depository institution's deposits are FDIC-insured, the FDIC may be appointed receiver or conservator for the institution in connection with any violation of law or regulation, or any "unsafe or unsound practice or condition" that is "likely to—(i) cause insolvency or substantial dissipation of assets or earnings; (ii) weaken the institution's condition; or (iii) otherwise seriously prejudice the interests of the institution's deposits or the deposit insurance fund." FDIA § 11(c)(5)(H). Under both the FDIA and the NYBL, other grounds for appointment of a receiver or conservator include problems or likely problems in meeting obligations or involving capitalization. *See, e.g.,* NYBL § 606(1)(e) & (f) & FDIA § 11(c)(4)(A), (F), (G) & (K). In addition, under the IBA, a creditor of a federally chartered branch or agency in the United States of a foreign bank may apply for the appointment of a receiver for the property and assets of the foreign bank in the U.S. by obtaining a judgment against the foreign bank's U.S. branch or agency in a state or federal court in this country and making an application to the OCC, accompanied by a certificate from the clerk of the court stating that the judgment has been rendered and remained unpaid for 30 days. IBA § 4(j)(1).

Bankruptcy and Insolvency Concerns

Proceedings are referred to as "Voluntary" if they are instituted by the Debtor and "Involuntary" if they are instituted against the Debtor or its property.[786] Whether Voluntary or Involuntary, Proceedings are referred to as involving "Liquidation" if their aim is to wind up the Debtor's business and conduct an orderly distribution of the Debtor's property or the proceeds of its liquidation. Proceedings are referred to as involving "Reorganization" if their aim is to enable the Debtor to obtain relief sufficient for it to emerge as a rehabilitated, viable concern—or at least for it to continue operations for the time necessary to arrange the sale of any viable business as a going concern, with the aim of generating proceeds greater than those likely to be produced in a Liquidation.

This chapter also adopts generic terminology to refer to some of the basic Insolvency Law issues that market participants usually analyze when they first consider entering into OTC derivatives transactions with a given counterparty. These issues relate primarily to the rights listed below, which are usually viewed as fundamental to the parties' dealings.[787] Uncertainty about whether these rights will be enforceable under the Insolvency Laws applicable to a potential counterparty may result in a decision not to trade with it at all or in dealings at a level far lower than that which would have been possible if the uncertainty did not exist:[788]

- The right (the "Close-Out Right") to terminate, liquidate or cancel transactions,[789] or to treat transactions as automatically terminated, liquidated or canceled,[790] if an Insolvency Event occurs with respect to the counterparty

---

[786] *See infra* pp. 839 & 965 for discussion of the ways in which Insolvency Events in standardized market contracts distinguish between Voluntary Proceedings and Involuntary Proceedings and for further distinctions (for example in the FEOMA, ICOM and IFEMA forms and in the *2001 ISDA Amendments*) between Involuntary Proceedings that are commenced in a Debtor's home jurisdiction by a governmental authority or self-regulatory organization with jurisdiction over the Debtor or its assets, on one hand, and anyone else, on the other.

[787] There are cases in which the parties bargain away some of these rights. When used in complex investment structures derivatives are, for example, often isolated from other dealings between the parties so that the parties' mutual claims under other dealings will not affect a derivatives cash flow that is central to the structure. *See infra* note 2101.

[788] In some cases these uncertainties do not constrain dealings with the counterparty. The risk of loss that may result from the counterparty's financial difficulties may be perceived to be acceptable (say in dealings with sovereign states), or the parties may agree to special termination rights (such as the right to close out transactions in the event of a downgrade of the counterparty's debt) that, it is assumed, can be exercised, or will automatically be exercised, in advance of default. *See infra* p. 907.

[789] In fact, although the practice, which we will follow below, is to refer to the transactions as being closed out, termination usually relates to the parties' obligations scheduled to fall due after close-out. *See* Annotation 2 to Section 6(c)(ii) of the sample master agreement, *supra* p. 857.

[790] The presumption in ISDA's 1987 master agreement forms was that the parties would want automatic early termination to apply. This presumption was reversed in ISDA's 1992 forms. The 1997 FEOMA (§ 8.1(a)), ICOM (§ 8.1(a)) and IFEMA (§ 5.1(a)) forms retain a presumption of automatic transaction close-out and liquidation in connection with insolvency-related events but make available a place in the schedule to the master agreement in which the parties may override the presumption. The 2000 Master OTC Options Agreement published by TBMA provides (in § 8(a)) for automatic cancellation, close-out and liquidation of options in connection with any "Act of Insolvency" and does not expressly contemplate the possibility that the parties may wish to override this rule. On the potential dangers involved in automatic close-out, *see* the discussion included in the annotations to Section 6(a) of the sample master agreement in Part 3, *infra* p. 850.

- The right (the "Right to Settle Net") to reduce to a single, net amount the mutual claims of the parties in respect of their derivatives dealings, whether by way of setoff, through a close-out settlement mechanism provided for in a master agreement[791] or pursuant to another framework for netting

- The right to be protected against what is often referred to as cherry-picking—actions by the counterparty or its Insolvency Representative that could diminish the benefits of the Right to Settle Net, such as selective assumption and transfer of transactions that are in the money to the defaulting Debtor and repudiation of the rest

- The right to retain payments and transfers, including collateral or other credit support, made by the counterparty before it becomes a Debtor in Proceedings or before the appointment of an Insolvency Representative for the counterparty or its property

- The right, through setoff or otherwise, to apply collateral or other credit support in respect of a claim against the Debtor for a close-out settlement or other unpaid obligations of the Debtor

Concerns about the enforceability of these rights are easily understood in the context of the credit limits that are applicable to the operations of market participants and the increased exposure to loss that a party may incur if its counterparty defaults and the rights are not enforced. Participants in the derivatives markets usually trade subject to internal credit limits that they set periodically for each counterparty (and, perhaps, to global limits for certain categories of risk). They may also be subject to limits imposed by supervisory agencies. Many are also subject to capital adequacy regulations that lead them to evaluate the projected return on possible dealings after adjustment for the capital charges that would be assessed on account of the risk of counterparty default.[792]

In the context of these risk limits and capital requirements, if a party must look at the value of each separate transaction with a counterparty as representing a potential total loss in the event of the counterparty's failure—say, because the Close-Out Right and Right to Settle Net would not be protected in Proceedings for the counterparty, or the counterparty or its Insolvency Representative would be entitled to engage in cherry-picking that could that diminish those rights—the volume of acceptable dealings with the counterparty may, logically, be much smaller than would the case if these rights were enforceable. On the other hand, if these rights are enforceable, the aggregate potential loss in that event could with substantial certainty be viewed as a smaller net amount equal in

---

[791] *See* Section 6(e) of the sample multicurrency master agreement and related annotations, *infra* p. 860, for discussion of this net claim, which may be calculated in various ways to capture the value of the payments scheduled to fall due after close-out along with payments that were scheduled to have been paid on or before the date of the close-out and certain other amounts.

[792] *See supra* p. 13 on the capital adequacy regimes applicable to many banks. Various techniques are used to analyze risk in these terms. *See, e.g.*, DICTIONARY OF FINANCIAL RISK MANAGEMENT 238 & 243, under "Return on Risk-Adjusted Capital (RORAC)," "Risk-Adjusted Return on Capital (RAROC)" and "Risk-Adjusted Return on Risk-Adjusted Capital (RARORAC)."

the simplest case, roughly speaking, to (1) the aggregate value of transactions, or transactions of specific types, that are in the money to the party less (2) the aggregate value of the transactions that are in the money to the failed counterparty and less (3) the aggregate value of the collateral or other credit support provided by the counterparty.

If there is doubt about the enforceability of these rights, the amount of the required credit support, or the expected return from the possible dealings with the counterparty, may have to be much higher than would otherwise be the case.[793] The results of the analysis would be similar or might even lead to a decision not to trade with a counterparty at all if potentially applicable Insolvency Law could impair the right to retain payments and collateral transfers received from the counterparty prior to the commencement of Proceedings, or if the law disallowed or permitted the counterparty or its Insolvency Representative to avoid obligations incurred prior to the commencement of Proceedings for the counterparty.

Concerns about the enforceability of contractual rights arise in connection with Insolvency Laws because these laws often override those rights or delay their exercise, in order to serve the public policy purposes reflected in the legislation. For example, some Insolvency Laws contain "automatic stay" provisions, which provide that, once a Debtor has become the subject of Proceedings or an Insolvency Representative has been appointed for the Debtor or any of its property, rights to close out at least some transactions and apply credit support to satisfy claims are stayed and may not be exercised unless the action is authorized by a court or by an Insolvency Representative, so that the Debtor's Estate is insulated pending an orderly and equitable disposition of all recognized creditor claims. Under another common approach, the appointment of an Insolvency Representative or commencement of Proceedings automatically results in the close-out of contracts with the Debtor, regardless of a provision in the contract permitting the other party to choose whether and when to close out.

Once Proceedings have been commenced, generally transfers of property of the Debtor are prohibited (and may be reversed) unless they have been approved by order of a court or other relevant authority or the transfer is expressly permitted by law. In addition, under some Insolvency Laws, Debtors or their Insolvency Representatives may be given special powers—which we refer to below generically as "Avoidance Powers"—to reverse transfers of property of the Debtor. These powers will generally relate to transfers made within a specified period leading up to the commencement of Proceedings. These Avoidance Powers may view the concept of "transfer of property" broadly for this purpose and, so, may involve the disavowal of obligations that the Debtor incurred during the specified period. These periods are often set on the presumption that transfers made and obligations incurred relatively shortly before a Debtor's insolvency may be suspect or may be conclusively presumed to favor one creditor over others unfairly. If a transfer benefits an insider, the "suspect period" may be longer, on the theory that those who are in a privileged position to know of the Debtor's troubles before they become public

---

[793]This statement of the measure is rough because it does not take into account, for instance, overdue payments or credit support from third parties. *See* Chapter 6, *supra* p. 219, on the various ways in which net settlements in connection with close-outs may be calculated.

through the commencement of Proceedings should not be allowed to use that position to obtain an advantage over other creditors.

Sometimes Avoidance Powers exist only when there is proof that a transfer was made, or an obligation was incurred, with the intent to defraud creditors or an Insolvency Representative, but this is not always the case. In addition to these intentional fraudulent transfers or conveyances, some Insolvency Laws recognize "constructive fraudulent conveyances," by extending Avoidance Powers to cases in which the Debtor is perceived as not having obtained fair value for the transfer that it made, or for the obligation that it incurred.[794] These Avoidance Powers relating to constructive fraudulent transfers are sometimes conditioned on a finding that the Debtor was insolvent at the time the transfer was made or the obligation was incurred or as a result of the transfer or obligation was left insolvent, unable to pay its debts as they matured or with capital that was unreasonably small in light of its then expected business or transactions.

Furthermore, when transfers are made by a Debtor within specified periods leading up to its Proceedings on account of obligations that were already outstanding at the time of the transfer, Avoidance Powers may turn on purely mathematical tests so that those who benefit from these transfers do not retain more than they would be entitled to receive in the Debtor's liquidation. A transfer of this kind on account of antecedent debt may simply be viewed by the law as an inappropriate preference to the beneficiary of the transfer, at least to the extent that the Debtor has not received a substantially contemporaneous exchange of new value, in the absence of other factors indicating that the transfer should not be viewed as preferential.[795] Similarly, although Insolvency Laws may generally preserve setoff rights arising out of the mutual claims of a Debtor and a creditor to the extent they existed prior to the commencement of Proceedings for the Debtor, exceptions may exist in respect of mutual claims that come into existence, and setoff rights that are exercised, shortly before the Proceedings commence.[796]

From jurisdiction to jurisdiction, and even within a single jurisdiction, Insolvency Laws can vary a good deal as to these and other matters. Within the laws of a single country, for example, separate legal regimes may apply to Proceedings for particular classes of Debtors, such as natural persons, local governmental bodies, general business organizations, domestic banks and financial institutions, local branches or agencies of foreign banks, insurance companies and securities brokers and others entrusted with customer funds. Sovereign states are a special class and are not subject to Proceedings under Insolvency Laws, and the same may be true for at least some political subdivisions.

Distinctions in Insolvency Laws may also be drawn on the basis of the nature of the creditor's claims. Some of these distinctions relate to priorities in the distribution of the Debtor's general assets and are founded on broad social or economic policies, or on the need to give preference to those who provide accommodations to a Debtor during Proceedings. So, for instance, tax and other statutory claims of the government or a governmental agency may come ahead of the claims of other creditors, in proceedings for

---

[794] *See infra* p. 302 on Section 548 of the Bankruptcy Code.

[795] *See infra* p. 299 on the avoidance of preferences under Section 547 of the Bankruptcy Code.

[796] *See infra* p. 300 on these issues under Section 553 of the Bankruptcy Code.

an insurance company, policyholders' claims may come ahead of other claims against the insurer and in what are referred to as debtor-in-possession Reorganization Proceedings under the Bankruptcy Code, creditors that supply funds to the Debtor to finance its operations during the Proceedings expect to be granted a special priority that puts their claims for this financing ahead of the claims of creditors arising out of their dealings with the Debtor during the Proceedings.

Other distinctions are more geographical and reflect the view that creditors whose claims arise out of local dealings with a Debtor should be given preference, in the distribution of the Debtor's local assets, to creditors (even the same creditors) whose dealings with the Debtor arise elsewhere. Concerns relating to these distinctions, often referred to as ring-fencing, often arise in connection with dealings with banks, which may engage in dealings with a single creditor from multiple offices of the bank.

Under one type of ring-fencing provision, a creditor's recoveries in the local Proceedings, from the Estate involved in those Proceedings, may not exceed the amount the creditor would be entitled to receive in respect of its local dealings with the Debtor. This is the partial ring-fencing approach taken in the provisions of the NYBL[797] relating to OTC derivatives and other qualified financial contracts in Proceedings for a New York branch or agency of a foreign bank that has acted from multiple offices under the same agreement—in ISDA parlance, as a multibranch party.[798]

Under another type of ring-fencing, the Debtor's assets available to creditor claims in the Proceedings may be applied only to claims of creditors who have dealt with a local branch or agency of the Debtor. Section 4(j) of the IBA has been thought to take this approach to the property in the United States of any bank organized outside this country if the Comptroller of the Currency, pursuant to that provision of the IBA, appoints a receiver for any branch or agency of the foreign bank in the U.S. Section 4(j) of the IBA suggests that the assets of the foreign bank involved in the receivership are subject only to claims arising out of dealings between the bank's U.S. branches and agencies and creditors, and any of those assets (or their proceeds) remaining after the distribution prescribed in the IBA are to be turned over to head office of the foreign bank or an Insolvency Representative conducting Proceedings in the foreign bank's home jurisdiction.[799]

---

[797] The general ring-fencing rule is set out as follows in Section 606(4)(a) of the NYBL: "Only the claims of creditors of such corporation arising out of transactions had by them with its New York agency or agencies, or with its New York branch or branches, shall be accepted by the superintendent for payment out of such business and property in this state as provided in this article." The more liberal rule for qualified financial contracts is discussed *infra* p. 325.

[798] On multibranch parties, *see* Section 10 of the sample master agreement and related annotations, *infra* p. 874.

[799] The IBA provides for this turnover after payment of all expenses of the receivership and payment of all but excluded claims of depositors and creditors, but only to the extent the claims arise out of "transactions had by them with any branch or agency of such foreign bank located in any State of the United States," subject to two exclusions: "(A) claims that would not represent an enforceable legal obligation against such branch or agency if such branch or agency were a separate legal entity, and (B) amounts due and other liabilities to other offices or branches or agencies of, and wholly owned (except for a nominal number of directors' shares) subsidiaries of, such foreign bank." IBA § 4(j)(2). This language has been thought to require treatment of transactions with the federally licensed branches and agencies of foreign banks in the U.S. as if they were transactions with a legal entity separate from the head office and other branches of the foreign bank. *See* "Differences in Treatment of

The special Insolvency Law provisions discussed below for OTC derivatives and other financial contracts involve yet a third kind of distinction. These product-specific provisions create exceptions to the rules that would otherwise apply under the Insolvency Laws, to protect the functioning, and promote the development, of the financial markets. In these markets, the bilateral dealings between the Debtor and its counterparty may be but one link in a chain: Party A pays fixed amounts to Party B in rate swap 1, Party B to Party C in swap 2, and so on. The special provisions relating to these products apply so as to reduce the risk—referred to as system, or systemic, risk—that Proceedings for a market participant will produce a ripple effect that will have adverse effects on others all along the chain. The following are examples:

1. Insolvency Law provisions may give a Debtor's counterparty greater certainty about the timing of the termination of its transactions with the Debtor and perhaps greater control over it. This makes it possible for the counterparty to adjust its transactions with others as necessary to reflect the termination of the transactions with the Debtor, for example, by terminating a hedge or adding a replacement transaction to its book. For the markets to function properly, intermediaries should not be locked into a position between a Debtor that may not perform and a third party, in a hedging position, which expects full performance from the intermediary. Nor can intermediaries function properly if they must face the risk of learning only after the fact that a transaction with the Debtor that they thought had terminated is going to be treated as remaining in place. In such a case, the intermediary could be left with an unnecessary replacement transaction or without a hedge for the transaction with the Debtor. Either way, it could incur substantial loss because of the mismatch. Insolvency Laws may protect intermediaries against these risks by permitting them, notwithstanding the commencement of Proceedings for a counterparty, to exercise a Close-Out Right and calculate any related settlement payment due from one party to the other as at the time the intermediary replaces the closed out transactions or unwinds its hedge.

2. Special Insolvency Law provisions may protect the Debtor's counterparty from the risk of having to return to the Estate payments or transfers received in good faith from the Debtor before the commencement of Proceedings, by creating exceptions from generally applicable Avoidance Powers. Such provisions permit market participants to rely on the finality of those payments and transfers and to use the funds,

---

United States Creditors under Bankruptcy and Receivership Laws," Appendix E to the "Subsidiary Requirement Study, made pursuant to Section 215 of FDICIA, conducted by the Secretary of the Treasury and the Board of Governors of the Federal Reserve System" (submitted to Senator Riegle on December 18, 1992). The Chief Counsel of the OCC has, however, indicated that this provision of the IBA and the related powers of a receiver in IBA Proceedings (many of which are derived from the NBA) should not interfere with the Right to Settle Net under an otherwise enforceable netting contract or a secured party's enforcement action against collateral under an otherwise enforceable security arrangement even though the netting or enforcement action against the collateral involves obligations of a non-U.S. office of the foreign bank involved in the IBA receivership Proceedings. *See infra* p. 320.

Bankruptcy and Insolvency Concerns 277

securities or other property received from the Debtor, or recovered through setoff, to fund or provide credit support in transactions with third parties who, naturally, have no obligation to give the money or property back merely because the Debtor has failed.

3. Special Insolvency Law provisions may seek to promote market liquidity by protecting setoff and other netting rights. That is, by ensuring that those rights will be enforceable notwithstanding the occurrence of an Insolvency Event with respect to the Debtor, and by ensuring that credit support may be applied to claims against the Debtor notwithstanding the commencement of Proceedings and the appointment of an Insolvency Representative, these provisions may enable market participants to make trading decisions on the basis of net, rather than gross, calculations of exposure to loss.[800]

Product-specific provisions of the Insolvency Laws may also seek to achieve each of the goals summarized above through provisions relating to dealings with multilateral clearing organizations, which are central to the existence of some of the most liquid markets for financial products. Simply stated, the liquidity in these markets—such as exchanges and other multilateral trading facilities—is possible because a clearing organization acts as the buyer to every seller in a financial contract, and as the seller to every buyer, so none of the organization's counterparties needs to evaluate the risk of default by any of the others, so long as the organization itself retains its ability to perform regardless of the failure of any of its counterparties. For this to be the case, special Insolvency Law provisions may protect Close-Out Rights and Rights to Settle Net arising out of the rules of clearing organizations and related rights to set off claims against the margin held within the clearing system or by those who deal directly within it to support their related dealings with their customers.[801]

SPECIAL INSOLVENCY TREATMENT OF OTC DERIVATIVES

The following subsections discuss the special insolvency protections applicable to OTC derivatives. As explained, they are available for specified categories of transactions and, under the Bankruptcy Code (unlike the FDIA and the NYBL), some of the special protections are available only if the creditor fits into a particular class. In the remainder of this chapter, we will sometimes refer to the classes of persons entitled to protection, collectively, as "Protected Persons."

---

[800] *Supra* p. 272.

[801] *See infra* pp. 285 & 304. For a succinct description of the market-based rationale for provisions of this kind, *see In re Amcor Funding Corp.*, 117 B.R. 549, 551–52 (D. Az. 1990) (quoting from legislative history of the Bankruptcy Code amendments introducing special provisions relating to securities contracts). Some clearing agencies operate differently. *See infra* p. 488.

CONTRACT CATEGORIES

In the Bankruptcy Code and the FDIA, the OTC derivatives transactions that may benefit from special protections of Close-Out Rights, Rights to Settle Net and other important rights and protections are grouped in the following categories:[802]

- swap agreements,
- securities contracts,
- forward contracts,
- commodity contracts and
- repurchase agreements.

We refer to all these categories collectively as "financial contracts" or as "qualified financial contracts," the term used to refer to them in the FDIA[803] and the NYBL.[804]

The definitions of the individual categories for purposes of the Bankruptcy Code and the FDIA are largely identical but not completely so.[805] H.R. 3211 would both expand

---

[802] The Bankruptcy Code definitions of these classes of contracts appear in Sections 101(25) (forward contract), 101(47) (repurchase agreement), 101(53B) (swap agreement), 741(7) (securities contract) and 761(4) (commodity contract). The Schedule of Bankruptcy Code Definitions at the end of this chapter sets out some of the key terms as they are defined in existing legislation and in the H.R. 3211 reform proposal. The definitions of these classes of contracts in the FDIA appear in the following clauses of Section 11(e)(8)(D) of the FDIA: cl. (ii): securities contract; cl. (iii): commodity contract; cl. (iv): forward contract; cl. (v): repurchase agreement; cl. (vi): swap agreement.

[803] For FDIA purposes, "qualified financial contract" is defined in Section 11(e)(8)(D)(i) to include any "securities contract, commodity contract, forward contract, repurchase agreement, swap agreement, and any similar agreement that the Corporation [the FDIC] determines by regulation to be a qualified financial contract for purposes of this paragraph."

[804] "Qualified financial contract" is defined in Section 618–a(1)(e) of NYBL to mean "any securities contract, commodity contract, forward contract (including spot and forward foreign exchange), repurchase agreement, swap agreement, and any similar agreement, any option to enter into any such agreement, including any combination of the foregoing, and any master agreement for such agreements (such master agreement, together with all supplements thereto, shall be treated as one qualified financial contract), provided that such contract, option or agreement, or combination of contracts, options or agreements is reflected in the books, accounts or records of the banking organization or a party provides documentary evidence of such agreement." The section also gives the New York banking superintendent the power to define certain terms used in the definition and to determine that other agreements are "qualified financial contracts."

[805] The FDIA originally borrowed the definitions from the Bankruptcy Code, at the time the FDIA was amended in 1991, through FIRREA, to address qualified financial contracts. However, subsequent expansions of the definitions of financial contracts in the Bankruptcy Code and the FDIA were not identical. In 1995, the FDIC adopted a rule expanding the definition of "qualified financial contract." 12 CFR § 360.5 (2002). "Repurchase agreements" under Section 11(e)(8)(D)(v) of the FDIA was expanded to include repos on foreign qualified government securities—direct obligations of, or obligations fully guaranteed by, the central governments of the OECD-based group of countries. The Bankruptcy Code's definition of "repurchase agreement" was not amended when the FDIC adopted this rule. The rule operates by reference to a list of the OECD countries in 12 CFR part 325, appendix A, as amended from time to time. The FDIC rule also expands "swap agreement" for purposes of Section 11(e)(8)(D)(vi) of the FDIA to include spot foreign exchange transactions, which were not covered by the definition of "swap agreement" in the Bankruptcy Code originally incorporated into the FDIA but were subsequently added to the Bankruptcy Code definition of the term. The FDIA (but not the Bankruptcy Code) defines "spot foreign exchange agreement" for this purpose to include "any agreement providing for or effecting the purchase or sale of one currency in exchange for

on the definitions in these statutes and restore the identity of the classes of financial contracts they cover.[806]

Some OTC derivatives may fall within more than one of these classes. For example, a deliverable FX forward transaction would qualify as a swap agreement and as a forward contract. Under H.R. 3211, there would be additional overlapping. The modified definitions would, for example, expressly provide that an option on a security is both a securities contract and a swap agreement, and that a forward on a security is a forward contract, a securities contract and a swap agreement. As noted below,[807] in some cases the overlap may be beneficial to the creditor, because the creditor may qualify for special protections relating to one category but not another.

The definition of "swap agreement" in both statutes is very expansive, in that it includes not only products listed in the statute, consisting of the kinds of products commonly engaged in by market participants at the time the definition was most recently amended (1991) but also any other similar agreement and any option to enter into any of the agreements captured by the definition. One of the purposes of the proposed reforms in H.R. 3211 is to make even clearer that this definition should be interpreted to include new products traded in the derivatives markets as they continue to evolve. H.R. 3211 seeks to achieve this goal by modifying the final part of the existing definition to treat as a swap agreement any agreement or transaction that is similar to, or involves any combination of, the listed products, that:

> (I) is of a type that has been, is presently, or in the future becomes, the subject of recurrent dealings in the swap markets (including terms and conditions incorporated by reference therein); and;
>
> (II) is a forward, swap, future, or option on one or more rates, currencies, commodities, equity securities, or other equity instruments, debt securities or other debt instruments, quantitative measures associated with an occurrence, extent of an occurrence, or contingency associated with a financial,

---

another currency (or a unit of account established by an intergovernmental organization such as the European Currency Unit) with a maturity date of two days or less after the agreement has been entered into, and includes short-dated foreign exchange transactions such as tomorrow/next day and same day/tomorrow transactions." 12 CFR § 360.5(c) (2002). These expansions would be brought into the Bankruptcy Code and the FDIA through the proposed reforms. H.R. 3211 §§ 1(f) & 8(a)(1).

[806]The special provisions of the NYBL relating to these contracts were adopted in 1993 incorporating the definitions given to "swap agreement" and the other financial contract terms listed above as they existed in the FDIA at the time. Any differences in the definitions may not, however, have an important practical effect. *See* the discussion of the NYBL, *infra* p. 293.

[807]*See infra* note 819 and accompanying text. The reach of some of these categories has been the subject of litigation in connection with Bankruptcy Code Proceedings. There have, for example, been questions over the reach of the definition of "forward contract" (*see, e.g., In re Olympic Natural Gas Co.,* 258 Bankr. 161 (Bankr. S.D. Tex. 2001); *Are Energy Deals Forward Contracts? IBM Says Yes; Compaq Drops Similar Tack,* ANDREWS DERIVATIVES LITIG. REP., Feb. 25, 2002, at 3 (on issues raised in the Proceedings for Enron Corp.) and over whether repos that do not qualify as repurchase agreements under the Bankruptcy Code can nonetheless be treated as securities contracts. *See, e.g.,* Motion of Citicorp Securities, Inc. for an Expedited Hearing under Section 555 of the Bankruptcy Code and Emergency Motion to Enforce Automatic Stay, for an Expedited Hearing and for Interim Relief (October 23, 1998), *In re Criimi Mae,* 251 B.R. 796 (D. Md. 2000).

commercial, or economic consequence, or economic or financial indices or measures of economic or financial risk or value.[808]

H.R. 3211 also expands the definitions of all the other classes of financial contracts listed above, as they appear in both the Bankruptcy Code and the FDIA. Two new features that expand the definitions are built into the definitions of all five of the categories as follows.

The first of these new features relates to the treatment of master agreements. "Swap agreement" is currently defined in the Bankruptcy Code and the FDIA to include a master agreement for any of the types of products covered by the definition, together with all supplements to such a master agreement. This language reflects the market's assumption that all transactions governed by the same master agreement should be treated as integral parts of the whole, and the wish of market participants to be protected against cherry-picking, through, say, selective assumption and repudiation of these transactions by an Insolvency Representative. The common practice is to treat the confirmation of each new transaction under a master agreement as a "supplement" to the master agreement.[809] Under H.R. 3211 each of the five relevant categories would be re-defined to include the listed kinds of products or agreements and a master agreement that provides for any of those products, together with all supplements to any such master agreement, without regard to whether the master agreement also covers other products or agreements. The proposed definitions go on to clarify that any such master agreement will be considered to be a swap agreement, a securities contract, a forward contract, a commodity contract or a repurchase agreement under the relevant definition only to the extent it relates to the itemized products and agreements covered by the definition.

This feature of H.R. 3211 would encourage increased use of a single agreement, or a smaller number of agreements, to govern the dealings in multiple financial products that two parties may currently document under many separate, and often inconsistent, agreements.[810] Say, for example, that prior to the filing of a petition commencing a Bankruptcy Code case for Party X, Party X and Party Y had entered into a single master agreement prepared using an ISDA form and that seven transactions were outstanding under it at the time the case commenced: an interest rate cap, two FX forwards, a commodity price swap, two short-term repos on U.S. Treasury obligations and one transaction that Party Y's legal counsel has said looks very much like a loan, although the parties documented it as another "Transaction" under their master agreement. Party Y consulted counsel when it received notice that a Bankruptcy Code case for Party X was commenced, wishing to confirm that it could exercise its Close-Out Right and Right to Settle Net in

---

[808]H.R. 3211 § 8(a)(1)(E)(ii).

[809]See, e.g., Paragraph 1 of the sample rate swap confirmation, infra p. 428.

[810]See generally the introduction to Part 6, infra p. 1281. H.R. 3211 would extend this approach to master netting agreements, a new category that would be introduced into the Bankruptcy Code to facilitate cross-product risk management, as discussed infra p. 329. Section 6 of the reform act proposed in H.R. 3211 would also add related clarifying language to Section 11(e)(8)(D)(vii) of the FDIA. The provision would expressly recognize as a single agreement an agreement covering different types of qualified financial contracts and provide that "[i]f a master agreement contains provisions relating to agreements or transactions that are not themselves qualified financial contracts, the master agreement shall be deemed to be a qualified financial contract only with respect to those transactions that are themselves qualified financial contracts."

respect of all the transactions under the special Bankruptcy Code provisions that protect those rights in respect of swap agreements and repurchase agreements. As the law now exists, counsel might feel the need to give a reasoned, qualified, opinion about the nature of the master agreement as a swap agreement or a repurchase agreement because of the mix of products. The proposed reform would remove uncertainty in this regard. Counsel would be able with certainty to advise Party Y that its master agreement with Party X will be a swap agreement insofar as it relates to the first four transactions and a repurchase agreement insofar as it relates to the short-term repos, so Party Y should be entitled to claim the benefits of the special protections described below relating to swap agreements and repurchase agreements in relation to those transactions. The proposed reform also makes clear that merely including that last transaction under the master agreement will not cause Party Y to lose those benefits for the other transactions.[811]

The second of these new features relates to the treatment of collateral and other credit enhancements. Each of the five categories would be re-defined to include any "security agreement or arrangement or other credit enhancement related to" any of the products or agreements itemized in that definition, as well as "any guarantee or reimbursement obligation by or to" a counterparty to the debtor under one of those itemized products or agreements." As they would be introduced into the Bankruptcy Code, these changes would be subject to the following limitations:

- The beneficiary of the relevant guarantee or reimbursement obligation must be an entity that, as described below, is entitled to claim the benefits of the special protections in the Bankruptcy Code relating to the relevant kind of financial contract.[812]

- The security and other credit enhancement agreements and arrangements and guarantee and reimbursement obligations would themselves qualify as swap agreements, securities contracts, forward contracts, commodity contracts or repurchase agreements only to the extent of damages in connection with any such agreement or transaction measured in accordance with a proposed new provision (proposed Section 562) of the Bankruptcy Code, which would clarify that if any of these kinds of financial contracts is liquidated, terminated or accelerated or

---

[811] However, Party Y might face other obstacles to the exercise of its rights. For example, master agreements often provide that a non-defaulting party may exercise the right to close out transactions in connection with a defaulting party's breach of contract only if the right is exercised with respect to all transactions under the master agreement, to prevent the non-defaulting party from cherry-picking among the transactions. If applicable insolvency law prevents, or delays, close-out of the loan, Party Y may be unable to close out the cap, swaps and repos under the hypothetical master agreement, unless the master agreement creates an exception, permitting Party Y to proceed with close-out of the transactions that can be closed out without risk of violating applicable law, while leaving in place transactions that cannot be closed out under applicable law at the relevant time. See infra p. 1321 for an illustration of this kind of exception, which is sometimes used in the market today.

[812] This limitation does not apply under the FDIA because, in Proceedings under that statute, a creditor need only be a counterparty to the Debtor in respect of the relevant kind of qualified financial contract when the Proceedings begin; there are no further qualifications for classes of parties protected under product-specific provisions, since all the special provisions in the FDIA discussed below in this chapter relate without distinction to all qualified financial contracts. See infra p. 312.

rejected in the Debtor's Bankruptcy Code case, damages will generally be measured as of the earlier of (1) the date of the rejection or (2) the date of the liquidation, termination, or acceleration.[813]

It is not unusual for market participants both to enter into financial contracts themselves and to act as guarantors for the financial contract obligations of their affiliates.[814] The effect of the revised provisions in such a case may be illustrated as follows. Say a creditor and a Debtor in Bankruptcy Code Liquidation Proceedings were parties to a swap agreement under which the creditor owed the Debtor a payment and, at the same time, the Debtor was in default on a payment due to the creditor as beneficiary of a guaranty issued by the Debtor to support the obligations of an affiliate under a second swap. Under a special provision on swap agreements,[815] a person who is a party to a swap agreement with the Debtor before the commencement of Bankruptcy Code Proceedings generally may set off its mutual claims against the Debtor under any swap agreement for a payment due from the Debtor against any payment due from that person to the Debtor under any swap agreement, notwithstanding the stay on the exercise of setoff rights that normally applies automatically when Bankruptcy Code Proceedings are commenced. No such exception to the automatic stay applies, however, to permit the setoff of a claim against the Debtor under a swap agreement against a mutual claim due to the Debtor under a contract of any other kind. The proposed expansion to the definition of "swap agreement" to include guaranties of swap agreements would enable the counterparty in our example to exercise its setoff rights notwithstanding the automatic stay.[816] As a general matter, the proposed change to the definitions of the various classes of financial contracts would facilitate better management of the risk of counterparty default.

PROTECTED PERSONS

As a participant in the derivatives markets considers the concerns discussed in this chapter relating to the Close-Out Right, the Right to Settle Net and the other basic rights and protections for financial contracts, a second threshold question is whether the

---

[813] *See supra* p. 261 for discussion of timing issues related to the measurement of damages. On other issues relating to the determination of damages claims under the Bankruptcy Code and other statutes discussed in this Chapter, *see infra* p. 1034.

[814] Indeed, foreseeing the possible need to reorganize business lines, shifting them from one entity to another within the same corporate group for regulatory or other reasons, some market participants provide in their agreements that they retain the right to transfer contract positions to affiliates so long as the entity effecting the transfer (or another affiliate acting as the initial guarantor) provides a guaranty for the obligations of the transferee. *See* the annotations to Section 7 of the sample master agreement in Part 3, *infra* p. 867, for discussion of these provisions and related conditions usually imposed on this right of transfer.

[815] *See infra* p. 307.

[816] The proposed amendment would also provide greater comfort to market participants who document their credit support arrangements for OTC derivatives with potential Bankruptcy Code Debtors using the title transfer approach of ISDA's 1995 bilateral Credit Support Annex prepared for use under English law or the similar provisions in the *2001 ISDA Margin Provisions*. This is so because these title transfer arrangements are treated in those standardized terms as transactions under the parties' master agreement. That approach has given rise to some concern over how the deemed transaction would be treated for purposes of the Bankruptcy Code's protections for claims relating to swap agreements, including setoff rights. The proposed amendment would eliminate the concern.

participant falls within one of the classes of persons intended to be protected by the special protections for financial contracts.

There is a fundamental difference between the approaches to Protected Persons taken in the Bankruptcy Code, on one hand, and the FDIA and the NYBL, on the other. The special protections for financial contracts in the Bankruptcy Code are limited to Protected Persons, while those in the FDIA and the NYBL are not—anyone, whether an individual or a legal entity, should qualify for the special protections relating to qualified financial contracts in those laws, if the counterparty is the subject of a receivership or conservatorship in which those special protections are applicable.

The categories of Protected Persons mentioned in the Bankruptcy Code's special protective provisions as intended to benefit from those provisions are as shown in the following table. H.R. 3211 would add another category, "financial participant," to each of the columns.

PROTECTED PERSONS FOR BANKRUPTCY CODE PURPOSES			
Swap Agreements	*Securities Contracts*	*Forwards and Commodity Contracts*	*Repurchase Agreements*
swap participants	stockbrokers financial institutions securities clearing agencies	commodity brokers forward contract merchants	repo participants

Under current law, any creditor that was a party to a swap agreement or repurchase agreement with the Debtor either at any time before the Debtor's Bankruptcy Code case was commenced (swap participants) or on any day during the period beginning 90 days before the commencement of the case (repo participants) can claim the benefit of these special protections. There are no further requirements to be satisfied. The definitions read as follows:

> "swap participant" means an entity that, at any time before the filing of the petition, has an outstanding swap agreement with the debtor.[817]

> "repo participant" means an entity that, on any day during the period beginning 90 days before the date of the filing of the petition, has an outstanding repurchase agreement with the debtor.[818]

The remaining categories of Protected Persons are more limited. However, even if a market participant concludes that it is not a Protected Person with respect to one class of

---

[817] Bankruptcy Code § 101(53C).

[818] Bankruptcy Code § 101(46).

financial contracts, it may nonetheless find that its dealings with a counterparty eligible to be a Bankruptcy Code Debtor also fall within another class and that it can benefit from the protections applicable to that class.[819] The proposed expansion of products treated as swap agreements in H.R. 3211 will, accordingly, produce a welcome result for some categories of market participants.

As shown in the preceding table, the special protections relating to commodity contracts and forward contracts are available to any commodity broker and any forward contract merchant. "Commodity broker" is defined to include the following:

> futures commission merchant, foreign futures commission merchant, clearing organization, leverage transaction merchant, or commodity options dealer, as defined in section 761 of this title [the Bankruptcy Code], with respect to which there is a customer, as defined in section 761 of this title.[820]

"Forward contract merchant" is defined to include:

> a person whose business consists in whole or in part of entering into forward contracts as or with merchants in a commodity, as defined or in section 761(8) of this title, or any similar good, article, service, right, or interest which is presently or in the future becomes the subject of dealing in the forward contract trade.[821]

The reforms proposed in H.R. 3211 would add Federal Reserve Banks to the list of persons treated as forward contract merchants.[822]

Although the classes of commodity brokers and forward contract merchants are limited, it should be remembered that some OTC transactions that constitute commodity contracts or forward contracts may also constitute swap agreements and, in some cases, securities contracts, and the special protections for those classes described below are available to the additional broad class of swap participants, discussed above, and to financial institutions, respectively.

"Financial institution" is defined in the Bankruptcy Code to include "a Federal reserve bank or an entity (domestic or foreign) that is a commercial or savings bank, industrial savings bank, savings and loan association, trust company or receiver or conservator

---

[819] Alternatively, to enjoy the benefits of the special financial contract protections, it may be possible to structure dealings in the relevant class of financial contracts so that the benefits flow through a Protected Person to a person who is not a Protected Person for that contract class. There can, however, be substantial drawbacks to this approach. This is because one of the principal benefits afforded by these special protections is the right to set off mutual claims in respect of the covered financial contracts and to set off those claims against margin and other property supporting related obligations. As discussed *infra* note 887, mutuality for this purpose requires that each party with obligations involved in the setoff be acting in the same capacity. In some structures aimed at obtaining the benefits of the Bankruptcy Code protections indirectly, the interposition of an intervening person may adversely affect the desired setoff benefits.

[820] Bankruptcy Code § 101(6). Section 761, in turn, supplies definitions for some of the terms used in Section 101(6) and defines others by reference to the CEA.

[821] Bankruptcy Code § 101(26).

[822] H.R. 3211 § 8(b).

for such entity and, when . . . [it] is acting as agent or custodian for a customer in connection with a securities contract, as defined in section 741 of this title, the customer."[823] For purposes of the Bankruptcy Code's special protections for securities contracts described below, "financial institution" also includes any investment company registered under the Investment Company Act.

Certain of the special protections of the Bankruptcy Code relating to financial contracts are available to natural persons engaged in these contracts only in limited ways. For example, an individual could be a Protected Person with respect to forward contracts and commodity contracts if the individual were a commodity broker or a forward contract merchant. Individuals who engage in these contracts through commodity brokers and futures commission merchants (FCMs) benefit only indirectly from the Bankruptcy Code's protections for these contracts. If the brokers or FCMs through which the individuals deal become Debtors, the individuals are not, however, Protected Persons in connection with their claims against the brokers and FCMs.

On the other hand, an individual would qualify as a Protected Person—a swap participant—with respect to a swap agreement with the Debtor so long as the swap agreement was outstanding between the parties at the time of the commencement of the relevant Bankruptcy Code Proceedings, as indicated above.[824]

Individuals also benefit indirectly from the Bankruptcy Code protections for financial contracts when they trade through financial intermediaries on exchanges. Under current law this is so with respect to securities contracts because, as noted above, financial institutions are Protected Persons in relation to that financial contract class and, if a financial institution is acting as agent or custodian for a customer in connection with a securities contract, the customer—including an individual—will be a Protected Person as a financial institution in relation to that securities contract. This is also true with respect to futures, options and options on futures that qualify as commodity contracts because, as noted earlier, a clearing organization qualifies as a Protected Person in connection with these contracts.

These indirect benefits would be extended through H.R. 3211 to other kinds of financial contracts by virtue of the creation of a new category of Protected Person identified as a financial participant. Under Section 8(b) of H.R. 3211, the term "financial participant" would be defined (in a new Section 101(22A) of the Bankruptcy Code) to include three broad categories: (1) any "clearing organization," as that term is defined in Section 402 of FDICIA, (2) any entity that either at the time it enters into a financial contract securities contract or at the time of the filing of the petition that commences the Debtor's Bankruptcy Code Proceedings has one or more financial contracts with the Debtor or with any other entity other than an affiliate and (3) any other entity that satisfies either of the following two tests on any day during the 15-month period ending at the time

---

[823]Bankruptcy Code § 101(22). The inclusion of customers can be important to preserve setoff rights they may have in connection with other dealings with the Debtor, whether direct or conducted though other financial institutions.

[824]Although a swap participant must be an entity with such an outstanding swap agreement with the Debtor, "entity" is defined (in Section 101(15) of the Bankruptcy Code) to include any person, and "person" is defined (in Section 101(41)) to include an individual.

it entered into a relevant financial contract with the Debtor or at the time of the filing of the petition that commenced the Debtor's Bankruptcy Code Proceedings:

(1) the entity had swap agreements, securities contracts, forward contracts, commodity contracts, repurchase agreements or master netting agreements with the Debtor or any other entity, except an affiliate, of a total gross dollar value of not less than U.S.$ 1 billion in notional or actual principal amount outstanding, or

(2) the entity had gross mark-to-market positions of not less than U.S.$ 100 million aggregated across counterparties in one or more such contracts.[825]

The clearing organizations covered by the definition of "financial participant" are those that have traditionally played an important role in the markets for exchange-traded derivatives as well as others that have, and are expected to have, an increasingly important role, as clearing of OTC derivatives becomes more prevalent. Section 402 of FDICIA defines "clearing organization" to include any "clearinghouse, clearing association, clearing corporation or similar organization" that (1) is registered with the CFTC as a derivatives clearing organization under Section 5b of the CEA or (2) provides clearing, netting, or settlement services for its members, is made up of financial institutions or other clearing organizations and is registered as a clearing agency under the Securities Exchange Act of 1934.

"Derivatives clearing organization" is the term added to the CEA by the CFMA to refer to clearers that are subject to supervision by the CFTC.[826] Although the term is new, the role is not. These DCOs will include the clearing organizations that have historically mutualized the credit risk involved in the trading of futures and options on organized exchanges designated as contract markets by the CFTC as well as independently organized

---

[825] These requirements are set out as follows in the proposed definition:

(A) an entity that, at the time it enters into a securities contract, commodity contract, swap agreement, repurchase agreement, or forward contract, or at the time of the filing of the petition, has one or more agreements or transactions described in paragraph (1), (2), (3), (4), (5), or (6) of Section 561(a) with the debtor or any other entity (other than an affiliate) of a total gross dollar value of not less than $1,000,000,000 in notional or actual principal amount outstanding on any day during the previous 15-month period, or has gross mark-to-market positions of not less than $100,000,000 (aggregated across counterparties) in one or more such agreements or transactions with the debtor or any other entity (other than an affiliate) on any day during the previous 15-month period.

[826] The definition of "derivatives clearing organization" is set out *supra* p. 96. A derivatives clearing organization is subject to supervision by the CFTC and must be registered with the CFTC if it clears futures, options on futures or options on commodities other than the excluded contracts or options listed in Section 5b(a)(1) of the CEA, unless it is a securities clearing agency registered with the SEC and the relevant transaction is a security futures product. CEA § 5b(a). The requirement operates through a prohibition on the direct or indirect use of the mails or any means or instrumentality of interstate commerce to perform the functions of a derivatives clearing organization "with respect to a contract of sale of a commodity for future delivery (or option on such a contract) or option on a commodity" unless the contract or option is excluded from CEA regulation under specified provisions of that act discussed in Chapter 3 of this book, *supra* p. 95, or is a security futures product cleared by a clearing agency registered with the SEC. DCOs that clear contracts excluded or exempted from CEA regulation as described in Chapter 2 may also voluntarily register with the CFTC. *See* CEA § 5b(b).

Bankruptcy and Insolvency Concerns

clearing organizations that contract to provide these services to contract markets. Similarly, clearing agencies that are registered under the Securities Exchange Act are those that have traditionally cleared exchange-traded options on securities. Both of these kinds of clearing organizations may be used in the future for the clearing of single stock futures and futures on narrow groups and indices of securities, when they trade as security futures products in the United States.[827]

H.R. 3211 would expand on the clearing organizations included as financial participants—and which, therefore, are Protected Persons for purposes of the Bankruptcy Code's special provisions on financial contracts discussed here—so as to add clearing agencies exempted from registration by order of the SEC, those exempted from registration under Section 4(c)(1) of the CEA, and multilateral clearing organizations.[828] Multilateral clearing organizations (MCOs) are newer features of the derivatives markets. Sometimes referred to as clearing banks,[829] MCOs are systems "utilized by more than two participants in which the bilateral credit exposures of participants arising from the transactions cleared are effectively eliminated and replaced by a system of guarantees, insurance, or mutualized risk of loss."[830]

Under U.S. law, a multilateral clearing organization may clear any contract that qualifies as an "over-the-counter derivatives instrument," a term that includes a broad list of product types, as well as

> any agreement, contract or transaction similar to any other agreement, contract, or transaction referred to in this clause that is presently, or in the future becomes, regularly entered into by parties that participate in swap transactions (including terms and conditions incorporated by reference in the agreement) and that is a forward, swap, or option on one or more occurrences of any event, rates, currencies, commodities, equity securities or other equity instruments, debt securities or other debt instruments, economic or other indices or measures of economic or other risk or value.[831]

In effect, any transaction that qualifies as a swap agreement for purposes of the Bankruptcy Code should also qualify as an over-the-counter derivatives instrument that may be cleared on an MCO.

The reforms proposed in H.R. 3211 also introduce another class of Protected Person: the master netting agreement participant.[832] The final section of this chapter discusses

---

[827] *See supra* p. 96.

[828] *See* H.R. 3211 § 7, including a proposed amendment to FDICIA § 402(2)(B).

[829] Under Section 409 of FDICIA, only a registered clearing agency, a registered DCO, or a national bank, a state member bank of the Federal Reserve System, a state-chartered FDIC-insured bank that is not a member of the Federal Reserve System, an affiliate of a national bank, a state member bank, or such an insured state nonmember bank, or an Edge Act corporation may operate a multilateral clearing organization.

[830] FDICIA § 408(1).

[831] FDICIA § 408(2).

[832] H.R. 3211, § 8(c), which would introduce a new Section 38B to the Bankruptcy Code.

this class and the related proposed class of master netting agreements in the context of netting contracts and related concerns under Insolvency Laws.[833]

IDENTIFYING THE APPLICABLE INSOLVENCY LAW

The parties' contractual choice of the law of a U.S. state to govern an OTC derivatives agreement will not make it subject to the provisions of the Bankruptcy Code, the FDIA or the NYBL if those statutes would not otherwise apply. Regardless of the governing law chosen, the laws applicable in connection with Proceedings for a party are likely to be those of the jurisdiction in which it is organized, principally engaged in business or domiciled or, in some instances, the laws of a jurisdiction in which it owns property. Therefore, market participants should consult with counsel to identify and analyze which law is likely to apply if an Insolvency Event involving a particular counterparty occurs.[834]

This analysis will of course be particularly important if it is not clear which legal regime will apply and there is a risk of different and conflicting results under the different regimes. This risk may arise, for example, in dealings with a counterparty that is acting from offices in more than one jurisdiction or from an office outside its home jurisdiction. Complexities may also exist even when the counterparty is acting from its home jurisdiction if it has provided security or other credit support that is held (or deemed to be held) elsewhere.[835] The risk of conflicting results in multiple proceedings and the related possible consequences are matters that must be assessed in each case in light of the particular facts relating to the parties and their dealings with each other.

The remainder of this section sets out some generalizations about Proceedings under the Bankruptcy Code, the FDIA or the NYBL, based on the assumption that Proceedings for the counterparty will be conducted under a legal framework that respects the counterparty's identity as a separate legal person. Market participants should consult with counsel about the circumstances in which a counterparty's legal identity might be disregarded under the potentially applicable Insolvency Laws.[836]

BANKRUPTCY CODE

Many derivatives market participants may be eligible to be Debtors[837] in Proceedings—called cases—of one kind or another under the Bankruptcy Code, if they have

---

[833] *Infra* p. 329.

[834] *See infra* p. 1089.

[835] *See, e.g., infra* p. 290 on ancillary proceedings under the Bankruptcy Code.

[836] When an entity's separate identity is disregarded in Proceedings, this process is often referred to as "substantive consolidation." Market participants must consider whether there is a real risk that the assets and liabilities of a prospective counterparty will be consolidated with those of another entity. If so, the risk may render the counterparty undesirable. For example, assets thought to belong to the counterparty might be treated as part of the Estate in Proceedings (under the same or even possibly different Insolvency Laws) for another entity and thus be subject to the potentially far greater claims of the creditors of that other entity. On substantive consolidation in Bankruptcy Code Proceedings, *see* 2 COLLIER ON BANKRUPTCY ¶ 105.9.

[837] In this discussion, we continue to use the capitalized term "Debtor" in the generic sense indicated earlier. The Bankruptcy Code itself refers to the subjects of Proceedings under the Code as "debtors."

Bankruptcy and Insolvency Concerns 289

a residence, a domicile, a place of business or property in the United States. There are, however, numerous exceptions and limitations, including the following notable cases:

- Domestic banks, savings banks, cooperative banks, savings and loan associations, building and loan associations, homestead associations, certain small business investment companies, credit unions, industrial banks and similar institutions that are FDIC-insured banks are not generally eligible to be Debtors in Bankruptcy Code Proceedings[838] (subject to an exception for an uninsured state bank that is a member of the Federal Reserve System or a corporation chartered under Section 25A of the Federal Reserve Act that operates, or operates as, a multilateral clearing organization for OTC derivative instruments, which may be a Debtor in Liquidation Proceedings under Chapter 7 of the Bankruptcy Code).[839]

- Foreign banks and financial institutions of the kinds listed above that are engaged in business as such in the United States are also ineligible to be Bankruptcy Code Debtors.[840] Proceedings in the U.S. for these Debtors may be subject to the law of the state in which the relevant branch or agency is licensed,[841] the FDIA, the IBA or other federal law.[842]

- Domestic insurance companies and foreign insurance companies engaged in business as such in the U.S. are ineligible to be Bankruptcy Code Debtors.[843]

---

[838]Bankruptcy Code § 109(b)(2).

[839]This exception (which was introduced into the Bankruptcy Code and the Federal Reserve Act by Section 112 of the CFMA) applies if a petition for one of these institutions is filed at the direction of the Board of Governors of the Federal Reserve System under Chapter 7 of the Bankruptcy Code. *See* Bankruptcy Code § 109(b)(2) and Federal Reserve Act § 9B(c).

[840]Bankruptcy Code § 109(b)(3).

[841]*See infra* p. 293.

[842]The Federal Reserve Act would apply in cases involving uninsured branches of state-chartered banks that are members of the Federal Reserve System and Edge Act corporations although, as indicated in the first listed category, when one of these entities operates or operates as a multilateral clearing organization pursuant to Section 409 of FDICIA, the Federal Reserve Board may instruct the Insolvency Representative for the relevant Debtor to file a petition commencing Liquidation Proceedings for these Debtors under the Bankruptcy Code. State law would apply if a foreign bank's branch or agency were state-chartered, although federal law (the FDIA), could also apply, if the branch or agency were federally insured and (1) the Insolvency Representative authorized to act under state law tendered the appointment to the FDIC or (2) the FDIC took over the Proceedings itself. *See infra* p. 293. The FDIA would also apply if the foreign bank's branch or agency were both FDIC-insured and federally chartered. The IBA would apply if the relevant U.S. branch or agency of a foreign bank were federally chartered or if the Comptroller of the Currency had appointed a receiver for another, federally chartered, branch or agency of the bank. IBA § 4(j)(1).

[843]Bankruptcy Code §§ 109(b)(2) & (3). Proceedings in the U.S. for these entities are subject to state laws dealing with the liquidation and rehabilitation of insurance companies. State law in this regard may differ from state to state. Efforts to address the insolvency-related concerns of those who act as counterparties to insurers have led to the endorsement by the NAIC—the National Association of Insurance Commissioners—of special protections relating to OTC derivatives and other financial contracts and netting agree-

- Municipalities—understood to mean political subdivisions or public agencies or instrumentalities of a U.S. state[844]—are eligible to be Bankruptcy Code Debtors only in Voluntary Proceedings for the adjustment of debts under Chapter 9 of the Bankruptcy Code, and only if certain other conditions are satisfied.[845]

- Except for municipalities, governmental units are not eligible to be Bankruptcy Code Debtors.[846]

- An entity that has property in the U.S. may be a Debtor in limited Proceedings that are ancillary to foreign Proceedings for that entity, if a representative in the foreign Proceedings files a petition with the bankruptcy court, even if the entity is domiciled abroad and has no place of business in the U.S.[847] Ancillary Proceedings may, for example, be commenced against a foreign bank not engaged in the business of banking in the United States if a foreign Proceeding for the bank is

---

ments in Section 46 of the Insurers Rehabilitation and Liquidation Model Act, which is set forth in volume III of the NAIC's *Model Laws, Regulations and Guidelines*. Section 46 includes measures aimed, among other things, at protection of an insurance company's counterparties against cherry-picking, protection of the Close-Out Right, the Right to Settle Net and rights relating to application of collateral as well as protection against the risk of avoidance of transfers made by the Debtor insurer prior to the commencement of Proceedings except in cases of transfers made with actual intent to hinder, delay or defraud the insurer, a receiver appointed for the insurer or existing or future creditors. The Model Act provisions endorsed by the NAIC do not, however, have the force of law. State law must be examined to determine whether a given state has adopted provisions based on those included in the Model Act. *See, e.g.,* CONN. GEN. STAT. ANN. § 38a-944a (2000).

[844] Bankruptcy Code §§ 101(40) & 101(52).

[845] For example, the municipality must be specifically authorized to be a debtor under Chapter 9 by state law or by a governmental officer or organization empowered by state law to grant the necessary authority. Chapter 9 proceedings must also satisfy other tests under Section 109(c) of the Bankruptcy Code. In addition, "[a] municipality that is eligible for relief under chapter 9 cannot be a debtor under any other chapter of the Bankruptcy Code." 2 COLLIER ON BANKRUPTCY ¶ 109.04[1].

[846] This follows from the fact that only a "person" or a municipality may be a Debtor in a Bankruptcy Code case (Bankruptcy Code § 109(a)), and (subject to a special exception for governmental units that acquire assets pursuant to the operation of a loan guaranty agreement) governmental units are not persons for this purpose. Bankruptcy Code § 101(41). Under Section 101(27) of the Bankruptcy Code, "'governmental unit' means United States; State; Commonwealth; District; Territory; municipality; foreign state; department, agency or instrumentality of the United States (but not a United States trustee while serving as a trustee in a case under this title), a State, a Commonwealth, a District, a Territory, a municipality, or a foreign state; or other foreign or domestic government."

[847] The scope of ancillary Proceedings in aid of a foreign proceeding is established in Section 304 of the Bankruptcy Code. "Foreign proceeding" is defined to include a "a proceeding, whether judicial or administrative and whether or not under bankruptcy law, in a foreign country in which the debtor's domicile, residence, principal place of business, or principal assets were located at the commencement of such proceeding, for the purpose of liquidating an estate, adjusting debts by composition, extension, or discharge, or effecting a reorganization." Bankruptcy Code § 101(23). "Foreign representative" is defined to mean "duly selected trustee, administrator, or other representative of an estate in a foreign proceeding." *Id.* § 101(24). It is possible for a Bankruptcy Code case to exist concurrently with foreign Proceedings for the same Debtor, although the foreign representative might seek dismissal or suspension of the Bankruptcy Code case if the interests of creditors and the Debtor would be better served by the dismissal or suspension. *Id.* § 305.

Bankruptcy and Insolvency Concerns 291

> pending and an appropriate petition is filed by the foreign representative.
>
> - Some classes of persons may be eligible to be Debtors only in a Liquidation under Chapter 7 of the Bankruptcy Code, or only in a Reorganization under Chapter 11, but others are eligible to be Debtors in either one or in additional kinds of cases, subject to the satisfaction of specified conditions.[848]

The special Bankruptcy Code provisions applicable to OTC derivatives and other financial contracts discussed below would apply in Proceedings for most potential Debtors. They are not, however, expressly made applicable to cases under Chapter 9 for the adjustment of debts of municipalities.[849] The reform legislation in H.R. 3211 would expressly extend those provisions to Chapter 9 cases involving municipalities.[850]

FEDERAL DEPOSIT INSURANCE ACT

Many of the major participants in the derivatives markets are financial institutions organized in the United States that take deposits insured by the FDIC. Many are organized under federal law, while others are organized under state law. If a receiver or conservator is to be appointed for an FDIC-insured institution organized under federal law—a "national" bank or savings association—the appointment will be made by the relevant federal supervisory authority for the institution.[851] If the supervisory authority decides to appoint a receiver to wind up or liquidate the affairs of the institution, the receiver will normally

---

[848] The intricate rules on what entities may be Debtors under what Chapters are set out in Section 109 of the Bankruptcy Code. Subject to certain exceptions, only a person eligible to be a Debtor in a Liquidation case under Chapter 7 may be a Debtor in a Reorganization under Chapter 11. Stockbrokers and commodity brokers are eligible to be Debtors only under Chapter 7, while railroads may be debtors only in reorganizations under Chapter 11. Qualifying individuals may be debtors in a case under Chapter 7 or Chapter 11. Proceedings for the adjustment of debts under Chapter 12 are available only for family farmers with regular annual income and Proceedings for the adjustment of debts under Chapter 13 are available only for individuals with regular income whose debts do not exceed stated amounts.

[849] *See* Bankruptcy Code § 103 and provisions identified therein.

[850] H.R. 3211 § 14. The proposals in H.R. 333 and S. 420 (which are not included in H.R. 3211 in this respect) would also involve substantial changes relating to ancillary Proceedings and (in Section 802) remove any doubt that might otherwise exist about whether the protections for derivatives and other financial contracts described below are applicable in ancillary Proceedings. Under Section 801 of those earlier acts, the Bankruptcy Code would incorporate, as a new Chapter 15, the UNCITRAL Model Law on Cross-Border Insolvency. U.N. COMM'N ON INT'L LAW, UNCITRAL MODEL LAW ON CROSS-BORDER INSOLVENCY WITH GUIDE TO ENACTMENT, *available at* www.uncitral.org/english/texts/insolven/insolvency.htm. The new Chapter 15 would deal more fully with ancillary Proceedings and would also provide rules applicable (1) when assistance is sought in a foreign country in connection with a case under the Bankruptcy Code, (2) when a foreign Proceeding and a case under the Bankruptcy Code with respect to the same Debtor are taking place concurrently and (3) when creditors or other interested persons in a foreign country have an interest in requesting the commencement of, or participating in, a Proceeding under the Bankruptcy Code. Within the proposed Chapter 15, Section 1521(f) would expressly extend to ancillary Proceedings certain provisions of Section 362 of the Bankruptcy Code, discussed *infra* p. 307, regarding the exercise of setoff rights relating to swap agreements and other financial products.

[851] This supervisory authority could be the Comptroller of the Currency, the Board of Governors of the Federal Reserve System or the Director of the OTS.

be the FDIC.[852] The supervisory authority could also, in its discretion, appoint the FDIC as conservator for the purpose of putting the insured institution in a sound and solvent condition, carrying on its business and preserving and conserving its assets and property.[853]

If the troubled institution is FDIC-insured but state-chartered, the FDIC can act as receiver or conservator if the appointment is tendered to it by the bank supervisory agency of the relevant state.[854] In certain other cases, the FDIC can appoint itself as receiver or conservator for a state-chartered institution.[855]

In each of these cases, if the FDIC acts as receiver or conservator in Proceedings for an institution, the special provisions of the FDIA discussed below relating to swap agreements and other qualified financial contracts will be applicable, and the powers and duties of the FDIC under the FDIA will be supplemented by those conferred or imposed by other laws on a receiver or conservator for the relevant kind of depository institution, to the extent the additional powers or duties do not derogate from those provided for in the relevant provisions of the FDIA.[856]

Depending on the circumstances, the FDIA's provisions on qualified financial contracts may not be applicable under the law (state or federal) that would be applicable to Proceedings in the U.S. for (1) uninsured national banks, (2) U.S. branches and agencies of foreign financial institutions,[857] (3) Edge Act corporations—subsidiaries of U.S. financial institutions that are organized to engage in international business activities as corporations chartered under Section 25A of the Federal Reserve Act—or (4) uninsured state member banks of the Federal Reserve System.[858] However, an Edge Act corporation or uninsured State member bank that operates, or operates as, a multilateral clearing organization may be a Debtor in Liquidation Proceedings under Chapter 7 of the Bankruptcy Code.[859] In such a case it appears that the Insolvency Representative (acting as trustee) would be required to exercise its powers subject to the special provisions on OTC derivatives and other financial contracts that are included in the Bankruptcy Code and, at

---

[852] FDIA §11(c)(2)(A)(ii). This is also the case for a District bank, a term defined in Section 3(a)(4) of the FDIA to mean a state bank operating under the Code of Law for the District of Columbia. As receiver for a national bank, the FDIC may also organize a new national bank or a bridge bank to assume the insured deposits of the bank in or in danger of default. *See* FDIA §§11(m) & 11(n).

[853] FDIA §11(c)(2)(A)(i). Ultimately a receiver could be appointed to liquidate the assets of the depository institution and wind up its affairs if efforts to return the institution to operation or selling it as a going concern proved unsuccessful.

[854] *See* FDIA § 11(c)(3)(A).

[855] *See* FDIA § 11(c)(4) & (5).

[856] *See* FDIA §§ 11(c)(2)(B) & 11(c)(3)(B) and, as to state law, *FDIC v. Wilhoit*, 180 S.W.2d 72, 73 (Ky. 1943).

[857] The IBA empowers the Comptroller of the Currency to appoint a receiver for any branch or agency in the United States of a foreign bank that has any federally chartered branch or agency. IBA § 4(j)(1).

[858] *See* Walter Eccard & Seth Grosshandler, *Qualified Financial Contracts with FDIC-Insured Banks and Thrifts*, 7 REV. BANK. & FIN. SERVS. 49 (1991), on some of these cases.

[859] *See supra* p. 289.

least to some extent, in the FDIA.[860] In addition, Section 9B of the Federal Reserve Act, as added by the CFMA, empowers the Board of Governors of the Federal Reserve System to appoint a receiver for an uninsured state bank that is a member of the Federal Reserve System that operates, or operates as, a multilateral clearing organization. In each of these cases, the Insolvency Representative appointed by the Comptroller or the Federal Reserve Board would have the same powers, functions, and duties and be subject to the same limitations, as a conservator or receiver for a national bank.

H.R. 3211 includes proposals under which, in Liquidation Proceedings for each of these four classes of financial institutions, the special provisions of the FDIA on swap agreements and other qualified financial contracts would apply.[861] Under these proposals, the result would be the same regardless of the identity of the Insolvency Representative authorized to conduct the Proceedings, although the Board of Governors of the Federal Reserve System would retain the right to direct the receiver or conservator appointed by it for an Edge Act corporation or an uninsured state bank operating, or operating as, a clearing organization to commence Liquidation Proceedings under Bankruptcy Code, and those Proceedings would be subject to the rules currently applicable under subchapter V of Chapter 7 of the Bankruptcy Code.

NEW YORK BANKING LAW

The NYBL applies to the liquidation of New York banking organizations. It also applies to the liquidation of New York branches and agencies of foreign banks other than those for which a receiver would be appointed by the Comptroller of the Currency pursuant to the IBA (which, as noted above, are the branches and agencies in the U.S. of a foreign bank that has any federal branch or agency in the U.S.). Also as noted, if a state supervisory official—in New York, the Superintendent of Banks—appoints a receiver or conservator for an insured depository institution and tenders the appointment to the FDIC, the FDIC may take over as receiver, and in some other cases the FDIC may appoint itself as receiver or conservator for a state-chartered insured depository institution.

---

[860] That is, in exercising the powers conferred by the Bankruptcy Code on a trustee in other Proceedings under Chapter 7, the trustee would be subject to the special provisions of the Bankruptcy Code protecting a counterparty's Close-Out Right, Right to Settle Net, setoff rights and other rights described *supra* p. 277. In addition, Section 783(b) of the Bankruptcy Code provides that the trustee in Liquidation Proceedings for a clearing bank (that is, an Edge Act corporation or uninsured State member bank that operates, or operates as, a multilateral clearing organization) may exercise the powers that the FDIA could exercise in Proceedings for an insured depository institution: the rights to sell the clearing bank to a depository institution or consortium of depository institutions, to merge it with a depository institution, to transfer its assets and liabilities to a depository institution or to a bridge bank, and "to transfer contracts [of the clearing bank] to the same extent" as could a receiver for a depository institution under paragraphs (9) and (10) of Section 11(e) of the Federal Deposit Insurance Act. In any such transfer of OTC derivatives and other specified financial contracts, the other party to the contracts would be protected against cherry-picking, because the provisions of the FDIA that are cited would, as discussed *infra* p. 314, require the trustee to transfer all "qualified financial contracts" between the clearing bank and a counterparty (or any affiliate of the counterparty) to the same transferee, along with all related credit support arrangements.

[861] The change would be effected through amendment of FDICIA to include a new Section 407, the text of which is set forth in Section 7(d) of the reform act proposed in H.R. 3211. The same change would be effected under Section 906(d) of the reform act proposed in H.R. 333 and S. 420.

BANKRUPTCY CODE

ISSUES

The discussion in this section first provides an overview of general Bankruptcy Code rules that give rise to concerns on the enforceability of contractual rights that are important to the functioning of the markets for OTC derivatives and other financial contracts.[862] The special exceptions to these general rules applicable in connection with financial contracts are then summarized in the second part of the section.

The Bankruptcy Code provisions reviewed in this section generally speak in terms of the powers of a trustee in a case under the Bankruptcy Code, and our discussion follows that approach. The reader should, however, note that, in Reorganization Proceedings under Chapter 11, a Debtor in possession of its own bankruptcy Estate has most of the rights and powers, and must perform most of the functions, of a trustee, subject to the same limitations as would apply to a trustee and other limitations and conditions prescribed by the court hearing the case.[863]

AUTOMATIC STAY

The petition that commences a Debtor's Bankruptcy Code case[864] generally operates, under Section 362 of the Bankruptcy Code, as a stay of broad categories of actions against the Debtor and its property,[865] unless the actions have first been approved by a court or other competent authority or an exception to the automatic stay applies.[866] Among the prohibited actions are the commencement or continuation of judicial and other proceedings to recover claims against the Debtor that arose before the commencement of the case, the enforcement of judgments obtained against the Debtor or property of the Estate before the commencement of the case, and any action to collect, assess, enforce or recover claims against the Debtor or the Estate, to create, perfect, or enforce any lien

---

[862] For fuller discussion of the matters summarized below and related complexities of the Bankruptcy Code, see 3 COLLIER ON BANKRUPTCY, ch. 362 (automatic stay) & ch. 365 (trustee's right to assume or reject); 5 COLLIER ON BANKRUPTCY, chs. 546–49 (avoidance powers) & ch. 553 (setoff).

[863] Bankruptcy Code § 1107(a).

[864] In Voluntary cases, the petition may be filed by the Debtor. Bankruptcy Code § 301. If the debtor is an individual, the individual may file a petition that commences a joint case for the individual and the individual's spouse. Id. § 302. In Involuntary cases, the petition may be filed, among others, by holders of specified kinds of claims against the debtor or by general partners, in the case of partnerships. Id. § 303(b)). As indicated earlier, in an ancillary case, the petition must be filed by a foreign Insolvency Representative (Bankruptcy Code § 304) and, in certain cases involving clearing banks, the petition may be filed by a receiver appointed by the Board of Governors of the Federal Reserve System. See supra note 839.

[865] If the Debtor is a stockbroker, the filing with SIPC, the Securities Investor Protection Corporation, of an application for protection under Section 5(a)(3) of the Securities Investor Protection Act of 1970, 15 U.S.C. § 78eee(a)(3), similarly operates as an automatic stay under Section 362 of the Bankruptcy Code. Special rules relating to the automatic stay in a case for the adjustment of debts of a municipality are set out in Section 922 of the Bankruptcy Code.

[866] In most cases, "[a]n individual injured by any willful violation of a stay provided by this Section [Section 362] shall recover actual damages, including costs and attorneys' fees, and, in appropriate circumstances, may recover punitive damages." Bankruptcy Code § 362(h). Although authority on the subject is split, most courts have held that actions in violation of the stay are void, not merely voidable. 3 COLLIER ON BANKRUPTCY ¶ 362.11[1].

Bankruptcy and Insolvency Concerns

against that property, or to obtain possession of or exercise control over that property, through setoff or otherwise.[867] Absent an applicable exception, the automatic stay would interfere with several of the fundamental rights referred to earlier in this chapter, including the Close-Out Right and the right to set off a claim for damages against credit support provided by a counterparty that has become a Debtor in a Bankruptcy Code case.

TRUSTEE'S RIGHT TO ASSUME OR REJECT

Under Section 365(a) of the Bankruptcy Code, the trustee in Bankruptcy Code Proceedings may, subject to court approval, elect to assume or reject executory contracts of the Debtor in certain circumstances. If the trustee elects to assume the contract, the trustee may also realize on its value by assigning the Debtor's position under the contract to a third party.[868] Generally speaking "executory contracts" are agreements involving unperformed obligations of both parties.[869] In many cases, the agreements relating to OTC derivatives transactions and other financial contracts with a Bankruptcy Code Debtor will be executory contracts.

The trustee's right to elect to assume and assign executory contracts under the Bankruptcy Code is subject to the satisfaction of conditions relating to the cure of the Debtor's payment defaults and provision for future performance under the relevant contract.[870] The trustee may not assume or assign agreements in cases in which applicable law other than the Bankruptcy Code excuses the other party from being compelled to accept performance from or render performance to anyone other than the Debtor, absent that party's consent.[871] The trustee may not assume or assign an executory contract, whether or not it or restricts assignment of rights or delegation of duties, if "such contract is a contract to make a loan, or extend other debt financing or financial accommodations, to or for the benefit of the debtor . . . ."[872] Subject to the applicable exceptions, the trustee's power

---

[867] Bankruptcy Code § 362(a).

[868] Bankruptcy Code § 365(k). The general qualifications to this right of election prohibit assumption as described in the following footnote.

[869] "An executory contract is one 'on which performance remains due to some extent on both sides.' *Griffel v. Murphy (In re Wegner)*, 839 F.2d 533, 536 (9th Cir. 1988), quoting from *NLRB v. Bildisco & Bildisco*, 465 U.S. 513, 522 n.6 (1983), in turn quoting from the legislative history of Bankruptcy Code § 365(a). More precisely, a contract is executory if 'the obligations of both parties are so unperformed that the failure of either party to complete performance would constitute a material breach and thus excuse the performance of the other.'" *Id.*, quoting from *Pacific Express, Inc. v. Teknetron Infoswitch Corp. (In re Pacific Exp., Inc.)*, 80 F.2d 1482, 1487 (9th Cir. 1986).

[870] Bankruptcy Code § 365(b)(1). If there has been a default in an executory contract, the trustee may not assume or assign the contract unless the trustee cures or provides adequate assurance that it will promptly cure the default, compensates or provides adequate assurance that it will promptly compensate the other party to the contract for its actual pecuniary loss resulting from the default and provide adequate assurance of future performance under the contract (Bankruptcy Code § 365(b)(1)), but these qualifications do not apply to defaults that are breaches of a provision relating to the insolvency or financial condition of the Debtor at any time prior to the closing of the case, or to the commencement of the Bankruptcy Code case, the appointment of or taking possession by a trustee in the case, or by a custodian before commencement of the case, or the satisfaction of any penalty rate or provision relating to a default arising from any failure by the Debtor to perform nonmonetary obligations under the contract (Bankruptcy Code § 365(b)(2)).

[871] Bankruptcy Code § 365(c)(1).

[872] Bankruptcy Code § 365(c)(2).

to assign the Debtor's position in assumed executory contracts overrides a provision in the agreement entitling the other party to terminate the contract in connection with the insolvency of the Debtor, the commencement of Proceedings under the Bankruptcy Code or similar circumstances, and this power also overrides a contractual provision prohibiting transfers by the Debtor without its counterparty's prior consent.

The general rules on the timing for exercise of this right are as follows: in Liquidation Proceedings under Chapter 7, an executory contract of the Debtor will generally be deemed rejected 60 days after the court's order for relief in the case, "or within such additional time as the court, for cause, within such 60-day period, fixes," if the trustee has not previously assumed or rejected the contract.[873] In a case under Chapter 9 (adjustment of debts of a municipality) or Chapter 11 (reorganization), the decision to assume or reject may be made at any time up to confirmation of a plan but the court, on request of a party to the relevant contract, may order the trustee to make the election within a period specified by the court.[874] In the Liquidation of a stockbroker (under subchapter III of Chapter 7), the trustee is required to assume or reject any executory contract of the Debtor for the purchase or sale of a security in the ordinary course of the Debtor's business within a reasonable time after the date of the order for relief but in any case within 30 days.[875]

If the trustee elects to reject an executory contract of the Debtor, or the contract is deemed rejected, the contract will be treated as if it had been breached by the Debtor. The breach could be treated as having occurred just before the filing of the petition that commenced the Proceeding, in a Liquidation Proceeding under Chapter 7, but the breach could also be treated as having occurred at a later time, including the time of the rejection, in some cases.[876]

When these rules relating to executory contracts apply and, because of the automatic stay, the Debtor's counterparty in an executory contract cannot take action to preempt the trustee's election, the Debtor's counterparty may not know for some time which of the two elections will be made. Accordingly, it will be left in doubt as to whether and when to treat the executory contract as terminated and cover the resulting open position.[877] This situation can, of course, leave the Debtor's counterparty exposed to further loss, as shown in the following example.

---

[873] Bankruptcy Code § 365(d)(1). Various actions are treated as constituting an order for relief in a case. The first is the filing of the petition that commences the case, in a Voluntary case. Bankruptcy Code § 301. In an Involuntary case, the court orders relief if the petition filed against the Debtor is not timely controverted or, it is controverted, in the circumstances specified in Section 303(h) of the Bankruptcy Code. Conversion of Proceedings from one type of case to another is also treated as an order for relief. Bankruptcy Code § 348(a).

[874] Bankruptcy Code § 365(d)(2). This second rule also applies in a case under chapter 12 (adjustment of debts of a family farmer with regular annual income) or Chapter 13 (adjustment of debts of an individual with regular income).

[875] *See* Bankruptcy Code § 744.

[876] Bankruptcy Code § 365(g).

[877] *See* Anthony C. Gooch & Albert S. Pergam, *United States and New York Law*, *in* HANDBOOK OF RISK MANAGEMENT 34–1, at 34–14.

Suppose that a financial intermediary has entered into an OTC derivatives transaction with a Debtor. The intermediary will normally have a hedge for the transaction.[878] Except in very unusual cases, the Debtor's insolvency will not excuse the intermediary from having to perform its ongoing obligations under the hedge. Generally, the options open to the intermediary at this point are (1) to maintain the hedge, in the belief that the trustee will ultimately assume the Debtor's transaction, (2) to remove the hedge or (3) to maintain the hedge and put on a new position to replace its transaction with the Debtor.[879] In each case, the intermediary may be exposed to loss, depending on market movements after the filing of the petition.

If the intermediary simply maintains the hedge without doing anything further and the market moves in favor of the intermediary on the transaction with the Debtor, there is an incentive for the trustee to reject that transaction. In such a case, during the period from the filing to the rejection, the intermediary will have suffered incremental loss on the hedge, which will not be covered from any source.

If the intermediary lifts the hedge and the market moves in favor of the Estate during the period between the filing and the assumption/rejection decision, the trustee will have an incentive to accept (and perhaps assign) the transaction with the intermediary. If it does so, the intermediary will suffer an incremental, unhedged, loss to the extent that the market moved against it. The Bankruptcy Code does not give the intermediary the right to make a claim in respect of a loss of this kind in the Debtor's Bankruptcy Code case.

If the intermediary puts on a new position to replace its transaction with the Debtor and the market moves in favor of the Estate during the period between the filing and the assumption/rejection decision, the trustee will have an incentive to accept (and perhaps assign) the transaction with the intermediary. If it does so, the intermediary will be left with an unnecessary replacement transaction, and the intermediary will not have a Bankruptcy Code claim for the balance of the loss.

The counterparty's position can become even more precarious if it has multiple transactions with the Debtor, because the right of the trustee to assume, assume and assign or reject executory contracts could expose the counterparty to the risk of cherry-picking, diminishing or destroying the benefits of a contract's terms providing for close-out netting. The trustee is given the right to make these elections regarding its executory contracts to preserve or realize on the value of contracts that are favorable to the Debtor and relieve it of those that constitute liabilities, in exchange for a claim for damages. Often those goals will be best preserved by picking and choosing among the Debtor's transactions and, as noted, there can be a lengthy period over which the election may be made, in light of changes in the value of the contract over that period.

---

[878]*See supra* p. 39.

[879]Another option theoretically open to the intermediary is to hedge the contingent loss with a swaption or termination option. For example, it could buy an option to terminate its hedge and exercise it if the Insolvency Representative rejects the transaction with the Debtor. If it does so, however, it will have to pay a premium for the swaption, and it should consult with counsel as to whether it will have recourse to the Debtor for the cost of the option.

Close-out of executory contracts with the Debtor seems the logical way for the counterparty to protect itself against exposure to these risks. The Bankruptcy Code creates two obstacles to close-out, however. The first, as indicated earlier, is the automatic stay. The second is a rule designed to protect the Debtor's interests under executory contracts pending the election to assume, assume and assign or reject. Under this rule, the Debtor's executory contracts and rights and obligations under them may not be terminated or modified once its Bankruptcy Code case has commenced through the operation a so-called *ipso facto* clause—a provision in the contract giving rise to a right to terminate or modify the contract that is conditioned on the insolvency or financial condition of the Debtor at any time before the closing of the case, the commencement of the case, the appointment of the trustee or certain related circumstances.[880]

The resulting concerns for a counterparty may be illustrated as follows. Suppose the Debtor and its counterparty have two executory contracts outstanding at the time the Debtor's Bankruptcy Code case commences and that immediate rejection of one, which is out of the money for the Debtor, would result in claim of $11 million against the bankruptcy Estate, while immediate assumption and assignment of the Debtor's position in the other, which is in the money to the Debtor, would generate $10 million for the Estate from the assignee. Suppose, further, that the transactions were documented under agreements providing for close-out in connection with the commencement of the bankruptcy case and for setoff of the parties' mutual settlement claims if close-out occurs. If the counterparty is permitted to exercise these rights, it will have a net claim of $1 million in the Debtor's case. On the other hand, if the automatic stay and Section 365(e)(1) of the Bankruptcy Code prevent the counterparty from exercising those rights and the trustee rejects the first transaction and assumes and assigns the second, the counterparty will have a gross claim of $11 million on account of the first transaction and nothing against which that claim may be set off. The $10 million generated for the Estate by the assignment will be available for application, as required by the Bankruptcy Code, to administrative costs involving the case and allocation among the Debtor's creditors generally.

AVOIDANCE POWERS AND LIMITATIONS ON SETOFF

As indicated above, insolvency regimes sometimes give Debtors and their Insolvency Representatives certain Avoidance Powers that permit them to recover transferred property of the Debtor and to disavow obligations incurred by the Debtor during specified periods leading up to the commencement of the Proceedings.[881] These transfers and obligations may be viewed as preferences, or as intentional or constructive fraudulent transfers. Insolvency Laws may also disallow setoffs in respect of claims obtained during the specified periods, at least to the extent the setoff results in an improvement in the position of the creditor. In addition, Insolvency Laws generally give Insolvency Representatives Avoidance Powers with respect to transfers of property of the Debtor made after its Proceedings have commenced or the Insolvency Representative has been appointed. Each of these Avoidance Powers and limitations on setoff exists under the Bankruptcy Code.[882]

---

[880] Bankruptcy Code § 365(e).

[881] *See supra* p. 273.

[882] Section 546 of the Bankruptcy Code sets out general rules relating to the various periods within which these avoidance powers may be exercised. Special rules relating to avoidance powers, and special

Preferences

Generally speaking, Section 547 of the Bankruptcy Code gives rise to a power to seek the return of payments made to a creditor, and to avoid security interests granted to or for the benefit of a creditor, if the payment or grant (1) was made on or within 90 days before the date of the filing of a petition commencing a Bankruptcy Code case, or within one year before the petition was filed, if the transfer was for the benefit of a creditor viewed as an insider with respect to the Debtor, (2) was made in respect of antecedent debt, (3) resulted in receipt by a creditor of more than it would have been entitled to receive in a liquidation of the Debtor under Chapter 7 of the Bankruptcy Code and (4) was made when the Debtor was insolvent. The Debtor is presumed to have been insolvent on the day of the filing of the petition that commences the case and each of the 90 days preceding the filing.[883]

There are various exceptions to the Bankruptcy Code rule on the avoidance of preferences. One involves inquiry into the parties' intent relating to the transfer and whether the Debtor received a substantially contemporaneous exchange of new value.[884] Another involves inquiry into whether the relevant antecedent debt was incurred by the Debtor, and the transfer was made, in the ordinary course of business or financial affairs of the Debtor and the transferee and whether the transfer was made according to ordinary business terms.[885] There are also other exceptions applicable to grants of security interests, which turn on such matters as the nature of the property subject to the interest and whether new value was given to the Debtor in connection with the grant.[886]

These general exceptions to the trustee's powers to avoid preferential transfers are not well designed to foster the development of a viable market for OTC derivatives, because of the excessively restrictive character of the inquiries required and conditions imposed. The normal functioning of an OTC derivatives transaction with the Debtor may well have involved payments and transfers right up to the time of the filing of the petition commencing a Bankruptcy Code case, including mark-to-market transfers of collateral and other credit support in respect of pre-existing transactions. The problems posed by these Avoidance Powers are seen most clearly by considering the position of a financial intermediary that has been dealing with the Debtor. In connection with those dealings, the intermediary is likely to have offsetting hedge positions. If it is required to return a payment or transfer made by the Debtor during the preference period, the intermediary is unlikely to have the right to look to those hedge positions to recoup the avoided payment or transfer. Similarly, if the intermediary uses collateral and other credit support transferred to it by the Debtor to secure or otherwise support its obligations under hedge positions,

---

exceptions, are applicable in the Liquidation of a stockbroker (Bankruptcy Code § 749) or a commodity broker (Bankruptcy Code § 764) or in the adjustment of debts of a municipality (Bankruptcy Code § 926). These rules are not discussed here. Usually "avoidance" refers to transfers before a case commences.

[883] This presumption is set forth in Section 547(f) of the Bankruptcy Code.

[884] See Bankruptcy Code § 547(c)(1).

[885] See Bankruptcy Code § 547(c)(2).

[886] See Bankruptcy Code § 547(c)(3)–(5). Section 547 also provides for other exceptions that are not relevant to the subject of this chapter.

avoidance of the Debtor's transfers may result in a need to close out other positions, undermining its ability to engage in market activities in a normal manner.

Limitations on Setoff

Section 553(a) of the Bankruptcy Code sets out as the general rule that the Bankruptcy Code "does not affect any right of a creditor to offset a mutual debt owing by such creditor to the Debtor that arose before the commencement of the case under this title [the Bankruptcy Code] against a claim of such creditor against the Debtor that arose before the commencement of the case."[887] This rule reflects a common sense view that the right of setoff, as described by the U.S. Supreme Court, "allows entities that owe each other money to apply their mutual debts against each other, thereby avoiding 'the absurdity of making A pay B when B owes A.'"[888] The exercise of preserved setoff rights may, however, be automatically stayed, as described above,[889] and there are important limitations to the general rule on setoff.

First, the setoff rights preserved under Section 553(a) do not apply to the extent that:

(1) the claim of such creditor against the debtor is disallowed;

---

[887] Under Section 101(12) of the Bankruptcy Code, "debt" is understood broadly to include any liability on a claim. Section 101(4)(A) broadly defines "claim" to include any "right to payment, whether or not such right is reduced to judgment, liquidated, fixed, contingent, matured, unmatured, disputed, undisputed, legal, equitable, secured, or unsecured. . . ." Under Section 502(c), if a claim is contingent or unliquidated, the contingent or unliquidated claim is to be estimated if the fixing or liquidation of the claim would unduly delay the administration of the case. Precisely what the courts may permit in connection with setoff of unmatured claims (*e.g.,* whether or not the full amount or only its present value may be set off) may depend on the nature of the claim. The rights of setoff in respect of mutual debts preserved under the Bankruptcy Code are those that existed prepetition, so that, for example, the amount of a creditor's deposit obligation to the debtor that may be reduced through setoff against a claim of the creditor against the debtor cannot include any amount that was not on deposit prior to the filing of the petition. *See, e.g., In re Orr* 234 B.R. 249, 254–55 (Bankr. N.D.N.Y. 1999) (discussing various cases on this point in finding that a creditor had willfully violated the automatic stay by denying the debtor access to funds deposited to the debtor's account after the filing of the petition). The concept of mutuality requires that the same person, acting in the same capacity, hold each of the claims being offset. As a result, an obligation owed to Party B and incurred by Party A as agent for, say, its affiliates, could not be set off against obligations owed by Party B to Party A acting as principal on its own behalf. In addition, the requirement of mutuality would generally preclude setoff by Party A of its obligation to Party B against an obligation of Party B to an affiliate of Party A (*see* 4 COLLIER ON BANKRUPTCY ¶ 553.04[2]), although courts have indicated that an express agreement providing for "triangular" setoff of this kind may be upheld. *See* 4 *Id.* ¶ 553.04[2]. In preserving setoff rights only for prepetition, mutual, claims, Section 553 in effect treats the prepetition Debtor and the Debtor in the case as different persons or as the same person acting in different capacities.

[888] *Citizens Bank v. Strumpf,* 516 U.S. 16, 18 (1995), quoting from *Studley v. Boylston Nat'l Bank,* 229 U.S. 523, 528 (1913). In *Strumpf,* the court found that a bank's temporary refusal to pay a deposit debt owed to the Debtor (characterized by the creditor as an administrative freeze) so as to protect its right of setoff against a debt owed to it by the Debtor was not a setoff in violation of the automatic stay where, within five days after commencement of the case, the creditor filed a motion for relief from the automatic stay so as to be able to exercise that setoff right. On the other hand, a creditor that maintained a hold on funds in a debtor's accounts for almost two months before seeking court authorization to exercise its setoff rights has been found to have violated the automatic stay. *See In re Orr,* 234 B.R. 249, 255 (Bankr. N.D.N.Y. 1999).

[889] *See supra* p. 294.

(2) such claim was transferred, by an entity other than the debtor, to such creditor—
  (A) after the commencement of the case; or
  (B) (i) after 90 days before the date of the filing of the petition; and (ii) while the debtor was insolvent; or
(3) the debt owed to the debtor by such creditor was incurred by such creditor—
  (A) after 90 days before the date of the filing of the petition;
  (B) while the debtor was insolvent; and
  (C) for the purpose of obtaining a right of setoff against the debtor.[890]

For all purposes of Section 553, as with Section 547 on preferences, the Debtor is presumed to have been insolvent during the 90 days immediately preceding the date of the filing of the petition that commences Bankruptcy Code Proceedings for the Debtor.[891]

The second general limitation on setoff rights preserved under Section 553(a) of the Bankruptcy Code is that, unless the setoff is otherwise protected by a special rule, setoffs during the period of 90 days before the commencement of Proceedings may be recovered by the trustee from the creditor that effected the setoff, to the extent the setoff enabled the creditor to obtain through setoff more than it would have obtained through setoff on the first day during that period on which the creditor's claims against the Debtor exceed the Debtor's claims against the creditor.

(1) . . . if a creditor offsets a mutual debt owing to the debtor against a claim against the debtor on or within 90 days before the date of the filing of the petition, then the trustee may recover from such creditor the amount so offset to the extent that any insufficiency on the date of such setoff is less than the insufficiency on the later of—
  (A) 90 days before the date of the filing of the petition; and
  (B) the first date during the 90 days immediately preceding the date of the filing of the petition on which there is an insufficiency.
(2) In this subsection, "insufficiency" means amount, if any, by which a claim against the debtor exceeds a mutual debt owing to the debtor by the holder of such claim.[892]

In addition, the benefit of these setoff rights may also be lost or substantially diminished if the trustee—pursuant to Section 365 of the Bankruptcy Code, as described above—elects to assume and assign executory contracts of the Debtor, cherry-picking among those that would otherwise have given rise to claims subject to permitted setoff.

---

[890] The rules on allowance of claims are set forth in Section 502 of the Bankruptcy Code. Among the claims that are disallowed are (under Section 502(b)(2)) claims for unmatured interest. As a general matter, interest accruing once the petition is filed accrues at the rate provided for by law (referred to as the legal rate), rather than the rate specified by the parties' contract. In a Liquidation, payment of this interest comes last (before distribution of the balance to the Debtor) among the claims to which property of the Estate may be applied. *See* Bankruptcy Code § 726(a). In Proceedings under other chapters of the Bankruptcy Code, allowed claims are disposed of in accordance with a plan prepared and confirmed pursuant to the rules of the particular chapter.

[891] Bankruptcy Code § 553(c).

[892] Bankruptcy Code §§ 553(b)(1) & (2).

That is, the value to the Debtor's counterparty of its setoff rights can be lost or diminished if the trustee assigns to third parties assumed contracts that are in the money to the Debtor while leaving the creditor with uncollectible claims on account of the contracts that are in the money to the Debtor's counterparty.

These limitations on setoff rights and the cherry-picking risk, like the Avoidance Powers for preferences described above, present obstacles to the conduct of a viable market for OTC derivatives. For the markets to function properly, those who enter into or obtain contract positions and related offsets in good faith need to be confident that they will be able to enter into and adjust the related hedging positions as necessary to manage their positions.

Fraudulent Transfers

Section 548 is the primary source in the Bankruptcy Code for the Avoidance Powers relating to intentional and constructive fraudulent transfers and agreements.[893] Generally speaking, an intentional fraudulent transfer under this provision is "any transfer of an interest of the debtor in property, or any obligation incurred by the debtor, that was made or incurred on or within one year before the date of the filing of the petition, if the debtor voluntarily or involuntarily . . . made the transfer or incurred the obligation with actual intent to hinder, delay, or defraud its creditors."[894] A constructive fraudulent transfer, on the other hand, involves a transfer of property of the Debtor, or the incurrence by the Debtor of an obligation, within that period in circumstances in which the Debtor received less than a reasonably equivalent value in exchange for the transfer or obligation and (1) was insolvent when the transfer was made or the obligation was incurred, or became insolvent as a result thereof, or (2) was left, after the transfer was made or the obligation was incurred, with an amount of capital that was unreasonably small to carry on its business or (3) intended to incur, or believed it would incur, debts that were beyond its ability to pay them as they matured.[895] The Avoidance Powers with respect to constructive fraudulent transfers under Section 548 of the Bankruptcy Code pose the same obstacles to the conduct of a viable market for OTC derivatives and other financial contracts as do the Avoidance Powers relating to preferences, as described above.

Postpetition Transactions

Section 549 of the Bankruptcy Code is the source of the general Avoidance Power relating to any transfer of property of the Debtor's Estate that is made after the commencement of the Debtor's Bankruptcy Code Proceedings. In Voluntary Proceedings, all

---

[893] Section 544(b) of the Bankruptcy Code gives a trustee the additional power to avoid any transfer of property of the Debtor made prior to the commencement of a case if the transfer is voidable under state laws by an unsecured creditor. Some of these state laws (including New York's Debtor and Creditor Law) permit creditors to avoid transfers made as much as six years before the commencement of a Bankruptcy Code case. *See, e.g.,* N.Y. DEBT. & CRED. L., Art. 10 & NYCPLR § 213.

[894] Bankruptcy Code § 548(a).

[895] Under Section 544(b) of the Bankruptcy Code, the trustee may also be entitled to avoid similarly defined kinds of transfers and obligations incurred under similar circumstances even if the transfer was made or the obligation incurred more than one year before the commencement of Bankruptcy Code proceedings if applicable state fraudulent conveyance law contemplates a longer period.

Bankruptcy and Insolvency Concerns 303

such transfers may be avoided if they are not authorized under the Bankruptcy Code or by the court.[896] In Involuntary Proceedings, a separate rule applies to postpetition transfers by the Debtor during the period beginning with the filing of the petition against the Debtor and ending with the court's entry of an order for relief. Unless and until the court, on request of a party in interest, orders the appointment of an interim trustee to preserve the property of the Estate or prevent loss to the Estate[897] during that period, the Debtor is permitted during the period to continue to operate, use, acquire and dispose of property.[898] The trustee's ability to avoid these transfers by the Debtor is, therefore, appropriately qualified.[899]

FINANCIAL CONTRACT EXCEPTIONS

Exceptions to the automatic stay, the general rules relating to *ipso facto* clauses in executory contracts, the limitations on setoff rights and the Avoidance Powers exist under the Bankruptcy Code with respect to swap agreements, securities contracts, commodity contracts, forward contracts and repurchase agreements. These exceptions are created by separate product-specific sets of provisions, under which the protections are available to specified classes of Protected Persons for each contract class, as shown in the table set out above.[900] H.R. 3211 would eliminate many of the inconsistencies in language that exist in the separate product-specific provisions reviewed in this section.

RIGHTS OF CLOSE-OUT AND RELATED MATTERS

Under the Bankruptcy Code, there are exceptions from the automatic stay and the rule on *ipso facto* clauses that permit Protected Persons to exercise contractual rights to close out financial contracts with a Bankruptcy Code Debtor even after the Debtor's case has commenced and even if the only ground for the close-out is the Debtor's insolvency, the commencement of the case, the appointment of the trustee or some other circumstance relating to the Debtor's financial condition. Set out below, by way of illustration, is Section 560 of the Bankruptcy Code, which relates to swap agreements:

> The exercise of any contractual right of any swap participant to cause the termination of a swap agreement because of a condition of the kind specified in section 365(e)(1) of this title [the Bankruptcy Code] or to offset or net out any termination values or payment amounts arising under or in connection with any swap agreement shall not be stayed, avoided, or otherwise limited by operation of any provision of this title or by order of a court or administrative agency in any proceeding under this title. As used in this section, the term "contractual right" includes a right, whether

---

[896] Bankruptcy Code § 549(a).

[897] *Id* § 303(g).

[898] *Id* § 303(f).

[899] *See* Bankruptcy Code §§ 549(b) & (c), protecting these transfers to the extent value is given in exchange and the transfer is not made to satisfy or secure a debt that arose before the commencement of the case, and certain transfers of real property for present fair value to a good faith purchaser without knowledge of the commencement of the case.

[900] *See supra* p. 283.

or not evidenced in writing, arising under common law, under law merchant, or by reason of normal business practice.[901]

Thus, Section 560 protects both Rights of Close-Out and Rights to Settle Net relating to any swap agreement. This protection is supplemented, as described below, by a separate exception from the automatic stay for specified setoff rights. In the context of standard market forms of agreement, the rights protected by Section 560 are, for example, the rights provided for in Section 6 of the ISDA master agreement forms, involving the designation or automatic occurrence of an Early Termination Date and the calculation of a single, net settlement amount, and the close-out and liquidation rights, and related provisions on the calculation of a single net settlement obligation provided for in Section 8.1 of the 1997 FEOMA form.

For example, if a Bankruptcy Code Debtor and a counterparty that qualifies as a "swap participant" have outstanding currency options and FX forwards at the time of commencement of the Debtor's Bankruptcy Code case and those transactions are documented under a master agreement prepared using an ISDA master agreement form or the FEOMA form, the automatic stay and the provisions of Bankruptcy Code on assumption and assignment of executory contracts and *ipso facto* clauses will not prevent the counterparty from exercising the early termination rights provided for in Section 6 of the ISDA form or the close-out and the liquidation rights provided for in Section 8.1 of the FEOMA form.

The proposed modifications to Section 560 in H.R. 3211 would add "financial participants" to the categories of Protected Persons, as discussed earlier in this chapter,[902] and also make clearer that (1) the rights protected by Section 560 may be exercised across contracts or transactions that qualify as swap agreements, (2) the Close-Out Right applies regardless of what terminology the parties use to refer to the right and (3) the protections of Section 560 apply in connection with close-out and net settlement rights for swap agreements provided for in the rules or by-laws of the various kinds of trading facilities on which swap agreements may be executed or cleared, as well as the rules of national securities associations, by amending Section 560 to read as follows:[903]

> The exercise of any contractual right of any swap participant or financial participant to cause the liquidation, termination, or acceleration of one or more swap agreements because of a condition of the kind specified in section 365(e)(1) of this title [the Bankruptcy Code] or to offset or net out any termination values or payment amounts arising under or in connection with the termination, liquidation, or acceleration of one or more swap agreements shall not be stayed, avoided, or otherwise limited by operation of any provision of this title or by order of a court or administra-

---

[901] Section 560, which relates to swap agreements, and the similar Bankruptcy Code provisions relating to other financial contracts are intended to protect Close-Out Rights of counterparties, not to give the Debtor Close-Out Rights, although the drafting has led to assertions to the contrary. *See, e.g., In re Amcor Funding Corp.,* 117 B.R. 549 (D. Az. 1990) (rejecting such an assertion in a case involving securities contracts and Section 555 of the Bankruptcy Code).

[902] *See supra* p. 285.

[903] H.R. 3211 §§ 8(j) & 8(o)(10).

tive agency in any proceeding under this title. As used in this section, the term "contractual right" includes a right set forth in a rule or bylaw of a derivatives clearing organization (as defined in the Commodity Exchange Act), a multilateral clearing organization (as defined in the Federal Deposit Insurance Corporation Improvement Act of 1991), a national securities exchange, a national securities association, a securities clearing agency, a contract market designated under the Commodity Exchange Act, a derivatives transaction execution facility registered under the Commodity Exchange Act, or a board of trade (as defined in the Commodity Exchange Act) or in a resolution of the governing board thereof and a right, whether or not evidenced in writing, arising under common law, under law merchant, or by reason of normal business practice.[904]

The Bankruptcy Code's similar contract-specific provisions for securities contracts (Section 555), forward contracts and commodity contracts (Section 556) and repurchase agreements (Section 559) generally operate in the same way in connection with a Protected Person's contractual rights to cause the "liquidation" of these kinds of contracts and agreements—each referring only to close-out of its own class or classes of financial contracts. However, where securities contracts are concerned, Section 555 provides that the order of a court or an administrative agency may stay a Protected Person's liquidation of securities contracts, if the order is authorized under the Securities Investor Protection Act of 1970 (SIPA).

H.R. 3211 would modify this rule and provide greater legal certainty for parties to securities contracts with stockbrokers, by adding to SIPA a new Section 5(b)(2)(C)(i) under which a creditor of a stockbroker could not be prevented by the automatic stay, by a court order obtained by SIPC—the Securities Investor Protection Corporation—or by an application for relief under SIPA, from liquidating, terminating, or accelerating any securities contract, commodity contract, forward contract, repurchase agreement or swap agreement, as those terms are defined in the Bankruptcy Code (or any master netting agreement, a new concept that would be introduced by H.R. 3211).[905]

As it would do for swap agreements under Section 560 of the Bankruptcy Code, H.R. 3211 would add financial participants to the classes of Protected Persons under each of these other provisions, would expand the reference to close-out to include "liquidation, termination, or acceleration" and would bring consistency to the references in the various sections to the sources of the relevant "contractual rights."

These provisions for securities contracts, commodity contracts, forward contracts or repurchase agreements do not refer to rights to offset or to net settlement values, but

---

[904]The CEA contemplates derivatives trading on various kinds of trading facilities, which are subject to varying degrees of oversight by the CFTC. The highest degree of supervision applies to contract markets designated by the CFTC for trading in commodity futures, commodity options and options on futures. Derivatives transaction execution facilities, or DTEFs, registered with the CFTC are subject to lesser supervision, and certain boards of trade may be completely exempt from CFTC oversight and regulation. The kinds of commodities that may be involved in transactions traded on these various facilities differ depending on the persons given access to the facility and the degree of CFTC oversight. *See generally supra* p. 96.

[905]*See infra* p. 329.

specified setoff rights are protected in the other ways described below. Section 556 of the Bankruptcy Code, which applies to commodity contracts and forward contracts, preserves "the right to a variation or maintenance margin payment received from a trustee with respect to open commodity contracts or forward contracts," and Section 559, which applies to repurchase agreements, effectively imposes a full two-way payments approach to close-out settlement (a ban on walkaway clauses),[906] so that the Estate is credited with and (subject to permitted setoff) actually receives any net value in the Debtor's favor resulting from the close-out.[907]

Although these protections are broad, they relate only to specific kinds of rights: Rights of Close-Out of the relevant kinds of financial contracts and, in certain cases, related Rights to Settle Net. Particularly in complex structures, the parties to derivatives and other financial products sometimes agree that other kinds of rights, or changes to their contract, will be triggered by a party's insolvency, the commencement of insolvency or similar proceedings, the appointment of an Insolvency Representative or some other event relating to the party's financial condition. When this is so, if one of the parties is eligible to become a Debtor under the Bankruptcy Code, the parties should consult with counsel about possible obstacles to the exercise of these rights or to the effectiveness of these changes, given the automatic stay of Section 362 or the general rule on termination or modification of executory contracts pursuant to *ipso facto* clauses in Section 365(e)(1) of the Bankruptcy Code. Counsel should also be consulted about problems that may arise under Section 541(c), pursuant to which an interest (legal or equitable) of the Debtor in property at the time of the commencement of Proceedings becomes property of the Estate notwithstanding an *ipso facto* clause that "effects or gives an option to effect a forfeiture, modification, or termination of the debtor's interest in property."

Finally, it should be noted that the Bankruptcy Code protections for swap agreements, securities contracts, forward contracts and commodity contracts and repurchase agreements in Sections 560, 555, 556 and 559 of the Bankruptcy Code do not eliminate the right of a trustee to elect to assume, assume and assign or reject executory contracts of the Debtor. These provisions merely permit the Protected Persons, as counterparties in financial contracts with the Debtor, to exercise the protected contractual rights. If the

---

[906]*See infra* p. 230, on ISDA terminology relating to full two-way payments, which is called the "Second Method" in ISDA's 1992 master agreement forms.

[907]This aspect of Section 559 is like the prohibitions against walkaway clauses that, as described *supra* p. 233, already apply under the NYBL and, pursuant to Section 3(a)(2), of H.R. 3211, would be made expressly applicable to all financial contracts in Proceedings under the FDIA, as discussed *infra* p. 337. Section 559 of the Bankruptcy Code imposes the requirement in relation to repurchase agreements by providing that, if a repo participant liquidates one or more repurchase agreements with the debtor and under the terms of one or more of those agreements has agreed to deliver assets subject to repurchase agreements to the debtor,

> any excess of the market prices received on liquidation of such assets (or if any such assets are not disposed of on the date of liquidation of such repurchase agreements, at the prices available at the time of liquidation of such repurchase agreements from a generally recognized source or the most recent closing bid quotation from such a source) over the sum of the stated repurchase prices and all expenses in connection with the liquidation of such repurchase agreements shall be deemed property of the estate, subject to the available rights of setoff.

Bankruptcy and Insolvency Concerns

counterparty delays in exercising those rights, it will remain subject to the cherry-picking risks associated with exercise of those assumption, assignment and rejection rights.[908]

SETOFF

The protections described above are supplemented by exceptions to the Bankruptcy Code's automatic stay that permit Protected Persons to set off mutual debts and claims under or in connection with financial contracts with a Bankruptcy Code Debtor. The exceptions are drafted somewhat differently in the various clauses of Section 362(b) that relate to securities contracts, commodity contracts and forward contracts (§ 362(b)(6)), repurchase agreements (§ 362(b)(7)) and swap agreements (§ 362(b)(17)). Generally speaking, however,[909] each of them permits a counterparty to set off a claim against the Debtor for a payment due from the Debtor in relation to a relevant class of financial contract against either (1) a payment due to the Debtor from that counterparty or (2) securities or other property of the Debtor held by or due from the counterparty to margin, guarantee, secure, or settle a relevant class of financial contract.[910]

To illustrate, the following is the exception relating to the setoff of mutual claims involving swap agreements:

> (b) The filing of a petition under section 301, 302, or 303 of this title [the Bankruptcy Code], or of an application under section 5(a)(3) of the Securities Investor Protection Act of 1970, does not operate as a stay—
>
> . . .
>
> (17) under subsection (a) of this section, of the setoff by a swap participant, of any mutual debt and claim under or in connection with any swap agreement that constitutes the setoff of a claim against the debtor for any payment due from the debtor under or in connection with any swap agreement against any payment due to the debtor from the swap participant under or in connection with any swap agreement or against cash, securities, or other property held by or due from such swap participant to guarantee, secure, or settle any swap agreement.

This provision goes a long way in providing that a swap participant may, notwithstanding the automatic stay, proceed through the exercise of otherwise enforceable setoff rights[911] to collect a payment due from the Debtor under any swap by setting off the

---

[908] These risks may, however, be attenuated in some circumstances by the Bankruptcy Code's treatment of a master agreement for swap agreements and all supplements to such an agreement as a swap agreement. See supra p. 280.

[909] This rule is subject to an exception if the Debtor is a stockbroker, as described infra p. 308.

[910] The references to margin are included in all of the relevant subsections of Section 362(b) other than the one relating to swap agreements. Those other subsections specifically refer to Sections 741 and 761, which spell out what is included in "margin payment." Section 362(b)(17), relating to setoff and swap agreements, refers generally to claims for payments due from the Debtor under or in connection with a swap agreement.

[911] See supra note 887 on mutuality of protected setoff rights. In this regard, it should be noted that Section 553(a)(3) of the Bankruptcy Code provides that a right of setoff asserted by a creditor will not be recognized when it is based on a debt owed to the Debtor by a creditor which was incurred by the creditor

amount of that payment against a payment due from the swap participant to the Debtor under a swap agreement or against credit support posted by the Debtor. The amendments to the Bankruptcy Code proposed in H.R. 3211 would, however, expand on these rights in various ways and provide desirable clarifications.

First, as noted above,[912] H.R. 3211 would extend to "financial participants" the special protections for financial contracts in the Bankruptcy Code, including the rights provided by Section 362(b)(17). In addition, if modified as provided in H.R. 3211, that section would be further clarified, to the effect that the permitted setoffs may involve "one or more swap agreements" and to provide that they include not only claims for payments due from a Debtor but also claims for any "other transfer of property" due from the Debtor under or in connection with one or more swap agreements.[913]

This clarification can be useful, for example, when the Debtor and a counterparty have entered into reciprocal credit support arrangements (like those contemplated in ISDA's forms of Credit Support Annexes) and the Debtor holds collateral thereunder at the time of its failure. In that case, the proposed change would eliminate any possible doubt about the counterparty's right to set off a payment owed by it against collateral that the Debtor was required to return, if the Debtor has failed to do so immediately.[914]

Second, H.R. 3211 would amend Section 362(b)(17) of the Bankruptcy Code to clarify that the permitted setoffs may be made not only against cash, securities, or other property "held by or due from such swap participant" but also against cash securities and other property that is "pledged to" or "under the control of" the party effecting the setoff, to "margin, guarantee, secure, or settle any swap agreement." This additional language is helpful in clarifying the position of secured parties who have disposed of collateral posted by a Debtor, as is commonly the case,[915] and the proposed reference to "control" is helpful in light of the many circumstances in which a party's security interest may be perfected through means other than possession.[916]

H.R. 3211 would also add to legal certainty relating to setoff rights in the Liquidation of a stockbroker. It would do so by adding to Section 5(b)(2) of SIPA a provision under which neither the filing of an application for relief under SIPA nor any court order

---

after 90 days before the date of filing of the petition, while the Debtor was insolvent and for the purpose of obtaining a right of setoff against the Debtor. In addition, under Section 553(a)(2), a right of setoff asserted by a creditor will not be recognized if it is based on a claim that was transferred to the creditor by a third party either after the commencement of the case or after 90 days before the filing of the petition and while the Debtor was insolvent.

[912] *Supra* p. 283.

[913] "Transfer" for this and other purposes includes all of the following under Section 101(54) of the Bankruptcy Code: "every mode, direct or indirect, absolute or conditional, voluntary or involuntary, of disposing of or parting with property or with an interest in property, including retention of title as a security interest and foreclosure of the Debtor's equity of redemption."

[914] *See* the annotation to Paragraph 8(b)(iii) of the sample credit support agreement, *infra* p. 1176, on this feature of ISDA's bilateral (that is, reciprocal) form of Credit Support Annex published in 1994 for use with agreements governed by New York law and on the parallel provision in the *Margin Provisions*.

[915] *See infra* p. 1072.

[916] On the concept of "control" in connection with the perfection of security interests under the Uniform Commercial Code, *see infra* p. 1095.

or decree obtained by SIPC could operate as a stay of any contractual rights of a creditor to offset or to net termination values, payment amounts or other transfer obligations arising under or in connection with one or more financial contracts, or to foreclose on any cash collateral pledged by the Debtor, whether or not the collateral was secured financial contracts.[917] It should be noted that the proposed protective provision applies only to cash collateral. Under SIPA, as so amended, the automatic stay imposed by Section 362(a) of the Bankruptcy Code would still apply to "the foreclosure on, or disposition of, securities collateral pledged by the debtor, whether or not with respect to one or more [financial contracts] . . . , securities sold by the debtor under a repurchase agreement, or securities lent under a securities lending agreement."[918]

AVOIDANCE POWERS

Section 546 of the Bankruptcy Code includes special provisions limiting a trustee's Avoidance Powers in relation to financial contracts. These limitations apply to the avoidance of payments and other transfers made by a Debtor, and to the disavowal of obligations incurred by the Debtor, that might otherwise have been treated as preferences or constructive fraudulent transfers. There is no limitation on Avoidance Powers based on intentional fraudulent transfers.

As with the special provisions for financial contracts described in the preceding paragraphs, these limitations on Avoidance Powers apply under separate clauses that refer to specific classes of financial contracts and the categories of Protected Persons entitled to the benefits of the particular limiting clause. By way of example, the following are the clauses of Section 546 of the Bankruptcy Code applicable to swap agreements.

> (g) Notwithstanding sections 544, 545, 547, 548(a)(1)(B) and 548(b) of this title [the Bankruptcy Code], the trustee may not avoid a transfer under a swap agreement, made by or to a swap participant, in connection with a swap agreement and that is made before the commencement of the case, except under section 548(a)(1)(A) of this title [on intentional fraudulent conveyances].[919]

The Bankruptcy Code provisions limiting Avoidance Powers in connection with securities contracts, forward contracts, commodity contracts and repurchase agreements appear in Sections 546(e) and (f) and, except for intentional fraudulent transfers, preclude avoidance of "a transfer that is a margin payment" or a "settlement payment," as defined in the relevant sections of the Bankruptcy Code, if the transfer is made to any of the relevant Protected Persons identified in the table set out earlier in this chapter.[920]

---

[917] H.R. 3211 § 12.

[918] Id.

[919] There is no need for Section 546 to refer to Section 549, which permits the avoidance of post-petition transfers, because Section 549 does not permit the avoidance of transfers of property of the Estate that are authorized by the Bankruptcy Code, and since the provisions discussed above relating to offset, netting and setoff expressly authorize those transfers under and in connection with financial contracts.

[920] Supra p. 283. In addition, various clauses of Section 548 of the Bankruptcy Code provide that, for purposes of that provision (on fraudulent transfers), Protected Persons that receive margin payments or

The amendments to these provisions proposed in H.R. 3211 would, as noted above, add financial participants to the Protected Persons and, in the provision applicable to swap agreements (Section 546(g)), would also clarify that the protected transfers are those made prior to the commencement of the Debtor's case "under or in connection with a swap agreement," and not merely *under* a swap agreement.[921]

FEDERAL DEPOSIT INSURANCE ACT

ISSUES

Under the FDIA, a receiver or conservator for an FDIC-insured depository institution will have avoidance, repudiation, transfer and other powers and rights very much like those given by the Bankruptcy Code to trustees and debtors in possession.[922] As indicated earlier in this chapter, the same powers may also apply in Proceedings conducted for Edge Act corporations and uninsured state member banks of the Federal Reserve System that operate, or operate as, multilateral clearing organizations.[923] Under the reforms proposed in H.R. 3211, these powers would be available to the Insolvency Representative for other uninsured financial institutions, including the U.S. branches and agencies of foreign banks subject to Proceedings pursuant to the IBA.[924]

Specifically, the FDIA grants the FDIC, as receiver or conservator for a Debtor, the right to repudiate or disaffirm burdensome contracts of the institution within a reasonable time after the FDIC's appointment as receiver or conservator, the right to enforce contracts notwithstanding their purported termination on the basis of the FDIA equivalent of *ipso facto* clauses, the power to transfer assets and liabilities of the institution without any approval, assignment or consent, and the right to avoid certain transfers by the institution.[925] The FDIA also provides that the FDIC, once it has been appointed as conserva-

---

settlement payments (securities contracts, forward contracts, commodity contracts and repurchase agreements) or transfers of any kind (swap agreements) will be treated as having taken for value. *See* Bankruptcy Code §§ 548(d)(2)(B)–(D). Under the proposed clause (E) that would be added by H.R. 3211, a master netting agreement participant is not treated as having taken for value with respect to a transfer under any individual contract covered by the master agreement "to the extent that such master netting agreement participant otherwise did not take (or is otherwise not deemed to have taken) such transfer for value." That is, the proposed master netting agreement clause of Section 548(d)(2) does not enlarge on the protection that a master netting agreement participant is entitled to obtain as a Protected Person in respect of the separate financial contracts covered by its master netting agreement.

[921] The limiting reference in transfers under swap agreements in Section 546(g) has led to the structuring of credit support documents so that they form part of swap agreements. *See, e.g., infra* p. 1906 on the structuring of ISDA's 1994 Credit Support Annex form as part of the schedule to a Master Agreement prepared using an ISDA form, the similar approach in the Credit Support Annex published for use with the FEOMA, ICOM and IFEMA forms for currency options and spot and forward FX contracts, the approach of the 1995 ISDA Credit Support Annex for use with ISDA Master Agreements governed by English law, where the credit support arrangements are treated as Transactions under the related Master Agreement, and the *Margin Provisions*, which provide that the parties may incorporate those provisions into any agreement through a supplement to the agreement.

[922] The provisions of the FDIA setting out these powers were enacted by FIRREA, with the result that OTC derivatives documentation sometimes makes reference to that statute. *See, e.g., infra* p. 900.

[923] *See supra* p. 289.

[924] H.R. 3211 § 7(d), which would add a new Section 407 to FDICIA.

[925] *See* FDIA §§ 11(e)(1)(A) (on repudiation of burdensome contracts to promote the orderly administration of the institution's affairs), 11(e)(12) (on the equivalent of *ipso facto* clauses—conditioning

tor or receiver for an institution, may request a stay of any judicial action to which the institution is or becomes a party, and the FDIC always obtains these stays, which may last for up to 45 days, when the FDIC is acting as conservator, and up to 90 days, when it is acting as receiver.[926]

The FDIC also has additional powers provided for in other laws applicable to the relevant institution's Proceedings, which would include the NBA, if the institution were a national bank or were an FDIC-insured branch in the U.S. of a foreign bank subject to Proceedings under the IBA.[927] The NBA provides that any payment or transfer of assets by a national bank that is made "after the commission of an act of insolvency, or in contemplation thereof" will be "utterly null and void" if made to the bank's shareholders or creditors "with a view to the preference of one creditor to another" or otherwise to prevent the application of the bank's assets in the manner prescribed by the NBA, which requires distribution of a national bank's assets to its creditors ratably.[928]

"Acts of insolvency" have been found to include the adoption by the directors of a national bank of a resolution to suspend its operations, the bank's failure to pay a deposit on demand or to meet its obligations at maturity and an admission by the bank or its officers that it is unable to satisfy its obligations when due.[929] In Proceedings under the NBA or Proceedings under the FDIA in which the powers of the FDIC include those available to a receiver or conservator under the NBA, payments and other transfers made prior to the Proceedings could be void as preferences without any knowledge on the part of the payee or transferee that the payment or transfer could be recovered as having been made "in contemplation of" the institution's insolvency.[930]

However, the FDIA extends to swap agreements and the other qualified financial contracts special protections for the Close-Out Right and the Right to Settle Net, as well as rights involving setoff against credit support and protections against the Avoidance Powers referred to in the preceding paragraphs of this section. These protections are similar but not identical to those afforded under the Bankruptcy Code in connection with the same kinds of financial contracts.

---

termination, default, acceleration or exercise of rights upon, or solely by reason of, the insolvency of the institution or the appointment of a conservator or receiver), 11(d)(2)(G)(i)(II) (on transfers of assets or liabilities) & 11(e)(11) (on avoidance of security interests taken in contemplation of the institution's insolvency or with the intent to hinder, delay, or defraud the institution or its creditors).

[926]FDIA § 11(d)(12).

[927]The IBA provides that a receiver appointed thereunder has "the same rights, privileges, powers, and authority" with respect to the entity in receivership "as are now exercised by receivers of national banks appointed by the Comptroller." IBA § 4(j)(1).

[928]NBA §§ 91 & 194.

[929]*See, e.g., Armstrong v. Chemical Nat'l Bank,* 41 Fed. 234 (C.C.S.D.N.Y. 1890).

[930]*Id.* (to the effect that a payment by a national bank could be viewed as made in contemplation of its insolvency at any time after it became "reasonably apparent to its officers" that the bank "will presently be unable to meet its obligations, and will be obliged to suspend its operations").

Exceptions for Qualified Financial Contracts

The special protections afforded under the FDIA are available to all who are parties to qualified financial contracts with a Debtor at the time a receiver or conservator for the Debtor is appointed, rather than only to the limited classes of Protected Persons identified in the Bankruptcy Code's special protections for financial contracts. The nature of the special protections afforded under the FDIA will, however, in some cases depend on whether the FDIC chooses to operate the failed or failing institution as a going concern, to carry out a merger or purchase and assumption transaction through which assets of the insolvent entity are transferred, or to liquidate the institution.

In addition, a creditor's right to the special protections afforded by the FDIA, which are described below, is available only in connection with agreements that satisfy special writing and authorization requirements of the FDIA described elsewhere in this book.[931] The remainder of this discussion will presume satisfaction of those requirements and, to the extent necessary, a creditor's filing of a necessary claim in its counterparty's FDIA Proceedings.

Close-Out with an Institution in Conservatorship

If a depository institution is placed in conservatorship under the FDIA, its counterparty in a qualified financial contract will be entitled to exercise a contractual right to terminate or liquidate the contract which is enforceable under noninsolvency law so long as there is a ground for the termination or liquidation that is not, and is not incidental to, the appointment of a conservator for the depository institution (or the insolvency or financial condition of the depository institution for which the conservator has been appointed). If, however, the contractual ground for termination or liquidation of the relevant qualified financial contracts is "upon, or solely by reason of, insolvency or the appointment of a conservator or receiver" the counterparty will be unable to exercise its contractual Close-Out Right,[932] and the conservator will be entitled to require continuing performance from the counterparty, repudiate the qualified financial contracts if they are burdensome, as described above, and transfer those contracts and related claims and collateral as described below.

In these circumstances, the counterparty will, as discussed below, (1) be protected against cherry-picking by the conservator,[933] (2) be entitled to exercise the counterparty's contractual Close-Out Right if the Debtor in conservatorship fails to perform its obligations under the relevant qualified financial contract, (3) have a claim for damages[934] if the conservator repudiates the qualified financial contract and (4) be entitled to liquidate collateral for the Debtor's obligations under a repudiated qualified financial contract, to the extent possible without need for judicial assistance, and exercise setoff rights against that

---

[931] See supra p. 51.

[932] FDIA §§ 11(e)(8)(a)(i) & 11(e)(12(A).

[933] See infra p. 314.

[934] See infra p. 338.

collateral or the proceeds of its liquidation, provided the relevant security interest and set-off rights are otherwise enforceable under the FDIA.[935]

CLOSE-OUT WITH AN INSTITUTION IN RECEIVERSHIP

If a depository institution is placed in receivership under the FDIA, the counterparty will be entitled to exercise a contractual right to terminate or liquidate its qualified financial contracts with the institution[936] subject to two conditions:

- The termination or liquidation may not occur prior to the close of business on the business day following the date of the appointment of the receiver, so as to enable the receiver to determine whether it will make a permitted transfer of the depository institution's qualified financial contracts, as described below.

- The termination or liquidation may not occur at all if at or prior to the close of business on the business day following the appointment, the receiver has notified the counterparty that such a transfer has been made.[937]

H.R. 3211 would make the FDIA references to the Close-Out Right relate more broadly to a right to cause the termination, liquidation or acceleration of qualified financial contracts—as would the parallel changes to the Bankruptcy Code. The changes would also clarify matters relating to the described conditions to exercise of the Close-Out Right. Under the proposed modification, the FDIA would provide that the right to cause the termination, liquidation or acceleration of a qualified financial contract may not be exercised until 5:00 p.m. (eastern time) on the business day following the date of the appointment of the receiver and may not be exercised at all after the counterparty has received notice that such a transfer has been made.[938]

---

[935] *See infra* p. 316 on these rights relating to collateral and setoff rights and *infra* p. 338 on provisions generally applicable to claims against the FDIC.

[936] FDIA § 11(e)(8)(A).

[937] This summary reflects a combination of the statutory provision and its refinement under FDIC policy. Section 11(e)(10)(A) of the FDIA merely requires the FDIC to use its best efforts to give notice of such a transfer by noon on the business day following the transfer. However, in the *Policy Statement regarding Qualified Financial Contracts*, FED. BANKING L. REP (CCH) ¶ 68–265 (Dec. 12, 1989), the FDIC stated that it interprets the provision to have the effect described above. The FDIC further stated that it would not view the counterparty's exercise of a Close-Out Right (and its exercise of other rights against collateral security for the failed depository's obligations under qualified financial contracts) as protected if they were exercised before the close of business on the business day following the appointment of the receiver. The FDIA does not deal expressly with whether the one-day waiting period applies when a receiver is appointed and the counterparty has a contractual right to close out on a ground other than the appointment of the receiver.

[938] H. R. 3211 § 4(c)(2). This change would be effected through the introduction of a new subparagraph (B) to Section 11(e)(10) of the FDIA. A related change would be effected to Section 11(e)(10)(A) of the FDIA, pursuant to which the conservator or receiver for a Debtor in FDIA Proceedings would be required to notify any person who is a party to any qualified financial contract with the Debtor of a transfer of the Debtor's qualified financial contracts by 5:00 p.m. (eastern time) on the business day following the date of the appointment of the receiver in the case of a receivership, or the business day following such transfer in the case of a conservatorship. H. R. 3211 § 4(b).

In addition, under the reform law contemplated in H.R. 3211, the FDIC, as receiver or conservator, will be deemed to have notified a person who is a party to a qualified financial contract with a depository institution about a transfer if the FDIC has taken steps reasonably calculated to provide notice to the party by the time indicated.[939]

PROTECTION AGAINST CHERRY-PICKING

The FDIA protects the counterparty to a depository institution that is a Debtor in FDIA Proceedings against cherry-picking of qualified financial contracts in two ways. First, the FDIA limits the power of a receiver or conservator to transfer qualified financial contracts. Second, the FDIA provides that any master agreement for any qualified financial contract, together with all supplements to the master agreement, must be treated as a single agreement and a single qualified financial contract,[940] thereby, limiting the power of a receiver or conservator to engage in selective repudiation of qualified financial contracts under the same master agreement.

The proposed reforms contemplated in H.R. 3211 would provide, as do the proposed parallel modifications to the Bankruptcy Code described above,[941] that, if a master agreement contains provisions relating to agreements or transactions that are not themselves qualified financial contracts, the master agreement will be deemed to be a qualified financial contract with respect to the transactions that are themselves qualified financial contracts. The provision would eliminate concerns over loss of the FDIA's protections for qualified financial contracts covered by a master agreement merely because the agreement was also used to document other kinds of dealings.

Under the FDIA, a conservator or receiver is not permitted to transfer any qualified financial contract of the relevant depository institution with a counterparty or any of the counterparty's affiliates unless the conservator transfers all of the following—which we will refer to collectively as "QFC Rights and Claims"—to one eligible financial institution:

- all qualified financial contracts between the counterparty or any affiliate of the counterparty and the depository institution in default;

- all claims of the counterparty or any affiliate of the counterparty against the depository institution under any qualified financial contract (other than any claim which, under the terms of any such contract, is subordinated to the claims of general unsecured creditors of the depository institution);

- all claims of the depository institution against the counterparty or any affiliate of the counterparty under any qualified financial contract; and

- all property securing or any other credit enhancement for any qualified financial contract between the counterparty or any of its affiliates and

---

[939]This change would codify FDIC policy as stated in December 1989 (*see supra* note 937) and would be incorporated into a new Section 11(e)(10)(B)(iii) of the FDIA. H. R. 3211 § 4(c)(2).

[940]*See* FDIA § 11(e)(8)(D)(vii).

[941]*Supra* p. 280.

the depository institution, or for any claim under any such contract (other than the subordinated claims referred to above).[942]

Under the reform proposal in H.R. 3211, if the receiver elects to make such a transfer, the transferee must be a "financial institution," understood to mean "a broker or dealer, a depository institution, a futures commission merchant, or any other institution, as determined by the Corporation [the FDIC] by regulation to be a financial institution."[943] The transferee may not be a financial institution that is "in default."[944]

The reforms contemplated in H.R. 3211 will also place two further limitations on transfers by the FDIC. First, they would provide that the transferee may not be a foreign bank, financial institution organized under the laws of a foreign country, or a branch or agency of a foreign bank or financial institution unless,

> under the law applicable to such bank, financial institution, branch or agency, to the qualified financial contracts, and to any netting contract, any security agreement or arrangement or other credit enhancement related to one or more qualified financial contracts, the contractual rights of the parties to such qualified financial contracts, netting contracts, security agreements or arrangements, or other credit enhancements are enforceable substantially to the same extent as permitted under this section [the protective provisions for qualified financial contracts set forth in Section 11(e) of the FDIA].[945]

Second, as amended by H.R. 3211, the FDIA would provide that, if the transfer included a qualified financial contract cleared by or subject to the rules of a clearing organization, as defined in Section 402 of FDICIA, the clearing organization would not be required to accept the transferee as a member by virtue of the transfer.[946]

The reform law contemplated in H.R. 3211 would also provide greater legal certainty that cherry-picking through repudiation will not occur in FDIA Proceedings. As indicated, the statute already provides some protection in this area through its identification of a master agreement for swap agreements as a single qualified financial contract. That approach does not expressly extend to selective repudiation of qualified financial contracts documented under separate master agreements or other contracts. The law does, however, expressly protect rights to offset or net out termination values, payment amounts and other transfer obligations arising under or in connection with one or more qualified financial contracts, as discussed in the following section. Since selective repudiation of separately documented qualified financial contracts would eviscerate those protected set-off rights, implicitly the law already appears to eschew cherry-picking among qualified financial contracts through selective repudiation. The reforms proposed in H.R. 3211 would provide greater legal certainty in this regard by providing that, under the FDIA, a

---

[942] *See* FDIA § 11(e)(9)(A).

[943] H.R. § 4(a).

[944] *Id.*

[945] *Id.*

[946] *Id. See also supra* p. 111 regarding these clearing organizations.

conservator or receiver may not repudiate or disaffirm any qualified financial contract between a depository institution in conservatorship or receivership and a counterparty or any of the counterparty's affiliates unless the conservator or receiver also repudiates and disaffirms all qualified financial contracts of the institution with that counterparty and its affiliates.[947]

Like the proposed reforms to the Bankruptcy Code described above, the proposed modifications to the FDIA would also extend to financial contracts other than swap agreements the rule that a master agreement providing for a particular class of financial contracts will, together with all supplements thereto, constitute a single agreement to the extent it provides for that class of financial contracts.

RIGHT TO SETTLE NET AND SETOFF RIGHTS

In a receivership or conservatorship for a depository institution under the FDIA, if the institution's counterparties in qualified financial contracts are permitted, under the rules described above, to exercise contractual rights to terminate or liquidate those contracts, the counterparties will also be entitled to exercise contractual rights to offset or net out all amounts payable in respect of qualified financial contracts with the insolvent institution, including the termination values of multiple transactions under a master swap agreement.[948] As a result, the counterparties of depository institutions subject to Proceedings under the FDIA may have broader protection for their setoff rights relating to the full array of qualified financial contracts exercisable notwithstanding the commencement of insolvency proceedings than do parties to the same array of transactions with Bankruptcy Code Debtors under the Bankruptcy Code provisions described above. This is so because the Bankruptcy Code provisions permitting the exercise of setoff rights notwithstanding the automatic stay apply separately to swap agreements, on one hand, and forward contracts and securities contracts or repurchase agreements, on the other.[949]

RIGHTS RELATING TO CREDIT SUPPORT

In many cases the counterparty of a depository institution subject to Proceedings under the FDIA will also be entitled to exercise its rights under security arrangements re-

---

[947] The modification would be added to the FDIA through redesignation of various subsections of Section 1821(e) and the introduction of a new subsection (11) on this subject.

[948] FDIA § 11(e)(8)(A)(iii). This provision is to the effect that a person may not be stayed or prohibited from exercising "any right to offset or net out any termination value, payment amount, or other transfer obligation arising under or in connection with 1 or more [qualified financial] contracts . . . , including any master agreement for such contracts."

[949] As described *infra* p. 332, however, the broader protections for cross-product netting available under the FDIA but not the Bankruptcy Code would also be available to a counterparty to a Bankruptcy Code Debtor if both it and the Debtor were financial institutions for purposes of FDICIA's provisions on netting contracts and they had entered into a netting contract covering all their financial contracts that qualified for the benefits of those provisions. In addition, as discussed *infra* p. 329, under proposed amendments to the Bankruptcy Code in H.R. 3211 relating to master netting agreements, any master netting agreement participant would be entitled to cross-product netting protections.

lating to qualified financial contracts,[950] (1) subject to the right, noted above, of a receiver or conservator to obtain a stay of all judicial actions involving the insolvent depository, for a period of 90 days, in the case of a receivership, and 45 days in the case of a conservatorship,[951] and (2) provided the security interest is enforceable and perfected under noninsolvency law and the agreement granting the interest satisfies the writing and related requirements referred to above that must be satisfied by all agreements that serve as the basis for claims against the FDIC.[952]

Therefore, assuming satisfaction of those requirements, if collateral is available to a creditor of a Debtor that is the subject of FDIA Proceedings without judicial action, the creditor will be able to apply the collateral without delay against the Debtor's obligations under qualified financial contracts, including obligations in respect of close-out settlement where the close-out was effected consistent with the FDIA—that is, in a conservatorship, provided the Close-Out Right was exercised on grounds other than the appointment of the conservator or the insolvency or financial condition of the depository institution for which the conservator has been appointed; and in a receivership, provided the Close-Out Right was exercised after the close of business on the business day following the day the receiver was appointed and the receiver had not given notice of a transfer to a single transferee of all the relevant QFC Rights and Claims as described above.[953]

As indicated above, the reforms proposed in H.R. 3211 would broaden the definitions of the various classes of financial contracts to include any security agreement or arrangement or other credit enhancement related to any agreement or transaction covered by the definition, or any guarantee or reimbursement obligation in connection with any such agreement or transaction. Like the parallel proposed changes to the Bankruptcy Code described earlier, these changes would benefit counterparties to Debtors in FDIA Proceedings in at least two important ways.

The first area of additional protection would benefit a creditor that was both a counterparty to the Debtor under qualified financial contracts and the beneficiary of a guaranty or letter of credit issued by the Debtor to support the obligations of a third party under qualified financial contracts. If the contracts entered into directly between the Debtor and this creditor were, say, in the money to the Debtor at the time of close-out, so that the creditor owed a close-out settlement payment to the Debtor, under the broadened definition of each of the classes of qualified financial contract, it would be clear that the Debtor could offset that close-out settlement obligation against the Debtor's obligations to it under the guaranty or letter of credit, without concern over a court ordered stay—assuming the close-out settlement obligation arose from the exercise of a Close-Out Right

---

[950] FDIA § 11(e)(8)(A)(ii). These rights are not protected in cases in which the qualified financial contract is transferred to another institution or the counterparty's economic rights are otherwise not impaired in circumstances in which a conservator keeps the contract in place. *Id.*

[951] *Id.* § 11(d)(12).

[952] These requirements are discussed *supra* p. 51.

[953] This subject was addressed shortly after the adoption of FIRREA in "Self-Help Liquidation of Collateral by Secured Claimants in Insured Depository Institution Receiverships," 1989 FDIC Interp. Ltr. LEXIS 69 (Dec. 15, 1989), an interpretive letter issued by the FDIC's general counsel.

permitted as described above and all the relevant claims satisfied the writing and authorization requirements applicable to all claims against the FDIC under the FDIA.[954]

The second chief area of additional protection would benefit creditors who take and give credit support for qualified financial contract obligations by way of title transfer rather than security interests, pursuant to mechanisms like those contemplated in ISDA's 1995 Credit Support Annex prepared for use with master agreements governed by English law and the similar provisions in the *2001 ISDA Margin Provisions*.[955] Say a creditor has transferred $75 million as credit support to the Debtor prior to the commencement of the Debtor's FDIA Proceedings and the balance of that amount of credit support has not previously been applied pursuant to the parties' agreement or reduced by title transfers made by the Debtor. At the time the FDIA Proceedings commence, these ISDA title transfer mechanisms would treat the $75 million transfer as a deemed Transaction under the parties' master agreement giving rise to a payment obligation of $75 million in favor the creditor. The creditor would expect to be entitled to take that amount into account as an offset to its obligations to the Debtor under qualified financial contracts (other Transactions) under the master agreement in calculating the net close-out settlement amount payable under the agreement.[956] By broadening the definitions of the classes of qualified financial contracts to cover credit enhancements generally, and not merely security agreements or arrangements, the proposed H.R. 3211 changes would provide the creditor with greater legal certainty that this net calculation would be enforceable in the Debtor's FDIA Proceedings—again, assuming the close-out settlement arose from the exercise of a Close-Out Right permitted as described above and all the relevant claims satisfied the writing and authorization requirements applicable to all claims against the FDIC under the FDIA.

These changes could confer a similar benefit on a creditor that had transferred collateral to the Debtor pursuant to a grant of a security interest and permitted the Debtor to use and dispose of the collateral freely. In such a case, say the collateral transferred by the creditor prior to the commencement of the Proceedings had a value of $75 million at the time the Proceedings commenced and the parties had documented their qualified financial contracts using an ISDA-based master agreement governed by New York law. Under the standard documentation of security arrangements published by ISDA for use with such agreements (the Credit Support Annex published in 1994 and the similar provisions in the *2001 ISDA Margin Provisions*), if the Debtor failed to return the same or equivalent property immediately upon the occurrence of the Event of Default that would exist pursuant to the parties' master agreement upon the commencement of the Debtor's FDIA Proceedings, the creditor would expect to be able to set off a claim for that $75 million against the amount payable by the creditor to the Debtor in connection with transactions under that master agreement, whether as a result of a close-out settlement calculation or otherwise. Again, by broadening the definitions of the classes of qualified financial contracts to cover credit enhancements generally, the proposed H.R. 3211 changes would

---

[954] *See supra* note 952. The offset right would be as permitted under Section 11(e)(8)(A)(iii) of the FDIA, as described *supra* p. 316.

[955] *See infra* p. 1065.

[956] As described *infra* p. 1065, the $75 million would be treated as an Unpaid Amount in the calculation of the net close-out settlement payment.

provide the creditor with greater legal certainty that this offset would be enforceable in the Debtor's FDIA Proceedings—assuming any relevant close-out settlement arose from the exercise of a Close-Out Right permitted as described above and the creditor's claims against the Debtor satisfied the writing and authorization requirements applicable to all claims against the FDIC under the FDIA.

In addition, as indicated above, the protections for rights of setoff and net settlement against credit support described in the preceding paragraphs would be further enhanced through the reforms proposed in H.R. 3211 as a result of a modification to the definition of the term "transfer" as used in the FDIA. "Transfer" would be redefined to mean "every mode, direct or indirect, absolute or conditional, voluntary or involuntary, of disposing of or parting with property or with an interest in property, including retention of title as a security interest and foreclosure of the [relevant] depository institution's equity of redemption."[957]

PROTECTION AGAINST AVOIDANCE POWERS

Finally, the FDIA protects the counterparties to qualified financial contracts with a depository institution in FDIA Proceedings against the avoidance powers of the institution's receiver or conservator referred to above.[958] Specifically, the FDIC, as receiver or conservator for a depository institution will have no power to avoid any transfer of money or other property of the institution in connection with any qualified financial contract, unless the FDIC determines the transfer was made with actual intent of the transferee to hinder, delay, or defraud the depository institution, its creditors or any conservator or receiver appointed for the institution.[959] The proposed reforms in H.R. 3211 will clarify that this limitation on the FDIC's avoidance powers applies not only to those given to the FDIC in provisions of the FDIA but also to the powers of a receiver or conservator appointed under the NBA, which supplement those provided for directly in the FDIA as noted above.[960]

OTHER FEDERAL BANKING LAWS

As noted above, the Bankruptcy Code and the FDIA as currently in effect, with their special protections for financial contracts, would not apply in all Proceedings in the U.S. for banks and other financial institutions organized in this country or for all branches or agencies in this country of banks and other financial institutions organized elsewhere. For example, those special protections would not be available in Proceedings under the NBA or the IBA for deposit-taking domestic institutions or domestic branches of foreign banks if their deposits are not FDIC-insured, nor would the special protections apply in Proceedings under the IBA for any agency in this country of a foreign bank.

---

[957] H.R. 3211 § 2(g). This change would be effected through Section 2(g), by amending Section 11(e)(8)(D)(viii) of the FDIA. *See supra* p. 913.

[958] *See supra* note 925.

[959] FDIA § 11(e)(8)(C).

[960] H.R. 3211 § 2(i). *See supra* p. 311 on these supplemental avoidance powers. The clarification would be made through an amendment to Section 11(e)(8)(C)(i) of the FDIA, which would expressly override supplemental powers under state or federal law to avoid preferential or fraudulent transfers.

The NBA and the IBA do not have special provisions relating to financial contracts. Therefore, to the extent that these laws may override or otherwise impair or delay the exercise of the Close-Out Right or the Right to Settle Net, or the other important rights outlined above in this chapter, the counterparties to Debtors that become subject to NBA or IBA Proceedings may have cause for concern. As indicated earlier, the powers of a receiver appointed by the Comptroller of the Currency in Proceedings under the IBA for an uninsured Debtor would be substantially the same as those of a receiver appointed for a national bank under the NBA.

If the Comptroller appoints a conservator in Proceedings under the NBA for an uninsured bank or branch and seeks a court order staying any judicial action or proceeding to which the bank or branch is or may be subject, the court will be required to grant the request, and the stay may apply for up to 45 days after the appointment of the conservator.[961] This power applies only to stays of judicial actions and proceedings, however, and only in the context of a conservatorship.

The NBA also authorizes a receiver for a national bank, with court approval, to sell a national bank's property.[962] As described above, the NBA also provides that any payment or transfer of assets by a national bank that is made "after the commission of an act of insolvency, or in contemplation thereof" will be "utterly null and void" if made to the bank's shareholders or creditors "with a view to the preference of one creditor to another" or otherwise to prevent the application of the bank's assets in the manner prescribed by the NBA, which requires distribution of a national bank's assets to its creditors ratably.[963] The NBA does not otherwise address the repudiation or avoidance of contracts, the enforceability of the Close-Out Right or the Right to Settle Net or limitations on otherwise enforceable setoff rights or security interests.

These subjects have, however, been addressed by the Chief Counsel of the OCC in the context of security interests and setoff rights relating to foreign exchange transactions of an uninsured federally licensed branch or agency of a foreign bank in IBA receivership Proceedings. The guidance was provided in response to an inquiry made on behalf of Exchange Clearing House Organization (ECHO) as it explored the U.S. Insolvency Law risks associated with the participation of such a branch or agency in ECHO.

Under the ECHO arrangements, as described in the letter of inquiry, ECHO would mutualize the credit risk involved in the transactions of its participants by acting as a substitute counterparty to each participant in each transaction, the payment obligations and entitlements among all the ECHO participants would be netted pursuant to agreements governed by English law, those agreements would provide for the termination of transactions after appointment of a receiver for a participant and the participants would pledge collateral to secure their obligations under the netting arrangements. The OCC was asked to confirm whether the right to exercise remedies against the collateral would be enforceable in a receivership conducted pursuant to Section 4(j) of the IBA for an uninsured federally licensed branch or agency of a non-U.S. bank participating in ECHO.

---

[961] The source of this rule is the Bank Conservation Act, 12 U.S.C. § 203(b)(2).

[962] *See* NBA § 192.

[963] *See supra* p. 311 for discussion of these provisions.

The response, set forth in Interpretive Letter No. 748, of September 13, 1996,[964] confirmed that a receiver acting under receivership authority of the NBA in those circumstances:

(1) would not have the right to stay, delay or hinder a secured party's remedies with respect to such collateral, assuming its security interest were valid and perfected under applicable U.S. law, the relevant security agreement was not entered into in contemplation of the foreign bank's insolvency or that of the branch or agency, and the security agreement provided for the relevant remedies; and

(2) would not have the right to prevent ECHO from liquidating and applying the collateral held in the U.S. without delay to the obligation of a non-U.S. office of the relevant foreign bank or otherwise stay, delay or hinder the exercise of remedies against the foreign bank and the collateral pledged to secure the foreign bank's obligations assuming the relevant netting contract was entered into by the head office or another non-U.S. office of the foreign bank, the non-U.S. office secured its obligations under the netting contract by a pledge of collateral located in the U.S. pursuant to an arrangement that constituted a valid and perfected security agreement under applicable U.S. law, the security arrangement at the time of its execution was not entered into in contemplation of the foreign bank's insolvency, or that of the branch or agency in receivership and the security arrangement provided for the relevant remedies.[965]

The second conclusion indicates that, although Section 4(j) of the IBA includes ring-fence features described at the outset of this chapter,[966] these features do not preclude the enforcement of netting provisions and security arrangements providing for the application of assets of a foreign bank held as collateral in the U.S. to obligations of the foreign bank's non-U.S. offices. In addressing the enforceability of a right of setoff in this context, Letter 748 states: "the cases and practice of receivership under the National Bank Act instruct that a Comptroller-directed receivership is subject to longstanding legal principles upholding the rights of . . . creditors with setoff rights."[967]

---

[964] [1996-1997 Transfer Binder] FED. BANKING L. REP. (CCH) ¶ 81-113.

[965] In an earlier interpretive letter, Interpretive Letter No. 768, of October 4, 1995, [1996-1997 Transfer Binder] FED. BANKING L. REP. (CCH) ¶ 81-132, the Chief Counsel of the OCC discussed at somewhat greater length the provisions of the NBA that would be relevant to the treatment of netting contracts and related collateral arrangements, as well as certain court decisions interpreting those provisions. The conclusions stated in Interpretive Letter 768 are consistent with those set forth in Interpretive Letter 748, although Interpretive Letter 768 also indicates that a security interest would be invalidated in receivership proceedings under the NBA if the interest were created with the intent to avoid the pro rata application of assets required in receiverships under the NBA or to prefer one creditor over another—principles explained by the Supreme Court in the *Armstrong* case referred to *infra* note 967.

[966] *See supra* p. 275.

[967] Interpretive Letter 748, *supra* note 964, at 90,347, citing, as to setoff rights, *Scott v. Armstrong*, 146 U.S. 499, 510 (1892) ("ratable payments by the receiver to claimants are made only 'from what belongs to the bank, and that which at the time of insolvency belongs of right to [a creditor with setoff rights] does not belong to the bank'").

Implicit in this guidance in Letter 748 is the conclusion that a receiver appointed by the Comptroller pursuant to the IBA for an uninsured federally licensed branch or agency in the U.S. of a foreign bank would not have the power to interfere with or disregard the right to terminate provided by the ECHO netting arrangements. Nothing in Letter 748 suggests that its guidance would be different in the context of a receivership for an uninsured bank conducted directly under the NBA, rather than pursuant to the IBA.[968]

H.R. 3211 would amend FDICIA to provide that the special protections for qualified financial contracts applicable in Proceedings conducted pursuant to the FDIA would also be applicable in Proceedings for an uninsured national bank or an uninsured federally chartered branch or agency of a foreign bank, as well as an Edge Act corporation or an uninsured state member bank that operates, or operates as, a multilateral clearing organization under Section 409 of FDICIA, even though the Proceedings would not be conducted pursuant to the FDIA and the FDIC would not be acting as conservator or receiver.[969] This change would eliminate legal uncertainty about the enforceability in these Proceedings of the Close-Out Right, the Right to Settle Net and the other important protections relating to setoff rights, security interests and Avoidance Powers discussed in this chapter.

NEW YORK BANKING LAW

ISSUES

AUTOMATIC STAY

Just as the filing of a petition to commence a Bankruptcy Code case operates as an automatic stay of many kinds of actions against the Debtor and its property, the New York banking superintendent's taking possession of the business and property in New York of a New York banking organization, including a New York branch or agency of a foreign bank, generally operates to stay, among other things, the following, unless the FDIC or a federal bank regulatory agency is appointed as receiver or liquidator:

(i) The commencement or continuation, including the issuance or employment of process, of a judicial, administrative, or other action or proceeding against the banking organization that was or could have been commenced before the taking of possession, or to recover a claim against the banking organization that arose before the taking of possession;

(ii) The enforcement, against the banking organization or the business and property of the banking organization in this state, of a judgment obtained before the taking of possession;

(iii) Any act to obtain possession of property of the banking organization or of property from the banking organization or to exercise control over property of the banking organization;

---

[968] The conclusions stated in Interpretive Letter 748 are not binding on a court in the United States, although, as stated therein, they are entitled to substantial deference, in light of the fact that the Comptroller is responsible for administering Section 4(j) of the IBA. It should also be noted that the positions enunciated in Interpretive Letter 748 are, as described therein, based on court decisions to a great extent.

[969] H.R. 3211 § 7(d). The change would be effected through the redesignation of Section 407 of FDICIA as Section 407A and the addition of a new Section 407 to deal with these subjects.

(iv) Any act to create, perfect, or enforce any lien against property of the banking organization;

(v) Any act to create, perfect or enforce against property of the banking organization any lien to the extent that such lien secures a claim that arose before the taking of possession; and

(vi) Any act to collect, assess, or recover a claim against the banking organization that arose before the taking of possession.[970]

In addition to specific exceptions relating to qualified financial contracts as discussed below, there are important general exceptions to this stay.

The NYBL's automatic stay does not apply to "the right of any secured creditor with a perfected security interest or other valid lien or security interest enforceable against third parties to retain collateral"[971] to the extent necessary to satisfy the creditor's claim. As a general rule, however, a creditor may seek to enforce such a security interest only with court permission.

The automatic stay also does not apply to "any right of setoff permitted under applicable law."[972] However, where the Debtor is the New York branch or agency of a foreign bank, the NYBL includes a general ring-fencing provision pursuant to which a creditor may not "set off the business and property in . . . [New York] of such foreign banking corporation" involved in the Proceeding "against liabilities of such foreign banking corporation other than those that arise out of transactions had by such entity or individual [creditor] with such branch or agency."[973]

REPUDIATION AND TRANSFERS

The NYBL generally authorizes the superintendent to repudiate burdensome contracts of the Debtor, if repudiation would promote the orderly administration of the Debtor's affairs.[974] The NYBL also authorizes the superintendent, with court permission, to sell the Debtor's assets and assign its contract rights notwithstanding contractual restrictions on transfers.[975] The NYBL does not expressly grant a receiver or liquidator in NYBL Proceedings Avoidance Powers.

Contracts that are not affirmatively assumed or repudiated by one month before the last date for filing claims against the Estate will be deemed repudiated.[976] A creditor may, however, demand in writing that the superintendent assume or repudiate a contract with the Debtor after the end of a period of 90 days beginning with the date the superintendent took possession of the Debtor. If the superintendent has not assumed or repudiated

---

[970] NYBL § 619(1)(d)(1).

[971] NYBL § 619(1)(d)(2).

[972] Id.

[973] Id. §§ 615(2) & 619(1)(d)(2).

[974] Id. § 618(1).

[975] Id. § 618–a(1).

[976] Id.

such a contract by within fifteen calendar days from the date of receipt of the demand, the creditor may seek to compel the superintendent to decide whether to assume or repudiate the contract by bringing a court action in the judicial district in which the principal office of the banking organization is located.[977]

EXCEPTIONS FOR QUALIFIED FINANCIAL CONTRACTS

Under the NYBL, special exceptions to these general rules apply to qualified financial contracts, including "any securities contract . . . repurchase agreement, swap agreement, and any similar agreement."[978] A creditor's right to these protections, and generally to collect on any claim in NYBL Proceedings, will only be available, however, if the agreement under which the claim arises is reflected in the books, accounts or records of the banking organization or a party provides documentary evidence of such agreement."[979] This discussion will assume satisfaction of this requirement.

CLOSE-OUT RIGHTS

The NYBL provides that the automatic stay imposed when the superintendent takes possession of the property and business of a banking organization does not apply to "any automatic termination in accordance with the terms of any qualified financial contract or any right to cause the termination or liquidation of any qualified financial contract, as defined in section six hundred eighteen-a of this article, in accordance with the terms thereof."[980] Thus, Close-Out Rights in respect of qualified financial contracts may be exercised by any counterparty, and not merely by specified classes of counterparties.

THE RIGHT TO SETTLE NET AND SETOFF

The NYBL also provides that this automatic stay does not apply to "any right to offset or net out any termination value, payment amount, or other transfer obligation arising under or in connection with one or more . . . qualified financial contracts."[981] By its terms this provision broadly protects the Right to Settle Net in respect of three kinds of claims involving qualified financial contracts: claims for termination values arising out of exercise of a Close-Out Right; claims for other payments; and claims in respect of transfer obligations, such as obligations in respect of property in physically settled qualified financial contracts or credit support to be delivered in connection with these contracts.

This special rule is, however, qualified in any case in which the Debtor in the NYBL Proceedings is a New York branch or agency of a foreign bank. As noted above, the NYBL generally ring-fences the claims against these Debtors that may be collected from their property involved in NYBL Proceedings, limiting those claims to those that

---

[977] *Id.*

[978] NYBL § 618–a(1)(e).

[979] *Id.* § 620–a.

[980] *Id.* § 619(1)(d)(2)(i).

[981] *Id.*

arise from dealings with the New York branch or agency.[982] Where claims arise out of qualified financial contracts, this general ring-fencing rule is modified if a counterparty has dealt with the foreign bank subject to a netting agreement that covers transactions entered into by the foreign bank from offices in and outside New York. That is, this rule would apply to transactions governed by a master agreement prepared using an ISDA form if the creditor's foreign bank counterparty had acted as a multibranch party from a New York branch and, say, the bank's head office outside the United States.

In these cases, the NYBL provides that, notwithstanding the automatic stay, the foreign bank's creditor may exercise otherwise enforceable setoff rights in respect of liabilities determined under the netting contract to be the lesser of two amounts calculated giving effect or partial effect to the netting provisions of the parties' contract.[983] The same rule is also expressed in a separate provision relating to the calculation of the maximum liability that the superintendent may have which arises out of qualified financial contracts subject to netting arrangements, regardless of whether the liability arises out of repudiation of the contracts by the superintendent or out of the counterparty's exercise of Close-Out Rights.[984]

The first of the two amounts is calculated on the basis of only the qualified financial contracts entered into with the New York branch or agency of the foreign bank. This is referred to in the NYBL as the "branch/agency net payment obligation."[985] The second amount, calculated on the basis of all of the qualified financial contracts covered by the netting agreement, is referred to in the NYBL as the "global net payment obligation."[986] If the global net payment obligation of the foreign bank multibranch party exceeds the branch/agency net payment obligation, the NYBL does not authorize the exercise of setoff with respect to the excess, nor does it permit the counterparty to claim the excess from the superintendent.

However, if the foreign bank's qualified financial contract obligations are secured, under a provision described in the following section, the secured creditor will be permitted to apply the collateral to the full extent of the foreign bank's liabilities calculated on a global basis—that is, taking into account all transactions under the parties' master agreement. What if the creditor's claim is unsecured, or if the collateral is insufficient to cover the entire amount of the creditor's claim calculated on a global basis? In such a case the creditor would have to seek to recover the balance of its claim outside the NYBL Pro-

---

[982] *See supra* p. 275.

[983] NYBL §§ 615(2) & 618-a(2)(c).

[984] *Id.* § 618–a(2)(c). Here the NYBL also provides that the liability of the superintendent is to be "reduced by any amount otherwise paid to or received by the party in respect of the global net payment obligation pursuant to such qualified financial contract which if added to the liability of the superintendent under this paragraph would exceed the global net payment obligation."

[985] NYBL § 618–a(2)(e)(iv): "'branch/agency net payment obligation' means with respect to a qualified financial contact [sic] the amount, if any, that would have been owed by the foreign banking corporation to a party after netting only those transactions entered into by the branch or agency and such party under such qualified financial contract."

[986] *Id.* § 618–a(2)(e)(ii): "'global net payment obligation' means the amount, if any, owed by a foreign banking corporation as a whole to a party after giving effect to the netting provisions of a qualified financial contract with respect to all transactions subject to netting under such qualified financial contract."

ceedings—that is, most likely, in Proceedings for the Debtor in its home jurisdiction, or in another jurisdiction out of which the Debtor acted in connection with the relevant qualified financial contracts.[987]

ENFORCEMENT AGAINST COLLATERAL

As indicated above, the NYBL generally permits a secured creditor with a perfected security interest or other valid lien or security interest enforceable against third parties to retain collateral and, with court permission, to enforce against that collateral if necessary. The superintendent has taken the position that leave of court is necessary for this purpose in connection with qualified financial contracts of New York banking organizations other than the New York branches and agencies of foreign banks.[988]

Where a creditor has entered into qualified financial contracts with a foreign bank acting as a multibranch party from offices in and outside New York, the NYBL expressly authorizes the creditor, notwithstanding the NYBL's automatic stay, to exercise its otherwise enforceable rights as secured party under any security arrangement related to a qualified financial contract to retain collateral for the foreign bank's obligations covered by the parties' multibranch netting agreement and apply the collateral up to the full amount of the foreign bank's global net payment obligation, calculated taking into account all the transactions covered by the parties' multibranch netting agreement as described above.[989] These rights may be exercised in connection with the termination or liquidation of the qualified financial contracts in accordance with their terms or upon repudiation of the contracts by the superintendent. The creditor may not retain or apply collateral to liabilities of the foreign bank that exceed the claims in respect of qualified financial contracts secured by the collateral.[990]

PROTECTION AGAINST CHERRY-PICKING

If a counterparty to qualified financial contracts with a Debtor in NYBL Proceedings has not exercised its Close-Out Rights, the superintendent will retain its right to repudiate the contracts if they are burdensome, as described above. However, the statute includes two kinds of protections against cherry-picking through selective repudiation.

First, the NYBL provides that any master agreement for qualified financial contracts, together with all supplements thereto, "shall be treated as one qualified financial contract."[991]

---

[987] *See* Section 10(a) of the ISDA Master Agreement (Multicurrency—Cross Border) form, *infra* p. 874, on a representation that may be requested of a party that is acting from an office other than its home office, or from multiple offices, regarding the obligations of the institution as a whole for the obligations incurred under the agreement, regardless of the booking office.

[988] *See* Rebecca J. Simmons, *Bankruptcy and Insolvency Provisions Relating to Swaps and Derivatives, in* NUTS AND BOLTS OF FINANCIAL PRODUCTS 2001: UNDERSTANDING THE EVOLVING WORLD OF CAPITAL MARKET & INVESTMENT MANAGEMENT PRODUCTS 323, 347 (PLI Corp. L. & Practice Course Handbook Series No. B-1229, 2001).

[989] *Id.* §§ 615(2) & 618–a(2)(d).

[990] *Id.* § 618–a(2)(d).

[991] *Id.* § 618–a(2)(e).

Like the parallel provisions on swap agreements in the Bankruptcy Code and on qualified financial contracts in the FDIA, this provision is widely viewed as protection against cherry-picking among transactions documented under a single master agreement, although it does not preclude selective repudiation of separately documented qualified financial contracts.

Second, the NYBL affords additional protection against cherry-picking in NYBL Proceedings for the New York branch or agency of a foreign bank. In these cases, the NYBL, as discussed above, generally endorses the otherwise enforceable netting provisions of a netting agreement between a counterparty and the foreign bank, although it limits the superintendent's liability to the lesser of the branch/agency net payment obligation of the Debtor and the global net payment obligation of the Debtor. The applicable provision also states as follows:

> In the event that netting under the applicable netting agreement or arrangement results in a branch/agency net payment entitlement, notwithstanding any provision in any such contract that purports to effect a forfeiture of such entitlement, the superintendent may make written demand upon the party to such contract under subdivision two of section six hundred fifteen of this article for an amount not to exceed the lesser of (x) the global net payment entitlement and (y) the branch/agency net payment entitlement. The liability of the party under this paragraph shall be reduced by any amount otherwise paid to or received by the superintendent or any other liquidator or receiver of the foreign banking corporation in respect of the global net payment entitlement pursuant to such qualified financial contract which if added to the liability of the party under this paragraph would exceed the global net payment entitlement. The liability of the party under this paragraph to the superintendent pursuant to such qualified financial contract also shall be reduced by the fair market value or the amount of any proceeds of collateral that secures and has been applied to satisfy the obligations of the party pursuant to such qualified financial contract to the foreign banking corporation.[992]

The NYBL does not protect a counterparty against the risk that the superintendent might selectively transfer a counterparty's qualified financial contracts with a Debtor in NYBL Proceedings. In this regard, the NYBL is like the Bankruptcy Code but unlike the FDIA, which, as described above, requires the FDIC, as receiver or conservator, to transfer to a single transferee all QFC Claims and Rights arising out of dealings between the Debtor and a counterparty or any of its affiliates.[993]

---

[992] *Id.* § 618–a(2)(c). "Branch/agency net payment entitlement" is defined to mean "with respect to a qualified financial contract the amount, if any, that would have been owed by a party to the foreign banking corporation after netting only those transactions entered into by the branch or agency and such party under such qualified financial contract," and "global net payment entitlement" is defined as "the amount, if any, owed by a party (or that would be owed if the relevant agreements provided for payments to either party, upon termination thereof under any and all circumstances) to a foreign banking corporation as a whole after giving effect to the netting provisions of a qualified financial contract with respect to all transactions subject to netting under such qualified financial contract." NYBL §§ 618–a(2)(e)(v) & 618–a(2)(e)(iii).

[993] *See supra* p. 314.

NETTING CONTRACTS

The Insolvency Laws reviewed in the preceding sections expressly recognize that participants in the various markets for financial contracts seek to manage the risk of counterparty default, in connection with Insolvency Events and otherwise, by entering into master agreements and other contracts that provide for close-out netting arrangements and other setoff rights. As described, these Insolvency Laws differ in the extent to which they permit a counterparty to exercise rights under arrangements of these kinds with an entity involved in Proceedings, without first seeking court permission.

The most expansive provisions in this regard are those applicable in FDIA receivership Proceedings if during the permitted period after appointment of the receiver all of the Debtor's QFC Rights and Claims have not been assigned to a single transferee.[994] In such a case the FDIA draws no distinctions among persons whose rights may be exercised or among the kinds of qualified financial contracts that may be covered by otherwise enforceable netting contracts. The Bankruptcy Code, on the other hand, does draw distinctions among classes of Protected Persons by financial contract class and does not expressly provide an exception from the automatic stay imposed under Section 362 for the setoff of the mutual claims of a Debtor and its counterparty arising out of all the different classes of financial contracts. Similarly, the Bankruptcy Code does not expressly permit a net settlement approach involving collateral or other credit support for all of the mutual obligations of a counterparty and the Debtor in respect of financial contracts, although counterparties to potential Bankruptcy Code Debtors could—and sometimes do—seek protection in this regard through arrangements under which all collateral for obligations under any financial contract with a potential Debtor secures the Debtor's obligations under all financial contracts.[995] The special Insolvency Law protections against cherry-picking reviewed above also fall short in preventing selective repudiation by an Insolvency Representative and, where the Bankruptcy Code and the NYBL are concerned, in protecting against cherry-picking through selective transfer of assumed contracts. For these and other reasons, the ability of a counterparty to exercise its Close-Out Rights may be critical.

The reforms proposed in H.R. 3211 would expand on these protections against selective repudiation in the Bankruptcy Code and the FDIA through amendments that, as discussed above, would recognize as a single agreement any master agreement for any of the described classes of financial contracts.[996] That is, the recognition accorded to master agreements for swap agreements would also be accorded to master agreements for securities contracts, forward contracts, commodity contracts and repurchase agreements, and under these amendments, if the parties chose to document multiple types of financial con-

---

[994] See supra p. 316.

[995] These arrangements can be complex because they involve not only the actual collateral posted by the potential Debtor but also the Debtor's rights against the counterparty under the relevant financial contracts, and the perfection of a security interest in these contractual rights in some jurisdictions may require filings. See infra p. 1095 on filings to perfect security interests under the UCC. Ultimately this approach leaves concerns about the effect of the automatic stay under Section 362 of the Bankruptcy Code on the ability of the counterparty to offset against each other and against any remaining collateral the net close-out settlement claims relating to, say, master agreements for securities contracts and swap agreements.

[996] See supra p. 280.

tracts under the same master agreement, the agreement would be treated as a swap agreement, to the extent it relates to swap agreements, as a securities contract, to the extent it relates to securities contracts, and so on.

Participants in the derivatives markets may continue to prefer to use separate product-specific master agreements, such as the FEOMA, ICOM or IFEMA forms for currency options and FX forwards and spot transactions, as well as proprietary agreements for individual transactions or for all their dealings with the counterparty in a particular segment of the derivatives market. This is often the case with dealings in at least some securities-linked derivatives. Market participants also generally prefer product-specific standardized forms for their securities lending and repo activities.

The risks the parties may encounter when they use multiple agreements and some of the approaches they take to manage these risks are subjects discussed to a limited extent in the annotations to the sample master agreement in this book.[997] These subjects are discussed in depth in Part 6, which also includes an annotated sample master netting agreement prepared using the form of Cross-Product Master Agreement published in 2000 by TBMA and other sponsoring associations.[998]

The next part of this section describes provisions in H.R. 3211 that would protect the contractual rights of parties to netting contracts of this and other kinds. Following that, the section discusses provisions of FDICIA under which the netting of mutual payment obligations and entitlements of two parties under contracts of this and other kinds are enforceable under U.S. law provided the netting contract satisfies specified criteria and the parties qualify as financial institutions under the statute or action taken by the Board of Governors of the Federal Reserve System. In the course of the discussion we also refer to proposed modifications of these FDICIA netting contract provisions.

MASTER NETTING AGREEMENTS

H.R. 3211 would amend the Bankruptcy Code to introduce a new category of contract, referred to as a master netting agreement, and a new, related class of Protected Persons for these agreements, referred to as a master netting agreement participant.[999] The provisions would largely parallel the special protections described above for the various classes of financial contracts, as those product-specific provisions would be modified under H.R. 3211, so as to protect Close-Out Rights and Rights to Settle Net of master netting agreement participants under master netting agreements with a Debtor in Bankruptcy Code Proceedings. The provisions would also deal with the other subjects addressed by the product-specific protections for financial contracts.

---

[997] See infra p. 1289 on standardized setoff provisions and bridges used by some market participants.

[998] Infra p. 1279. A second and much modified version of that Cross-Product Master Agreement is in preparation. It is expected, among other things, to include various approaches aimed at enabling market participants to reduce the risks that arise not only as a result of multiple agreements between the same two parties but also as a result of dealings with the same counterparty through more than one entity in a corporate family.

[999] H.R. 3211 § 8(c).

For purposes of these proposed provisions, "master netting agreement participant" would mean "an entity that, at any time before the filing of the petition [commencing a case under the Bankruptcy Code] is a party to an outstanding master netting agreement with the debtor,"[1000] and "master netting agreement" would mean:

>   (A) . . . an agreement providing for the exercise of rights, including rights of netting, setoff, liquidation, termination, acceleration, or close out, under or in connection with one or more contracts that are described in any one or more of paragraphs (1) through (5) of section 561(a), or any security agreement or arrangement or other credit enhancement related to one or more of the foregoing, including any guarantee or reimbursement obligation related to 1 or more of the foregoing; and:
>
>   (B) if the agreement contains provisions relating to agreements or transactions that are not contracts described in paragraphs (1) through (5) of section 561(a), shall be deemed to be a master netting agreement only with respect to those agreements or transactions that are described in any one or more of paragraphs (1) through (5) of section 561(a).[1001]

The proposed Section 561 referred to in the definition would largely parallel Section 560 of the Bankruptcy Code and provide that the provisions of Section 365(e) of the Bankruptcy Code on *ipso facto* clauses will not prevent a master netting agreement participant from the exercise of rights, including rights of netting, setoff, liquidation, termination, acceleration, or close-out, under or in connection with one or more financial contracts—swap agreements, securities contracts, repurchase agreements, commodity contracts, forward contracts—or one or more master netting agreements, or any security agreement or arrangement or other credit enhancement or any guarantee or reimbursement obligation related to one or more of the foregoing.

Proposed Section 561 would also provide that an agreement will qualify as a master netting agreement insofar as it relates to financial contracts and master netting agreements and related security and other credit enhancement agreements and arrangements and guarantee and reimbursement obligations, even if the same agreement also applies to transactions that do not benefit from the Bankruptcy Code's special protections for financial contracts and master netting agreements.

The structure, thus, would protect the exercise, notwithstanding the automatic stay, of Close-Out Rights and Rights to Settle Net under or in connection with the identified classes or financial contracts as well as provisions in master netting agreements under which, say, a default under any financial contract between the parties would give rise to a Close-Out Right under all the others between the same parties, and a provision under which the parties' mutual claims under all such contracts would be settled net. The provision would not expand the classes of Protected Persons entitled to exercise Close-Out Rights under the separate Bankruptcy Code provisions relating to swap agreements, securities contracts, forward contracts, commodity contracts and repurchase agreements.

[1000] As proposed in H.R. 3211, the definition would be added as Section 101(38B) of the Bankruptcy Code.

[1001] H.R. 3211 § 8(c). The definition would be added as a new Section 101(38A) of the Bankruptcy Code.

Rather, the proposed Section 561 would operate so that, if a party is permitted by those product-specific provisions to exercise a Close-Out Right or Right to Settle Net, it may also proceed to engage in cross-product netting of claims arising out of the exercise of those rights.

The proposed provision goes beyond the parallel provisions on swap agreements and other financial contracts by protecting the right of a master netting agreement participant to cause the termination, liquidation, or acceleration of or to offset or net "transfer obligations."[1002] The intended reach of this reference to "transfer obligations" is not clear. At a minimum, however, these words appear aimed at protecting the kinds of offset and netting of credit support transfer obligations contemplated in standard credit support documents used in the derivatives market.

For example, when the parties to OTC derivatives adopt ISDA's 1994 Credit Support Annex prepared for use with agreements governed by New York law, they agree, in its Paragraph 8(b) that, if an Early Termination Date is designated or occurs in connection with an Event of Default or certain other conditions relating to a Secured Party, the Secured Party will be obligated immediately to Transfer all Posted Credit Support and certain other amounts to the Pledgor and that, to the extent the Posted Collateral is not so Transferred, the Pledgor may setoff its own obligations to the Secured Party against that Posted Collateral not Transferred, its cash equivalent or the obligation to have made the Transfer. In this regard, as indicated above, the Bankruptcy Code's definition of "transfer" broadly includes "every mode, direct or indirect, absolute or conditional, voluntary or involuntary, of disposing of or parting with property or with an interest in property, including retention of title as a security interest."[1003]

Like its parallels in the product-specific Sections 555, 556, 559 and 560 of the Bankruptcy Code, the proposed Section 561 on master netting agreements would protect specified "contractual rights." As in these other provisions, "contractual right" would include rights set forth by way of agreement as well as rights that may arise by virtue of normal business practice.[1004]

As a result, if a Protected Person has just concluded a financial contract with a counterparty that has become the subject of a Bankruptcy Code case, even though a master agreement or the relevant confirmations are not yet in place for all relevant financial contracts, a master netting agreement participant may be entitled to invoke the established

---

[1002] When the Debtor is a commodity broker, proposed Section 561(b) of the Bankruptcy Code sets out special limitations on these setoff rights contemplated in Section 561(a). First, if a counterparty has dealings with the Debtor in commodity contracts traded on or subject to the rules of a contract market designated under the CEA or a derivatives transaction execution facility registered under the CEA, the maximum amount that may be setoff against any claim arising under, or in connection with, other financial contracts or master netting agreements is the party's positive net equity in its commodity accounts maintained at the Debtor. Second, another commodity broker may not net or offset an obligation to the Debtor arising under, or in connection with, a commodity contract entered into or held on behalf of a customer of the Debtor and traded on or subject to the rules of a contract market designated under the CEA or a derivatives transaction execution facility registered under the CEA against any claim arising under, or in connection with, other financial contracts or master netting agreements.

[1003] See supra note 913.

[1004] H.R. 3211 § 8(k)(1).

normal business practice in the relevant markets to close out transactions and calculate a single net close-out settlement amount in respect of all the financial contacts covered by a master netting agreement between the parties. In addition, "contractual right" would include rights that arise by operation of common law and law merchant as well as rights established by the rules and bylaws, or by resolution of the governing board, of a clearing organization, exchange or other trading facility used by the parties to manage the credit risk of their mutual dealings or execute their transactions. These features parallel the proposed expansions on the concept of "contractual right" in Sections 555, 556, 559 and 560 of the Bankruptcy Code.

NETTING CONTRACTS UNDER FDICIA

In light of limitations like those described above on the enforceability of netting arrangements under Insolvency Laws, FDICIA, as enacted in 1991, included provisions aimed at providing greater legal certainty regarding the enforceability of bilateral netting arrangements between institutions with significant activities in the financial markets and multilateral netting arrangements under which clearing organizations and their members are required to make payments to each other. The key element of FDICIA's netting provisions is their preemption of all other provisions of applicable law to the extent necessary to recognize the enforceability of "netting contracts" between "financial institutions."[1005] Section 405 of FDICIA also provides that "[n]o stay, injunction, avoidance, moratorium, or similar proceeding or order, whether issued or granted by a court, administrative agency, or otherwise, shall limit or delay application of otherwise enforceable netting contracts" in accordance with Sections 403 and 404 of FDICIA. These provisions are stated to apply regardless of whether a party to the protected netting arrangements is a "failed financial institution" or a "failed member." The first of these terms is defined in Section 402(7) of FDICIA to mean a financial institution that "(A) fails to satisfy a covered contractual payment obligation when due; (B) has commenced or had commenced against it insolvency, liquidation, reorganization, receivership . . . conservatorship, or similar proceedings; or (C) has generally ceased to meet its obligations when due." A member of or participant in a clearing organization would be a "failed member" if it failed to satisfy a covered clearing obligation when due of if any of the events described in clauses (B) and (C) of the definition of "failed financial institution" occurs with respect to the clearing organization member or participant.

Sections 403 and 404 of FDICIA include the two operative provisions relating to bilateral netting according to which, if two financial institutions are parties to a netting contract, neither will be required to pay the other more than its net obligation (if any) in respect of all covered payment obligations, and each will be entitled to receive its net entitlement (if any) in respect of all covered payment obligations, even if one or both of the financial institution parties to the agreement is a failed financial institution. For these purposes, "covered contractual payment obligation" is defined quite simply to be a financial institution's obligation "to make payment, subject to a netting contract to another financial institution,"[1006] and "covered contractual payment entitlement" is similarly defined to

---

[1005] The preemption language appears in Sections 403(a) and 404(a) of FDICIA.

[1006] FDICIA § 402(5).

Bankruptcy and Insolvency Concerns 333

be a financial institution's entitlement "to receive a payment, subject to a netting contract from another financial institution."[1007]

The protection of the FDICIA netting contract provisions is extended to multilateral arrangements among clearing organization members and participants (referred to collectively as members) by defining "covered contractual payment obligation" in such a way that it also includes the similar right of a member to receive payment of a covered clearing obligation from another member. These covered clearing obligations include all obligations of a member to make payment to another member pursuant to a netting contract.[1008] As discussed above,[1009] FDICIA's definition of "clearing organization" includes derivatives clearing organizations registered with the CFTC and clearing agencies registered with the SEC, and the reform legislation proposed in H.R. 3211 would expand the definition to include clearing systems that have been granted exemptions from registration by either of these agencies as well as multilateral clearing organizations.

The term "netting contract," as defined in Section 402(14)(A) of FDICIA, is a contract, including the rules of a clearing organization, between two or more financial institutions or members that is governed by the laws of the United States or any state or political subdivision of any state and "provides for netting present or future payment obligations or payment entitlements (including liquidation or close-out values relating to the obligations or entitlements) among the parties to the agreement."[1010] "Payment obligations" is not defined in the Act and seems to be intended to encompass all kinds of obligations, so long as they exist between financial institutions.

Although quite broad, these protections are subject to an exception and to important limitations. The exception is that contracts that are considered invalid under or precluded by federal law are not considered netting contracts.[1011] As the definition of "netting contract" in FDICIA would be amended pursuant to the reform legislation proposed in H.R. 3211, this exception would be removed and, instead, the relationship between the FDICIA netting contract provisions and certain other provisions of federal law would be clarified, as discussed below.[1012]

The first limitation is that, as noted, FDICIA requires that a netting contract be governed by the laws of the United States or a U.S. state. An amendment to FDICIA proposed in H.R. 3211 would also eliminate this requirement.[1013] The second limitation relates to the reach of the definition of "financial institution." That term is defined for these purposes in Section 402(9) of FDICIA to include depository institutions (national and state banks, credit unions, thrifts, U.S. branches and agencies of foreign banks, and corpo-

---

[1007] *Id.* § 402(4).

[1008] *Id.* § 402(3).

[1009] *See supra* p. 286.

[1010] FDICIA § 402(14)(A).

[1011] FDICIA § 402(14)(B). On this limitation, see Ernest T. Patrikis & Karen Walraven, *The Netting Provisions of the Federal Deposit Insurance Corporation Improvement Act of 1991*, 12 FUTURES INT'L LETTER 1, 4 (1992).

[1012] *See infra* p. 336.

[1013] H.R. 3211 § 7(a)(4).

rations organized under the Edge Act), brokers or dealers (including any company registered or licensed under U.S. federal or state law to engage in the business of brokering, dealing or underwriting securities in the U.S., as well as affiliates of a broker or dealer that are engaged in the business of entering into netting contracts, to the extent consistent with FDICIA, as determined by the Board of Governors of the Federal Reserve System), futures commission merchants (companies registered or licensed under U.S. law to engage in the business of selling futures and options in commodities), and any other institution determined by the Board to be a "financial institution" for purposes of FDICIA.

In 1994, the Board of Governors adopted Regulation EE, which expanded the definition of "financial institution" because, as stated in the rule proposal, "the Board believes that . . . the netting provisions of the Act [FDICIA] should extend to all financial market participants that regularly enter into financial contracts, both as buyers and sellers, where the failure of the participant could create systemic problems in the financial markets."[1014] Under the expanded definition:

> (a) A person qualifies as a financial institution for purposes of sections 401–407 of the Act [FDICIA] if it represents, either orally or in writing, that it will engage in financial contracts as a counterparty on both sides of one or more financial markets and either—
>
> (a)(1) Had one or more financial contracts of a total gross dollar value of $1 billion in notional principal amount outstanding on any day during the previous 15-month period with counterparties that are not its affiliates; or
>
> (2) Incurred total gross mark-to-market positions of at least $100 million (aggregated across counterparties) in one or more financial contracts on any day during the previous 15-month period with counterparties that are not its affiliates.[1015]

Regulation EE broadly defines "person" to include "any legal entity, foreign or domestic, including a corporation, unincorporated company, partnership, government unit or instrumentality, trust, natural person, or any entity or organization,"[1016] and defines "financial contract" to mean any qualified financial contract as defined in the FDIA, as well as a spot FX transaction.[1017] For purposes of measuring satisfaction of the quantitative tests, the regulation defines "gross mark-to-market positions" in one or more financial contracts to mean "the sum of the absolute values of positions in those [financial] con-

---

[1014] Board of Governors of the Federal Reserve System, Netting Eligibility for Financial Institutions, Proposed Rule, 58 Fed. Reg. 29,149 (1993).

[1015] 12 C.F.R. § 231.3 (2002). If a person qualifies under one of the quantitative tests, it will be considered to be a financial institution for purposes of any contract entered into during the period in which it qualifies, even if it subsequently fails to qualify. 12 C.F.R. § 231.3.(b). Any person that qualified as a financial institution on March 7, 1994 (the effective date of the regulations) is considered to qualify for purposes of all contracts entered into before that date and outstanding on that date. 12 C.F.R. § 231.3.(c).

[1016] 12 C.F.R. § 231.2(f).

[1017] 12 C.F.R. § 231.2(c).

Bankruptcy and Insolvency Concerns

tracts, adjusted to reflect the market values of those positions in accordance with the methods used by the parties to each contract to price the contract."[1018]

In proposing this regulation, the Board confirmed its willingness to consider requests from applicants that they be determined to be financial institutions for purposes of the netting provisions of FDICIA even if they do not meet the quantitative tests, provided the request includes "a statement as to how a determination that the person is a financial institution would enhance efficiency and reduce systemic risk in financial markets."[1019] The Board also noted that it may certify persons as financial institutions "for general purposes (e.g., for all types of netting contracts entered into by the institution) or for limited purposes (e.g., for netting contracts within a certain clearing corporation)."[1020]

As a result of the netting provisions of FDICIA as they now exist, it would seem that two financial institutions, as defined in that Act, may, for example, enter into a single master agreement qualifying as a netting contract to document all their payment obligations to each other and provide therein that, in the event of a default under any of those obligations, or in the event either of them otherwise became a failed financial institution, all the transactions giving rise to obligations thereunder could be terminated or liquidated at the request of the other party and only the net covered contractual payment obligation determined as damages in respect of the termination or liquidation would be payable. In the alternative, if the parties had multiple agreements with each other, under the netting provisions of FDICIA, they could enter into an "umbrella" master netting contract providing for netting of all the obligations arising under the various agreements, whether in connection with their early termination, liquidation or otherwise.[1021] Under the netting provisions of FDICIA, both of these kinds of netting arrangements would be enforceable notwithstanding the insolvency of either or both of the parties.

Amendments proposed in H.R. 3211 would further expand the definition of "financial institution" to include any uninsured national bank and any uninsured State bank that is a member of the Federal Reserve System, if the national bank or State member bank is not eligible to make an application to become an insured bank under the FDIA, as well as foreign banks that have established a branch or agency that is subject to Proceedings under the IBA.[1022]

[1018] 12 C.F.R. § 231.2(e).

[1019] 58 Fed. Reg. at 29,151.

[1020] Id.

[1021] See Patrikis, supra note 1010, at 7.

[1022] This second change can be important in many derivatives market dealings because, although the branches and agencies in the United States of non-U.S. banks are financial institutions for purposes of FDICIA's netting provisions as originally adopted and, therefore, can be parties to netting contracts validated by the law, the offices of those institutions outside the United States are not. Therefore, to the extent a market participant has, say, entered into a master agreement of the kind illustrated in Part 3 of this book with a foreign bank acting as a multibranch party out of offices both in and outside the United States, in analyzing whether the benefits of the netting provisions of FDICIA would apply to claims against offices of the foreign bank other than its U.S. branches and agencies, the market participant might have to determine whether the foreign bank qualified as a financial institution under Regulation EE.

Amendments to FDICIA proposed in H.R. 3211 would also clarify doubts that have existed over FDICIA's preemptive effect and expand the protections of FDICIA's netting contract provisions in two important ways. The principal doubt in this regard for the OTC derivatives market has been whether FDICIA overrides the provisions described earlier[1023] that limit Close-Out Rights relating to qualified financial contracts in Proceedings under the FDIA. Another doubt has been whether the FDICIA preemption overrides an order of SIPC, issued pursuant to SIPA, staying the liquidation of securities contracts in Proceedings for a securities firm.[1024] Amendments contemplated in H.R. 3211 would codify the views of the FDIC and SIPC that the FDICIA's netting contract provisions do not override those FDIA limitations on Close-Out Rights or SIPC orders.[1025]

The two principal further expansions would bring within the protections of FDICIA's netting contract provisions netting arrangements involving noncash deliveries and security agreements and other credit enhancements for netting contracts. The first of these expansions would be made through the addition of a definition of the term "payment" as follows: "The term 'payment' means a payment of United States dollars, another currency, or a composite currency, and a noncash delivery, including a payment or delivery to liquidate an unmatured obligation."[1026] Given this change, in defining "netting contract" by reference to agreements between or among financial institutions, clearing organizations or their members, if they provide for netting of "present or future payment obligations or payment entitlements," FDICIA will now sweep within its protective provisions many arrangements that would not previously have been covered. The second expansion would be effected through the addition of a new Section 403(f), as follows:

> ENFORCEABILITY OF SECURITY AGREEMENTS–The provisions of any security agreement or arrangement or other credit enhancement related to one or more netting contracts between any 2 financial institutions shall be enforceable in accordance with their terms (except as provided in section 561(b)(2) of title 11, United States Code), and shall not be stayed, avoided or otherwise limited by any State or Federal law (other than paragraphs (8)(E), 8(F), and (10)(B) of section 11(e) of the Federal Deposit Insurance Act and section 5(b)(2) of the Securities Investor Protection Act of 1970).[1027]

The first two exceptions to the preemptive effect of this proposed provision are the same as those described above, which would be added to FDICIA's provision validating netting contracts; that is, they are exceptions making clear that FDICIA does not override the limitations on Close-Out Rights described above in this chapter that are im-

---

[1023] See supra p. 313 for discussion of these FDIA limitations on the Close-Out Right.

[1024] See supra p. 305 on amendments to SIPA proposed in H.R. 3211 which would, however, protect the Close-Out Right in respect of securities contracts, notwithstanding an application for relief under SIPA or a court order obtained by SIPC.

[1025] H.R. 3211 § 7(b)(1) includes the amendment to Section 403(a) that effect this change, by clarifying that preemption does not extend to paragraphs 8(e), (8)(F) and (10)(B) of Section 11(e) of the FDIA or to any order authorized under Section 5(b)(2) of SIPA.

[1026] H.R. 3211 § 7(a)(5). The definition would become Section 402(15) of FDICIA.

[1027] Id. § 7(b)(2).

posed by the FDIA or orders issued or obtained by SIPC to stay certain foreclosure actions in Proceedings for securities firms subject to SIPA.[1028] The other exception makes clear that FDICIA would not override the limitations on cross-product netting imposed by Section 561 of the Bankruptcy Code, as described above.[1029] Subject to these exceptions, this sweeping new provision of FDICIA appears to eliminate all uncertainties that might otherwise exist with respect to security and other credit enhancements for bilateral and multilateral netting contracts between financial institutions, clearing organizations and members of or participants in clearing organizations.[1030]

CLAIMS FOR DAMAGES AND WALKAWAY CLAUSES

WALKAWAY CLAUSES

We have described in detail in Chapter 6 the distinction that is made in OTC derivatives documentation between terminations of OTC derivatives transactions that come about because a party defaults, on one hand, and so-called "no-fault" terminations, on the other.[1031] As noted there, bankruptcy and other insolvency events have traditionally been included in the "fault" category. The "walkaway" clauses that were common in the earlier days of the market were structured to permit the non-defaulting party to retain any benefits that it might derive from early termination of its OTC derivatives transactions with a defaulting counterparty in all cases, including cases where the default consisted of an insolvency-related event.[1032] This feature of the walkaway clause was subject to substantial criticism by bank supervisors and others, and it has led to actual and proposed legislative reform prohibiting the application of the clause, particularly in cases of insolvent financial institutions, and to regulatory discouragement of use of these clauses, principally through rules under which close-out netting provisions will not be recognized within capital adequacy regimes if the contract includes a walkaway clause.[1033] The reform proposal in H.R. 3211 would provide that walkaway clauses in qualified financial contracts (including OTC derivatives, repos, commodity contracts and securities contracts) will not be en-

---

[1028] *See supra* p. 309 on amendments to SIPA proposed in H.R. 3211 which would, however, narrow the application of the relevant portion of SIPA.

[1029] *See supra* p. 330.

[1030] Given the sweeping nature of the proposed amendment, if it is adopted there may be challenges.

[1031] *Supra* p. 225.

[1032] For discussion of the treatment of this subject in ISDA's forms, *see supra* p. 229.

[1033] *See supra* p. 232. Reflecting this trend, both the Model Netting Act published by ISDA (*available at* www.isda.org), and the Insurers Rehabilitation and Liquidation Model Act published by the NAIC (*see supra* note 843) expressly state that a person subject to Proceedings of the kinds contemplated in those model laws, or the Insolvency Representative acting for it, will have a claim against the other party in respect of any net settlement entitlement favoring the Debtor. On the ISDA Model Netting Act, as it has evolved and been recommended for adoption in many jurisdictions whose Insolvency Laws had not previously protected close-out netting, *see* Daniel P. Cunningham & Thomas J. Werlen, *The Model Netting Act: A Solution for Insolvency Uncertainty*, FUTURES & DERIVATIVES L. REP., Nov. 1996, at 7-15; Thomas J. Werlen & Sean M. Flanagan, *The 2002 Model Netting Act: A Solution for Insolvency Uncertainty*, 17 BUTTERWORTH'S J. INT'L BANK. & FIN. L. 154 (2002).

forceable against any entity subject to proceedings under the FDIA, and would extend the reach of the FDIA to a broader group of institutions.[1034]

DAMAGES PROVISIONS IN INSOLVENCY PROCEEDINGS

Chapter 6 also considers in detail the quantification of claims arising upon early termination of OTC derivatives transactions.[1035] The principal focus of U.S. insolvency laws relating to this aspect of OTC derivatives is on enforcement of the terms of the related agreements once one of the parties to the agreement has become insolvent, assuming the agreements are otherwise enforceable under noninsolvency law. However, the FDIA also includes a provision (added under FIRREA) that directly addresses the measurement of enforceable claims for damages in connection with the repudiation of derivatives that constitute qualified financial contracts. Under the FDIA, if an insolvent depository's qualified financial contracts are repudiated by a receiver or conservator, the damages payable to the other party to the transactions will be limited to "actual direct compensatory damages" determined as of the date of the appointment of the conservator or receiver or, in the case of a claim based on a qualified financial contract that is disaffirmed or repudiated, the date of the disaffirmance or repudiation, and, for these purposes, "normal and reasonable costs of cover or other reasonable measures of damages utilized in the industries for such contract" will be deemed to be compensatory.[1036] This statutory provision is important, given the fact that the FDIC "has maintained a longstanding position that contingent obligations have no provable damages under the FDI Act's statutory damages limitation, if repudiated by the receiver or conservator, because the damages are not fixed and certain as of the date of the appointment of the receiver or conservator."[1037]

Similarly, the NYBL provides that the superintendent's liability in respect of a claim based on exercise of a Close-Out Right and a Right to Settle Net is limited to "actual direct compensatory damages . . . determined as of the date the superintendent took possession of the banking organization" but goes on to provide that compensatory damages, for this purpose, are deemed to include "normal and reasonable costs of cover or other reasonable measures of damages utilized among participants in the market for qualified financial con-

---

[1034]*See* H.R. 3211 § 3(a)(2), which would add a new clause (G) to Section 11(e)(8) of the FDIA.

[1035]*See supra* p. 235.

[1036]FDIA §§ 11(e)(3)(A) & 11(e)(3)(C)(i). These provisions by their terms deal only with qualified financial contracts that are repudiated or disaffirmed by the receiver or conservator. They are, however, widely believed to mean that a counterparty to a financial institution involved in FDIA Proceedings should also be able to assume its claim for damages will be viewed as compensatory in other cases (*i.e.*, close-out by the counterparty itself) if calculated according to a reasonable measure of damages utilized in the relevant contract industry. The market also widely assumes that the statutory reference to "normal and reasonable costs of cover and other reasonable measures of damages" is meant to include the reasonable timing features customarily included in industry measures of damages. In this regard, it should be noted that this language in the quoted FDIA provision speaks only to whether damages will be viewed as compensatory, but the statutory provision also requires that damages be actual and direct. *See supra* p. 251 for discussion of actual damages and *supra* p. 261 on how timing issues might have a bearing on whether damages are direct.

[1037]*See* FDIC, Statement of Policy Regarding Treatment of Collateralized Put Obligations After Appointment of the Federal Deposit Insurance Corporation as Conservator or Receiver (Jul. 9, 1991), 56 Fed. Reg. 36152 (Jul. 31, 1991), *available at* http://www.fdic.gov/regulations/laws/rules/5000-2800.html.

tract claims, calculated as of the date of the . . . termination of such qualified financial contract in accordance with its terms."[1038]

The Bankruptcy Code does not include provisions like these regarding the calculation of damages, but the reforms contemplated in H.R. 3211 would, as indicated above,[1039] introduce into the Bankruptcy Code a new Section 562 on the timing of the calculation of damages. The provision would apply if a Trustee rejected a financial contract or if a Protected Person exercised a right to liquidate, terminate or accelerate a financial contract. In either such case, under the new provision, damages would generally be measured as of the earlier of the (1) the date of the rejection or (2) the date of the liquidation, termination or acceleration.[1040] As proposed, Section 562 would go on to provide that, if "there are not any commercially reasonable determinants of value" as of these specified dates, "damages shall be measured as of the earliest subsequent date or dates on which there are commercially reasonable determinants of value."[1041] A Protected Person will, under the proposed provision, have the burden of proving "that there were no commercially reasonable determinants of value" as of the date prescribed by Section 562 for the determination of damages.[1042] Market participants who consider adopting an approach (like the Replacement Value approach contemplated in the *2001 ISDA Amendments*) that permits the use historical data relating to a date prior to close-out should consider with counsel issues that may be raised by the approach if this proposed amendment to the Bankruptcy Code becomes law.

As a general matter, however, at least in the United States, the enforceability against an insolvent counterparty of a contractual provision relating to payments in connection with early termination will be governed by the same nonbankruptcy law in the field of contracts that would apply in an action brought outside insolvency proceedings, including principles of contract law that render penalty provisions unenforceable.[1043]

[1038]NYBL § 618–a(2). *See supra* p. 281 on the proposed Section 562 on the timing of calculation of damages that would be added to the Bankruptcy Code by H.R. 3211 § 11(a).

[1039]*See supra* p. 281.

[1040]H.R. 3211 § 11(a). The quoted language is in proposed Section 562(a).

[1041]*Id.* These words, which are in proposed Section 562(b), are followed by another subparagraph (Section 562(c)) under which a Protected Person will have the burden of proving "that there were no commercially reasonable determinants of value" as of the date prescribed by proposed Section 562(a).

[1042]*Id.* The burden would be imposed by Section 562(c).

[1043]*See supra* p. 249.

SCHEDULE OF BANKRUPTCY CODE DEFINITIONS

Commodity Contract *Bankruptcy Code § 761(4)*	
Existing Law at July 15, 2002	*Proposed Insolvency Law Reform*
"commodity contract" means— (A) with respect to a futures commission merchant, contract for the purchase or sale of a commodity for future delivery on, or subject to the rules of, a contract market or board of trade; (B) with respect to a foreign futures commission merchant, foreign future; (C) with respect to a leverage transaction merchant, leverage transaction; (D) with respect to a clearing organization, contract for the purchase or sale of a commodity for future delivery on, or subject to the rules of, a contract market or board of trade that is cleared by such clearing organization, or commodity option traded on, or subject to the rules of, a contract market or board of trade that is cleared by such clearing organization; or (E) with respect to a commodity options dealer, commodity option;	"commodity contract" means— (A) with respect to a futures commission merchant, contract for the purchase or sale of a commodity for future delivery on, or subject to the rules of, a contract market or board of trade; (B) with respect to a foreign futures commission merchant, foreign future; (C) with respect to a leverage transaction merchant, leverage transaction; (D) with respect to a clearing organization, contract for the purchase or sale of a commodity for future delivery on, or subject to the rules of, a contract market or board of trade that is cleared by such clearing organization, or commodity option traded on, or subject to the rules of, a contract market or board of trade that is cleared by such clearing organization; or (E) with respect to a commodity options dealer, commodity option; or (F) any other agreement or transaction that is similar to an agreement or transaction referred to in this paragraph; (G) any combination of the agreements or transactions referred to in this paragraph; (H) any option to enter into an agreement or transaction referred to in this paragraph; (I) a master agreement that provides for an agreement or transaction referred to in subparagraph (A), (B), (C),

Commodity Contract Bankruptcy Code § 761(4)	
Existing Law at July 15, 2002	*Proposed Insolvency Law Reform*
	(D), (E), (F), (G), or (H), together with all supplements to such master agreement, without regard to whether the master agreement provides for an agreement or transaction that is not a commodity contract under this paragraph, except that the master agreement shall be considered to be a commodity contract under this paragraph only with respect to each agreement or transaction under the master agreement that is referred to in subparagraph (A), (B), (C), (D), (E), (F), (G), or (H); or
	(J) any security agreement or arrangement or other credit enhancement related to any agreement or transaction referred to in this paragraph or any guarantee or reimbursement obligation by or to a commodity broker or financial participant in connection with any agreement or transaction referred to in this paragraph, but not to exceed the damages in connection with any such agreement or transaction measured in accordance with section 562 of this title.

Forward Contract Bankruptcy Code §101(25)	
Existing Law at July 15, 2002	*Proposed Insolvency Law Reform*
"forward contract" means a contract (other than a commodity contract) for the purchase, sale, or transfer of a commodity, as defined in section 761(8) of this title, or any similar good, article, service, right, or interest which is presently or in the future becomes the subject of dealing in the forward contract trade, or product or byproduct thereof, with a maturity date more than two days after the date the contract is entered into, including, but not limited to, a repurchase transaction, reverse repurchase transaction, consignment, lease, swap, hedge transaction, deposit, loan, option, allocated transaction, unallocated transaction, or any combination thereof or option thereon;	"forward contract" means— (A) a contract (other than a commodity contract) for the purchase, sale, or transfer of a commodity, as defined in section 761(8) of this title, or any similar good, article, service, right, or interest which is presently or in the future becomes the subject of dealing in the forward contract trade, or product or byproduct thereof, with a maturity date more than two days after the date the contract is entered into, including, but not limited to, a repurchase transaction, reverse repurchase transaction, consignment, lease, swap, hedge transaction, deposit, loan, option, allocated transaction, unallocated transaction, or any combination thereof or option thereon; (B) any combination of agreements or transactions referred to in subparagraphs (A) and (C); (C) any option to enter into an agreement or transaction referred to in subparagraph (A) or (B); (D) a master agreement that provides for an agreement or transaction referred to in subparagraph (A), (B), or (C), together with all supplements to any such master agreement, without regard to whether such master agreement provides for an agreement or transaction that is not a forward contract under this paragraph, except that such master agreement shall be considered to be a forward contract under this paragraph only with respect to each agreement or transaction under such master agreement that is referred to in subparagraph (A), (B), or (C); or

Forward Contract Bankruptcy Code §101(25)	
Existing Law at July 15, 2002	*Proposed Insolvency Law Reform*
	(E) any security agreement or arrangement, or other credit enhancement related to any agreement or transaction referred to in subparagraph (A), (B), (C), or (D), or any guarantee or reimbursement obligation by or to a forward contract merchant or financial participant in connection with any agreement or transaction referred to in any such subparagraph, but not to exceed the damages in connection with any such agreement or transaction measured in accordance with section 562 of this title.

Repurchase Agreement Bankruptcy Code §101(47)	
Existing Law at July 15, 2002	*Proposed Insolvency Law Reform*
"repurchase agreement" (which definition also applies to a reverse repurchase agreement) means an agreement, including related terms, which provides for the transfer of one or more certificates of deposit, eligible bankers' acceptances, or securities that are direct obligations of, or that are fully guaranteed as to principal and interest by, the United States or any agency of the United States against the transfer of funds by the transferee of such certificates of deposit, eligible bankers' acceptances, or securities with a simultaneous agreement by such transferee to transfer to the transferor thereof certificates of deposit, eligible bankers' acceptances, or securities as described above, at a date certain not later than one year after such transfers or on demand, against the transfer of funds;	"repurchase agreement" (which definition also applies to a reverse repurchase agreement)— (A) means— (i) means an agreement, including related terms, which provides for the transfer of one or more certificates of deposit, mortgage-related securities (as defined in section 3 of the Securities Exchange Act of 1934), mortgage loans, interests in mortgage-related securities or mortgage loans, eligible bankers' acceptances, qualified foreign government securities (defined as a security that is a direct obligation of, or that is fully guaranteed by, the central government of an OECD member), or securities that are direct obligations of, or that are fully guaranteed by, the United States or any agency of the United States against the transfer of funds by the transferee of such certificates of deposit, eligible bankers' acceptances, securities, mortgage loans, or interests, with a simultaneous agreement by such transferee to transfer to the transferor thereof certificates of deposit, eligible bankers' acceptances, securities, mortgage loans, or interests of the kind described in this clause, at a date certain not later than 1 year after such transfers or on demand, against the transfer of funds; (ii) any combination of agreements or transactions referred to in clauses (i) and (iii); (iii) an option to enter into an agreement or transaction referred to in clause (i) or (iii); (iv) a master agreement that provides for an agreement or transaction referred to in clause (i), (ii), or (iii), together with all

Repurchase Agreement
Bankruptcy Code §101(47)

Existing Law at July 15, 2002	Proposed Insolvency Law Reform
	supplements to any such master agreement, without regard to whether such master agreement provides for an agreement or transaction that is not a repurchase agreement under this paragraph, except that the master agreement shall be considered to be a repurchase agreement under this paragraph only with respect to each agreement or transaction under the master agreement that is referred to in clause (i), (ii), or (iii); or
	(v) any security agreement or arrangement or other credit enhancement related to any agreement or transaction referred to in clause (i), (ii), (iii), or (iv), including any guarantee or reimbursement obligation by or to a repo participant or financial participant in connection with any agreement or transaction referred to in any such clause, but not to exceed the damages in connection with any such agreement or transaction, measured in accordance with section 562 of this title; and
	(B) does not include a repurchase obligation under a participation in a commercial mortgage loan;

Securities Contract Bankruptcy Code § 741(7)	
Existing Law at July 15, 2002	*Proposed Insolvency Law Reform*
"securities contract" means contract for the purchase, sale, or loan of a security, including an option for the purchase or sale of a security, certificate of deposit, or group or index of securities (including any interest therein or based on the value thereof), or any option entered into on a national securities exchange relating to foreign currencies, or the guarantee of any settlement of cash or securities by or to a securities clearing agency;	"securities contract" (A) means— (i) a contract for the purchase, sale, or loan of a security, a certificate of deposit, a mortgage loan or any interest in a mortgage loan, a group or index of securities, certificates of deposit, or mortgage loans or interests therein (including an interest therein or based on the value thereof), or option on any of the foregoing, including an option to purchase or sell any such security, certificate of deposit, mortgage loan, interest, group or index, or option, and including any repurchase or reverse repurchase transaction on any such security, certificate of deposit, loan, interest, group or index, or option; (ii) any option entered into on a national securities exchange relating to foreign currencies; (iii) the guarantee by or to any securities clearing agency of a settlement of cash, securities, certificates of deposit, mortgage loans or interests therein, group or index of securities, or mortgage loans or interests therein (including any interest therein or based on the value thereof), or option on any of the foregoing, including an option to purchase or sell any such security, certificate of deposit, loan, interest, group or index, or option; (iv) any margin loan; (v) any other agreement or transaction that is similar to an agreement or transaction referred to in this subparagraph; (vi) any combination of the agreements or transactions referred to in this

Bankruptcy and Insolvency Concerns

Securities Contract Bankruptcy Code § 741(7)	
Existing Law at July 15, 2002	*Proposed Insolvency Law Reform*
	subparagraph; (vii) any option to enter into any agreement or transaction referred to in this subparagraph; (viii) a master agreement that provides for an agreement or transaction referred to in clause (i), (ii), (iii), (iv), (v), (vi), or (vii), together with all supplements to any such master agreement, without regard to whether the master agreement provides for an agreement or transaction that is not a securities contract under this subparagraph, except that such master agreement shall be considered to be a securities contract under this subparagraph only with respect to each agreement or transaction under such master agreement that is referred to in clause (i), (ii), (iii), (iv), (v), (vi), or (vii); or (ix) any security agreement or arrangement or other credit enhancement related to any agreement or transaction referred to in this subparagraph or any guarantee or reimbursement obligation by or to a stockbroker, securities clearing agency, financial institution or financial participant in connection with any agreement or transaction referred to in this subparagraph, but not to exceed the damages in connection with any such agreement or transaction measured in accordance with section 562 of this title; and (B) does not include any purchase, sale, or repurchase obligation under a participation in a commercial mortgage loan.

Swap Agreement Bankruptcy Code § 101(53B)	
Existing Law at July 15, 2002	*Proposed Insolvency Law Reform*

"swap agreement" means—
 	
(A) an agreement (including terms and conditions incorporated by reference therein) which is a rate swap agreement, basis swap, forward rate agreement, commodity swap, interest rate option, forward foreign exchange agreement, spot foreign exchange agreement, rate cap agreement, rate floor agreement, rate collar agreement, currency swap agreement, cross-currency rate swap agreement, currency option, any other similar agreement (including any option to enter into any of the foregoing);
 	
(B) any combination of the foregoing;
 	
(C) a master agreement for any of the foregoing together with all supplements;
	"swap agreement"—
	
	(A) means—
	    (i) any agreement, including the terms and conditions incorporated by reference in such agreement, which is—
	        (I) an interest rate swap, option, future, or forward agreement, including a rate floor, rate cap, rate collar, cross-currency rate swap, and basis swap;
	        (II) a spot, same day-tomorrow, tomorrow-next, forward, or other foreign exchange or precious metals agreement;
	        (III) a currency swap, option, future, or forward agreement;
	        (IV) an equity index or equity swap, option, future, or forward agreement;
	        (V) a debt index or debt swap, option, future, or forward agreement;
	        (VI) a total return, credit spread or credit swap, option, future, or forward agreement;
	        (VII) a commodity index or a commodity swap, option, future, or forward agreement; or
	        (VIII) a weather swap, weather derivative, or weather option;
	    (ii) any agreement or transaction that is similar to any other agreement or transaction referred to in this paragraph and that—
	        (I) is of a type that has been, is presently, or in the future becomes, the subject of recurrent dealings in the swap markets (including terms and conditions incorporated by reference therein); and
	        (II) is a forward, swap, future, or option on one or more rates, currencies, commodities, equity securities, or other

Swap Agreement Bankruptcy Code § 101(53B)	
Existing Law at July 15, 2002	*Proposed Insolvency Law Reform*

	equity instruments, debt securities or other debt instruments, quantitative measures associated with an occurrence, extent of an occurrence, or contingency associated with a financial, commercial, or economic consequence, or economic or financial indices or measures of economic or financial risk or value;
	    (iii) any combination of agreements or transactions referred to in this subparagraph;
	    (iv) any option to enter into an agreement or transaction referred to in this subparagraph;
	    (v) a master agreement that provides for an agreement or transaction referred to in clause (i), (ii), (iii), or (iv), together with all supplements to any such master agreement, and without regard to whether the master agreement contains an agreement or transaction that is not a swap agreement under this paragraph, except that the master agreement shall be considered to be a swap agreement under this paragraph only with respect to each agreement or transaction under the master agreement that is referred to in clause (i), (ii), (iii), or (iv); or
	    (vi) any security agreement or arrangement or other credit enhancement related to any agreements or transactions referred to in clause (i) through (v), including any guarantee or reimbursement obligation by or to a swap participant or financial participant in connection with any agreement or transaction referred to in any such clause, but not to exceed the damages in connection with any such agreement or transaction, measured in accordance with section 562 of this title;

CHAPTER 8

U.S. WITHHOLDING TAX ISSUES

Introduction	350
Documentation Challenges	351
U.S. Withholding Taxes	353
Evolution of Rules	356
Notional Principal Contract Income	358
Other Exemptions and Reduced Rates and Related Certifications	362

INTRODUCTION

Since the inception of the market for interest rate swaps, the documentation for these and similar transactions between parties organized in or acting from different jurisdictions has reflected two basic and related concerns about withholding taxes: (1) how to reduce to a tolerable level each party's risk that it might be required to make gross-up payments on account of withholding taxes, or receive payments reduced by withholding taxes without the benefit of a gross-up, in amounts that would render participation in the transaction uneconomical; and (2) how fairly to allocate to the parties responsibilities for the identification and delivery of information—whether as representations in their agreement or as separate documents required by a revenue or taxing authority—that will enable each party, with minimal effort, to discharge its duties as a withholding agent for a government imposing withholding taxes.

This chapter briefly reviews the functions that the documentation often serves in addressing these and associated concerns and provides some background about how withholding tax concerns most commonly arise under U.S. tax law, as reflected in the IRC and Treasury regulations. Market participants should consult their tax advisers about the withholding and other tax issues that may be relevant in connection with the derivatives transactions in which they engage.[1044]

[1044] Other important tax issues include questions as to (1) the point at which, or period over which, a party may be required to recognize as income certain kinds of payments (such as lump sum payments) received by it in connection with derivatives; (2) the point at which, or period over which, payments may be deductible for tax purposes; (3) the characterization of deductions as ordinary or capital; (4) the characterization and timing of recognition (as income or deductible expense or as gain or loss) of payments received or made in connection with the transfer or early termination of derivatives (and whether certain alterations to the structure of a transaction may be deemed to constitute a transfer or early termination, for these purposes); (5) the tax effects, if any, of a transfer on the party that is neither the transferor nor the transferee; and (6) whether or not derivatives payments may be integrated with payments on borrowings or investments for purposes of determining interest income or expense when the derivatives are entered into as hedges against risks associated with the borrowing or investment or otherwise to alter the structure of the borrowing or investment synthetically. The tax concerns may be far more numerous and complex for financial institutions that run a "global book" of derivatives transactions and have offices in different jurisdictions that enter into transactions with each other. Market participants that are generally exempt from tax also have special concerns, typically relating to taxes on business income not deemed to be related to their tax-exempt purposes. The

DOCUMENTATION CHALLENGES

The first withholding tax question to be resolved in documenting a derivatives transaction is which party will bear the burden if withholding taxes are imposed on a payment under the transaction. When will the payer be required to make gross-up payments on account of the taxes, and when will the payee be required to receive the payments as reduced by the taxes without the benefit of a gross-up? If withholding taxes are imposed, will the party that bears the burden of the taxes (by having to gross up or receive a reduce payment) be contractually entitled to close out the transaction and, if so, on what terms?[1045] If close-out is permitted, how will the legitimate interests of the other party be protected? [1046] Assuming that other party has a continuing need for the protection of the transactions being closed out, will it be able to obtain replacement transactions and will a close-out settlement payment compensate it for all the adverse effects of the close-out?

The second, related, set of questions often addressed in the documentation focuses, as noted, on the concerns a party may have if it is required by applicable law to act as withholding agent for a taxing authority. In these cases the party's concerns typically arise if a withholding agent may be liable for a tax it fails to withhold or if it may incur liability for failure to file a required report. These concerns can be exacerbated if the

---

U.S. tax law issues are discussed in ANDREA S. KRAMER, FINANCIAL PRODUCTS: TAXATION, REGULATION, AND DESIGN (Aspen Publishers, Inc., 3rd ed. 2000 & Supps. 2001 & 2002) and the sources cited therein. For discussion focused on issues that arise for U.S. taxpayers in connection with particular classes of derivatives, derivatives used for hedging and derivatives documented using ISDA forms, *see,* Edward D. Kleinbard, *Equity Derivative Products: Financial Innovation's Newest Challenge to the Tax System,* 69 TEXAS L. REV. 1319 (1991), *reprinted in* ADVANCED STRATEGIES IN RISK MANAGEMENT 327; Robert J. Mackay & Phoebe A. Mix, *Uncertain Futures: The Tax Treatment of Hedging, in* ADVANCED STRATEGIES IN RISK MANAGEMENT 377; Erika W. Nijenhuis & David E. Arroyo, *ISDA Master Agreement Tax Issues, in* PLI 2000, at 107; Andrew T. Chalnick, *SWAPs & Other Derivatives in 2001–A Tax Primer, in* PLI 2001, at 123; Bruce Kayle, *The Federal Income Tax Treatment of Credit Derivative Transactions, in* HANDBOOK OF CREDIT DERIVATIVES 221; and David Z. Nirenberg & Steven L. Kopp, *Credit Derivatives: Tax Treatment of Total Return Swaps, Default Swaps, and Credit-Linked Notes,* 87 J. TAX'N 82 (1997).

[1045] As illustrated *infra* p. 797, ISDA's 1992 Master Agreement (Multicurrency—Cross Border) form allocates to the payer the burden of making additional, gross-up payments to its counterparty for Indemnifiable Taxes, subject to specified exceptions (*see infra* p. 811). The critical threshold issue, therefore, is whether the definition of that term in the ISDA form, or in any proposed modification of that definition, fairly allocates to the payer the risk of gross-up for taxes that would not have been imposed but for connections between the taxing jurisdiction and the payee or an entity related to it other than the payee's merely being a party to the agreement and transactions under it. Under this ISDA form (as under ISDA's 1987 master Interest Rate and Currency Exchange Agreement before it), a payer required to make gross-up payments may or may not have close-out rights, depending on the circumstances, and the same is true of a payee that receives payments reduced by withholding taxes and without the benefit of gross-up payments (*see infra* p. 842). The ISDA form does not provide for contractual close-out rights relating to withholding taxes imposed in respect of interest payments expressly contemplated in enumerated provisions of the form, and neither it nor the standard ISDA credit support terms discussed in Part 5 of this book (*infra* p. 1055) relieves a party from gross-up obligations that it may have in respect of payments of income to the other party in relation to collateral (*see infra* p. 1167).

[1046] Whether these risks are significant may turn on a variety of factors, depending on the context in which the party not seeking close-out has engaged in the transaction. Dealers who mark their transactions to market daily for tax and accounting purposes may, in normal circumstances, be largely indifferent to certain risks, whereas end-users may suffer adverse tax or accounting consequences as a result of close-out of a transaction at an unintended time.

withholding agent may also be liable for interest on a relevant tax from the date the withholding should have been made, or, possibly, for penalties. When these risks exist, the parties will usually ask questions like the following to identify how their agreement allocates the risks:

- Which of the parties is responsible for determining what procedures should be followed and which forms or representations, if any, should be obtained from each party as payee, in order for the payer to be protected against these risks?[1047]

- Which of the parties is required to monitor the need for additional procedures or forms, either as a matter of contract or as a matter of law?[1048]

- What are the potential consequences under the terms of the parties' contract and as a matter of law if a party fails to call for, or deliver, a form or make a representation or follow another procedure necessary to permit its counterparty, as payer, to make a payment without withholding or subject to withholding taxes at a reduced rate?

- Is the payer required to inquire into the payee's circumstances, or does applicable law permit it to rely on information given to it by the payee? If reliance is permitted, is it permitted in all circumstances, or only if the facts as they appear would not give the payer reason to wonder about the reliability of the payee's forms or representations?

- What presumptions, if any, should a payer apply if it lacks sufficient, reliable information about the status of the payee or the appropriate treatment of some or all payments under the parties' contract?

[1047] As illustrated *infra* p. 797, ISDA's 1992 Master Agreement (Multicurrency—Cross Border) form assumes that each party, standing in the position of a potential payer under the agreement, will analyze applicable law in its own Relevant Jurisdictions (*see infra* p. 892) to determine what it must learn from the other party, as payee, by way of representation, and what forms, if any, it must receive from that party, so as not to have to withhold on account of taxes imposed in that jurisdiction.

[1048] *See infra* p. 825 for an illustration of one of the ways in which users of ISDA's 1992 Master Agreement (Multicurrency—Cross Border) form establish an obligation of their counterparties to deliver replacements for forms initially required. As discussed *infra* p. 916, when the parties do not expressly contract for these obligations, the standard ISDA approach (in Section 4(a)(iii) of that form) would not result in a party's obligation to deliver a form to a payer without request from the payer and, even if a request is made, will not necessarily result in an obligation to deliver the form. However, if a change in circumstances—rather than a change in law—renders a representation that is relevant to a party's status as a payee incorrect, and if that party does not correct the representation and its counterparty is required to withhold on account of taxes that would not have been imposed if the representation had continued to be correct, the payer will not be required to make gross-up payments to the payee in respect of the relevant taxes and the payee will not have a contractual right to close out the transactions under which the payments reduced by withholding are made. The instructions to the IRS forms (*e.g.*, W-8BEN and W8ECI), on the other hand, expressly provide that if a change in circumstances makes any information in the form incorrect, the person submitting the form must, within 30 days of the change in circumstances, give the withholding agent notice of the change and file a new, appropriate form.

- Will a payer be entitled to indemnification from the payee if the payer does not make a required withholding and is later assessed the tax and interest or penalties?[1049]

When market participants negotiate their documentation, they will normally do so in the context of a master agreement. Accordingly, they will be required to make broad assumptions about their expected dealings with each other—the types of income those dealings are likely to generate under the master agreement and the related credit support arrangements, the places from which payments will be made, the tax status of each of the parties (or its agent) in each office that may be relevant to those dealings, and withholding tax exemptions that might be available. In light of these assumptions, typically the parties then seek to prepare their documents so as to enhance the likelihood that neither will be required to withhold taxes, and so as to minimize the reporting and other duties that they will be required to perform.

This documentation work is done in the light of the law as it exists when the parties negotiate their master agreement and in the context of their circumstances at the time. Since they are creating a framework for ongoing future dealings, however, they must also allocate between them the risks that that may arise if the applicable law or their circumstances change, or if their initial assumptions about applicable law as applied to their circumstances prove wrong.

The standardized derivatives documents published by ISDA have embodied an intricate allocation of these risks between the parties. The ISDA conventions are complex precisely because they involve allocations of future and contingent risks. These market conventions are illustrated in the sample master agreement in Part 3 of this book and discussed in the related annotations.[1050] The annotations to the sample Credit Support Annex in Part 5 point to issues that may be raised by the application of these matters to collateral arrangements.[1051]

U. S. WITHHOLDING TAXES

When participants in the derivatives markets analyze the concerns summarized above in the context of U.S. withholding taxes and the related rules applicable to withholding agents, they usually begin with a few basic rules of thumb. The first is that U.S. withholding taxes—taxes required to be withheld under Section 1441, 1442 or 1443 of Chapter 3 of the IRC and related Treasury regulations—may become an issue for derivatives transactions when:

- the payer is subject to U.S. tax jurisdiction,
- the payment is of a type that is subject to U.S. withholding taxes,
- the payment is treated as having a U.S. source,

[1049]See Section 2(d)(i)(4)(A) of the sample master agreement and the related annotation, *infra* p. 812.

[1050]See *infra* pp. 812, 823 and 826, for the annotations to Sections 2(d), 3(e), 3(f) and 4(d) of the sample master agreement, and to some of the defined terms used in those provisions.

[1051]See *infra* pp. 1167 & 1182.

- the payee, or the beneficial owner of the income for which the payee is receiving the payment is subject to U.S. withholding taxes, and

- no exemption from U.S. withholding taxes is available for the payment.

Generally speaking, in the absence of an exemption or reduction of the rate,[1052] U.S. withholding tax is imposed, under Section 1441, 1442 or 1443 of the IRC, at a rate of 30% on certain kinds of fixed or determinable, annual or periodic payments—commonly referred to as *"FDAP"*—that have a U.S. source, if those payments are made to a nonresident alien or a foreign partnership or corporation.[1053]

The second basic rule of thumb is that "any person, U.S. or foreign, that has the control, receipt, custody, disposal, or payment of an item of income of a foreign person subject to withholding" will be treated as a withholding agent for purposes of U.S. withholding taxes.[1054] The third general rule is that a withholding agent is liable[1055] for a tax required to be withheld under Chapter 3 of the IRC and the regulations thereunder if the withholding agent "cannot reliably associate a payment" with prescribed documentation (usually IRS forms referred to as withholding certificates but sometimes other certifications) on the date of payment and the withholding agent "does not withhold" or withholds at a rate lower than the prescribed rate, subject to exceptions that apply if (1) the withholding agent has appropriately relied on presumptions prescribed by Treasury regulations in order to treat the payee as a U.S. person or to treat the payment as income effectively connected with a trade or business conducted in the U.S.,[1056] or (2) the withholding agent can demonstrate that the proper amount of tax, if any, was paid to the IRS or (3) no documentation is required for a reduced rate of withholding to apply.[1057] If under that rule it is liable for a tax that should have been but was not withheld, the withholding agent may also be liable for interest and penalties.[1058]

[1052] Section 1.1441-1(b)(4) of the Treasury regulations is a list of exemptions from, and reduced rates of, withholding taxes.

[1053] Section 1441 of the IRC deals with payments to nonresident alien individuals and foreign partnerships, Section 1442 with payments to foreign corporations and Section 1443 with certain payments to foreign tax-exempt entities. Except for references to appropriate tax forms, the discussion in this chapter does not address withholding from payments to foreign tax-exempt entities, nor does it deal with issues involving payments to an entity acting as an intermediary, to a business entity that has a single owner (and, therefore, may be disregarded for purposes of tax analysis as an entity separate from its owner), or a to hybrid entity, understood to mean a legal entity treated as fiscally transparent (not as a taxable entity) by a country with which the U.S. has an income tax treaty. The tax representations requested from payees in connection with OTC derivatives sometimes seek to establish that the payee is not a business entity with a single owner, and that the entity is not treated as fiscally transparent for purposes of a potentially relevant income tax treaty.

[1054] Treas. Reg. § 1.1441-7(a) states this rule regarding withholding agents for purposes of Chapter 3 of the IRC and regulations thereunder. The same provision deals with the obligation of such a withholding agent to pay over tax withheld and to file returns.

[1055] The liability arises under Section 1461 of the IRC.

[1056] *See* Treas. Reg. § 1.1441-1(b)(3).

[1057] *See* Treas. Reg. § 1.1441-1(b)(7)(1).

[1058] *See* Treas. Reg. § 1.1441-1(b)(7)(iii) on interest and penalties.

Various Treasury regulations address a withholding agent's ability to rely on information or certificates furnished to it and related matters.[1059] As a general matter, a withholding agent must withhold at the full rate applicable under Section 1441, 1442 or 1443 of the IRC if it has actual knowledge or reason to know that a claim of U.S. status, or a claim to entitlement to a reduced rate of withholding, is unreliable or incorrect.[1060] For purposes of the Treasury regulations under those sections of the IRC,

> a withholding agent may rely on information or certifications contained in, or associated with, a withholding certificate or other documentation furnished by or for a beneficial owner or payee unless the withholding agent has actual knowledge or reason to know that the information or certifications are incorrect or unreliable and, if based on such knowledge or reason to know, it should withhold . . . an amount greater than would be the case if it relied on the information or certifications.[1061]

For these purposes, a withholding agent "shall be considered to have reason to know if its knowledge of relevant facts or of statements contained in the withholding certificates or other documentation is such that a reasonably prudent person in the position of the withholding agent would question the claims made."[1062] There are also presumptions that withholding agents are required to apply when required certifications are not obtained or are unreliable.[1063] In addition, as discussed in the section on notional principal contract income,[1064] there are special rules under which a withholding agent may not be required to withhold on certain payments under OTC derivatives regardless of whether it has obtained a withholding certificate.

As the parties to OTC derivatives document their agreements on allocating the risks of U.S. withholding taxes, they should note the important distinction between these taxes and U.S. backup withholding. As indicated, U.S. withholding taxes, generally speaking, are imposed on U.S.-source payments made to nonresidents in the absence of an applicable exemption. Backup withholding and related reporting requirements, on the other hand, may exist in connection with payments made to U.S. persons if they are not exempt recipients—as are, for example, corporations organized in the United States.[1065]

Often this distinction is not readily apparent in the documents. That is, in adapting the standardized market documents for their use, when both U.S. withholding taxes and backup withholding (and related reporting) may be issues, the parties simply identify in

---

[1059] See, e.g., Treas. Reg. §§ 1.1441-1(b)(3)(ix) & 1.1441-7(b).

[1060] Treas. Reg. § 1.1441-7(b)(1).

[1061] Treas. Reg. § 1.1441-7(b)(1). The same rule applies to reporting by a withholding agent to the IRS.

[1062] Treas. Reg. § 1.1441-7(b)(2). Special rules apply to the knowledge of financial institutions acting as withholding agents in relation to payments to account holders.

[1063] See Treas. Reg. § 1.1441-7(b)(3). These presumptions do not, however, excuse the payee from furnishing documentation if the documentation is required to obtain a reduced rate of withholding. Id.

[1064] Infra p. 358.

[1065] Backup withholding and related reporting requirements are addressed in Chapter 61 and Section 3406 of the IRC and related regulations.

the same place the representations and tax forms that they are seeking from each other. The forms relevant where U.S. withholding taxes are concerned are generally one variant or another of IRS W-8 form described below,[1066] all of which are, naturally, focused on payees and beneficial owners who are foreign persons. Where backup withholding and related reporting to the IRS are concerned, the documentation for OTC derivatives generally includes a requirement that the payee deliver to the payer an IRS Form W-9, which cannot be used by a foreign person. Form W-9 sets forth the payee's tax payer identification number and attests that the payee is a domestic entity. In addition, to establish that the payee is not subject to backup withholding or related reporting, a foreign payee will generally be asked to represent as to its foreign status for U.S. federal income tax purposes.[1067]

Generally, the risk of U.S. backup withholding will be allocable to the payee, since backup withholding is imposed because of a connection between the taxing jurisdiction—the United States—and the payee, and taxes of this kind are conventionally excluded from those that give rise to a gross-up obligation on the part of the payer, referred to in ISDA documentation as "Indemnifiable Taxes."[1068] Similarly, as a matter of customary practice, a payee that receives payments reduced by backup withholding would not be expected to have a contractual right to close out transactions. To the extent that the parties' documents leave any doubt on this subject, they may wish to clarify the matter.

EVOLUTION OF RULES

The market for derivatives products, and related documentation practices, initially developed in an environment of legal uncertainty on U.S. withholding tax issues. Most of those uncertainties have been resolved at different stages and in different ways through Treasury regulations on notional principal contract income—a category that includes payments of the basic cash flows under many swaps and similar transactions, but not interest or nonperiodic payments treated as interest[1069]—and separate rules relating to payments under other derivatives, such as currency options and FX forwards.[1070]

The withholding tax issues have not related to true interest that may be payable under an agreement between the parties if, say, one of the parties is late in making a payment under a swap or similar transaction, or if a party exercises a contractual right to

---

[1066] *Infra* p. 362.

[1067] *See* Chalnick, *supra* note 1044, at 159–61. *See also* ISDA, *Memorandum: New US Tax Representations for Schedule to ISDA Master Agreement*, October 25, 2001, and *Explanatory Note for New US Tax Representations,* October 25, 2001, *available at* www.isda.org/whatsnew/index.html.

[1068] *See infra* p. 886 on the ISDA definition of "Indemnifiable Taxes."

[1069] *See infra* p. 358 on notional principal contract income and these regulations, which were made generally applicable to payments made after December 31, 2000, regardless of whether the transactions giving rise to the income were entered into before that date.

[1070] The separate, and earlier, clarification of the rules applicable to these FX derivatives transactions is reflected in the fact that, although ISDA's standardized documents, originally developed for use with swaps and similar derivatives, have from the outset included provisions on withholding taxes like those referred to *supra* note 1045, the standard ICOM and IFEMA terms used to document currency options and FX forwards (and spot FX transactions in the latter case), and the subsequently developed FEOMA form used to document all these products, have not dealt with withholding tax issues.

withhold a payment and later makes the payment with interest, or if the party pays interest on cash collateral posted with it by a counterparty.[1071] It has always been clear that, in the absence of an applicable exemption, this interest income would be subject to U.S. withholding tax if paid from a U.S. source to a person subject, in the circumstances, to U.S. withholding tax—referred to generically in the remainder of this discussion as a "nonresident" or a "foreign person." The parties have generally negotiated their agreements assuming that some interest may be payable, and there has been little debate about market practices in allocating as between the parties the risk of withholding taxes on interest, understood, as it traditionally has been for purposes of U.S. tax analysis, as the compensation that a person pays for the use someone else's money or the equivalent.[1072]

Rather, the withholding tax concerns have usually related to the possible taxation of the basic payment streams of the derivatives transaction. These payments are frequently calculated by applying a percentage rate, such as an interest rate observed in the debt markets or a commodity price, to a notional amount. This has sometimes led to concerns that the IRS or the courts could characterize the payments as interest or some other category of FDAP subject to withholding taxes.[1073]

In conventional transactions, the key factor that distinguishes the basic derivatives payments from interest, of course, is that the notional amount, unlike the principal in a loan or other financing, never changes hands. Nonetheless, when there have been, or continue to be, concerns over the characterization of payments for purposes of withholding taxes, the parties to derivatives transactions have included provisions in their documents that would allocate, as between them, whatever risk has existed on this score. A related issue has been how those payments would be treated for purposes of tax treaties between the United States and other countries, since those treaties may, given the necessary circumstances, reduce an otherwise applicable withholding tax rate partially in respect of some kinds of income but all the way to zero for others.

Over time, the IRC and Treasury regulations have, in three principal ways, clarified how some basic payments under OTC derivatives will generally be characterized for purposes of U.S. withholding taxes, by establishing the following:

- Some payments will not be treated as FDAP but, rather, will be analyzed for purposes of U.S. taxes as gain, where applicable. This is so, for example, with foreign currency gain or loss on a forward contract

---

[1071]These are cases in which interest is, at least to some extent, conventionally provided for under the ISDA forms of master agreements and some ISDA forms of credit support documents. *See infra* pp. 814, 896 & 1165.

[1072]*See, e.g.,* 3 Kramer, *supra* note 1044, § 78.03[C][1], at 78-13 to 78-14, discussing the Supreme Court cases on which this classic tax-law view of interest is based and the following observation in legislative history of IRC amendments relating to swap payments: "Although in an interest rate swap . . . payments are measured by interest payments, they are not viewed as interest because these are not paid as compensation for the use or forbearance of money" (quoting from Staff of the Joint Comm. on Taxation, 99th Cong., 2d Sess., General Explanation of the Tax Reform Act of 1986, at 1077 (Joint Comm. Print 1986)).

[1073]Where this concern has existed, the drafters of documents for swaps and similar derivatives transactions have, therefore, traditionally avoided any suggestion in the document that the basic payments contemplated by the transactions were or should be treated as interest, noting that these basic payments are calculated on the basis of a notional amount but do not involve a charge for the use of actual principal.

or a conventional option, including an option to enter into or terminate a swap or other notional principal contract.[1074] In these cases, if the payments are made to nonresidents, they will be treated as having their source in the place of the payee's tax residence.[1075]

- Other payments, although considered to be FDAP, will not be subject to U.S. withholding taxes even if made to nonresidents because they too will be treated as having their source in the payee's tax jurisdiction. Under Treasury regulations discussed in the next section, this is the general rule applicable to a broad class of derivatives payments that qualify as notional principal contract income, provided the notional principal contract is properly reflected on the payee's books.[1076] This special foreign sourcing is also the rule for conventional currency swap payments under Section 988(a)(3)(A) of the IRC and related Treasury regulations.[1077]

- Still other derivatives payments will be treated as interest and, when paid to nonresidents, will be subject to U.S. withholding taxes at the generally applicable rate in the absence of an applicable exemption or reduction of the rate. For example, some payments under notional principal contracts are characterized as interest under the Treasury regulations applicable to what are referred to as "nonperiodic payments,"[1078] as discussed in the next section.

NOTIONAL PRINCIPAL CONTRACT INCOME

A withholding agent that makes payments attributable to a notional principal contract of the kind defined in applicable Treasury regulations[1079] will not be obligated to withhold on certain payments, regardless of whether a withholding certificate is provided to the withholding agent. This is because notional principal contract income payments made to a nonresident payee will be treated as having their source where the payee is resi-

---

[1074] See IRC § 988(a).

[1075] See, e.g., 1 Kramer, supra note 1044, § 6.11[F][8][b][ii], at 6-111.

[1076] See Treas. Reg. § 1.863-7. This approach to the issue of withholding taxes through sourcing rules is consistent with that generally accorded under U.S. withholding tax rules to payments treated as gain on currency options and FX forwards, as indicated above, and to gain on interest rate futures contracts. If the payments made to the nonresident are effectively connected with a trade or business conducted in the United States, the payments will be subject to taxation (but not withholding tax) in the U.S.

[1077] These rules are the outgrowth of guidance previously given by the IRS regarding the sourcing of conventional periodic payments under swaps. The first significant step in this regard was Notice 87-4, released in December 1986, 1987-1 C.B. 416, where the IRS clarified that the basic periodic payments made by a U.S. entity having the U.S. dollar as its functional currency on a conventional U.S. dollar denominated rate swap to a nonresident acting from outside the United States would be treated as having their source in the place of the payee's residence and, therefore, would not be U.S.-source income subject to U.S. withholding tax if the U.S. entity made an irrevocable election to apply the rules to all the entity's swap income. See also Rev. Rul. 87-5, 1987-1 C.B. 180.

[1078] See Treas. Reg. § 1.1441-4(a)(3)(i), referring to Treas. Reg. § 1.446-3(g)(4).

[1079] These are Sections 1.863-7(a) and 1.988-2(e) of the Treasury regulations.

dent for tax purposes, except where the payments are effectively connected with a trade or business conducted in the United States, provided the notional principal contract is properly reflected on the payee's books.[1080] For purposes of these regulations, a notional principal contract is "a financial instrument that provides for the payment of amounts by one party to another at specified intervals calculated by reference to a specified index upon a notional principal amount in exchange for specified consideration or a promise to pay similar amounts."[1081] It should be noted that notional principal contract income does not include any amount characterized as interest under the regulations applicable to what are referred to as "swaps with significant nonperiodic payments."[1082]

No withholding under Section 1441 of the IRC is required if the income is effectively connected with a trade or business conducted in the United States. A withholding agent must treat as effectively connected all notional principal contract income that it pays to, or to the account of, a qualified business unit of a foreign person located in the United States (e.g., the U.S. branch of a foreign bank). The withholding agent must also treat notional principal contract income as effectively connected with the conduct of a U.S. trade or business if it knows or has reason to know that the payment is effectively connected with the conduct of a trade or business within the United States.[1083]

A withholding agent will generally be required to file returns with the IRS reporting the notional principal contract income that it pays if it is required, as described above, to treat the income as effectively connected with the conduct of a trade or business in the United States.[1084] Where applicable, these returns must be filed on IRS Form 1042-S. However, the Treasury regulations expressly provide for an exception to these filing requirements

> if the payee provides a representation in a master agreement that governs the transactions in notional principal contracts between the parties (for example an International Swaps and Derivatives Association (ISDA) Agreement, including the Schedule thereto) or in the confirmation on the particular notional principal contract transaction that the payee is a U.S. person or a non-U.S. branch of a foreign person.[1085]

ISDA has published standard forms of representations that may be used for this purpose, along with a memorandum explaining these subjects.[1086]

[1080] Treas. Reg. § 1.863-7.

[1081] Treas. Reg. § 1.863-7(a)(1). The definition of "notional principal contract" for other purposes of the IRC may not be identical. See, e.g., Treas. Reg. § 1.988-1(a)(2)(iii)(B)(2). A "notional principal amount" is "any specified amount of money or property that, when multiplied by a specified index, measures a party's rights and obligations under the contract, but is not borrowed or loaned between the parties to the contract." Treas. Reg. § 1.446-3(c)(3).

[1082] Treas. Reg. § 1.1441-4(a)(3)(i), referring to Treas. Reg. § 1.446-3(g)(4). See also infra note 1093.

[1083] Treas. Reg. § 1.1441-4(a)(3)(i).

[1084] Id.

[1085] Treas. Reg. § 1.1441-4(a)(3)(ii).

[1086] ISDA, supra note 1067.

When they analyze U.S. withholding tax and information reporting considerations related to an OTC derivatives transaction in the context of these rules, the parties should take into account whether it has each of the characteristics required for identifying it as a notional principal contract under the quoted definition and whether it is expressly excluded by the Treasury regulations from the definition of that term. In this connection, it should be noted that the withholding regulations are less detailed on what constitutes a notional principal contract than the regulations under Section 446, which deal with the timing of income and deductions. The Section 446 regulations appear likely to be applied to decisions as to what constitutes a notional principal contract for withholding purposes.

In connection with the treatment of notional principal contracts for purposes of these Section 446 regulations, for example, "specified index" includes:

(1) a fixed rate, price or amount,

(2) a fixed rate, price or amount applicable in one or more specified periods followed by one or more different fixed rates, prices or amounts in other periods,

(3) an index based on objective financial information—defined to mean any current objectively determinable financial or economic information that is not within the control of a party to the contract and is not unique to the circumstances of one the parties—and

(4) an interest rate index regularly used in normal lending transactions between a party and unrelated persons.[1087]

In addition, the conclusions on the timing of income and deductions may turn on whether payments are regarded as "periodic" or "nonperiodic," and in this context, a periodic payment under a notional principal contract, generally, is defined as a payment that is made at least annually, is based on a specified index and is calculated on a notional amount that is the same as the one used to calculated the payment or payments due from the other party or varies in the same proportion as the notional amount used to calculate the other party's payments.[1088]

Generally speaking, conventional interest rate swaps, currency swaps, basis swaps, interest rate caps, interest rate floors, commodity swaps and equity swaps,[1089] as well as conventional caps and floors relating to a specified index, will be notional principal contracts. The following are, however, some of the issues that commentators have raised in connection with determinations about whether OTC derivatives will qualify as notional principal contracts.

- The definition refers to transactions providing for payments by one party at specified intervals calculated by reference to a specific index in exchange for specified consideration or a promise to pay similar

---

[1087]Treas. Reg. § 1.446-3(c)(2).

[1088]Treas. Reg. § 1.446-3(e).

[1089]For an extensive discussion of issues relating to credit derivatives under U.S. tax laws, including analysis of whether particular kinds of credit derivatives may be viewed as notional principal contracts, *see* Kayle, *supra* note 1044, at 221.

U. S. Withholding Taxes 361

amounts. Would provision for physical settlement disqualify a transaction as a notional principal contract?[1090]

- The definition refers to multiple amounts payable by a party at specified intervals. Do transactions providing only for a one-time payment by each of the parties qualify as notional principal contracts?[1091]

- The definition requires that at least one of the parties have payment obligations calculated by reference to a specified index. Are weather derivatives captured by this definition? If a party's own dividends or profits or the value of its stock are treated for this purpose as within the party's control and, therefore, may not be the subject of a notional principal contract entered into by that party, how would such transactions be treated?[1092]

In addition, in any analysis of the U.S. withholding tax questions, the parties must take into account that their characterization of a transaction as a notional principal contract will not be dispositive if the transaction in fact involves a financing. This concern may arise, for example, if a party makes a significant initial, final or other payment—say because the transaction is executed at an off-market rate.[1093]

Therefore, as market participants review potential U.S. withholding tax concerns relating to their OTC derivatives and negotiate their documents in light of those concerns, they should take into account that not all their derivatives transactions, and not all payments made by or to them in connection with those transactions, will necessarily be treated in the same way in all circumstances.

[1090] *See* 3 Kramer, *supra* note 1044, § 78.02[A][1], at 78-7. For example, in preparing new definitions for equity derivatives, ISDA is considering terms that would permit physically settled equity swaps. Say the periodic payments under such a transaction involved exchanges of amounts calculated by reference to an interest rate for payments calculated by reference to dividends paid on the underlying stock during the swap's specified periods but at the end of the transaction's term the parties agreed that one or the other of them would deliver a number of shares of stock calculated by reference to the increase or decline in value of the stock over a specified period, rather than a cash payment so calculated. Would some part or none of the transaction be treated as a notional principal contract under the quoted definition?

[1091] *See* 3 Kramer, *supra* note 1044, § 78.02[A][2], at 78-7 ("At least one party must have an obligation to make more than one payment if the conditions of the contract are satisfied").

[1092] These issues are pointed to in 3 Kramer, *supra* note 1044, § 78.02[D][3], at 78-9 to 78-10. Referring to Treas. Reg. § 1.446-3(c)(4)(ii), the author notes that a contract would not qualify as a notional principal contract for Section 446 purposes if the underlying were the stock value, dividends or profits of a party. The author states that the same rule would apply if the stock value, dividends or profits of a member of the same consolidated corporate group as a party were the underlying, because these entities are treated as related persons, and related persons are treated as if they were parties for purposes of determining whether the contracts have amounts calculated by reference to a permitted specified index. *Id.* § 78.02[F], at 78-11.

[1093] *See supra* p. 222 for discussion of at-the-market and off-market transactions. An off-market transaction is discussed in another context (currency swaps under Section 988 of the IRC) in the Treasury regulations as a transaction "under which the present value of the payments to be made is not equal to that of the payments to be received on the day the taxpayer enters into or acquires the contract (absent the swap premium or discount . . .)." Treas. Reg. § 1.988-2(e)(3)(i). On analysis of swaps and other OTC derivatives as having imbedded loans, *see* Treas. Reg. § 1.446-3(g)(4). In this regard, the result is likely to turn on whether the payment is "significant," a concept that is not clearly defined, although some guidance is given in examples in the Treasury regulations. *See* Treas. Reg. § 1.446-3(g)(6).

OTHER EXEMPTIONS AND REDUCED TAX RATES AND RELATED CERTIFICATIONS

A broad exemption from U.S. withholding tax applies when the withholding agent can reliably establish in a recognized manner that the relevant payment is income effectively connected with a trade or business conducted in the United States and is includible in the gross income subject to taxation in the U.S. in the relevant tax year of the beneficial owner of that income.

Reduced, or zero, rates may apply when the withholding agent can reliably establish that the beneficial owner of the income is entitled to the benefits of an income tax treaty between the United States and the country where the beneficial owner is resident for tax purposes. An additional requirement, in these cases, is that the relevant income not be effectively connected with a trade or business conducted in the United States.

As noted above, if a payment constitutes FDAP potentially subject to U.S. withholding tax, the payer, as withholding agent, will be required to report the payments it makes to a nonresident and withhold the tax, unless the withholding agent is able to determine in a manner recognized by applicable law that the reporting or withholding is not required. For purposes of determining whether withholding on account of U.S. withholding taxes is required and, if so, at what rate, on payments in connection with privately negotiated OTC derivatives, the withholding agent will generally rely on a certificate delivered by or on behalf of the beneficial owner of the relevant income on an IRS form. The certifications in these forms are made to the best of the knowledge and belief of the person making the certification and are made under penalties of perjury.

Which form is appropriate will depend on various factors. One is the nature of the payee and whether it is acting on its own behalf or as an intermediary (say, as the nominee or agent for another person) in receiving the payments. Another is whether the claim to zero or reduced withholding is based on a tax treaty or a claim that withholding is not required because the payments should be treated as income effectively connected with a trade or business conducted by the payee in the United States.

Each of the forms now used for certifications by foreign persons is a variant of IRS Form W-8.[1094] An extension at the end of the form's designation indicates the appropriate use. The following gives some examples, without seeking to provide an exhaustive list of all the relevant forms or their purposes:

- W-8IMY is designed for use, among others, by a payee certifying as to relevant matters in its capacity as an intermediary or as a foreign partnership. The nature of the certifications and the information that the intermediary or partnership must obtain and attach to the form or supply to the IRS depend in part on whether the payee is acting as a qualified intermediary,[1095] a nonqualified intermediary,[1096] a withholding foreign part-

---

[1094] The forms are available at www.irs.gov/forms_pubs/forms.html, with substantial sets of instructions.

[1095] Qualified intermediaries include foreign financial institutions and clearing organizations and may also include non-U.S. branches of U.S. financial institutions. They become qualified intermediaries by agreeing with the IRS (among other things) to collect information relating to the persons for whom they are acting (that is, their account holders or principals) and furnish it to the IRS. A qualified intermediary does not need to attach the certificates and other documentation that it obtains to a W-8IMY. Rather, it furnishes to

U. S. Withholding Taxes

nership[1097] or a nonwithholding foreign partnership,[1098] and the related responsibilities of the payer, as withholding agent, may also be affected by these variables.

- W-8EXP is designed for use by foreign governments and certain other foreign entities that are exempt from U.S. withholding taxes, when the income covered by the form is not effectively connected to the conduct of a trade or business carried on in the United States.[1099]

- W-8BEN is designed for use by a foreign person—other than one who would use one of the forms identified above—when claiming a reduced rate of, or an exemption from, U.S. withholding tax as a resident of a foreign country with which the United States has an income tax treaty. The form is submitted by the beneficial owner of the income referred to in the form, or a person authorized to act on its behalf, who certifies, among other things, as to the relevant country, that the beneficial owner of the income covered by the form is a foreign person, that the income is not effectively connected with the conduct of a trade or business in the United

---

the payer, as withholding agent, only the information sufficient to enable the payer to determine the correct amount to be withheld from amounts paid to the intermediary and reported to the IRS. It agrees to update that information as required. In a W-8IMY, a qualified intermediary certifies that it has assumed primary withholding responsibility with respect to the amounts covered by the form that are payable to the intermediary's account holders or principals. A payer making a payment to a qualified intermediary is entitled to rely on these certifications to determine whether withholding is required, and if so, at what rate, in connection with payments to the beneficial owners or payees for which the intermediary is acting. *See* IRS Form W-8IMY, Part II, and *see* 3 Kramer, *supra* note 1044, § 77.05[B][1] & [2]. There may also be agreements between a payer, as withholding agent, and U.S. branches of foreign banks and foreign insurance companies under which the latter assumes responsibility for withholding and reporting relating to payments received from the payer, and in these cases the payer will not be responsible for withholding. *See id.* § 77.05[B][4], at 77-57.

[1096]Nonqualified intermediaries are required to transmit to the payer, acting as withholding agent, the withholding certificates and other documentation obtained in support of the statements they supply to the payer, to enable the latter to determine the correct amount to be withheld from amounts paid to the intermediary and reported to the IRS. *See* IRS Form W-8IMY, Part III, and *see* 3 Kramer, *supra* note 1044, § 77.05[B][2][b], at 77-54.

[1097]Like qualified intermediaries, withholding foreign partnerships enter into agreements with the IRS. A withholding foreign partnership agrees, among other things, to act as withholding agent with respect to payments to the relevant partners and report withholdings to the IRS. It is not required to attach the certifications and other documentation it obtains from partners to the W-8IMY it gives to the payer, but it is required to file a partnership return with the IRS. *See* IRS Form W-8IMY, Part V, and *see* 3 Kramer, *supra* note 1044, § 77.05[B][3], at 77-55.

[1098]A nonwithholding foreign partnership uses W-8IMY only in cases where it can certify that the payments covered by the form are not effectively connected with the conduct of a trade or business in the United States and the partnership has provided or will provide to the payer a statement with information sufficient for the payer to determine the correct amount required to be withheld from amounts paid to the partnership and reported to the IRS. It must agree to update the statement. *See* W-8IMY, Part VI, and *see* 3 Kramer, *supra* note 1044, § 77.05[B][3], at 77-55.

[1099]*See* IRS Form W-8EXP. In addition to foreign sovereigns, central banks of issue wholly owned by foreign sovereigns may use this form, and central banks of issue not wholly owned by sovereigns may use this form for certain kinds of income. *Id.* Part II.

States[1100] and, when the form is used in connection with notional principal contracts, that the person submitting the form has provided, or will provide, and as required will update, a statement identifying those notional principal contracts the income from which is not effectively connected with the conduct of a U.S. trade or business.[1101]

- W-8ECI is designed for use by a foreign persons—other than one who would use one of the forms identified above—seeking to establish that the income covered by the form is not subject to U.S. withholding tax because the income is effectively connected with the conduct of a trade or business in the United States and is includible in gross income for the relevant taxable year. The form is submitted by the beneficial owner of the income referred to in the form or a person authorized to act on behalf of the beneficial owner, who certifies as to the foregoing and that the beneficial owner is a foreign person.[1102]

A payer treated as a withholding agent in respect of U.S. withholding tax cannot elect not to fulfill this function and, as indicated above, it may be liable for taxes that it should but does not withhold, as well as related interest and penalties, if it did not have documentation on which it could, in the circumstances, rely to determine the existence of an exemption from the tax.[1103]

In effect, if either of the parties to an OTC derivatives agreement would be required to act as a withholding agent for U.S. withholding tax purposes and to file related reports with the IRS, the IRC and Treasury regulations make it incumbent on the payee to make representations and deliver IRS forms to the payer as necessary to establish that the withholding is not required or, where relevant, to establish that payments, although subject to U.S. withholding taxes, are subject to withholding at a reduced rate.

Situations that introduce complexity into these questions arise with some frequency. The most common arises when a counterparty reserves the right to act from multiple offices in and outside the United States. Another arises when a withholding agent's counterparty is a market professional organized outside the U.S. that treats payments under transactions booked in an office outside the United States as income effectively connected with a trade or business carried on in the United States, perhaps because of a role played by the U.S. office in the negotiation or administration of the agreement.

In the first of these cases, the preference of the withholding agent will be to have an agreement that enables it clearly to identify which payments it should treat as income

---

[1100]*See* IRS Form W-8BEN, Parts II & IV.

[1101]*Id.*, Part III. The type of beneficial owner (*e.g.,* individual, corporation, partnership, trust, estate) must be completed, and additional information, including a U.S. TIN—taxpayer identification number—or a similar number issued by the beneficial owner's country of residence for tax purposes, may also be required.

[1102]*See* IRS Form W-8ECI, Part II. Other information that must be supplied includes the type of beneficial owner (*e.g.,* individual, corporation, partnership, trust, estate), the beneficial owner's U.S. taxpayer identification number and a specification of each item of income that is, or is expected to be, received from the payer that is effectively connected with the conduct of a trade or business in the U.S. *Id.* Part I.

[1103]*See supra* p. 352 on this subject and rules regarding the ability of a withholding agent to rely on certifications received by it and related matters.

received by the counterparty in connection with a trade or business conducted in the United States. In the second, the withholding agent may want further information to understand why the counterparty is so treating the income, even though it consists of payments to be made under transactions booked by the counterparty outside the United States, so that the withholding agent is comfortable that it has taken the action that a reasonably prudent withholding agent would take in the circumstances.

The withholding agent is put in a particularly uncomfortable position when a non-U.S. counterparty proposes to represent that one of two alternatives may apply to each payment it is entitled to receive under the agreement: either the payment will be income effectively connected with a trade or business conducted in the United States or the counterparty will be entitled to the benefits of an income tax treaty between the United States and another country in connection with the payments. If the counterparty proposes to stop at that and supply the withholding agent with the IRS forms that would be needed by the withholding agent in connection with both alternatives, the withholding agent is left without guidance about how it should determine the extent to which one or the other of the alternatives applies in connection with a particular payment. The difficulty, from the perspective of the withholding agent, can be illustrated by reference to the following rule stated in Treasury regulations applicable to withholding agents:

> Generally, a withholding agent can reliably associate a payment with valid documentation if, prior to the payment, it holds valid documentation (either directly or through an agent), *it can reliably determine how much of the payment relates to the valid documentation,* and it has no actual knowledge or reason to know that any of the information, certifications, or statements in, or associated with, the documentation are incorrect.[1104]

This approach may leave the withholding agent uncomfortable on the point that is italicized in the quoted language.

Especially in their dealings with non-U.S. counterparties whose circumstances pose unusual issues, withholding agents may engage in quite deliberate negotiations over the representations and tax forms that the counterparty will provide. From the perspective of the withholding agent, reaching an appropriate level of comfort on these matters is a serious matter, given the legal duties imposed by U.S. law on withholding agents and the associated risks they are exposed to if they fail to perform those duties. When the parties are documenting their relationship on an ISDA-based master agreement, they should note that the protections for withholding agents are somewhat limited.

Essentially, these protections consist in: (1) being excused from having to make gross-up payments to a counterparty to the extent of Indemnifiable Taxes that would not have been imposed but for certain circumstances involving a breach of covenant or representation as to tax matters by the counterparty;[1105] and (2) being entitled to an indemnity for taxes and interest imposed on the withholding agent—and in some cases, related penalties—if it has not made a required deduction or withholding, the liability is assessed directly against it, the counterparty itself has not paid the tax or interest and the withholding

---

[1104]Treas. Reg. § 1.1441-1(b)(2)(vii) (emphasis added).

[1105]*See* the annotation to Section 2(d)(i)(4)(A) of the sample master agreement, *infra* p. 812.

agent would not, under the parties' contract, have been required to make a gross-up payment to the counterparty if it had made the deduction or withholding.[1106] The ISDA master agreement form does not, however, include a provision that directly addresses the costs and expenses that the withholding agent may incur in, say, dealing with tax authorities over claims of under-withholding, nor does it deal with the costs and expenses associated with filing information reports with tax authorities.[1107]

[1106] *See* Section 2(d)(ii) of the sample ISDA-based agreement, *infra* p. 811.

[1107] The general provision on expenses in the ISDA master agreement forms (*see infra* p. 876) imposes indemnification obligations only on Defaulting Parties, and only in connection with the other party's enforcement or protection of its rights under the parties' agreement.

Part 2

Sample Confirmations and Product Descriptions

CONTENTS OF PART 2

Introduction to Part 2 369
Interest Rate Products
    Introduction 408
    Rate Swaps 421
    Sample Rate Swap Confirmation 427
    Caps and Floors 439
    Sample Rate Cap Confirmation 444
    Collars and Corridors 448
    Sample Rate Collar Confirmation 451
    Options on Swaps ("Swaptions") 455
    Sample Swaption Confirmation 464
    Forward Rate Agreements (FRAs) 476
    Sample FRA Confirmation 479
Currency Derivatives
    Introductory Note 484
    Currency Swaps 505
    Sample Cross-Currency Rate Swap Confirmation 508
    Forward Foreign Exchange Contracts 515
    Currency Sample Confirmation for a Deliverable FX Transaction 518
    Options 524
    Sample Confirmation for a Non-Deliverable Currency Option 531
Commodity Derivatives
    Introductory Note 543
    Sample Confirmation for a Cash-Settled Commodity Swap 574
    Sample Confirmation for a Cash-Settled Commodity Price Floor 588
    Sample Confirmation for a Cash-Settled Bullion Swap 594
    Sample Confirmation for a Physically Settled Bullion Trade 601
Credit, Debt and Equity Derivatives
    Introductory Note 605
    Shared Issues in Credit, Debt and Equity Derivatives 608
        Documentation Features Addressing Regulatory Issues 608
        Documentation Features Addressing Market Conventions
            and Problems 610
        Valuation and Settlement Conventions and Market Disruptions .. 611
            The Standard ISDA Approaches 611
            Issues Raised by the Standard Approaches 619
        Events Affecting the Underlying Debt or Equity 627
        Extraordinary Events Affecting a Reference Entity
            Credit Derivatives 630
            Equity Derivatives 632
        Early Termination in Other Special Cases 636
    Credit Default Swaps 639
        Sample Confirmation for a Credit Default Swap 687
    Equity Derivatives 717
        Sample Confirmation for an Equity Index Swap 736
    Weather Derivatives
        Introductory Note 756
        Sample Confirmation for an HDD Swap 765
        Sample Confirmation for an ATDD Cap 779

INTRODUCTION TO PART 2

This part of *Documentation for Derivatives* includes introductory notes on various segments of the OTC derivatives markets, product descriptions and sample confirmations. The aim in this progression from the general to the specific is to assist those involved with documentation in several ways.

The introductory notes seek to identify issues that arise out of the need for the derivatives structures and documentation to take into account distinctive realities of the underlying assets or instruments. So, for instance, those who engage in interest rate derivatives must consider conventions on the setting of rates and the calculation of interest in the markets for bonds, loans, deposits and other fixed-income assets. These conventions may vary depending on the currency in which the assets or instruments are denominated and the market in which they are offered. Parties dealing in credit, debt and equity derivatives must consider conventions on pricing, coupon or dividend payments and settlement in the markets for the underlying securities or other obligations, as well as the procedures for dealing with extraordinary events involving the securities or obligations and their issuers (such as bond redemptions or stock splits or combinations, mergers, spinoffs and the like). We address these special concerns in the following introductory notes on derivatives in various market segments. Each introductory note focuses on issues that are of common concern for derivatives of various kinds in the relevant market segment.

The individual product descriptions explain in general terms how the basic types of OTC derivatives are most commonly used and how they differ from other, more complex products. In this way, the product descriptions both serve as background for the sample confirmations and seek to shed light on how the basic derivatives serve as building blocks that market professionals combine to create transactions with highly refined risk/reward profiles and price structures.[1108] There is always danger in discussing OTC derivatives in general terms because they are often highly tailored to customer needs and because different names may be used for the same or similar products.[1109] The product descriptions, therefore, also identify some of this commonly used terminology.

The sample confirmations illustrate how the basic products may be documented. Most of the confirmations are prepared using forms published in the *1993/2000 ISDA Commodity Derivatives Definitions*, the *1996 Equity Derivatives Definitions*, the *1997 ISDA Bullion Definitions*, the *1997 Short Form Bullion Definitions*, the *1998 FX and Cur-*

[1108] A useful general introduction to the products is Charles W. Smithson, *A Building Block Approach to Financial Engineering: Introduction to Forwards, Futures, Swaps, Options, and Hybrid Securities*, in PLI 2001, at 9. *See also* Charles W. Smithson, *A LEGO® Approach to Financial Engineering: An Introduction to Forwards, Futures, Swaps and Options*, in HANDBOOK OF RISK MANAGEMENT 3–1.

[1109] Specialized periodicals relating to derivatives frequently report on new OTC derivatives products. A regular source for such information is the "Learning Curve" column that appears in each issue of DERIVATIVES WEEK, a publication of Institutional Investor. Selections from the column are referred to below, as are the brief descriptions of various kinds of transactions included in DICTIONARY OF RISK MANAGEMENT.

rency Option Definitions, the *1999 Credit Derivatives Definitions* with their various supplements published in 2001, and the *2000 ISDA Definitions.* The sample confirmations for weather derivatives illustrate features of forms published by WRMA but also include our own formulations on many matters.

In each case, the sample confirmation assumes the parties are documenting the illustrated transaction under a master agreement prepared using one of the forms published by ISDA in 1992. Annotated versions of ISDA's two 1992 master agreement forms appear in Parts 3 and 4 of this book.[1110] The remainder of this Introduction addresses the function of the confirmation as a supplement to a master agreement and the use of a confirmation prior to the parties' execution of a master agreement.[1111] We then turn to some of the basic concepts underlying the terminology used in ISDA's definitions and forms of confirmation.[1112] Terminology relevant for specific market segments is addressed in the introductory note for that segment, and terminology that is specific to a product is taken up in the relevant product description and annotations.

THE FUNCTIONS OF THE CONFIRMATION UNDER ISDA MASTER AGREEMENTS

Bringing the Transaction Under the Master Agreement

General. As discussed further below,[1113] the 1992 ISDA forms of master agreement adopt the "single agreement" approach to the documentation of multiple derivatives transactions. Under this approach, the master agreement sets forth the basic terms governing all transactions the parties choose to document under the master, and the confirmation is the mechanism by which the financial terms of each transaction are added to the master. Since the operative terms giving rise to the parties' rights and obligations are generally contained in the body of the master agreement, it is critical that the confirmation process provided for in the master agreement be followed.[1114] If the parties' dealing practices depart from those assumed in the standard master agreement terms, it is equally critical that they customize those terms to reflect their practices.[1115]

The Required Exchange of Confirmations. Each of the confirmation forms published by ISDA includes either introductory or concluding language that operates, together with various provisions of an ISDA-based master agreement form, to bring transactions documented using that confirmation form under the master agreement. For example, the following language appears in the opening of the form of confirmation included in the *2000 ISDA Definitions*:

[1110] *Infra* pp. 787 & 1003, respectively.

[1111] *Infra* p. 378.

[1112] *Infra* p. 381.

[1113] *See infra* p. 794. *See* the discussion of the master agreement approach to the documentation of OTC derivatives in the Introduction to Part 3, *infra* p.794, and the annotations to the recital and to Section 9(e)(ii) of the sample master agreement in Part 3, *infra* pp. 797 & 872.

[1114] *See, e.g.*, Section 2(a)(i) of the sample master agreement, in Part 3, *infra* p. 800.

[1115] *See* ISDA 2002 Operations Survey 13 on confirmation practices prevailing in the market.

Introduction to Part 2 371

> The purpose of this [letter agreement/telex] is to confirm the terms and conditions of the Transaction entered into between us on the Trade Date specified below (the "Transaction"). This letter agreement constitutes a "Confirmation" as referred to in the Agreement specified below.
>
> The definitions and provisions contained in the 2000 ISDA Definitions, as published by the International Swaps and Derivatives Association, Inc., are incorporated into this Confirmation.[1116] In the event of any inconsistency between those definitions and provisions and this Confirmation, this Confirmation will govern.
>
> This Confirmation constitutes a "Confirmation" as referred to in, and supplements, forms part of and is subject to, the ISDA Master Agreement dated as of [date], as amended and supplemented from time to time (the "Agreement") between [Name of Party A] ("Party A") and [Name of Party B] ("Party B"). All provisions contained in the Agreement govern this Confirmation except as expressly modified below.

This standard language operates with the opening recital[1117] and the section on confirmations[1118] in the relevant 1992 ISDA master agreement form to bring the Transaction reflected in the Confirmation under the master agreement. Those provisions require that the Confirmation take the form of a document executed and delivered by the parties (which may be in counterparts and may be transmitted by facsimile) or of an exchange[1119] of telexes or electronic messages, in each case that is stated (in the Confirmation itself or elsewhere) to be a "Confirmation" for purposes of the master agreement. Therefore, unless the parties agree otherwise by modifying the printed terms of the ISDA master agreement forms, without some sort of execution or exchange of confirmations identified as such, the parties' attempt to bring a transaction between them under the terms of their master agreement prepared on one of those ISDA forms may not succeed.[1120]

Out of concern over the consequences of a failure to complete the process of exchanging confirmations, some market participants modify the ISDA formulation that requires an exchange with a provision of the following sort included in the schedule to their master agreements:

[1116] A footnote to this standard language clarifies that incorporation of the *2000 ISDA Definitions* automatically constitutes incorporation of the version of the Annex to those definitions most recently published at the date the parties enter into the relevant transaction, so the parties should vary this language if they wish to incorporate a specific version of that Annex. On the contents of the *Annex to the 2000 ISDA Definitions*, see *infra* note 1192.

[1117] *See infra* p. 797 (Multicurrency—Cross Border form) and p. 1014 (Local Currency—Single Jurisdiction form).

[1118] Section 9(e) of the Multicurrency—Cross Border form, *infra* p. 872, and Section 8(e) of the Local Currency—Single Jurisdiction form, *infra* p. 1028.

[1119] *See* ISDA 2002 OPERATIONS SURVEY 13 on the methods of confirming trades that prevail in the market.

[1120] This appears to be so even though Section 9(e)(ii) of the Multicurrency—Cross Border form and Section 8(e)(ii) of the Local Currency—Single Jurisdiction form provide that the parties intend to be legally bound with respect to each Transaction "from the moment they agree" to its terms "whether orally or otherwise."

The parties hereby amend Section 9(e)(ii) of this Agreement by adding the following sentences at the end thereof: "Each party shall respond promptly to each Confirmation sent by the other party as provided herein, indicating whether the Confirmation contains any error and, if so, how the error should be corrected so that the Confirmation correctly reflects the parties' agreement with respect to the Transaction referred to in the Confirmation. A party's failure to respond [promptly] [within three Local Business Days][1121] to a Confirmation sent to it as provided in Section 12 that has become effective as provided therein shall constitute its acknowledgment that the Confirmation correctly reflects the parties' agreement on the terms of the Transaction referred to herein. The requirement of this Section and elsewhere in this Agreement that the parties exchange Confirmations shall for all purposes be deemed satisfied by a Confirmation sent and an acknowledgment deemed given as provided in this Section.[1122]

In a more general approach to the same concern, some market participants may choose to modify the standard recital to the 1987 and 1992 ISDA master agreement forms to indicate that the parties' agreement will treat as Transactions those provided for in "documents and other confirming evidence" if they are either exchanged between the parties or are otherwise effective under the terms of their agreement or applicable law to evidence the existence of a transaction between the parties. In its projected revision to the 1992 master agreement forms, ISDA is considering an approach along these lines.

Users of the ISDA forms of master agreement should consult with counsel about whether any such alternative approach, without an exchange of confirmations, will satisfy a potentially applicable statute of frauds.[1123] Market participants should also consider whether the ISDA 1992 agreement approach to bringing a transaction under a master agreement may require modification, through part 5 of the schedule to their master agreements, in light of the ways in which they conduct their derivatives dealings, including electronic messaging and trade matching systems.[1124]

Given the widespread practice in the OTC derivatives markets of reaching agreement orally and then recording the terms agreed to in a confirmation, it is important to

---

[1121] Three Business Days is the period provided for in a provision on this subject included in the FEOMA (§ 11.15), ICOM (§ 11.15) and IFEMA (§ 8.15) forms prepared for use with FX spot and forward transactions and currency options. *See supra* p. 48 on the period contemplated in special provisions of New York's statutes of frauds applicable to many OTC derivatives.

[1122] The references to section numbers in the sample language assume use of the Multicurrency—Cross Border ISDA form of master agreement.

[1123] *See* the annotations to Section 9(e)(ii) of the sample agreement in Part 3, *infra* p. 872. *See also* Chapter 2, *supra* p. 39.

[1124] One of the methods contemplated for exchanges of confirmations in the 1992 ISDA forms is electronic messaging. Because of the concern that the limitations of electronic messaging systems might make it difficult for the parties to satisfy the requirement that the confirmation identify itself as a confirmation under a specific master agreement, market participants often modify the standard ISDA provisions on confirmations when they intend to use these systems to execute transactions. On this and related subjects, *see* Part 5(c) of the schedule to the sample agreement in Part 3 and related annotations, *infra* p. 930.

draw a distinction between the confirmation process and the process of contract formation, which consists of offer and acceptance. When agreement on a derivatives transaction is reached orally by the parties, the process of contract formation is complete unless the parties' understanding is to the contrary, assuming the oral offer and acceptance express terms sufficient for an agreement with respect to the relevant kind of transaction. The confirmation memorializes that oral contract and may be required to satisfy a statute of frauds for the contract to be enforceable as such, as described more fully in Chapter 2.[1125] The confirmation is not an offer that still requires acceptance for a contract to exist. The distinction is important because market practice is to treat a contract as in existence, and to rely on its existence, from the moment the "trade" is completed, orally or otherwise.[1126]

As noted above, under the approach prescribed by the standard provisions in ISDA's 1987 and 1992 master agreement forms, a Confirmation must be identified by the parties as such. The mere fact that the parties have entered into a master agreement using a 1987 or 1992 ISDA form does not give rise to a contractual presumption that all OTC derivatives between the parties will necessarily be documented under that master agreement, although the parties' unwritten understanding may be that this will be the case, or that it will be the case for all derivatives of certain types. Therefore, in using one of these forms, the parties must either modify the standard rule or be extremely careful to include in their confirmations (or elsewhere in the documentation) the following sentence, or a variant, tying the confirmation to the master agreement: "This [letter agreement] [document] [Confirmation] constitutes a 'Confirmation' as referred to in the ISDA Master Agreement dated as of [date], as amended and supplemented from time to time (the "Agreement") between [Name of Party A ('Party A') and [Name of Party B] ('Party B')."

This feature of the 1987 and 1992 ISDA master agreement forms reflects their design for use with any kind of transaction that the parties choose to bring under their master agreement. Other, product-specific standard master agreements—such as the FEOMA, ICOM and IFEMA forms—operate with a contractual presumption that all transactions between the parties, when acting from offices specified by them in their master agreement, will be governed by that agreement so long as the transactions are of a type that the agreement covers, unless the parties otherwise expressly agree in connection with the transaction.[1127] The EMA form is something of a hybrid in this regard since, like the

---

[1125] *Supra* p. 39.

[1126] *See* the annotation to Section 9(e) of the sample master agreement in Part 3, *infra* p. 872, and Chapter 2, *supra* p. 39. The Australian Bankers' Association, the Australian Society of Corporate Treasurers Limited and the Australian Financial Markets Association have published a Telephone Dealing Supplement for use with master agreements, including agreements on ISDA's forms, to clarify the parties' understanding on procedures to be followed in effecting trades by telephone.

[1127] Section 2.1 of each of the FEOMA, ICOM and IFEMA forms states this rebuttable presumption. Like the ISDA master agreement forms, the EMA form was prepared to accommodate unlimited types of transactions and, therefore, does not include any presumption about the transactions that will be governed by a master agreement prepared using that form. Section 1(a) of the EMA General Provisions states that "[t]he provisions of a Master Agreement [prepared using those EMA General Provisions] shall apply to the extent that they are incorporated by the parties into the terms of a Transaction or type of Transactions between them." The reference to the incorporation of the General Provisions into Transactions facilitates use of the form in cases in which the General Provisions are presumed to apply to all transactions between the parties that fall within any of the categories covered by a product-specific Annex adopted by the parties for purposes of their master agreement.

ISDA master agreement forms, the EMA form contemplates the application of its basic terms, as embodied in its General Provisions, to any "financial transaction" to the extent the General Provisions are incorporated by the parties into that transaction's terms, but it also provides for the application of the General Provisions to agreed types of transactions. Each product-specific Annex includes the presumption that, if the parties (using Special Provisions that function like the schedule to an ISDA master agreement) adopt the Annex as part of their master agreement, all their mutual dealings in that product through the specified booking offices will be governed by that master agreement.[1128]

Users of the ISDA master agreement forms can easily customize their agreements to have their master agreement automatically apply to their mutual dealings in specified kinds of transactions unless they expressly override that presumption in connection with a particular transaction. The schedule to the sample agreement in Part 3 of this book illustrates one way in which this may be done.[1129]

Identifying the Transaction as Covered by the Definitions Incorporated in the Confirmation. As part of the process of bringing an OTC derivatives transaction under a master agreement prepared using one of the 1992 ISDA forms, the parties are likely to identify the transaction referred to in the confirmation as a "Transaction," because this is the way the transactions covered by the form are referred to in the form.[1130] Identification of the derivatives transaction being confirmed must, however, also be done so that the transaction is properly identified for purposes of any set of definitions or terms that the parties incorporate by reference into the confirmation. The various sets of definitions refer in their own ways to the kinds of derivatives they cover:

ISDA Definitions	Transactions Covered
1991 ISDA Definitions	Swap Transactions, including those identified as Options Transactions
1992 ISDA U.S. Municipal Counterparty Definitions	Transactions; these definitions do not include provisions on options applicable for "swaptions"
1992 ISDA FX and Currency Option Definitions	FX Transactions, Currency Options

---

[1128] This framework is created through Section 1(a) of the EMA General Provisions and the provision on "Applicability" in the relevant Product Annex. EMA Section 1(a) states that "[t]he provisions of a Master Agreement [prepared using those EMA General Provisions] shall apply to the extent that they are incorporated by the parties into the terms of a Transaction or type of Transactions between them."

[1129] *See* Part 5(a) of the sample schedule in Part 3 and related annotations, *infra* p. 926.

[1130] The analogous terms under ISDA's 1987 Interest Rate and Currency Exchange Agreement form and Rate Swap Agreement form were "Swap Transaction" and "Rate Swap Transaction."

Introduction to Part 2

ISDA Definitions	Transactions Covered
1993/2000 ISDA Commodity Derivatives Definitions	Transactions, including any commodity swap transaction, cross-commodity swap transaction, commodity cap, floor or collar transaction, commodity option transaction or any other similar transaction, including any Option with respect to any such transaction (understood to include a cash-settled option transaction in respect of commodity prices, a Swaption to enter into, or to pay a Cash Settlement Amount in respect of, any such Transaction and other transactions identified as Options)
1996 Equity Derivatives Definitions	Transactions, including Index Option Transactions, Share Option Transactions, Index Basket Option Transactions, Share Basket Option Transactions, Index Swap Transactions, Share Swap Transactions, Index Basket Swap Transactions and Share Basket Swap Transactions
1997 ISDA Bullion Definitions	Transactions, including bullion trades, bullion options, bullion swaps and swaptions
1998 FX and Currency Option Definitions	Transactions, including Deliverable FX Transactions, Non-Deliverable FX Transactions, Deliverable Currency Option Transactions and Non-Deliverable Currency Option Transactions
1997 Government Bond Option Definitions	Government Bond Option Transactions, including OTC options relating to bonds or any other debt securities issued by a government, governmental entity, agency or subdivision or a transactional or supranational organization
2000 ISDA Definitions	Swap Transactions, including Swaptions and Swap Transactions subject to Optional Early Termination (but not including commodity swaps, or options, currency options or caps, floors or collars other than on interest rates)

Because each of these sets of definitions, with its special nomenclature, is carefully tailored to fit a particular type or types of transactions, it is of course important to ensure that each transaction documented using the terminology from a particular set of definitions satisfies the criteria set forth in those definitions. For example, although the *2000 ISDA Definitions* refer to "Option Transactions," the term is intended only to refer to transactions that create rights to enter into, terminate early or otherwise modify other Swap Transactions. The definitions do not include provisions that would normally be used in documenting other kinds of options, or synthetic options, and the parties may find that they have not succeeded in achieving their goals if they choose to document one of these other kinds of options using those definitions rather than, say, the *1996 Equity Derivatives Definitions* or the *1997 Government Bond Option Definitions.*

The *2000 ISDA Definitions* are stated to cover listed types of "Swap Transactions," "similar" transactions and other transactions identified in confirmations as Swap Transactions. If the parties wish to use those definitions to document a Transaction that is neither clearly included in the list nor necessarily similar to the listed transactions, for the confirmation should state that the transaction is a "Swap Transaction." It should be noted, however, that the 1992 ISDA master agreement forms refer to "Transactions" and not to "Swap Transactions," so that Confirmations of Transactions under agreements based on those forms normally describe the transactions they cover as "Transactions" rather than "Swap Transactions." Therefore, when market participants incorporate the *2000 ISDA Definitions* into a confirmation, they often add language like that set forth in the second sentence below to clarify the linkage between the Transaction being confirmed and those definitions:

> The definitions and provisions contained in the *2000 ISDA Definitions* (as published by the International Swaps and Derivatives Association, Inc.) are incorporated into this Confirmation. For these purposes, all references in those Definitions to a "Swap Transaction" shall be deemed to apply to the Transaction referred to herein.

The modification is not necessary or appropriate when definitions other than the *1991 ISDA Definitions* or the *2000 ISDA Definitions* are incorporated by reference into a confirmation and, as noted, it is also not necessary when those definitions are used if the Transaction being confirmed is clearly within their definition of "Swap Transaction."

Modifying the Terms of the Master Agreement

A confirmation may also be used to modify the terms of a master agreement. If the parties wish to use a confirmation for that purpose, they may do so by adding a provision along these lines before the standard closing for confirmations recommended in the ISDA forms:

> 3. The terms of the Agreement specified below are hereby amended as set forth below [for purposes of the Transaction confirmed herein]:
>
> (a) [Section __ of the Agreement][The definition of the term "___" set forth in Section __ of [the Agreement][, as modified in Part __ of the Schedule,] is hereby amended. . . .

(b) The following is hereby made a part of the Agreement: . . .

(c) Section __ shall have no effect for purposes of the Transaction confirmed herein.

The use of the confirmation for this purpose is expressly contemplated in ISDA's standard forms of confirmation, each of which includes some variant of the following sentence: "All provisions contained in the Agreement govern this Confirmation except as expressly modified below."[1131] The use of a confirmation to modify a master agreement's terms is also contemplated in Section 1(b) of the 1992 ISDA master agreement forms, the second part of which provides: "In the event of any inconsistency between the provisions of any Confirmation and this Master Agreement (including the Schedule), such Confirmation will prevail for the purpose of the relevant Transaction."

The rule on inconsistencies is not the same under other standard market agreements for OTC derivatives. The FEOMA, ICOM and IFEMA forms provide, for example, that as to some matters a confirmation will not override the terms of a master agreement to the extent there are inconsistencies between the two.[1132] Those who use confirmations to modify the terms of a master agreement prepared using an ISDA form should also remember that, as discussed above, the 1992 ISDA forms require execution or an exchange of confirmations, unless the parties have created an exception to the standard ISDA rule on this subject.[1133]

[1131] *See, e.g., infra* pp. 508 & 575.

[1132] Section 2.4 of the FEOMA form provides: "In the event of any inconsistency between the terms of a Confirmation and the other provisions of the Agreement, (i) in the case of an FX Transaction, the other provisions of the Agreement shall prevail, and the Confirmation shall not modify the other terms of the Agreement and (ii) in the case of an Option, the terms of the Confirmation shall prevail, and the other terms of the Agreement shall be deemed modified with respect to such Option, except for the manner of confirmation under Section 2.3 and, if applicable, discharge of Options under Section 4." Parallel provisions appear in Section 2.4 of the ICOM and IFEMA forms. *See infra* p. 947 on the FEOMA and ICOM provisions on the discharge of Options. ISDA, EMTA and the Foreign Exchange Committee have published forms of Addendum that may be used to vary these rules and to adopt the *1998 FX and Currency Option Definitions* as applicable to the parties' FX spot and forward transactions (FX Transactions and currency options (Options) governed by their master agreement. *See, e.g., http://www.newyorkfed.org/fmlg/feomaadd.pdf.* Under the approach set out in Section 3 of the Addendum for use with a FEOMA-based agreement, in the event of any inconsistency between the terms of a Confirmation for a Non-Deliverable FX Transaction and the terms of the parties' master agreement, the terms of the Confirmation would prevail, but the same would be true with respect to a Deliverable FX Transaction only if "either the Confirmation explicitly states that it shall so prevail and has been signed by both Parties or Confirmations so stating have been exchanged" by the parties as provided in their master agreement.

[1133] *See supra* p. 370. An agreement to override the master agreement's requirement of an exchange of confirmations for this purpose would itself have to satisfy the master agreement terms providing that effective amendments and modifications of the master agreement must be in writing and executed by the parties or confirmed by an exchange of telexes or electronic messages on an electronic messaging system. *See* Section 9(b) of the Multicurrency—Cross Border form, *infra* p. 871, and Section 8(b) of the Local Currency—Single Jurisdiction form, *infra* p. 1028.

Completing the Terms of the Master Agreement

The confirmation sometimes serves the additional function of supplying information called for by the terms of the master agreement. For example, Section 2(c) of each of the 1992 ISDA master agreement forms indicates how the parties may elect to implement cross-transaction netting in the schedule to their master agreement or in a confirmation. If they are silent on the subject, these master agreement forms do not provide for payment netting across transactions—that is, an obligation of Party A to make a payment due under one transaction will (subject to setoff rights that might otherwise be available) be payable as a gross amount even though on the same day Party B owes Party A an amount in the same currency under a second transaction.

When the parties wish to provide for cross-transactional netting of some but not all of the kinds of transactions between them, they often express their decision in both the schedule and the confirmation. For example, if the parties have elected that cross-transactional netting will apply to all their rate swaps, caps, collars and floors, as a group, and to all their commodity swaps, caps, collars and floors, as a group, but not otherwise, they might so indicate in paragraph (i) of Part 4 of the schedule to their master agreement and use each confirmation to identify the specific transaction as falling within one of those groups. This is often done either as a heading to the confirmation (as illustrated in the sample confirmations set forth below) or through a modification to paragraph 2 of the form of confirmation, as follows:

> [For purposes of paragraph (i) of Part 4 of the Schedule to the Agreement,] the Transaction to which this Confirmation relates is a _____. The terms of this Transaction are as follows:]

The same format, or a heading to a confirmation, may also be used if the transaction being confirmed must be identified in a particular way for purposes of the set of definitions incorporated by reference into the confirmation. For example, the *2000 ISDA Definitions* define the term "Swaption" to be a transaction identified as such in a confirmation. Some market participants also use the confirmation as a means of identifying the transaction it documents as one covered by (or excluded from the coverage of) a credit support document, or of supplying information that may be relevant under a credit support document.

USE OF THE CONFIRMATION BEFORE EXECUTION OF A MASTER AGREEMENT

It is not unusual for the first OTC derivatives transaction between two parties to be agreed to before they have entered into a written agreement. In these circumstances, market participants often use a modified version of an ISDA form of confirmation to express their binding agreement with respect to the transaction until the confirmation is superseded by or made part of a master agreement executed by the parties.

No change will be required to the second part of the standard form of confirmation, which is used to state the financial terms of the transaction, if one of ISDA's sets of definitions is incorporated by reference into the confirmation and the terminology of those definitions is used to state the financial terms in short form, as illustrated in the sample confirmations included below. However, the standard form of confirmation must be expanded to include basic operative provisions that would normally have been supplied by

Introduction to Part 2 379

the master agreement.[1134] At a minimum, the confirmation must include a statement of the parties' basic payment obligations, which can be modeled on Section 2(a) and Section 2(c) of the ISDA master agreement forms or can be stated simply along the following lines, if the parties' names have been set forth earlier in the confirmation. Market participants also often include a netting formulation along these lines, if it satisfies the requirements of applicable law, and make their obligations subject to the conditions precedent suggested below:

> Each of the parties shall pay each amount stated herein to be payable by it for value on the date that amount is stated herein to be payable by it, and in the specified currency, to the account specified below for the intended payee, or such other account as may be specified by notice to the other party, subject to the following: (a) any amounts otherwise payable hereunder by each of the parties to the other in the same currency on the same date shall be netted and payable only to the extent they do not cancel each other out through netting; and (b) neither party shall be under any obligation to make any payment hereunder on any date (i) if it has designated an early termination date as provided herein on the ground of any Event of Default with respect to the other party or (ii) any amount payable hereunder to it by that other party on or before that date has not been tendered or paid, together with interest at the Default Rate specified below and calculated as specified below.[1135]

If withholding tax concerns exist[1136] some form of the "gross-up" obligation stated in Section 2(d) of the ISDA Multicurrency—Cross Border form should be included, with appropriate exceptions.[1137] Any applicable requirement that a party deliver any form required to enable the other party to make payments in respect of the transaction without withholding, or subject to withholding at a reduced rate, should also be reflected. Moreover, as suggested by the formulation set forth above, the parties should consider including abbreviated versions of provisions (including Events of Default) relating to the right to designate an early termination date, payments to be made in connection with early termination, any applicable conditions to a party's obligation to making payments, the parties' choice of the law to govern their agreement, a choice of forum and submission to the ju-

---

[1134] *See* Barry Taylor-Brill, *Negotiating and Opining on ISDA Masters*, *in* PLI 2000, at 71, 83.

[1135] USER'S GUIDE TO THE ISDA 1992 MASTER AGREEMENTS 38 includes a similar suggested approach. To state the Default Rate and interest obligation contemplated in this formulation the parties might include in their confirmation a paragraph like the following, which has been drafted using terminology from the *2000 ISDA Definitions*: "Interest on Overdue Amounts: If any amount is not paid as and when due hereunder, interest shall accrue thereon (both before and after judgment) for each day from and including the due date stated herein and to but excluding the day the amount is paid in full at a rate per annum equal to the sum of 1% and the Relevant Rate for that day determined using the USD-Federal Funds H.15 Floating Rate Option and treating that day as a Reset Date. Such interest shall be payable from time to time on demand and calculated on the basis of an Actual/360 Day Count Fraction."

[1136] *See* Chapter 8, *supra* p. 350, and the annotations to Section 2(d) to the sample master agreement in Part 3, *infra* p. 812.

[1137] In addition to the discussion referred to in the preceding footnote, *see infra* p. 1167 on taxes that may have to be withheld from payments made in respect of collateral.

risdiction of the appropriate courts, as well as any appropriate provisions relating to required credit support documents.

Some market participants deal with these subjects by incorporating specific terms of an ISDA form of master agreement into the interim confirmation or by spelling out their own formulations on the subjects they believe critical. The prevailing market practice is to deal with these subjects by temporarily adopting an ISDA form of master agreement as published, with only a minimal statement of critical choices, pending execution of the parties' definitive master agreement. The *User's Guide to the 1992 ISDA Master Agreements*[1138] discusses one such approach, and other formulations of the approach are included in footnotes to the forms of confirmation included in many of the sets of ISDA definitions.[1139] The following is an example from the second footnote to Exhibit I to the *2000 ISDA Definitions:*

> This Confirmation evidences a complete and binding agreement between you and us as to the terms of the Swap Transaction to which this Confirmation relates. In addition, you and we agree to use all reasonable efforts promptly to negotiate, execute and deliver an agreement in the form of the ISDA Master Agreement (Multicurrency—Cross Border) (the "ISDA Form"), with such modifications as you and we will in good faith agree. Upon the execution by you and us of such an agreement, this Confirmation will supplement, form a part of and be subject to that agreement. All provisions contained in or incorporated by reference in that agreement upon its execution will govern this Confirmation except as expressly modified below. Until we execute and deliver that agreement, this Confirmation, together will all other documents referring to the ISDA Form (each a "Confirmation") confirming transactions (each a "Transaction") entered into between us (notwithstanding anything to the contrary in a Confirmation) shall supplement, form a part of, and be subject to, an agreement in the form of the ISDA Form as if we had executed an agreement in such form (but without any Schedule except for the election of [English law] [the laws of the State of New York] as the governing law and [specify currency] as the Termination Currency) on the Trade Date of the first such Transaction between us. In the event of any inconsistency between the provision of that agreement and this Confirmation, this Confirmation will prevail for purposes of this Swap Transaction.

Many variants of this provision are used in the market. When the parties use one of these clauses, they should pay close attention to how the confirmation refers to their intention to enter into a master agreement at a later time. It is usual, as illustrated, for the parties to state their intention and to promise to use "all reasonable efforts" to conclude

---

[1138] At 38–39.

[1139] Using this approach over time without ever executing a master agreement can prove problematic when the formulation used differs from transaction to transaction. *See Indosuez Int'l Fin. B.V. v. National Reserve Bank,* 2002 N.Y. LEXIS 1097 (N.Y. 2002), a case where 10 of the 14 confirmations of the parties' NDF transactions included a choice of New York law while the others included a choice of English law, and six included New York forum selection clauses while the other eight either contained no forum selection clause or contained clauses designating English or other courts.

Introduction to Part 2 381

their negotiations and execute the agreement promptly. Nothing should be stated that might give rise to an inference that execution of the master agreement is a condition precedent to the parties' obligations with respect to the transaction being confirmed, or that their failure to enter into the agreement by a certain date will give rise to a right to terminate the transaction. Indeed, the parties usually state—as in the quoted ISDA text—that the confirmation (as supplemented by the terms, if any, incorporated by reference into it) constitutes a complete and binding expression of the parties' agreement with respect to the subject matter set forth therein.[1140]

Those who take the general approach suggested by the quoted ISDA provision should also consider how to deal with the possibility that they may enter into multiple transactions before executing a master agreement. As illustrated, the standard ISDA text seeks to establish that, if the parties enter into multiple confirmations temporarily adopting the same ISDA master agreement form before they have executed their definitive master agreement, all those confirmations will form part of a single master agreement, rather than a series of separate agreements, each with its own incorporation of the same published ISDA terms. Although this is generally the parties' intent, that is not necessarily the case, so it may be appropriate to modify the standard ISDA language to deal with cases in which the parties may wish to isolate a transaction from their other dealings with each other.

CERTAIN BASIC CONCEPTS APPLICABLE IN CONFIRMING TRANSACTIONS

As illustrated in the sample confirmations included below, the ISDA sets of definitions make it possible to use certain basic concepts to set forth the financial terms of many different kinds of OTC derivatives. This section includes a brief description of some of those common concepts and of how they are generally used within the framework of the ISDA definitions.[1141] If the parties wish to use an ISDA term in a manner other than that contemplated in ISDA's definitions, they may modify the definition of that term in the relevant confirmation.

TERM

The concept of a Transaction's Term is relevant to many, but not all, derivatives products commonly documented using standard definitions published by ISDA and others. Most swaps and related products (such as caps, floors and FRAs) are documented within the ISDA framework described below, which involves the Term concept. The concept is not, however, used in documenting spot, forward and option transactions under the

---

[1140] *See supra* p. 59.

[1141] When we use capitalized terms in the following descriptions, we intend them to have the meanings given to them in the *2000 ISDA Definitions*, unless we expressly say otherwise. A general exception to this rule is our use of the term "Transaction." As noted above, the *2000 ISDA Definitions* are stated to apply to "Swap Transactions." Since the 1992 ISDA master agreement forms both use "Transaction" to refer to any transaction documented using either such form, we will be using that term and assume that the reader understands that a technical correction might be required, as described in the preceding discussion in this Introduction, for some kinds of Transactions documented under a 1992 ISDA form to be treated as "Swap Transactions" for purposes of the *2000 ISDA Definitions*.

1998 FX and Currency Option Definitions, nor is it used in the *1996 Equity Derivatives Definitions.*

Where "Term" is used, it is the period that begins on the Effective Date and ends on the Termination Date of the Transaction. This is the case under the *2000 ISDA Definitions* (as it was under the *1991 ISDA Definitions*) and is also the case under the *1993/2000 ISDA Commodity Derivatives Definitions.* The parties generally do not identify the Term of their Transactions as such in their confirmations. They simply specify an Effective Date and a Termination Date.

Definitions that relate to calculating the basic amounts payable in connection with certain kinds of Transactions may operate by reference to the Transaction's Term. For example, in interest rate and currency swaps and similar products, Floating Amounts and Fixed Amounts are often stated to be payable with respect to Calculation Periods, and every Calculation Period must begin and end within the Term of the relevant Transaction, under the ISDA approach. This presumption generally works as the parties expect in simple transactions documented using the ISDA definitions that adopt the concept of the Term. For example, in a conventional Fixed/LIBOR U.S. dollar interest rate swap, both the fixed-rate payer and the floating-rate payer would expect the last of their obligations to be calculated on the agreed notional amount in respect of a final Calculation Period ending on and excluding the stated Termination Date. Their transaction reallocates risks related to changes in interest rates over that period.[1142]

Similarly, in a simple credit default swap, the payments due periodically to the Seller of the protection are calculated in respect of Calculation Periods over the swap's Term, which ends either on the Specified Termination Date or, in some cases, on an earlier date—the Event Determination Date—if a Credit Event has occurred in relation to a Reference Entity and the agreed Conditions to Payment for a settlement with the Buyer have been satisfied.[1143] The Seller is, generally speaking, assuming risks associated with Credit Events that occur during the Term[1144] and the Buyer, in exchange for protection against those risks, agrees to pay the Seller Fixed Amounts—the premium for the protection—calculated through, and including, the last day of that Term (that is, including the last day on which there can be an event that may give rise to a payment from the Seller to the Buyer).

The approach will not, however, necessarily work exactly as the parties—or one of them—may intend in more complex products. Take, for example, a complex credit default swap involving multiple Reference Entities, where the total exposure that the Seller is agreeing to assume in exchange for premium is viewed on a portfolio basis, rather than as the simple sum of the individual exposures being assumed in respect of the Reference Entities. For example, the Seller might agree to make an aggregate amount of payments of

---

[1142]*See infra* p. 421 for the product description of interest rate swaps.

[1143]*See infra* p. 668 on the various possibilities in this regard under the *1999 Credit Derivatives Definitions.*

[1144]In cases involving the Credit Event referred to as "Failure to Pay," the Seller may also be assuming risks associated with missed payments that occur during the Transaction's Term but do not actually ripen into Credit Events until later because the end of the Term occurs before an applicable grace period has expired. *See infra* p. 647.

up to $50 million in connection with Credit Events affecting any of 100 Reference Entities, not to exceed $5 million for any individual Reference Entity. If the Seller has negotiated for its premium (the Fixed Amounts) by reference to the total, blended risk represented by the pool of Reference Entities—given its analysis of such factors as the diversification of the risk represented by the pool (by Reference Entity debt ratings, industry, region, etc.) and any portion of the pool risk that the Buyer is retaining before the Seller is ever required to make a payment—the Seller's view could logically be that the Fixed Amounts it is entitled to receive should be reduced only as, and to the extent that, the actual amounts payable by it are determined, if after any particular Credit Event it will still be exposed to having to make payments in respect of Credit Events affecting other Reference Entities. Viewing the Transaction as if it were the simple sum of separate credit default derivatives relating to the individual Reference Entities and applying the standard ISDA presumptions relating to Term, Termination Date and the calculation of Fixed Amounts would not produce this result.[1145]

Floating Amounts and Fixed Amounts can also be stated to be payable with respect to Payment Dates. When the ISDA concept of Term applies, each Payment Date too must fall within the Term of a Transaction or be a specified number of days after the end of the last Calculation Period for the Transaction—that is, after the Termination Date. There are exceptions to these rules. A Fixed Amount payable in connection with a Transaction involving a cap rate or a floor rate may, for example, be payable on a Payment Date stated to occur prior to the Effective Date of the Transaction.

Because the Term of a Transaction does not begin until its Effective Date, for some purposes some market participants adopt another term—such as "Outstanding Transaction"—to refer to Transactions whose Trade Dates have occurred but whose Effective Dates have not. This need may arise in the context of provisions that are meant to apply at all times when a Transaction involves credit exposure, because the potential for loss to a party arises once the Trade Date has occurred, as further discussed below under "Trade Date." For example, because of this potential for loss, the Trade Date, and not the Effective Date, is the point at which guaranty or other credit support coverage should begin to apply, or at which the parties should begin to determine any obligations they may have to deliver credit support from time to time, in cases in which the delivery obligation does not arise until exposure to loss has surpassed an agreed *de minimis* threshold.

By the same token, credit exposure does not necessarily end on the last day of the Term of a Transaction (its Termination Date) or on its Early Termination Date, when a Transaction is wound up prematurely. A Transaction continues to involve credit exposure so long as either party has any remaining obligations in respect of the Transaction. Therefore, when market participants find a term like "Outstanding Transaction" useful in their derivatives documentation (say, for purposes of the applicability of financial covenants or the like or for purposes of a credit support document), the term may appropriately be defined to be each Transaction whose Trade Date has occurred and in respect of which either party has any remaining payment or delivery obligations, whether under Section 2(a) of an ISDA-based master agreement, under the provisions of Section 6 relating to early

---

[1145]*See infra* p. 642 on the calculation of the Fixed Amounts under the *1999 Credit Derivatives Definitions*.

termination or under other provisions relating to tax gross-up or indemnity payments, interest on overdue amounts or expenses related to enforcement of rights.

EFFECTIVE DATE AND TERMINATION DATE

As indicated above,[1146] these ISDA terms define the limits of the Term of a Transaction, when the concept of Term is relevant. In the context of many OTC derivatives, the Effective Date and the Termination Date are like the disbursement date and the maturity date of a loan. Just as interest on a loan usually begins to accrue on the loan's disbursement date and is generally calculated to but excluding its maturity date, the Floating Amounts and Fixed Amounts for certain kinds of derivatives transactions are calculated from and including the Effective Date and to but excluding the Termination Date of the Transaction, subject to earlier termination of the Transaction.[1147] There is a presumption in the ISDA framework that the Termination Date for a Transaction will be fixed on a stated day, even if that day falls in a weekend or on a bank holiday. To overcome that presumption, it is not enough for the parties to state that a particular Business Day Convention is applicable to a Transaction; they must also expressly indicate that the convention is applicable for purposes of adjusting the Termination Date. *See* Section 3.3 of the *1992 ISDA U.S. Municipal Counterparty Definitions*, Section 3.3 of the *2000 ISDA Definitions* and Section 3.5 of the *1993/2000 ISDA Commodity Derivatives Definitions*.

Although the Termination Date is the last day considered in calculating basic payments in respect of a Transaction for which the term has relevance, the Termination Date is not necessarily the last day on which such a Transaction may involve credit exposure, as discussed above.

TRADE DATE

Under the *1992 ISDA U.S. Municipal Counterparty Definitions*, the *1993/2000 ISDA Commodity Derivatives Definitions*, the *1997 ISDA Bullion Definitions*, the *1997 Government Bond Option Definitions*, the *1998 FX and Currency Option Definitions*, the *1999 Credit Derivatives Definitions* and the *2000 ISDA Definitions* the Trade Date for a Transaction is the day the parties enter into the Transaction. In connection with FX Transactions, "Trade Date," "Contract Date," "Create Date," and "Deal Date" can be used interchangeably to express the same concept. Under the *1997 ISDA Bullion Definitions*, "Trade Date" and "Contract Date" are synonymous.

In American style options documented under many of the sets of ISDA standard terms, unless the parties agree otherwise, the Trade Date of a Transaction is also automatically the first day of the Exercise Period—also called the Commencement Date—during which the option may be exercised. This is the case under the *1996 Equity Derivatives Definitions*, the *1997 ISDA Bullion Definitions*, the *1997 Government Bond Option Definitions* and the *1998 FX and Currency Option Definitions*. There is no presumption on this subject in the *1993/2000 ISDA Commodity Derivatives Definitions*,

---

[1146] *Supra* p. 381.

[1147] *Cf.* Annotation 11 to the sample annotated credit default swap confirmation, *infra* p. 691, discussing why the final Fixed Rate Payer Calculation Period in a transaction of that kind includes the Scheduled Termination Date (or, if earlier, the Event Determination Date).

however, so when they use these definitions to document an American style option, the parties must specify when the Exercise Period begins.

In cases in which the ISDA concept of Term is relevant to the calculation of the parties' basic obligations, as described above, the Trade Date does not necessarily need to be within the Transaction's Term. Indeed, the Effective Date of a Transaction often occurs after the Transaction's Trade Date. This is so, for example, with "delayed start" swaps, caps, floors and similar Transactions (including some varieties referred to as "spread-lock transactions."[1148] The Effective Date also always occurs after the Trade Date in FRA Transactions[1149] and similar transactions involving foreign exchange, forward exchange agreements or "FXAs".[1150] In addition, in swap Transactions that involve a U.S. dollar LIBO rate, the Effective Date is often two London Business Days after the Trade Date, and the Floating Rate for the first Calculation Period is set on the Trade Date. *See* the introductory note on interest rate derivatives[1151] with respect to related rate setting conventions in the London interbank market.

Once the parties have entered into a Transaction, it is assumed that they may enter into other arrangements in reliance on the existence of a binding agreement between them relating to the Transaction, whether or not the Effective Date of the Transaction has occurred. As a result, once the Trade Date for a Transaction has occurred (assuming the Transaction has been correctly brought under an ISDA-based master agreement), the provisions on early termination will apply to the Transaction, whether or not the Term of the Transaction has begun, since it is assumed that one or the other of the parties may incur damages (*e.g.*, in replacing the Transaction or unwinding related arrangements entered into on the Trade Date) if the Transaction is terminated prematurely, whether or not its Effective Date has occurred.

The Trade Date is also important for purposes of the section on representations in the ISDA master agreement forms (Section 3): that section provides that the representations made by the parties in the master agreement are repeated on each date on which they enter into a Transaction.

NOTIONAL AMOUNT, NOTIONAL QUANTITY AND CURRENCY AMOUNT

The Fixed Amounts and Floating Amounts calculated in connection with some kinds of Transactions within the ISDA framework are calculated by reference to the Notional Amounts, Notional Quantities or Currency Amounts agreed for the Transactions. The analogous concept in the loan context is the principal amount, in that the notional concept is used to calculate periodic payments due in many derivatives transactions in the manner in which the principal amount of a loan is used as the base for calculating interest. Notional Amounts are used in connection with interest rate and currency swaps and

---

[1148]*See* DICTIONARY OF RISK MANAGEMENT 259.

[1149]*See* the sample FRA confirmation, *infra* p. 479.

[1150]*See Forward Exchange Agreements*, DERIVATIVES WEEK, Sept. 21, 1992, at 9 (Learning Curve column).

[1151]*Infra* p. 408.

similar OTC derivatives and in what are often referred to as the interest rate legs of other kinds of derivatives, such as total return swaps.

Notional Amounts (and, sometimes, Equity Notional Amounts) are used in equity-linked index derivatives. Notional Quantities are used in commodity swaps and the like, and Currency Amounts are used in currency swaps.[1152] There may be different Notional Amounts or Notional Quantities or Currency Amounts for different Calculation Periods during the Term of a Transaction,[1153] and the relevant amounts or quantities may decline, may increase or may go up and down in accordance with a fixed schedule or by reference to changes in a specified index.[1154] When a Transaction involves changes of this sort, the amount for each Calculation Period, or the method for determining incremental changes, is often shown in a table in the confirmation (and referred to on the line allocated for completion of the Notional Amount, Notional Quantity or Currency Amounts). However, when equity swaps are documented under the *1996 Equity Derivatives Definitions,* the parties may also adopt conventions referred to with the terms "Equity Notional Reset" and "Re-investment of Dividends" to signal their agreement to adjust the swap's Notional Amount periodically so that it mimics an investment in an underlying stock or basket of stocks over the swap's Term, as the stock value rises and falls and as if dividends paid were reinvested.

The Notional Amounts, Notional Quantities or Currency Amounts for the two parties to the Transaction are not necessarily identical; in fact, they are always different in a conventional currency swap, where one party's payment obligations are denominated in one currency and its counterparty's payment obligations are denominated in a second currency, and both parties will have payment obligations in both currencies involved in the transaction if the currency swap involves an initial exchange.[1155]

Under the *1998 FX and Currency Option Definitions,* a Notional Amount is used somewhat differently in connection with Non-Deliverable FX Transactions (NDFs). Widely used, as discussed below,[1156] to manage exchange rate risk in connection with currencies that are, or may be, subject to exchange controls, these transactions are modeled on more traditional, deliverable forward foreign exchange contracts in which the parties agree at the outset on a forward rate at which, on a specified date, one will buy and the other will sell a specified amount of one currency for a second currency, regardless of

---

[1152]Within the ISDA framework, a party's Currency Amount will be used to calculate the party's periodic payment obligations in connection with a Transaction. Different terms—"Initial Exchange Amount" and "Final Exchange Amount"—are used to refer to the amounts, if any, to be exchanged at the outset and conclusion of a currency swap transaction.

[1153]In fact, "Notional Quantity per Calculation Period" is an alternative to "Notional Quantity" under the *1993/2000 ISDA Commodity Derivatives Definitions.*

[1154]*See, e.g.,* the definitions of "Accreting Principal Swap," "Amortizing Swap," "CMO Swap," "Indexed Principal Swaps," "Mortgage Replication Swap," "Rollercoaster Swap," "Step-Down Swap" and "Step-Up Swap" *in* DICTIONARY OF RISK MANAGEMENT, and *see Index Amortizing Notes and Swaps,* DERIVATIVES WEEK, Jan. 25, 1993, at 9 (Learning Curve column). *See also* the discussion of this sort of transaction in the product description for rate swaps, *infra* p. 421.

[1155]*See* the introductory note on currency swaps, *infra* p. 505, and the sample currency swap confirmation, *infra* p. 508, on currency swaps involving initial exchanges.

[1156]*Infra* p. 488.

whether that forward rate is different from the actual spot rate of exchange at which the transaction could be done in the market at the time, and the two currency amounts will be delivered. The NDF cash settles this kind of forward arrangement in a single Settlement Currency, and the Notional Amount is used for purposes of calculating the amount of the settlement.[1157]

PAYMENT DATE

This is only one of the many ISDA terms used to refer to the due date or dates for certain of the basic payment obligations of the parties to various kinds of OTC derivatives. For example,

- Under the *1993/2000 ISDA Commodity Derivatives Definitions*, "Payment Date" and "Settlement Date" are synonymous.

- The *1997 ISDA Bullion Definitions, 1997 Short Form Bullion Definitions* and *1998 FX and Currency Option Definitions* all use the term "Settlement Date."[1158] The *1997 ISDA Bullion Definitions* also use "Payment Date" for payments under Bullion Swaps.

- In the *1996 Equity Derivatives Definitions*, "Settlement Date" is used in connection with physical settlement of options, whereas "Cash Settlement Payment Date" is used in connection with cash settlement of options and "Equity Payment Date" is used in connection with payments under equity swaps.[1159]

- Under the *1999 Credit Derivatives Definitions*, "Settlement Date" is used in connection with the payments that may become due, through Cash Settlement or Physical Settlement, if a Credit Event occurs and the applicable Conditions to Payment are satisfied but the scheduled periodic payments—the Fixed Amounts—payable to the Seller of credit default protection are due on Fixed Rate Payer Payment Dates.

"Premium Payment Date" is used in many of these sets of definitions for the payment of option premium but some payments that the market thinks of as premium are referred to as Fixed Amounts payable on Payment Dates, or Fixed Rate Payer Payment Date (*e.g.*, the Fixed Amounts payable under interest rate and commodity price caps and floors and under credit derivatives).

[1157]The formula for the calculation is set out in Section 2.2(b) of the *1998 FX and Currency Option Definitions* as Settlement Currency Amount = [Notional Amount x (1–Forward Rate/Settlement Rate)].

[1158]"Settlement Date" is used in these definitions in place of "Value Date," the term that had been used in the *1992 ISDA FX and Currency Option Definitions*. For examples of the use of the term "Value Date" in the ICOM, IFEMA and FEOMA forms, *see* Part 6 of the sample schedule in Part 3, *infra* p. 945.

[1159]In Section 7.1 of those definitions, obligations payable in respect of an "equity leg" of an equity swap, that is payments calculated by reference to change in the market value of stock or change in the level of an equity index, are stated to be payable on each Equity Payment Date together with any other obligations that may be payable at the same time. Therefore, if the swap has both an equity leg and an interest rate leg, as is often the case (*see infra* p. 729), the parties generally use the Payment Date conventions in the *2000 ISDA Definitions* to provide for the non-equity payments.

As contemplated in the *1992 ISDA U.S. Municipal Counterparty Definitions* and the *2000 ISDA Definitions*, Payment Dates must be dates within the Term of a Transaction, with two exceptions. The first exception relates to Payment Dates that may occur before the Effective Date; this exception applies to payments to be made by the Fixed Rate Payer in a Transaction involving a cap rate or a floor rate and is intended to accommodate the buyer's payment of the price (documented as the Fixed Amount) for a cap or floor on or about the Trade Date when the Effective Date occurs later (a "delayed-start" cap or floor). The other exception relates under the *2000 ISDA Definitions* to the payment due in respect of the final Calculation Period in a Transaction for which the parties have agreed that the "Delayed Payment" convention will apply. Where the parties have so agreed, the final Payment Date for a Transaction will occur after the end of the Transaction's Term, so long as they have also agreed on the relevant number of days of delay. (*See* the commentary below on the "Early Payment," "Delayed Payment" and "Rate Cut-off Date" ISDA conventions.)

Subject to the stated exception for the Fixed Amount payable in connection with certain caps and floors, the *1992 ISDA U.S. Municipal Counterparty Definitions* and the *2000 ISDA Definitions* do not contemplate the use of the term "Payment Date" for identifying the due date of any amount payable before the beginning of a Transaction's Term, such as a fee payable prior to the Effective Date of a Transaction. If such a fee is payable, the confirmation may simply state the "Due Date" for the fee. In the alternative, the parties may modify the existing ISDA term, such as "Payment Date," by placing the word "Fee" in front of it; so long as the method they choose clearly indicates which of the parties is required to make the payment and when, the approach chosen should suffice under Section 2(a)(i) of the ISDA forms of master agreement, which broadly states that each party agrees thereunder to "make each payment or delivery specified in each confirmation to be made by it," subject to the other provisions of the master agreement.

The *1993/2000 ISDA Commodity Derivatives Definitions* permit the designation of any day as a Payment Date or Settlement Date, for purposes of any kind of Transaction documented incorporating the terms of those definitions. Therefore, a day prior to the Effective Date of a commodity swap, cap or floor, for example, can be specified as the Payment Date or Settlement Date for a Fixed Amount payable as a fee or premium in respect of that swap, and any day may be specified as the Premium Payment Date for an Option or the Payment Date or Settlement Date for the payment of a Total Premium or Cash Settlement Amount in respect of an Option (including a cap or floor documented as an Option under those definitions). Similarly, the *1999 Credit Derivatives Definitions* place no restrictions on the parties' freedom in specifying Fixed Rate Payer Payment Dates.[1160]

[1160] However, Section 2.10 of those definitions makes clear that, whether or not the parties so specify, the Seller will be entitled to its first Fixed Amount on a Transaction's Termination Date or first Settlement Date, if either of those dates occurs before the first scheduled Fixed Rate Payer Payment Date. This provision reflects the necessary linkage between the accrual of the Fixed Amounts and the Seller's exposure to risk, as discussed *infra* p. 668.

Introduction to Part 2 389

PERIOD END DATE AND CALCULATION PERIOD

As indicated above, for various kinds of OTC derivatives, the parties' basic payment obligations are expressed as Floating Amounts and Fixed Amounts, and those amounts may relate to Payment Dates or Settlement Dates or, in the alternative, to Calculation Periods. The Fixed Amounts payable in respect of the Payment Dates or Settlement Dates for a Transaction may be known at the outset of some Transactions. When this is the case, the parties may simply state the Fixed Amount for each Payment Date or Settlement Date. Floating Amounts, however, must be determined in accordance with an agreed formula, at an agreed Floating Rate or Floating Price for each Calculation Period.

Generally, where Calculation Periods are relevant, the first begins on the Transaction's Effective Date and the last ends on the Transaction's Termination Date, and each other Calculation Period begins on the Period End Date, that is, the last day, of the preceding Calculation Period for the Transaction. Therefore, the confirmation of each Transaction involving a Floating Amount must somehow specify or allow the parties to determine the Period End Dates for all Calculation Periods other than the last, either through incorporation of rules on this subject in ISDA definitions or otherwise. The sample confirmations included in this Part illustrate how Period End Dates may be identified in circumstances in which the parties' payments are due on the final day of each Calculation Period,[1161] before the end of each Calculation Period,[1162] and after the end of each Calculation Period.[1163]

EXERCISE PERIOD, COMMENCEMENT DATE, EXPIRATION DATE,
EXPIRATION TIME AND LATEST EXERCISE TIME

"Exercise Period" is the term generally used to refer to the period within which an option may be exercised. The period always ends on the option's "Expiration Date" at the "Expiration Time." Other matters relevant to the Exercise Period vary, however, with the "style" of option involved.

The various sets of ISDA definitions provide for some or all of the following styles of options:[1164]

- European—which are exercisable at one time only, on the Expiration Date,

- American—which are exercisable on any day during an Exercise Period usually presumed to begin on the Trade Date and end on the Expiration Date,

- Bermuda—which are exercisable during an Exercise Period consisting of specified dates and

---

[1161]*See* the sample confirmation for a rate swap, *infra* p. 427.

[1162]*See* the sample confirmation for a currency swap, *infra* p. 508.

[1163]*See* the sample confirmation for a commodity swap, *infra* p. 574.

[1164]The *1997 Government Bond Option Definitions* refer only to American and European options. Bermuda style options are only contemplated in the *1998 FX and Currency Option Definitions* but will be included in the proposed revision to the *1996 Equity Derivatives Definitions*.

- Asian—which, like European options, are usually presumed to be exercisable only on the Expiration Date but are distinguished by their valuation terms, which always involve the comparison of an agreed strike price with a price determined by averaging the price or value of the option's "underlying" on multiple dates.

In many cases ISDA uses the term "Commencement Date" for the first day of the Exercise Period. This is so in the *1996 Equity Derivatives Definitions,* the *1997 ISDA Bullion Definitions,* the *1997 Government Bond Option Definitions* and the *1998 FX and Currency Option Definitions.* As noted in the previous discussion of the term "Trade Date," under each of these sets of definitions, the Exercise Period for an American style option will automatically begin on the option's Trade Date unless the parties specify otherwise. In American style options documented under the *1993/2000 ISDA Commodity Price Derivatives,* however, there is no presumption on this matter, so the parties must specify when the Exercise Period begins.

The various sets of definitions differ in their treatment of the time at which the Exercise Period begins and ends. The former, although not given a name, is specified in the *1996 Equity Derivatives Definitions* and the *1998 FX and Currency Option Definitions* to be 9:00 a.m. local time in a specified location of the Seller. This was also the approach in the *1998 Supplement to the 1991 ISDA Definitions* for Option Transactions covered by those definitions (Swaptions and Swap Transactions involving Optional Early Termination). Other sets of definitions (including the *2000 ISDA Definitions,* where Swaptions and the same kinds of Swaptions and other Option Transactions are concerned) leave it to the parties to specify the earliest time of day at which an option can be exercised on a day during the Exercise Period.

As a general matter the parties must also specify the latest time for exercise—the "Expiration Time"— on the Expiration Date, although the *1997 ISDA Bullion Definitions* include a presumptive Expiration Time of 9:30 a.m., in New York City. When an option can be exercised on a day other than the Expiration Date, some of the definitions use the term "Latest Exercise Time" to refer to the cut-off by which exercise must occur on such a day. This is the case, for example, with the *1996 Equity Derivatives Definitions,* the *1997 Government Bond Definitions* and the *1998 FX and Currency Option Definitions.*

These rules, naturally, can be critical if failure to comply with them can result in a buyer's loss of its option rights. Users of these definitions should, therefore, carefully check the relevant rules in light of other possibly relevant provisions, such as those relating to the treatment of a notice of exercise given before the earliest, or after the latest, permitted time for exercise on a date on which exercise is permitted and provisions on automatic exercise, or the equivalent.[1165] Where provisions on automatic exercise or the equivalent may apply, or notice of exercise may be effective even if the option seller is not open for business, the parties should also study how the rules on these subjects operate with provisions relating to settlement (*e.g.,* whether the time before settlement, counted from effective notice of exercise, will be sufficient for the seller and whether normally

---

[1165] *See* Annotations 12 & 17–19 to the sample Swaption confirmation, *infra* pp. 468 & 470, for further discussion of these matters.

Introduction to Part 2 391

applicable provisions on valuations of the underlying, again counted from effective notice of exercise, will operate sensibly).

INITIAL EXCHANGE DATE, INITIAL EXCHANGE AMOUNT,
FINAL EXCHANGE DATE AND FINAL EXCHANGE AMOUNT

Under the sets of definitions illustrated in this book, these terms are generally used only in connection with currency swaps.[1166] Their usage is discussed and illustrated in the sample currency swap confirmation[1167] and its accompanying product description.

BUSINESS DAY AND COMMODITY BUSINESS DAY CONVENTIONS

In a loan or investment transaction, if a payment is stated to be due on a specified day and that day falls on a Saturday, Sunday or bank holiday, another provision in the documentation should state whether the payment will be made before or after the specified day and whether the amount to be paid will be adjusted accordingly. With limited exceptions,[1168] the various booklets of ISDA definitions deal with this subject in a variety of ways that differ in terms of the alternatives presented, the situations in which they are stated to apply and the default choices that will apply in various circumstances in the absence of an express choice by the parties.

Under many of these sets of ISDA definitions,[1169] there are three basic Business Day Conventions that the parties to a Transaction may elect if they wish to adjust dates of various sorts falls during a weekend or on a holiday:

- The Following Business Day Convention moves the relevant date to the following Business Day in the agreed cities.

- The Preceding Business Day Convention moves the relevant date to the preceding Business Day in the agreed cities.

- The Modified Following Business Day Convention moves the relevant date to the following Business Day in the agreed cities unless the result would be to cause the date to fall in a new calendar month, in which case it will be moved to the preceding Business Day in the agreed cities.

[1166] Under proposed modifications to the *1996 Equity Derivatives Definitions*, the covered products would be expanded to include swaps and similar products subject to physical settlement. Initial and final exchanges, and related terminology, would be introduced in connection with these expansions.

[1167] *Infra* p. 508.

[1168] The *1996 Equity Derivatives Definitions* do not offer adjustment conventions for some of the payments normally required in connection with some products that they cover because the due dates are self-adjusting (that is, they must always be Currency Business Days or Seller Business Days). In other cases, the presumption is that the parties will state their payment obligations so as to include a rule on adjustment, either through incorporation by reference of conventions from another set of definitions or otherwise. There are also self-adjusting due dates under other sets of definitions, including the *1997 Short Form Bullion Definitions* and the *1999 Credit Derivatives Definitions*.

[1169] The *1999 Credit Derivatives Definitions* do not offer the Preceding Business Day choice.

The *2000 ISDA Definitions* (like the *1991 ISDA Definitions* but unlike the other sets of definitions) also allow the parties to agree to the FRN Convention, also known as the Eurodollar Convention. If they do so, the result will be the same as if they had selected the Modified Business Day Convention, except that, if a Payment Date or Period End Date is once adjusted to fall on the final Business Day in a calendar month, all subsequent Payment Dates or Period End Dates prior to the Termination Date of the Transaction will fall on the last Business Days of the relevant calendar months. For example, a one-month Calculation Period beginning on January 31, 2003 (the Effective Date for the Transaction)[1170] would end on February 28, 2003; the following Calculation Period would end on (1) March 28, 2003 under the Modified Following Business Day Convention or (2) March 31, 2003 under the Eurodollar (or FRN) Convention.

The *1993/2000 ISDA Commodity Derivatives Definitions* and the *1998 FX and Currency Option Definitions* (but not the other booklets) contemplate a further convention: the Nearest Business Day Convention. Under this convention, if a date specified to be subject to adjustment is not a Business Day (the *1998 FX and Currency Option Definitions*) or is not a Commodity Business Day or Business Day (the *1993/2000 ISDA Commodity Derivatives Definitions*), it will be adjusted to the preceding Business Day (or Commodity Business Day), unless that would be a Friday, in which case the date will be adjusted to the following Business Day (or Commodity Business Day).

These adjustment conventions are used to adjust dates specified in the definitions or in the documentation applicable to particular transactions. Under the *2000 ISDA Definitions*, they are made applicable to Payment Dates, the ends of Calculation Periods (Period End Dates) and any other designated dates. Accordingly, they may be made to apply to the Initial Exchange Date and Final Exchange Date for a currency swap. Any resulting shortening or lengthening of a Calculation Period will be taken into account in calculating each Floating Amount and Fixed Amount to be calculated in respect of the period. Under the *2000 ISDA Definitions* (like the *1991 ISDA Definitions* and the *1992 ISDA U.S. Municipal Counterparty Definitions*), these conventions may also be used to adjust the days specified as Reset Dates on which each new Relevant Rate to be used in determining the Floating Rate for a Calculation Period will take effect.

Under the *1993 Commodity Derivatives Definitions*, the same conventions may be adopted as "Commodity Business Day Conventions" to adjust the days specified as Pricing Dates for purposes of setting the Relevant Prices to be used to determine the Floating Price for a Calculation Period (*e.g.*, in connection with a commodity swap) or the Floating Price relevant for purposes of determining the Strike Price Differential for a Commodity Option. The adjustment occurs if any of those specified days is not a Commodity Business Day in relation to the Exchange or Price Source to which the parties will look to determine the Floating Prices for the Transaction (*i.e.*, the day is not a scheduled trading date for the Exchange or a normal publication date for a published Price Source).

[1170]The result could be different if the January date itself had been adjusted as the result of the operation of one of the conventions being discussed. If, for example, the Transaction had begun on December 30, 1992, the next two Calculation Periods would end on January 29 and February 26, 1993, respectively, under all the conventions under discussion, and the following period would end on March 30, 1993 under the Modified Following Business Day Convention or March 31, 1993 under the Eurodollar Convention.

Introduction to Part 2

The *Swaps Code* and the *1987 ISDA Definitions* made the Following Business Day convention apply unless the parties agreed otherwise. The default choices under the current ISDA frameworks for various transactions and dates are as follows:

1991 ISDA Definitions	
Type of Date	**Default Choice for Convention**
Payment Dates	Modified Following Business Day
Period End Dates except Termination Date	Modified Following Business Day
Initial Exchange Dates	Following Business Day
Final Exchange Dates	Modified Following Business Day
Maturity Dates	Modified Following Business Day
Value Dates for FX Transactions	Modified Following Business Day
Premium Payment Dates for Options	Modified Following Business Day
Cash Settlement Payment Dates for Options	Modified Following Business Day
Expiration Dates for Options	Following Business Day
Compounding Dates	Same as for Period End Dates for the party
Reset Dates for Transactions involving Price Options[1171]	Following Business Day
Reset Dates for Transactions involving other Floating Rate Options	Same as for the relevant Floating Rate Payer's Payment Dates, unless that would cause the Reset Date to fall on the Payment Date for the Calculation Period to which the Reset Date relates, in which case, Preceding Business Day

---

[1171] These are listed in Section 7.2 of the *1991 ISDA Definitions* are: S&P 500; FT-SE 100; NIKKEI 225; TOPIX; DAX; CAC-40; and OIL-WTI-NYMEX, as those terms are there defined. These Price Options were not included in the *2000 ISDA Definitions*.

1992 ISDA U.S. Municipal Counterparty Definitions	
Type of Date	**Default Choice for Convention**
Payment Dates	Modified Following Business Day
Period End Dates except Termination Date	Modified Following Business Day
Reset Dates	Same as for relevant Floating Rate Payer's Payment Dates, unless the Reset Date would fall on the Payment Date for the Calculation Period to which it relates, in which case, Preceding Business Day

1992 ISDA FX and Currency Option Definitions	
Type of Date	**Default Choice (without Defined Conventions)**[1172]
Value Date for FX Transactions	Following Banking Day
Expiration Date for Currency Options	Following Banking Day
Premium Payment Date for Currency Options	Following Banking Day

1993/2000 ISDA Commodity Derivatives Definitions	
Type of Date	**Default Choice for Convention**
Payment Dates and Settlement Dates	Following Business Day
Premium Payment Dates for Options	Following Business Day
Expiration Dates for Options	Last Day of the Exercise Period or, if that is not a Commodity Business Day, the Following Commodity Business Day

---

[1172] In their terminology (somewhat modified in the 1998 version), the definitions simply stated (in Sections 1.2(b), 2.2(h) and 2.2(m)) that, if the Value Date for an FX Transaction or the Expiration Date or Premium Payment Date for a Currency Option fell on a day that was not a Banking Day in the agreed cities, it would be moved to the next following Banking Day in those cities. For Currency Options, this result was different from the one that would have applied automatically under the *1991 ISDA Definitions*, where (absent agreement to the contrary) the Modified Following Business Day Convention would apply to the Value Date the stated Value date was not a Business Day in the agreed cities.

Introduction to Part 2

1996 Equity Derivatives Definitions	
Type of Date	*Default Choice for Convention*
Valuation Dates for Equity Swap Transactions	following Exchange Business Day (subject to the Market Disruption Events provisions summarized in tables *infra* p. 612)
Valuation Dates for Options	Self-adjusting, because they must be Exercise Dates, and these must be Exchange Business Days
Valuation Dates where Futures Price Valuation is specified to be applicable	Self-adjusting, because they must always be the day on which the Official Settlement Price is published
Averaging Dates in respect of Valuation Dates	following Exchange Business Day
Premium Payment Dates for Options	following Currency Business Day
Expiration Dates for Options	following Exchange Business Day
Cash Settlement Payment Dates for Options	In relation to an Exercise Date, if the parties are silent, as many Exchange Business Days after the Valuation Date (or last Valuation Date) as the Premium Payment Date falls after the Trade Date or, if that day is not a Currency Business Day, the following Currency Business Day. (The reference to the last Valuation Date applies to Index Basket Options, where a Market Disruption Event results in multiple Valuation Dates.) No default choice if the parties have specified a number of calendar days (rather than Currency Business Days) after the Exercise Date

1996 Equity Derivatives Definitions	
Type of Date	**Default Choice for Convention**
Settlement Date for Options subject to Physical Settlement	Self-adjusting to fall on the first day on which settlement of a sale of the Shares executed on the applicable Exercise Date would customarily take place through the relevant Clearance System[1173]
Equity Payment Date for Equity Swap Transactions	No default choice
Floating Rate Payer Payment Dates for Equity Swap Transactions	No default choice

1997 ISDA Bullion Definitions	
Type of Date	**Default Choice for Convention[1174]**
Expiration Date	In effect, the Preceding Business Day Convention, by providing that the default choice will be the Standard Date for the relevant month and defining "Standard Date" as indicated below
Payment Date	Following Business Day Convention
Period End Date	Following Business Day Convention
Standard Date	In effect, the Preceding Business Day Convention, by providing that the Standard Date for a month will be the day that is two Bullion Business Days preceding the last Bullion Business day of the month

---

[1173] Subject to rules on Settlement Disruption Events specified in Section 6.2 of these definitions.

[1174] Other important dates (such as Settlement Dates for Bullion Options and Pricing Dates for any Bullion Trade (spot or forward sale of Bullion) are always presumed to be a specified number of Bullion Business Days before or after one of these days or before a Value Date, which will also always be a Bullion Business Day under the conventions as published in the *1997 ISDA Bullion Definitions*.

Introduction to Part 2

1997 ISDA Bullion Definitions	
Type of Date	*Default Choice for Convention[1174]*
Premium Payment Date	The Premium Payment Date is presumed to be the second Bullion Business Day after the Trade Date, unless the parties specify otherwise, and no default choice is supplied if the parties choose another day which is not a Bullion Business Day

1997 Government Bond Option Definitions	
Type of Date	*Default Choice for Convention*
Premium Payment Date	Following Business Day
Expiration Date	The following day that is both an Exchange Business Day and a Seller Business Day
Settlement Date	Following Business Day

1998 FX and Currency Option Definitions	
Type of Date	*Default Choice for Convention*
Averaging Date for FX Transactions or Currency Option Transactions	Preceding Business Day Convention
Expiration Date for Currency Option Transactions	Following Business Day Convention
Premium Payment Date for Currency Option Transactions	Following Business Day Convention
Settlement Date for FX Transactions or Currency Option Transactions	Following Business Day Convention
Specified Payment Date for Bermuda style Currency Option Transactions	Following Business Day Convention
Valuation Date for FX Transactions or Currency Option Transactions	Preceding Business Day Convention

1999 Credit Derivatives Definitions	
Type of Date	*Default Choice for Convention*
Any date	Modified Following Business Day

2000 ISDA Definitions	
Type of Date	*Default Choice for Convention*
Payment Dates[1175]	Modified Following Business Day
Period End Dates other than the Termination Date	Modified Following Business Day
Initial Exchange Dates	Following Business Day
Interim Exchange Dates	Modified Following Business Day
Periodic Exchange Dates	Modified Following Business Day
Final Exchange Dates	Modified Following Business Day
Exchange Dates	Modified Following Business Day
Maturity Dates	Modified Following Business Day
Premium Payment Dates for Options	Following Business Day
Cash Settlement Payment Dates for Options	Modified Following Business Day
Expiration Dates for Options	following Exercise Business Day[1176]

[1175] Although not a default choice in the sense indicated for the following dates, an important rule specified in these definitions is that the Effective Date and Termination Date will not be subject to adjustment in accordance with a Business Day Convention that is merely stated to apply generally to the relevant Transaction. If a convention is to apply, it must be expressly stated to apply to these two dates.

[1176] For purposes of Cash Settlement, an Exercise Business Day must be a Banking Day in each place specified in the relevant Confirmation or, if the parties are silent, will depend on the Cash Settlement Currency and will be (1) TARGET Settlement Days, if the euro is involved; (2) a Banking Day in the Financial Center specified in a list in Section 1.5 of these definitions for the relevant currency; or (3) in any other case, the principal financial center for the relevant currency.

2000 ISDA Definitions	
Type of Date	***Default Choice for Convention***
Bermuda Option Exercise Dates for Option Transactions (largely Swaptions and options to terminate Swap Transactions) that qualify as Bermuda style transactions	following Exercise Business Day
Compounding Dates	Same as for Period End Dates for the relevant party
Reset Dates for Transactions involving other Floating Rate Options	Same as for relevant Floating Rate Payer's Payment Dates, unless that would cause the Reset Date to fall on the Payment Date for the Calculation Period to which the Reset Date relates, in which case, Preceding Business Day

To overcome any of these listed default choices on adjustment to Calculation Periods, "No Adjustment" may be specified in connection with a Transaction documented using the *1991 ISDA Definitions*, the *1992 ISDA U.S. Municipal Counterparty Definitions*, or the *2000 ISDA Definitions*. Neither the *1991 ISDA Definitions* nor the *1992 ISDA U.S. Municipal Counterparty Definitions* supplies a default choice for how to deal with the Effective Date of a Transaction if it falls on a day other than a Business Day, and the *2000 ISDA Definitions* includes a presumption that a Transaction's Effective Date will not be subject to adjustment. The handling of an Effective Date that falls on a holiday may be a concern in delayed start swaps, and the possibility of an unexpected holiday may be of somewhat greater concern in transactions such as FRAs and SAFES (ERAs and FXAs), in which the period in respect of which an amount may be payable always occurs after the Trade Date. Finally, as noted in the foregoing commentary on the concept of "Term" and the preceding tables, each of the *1991 ISDA Definitions*, the *1992 ISDA U.S. Municipal Counterparty Definitions*, or the *2000 ISDA Definitions* includes the presumption that the Termination Date for a Transaction will not be adjusted.

EARLY PAYMENT, DELAYED PAYMENT AND RATE CUT-OFF DATE CONVENTIONS

These conventions are available under the *2000 ISDA Definitions*, as they were under the *1991 ISDA Definitions*.

"Early Payment" is a convention designed to allow the parties to call for payment of the Floating Amount or Fixed Amount for a Calculation Period, calculated in respect of the entire Calculation Period, on an agreed Business Day before the last day of the Calculation Period. This convention is, for example, useful in connection with derivatives entered into in connection with capital markets transactions under which an issuer is required to make funds available to a paying agent or trustee one or more days before an interest payment date but the amount of funds required is the full amount calculated with respect to the interest period ending on that interest payment date. The sample currency swap confirmation[1177] illustrates how the convention may be used.

The "Rate Cut-off Date" convention is designed to deal with circumstances in which parties want to designate the last day of a Calculation Period as the Payment Date for the period but find that, if they do so, the Calculation Agent may be unable to calculate the Floating Amount for the full period (*i.e.*, the "Relevant Rate" for each "Reset Date" in the period) on the basis of the agreed Floating Rate Option and still report the amount in advance of the Payment Date as required by the ISDA framework. *See, e.g.,* Sections 4.14 and 4.15 of the *2000 ISDA Definitions,* on the Calculation Agent and the Calculation Date, respectively, which together operate, among other things, to require the Calculation Agent to report the Floating Amounts and Fixed Amount, if any, for each Calculation Period no later than the close of business on the Business Day before the Payment Date for the Calculation Period.

This kind of situation may arise in connection with a rate swap involving a freely floating rate base, that is, a rate that may be reset daily during each Calculation Period. Comparable circumstances can arise in connection with prime-based lending transactions and, as a result, the parties to such loans sometimes agree that the interest payment to be made by the borrower on a particular interest payment date will be calculated on the basis of prime for each day through but excluding, say, the fifth New York banking day before that interest payment date. Within the ISDA framework, if the parties agree on a Rate Cut-off Date for purposes of calculating the relevant Floating Amount payable on a Payment Date, they agree that the Relevant Rate for each Reset Date in a Calculation Period falling on or after that Rate Cut-off Date will be assumed to be the Relevant Rate in effect on the agreed Rate Cut-off Date. If the assumption proves not to have been correct and the parties wish to make an appropriate adjustment after the Payment Date, they must state their own rule for settlement of the adjustment in their agreement or the relevant confirmation if the Rate Cut-off Date convention applies to their dealings. A simpler alternative is for the parties to choose the Delayed Payment convention, which is described below, but that alternative would involve a settlement payment after the end of the relevant Calculation Period.

Users of the *2000 ISDA Definitions* should pay particular attention to this issue in connection with transactions involving U.S. commercial paper, federal funds and prime rates because, under Section 6.2(d)(i) of those definitions, there is a presumption that the second New York City Banking Day before a Period End Date (or before the Termination Date, in the case of the last Calculation Period) will be the Rate Cut-off Date for a transaction whenever the parties have selected any of the Floating Rate Options specified in Section 6.2(e) of the definitions, which are USD–CP–H.15, USD–Federal Funds–H.15 and USD–Prime–H.15.[1178]

[1177]*Infra* p. 508.

[1178]This presumption would not apply if the parties chose to base their transaction's U.S. dollar commercial paper, federal funds or prime rate determinations on quotations obtained from reference dealers or reference banks, even though the presumption would automatically apply if they chose any of the indicated Floating Rate Options and were required to fall back to using quotations supplied by reference dealers or reference banks because a relevant day's rate could not be determined in a timely manner from H.15(519), a statistical release published by the Federal Reserve Bank of New York, or the daily update to that release, a

Introduction to Part 2 401

The "Delayed Payment" convention too is designed to deal with circumstances involving freely floating rates or prices, or rates or prices that may be determined at or towards the end of a Calculation Period. In these circumstances, if the parties want the Floating Amount for the Calculation Period determined on the basis of the actual rate or price set for each Reset Date in the Calculation Period and are willing to settle in respect of the period after it has ended, under the Delayed Payment approach they merely designate a day, or Business Day, after the end of the Calculation Period as the Payment Date for the period. The ISDA practice is not to have the amount paid bear interest from the end of the relevant Calculation Period to the Payment Date for that period set in accordance with the Delayed Payment convention. The sample confirmations for a commodity swap and for weather derivatives illustrate how the Delayed Payment convention approach is achieved quite simply without use of the Delayed Payment convention.[1179]

FIXED RATE PAYER OR FIXED PRICE PAYER AND FLOATING RATE PAYER OR FLOATING PRICE PAYER

These terms are used to identify the parties whose payment obligations in connection with a Transaction are determined on the basis of "Fixed Amounts" and "Floating Amounts," respectively. They are used in connection with swaps, caps, floors, collars and other combinations of caps and floors, and in connection with FRAs and other similar Transactions. In some Transactions both parties agree to make payments calculated by reference to floating rates or prices. In these cases, which often arise in connection with products documented using the *2000 ISDA Definitions* or the *1993/2000 ISDA Commodity Derivatives Definitions,* a common practice is to tie a party's name to obligations relating to First Floating Amounts and a Second Floating Amounts, although we prefer the simple approach—suggested in the ISDA definitions—of using a party's name (or a short form of its name) in identifying its obligations. The product description for equity swaps discusses ISDA conventions, in the *1996 Equity Derivatives Definitions,* involving Equity Amount Payers and cases in which one leg of a transaction may involve payments calculated on the basis of a price index and a second leg will involve payments calculated on the basis of a floating interest rate.[1180]

FIXED AMOUNT, OR FIXED PRICE, FLOATING AMOUNT AND FLOATING PRICE

These terms are used for purposes of referring to the parties' basic payment obligations, payable on Payment Dates, or in commodity price derivatives, Settlement Dates, in connection with derivatives such as swaps, caps, floors and combinations of these products.

Fixed Amounts may be stated and immutable, if they are known at the outset of the Transaction, or they may be determined by multiplying a Fixed Rate or Fixed Price for the relevant Calculation Period (or Payment Date or Settlement Date) by a Notional

---

successor publication, or the appropriate extension of the Web site of the Board of Governors of the Federal Reserve System, www.bog.frb.us.

[1179] *Infra* pp. 578 & 768.

[1180] *See infra* p. 717.

Amount or Notional Quantity for that period and then multiplying the result by any applicable Day Count Fraction (a term whose use is described below).

The Floating Amounts calculated by reference to interest rates and commodity prices are always determined in accordance with a formula, except in cases in which the Floating Amount for the initial Calculation Period is known at the outset of the period. When the Transaction does not involve Compounding, the formula requires the multiplication of the Floating Rate for the Calculation Period (plus or minus a Spread, where applicable) by the Notional Amount or Notional Quantity for the period and the applicable Day Count Fraction.

Where the ISDA conventions on Compounding are applicable—that is, under the *2000 ISDA Definitions* and the *1991 ISDA Definitions*—a similar formula must be used to determine a Compounding Period Amount for each of the Compounding Periods in each Calculation Period,[1181] and the Floating Amount for each Calculation Period is the sum of the Compounding Period Amounts for all the Compounding Periods in the Calculation Period. The *2000 ISDA Definitions* also include self-compounding Floating Rate Options. For these cases, the parties need only specify a single Reset Date at the end of each Calculation Period. This choice operates with a formula included in the Floating Rate Option to specify how the Calculation Agent should calculate a rate of return that will be the Floating Rate for the Calculation Period. These self-compounding Floating Rate Options include provisions for the calculation of rates of return assuming daily compound interest investments and monthly compound interest investments renewed at the end of each month over a period of 12 months leading up to the Reset Date.[1182]

[1181] The formula requires the multiplication of an Adjusted Calculation Amount for the Compounding Period by the Floating Rate for the period and the further multiplication of the result by the appropriate Day Count Fraction. For the first Compounding Period in a Calculation Period, the Adjusted Calculation Amount is simply a Notional Amount. For each subsequent Compounding Period in the same Calculation Period, the Adjusted Calculation Amount is that original Notional Amount adjusted upwards to reflect the effects of mathematical compounding in each of the preceding Compounding Periods in the Calculation Period, that is, as if the Notional Amount were principal being invested at the Floating Rate for the first Compounding Period, and then principal and interest were reinvested during the second Compounding Period at the Floating Rate for the second Compounding Period, and so on. The *2000 ISDA Definitions* and the *1991 ISDA Definitions* also provide a second method of Compounding, called Flat Compounding. There would be no difference between the two approaches in a transaction involving a compound floating rate determined on the basis of a straight reading from a floating rate index, such as one-month LIBOR. However, if the parties have agreed to a transaction involving the use of LIBOR plus or minus a spread, the distinction between Compounding and Flat Compounding becomes relevant. Under the Compounding approach, the spread would be taken into account for purposes of compounding as described in the foregoing example (that is, each hypothetical investment for a Compounding Period would be at one-month LIBOR for that period plus or minus the agreed spread). Under the Flat Compounding approach, the spread would be taken into account for a hypothetical investment of the Notional Amount but not the successive hypothetical reinvestments of interest.

[1182] The Floating Rate Options included in Section 7.1(c) of the *2000 ISDA Definitions* to accommodate this approach use "OIS" to identify them as involving the compounding of overnight interest rates for transactions in euros in the Euro-zone interbank euro money market (EUR–EONIA–OIS–COMPOUND) and the day-to-day interbank money market in London (EUR–EURONIA–OIS–COMPOUND). There are also Floating Rate Options (EUR–TAM–CDC and EUR–TMM–CDC–COMPOUND) that are used in Transactions involving the rate of return on a monthly compound interest investment renewed at the end of each month over the period of 12 months preceding the Reset Date identified by the parties.

Introduction to Part 2 403

The following are some general concepts used in connection with the determination of the Floating Rate or Floating Price for a Calculation Period:

RESET DATES, PRICING DATES AND VALUATION DATES

The first of these terms is used in connection with the calculation of Floating Amounts: "Reset Date" in the *1991 ISDA Definitions*, the *1992 ISDA U.S. Municipal Counterparty Definitions* and the *2000 ISDA Definitions*. "Pricing Date" is the term used for the same purpose in the *1993/2000 ISDA Commodity Derivatives Definitions* and the *1997 ISDA Bullion Definitions*. As discussed in the product description for equity swaps,[1183] when those Transactions involve both an equity leg and an interest-rate leg, the general practice is to incorporate the *2000 ISDA Definitions* or the *1991 ISDA Definitions*, including the concept of Reset Date, for purposes of calculating the amounts payable on the interest-rate leg. The *1997 ISDA Bullion Definitions* contemplate the possibility that the parties would wish to take the same approach in connection with a bullion swap involving a price leg and an interest-rate leg by incorporating the concept of Reset Date (among other terms) from the *1991 ISDA Definitions*.

If the Floating Rate or Floating Price for a Calculation Period (or under the *1993/2000 ISDA Commodity Derivatives Definitions*, for a Settlement Date or Payment Date) is based on a single rate setting or price fixing, each Calculation Period for the relevant Floating Rate Payer or Floating Price Payer (or the Settlement Date or Payment Date, under the *1993/2000 ISDA Commodity Derivatives Definitions*) will have only one related Reset Date or Pricing Date. As illustrated in the sample rate swap confirmation,[1184] this would be the case in a simple fixed/LIBOR rate swap. However, many OTC derivatives involve Floating Rates or Floating Prices calculated by reference to Relevant Rates or Relevant Prices for multiple Reset Dates or Pricing Dates per Calculation Period. The confirmation for each Transaction must specify the Reset Dates or Pricing Dates applicable for determining the Floating Amount obligations of each Floating Rate Payer or Floating Price Payer. As noted above, Reset Dates may be adjusted in accordance with a Business Day Convention or a Commodity Business Day Convention if they do not fall on a Business Day or a Commodity Business Day. If the parties fail to specify an applicable convention, the various booklets of definitions supply the default choices indicated in the preceding tables.

The *1993/2000 ISDA Commodity Derivatives Definitions* also use the term "Pricing Date" in another sense, in connection with Options documented using those definitions. In this sense, the term is used as is the term "Valuation Date" in connection with other options, including those documented under the *1996 Equity Derivatives Definitions* and the *1998 FX and Currency Option Definitions*.[1185] Under the *1993/2000 ISDA Commodity Derivatives Definitions*, if the parties fail to specify Pricing Dates for their Options, the Pricing Date for a European style Option will be its Expiration Date and the Pricing Date for an American style Option will be its Exercise Date, and each Commodity

---

[1183]*Infra* p. 717.

[1184]*Infra* p. 508.

[1185]The complex rules relating to valuation and Valuation Dates under the *1999 Credit Derivatives Definitions* are summarized in the table *infra* p. 612.

Business Day during the Calculation Period for an Asian style Option will be a Pricing Date for that Option. The presumption under the *1997 Government Bond Option Definitions,* the *1998 FX and Currency Option Definitions* and the *1996 Equity Derivatives Definitions* is that each Exercise Date is a Valuation Date for an option.

See the introductory note on interest rate derivatives[1186] with respect to certain London interbank conventions that should be considered in specifying Reset Dates for Transactions involving a LIBOR-based Floating Rate Option.

FLOATING RATE OPTIONS AND COMMODITY REFERENCE PRICES

Under the *1991 ISDA Definitions,* the *1992 ISDA U.S. Municipal Counterparty Definitions* and the *2000 ISDA Definitions,* "Floating Rate Option" is the term used to refer to the various floating rate indexes on the basis of which Floating Rates may be calculated. In the *1991 ISDA Definitions* and the *1998 Supplement* to those definitions, the same term was used to refer to several price indexes for commodity and equity-linked transactions. Those price options have been eliminated from the *2000 ISDA Definitions*.

Where Floating Rate Options are used, the first step is the choice of the option for each Floating Rate Payer in the Transaction. Then that party's Floating Amount obligation with respect to each Calculation Period for a Transaction is calculated on the basis of the Floating Rate for that Calculation Period determined in accordance with the chosen Floating Rate Option. For this purpose, each of the Floating Rate Options is drafted so as to explain how the Calculation Agent should determine a Relevant Rate for each Reset Date for a Calculation Period if that Floating Rate Option is applicable.

The *1993/2000 ISDA Commodity Derivatives Definitions* use Commodity Reference Prices in much the same way as the *2000 ISDA Definitions* use Floating Rate Options. This subject is explored in depth below.[1187] The *1996 Equity Derivatives Definitions* leave it to the parties to specify how they wish to determine the "Reference Price" that will be used in calculating equity swap or similar payments and the "Settlement Price" that will be used in connection with cash-settled options.

FLOATING RATE AND RELEVANT RATE; FLOATING PRICE AND RELEVANT PRICE

"Floating Rate" is a term used in the *2000 ISDA Definitions* (as in the *1991 ISDA Definitions*[1188]) and the *1992 ISDA U.S. Municipal Counterparty Definitions*. The *1993/2000 ISDA Commodity Derivatives Definitions* use the term "Floating Price" instead. A Floating Rate or Floating Price is determined for each Calculation Period for a Floating Rate Payer or Floating Price Payer or, under the *1993/2000 ISDA Commodity Derivatives Definitions*, may be determined instead in respect of each Settlement Date or

---

[1186] *Infra* p. 508.

[1187] *Infra* p. 561.

[1188] Under the *1991 ISDA Definitions*, but not the *2000 ISDA Definitions*, however, the term may be used in connection with all Transactions for which a Floating Rate Option is applicable, whether that Floating Rate Option is rate based or price based. That is, the same term is used for, *e.g.*, a fixed/LIBOR rate swap and a commodity swap involving the OIL-WTI-NYMEX Price Option. As noted earlier, the *2000 ISDA Definitions* omit reference to commodity derivatives, and Commodity Reference Prices are included in the *1993/2000 ISDA Commodity Derivatives Definitions*.

Payment Date for a Floating Price Payer. If a Transaction is documented using the *2000 ISDA Definitions* or the *1991 ISDA Definitions* and involves the ISDA Compounding conventions, each Calculation Period for the relevant Floating Rate Payer will consist of Compounding Periods, and a Floating Rate will be determined for each Compounding Period.[1189] In all cases, the Floating Rate or Floating Price is a number—a rate per annum or amount stated as a price—and it is determined on the basis of the Relevant Rate or Relevant Price for each Reset Date or Pricing Date in the Calculation Period or Compounding Period, where applicable.

In swaps and similar products that involve the use of a Floating Rate Option, if there is a single Reset Date, the Relevant Rate for that date will be the Floating Rate. If there is more than one Reset Date in the period (or relating to a Payment Date), the Relevant Rates will be averaged. Under the *2000 ISDA Definitions* (like the *1991 ISDA Definitions*) and the *1992 ISDA U.S. Municipal Counterparty Definitions*, the parties may choose an Unweighted Average or a Weighted Average approach, and in the absence of an express choice, the Unweighted Average approach will apply. *See* the annotations to the sample rate cap confirmation[1190] for discussion of Floating Rates and Floating Prices in Transactions involving caps and floors.

Similarly, in commodity price swaps and similar products documented under the *1993/2000 ISDA Commodity Derivatives Definitions,* if there is a single Pricing Date in a Calculation Period, the Relevant Price for that date will be the Floating Price. If there is more than one Pricing Date in the period (or relating to a Payment Date or Settlement Date), the Relevant Prices will be averaged, and there is a built-in assumption that the Floating Price for the Calculation Period will be the arithmetic average of the Relevant Prices for all the Pricing Dates. *See* the annotations to the sample commodity price floor confirmation[1191] for discussion of Floating Prices in Transactions involving caps and floors.

DAY COUNT FRACTIONS

The Day Count Fraction is used to calculate payments in respect of periods shorter than a year when the applicable rate is stated as a rate per annum (as Fixed Rates and Floating Rates are in the ISDA framework). The *Annex to the 2000 ISDA Definitions*[1192] and Section 4.10 of the *1992 ISDA U.S. Municipal Counterparty Definitions* set out the

---

[1189]Compounding calls for dividing each Calculation Period into a series of Compounding Periods. Part of the Floating Amount for the Calculation Period is calculated with respect to each of the Compounding Periods in the Calculation Period. The amount calculated for each Compounding Period is added to the Notional Amount for the purpose of computing the additional part of the Floating Amount for each subsequent Compounding Period in the same Calculation Period. *See supra* note 1181 for further details on how this Compounding convention operates, and on the ISDA self-compounding Floating Rate Options, which operate differently.

[1190]*Infra* p. 508.

[1191]*Infra* p. 590.

[1192]The *Annex* was published at the same time as the definitions and includes sections on day count fractions, currencies and floating rate options, and related definitions. It is expected to be supplemented with some frequency. The parties are presumed to have intended to adopt the *Annex* as supplemented and amended through the Trade Date for each Transaction unless they indicate otherwise.

various choices of Day Count Fractions (such as Actual/360 and 30/360)—which may be specified in a confirmation as Fixed Rate Day Count Fractions and Floating Rate Day Count Fractions. Some of these choices are illustrated and commented on in the following sample confirmations.

Sections 5.1 and 6.1 of the *2000 ISDA Definitions* (like the same sections of the *1991 ISDA Definitions*) require the use of a Fixed Rate Day Count Fraction or a Floating Rate Day Count Fraction for purposes of calculating a Fixed Amount or a Floating Amount, respectively.[1193] Section 6.2(f)(ii) of the *2000 ISDA Definitions* provides a generally-applicable default choice of Actual/360 for Floating Rate Options, and Section 6.2(g) of those definitions (found in the *Annex*) supplies other default choices as excepttions to that general rule. If the parties do not wish to select the applicable default choice for the Floating Rate Option in a given Transaction, they should specify the agreed Day Count Fraction in confirming the Transaction.

The *1993/2000 ISDA Commodity Derivatives Definitions* do not contemplate the use of Day Count Fractions; therefore, if a commodity price Transaction is documented using those definitions and involves the calculation of an amount using an interest rate base, instead of a price base, the parties should consider incorporating the appropriate parts of the *2000 ISDA Definitions* to use a term related to a Day Count Fraction supplied there or a rule regarding the calculation of the relevant Floating Amount or Fixed Amount using the agreed Day Count Fraction. The same would be true if the parties were documenting an interest-rate leg to, say, an equity swap or debt-linked total return swap.

CONCLUSION

As indicated earlier, the preceding discussion is limited to basic concepts and terminology commonly used in multiple segments of the OTC derivatives market. The introductory notes, product descriptions and sample confirmations below review other conventions used in connection with specific kinds of transactions and the documentation and structuring concerns that some of these conventions may raise.

Throughout the preceding discussion and in the remainder of this Part 2 we point to some of the ways in which conventions may differ from one set of standard definitions to the next. In many cases these differences reflect actual disparities in practice in the markets for the underlying risks, but market participants should not assume that this is always so. The conventions in the definitions published by ISDA and other trade groups often reflect compromises among those involved in the drafting discussions when consensus does not exist, or even a compromise among those who represent a bare majority view on a subject at a particular time. Even when these views reflect prevailing practice in a product market broadly defined, they do not necessarily correspond to practice in narrower regional markets. Market practices change over time, and sometimes quite suddenly, as a result of disruptions that reveal weaknesses in previously existing practices or

---

[1193] Unlike the *2000 ISDA Definitions*, the *1991 ISDA Definitions* were designed to cover commodity swaps. Since Day Count Fractions are irrelevant for purposes of calculating Fixed Amounts and Floating Amounts using certain Price Options for commodity and equity-linked transactions, the *1991 ISDA Definitions* also provide (in Sections 5.2(b) and 6.2(f)(ii)) that the Fixed Rate Day Count Fraction and Floating Rate Day Count Fraction will be 1/1 if a Fixed Amount or Floating Amount is calculated using a Price Option and the parties have not specified a Day Count Fraction).

Introduction to Part 2 407

as a result of disputes that bring into focus important disagreements over what existing conventions mean. These changes are often reflected in new editions or versions of a product-specific set of definitions or in supplements to an existing set, but there can be substantial lags between a change in general market practice and the publication of a new set of definitions or supplement that will reflect the change. In addition, market conventions simply will not always suit a party's aims.

Those who have been involved with the derivatives markets for some time will not need to reach far into their memories to find examples of these phenomena. Those involving the *1999 Credit Derivatives Definitions* are perhaps the most widely known, because they have involved major financial institutions in numerous law suits and led to the publication of multiple supplements to those definitions. In some cases, as discussed below, the supplements themselves have failed to achieve the harmony across regional markets despite lengthy consultations.[1194] In other cases, they are acknowledged to offer solutions that have been adopted because they are simple to administer, even though they may prove less than ideal in important cases.[1195] Those involved with the equity and FX derivatives market can, similarly, point to features of the *1996 Equity Derivatives Definitions* and *1998 FX Transaction and Currency Option Definitions* that simply no longer reflect market practice, at least for some products.[1196]

These are merely some of the instances that highlight the need for the parties to look with critical eyes at standard terms that may fall short as tools for achieving their desired business result and to be alert to changes in market practices and ongoing market debates, both at the time a trading decision is made and later on, if the adopted standard terms are tested in connection with unforeseen events.

[1194] This is the case on the issue of the Restructuring Credit Event.

[1195] This is the case with the treatment of Successors in connection with corporate restructurings involving spinoffs, demergers and the like.

[1196] *See, e.g.* the discussion of non-deliverable forwards (NDFs) in the introductory note on currency derivatives, *infra* p. 488, on some differences between EMTA's recommended practices for NDFs and the *1998 FX Transaction and Currency Option Definitions.*

INTEREST RATE PRODUCTS

INTRODUCTION

The OTC derivatives reviewed in this section are used in many ways to transfer and assume risks associated with changes in the interest rate environment. The product descriptions relate to rate swaps, caps, floors, collars, corridors and their variants, forward rate agreements, or FRAs, as they are widely called, and swaptions, the term broadly used to refer to options to enter into swaps and similar derivatives, as well as options to terminate derivatives. The product descriptions also discuss differences between these derivatives and when some end-users may prefer one to another.

For most, interest rate risk is an ever-present reality since it is inherent in investment and financing activities of every kind. The motivations to manage one or another of the manifestations of interest rate risk vary considerably among users of these derivatives, and may vary for a particular end-user over time. A U.S. manufacturer may, for example, be most concerned with changes in the absolute level of domestic interest rates if it funds production with floating-rate debt, because its ability to raise prices may not keep pace with rising interest rates. By way of comparison, a bank that depends on customer deposits to fund a mortgage lending business will have more complex concerns relating to changes in the interest rate environment. Its success will be more closely tied than will the fortunes of the manufacturer to changes in the shape of the yield curve over time. The bank's profit margins on its mortgage assets will be directly linked to the difference between its cost of funding and the return on the mortgage assets and both will be sensitive, in varying degrees, not only to whether interest rates generally rise or fall but also to where along the yield curve they seem most attractive.[1197] Professional asset managers have similar concerns and still others, about the ways in which changes in the interest rate environment can result in undesirable volatility in the portfolios they manage.

The following are some of the most common uses of OTC interest-rate derivatives:

- Hedging against Rising Costs of Servicing Debt

    Many users of rate swaps and caps, and sometimes collars, are borrowers and issuers of floating-rate debt that use OTC derivatives to protect themselves against rising interest rates, often to

---

[1197] For instance, depositor preferences could shift substantially to shorter-term deposits in an environment in which the yield curve is inverted, so the bank may be exposed to greater than expected mismatches between the cost of funding and the return on its variable rate mortgages (since depositors are free to choose the maturities of their deposits but the bank will have agreed on specific reset points for the interest rate on the variable-rate mortgage loans). In addition, given a significant decline in the rates charged for new fixed-rate mortgage loans, prepayments of existing loans may be greater—and, therefore, absolute returns on those assets lower—than expected.

satisfy requirements of their lenders.[1198] In many secured lending facilities, the borrower will covenant to seek protection against rising interest rates with respect to at least a stated percentage of its debt incurred under the credit agreement, and the borrower's rights to receive payments under the swaps or caps will be part of the lenders' security.[1199]

- Balancing the Mix and Managing the Duration of Liabilities

    Borrowers and issuers with fixed-rate debt also use interest-rate derivatives, usually swaps but sometimes collars, to alter the mix of their floating- and fixed-rate liabilities, and to change the tenor of these liabilities synthetically, when prepayment or redemption of their fixed-rate debt to take advantage of declining interest rates would result in an obligation to pay a premium or "make-whole" indemnity.[1200] It is not, in fact, unusual to find references to major corporations using interest rate derivatives for the first time for this purpose.[1201]

- Locking in the Return or Cost on Fixed-Income Assets or Liabilities

    Lenders and investors often engage in rate swaps so as, synthetically, to protect their return on interest-bearing assets, measured by reference to their cost of carrying the asset over its term—that is, their own funding costs.[1202]

- Asset Swaps and Synthetic Assets

    Investors engage in rate swaps and similar derivatives to diversify their portfolios of fixed-income assets (say, to change the mix of

---

[1198]*See infra* p. 421 on this use of interest rate swaps and similar derivatives. On lender requirements relating to borrower use of derivatives, *see* GOOCH & KLEIN, LOAN DOCUMENTATION 372–74.

[1199]*See, e.g.,* Christian A. Johnson, *Banking, Antitrust, and Derivatives: Untying the Antitying Restrictions,* 49 BUFFALO L. REV. 1, 16 (Winter 2001), where the author reported having reviewed the documentation for "200 large multi-lender agented loan transactions that were entered into between 1995 and 1999" with more than 38 agents and having found that "more than 180 of these loan agreements contained detailed provisions regarding the borrower's derivatives activities." The author discusses some of the public-policy concerns that may arise under U.S. law as a result of these arrangements and refers to other discussions of these matters. *Id.* at 1 n.1.

[1200]These indemnities are, naturally, charged because the prepayment represents a loss of bargain for the fixed-rate lender; when it seeks to reinvest the amount prepaid, it will earn a lower rate than the rate applicable to the loan prepaid. On the difference between these make-whole clauses, as they have traditionally been used by institutional lenders in the U.S. market in note private placements, and the "broken funding" clauses traditionally used in LIBOR financing, *see* GOOCH & KLEIN, LOAN DOCUMENTATION 383–86.

[1201]This is so particularly when the yield curve is steep. *See, e.g., Houston Oil and Gas Co. Looks at First Interest-Rate Swap,* DERIVATIVES WEEK, May 6, 2002, p. 1 (referring to a strategy involving a mix of long-dated swaps, in which the company would receive fixed and pay floating, and short-dated swaps in which it would do the reverse, to take advantage of a steep yield curve). *See also Foam Manufacturer Eyes First I-Rate Swap,* DERIVATIVES WEEK, Apr. 22, 2002, p. 1.

[1202]*See also infra* p. 477 in the product description of FRAs, *infra* p. 1009 on the use of "rate lock" agreements by issuers that expect to be issuing fixed-rate debt.

fixed and floating-rate instruments in the portfolio, to alter the portfolio's sensitivity to a particular part of the yield curve) and to take on floating-rate exposure to an issuer whose publicly traded obligations are all bonds or notes with fixed rates.

- Arbitrage of Differentials in Market Pricing of Rate Risk

    Investors in FRNs and the OTC derivatives market sometimes value protection against falling and rising interest rates differently. When this is so, issuers may be able to combine an issuance of debt in the capital markets with OTC derivatives at overall cost savings.[1203]

In these and the other myriad uses of interest-rate derivatives referred to in the following product descriptions, many of the most critical challenges involve the need to identify differences in conventions and documentation practices in the various markets for fixed- and floating-rate obligations that can adversely affect a party's ability to achieve its desired objectives.

As background for the more detailed discussion of product-specific documentation issues in the annotations to the sample confirmations below, this Introduction deals with a few of the ways in which these critical differences typically arise. We deal first with special conventions of the London interbank deposit market and how they are reflected in, or differ from, practices used in documenting OTC derivatives with a LIBOR-based floating rate payment stream. The Introduction then concludes with common issues relating to the calculation of fixed rates.

ISSUES RELATING TO LIBOR CONVENTIONS

Banks in London take deposits from their customers in many currencies. If a bank has excess funds in a given currency, it may seek to employ them by placing them with another bank. The bank with excess funds in a given currency will offer them to other banks in the "London interbank market"; the rate at which they are offered for deposit is known as the London Interbank Offered Rate—"LIBOR" or the "LIBO Rate." A bank that needs funds in a particular currency may seek to obtain them in the interbank market. The rate at which that bank in need of funds offers to accept deposits is known as "LIBID." The average of LIBOR and LIBID is referred to as "LIMEAN."

The floating amounts in FRA, swap and related derivatives are often calculated on the basis of a LIBO Rate determined for successive Calculation Periods, most often of three months each. When one of these products is used in connection with an asset or liability that observes LIBOR market conventions, it is important that the rate-setting mechanics in the derivatives documentation accurately reflect the same conventions, or that the party seeking to manage risk associated with the asset or liability have evaluated the potential impact of the mismatch. Mistakes in this area most commonly occur in connection with conventions regarding rate settings, Calculation Periods and adjustments to the length of these periods for weekends and holidays.

[1203] See *infra* note 1254 and accompanying text on floors and collars.

LONDON INTERBANK DEPOSITS AND CALCULATION PERIODS FOR OTC DERIVATIVES

LIBOR deposits are routinely offered on an overnight basis and for periods of one week, one month, three months, six months and one year. Deposits for longer periods may also be available but in a much less liquid market. Banks will also quote rates for non-standard periods, but market participants generally prefer to avoid basing swap payments on such specially-tailored quotations, which do not necessarily reflect a broad cross-section of the market.

Absent problems with weekends or holidays, the term of a deposit in the London interbank market runs from the day the deposit is made until the same day of the next week (in the case of one week deposits) or until the numerically corresponding day in the month in which the deposit matures (in the case of deposits for a term of months). When a bank funds a transaction on a rolling basis in the market, for example, if a five-year term loan is funded with three-month deposits, the successive funding periods will overlap by one day. If a loan is funded for three months on January 15, for example, that funding will be repaid on April 15 and new funding will be obtained for the period from April 15 through July 15. Within the framework of the ISDA definitions published for use in connection with interest rate swaps, the same convention is used to make Calculation Periods overlap; the Calculation Periods for a transaction run from and including one Period End Date and to but excluding the next following Period End Date, with the exception of the first Calculation Period, which begins on the transaction's Effective Date, and the last Calculation Period, which ends on the transaction's Termination Date. *See* the commentary on the definitions of "Calculation Period" and "Term" in the Introduction to this Part.[1204]

Weekends and Holidays. Banks in London quote rates for U.S. dollar deposits for value (*i.e.*, availability) on days that are working days both in London, where those banks are located, and in New York, where payments in U.S. dollars are usually settled. Similarly, repayment of a U.S. dollar-denominated deposit taken in the London interbank market has to be made on day that is a working day in both London and New York.[1205] In ISDA's framework for documenting swaps and related OTC derivatives, adjustments for weekends and holidays are made through the selection of an appropriate Business Day Convention.

One rule for adjustments—the Following Business Day Convention—provides for extending the period if banks in the relevant cities are not open on the scheduled last day of the period, and another—the Preceding Business Day Convention—calls for shortening the period in that event. The Modified Following Business Day Convention provides for extending the period unless doing so would cause it to end in the following calendar month, in which case the convention calls for shortening the period.[1206] This is the convention generally used when a floating rate for a derivatives transaction is determined

---

[1204] *Supra* pp. 381 & 389.

[1205] For a discussion of the Euromarket generally, the operations of banks in the market and the mechanics of Eurodeposits and loans, see MARCIA STIGUM, THE MONEY MARKET 199–311 (3rd ed. 1990).

[1206] *See supra* p. 393 for tables showing which of these conventions is automatically deemed applicable in the various sets of ISDA definitions if the parties fail to specify their choice.

with reference to LIBOR, because the practice in the London interbank deposit market is not to extend the term of a deposit into a new calendar month. Where a U.S. dollar LIBOR-based rate is a Floating Rate Option involved in a transaction documented using ISDA terminology, the term "Business Day" itself is automatically deemed to involve good banking days in both London and New York, so as to conform to the convention in the London interbank market for U.S. dollar-denominated deposits.[1207]

The *2000 ISDA Definitions* also include a special "Eurodollar Convention" or "FRN Convention," under which, if the final day of a Calculation Period is not a good Business Day in the relevant cities, the period will be extended unless the extension would take the period into another calendar month, in which case the period will be shortened, and once a Calculation Period is adjusted to end on the last Business Day of a calendar month, all subsequent Calculation Periods will end on the last Business Day of each relevant calendar month. This variant on the London interbank convention described above may be appropriate with derivatives related to some FRNs.

When derivatives—often LIBOR/fixed rate swaps—are used to manage risks associated with assets and liabilities that follow these conventions, problems may arise if these standard conventions are observed in the derivatives documentation but holidays in other cities may be taken into account in the agreement or instrument governing the asset or liability. As described below, the potential problem is not merely that the swap payment may be due on the last day of a Calculation Period that ends on a day different from the adjusted end of the interest period on the related asset or liability. Rather, potentially more important is the fact that the next rate setting for the swap and the asset or liability will occur on different days.

The prevailing practice for documenting swaps and related derivatives is to state a specific day in each of the appropriate months (for example, each January 15 and July 15) as the last day of each Calculation Period and then to adjust the end of each Calculation Period other than the final one for weekends and holidays in the relevant cities. For example, if the 15th of January, April, July and December are selected as the last days of the Calculation Periods for a swap transaction and the 15th of January in a particular year during the term of the transaction is not a Business Day in the appropriate cities, the Calculation Period scheduled to end on that January 15 will be adjusted in accordance with the Business Day Convention selected by the parties, but the following Calculation Period will nonetheless end on March 15 of that year (subject to further adjustment if that day is a Saturday, Sunday or holiday in a relevant city).

Potential problems in this area can arise if interest-rate derivatives are used in connection with assets or liabilities for which LIBOR is set in respect of what are sometimes referred to as progressively creeping interest periods—that is, where each successive interest period begins on the last day of the preceding interest period and ends on the same numerical day in the relevant calendar month. Thus, looking again at the preceding example, say the 15th of January in a particular year during the term of a loan is not a Business Day in the appropriate cities. In a fully creeping approach to the definition of interest periods, the interest period scheduled to end on that January 15 would be adjusted in accordance with loan agreement's rules for holiday adjustments—normally to January

---

[1207]See *Annex to the 2000 ISDA Definitions* § 1.6(c).

16—and the following interest period would, therefore, end on March 16 of that year (subject to further adjustment if that day is a Saturday, Sunday or holiday in a relevant city), and so on. Again, if a related swap observed the derivatives market convention described above, the swap's Calculation Periods would cease to match the interest periods on the loan (and, therefore, as discussed below, the dates for LIBOR settings would not match).

The practice in the derivatives market, as noted, is also to fix the last day of a Transaction's Term on a specific day, whether or not it falls on a bank holiday or during a weekend. This approach was adopted because Floating Amounts for OTC derivatives are generally calculated on the basis of the actual number of days in the relevant Calculation Period, while the Fixed Amounts for which they are exchanged are sometimes stated as set amounts or amounts calculated so that they do not increase if the length of a Calculation Period is adjusted for a weekend or holiday. If the final Calculation Period were extended or shortened in such a case, the Floating Amount for that period would increase or decrease, but the Fixed Amount would not be adjusted accordingly. To avoid this result, the practice is to "freeze" the Termination Date (that is, the end of the Term) of rate swaps and similar derivatives under ISDA conventions.[1208] As a result of this mechanism, if the parties to a transaction want the Termination Date specified by them to be adjusted in accordance with a particular Business Day Convention, they must expressly so indicate in connection with their designation of the Termination Date. Otherwise, their general designation of that Business Day Convention will not operate to cause the adjustment of the Termination Date. (As noted in the preceding paragraph, the Termination Date for the derivatives transaction should expressly be made subject to this convention, if appropriate; otherwise, a general statement that the FRN Convention applies will not result in its application to the final Calculation Period.)

LIBOR SETTINGS AND CALCULATIONS

Rate Determination Dates. The U.S. dollar LIBO Rate applicable for each Calculation Period in a swap or similar transaction is generally determined on the second London Banking Day before the beginning of that period, because the convention in the London interbank market for deposits in U.S. dollars is to quote for value two days later or, if that day is not a banking day in London and New York, the following banking day in those cities. The conventional delay between a bank's commitment to take a deposit and the value date for the deposit (on which the deposit will be available) facilitates the processing of payments, which are settled in New York, the principal financial center for U.S. dollars. Where these geographical and time zone concerns do not exist, the two-day delay is not necessary. For example, quotations for deposits in Pounds Sterling in the London interbank market are for value on the same day and, so, are obtained on the first day of each relevant Calculation Period in swaps involving Sterling LIBOR.

In ISDA's terminology for rate-based derivatives transactions (under the *2000 ISDA Definitions* (as in the *1991 ISDA Definitions* and their *1998 Supplement* and the *1992 ISDA U.S. Municipal Counterparty Definitions*), the day in respect of which a rate, or a new rate, is set and takes effect is known as the "Reset Date." In transactions involv-

---

[1208]This practice is reflected in the definitions of the terms "Calculation Period" and "Termination Date" in Sections 3.3 and 4.13 of the *2000 ISDA Definitions*.

ing U.S. dollar LIBOR that is set once for each Calculation Period, that day will not be the same as the day the rate is determined, since, as noted, the convention in the London interbank market is to set the rate for a U.S. dollar deposit on the second London Banking Day before the value date for the deposit.

When swaps and similar derivatives are entered into in connection with assets and liabilities priced by reference to LIBOR, mistakes are often made in attempts to have the rate settings coincide because those involved in the documentation are not familiar with the intricacies of the ISDA Reset Date conventions. In particular, they do not realize that that the ISDA Floating Rate Options involving LIBOR state the rule described in the preceding paragraph, so that U.S. dollar LIBOR is set on the second London Banking Day before a Reset Date. When this occurs, the swap confirmation is incorrectly prepared identifying the Reset Date for each Calculation Period as the second London Banking Day before the first day of that Calculation Period, an approach that would operate perversely with the ISDA definitions of U.S. dollar LIBOR-based Floating Rate Options, resulting in LIBOR settings four (instead of two) London Banking Days, before the first day of a Calculation Period. Another common mistake is to state that these settings will occur by reference to Business Days rather than London Banking Days, as is the standard practice in the derivatives market, as indicated.

LIBO Rate Sources. In swaps and similar transactions, the parties generally use a published rate as the basis for determining floating-rate payment obligations. The rate base is often taken from a display screen of a rate quotation service such as Moneyline's Telerate Service, the Reuters Money 3000 Service or Reuters pages published for ISDA. The *Annex to the 2000 ISDA Definitions* includes LIBO Rate definitions based on data from all these sources, which generally use LIBOR quotations collected by the British Bankers' Association.[1209]

This derivatives market practice can be contrasted with the practice traditionally used in Eurocurrency loan agreements, which rarely used LIBOR as obtained from a published source. In single-bank eurocurrency credit agreements, the traditional practice has been to set the interest rate with reference to the rate at which the lender itself would offer deposits to major banks in the London interbank deposit market.[1210] Historically there was a reluctance on the part of lenders to look to published rates, quite possibly because the lender was often actually obtaining matched funding for each loan and wanted to pass through the precise cost of that funding. For syndicated loans, the traditional practice has been to name several "Reference Banks" in the loan documentation and to average the

---

[1209] The BBAIRS terms of the British Bankers' Association (*see supra* p. 20) have provided for the determination of LIBOR on the basis of quotations furnished by a panel of not fewer than 12 banks designated by the association for the purpose. The association appoints an information vendor charged with calculating LIBOR (which is referred to in the BBAIRS terms as the "BBA interest settlement rate") by obtaining rate quotations from eight of the panel members and averaging the middle four (and rounding up, if necessary, to five decimal places). The rate to be furnished by each panel member is described as the rate that in its view is the offered rate at which deposits in the relevant currency for the relevant term are being quoted to prime banks in the London interbank market at 11:00 a.m. London time on the relevant date. The association's information vendor (currently Moneyline Telerate) is required to publish the average through its screen service.

[1210] *See* GOOCH & KLEIN, LOAN DOCUMENTATION 41.

rates at which they would offer deposits in the market.[1211] The practice has involved selecting Reference Banks that are generally representative of the banks making up the syndicate, in terms of their currency base and overall size. In derivatives that are executed to hedge risks or reduce costs associated with a specific transaction, such as a LIBOR-priced loan, it is common for the derivative to incorporate the same rate base definition as the associated transaction. No doubt influenced by the derivatives market, many credit agreements use rates from published sources, at least where the rates are available from those sources.[1212]

Fall-Back Provisions. In loans and in derivatives transactions, the documentation will usually provide for a fallback method for obtaining a required rate or price if it cannot be obtained from the primary source designated in the confirmation for the relevant transaction. In the case of LIBOR, for example, under the approach taken in the *Annex to the 2000 ISDA Definitions*[1213] (and the *1991 ISDA Definitions* with their *1998 Supplement* and the *1992 ISDA U.S. Municipal Counterparty Definitions*), when the parties have selected the "USD-LIBOR-LIBO" Floating Rate Option, which is based on quotations that appear on the Reuters LIBO Page screen, a fallback method for determination of LIBOR will apply if fewer than two rate quotations appear on that screen display at the appropriate time. If the selected Floating Rate Option is USD-LIBOR-BBA (a rate taken from a screen on the Telerate service) or USD-LIBOR-ISDA (a rate taken from a screen on the Reuters service), the fallback method will apply if the relevant rate is not available from the selected source at the appropriate time.

In each of these cases, the first fallback is USD-LIBOR-Reference Banks, which means that the rate will be determined by obtaining and averaging actual rate quotations sought from four major banks in the London interbank market selected by the Calculation Agent. If actual LIBOR quotations cannot be obtained from at least two of the Reference Banks, a second fallback calls for looking to the "lending rate" in New York City, which many financial professionals believe should closely approximate what LIBOR would have been if it could have been determined. It should be noted, however, that, if there had been a "Eurodollar disaster" that made it impossible to determine LIBOR, major banks in New York may not be conducting their business of lending to foreign banks in their usual manner, so this fallback rate may not be a reliable substitute. Efforts to develop a better "surrogate" for U.S. dollar LIBOR have not been successful to date. The same sequence of fallback approaches applies for purposes of determining LIBOR-based Floating Rate Options in other currencies under the *2000 ISDA Definitions*.

When quotations from Reference Banks (or Reference Dealers) are used to set a rate or price, borrowers and derivatives end-users want to ensure that the institutions chosen as sources will in fact provide quotations that fairly reflect the rates or prices prevailing in the relevant market. This has led them to question the practice of leaving the selection to the Calculation Agent, in cases where their counterparty is designated as the Calculation Agent. (An analogous question arises in the loan context, if the selection is (as it usually is) made by an agent bank that is a lender or an affiliate of a lender.) Derivatives

---

[1211]*See* GOOCH & KLEIN, LOAN DOCUMENTATION 145-48.

[1212]*See id.* at 42.

[1213]Section 7.1(w)(xvii)–(xix).

documentation[1214] and the applicable general legal principles of New York law[1215] require that the entity selecting the quotation sources act in a fair and reasonable manner.[1216]

In the documentation for FRNs, customary practice has been to provide that, if LIBOR cannot be determined for a particular Calculation Period from the primary source or the fallback source, LIBOR from the preceding interest period will be used again. This approach, of course, makes sense as between an issuer and passive investors, who are simply not expected to engage in discussions with the issuer over a substitute rate. In the derivatives market, on the other hand, this ultimate fallback is not used, even when derivatives are entered into in connection with FRNs, since it is virtually certain to give a windfall to one of the parties. The derivatives market simply operates on the assumption that the ultimate fallback to a local lending rate will be available if all else fails. As a result, even if the primary and second choices of rate sources are the same in the swap and FRN documents, it is theoretically possible to have a mismatch in the event of a major disaster in both London and New York (where U.S. dollar LIBOR is concerned).[1217]

Rounding. The rounding convention used in the *2000 ISDA Definitions* and the *1991 ISDA Definitions*, the *1992 ISDA U.S. Municipal Counterparty Definitions* and the BBAIRS Terms before them, have become the prevailing derivatives market convention for interest rate derivatives, subject to certain special rules described below. That convention provides for the rounding of fractions of a percent, if necessary, to the nearest one hundred-thousandth of a percentage point (with .000005% rounded up) and for rounding of U.S. dollar amounts to the nearest cent, with one-half cent rounded up. If a rate swap or other OTC derivatives transaction is written in connection with a related LIBOR-priced loan agreement or FRN issue, the need to match the rounding convention in the related financing transaction should be carefully examined, since the impact of using a different convention can be quite significant.[1218]

[1214] *See, e.g.*, Section 4.14 of the *2000 ISDA Definitions*.

[1215] *See supra* note 569.

[1216] In special cases, if there are concerns about leaving the choice to the Calculation Agent, a third party can be employed to make the selection, either by naming it as the Calculation Agent for all purposes of the transaction or by appointing it as a rate determination agent. The drawback, of course, is the cost of the third-party services. It is also possible to name the sources and backup sources in the documentation, but this approach has generally not found favor, given the chances that a named source may cease to be suitable if its circumstances change. As noted above, another approach, as exemplified in the BBAIRS Terms, is to use as sources institutions named by a panel, or those selected by an information vendor such as Reuters or Moneyline Telerate as its own sources, as they may change from time to time. *See also infra* note 1484 on the possible need to deal in the documentation with changes in circumstances of the rate or price quotation sources.

[1217] It would, of course, be possible in the derivatives documentation to provide as an ultimate fallback that the parties will negotiate in good faith to agree upon a substitute rate and, if they fail to agree within a stated period, one or the other—presumably the party most interested in matching the floating rate payment to the FRN—will be entitled to treat the circumstances as an Additional Termination Date in respect of the particular transaction. *See* the annotations to Section 5 in the sample master agreement in Part 3, *infra* p. 827, and the other annotations referred to therein, and *see supra* p. 246, on no-fault termination. *See also* GOOCH & KLEIN, LOAN DOCUMENTATION 53–54, 152–53, for a more extensive discussion of "Eurodollar disaster" situations.

[1218] In the lending market, the rounding conventions are often less precise, and rounding to the nearest, or next higher, 1/16 of 1% is common. *See* the LIBOR definition and related annotations in GOOCH & KLEIN, LOAN DOCUMENTATION 41–42, 145–46.

Sections 8.1 and 8.2 of the *2000 ISDA Definitions* also include refinements and rules relating to rounding involving other currencies. For example, under Section 8.1 there is a special rule for cases in which rounding should occur for purposes of determining an applicable rate by interpolating between two published rates. In such a case, the rate obtained by interpolation is to be rounded "to the same degree of accuracy used in the relevant publication (subject to a minimum level of accuracy equivalent to three decimal places)."[1219] Section 8.1 further provides that currency amounts are to be rounded in accordance with Section 8.2, which in turn refers to the *Annex to the 2000 ISDA Definitions* for the conventions on rounding of amounts in certain listed currencies. For currencies that are not listed, Section 8.1 requires rounding to the nearest two decimal places in "the relevant currency," with .005 being rounded upwards. For amounts in U.S. currency—which is not listed in the *Annex*—the "relevant currency" is presumably the dollar and not the cent. For the currencies listed in the *Annex* as first published, the rule is that rounding is to the nearest currency unit, with half a unit rounded up, except for the Japanese Yen, which is to be rounded "to the next lower whole Japanese Yen."[1220]

THE ISDA NEGATIVE INTEREST RATE METHOD

To those who enter the derivatives world to manage risks associated with debt and other fixed- and floating-rate obligations, concerns relating to "negative interest rates" seem nonsensical. Depositors are sometimes charged fees by the banks with which they maintain accounts and those fees can erode principal, thereby reducing the base on which principal is calculated, but these and similar types of arrangements involving fees are not what the ISDA "Negative Interest Rate Method" is about. This method, in fact, does not involve negative interest rates but, rather, negative Floating Amounts understood, in the context of the ISDA conventions, to be amounts that can be produced if a Notional Amount is multiplied by a negative Floating Rate[1221] or by a positive Floating Rate minus a Spread.

Under the *2000 ISDA Definitions,* if a negative Floating Amount were determined for a party in this way, its counterparty's obligations could be increased by the absolute value of the negative Floating Amount. This would be the case for interest rate swaps under the Negative Interest Rate Method provided for in Section 6.4 of the *2000 ISDA Definitions,* as it would under Section 8(f) of the *1998 Supplement to the 1991 ISDA Definitions.* (The *1991 ISDA Definitions* and the *1992 U.S. Municipal Counterparty Definitions* do not include this convention.) The Negative Interest Rate Convention will not, however, apply to transactions for which a floor rate is specified or transactions in which obliga-

---

[1219] *2000 ISDA Definitions*, at viii.

[1220] The simpler rules in the *1998 FX and Currency Option Definitions* (Section 1.23) provide for rounding of currency amounts in accordance with the relevant market practice and for the rounding of rates using the same approach as the *2000 ISDA Definitions* (but without any rule for interpolation, which is not normally relevant to the transactions documented using these FX and option definitions).

[1221] Although the ISDA definitions refer to cases involving a quoted negative Floating Rate, if a party's Floating Amount obligations are not calculated to take into account a negative Spread, negative Floating Rates are likely to be produced only in complex transactions in which the Floating Rate is otherwise calculated by subtracting one rate index from another.

tions are calculated applying ISDA's Discounting formula.[1222] To provide that the parties do not wish the Negative Interest Rate Method to apply in connection with an interest rate swap, the *2000 ISDA Definitions* (and the *1998 Supplement to the 1991 ISDA Definitions*) provide that the parties should specify that the "Zero Interest Rate Method" will apply.

OTHER ISSUES RELATING TO FIXED AND FLOATING AMOUNT CONVENTIONS

The preceding discussion has focused on issues that arise in connection with the need to coordinate derivatives conventions with those applicable to floating-rate assets and liabilities calculated by reference to LIBO Rates, which are by far the most commonly used benchmarks in interest rate derivatives and cross-currency interest rate swaps. Similar issues can, of course, apply in connection with other Floating Rate Options, and when each of the parties will have Floating Amount obligations calculated by reference to different market conventions.

A frequently encountered issue of this kind arises when one party's obligations are calculated in arrears by reference to LIBOR as set before the beginning of each Calculation Period—as is customary in conventional transactions—but the other party's obligations are calculated by reference to an interest rate base that may change daily—such as a federal funds, commercial paper or prime rate—and therefore may not be known until the close of the day before the end of each Calculation Period. The Introduction to this Part discusses ISDA's two approaches to dealing with freely floating rates, which are identified with the terms "Delayed Payment" and "Rate Cut-off Date."[1223] A tension between the parties' interests can arise if one of them has obligations calculated by reference to a freely floating rate and the other, making payments by reference to LIBOR, would like to settle up for each Calculation Period at the period's end, because that is when it will be required to make a payment in connection with a liability that it is seeking to hedge through the derivatives transaction. In addition, normal conventions related to the floating rate applicable in determining one of the parties' obligations may have to be ignored to accommodate the conventions applicable for the other party. For instance, holidays in both London and New York are, as indicated earlier, normally taken into account in deciding whether a day will be treated as a Business Day for purposes of determining the length of a Calculation Period, but only holidays in New York would normally be relevant in connection with payments calculated by reference to a prime, commercial paper or federal funds Floating Rate Option. Where these issues arise, the parties can always make their payments gross, on different Payment Dates, but other solutions are usually preferable.

Issues of the same kinds can, naturally, arise in a transaction when one of the parties will make payments calculated at a fixed rate and the other on a floating-rate basis. In

---

[1222] Section 8.4(a) of the *2000 ISDA Definitions* supplies a simple formula for cases in which the parties wish to provide for discounting of a Fixed Amount or a Floating Amount in respect of a Calculation Period not longer than one year. The provision operates with Section 8.4(c), which provides that the applicable Discount Rate will be as specified by the parties or, if they are silent, the Fixed Rate or Floating Rate used to calculate the amount being discounted. This Discounting method is different from FRA Discounting, which is discussed in Annotation 7 to the sample FRA confirmation, *infra* p. 482.

[1223] *See supra* pp. 400 & 401.

Interest Rate Products 419

these transaction an additional common concern relates to the method used to calculate the Fixed Amounts, and how the method selected may have an impact on the way the parties choose to define the Calculation Periods in their transactions.

As discussed in the Introduction to this Part, there are various Day Count Fractions used in the ISDA standard terms for the calculation of interest for periods shorter than one year, when the interest rate applicable is—as it usually is—stated as a rate per annum. Where Floating Amounts are concerned, the Actual/360 Day Count Fraction is most often applied, at least with U.S. dollar rates, reflecting conventions in the underlying markets—for example, the London interbank market and the federal funds market. When Actual/360 is used, if a Calculation Period is extended or shortened, the increase or decrease in the number of days will be directly reflected in the Floating Amount calculated in respect of the period. Therefore, applying any of the ISDA Business Day Conventions normally followed in an underlying deposit or other market is not problematic, except to the extent the conventions followed in the two markets relevant to the parties' obligations differ.

The Actual/360 convention is also often used in calculating Fixed Amounts, and when this is so it is rare for a problem to arise out of possible timing or calculation mismatches for fixed and floating obligations in an interest rate swap, so long as both parties are willing to define Business Days relevant to their payments by reference to the same cities. It is, however, often the case that the Fixed Amounts will be calculated applying an alternative Day Count Fraction, referred to as the 30/360 Day Count Fraction or the Bond Basis.

This approach is commonly used because it is followed in the calculation of interest on many bonds. Under the approach, a year is treated as consisting of 12 months of 30 days each and, depending on the choices made by the parties, the amount payable in respect of a Calculation Period can differ depending on whether or not the period is adjusted if it ends on a weekend or a holiday. If every Calculation Period ends on its scheduled final day, as a general matter the Fixed Amounts for a year consisting of two Calculation Periods of six months each will be equal, each being one half of a full year's interest calculated at the fixed rate, even though one of the periods is shorter than the other. If a Calculation Period's length is adjusted for a weekend or a holiday, however, the amounts for the two periods will differ. ISDA has explored these complexities in great depth in a memorandum dated June 3, 1999, which includes examples of the different results that may be produced during normal years and leap years, and in cases in which transactions have Terms that are not divisible into Calculation Periods of approximately equal length—that is, if there is a "stub" period somewhere during the Transaction's Term.[1224] Those who document interest rate swaps using this Day Count Fraction must take these issues into account when their objective is to have Fixed Amounts equal to coupon payments on bonds or other instruments. To achieve their objective, it may be necessary to disregard weekends and holidays in establishing the Calculation Periods applicable in calculating the Fixed Amounts, even though the Calculation Periods

---

[1224] The Introduction to the *2000 ISDA Definitions* at x states that this memorandum may be obtained by members from ISDA's executive offices.

applicable on the floating-rate side of the same transaction are subject to adjustment in connection with a Business Day Convention.[1225]

Conclusion

The development of the OTC derivatives market and of standardized terms to document derivatives have, to a great extent, been prompted by growth in the recognition of interest-rate derivatives as powerful tools to transfer and assume selected aspects of the many risks associated with change in the interest rate environment and, then, the further application of these lessons to other risks. Therefore, concerns similar to those outlined above and related documentation issues highlighted in the sample confirmations in this section also arise in connection with OTC derivatives described in other sections of this book.

In addition, the foregoing considerations relating to conventions in the fixed-income markets are often relevant in derivatives in which one of the parties is required to make payments calculated on a notional amount on the basis of a fixed or floating interest rate—the transaction's interest-rate "leg," as it is called—while other cash flows in the transaction are calculated on the basis of other contingencies, such as changes in stock prices, in the case of equity swaps. When this is so, special problems may arise out of the wish of one or both of the parties to address conventions in one market that conflict with conventions in another.

[1225] *See supra* p. 399 on the ISDA convention of providing for "No Adjustment" to Period End Dates or Calculation Periods. This does not mean the parties' Payment Dates need differ; only that, in calculating the Fixed Amounts, the amount itself will not change when the day a payment is due falls on a weekend or a holiday.

RATE SWAPS

In its conventional form, the rate swap (or interest rate swap transaction) is a bilateral agreement in which each party promises to make periodic payments to the other calculated as one would calculate interest payments on the principal amount of a debt obligation, but no actual principal payments are involved and the periodic payment obligations of the parties are calculated using different rate bases and are made in the same currency.[1226] For example, the transaction documented in the following confirmation is a rate swap with a five-year Term in which the quarterly U.S. dollar payment obligations of the Company are calculated at a fixed rate per annum, the semiannual U.S. dollar payment obligations of the Bank are calculated at a London interbank offered rate (LIBOR), expressed as an annual rate, for six-month deposits and both sets of payment obligations are calculated on a Notional Amount of U.S.$ 50 million. The transaction may be illustrated as shown in Figure 1.

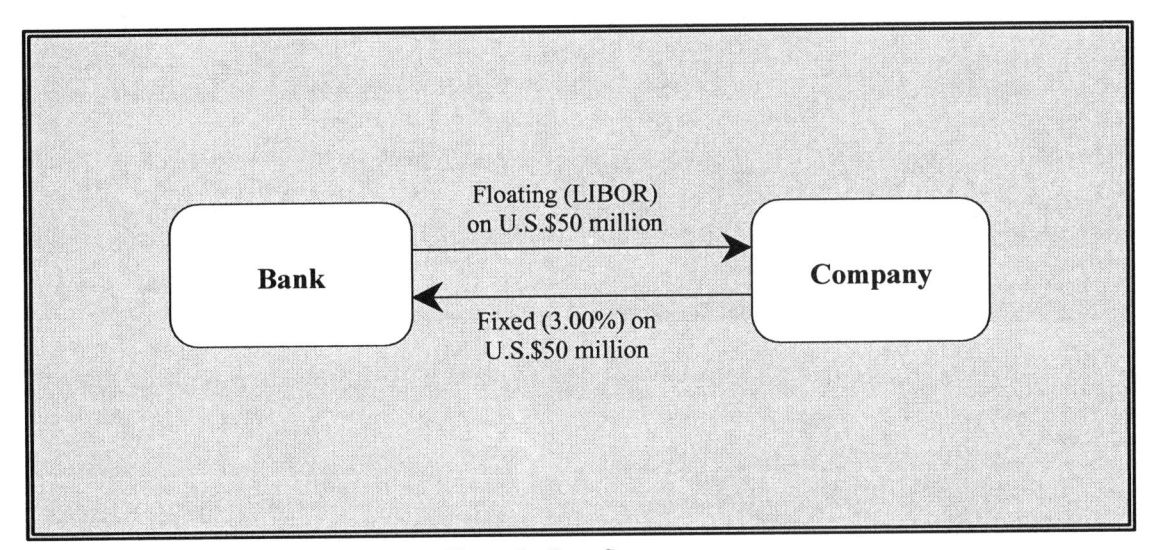

```
        Floating (LIBOR)
        on U.S.$50 million
  Bank ─────────────────▶ Company
       ◀─────────────────
        Fixed (3.00%) on
        U.S.$50 million
```

Figure 1. Rate Swap

The Company might have entered into this swap to hedge against the risk of rising interest rates. For instance, as illustrated in Figure 2, if the Company had entered into a U.S.$ 50 million Eurodollar loan agreement and was obligated to make semiannual interest payments on the loan at a rate of six-month LIBOR plus 1%, through the rate swap it could synthetically "convert" its floating-rate loan interest obligations to a fixed rate equal to the swap fixed rate plus the loan margin of 1% (assuming the interest periods on the

---

[1226] *See generally* Clifford W. Smith, Jr., Charles W. Smithson & Lee Macdonald Wakeman, *The Evolving Market for Swaps*, in HANDBOOK OF RISK MANAGEMENT 6–1 to 6–6 & 6–10 to 6–15; Rod A. Beckstrom, *Fundamental Models for Pricing Swaps*, in HANDBOOK OF RISK MANAGEMENT 7–1; Thomas E. Francois, *A Senior Credit Officer's View on Credit Issues*, in HANDBOOK OF RISK MANAGEMENT 22–1, 22–11 to 22–12.

loan and the Bank's swap Calculation Periods matched and LIBOR was determined in the same way for both the swap and the loan).

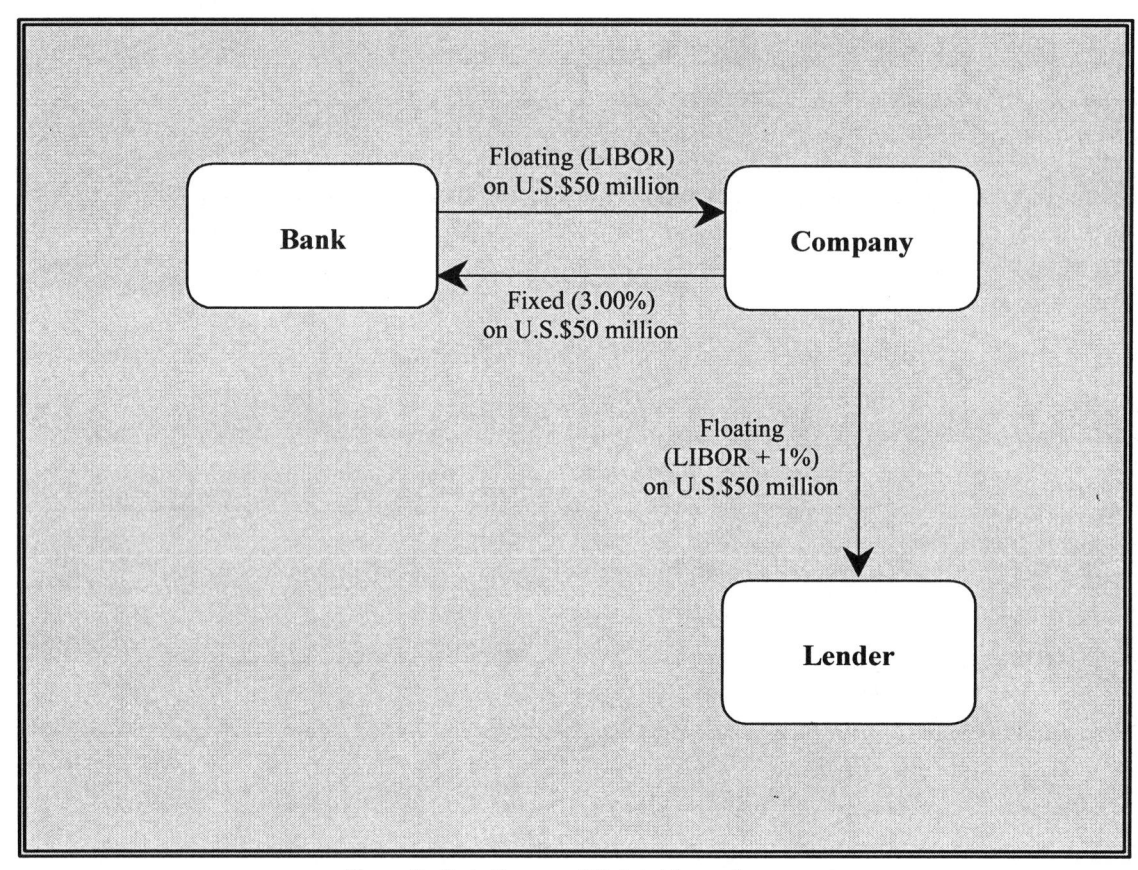

```
                Floating (LIBOR)
                on U.S.$50 million
       Bank  ───────────────────▶  Company
            ◀───────────────────
                Fixed (3.00%)
                on U.S.$50 million
                                        │
                                        │ Floating
                                        │ (LIBOR + 1%)
                                        │ on U.S.$50 million
                                        ▼
                                      Lender
```

Figure 2. Rate Swap and Related Loan Agreement

OTC rate swaps are commonly used in this way as liability-management tools by entities that can readily raise funds by issuing floating-rate debt but either do not have access to providers of fixed-rate funds or can obtain fixed-rate funding synthetically, by combining a swap and the issuance of floating-rate debt, more cheaply, or for a longer term, than would be possible through the issuance of fixed-rate obligations. As discussed in their respective descriptions in this section,[1227] rate caps, collars and corridors are other OTC derivatives that are used with the same objective of hedging against rising rates as alternatives to rate swaps.

Rate swaps are also used as liability management tools by borrowers that have fixed rate debt obligations when they want to take advantage of an environment of declining interest rates without prepaying their fixed-rate debt, either because the debt instrument or agreement does not permit optional prepayment or redemption or because it does so subject to payment of a premium or a make-whole indemnity. Also, in some cases a company may have ready access to the capital markets through the issuance of notes or bonds with a fixed-rate coupon but may prefer to have floating rate debt at the time. In these cases, the company might use a rate swap to synthetically convert its debt obliga-

---

[1227] *Infra* pp. 439 & 448.

tions to a floating rate, by agreeing to be the Floating Rate Payer under a swap, in return for Fixed Amount payments from its swap counterparty.[1228]

Rate swaps are also used in asset management. For example, investors use them to create "synthetic assets" with characteristics that are not at the time available in the money markets or capital markets. Thus, an investor seeking a medium-term fixed-rate obligation of a blue chip company in a particular industry might find that only floating-rate paper of that kind was available at the time. As shown in Figure 3, it might, however, find that it could achieve its objective by investing in the floating-rate paper and passing on the coupon, as its Floating Amount obligations under a rate swap, to an equally credit-worthy counterparty that would agree to make Fixed Amount swap payments at a desirable rate for the term of the floating-rate investment.

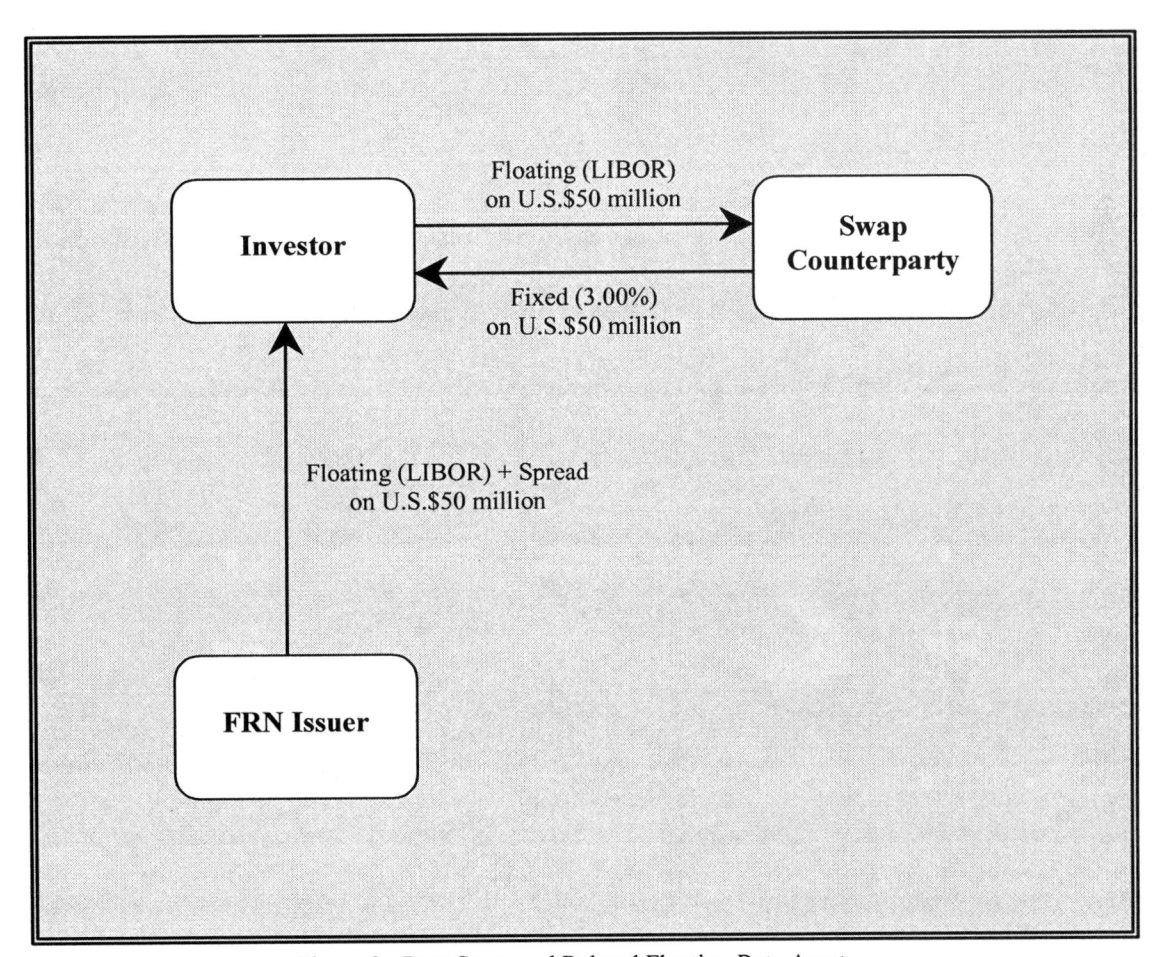

Figure 3. Rate Swap and Related Floating Rate Asset

Similarly, as shown in Figure 4, a rate swap of the kind commonly referred to as a "basis swap" might be used to create a floating-rate asset priced at one rate base from a floating-rate asset priced at another (*e.g.*, to exchange the stream of payments at six-

---

[1228] *See supra* note 1201.

month LIBOR plus a spread for a swap stream of payments calculated at a spread over 90-day commercial paper rates).

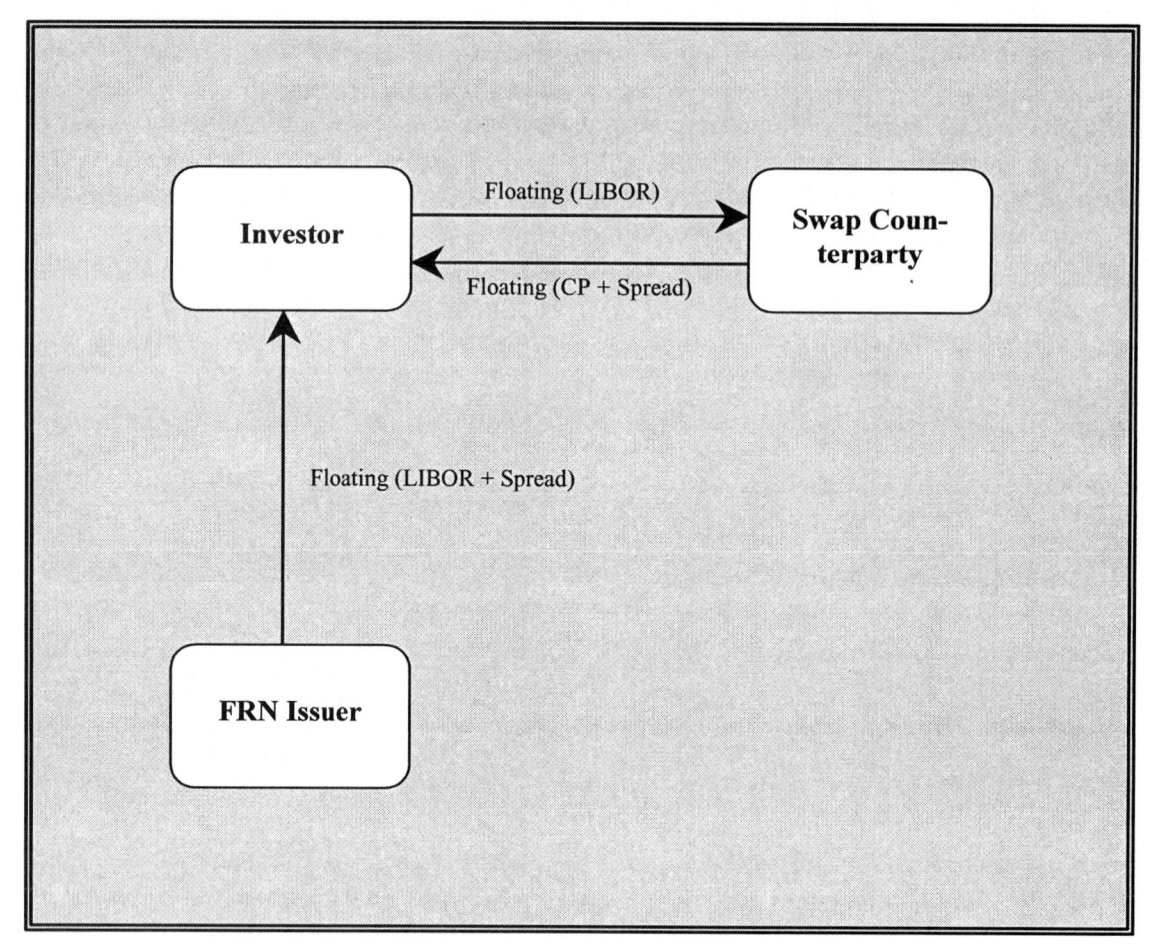

Figure 4. Basis Swap and Related Floating Rate Asset

Each of the foregoing examples involves a simple rate swap structure. The more complex variants available are far too many to name and their number increases each time the market discovers another need that can be met through a swap. Some of the more common variants are swaps in which the Notional Amount changes, to match the known amortization or drawdown schedule of an asset or liability. So, for example, a company with an amortizing floating-rate loan obligation might enter into a rate swap of the kind referred to as a "step-down" or "amortizing swap," a company with a multiple disbursement loan facility that knew its schedule for drawdowns thereunder might enter into a "step-up" rate swap, and a company with known debt obligations scheduled to go up and down might enter into a "roller coaster" rate swap.[1229] Similarly, rate swaps with varying Notional Amounts are used to try to replicate expected prepayments on interest-rate sensitive assets. These customized swaps, which are often used to manage investments in mortgage-backed securities or hedge against declines in mortgage servicing fees, are often

---

[1229] See, e.g., the definitions of "Accreting Principal Swap," "Amortizing Swaps," "Rollercoaster Swap," "Step-Down Swap" and "Step-Up Swap," in DICTIONARY OF RISK MANAGEMENT.

called "mortgage swaps" or "index amortizing" or "indexed-principal" (IP) swaps, and in them the Notional Amount can be designed to go up and down with corresponding changes of agreed magnitudes in an agreed rate index.[1230]

Other variants of the rate swap differ from the "plain vanilla" transaction[1231] in their use of a customized floating-rate stream created through the manipulation of the Reset Dates on which rate fixings take effect. An example is the "LIBOR-in-arrears" or "delayed LIBOR reset" swap, which involves calculating the Floating Amount for each Payment Date on the basis of LIBOR fixed at the end of the relevant Calculation Period.[1232] There are also transactions, sometimes referred to as Asian style swaps, in which the Floating Amount for a Payment Date is calculated on the basis of a rate determined by averaging rate settings. For example, an investor interested in replicating the return on an actively managed portfolio of floating-rate obligations might enter into a swap as the receiver of Floating Amounts calculated and payable quarterly at a rate equal to the average of three-month LIBO rates quoted every London business day during the relevant quarter. Or a borrower "might view its objective as hedging its average cost of funds during an accounting cycle, rather than hedging individual payments" and, so, might choose to enter into an Asian style swap entitling it to payments that would simulate that average funding cost.[1233] Other investor-driven variants structure a floating-rate leg of a swap to create enhanced yields in certain rate environments.[1234]

[1230] See *Index Amortizing Notes and Swaps*, DERIVATIVES WEEK, Jan. 25, 1993, at 9 (Learning Curve column); David Shirreff, *Making ends meet*, RISK, Feb. 1993, at 16 (on index amortizing swaps); and the definitions of "CMO Swap," "Indexed Principal Swap" and "Mortgage Replication Swap" *in* DICTIONARY OF RISK MANAGEMENT. See also Stephen Miller, *Interest amortizing swaps*, *in* DERIVATIVES 25, a supplement published with the May 1993 edition of CORPORATE FINANCE. These swaps are also entered into by issuers of mortgage-backed securities to manage their coupon liability in respect of those instruments. Stated simply, the theory behind the swaps is that, as interest rates fall by certain increments, fixed-rate mortgages are likely to be prepaid—so the Notional Amount of the swap (and thereby its average life) should be reduced—and as interest rates rise by certain increments, prepayments on fixed-rate mortgages will decline—so the Notional Amount of the swap (and thereby its average life) should increase.

[1231] Simple transactions have long been known in the market as "plain vanilla," in the common slang use of the expression. See, e.g., ROBERT L. CHAPMAN, NEW DICTIONARY OF AMERICAN SLANG 328 (1986). More recently, market participants have begun to use the term "vanilla" to mean a contract that "is *capable* of being electronically matched by a commercially available auto-marching engine, regardless of whether the . . . [participant] actually uses the electronic capability." ISDA 2002 OPERATIONS SURVEY 2.

[1232] See *LIBOR-in-Arrears Swaps*, DERIVATIVES WEEK, Dec. 14, 1992, at 9 (Learning Curve column).

[1233] See Chuang-Chang Chang & San-Lin Chung, *Pricing Asian-Style Interest Rate Swaps*, 9 J. OF DERIVATIVES 45 (Summer 2002).

[1234] For example, "diff" or "differential" swaps can be used by asset managers to take a position on the differential between short-term rates in two different currencies in order to obtain yield "pick up." As described in one pre-euro discussion of this kind of transaction, the asset manager may have a U.S. dollar-denominated investment priced over six-month LIBOR and may want to pay that coupon through in a rate swap to a counterparty that, in exchange, will pay six-month DM LIBOR minus a margin, but payable in U.S. dollars. In that example, so long as the DM LIBOR exceeded the USD LIBOR by more than the margin, the asset manager would have enhanced the yield on the U.S. dollar investment without taking on the settlement and other risks involved in an actual DM investment. See Satyajit Das, *Differential Operators*, RISK, July–Aug. 1992, at 51–53. Rate swaps are also combined with FRNs to produce "inverse floaters"—investment securities whose coupon increases as rates decline (*see Inverse Floaters*, DERIVATIVES WEEK, Aug. 31, 1992, at 8 (Learning Curve column)). "Inverse floater swaps" are structured so that the recipient of Floating

There are also transactions in which a party agrees to limit its protection against adverse interest rate movements in order to retain at least part of the potential benefits of favorable rate movements. These products, which have many different names, including "participating swaps," might, for example, cap the rate at which the fixed-rate payer will receive protection against rising rates, or lower the notional amount at which it obtains that protection once rates rise to a specified level, so that this party also enjoys a fractional "participation" in the benefits of declining interest rates.[1235]

In all cases, the liabilities and assets being managed through the use of a rate swap remain unaffected and nothing that happens in the relationship of the parties to the swap affects their rights or obligations with respect to the managed liabilities or assets. For example, the Company with the LIBOR-based debt in our first example will have to continue servicing that debt whether or not its swap with the Bank produces the stream of LIBOR Floating Amounts expected by the Company.[1236] Therefore, in weighing the desirability of an OTC swap as an asset or liability management tool, a market participant must recognize that the benefit of the swap depends on continuing performance by its counterparty;[1237] each of the parties must carefully analyze the credit implications of the particular rate swap structure it is considering,[1238] as well as all issues relating to its power and authority to enter into the transaction and all the tax, accounting and regulatory questions that may be associated with the swap.

Amounts receives higher payments as LIBOR or another reference rate declines (in accordance with an agreed schedule) and smaller payments as it rises (in accordance with the schedule), but the recipient's own swap payment obligations remain based on the agreed reference rate at all times.

[1235] *See* DICTIONARY OF RISK MANAGEMENT 208–09, on the Participating Swap and the Participating Interest Rate Agreements, or PIRA. *See infra* p. 439 for our production description of rate caps.

[1236] For an example of an unsuccessful challenge to the separateness of OTC derivatives and related transactions, *see, e.g., In re Thrifty Oil Co.,* 212 B.R. 147 (Bankr. S.D. Cal. 1997), *aff'd,* 149 B.R. 537 (S.D. Cal. 2000) (in which the debtor in Bankruptcy Code proceedings, which had provided guaranties for another company's obligations under interest rate swaps, argued the swaps and related floating-rate loans should be viewed together as integral parts of a fixed rate loan and that the swap counterparty's claim for damages in connection with close-out of the swaps should be disallowed under Section 502(b)(2) of the Bankruptcy Code, which disallows claims for unmatured interest). For discussion of the court's treatment of the arguments made in this case, *see* Johnson, *supra* note 1199, at 26–29.

[1237] This risk does not exist in "prepaid" swap transactions, in which the Fixed Rate Payer makes a single payment at the beginning of the swap Term equal to the present value of the periodic payments it would have made over the Term in a conventional fixed/floating transaction. Such transactions are not, however, common, precisely because they require a large initial payment. Market participants considering prepaid swaps should consult their counsel and accountants about the tax and other implications of these transactions. *See supra* p. 263 for discussion of an English court decision in an unusual dispute involving what appears to have been a prepaid swap.

[1238] The weight given to these credit concerns may, of course, depend on the term of the swap. As noted in the General Introduction, the BBAIRS terms were prepared for use in the London interbank market in connection with short-term rate and currency swaps and, accordingly, include fewer credit protections than the parties would normally require in documenting derivatives under which either of the parties might owe the other obligations. As professional participants in the derivatives markets have increasingly sought ways of netting as much of their mutual exposure as possible, transactions that would formerly have been documented under the BBAIRS terms have increasingly been documented under ISDA-based master agreements or been brought under them using an ISDA/BBAIRS Bridge published in 1996. Part 6 of this book discusses the use of bridges, including the ISDA/BBAIRS Bridge, among other tools for managing the risks that can arise from the use of multiple contracts to document the parties' mutual dealings. *See infra* p. 1298.

[Letterhead of Big Bank, N.A.]

April 16, 2002

Rate Swap Transaction

English Company PLC
Company House
Company Lane
London AB1C 2DE

Ladies and Gentlemen:

The purpose of this communication (the "Confirmation") is to confirm the terms and conditions of the transaction entered into between us on the Trade Date specified below (the "Transaction").

The definitions and provisions contained in the 2000 ISDA Definitions, as published by the International Swaps and Derivatives Association, Inc., are incorporated into this Confirmation. For these purposes, all references in those Definitions to a "Swap Transaction" shall be deemed to apply to the Transaction. In the event of any inconsistency between those definitions and provisions and this Confirmation, this Confirmation will govern.

> Annotation 1. This sample confirmation has been prepared using the forms supplied as Exhibits I and II-A to the *2000 ISDA Definitions*. Under Section 1.2 of those definitions and the 1992 ISDA master agreement forms (Sections 9(e)(ii) and 8(e)(ii) of the Multicurrency—Cross Border and the Local Currency—Single Jurisdictions forms), a confirmation sent by one of the parties will not constitute a binding "Confirmation" sufficient to document a transaction unless there has been an actual exchange of communications between the parties. *See supra* p. 372 for discussion of provisions that the parties sometimes use to indicate their understanding that all their transactions of specified types will be treated as subject to the master agreement between them regardless of whether they have yet had an exchange of Confirmations in this sense. A sample of such a provision is included in Part 5(a) of the schedule to the sample agreement in Part 3, *infra* p. 926. *See also* the discussion of related issues under statutes of frauds in Chapter 2, *supra* p. 48. The rate swap confirmed in this sample is referred to as a "Transaction" because that is the term used in the related master agreement. Since the *2000 ISDA Definitions* incorporated into the sample confirmation use the term "Swap Transaction" and not "Transaction," the penultimate sentence in this paragraph has been added for the sake of clarity. As a technical matter, the sentence is not necessary for trades of the kind documented in the sample confirmation, although it may be necessary in connection

> with other kinds of transactions documented using terms incorporated from those definitions. *See supra* p. 374. *See also 2000 ISDA Definitions* vii.

    This Confirmation constitutes a "Confirmation" as referred to in, and supplements, forms part of, and is subject to, the Master Agreement dated as of April 16, 2002, as amended and supplemented from time to time (the "Agreement"), between Big Bank, N.A. (the "Bank") and English Company PLC (the "Company"). All provisions contained in the Agreement govern this Confirmation except as expressly modified below.

> **Annotation 2.** The standard ISDA terms on the confirmation process provide that the parties should identify the confirmation as a Confirmation under the parties' master agreement. *See supra* p. 371. The first sentence of this paragraph reflects that requirement and is part of the standard ISDA form of confirmation. *See supra* p. 378 on the confirmation of a transaction prior to the existence of an executed master agreement.

    1. The terms of the particular Transaction to which this Confirmation relates—which is a rate swap—are as follows:

> **Annotation 3.** The nature of the transaction being confirmed in the sample is specified here and at the top of the sample confirmation. As explained in the Introduction to this Part, *supra* p. 374, in some cases it is necessary to include such an identification for purposes of substantive provisions of the related master agreement, or a related credit support document, which apply only to certain listed kinds of transactions.

Reference No: 00000-00

Notional Amount: USD 50,000,000

> **Annotation 4.** Incorporation of the *2000 ISDA Definitions* into the sample confirmation gives content to the term "Notional Amount" and the other capitalized terms used in part 1 of the sample confirmation. In specifying the Notional Amount, the parties can use one of the acronyms or currency names listed in Section 1.7 of the *Annex to the 2000 ISDA Definitions*. If the parties do not agree otherwise, by identifying one of those currencies, they will also indirectly be agreeing to the city or cities to be taken into account for purposes of determining whether the Payment Dates are Business Days and, therefore, whether the selected Payment Dates should be adjusted in accordance with a Business Day Convention selected by the parties or supplied by default by the *2000 ISDA* Definitions. (*See* the table *supra* p. 393, for the fallback choices prescribed in those definitions.) This is so because Sections 1.5 and 1.6 of the *Annex to the 2000 ISDA Definitions* specify the cities to be

considered for these purposes for each of the currencies (and, in some cases, Floating Rate Options) listed there, in the absence of an agreement of the parties to the contrary. (*See* Annotation 10 to this sample confirmation with respect to the default choice applicable for the transaction confirmed in the sample confirmation.)

Trade Date: April 16, 2002

Annotation 5. This is the date the parties reached agreement on the transaction being confirmed. It is also the date the sample confirmation is sent (reflecting the obligation in Section 9(e)(ii) of the sample agreement in Part 3, *infra* p. 872, that the confirmation process occur as soon as practicable after agreement is reached). *See supra* p. 384 on the importance of the Trade Date.

Effective Date: April 18, 2002

Annotation 6. For each of the parties, the first Calculation Period for the transaction being confirmed begins on this date. Therefore, as described in the Introduction to this Part, *supra* p. 381, the first Floating Amount and the first Fixed Amount payment obligations of the parties are calculated by reference to this date, not the Trade Date.

Termination Date: April 18, 2007

Annotation 7. This is the last day of the final Calculation Period for each of the parties, and it is the last day of the Term of the transaction being confirmed. Because the parties did not specify otherwise, the final Calculation Period (and, therefore, the final Fixed Amount and Floating Amount payment obligations) will be cut off on this date (and calculated through but excluding the Termination Date), regardless of whether it is a working day. The parties have specified that their agreement on the Payment Dates for the transaction will be subject to the Modified Following Business Day Convention. Therefore, if the Termination Date is not a Business Day, the payment due in respect of the final Calculation Period will not be due until the following Business Day. If the parties had wanted the length of the final Calculation Period to be extended to the following Business Day if the Termination Date were not a Business Day, they would have had to specify "subject to the Modified Following Business Day Convention" in completing the Termination Date.

Fixed Amounts:

    Fixed Rate Payer: The Company

    Company Period End Dates: January 18, April 18, July 18, and October 18 in each year, commencing with July 18, 2002 and ending with the Termination Date, subject to No Adjustment

    Company Payment Dates: January 18, April 18, July 18, and October 18 in each year, commencing with July 18, 2002 and ending with the Termination Date, subject to the Modified Following Business Day Convention.

> Annotation 8. As in the *1991 ISDA Definitions*, the recital preceding Article 1 of the *2000 ISDA Definitions* states that, when any of the terms defined in those definitions is used together with the name of a party, the term will have meaning in respect of that party only. Hence, the illustrated designation of the quarterly payment dates for the Fixed Amounts as Company Payment Dates, to distinguish them from the semiannual payment dates for the Bank's Floating Amount payments.
>
> Annotation 9. Here the parties have specified Period End Dates for the Fixed Rate Payer because they wish to make clear that the Fixed Amounts will be calculated in respect of Calculation Periods that are not subject to adjustment if they end on Saturdays, Sundays or holidays. The parties have chosen this approach so that each of the Fixed Amounts in a year will be one quarter of a full year's interest calculated at the Fixed Rate, calculated applying the Fixed Rate Day Count Fraction specified by the parties and discussed in Annotation 11. If the parties had not specified Period End Dates, each Calculation Period would end on each of the specified Payment Dates, and those periods would have been subject to adjustment applying the Business Day Convention selected to be applicable to Payment Dates. *See* the Introduction to this Part, *supra* p. 391. For illustrations of other approaches that may be used when the parties agree that Payment Dates will be before or after the end of a Calculation Period, *see* the sample currency swap and commodity swap confirmations, *infra* pp. 509 & 577.
>
> Annotation 10. For the sake of clarity, the authors' preference is always to specify the Business Day Convention agreed to by the parties, as illustrated. If the parties had been silent about their choice of Business Day Convention, under the *1991 ISDA Definitions and the 2000 ISDA Definitions* (Section 4.9 in both), the Modified Following Business Day Convention would automatically have applied to the specified Payment Dates.

Fixed Rate:	3.00% per annum
Fixed Rate Day Count Fraction:	30/360

> Annotation 11. In some fixed/floating rate swaps, the parties state the Fixed Amount for each Calculation Period as an immutable amount. By contrast, in this sample confirmation, the Fixed Rate and Fixed Rate Day Count Fraction have been specified. As a result, pursuant to the formula in Section 5.1 of the *1991 ISDA Definitions* and the *2000 ISDA Definitions*, the Fixed Amount for each Calculation Period for the Company, as Fixed Rate Payer, will be the Notional Amount of USD 50 million multiplied by the Fixed Rate of 3.00% per annum, calculated in accordance with the Day Count Fraction convention referred to as "30/360" or "360/360" or "Bond Basis." According to that convention, each full month in the Calculation Period will be counted as 30/360 of a year and each day in a short period will be counted as 1/360 of a year, with exceptions for Calculation Periods or Compounding Periods that (1) end on the 31st of a month but do not begin on the 30th or 31st of a month or (2) end on the last day of February. *Annex to the 2000 ISDA Definitions* § 4.16(e). The application of this convention can be complex, as discussed *supra* p. 419.

Floating Amounts:

Floating Rate Payer:	The Bank
Bank Payment Dates:	April 18 and October 18 in each year, commencing with October 18, 2002 and ending with the Termination Date, subject to the Modified Following Business Day Convention.

> Annotation 12. The *2000 ISDA Definitions* (like the *1991 ISDA Definitions* before them) provide that where, as here, the parties have specified Payment Dates for a party and have not otherwise specified rules for determining the length of Calculation Periods for the party's obligations, the Payment Dates will define the ends of the Calculation Periods. Annotation 9 explains why the parties have taken a different approach in defining the Calculation Periods applicable to the calculation of the Fixed Amounts payable by the Company under the sample confirmation. The transaction being confirmed calls for "mismatched" payments—the Floating Amounts are payable semiannually but the Fixed Amounts are payable quarterly. The first and third Fixed Amount scheduled for payment in each year must therefore be paid without netting, while the second and last Fixed Amount for a year are netted against the Floating Amounts payable on the same day, by virtue of Section 2(c) of the master agreement.
>
> Annotation 13. Transactions with mismatched Payment Dates involve increased credit exposure for the party scheduled to make payments more frequently. If an Event of Default or Potential Event of Default with respect to the other party

were continuing, Section 2(a)(iii) of the 1992 ISDA master agreement forms would afford protection to the party with the more frequent payment obligations, because (subject to applicable bankruptcy and similar laws) it would be entitled, under that provision, to withhold its own payments pending cure of the problem or settlement in connection with early termination. *See* Section 2(a)(iii) of the sample master agreement in Part 3, *infra* p. 803, and the related annotations. So, for example, if the Bank under the sample agreement defaulted on its debt obligations in a way that triggered the Cross Default provision (Section 5(a)(vi), *infra* p. 836), the Company would be under no obligation to make its next scheduled quarterly Fixed Amount payment on the relevant Payment Date. However, if a circumstance short of an Event of Default or Potential Event of Default occurred, the Company would have no contractual right to withhold that Fixed Amount payment under an ISDA-based master agreement.

Annotation 14. Since agreements for OTC derivatives tend to include few Events of Default, when market participants expect to enter into transactions with mismatched Payment Dates, they sometimes seek protection against these kinds of circumstances. The most common approach is to seek the protection through credit support for all transactions under the master agreement. Another approach, which is sometimes used in the market for swaps and related derivatives but has been more widely adopted in currency options market, is to expand the Events of Default to include the failure by a party to give adequate assurances of its ability to perform its obligations with respect to a covered transaction within an agreed number of Business Days after notice from the other party requesting such assurance, in circumstances in which that other party has reasonable grounds for insecurity. Depending on the circumstances, adequate assurances may consist of something less than credit support. The ICOM form for currency options adopts this approach, which is also embodied in New York law applicable to certain kinds of contracts for the sale of goods (which, as described *infra* p. 43, can include foreign currency in some cases). *See* Section 2–609 of the NYUCC and *see* the annotation to Section 2(a)(iii) of the sample master agreement in Part 3, *infra* p. 803.

Annotation 15. When neither of these approaches is possible, an alternative is to seek protection specifically for transactions involving mismatched Payment Dates through deferral of the obligations of the party with the more frequent payment dates. Another alternative is to require the party affected by a material adverse change to accelerate payment of a portion of the amount that would otherwise be payable by it on a later Payment Date. If this approach is chosen, an adjustment to the rate at which the accelerated payment is determined will be required to take account of the acceleration.

Annotation 16. Either of these alternatives may worsen the predicament of the financially troubled party. Under the approach providing for deferral, that party may have to obtain other funding in the amount of the deferred payment if it expected to pass that payment through to a third party (such as a creditor under a related loan agreement). Under the installment payment approach, the troubled party may require funding to make the installment payment, and that unexpected funding need may be difficult to meet given its situation. As a result—and because general credit support arrangements are simpler—it is more common for parties concerned about the risk entailed in mismatched Payment Dates to require the delivery of collateral or other credit support by the party with the less frequent Payment Dates or generally in relation to the parties' dealings, as discussed in Part 5, *infra* p. 1055.

Floating Rate for initial Calculation Period: 2.50% per annum

Annotation 17. In the transaction being confirmed, the Floating Rate for each Calculation Period for the Bank is determined before the beginning of that period, in accordance with the convention in the London interbank market for U.S. dollar deposits. *See* the introductory note on interest rate derivatives, *supra* p. 408. The Floating Rate for the first Calculation Period in a swap involving LIBOR-based Floating Amount obligations in U.S. dollars is often set on the Trade Date of the transaction, and the Trade Date is the second London Business Day before the first day of that Calculation Period (*i.e.*, before the Effective Date of the transaction).

Floating Rate Option: USD-LIBOR-LIBO

Annotation 18. USD-LIBOR-LIBO is one of the four U.S. dollar Floating Rate Options involving London interbank offered rates available under the *Annex to the 2000 ISDA Definitions*. By choosing USD-LIBOR-LIBO, the parties have agreed that the Floating Rate for each Calculation Period for the Bank will normally be the average of the rates appearing on the LIBO Page screen display of the Reuters Money 3000 Service as of 11:00 a.m. London time on the second London Banking Day before the first day of the Calculation Period, for deposits of U.S. dollars with a term equal to the Designated Maturity specified in the next line of the sample confirmation, *i.e.*, six-month deposits. If this Floating Rate Option is chosen and the parties do not agree otherwise, the average of the rates so obtained will, if necessary, be rounded in accordance with Section 8.1 of the *2000 ISDA Definitions*, which provides in this case for rounding of percentages to the nearest 1/100,000 of 1%. *See* the introductory note on interest rate derivatives, *supra* p. 416, for discussion of rounding conventions in the London interbank market.

Annotation 19. Two of the LIBOR alternatives, USD-LIBOR-ISDA and USD-LIBOR-BBA, are based on a single, average rate, the first published on the Reuters ISDA Page and the second on Telerate Page 3750.

Annotation 20. Each of these Floating Rate Options—and the similar options available for LIBOR-based rates involving other currencies—provides for a fallback to another method of determining the Floating Rate for a Calculation Period if the chosen source is unavailable or, in the case of USD-LIBOR-LIBO, if fewer than two rates appear on the LIBO Page at the appropriate time. For many of the Floating Rate Options available under those ISDA definitions, the fallback method is to seek rates from Reference Banks or Reference Dealers. *See* "USD-LIBOR-Reference Banks" in Section 7.1(w)(xix) of the *Annex to the 2000 ISDA Definitions* (Section 7(s)(iv) in the *1991 ISDA Definitions* and Section 7(ag)(iv) in the *1998*

Supplement to those definitions) for an example of a Floating Rate Option using Reference Banks (which they parties may select in the first instance, and not merely as an alternative if their first choice is not available). In most instances the Calculation Agent chooses these Reference Banks or Reference Dealers in accordance with the guidelines set forth in Sections 7.3(c) ("Reference Banks") and 7.3(f) ("Reference Dealers") of the *2000 ISDA Definitions* (Sections 7.4(c) and 7.4(d) of the *1991 ISDA Definitions* and the *1998 Supplement* to those definitions). In some cases the applicable guidelines identify the Reference Banks, since they are to be banks authorized to provide quotations for a particular screen display or banks nominated by a national banking association. When the LIBOR-based payments involved in a swap should match those due under a related asset or liability (such as a Eurodollar loan agreement or an FRN), the parties generally craft their own Floating Rate Option to match the terms—including the identification of the Reference Banks—for the related asset or liability.

Designated Maturity: 6 months

Annotation 21. As indicated in the preceding annotation, the Designated Maturity is the term of the U.S. dollar deposits that serve as the basis for the USD-LIBOR-LIBO Floating Rate Option. Although most Floating Rate Options available under the *Annex to the 2000 ISDA Definitions* to document OTC derivatives require the specification of a Designated Maturity, not all do. For example, those based on LIBOR and CD, T-Bill, bankers acceptance and commercial paper rates, do, but those based on federal funds and prime rates do not.

Spread: None

Floating Rate Day Count Fraction: Actual/360

Annotation 22. As described in the introductory note on interest rate derivatives, *supra* p. 408, Actual/360 is used as the Floating Rate Day Count Fraction to calculate LIBOR-based Floating Amounts because the convention in the London interbank market is that interest on deposits in that market is calculated on the basis of the actual number of days in the term of the deposit and a year of 360 days. If the parties had not specified a Floating Rate Day Count Fraction, Section 6.2(g) of the *2000 ISDA Definitions* would have supplied Actual/360 as the "default choice," because this is not one of the rates for which a different default choice is specified in Section 6.2(h) of the *Annex to the 2000 ISDA Definitions*. Actual/365 and Actual/365 (Fixed) are the default choices for most of the rates listed there. The authors' practice is to recommend that the parties state their choice in the confirmation. *See* the Introduction to this Part, *supra* p. 402, on how the Floating Amount is calculated for each Calculation Period on the basis of the formula set forth in Article 6 of those definitions.

Reset Dates: First day of each Calculation Period for the Bank

> Annotation 23. As described in the Introduction to this Part, *supra* p. 403, under Article 6 of the *2000 ISDA Definitions* (like the *1991 ISDA Definitions*), in order to determine the Floating Rate for a Calculation Period, a Relevant Rate must be determined for each Reset Date in the Calculation Period. As illustrated in the sample confirmation, when the floating leg of fixed/LIBOR rate swap is intended to parallel the London interbank offered rate for deposits with a maturity of the same length as the Calculation Period for the Floating Rate Payer, there is a single Reset Date per Calculation Period and that occurs on the first day of the period. Although rate settings in the London interbank market for U.S. dollar deposits occur on the second London Banking Day before the value date for the deposit—that is, the first day of the term of the deposit—as described in the introductory note on interest rate derivatives, *supra* p. 408, within the framework provided by the *2000 ISDA Definitions* (and the *1992 ISDA U.S. Municipal Counterparty Definitions*) it would be a mistake to specify that the Reset Date for the LIBOR leg of the swap is the second London Banking Day before the first day of each Calculation Period for the party making LIBOR-based payments. This is so because the various Floating Rate Options based on USD-LIBOR already take the London market rate setting convention into account. Therefore, as illustrated, in a simple fixed/ USD LIBOR swap, the parties must specify that the Reset Date for each Calculation Period for the LIBOR-based Floating Amounts is the first day of that Calculation Period. This is also the case with other Floating Rate Options based on interbank offered rates for deposits; however, most of the other Floating Rate Options provide that the Relevant Rate for each Reset Date is a rate set on that Reset Date itself, by reference to the appropriate source. Therefore, in a simple USD LIBOR/USD commercial paper rate swap, the Reset Date for each Calculation Period for both parties would be specified as the first day of the Calculation Period, but, by operation of the two different Floating Rate Options, the LIBOR setting for the party making LIBOR-based payments would occur on the second London Banking Day before that Reset Date, whereas the commercial paper rate setting would occur on the Reset Date itself.

Rate Cut-off Dates: None

> Annotation 24. *See supra* p. 400 for discussion of the use of this term in circumstances in which parties want to designate the last day of a Calculation Period as the Payment Date for the period but, if they do so, the Calculation Agent may be unable to calculate the Floating Amount for the full period.

Compounding: Inapplicable

Annotation 25. If Compounding were applicable, it would also be necessary to specify Compounding Dates. *See supra* pp. 402 & 405 for discussion of compounding as provided for in ISDA's booklets of definitions.

Business Days:	London and New York City

Annotation 26. Section 1.4 of the *2000 ISDA Definitions* (like the same section of the *1991 ISDA Definitions*), which deals with the term "Business Day," specifies the cities to be taken into account in determining Business Days if the parties are silent about the matter and if the payments to be made in connection with the transaction are denominated in one of the listed currencies. (In the *2000 Definitions* the list appears in Section 1.5 of the *Annex*.) If payments are to be made in another currency, the parties must specify the cities to be taken into account. When a transaction involves a payment obligation in U.S. dollars calculated by reference to any LIBOR Floating Rate Option, as is the case in the example, Section 1.6(c) of the *Annex to the 2000 ISDA Definitions* (Section 1.4(a)(i)(B) of the *1991 ISDA Definitions* and Section 1.4(a)(i)(D) of the *Supplement* to those definitions) provides that holidays in both London and New York City should be taken into account. Therefore, the parties to the transaction documented in the sample confirmation could have remained silent on the issue of Business Days. However, many market participants feel more comfortable specifying their choices in all instances, as illustrated.

Annotation 27. Parties located in cities other than those that would ordinarily be taken into account for purposes of determining Business Days sometimes request that bank holidays in their cities be taken into account. In most cases, inclusion of other cities adds a needless complication (particularly for a financial intermediary counterparty that may wish to enter into an offsetting transaction with a party from a different jurisdiction), since a party can always make advance arrangements for payments due from it when it sees that the payment is due on a bank holiday in its own jurisdiction.

Calculation Agent:	The Bank

Annotation 28. *See* the annotations to Section 4(e) of the sample annotated schedule, *infra* p. 922, for discussion of the role of the Calculation Agent and for language that market participants sometimes use to provide that, if the selected Calculation Agent is a Defaulting Party, it may be replaced in that function by the other party or a third party designated by it.

Negative Interest Rate Method:	Applicable

> Annotation 29. *See supra* p. 417 on the ISDA Negative Interest Rate Method. In the illustrated transaction, although the parties have specified that this convention will apply, it should have no impact on their dealings. If the Bank's Floating Amounts were to be calculated on the basis of a Floating Rate Option minus a Spread, the convention would have an impact in a Calculation Period in which subtracting the Spread from the Floating Rate for the period produced a negative number. As discussed earlier, the Negative Interest Rate Method will automatically apply to many transactions documented using the *2000 ISDA Definitions* and the *1991 ISDA Definitions* as supplemented by the *1998 Supplement to the 1991 ISDA Definitions* unless the parties agree otherwise. We have inserted the line item in the sample confirmation to remind market participants of this fact. The forms of confirmation appended to the ISDA definitions do not include a spot.

2. Account Details

Account for Payments to the Bank:

    Big Bank, N.A., New York, N.Y., ABA No. 000, CHIPS No. 000, Attention: Swaps Division

Account for Payments to the Company:

    Account No. 00000 with Big Bank, N.A., New York, N.Y.

3. Offices. The Office of the Bank for the Transaction is its head office in New York. The Office of the Company for the Transaction is its office at the address specified for notices to it in the Schedule to the Agreement.

Please confirm that the foregoing correctly sets forth the terms of our agreement by executing the copy of this Confirmation enclosed for that purpose and returning it to us or by sending to us a communication substantially similar to this letter, which sets forth the material terms of the Transaction to which this Confirmation relates and indicates your agreement to those terms. If you believe the foregoing does not correctly reflect the terms of our agreement, please give us notice as soon as possible of what you believe to be the necessary corrections.

                              Yours sincerely,

                              BIG BANK, N.A.

                              By: _____
                                  Name:
                                  Title: Vice President

> Annotation 30. The standard ISDA closing does not include the final sentence. Market participants should carefully review the closing text of the confirmations that they receive, because some professional participants in the market include in this spot an indication of the time by which they will treat the recipient as bound if it fails to reply and statements to the effect that the sender will withhold payments

> from a counterparty that has not replied or that the sender may treat the recipient's failure to reply as grounds for terminating the transaction being confirmed. *See supra* p. 53, on the importance of having an officer with the rank of vice president or higher execute the agreements relating to qualified financial contracts, including swaps, on behalf of federally insured U.S. depository institutions.

Confirmed as of the date first
above written on   ,   :

ENGLISH COMPANY PLC

By: _____
    Name:
    Title:

> Annotation 31. *See* the annotation to the recital of the sample master agreement in Part 3, *infra* p. 797, on certain English law concerns relating to the desirability of indicating the actual date on which an agreement is executed when it is to have effect as of a different date.

CAPS AND FLOORS

COMPARING CAPS, SWAPS AND FLOORS

RATE CAPS

In a conventional rate cap transaction, one party, usually called the "seller," agrees to make a series of payments to the other measured by the excess of an index rate[1239] over an agreed "cap rate" or "strike rate." For this protection against rate increases, the "buyer" pays a premium, which, in a conventional cap, takes the form of a single payment made at inception.[1240] Thus, in the transaction documented in the following confirmation, the Company has agreed to pay a one-time premium—treated as a "Fixed Amount" following ISDA methodology—in return for the Bank's promise to make quarterly payments—the "Floating Amounts"—to the Company for five years calculated on the basis of the excess of the London interbank offered rate for three-month U.S. dollar deposits over an agreed cap rate.[1241]

RATE CAPS AND SWAPS COMPARED

This hypothetical cap Transaction can be compared with the Transaction documented in the sample rate swap confirmation.[1242] The Company's motivation for entering into the rate cap Transaction might be identical to its motivation for entering into the rate swap Transaction—to hedge against the risk of rising interest rates. For instance, as illustrated in Figure 5, if the Company had entered into a U.S.$ 50 million Eurodollar loan agreement and was obligated under that agreement to make quarterly interest payments at a rate equal to three-month LIBOR plus a margin of 1%, it could ensure through the sample rate cap that its costs on the financing (assuming the Bank performs its obligations under the cap) will be limited to a fixed rate equal to the cap rate plus the loan margin of 1%, adjusted to take into account the premium paid to obtain the hedge.

[1239] See *Caps, Floors and Collars*, DERIVATIVES WEEK, May 4, 1992, at 9 (Learning Curve column). Caps (and floors, which are described below).

[1240] See *infra* p. 442 on variants.

[1241] In the U.S. dollar market, rate caps (and floors) most often relate to LIBO rates, but commercial paper and prime rates are also used in these derivatives products, and the cash flows in these other U.S. dollar interest-rate derivatives are often also calculated by reference to rate indexes. For example, they may be "CMT-linked"; that is, the reference rate to which they relate can be the rate for U.S. government securities having a particular maturity taken from the estimated constant-maturity Treasury rates calculated daily by the Federal Reserve. See *CMT-Based Derivatives*, DERIVATIVES WEEK, Nov. 23, 1992, at 9 (Learning Curve column). The *2000 ISDA Definitions* include two Floating Rate Options for such constant maturity derivatives. Those definitions also include Floating Rate Options that reflect "COF," or "COFI," rates—acronyms used to refer to the monthly weighted average cost of funds paid by member institutions of the Eleventh District of the U.S. Federal Home Loan Bank System—and "DISCO" rates—the acronym used to refer to the bond equivalent yield of an index reflecting the discounts at which notes are sold in the Federal Farm Credit Banks Funding Corporation Consolidated Systemwide Discount Note Selling Group.

[1242] *Supra* p. 427.

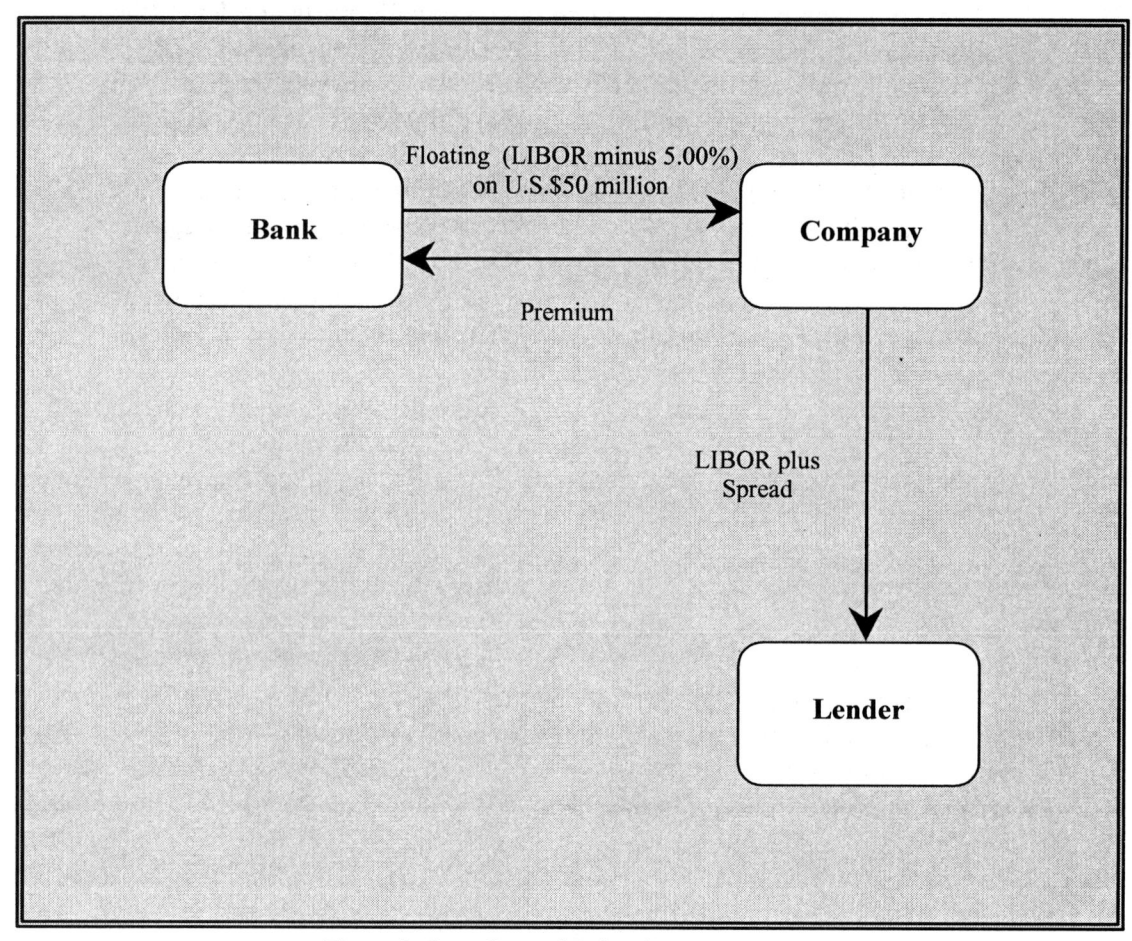

Figure 5. Rate Cap and Related Loan Agreement

From the Company's point of view, the most significant differences between the rate swap approach and the rate cap approach to hedging against the risk of rising interest rates are as follows:

1. With the cap, the Company has retained the potential savings that it would realize if the three-month LIBO rate drops rather than rising; under the swap, the Company gives up those potential savings, since it must pay over to the counterparty the excess of the Fixed Rate over three-month LIBOR for any Calculation Period for which such an excess exists.

2. To obtain the cap, the Company has been required to pay an up-front premium reflecting, among other things, the market's expectations about the likelihood that three-month LIBOR will exceed the cap rate; the conventional rate swap involves no such up-front premium, since its cost, effectively, is the potential for savings that the Company gives up by agreeing to pay the excess of the swap Fixed Rate over three-month LIBOR when such an excess exists.

Caps and Floors

3. The cap's protection against rising rates normally starts at a level (the cap or strike rate) higher than the current fixed rate for a fixed/LIBOR swap of the same Term. The Company selects that strike rate after considering the level at which it believes protection will be desirable and weighing the cost of protection at that level against the cost of protection at other levels.[1243] That is, cap rates are set "out of the money." The protection afforded by the rate swap is measured against the swap fixed rate, which is generally set "at market," that is, at a spread over the current yield on the swap's trade date of a benchmark fixed-rate debt instrument (or hypothetical instrument) with a term equal to the swap term.[1244]

4. Because the credit characteristics of the cap are different from those of the swap, the cap is available to a larger pool of potential buyers. In a conventional cap, the seller's credit exposure to the buyer ends with the payment of the premium.[1245] In a swap, either party may be required to make payments from time to time over the term of the transaction, so each party must satisfy itself with respect to its counterparty's creditworthiness. Parties with credit ratings below certain levels may be unable to obtain the protection of a swap without providing collateral or some other form of credit support.[1246] The cap may be a more attractive alternative for this group. Of course the Company, as buyer, must nonetheless satisfy itself as to the creditworthiness of the Bank before entering into the cap.

Because of this last difference between the cap and swap, when the buyer's obligation in respect of premium is paid in full at the outset, in some cases caps are documented differently from swaps. Whereas the documentation for a swap will include the full panoply of credit protections that each of the parties feels necessary, if the cap is the only transaction between the parties, or is intended to be insulated from their other dealings, it can be documented so that, once the premium is paid, the seller of cap protection will have no rights, or only limited rights, to terminate the cap, although the buyer, naturally, will retain all the usual close-out rights.[1247]

[1243] *See* the discussion *infra* note 1249 on variants designed to reduce the cost through periodic resets or other adjustment to the cap rate. On the pricing of caps generally, *see* Lee Macdonald Wakeman, *Option-Based Rate Risk Management Tools*, in HANDBOOK OF RISK MANAGEMENT 11–8. *See also* Steve Oakes, *Mechanics of caps and collars*, in MANAGEMENT OF RATE RISK 243, 247–48, on the importance of the shape of the yield curve (and the implied forward curve used in pricing swaps and caps) in setting cap rates and other considerations in comparing swap fixed rates and cap strike rates.

[1244] On the pricing of swaps, *see* PAUL MIRON & PHILIP SWANNELL, PRICING AND HEDGING SWAPS (Euromoney Publications 1991); Carl R. Beidleman, FINANCIAL SWAPS 29–41 (Dow Jones-Irwin 1985); Rod A. Beckstrom, *Fundamental Models for Pricing Swaps*, in HANDBOOK OF RISK MANAGEMENT 7–1 to 7–26.

[1245] In some jurisdictions there may be some risk that the cap seller could be required to pay back the premium in the event of the bankruptcy of the cap buyer. *See supra* p. 299.

[1246] *See Caps, Floors and Collars*, DERIVATIVES WEEK, May 4, 1992, at 9 (Learning Curve column).

[1247] When two parties enter into a master agreement for all their derivatives dealings and one of them believes that there may be times when its only positions will be caps or other transactions in respect of which it will have fully discharged all its obligations, it may ask that the master agreement include a provi-

RATE FLOORS

"Caps hedge against rates moving up and floors protect holders from rates moving down."[1248] The structure of the rate floor is much like that of the cap: the seller agrees to make a series of payments to the buyer measured by the extent to which a given index rate drops below the agreed "floor rate"; the buyer pays a premium, usually in the form of a single, up-front payment. The rate floor is used primarily by holders of floating-rate assets to protect themselves against falling rates. Examples are banks and other lenders that make floating-rate loans and investors in FRNs. When FRNs are sold with minimum interest rates, as described in the next section, investors in FRNs may also act as sellers of OTC floors, to obtain the premium a derivatives market participant will pay for the protection against falling rates.

VARIANTS ON THE CAP AND THE FLOORS

The protection afforded by a cap or a floor can be expensive. As a result, market professionals have designed products of varying levels of complexity to reduce the buyer's premium cost. All, naturally, require that the buyer give up some of the protection a conventional transaction would provide, or that the buyer itself take on added risk. The following are some of the techniques used in caps, although the same techniques can be used with floors.

In the "periodic" or "variable strike" cap, the cap or strike rate is reset periodically, at an agreed spread above the reference index for each successive "caplet" period.[1249] In an alternative, sometimes called a "step-up cap," the cap rate goes up at predetermined levels.[1250] In each case, the buyer of the cap does not obtain the absolute protection against rate increases that the buyer of a conventional cap does. These cheaper variants may, however, be sufficient hedging tools for end-users that expect to be able to pass on to their customers part, if not all, of their increased expense resulting from higher funding costs in a rising interest rate environment.[1251] To reduce premium cost, as dis-

---

sion that, in such circumstances, reduces the other party's right to designate an Early Termination Date. Provisions of this kind are often modeled on clauses included in the addenda published by ISDA in 1989 and 1990 to facilitate the documentation of caps, floors and swaptions under the 1987 forms of ISDA master agreements.

[1248] *Caps, Floors and Collars*, DERIVATIVES WEEK, May 4, 1992, at 9 (Learning Curve column).

[1249] These variants are designed to reduce premiums through resets of the cap or strike rate. Each reset is effected at an agreed spread above the reference index for each successive caplet period. These cheaper variants may be sufficient hedging tools for end-users that expect to be able to pass on to their customers part, if not all, of their increased expense resulting from higher funding costs in a rising interest rate environment. *See Periodic Caps*, DERIVATIVES WEEK, Feb. 22, 1993, at 7 (Learning Curve column) and *New Cap Structure Emerges*, SWAPS MONITOR, June 29, 1992, at 1.

[1250] *See Periodic Caps*, DERIVATIVES WEEK, Feb. 22, 1993, at 7 (Learning Curve column) and *New Cap Structure Emerges*, SWAPS MONITOR, June 29, 1992, at 1.

[1251] *See also* DICTIONARY OF RISK MANAGEMENT 154, under "Index Strike-Cap," for an example of an N-cap (so called "because of the shape of its payoff pattern") in which knock-in and knock-out features are incorporated into a cap to grade the buyer's protection against rising rates and premium cost as rates climb: "The logic is that a borrower will be able to pay higher rates in an . . . [agreed] rate environment because business will be stronger and competitors will also be paying high rates."

Caps and Floors 443

cussed elsewhere in this Part 2, caps are also combined to produce corridors, caps are combined with floors to produce collars and participating caps, and caps are combined with swaps, to produce what are sometimes called participating swaps.[1252]

IMBEDDED CAPS AND FLOORS

Capital markets instruments are often issued with "imbedded" caps and floors, which permit the issuer or investor to enter into a related transaction that is thought of as "selling" or "stripping" the imbedded derivative. Say, for example, that a floating-rate note provides for interest payable at a rate set periodically to equal LIBOR plus a spread, subject to a guaranteed minimum rate. The issuer in this sense has sold the investor an imbedded floor. The investor might decide to reduce the cost of the investment to it (or, viewing it in another way, synthetically enhance the yield on the FRN) by selling all or a part of the imbedded floor protection in a separate transaction to a buyer willing to pay an attractive premium. If LIBOR dropped below the floor rate, the investor would expect to pass through to the floor buyer the floor differential (the floor rate minus LIBOR on the principal of the FRN) received by the investor from the issuer of the FRN.[1253]

Similarly, the FRN might be issued with a cap on the rate that the issuer will have to pay. The investor, naturally, would expect a higher yield (say, as a spread over LIBOR) in return for providing the issuer with the imbedded protection against rising interest rates. However, the issuer might be able to sell a cap at the same strike price in the OTC derivatives market for a premium higher the yield "pick up" demanded by the investor. When these arbitrage opportunities exist, issuers sometimes issue capped FRNs and sell the cap benefits for a cash premium in the OTC derivatives market.[1254]

SYNTHETIC INVESTMENTS CREATED WITH CAPS AND FLOORS

Investors can also combine purchases of capital markets instruments with cap or floor transactions to obtain "synthetic" assets with characteristics different from those available in the market, or to enhance the yield over that which would be available on a straightforward investment. Thus, the investor might find it attractive to purchase a floating rate investment and, as noted above, (1) buy a floor, to ensure that the yield will not drop below a certain point or (2) sell a cap, in order to reduce the initial investment required by selling off part of the upside potential of the investment.

[1252]On participating caps and swaps, *see infra* p. 554.

[1253]In selling or "stripping" the imbedded floor in this way, the investor would, however, be promising to pay the floor buyer the floor differential whether or not the investor received payment from the issuer of the FRN.

[1254]There are sophisticated variations on this theme. *See, e.g., Periodic Caps*, DERIVATIVES WEEK, Feb. 22, 1993, at 7 (Learning Curve column), describing the issuance of "one-way floaters" combined with selling a periodic cap and buying a floor. There are also FRNs that imbed both caps and floors in what are often referred to Mini-Max Floaters. If these instruments are issued when the investor perceives the respective values of the cap and the floor to be equal (so that the issuer is paying no more in yield than it would on a conventional FRN) but the derivatives market places a higher value on the cap, again, the issuer may choose to "sell" the cap in a separate transaction.

> The Introduction to this Part, *supra* p. 369, and the annotations to the sample rate swap confirmation, *supra* p. 427, contain general commentary about the confirmation process and the use of ISDA's confirmation forms both before and after the parties have entered into a master agreement that is not repeated or expressly referred to in the annotations to the other sample confirmations in this book.

[Letterhead of Big Bank, N.A.]

April 16, 2002

Rate Cap Transaction

English Company PLC
Company House
Company Lane
London AB1C 2DE

Ladies and Gentlemen:

The purpose of this communication (the "Confirmation") is to confirm the terms and conditions of the transaction entered into between us on the Trade Date specified below (the "Transaction").

The definitions and provisions contained in the 2000 ISDA Definitions, as published by the International Swaps and Derivatives Association, Inc., are incorporated into this Confirmation. For these purposes, all references in those Definitions to a "Swap Transaction" shall be deemed to apply to the Transaction. In the event of any inconsistency between those definitions and provisions and this Confirmation, this Confirmation will govern.

This Confirmation constitutes a "Confirmation" as referred to in, and supplements, forms part of, and is subject to, the Master Agreement dated as of April 16, 2002, as amended and supplemented from time to time (the "Agreement"), between Big Bank, N.A. (the "Bank") and English Company PLC (the "Company"). All provisions contained in the Agreement govern this Confirmation except as expressly modified below.

1. The terms of the particular Transaction to which this Confirmation relates—which is a rate cap—are as follows:

Reference No.:	00000-00
Notional Amount:	USD 50,000,000
Trade Date:	April 16, 2002
Effective Date:	April 18, 2002

Termination Date: April 18, 2007

> Annotation 1. The Notional Amount is used, as described in Annotation 4 to the sample rate swap confirmation, *supra* p. 428, to calculate the amounts that may be payable to the buyer of the illustrated cap. On the way in which the Trade Date, Effective Date, and Termination Date affect the calculations, *see supra* p. 384

Fixed Amounts:

    Fixed Rate Payer: The Company

    Company Payment Date: April 16, 2002

    Fixed Amount: USD 500,000

> Annotation 2. As illustrated, within the framework of the *2000 ISDA Definitions* the premium payable by the Company, as buyer of the cap, is expressed as a Fixed Amount payable on a Company Payment Date. That Payment Date coincides with the Trade Date of the Transaction and falls before the beginning of the Transaction's Term. If the Company were the buyer of a floor, the terminology on its fixed-rate side would be the same. *See* the discussion of the term "Payment Date" *supra* p. 387, on the use of the term in this way in connection with caps, floors and other OTC derivatives that involve the use of cap rates or cap prices and floor rates or floor prices.

Floating Amounts:

    Floating Rate Payer: The Bank

    Cap Rate: 5.00% per annum

    Bank Payment Dates: January 18, April 18, July 18 and October 18 in each year, commencing with July 18, 2002 and ending with the Termination Date, subject to the Modified Following Business Day Convention.

    Floating Rate for initial Calculation Period: 2.50% per annum

    Floating Rate Option: USD-LIBOR-LIBO

    Designated Maturity: 3 months

Floating Rate Day Count Fraction: Actual/360

Reset Dates: First day of each Calculation Period

Compounding: Inapplicable

> Annotation 3. The specification of the Bank's cap rate is the only difference between this part of the sample confirmation and the same part of the sample rate swap confirmation. Because the parties have specified a cap rate for the Bank, under Section 6.1(a) and Section 6.2(a)(i) of the *2000 ISDA Definitions* (as would have been the case under the same sections of the *1991 ISDA Definitions*), the Bank's Floating Amount for each Calculation Period will be calculated at a Floating Rate determined by subtracting the specified cap rate from a Floating Rate for that Calculation Period determined in accordance with the specified USD-LIBOR-LIBO Floating Rate Option, as described in Annotation 18 to the sample rate swap confirmation, *supra* p. 432. Because Section 6.2(a)(i) specifies that the excess, if any, will be the Floating Rate for the provider of the cap (the Bank, here), if the cap rate is equal to or higher than the Floating Rate determined at the Floating Rate Option for a Calculation Period, there can be no Floating Amount payable by the provider of the cap.
>
> Annotation 4. If the parties were documenting a rate floor, they would simply specify a floor rate instead of a cap rate, along with the Floating Rate Option for the Bank, and Section 6.2(a)(ii) would operate with Section 6.1 of the *2000 ISDA Definitions* so that the Bank's Floating Amount obligation for each Calculation Period would be calculated at a Floating Rate equal to the excess, if any, of the floor rate over the Floating Rate for the Calculation Period determined using the Floating Rate Option.
>
> Annotation 5. These provisions of Section 6.2(a) of the *1991 ISDA Definitions* and the *2000 ISDA Definitions* are patterned on paragraph 2 of the addenda published by ISDA in May 1989 to enable users of the 1987 ISDA master agreement forms to document rate caps, collars and floors under those master agreements.
>
> Annotation 6. *See* the introductory note on interest rate derivatives, *supra* p. 408, and the annotations to the sample rate swap confirmation, *supra* p. 433, for discussion of LIBOR generally and of conventions in the London interbank market and how the Reset Date operates with these conventions and related matters. *See supra* pp. 402 & 405 on the ISDA compounding conventions.

Calculation Agent: The Bank

2. Account Details

Account for Payments to the Bank:

> Account No. Big Bank, N.A., New York, N.Y., ABA No. 0000, CHIPS No. 0000, Attention: Swaps Division

Account for Payments to the Company:

    Account No. 00000 with Big Bank, N.A., New York, N.Y.

3. Offices

The Office of the Bank for the Transaction is its head office in New York. The Office of the Company for the Transaction is its office at the address specified for notices to it in the Schedule to the Agreement.

Please confirm that the foregoing correctly sets forth the terms of our agreement by executing the copy of this Confirmation enclosed for that purpose and returning it to us or by sending to us a communication substantially similar to this letter, which sets forth the material terms of the Transaction to which this Confirmation relates and indicates your agreement to those terms. If you believe the foregoing does not correctly reflect the terms of our agreement, please give us notice as soon as possible of what you believe to be the necessary corrections.

                                  Yours sincerely,

                                  BIG BANK, N.A.

                                By: _____
                                    Name:
                                    Title: Vice President

Confirmed as of the date first
above written on   ,   :

ENGLISH COMPANY PLC

By: _____
   Name:
   Title:

COLLARS AND CORRIDORS

COLLARS

A rate collar transaction can be best understood as a combination of a cap and a floor in a single transaction. One party, the "seller" of the cap element of the collar, agrees to make a series of payments to the other measured by the excess of an index rate over an agreed "cap rate" or "strike rate," and the "buyer" of the cap also sells back a floor. That is, it agrees to make a series of payments measured by the extent to which the same index rate drops below an agreed "floor rate" lower than the cap rate.[1255] One of the parties, usually the buyer of the cap, also pays a premium,[1256] normally in the form of a single payment at the beginning of the transaction, unless the floor rate and cap are set so that the premiums otherwise payable in respect of the cap and floor components cancel each other out.[1257] The collar has its origins in efforts of market professionals to make caps more affordable for end-users by combining the caps with floors sold back by the end-users and crediting the end-users with the value of the floors.

In the Transaction documented in the following confirmation, the Bank promises to make quarterly payments (the "Bank Floating Amounts") to the Company for five years calculated on the basis of the excess of the three-month U.S. dollar LIBOR over an agreed cap rate, and the Company promises to make quarterly payments (the "Company Floating Amounts") to the Bank for five years calculated on the basis of the excess of an agreed floor rate over three-month U.S. dollar LIBOR. There is no premium, or "Fixed Amount." The Transaction may be illustrated as shown in Figure 6.

[1255] A variant, the "participating cap," involves setting the cap and the floor rate at the same level, but agreeing that, while the buyer of the cap will receive 100% of the excess of the index over the cap price, it will give up only an agreed percentage of the savings it receives when the index falls below the floor level. "This percentage, or 'participation' rate, is usually set so that the value of the participation in the floor equals the value of the cap." Lee Macdonald Wakeman, *Option-Based Risk Management Tools*, in HANDBOOK OF RISK MANAGEMENT 11–1, 11–15.

[1256] It is possible that the value of the floor may exceed that of the cap, requiring an up-front payment to the party that is the seller of the floor and the buyer of the cap. *Id.* at 11–12.

[1257] This zero-premium cap is often loosely called a "free" or "zero cost" collar. *Id.* It and similar structures involving currency put and call options are also referred to with many other names, including the "range forward." *See Range Forwards*, DERIVATIVES WEEK, Oct. 12, 1992, at 13 (Learning Curve column). The conventional approach to collars that eliminate the cap premium involves narrowing the band, range or collar between the cap rate and the floor rate. The "knock-in collar" is a variant designed to preserve a somewhat wider band of potential savings for the cap buyer in a level or declining rate environment but also involves the cap buyer's agreement to give up all the savings below the cap rate if the index rate used in the transaction (say LIBOR) falls below the floor rate. An example of such a transaction was described in *SOCGEN Does Knock-in Sterling Collar Deal*, DERIVATIVES WEEK, Feb. 15, 1993, at 2, as follows: a U.K. corporation bought a £20 million cap with a cap rate of 6.25% from Société Générale in London and sold the bank a "down-and-in floor . . . activated if rates [Sterling LIBOR] fall below 5.25%"; "the corporate pays the bank the difference between 6.25% and LIBOR if rates fall below 5.25%" at a time when "[a] plain vanilla collar with a 6.25% cap of similar maturity would require a 5.65% floor to be zero cost . . . ."

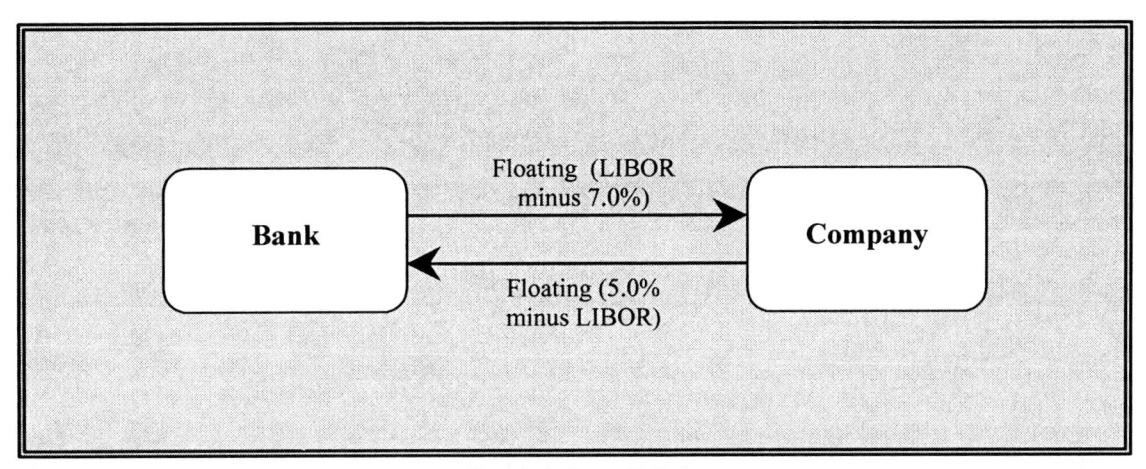

Figure 6. Rate Collar

The Company's motivation in entering into the rate collar might well be identical to its motivation for entering into the rate swap or the rate cap documented in sample confirmations appearing earlier in this book[1258]—to hedge against the risk of rising interest rates on floating-rate debt. The collar is more like the cap, in that the Company has retained some of the potential savings from a drop in rates, but it has eliminated the premium cost of the cap by giving up some of that potential through the collar technique. It should be noted that, in the typical collar, as in the cap, the Company's protection against rising rates starts at a level higher than the fixed rate for a swap of the same term against the same index. This cap rate is set at a level chosen by the Company after balancing its need for protection against the premium cost for protection at various levels.[1259]

CORRIDORS

The term "corridor" is used to refer to various kinds of derivatives products[1260] but is most commonly applied to a transaction that consists of two rate caps in which the buyer of the first is also the seller of the second, set at a higher cap rate.[1261] These transactions are tools used to reduce the cost of a cap to the buyer of cap protection. The buyer seeking cap protection at the lower strike rate effectively agrees to limit that protection at the higher strike: it will enjoy the full protection of the cap it bought so long as the relevant index rate is above the lower strike and at or below the higher strike but, because it sold the second cap, if the index rate rises above the higher strike rate, it will owe a payment calculated by reference to the excess. The value of the protection it sells through the second cap reduces the premium it must pay on the first.

[1258] *See supra* pp. 427 & 444.

[1259] *See supra* note 1243 and sources cited therein.

[1260] *See, e.g.,* BIS, FOREIGN EXCHANGE AND DERIVATIVES MARKET ACTIVITY IN 2001 at 36 (March 2002), using the term "interest rate corridor" to refer to the kind of transaction described in this sentence as well as "A collar on a swap created with two swaptions—the structure and participation interval is determined by the strikes and types of the swaptions" and "A digital knockout option with two barriers bracketing the current level of a long-term interest rate."

[1261] *See* DICTIONARY OF RISK MANAGEMENT 73. Transactions with the same structure as the described corridor are sometimes also referred to as call spreads. For a discussion of a strategy using a call spread on gas oil prices, *see Icelandair Hedges Fuel Exposure,* DERIVATIVES WEEK, Apr. 16, 2001, p. 4.

For example, if a corporation wished to buy a cap on 3-month LIBOR at 6%, it might reduce the cost of that cap by selling back a cap at 8%; at any time when 3-month LIBOR is above 8%, the payment due on the second cap will be reduced by the payment due on the first. The corridor may be illustrated as shown in Figure 7.

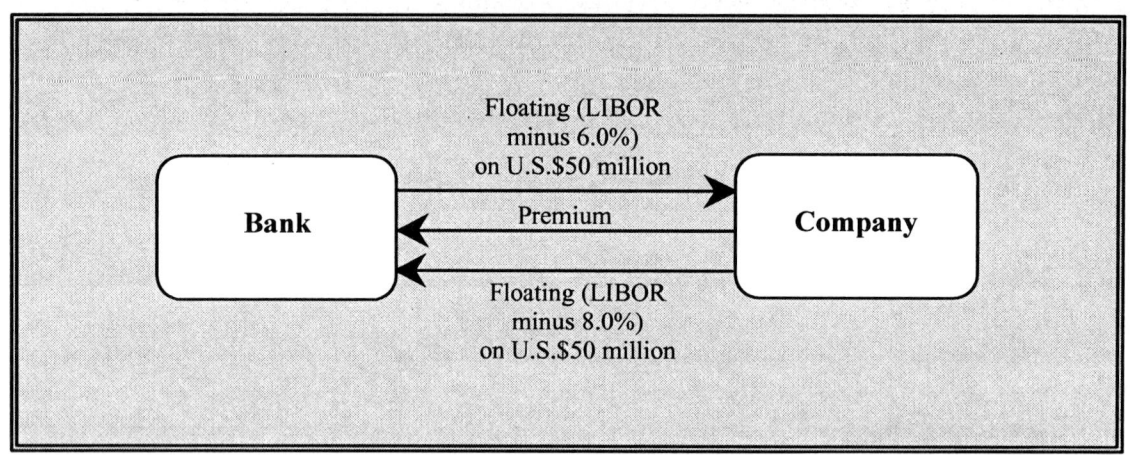

Figure 7. Rate Corridor

CREDIT RISK IN COLLARS AND CORRIDORS

As described in the description of caps and floors,[1262] the credit characteristics of a conventional cap or floor, on one hand, and a conventional swap, on the other, are fundamentally different. This is so because the cap or floor seller's risk with respect to default on the transaction ends once the buyer has paid the premium in full (assuming no risk that all or part of the premium may be recovered by the buyer or a receiver, trustee or similar official appointed for it or its property), whereas in a swap either party may be required to make payments from time to time over the entire term of the transaction.

The collar and the corridor are like the swap and unlike an independent cap or floor in this regard. Both the collar and the corridor are structures that always involve the potential that one party or the other will be required to make payments. As a result, each party to a collar or corridor must satisfy itself with respect to its counterparty's creditworthiness, and the documentation for these OTC derivatives will reflect the existence of mutual credit risk, even when the collar or corridor is documented in a separate agreement (as opposed to under a master agreement).

When these derivatives are entered into by a party from a jurisdiction where there is risk that in insolvency or similar proceedings a receiver, trustee or similar official may pick and choose among the party's executory transactions,[1263] the documentation should also clearly convey the parties' intention that the collar or corridor be treated as a single transaction, and not merely as a cap and a floor (in a collar) or two caps (in a corridor) that happen to be documented together and can be picked apart.

[1262] *Supra* p. 427.

[1263] *See supra* p. 272.

> The Introduction to this Part, *supra* p. 369, and the annotations to the sample rate swap confirmation, *supra* p. 427, contain general commentary about the confirmation process and the use of ISDA's confirmation forms both before and after the parties have entered into a master agreement that is not repeated or expressly referred to in the annotations to the other sample confirmations in this book.

[Letterhead of Big Bank, N.A.]

April 16, 2002

Rate Collar Transaction

English Company PLC
Company House
Company Lane
London AB1C 2DE

Ladies and Gentlemen:

The purpose of this communication (the "Confirmation") is to confirm the terms and conditions of the transaction entered into between us on the Trade Date specified below (the "Transaction").

The definitions and provisions contained in the 2000 ISDA Definitions, as published by the International Swaps and Derivatives Association, Inc., are incorporated into this Confirmation. For these purposes, all references in those Definitions to a "Swap Transaction" shall be deemed to apply to the Transaction. In the event of any inconsistency between those definitions and provisions and this Confirmation, this Confirmation will govern.

This Confirmation constitutes a "Confirmation" as referred to in, and supplements, forms part of, and is subject to, the Master Agreement dated as of April 16, 2002, as amended and supplemented from time to time (the "Agreement"), between Big Bank, N.A. (the "Bank") and English Company PLC (the "Company"). All provisions contained in the Agreement govern this Confirmation except as expressly modified below.

1. The terms of the particular Transaction to which this Confirmation relates—which is a rate collar—are as follows:

Reference No.:	00000-00
Notional Amount:	USD 50,000,000
Trade Date:	April 16, 2002
Effective Date:	April 18, 2002

Termination Date: April 18, 2007

Bank Floating Amounts:

    Floating Rate Payer: The Bank

    Cap Rate: 5.0% per annum

    Payment Dates: January 18, April 18, July 18 and October 18 in each year, commencing with July 18, 2002 and ending with the Termination Date, subject to the Modified Following Business Day Convention.

    Floating Rate for initial Calculation Period: 2.50% per annum

    Floating Rate Option: USD-LIBOR-LIBO

    Designated Maturity: 3 months

    Floating Rate Day Count Fraction: Actual/360

    Reset Dates: First day of each Calculation Period

    Compounding: Inapplicable

Company Floating Amounts:

    Floating Rate Payer: The Company

    Floor Rate: 2.00% per annum

    Payment Dates: Same as Payment Dates for Bank Floating Amounts

    Floating Rate for initial Calculation Period: 2.50% per annum

    Floating Rate Option: USD-LIBOR-LIBO

    Designated Maturity: 3 months

    Floating Rate Day Count Fraction: Actual/360

    Reset Dates: Same as Reset Dates for Bank Floating Amounts

Sample Rate Collar Confirmation

Compounding: Inapplicable

> Annotation 1. In the transaction illustrated in this sample confirmation, neither party is required to pay a premium for the cap or floor protection afforded by the collar. The buyer of the cap has agreed to sell a floor with a floor rate, or strike price, at a level set with the purpose of having the premium otherwise payable for the floor equal the premium otherwise payable for the cap. Therefore, confirmation of the Transaction does not require the designation of a Fixed Amount or Fixed Amount Payer. If the premiums for the two legs of the Transaction did not cancel each other out, the Transaction would be documented with three kinds of obligations: the Floating Amount obligations of each of the parties and the Fixed Amount obligation of the party required to pay the premium, documented as illustrated in the sample rate cap confirmation, *supra* p. 444.
>
> Annotation 2. If the parties were documenting a corridor, the Transaction would be documented as having two Floating Amount legs, both of which would be cap obligations, like those of the Bank in the cap illustrated in the sample rate cap confirmation, *supra* p. 444, and the premium, if any, would be documented as a Fixed Amount, as described in the preceding paragraph.
>
> Annotation 3. *See* the annotations to the sample rate swap and rate cap confirmations, *supra* pp. 431 & 446, for explanations about how the *2000 ISDA Definitions* work with the terminology set out above in establishing the Floating Amount obligations of the parties to the illustrated collar.

Calculation Agent: The Bank

2. Account Details

Account for Payments to the Bank:

    Big Bank, N.A., New York, N.Y., ABA No. 000, CHIPS No. 000, Attention: Swaps Division

Account for Payments to the Company:

    Account No. 00000 with Big Bank, New York, N.Y.

3. Offices.

The Office of the Bank for the Transaction is its head office in New York. The Office of the Company for the Transaction is its office at the address specified for notices to it in the Schedule to the Agreement.

Please confirm that the foregoing correctly sets forth the terms of our agreement by executing the copy of this Confirmation enclosed for that purpose and returning it to us or by sending to us a communication substantially similar to this letter, which sets forth the material terms of the Transaction to which this Confirmation relates and indicates your agreement to those terms. If you believe the foregoing does not correctly reflect the terms of our agreement, please give us notice as soon as possible of what you believe to be the necessary corrections.

                                                  Yours sincerely,

                                                  BIG BANK, N.A.

                                                  By: _____
                                                        Name:
                                                        Title: Vice President

Confirmed as of the date first
above written on   ,   :

ENGLISH COMPANY PLC

By: _____
    Name:
    Title:

Options on Swaps ("Swaptions")

Options to Enter into Swaps and Other Derivatives

Options to enter into swaps are commonly referred to as swaptions.[1264] They are particularly useful in cases in which a party is seeking to create a structure that requires combining a financing with one or more OTC derivatives. In such cases, there often comes a time in the pre-closing period when that party wants to lock in the economics of the entire transaction, but the financing remains subject to a number of conditions that the party is not certain it will be able to fulfill or contingencies that are not within its control, such as the underwriters' "market out" in a securities issue, which permits the underwriters to terminate their commitments if certain adverse economic or political developments make it impracticable to complete the transaction. The swaption is designed to permit that party to lock in the economics without being committed to go forward with the derivative if the financing transaction fails to close. Swaptions are also used in asset management, where their applications include management by investors of portfolio duration.[1265]

As a tool for locking in the cost of a swap or similar transaction or seeking protection against changes in the market rates for those transactions, the swaption is an alternative to the forward, or forward-starting, swap. The critical difference between the alternatives is the same as the difference between an interest rate swap and an interest rate cap as tools to obtain protection against rising rates. The swap and the forward swap, when executed at market,[1266] involve no upfront payment, but the party seeking protection against rising rates (interest rates in the swap and swap rates in the forward swap) obtains that protection at the cost of giving up the potential advantages of declining rates. The cap and the swaption, on the other hand, involve the payment of a premium for the agreed protection at a cost that is always limited to the premium paid.

So, for example, if a party seeking protection against rising swap rates for a three-year fixed/LIBOR U.S. dollar rate swap enters into a forward swap, it actually commits to enter into the swap on the agreed start date, with fixed-rate obligations at the agreed rate, say 3%, or to pay a cash-settlement amount to terminate the swap at the inception of its term if the then current market rate for the same three-year transaction is below 3%. It has, in effect, given up the benefit of favorable changes (a decline in swap rates) without knowing what the ultimate cost of the protection will be. If the same party, instead, pays a

---

[1264] *See generally* Brian John Crowe, *Swaptions: Tailoring Interest Rate Swaps*, in Handbook of Risk Management 12–1; Lee Macdonald Wakeman, *Option-Based Risk Management Tools*, in Handbook of Risk Management 11–1.

[1265] *See* Brian John Crowe, *Swaptions: Tailoring Interest Rate Swaps*, in Handbook of Risk Management 12–1, 12–8 to 12–15 on this use of swaptions, as well as their use by mortgage lenders to cover imbedded options risk and their use by asset-liability managers to manage rate and volatility risk.

[1266] For further discussion of this subject, *see supra* p. 222.

premium for a swaption entitling it to enter into the fixed-floating swap transaction,[1267] it knows that the maximum cost it will incur for the protection is the premium. If the market rate for the swap is 2.85% on the swaption's expiration date, the swaption will simply expire unexercised. If the party still needs the protection of a fixed-floating swap at the time, it can enter into a swap at the current market rate, and the savings derived from the decline in market rates acts to offset the cost of the premium for the expired swaption. If, on the other hand, the market rate for the swap is 3.5% on the swaption's expiration date, the party can either enter into the swap at the agreed 3% fixed rate (assuming the swaption provided for physical settlement) or receive a cash settlement reflecting the difference between the agreed 3% fixed rate and the 3.5% market rate current at the time.

There are also "captions" on rate caps and "floortions" on rate floors.[1268] As suggested, in an option to enter into a swap, if the option is exercised and settled physically, the underlying swap will simply come into effect on the terms agreed when the swaption was executed and, except for the premium it paid to purchase the swaption, the buyer will have no further payment to make at the time of exercise. In an option to enter into a cap or a floor, the buyer pays the option premium to have the right to enter into the cap or floor with the agreed cap rate or floor rate for a premium set at the time the option is executed. Therefore, if the buyer exercises the option for physical settlement, it will still be required to pay the agreed premium for the cap or floor at the time. In each case, however, the swaption (or, for those who use the terms, caption or floortion) premium is the price paid for the right, but not the obligation, to enter into another transaction.

OPTIONS TO TERMINATE SWAPS

Options to terminate swaps are useful in cases in which an issuer enters into a swap as a hedge in connection with its issuance of "callable" debt or floating-rate debt convertible at the issuer's option to a fixed rate. In such cases, if the issuer exercises its right to redeem the debt or convert the coupon, it will not want to be left with the swap on its books after the redemption or conversion. An option to terminate the swap in those circumstances secures for the issuer a clear right to terminate the swap in accordance with an agreed settlement mechanism, removing any concerns it might otherwise have about negotiating a termination with the swap counterparty at the time of the redemption or conversion.

Alternatively, an issuer of callable bonds might improve the economics of the transaction by entering into a swap that gives its counterparty the right to terminate the swap at the same time or times the bonds can be called. If the counterparty exercises that right, the issuer can then redeem the debt.[1269] It has been said that "[t]he swaptions market developed from this [kind of transaction] because the [provider of the swap] . . . would pay the issuer more for the call feature than the investor had charged."[1270]

[1267]"Payer's swaption" and "receiver's swaption" are terms sometimes used to refer, respectively, to swaptions in which the buyer pays for the right to be the fixed-rate payer in the underlying transaction, or for the right to be the receiver of fixed amounts in the underlying transaction.

[1268]*See* the definitions of "caption" and "floortion" in DICTIONARY OF RISK MANAGEMENT 50, 128.

[1269]*See* Wakeman, *supra* note 1264, at 11-1, 11-16.

[1270]Crowe, *supra* note 1265, at 12-1, 12-6.

Swaptions

In addition, options to terminate transactions are sometimes used to manage exposure to credit risk when parties want to transact for terms longer those permitted by limits in place under their policies at the time they transact. Since the 1990s options to terminate have been used in this way in what are often referred to as mutual puts.[1271]

DOCUMENTATION

In the *2000 ISDA Definitions,* options to enter into and to terminate swaps are referred to as Option Transactions. Options to enter into Swap Transactions are Swaptions, as are other Swap Transactions the parties identify as Swaptions. Options to terminate Swap Transactions are simply Swap Transactions that are subject to Optional Early Termination. The parties are free to refer to other transactions as Option Transactions, but this freedom, and that of designating transactions as Swaptions, should be used with care because the provisions of the *2000 ISDA Definitions* relating to Swaptions and Option Transactions are designed to work in limited cases.

For example, the provisions relating to Swaptions all operate on the assumption that a Swaption will be an option of the Buyer to enter into a Swap Transaction—the Underlying Transaction—or to receive a Cash Settlement Amount that, generally speaking, approximates the amount that the Buyer could receive by entering into the Underlying Transaction and simultaneously closing it out at an agreed measure of its market value. Also, as indicated below, some of the provisions on calculating Cash Settlement Amounts may work well only for single currency fixed/floating interest rate swaps. Furthermore, unlike the *1991 ISDA Definitions,* the *2000 ISDA Definitions* are not designed to accommodate options or synthetic options on commodity prices, equity indices or currencies.

When an Option Transaction involves a right to enter into a Swap Transaction, the latter is, as noted, referred to in the *2000 ISDA Definitions* as the Underlying Transaction. That term is not used to refer to a Swap Transaction that is subject to Optional Early Termination (or, for that matter, to Mandatory Early Termination). As the sample confirmation illustrates, the ISDA conventions assume that a single Confirmation will set out the terms of a Swaption and the Underlying Transaction. Similarly, if a Swap Transaction provides for Optional Early Termination, the assumption is that all terms relevant to that option will be set out in confirming that Swap Transaction. Exhibits II-E and II-F to the *2000 ISDA Definitions* set out the special provisions that would normally be included in documenting either of these classes of Option Transactions under those definitions.

OPTION STYLES

The *2000 ISDA Definitions* provide for three styles of Option Transactions:

- A European style Option Transaction, exercisable at one time only, on the Expiration Date,

---

[1271]*See As Mutual Puts become Commonplace, Will There Be Any Unexpected Consequences?* SWAPS MONITOR, Nov. 6, 1995, at 1.

- An American style Option Transaction, exercisable on any of the days in a specified Exercise Period, which is presumed to begin on the first Premium Payment Date if the parties are silent on the matter,[1272] and

- A Bermuda style Option Transaction, exercisable during an Exercise Period consisting of specified dates.

There are, however, more complex exercise terms available in the market.[1273]

CASH SETTLEMENT AND PHYSICAL SETTLEMENT

Under the *2000 ISDA Definitions*, Swaptions may be subject to Physical Settlement or Cash Settlement. Accordingly, in documenting a Swaption under those definitions, the parties must specify either Physical Settlement or Cash Settlement. If "Physical" or "Physical Settlement" is specified and the Swaption is exercised or deemed to have been exercised, under Section 14.1 of those definitions, the Underlying Transaction will become effective, and the Notional Amount specified in the notice of exercise will be the Notional Amount of the Underlying Transaction.[1274] If "Cash" or "Cash Settlement" is specified to be applicable, the Buyer will (under Section 13.1 of those definitions) have the right to receive the Cash Settlement Amount (if any) from the Seller on the Cash Settlement Payment Date.

In the case of Swap Transactions to which Optional Early Termination applies, if Cash Settlement is specified to be applicable, the party that is out-of-the-money on the Optional Early Termination Date will be required to pay the absolute value of the Cash Settlement Amount to the other party on the Cash Settlement Payment Date. That Cash Settlement Amount will be calculated (as described in the following section) by reference to the portion of the Notional Amount of the relevant Swap Transaction that is being terminated early. Cash Settlement is deemed to apply to these transactions unless the parties specify otherwise[1275] This would also be the economic result if the parties had chosen to make a Swap Transaction subject to Mandatory Early Termination.[1276]

However, if the parties have made a Swap Transaction subject to Optional Early Termination and have also affirmatively specified that Cash Settlement will be inapplicable, in the event of exercise the Swap Transaction's Notional Amount will simply be re-

---

[1272] Section 11.2 of the *2000 ISDA Definitions*, in defining the term "Commencement Date," operates with Section 11.2(a), which defines the "American" option style, and Section 12.1(a), which defines "Exercise Period," to create this "default choice."

[1273] *See* Lee Macdonald Wakeman, *Option-Based Rate Risk Management Tools, in* HANDBOOK OF RISK MANAGEMENT 11-1, at 11-16, describing as an "American window" transaction a caption that is "considerably cheaper than the American caption because the option exercises into a cap with a decreasing term; that is, the Termination Date of the cap will be the same regardless of when the option is exercised." *See also supra* note 646 and sources cited therein on the pricing of options.

[1274] This general rule is qualified by special rules applicable in cases in which the parties have agreed to terms relating to partial exercise and multiple exercise, subjects discussed in the annotations to the following sample confirmation.

[1275] *2000 ISDA Definitions* § 15.1.

[1276] *Id.* § 16.1 (which states that the Cash Settlement Amount will be payable on the Mandatory Early Termination Date, subject to the satisfaction of any applicable conditions precedent).

duced by the amount involved in the exercise of the Optional Early Termination feature, with effect on the Optional Early Termination Date, and neither party will have any further Fixed Amount or Floating Amount obligation in respect of that exercised portion of the Notional Amount. This is a choice the parties would make only if the parties' intention was to simply end their mutual obligations, without any settlement in respect of the value of the swap being terminated.[1277]

CASH SETTLEMENT COMPUTATIONS

The *1991 ISDA Definitions* did not supply rules on calculating the amount to be paid in cash settlement of options. Rules for calculating cash settlement of particular types of products were introduced in the *1993 ISDA Commodity Derivatives Definitions*,[1278] the *1994 ISDA Equity Option Definitions*,[1279] the *1998 FX and Currency Option Definitions*[1280] and the *1999 Credit Derivatives Definitions*.[1281] Rules tailored to cash settlement of Swaptions on some interest rate derivatives and currency swaps were established in the *1998 Supplement to the 1991 ISDA Definitions* and now appear in the *2000 ISDA Definitions*.

Regardless of whether they are calculating a Cash Settlement Amount for a Swaption or for a Swap Transaction subject to Optional Early Termination or Mandatory Early Termination, the preferred method of determining the Cash Settlement Amount under the *2000 ISDA Definitions* (Section 17.2) is for the parties to agree on an amount by the Cash Settlement Valuation Time on the Cash Settlement Valuation Date. The parties will, however, specify in the applicable Confirmation a Cash Settlement Method that will apply if they are unable to reach agreement.

The choices of Cash Settlement Methods in the *2000 ISDA Definitions* are:

- Cash Price
- Cash Price–Alternate Method
- Par Yield Curve–Adjusted
- Zero Coupon Yield–Adjusted
- Par Yield Curve–Unadjusted

Cash Price. This method is appropriate for all three types of Option Transactions and is calculated in the same manner for all of them. The basic methodology, set forth in Section 17.3(a) of the *2000 ISDA Definitions*, is to calculate the Cash Settlement Amount

---

[1277] Market participants sometimes refer to this as "settling flat" or "without swap breakage." It should be noted that under this ISDA convention, if the Optional Early Termination Date is not a scheduled Payment Date under the transaction being terminated, no payment will be required in respect of the portion of the Calculation Period preceding the Optional Termination Date.

[1278] See infra p. 559.

[1279] See infra p. 721.

[1280] See infra p. 528.

[1281] See infra p. 647.

(as of the Cash Settlement Valuation Time on the Cash Settlement Valuation Date) by obtaining quotations in the market, as would be done to calculate an early termination payment under Section 6(e)(ii) of a 1992 ISDA Master Agreement form using the Market Quotation payment measure.[1282] For this purpose, the parties are to refer to their own master agreement, if they have one in place and have referred to it in confirming the relevant Transaction and, in any other case, they are supposed to apply this methodology in accordance with the terms printed by ISDA in the 1992 Master Agreement (Multicurrency—Cross Border) form.[1283] In any case, certain terms in Section 6(e) of the 1992 ISDA Master Agreement forms are redefined for purposes of calculating a Cash Settlement Amount as follows:

Section 6(e) Term	Cash Settlement Term
Terminated Transaction	Relevant Swap Transaction
Early Termination Date	Cash Settlement Payment Date, Optional Early Termination Date Payment Date or Mandatory Early Termination Date, as the case may be
Reference Market-makers	Cash Settlement Reference Banks
Termination Currency	Cash Settlement Currency

In addition, the quotations used in Cash Price calculations are obtained by the Calculation Agent, whereas they would be obtained by one or both of the parties in an actual early termination pursuant to Section 6(e) of a master agreement prepared using one of these ISDA forms.[1284]

The Cash Settlement Reference Banks may be identified in the relevant Confirmation. If they are so identified and any of them ceases to exist or to quote the relevant rates or prices, that institution will be dropped form the list, and the parties may agree on a replacement.[1285] If Cash Settlement Reference Banks are not identified in the Confirmation, the parties may agree on them at the relevant time and, if the parties fail to reach agreement, the Cash Settlement Reference Banks are to be leading dealers selected by the Calculation Agent from the list of dealers whose rates are used in deriving the rates on the relevant ISDAFIX page—a screen page of the Reuters Money 3000 Service used to display par swap rates for swaps in the relevant currency.

[1282] See supra p. 241.

[1283] These rules are supplied by Section 17.1(i) of the *2000 ISDA Definitions* and would apply even if the parties had chosen Loss or Replacement Value as the appropriate measure of damages in connection with an early termination under their master agreement in connection with an Event of Default or Termination Event.

[1284] See infra p. 890.

[1285] See Section 17.2(g)(ii) of the *2000 ISDA Definitions*.

The parties will also specify a Quotation Rate in their Confirmation. The Quotation Rate may be a "bid" rate, an "ask" rate or a "mid" (midmarket) rate. This choice identifies the basis on which the Cash Settlement Reference Banks will be asked to provide their quotations.

Section 17.3(a) provides that the Cash Settlement Reference Banks should be asked, in providing their quotations, to assume that the counterparty on the transaction for which they are quoting would be "a dealer in the relevant market of the highest credit standing which satisfies all the credit criteria which such Cash Reference Banks apply generally at the time in deciding whether to offer or make an extension of credit" and to disregard any existing credit support.[1286] Section 17.3(a) departs further from the Section 6(e) mechanics applicable in calculating early termination settlement amounts in connection with Events of Default and Termination Events by providing that, if fewer than three quotations are received, the Calculation Agent will determine the Cash Settlement Amount. In making such a determination, the Calculation Agent would be required "to do so in good faith and in a commercially reasonable manner," under Section 4.14 of the *2000 ISDA Definitions*.

Cash Price–Alternate Method. Like Cash Price, this Cash Settlement Method is appropriate for Swaptions, Swap Transactions to which Optional Early Termination applies and Swap Transactions to which Mandatory Early Termination applies and is calculated in the same way for all three types of transaction. The difference in the basic methodology, set forth in Section 17.3(b) of the *2000 ISDA Definitions*, as compared with Cash Price, is that the Cash Settlement Amount is calculated as if it were an early termination payment under Section 6(e)(ii)(2) of an ISDA-based master agreement using the Market Quotation payment measure. That is, the calculation is always made as if there were a no-fault Termination Event involving two Affected Parties.[1287]

In this case, the quotations are obtained by the parties, rather than a Calculation Agent, and, if fewer than three quotations are received by a party, that party will determine an amount "in good faith and in a commercially reasonable manner." The amounts obtained by the parties are averaged in order to calculate the Cash Settlement Amount.

As in the case of Cash Price, the Cash Settlement Reference Banks are to be asked to use the agreed Quotation Rate (bid, ask or mid) and to assume in giving their quotations that the counterparty on the transaction they are quoting for would be a suitable dealer of the highest credit standing, disregarding the existence of any credit support. These features of Section 17.3(b) have the effect of eliminating the essential distinguishing characteristics of the Section 6(e)(ii)(2) mechanism. As a result, a Cash Settlement Amount determined in accordance with the Cash Price–Alternate Method for a given Transaction at a given time should be very close to one determined in accordance with the Cash Price method, except in very unusual cases.

[1286] This approach is similar to that taken in the provisions of the *2001 ISDA Amendments* that relate to Force Majeure Events and Illegality, although those provisions also always require the use of midmarket quotations. *See infra* p. 865. *See also supra* p. 224 on the relevance of the credit standing of the parties in calculating damages under the Loss, Market Quotation and Replacement Value methods.

[1287] *See supra* note 723 and Example 3 on p. 248.

Par Yield Curve–Adjusted. This Cash Settlement Method is appropriate for Swaptions, Swap Transactions to which Optional Early Termination applies and Swap Transactions to which Mandatory Early Termination applies and is calculated in the same way for all three types of transaction, although certain refinements are introduced if Optional Early Termination or Mandatory Early Termination applies and there are mismatches between the Fixed Rate Payer Payment Dates and the Floating Rate Payer Payment Dates under the transaction being terminated.

This method calls for calculating the present value of an annuity that would pay the difference between the remaining amounts scheduled to be paid by the Fixed Rate Payer under the transaction being terminated and the payments that the Fixed Rate Payer would make if the Fixed Rate were the Settlement Rate. The Settlement Rate is the par swap rate that appears on a designated price source for swaps in the relevant currency and for a period "equivalent" to the remaining Term of the Relevant Swap Transaction. The discount rate to be used under this approach is the Settlement Rate. The Business Day Convention to be used is the one applicable to Fixed Rate Payer Payment Dates under the Relevant Swap Transaction.

The applicable provision (Section 17.2(f) of the *2000 ISDA Definitions*) contemplates that the Confirmation for the relevant Transaction will specify one of three sources for a par swap rate: "ISDA Source," "Other Price Source" (along with the selected source) or "Reference Banks." If ISDA Source or Other Price Source is specified but the relevant rate does not appear in the specified source, the fallback is to Reference Banks. If Reference Banks applies, quotations are obtained from the Cash Settlement Reference Banks following the procedures that would have been followed if Cash Price or Cash Price–Alternate Method had been specified by the parties.

The application of this method may be illustrated as follows, assuming a fixed-floating swap with South American Company paying a fixed rate of 3.25% on a Notional Amount of U.S. $100 million and Dealer paying 3-month LIBOR on the same amount. Suppose that the specified Quotation Rate is "mid," that there is one year left to run on the swap and that the Settlement Rate—the par swap rate obtained from the relevant price source—is 2.75%, because of a fall in rates since the transaction began (that is, 2.75% is the average of midmarket quotations of the fixed rate that would be paid by the Cash Settlement Reference Banks to a suitable counterparty of the highest credit standing in a fixed-floating swap with the counterparty paying 3-month LIBOR). The amounts that would be paid by the Fixed Rate Payer under the Relevant Swap Transaction would be four quarterly payments calculated at the rate of 3.25% per annum on U.S.$100,000,000. The amounts that would be paid by the Fixed Rate Payer if the fixed rate were the Settlement Rate would be four quarterly payments calculated at the rate of 2.75% per annum on U.S.$100,000,000. The amounts of the two payment streams and the difference between them might be as shown in the following table, after adjustment for non-working days. Accordingly, the Cash Settlement Amount would be about U.S. $492,000—the present value of a flow of four quarterly annuity payments in amounts equal to the differences between payments calculated at 3.25% per year and payments at 2.75% per year, discounted to present value at the Settlement Rate (2.75% per year).

Payments @ 3.25% per annum	Payments @ 2.75% per annum	Difference
$810,274	$687,616	$124,658
$810,274	$687,616	$124,658
$810,274	$687,616	$124,658
$819,178	$693,151	$126,027

The Introduction to the *2000 ISDA Definitions*[1288] notes that this method may be inappropriate for transactions other than fixed-floating rate swaps in a single currency, because of its reliance on valuation through a comparison of the fixed rate in the transaction with a prevailing market rate.

Zero Coupon Yield–Adjusted. The Zero Coupon Yield–Adjusted Cash Settlement Method is generally similar to the Par Yield Curve–Adjusted method, with the present value calculated by using a set of discount factors calculated from a current zero coupon curve agreed to by the parties. If the parties fail to agree on a curve, there is a fallback to the Cash Price method of determining the Cash Settlement Amount. Depending on the shape of the selected curve at the time, the Cash Settlement Amount could be somewhat larger or somewhat smaller than the amount calculated using the Par Yield Curve–Adjusted method. The Introduction to the *2000 ISDA Definitions* notes that this method, like Par Yield Curve–Adjusted, may be inappropriate for transactions other than fixed-floating rate swaps in a single currency, for the reason stated above.

Par Yield Curve–Unadjusted. This Cash Settlement Method is identical to the Par Yield Curve–Adjusted method, except that the annuity payments and discounting are both calculated based on the Fixed Rate Payer Payment Dates under the Relevant Swap Transaction without adjustment for non-working days. In the above example, the Cash Settlement Amount would be slightly higher under the Unadjusted method, because the first three "difference" amounts would each be somewhat larger (U.S.$250,000) and the last would be correspondingly smaller. On other assumptions, the Cash Settlement Amount could be the same under the two methods or lower without the adjustment. The Introduction to the *2000 ISDA Definitions* further notes that this method, like Par Yield Curve–Adjusted and Zero Coupon Yield–Adjusted, may be inappropriate for transactions other than fixed-floating rate swaps in a single currency, for the reason stated above.

The following sample confirmation illustrates the documentation for a European style Swaption that gives the Buyer the right to receive a Cash Settlement Amount in respect of the midmarket value of a fixed/LIBOR U.S. dollar rate swap.

[1288] At xiv.

> The Introduction to this Part, *supra* p. 369, and the annotations to the sample rate swap confirmation, *supra* p. 427, contain general commentary about the confirmation process and the use of ISDA's confirmation forms both before and after the parties have entered into a master agreement that is not repeated or expressly referred to in the annotations to the other sample confirmations in this book.

[Letterhead of Big Bank, N.A.]

April 16, 2002

Swaption

English Company PLC
Company House
Company Lane
London AB1C 2DE

Ladies and Gentlemen:

The purpose of this communication (the "Confirmation") is to confirm the terms and conditions of the transaction entered into between us on the Trade Date specified below (the "Transaction").

The definitions and provisions contained in the 2000 ISDA Definitions, as published by the International Swaps and Derivatives Association, Inc., are incorporated into this Confirmation. For these purposes, all references in those Definitions to a "Swap Transaction" shall be deemed to apply to the Transaction. In the event of any inconsistency between those definitions and provisions and this Confirmation, this Confirmation will govern.

This Confirmation constitutes a "Confirmation" as referred to in, and supplements, forms part of, and is subject to, the Master Agreement dated as of April 16, 2002, as amended and supplemented from time to time (the "Agreement"), between Big Bank, N.A. (the "Bank") and English Company PLC (the "Company"). All provisions contained in the Agreement govern this Confirmation except as expressly modified below.

The terms of the particular Transaction to which this Confirmation relates—which is a Swaption on the Underlying Transaction referred to below—are as follows:

> Annotation 1. This sample confirmation has been prepared using the forms supplied as Exhibits I and II-E to the *2000 ISDA Definitions*. As illustrated in this sample, the confirmation of a swaption must describe two Transactions. The first is the Option Transaction itself, and its terms are described in numbered paragraphs 1–3 of ISDA's form of confirmation for Swaptions. The second is the Underlying Transaction that will be entered into, or settled in cash, if the Swaption is exercised.

Sample Swaption Confirmation

> The Underlying Transaction is described in numbered paragraph 4 of the ISDA form. If the Swaption is exercised, it is not necessary to document the Underlying Transaction anew at the time of exercise.
>
> Annotation 2. As illustrated here, some market participants like to specify the nature of the Option Transaction being confirmed at the beginning of the confirmation. Since the Swaption contemplated in the sample confirmation is being documented using a 1992 ISDA master agreement form, we have clarified in the second introductory paragraph of the sample confirmation that references in those definitions to "Swap Transaction" are to be understood to be references to the Underlying Transaction described in the confirmation. This may be particularly useful if the parties wish to document an option to enter into a kind of Transaction that does not clearly fall within the definition of "Swap Transaction" in the *2000 ISDA Definitions*. *See* Annotation 1 to the sample rate swap confirmation, *supra* p. 427.

Reference No.: 00000-00

1. Swaption Terms

Trade Date: April 16, 2002

Option Style: European

> Annotation 3. By specifying "European," the parties have indicated that the Buyer will be entitled to exercise its rights only on a single specified day, the Expiration Date. Section 11.2(c) of the *2000 ISDA Definitions*, unlike Section 8.2(h) of the *1991 ISDA Definitions*, specifies that the single day is presumed to be the Expiration Date of the Option—as is the common understanding with options of this style—so it is not be necessary for parties using the *2000 ISDA Definitions* for this purpose to specify the day by completing a line relating to the Exercise Period unless they wish to adopt some different rule. If the Transaction being documented could be exercised on more than one day, the parties would complete this line of the confirmation with the word "American" or "Bermuda." *See* Annotation 10.

Seller: The Bank

Buyer: The Company

Premium: USD 250,000

Premium Payment Date: April 18, 2002

Business Day Convention for Premium Payment Date: Following Business Day Convention

Annotation 4. Under Section 11.3(b) of the *2000 ISDA Definitions*, the Following Business Day Convention applies automatically if the parties do not specify a Business Day Convention for the Premium Payment Date. This is different from the result under Section 8.5(b) of the *1991 ISDA Definitions*, under which the Modified Following Business Day Convention is the default choice. *See supra* p. 391, on Business Day Conventions. In the sample, the parties have chosen the same Business Day Convention for the Premium Payment Date and the Cash Settlement Payment Date. They could have documented this choice on a single line. In setting out in brackets various line items that the parties may use to specify their agreement on Business Days and Business Day Conventions in Swaptions, the confirmation template in Exhibit II-E to the *2000 ISDA Definitions* points out that the parties should consider in connection with each transaction, whether the choices should be uniform.

Annotation 5. The templates attached to the *1998 Supplement to the 1991 ISDA Definitions* as Exhibits II and III include a bracketed line item for "Seller Business Day." This item is not included in the templates in the *2000 ISDA Definitions*. This reflects a change in the definition of Exercise Period for an American style Option Transaction. Under Section 13.1 of the *1998 Supplement*, the Exercise Period is presumed to include all Seller Business Days from, and including, the Commencement Date (beginning on that date at 9:00 a.m. local time in the specified location of the Seller or, if so designated in a confirmation, the Seller's Agent) to, and including, the Expiration Date. Section 12.4 of the *1998 Supplement* also provides that, if the parties fail to specify a meaning for "Seller Business Day," it will be a Banking Day in the city where the Seller, or the Seller's Agent, is to receive notices. Section 12.1 of the *2000 ISDA Definitions* makes no presumptions regarding the time at which the Exercise Period will begin on the Commencement Date of an Option Transaction. The parties must specify the Earliest Exercise Time for the Commencement Date and any other Exercise Date during the Exercise Period. Similarly, the *2000 ISDA Definitions* do not provide that Option Transactions may be exercised only on days that are business days for the Seller. Instead, for each style of Option Transaction the Exercise Period is defined to include only Exercise Business Days, and if the parties fail to identify cities to be taken into account in defining Exercise Business Days, Section 11.4 supplies a default choice.

Business Days for Payments: London and New York

Annotation 6. In the sample transaction, if the parties had not specified a place or places here, Business Day for Payments would mean any day "on which commercial banks and foreign exchange markets settle payments and are open for general business (including dealings in foreign exchange and foreign currency deposits) in the same currency as the payment obligation" in New York, under a default choice specified in Section 1.6(d) for the Cash Settlement Currency, U. S. dollars.

Exercise Business Day: London and New York

> Annotation 7. In the sample transaction, if the parties did not specify a place or places here, Exercise Business Day would mean any day that is a Banking Day in New York, the specified financial center for the Cash Settlement Currency, U.S. dollars. "Banking Day" means "any day on which commercial banks are open for general business (including dealings in foreign exchange and foreign currency deposits)" in the relevant city.

Calculation Agent: The Bank

> Annotation 8. The specification of the Calculation Agent is sometimes regarded as a detail, particularly in transactions between dealers and end-users, where the dealer is almost always specified. As noted *infra* p. 922, however, the specification takes on added importance as the discretion given to the Calculation Agent increases, particularly in complex transactions. Section 4.14 of the *2000 ISDA Definitions* provides a useful enumeration of the duties of the Calculation Agent in transactions documented under those definitions. In cash-settled Option Transactions where Cash Price is selected as the Cash Settlement Method, the role of the Calculation Agent takes on even greater importance, as discussed *supra* p. 459.

2. Procedure for Exercise

Expiration Date: April 18, 2003

> Annotation 9. Since the illustrated transaction is a European style Option Transaction documented under the *2000 ISDA Definitions*, the Exercise Period will be the Expiration Date, from and including the Earliest Exercise Time, to and including the Expiration Time (Section 12.1). If the date specified is not an Exercise Business Day, it will be extended to the following Exercise Business Day. In Physical Settlement Swaptions, Buyers should carefully consider whether they would want the hedge protection of the Underlying Transaction to be adjusted to begin on an earlier or later day if the Expiration Date turned out to fall on an unexpected holiday. In a conventional interest rate swap documented under the *2000 ISDA Definitions,* if the Effective Date specified by the parties fell on a day that was not a Business Day, that day would nonetheless be the first day of the swap's Term.
>
> Annotation 10. If the parties were documenting a Bermuda style Option Transaction, a series of Bermuda Option Exercise Dates would be indicated here, and the Exercise Period would consist of each Bermuda Option Exercise Date and the Expiration Date, from and including the Earliest Exercise Time, to and including the Latest Exercise Time (*2000 ISDA Definitions,* § 12.1) on each of those

dates. If they were documenting an American style Option Transaction, the Exercise Period would consist of all Exercise Business Days from and including the Commencement Date to and including the Expiration Date, between those times. The ISDA confirmation template supplies a place here for designating the Commencement Date but, if none were specified, the Commencement Date would be presumed to be the first Premium Payment Date, under Section 12.1(g) of the *2000 ISDA Definitions*.

    Earliest Exercise Time: 9:00 a.m. New York City time

    Expiration Time: 3:00 p.m. New York City time

Annotation 11. Section 12.2 of the *2000 ISDA Definitions* deals with the procedures for exercising Option Transactions. Except where Automatic Exercise or Fallback Exercise applies (as discussed in Annotations 17 through 19), and absent contrary agreement of the parties, Option Transactions are exercised by giving notice of exercise (which may be oral) during the Exercise Period. Absent agreement to the contrary, in transactions documented under a master agreement prepared using an ISDA form, the rules on permitted means of giving notices and the effectiveness of notices generally will be those found in Sections 11 and 12, respectively, of the Local Currency—Single Jurisdiction and Multicurrency—Cross Border forms of ISDA Master Agreement published in 1992. *See infra* p. 876.

Annotation 12. Under Section 12.2 of the *2000 ISDA Definitions*, a notice of exercise for an Option Transaction will be ineffective if given after the Expiration Time. A notice of exercise given after the Latest Exercise Time on any day other than the Expiration Date will also be deemed ineffective if given for a European or Bermuda style Option Transaction but will be deemed given on the following day in the Exercise Period if given for an American style Option Transaction. Any notice of exercise given before the Earliest Exercise Time on a day in the Exercise Period will be deemed given at the Earliest Exercise Time on that day. *See* Annotation 23, *infra* p. 472, on the relationship between the Expiration Time and the Cash Settlement Valuation Time in the illustrated Swaption.

Annotation 13. In American and Bermuda style Swaptions, the parties would also specify a Latest Exercise Time, to apply on days in the Exercise Period other than the Expiration Date. The common working hours for the Buyer and the Seller, naturally, offer the most logical timeframe for the Earliest Exercise Time and the Latest Exercise Time, but that period may not necessarily be the most advantageous in timing any valuation required in connection with cash-settled Option Transactions, and the parties will not always have overlapping business days. Hence the rules referred to in the preceding annotation regarding notices of exercise given before the Earliest Exercise Time and after the Latest Exercise Time on a day.

    Partial Exercise: Inapplicable

Sample Swaption Confirmation

> Annotation 14. Under Section 12.3 of the *2000 ISDA Definitions*, the parties may specify that Partial Exercise will apply to a European style Option Transaction, in which case the Buyer may exercise less than the full Notional Amount of the Underlying Transaction (or elect to terminate less than the full notional amount of a Transaction to which Optional Early Termination applies). If Partial Exercise were applicable, the parties might choose to specify a Minimum Notional Amount or to specify "Integral Multiple" and a currency amount, so that the Partial Exercise would be required to be in an integral multiple of the amount specified. If the parties are silent on the subject in a transaction governed by the *2000 ISDA Definitions*, Partial Exercise will not be applicable. This is a reversal of the presumption expressed in Section 13.3 of the *1998 Supplement to the 1991 ISDA Definitions*.
>
> Annotation 15. In the case of an American style or Bermuda style Option Transaction, Section 12.4 of the *2000 ISDA Definitions* sets forth rules that provide for Multiple Exercise. Under these rules, the parties may elect to specify a Minimum Notional Amount, a Maximum Notional Amount or an Integral Multiple that will limit the amount that can be exercised on any Exercise Day during the Exercise Period, subject to an exception so that the Buyer may exercise its rights with respect to all the remaining Notional Amount on the Expiration Date. Multiple Exercise will not apply if the parties are silent in a transaction governed by the *2000 ISDA Definitions*. As with Partial Exercise, this represents a reversal of the rule stated in the *1998 Supplement to the 1991 ISDA Definitions* (Section 13.4).

Written Confirmation of   Applicable
Exercise:

> Annotation 16. By specifying that Written Confirmation of Exercise is applicable, the parties have indicated that the Buyer is obligated to give written confirmation of the substance of the notice of exercise within one Exercise Business Day after the notice becomes effective (which would also be the result, under Section 12.2 of the *2000 ISDA Definitions*, if the confirmation were silent on the question). Failure to give written confirmation does not affect the validity of the notice of exercise. These provisions of the *2000 ISDA Definitions* reflect refinements to the exercise procedures introduced by the *1998 Supplement to the 1991 ISDA Definitions*, and somewhat different provisions are applicable (under Section 8.4(b)) to transactions governed by the *1991 ISDA Definitions*. The various alternative means for giving written notice—including telexes, facsimiles and electronic transmissions—are found in Sections 11 and 12, respectively, of the Local Currency—Single Jurisdiction and Multicurrency—Cross Border forms of ISDA Master Agreements published in 1992. *See infra* p. 876.

Automatic Exercise: Applicable

Annotation 17. Section 12.7 of the *2000 ISDA Definitions* provides the rules to be followed if the parties have specified that Automatic Exercise will apply to their Transaction. There was no concept of Automatic Exercise for Swaptions under the *1991 ISDA Definitions*, so a Swaption documented using those definitions could not be exercised without a Notice of Exercise, given either orally (*e.g.*, by telephone) or in writing. The *1998 Supplement to the 1991 ISDA Definitions* introduced the concept of Automatic Exercise, which has been further refined in the *2000 ISDA Definitions*.

Annotation 18. The *2000 ISDA Definitions* introduced a limited "safety net for buyers of swaptions that are deeply in-the-money at the expiration date, but who forget to exercise the option." *Id.* at xiii. This protection, known as Fallback Exercise, applies to a limited category of "Interest Rate Swaps," defined in Section 12.1(j) of those definitions to mean non-amortizing fixed/floating swaps in a single currency, even if the parties do not specify that Automatic Exercise will apply, and results in deemed exercise of a Swaption that is in-the-money to the Buyer, unless the difference between the Fixed Rate in the Relevant Swap Transaction and the Settlement Rate current at the time of expiration is less than one tenth of one percent or unless the Buyer notifies the Seller that the Buyer does not want the Fallback Exercise to apply. Similar results apply under Section 3.6(c) of the *1998 FX and Currency Option Definitions* and Section 2.6(b) of the *1997 ISDA Bullion Definitions*, which provide that a Currency Option Transaction or a Bullion Option will be deemed exercised at the applicable Expiration Time if it is in the money to the Buyer to at least a certain extent (currency option) or at all (Bullion Option) unless the Buyer has otherwise instructed the Seller or has already exercised the Option. *See* Annotation 22 to the sample currency option confirmation, *infra* p. 537.

Threshold:	USD 2,500

Annotation 19. Automatic Exercise will take place only if the Cash Settlement Amount that would be payable to the Buyer is equal to or greater than the specified Threshold amount.

Contact Details for Purpose of Giving Notice:	Timely notice of exercise of this Option Transaction should be given to the Bank at 1 Vault Street, New York, New York 00000, attention Swaptions Group—Cash Settlement, if by telex, to 00000—answerback: BB; if by facsimile transmission, to 212-000-000; if by electronic transmission, to swaptions.group@bbank.com; and, if by telephone, to 212-000-0000.

Annotation 20. Buyers of Option Transactions documented under the *2000 ISDA Definitions* should consider whether their confirmations should include a reminder of the address at which the Seller receives notices under the master agreement between the Buyer and the Seller. Where the Seller has designated more than one address for notices in the master agreement, the confirmation should make clear which of the addresses will apply for purposes of a notice of exercise or, indeed, whether a different address will apply for this purpose. The *2000 ISDA Definitions* contemplate the possibility that the Seller may have designated an agent—referred to as "Seller's Agent"—to receive notice of exercise in some cases (because, say, of applicable regulatory requirements or because the Seller has hedged its position in the Option Transaction with a mirror image transaction with an affiliated entity and, to protect itself against inconsistent results from exercise, or nonexercise, in the two transactions, has in place arrangements under which receipt by that affiliate, in its capacity as Seller's Agent, of a notice of exercise from the Buyer under the illustrated Swaption will be treated as simultaneous notice of exercise delivered to that affiliate, in its capacity as principal and Seller, under the second Swaption). This line item in the ISDA confirmation template is the place contemplated for the designation of Seller's Agent.

Exercise Business Days: Banking Days in New York City and London

Annotation 21. Under Section 11.4 of the *2000 ISDA Definitions*, if the parties do not specify otherwise, Exercise Business Day will mean either (1) a Banking Day for the Cash Settlement Currency in the financial center indicated in Section 1.5 of the *Annex to the 2000 ISDA Definitions*, in the case of a currency listed in Section 1.7 of the *Annex*, (2) a TARGET Settlement Day, if the Cash Settlement Currency is the euro, or (3) a Banking Day in the principal financial center for the Cash Settlement Currency, in the case of a currency not listed in Section 1.7 of the *Annex*. For Option Transactions that are not to be cash-settled, there is no presumption about Exercise Business Days under the *2000 ISDA Definitions*. *See* Annotation 5 to this sample confirmation, *supra* p. 466.

3. Settlement Terms

Settlement: Cash

Annotation 22. If the parties had specified "Physical" or "Physical Settlement," they would have indicated that, if the Swaption were exercised, the Underlying Transaction would become effective. In a sense, the date the Swaption is exercised is the Trade Date for the Underlying Transaction in such cases. *See generally* p. 458. *See* Annotations 17 through 19 to this sample confirmation on the cases in

> which the illustrated Swaption would have resulted in an obligation of the Seller to pay a Cash Settlement Amount if the Buyer inadvertently failed to give timely notice of exercise, even if the parties' chosen settlement method had been Physical.

    Cash Settlement Valuation Time: 9:00 a.m. New York City time

    Cash Settlement Valuation Date: Expiration Date

    Valuation Business Days: Same as Exercise Business Days

> Annotation 23. In this Swaption, the window within which the Buyer may give notice of exercise (or at the end of which Automatic Exercise may occur if it fails to give the notice in certain circumstances) is 9:00 a.m. through 3:00 p.m., New York City time on the Expiration Date. In completing these lines as illustrated, the parties have indicated that whether or not the Swaption is in-the-money to the Buyer will be determined as at the earliest point in that window. This determination is made through comparison of the Settlement Rate, which is determined as of the Cash Settlement Valuation Time on the Cash Settlement Valuation Date, and the Fixed Rate specified for the Underlying Transaction in paragraph 4 of the sample confirmation. To ensure that the dates will be the same, the parties have specified that the Expiration Date will also be the Cash Settlement Valuation Date, and they have adopted identical conventions for determining when the two dates will occur if the specified Expiration Date, which is a Friday, falls on an unexpected holiday. *See supra* p. 393 for the default choice on Valuation Business Days, which would apply—by reference to the Cash Settlement Currency and pursuant to Section 17.2(m)(i) of the *2000 ISDA Definitions* and Section 1.5(d) of the *Annex to the 2000 ISDA Definitions*—if the parties had been silent on this matter. Where either Automatic Exercise or Fallback Exercise applies (to protect the Buyer against inadvertent failure to exercise an Option Transaction that is in-the-money to it by at least the minimum required, as discussed in Annotations 17 through 19), the Settlement Rate is always determined at approximately the Expiration Time on the Expiration Date (under Section 12.9 of those definitions).

    Cash Settlement Payment Date: April 22, 2003

    Business Day Convention for   Following Business Day Convention
    Cash Settlement Payment Date:

> Annotation 24. The Following Business Day Convention would have applied even if the parties had been silent on the subject, under Section 17.2 (e) of the *2000 ISDA Definitions*. Under their specified terms, if the Swaption is exercised or deemed exercise on the Expiration Date, the Cash Settlement Amount payable to the Buyer will be due on same date the parties chose (in paragraph 4) as the Effec-

tive Date of the Underlying Transaction—the date as of which the parties would have begun to calculate the Fixed Amounts and Floating Amounts for that transaction if they had chosen to settle the Swaption physically.

        Cash Settlement Method: Cash Price

        Cash Settlement Currency: USD

Annotation 25. Section 17.3 of the *2000 ISDA Definitions* specifies five alternative Cash Settlement Methods: Cash Price, Cash Price–Alternate Method, Par Yield Curve–Adjusted, Zero Coupon Yield–Adjusted, Par Yield Curve–Adjusted and Par Yield Curve–Unadjusted. *See supra* p. 459. In defining "Cash Settlement Method," Section 17.2(l) of those definitions also indicates that the parties may define their own Cash Settlement Method in the Confirmation of their Transaction.

Annotation 26. If the parties had selected Par Yield Curve–Adjusted, Zero Coupon Yield–Adjusted or Par Yield Curve–Adjusted as their Cash Settlement Method, under the confirmation template provided by ISDA, the parties would indicate here, on a Settlement Rate line, a price source to be used for purposes of calculating that rate, which might be ISDA Source, Other Price Source or Reference Banks.

        Cash Settlement Reference Banks: Bank V, Bank W, Bank X, Bank Y and Bank Z

Annotation 27. Since the parties have selected Cash Price, to determine the Settlement Rate (and, thus, whether the Swaption is in-the-money to the Buyer and there is a Cash Settlement Amount) it will be necessary to seek quotations from Cash Settlement Reference Banks if they are unable to reach agreement on the Cash Settlement Amount. If the confirmation were silent on the Cash Settlement Reference Banks and they could not agree on five institutions at the relevant time, the Calculation Agent would pick five leading dealers from the panel whose rates are used in deriving the rates shown on the ISDAFIX Page of the Reuters Money 3000 Service used at the time to post par swap rates for transactions like the Underlying Transaction. If there were no relevant ISDAFIX Page, the Calculation Agent would select the Cash Settlement Reference Banks "in good faith and in a commercially reasonable manner." *2000 ISDA Definitions*, § 17.2(g)(iv) & (v).

        Quotation Rate: Mid, consisting of the arithmetic mean of the bid and the ask rates quoted by the Cash Settlement Reference Bank at the relevant time

> Annotation 28. The parties specify here the type of quotation the Cash Settlement Reference Banks are to be asked to supply. Section 17.2(j) of the *2000 ISDA Definitions* indicates that the specified rate "may be a 'bid', 'ask' or 'mid' rate." As illustrated, when the parties choose "mid," they may wish to spell out what they intend, because terms like "midmarket" are used in various ways in the market. *See, e.g.,* DICTIONARY OF RISK MANAGEMENT 185 (defining "Middle Market (or Mid-Market) Price or Quotation" as "(1) The mean between the best bid and the best offer quoted by market makers. (2) The mean of two or more recent prices."

4. The particular terms of the Underlying Transaction to which the Swaption relates are as follows:

> Annotation 29. *See* the product description on rate swaps and the annotations to the sample rate swap confirmation, *supra* pp. 421 & 427, for explanations of the ways in which the terms set out below by the parties would operate.

Notional Amount:	USD 50,000,000
Effective Date:	April 22, 2003
Termination Date:	April 22, 2007
Fixed Amounts:	
Fixed Rate Payer:	The Company
Payment Dates:	January 19, April 19, July 19 and October 19 in each year, commencing with July 19, 2002 and ending with the Termination Date, subject to the Modified Following Business Day Convention.
Fixed Rate:	3.00% per annum
Fixed Rate Day Count Fraction:	Actual/360
Floating Amounts:	
Floating Rate Payer:	The Bank
Payment Dates:	Same as Payment Dates for Fixed Amounts
Floating Rate Option:	USD-LIBOR-LIBO

Designated Maturity:	3 months
Spread:	None
Floating Rate Day Count Fraction:	Actual/360
Reset Dates:	First day of each Calculation Period
Compounding:	Inapplicable

5. Account Details

   Account for Payments to the Bank:

   Big Bank, N.A., New York, N.Y., ABA No. 000, CHIPS No. 000, Attention: Swaps Division

   Account for Payments to the Company:

   Account No. 00000 with Big Bank, N.A., New York, N.Y.

6. Offices

   The Office of the Bank for the Transaction is its head office in New York. The Office of the Company for the Transaction is its office at the address specified for notices to it in the Schedule to the Agreement.

   Please confirm that the foregoing correctly sets forth the terms of our agreement by executing the copy of this Confirmation enclosed for that purpose and returning it to us or by sending to us a communication substantially similar to this letter, which sets forth the material terms of the Transaction to which this Confirmation relates and indicates your agreement to those terms. If you believe the foregoing does not correctly reflect the terms of our agreement, please give us notice as soon as possible of what you believe to be the necessary corrections.

Yours sincerely,

BIG BANK, N.A.

By: _____
    Name:
    Title: Vice President

Confirmed as of the date first
above written on   , :

ENGLISH COMPANY PLC

By: _____
    Name:
    Title:

Forward Rate Agreements (FRAs)

A conventional forward rate agreement (FRA) can be thought of as being like a delayed start fixed/LIBOR rate swap (generally beginning one, two, three or six months after the Trade Date) with a single Calculation Period and cash settlement at the beginning of the FRA Calculation Period in an amount calculated so as to be equal to the present value of the amount that would have been payable at the end of the Calculation Period in a conventional swap.[1289]

An FRA can also be thought of as a cash-settled forward contract on a Eurocurrency deposit in which the seller and buyer agree at the outset on the rate of interest at which the seller would place the deposit with the buyer at a specified time in the future but, instead of actually transferring the funds to be deposited and repaying them with interest at the end of its term (as would happen with a so-called "forward"), the parties agree to a net settlement at the beginning of the deposit term equal to the present value of the difference between the amount of interest that would have accrued on the deposit (1) at the FRA rate and (2) at the rate prevailing in the market for such a deposit (LIBOR) just before the settlement date—the beginning of what would have been the deposit term if an actual deposit had been made.[1290]

The FRA Transaction documented in the following sample confirmation illustrates the structure of what the market would call a 3s against 6s FRA, an FRA relating to a three-month deposit with a term beginning three months later. If market LIBOR for a three-month U.S. dollar deposit for value (*i.e.*, placed) three months after the FRA trade is done is lower than the Fixed Rate specified in the confirmation, at the beginning of what would have been the term of that deposit (its value date and the Effective Date for the FRA's Calculation Period), the Company must make a payment to the Bank, and if that LIBO rate is higher than the Fixed Rate, the Bank must make a payment to the Company on that value date. The amount of the payment is equal to the amount of interest that would have accrued on the deposit at a per annum rate equal to the difference between the Fixed Rate and LIBOR for the FRA's sole Calculation Period, discounted back to present value from the end of the deposit term to the value date on which the payment is due (referred to as the Payment Date for the FRA) at a discount rate equal to that LIBO rate.

[1289] On delayed start or "forward" swaps, their uses and their advantages and disadvantages as compared with swaptions, *see Forward Swaps*, Derivatives Week, Mar. 15, 1993, at 9 (Learning Curve column).

[1290] In the Australian market, "FRBs" are like FRAs in the respects mentioned except that a party to an FRB may be required to make physical delivery of a bank negotiable certificate of deposit or bank bill in settlement of an FRB. Part 9 of the *1992 Australian AFMA/ISDA Guide* describes FRBs and is followed by the September 1992 Australian Addendum No. 7, prepared for documenting FRBs in the Australian market under an agreement using an ISDA form. In both that Addendum for FRBs and Addendum No. 6 for Australian dollar FRAs in that market prepared under such a master agreement, the forward period in respect of which payment is calculated is referred to as the "Settlement Period" and the amount, if any payable, is the "Settlement Sum." Under the FRABBA terms for FRAs in the London interbank market, the terms are "Contract Period" and "Settlement Sum."

As an OTC tool for hedging against rising interest rates, structurally the FRA is like a swap,[1291] in that both the FRA and the swap are bilateral agreements under which either of the parties may be obligated to make a payment, and the party that buys protection against rising rates gives up the potential benefit if rates decline below the agreed FRA fixed rate. In that sense the FRA is unlike a conventional rate cap, in which the buyer of protection against rising rates fully discharges its obligations at the outset of the transaction through the payment of a premium, in return for the promise of the cap seller to make it a payment if the agreed rate index, set at the agreed time for the agreed period, exceeds the cap rate.

Similarly, as an OTC tool for hedging against declining interest rates[1292]—say, for locking in the benefit of today's LIBOR market rates against the risk that deposits in that market will be less attractive assets in three or six months hence—the FRA is like a swap, in that the party that buys protection against declining rates gives up the potential benefit if rates rise above the agreed FRA fixed rate. Thus, the FRA is unlike a conventional rate floor, in which the buyer of protection against declining rates fully discharges its obligations at the outset of the transaction through the payment of a premium, in return for the promise of the floor seller to make it a payment if the agreed rate index, set at the agreed time for the agreed period, is below the floor rate.

Although the sample confirmation contemplates an FRA between a bank and a corporation, in fact the FRA market developed in London as—and largely remains—an interbank market[1293] used as a flexible alternative to exchange-traded Eurodollar futures contracts, which may have standard terms that do not suit a party's needs and, like other futures contracts, require initial margin and daily marks-to-market.[1294] FRAs are also important hedging instruments for the swaps professional. The FRA is generally executed as a short-term transaction for contract periods of three, six, nine or twelve months, although FRAs can be done for different or longer periods, whereas rate swaps are primarily executed for longer terms.[1295]

[1291]Or more properly perhaps, the swap is like a strip of FRAs which, however, often has a term that goes much farther out along the yield curve than does the FRA market. The comparison of the rate swap with a strip or portfolio of FRAs is standard. *See, e.g.*, ALAN L. TUCKER, FINANCIAL FUTURES, OPTIONS AND SWAPS 489–90 (1991).

[1292]On this and other uses of FRAs, *see* Daniel-Yves Treves & Graham Wandrag, *Case study: Future rate agreements*, in MANAGEMENT OF RATE RISK 237–40 (referring, for example, to bank use of these products to increase yields on deposits, to reduce borrowing costs and to profit from an arbitrage between exchange-traded Euro futures and LIBOR expressed by the FRA market, or between the fixed/LIBOR rate swap market and the market for FRAs).

[1293]For a brief description of the FRABBA terms, *see* Anthony C. Gooch & Linda B. Klein, *Documentation of forward rate agreements*, in MANAGEMENT OF RATE RISK 227–28.

[1294]*See* R. D. Bown, *Mechanics of forward rate agreements*, in MANAGEMENT OF RATE RISK 219–21 and MARCIA STIGUM, THE MONEY MARKET 257–63 (3d ed. 1990) (comparing Euro futures with FRAs and describing the jargon in the market as well as liquidity for the instruments).

[1295]"However, pricing will almost invariably be affected by the less liquid state of the market for such non standard periods." Marcus Money-Chappelle, *Forwards, FRAs and SAFEs: an exposition*, in DERIVATIVES 10, a supplement published with the May 1993 edition of CORPORATE FINANCE.

As noted in the General Introduction, the FRABBA terms became the standard for documenting FRAs in the London interbank market in the mid-1980s. When the parties use these terms, they do so by effectively adopting them in confirming each separate FRA. The separate confirmations subject to the FRABBA terms are not, however, made part of a master agreement by virtue of the FRABBA terms. These terms do not, for example, treat a default under one FRA between the parties as a default under another, nor do they include a mechanism for close-out netting in the event of a party's default. Therefore, if the parties have, say, executed three FRAs with each other and two are in-the-money to Party A by an aggregate amount of U.S. $100,000 while the third is out-of-the-money to it by U.S.$ 25,000 at the time its counterparty, Party B, becomes the subject of insolvency or similar proceedings, there is no contractual mechanism in the FRABBA terms that would enable Party A to withhold payment on the third FRA pending receipt of payment on the first two, so as to protect setoff rights, nor is there a contractual mechanism that would enable Party A to reduce its exposure to loss by closing out all of the FRAs and reducing to a single net sum (U.S.$ 75,000) the amount payable to it by Party B (and, in the same way, protect itself against the risk that a receiver or similar official might seek to collect the U.S. $25,000 from Party A, or transfer that third FRA to a party willing to pay approximately that amount, leaving Party A with a claim of U.S.$ 100,000, which could be worthless).[1296]

As professional participants in the derivatives markets have increasingly sought ways of netting their exposure to each other with respect to as much of their mutual business as possible, FRAs have increasingly been brought under master agreements prepared using ISDA forms, often through an ISDA/FRABBA Bridge published in 1996. Part 6 of this book discusses that and other standardized bridge provisions, among other tools for the management of the risks that may arise when the parties document their dealings with each other under multiple contracts.[1297] The annotations to the following sample FRA confirmation point to some features of the FRABBA terms that the parties may wish to preserve or to take into account in documenting FRAs under standard ISDA terms.

[1296] On the risks that close-out settlement mechanisms are used to manage and how they can arise in a counterparty's insolvency proceedings, *see supra* p. 271.

[1297] *Infra* p. 1279.

> The Introduction to this Part, *supra* p. 369, and the annotations to the sample rate swap confirmation, *supra* p. 427, contain general commentary about the confirmation process and the use of ISDA's confirmation forms both before and after the parties have entered into a master agreement that is not repeated or expressly referred to in the annotations to the other sample confirmations in this book.

[Letterhead of Big Bank, N.A.]

April 18, 2002

FRA Transaction

English Company PLC
Company House
Company Lane
London AB1C 2DE

Ladies and Gentlemen:

The purpose of this communication (the "Confirmation") is to confirm the terms and conditions of the transaction entered into between us on the Trade Date specified below (the "Transaction").

The definitions and provisions contained in the 2000 ISDA Definitions, as published by the International Swaps and Derivatives Association, Inc., are incorporated into this Confirmation. For these purposes, all references in those Definitions to a "Swap Transaction" shall be deemed to apply to the Transaction. In the event of any inconsistency between those definitions and provisions and this Confirmation, this Confirmation will govern.

This Confirmation constitutes a "Confirmation" as referred to in, and supplements, forms part of, and is subject to, the Master Agreement dated as of April 16, 2002, as amended and supplemented from time to time (the "Agreement"), between Big Bank, N.A. (the "Bank") and English Company PLC (the "Company"). All provisions contained in the Agreement govern this Confirmation except as expressly modified below.

1. The terms of the particular Transaction to which this Confirmation relates—which is an FRA—are as follows:

Reference No.:	00000-00
Notional Amount:	USD 50,000,000
Trade Date:	April 18, 2002

Effective Date: July 18, 2002, subject to the Modified Following Business Day Convention

Termination Date: October 18, 2002, subject to the Modified Following Business Day Convention

> Annotation 1. As indicated in the Introduction to this Part, *supra* p. 413, the prevailing practice in the derivatives market has been to "freeze" the end of the Term of a swap, that is, its Termination Date, for purposes of calculating the final Fixed Amount and Floating Amount obligations of the parties. The market practice is reflected in Section 3.3 of both the *2000 ISDA Definitions* and the *1991 ISDA Definitions*, which require the parties to provide expressly that the Termination Date of a Transaction will be adjusted in accordance with a Business Day Convention, if they wish adjustment to occur.
>
> Annotation 2. The parties to the FRA Transaction illustrated in the sample confirmation have elected to adjust the Termination Date of the FRA Transaction documented here under the *2000 ISDA Definitions*. Since the convention in the FRA market, as described in the product description preceding this sample confirmation, is for payment in respect of the FRA contract period (the Calculation Period, using ISDA terminology) to be made at the beginning of the period, as illustrated below, an unexpected bank holiday coinciding with the last day of that period (the Termination Date of a single period FRA) might not be taken into account if it were declared after the payment were made. If the buyer of the FRA protection against rising rates (the Fixed Rate Payer) would like the declaration of any such bank holiday taken into account in the calculation of the amount payable for the period if the bank holiday is declared prior to the Payment Date for the FRA, a rule on adjustment of the Termination Date to this effect would have to be added to this line of the confirmation as illustrated. Both the FRABBA terms and the September 1992 Australian Addendum No. 6 for Australian dollar forward rate agreements provide for adjustment of both the first day and the last day of the Settlement Period for an FRA (the "Settlement Date" and the "Maturity Date," respectively) in accordance with the equivalent of the Modified Following Business Day Convention.

Fixed Rate Payer: The Company

Fixed Rate: 2.5% per annum

Floating Rate Payer: The Bank

Payment Date: The Reset Date

> Annotation 3. The parties' choice of the Payment Date reflects the convention in the FRA market of setting the Payment Date (referred to as the Settlement Date

in the FRABBA terms and the Australian Addendum No. 6 discussed above) for the FRA shortly after the determination of LIBOR for the FRA contract period (*i.e.*, the Calculation Period, using ISDA terminology). Since the Floating Rate for the Transaction illustrated here will be determined on the basis of USD-LIBOR-BBA, and that Floating Rate Option provides, as is customary in the market, that LIBOR will be set on the second London Banking Day before the first day of the FRA Calculation Period scheduled to begin on the Reset Date specified in the confirmation (*see* the introductory note on interest rate products, *supra* p. 408), the first day of that period can be selected as the Payment Date for settlement of the FRA Amount for the Transaction.

Annotation 4. Under the *2000 ISDA Definitions* and the *1991 ISDA Definitions*, specifying the Reset Date as the Payment Date for the illustrated Transaction is consistent with the general rule of Section 4.9 of each of those sets of definitions that a Payment Date must fall within a transaction's Term, since the beginning of the Term of the illustrated FRA is the same as its Reset Date. Although there is an exception to that general rule for amounts payable by Fixed Rate Payers in transactions involving cap rates and floor rates (to accommodate premium payments prior to the Effective Date of a cap, floor or combination of such derivatives), there is no exception to the general rule contemplating payment of an FRA Amount prior to the Effective Date of an FRA. Therefore, if the parties to an FRA documented under those definitions wish to provide for payment of the FRA Amount prior to the Effective Date of the Transaction (*e.g.*, the Business Day after LIBOR for a U.S. dollar FRA contract period is set), the parties must override the rule of Section 4.9 of the *2000 ISDA Definitions*.

Annotation 5. Since the parties have specified that the Payment Date will be the Reset Date, and that term is defined to be the Effective Date, which is already made subject to the parties' choice of Business Day Convention, there is no need to establish a Business Day Convention rule specifically for the Payment Date. If, however, the parties had defined the Payment Date in terms of a calendar date (July 18, 2002), for the reasons specified in the next annotation, it would have been necessary for them to supply their choice of Business Day Convention to deal with the possibility of a bank holiday on that date.

Floating Rate Option:	USD-LIBOR-BBA
Designated Maturity:	3 months
Spread:	None
Floating Rate Day Count Fraction:	Actual/360
Reset Date:	The Effective Date

Annotation 6. *See* Annotations 12–21 to the sample rate swap confirmation, *supra* p. 431, on documenting Floating Amount obligations using the *2000 ISDA Definitions*. The parties to an FRA documented using those definitions should specify their choice of Business Day Convention for a Reset Date, because Section 6.2(b) of those definitions (like Section 6.2(b) of the *1991 ISDA Definitions*), which supplies default choices for adjusting Reset Dates, does not provide a rule directly applicable to FRA Amounts. Section 6.2(b) does provide a default choice, but it ties adjustment of Reset Dates to the Business Day Convention applicable to Floating Rate Payer Payment Dates for the relevant Transaction. An FRA Transaction involves a single Payment Date and, at the time of its confirmation, it is impossible to know whether the Payment Date will be a Fixed Rate Payer Payment Date or a Floating Rate Payer Payment Date. For the sake of clarity, the parties should, therefore, specify their choice of Business Day Convention for Reset Dates for FRAs documented under either of those sets of definitions. In the sample, they have accomplished this by stating that the Reset Date is the Effective Date and specifying the Business Day Convention applicable to the Effective Date.

FRA Discounting:　　　　　　　　　　　Applicable

Annotation 7. The key provision in documenting a conventional FRA under the *2000 ISDA Definitions* or the *1991 ISDA Definitions* is the term "FRA Discounting." By specifying "FRA Discounting," designating a Payment Date shortly after the fixing of LIBOR for the Transaction and incorporating Section 8.4(b) of the *2000 ISDA Definitions* (Section 9.3(b) of the *1991 ISDA Definitions*), the parties have agreed that the amount, if any, payable in respect of their FRA Transaction— the "FRA Amount"—will be the present value on the Payment Date (discounted back from the last day of the Transaction's Calculation Period) of the difference between the respective amounts of interest that would accrue during that period on the Notional Amount at the Fixed Rate and at the Floating Rate set in respect of the agreed Reset Date. By specifying "FRA Discounting" the parties have also agreed that the FRA Amount will be payable by the Fixed Rate Payer, if the Fixed Rate exceeds the Floating Rate, and by the Floating Rate Payer, if the Floating Rate exceeds the Fixed Rate, and they have (through Section 8.4(c) of the *2000 ISDA Definitions* or Section 9.3(c) of the *1991 ISDA Definitions*) agreed that the discount rate used to determine the FRA Amount will be the Floating Rate (plus or minus the Spread, if the parties had agreed to one) for the Transaction's Calculation Period. They have also agreed in this way that the Discount Rate Day Count Fraction will be the Floating Rate Day Count Fraction.

Business Day Convention:　　　　　　　As set out above

Sample FRA Confirmation

> Annotation 8. This ISDA confirmation template for FRAs includes this item for use by parties that wish to specify in one place a single Business Day Convention for the transaction.

Calculation Agent: The Bank

2. Account Details

Account for Payments to the Bank:

>Big Bank, N.A., New York, N.Y., ABA No. 000, CHIPS No. 000, Attention: Swaps Division

Account for Payments to the Company:

>Account No. 00000 with Big Bank, New York, N.Y.

3. Offices

The Office of the Bank for the Transaction is its head office in New York. The Office of the Company for the Transaction is its office at the address specified for notices to it in the Schedule to the Agreement.

Please confirm that the foregoing correctly sets forth the terms of our agreement by executing the copy of this Confirmation enclosed for that purpose and returning it to us or by sending to us a communication substantially similar to this letter, which sets forth the material terms of the Transaction to which this Confirmation relates and indicates your agreement to those terms. If you believe the foregoing does not correctly reflect the terms of our agreement, please give us notice as soon as possible of what you believe to be the necessary corrections.

>Yours sincerely,
>
>BIG BANK, N.A.
>By: _____
>   Name:
>   Title: Vice President

Confirmed as of the date first
above written on   ,   :

ENGLISH COMPANY PLC

By: _____
   Name:
   Title:

CURRENCY DERIVATIVES

INTRODUCTION

The product descriptions and sample confirmations in this section deal with currency swaps, forward foreign exchange agreements and currency options, all of which are derivatives products used to manage and assume risks associated with changes in foreign exchange rates. Of these transactions, the most ancient[1298] and most widely used is the forward foreign exchange agreement, or FX forward. In fact, the history of the development of the modern derivatives markets is very much the story of the changes that, beginning in the early 1970s, led from the traditional use of the FX forward to protect cash flows and earnings against adverse changes in exchange rates for periods of up to one year to the development of longer-dated forwards, futures on foreign exchange, currency swaps and, then, currency options.[1299] For decades, foreign exchange rates had been fixed through international monetary arrangements known as the Bretton Woods system and, when that system collapsed, "[t]o stay unhedged became a risky, expensive and sometimes painful experience."[1300] The classic example generally given is that of the Herstatt Bank, "whose foreign exchange losses brought it under . . . ."[1301]

The sample confirmations in this section illustrate how some of these products may be documented using the *2000 ISDA Definitions* (currency swaps) and the *1998 FX and Currency Option Definitions* (FX forwards and currency options), when the parties use the templates published as exhibits to those definitions.[1302] Many of the most active participants in the FX markets are, however, shifting or have already shifted from the traditional environment in which oral trades are followed by confirmations of these kinds to electronic trades followed by automated, or straight-through, processing of confirmations for at least some of these products. In these cases, the initial electronic affirmation of the parties' trades and the confirmations subsequently produced automatically by the proc-

---

[1298] The FX forward is believed to have existed as long ago as the 12th century. S. Waite Rawls III & Charles W. Smithson, *The Evolution of Risk Management Products*, in HANDBOOK OF RISK MANAGEMENT 2–1, 2–16, citing RICHARD J. TEWELES & FRANK J. JONES, THE FUTURES GAME (2d ed. 1987).

[1299] *See, e.g.,* Rawls, *supra* note 1298, at 2–1. *See infra* p. 515 on uses of the FX forward.

[1300] George Handjinicolaou, *The Forward Foreign Exchange Market: An Alternative for Hedging Currency Risks, in* HANDBOOK OF RISK MANAGEMENT, at 13–1.

[1301] *Id.*

[1302] Additional confirmation forms or samples are available from other sources. EMTA has published numerous templates for non-deliverable forwards, for example, as discussed *infra* p. 489, and the *User's Guide to the 1998 FX Transaction and Currency Option Definitions* includes six sample confirmations illustrating deliverable and non-deliverable transactions involving many of the Disruption Events and Disruption Event Fallbacks included in those definitions and discussed below.

essing systems may look quite different from those illustrated here. These developments and their impact on documentation practices are referred to elsewhere in this book.[1303]

The commercial bank segment of the currency derivatives market has been at the forefront in developing special documentation and trading practices involving many products. Banks have traditionally been the most substantial and active actors in these markets, for their own account and as providers of products to their customers.[1304] Indeed, some of the distinctive features of the documents for FX forwards, currency options and spot FX transactions, were developed by associations of bankers working with the Foreign Exchange Committee, with the support of the Federal Reserve Bank of New York.

This is the case with the provisions on novation netting of FX transactions and the discharge of currency options by offset illustrated in Part 3.[1305] These features have figured since the 1980s in standardized terms that evolved into the IFEMA form, for spot and FX forward transactions, and the ICOM form, for currency options, and in 1997 into the FEOMA form, a single master agreement that can be used to document all these transaction types. Much of the terminology used in the 1997 versions of the FEOMA, ICOM and IFEMA forms was reflected in the *1998 FX and Currency Option Definitions*, and it is not unusual for institutions that have customarily preferred the ICOM and IFEMA forms for these transactions importing certain features of those forms into master agreements prepared using an ISDA form, as those institutions seek to bring more of their derivatives dealing with each counterparty under a single agreement.[1306]

The Foreign Exchange Committee also publishes other standard terms, forms of confirmations and statements of best practices. Examples are the standard terms and forms of confirmations for knock-in and knock-out options endorsed by the Foreign Exchange Committee, its *Barrier Options: New Best Practices*[1307] and its *Guidelines for Foreign Exchange Trading Activities January 2001*,[1308] which also refer to other Committee publications on trading and documentation practices and about the market and the credit, liquidity, operational, legal and settlement risks associated with activities in currency derivatives. Most, if not all, of these risks may also arise in connection with other OTC derivatives, but currency derivatives in their traditional forms usually involve far greater

---

[1303] *See, e.g., supra* note 1132 and accompanying text on whether a subsequent confirmation should be viewed as evidence that the parties have agreed to modify terms executed electronically, and *see* Part 5(b) of the schedule to the sample master agreement in Part 3 and related annotations, *infra* p. 928, on presumptions that transactions executed electronically are intended to be subject to the parties' master agreement.

[1304] The BIS Triennial Central Bank Surveys are valuable resources on the composition of and trends in the FX markets. *See, e.g., BIS 2001 FX and Derivatives Market Survey* 2 & 4, which reflects data gathered from 48 central banks and monetary authorities in April–June 2001 and analyzes a marked decline in FX market activity in 1998–2001, ascribing it to various factors, including the introduction of the euro and reductions by banks in their internal credit limits following the market turbulence in the autumn of 1998.

[1305] *See infra* pp. 946 & 949.

[1306] *See infra* p. 1287 on the risks associated with the use of multiple agreements with the same counterparty

[1307] On these products, *see infra* note 1383.

[1308] The Guidelines and certain other sources referred to therein, as well as the materials on barrier options referred to above, are available at www.ny.frb.org/fxc.

levels of settlement risk, understood as the risk of loss that a party may incur if it delivers an amount of currency due from it under a contract but does not receive the corresponding payment due from the other party. The remainder of this introductory note looks briefly at this risk and at some of the ways in which it has been addressed in the OTC currency derivatives market, including the development of the transactions called non-deliverable forwards (NDFs), and non-deliverable options (NDOs). This introductory note also explores the conventions used in the *1998 FX Transaction and Currency Option Definitions* to deal with concepts referred to as Disruption Events and Disruption Fallbacks, which may be used in connection with both deliverable and non-deliverable currency derivatives.[1309] Certain legal concerns relating to the currency derivatives discussed—many of which also arise in connection with derivatives of other kinds—are addressed in the chapters in Part 1 of this book. In particular, Chapter 3 on commodities laws covers issues that have arisen in connection with the treatment of FX forwards and currency options under U.S. commodity law and regulation.[1310]

SETTLEMENT RISK

As discussed in the following descriptions of currency swaps[1311] and FX forwards,[1312] settlement risk arises in those transactions because each of the parties is obligated to make one or more payments (one in a forward, and usually several in a swap) in one currency in exchange for one or more payments in a second currency. Traditional currency options[1313] involve the same risk if the option is exercised. The duration of this settlement risk can be significant. This is so because, even though the parties' payments may be due on the same day, they may not be due at the same time. Indeed, because of time zone differences, it may not be possible for the parties to make their payments at the same time using conventional settlement methods.[1314] In addition, a party's arrangements with its correspondent banks may result in its giving irrevocable (or effectively irrevocable) instructions to make a payment well in advance of the time it can expect to receive the corresponding payment from its counterparty.[1315]

At one time settlement risk in the currency markets was referred to as Herstatt risk because, as noted above, in the early 1970s a bank of that name collapsed, leading to sub-

---

[1309] Other concepts relevant to currency swaps are discussed in the Introduction to Part 2, *supra* p. 369.

[1310] *Supra* p. 74.

[1311] *Infra* p. 505.

[1312] *Infra* p. 515.

[1313] *Infra* p. 524.

[1314] Where the currency pair involves Japanese yen and U.S. dollars, for example, even though both payments are due on the same calendar day, the party required to deliver the yen will have to do so at a time in Tokyo before the opening of traditional settlement systems for U.S. dollars in New York,

[1315] These subjects are discussed at length in BIS, SETTLEMENT RISK IN FOREIGN EXCHANGE TRANSACTIONS (1996), and BIS, REDUCING FOREIGN EXCHANGE SETTLEMENT RISK: A PROGRESS REPORT (1998). The court opinion referred to in the following footnote, in a case involving the collapse of Herstatt, illustrates the kinds of circumstances in which a payment instruction, although not irrevocable, may not as a practical matter be revocable.

Currency Derivatives 487

stantial losses by that bank's customers and other major financial institutions in connection with FX transactions.[1316] Settlement risk can, however, also arise in many other contexts. The cases that most readily come to mind are the imposition of exchange controls or transfer restrictions and other governmental actions that make it impossible or illegal for a party to deliver a required amount of currency when it falls due. The criminal proceedings that led to the sudden global shutdown of BCCI in 1991 and the fallout from Baring Brothers' massive losses owing to rogue trading suggest other possibilities. In the wake of that event a number of major financial institutions brought actions in which they sought to obtain funds in BCCI accounts that were subject to a U.S. forfeiture order because they had made their own payments under currency swaps and FX forwards but did not receive the expected counterpayment from a BCCI entity because of the shutdown.[1317]

Because financial institutions often have significant exposure to loss in FX transactions, banks and their supervisory agencies have long been concerned with settlement risk and the potential impact a substantial failure could have on individual institutions and on the international settlement systems in which they participate. In particular, the Committee on Payment and Settlement Systems of the central banks of the Group of Ten (G-10), has worked for decades under the auspices of the Bank for International Settlements to promote better understanding of FX settlement risk among banks and their supervisory agencies, to give guidance on important principles that should be observed in settlement and netting systems, to measure bank progress in the management of settlement risk and to encourage individual banks and industry groups to manage settlement risk through the use of collateral,[1318] bilateral and multilateral netting of obligations and otherwise.[1319]

Settlement risk has led many market participants to include escrow provisions of the kind illustrated in Part 3 of this book[1320] in their master agreements. The usefulness of these provisions, naturally, depends on the party's having sufficient advance notice of the problems that may lead to a counterparty's inability to pay. Settlement risk also prompted the market's development of novation netting in the 1980s[1321] and, since that time, has led

---

[1316] *See, e.g., Delbrueck & Co. v. Manufacturers Hanover Trust Co.,* 464 F. Supp 989 (S.D.N.Y. 1979), for a description of some of the complex relationships giving rise to settlement risk that led to litigation following the collapse of Bankhaus I.D. Herstatt, K.G.a.A.

[1317] *See, e.g., United States v. BCCI Holdings, S.A.,* 833 F. Supp. 22 (D.D.C. 1993).

[1318] On the use of collateral generally, *see* the Introduction to Part 5, *infra* p. 1057, which includes references to the *FX Collateral Annex* published by the Foreign Exchange Committee in 1999.

[1319] These matters are discussed in a succession of important BIS publications. *See, e.g.,* BIS, SETTLEMENT RISK IN FOREIGN EXCHANGE TRANSACTIONS (1996), and BIS, REDUCING FOREIGN EXCHANGE SETTLEMENT RISK: A PROGRESS REPORT (1998). *See also* BASEL COMMITTEE ON BANKING SUPERVISION, SUPERVISORY GUIDANCE FOR MANAGING SETTLEMENT RISK IN FOREIGN EXCHANGE TRANSACTIONS (2000). Appendix 3 to the last of these documents includes further bibliography on these and related subjects, such as the standards for payment and netting systems. One early source was the *Report on Netting Schemes,* published in February 1999 by the Group of Experts on Payment Systems of the central banks of the Group of Ten countries, *available at* http://www.bis.org/publ/cpss02.htm. The report is often referred to for its useful, straightforward explanation of informal and formal netting arrangements and some of the concerns they may raise.

[1320] *See infra* p. 941.

[1321] For many years, spot and forward FX transactions were documented on "deal tickets" confirming the financial terms of the transaction, with little if anything more. By 1980 participants in the interbank

market professionals to devote very significant resources to the development of bilateral and multilateral netting systems or services[1322] and, more recently, to the development of a "continuous linked settlement" bank, the CLS Bank, whose services as a settlement intermediary would enable counterparties to settle their FX settlement exposures to each other simultaneously, on a payment-versus-payment basis.[1323]

Settlement risk has also led to product innovation. The principal focus in this regard has been the creation of derivatives that enable a party to manage exchange rate risk without an actual exchange of the currencies involved. Over the years these efforts have led to the use of products referred to as "diff" or "differential swaps," exchange rate agreements, or ERAs, and forward exchange agreements, or FXAs—the last two collectively referred to as "SAFEs"—but the products of this kind that have gained the broadest acceptance are NDFs and NDOs.

NON-DELIVERABLE CURRENCY DERIVATIVES

Non-deliverable derivatives products are chiefly used to manage exchange rate risk involving emerging market currencies. In some cases a non-deliverable product will be chosen because the relevant currency is subject to convertibility and remittance restrictions at the time the parties trade. In other cases, even though such restrictions do not exist at the time of the trade, one of the parties may be concerned over settlement risk if restrictions of these or other kinds are imposed at a later date or, simply, if the foreign exchange market for transactions in the relevant currency is illiquid.

---

market in New York had formed a Foreign Exchange Committee to work in an advisory capacity with the Federal Reserve Bank of New York to consider various aspects of market practice and of the management of FX trading operations. The Committee and, at the same time, participants in the London market, considered the development of a netting procedure that might reduce some of the strain and risk involved in the high volume of transactions being executed. Both groups concluded that model bilateral FX netting agreements should be developed for these transactions. The New York committee completed a model interbank FX netting agreement in 1985. It provided for the netting of two banks' mutual FX obligations in each agreed pair of currencies. The London project produced a similar but broader approach, which contemplated bilateral netting of all FX obligations in each currency, regardless of the second currency involved in each transaction. These approaches came to be reflected in the matched-pair novation netting and by-currency novation netting conventions discussed *infra* p. 950.

[1322]These include FXNET, Valuenet and S.W.I.F.T. Accord. FXNET was the first of the bilateral arrangements to gain substantial support and was developed as a London-based limited partnership of subsidiaries of banks active in FX trading, to licenses an electronic system for the automated implementation of bilateral netting and close-out of FX contracts. Model netting agreements were prepared for execution by FXNET banks. The fundamental concept of the agreements was the creation of series of running accounts that two parties would have with each other for each currency involved in their FX transactions. As a result of netting by novation, the parties' obligations to each other are netted and change each time a new transaction between them is confirmed and matched in the automated system, so that each new transaction discharges the parties' previously existing rights and obligations vis-à-vis each with respect to the two currencies involved in the new transaction and replaces those previously existing obligations with new, net obligations that take the new transaction into account. As a result, each party is always obligated to make, or has the right to receive, only a single payment for each currency involved in their FX transactions with each other that have the same settlement date.

[1323]For some background about these bilateral and multilateral netting and settlement services, *see* BIS, REDUCING FOREIGN EXCHANGE SETTLEMENT RISK: A PROGRESS REPORT 2 & 18–20 (1998). On CLS Bank, *see* http://www.cls-services.com/; Robert Bogusz, *FX Risk Reduction Through CLS*, AFP EXCHANGE 58 July-Aug. 2001.

Currency Derivatives

The main source of standardized templates for non-deliverable derivatives products is EMTA, which has also published numerous recommended market practices for these derivatives, both generally and for transactions involving only particular currencies. For most transactions, the norm is to document NDFs and NDOs using the *1998 FX and Currency Option Definitions* but subject to modifications that reflect EMTA's recommended practices, where they require modifications to the standard terms in those definitions. The following is an overview of terminology and conventions used in documenting NDFs and NDOs under these definitions and refers to some of these EMTA practices and modifications. This review also touches on cases in which Disruption Events and Disruption Fallbacks developed primarily for use in connection with non-deliverable transactions may be used in connection with traditional deliverable transactions.

GENERAL

The *1998 FX and Currency Option Definitions* cover FX Transactions and Currency Option Transactions. They distinguish between Deliverable and Non-Deliverable transactions. In order to indicate that the parties intend their transaction in respect of a currency pair to be non-deliverable, they may use any of three expressions: "Non-Deliverable," "Cash Settlement" or "In-the-Money Settlement."[1324] If a Confirmation applies any of these terms to a Transaction, the amount payable in settlement of the Transaction will, generally speaking, be determined in a single currency (the Settlement Currency), by the application of a formula. The formula is designed to produce a Settlement Currency Amount, in the case of a Non-Deliverable FX Transaction, or an In-the-Money Amount, in the case of a Non-Deliverable Currency Option Transaction. In all cases, for the formula to work, it must be possible to determine a Settlement Rate—a rate of exchange of the relevant Reference Currency for the Settlement Currency in which the Settlement Currency Amount or In-the-Money Amount will be payable.

As discussed in the following product descriptions, this Settlement Rate is compared with the Forward Rate agreed by the parties, in connection with Non-Deliverable FX Transactions, and with the Strike Price agreed by the parties, in connection with Non-Deliverable Currency Option Transactions. If the parties are silent regarding the determination of the Settlement Rate, it will be the Spot Rate of exchange of the Reference Currency for the Settlement Currency, determined by the Calculation Agent in good faith and in a commercially reasonable manner.[1325] However, generally speaking the parties will identify the way in which the Settlement Rate should be determined by specifying a Settlement Rate Option.

Section 4.5, in *Annex A to the 1998 FX and Currency Option Definitions*,[1326] supplies currency-specific Settlement Rate Options from which the parties may choose for

---

[1324] *1998 FX and Currency Option Definitions* § 1.13.

[1325] *1998 FX and Currency Option Definitions* § 1.16(e).

[1326] *Annex A* is a loose-leaf booklet that was published at the same time as the definitions and includes sections on identification of currencies, principal financial centers for those currencies, Settlement Rate Options and related definitions, and corrections to published and displayed rates. It is supplemented with some frequency. As noted in Annotation 3 to the sample currency option confirmation, *infra* p. 532, the parties are presumed to have intended to adopt *Annex A* as supplemented and amended through the Trade Date for each Transaction unless they indicate otherwise.

non-deliverable transactions involving many currencies. Unless they specify their intention to be different, when the parties to a Transaction incorporate these definitions they will automatically be adopting *Annex A* as amended through the date on which they enter into their FX Transaction or Currency Option Transaction.[1327]

To facilitate either oral or electronic trading, the Settlement Rate Options in *Annex A* are identified in two ways. One includes an identification of the relevant currency followed by words or an acronym that indicates the underlying source of exchange rate data. The other simply identifies the currency and refers to the number assigned by the definitions to the particular Settlement Rate Option. Thus, for example, "TWD Telerate 6161" and "TWD01" both mean that a Settlement Rate is to be determined by reference to the spot rate of exchange of Taiwanese Dollars per one U.S. dollar for settlement in two Business Days as reported by the Taipei Forex Inc, as it appears on Telerate Page 6161 under heading "Spot" as of 11:00 a.m., Taipei time, on the relevant date of calculation. Some of these currency-specific choices are the official rates for a spot exchange of local currency for the U.S. dollar as reported by the central bank of the jurisdiction for which the Reference Currency is legal tender.

Section 4.5 of the *1998 FX and Currency Option Definitions* also includes five general choices of means for determining a Settlement Rate.[1328] One calls for setting the Settlement Rate by agreement of the parties ("Currency–Mutual Agreement"), and another for doing so by reference to the Calculation Agent's determination of the relevant day's rate in a customary wholesale market in which there is minimal or no control or interference by a Governmental Authority from the Reference Currency Jurisdiction ("Currency–Wholesale Market").

Two others involve implied rates derived from asset prices. The first of these is known as "Currency–Implied Rate (ADR)." It involves finding the Settlement Rate to be the Reference Currency/U.S. dollar exchange rate determined on the basis of quotations provided by Reference Dealers for the relevant day's price of a Specified Company's American Depositary Receipts and the price of the local share or shares of the Specified Company underlying those ADRs. If the Specified Company is not identified in the parties' confirmation, the Calculation Agent chooses the Specified Company.

The second asset-based Settlement Rate Option is known as "Currency–Implied Rate (Local Asset)." It involves obtaining from Reference Dealers their firm quotation bid and offer prices for a debt security that is traded both locally, in the Reference Currency, in the jurisdiction where the Reference Currency is the lawful currency, and internationally, in the Settlement Currency. If at least one quotation is obtained, the Settlement Rate is determined by dividing (A) the arithmetic mean of the midpoint of the bid and offer prices quoted in the Reference Currency by (B) the arithmetic mean of the midpoint of the bid and offer prices quoted in the Settlement Currency.

The last of these general Settlement Rate Options is "Currency–Reference Dealers." The method applied to determine a Settlement Rate following this alternative depends on whether it is being used as the parties' primary choice or as a fallback—a Fall-

---

[1327] *Id.* at 1.

[1328] *Id.* § 4.5(e).

Currency Derivatives

back Reference Price Settlement Rate Option—because the parties are unable to determine the Settlement Rate using another choice, as a result of a Disruption Event.

When selected as the parties' primary choice for determining the Settlement Rate, Currency–Reference Dealers requires the Calculation Agent to poll the Specified Offices of four entities named as Reference Dealers in the transaction's confirmation or, if none are named, four leading dealers in the relevant market selected by the Calculation Agent. The relevant spot rate quotations are sought at a time identified by the parties as the "Specified Time," or, if none is indicated in the Confirmation, at a time chosen by the Calculation Agent. If four quotations are obtained, the highest and lowest are disregarded and the Settlement Rate is the arithmetic average of the remaining two. If two or three quotations are obtained, their arithmetic average is used. If fewer than two quotations are obtained, a Disruption Event, known as Price Source Disruption, will be deemed to have occurred.

When Currency–Reference Dealers is used as a fallback, the Calculation Agent is required to request the Specified Office of each of the Reference Dealers to provide a quotation of what the primary choice—the Specified Rate at the Specified Time—would have been had it been published, reported or available for the relevant date, based on that Reference Dealer's "experience in the foreign exchange market for the Reference Currency and general activity in such market" on that date. The request is supposed to be made at or as soon as practicable after it is determined that the Specified Rate was not available.

Currency–Reference Dealers is often the only or ultimate Fallback Reference Price Settlement Rate Option in non-deliverable transactions. Participants in the market should be aware that when it is used in inter-dealer trades, the parties sometimes agree that they will both be Calculation Agents—EMTA uses the term "Joint Calculation Agents" for these cases—and, further, spell out as follows the approach that they will take to determine a Settlement Rate if they are unable to agree on it within one Business Day:

> [E]ach party agrees to be bound by the determination of an independent leading dealer in Reference Currency/Settlement Currency Transactions not located in the Reference Currency jurisdiction ("independent leading dealer"), mutually selected by the parties, who shall act as the substitute Calculation Agent, with the fees and expenses of such substitute Calculation Agent (if any) to be met equally by the parties. If the parties are unable to agree on an independent leading dealer to act as substitute Calculation Agent, each party shall select an independent leading dealer and such independent dealers shall agree on an independent third party who shall be deemed to be the substitute Calculation Agent.

DISRUPTION EVENTS AND DISRUPTION FALLBACKS

Many of the potential complexities of Non-Deliverable Transactions relate to cases in which the Settlement Rate cannot be determined, or cases in which the parties agree that the Settlement Rate should be disregarded or that, regardless of the Settlement Rate, their transaction should be settled in some way other than a payment in the Settlement Currency. The *1998 FX and Currency Option Definitions* refer to these cases as Disruption Events and use the term "Disruption Fallback" to refer to the ways in which the parties may determine the Settlement Rate if it cannot be determined using a preferred method, or if the parties have agreed in the circumstances to disregard the rate determined using that preferred method.

Disruption Events. There are 12 different types of Disruption Events under these definitions: Benchmark Obligation Default; Dual Exchange Rate; General Inconvertibility; General Non-Transferability; Governmental Authority Default; Illiquidity; Material Change in Circumstance; Nationalization; Price Materiality; Price Source Disruption; Specific Inconvertibility; and Specific Non-Transferability.[1329] There is also a further choice, Inconvertibility/Non-Transferability, which is simply shorthand to indicate that four of the Disruption Events will apply: General Inconvertibility; General Non-Transferability; Specific Inconvertibility and Specific Non-Transferability.[1330] The *1998 FX and Currency Option Definitions* also provide other shorthand mechanisms for indicating that these two "General" or "Specific" Disruption Events will apply: General Inconvertibility/Non-Transferability, and Party Specific Events.[1331]

The parties to Deliverable Transactions are free to specify that Disruption Events and Disruption Fallbacks will apply to these transactions too. If they are silent on the matter, however, none of the Disruption Events will be deemed applicable to their Deliverable Transactions. On the other hand, if the parties enter into a Non-Deliverable Transaction and are silent on the matter of Disruption Events, Price Source Disruption will automatically be deemed to apply.[1332]

This default choice reflects the prevailing practice, under which Price Source Disruption is generally the only Disruption Event that the parties choose, as is reflected in EMTA's NDF confirmation templates. Price Source Disruption occurs when it becomes impossible to obtain the Settlement Rate on the relevant Valuation Date, "or, if different, the day on which rates for the Valuation Date would, in the ordinary course, be published or announced by the relevant price source."[1333]

[1329] *Id.* § 5.1(d).

[1330] *Id.*

[1331] *Id.* §§ 5.1(e)(ii) & (iii).

[1332] Both of these rules are set out in Section 5.1(e)(i)) of the *1998 FX and Currency Option Definitions.* Under related rules, in Section 5.1(e)(iv) of these definitions, if the parties specify that particular Disruption Events will apply to their transaction—whether Deliverable or Non-Deliverable, those specified Disruption Events will apply and, if the transaction is Non-Deliverable, Price Source Disruption will apply, regardless of whether it was specified by the parties.

[1333] *Id.* § 5.1(d)(xi). Under another rule, in Section 4.1(a) of these definitions, if the currency exchange rate specified to be applicable for determining the Settlement Rate is published or announced by multiple price sources and the source specified by the parties as the Settlement Rate Option fails to publish or announce the rate on the Rate Calculation Date (or another relevant date), but another source actually publishes or announces that exchange rate, a Price Source Disruption will not be treated as having occurred, because there is an automatic fallback to the other, available source. There is also another fallback, which applies (under Section 4.1(b) of these definitions) if the parties have chosen as their Settlement Rate Option a currency exchange rate "reported, sanctioned, recognized, published, announced or adopted (or other similar action)" by a relevant Governmental Authority, and that exchange rate ceases to exist and is replaced by a successor currency exchange rate recognized by the same Governmental Authority—an Official Successor Rate. In this event, use of the Official Successor Rate automatically becomes the Settlement Rate Option in the parties' transaction.

Currency Derivatives 493

Unscheduled bank closures can give rise to somewhat difficult issues in connection with this approach to Price Source Disruption, because the *1998 FX Transaction and Currency Option Definitions* provide that Valuation Dates are to be adjusted in accordance with the Preceding Business Day Convention unless another Business Day Convention is specified to be applicable, and the definition of "Business Day" (in Section 1.1(b) of those definitions), as it relates to Valuation Dates, views as a Business Day a day on which "commercial banks are open (or, but for the occurrence of any Disruption Event applicable to a Transaction, would have been open) for business (including dealings in foreign exchange in accordance with the market practice of the foreign exchange market) in the place(s) specified for that purpose in a Confirmation generally or specifically for purposes of the Valuation Date."[1334]

The *User's Guide to the 1998 FX and Currency Option Definitions* notes that there "is no bright line" about treatment of unscheduled bank closures for purposes of determining whether or not a Price Source Disruption exists. It encourages market participants to consider whether, in the context of a particular transaction, they should deal with this question, or whether they prefer to leave such matters to ad hoc negotiations if the need arises.[1335] EMTA recommended practices adopted in October 2000 to reduce the uncertainties surrounding these questions through various changes that, generally speaking, reflect a consensus among traders that unscheduled bank holidays should not be viewed as Disruption Events unless they continue for at least eight consecutive days.[1336]

[1334] The provision goes on to supply a rule if the parties have failed to specify a relevant place or places.

[1335] *User's Guide to the 1998 FX and Currency Option Definitions* 23.

[1336] This general recommended NDF market practice was published, along with others related to it, on October 2, 2000, when it reflected a compromise in light of the five to ten day periods advocated by a majority of market participants in New York, London and Asia involved in the deliberations. EMTA has, however, subsequently recommended more prolonged deferrals of Valuation Dates in light of particular currency market crises. Examples are successive recommendations of deferrals during 2002 in connection with Argentina's decision to permit the Peso/USD exchange rate to float. Documentation of the October 2, 2000 recommended general practice involves the adoption of definitions that distinguish between Scheduled Holidays and Unscheduled Holidays, viewing the latter as occurring when the market is not aware "by means of a public announcement or by reference to other publicly available information" that a day will not be a Business Day until after 9:00 a.m. local time in the Principal Financial Center(s) for the Reference Currency two Business Days before the scheduled Valuation Date. If greater advance notice is given to the market, a Scheduled Holiday is treated as having occurred. Related EMTA modifications to the *1998 FX Transaction and Currency Option Definitions* require statements to the effect that, if a Valuation Date falls on a Scheduled Holiday, the Valuation Date is moved to the preceding Business Day and, in connection with an Unscheduled Holiday, a Settlement Date will occur as soon as practicable after the scheduled Valuation Date, but in no event later than two Business Days after the scheduled Valuation Date subject to the indicated rule that, if an Unscheduled Holiday continues for eight consecutive days, the eighth day will be treated as the Valuation Date if, but for the Unscheduled Holiday, it would have been a Business Day. Thus, on that eighth day, or on the next following day that, but for the Unscheduled Holiday would have been a Business Day, the parties look to their agreement on Disruption Fallbacks. Market participants should also be aware that EMTA more generally recommends a change to the presumption in the *1998 FX Transaction and Currency Option Definitions* regarding the cities that will be considered in determining whether a day that would otherwise be a Valuation Date is a Business Day. The EMTA recommended practice looks at good working days in any Principal Financial Center for the Reference Currency, overriding the presumption in those definitions that the Principal Financial Centers relevant to both parties and the Reference Currency should be considered, in the absence of contrary agreement of the parties.

Price Materiality is a second Disruption Event that is sometimes used in non-deliverable transactions documented using EMTA templates. It was, for example, added to Price Source Disruption in the template for NDFs involving the Argentine Peso after Argentina abandoned the 1:1 exchange rate peg of its currency to the U.S. dollar in 2002. As explained in the *User's Guide to the 1998 FX and Currency Option Definitions,* this Disruption Event was created because "it is possible that the parties to a Transaction may be able to obtain the Settlement Rate but are unable to trade at such rate because it is not reflective of the rate at which trades are being settled in the market."[1337] When they opt to have this Disruption Event apply, the parties normally specify a Primary Rate and a Secondary Rate for determining a Settlement Rate along with a Price Materiality Percentage. If the two rates differ by at least that percentage, Price Materiality will be deemed to have occurred.[1338]

The Illiquidity Disruption Event is similar to Price Materiality, in that it applies if on a relevant date it is "impossible to obtain a firm quote of the Settlement Rate" for an agreed Minimum Amount, "either in one transaction or a commercially reasonable number of transactions that, when taken together, total the Minimum Amount."[1339] However, whereas the Price Materiality Disruption Event is designed so that parties' chosen Disruption Fallbacks immediately apply if a Price Materiality occurs, the Illiquidity Disruption Event is designed so that, in the event of Illiquidity, they can agree on a day—the Illiquidity Valuation Date—to which determination of the Settlement Rate will be deferred.

The Dual Exchange Rate Disruption Event is triggered only if the currency exchange rate chosen as the Settlement Rate Option splits into dual or multiple exchange rates after the Trade Date of the parties' Transaction. This Disruption Event is not triggered merely by virtue of the introduction of a new exchange rate, even if the new rate replaces the rate originally specified as the commercial rate of choice. The *User's Guide to the 1998 FX Transactions and Currency Option Definitions* discusses[1340] how market participants can make choices involving the Price Materiality Disruption Event so as to seek to capture the introduction of such a new rate as a Disruption Event.[1341]

The general and specific inconvertibility Disruption Events relate to exchange controls and similar regulations. General Inconvertibility arises when, as a result of any event, it is "impossible to convert the Event Currency into the Non-Event Currency in the

---

[1337] At 24.

[1338] It should be noted that, if the parties have specified Price Materiality and a Primary Rate and a Price Materiality Percentage but not a Secondary Rate, it appears that the Secondary Rate will be determined applying the Currency–Reference Dealers convention described above. *See User's Guide to the 1998 FX Transaction and Currency Option Definitions* 25 & *1998 FX Transaction and Currency Option Definitions* § 5.2(e)(i)(D).

[1339] *Id.* § 5.1(d)(vi). The relevant test date is presumed to be the Valuation Date unless the parties have specified an "Illiquidity Valuation Date." If they have made such a specification, that Illiquidity Valuation Date is also used in connection with the Disruption Fallbacks.

[1340] At 24.

[1341] *See also id.* at 42, for discussion of a split in a screen rate for the Thai baht that would have fallen within the Dual Exchange Rate Disruption Event.

Event Currency Jurisdiction through customary legal channels."[1342] Specific Inconvertibility applies if it is impossible for one of the parties to the relevant transaction, or for any person in a Relevant Class of persons identified by the parties, to convert at least a stated Minimum Amount of the Event Currency into the Non-Event Currency, but subject to certain exceptions. Specific Inconvertibility will not be found to exist if the impossibility "is due solely to the failure by that party (or Relevant Class, as the case may be) to comply with any law, rule or regulation enacted by any Governmental Authority (unless such law, rule or regulation is enacted after the Trade Date of the Transaction and it is impossible for such party (or Relevant Class, as the case may be), due to an event beyond the control of that party (or relevant Class) to comply with such law, rule or regulation."

Similarly, General Non-Transferability applies when any event "generally makes it impossible to deliver (A) the Non-Event Currency from accounts inside the Event Currency Jurisdiction to accounts outside the Event Currency Jurisdiction or (B) the Event Currency between accounts inside the Event Currency Jurisdiction or to a party that is a non-resident of the Event Currency Jurisdiction.[1343] On the other hand, Specific Non-Transferability must affect one of the parties to the transaction or a Relevant Class identified by the parties and must not be due solely to the failure by that party (or Relevant Class) to comply with applicable law, rule or regulation, unless the law, rule or regulation was adopted after the transaction's Trade Date and it is impossible for the party (or Relevant Class, as the case may be), due to an event beyond the control of that party (or relevant Class) to comply with such law, rule or regulation.[1344]

The remaining Disruption Events are unlike those described above, in that they are not triggered by conditions in or directly affecting the foreign exchange markets. Rather, two relate to events and circumstances that affect one of the parties to the relevant Transaction or its assets and the others relate to defaults that are likely to be followed by disruptions in the foreign exchange markets in the country where the Reference Currency is the lawful currency—referred to as the Event Currency Jurisdiction.

The first group includes Nationalization and Material Change in Circumstances. Nationalization involves "any expropriation, confiscation, requisition, nationalization or other action by any Governmental Authority which deprives a party to the Transaction (or any of its Relevant Affiliates) of all or substantially all of its assets" in that jurisdiction. Material Change in Circumstances means any event, other than those covered by another Disruption Event, if it occurs in the Event Currency Jurisdiction and makes it impossible for a party to the relevant Transaction to fulfill its obligations thereunder or generally to fulfill obligations similar to those obligations.

Benchmark Obligation Default and Governmental Authority Default involve payment failures, reschedulings, repudiations and other defaults with respect to specified obligations (Benchmark Obligation Default) or any security or indebtedness for borrowed money of, or guaranteed by, any Governmental Authority in that jurisdiction

---

[1342] *Id.* § 5.1(d)(iii).

[1343] *Id.* § 5.1(d)(iv).

[1344] *Id.* § 5.1(d)(xiii).

(Governmental Authority Default). Like the Credit Events covered by the *1999 Credit Derivatives Definitions,* these Disruption Events will be treated as having occurred regardless of whether the underlying payment failure, rescheduling, repudiation or other default is allegedly defensible because the issuer of the Benchmark Obligation or the relevant Governmental Authority lacked authority or capacity to have issued the relevant obligation.

All the Disruption Events are drafted in objective terms and do not presume that their existence or nonexistence will be determined by the Calculation Agent. However, if the parties wish to give the Calculation Agent the authority to make the determination, under Section 5.1(g) of the *1998 FX and Currency Option Definitions,* the parties may do so by specifying that "Calculation Agent Determination of Disruption Event" applies to their transaction. In this event, the Calculation Agent will be required to make the determination in good faith.

Generally speaking, only Price Source Disruption and, on occasion, Price Materiality, are chosen as Disruption Events when NDFs and NDOs are used merely to manage a company's exchange rate risk associated with expenses incurred in connection with operations in the Reference Currency jurisdiction or receivables generated by sales in that jurisdiction, when they are payable in the Reference Currency. The remaining Disruption Events, generally speaking, are most often used in connection with specific investments linked to emerging market debt instruments and investments of other kinds that are made in the country that issues the Reference Currency—which may be referred to as the Event Currency Jurisdiction in connection with Disruption Events and Disruption Fallbacks.

These other Disruption Events are, for example, commonly found in both Deliverable and Non-Deliverable FX Transactions entered into with special purpose vehicles that issue notes secured by sovereign debt, when the issuer of these notes passes along to the note holders the credit, convertibility, remittance and other country risks underlying these Disruption Events. That is, in exchange for an attractive note coupon linked to the yield on the collateral, the investor effectively agrees to assume these risks by agreeing that the notes will be redeemed (or perhaps settlement on the notes will be postponed or modified) if a Disruption Event occurs. If redemption does occur, the related FX transaction is also closed out, the collateral is liquidated, the provider of the FX Transaction is paid what it is owed as close-out settlement if the FX Transaction is in the money to it at the time, and the remaining proceeds of liquidation of the collateral are available for payments to the holders of the notes, after satisfaction of transaction costs that may be owed to a trustee in connection with the redemption, collateral liquidation or otherwise. In other variants, if a Disruption Event occurs the collateral may be distributed to the investors in full discharge of the issuer's note obligations, as would occur in a physically settled credit default swap or a structured note with embedded features of credit default swaps.[1345]

These and other uses of Disruption Events involving circumstances other than Price Source Disruption and Price Materiality are suggested by several of the Disruption

---

[1345] *See infra* p. 643.

Fallbacks included in the *1998 FX and Currency Option Definitions,* as described below.[1346]

DISRUPTION FALLBACKS

These definitions provide ten Disruption Fallbacks for Non-Deliverable Transactions, in the following alphabetical order: Assignment of Claim; Calculation Agent Determination of Settlement Rate; Deliverable Substitute; Escrow Arrangement; Fallback Reference Price; Local Asset Substitute Gross; Local Asset Substitute Net; Local Currency Substitute; No Fault Termination; Non-Deliverable Substitute; and Settlement Postponement. The definitions also contemplate the possibility that the parties to a Deliverable Transaction may wish to specify that, if a Disruption Event occurs, their transaction will be settled as if it were a Non-Deliverable Transaction.[1347]

The possible combinations of these Disruption Fallbacks, and their complexities, are numerous. As with the Disruption Events, the *1998 FX and Currency Option Definitions* supply default choices if the parties are silent regarding Disruption Fallbacks and provide that, if the parties specify their choices, those choices will apply, in the order specified.[1348]

No Fault Termination. It is important to note that in all cases, including those in which the parties have specified other Disruption Fallbacks, No Fault Termination is the ultimate fallback, if all others fail to lead to settlement otherwise. If No Fault Termination becomes the applicable Disruption Fallback, on the date this occurs either of the parties may designate an Early Termination Date for the relevant Transaction and, regardless of which of the parties does so, the amount payable by or to it will be determined as provided in Section 6 of the ISDA Master Agreement (Multicurrency—Cross Border) form, using Loss as the measure of damages (unless the parties have agreed otherwise for this particular purpose) and as if the Transaction were the sole Affected Transaction being closed out in connection with an Additional Termination Event affecting both parties. As

---

[1346] NDFs and NDOs including disruption events of these kinds—but predating the publication of the *1998 FX Transaction and Currency Option Definitions*—were widely used in the 1990s in transactions involving the Russian ruble. The *User's Guide to the 1998 FX Transaction and Currency Option Definitions* (at 39) discusses how Russia's announcement in August 1998 of a plan to convert public debt obligations into other securities and ensuing events, including a moratorium on bank payments, would have been treated under those definitions applying various of these other Disruption Events.

[1347] See *1998 FX and Currency Option Definitions* § 5.2(c)(x). This choice carries with it an obligation to pay interest to the party that would have been entitled to payment treating the transaction as non-deliverable, at that party's cost of funds (without proof or evidence of such cost). For purposes of determining what that non-deliverable settlement should be, the parties determine the Settlement Rate on the basis of quotations from Currency-Reference Dealers.

[1348] Users of these definitions should consider issues that may arise in connection with their transactions if multiple Disruption Events apply and the chosen or presumed Disruption Fallbacks for these events differ, or are applicable in a different order. Section 5.2(g) of the definitions sets out a presumed order in which Disruption Events must be remedied, in the absence of other rules agreed to by the parties, and these presumptions must be read in light of Section 5.1(f), which identifies, in relation to the various Disruption Events, the day on or as of which the Settlement Rate, or the appropriate alternative means of settlement of a transaction, will be determined, again, unless the parties agree otherwise.

described elsewhere in this book,[1349] this approach should lead to a settlement at the arithmetic mean of the absolute amounts of the Loss determinations (positive for one party's loss and negative for the other's gain) which are to be made by each of the presumed Affected Parties as at or as soon as practicable after the date No Fault Termination became the applicable Disruption Fallback.

In entering into Transactions that could ultimately be closed out under this ultimate Disruption Fallback, the parties should examine the related risks that this approach to settlement may involve. For example, as a result of the same circumstances that lead to No Fault Termination, each of the parties may be determining its Loss on the basis of its own particular losses, costs and expenses, including its cost of funding reflecting its own financial condition (as, possibly, affected by the underlying Disruption Event or Events) and the party's own costs involved in liquidating or unwinding a hedge or related position if, as may very well be the case, a replacement transaction is not available or, even if it is available, the party chooses to look to these unwind costs. A market participant might conclude that this result involves risks it does not wish to assume, particularly if it has not reached a more precise agreement with the other party about hedge or related unwind costs that may be taken into account or if there is reason for concern over the way in which the other party's cost of funding, in the midst of a Disruption Event, might have an impact on the ultimate settlement through No Fault Termination. The parties may wish to adopt an approach aimed at eliminating exposure to some of these risks.[1350]

Fallback Reference Price and Calculation Agent Determination. For Price Source Disruption, the initial presumed Disruption Fallback is Fallback Reference Price, calling for the determination of the Settlement Rate as if the parties had specified Currency–Reference Dealers as the fallback Settlement Rate Option for their Transaction. This is the Disruption Fallback specified in EMTA's NDF confirmation templates as well.

If that fallback does not result in the determination of a Settlement Rate, under the *1998 FX Transaction and Currency Option Definitions,* the remaining fallback before No Fault Termination is to seek to determine the Settlement Rate as if the parties had chosen Calculation Agent Determination of Settlement Rate.

The same two fallbacks are presumed to apply in connection with Illiquidity. On the other hand, if the relevant Disruption Event is Price Materiality or Dual Exchange Rate, No Fault Termination will apply unless the parties are able, by way of fallback, to determine the Settlement Rate using Currency–Reference Dealers (Price Materiality) or Calculation Agent Determination of Settlement Rate (Dual Exchange Rate). As noted earlier, in each of these cases, if the parties had designated a Fallback Reference Price, it would apply (subject to No Fault Termination as the ultimate Disruption Fallback).

Other Disruption Fallbacks. The *User's Guide to the 1998 FX Transaction and Currency Option Definitions* includes a flow chart showing how the presumed and specified Disruption Fallbacks operate under those definitions in connection with all published

---

[1349] *See supra* p. 246 on the Loss measure of damages and the calculation of close-out amounts involving two Affected Parties under this ISDA form.

[1350] By way of example, *see infra* p. 983 on the ISDA approach to close-out settlement calculations in connection with Force Majeure Events under the *2001 ISDA Amendments.*

Disruption Events.[1351] The *User's Guide* also discusses how the Disruption Fallbacks that are not summarized above work in isolation and, in some cases, together,[1352] and usefully puts the Disruption Events and Disruption Fallbacks into context by giving historical examples involving Indonesia, New Zealand, Russia, South Africa, Thailand and Venezuela and explaining how the relevant disruptions in the 1980s and 1990s might have been treated in connection with a transaction documented under the *1998 FX Transaction and Currency Option Definitions.*

When the parties have chosen Disruption Fallbacks involving inconvertibility, non-transferability, reschedulings and defaults under specific Benchmark Obligations or obligations of Governmental Authorities in the Event Currency Jurisdiction more generally, they are, as suggested earlier, likely to be seeking a very specific set of results in connection with Disruption Events. Whether or not the standard Disruption Fallback definitions will operate to produce these results is a matter that deserves close attention in each particular case. The following are some examples.

Non-Deliverable Substitute. Where the affected Transaction is Deliverable, the parties' aim may be settlement in the Settlement Currency, as if it were Non-Deliverable. The standard Disruption Fallback that provides for this approach is Non-Deliverable Substitute, and it is the presumed Disruption Fallback for Deliverable Transactions when the parties have selected any of the inconvertibility or non-transferability Disruption Events as applicable to their Transaction. The Non-Deliverable Substitute approach spells out presumptions that should be applied to calculate the Cash Settlement Amount (Deliverable FX Transaction) or In-the-Money Amount (Deliverable Currency Option Transaction) to be paid as if the Transaction had been Non-Deliverable. These presumptions include determining the Settlement Rate by treating as the Valuation Date the date that, but for a Disruption Event, would have been the Settlement Date for the affected Deliverable Transaction. Those who adopt this fallback should, naturally, review these presumptions carefully and also examine whether they agree to the related requirement that the party required to pay the settlement should indemnify the other party for its cost of funding the settlement amount, "without proof or evidence of such cost," for the period beginning with the date that would have been the Settlement Date but for the occurrence of Disruption Events.

Deliverable Substitute. In some cases the parties' aim may, conversely, be settlement of a Non-Deliverable Transaction as if it had been executed on a Deliverable basis. The Disruption Fallback that would produce this result is Deliverable Substitute. This fallback presumes that the settlement will involve payment of the Reference Currency Notional Amount to an account designated by the Reference Currency Buyer and payment by that party of the Notional Amount (stated in the Settlement Currency) to an account designated by the Reference Currency Seller. This gross settlement, as if the parties had entered into a Deliverable FX Transaction or Currency Option Transaction, may not take into account adjustments that would be required to achieve the parties' aim, in light of related transactions. In addition, as presented, this fallback involves settlement risk, which the parties may, as described below, seek to deal with by adopting the Escrow Arrange-

---

[1351] At 56–57.

[1352] At 30–34.

ment fallback. The Deliverable Substitute fallback is not a presumed Disruption Fallback in connection with any of the Disruption Events.

Local Currency Substitute. Another possibility is that the parties' agree to settle their Deliverable or Non-Deliverable Transaction in the Reference Currency. The standard Disruption Fallback that would produce this result is called Local Currency Substitute. This is the presumed primary Disruption Fallback for Non-Deliverable Transactions involving the general and specific inconvertibility and non-transferability Disruption Events. Naturally, for it to operate there must be a method acceptable to both parties for determining the spot rate of exchange at which the Settlement Currency Amount (FX Transaction) or In-the-Money Amount (Currency Option Transaction) should be translated to the Reference Currency. For Deliverable Transactions, operation of this fallback requires two steps. Under the first, the parties follow the procedure that would have been applicable if they had chosen Non-Deliverable Substitute (as described above), and then they translate the amount in the Settlement Currency determined in that manner to the Reference Currency.

Fallbacks involving Delivery of Local Assets. Where the Transaction is entered into to shift risks associated with a particular Benchmark Obligation or class of obligations from the Reference Currency Seller to the Reference Currency Buyer, the parties may find that the Disruption Fallback called Local Asset Substitute–Gross or Local Asset Substitute–Net serves their purposes. In connection with a Deliverable Transaction, the first of these fallbacks would call for Delivery by the Reference Currency Seller to an account designated by the Reference Currency Buyer of Benchmark Obligations with a Specified Value equal to the Event Currency Amount, and for payment by the latter of an amount in the Non-Event Currency equal to the Non-Event Currency Amount. In a Non-Deliverable Transaction, the approach, similarly, requires the same Delivery of Benchmark Obligations by the Reference Currency Seller and payment by the Reference Currency Buyer of the Notional Amount in the Settlement Currency (where the Event Currency is the Reference Currency) or in the Reference Currency (where the Event Currency is the Settlement Currency). Local Asset Substitute–Gross is the presumed Disruption Fallback for cases involving the Disruption Events known as Benchmark Obligation Default and Governmental Authority Default, when the obligation involved in the underlying default must be delivered in accordance with the parties' agreement.

The Specified Value of the Benchmark Obligation and the Event Currency Amount used in connection with these fallbacks are amounts determined by reference to definitions in Section 5.4 of the *1998 FX Transaction and Currency Option Definitions.*[1353] The Non-Event Currency Amount or Notional Amount (as required) must be specified in the relevant Transaction's Confirmation. The Local Asset Substitute–Gross fallback also involves settlement risk (one party may not make the required Delivery or payment, and the provision does not call for payment vs. delivery). This risk may be pronounced because of the very Disruption Events that have led to use of the fallback. The Local Asset Substitute–Net alternative requires the same attention to detail regarding settlement but eliminates the settlement risk by providing for settlement through Delivery of Benchmark Obligations with a Specified Value equal to the Event Currency Amount by the party that would have been obligated to pay the Settlement Currency Amount (FX

[1353] *See infra* p. 501 on the Event Currency Amount.

Transaction) or In-the-Money Amount (Currency Option Transaction). Users of both fallbacks involving Delivery of Local Assets may encounter obstacles to settlement applying the fallbacks under applicable securities laws or restrictions on transfer in the relevant instruments or agreements governing them.

Fallbacks involving Escrow Arrangements. The Disruption Fallback called Escrow Arrangement can be used to deal with settlement risk in the context of Disruption Events in connection with Deliverable Transactions and Non-Deliverable Transactions that are being settled through the Deliverable Substitute fallback. The Escrow Arrangement fallback is not drafted to deal with settlement involving payment of currency by one party and delivery of assets other than currency by the other. Under this fallback, the parties are required to use their reasonable efforts to deposit, or cause an escrow agent to deposit, the amounts they are obligated to pay in a segregated, interest-bearing account or otherwise invest the amounts in an investment acceptable to both parties. These escrow arrangements must be spelled out in the parties' Confirmation. The parties also specify as the Maximum Days of Disruption a number of consecutive Business Days during which these arrangements will remain in place. If the Disruption Events cease to exist during that period, the escrowed funds and interest or investment return are released to the relevant parties. If a relevant Disruption Event is continuing at the end of this period, the party obligated to pay the Non-Event Currency is entitled to release of the funds due to it (plus interest or investment return) but it is not required to pay the other party the amount owed to it in the Event Currency (plus interest or return on the agreed investment of the escrowed fund) until the applicable Disruption Event has ceased to exist. Escrow arrangements also automatically apply, as described in the next paragraph, if Settlement Postponement is an applicable Disruption Fallback.

Fallbacks involving Settlement Postponement. The *1998 FX Transaction and Currency Option Definitions* presume that, in some cases, the parties will wish to postpone settlement of their Transactions as a primary or secondary Disruption Fallback, before they ultimately lapse into No Fault Termination. The presumption applies as the primary presumed Disruption Fallback in connection with the Nationalization Disruption Event and as the secondary presumed Disruption Fallback when any of the inconvertibility or non-transferability Disruption Events applies and when Benchmark Obligation Default or Governmental Authority Default applies. As with Escrow Arrangement, the parties must specify a number of Maximum Days of Disruption during which settlement will be postponed. During the period of postponement, each of the parties must either follow the rules applicable to Escrow Arrangement, if they are using that Disruption Fallback too, or they must use reasonable efforts to deposit the amounts they would be required to pay in an ultimate settlement into an interest bearing escrow account, or otherwise invest the amounts in an investment acceptable to both parties. As under the Escrow Arrangement Disruption Fallback, the escrow arrangements contemplated in this Settlement Postponement fallback were not drafted to apply in cases in which settlement is to occur through Delivery of Local Assets by one of the parties and a payment by the other party.

Assignment of Claim. Assignment of Claim is a Disruption Fallback presumed to apply as a secondary fallback in connection with Nationalization—a Disruption Event that, as noted above, only applies if all or substantially all of the assets in the Event Currency Jurisdiction of a party or a Relevant Affiliate of a party are expropriated, confiscated, requisitioned, nationalized or subjected to other Governmental Authority action that deprives the party or Relevant Affiliate of the assets. Under this fallback settlement occurs through assignment by that party or Relevant Affiliate of a relevant amount of its official claim (referred to as a "Claim") against any Governmental Authority with respect to the expropriation or other event, if the assignment is permitted under applicable law. If applicable law does not permit the assignment, the party or Relevant Affiliate must, instead, transfer a beneficial interest in the Claim. Where a Deliverable Transaction is involved, the amount of the Claim in either case is to be equal to the Event Currency Amount specified in the relevant Confirmation or, if no such amount is so specified, determined to be the amount of the Event Currency owed by the Event Currency Seller on the Settlement Date. Where a Non-Deliverable Transaction is involved, if the Event Currency is not the Settlement Currency, the amount of the Claim is determined by using the Settlement Rate to translate the applicable settlement amount (Settlement Currency Amount, for an NDF, or In-the-Money Amount, for an NDO) to the Event Currency or, if the Event Currency is the Settlement Currency, the amount of the claim is the relevant settlement amount (Settlement Currency Amount or In-the-Money Amount).

Negotiation as a Disruption Fallback. As noted, Material Change in Circumstance is a broadly drafted Disruption Event that applies if there is any event, other than one that would be covered by another of the Disruption Events, that is beyond the control of the parties and makes it impossible for a party to fulfill its obligations under the Transaction or generally under similar Transactions—even if the parties' own Transaction is not affected. Since the Disruption Event will, by definition, involve events that the parties do not foresee when they enter into their Transaction, the presumed Disruption Fallback simply requires each party, promptly upon becoming aware of the underlying event, to negotiate with its counterparty in good faith and in a commercially reasonable manner to seek to determine an alternative basis for determining the Settlement Rate or for settling the Transaction in accordance with prevailing market practice. The parties must specify a number of Maximum Days of Disruption during which these negotiations should occur. If agreement is not reached during that period, No Fault Termination will apply.

DISRUPTION EVENTS, ILLEGALITY AND FORCE MAJEURE EVENTS

Users of the *1998 FX Transaction and Currency Option Definitions* in connection with a particular Transaction should consider how the provisions on Disruption Events and Disruption Fallbacks in these definitions will operate with other terms in the agreement governing the Transaction. This issue typically arises in connection with master agreement provisions relating to supervening illegality, force majeure and impossibility.

The *1998 FX Transaction and Currency Option Definitions* are quite precise (in Section 5.1(c)) on this point in their references to the provision on Illegality in the 1992 ISDA Master Agreement (Multicurrency—Cross Border) form. The rule is that, if an event would constitute both a Disruption Event and an Illegality, it will be treated as a Disruption Event. Those definitions apply the same rule in a case in which the parties have added to the schedule to their agreement a provision on Impossibility, like the one illustrated in the *User's Guide to the 1992 ISDA Master Agreements.* Assuming that they intend to adopt this rule, if the parties adopt ISDA's provisions on Force Majeure Events, as made available in the *2001 ISDA Amendments* and, when it is published, as set out in the proposed new ISDA master agreement, they may find it appropriate to expand the rule to apply to Force Majeure Events.[1354]

Under Section 5.1(c), the same rule will apply to the parties to agreements prepared using a FEOMA, ICOM or IFEMA form who adopt those definitions. That is, if an event constitutes both a Disruption Event and a force majeure event, act of state, illegality or impossibility for purposes of the relevant IFEMA, ICOM or FEOMA provisions as published in 1992, 1993 or 1997, the event will be treated as a Disruption Event. The Foreign Exchange Committee subsequently (in December 1999) published new provisions on Force Majeure Events that prefigure many of the features included in the ISDA approach to the subject.[1355] Many of those who use the *1998 FX Transaction and Currency Option Definitions* with a FEOMA, ICOM or IFEMA form do so under the terms of a bridge (called the *1998 FX and Currency Option Definitions Addenda for the IFEMA, ICOM and FEOMA Agreements*) published by the Foreign Exchange Committee. The bridge included a presumption about the automatic application of certain Disruption Events and Disruption Fallbacks to all transactions under an IFEMA, ICOM or FEOMA form. Users of these forms that also adopt the 1999 provisions on Force Majeure Events published by the Foreign Exchange Committee should note that this presumption was reversed in the form of amendment published by the committee to facilitate adoption of the 1999 provisions. As a result, if they have used that form of amendment, the parties must agree on specific Disruption Events and Disruption Fallbacks that they wish to have apply in lieu of the 1999 provisions on Force Majeure Events.[1356]

CONCLUSION

As will be apparent from the preceding discussion, many of the provisions in the *1998 FX Transaction and Currency Option Definitions* can require or result in complex choices. Many of them are, however, used infrequently and only in connection with highly tailored transactions. In most cases, both deliverable and non-deliverable FX forwards and currency options can be documented using these definitions with relative ease.

Those who adopt these definitions should, however, take care to understand the default choices that will apply if the parties do not specify otherwise, even in cases where they are used for relatively simple transactions. The *User's Guide* to these definitions includes a helpful table of these presumptions,[1357] which market participants should consult. They may also wish to compare the presumptions in the table with presumptions used under other sets of ISDA definitions identified in tables in this book.

In using the *1998 FX Transaction and Currency Option Definitions* with Non-Deliverable Transactions, market participants generally should also bear in mind that not all portions of these definitions will necessarily reflect current market practices when they

---

[1354]Whether or not an expansion may be appropriate will depend on the parties' choices of Disruption Events. If Price Source Disruption and Price Materiality are the only applicable choices, an expansion may not be necessary.

[1355]The amendments are available at http://www.ny.frb.org/fxc/fmagagree.pdf.

[1356]Foreign Exchange Committee, *User's Guide: Revised Force Majeure Provisions* 3 (1999), *available at* www.ny.frb.org/fxc.

[1357]Pp. 45–55.

transact. As discussed in this introductory note, EMTA has published and continues to release recommended market practices and transaction templates that the parties should consider in preparing their documents.

The Foreign Exchange Committee, similarly, has published confirmation forms and best practices for use with barrier options. Users of the *1998 FX Transaction and Currency Option Definitions* should take into account these and other standards and recommended practices published by the Foreign Exchange Committee and by bankers' associations in jurisdictions relevant to the parties' transactions.

Finally, as illustrated in the following sample confirmation, currency swaps are generally documented using the *2000 ISDA Definitions,* and not the *1998 FX Transaction and Currency Option Definitions*. Nonetheless, there are cases in which features of nondeliverable products are grafted onto currency swaps. In these cases, care must be taken that all appropriate provisions from the 1998 definitions are adopted and inconsistencies between the two sets of definitions are avoided or appropriately resolved. Examples of areas in which inconsistencies often arise include concepts of Business Day (particularly taking into account EMTA distinctions between Unscheduled Holidays and Scheduled Holidays, as described above) and provisions on the role of the Calculation Agent.

CURRENCY SWAPS

Like the single-currency interest rate swap, the conventional currency swap is a bilateral agreement in which each of the parties promises to make periodic payments to the other calculated as one would calculate interest on a debt obligation. The key difference is that the parties' periodic payment obligations in a currency swap are denominated in different currencies. This exchange of interest-rate streams in different currencies distinguishes the currency swap from what is sometimes called a "foreign exchange swap," a transaction involving an initial exchange of two currencies at an agreed rate and a reverse exchange of the same currencies at a later date, usually at a different rate.[1358] In fact, many currency swap transactions combine a foreign exchange swap, understood in this sense, with the hallmark periodic interest-rate exchanges of a currency swap, or combine these periodic interest-rate exchanges with a final exchange of the amounts—in ISDA terminology, the Currency Amounts—used in their calculation.

As with other OTC derivatives, there is considerable variety in the terminology used in market to refer to currency swaps. For example, when a currency swap involves fixed amount payments in one currency and floating amount payments in the other, it is sometimes referred to as a "circus swap," a "currency coupon swap"[1359] or a cross-currency swap, to distinguish the transaction from a simple currency swap, in which both interest-rate streams are calculated at fixed rates.

The currency swap had its origins in parallel loan and back-to-back loan transactions,[1360] which can be described in simple terms as follow: Corporation A, organized in one jurisdiction (the United States, for example), makes a loan—Loan A—in domestic currency to the local subsidiary of Corporation B, a foreign corporation (organized in England, for example). In a parallel transaction, Corporation B makes a loan—Loan B—in its home currency to the local subsidiary of Corporation A. These transactions were widely used when the United Kingdom had exchange controls in place, as a mechanism to permit U.K. corporations to obtain funding for their offshore affiliates. They presented difficult structuring, legal and accounting issues: Should the loan in one currency be "topped-up" if that currency weakened in terms of the other? Would there be a right of offset on Loan A if there were a default on Loan B? In a consolidated balance sheet, would the loans cancel each other out? The cash flows in the parallel loans are identical to the flows on the currency swap described and illustrated below, if the parts of the parallel loan transaction are looked at together.

[1358] *See, e.g.*, BIS, FOREIGN EXCHANGE AND DERIVATIVES MARKET ACTIVITY IN 2001, AT 35 (2002), *available at* http://www.bis.org/publ/rpfx02.htm.

[1359] *See* DICTIONARY OF RISK MANAGEMENT 55, 82.

[1360] *See* Smith, *supra* note 1226, at 6–4 to 6–5. There are conflicting views on who originated the currency swap, but the product first received wide publicity on the occasion of the World Bank-IBM World Trade transaction in 1981. *See* Rawls, *supra* note 1298, at 2–7.

The currency swap documented in the following sample confirmation is a cross-currency rate swap with a five-year Term providing for (1) an initial exchange in which the Company pays an amount in Pounds Sterling in return for an amount in U.S. Dollars, (2) semiannual payments by the Company in U.S. Dollars calculated at 6-month LIBOR, (3) annual payments by the Bank in Pounds Sterling calculated at a fixed rate and (4) a final exchange in which the Company pays an amount in U.S. Dollars in return for an amount in Pounds Sterling. The transaction might be of interest to the Company because it had a need for funding in U.S. Dollars but could obtain a better all-in rate by issuing bonds in Pounds Sterling and "converting" the obligation to U.S. Dollars through the swap.[1361] Thus, separately from the swap, the Company might raise GBP 100 million in the bond market, with the intention of using the proceeds to make the initial payment on the swap. It would then apply the annual payments it received under the swap to pay interest on the bonds and apply the Sterling payment it received at the end of the swap to repay principal on the bonds (designating the Payment Dates for these periodic payments and the Final Exchange Date for the final exchange due to it as the dates funds are due to the fiscal agent for the bonds in London). From the point of view of the Bank, the transaction is simply one more swap added to its portfolio, to be taken into account in its overall management of that portfolio.[1362] The transactions may be illustrated as shown in Figure 8 on the following page

Cross-currency interest rate swaps of the kind illustrated here are often entered into without the initial exchange, to hedge existing indebtedness. Similar transactions may be entered into to manage assets as well as liabilities or to create "synthetic assets," as discussed in the description of rate swaps.[1363]

[1361] *See, e.g., Ford Credit Canada Enters Currency Swap,* in the "User Strategies" column in DERIVATIVES WEEK, May 6, 2002, at 7. In some cases, the currency swap is used both to lower the cost of the financing and to lengthen its term, as described in the "User Profile" column in DERIVATIVES WEEK, Jan. 11, 1993, at 8, detailing a five-year borrowing in U.S. dollars swapped into Thai baht at a time when direct fixed-rate financing in baht would have been available to the end-user for a maximum term of three months. *See also Swedish Company Enters FX Swap* and *French Rail Operator Converts Sterling Bond,* DERIVATIVES WEEK, Mar. 11, 2002, at 5 & 6, respectively, describing a 25-year sterling/euro cross-currency interest rate swap related to an SNCF bond stated at the time to have been "issued in sterling because it affords longer maturities than the euro market," and a 10-year swap by Investor, a Swedish industrial holding company, to convert the proceeds of a 500 million euro bond offering into Swedish krona, at a time when "[a] treasury official at the company . . . said it converted the deal into its local currency because it maintains all of its debt in the Swedish currency, but chose to issue in euros because it wanted to extend its maturity curve and would not be able to raise that much long-term money in the Swedish market."

[1362] As discussed in the introductory note on currency derivatives, currency swaps involve substantial settlement risk because the parties' obligations are denominated in different currencies and, therefore, are not paid net. These greater risks have historically been reflected in capital requirements under the Basel Accord, applicable to many of the major financial institutions that participate in the market for currency swaps, which are much higher than those applicable to rate swaps. As mentioned *supra* note 642, this is so in part because, for purposes of capital requirements relating to credit risk, bank exposure includes possible loss of the entire currency amount customarily payable at the end of the term of a conventional currency swap, as well as the risk of loss associated with each of the periodic exchanges.

[1363] *Supra* p. 427.

Currency Swaps

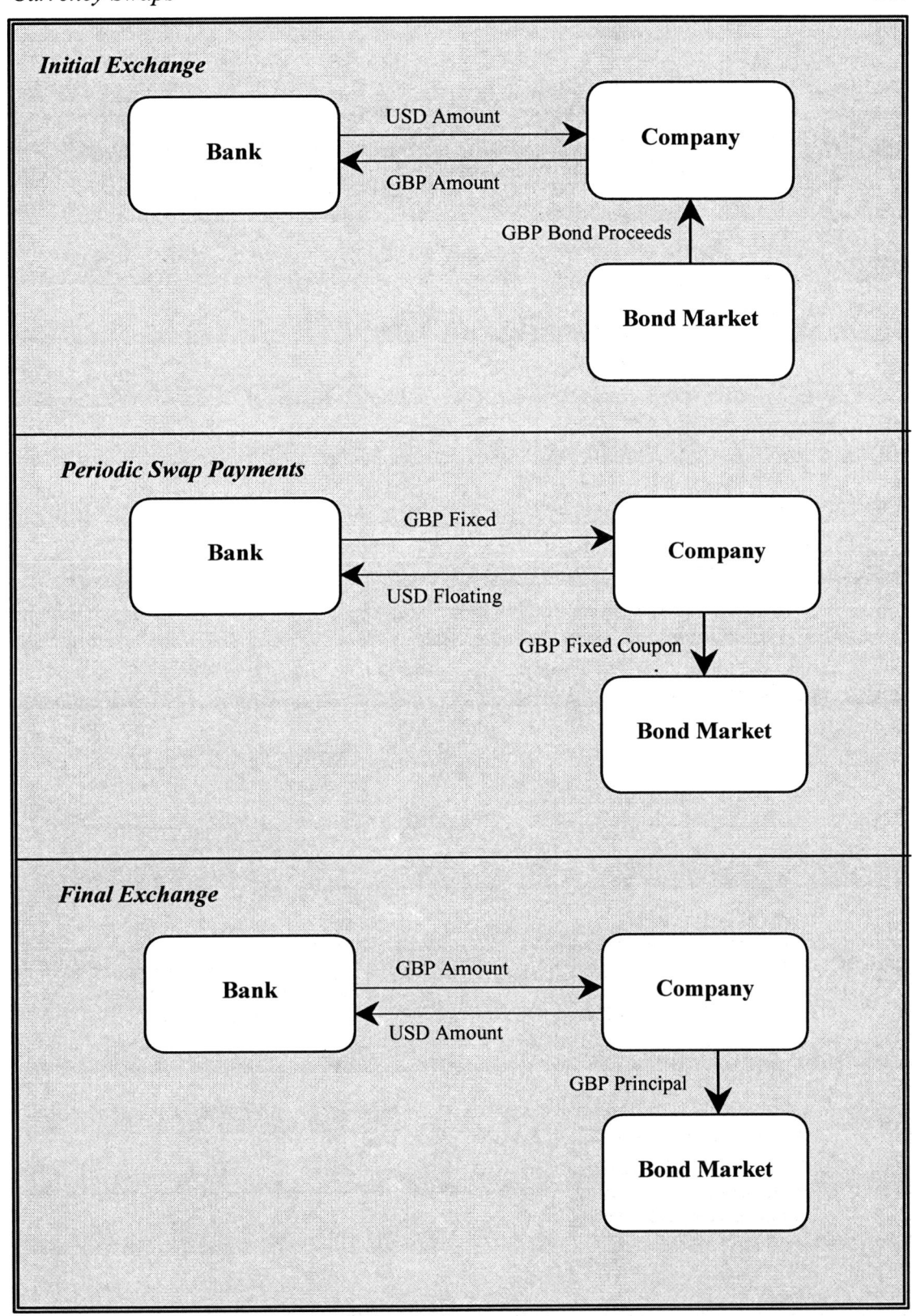

Initial Exchange

Bank → USD Amount → Company
Bank ← GBP Amount ← Company
Company ← GBP Bond Proceeds ← Bond Market

Periodic Swap Payments

Bank → GBP Fixed → Company
Bank ← USD Floating ← Company
Company → GBP Fixed Coupon → Bond Market

Final Exchange

Bank → GBP Amount → Company
Bank ← USD Amount ← Company
Company → GBP Principal → Bond Market

Figure 8. Cross Currency Rate Swap and Related Bond Issue

> The Introduction to this Part, *supra* p. 369, and the annotations to the sample rate swap confirmation, *supra* p. 427, contain general commentary about the confirmation process and the use of ISDA's confirmation forms both before and after the parties have entered into a master agreement that is not repeated or expressly referred to in the annotations to the other sample confirmations in this book.

[Letterhead of Big Bank, N.A.]

April 16, 2002

Cross-Currency Rate Swap Transaction

English Company PLC
Company House
Company Lane
London AB1C 2DE

Ladies and Gentlemen:

The purpose of this communication (the "Confirmation") is to confirm the terms and conditions of the transaction entered into between us on the Trade Date specified below (the "Transaction").

The definitions and provisions contained in the 2000 ISDA Definitions, as published by the International Swaps and Derivatives Association, Inc., are incorporated into this Confirmation. For these purposes, all references in those Definitions to a "Swap Transaction" shall be deemed to apply to the Transaction. In the event of any inconsistency between those definitions and provisions and this Confirmation, this Confirmation will govern.

This Confirmation constitutes a "Confirmation" as referred to in, and supplements, forms part of, and is subject to, the Master Agreement dated as of April 16, 2002, as amended and supplemented from time to time (the "Agreement"), between Big Bank, N.A. (the "Bank") and English Company PLC (the "Company"). All provisions contained in the Agreement govern this Confirmation except as expressly modified below.

1. The terms of the particular Transaction to which this Confirmation relates—which is a cross-currency rate swap—are as follows:

Reference No.:	00000-00
Trade Date:	April 16, 2002
Effective Date:	April 18, 2002
Termination Date:	April 18, 2007

Annotation 1. To this point, most of the sample confirmation is substantively identical to the sample rate swap confirmation, *supra* p. 427. However, whereas the parties must specify a Notional Amount in confirming a rate swap under the *2000 ISDA Definitions* (or the *1991 ISDA Definitions*), in confirming a currency swap—including a cross-currency rate swap—they must instead specify a Currency Amount for each of the parties. *See* the Introduction to this Part, *supra* p. 385.

Fixed Amounts:

    Fixed Rate Payer: The Bank

    Bank Currency Amount: GBP 100,000 000

Annotation 2. Under the formula set forth in Section 5.1 of the *2000 ISDA Definitions* (and the same section of the *1991 ISDA Definitions*), the specified Currency Amount of Pounds Sterling will be multiplied by the specified Fixed Rate to in order to calculate the Fixed Amount payable by the Bank in respect of each Calculation Period. The 30/360 Fixed Rate Day Count Fraction will be applied as explained in Annotation 11 to the sample rate swap confirmation, *supra* p. 431.

    Bank Period End Dates: April 18 in each year prior to and including the Termination Date, commencing on April 18, 2003; No Adjustment

Annotation 3. The approach shown here should be contrasted with the approach to defining the Calculation Periods for the Bank's Floating Rate payments illustrated in the sample rate swap confirmation, *supra* p. 431. There, the parties specified Payment Dates for the Bank and did not specify other rules for determining the length of the Calculation Periods for the Bank's obligations, so the Payment Dates define the ends of the Calculation Periods. In such a case, the *2000 ISDA Definitions* automatically operate to adjust the Calculation Periods for weekends and holidays. *See* the discussion of "Calculation Period" in the Introduction to this Part, *supra* p. 389. In the Transaction confirmed here, the rules regarding the length of the Bank's Calculation Periods—defined by reference to the specified Period End Dates—must be set forth separately from the Bank's Payment Dates. This is so for two reasons. First, the Bank's Fixed Amount obligations are due annually, whereas the Floating Amount obligations of the Company are payable semiannually. Second, the Fixed Amount payable by the Bank in respect of each of its Calculation Periods is due on the second London Business Day before the last day (the Period End Date) of that Calculation Period, a result produced by the illustrated indication of how the Bank's Payment Dates will be set in accordance with the "Early Payment" convention. This approach could be required in connection with currency swap payments that the payee expects to apply to service its obligations under a related bond or FRN transaction, where the payment due under the bond or FRN in respect of the related interest period must be made in advance to the fiscal or paying agent. The parties have specified "No Adjustment" in stating the Bank's Period End Dates because the length of the Bank's Calculation Periods is not to change even if a Period End Date falls on a weekend or a bank holiday in the city specified for the GBP payments to be made by the Bank. This can be important if the payee of the Fixed Amounts is seeking to have them exactly match the amounts of interest it will be required to pay in respect of "frozen" interest periods under a related bond. If the parties had not specified "No Adjustment," Section 4.10 of the *2000 ISDA Definitions* would have operated to result in adjustment of the Bank's Period End Dates in accordance with the Modified Following Business Day convention.

> Bank Payment Dates: Early Payment, on the second Business Day in London before each Bank Period End Date

Annotation 4. This item has been completed in accordance with Section 4.9(d) of the *2000 ISDA Definitions* to indicate that the Bank's Payment Date for the Fixed Amount with respect to each of its Calculation Periods will be the second London Business Day before the Period End Date for that Calculation Period. *See* the preceding annotation for a description of circumstances in which this approach may be appropriate. The same convention would apply under the same provision in the *1991 ISDA Definitions*.

> Fixed Rate: 7.00% per annum
>
> Fixed Rate Day Count Fraction: 30/360

Annotation 5. In some currency swaps the parties state the Fixed Amount for each Calculation Period as a fixed amount. By contrast, in this sample confirmation, the Fixed Rate and Fixed Rate Day Count Fraction have been specified. As a result, pursuant to the formula in Section 5.1 of the *2000 ISDA Definitions* (and the same section of the *1991 ISDA Definitions*), the Fixed Amount for each Calculation Period for the Bank, as Fixed Rate Payer, will be the Bank Currency Amount of GBP100,000,000 multiplied by the Fixed Rate of 7.00% per annum, calculated in accordance with the Day Count Fraction convention referred to as "30/360" or "360/360" or "Bond Basis." *See* the Introduction to this part, *supra* p. 405, on this convention.

Floating Amounts:

> Floating Rate Payer: The Company

Sample Currency Swap Confirmation

    Company Currency Amount: USD 145,000,000

    Company Payment Dates: April 18 and October 18 in each year, commencing with October 18, 2002 and ending with the Termination Date, subject to the Modified Following Business Day Convention.

> Annotation 6. The Company's Floating Amount obligations are semiannual, whereas the Bank's Fixed Amounts are to be paid annually. Annotations 12–16 to the sample rate swap confirmation, *supra* p. 431, discuss concerns for parties, like the Company in this example, that are required to make payments more frequently than their counterparties. In the illustrated transaction, there is a second kind of payment mismatch, favorable to the Company, in connection with the payments due in October of each year because, as explained in Annotations 3 and 4, the Fixed Amounts due from the Bank will be due on Payment Dates set in accordance with the Early Payment convention, whereas the Company's Payment Dates are set in accordance with standard practice for Floating Amounts calculated using a LIBOR-based Floating Rate Option. *See supra* p. 419. (It would of course be possible to make the Company's Payment Dates match the Bank's.) As a result, and because the Floating Amounts and the Fixed Amounts are due in different currencies, the payments cannot be netted. Timing mismatches often exist in connection with currency swaps, even if the parties' Payment Dates match, since the parties' payments may be made at different times because of time zone differences. Therefore, in currency swaps, one of the parties may take on significantly greater risk in connection with possible counterparty default. In the illustrated swap, even if the Company's Payment Dates and the Bank's Payment Dates matched, the Bank would run this risk since it would be required to make GBP payments at a time when banks in New York City, where the Floating Amount payments would be made, would not yet be open. *See supra* p. 486 on this settlement risk in currency derivatives.
>
> Annotation 7. The 1992 ISDA Multicurrency—Cross Border form does not specify a time by which payments must be made; it merely requires payment for value on the due date. A simple solution available in some cases is to specify a time for both payments when banks in both relevant cities will be open for business, so that neither of the parties need tender payment before the other. In practice, market participants do not monitor payments in this fashion, however, and in any event this approach is not available in all cross-currency transactions. For example, in a Yen/USD currency swap, banks would be closed in Tokyo—the place for payment of the Yen—by the time banks in New York City opened on the same day. Therefore, some market participants include provisions—like the one illustrated in Part 5(k) of the schedule to the sample master agreement in Part 3, *infra* p. 941—that enable them to use an escrow arrangement to protect themselves against settlement risk. An alternative is to give either party, or the party expecting to have to make its payment first in light of time zone differences, a right to elect to discharge its obligation by paying the equivalent, at the prevailing spot rate, in the currency in which the payment to it is due and to net the payment obligations.

Floating Rate for Initial Calculation Period:	2.50%
Floating Rate Option:	USD-LIBOR-BBA
Designated Maturity:	6 months
Spread:	None
Floating Rate Day Count Fraction:	Actual/360
Reset Dates:	First day of each Calculation Period
Compounding:	Inapplicable

> Annotation 8. For discussion of the ISDA conventions on the calculation of Floating Amounts, *see supra* p. 402, in the Introduction to this Part, and *see* Annotations 17–23 to the sample rate swap confirmation, *supra* p. 433.

Initial Exchange:

Initial Exchange Date:	April 18, 2002
Bank Initial Exchange Amount:	USD 145,000,000
Company Initial Exchange Amount:	GBP 100,000,000

Final Exchange:

Bank Final Exchange Date:	The final Payment Date for the Bank
Company Final Exchange Date:	April 18, 2007
Bank Final Exchange Amount:	GBP 100,000,000
Company Final Exchange Amount:	USD 145,000,000

> Annotation 9. As noted *supra* p. 506, the currency swap does not necessarily involve an Initial Exchange. When it does, generally the Initial Exchange Amount payable by each party will be the same as the Final Exchange Amount payable to it by the other at the end of the Term. This will not be so, however, if the Initial Exchange Amounts are adjusted to take account of the expenses associated with a capital markets transaction related to the swap.

> Annotation 10. In this sample confirmation, the parties have not specified what will occur if the Initial Exchange Date or the Final Exchange Date is not a Business Day. As a result, if that happens, Sections 3.4 and 3.6 of the *2000 ISDA Definitions* supply the rules that the Initial Exchange Date will be adjusted in accordance with the Following Business Day Convention and the Final Exchange Date will be adjusted in accordance with the Modified Following Business Day Convention. Under those provisions, if the parties had indicated that there was to be an Initial Exchange but had not specified the Initial Exchange Date, they would be deemed to have designated the Effective Date as the Initial Exchange Date. Similarly, if there were a Final Exchange but no date was indicated, they would be deemed to have designated the Termination Date as the Final Exchange Date. Although there is some ambiguity on the subject in Section 3.6, it appears that the intention of the drafters was to provide that, if the Termination Date is the Final Exchange Date and the Termination Date turns out not to be a Business Day, and even though the parties have not provided for adjustment of the Termination Date, the Final Exchange Date will be adjusted, since otherwise the payments due on that date could not be made. The extra day or days would not alter the agreed length of the final Calculation Period, but the Final Exchange Amounts would be payable in accordance with the applicable Business Day Convention, as will the Fixed Amount and Floating Amount due on the Termination Date.

Business Days for USD: New York City and London

Business Days for GBP: London

> Annotation 11. In the example, the parties have designated different cities for purposes of defining Business Days in connection with the GBP and USD payments. This is because the Bank is paying early so that its Fixed Amount GBP payments will be received by the fiscal agent for the Company's bonds as required by the bond documents. When swaps are entered into in connection with financings, the definition of "Business Day" for the swap may have to be reconciled with the payment provisions of the documentation for the financing. The usual practice in currency swaps is to define Business Day for both parties to take into account bank holidays in both of the cities where payments are to be made, but this is not universally so. Unless the parties expressly provide otherwise, Section 1.4 of the *2000 ISDA Definitions* would result in consideration of different holidays for the parties' payments because the payments are due in different currencies and cities. In the illustrated swap, London is also relevant because the Company's Floating Amounts are calculated on the basis of LIBOR. *See* the introductory note on interest rate derivatives, *supra* p. 413, on the reasons for taking London bank holidays into account in derivatives involving a LIBOR Floating Rate Option.

Calculation Agent: The Bank

2. Account Details

Payments to the Bank:
> Payments in USD: Big Bank, N.A., New York, N.Y., ABA No. 000, CHIPS No. 000, Attention: Swaps Division
> Payments in GBP: Account No. 0000 with Big Bank London, Bank Street, London

Payments to the Company:
> Payments in USD: Account No. 00000 with Big Bank, N.A., New York, N.Y.
> Payments in GBP: Account No. 0000 with Big Bank London, Bank Street, London

3. Offices

The Office of the Bank for the Transaction is its head office in New York. The Office of the Company for the Transaction is its office at the address specified for notices to it in the Schedule to the Agreement.

Please confirm that the foregoing correctly sets forth the terms of our agreement by executing the copy of this Confirmation enclosed for that purpose and returning it to us or by sending to us a communication substantially similar to this letter, which sets forth the material terms of the Transaction to which this Confirmation relates and indicates your agreement to those terms. If you believe the foregoing does not correctly reflect the terms of our agreement, please give us notice as soon as possible of what you believe to be the necessary corrections.

Yours sincerely,

BIG BANK, N.A.
By: _____
   Name:
   Title: Vice President

Confirmed as of the date first
above written, on   ,

ENGLISH COMPANY PLC

By: _____
   Name:
   Title:

Forward Foreign Exchange Contracts

The foreign exchange agreement has a venerable history, dating back at least to the middle ages.[1364] Given its substantial use worldwide for the management of exchange rate risk, it has been among the first OTC derivatives to be widely traded electronically. In its simplest form—sometimes referred to as an outright forward—the FX forward is an agreement by one party to deliver a specified amount in one currency on a specific future date against delivery of a specified amount in another currency.

The traditional FX forward has a settlement date not too far removed from the trade date but further removed than two business days forward, which is generally the value date for spot FX transactions.[1365] These transactions, with maturities of up to a year, are often referred to as short-dated transactions, to distinguish them from "long-dated forwards," which have terms in excess of a year and began to appear in the late 1970s and early 1980s with terms of up to 10 years.[1366] According to a survey published by the BIS on the basis of data reported in 2001, there appears to be "an overall lengthening in the maturity of outstanding positions" in foreign exchange contracts.[1367]

Because of the credit sensitivity of the FX forward,[1368] it grew up primarily as an interbank instrument. The principal categories of participants in today's short-dated FX market are described as including central banks, corporations and governmental entities and foreign exchange brokers (who act as intermediaries between banks and collect their commissions half from the buyer and half from the seller of the currency pair), as well as commercial banks and other financial institutions.[1369]

[1364] *See supra* note 1298.

[1365] "Although, in theory, forward FX contracts can have *any* maturity, the market typically exists for standard maturities such as exactly a week, a month, two months, and so on (so-called 'even' dates). Maturities such as one month and six days are referred to as 'odd' or 'broken' dates. Active trading in the interbank market is ordinarily limited to even dates for maturities longer than a week." Satyajit Das, *Forward foreign exchange contracts*, in 1 MANAGEMENT OF CURRENCY RISK 245, 246.

[1366] *See* George Handjinicolaou, *The Forward Foreign Exchange Market: An Alternative for Hedging Currency Risks*, in HANDBOOK OF RISK MANAGEMENT 13–1, 13–5 to 13–7 ("The Origin of the Long-Dated Forward Exchange Markets"); Satyajit Das, *supra* note 1365, at 245, 248 (comparing long-term forwards (LTFX) and currency swaps and their respective optimal uses).

[1367] *BIS 2001 FX and Derivatives Market Survey* 4 (reporting the same phenomenon in interest rate derivatives). The principal shift in the maturity structure observed involved a "significant drop in short-term foreign exchange contracts (up to one year) and robust growth in longer-term foreign exchange and interest rate contracts (over five years)." *Id.* at 26.

[1368] *See supra* p. 486 on settlement risk in FX forwards and other currency derivatives.

[1369] Satyajit Das, *Forward foreign exchange contracts*, in 1 MANAGEMENT OF CURRENCY RISK 245, 259. *BIS 2001 FX and Derivatives Market Survey* 7 reports some shifts in the relative importance of trading between different types of counterparties, involving declines in the share of interbank trading and trading between banks and non-financial customers and an increase in the share of trading between banks and non-bank financial customers, such as asset managers.

Short-dated FX transactions are widely used to manage exchange risk related to international trade transactions. For example, a U.S. importer may have bought goods from Japan, invoiced in yen, payable in 30 days. To eliminate the risk of a strengthening of the yen relative to the dollar and also to have the basis for an exact price calculation, the U.S. importer can buy the yen 30 days forward (outright) to lock in a dollar cost of the purchase. Similarly, a U.S. exporter who has yen receipts in payment for its exports can eliminate the related exchange risk by selling the yen three months forward (outright).[1370] Failure to hedge in these cases is speculative as the importer is then "betting" on a fall of the yen while the exporter is "expecting" a rise of the yen.[1371]

Short-dated FX forwards are also widely used to speculate on rate movements. Short-dated and long-dated FX forwards are used to serve the same kinds of asset and liability management goals as currency swaps.[1372] Long-dated forwards have been described as better suited than currency swaps to manage uneven currency cash flows.[1373]

There is an interesting relationship between the FX forward and the currency swap, since the currency swap can be thought of as a series of FX forwards wrapped into a single transaction,[1374] together with a spot FX transaction at the outset, in the case of a currency swap involving an initial exchange. Like the FRA, the FX forward has characteristics in common with financial futures contracts but can be distinguished from them. The futures require initial margin and daily marks-to-market in a clearing environment, whereas, in OTC foreign exchange forward dealing, any applicable credit support will be privately negotiated. Also, where conventional futures are concerned, the settlement dates are standard, while the settlement terms of the OTC transaction can be adapted to the needs of an end-user in light of the characteristics of the risk it is seeking to hedge.[1375]

In its traditional form, the FX forward transaction is often referred to as a deliverable transaction, to distinguish it from a non-deliverable forward (NDF), in which the value of the parties' forward exchange rate bargain is settled on a net basis through a single payment in a settlement currency, rather than through gross payments in the currencies involved. Using the terminology of the *1998 FX Transaction and Currency Option Definitions,* in a Deliverable FX Transaction, one of the parties agrees to pay an amount of one currency in exchange for an amount of the second currency that is either stated or determined at a stated exchange rate—the Forward Rate. This settlement occurs on the agreed Settlement Date. To translate this bargain into a Non-Deliverable FX Transaction,

---

[1370]These examples assume that the importer and exporter can be precise about the quantity in respect of which they need exchange rate protection. If precision is not possible, as is often the case, a parties sometimes enter into products that are referred to as quanto, or quantity-adjusting derivatives. *See infra* p. 526 for discussion of these products in connection with currency options.

[1371]*Id.* at 258. *See also* Boris Antl, *Forward foreign exchange contracts, in* 2 MANAGEMENT OF CURRENCY RISK 3–4.

[1372]*Supra* p. 505. *See also* Boris Antl, *Forward foreign exchange contracts, in* 2 MANAGEMENT OF CURRENCY RISK 5–8, describing the hedging of long-term debt with a "tailored" FX contract.

[1373]Satyajit Das, *supra* note 1369, at 258–60.

[1374]*See* Smith, *supra* note 1360, at 6–5 ("Swaps as Packages of Forward Contracts").

[1375]*See* David M. Modest, *Currency forwards and futures, in* 1 MANAGEMENT OF CURRENCY RISK 285, 286–93 (describing and comparing these derivatives).

one of the currencies is identified as a Reference Currency and the other is the Settlement Currency. One of the parties is identified as the Seller, and the other as the Buyer, of the Reference Currency. Settlement of the Non-Deliverable FX Transaction involves payment of a Settlement Currency Amount by the Buyer to the Seller or by the Seller to the Buyer, depending on whether the Reference Currency has increased in value relative to the Settlement Currency (the Seller pays) or has declined in value relative to the Settlement Currency (the Buyer pays). This Settlement Currency Amount is determined using a spot exchange rate identified as the Settlement Rate, which is generally determined in respect of a Valuation Date. Unless the parties agree otherwise, the Valuation Date is two Business Days before the Settlement Date for the NDF.

The conventions used in the documentation of NDFs are described in the introductory note on currency derivatives,[1376] which also discusses conventions relating to the handling of events—known as Disruption Events—in which the Settlement Rate cannot be determined in the parties' preferred manner or in which they agree to disregard the Settlement Rate determined in this manner. The various choices they may make regarding alternative methods for determining the Settlement Rate, or alternative means of settling their transactions, are referred to as Disruption Fallbacks.

The following sample confirmation illustrates the documentation of a Deliverable FX Transaction, and the annotations explain how the transaction could have been documented if it had been executed as an NDF.

[1376] *See supra* p. 488.

> The Introduction to this Part, *supra* p. 369, and the annotations to the sample rate swap confirmation, *supra* p. 427, contain general commentary about the confirmation process and the use of ISDA's confirmation forms both before and after the parties have entered into a master agreement that is not repeated or expressly referred to in the annotations to the other sample confirmations in this book.

[Letterhead of Big Bank, N.A.]

April 16, 2002

Deliverable FX Transaction

> Annotation 1. This sample confirmation is based on Exhibits I, II-A and II-E to the *1998 FX Transaction and Currency Option Definitions*. The Transaction is designated as Deliverable because the parties intend that it be settled by actual delivery of the two currencies, as is usual in transactions involving currencies of OECD countries. The standard templates for Non-Deliverable Transactions (including Exhibit II-B to those definitions and EMTA's templates for NDFs in various currencies) include a line item, on "Settlement," where the parties may identify the transaction as Non-Deliverable. Market participants often employ automated systems to execute and confirm both Deliverable and Non-Deliverable FX Transactions. *See User's Guide to the 1998 FX and Currency Option Definitions*, §§ II.B & III.B.1. An FX Transaction will be deemed to be Deliverable unless the parties specify "Non-Deliverable," "Cash Settlement" or "In-the-Money Settlement" in the Confirmation. *1998 FX Transaction and Currency Option Definitions* § 1.7.

English Company PLC
Company House
Company Lane
London AB1C 2DE

Ladies and Gentlemen:

The purpose of this letter agreement is to confirm the terms and conditions of the transaction entered into between us on the Trade Date specified below (the "Transaction"). This letter agreement constitutes a "Confirmation" as referred to in the Master Agreement specified below.

The definitions and provisions contained in the 1998 FX Transaction and Currency Option Definitions (as published by the International Swaps and Derivatives Dealers Association, Inc., EMTA (formerly the Emerging Markets Traders Association) and The Foreign Exchange Committee) are incorporated into this Confirmation. In the event of any inconsistency between those definitions and provisions and this Confirmation, this Confirmation will govern.

> Annotation 2. Some market participants incorporate the *2000 ISDA Definitions* into all Transactions they document under their master agreements, through Part 5 of the schedule. If this is done but other definitions—like the *1998 FX Transaction and Currency Option Definitions*—are then incorporated into the confirmations of particular products, the parties should be careful to determine whether any inconsistency may result and, if so, to indicate which of the inconsistent terms will apply. *See, e.g.*, the method used in paragraph (a) of Part 5 of the schedule to the sample master agreement, *infra* p. 926. The final paragraph of the sample confirmation also reaffirms this principle of having the definitions incorporated into a confirmation override inconsistent provisions in a master agreement, including terms incorporated by reference therein from another booklet of definitions.

1. This Confirmation supplements, forms part of, and is subject to, the Master Agreement dated as of April 16, 2002, as amended and supplemented from time to time (the "Agreement"), between Big Bank, N.A. (the "Bank") and English Company PLC (the "Company"). All provisions contained in the Agreement govern this Confirmation except as expressly modified below.

2. The terms of the particular Transaction to which this Confirmation relates—which is a Deliverable FX Transaction—are as follows:

(a) General Terms:

    Reference No.:   00000-00

    Trade Date: April 16, 2002

> Annotation 3. Participants in the FX market use a variety of terms other than "Trade Date" to refer to the date they enter into an FX transaction. The *1998 FX Transaction and Currency Option Definitions* provide (in Section 1.25) for "Contract Date," "Create Date" and "Deal Date" as alternatives to "Trade Date."

    Amount and currency payable by   GBP100,000,000
    the Bank:

> Annotation 4. Section 4.3 of *Annex A to the 1998 FX and Currency Option Definitions* includes acronyms and abbreviated names for numerous currencies. That section also provides rules relating to successor currencies with respect to currencies other than the Euro, which will apply unless the parties agree otherwise.

Amount and currency payable by the Company:	USD 150,000,000

> Annotation 5. If the parties were documenting a Non-Deliverable FX Transaction they would not specify the amount and currency payable by each of the parties. Instead, they could either set out (1) a Notional Amount and a Reference Currency Notional Amount or (2) a Forward Rate and a Notional Amount or a Reference Currency Notional Amount. Either approach works with the formula set out in Section 2.2(b) of the *1998 FX Transaction and Currency Option Definitions* to make it possible to determine which of them—the one identified as the Reference Currency Buyer or the one identified as the Reference Currency Seller—will be required to pay the Settlement Currency Amount on the agreed Settlement Date. Under that formula, the Settlement Currency Amount is (x) the Notional Amount (which is stated in the Settlement Currency) multiplied by (y) 1 minus the Forward Rate divided by the Settlement Rate), where both the Forward Rate and the Settlement Rate are quoted in terms of an amount of Reference Currency per unit of Settlement Currency. Thus, the payer will be the Reference Currency Buyer, if the Reference Currency weakens, or the Reference Currency Seller, if the Reference Currency strengthens, against the Settlement Currency, as measured by comparing the Forward Rate with the Settlement Rate. If the parties choose to state a Notional Amount and a Reference Currency Notional Amount, rather than a Forward Rate, under Section 2.1(a) of those definitions, the Forward Rate will automatically be the currency exchange rate obtained by dividing the Reference Currency Notional Amount by the Notional Amount.

Settlement Date:	May 18, 2002

> Annotation 6. By incorporating the *1998 FX Transaction and Currency Option Definitions* into the confirmation, the parties have agreed that, barring applicable conditions precedent, each will pay the amount specified in the confirmation as payable by it on the Settlement Date. *See* Sections 2.2 and 3.7 of those definitions.
>
> Annotation 7. The Settlement Date must be a day on which commercial banks effect delivery of the relevant currencies in the relevant cities (Section 1.1). If the agreed Settlement Date is not a Business Day in the specified cities, the Settlement Date will automatically become the following day that is such a Business Day (Section 1.24), unless the parties have specified a different Business Day Convention. There are slight differences in the definition of "Business Day," depending on the purposes for which it is used.
>
> Annotation 8. In a Non-Deliverable FX Transaction, the Settlement Date may be further adjusted if a Disruption Event results in the determination of the Settlement Rate on a day other than the scheduled Valuation Date specified in the confirmation, depending on which Disruption Events and Disruption Fallbacks apply.
>
> Annotation 9. Under EMTA's recommended NDF practices, the parties would state, after the Settlement Date: "*provided, however,* that, if the Scheduled Valua-

tion Date is adjusted in accordance with the Following Business Day Convention, then the Settlement Date shall be as soon as practicable after the Valuation Date, but in no event later than two Business Days after such date." To complete the arrangements, they would, in the line items following the Settlement Date, identify their first choice of Settlement Rate Option for determining the Settlement Rate (*see supra* p. 489) and the Scheduled Valuation Date and, adopting EMTA's recommendation, state that this Scheduled Valuation Date is "subject to adjustment in accordance with the Preceding Business Day Convention; *provided, however,* that the adjustment shall be made in accordance with the Following Business Day Convention in the event of an Unscheduled Holiday." On these EMTA practices and how they differ from the conventions in the *1998 FX Transaction and Currency Option Definitions, see supra* note 1336.

Annotation 10. The confirmation of a Non-Deliverable FX Transaction would typically go on to identify agreed Disruption Events and Disruption Fallbacks, in the order in which the parties wish them applied, usually beginning with a Fallback Reference Price. If they are silent on these matters, the *1998 FX Transaction and Currency Option Definitions* would supply default choices. Price Source Disruption would be the only presumed Disruption Event. The first presumed Disruption Fallback would be Fallback Reference Price determined as if the parties had chosen to determine the Settlement Rate on the basis of quotations from Reference Dealers (the term is Currency–Reference Dealers). The second presumed choice would be Calculation Agent Determination of Settlement Rate. On these and other Disruption Fallbacks, *see supra* p. 491.

(b) Other terms and conditions:

Annotation 11. In EMTA's NDF templates, the parties include here a definition of the term "Unscheduled Holiday" used, as described above, to deal with possible adjustments of the Scheduled Valuation Date. *See* Annotation 9. The EMTA recommended practices then also provide for a presumption under which the parties' choices regarding Disruption Fallbacks would come into play, if an Unscheduled Holiday continued for eight consecutive days. These practices (and circumstances in which this period may be lengthened) are discussed *supra* p. 493.

Annotation 12. In a Non-Deliverable FX Transaction, the parties would probably identify a Calculation Agent or identify the parties as joint Calculation Agents. On the related EMTA convention, *see supra* p. 491. *See* Exhibit II-E to the *1998 FX Transaction and Currency Option Definitions* for the recommended format for stating matters relevant to various choices of Disruption Events and Disruption Fallbacks. *See also* the sample confirmations in Appendix A to the *User's Guide to the 1998 FX Transaction and Currency Option Definitions.*

Account Details
: Account for Payments to the Bank:

: : Big Bank, N.A., New York, N.Y., ABA No. 000, CHIPS No. 000, Attention: Forex Division

: Account for Payments to the Company:

: : Account No. 00000 with Big Bank Frankfurt, Frankfurt

Offices:
: The Office of the Bank for the Transaction is its head office in New York City.

: The Office of the Company for the Transaction is its office at the address specified for notices to it in the Schedule to the Agreement.

Business Days: London and New York City

> Annotation 13. If the parties to an FX Transaction documented under the *1998 FX Transaction and Currency Option Definitions* do not indicate the cities to be taken into account in identifying Business Days, the definitions (in Section 1.1) supply extensive default choices, keyed to the Principal Financial Center of each jurisdiction that is relevant for the particular definition. The Principal Financial Center may be specified in the applicable confirmation. If it is not, a list of default choices for many currencies is supplied in Section 4.4 of *Annex A to the 1998 FX and Currency Option Definitions*. As noted above, the definition of "Business Day" in Section 1.1 for purposes of the term "Settlement Date" differs slightly from that which applies in connection with certain other terms.
>
> Annotation 14. For NDFs, EMTA's recommended practice is to specify the cities relevant for determining Business Days separately for the Valuation Date and the Settlement Date, since the relevant cities in the two cases are likely to be different. Only holidays in a Principal Financial Center for the Reference Currency will generally be treated as relevant for purposes of determining the Settlement Rate on the Valuation Date, whereas only the Principal Financial Center for the Settlement Currency would generally be specified for the Settlement Date.

Business Day Convention: Following Business Day Convention

> Annotation 15. Section 1.2 of *1998 FX Transaction and Currency Option Definitions* sets forth four choices of Business Day Conventions—Following, Modified Following (or Modified), Nearest and Preceding. *See supra* p. 391 for discussion of these conventions. If the parties had not specified a Business Day Convention, the Settlement Date would be the one illustrated here (Section 1.24). For Non-Deliverable Transactions, the default choice supplied by these definitions (under Section 1.16(f)) for the Valuation Date is the Preceding Business Day

Sample FX Forward Confirmation

> Convention. As noted in Annotation 9, the EMTA recommended practices instead adopt the Following Business Day Convention in connection with Unscheduled Holidays.

This Confirmation supersedes and replaces any earlier confirmation (including a SWIFT MT300 or phone confirmation), if any, sent in connection with this Transaction.

> Annotation 16. This language is based on a model in Exhibit I to the *1998 FX Transaction and Currency Option Definitions*. "SWIFT MT300" refers to a method used for electronic execution of FX Transactions.

Please confirm that the foregoing correctly sets forth the terms of our agreement by executing the copy of this Confirmation enclosed for that purpose and returning it to us or by sending to us a letter or telex substantially similar to this letter, which letter or telex sets forth the material terms of the Transaction to which this Confirmation relates and indicates agreement to those terms. If you believe the foregoing does not correctly reflect the terms of our agreement, please give us notice as soon as possible of what you believe to be the necessary corrections.

> Annotation 17. This language, from Exhibit I of the *1998 FX Transaction and Currency Option Definitions*, differs from that in other ISDA confirmation forms. *See, e.g., supra* p. 437. When the parties use manually generated confirmations for FX Transactions (rather than using automated processing systems), they generally send each other confirmations by facsimile transmission.

BIG BANK, N.A.

By: _____
    Name:
    Title: Vice President

Confirmed as of the date below:

ENGLISH COMPANY PLC

By: _____
    Name:
    Title:

CURRENCY OPTIONS

A currency option gives one party, the buyer, the right, but not the obligation, to enter into a transaction relating to that currency at a later date. In the most traditional of currency options, the buyer acquires the right to buy or sell one currency for another at an agreed "strike price,"[1377] or exchange rate. In this respect, the currency option is fundamentally different from a forward contract, which, in the most traditional case, obligates both parties to consummate an exchange of one currency for another at a price fixed at the outset, as discussed in the preceding product description.[1378] In the option, the maximum amount the buyer can lose is the premium it pays for its option right.[1379] In the forward, each of the parties takes on theoretically unlimited risk of adverse changes in the rate of exchange for the currency pair. Currency options are an important tool for investors who want to take a position in a foreign currency or to hedge against foreign currency exposure.

By way of example, take an English company that is about to sign a contract to acquire equipment from a manufacturer in Chicago a year from now. If the company generates all its earnings in sterling, it might buy a call option giving it the right to acquire the necessary amount in dollars for sterling one year later at the rate of U.S.$1.50 per £1, because the company finds the equipment attractively priced only if its cost of buying dollars with sterling at the time (that is, at the spot rate of exchange a year later) does not exceed that strike price. If more than U.S.$1.50 can be acquired for £1 at the time the English company has to pay for the equipment, the company will let the option expire without exercising it (that is, it would expire worthless). In this case, the company's cost for the protection it acquired through the option is the premium it paid, and that is its maximum exposure. The seller of the option, on the other hand, has theoretically unlimited exposure to the risk that the pound will weaken against the dollar.

If, instead of buying the option, the company had entered into a forward contract to buy U.S. dollars with sterling at an exchange rate of U.S.$1.50 per £1, both parties

---

[1377] A "cash currency option" of this kind should be distinguished from a "futures currency option," which "is the right to buy or sell a traded futures contract at a specified futures price at or before a specific date in the future." M. Desmond Fitzgerald, *Currency options*, in 1 MANAGEMENT OF CURRENCY RISK 301.

[1378] *See supra* p. 515. The protection afforded by a conventional FX forward requires the parties to agree on a specific future date at which settlement will occur whereas, as discussed below, with some styles of option the buyer has greater flexibility in choosing the time for exercise. The basic difference between the currency option and the forward foreign exchange transaction is analogous to the difference between a rate cap and an FRA, as described in the introductory notes to the sample cap and FRA confirmations included in this book, although the FRA involves a special settlement mechanism. *See supra* pp. 439 & 476.

[1379] For a discussion of the relationship of the premium amount to the value of the option if exercised immediately (the "intrinsic value" of the option), *see* Rene M. Stulz, *The Pricing of Currency Options: A Review*, in HANDBOOK OF RISK MANAGEMENT 5-1, 5-7. The difference between the premium and the intrinsic value is called the "time value" of the option. *See also* M. Desmond Fitzgerald, *Currency options*, in 1 MANAGEMENT OF CURRENCY RISK 301, 305-09. *See also* HULL, *supra* note 646, at 154.

would be obligated to consummate a purchase and sale of the currency pair at the agreed forward rate, so both parties would have theoretically unlimited exposure to changes in the GBP/USD exchange rate—with the company exposed to the risk that the pound would strengthen (resulting in an obligation on its part to pay) and the forward counterparty exposed to the risk that the pound would weaken (resulting in a right of the company to receive a payment), always as compared with the agreed forward rate.[1380]

Conversely, a conventional currency "put" option is a right of the buyer to cause the seller to buy a designated amount of a given currency at the strike price. In the case of the put, the premium paid is the maximum amount the buyer can lose if instead of weakening (as the buyer fears), the put currency retains or improves on its strength with the result that, at the time the option expires, the buyer can use the amount of the put currency covered by the option to obtain more of the other currency than the option seller would have been required to deliver, or the same amount.

Thus, assume, that the manufacturer in our previous example can only obtain the contract from the English company by agreeing to sell its equipment for sterling. In this case, if the manufacturer's costs are all in U.S. dollars, it will have no use for the sterling as such, so it may decide to protect itself against a decline in the value of its expected sterling receipts by paying a premium for an option giving it the right to put sterling to the option seller if, a year from now, the sterling received from the English company, in spot rate terms, is worth less than U.S.$1.50 per £1. The manufacturer would let the option expire worthless if more dollars, in fact, could be acquired with one pound because, in that case, it would simply use the sterling paid by the English company to buy dollars in the spot market. If the manufacturer had, instead, entered into a forward contract to buy U.S. dollars with sterling at an exchange rate of £1 per U.S.$1.50, it would be required to make a payment to its counterparty in the forward.

Each of these examples describes a simple European style option, which is an option that can only be exercised on the option's expiration date. In currency options, as with options on other "underlyings," there are other option styles, using the term "style" in all cases to refer to the option's flexibility in exercise terms. An American Style option can be exercised at any time during an agreed exercise period, and a Bermuda Style option—also called a Mid-Atlantic style option—is exercisable on one or more specified exercise dates.[1381] These are the three styles of option contemplated in the *1998 FX*

[1380] In the conventional forward executed "at market," no premium is paid.

[1381] "[B]ecause the American foreign currency call option gives its holder an additional right, namely the right to exercise early, its value can never be less than the value of a European foreign currency call option, but can be more." Rene M. Stulz, *The Pricing of Currency Options: A Review*, in HANDBOOK OF RISK MANAGEMENT 5–1, 5–6. A "chooser option" is effectively an option on two options; it gives the buyer the right to buy either a call or a put option on the underlying asset at an agreed time (the "choice date") during the life of the option. For investors who want to protect themselves against adverse movements in a cash market but are uncertain about the nature of the protection they will need, this kind of option is said to be a cheaper alternative to a straddle—which involves the purchase of both a put and a call and, therefore, involves payment of two premiums; the lower premium for the chooser option reflects the fact that the buyer of the straddle is entitled to exercise the put or the call in the straddle at any time during the exercise period (in an American style put and call) or on the expiration date (in a European style put and call), whereas the buyer of the chooser option must make its election earlier, on the agreed date. *See Chooser Options*, DERIVATIVES WEEK, Apr. 12, 1993, at 7 (Learning Curve column).

Transaction and Currency Option Definitions. Options with more complex exercise rights may, however, be created.[1382]

For example, a call option can be written so that it expires if the spot price of the relevant currency falls to an agreed "outstrike" price within a specified period—in which case the option may be referred to as a "down-and-out call." Similarly, a call option can be written so that it is activated, that is, it becomes a conventional call, only if the spot price of the relevant currency falls to an agreed "instrike" price within a specified period—in which case the option may be referred to as an "down-and-in call." These are two variants of transactions more generally referred to as knock-out and knock-in, or barrier, options.[1383] As mentioned in the introductory note on currency derivatives, the Foreign Exchange Committee has published standard terms, confirmation templates and best practices for options of these types.[1384]

Options may also depart from the conventional mold through adjustments to the strike price at various stages over the option's life, or in response to specified contingencies, and through variations on the terms applicable to the time of payment, or method of calculating, the premium. There are also quanto, or quantity adjusting, options, for cases in which the buyer is uncertain about the amount of protection it may require.

The classic example is a currency option used by the buyer to protect against loss, measured in U.S. dollar terms, on the future disposal of an offshore equity investment.

[1382] On "exotic options," *see generally* HULL, *supra* note 646, at 458 (ch. 18, "Exotic Options"). If an option with the desired characteristics is not generally available in the market, a "synthetic option" can be designed to create the position. A synthetic option is "a portfolio of instruments none of which is identical to the desired position, but which collectively replicate the way the desired position changes in value as market conditions change." Richard A. Laden, *Synthetic currency options*, in 1 MANAGEMENT OF CURRENCY RISK 313. Synthetic options may also be used to obtain a position more cheaply than it could be obtained by purchasing a straightforward option. *See, e.g., Synthetic Options*, DERIVATIVES WEEK, Oct. 5, 1992, at 6 (Learning Curve column), discussing the creation of a synthetic call option below market cost by combining a futures contract with a put option.

[1383] In some cases there is a requirement only that the outstrike or instrike barrier be touched. In other cases, the currency must "trade through" the barrier for the option to be activated or expire. *See* "Barrier Discontinuity," "Barrier Options," "Barrier Price" "Down-and-In Call," "Down-and-Out Call," "Knock-in Option," "Knock-Out Option," "Touch Option," "Up-and-Out Call" and "Up-and-Out Put," in DICTIONARY OF RISK MANAGEMENT. *See also* the definition of "Exploding Option" in the same book on a variant that involves the maximum pay-off of an option if the agreed level is touched or traded through. The terms "digital option" and "binary option" are sometimes used to refer to an option that has a predetermined pay-off at expiration or when the agreed strike is touched, regardless of how far in the money the option is. *See Digital Options*, DERIVATIVES WEEK, Apr. 26, 1993, at 9 (Learning Curve column). *See also European Bank Snaps Up Big One-Touch Dollar/Yen Option*, DERIVATIVES WEEK, Mar. 12, 2001, at 1, reporting on what was at the time said to be the largest barrier option trade in the preceding five years, providing for a payout of U.S.$ 20 million if the yen/dollar spot rate hit JPY 170 per U.S.$ 1.00 over the following 12 months.

[1384] *See supra* p. 485. The Foreign Exchange Committee's terms were first published in 1997 as an Addendum for use with a short-form barrier option confirmation or a master agreement prepared on the ICOM or FEOMA forms and as a long-form barrier option confirmation which includes the Addendum terms. Then, in 2000, the Committee recommended to the foreign exchange community new best practices, with important information about transactions that will and will not be taken into account in determining whether one of these breaches—a knock-in or knock-out event—has occurred, taking into account an extension of the period recognized in the global financial markets as the opening of trading in the Sydney spot market as well as the fact that practices will differ depending on what, at the relevant time, is viewed as a transaction of a commercial size for the currency pair in question.

The dollar value of the investment would suffer erosion if the dollar strengthened against the relevant foreign currency. If the investor knew exactly what the proceeds in foreign currency would be, it would buy a conventional put option, but the sale proceeds will depend on the investment's market value at the time of sale, so the investor cannot know precisely how much protection to buy. Quanto options may be used in cases like these when the option buyer is comfortable that an adequate model for automatically adjusting the quantity of foreign currency to be hedged exists.[1385]

As indicated above, the buyer of a conventional option pays a one-time premium at the outset of the transaction. The option is said to be "at-the-money" if the strike price is set at the price that the market expects to prevail for the option at the time it is written. The premium will be reduced if the buyer is willing to accept the additional exposure implied by an "out-of-the-money" option.[1386] The obligation to pay the premium can be postponed to the exercise date through a deferred premium option, in which the strike price is set at a level that builds in the future value of the premium, or the obligation to pay the premium can be made contingent on whether the option expires in the money.[1387]

Currency options are also sometimes structured so that the amount to be settled upon exercise is calculated by comparing the strike price with an average of spot prices for the currency pair over a specified period, rather than the spot price on the expiration date or another exercise date. Referred to as averaging rate options or, more commonly, Asian options,[1388] one of these products might be attractive to a company that needed to buy a given currency at regular intervals over a particular period; through an Asian currency call option it could set an upper limit on its average cost of the currency over that period.[1389]

As discussed in the introductory note on currency derivatives, currency options are also classified by reference to their settlement terms. In this context, conventional currency options are referred to as deliverable, to distinguish them from the non-deliverable option products. In a conventional deliverable currency option, settlement after exercise requires delivery of amounts of each of the currencies in the relevant currency pair. So,

---

[1385]In the example, the model adjusts the amount of currency to be hedged on the basis of principles applied to hedge in respect of the stock's market price. *See, e.g.,* NARU PAREKH, THE FINANCIAL ENGINEER 392 (Euromoney Books 1995).

[1386]*See* Smithson, *A LEGO® Approach to Financial Engineering: An Introduction to Forwards, Futures, Swaps and Options*, *supra* note 1108, at 3–12 to 3–19; Smithson, *A Building Block Approach to Financial Engineering: An Introduction to Forwards, Futures, Swaps and Options*, *supra* note 1108, at 17–20. *See also* Rene M. Stulz, *The Pricing of Currency Options: A Review*, *in* HANDBOOK OF RISK MANAGEMENT 5–1, and the sources cited *supra* note 646. *See also* HULL, *supra* note 646, at 154.

[1387]A "contingent premium" option will be more costly than an ordinary option, but the premium will only be payable if the option is exercised in-the-money. *See* DICTIONARY OF RISK MANAGEMENT 65. According to *Break Forwards*, DERIVATIVES WEEK, Dec. 28, 1992, at 13 (Learning Curve column), the cost of a contingent premium option can be roughly double that of the cost of an ordinary option.

[1388]*See* "Asian Options," *in* DICTIONARY OF RISK MANAGEMENT 29. *See also* HULL, *supra* note 646, at 467–69; *Average-Rate Options*, DERIVATIVES WEEK, July 27, 1992, at 9 (Learning Curve column); Ritchken, L. Sankarasubramanian & A. Vijh, *Averaging Options for Capping Total Costs*, 19 FIN. MGMT. 35 (Winter 1990).

[1389]Another variant is the "lookback option," which gives the buyer the right to buy the relevant currency at its lowest price, or to sell it at its highest price, during the lookback period.

under Section 3.7(a) of the *1998 FX Transaction and Currency Option Definitions,* and using terminology from those definitions, on the Settlement Date for a Deliverable Currency Option the Buyer must pay the Seller the Put Currency Amount and the Seller must pay the Buyer the Call Currency Amount (subject to the satisfaction of any applicable conditions precedent and applicable terms relating to Disruption Events).

In the alternative, a currency option can be settled at what is referred to as its In-the-Money Amount in a single currency, the Settlement Currency. Simply stated, this is settlement at the value of the option measured as if it were exercised at its expiry time, if at that time the option has value—is "in the money"—to the buyer. There are various ways in which this approach to settlement may become applicable in the parties' dealings under common documentation practices.

Under the FEOMA and ICOM forms (Section 5.3), and using the terminology of those forms, unless the parties have agreed otherwise or the Seller is otherwise instructed by the Buyer, if an Option has an In-the-Money Amount at its Expiration Time that equals or exceeds the product of (x) 1% of the Strike Price (or another agreed percentage) and (y) the amount of the Put Currency or Call Currency relevant in the Option, the Option will be deemed automatically exercised and the Seller has the right to elect whether settlement should occur through gross payments of the Put Currency and the Call Currency or through payment of the In-the-Money Amount. The Seller is required to notify the Buyer of the Seller's election as soon as practicable after the Expiration Time. Similarly, under the *1998 FX Transaction and Currency Option Definitions* (Section 3.6(c)), the parties may indicate that Automatic Exercise will apply and, if they are silent on the subject, settlement at the In-the-Money Amount will be deemed to apply, as under FEOMA and ICOM forms, if the option is in the money to the Buyer by an amount at least equal to 1% of the Strike Price multiplied by the relevant currency amount.[1390] These results are produced by rules that apply automatic exercise, not because an option is designated as nondeliverable.

Using the terminology of the *1998 FX Transaction and Currency Option Definitions*, settlement for the In-the-Money-Amount as applied to a Call Option Transaction means that, when the Option Transaction is exercised because the Settlement Rate exceeds the Strike Price—that is, the Call Currency has appreciated against the Put Currency, usually as measured by reference to a spot exchange rate—if the Settlement Currency is the Call Currency, the Seller will be required to pay the Buyer an amount in the Call Currency determined by multiplying the agreed notional, or Call Currency Amount, by the difference (Settlement Rate minus Strike Price) and then dividing the result by the Settlement Rate.

Similarly, in the case of a Deliverable Put Option that is exercised because the Strike Price exceeds the Settlement Rate—that is, the Put Currency has weakened against the Call Currency, again, as measured by reference to an agreed spot exchange rate—if the Settlement Currency is the Put Currency the Seller will be required to pay the Buyer

---

[1390]This is true regardless of whether Automatic Exercise applies by default or by virtue of an affirmative choice made by the parties in confirming their transaction. As in Section 5.3 of the ICOM and FEOMA forms, Section 3.6(c) of the *1998 FX Transaction and Currency Option Definitions* contemplates the possibility that the Buyer may wish to override the application of the Automatic Exercise terms, and permits it to do so by notice given to the Seller prior to the option's Expiration Time.

Currency Options

an amount in the Put Currency determined by multiplying the agreed notional, or Put Currency Amount, by the difference (Strike Price minus Settlement Rate) and then dividing the result by the Settlement Rate.

Section 3.7(c) of the *1998 FX and Currency Option Definitions* sets out these calculation formulas for the In-the-Money Amount along with rules to be applied to to determine In-the-Money Amount, if the parties have not stated the Settlement Currency. So, for example, in a call, where both the Strike Price and the Settlement Rate are quoted in terms of the amount of the Put Currency to be paid per one unit of Call Currency, the In-the-Money Amount will be the positive amount determined by multiplying the Call Currency Amount by the excess of the Settlement Rate over the Strike Price. The sample confirmation illustrates how the various relevant terms may be stated.

A Non-Deliverable Currency Option that is exercised, or deemed exercised, is always settled at its In-the-Money Amount in a single Settlement Currency (unless there is a Market Disruption and the parties' agreement provides for a different settlement method in such a case).[1391] This reflects the fact that Non-Deliverable Currency Options—like Non-Deliverable FX Transactions—are often entered into precisely because one of the currencies in the currency pair—the Reference Currency—is not fully convertible (or if converted, may not be remitted from the jurisdiction where it is issued) or because the Buyer is concerned that, at the time when settlement would occur if the option were exercised, exchange controls or other conditions beyond the parties' control may prevent conversion or remittance of that currency. The *1998 FX and Currency Option Definitions* presume that, with Non-Deliverable Currency Options, the parties may wish to provide that the In-the-Money-Amount will be payable automatically regardless of whether the option is the money to be buyer by at least 1% of the Strike Price multiplied by the relevant currency amount—the presumed test for automatic exercise of Deliverable Option Transactions, as noted above.[1392]

Currency options are sometimes imbedded in securities so that the value of the security at maturity is linked to a currency spot rate at that time. An issuer might decide to sell this kind of security—often referred to as a hybrid[1393]—if it were able to hedge the risk of the imbedded option at a cost that produced a lower all-in cost of funds than a straight debt issuance. Investors may be motivated to buy the hybrid for various reasons, including regulatory constraints that might otherwise prevent their taking on the currency "play" and their ability through the hybrid to obtain the desired exposure to the currency for a period longer than would otherwise be available.[1394]

[1391] The alternative methods for settlement of these non-deliverable products are discussed above in the introductory note on currency derivatives, *supra* p. 489.

[1392] *See* Section 3.7(b) of the *1998 FX and Currency Option Definitions*. The FEOMA and ICOM forms apply the 1% test for automatic exercise of deliverable and non-deliverable options.

[1393] *See supra* note 200 on the use of this term under the CEA and the U.S. banking and securities laws.

[1394] *See* Satyajit Das, *Securities embedded with currency options*, *in* 2 MANAGEMENT OF CURRENCY RISK 27. The author also discusses securities issues presented by instruments with currency warrants attached. *Id.* at 28. Examples of securities with imbedded currency options discussed in the article are indexed

In the transaction illustrated in the following sample confirmation, the Company has bought from the Bank a Non-Deliverable Currency Option Transaction under which the Brazilian Real is the Put Currency and the Reference Currency, the Settlement Currency is the U.S. dollar and the Strike Price is BRL 2.90 per U.S.$ 1.00. The option is American Style and, because it is a Non-Deliverable, it will only be cash-settled, for the In-the-Money Amount, through a payment by the Bank to the Company if the Real weakens to a level below the Strike Price. The Company has agreed to pay a one-time premium for the option at the beginning of the Transaction. If the option expires out-of-the-money (because the Real strengthens against the Dollar or continues to trade in the spot market at levels more favorable than the Strike Price), the Company's loss is limited to the amount of the premium. From the Bank's point of view, the currency option is not credit-sensitive once the Company has paid the option premium (except for the theoretical possibility that the premium might be "clawed back" if the Company becomes insolvent during the course of the Transaction). On the other hand, if the parties had entered into a Deliverable Option Transaction, as discussed above, the Bank would be exposed to settlement risk if the option were exercised.[1395]

---

currency option notes ("ICONS"), "heaven and hell" bonds, reverse dual currency notes and "duet bonds." *Id.* at 29–37.

[1395]*See supra* p. 486.

> The Introduction to this Part, *supra* p. 369, and the annotations to the sample rate swap confirmation, *supra* p. 427, contain general commentary about the confirmation process and the use of ISDA's confirmation forms both before and after the parties have entered into a master agreement that is not repeated or expressly referred to in the annotations to the other sample confirmations in this book.

[Letterhead of Big Bank, N.A.]

April 16, 2002

Non-Deliverable Currency Option

> Annotation 1. The form of this sample confirmation is taken from Exhibits I, II-D and II-E to the *1998 FX Transaction and Currency Option Definitions* and is similar to and patterned on the form of confirmation published as an exhibit to the ICOM form for currency options. As discussed above (*see supra* p. 528), under both the ICOM form (Section 5.3) and the *1998 FX and Currency Option Definitions* (Section 3.7(b)), the parties may agree that settlement of a Currency Option Transaction will be effected (subject to any applicable conditions precedent) by payment from the Seller to the Buyer of the Option's In-the-Money Amount, if positive, rather than by actual delivery of the Call Currency Amount and Put Currency Amount. As illustrated here, the parties have elected something like that result by agreeing that their Currency Option Transaction is Non-Deliverable. The difference is that, in treating their transaction as Non-Deliverable, the parties have also agreed that the In-the-Money Amount will be payable regardless of the amount by which the option is in the money to the Buyer of protection.

English Company PLC
Company House
Company Lane
London AB1C 2DE

Ladies and Gentlemen:

The purpose of this letter agreement is to confirm the terms and conditions of the transaction entered into between us on the Trade Date specified below (the "Transaction"). This letter agreement constitutes a "Confirmation" as referred to in the Master Agreement specified below.

The definitions and provisions contained in the 1998 FX and Currency Option Definitions (as published by the International Swaps and Derivatives Dealers Association, Inc., EMTA (formerly the Emerging Markets Traders Association) and The Foreign Exchange Committee) are incorporated into this Confirmation. In the event of any inconsistency between those definitions and provisions and this Confirmation, this Confirmation will govern.

1. This Confirmation supplements, forms part of, and is subject to, the Master Agreement dated as of April 16, 2002, as amended and supplemented from time to time (the "Agreement"), between Big Bank, N.A. (the "Bank") and English Company PLC (the "Company"). All provisions contained in the Agreement govern this Confirmation except as expressly modified below.

2. The terms of the particular Transaction to which this Confirmation relates—which is a Non-Deliverable Currency Option—are as follows:

General Terms

Reference No.: 00000-00

Trade Date: 16/APR/2002

> Annotation 2. This is the date the parties entered into the Currency Option Transaction documented in the sample confirmation. The format used to set forth the dates is different from that used in the other sample confirmations in this Part, but is described in Section III(M)(3) of the *ICOM Guide* as the market convention for Currency Options: day (expressed in two numbers)/month (abbreviated with three letters)/year (indicated by its last two numbers).

Date of Annex A:

> Annotation 3. The *1998 FX Transaction and Currency Option Definitions* (which the parties have incorporated into the sample confirmation) establish a presumption (in Section 4.2) that the parties intend to adopt *Annex A* as amended through the Trade Date unless the parties indicate another date for this purpose.

Commencement Date: 16/APR/2002

Buyer: The Company

> Annotation 4. The key operative terms relating to options in the *1998 FX Transaction and Currency Option Definitions* give substantive content to the term "Buyer." Thus, under Section 3.1(a) of those definitions, the party designated as Buyer is required to pay the indicated Premium on the Premium Payment Date, and under Section 3.7(b), in a Non-Deliverable Currency Option Transaction like the one illustrated here, Seller is required, on the Settlement Date, to pay Buyer the In-the-Money Amount, if it is positive.

Seller: The Bank

> Annotation 5. Similarly, Section 3.1(f) of the *1998 FX Transaction and Currency Option Definitions* gives substantive content to the term "Seller" as used in documenting a Currency Option Transaction. Under that definition, the Seller is the party that grants to the Buyer the option (subject to the applicable conditions) to receive the Call Currency Amount on the Settlement Date (if the option is a Deliverable Transaction) or to receive the In-the-Money Amount, if positive (if the option is a Non-Deliverable Transaction).

Currency Option Style: American

> Annotation 6. This line must be completed to indicate when the Buyer may exercise its rights under the Transaction. The sample confirmation indicates that the parties are documenting an American Style Option—one that can be exercised during an Exercise Period that consists of more than one day. The *1998 FX Transaction and Currency Option Definitions* include a presumption that the Exercise Period begins at 9:00 a.m. (local time in the place where the office through which the Seller is transacting is located) on the Commencement Date of a Currency Option Transaction and another presumption that the last possible time for exercise will be the Expiration Time on the Expiration Date (Section 3.5(c)). The presumption under the ICOM form is identical and is built into the definition of "American Style Option." Since the *1998 FX Transaction and Currency Option Definitions* have been incorporated into the sample confirmation and those presumptions have not been altered, the Buyer may exercise its rights under the Transaction during that period, subject to the rules of Section 3.6(b) on the effectiveness of a Notice of Exercise of an American Style Option, which are described in Annotation 20.
>
> Annotation 7. Unless the parties agree otherwise, a Currency Option Transaction—including an American Style Option—may be exercised only in whole, and not in part (Section 3.6(a) of the *1998 FX Transaction and Currency Option Definitions* and Section 5.2 of the ICOM form). If the parties enter into options—whether Deliverable or Non-Deliverable—using the provisions on Disruption Events and Disruption Fallbacks in those definitions, they should consider whether the chosen provisions require modification to accommodate partial exercise.
>
> Annotation 8. If the parties had specified "European" here, under Sections 3.2(c) and 3.5(c) of the *1998 FX Transaction and Currency Option Definitions* they would have indicated that the Buyer may exercise its rights only on the Expiration Date, between 9:00 a.m. (local time in the place where the office through which the Seller is transacting is located) and the specified Expiration Time, unless the parties agree otherwise. Therefore, to document a European Style option under those definitions, the parties need only indicate the Expiration Date and the Expiration Time to set forth the terms relating to the timing of exercise. The result and approach to documentation under the ICOM form would be identical.

Currency Option Type: BRL Put /USD Call

> Annotation 9. When the parties specify (as they have here) which of the currencies involved in their Transaction is the Settlement Currency for purposes of determining the In-the-Money Amount that may be payable on settlement, they are applying one of two formulas set out in Section 3.7(c)(i) of the *1998 FX and Currency Option Definitions*. One applies when the Reference Currency is the Put Currency and the Settlement Currency is the Call Currency. The other applies when the Reference Currency is the Call Currency and the Settlement Currency is the Put Currency. These same formulas are used when the Settlement Currency is determined by application of a Disruption Fallback in connection with a Disruption Event. If a Settlement Currency is not specified or deemed specified—which appears often to be the case when the parties document Non-Deliverable Currency Options involving OECD currencies—Section 3.7(c)(ii) works with the option type specification to determine how the In-the-Money Amount is computed. In the case of a Call, it would be the excess of the Settlement Rate over the Strike Price, multiplied by the Call Currency Amount, with both the Strike Price and the Settlement Rate stated in terms of an amount of Put Currency per one unit of Call Currency. In the case of a Put, the In-the-Money Amount would be the excess of the Strike Price over the Settlement Rate, multiplied by the Put Currency Amount, with both the Strike Price and the Settlement Rate stated in terms of an amount of Call Currency per one unit of the Put Currency.
>
> Annotation 10. If the Buyer of a currency option documented on the ICOM form wishes to avail itself of the provisions on automatic exercise, the parties must specify whether the transaction is a Put or a Call, because those provisions operate by reference to the In-the-money Amount, and that term has meaning only by reference to a Put or a Call. The structure of the transaction is, of course, easier to grasp if the parties indicate the Buyer's objective by completing this line.

Call Currency and Call Currency Amount: USD 25,000,000

Put Currency: BRL

> Annotation 11. The notes to the sample confirmation provisions included with the *1998 FX Transaction and Currency Option Definitions* state that the parties should specify a Strike Price and either a Call Currency Amount or a Put Currency Amount. This should be understood in the context of the formulas and methods referred to in Annotation 9, which are used to calculate the In-the-Money Amount, and depend on whether the transaction is a Put or a Call. Here the Bank has sold the Company a Put and the parties have specified the Real as the Put Currency. Therefore, the formula in Section 7.1(c)(i) determines the amount in U.S. dollars, as the Call Currency Amount, that the Company will be entitled to purchase with Reais if the option is exercised because the Real weakens beyond the Strike Price.

Sample Currency Option Confirmation 535

Strike Price: 2.90 BRL per 1 USD

> Annotation 12. In a Put, the In-the-Money Amount will be payable if the option is exercised because a number of Reais greater than the number shown in the Strike Price will be required to purchase one U.S. Dollar at a time when exercise is permitted—that is, during the Exercise Period. The determination is made by comparing the Strike Price with the Settlement Rate determined applying the Settlement Rate Option specified below. If the Company had, instead, purchased a Call on the Real, the In-the-Money Amount would be payable if the option was exercised because fewer Reais than the number shown in the Strike Price were required to acquire one U.S. Dollar.

Reference Currency: BRL
Settlement Currency: USD

> Annotation 13. In addition to their relevance to the calculation of the In-the-Money Amount, as discussed in the two preceding Annotations, the Reference Currency and Settlement Currency are critical to the application of the Disruption Events and Disruption Fallbacks in connection with Non-Deliverable Transactions. *See supra* p. 491.

Settlement Rate Option: BRL PTAX

> Annotation 14. Section 4.5 of the *1998 FX Transaction and Currency Option Definitions* includes terms like the one used here as shorthand to indicate screens and other sources that the parties may look to in determining the Settlement Rate applicable in calculating the In-the-Money Amount. These currency-specific Settlement Rate Options and others, which provide for the use of implied rates and rates determined on the basis of quotations from Reference Dealers, are discussed in the introductory note on currency derivatives, *supra* p. 489. The particular Settlement Rate Option illustrated here calls for the use of a Brazilian Real/U.S. Dollar offered rate for U.S. Dollars, expressed as an amount of Brazilian Reais per one U.S. Dollar, for settlement in two Business Days, reported by Banco Central do Brasil on its SISBACEN Data System under transaction code PTAX-800 ("Consulta de Câmbio"), Option 5, which relates to rates for accounting purposes, at approximately 8:30 p.m., Sao Paulo time, on the relevant Rate Calculation Date.

Expiration Date: 16/OCT/2002

Annotation 15. As noted, in an American Style Option, this is the last day on which the Buyer may exercise its option. The parties have stated a specific date—the approach contemplated in the *1998 FX Transaction and Currency Option Definitions*. During the actual telephonic trade of the transaction, however, they might simply have agreed that the Expiration Date would be a specific number of months later. This is sometimes referred to as quoting for "straight periods." As described in the *ICOM Guide* (Section II(B)), another market practice is to quote Currency Options for expiration in a particular month, without reference to a day. According to that source, this is understood to mean that the option's Expiration Date will be the Monday before the third Wednesday of that month. The *1998 FX Transaction and Currency Option Definitions* do not contemplate this approach—that is, they do not supply a rule under which "Expiration Date: March 2003" would be understood to mean that the Expiration Date would be the Monday before the third Wednesday of March 2003.

Annotation 16. The Expiration Date must be a day on which commercial banks are open for business (including dealings in foreign exchange in accordance with the market practice of the foreign exchange market) in the relevant cities. *1998 FX and Currency Option Definitions* § 1.1. If the agreed Expiration Date is not a Business Day in those cities, it will automatically become the following day that is such a Business Day, under Section 3.5(d) of those definitions, unless the parties have specified a different Business Day Convention. *ICOM Guide* 5 notes that, although the ICOM form does not provide that the Expiration Date must be a Business Day in the place of the office from which the Seller is transacting for purposes of an option, this will usually be the case.

Expiration Time: 10:00 a.m., local time in New York City

Annotation 17. The *ICOM Guide* indicates that market practice when it was published in 1997 was to provide for expiration of Currency Options at 10:00 a.m., New York time, except for transactions entered into in the Pacific rim, for which the standard was 3:00 p.m., Tokyo time. The definitions of the term "Expiration Time" in the ICOM form and the *1998 FX Transactions and Currency Option Definitions* do not supply a "default choice" if the parties fail to specify an Expiration Time. However, it is possible that Section 5.1 of the ICOM form could be read to mean that, if the parties are silent on this subject, a Notice of Exercise could be given on the Expiration Date at any time up to and including 3:00 p.m., local time, at the Seller's designated office and still be effective. Since that does not seem to reflect market practice except for Pacific rim transactions, according to the *ICOM Guide*, and since it does not appear that the provision was meant to be read in this manner, the parties should be careful to specify an Expiration Time.

Annotation 18. As indicated above, the Expiration Time on the Expiration Date is the last time at which the Seller is required to accept a Notice of Exercise of a Currency Option. If the parties had merely specified an hour, under the ICOM form (Section 11.9) the reference would be understood to mean that time in the

Sample Currency Option Confirmation

agreed location of the Seller. Therefore, the Buyer of a Currency Option may wish to ensure that the confirmation clearly identifies that location. One way of doing so is illustrated below in Part 6 of this sample confirmation.

Annotation 19. Under the rules on Automatic Exercise of the ICOM form (Section 5.3) and the *1998 FX Transaction and Currency Option Definitions* (Section 3.6(c)), the Expiration Time is also the time at which one determines whether a currency option will be deemed to have been exercised, unless the Buyer otherwise instructs the Seller or the option has previously been exercised.

Latest Exercise Time: 10:00 a.m., New York City time

Annotation 20. Under the *1998 FX Transaction and Currency Option Definitions,* Latest Exercise Time on the Expiration Date of an option is the same as the Expiration Time. On any other day on which the option can be exercised, it is the last time on that day when a Notice of Exercise can effectively be given. With American Style Options, under Section 3.6(b) of those definitions, if a Notice of Exercise is received after the Latest Exercise Time, it will be treated as effective "at 9:00 a.m., local time in the place where the office through which Seller is transacting is located" on the following Business Day, if any, during the Exercise Period.

Automatic Exercise: Applicable

Annotation 21. Even if Automatic Exercise is not specified, it will be deemed to be applicable, under the last sentence Section 3.6(c) of the *1998 FX Transaction and Currency Option Definitions*, unless the parties provide otherwise.

Annotation 22. As expressed in Section 3.6(c) of those definitions, a Currency Option will not be deemed automatically exercised unless it is in the money to the Buyer by an amount at least equal to 1% of the amount of the Call Currency that could be purchased at the Strike Price, in the case of a Call, or an amount at least equal to 1% of the amount of the Put Currency that could be sold at the Strike Price, in the case of a Put. When Automatic Exercise applies to a Deliverable Currency Option Transaction, the Seller is entitled to choose how settlement will be effected—by delivery of the Put Currency Amount and the Call Currency Amount, or by payment of the In-the-Money Amount, unless the parties have expressly agreed otherwise. Under a Non-Deliverable Currency Option Transaction like the one illustrated, settlement is always in the Settlement Currency.

Settlement: Non-Deliverable

Annotation 23. Unless identified as Non-Deliverable, a Currency Option Transaction will always be deemed to be Deliverable, under Section 1.13 of the

1998 FX Transaction and Currency Option Definitions. Under that provision, the parties could have used the expressions "Cash Settlement" or "In-the-Money Settlement" as alternatives to indicate that the transaction is Non-Deliverable.

Settlement Date: The second Business Day after the Exercise Date

Annotation 24. Under the ICOM form, it is not necessary to specify a Settlement Date unless the parties wish to deviate from the rule that settlement will occur on the spot delivery date for a trade in the relevant Currency Pair executed on the date of exercise of the Currency Option, in accordance with customary market usage. For most Currency Pairs, this means that the Settlement Date will be the second Business Day after the currency option is exercised, as is reflected in the sample confirmation. Under the *1998 FX Transaction and Currency Option Definitions,* the parties must generally state their own rule, although the Settlement Date will be determined by operation of certain Disruption Fallbacks in connection with Disruption Events. *See User's Guide to the 1998 FX Transaction and Currency Option Definitions* 12.

Valuation Date: The Exercise Date

Annotation 25. If the parties had been silent on the question, this choice would have been the applicable rule, under Section 1.16(f) of the *1998 FX Transaction and Currency Option Definitions.*

Averaging Dates: Not applicable

Annotation 26. In some circumstances, the Buyer might prefer to have the Settlement Rate calculated on the basis of an average of the rates at several times on a particular day, or at a specified time on several different days, to reduce the possibility that the transaction might be affected by a price aberration at a particular time. The averaging approach can also facilitate the handling of Disruption Events by making it possible to determine a rate even if one or more of the scheduled readings of the rate has to be dropped from the calculation. *See* the discussion of the use of Averaging Dates in Annotations 38 and 39 to the sample equity index swap, *infra* p. 748.

Annotation 27. The *1998 FX Transaction and Currency Option Definitions* provide (in Section 3.8(c)) that, if it is not possible to determine the rate on a particular Averaging Date, that day is to be disregarded, thus obtaining a result similar to that which is obtained in an equity-linked derivative by specifying "Omission" as the Averaging Date Disruption Fallback. *See infra* p. 748.

Exercise Period:

> Annotation 28. This line item could be used to vary the general rule applicable to American Style Options, which is described in Annotation 6.

Premium: USD 250,000

Premium Payment Date: 18/APR/ 2002

> Annotation 29. Neither the ICOM form nor the *1998 FX Transaction and Currency Option Definitions* supplies a default choice if the parties fail to specify when the Premium will be payable. As illustrated, in conventional currency options the Premium Payment Date is generally the date for spot delivery of the relevant Currency Pair at the time the trade is done. Some options do not require the payment of any premium unless the option is exercised. In these "contingent premium" options, the premium is generally payable on the date of exercise.

3. The Disruption Events and Disruption Fallbacks applicable to the particular Transaction to which this Confirmation relates are as follows:

Disruption Events: Price Source Disruption

> Annotation 30. The choice specified would apply if the parties had been silent. This choice also reflects standard EMTA practices in Non-Deliverable transactions involving Brazilian currency. For discussion of other Disruption Events, *see supra* p. 491.

Disruption Fallbacks:

Fallback Reference Price: BRL Industry Survey Rate

> Annotation 31. Where a survey rate of this kind is available, it is generally the preferred Disruption Fallback. This rate is calculated by the Chicago Mercantile Exchange pursuant to a BRL Methodology dated November 8, 1999, establishing a centralized industry-wide survey of financial institutions in Brazil that are active participants in the Brazilian Real/U.S. Dollar spot markets, for the purpose of determining the BRL Industry Survey Rate. The BRL Methodology is available at http://www.newyorkfed.org/FXC/fxann000314.pdf. By choosing this fallback, the parties have agreed, if a Disruption Event occurs, to determine the Settlement Rate based on that rate as displayed on the Reuters Screen EMTA Page at approximately 12:30 p.m., São Paulo time, or as soon thereafter as practicable, on the first Business Day following the date the Disruption Event occurs.

Calculation Agent Determination of
Settling Rate

> Annotation 32. On the use of this Disruption Fallback, *see supra* p. 498.

    4. Calculation Agent: The Company and the Bank

        If the parties are unable to agree on a determination within one Business Day, each party agrees to be bound by the determination of an independent leading dealer in Reference Currency/Settlement Currency Transactions not located in the Reference Currency jurisdiction ("independent leading dealer"), mutually selected by the parties, who shall act as the substitute Calculation Agent, with the fees and expenses of such substitute Calculation Agent (if any) to be met equally by the parties. If the parties are unable to agree on an independent leading dealer to act as substitute Calculation Agent, each party shall select an independent leading dealer and such independent dealers shall agree on an independent third party who shall be deemed to be the substitute Calculation Agent.

> Annotation 33. The approach of having both parties act as Calculation Agent is most often found when both parties are dealers in the derivatives market. The provision on the resolution of disagreements over the Settlement Rate was published by EMTA as a recommended practice for cases involving NDFs in which joint Calculation Agents are used.

    5. Account Details

        Account for Payments to the Bank:

            Big Bank, N.A. New York, N.Y., ABA No. 000, CHIPS No. 000, Attention: Forex Division

        Account for Payments to the Company:

            Account No. 00000 with Big Bank Frankfurt, Frankfurt

6. Offices and Information on Notice of Exercise

The Office of the Bank for the Currency Option Transaction confirmed herein is its head office in New York. The Bank's address and telephone number for Notice of Exercise are as follows: 100 Vault Street, New York, New York; telephone: 212-000-0000; attention FX Department.

Oral Notice of Exercise should be confirmed in writing. Notice of Exercise may not be given by facsimile transmission.

The Office of the Company for the Currency Option Transaction confirmed herein is its office at the address specified for notices to it in the Schedule to the Agreement.

> Annotation 34. As indicated in Annotation 18, Buyers of Currency Options should consider having their confirmations specify the office through which the Seller is acting, as illustrated here, because the Expiration Time for exercise of a Currency Option is an agreed time of day at the agreed location for the Seller. An alternative is to refer to the relevant city in stating the Expiration Time.
>
> Annotation 35. The parties have indicated here that Notice of Exercise by telecopy will not be acceptable. That rule is built into the definition of "Notice of Exercise" in the ICOM form whereas the *1998 FX Transaction and Currency Option Definitions*, which are incorporated into the confirmation in its final paragraph, permit facsimile transmission of Notice of Exercise (*see* Section 3.5(g) of those definitions). However, the opening text of the confirmation expressly provides that the terms of the confirmation will prevail to the extent they are inconsistent with those definitions.

Business Days:

    Relevant City for Exercise Dates: Any of Sao Paulo, Brasilia or Rio de Janeiro and New York City

    Relevant City for Settlement Date: New York City

> Annotation 36. As noted in Annotation 13 to the preceding sample confirmation, *supra* p. 522, if the parties to an FX Transaction under the *1998 FX Transaction and Currency Option Definitions* do not indicate cities to be taken into account for purposes of the Business Day definition, the definitions supply extensive default choices. For some purposes the presumption is that, in determining whether a day is a Business Day, commercial bank holidays in the cities from which both parties are transacting will be taken into account. In the sample provisions, the parties have selected any of three cities in Brazil for purposes of determining whether an Exercise Date is a Business Day, reflecting the practice in EMTA's standard template for NDFs involving Brazilian currency. The parties have also included New York City because that is the city from which the Seller is acting. Only New York City is

selected for purposes of settlement, because settlement will be in U.S. Dollars. Buyers sometimes wish to have the cities from which they are acting included as well.

Business Day Convention:				Following Business Day Convention

>   Annotation 37. Section 1.2 of *1998 FX Transaction and Currency Option Definitions* sets forth four choices of Business Day Conventions—Following, Modified Following (or Modified), Nearest and Preceding. *See supra* p. 391. If the parties do not specify a convention, the Settlement Date will be adjusted in accordance with the Following Business Day Convention (Section 1.24). This is also true of the Expiration Date (Section 3.5(d)), the Premium Payment Date (Section 3.4(b)) and the Specified Exercise Date for Bermuda style Currency Options Transactions (Section 3.5(h)). The default choice for the Averaging Date and the Valuation Date is the Preceding Business Day Convention, under Sections 1.16(f) and 3.8(a).

Please confirm that the foregoing correctly sets forth the terms of our agreement by executing the copy of this Confirmation enclosed for that purpose and returning it to us or by sending to us a letter or telex substantially similar to this letter, which letter or telex sets forth the material terms of the Transaction to which this Confirmation relates and indicates agreement to those terms. If you believe the foregoing does not correctly reflect the terms of our agreement, please give us notice as soon as possible of what you believe to be the necessary corrections.

>   Annotation 38. *See* Annotation 17 to the sample FX forward confirmation, *supra* p. 523.

BIG BANK, N.A.

By: _____
   Name:
   Title: Vice President

Confirmed as of the date below:

ENGLISH COMPANY PLC

By: _____
   Name:
   Title:

COMMODITY DERIVATIVES

INTRODUCTION

COMMODITY SWAPS

The term "swap" is sometimes used in the commodities markets to refer to an exchange of one grade or type of a commodity for another, with compensation for location or quality differences.[1396] As generally used in the OTC derivatives market, however, the "commodity swap," "commodity price swap" or "commodity price-index swap" is a purely financial transaction modeled on the interest rate swap. A conventional commodity swap of this kind—which the commercial market might call a "paper" transaction—treats a specified amount, or Notional Quantity, of the relevant commodity as the basis for calculating the parties' respective payment obligations but does not involve the delivery of the commodity.

Just as rate and currency swaps are used as flexible, privately negotiated tools for the management of interest-rate and exchange-rate risk, commodity swaps are used to manage the risks associated with commodity price volatility through customized transactions. In fact, in order for a derivatives market to develop in a particularly commodity, it must experience significant price volatility.[1397] As a general matter, for a commodity to be the subject of derivative products, there must also be "a deep and efficient market" for the commodity and "a readily available" price source,[1398] that is, a price benchmark acceptable in the marketplace for its "reliability" and "objectivity" and for the frequency with which it is made available.[1399]

[1396] *See* Arnold E. Safer & Benjamin Schlesinger, *Energy Commodity Brokerage, Spot and Futures Trading, in* 3 ENERGY LAW AND TRANSACTIONS § 87.01[2] n.11 (David J. Muchow & William A. Mogel eds. 1996).

[1397] "The major criterion for a commodity to be 'swappable' is price volatility .... If both sides expect the price of corn to be stable over the next five years, the product could be bought or sold on the spot, or cash, market. This was the case for many commodities prior to 1972. But broad fluctuations in commodity prices since this time have forced both producers and users to think more about leveling cash flows, at least for a portion of their exposure." Mary L. Shelman, *The Chase Manhattan Bank: Commodity Swaps* (Harvard Business School case study N9-588-056 1988), prepared under the supervision of Prof. Ray A. Goldberg, with the assistance of Gaylen Byker and The Chase Manhattan Bank. *See* Rawls, *supra* note 1298, at 2–11:

> Much of the increase in basic commodity prices in the 1970s was driven by inflation. The declining purchasing power of dollars increased the demand for commodities as assets, with the result that the prices of real goods were bid up relative to financial assets. . . . But when real interest rates rose sharply after . . . October 1979 . . . , the opportunity cost of holding inventories of commodities also rose. Thus, the real value of commodities fell . . . . [T]he relative prices of commodities have fallen dramatically from their peaks in 1974 and 1979.

[1398] *Shelman, supra* note 1397, at 3.

[1399] J.P. Morgan, *OTC products, in* COMMODITY-LINKED FINANCE 5 (J.P. Morgan & Co. ed. 1992).

The world of end-users of commodity swaps naturally includes commodity producers, refiners and traders, as well as major consumers. Where crude oil, natural gas and other fuels are concerned, for example, the consumers include such obvious and not-so-obvious participants as airlines, shipping companies, public utilities and municipalities and their transit authorities. Commodity swaps may also be entered into as hedges by institutions that issue or invest in commodity price-indexed instruments or limited partnerships or funds created to enable investors to take on exposure to commodity prices.[1400] These indexed instruments, which are also referred to as hybrids,[1401] are designed in various ways so that their coupon or their redemption value at maturity reflects commodity price change. As a result, an investment in the hybrid instrument simulates the return on an investment in the commodity, or in commodity futures or options.[1402]

For producers, the swap may operate as a hedge against declining prices. For example, an oil producer may be concerned about its ability to service its debt and still achieve an acceptable profit margin if the price it obtains for its oil declines.[1403] It might seek to protect itself by entering into a four-year crude-oil price swap (which is illustrated in Figure 9,[1404] together with related transactions entered into by the counterparty), under which it would be entitled to receive a stream of monthly Fixed Amount payments calculated on a Notional Quantity representing a portion of its production (say 25,000 barrels each month) at a fixed price per barrel.[1405] In return, the producer would agree to make a

---

[1400] "Investors are mostly large institutions who want to invest in a commodity index because they are 'negatively correlated with stocks and bonds. . . .'" *Commodity Swaps*, DERIVATIVES WEEK, Sept. 14, 1992, at 8 (Learning Curve column). *Torch Plans Hedging Program for New Oil & Gas L.P*, DERIVATIVES WEEK, July 27, 1992, at 6, includes a description of oil and gas limited partnership interests with a built-in commodity swap hedging program designed to enable institutional investors in the partnerships to reduce the commodity price risk involved in the investment. For an example of the use of a swap by an issuer of oil-linked notes, *see* J.P. Morgan, *Applications of commodity hedging techniques for fund managers*, *in* COMMODITY-LINKED FINANCE, *supra* note 1399, at 85, 90–91.

[1401] *See supra* note 368 and the source cited therein on the treatment of hybrid instruments under the CEA and related provisions of U.S. law.

[1402] *See generally* SATYAJIT DAS, STRUCTURED NOTES AND DERIVATIVE EMBEDDED SECURITIES, ch. 8 (1996) ("Commodity-linked Notes"). When these indexed investments are listed on securities exchanges, the exchanges often provide brief fact sheets that describe in simple terms how the indexation operates and the extent to which a change in commodity, commodity futures or commodity option prices would result in a loss of the invested principal or, in a "principal protected" instrument, would affect the coupon.

[1403] *See* Mark E. Taylor, *Commodity Derivatives*, *in* PLI 2000, at 495, 499–500, for an example of a swap used by an independent oil producer to increase the predictability of its cash flows in connection with planning its exploration and development programs. Others whose interests are like those of the producer may use the swap to seek protection against declining prices or, viewed another way, to add predictability to production revenues. Examples are governments that rely on tax revenues on production revenues. *See* Shelman, *supra* note 1397, at 5. Refiners are in the same position as producers with respect to their refined product, although they are also consumers with respect to the crude oil they refine. *See also* Mark E. Haedicke & Alan B. Aronowitz, *Gas Commodity Markets*, *in* 3 ENERGY LAW AND TRANSACTIONS § 88.01[4][a][1] (David J. Muchow & William A. Mogel eds. 1996), for examples of use of what they refer to as "producer-oriented" swaps involving natural gas.

[1404] *Infra* p. 547.

[1405] "The fixed price on a commodity swap is set upfront by reference to the prevailing swap or forward price market for a transaction of the duration under discussion." J.P. Morgan, *OTC Products*, *in* COMMODITY-LINKED FINANCE, *supra* note 1399, at 5. On commodity curves, the factors that determine the pure forward commodity price (the spot price, current interest rates and the yield curve, and the costs of stor-

stream of Floating Amount payments, due on the same dates—referred to as Settlement Dates or Payment Dates—to the counterparty, calculated on the same Notional Quantity but at a floating price that tracks and fluctuates with published prices for the relevant crude in a cash market or prices for exchange-traded futures contracts on the crude. Because the U.S. dollar is the principal currency in both the futures and the cash markets for crude oil (and most other actively traded commodities), both streams of payment (the Fixed Amounts and the Floating Amounts) will be in U.S. dollars. The two amounts for each period—referred to as Calculation Periods or Settlement Periods—will be settled on a net basis.[1406]

The swap will not affect the producer's rights or obligations under its agreements with its lenders or its "physical" contracts with purchasers of its crude, but if crude prices decline, and provided the swap counterparty performs its obligations, the producer will know that the price it obtains for its crude, together with the payments made by the swap counterparty, will be at a level that will enable it to meet the debt service and profit objectives described above. If crude prices rise above the swap fixed price, the producer will be required to make net payments to the swap counterparty but—assuming away production problems—it will be in a position to pay that cost of the swap protection because the sale proceeds for its crude will have risen too. This swap will not, of course, protect the producer against risks to its production or sales volume. To some extent, however, it might be able to obtain protection against the risk of reduced sales volumes through a weather derivatives transaction of the kind discussed in this book.[1407]

End-users of commodity swaps—*e.g.*, producers and consumers—sometimes enter into swaps, caps, floors and collars with each other directly.[1408] It is, however, more common, as illustrated in Figure 9, for end-users to engage in commodity swaps and

---

age, holding and location or transport costs for the commodity), and the impact that these and other factors have on the pricing of OTC commodity swaps and similar derivatives, *see, e.g.*, *Commodity Swaps*, DERIVATIVES WEEK, Sept. 14, 1992, at 8 and *Commodity Curves*, DERIVATIVES WEEK, Jan. 18, 1993, at 9 (Learning Curve columns), and Satyajit Das, *Forward March*, RISK, Feb. 1993, at 41 (commodity swaps section).

[1406] As in a rate swap, the parties' Payment Dates or Settlement Dates in a commodity price swap can be "mismatched," and the Notional Quantity need not remain the same for each Calculation Period. In addition, different commodities or commodity price indexes may be used to calculate the parties' payment obligations. Both parties may be Floating Price Payers, as in a "basis swap." For example, one party's payments may be calculated at an agreed crude oil futures contract price and the counterparty's payments may be calculated at a cash-market price for crude oil delivered at a different location. *See also infra* p. 548, for discussion of the "crack-spread" transaction, a kind of basis swap often used by crude oil refineries. For examples of the kinds of basis risk that can be managed with derivatives, *see* John Shapiro, *The Importance of Basis Risk in Commodity Price Risk Management*, INTERNATIONAL OIL & GAS FINANCE REVIEW 1997, at 96 (Michaella Crisell ed. Euromoney Publications).

[1407] *See infra* p. 756.

[1408] For a time in the late 1980s, commodity users, producers and trading companies sought through ERMA, the Energy Risk Management Association, to develop common terms that would facilitate development of this kind of direct derivatives dealing. ERMA produced a form of master agreement for transactions among these kinds of market participants and their affiliates. The ERMA form no longer has any notable following, however. Therefore, although the third edition of *Documentation for Derivatives* referred to the ERMA form and compared its terms and conventions with those published by ISDA, we have not included those references in this edition.

similar derivatives transactions with intermediaries, which include financial institutions and professional risk-management or trading arms of energy companies and major commodity producers. As with other OTC derivatives, the intermediary's business generally is to provide transactions tailored to its customers' needs, hedge itself against the risks, or at least the commodity price and other market risks, generated by those transactions and profit from the difference between its hedging and other costs and what it is able to charge its customers.

In the simplest and, from the perspective of the intermediary, the best case, the intermediary's hedge may be an off-setting derivative with an end-user with the opposite needs. That is, as illustrated in Figure 9, the intermediary may stand between a producer and a consumer of the same commodity, each of which itself is using a commodity swap to manage risks associated with its cash-market dealings in the relevant commodity.[1409]

From the consumer's point of view, the commodity swap can be attractive as a means of hedging against rising prices.[1410] Thus, the crude-oil swap described above would have the same economic effect as a medium-term fixed price supply contract entitling it to purchase 25,000 barrels of crude oil monthly at a fixed price—a type of supply contract that may not be available in the cash market. If the swap Floating Price (reflecting actual cash-market prices or futures prices) exceeded the swap Fixed Price for any of the monthly Calculation Periods, the consumer would look to its swap counterparty for the excess. If the swap Floating Price fell below the Fixed Price in the swap for a Calculation Period, the consumer would be required to make a net payment under the swap, but lower costs in the cash market could be expected to offset the swap expense.[1411]

[1409] Perfect matches of this kind, for precisely the same quantities and with payments at precisely the same times, can be unusual, however, so the intermediary may hedge itself with exchange-traded futures or with cash forward or options contracts. These hedges are available for limited periods and can be illiquid at the longer end of the available OTC derivatives spectrum. Their use, therefore, requires active management for medium- and long-term swaps and similar derivatives and can involve substantial risk. For a description of the problems involved in hedging OTC commodity price derivatives with exchange-traded futures and techniques used by professional providers of these products, *see* David Aspel, Jack Cogen & Michael Rabin, *Hedging Long Term Commodity Swaps with Futures*, 1 GLOBAL FIN. J. 77 (1989). The risks associated with these strategies were widely debated after MG Refining and Marketing, Inc., a U.S. affiliate of Metallgesellschaft AG, recorded losses of approximately U.S.$ 1.3 billion at year end in 1993 from its use of one such strategy. Part Seven of DERIVATIVES HANDBOOK includes several chapters on the Metallgesellschaft debacle. *See, e.g.*, Christopher L. Culp & Merton H. Miller, *Metallgesellschaft and the Economics of Synthetic Storage*, Franklin R. Edwards & Michael S. Canter, *The Collapse of Metallgesellschaft: Unhedgeable Risks, Poor Hedging Strategy, or Just Bad Luck?*, Antonio S. Mello & John E. Parsons, *Maturity Structure of a Hedge Matters: Lessons from the Metallgesellschaft Debacle*, and Anatoli Kuprianov, *Derivatives Debacles: Case Studies of Large Losses in Derivatives Markets*, in DERIVATIVES HANDBOOK 527, 548, 575 & 605, respectively. *See also supra* p. 77.

[1410] For examples and discussion of the uses of OTC commodity price swaps and other derivatives by various kinds of producers and consumers, and the questions of risk management to be resolved by them in deciding whether or how to use these derivative products, *see* Chapters 4 ("Issues in risk management") and 5 ("Application of commodity hedging techniques for users, producers and refiners") in COMMODITY-LINKED FINANCE, *supra* note 1399, at 39–52 & 53–71, respectively.

[1411] Whether this is so will, of course, depend on how the consumer makes its crude oil purchases. On crude oil pricing mechanisms, "posted prices" for immediate delivery of crude oil, the relationship between these posted prices and spot prices for conventional purchases for delivery the following month, and the further relationship between the spot price and the futures market price, *see* Safer & Schlesinger, *supra* note 1396, at § 87.01[1].

Commodity Derivatives   547

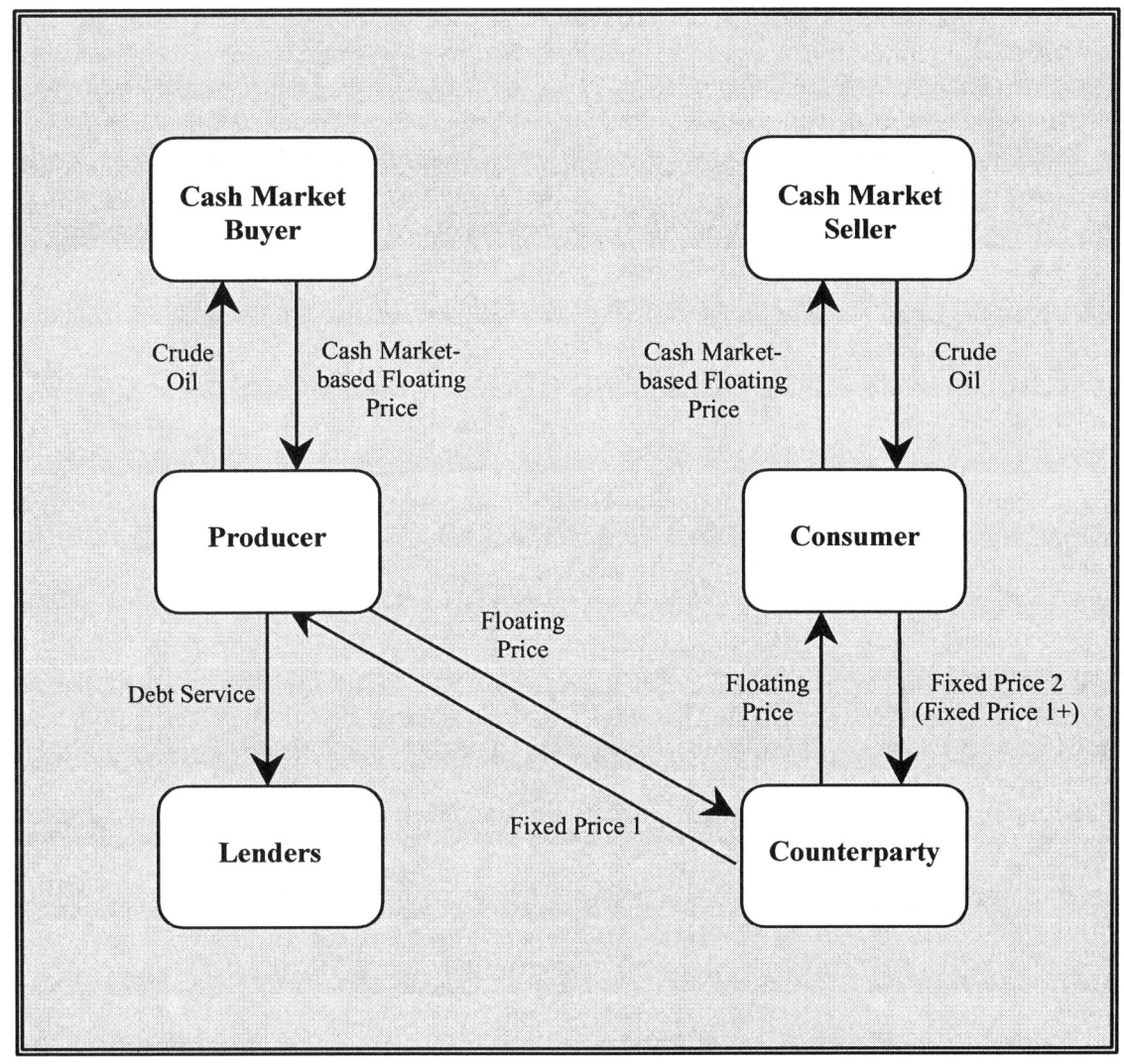

Figure 9. Commodity Swap and Related Transactions

The swap is not, of course, the only tool available to producers and consumers to hedge against volatile prices. For example, the producer might achieve the desired economic effect through a cash forward sale of crude oil or it might hedge itself in the futures market. The swap may, however, be preferable for various reasons. One is term—the producer may be able to obtain medium- or long-term price protection through a single swap, but the longest-dated of the available futures contracts may not go out as far as the hedge that the producer wants to execute.[1412] Similarly, the cash forward is a shorter-term hedging vehicle. The terms of the futures contract—commodity type or grade, delivery point and date, quantity, and the like—are largely standardized and established by the exchange,[1413] whereas the producer may be able to obtain a privately negotiated swap tai-

---

[1412] *See* Annotation 21 to the sample commodity swap confirmation, *infra* p. 581.

[1413] Some exchanges have developed products, often referred to as flex options, that permit the parties to choose at least some nonstandard terms or to provide for customized delivery, settlement or contract initiation mechanisms, sometimes referred to as alternate delivery procedures (ADP), exchange of futures for, or in connection with, physicals (EFP), and exchange of futures for swaps (EFS). ADPs and EFPs for the

lored far more closely to its needs. In addition, the producer is likely to have established channels for substantial portions of its physical sales contracts and may wish to continue with those arrangements undisturbed while using financial swaps to seek price protection at different levels with respect to discrete portions of its projected production.

The intermediary might also choose to hedge a swap with a producer or consumer in the cash markets. Not all market professionals can do so, however, nor can all do so equally favorably. The laws of some jurisdictions may, for example, restrict the power or authority of financial institutions to make and take delivery of some commodities.[1414] Such laws may nonetheless permit these institutions to participate indirectly in the physical markets for these commodities by investing in commodity trading companies.[1415]

The producer might use a swap transaction to hedge the relative costs of its principal raw material and its main finished products. An example is a crack-spread, or "refiner's margin" transaction, which is often used when spreads between the prices of crude oil and refined products are volatile.[1416] In this kind of swap, a crude oil refiner might contract to receive payments calculated periodically on the changing price for futures on a specified quantity of a blend of crude oil actually used in its own production facilities. In exchange, the refiner could agree to make payments calculated at an agreed spread below the futures prices for the main refined petroleum products that it produces from the crude, say heating oil and unleaded gasoline. Figure 10 illustrates what the agreed gross cash flows for each Calculation Period during the swap's term might look like (although, as noted above, the swap payments would actually be settled on a net basis).[1417] The diagram also illustrates how the gross amounts payable to the refiner under the swap could, at least theoretically, offset the amounts payable by it for its physical supply of crude oil, al-

---

NYMEX Henry Hub natural gas futures and the EFS for Middle East crude oil futures are described at www.nymex.com/markets/cont_all and http://208.206.41.61/sourmarker/mecspec.htm.

[1414] Although some commercial banks have the authority to own and deal in commodities, generally U.S. commercial banks are subject to restrictions on ownership of nonfinancial commodities other than those traded in the bullion markets and, therefore, on activities as principal in derivatives providing for their taking physical delivery of nonfinancial commodities. *See, e.g.,* Regulation Y of the Board of Governors of the Federal Reserve System (applicable to bank holding companies and their subsidiaries), 12 C.F.R. § 225.28(b)(8)(ii)(B) (2002).

[1415] *See* TORTORIELLO, *supra* note 462, at II–90 on direct and indirect hedging in physical commodities by banks regulated in the U.S.

[1416] In describing crack spreads executed with its exchange-traded futures and crack-spread options first launched in 1994, the NYMEX explains: "In recent years, the use of crack spreads has become more widespread as crude and product prices have fluctuated dramatically in response to extreme weather conditions or political crises. The spreads have displayed related volatility . . . sometimes generating high margins for refiners and marketers, but at other times severely squeezing their profitability." NEW YORK MERCANTILE EXCHANGE, CRACK SPREADS (1998), *available at* www.nymex.com /markets/cont_all.

[1417] Crack-spread hedges are also executed with exchange-traded futures. When so executed on the NYMEX, "[a] futures crack spread is treated as a single transaction for the purpose of determining a market participant's margin requirement. Specifically, the minimum margin requirement takes into account that the risk on one side of the spread is generally reduced by the other leg of the spread. Crack spread options and another commonly used spread uses a 5-3-2 ratio. Similarly, crack spread options [which trade on the NYMEX as two separate contracts with a one-to-one-ratio of crude oil to the New York Harbor unleaded gasoline and to heating oil], allow the hedge to be accomplished with the payment of one option premium instead of two." *Id.*

Commodity Derivatives 549

though in all likelihood the payment dates under the swap and the due dates for payment under the physical supply contract would differ.

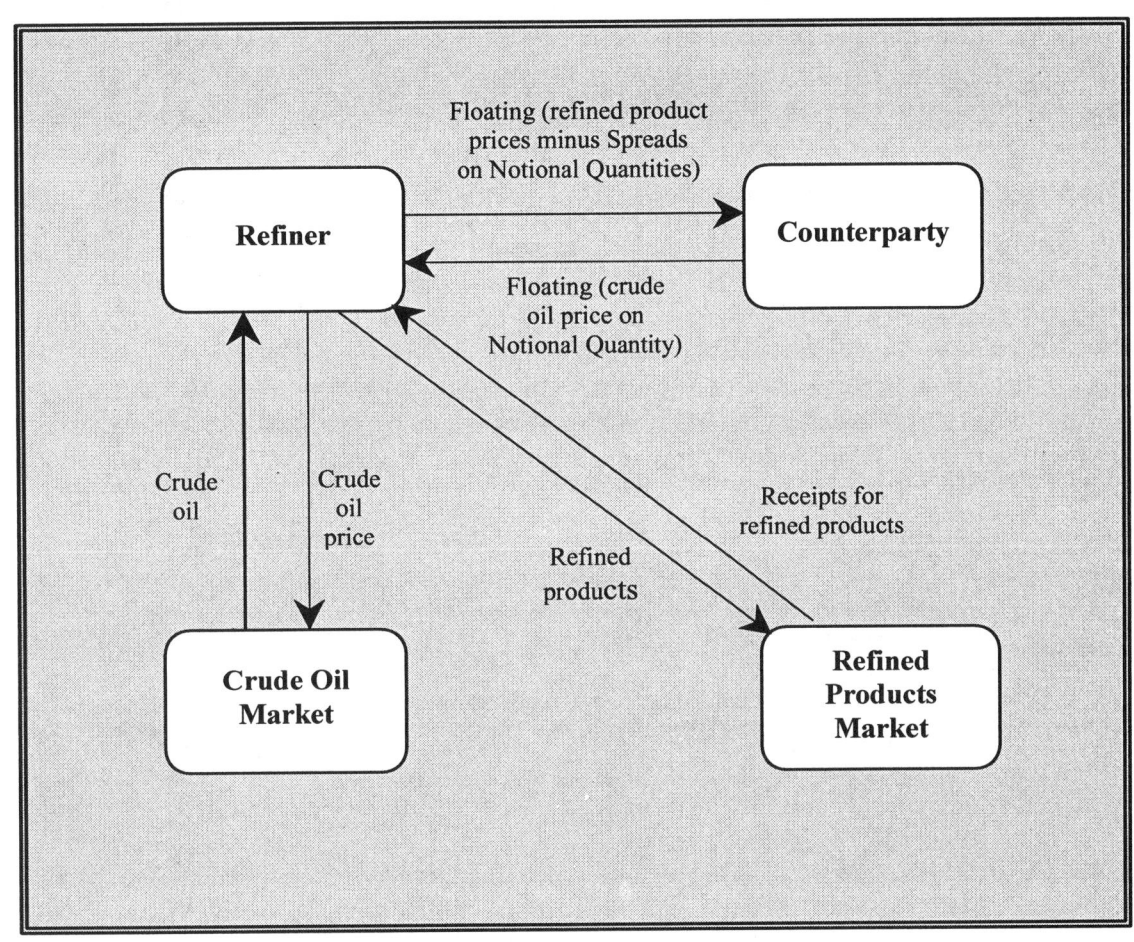

Figure 10. Crack-Spread Swap

Assuming the swap provider performs its obligations, a swap like this could be used by the refiner to lock in a theoretical refining margin for its production of heating oil and unleaded gasoline—the spread deducted, as shown, under the swap in calculating the refiner's payment obligations based on the combined refined products futures price index. The swap only operates roughly to this effect for many reasons, of course, including the fact that the swap is structured on the basis of necessary assumptions that may be inaccurate or may only approximate reality, such as the ratio of crude oil supply to gasoline and heating oil produced and the assumption that the benchmark prices used to calculate the swap payments (the Platt's crude oil price and the NYMEX futures prices for unleaded gasoline and heating oil) match the refiner's actual cost of physical crude oil supply and actual sales prices for its products for any given period.[1418] The swap's usefulness to the

---

[1418] According to the NYMEX, a popular crack spread uses a 3-2-1 ratio—three barrels of crude, two of gasoline and a barrel of heating oil—although a 5-3-2 ratio is also popular and other ratios are also used. As indicated in the preceding footnote, the standardized NYMEX crack spread options use a one-to-one ratio of light sweet crude oil to unleaded gasoline or heating oil.

refiner as a tool for risk and revenue management will, naturally, improve the closer the terms of the financial transaction relating to the crude-oil leg can be brought to the terms of the refiner's contract for physical supply. This may be easier to achieve if the two contracts are negotiated at the same time with the same entity. In addition, if the refiner would be required to post a bond, letter of credit or collateral to secure its performance on both the physical leg and the financial leg of its dealings, it may be able to achieve savings by dealing with a single entity that its willing to calculate its exposure on a net basis.[1419]

The particular goal an end-user is seeking to serve when it engages in a commodity swap or similar derivative may lead it to prefer a particular segment of the dealer community or, price being roughly equal, a particular intermediary. For example, commercial users of a commodity may seek to have their swaps, caps or collars tailored to hedge price risk associated with their physical supply contracts. In these cases, if the commodity supplier also offers financial derivatives, it may be the natural source for the derivatives, since it may be in the best position to tailor the hedge to suit its customer and, at the same time, to manage the risks associated with the physical and financial sides on a combined basis.

Commodity producers often link swaps and similar derivatives to a financing and in these cases one of the financial institutions involved in the financing may be best able to tailor the derivative to suit the producer's needs and to manage the associated risks on a combined basis.

The classic example is the U.S.$ 210 million three-year fixed-rate loan made in 1989 by a syndicate of lenders to Mexicana de Cobre, S.A. de C.V., a Mexican copper mine owner. The security for the lenders included an assignment of Mexcobre's rights to receive monthly payments under a commodity swap in which one of the lenders was the fixed price payer and Mexcobre was the floating price payer.[1420] Mexcobre's swap obligations were calculated at an average spot price for copper on the London Metals Exchange, which tracked the price payable to Mexcobre under a copper supply contract with a European trading company, and both the copper buyer's payments and any payments due to Mexcobre under the swap, if that market-based price dropped below the swap fixed price, were made into a collateral account outside Mexico. The lenders' security package also included an assignment of rights in that account and in Mexcobre's rights under the supply contract, and the amounts of the loan principal and interest and the terms of the supply contract and the swap were designed so that the lenders would be paid, assuming (1) Mexcobre actually shipped copper sufficient to meet its supply contract obligations,

---

[1419]This would be true if the refiner were entitled to reduce the amount of required support for its payment obligations under the physical contract by the mark-to-market value of the swap at times when the swap was out of the money for the swap provider. It would also be true more generally if in the normal course the amounts of credit support it was required to post would be rounded up, and the rounding could be done only once, on a net basis. Naturally, as a result, there is a substantial and increasing interest in frameworks that facilitate the netting of exposures across physical and financial commodity contracts, as well as across diverse financial contracts. *See infra* p. 1298 for discussion of the ISDA bridging approach to this objective, and a comparison of that and other ISDA approaches with that taken by the CPMA—the Cross-Product Master Agreement—published by The Bond Market Association and other industry groups. Part 6, *infra* p. 1279, includes an annotated version of the CPMA.

[1420]BNP-Paribas (then Banque Paribas) was the swap provider and the leader of the bank syndicate.

(2) the buyer paid for the copper and (3) the swap provider made any required swap payments.[1421]

Major producers of one commodity are often major users of another. This is the case, for example, of major energy consumers. Entities that fit this description sometimes enter into a combination of commodity swaps referred to as a "terms-of-trade" structure. As shown in the following diagram, in the first leg, the entity, say a producer of aluminum, might use a swap to fix its revenues on a portion of its production over a number of years by becoming the receiver of Fixed Amounts on a swap. In the second leg, the aluminum producer could enter into a crude oil price swap, as payer of the Fixed Amounts, to lock in a stable price for a commodity whose cost constitutes a significant production expense. By entering into the two transactions illustrated in Figure 11 on the following page, the producer would synthetically have fixed the price of its oil in terms of aluminum prices. Instead of the oil being denominated in dollars, it would effectively be denominated in aluminum through the two swaps. "This swap is a method of tying expenses to actual revenues."[1422]

Caps, Floors, Collars and Participation Derivatives Products

As is the case with interest-rate derivatives, the swap is only one of the cash-settled products used to manage or take on exposure to changes in commodity prices. The same alternatives—principally caps and floors and the combinations of these transactions that are often called collars and corridors—exist for commodity derivatives.[1423] As with interest-rate derivatives, they are generally used to enable a party to obtain some protection against adverse commodity price movements without giving up all the potential benefits of favorable movements.

For example, if a producer of a commodity enters into a conventional swap transaction, the counterparty promises to make a payment to the producer if the average price for the commodity over the agreed period and measured in the agreed way falls below the agreed level, and the producer also promises to make a payment to the counterparty if the average price rises. The converse is true in a commodity consumer's swap, where the consumer promises to make a payment if the average cash-market or futures measure of the commodity's price falls below the swap fixed price for a period in exchange for the counterparty's promise of a payment if the average cash-market or futures price for the period is above the swap fixed price. So, in each case the end-user party to the swap gives up the potential benefit of favorable commodity price movements in order to obtain protection against unfavorable movements.

[1421] For a further description of this transaction, *see* Robert S. Mancini, *Commodity Price Swaps*, in THE FUTURE OF DERIVATIVES 39, a supplement published with the November 1991 issue of INSTITUTIONAL INVESTOR.

[1422] *See Shelman, supra* note 1397, at 5, describing a terms-of-trade swap by a copper producer.

[1423] Some of the alternative uses of these products in the market for interest-rate derivatives are discussed *supra* pp. 439 (caps and floors) and 448 (collars and corridors).

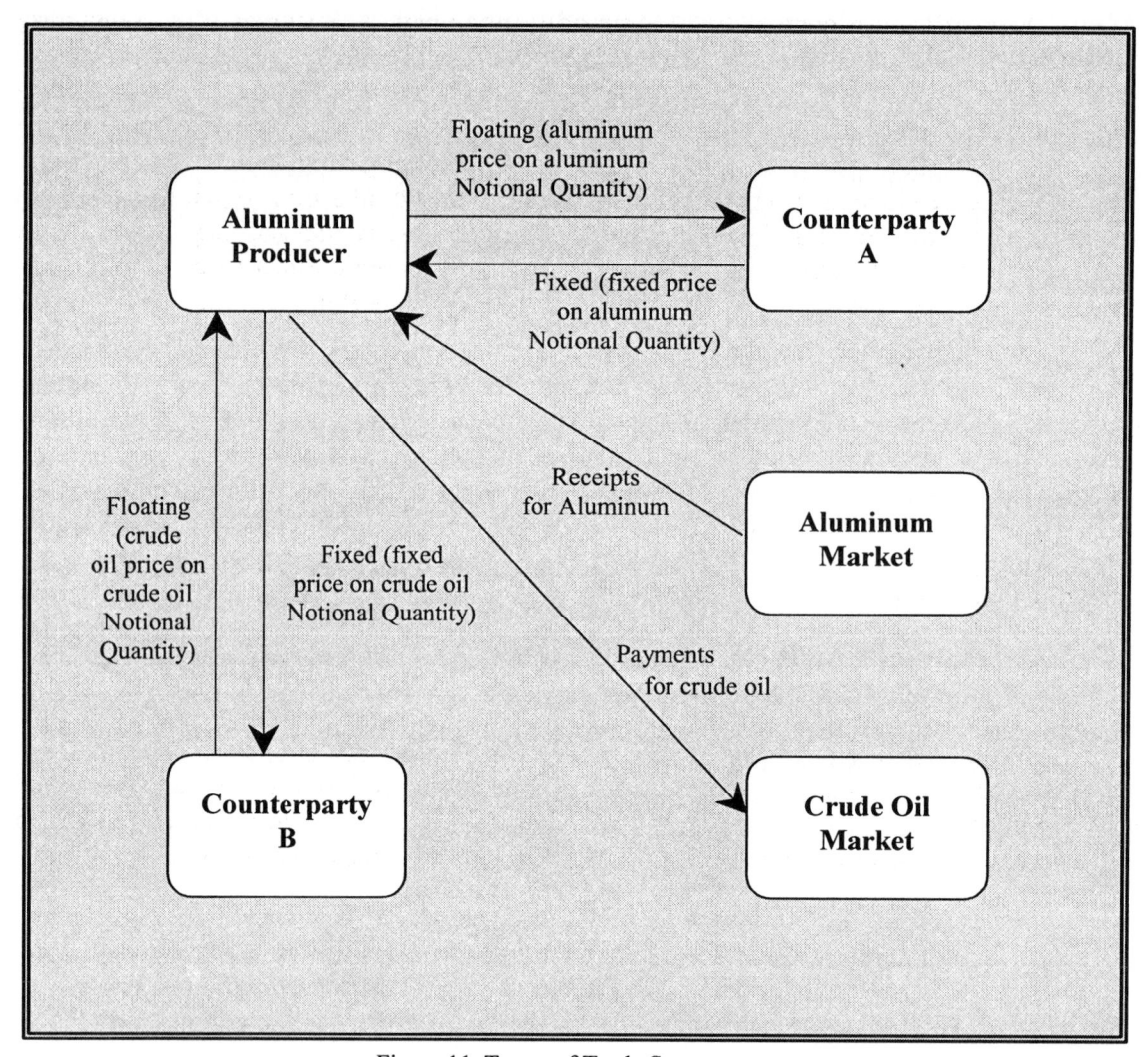

Figure 11. Terms of Trade Swap

      Commodity price floors and caps and combinations of these transactions are used by producers and consumers when they do not want to give up all of the potential benefit of favorable movements in commodity prices to obtain protection against adverse price changes. In a conventional floor transaction—using ISDA terminology—a producer would pay a Fixed Amount (the equivalent of a premium) at the outset of the Term of the Transaction in return for the agreement of its counterparty to make a Floating Amount payment at the end of each Calculation Period if the specified measure of the commodity's price in the cash or futures market over that period declined below an agreed Floor Price.[1424] The payment due from the floor seller, or Floating Price Payer, would be calculated on the agreed Notional Quantity at a price equal to the difference between the period's Floating Price for the commodity and the Floor Price.

[1424] As described in connection with interest-rate caps, the floor may also be structured so that the Fixed Amount, or premium, is payable in arrears at the end of each covered period, or so that the Floor Price differs from period to period. *See supra* note 1249.

Similarly, in a conventional commodity price cap, a consumer of a commodity might pay a Fixed Amount at the beginning of the cap's term in exchange for the agreement of its counterparty to make a Floating Amount payment at the end of each Calculation Period if the specified measure of the commodity's price over the period rose above an agreed Cap Price. The payment due from the cap seller, again called the Floating Price Payer, would be calculated on the agreed Notional Quantity at a price equal to the difference between the period's Floating Price for the commodity and the Cap Price. These simple cap and floor transactions may have the same economic effect as commodity options, but they do not involve physical delivery of the underlying commodity and may have terms that are more closely tailored to the needs of the buyer of the protection than are available with standardized, exchange-traded commodity options.

The premium payable by the buyer of the cap or floor protection will of course depend on the level at which the Cap Price or Floor Price is set. There are also other techniques available to the buyer of the cap or floor protection in order to manage premium cost.[1425] The simplest and most common of the conventional variants is the collar, sometimes referred to as a "range forward," which combines a cap and a floor. If a commodity producer entered into a collar to obtain protection against falling prices for its product, but at a lower cost than a swap, the producer would buy a floor from its counterparty and simultaneously sell a cap, thus giving up part of the upside potential from rising prices in order to reduce the premium cost of the floor.

The collar differs from the swap in that the Floor Price and the Cap Price are different, so neither party is required to make a payment for a period if the agreed measure of the commodity's price in the cash or futures market is within the range that begins at the Cap Price and ends at the Floor Price. If the initial value of the cap protection sold by the producer in the collar equals the initial value of the floor protection that it buys in the collar, the transaction may be referred to loosely as a "costless" or "zero cost" collar because the cap and floor premiums, or Fixed Amounts, will be netted, so that the producer is not required to make an initial payment. The collar is, of course, not ultimately "costless" if prices move outside the agreed range, so that one of the parties has to make a payment.[1426]

The theory behind the structure sometimes called a corridor is similar to that underlying the collar, in that the party seeking protection against unfavorable changes in the price of a commodity gives up a portion of that protection by selling back protection that begins at a different price level. However, whereas the collar combines a cap and floor, the corridor combines two caps, or two floors. For example, in a corridor entered into by a party exposed to the risk of declining commodity prices, that party would buy a floor at an

---

[1425] As applied to interest rate derivatives, some of these techniques are also discussed *supra* p. 442. *See also supra* note 1382 on exotics, a term often used to refer generically to options and other transactions with embedded options or complicated payoff structures, such as single transactions that package the effects of multiple conventional derivatives—like the collars and corridors discussed below—or that depart from the norm in a conventional transaction of a similar type by, say, providing for deferred payment or making the exercise price or payoff depend on multiple contingencies.

[1426] In addition to being called range forwards and costless or zero cost collars, these transactions are also sometimes referred to as flexible forwards, min-max transactions and forward bands. *See* HULL, *supra* note 646, at 458.

agreed Floor Price. At the same time, in order to reduce its premium cost, that party would also sell a floor to its counterparty at an even lower Floor Price, in effect giving up its protection if prices moved below that lower price. As a result, the protection bought in the corridor is limited to the range of commodity prices that begins at the higher floor level and ends at the lower floor level. This kind of transaction is more likely to appeal to parties who are exposed to price risk through commodity-indexed investments than it is to commodity producers, since an investor may take a "view" on price risk that makes selling the lower floor seem quite reasonable as a speculative matter whereas, in the normal course, if the price of the relevant commodity falls below the lower floor level, a producer would be ill equipped to make a payment under the corridor because its revenues from actual sales of its production in the cash market would, at the same time, have fallen.

Often appealing to commodity producers and consumers as end-users are "participating," or "participation" swaps, caps and floors in which the buyer of protection against declining or rising commodity prices shares part of the upside of favorable price changes with the seller. One variant of these transactions combines elements of a cap or floor with elements of a swap. For example, in order to obtain protection against rising prices but reduce its cost of a commodity-price cap, a commodity consumer might agree that, if the commodity's average price during a period were below the cap price, the consumer would make a payment to its counterparty equal to fifty percent of the excess of the cap price over the commodity price times the notional quantity, but if the average price were above the cap price, the counterparty would pay 100% of the difference times the notional quantity. Alternatively, the obligation to share the benefits of declining prices could be measured at a single time during the life of the cap, or the calculation period for the participation payment could be a shorter period carved out of the total term of the cap or floor.[1427]

DOCUMENTATION

The documentation for commodity derivatives of the kinds described above often has special features that the parties include in light of gaming laws, bucket-shop laws and laws that restrict trading in commodity futures and options. These features, largely representations, are discussed at length in Chapter 3.[1428]

The following discussion is an overview of documentation issues that commonly arise in using ISDA's standardized terms for commodity derivatives involving commodities other than currencies. These issues, and others, are also explored in detail in the annotations to the sample confirmations that follow the discussion. The use of the *2000 ISDA Definitions* in currency swaps and similar transactions is discussed and illustrated elsewhere in this Part,[1429] as is the use of ISDA's specialized terms for foreign exchange forward and spot transactions and currency options.[1430]

[1427] On these participation derivatives transactions, *see, e.g.*, Mark E. Haedicke & Alan B. Aronowitz, *Gas Commodity Markets, in* ENERGY LAW AND TRANSACTIONS § 88.01[4][a].

[1428] *See supra* p. 83.

[1429] *See supra* p. 505.

[1430] *See supra* pp. 515 & 524.

THE 1993/2000 ISDA COMMODITY DERIVATIVES DEFINITIONS

ISDA-based documentation for commodity price derivatives used the *1991 ISDA Definitions*, with appropriate adaptations, until the publication of the *1993 ISDA Commodity Derivatives Definitions*. The 1993 definitions were expanded on in the *2000 Supplement to the 1993 ISDA Commodity Derivatives Definitions*. The *2000 ISDA Definitions* are designed for use with interest-rate and currency swaps and similar transactions, and not commodity derivatives products.

The *1993/2000 ISDA Commodity Derivatives Definitions* are designed to be used in documenting cash-settled, but not physically settled,[1431] OTC commodity swaps, options, caps, collars, floors and swaptions and other cash-settled commodity derivatives transactions.[1432] The *2000 Supplement* added to and, in some cases, updated the definitions provided in the *1993 ISDA Commodity Derivatives Definitions* for the "Commodity Reference Prices" that may be used in the calculation of Floating Amounts, as described below. The *2000 Supplement* also completely replaced Article 7 of the *1993 ISDA Commodity Derivatives Definitions* to add new ways in which the parties may set out a transaction's terms relating to commodity prices as well as disruptions in the cash and futures market used as sources for those prices.[1433]

THE *1997 ISDA BULLION DEFINITIONS*

Between the publication of the *1993 ISDA Commodity Derivatives Definitions* and its *2000 Supplement*, ISDA published the more specialized *1997 ISDA Bullion Definitions* and *1997 Short Form Bullion Definitions*. In both of these sets of definitions, "Bullion" is defined (through definitions of "Gold," "Silver," "Platinum" and "Palladium") to include gold and silver bars, if they comply with the rules of the London Bullion Market Association (LBMA), and platinum and palladium ingots and plate, if they comply with the rules of the London Platinum and Palladium Market (LPPM), as well as gold, silver, platinum and palladium that is credited to an unallocated account complying with the relevant LBMA or LPPM rules.[1434] The LBMA participated in the working group that produced

---

[1431] Although some of the terminology could be used to document physically settled transactions, the *1993/2000 ISDA Commodity Derivatives Definitions* do not deal with important issues raised by those contracts, such as what constitutes good delivery, the general consequences of failure to make good delivery in a timely manner and how any of those consequences should be treated differently if the failure is attributable to force majeure or similar circumstances beyond the control of the party required to make delivery. The physical markets for individual commodities or commodity classes may, naturally, have their own customs and standard terms relating to these and other issues, which reflect, among other things, the nature of the relevant commodity, the ways in which it is normally delivered and the possible availability of substitute sources of supply when force majeure is an issue. Within the specialized markets there are ongoing efforts among major market participants to standardize dealing terms.

[1432] Under the *1993/2000 ISDA Commodity Derivatives Definitions*, a cap or floor structure for a single period can be documented as an Option under Article 8 or as a cap or floor, using the appropriate terminology described in Section 6.2 of those definitions.

[1433] The *2000 Supplement* describes these changes at ii–v.

[1434] As described by the LBMA, in an unallocated account, "specific bars are not set aside and the customer has a general entitlement to the metal" and is an unsecured creditor. LONDON BULLION MARKET ASSOCIATION, GLOSSARY OF TERMS 12, *available at* www.lbma.org.uk/london_glossary.html. The use of unallocated accounts is described by the LBMA as "the most convenient, cheapest and most commonly used method of holding metal." *Id.* By way of contrast, delivery to an allocated account of a member of the

these sets of 1997 ISDA definitions and, as indicated in the ISDA introductions to the definitions, the 1994 International Bullion Master Agreement Terms (IBMA), published for the London and U.S. markets by the LBMA and the Foreign Exchange Committee, served as the basis for many of ISDA's bullion terms and provisions.[1435]

As discussed in more detail below, the long-form bullion definitions are designed for documenting what are referred to as "Bullion Trades," "Bullion Options," "Bullion Swaps" and "Swaptions." The Bullion Trades (Section 2.1) include both cash-settled and physically settled[1436] bullion spot and forward sales transactions. "Bullion Options" (Section 2.4) are traditional puts or calls, involving "the right, but not the obligation, of the Buyer to purchase from or, as the case may be, to sell to the Seller a specified number of Ounces of Bullion at the Strike Price." Bullion Swaps (Section 6.1) include cash-settled swaps, caps, collars and floors in respect of Bullion,[1437] and Swaptions (Section 6.10) include only options to cause a Bullion Swap to become effective. The short-form bullion definitions cover only physically settled spot and forward trades and options and only contemplate delivery of bullion on an unallocated basis.[1438]

LBMA occurs when a person "requires metal to be physically segregated and needs a detailed list of weights and assays," and if delivery is made to an allocated account, "the owner of the metal is a secured creditor." *Id.* at 1.

[1435] On the Foreign Exchange Committee, *see supra* note 58. The IBMA was preceded by the Bullion Option Guidelines published by the LBMA in 1990. The IBMA was produced by a working party established by the Management Committee of the LBMA and a working party in the U.S., which involved the Financial Markets Lawyers Group, a group of lawyers representing U.S. financial institutions, which was also involved in the preparation of the ICOM and IFEMA terms for FX spot and forward transactions and currency options. The Bank of England and the Federal Reserve Bank of New York were represented as observers on these working parties. The IBMA was published in 1994 in two versions: one governed by English law and one governed by New York law. The *Guide to the 1994 International Bullion Master Agreement* published at the same time (June 1994) describes the process and explains various provisions of the IBMA.

[1436] The general rule in the long-form definitions (Section 3.1) calls for delivery by credit to an unallocated account. Section 3.3 sets forth special rules for transactions where the parties agree that delivery will be made on an allocated basis. As described by the London Bullion Market Association, delivery to an allocated account of a member of the LBMA occurs when a person "requires metal to be physically segregated and needs a detailed list of weights and assays," and if delivery is made to an allocated account, "the owner of the metal is a secured creditor." LONDON BULLION MARKET ASSOCIATION, GLOSSARY OF TERMS p.1, *available at* www.lbma.org.uk/london_glossary.html. *Supra* note 1434 refers to the important differences when delivery is made to an unallocated account, as is the more common practice.

[1437] As used in connection with cash-settled swaps, caps, floors and collars with payment terms that are wholly dependent on futures traded on the NYMEX, and swaptions on these "Bullion Swaps," the 1997 definitions' reference to "Bullion" as defined to refer only to LBMA and LPPM rules is something of a technical anomaly, given the fact that the NYMEX has its own specifications for the underlying. The anomaly does not exist under the *1993/2000 ISDA Commodity Derivatives Definitions*.

[1438] Both of the 1997 sets of bullion definitions (Article 5 in the long-form definitions and Article 4 in the short-form definitions) provide that Bullion delivery obligations under transactions documented using those definitions will be treated as if they were obligations to make payments for purposes of Section 2(c)(ii) of the ISDA master agreement forms. As a result, if the parties have specified in their ISDA-based master agreement that their respective obligations due on the same date under different transactions will be netted, their Bullion delivery obligations will also be treated in this manner. Both sets of definitions also provide for

Commodity Derivatives 557

The *2000 Supplement* to the *1993 ISDA Commodity Derivatives Definitions* was not designed to be used as a supplement to the 1997 sets of ISDA bullion definitions but does update provisions that are useful for bullion market transactions. As a result, if the parties to these transactions have a preference for using the sets of ISDA bullion product-specific definitions published in 1997, they may in some cases find it useful to use those definitions along with updated provisions from the *2000 Supplement*.

FIXED AMOUNTS AND FLOATING AMOUNTS

The *1993/2000 ISDA Commodity Derivatives Definitions* provide terms that may be used in indicating how a party's payment obligations under a transaction will be calculated.[1439] In this respect, they are modeled on the terminology available in the *1991 ISDA Definitions* and *2000 ISDA Definitions* for documenting interest-rate and currency swaps and similar derivatives.

Fixed Amounts. As illustrated in the sample commodity swap confirmation below, if the parties have incorporated the *1993/2000 ISDA Commodity Derivatives Definitions* into the confirmation of a fixed/floating commodity price swap, and if they have specified the swap's Calculation Periods and Unit, and the Notional Quantity applicable for each of those periods, only one other thing must be stated in the confirmation to ensure that the Fixed Amount obligations of the Fixed Price Payer for each period will be determinable: the Fixed Price.[1440]

Under the formula in Section 5.1 of the *1993/2000 ISDA Commodity Derivatives Definitions*, the Fixed Price will automatically be applied to the Notional Quantity to determine the Fixed Amount for the Calculation Period. If the confirmation supplements an agreement prepared using an ISDA master agreement form, the Fixed Price Payer will automatically be obligated to pay the Fixed Amount on the relevant Payment Date, subject to netting against a Floating Amount payable by the other party on the same day—

---

novation netting of obligations in respect of transactions at the time they are executed, in much the same way as novation netting is provided for in the FEOMA, ICOM and IFEMA forms. *See infra* p. 950.

[1439] The kinds of provisions described below, which are included in the various sets of ISDA terms, for the determination of commodity prices are not included in the IBMA, which was designed primarily for use in documenting spot, forward and option transactions in bullion. Except for cash-settled options, those transactions do not require the determination of a bullion price in connection with settlement; the parties will have specified the contract price at which settlement is to occur, or the strike price relevant in connection with a physically settled option. Where cash-settled options are concerned, it is necessary to compare the agreed Strike Price with a Spot Price for the relevant metal to determine any "In-the-Money Amount" that will be payable. The IBMA as published in 1994 provides that, unless the option buyer specifies otherwise, the spot price of the relevant metal will be as determined in good faith by the seller. *See IBMA Guide* 24 ("The Buyer should, therefore, ascertain at the outset how the Seller will determine the Spot Price"). Under Section 5.5 of the IBMA, the buyer is entitled, when giving its Notice of Exercise of the option, to "require that the In-the-Money Amount of the Bullion Option be ascertained with reference to the U.S. dollar bid or offer price, as appropriate, per Ounce quoted by the Seller to the Buyer at 9:30 a.m. New York time on the Exercise Date (in the case of an American Style Option) or the Expiration Date (in the case of a European Style Option) converted, if necessary, into the Option Currency at the price at which, at such time, the Seller could enter into a contract in the foreign exchange market to buy the Option Currency in exchange for U.S. dollars."

[1440] *See* Annotation 15 to that sample confirmation, *infra* p. 579.

and other qualifications in the master agreement, on matters such as conditions precedent and early termination.[1441] The third sample confirmation following this Introduction and its annotations illustrate how the same conventions apply to Bullion Swaps under the *1997 ISDA Bullion Definitions*.[1442]

Floating Amounts. Under the *1993/2000 ISDA Commodity Derivatives Definitions*, the Floating Amounts, like the Fixed Amounts, are calculated on the Notional Quantity specified for the relevant Calculation Period. The terminology used to specify how Floating Amounts should be determined, applying the formula and rules in Article 6 of those definitions, is somewhat complex. The same may be said for the rules regarding "Market Disruption Events" and "Additional Market Disruption Events," which may operate to alter the parties' preferred method for determining Floating Amounts, as discussed in the next section,

In each case, the Floating Amounts will be determined using a Commodity Reference Price. The term "Commodity Reference Price" is shorthand for the parties' choice of means for determining a Relevant Price for each Pricing Date in the Calculation Period. These terms in the *1993/2000 ISDA Commodity Derivatives Definitions* can be thought of as serving the same function as the Relevant Rate for each Reset Date in a Calculation Period under the *1991 ISDA Definitions* or the *2000 ISDA Definitions*. Under the *1997 ISDA Bullion Definitions*, the equivalent framework for Floating Amounts for Bullion Swaps involves the choice of a "Bullion Reference Price" as the means for determining a Relevant Price for each Pricing Date in a Calculation Period.

Determining Commodity Reference Prices or Bullion Reference Prices requires that quotations be obtained from Reference Dealers or prices obtained from a specified Price Source—an electronic or print publication or an Exchange on which a relevant futures contract is listed. The Reference Dealers must be polled or the Price Source must be consulted for a "Specified Price."

Under the *1993/2000 ISDA Commodity Derivatives Definitions*, the parties choose this Specified Price by indicating whether they wish to use, say, a Pricing Date's opening or closing price, bid or asked price, high or low price, morning or afternoon fixing, an average of any of these alternatives or any other price for the commodity or futures contract specified by the parties in the transaction's confirmation. The *1997 ISDA Bullion Definitions* do not use the term "Specified Price" and offer a more limited range of choices, involving only morning or afternoon fixing prices and the relevant futures settlement price published by the COMEX or the NYMEX.

The Relevant Prices determined from these data for the Pricing Dates in a period—and the parties must specify what those Pricing Dates will be—are automatically used to determine the particular period's Floating Price, giving effect to any applicable Method of Averaging if there is more than one Pricing Date in the period. The averaging approach will be as specified by the parties or, if they fail to specify their choice, will

---

[1441] *See* Sections 2(a) & 2(c) of the sample master agreement included in Part 3, *infra* pp. 800 & 807.

[1442] The formula and related provisions involving the determination of Fixed Amounts are included in Section 8.1 of the *1997 ISDA Bullion Definitions* and work with the definitions in Articles 6 and 7.

automatically involve taking the arithmetic mean of the Relevant Prices determined for the Pricing Dates in the particular Calculation Period.[1443]

Under the *1993/2000 ISDA Commodity Derivatives Definitions* and the *1997 ISDA Bullion Definitions*, all of the terminology and mechanisms used to determine a Floating Price for a swap, cap, floor or collar are also used in connection with cash-settled options. The applicable provisions are Sections 8.7 and 8.8 of the *1993/2000 ISDA Commodity Derivatives Definitions* and Sections 4.2 and 4.3 of the *1997 ISDA Bullion Definitions*. Under the former, this is so because cash settlement requires the payment of a Cash Settlement Amount calculated on the Notional Quantity at the "Strike Price Differential," the amount, if positive, by which the agreed Strike Price exceeds the Floating Price for the agreed Settlement Date. Similarly, under the *1997 ISDA Bullion Definitions* cash settlement requires the payment of an In-the-Money Amount calculated on the relevant number of Ounces of Bullion to be purchased at the difference between the Relevant Price and the agreed Contract Price, if the Relevant Price exceeds the Contract Price. The approach is also similar under the *1997 Short Form Bullion Definitions* (Section 2.7) for Bullion Options that are treated as automatically exercised.[1444] That is, the In-the-Money Amount is defined in the same terms but, unless the parties have agreed otherwise, the Relevant Price is left to the option seller to determine in good faith,[1445] since these short-form definitions were designed for use only in connection with physically settled transactions and, therefore, do not include defined terms or other procedures for determining a Relevant Price.

COMMODITY REFERENCE PRICES

Under the *1993/2000 ISDA Commodity Derivatives Definitions*, there are three ways in which the parties may specify the Commodity Reference Price to be used in determining Floating Amounts. The first two are identified using the terms "COMMODITY-REFERENCE DEALERS" and "COMMODITY REFERENCE PRICE FRAMEWORK."[1446] The third approach involves the adoption of Commodity Reference Price nomenclature listed in subsection (a) or (b) of Section 7.1 of these ISDA definitions. Each of the approaches is summarized below. Under the *1997 ISDA Bullion Definitions*, only

---

[1443] *See* Annotation 23 to the sample commodity swap confirmation, *infra* p. 581, and Annotation 5 to the sample commodity floor confirmation, *infra* p. 590, for illustrations using the *1993/2000 ISDA Commodity Derivatives Definitions* and the *1997 ISDA Bullion Definitions*, respectively.

[1444] Under those definitions, a Bullion Option will be deemed exercised, under Section 2.6(b)), unless the parties have agreed otherwise, if the In-the-Money Amount at the Expiration Time equals or exceeds the product of one percent (or another agreed percentage) of the Strike Price and the number of Ounces of Bullion which are the subject of the Bullion Option.

[1445] The seller must use the price that it determines in good faith would be quoted by it "to market counterparties at the Expiration Time as being (i) the bid price for a Bullion spot or forward transaction for delivery on the Settlement Date (where the Bullion Option is a Call Option) or (ii) the offer price for a Bullion spot or forward transaction (where the Bullion Option is a put Option) for delivery on the settlement date, such price to be quoted in the same currency as the Strike Price and to be in respect of one Ounce of the relevant type of Bullion." *1997 Short Form Bullion Definitions* § 2.7(a). *See supra* note 1439 on the similar formulation in the IBMA as published in 1994.

[1446] In the *1993 ISDA Commodity Derivatives Definitions*, the methodology to be applied using these two approaches was set out in Sections 7.1(c)(i) and (ii); under those definitions as supplemented by the *2000 Supplement*, the applicable rules are set out in Sections 7.1(d)(i) and (ii).

the first and third alternatives are available. They are identified in those 1997 definitions through a choice of "BULLION-REFERENCE DEALERS" or a specified Bullion Reference Price.

Commodity Reference Dealers. Under the first of the three alternatives available under the *1993/2000 ISDA Commodity Derivatives Definitions*, the parties may adopt the approach detailed in Section 7.1(d)(i), which uses price quotations (of the Specified Price for the relevant commodity) sought on each Pricing Date from four Reference Dealers to determine that Pricing Date's Relevant Price. If the confirmation does not identify the Reference Dealers, they will be leading dealers in the relevant commodity market chosen by the Calculation Agent.

If three or more quotations are obtained, they are averaged to produce the day's Relevant Price, after disregarding the highest and lowest quoted values. If fewer than three are obtained, a "Price Source Disruption" (one of several "Market Disruption Events") will be treated as having occurred.[1447] The consequences of this disruption will, as described below,[1448] depend on the Disruption Fallbacks chosen by the parties.

Section 11.2 of the *1997 ISDA Bullion Definitions* provides the equivalent approach of using quotations from reference dealers for Bullion Swaps documented using those definitions. One difference from the approach in the *1993/2000 ISDA Commodity Derivatives Definitions* is that the quotations must be sought from the principal London office of each of the Reference Dealers, since the presumption in the 1997 product-specific definitions for bullion transactions is that the relevant market for all the transactions will be in London.

The Commodity Reference Price Framework. The Commodity Reference Price Framework set out in Section 7.1(d)(ii) of the *1993/2000 ISDA Commodity Derivatives Definitions* is, as indicated, a second approach that may be used to identify how the parties will go about determining Floating Amounts under the *1993/2000 ISDA Commodity Derivatives Definitions*. This approach may be used to identify the parties' choice of a futures-based or cash-market-based price benchmark, if Section 7.1 of those definitions does not include ISDA nomenclature for the particular benchmark. Although Section 7.1(d)(ii) does not so contemplate, the approach may also be used if the parties simply prefer to spell out key relevant features of their price benchmark rather than using one of ISDA's listed defined terms.

The Commodity Reference Price Framework applicable under Section 7.1(d)(ii) is implemented somewhat differently depending on whether the Relevant Price for a Pricing Date will be a Specified Price for a futures contract or a Specified Price in the cash market for the underlying Commodity, and whether the relevant Price Source will, therefore, be an Exchange or a published print or electronic source. In effect, there is a Futures Exchange Framework and there is also a Cash Market Framework. In all cases, the Commodity must be specified with all relevant details involving grade or type and Delivery Date. Defined terms elsewhere in the *1993/2000 ISDA Commodity Derivatives Definitions* may be used to identify the Price Source, Delivery Date and other necessary

---

[1447] Market Disruption Events are discussed in detail *infra* at p. 564.

[1448] *Infra* p. 569.

Commodity Derivatives 561

details. The following examples illustrate how the details could be completed in a confirmation using ISDA's Commodity Reference Price Framework alternatives.

Futures Exchange Framework (Section 7.1(d)(ii)(A))	
Commodity:	Oil, light sweet crude (NYMEX WTI)
Unit:	Barrel
Exchange:	NYMEX
Relevant Currency:	USD
Specified Price:	Closing price
Delivery Date:	First Nearby Month[1449]

Cash Market Framework (Section 7.1(d)(ii)(B))	
Unit:	Barrel
Price Source:	APPI[1450]
Heading:	"Crude Oils: Code/Crude: 2(B) Tapis"
Relevant Currency:	USD
Specified Price:	Average of high and low
Delivery Date:	First Nearby Month

Listed Commodity Reference Prices. Under the *1993/2000 ISDA Commodity Derivatives Definitions*, as indicated, the third approach to specifying Commodity Reference Prices involves using ISDA nomenclature listed in Section 7.1. This nomenclature generally has two or three parts, separated by dashes, which together serve as shorthand for the ISDA descriptions of the relevant futures-based or cash-market based benchmarks for the commodity chosen.

So, for example, OIL–WTI–NYMEX is the ISDA term for the Commodity Reference Price that prescribes determining the Relevant Price for a barrel of crude oil for a Pricing Date by looking at the Specified Price (*e.g.*, Closing Price) in U.S. dollars for the

---

[1449]*See* Annotation 21 to the first sample confirmation following this introduction for explanation of the illustrated approach to specifying the Delivery Date, *infra* p. 581.

[1450]This term is defined in the *2000 Supplement* (§ 7.2(a)(i)) to mean "Asian Petroleum Price Index, or any successor report, prepared by KPMG Corporate Services Limited, Hong Kong or its successor and reported in the Energy Market Information Service or its successor." Use of the defined term eliminates the need to specify rules about successor publications, but the parties are free to identify the Price Source in any way that will clearly indicate their intent.

NYMEX futures contract with a specified Delivery Date (*e.g.*, the First Nearby Month's contract on that particular Pricing Date), for the light sweet crude oil commonly referred to as WTI, or West Texas intermediate, which meets the applicable NYMEX specifications.

When the parties choose this approach, they simply set out the ISDA term in their confirmation, generally with little more in the way of details, to specify a choice of Commodity Reference Price for determining Floating Amounts. The following examples illustrate how the details could be completed in a confirmation using ISDA's Listed Term approach, for the same two transactions assumed in the preceding illustrations of the Commodity Reference Price Framework approach:

Listed Term Approach Futures Market-based Specified Price (Section 7.1(a) or (b), depending on commodity)	
Commodity Reference Price:	OIL–WTI–NYMEX
Specified Price:	Closing price
Delivery Date:	First Nearby Month

Listed Term Approach Cash Market-based Specified Price (Section 7.1(a) or(b), depending on commodity)	
Commodity Reference Price:	OIL–TAPIS–APPI
Specified Price:	Average of high and low
Delivery Date:	First Nearby Month

As illustrated in the following sample confirmation for a commodity floor transaction,[1451] when the parties establish a Commodity Reference Price for a transaction using one of the Commodity Reference Price Frameworks, they must be careful to specify all key terms, including some that need not be mentioned when the parties, instead, use one of ISDA's listed defined terms for Commodity Reference Prices. The defined term approach, for example, already includes the unit and currency in which price reports are provided, the grade or type of commodity and, where relevant, the identifying delivery point, as well as the way in which the relevant price appears on the relevant electronic or print source. These are details that the parties themselves may have to specify using one of the ISDA Commodity Reference Price Frameworks. Some institutions nonetheless prefer the Commodity Reference Price Framework approach precisely because it requires identification of the terms that traders discuss when they negotiate and execute transac-

---

[1451] *Infra* p. 590.

tions, whereas the listed ISDA nomenclature for Commodity Reference Prices is less transparent.

Regardless of the method chosen by the parties for specifying the Commodity Reference Price, they must always consider whether the relevant Price Source supplies pricing data in a currency other than that used in their transaction for the relevant Floating Amount payments. If the currencies are different, the parties will have to provide a rule for translating the reported prices to the currency in which the payments will be due. They may find it convenient to do this in stating the Specified Price (*e.g.*, "Specified Price: the USD equivalent (calculated as provided below) of the average of the reported high and low prices").

The list of Commodity Reference Prices in subsections (a) and (b) of Section 7.1 of the *1993/2000 ISDA Commodity Derivatives Definitions*, as broadened in the *2000 Supplement*, is quite comprehensive for transactions in tangible energy products and metals and, as noted, includes updated versions of the Bullion Reference Prices included in the *1997 ISDA Bullion Definitions*. Section 7.1 also lists a futures-based Commodity Reference Price for woodpulp and various choices for electricity. The following is a summary of these listed choices.

Energy. The energy-related indexes in the *1993/2000 ISDA Commodity Derivatives Definitions* include benzene, diesel fuel, fuel oil, gas oil, gasoline, heating oil, jet fuel, kerosene, methanol, naphtha, natural gas, natural gas liquids and various blends and types of crude oil (Brent, Tapis, Dubai and West Texas Intermediate). The price sources for Commodity Reference Prices based on cash-market prices of these commodities comprise various *Platt's* reports (including *Platt's Crude Oil Marketwire* and *Platt's Oilgram Price Report*) and other publications of The McGraw-Hill Companies, *Argus* publications, the Asian Petroleum Price Index reported on the Energy Market Information Service, *Inside F.E.R.C.'s Gas Market Report*, *LOR World Crude Report*, *Natural Gas Intelligence*, *Natural Gas Week*, specialized sources for benzene and ethanol prices, and several U.K. sources for natural gas prices. The price sources for Commodity Reference Prices based on futures contract prices of these tangible energy products include the NYMEX (the New York Mercantile Exchange), the IPE (The International Petroleum Exchange of London Ltd.) and the Kansas City Board of Trade. Numerous electricity indexes are also included, with *Power Markets Week*, CEPI Market Report, www.apx.nl (posted by the Amsterdam Power Exchange) and Telerate as price sources for cash-market prices and NYMEX for futures contract prices.

Metals. The metals included in the *1993/2000 ISDA Commodity Derivatives Definitions* are aluminum, copper, gold, lead, nickel, platinum, silver, tin and zinc, of specified grades and for delivery at specified places. The price sources for these metals are cash-market and futures-contract based and include the *Financial Times*, *Metal Bulletin*, the Reuters Money Rates Service, the COMEX (the Commodity Exchange Inc., New York), the LBMA, the LPPM, the LME (The London Metal Exchange Limited) and the NYMEX.

Where metals are concerned, these sources expand on those provided in the *1997 ISDA Bullion Definitions* for gold, palladium, platinum and silver.[1452] The *1997 Short Form Bullion Definitions* cover the same four metals, but, as noted above, only for bullion spot and forward trades and options to be physically settled through delivery to an unallocated account.

Pulp and Paper. Only one index is included in this category in the *1993/2000 ISDA Commodity Derivatives Definitions*: a Commodity Reference Price based on the price for the futures contract on northern bleached softwood kraft pulp traded on the OM London Exchange, Ltd., as published on a Reuters screen.

MARKET DISRUPTION EVENTS

Market disruptions and similar circumstances pose particularly important documentation concerns for those involved with swaps and similar commodity derivatives and for options subject to cash settlement. This is so because, if a "Market Disruption Event" or "Additional Market Disruption Event" occurs, the parties' first choice of Commodity Reference Price may be replaced by another, a Relevant Price may be ignored or adjusted, the Pricing Date may be deferred or, ultimately, the transaction may be terminated prematurely. If the parties are silent with respect to their choice of Market Disruption Events, they will be deemed to have chosen a standard list of events and circumstances specified in Section 7.4(d) of the *1993/2000 ISDA Commodity Derivatives Definitions* or in Section 10.1(d) of the *1997 ISDA Bullion Definitions*.[1453]

These consequences flow from Market Disruption Events and Additional Market Disruption Events because the relevant events and circumstances may have made it impossible to determine a Relevant Price for a Pricing Date using the parties' preferred method or, in some cases, because the agreed method may not be reliable or cannot be relied on to reflect the economics of the transaction bargained for by the parties.

Eight types of Market Disruption Events are covered in Section 7.4 of the *1993/2000 ISDA Commodity Derivatives Definitions*:

[1452]In those 1997 definitions, the available alternatives were the morning and afternoon fixing prices as determined by the "London Gold Market" and the "London Silver Market" (defined (in Sections 1.12 and 1.13) to refer to the market in London on which members of the LBMA, among other things, quote prices for the buying and selling of gold or silver complying with LBMA requirements) or the London Platinum and Palladium Market. The LBMA is the updated source for the gold and silver fixings under the *2000 Supplement* to the *1993 ISDA Commodity Derivatives Definitions*. For transactions based on futures contract prices, the alternatives under the 1997 definitions are COMEX prices for gold and silver and NYMEX prices for platinum and palladium. The *1993 ISDA Commodity Derivatives Definitions* as originally published included three price sources for gold and silver—market prices as published in the *Financial Times* (in the case of gold) or the *Metal Bulletin* (in the case of silver); delivery prices made public by COMEX on the relevant Pricing Date for delivery on the relevant Delivery Date; and prices calculated by the LBMA and displayed on a Reuters screen (in the case of gold) or published in the *Financial Times* (in the case of silver). For platinum, the two sources included were market prices as published in the *Metal Bulletin* for cash-market prices and futures contract prices as made public by NYMEX on the relevant Pricing Date. Palladium was not covered.

[1453]Similarly, if the parties document a non-deliverable currency forward under the *1998 FX and Currency Option Definitions* and are silent about disruption events, they will be deemed to have specified that "Price Source Disruption" as defined in that set of definitions will apply to their transaction. *See supra* p. 491.

Price Source Disruption—Generally speaking, the temporary or permanent unavailability of an agreed Price Source or of the information necessary for determining the Specified Price. The *1993/2000 ISDA Commodity Derivatives Definitions* provide for four sorts of Price Source Disruption: (1) Failure of the Price Source to announce or publish the Specified Price or the information necessary to calculate the Specified Price for the relevant Commodity Reference Price; (2) temporary or permanent discontinuance or unavailability of the Price Source; (3) in the case of "COMMODITY-REFERENCE DEALERS," the failure to obtain at least three of the requested quotations; and, (4) if the Parties specify Price Materiality and the Specified Price as determined in accordance with the Commodity Reference Price differs from what it would have been if it had been determined in accordance with "COMMODITY-REFERENCE DEALERS" by a specified "Price Materiality Percentage" (or, presumably, more).

Trading Suspension—A lesser, but still material, suspension of trading in the relevant Futures Contract or Commodity on the applicable Exchange or in any additional market specified.

Disappearance of Commodity Reference Price—The disappearance of the relevant Commodity or the cessation of trading in that Commodity; or the failure of trading to commence, or the permanent discontinuation of trading, in the relevant Futures Contract on the applicable Exchange.

Material Change in Formula—A material change after the relevant Trade Date in the formula or method used to calculate the applicable Commodity Reference Price.

Material Change in Content—A material change after the relevant Trade Date in the content, composition or constitution of the relevant Commodity or Futures Contract.

***De Minimis* Trading**—Trading in the relevant Futures Contract becomes so limited (defined by reference to a specified Minimum Futures Contracts number) that the parties wish to treat the circumstance as tantamount to a discontinuation of trading.

Tax Disruption—The imposition or removal of or a change in certain kinds of taxes on the relevant Commodity, if the direct result is to raise or lower the Relevant Price.

Trading Limitation—A material limitation imposed on trading in the relevant Futures Contract or Commodity on the applicable Exchange or in any additional market specified.

Some of these events will automatically apply unless the parties specify otherwise, and there are various ways in which the parties may specify which they wish to have apply or not apply. Also, the parties may wish to identify the consequences of disruptive events and circumstances that are not covered by the ISDA definitions, if the event or circumstance, or its nonoccurrence, is critical to the parties' bargain. When this is the case, the parties may use the term "Additional Market Disruption Event" to identify the relevant event or circumstance.

The *1997 ISDA Bullion Definitions* (Section 10.1) contain a somewhat abbreviated version of the Market Disruption Events found in the *1993/2000 ISDA Commodity Derivatives Definitions*. Three types of Market Disruption Events are covered:

> **Price Source Disruption**—Like the *1993/2000 ISDA Commodity Derivatives Definitions*, these definitions provide for (1) Failure of the Price Source to announce or publish the Specified Price or the information necessary to calculate the Specified Price for the relevant Commodity Reference Price; (2) temporary or permanent discontinuance or unavailability of the Price Source; and (3) in the case of "BULLION-REFERENCE DEALERS," the failure to obtain at least three of the requested quotations. The bullion version does not, however, contain provisions relating to the effects of specifying Price Materiality.
>
> **Trading Suspension or Limitation**—As the name suggests, this Market Disruption Event combines Trading Suspension and Trading Limitation as included in the *1993/2000 ISDA Commodity Derivatives Definitions*.
>
> **Disappearance of Bullion Reference Price**—The disappearance of the relevant commodity or the cessation of trading in that commodity; or the failure of trading to commence, or the permanent discontinuation of trading, in the relevant Futures Contract on the applicable Exchange.

The *1997 ISDA Bullion Definitions* and the *1997 Short Form Bullion Definitions* do not treat the imposition of taxes as a possible Market Disruption Event and, in fact, expressly allocate as between the parties to a transaction the burden of value added taxes that may be imposed either on a party, as a supplier of Bullion subject to VAT, or on a third party treated by applicable law or by the practice of a relevant fiscal authority as chargeable for purposes of VAT with a supply made under a transaction, on account of a party's delivery obligations.[1454]

Both the *1997 ISDA Bullion Definitions* and the *1997 Short Form Bullion Definitions* contain (in Section 3.4) a definition of "Settlement Disruption Event" and a set of rules on how to deal with Settlement Disruption Events affecting transactions to which Settlement by Delivery (physical settlement) applies. For these purposes, a Settlement Disruption Event is "an event beyond the control of the parties as a result of which delivery cannot be effected by the method of delivery specified by the parties."[1455]

[1454]For background on these provisions relating to VAT, *see IBMA Guide* 18.

[1455]The equivalent provision in Section 9 of the IBMA is applicable if either party "is prevented from or hindered or delayed by reason of force majeure or act of State in the delivery or receipt of any Bullion or Currency in respect of a Bullion Obligation or Bullion Option." That provision simply calls for close-out and liquidation of the relevant transactions, at the election of either party. The IBMA does not address the kinds of events or circumstances that the ISDA definitions treat as Market Disruption Events because, as

Selecting the Applicable Market Disruption Events.—Under Section 7.4(d)(i) of the *1993/2000 ISDA Commodity Derivatives Definitions*, the first five events listed above will automatically be deemed to be Market Disruption Events applicable to a transaction unless the parties agree otherwise. Similarly, under the *1997 ISDA Bullion Definitions* (Section 10.1(d)), all three listed events will apply if the parties are silent on the subject. Therefore, market participants that adopt these ISDA definitions must be aware of these default choices and, if they wish only part of the standard package to apply, they must specify their choice or choices.[1456] If the parties have agreed that all those "default" choices should apply and have also agreed on other Market Disruption Events, those other events may be listed as "Additional Market Disruption Events." Under the *1993/2000 ISDA Commodity Derivatives Definitions*, the statement "Market Disruption Event: Inapplicable," will mean that none of the ISDA default choices will apply and that the parties have not agreed on any Additional Market Disruption Events;[1457] no similar rule is stated in the *1997 ISDA Bullion Definitions*.

Some of the listed events or circumstances relate to both futures-contract based and cash-market based Price Sources. Others may be most appropriate in transactions using Commodity Reference Prices based on commodity price indexes or futures on such indexes, and the parties may wish to avoid choosing those Market Disruption Events if they are concerned that the choice could produce an unintended result. For example, Material Change in Formula in the *1993/2000 ISDA Commodity Derivatives Definitions* is defined as "the occurrence since the Trade Date of the Transaction of a material change in the formula for or the method of calculating the relevant Commodity Reference Price." Although appropriate where the Commodity Reference Price is based on a commodity price index or futures on such an index, this event should not, presumably, be applied to published Price Sources, like the *Platt's Oilgram Price Report*, that report prices based on the publisher's judgment reached after making inquiries of participants in the cash market. In these cases, an objective description of the method used may not be available.

Adapting ISDA's Definitions of Market Disruption Events. One area where market participants consider modifications to ISDA's standard terms relates to the time at which the problem condition must exist in order to constitute a Market Disruption Event. Generally speaking, a Market Disruption Event is triggered under Section 7.4(a) of the *1993/2000 ISDA Commodity Derivatives Definitions* and Section 10.1(c) of the *1997 ISDA Bullion Definitions* if the event or condition occurs or exists "on a day that is a Pricing Date" for the relevant transaction, or "if different, the day on which prices for that Pricing Date would, in the ordinary course, be published or announced by the Price Source."

By its own terms, however, the Price Source Disruption event is somewhat narrower because it only exists if the agreed Price Source does not announce or publish the

---

indicated *supra* note 1439, the IBMA does not generally provide guidelines for how the parties may determine bullion prices.

[1456] *See* Section 7.4(d)(ii) of the *1993/2000 ISDA Commodity Derivatives Definitions* and Section 10.1(d)(ii) of the *1997 ISDA Bullion Definitions*, which provide that, if a confirmation specifies one or more Market Disruption Events as applicable to a transaction, only those specified will apply.

[1457] *See* Section 7.4(c) of the *1993/2000 ISDA Commodity Derivatives Definitions*.

Specified Price (or information necessary to determine the Specified Price) for the relevant Commodity Reference Price. Therefore, if the parties have, say, indicated that the Specified Price for a transaction will be the closing price for a futures contract on an agreed Exchange, under the narrower test just described a Price Source Disruption would have occurred if the closing price for the specified Futures Contract were not announced and the information necessary for determining it were not made available by the Exchange, but it would not have occurred if the opening price was not available but the closing price was. If this is the parties' intention and they would not wish to treat a temporary problem on the Exchange earlier in the day as Price Source Disruption, they may want to clarify the matter in their documents.

Similar limitations may be appropriate for other Market Disruption Events. For example, when the parties' agreed Specified Price is a closing price, they may wish to narrow the definition or applicability of Trading Suspension so that a material suspension of trading in the relevant Futures Contract early in the day on a Pricing Date will not result in recourse to a fallback Price Source if trading resumes later in the day. Similarly, where the Specified Price is the opening price, it may be inappropriate to treat a material suspension later in the day as a Trading Suspension.

Market participants sometimes also consider changes aimed at giving more objective content to the concepts of material suspension or material limitation. In this area, where futures are concerned, exchange rules about "circuit breaker" trading halts and existing contract specifications about daily price limits may be relevant. Under the *1993/2000 ISDA Commodity Derivatives Definitions* and the *1997 ISDA Bullion Definitions*, the decision on whether an event or circumstance is material ultimately falls to the Calculation Agent, after consultation with the other party or, if the Calculation Agent is a third party, after consultation with both parties. If the parties cannot agree at the outset on objective tests for materiality, and if—as is generally the case—the Calculation Agent is one of the parties, it is sometimes agreed that the Calculation Agent's determination of the existence of Market Disruption Events (or of some such events) will be subject to a dispute resolution mechanism involving a third party.

These issues relating to the possible narrowing, or definition, of material suspension or material limitation, should naturally be considered in the context of the particular commodity and futures contract and the parties' expectations. For example, where the NYMEX Henry Hub natural gas futures contracts are concerned, the exchange sets a maximum daily price fluctuation of $1.00 per mmBtu ($10,000 per contract) for all delivery months, if a contract is traded, bid or offered at the limit for five minutes, trading is halted for 15 minutes and, when trading resumes, expanded limits apply and the price is permitted to fluctuate by $2.00 in either direction of the previous day's settlement price. Those are the general rules, but they do not apply during the last three days of trading in the spot month.[1458] The ISDA rules on material trading suspensions do not indicate whether or at what point a trading suspension during those last three days of trading might be treated as a Market Disruption Event.

[1458] *See* NEW YORK MERCANTILE EXCHANGE, HENRY HUB NATURAL GAS, *available at* www.nymex.com/markets/cont_all.cfm (visited on March 21, 2001).

Other issues may also arise given the particular nature of the parties' transaction. For example, if a transaction has a relatively long term and involves a depleting commodity, parties that might otherwise not choose the *De Minimis* Trading Market Disruption Event might find it an appropriate choice if modified so that it would only trigger recourse to a Fallback Reference Price or other Market Disruption Fallback (as described below) if fewer than the Minimum Futures Contracts specified by the parties traded on a succession of Pricing Dates.

Finally, the parties may not want to treat a Tax Disruption Event as a Market Disruption Event if the payment obligations of the parties are equally affected by the event, and, if they have looked to commodity dealers to determine a Pricing Date's Relevant Price, either as their primary Commodity Reference Price or as a fallback, they may not wish to treat the dealer poll as having been unsuccessful merely because fewer than three quotations have been obtained. This would be especially so if the consequence would be a disruptive postponement or, ultimately, the premature termination of the transaction.

DISRUPTION FALLBACKS

Section 7.4(e) of the *1993/2000 ISDA Commodity Derivatives Definitions* provides that the Relevant Price for a Pricing Date will be determined in accordance with the first applicable Disruption Fallback if the Calculation Agent, after consultation with the parties (or the other party, if the Calculation Agent is one of the parties), determines in good faith that a Market Disruption Event or Additional Market Disruption Event has occurred or exists on a Pricing Date for the relevant Transaction, or "if different, the day on which prices for that Pricing Date would, in the ordinary course, be published or announced by the Price Source."

Section 7.5 of the *1993/2000 ISDA Commodity Derivatives Definitions* specifies various types of Disruption Fallbacks that the parties can choose to have apply in the case of a Market Disruption Event or Additional Market Disruption Event. Eight types of Disruption Fallbacks are covered:

Fallback Reference Dealers—The effect of selecting this fallback is to have the Relevant Price for the applicable Pricing Date determined using the average of dealer quotations, after disregarding the high and low values quoted if at least three quotations are obtained. This fallback is of course appropriate only if the parties' first choice of Commodity Reference Price does not itself rely on dealer quotations.

Fallback Reference Price—In order to use this Disruption Fallback, the parties must specify the same sorts of details for the fallback Commodity Reference Price as they would have to supply for their primary choice. The definition of "Fallback Reference Price" requires that the appropriate details be specified as relating to an "alternate Commodity Reference Price" specified by the parties. If more than one alternate is specified, they are to be tried in the order in which they are listed, in the effort to obtain the Relevant Price.

Postponement–Fallback Reference Price—This fallback combines Postponement (described below) with elements of Fallback Reference Dealers and Fallback Reference Price. If the postponements prescribed by the Postponement method would otherwise go beyond the specified Maximum Days of Disruption, and if the parties have specified one or more alternate Commodity Reference Prices, the last Commodity Business Day in the period of Postponement will become the applicable Pricing Date and the Calculation Agent will determine the Relevant Price using the applicable alternate Commodity Reference Price. If the parties have not specified an alternate Commodity Reference Price, the Relevant Price will be determined on the basis of quotations from dealers in accordance with the methodology summarized above.

Negotiated Fallback—Negotiated Fallback calls for good faith negotiations between the parties for a period ending not later than the fifth Business Day after the first Pricing Date on which a Market Disruption Event occurred or existed. If agreement on a Relevant Price, or method for determining it, is not reached by the end of that period, the next applicable Disruption Fallback is to be used.

No Fault Termination—This fallback results in early termination of the affected Transaction as if both parties were Affected Parties.[1459] Since the Market Disruption Event that has given rise to the need for a Disruption Fallback by definition has made it difficult or impossible to determine a Floating Price for the affected transaction, the determination of the Settlement Amount with respect to that transaction for the Floating Rate Payer (or the affected Floating Rate Payer) is likely, at best, to be difficult. Therefore, Market Disruption Events and Disruption Fallbacks should be drafted so as to minimize the possibility that No Fault Termination will occur.

Postponement—Postponement calls for the parties to specify Maximum Days of Disruption. Under this fallback, a Pricing Date affected by a Market Disruption Event will be postponed for consecutive Commodity Business Days until a Relevant Price can be determined, but the postponement cannot go beyond the Maximum Days of Disruption. If it would, the next applicable Disruption Fallback will apply. If the Floating Price for a Floating Amount payable on a Settlement Date or Payment Date cannot be determined as a result of Postponement, the Settlement Date or Payment Date will be postponed to the same extent as the relevant Pricing Date. Postponement may not be an appropriate choice for all transactions. Market participants may find it appropriate to define Maximum Days of Disruption as consecutive Commodity Business Days in a single Calculation Period, so as to limit the occasions on which they may have to postpone Settlement Dates or Payment Dates.

Calculation Agent Determination—This fallback calls for the Calculation Agent to determine the Relevant Price for the affected Pricing Date on the basis of "the latest available quotation for the rele-

---

[1459] *See supra* p. 246.

vant Commodity Reference Price and any other information that in good faith it deems relevant."

Average Daily Price Disruption—Like Postponement, this fallback requires that the parties specify Maximum Days of Disruption. It provides that a Pricing Date affected by a Market Disruption Event will not be included in the calculation of a Floating Amount, but the limit placed on Pricing Dates in the same Calculation Period that can be treated in this manner is the number specified as "Maximum Days of Disruption." If Market Disruption Events affect more than that number of Pricing Dates in a Calculation Period, the definition of this Disruption Fallback automatically provides that an applicable "alternate Commodity Reference Price" must be used for additional affected Pricing Dates. Average Daily Price Disruption may not be an appropriate choice for all transactions and, even if appropriate, it may require completion with a different number of Maximum Days of Disruption from that specified for Postponement. For example, in a Transaction with a small number of Pricing Dates, or only a single Pricing Date, in a Calculation Period, disregarding even one Pricing Date may be inappropriate, or the parties may agree to specify that one Commodity Business Day is the Maximum Days of Disruption for that Disruption Fallback but specify a greater number for Postponement.

The *1997 ISDA Bullion Definitions* (Section 10.2) contains a shorter list of Disruption Fallbacks, very similar to those found in the *1993 ISDA Commodity Derivatives Definitions* before the publication of the *2000 Supplement*; that is, they include the fallbacks listed above, but without Fallback Reference Dealers or Postponement–Fallback Reference Price. These bullion definitions differ further in two respects: No Fault Termination is to be calculated as if the affected Bullion Transaction "were the sole Terminated Transaction," and Average Daily Price Disruption is to apply only when more than one Pricing Date is applicable to the affected Calculation Period or Payment Date.

Market participants that adopt these sets of ISDA definitions should of course be familiar with these fallback choices and expressly include those they find appropriate for a particular transaction, for a particular Market Disruption Event or as a general matter. In establishing institutional guidelines for Disruption Fallbacks, market participants should consider the possibility that different templates of choices may be appropriate for different transaction classes. For example, fallbacks involving postponement of the determination of a Relevant Price and No Fault Termination are unlikely to be satisfactory choices for option transactions. The parties can also craft their own Disruption Fallbacks for use in lieu of or in addition to those listed in the applicable definitions. This is frequently an area of significant negotiation in transactions between dealers and end-users. The end-user will, naturally, seek to relate the fallbacks to the nature of the risk it is seeking to hedge. The dealer will press for adoption of its standard fallback mechanisms, to avoid basis risk between the particular transaction being negotiated and the aggregate obligations on the other relevant transactions in its portfolio, including the transaction or transactions designed to provide its hedge for the transaction being negotiated.

Section 7.5(d)(i) of the *1993/2000 ISDA Commodity Derivatives Definitions* lists the Disruption Fallbacks that will be deemed applicable, in the order there specified, if the parties do not override that provision by specifying the particular Disruption Fallbacks they have chosen. The three default choices supplied by Section 7.5(d)(i) are Fallback Reference Price (if the parties have specified an alternate Commodity Reference Price), Negotiated Fallback and No Fault Termination. As noted above, the existence of the Market Disruption Event that has given rise to the need for a Disruption Fallback may render it difficult to apply ISDA's No Fault Termination method.

Section 10.2(d) of the *1997 ISDA Bullion Definitions* reflects quite a different approach to the default choices. Here, if the parties do not override that provision, only two Disruption Fallbacks will apply: Fallback Reference Price (if the parties have specified an alternate Bullion Reference Price) and Calculation Agent Determination.

Pursuant to both sets of definitions, if the parties do specify Disruption Fallbacks, the Relevant Price will of course be determined in accordance with their choices, in the order specified. If this mechanism fails, and if the confirmation or agreement provides for the termination of the relevant Transaction in those circumstances, the Transaction will be terminated in accordance with the parties' agreement on the subject.

The *1997 ISDA Bullion Definitions 1997* and the *1997 Short Form Bullion Definitions* (Section 3.4(b)(i) in each case) deal with the consequences of the occurrence of a "Settlement Disruption Event" with respect to a physical-delivery transaction governed by those definitions. Two "Consequences of Settlement Disruption Events" are contemplated:

Negotiation—The Value Date—that is, the Bullion Business Date on which Bullion or Currency is to be delivered—is postponed until the first day on which delivery can be effected in accordance with the parties' original agreement, unless the Settlement Disruption Event prevents delivery for ten Bullion Business Days, in which case the definitions call for delivery in some other commercially reasonable manner, if one is available, or settlement of the transaction in some other commercially reasonable manner agreed to by the parties. No provision is made as to the course to be followed if there is no commercially reasonable way to make delivery (or if there is more than one), or as to what will happen if the parties fail to agree in the latter case.

Cancellation and Payment—The Value Date is postponed to a day on which delivery can be effected through a means agreed to by the parties, unless the Settlement Disruption Event prevents delivery for two Bullion Business Days, in which case an Early Termination Date will be deemed to have occurred, with the relevant Bullion Transaction as the sole Terminated Transaction and the party that was required to make the delivery as the Affected Party. The effect of having only one Affected Party in these circumstances is to value the transaction at the end of the bid-asked spread that is most favorable to the party that is to receive delivery.

Under Section 3.4(c) of both sets of ISDA's 1997 bullion definitions, Cancellation and Payment will be deemed to have been specified by the parties, if the parties do not override that provision by specifying the fallbacks they have chosen.

After the terrorist attack on the World Trade Center on September 11, 2001, there was a brief period during which both exchange and print sources widely used in connection with commodity derivatives (including the NYMEX and Platt's) did not announce or publish prices. To promote orderly valuation and settlement of derivatives, ISDA issued a statement of best practices that market participants were encouraged to follow—and generally did follow—in handling the resulting Market Disruption Events, irrespective of whether their applicable confirmations provided otherwise.

SAMPLE CONFIRMATIONS

Four sample confirmations follow this introductory note: one illustrating the documentation of a fixed/floating commodity swap using the *1993/2000 ISDA Commodity Derivatives Definitions*, the second illustrating a commodity-price floor documented under the same ISDA terms, the third illustrating a cash-settled bullion swap documented under the *1997 ISDA Bullion Definitions* and the fourth illustrating a physically settled bullion option documented using the *1997 Short Form Bullion Definitions*.

> The Introduction to this Part, *supra* p. 369, and the annotations to the sample rate swap confirmation, *supra* p. 427, contain general commentary about the confirmation process and the use of ISDA's confirmation forms both before and after the parties have entered into a master agreement that is not repeated or expressly referred to in the annotations to the other sample confirmations in this book.

[Letterhead of Big Bank, N.A.]

April 16, 2002

Commodity Swap Transaction—Cash-Settled

Oil Consumer Company
Refinery Lane
Houston, TX 00000-0000

Ladies and Gentlemen:

The purpose of this letter agreement is to confirm the terms and conditions of the transaction entered into between us on the Trade Date specified below (the "Transaction"). This letter agreement constitutes a "Confirmation" as referred to in the Master Agreement specified below.

> Annotation 1. This sample confirmation has been prepared using the forms supplied as Exhibits I and II-A to the *1993/2000 ISDA Commodity Derivatives Definitions*.

The definitions and provisions contained in the 1993 ISDA Commodity Derivatives Definitions (as supplemented by the 2000 Supplement), as published by the International Swaps and Derivatives Association, Inc., are incorporated into this Confirmation. In the event of any inconsistency between those definitions and provisions and this Confirmation, this Confirmation will govern.

> Annotation 2. The *2000 Supplement* specifies the formulation illustrated above for indicating that the parties are incorporating the *1993 ISDA Commodity Derivatives Definitions* as supplemented by the *2000 Supplement*. *Id.* at i. Those definitions as so supplemented provide a fairly comprehensive list of "Commodity Reference Prices" that the parties may use in confirming their transactions as well as alternative frameworks described in the description of commodity derivatives. *See supra* p. 561. In certain circumstances, concepts dealt with in the *2000 ISDA Definitions* and not covered in the *1993/2000 ISDA Commodity Derivatives Definitions* may be relevant in documenting a commodity derivatives transaction. For example, as observed in footnote 2 to the ISDA form of confirmation included in Exhibit I to

Sample Commodity Swap Confirmation 575

> those definitions, if one of the legs of a commodity swap involves payments calculated on a rate base (such as LIBOR), instead of a commodity price, the parties may wish to incorporate in the confirmation the portions of the *2000 ISDA Definitions* that relate to the calculation of interest rate-based payments. Before incorporating all or part of two different sets of ISDA definitions into the same master agreement or confirmation, the parties should carefully consider the potential for inconsistency and should state a rule about which of the sets of definitions will prevail with respect to the transaction, a particular issue or the obligations of a particular party, where appropriate.

1. This Confirmation supplements, forms part of, and is subject to, the Master Agreement dated as of April 16, 2002, as amended and supplemented from time to time (the "Agreement"), between Big Bank, N.A. (the "Bank") and Oil Consumer Company (the "Company"). All provisions contained in the Agreement govern this Confirmation except as expressly modified below.

2. The terms of the particular Transaction to which this Confirmation relates—which is a cash-settled commodity swap—are as follows:

Reference No.:	00000-00
Commodity:	Light Sweet Crude Oil (as that term is used by the NYMEX)

> Annotation 3. This line item is meant to capture an appropriate identification of the type of commodity involved in the transaction (by, *e.g.*, kind, grade or other measure of quality and delivery location or, in the illustrated case, the name assigned by the relevant Exchange to the agreed futures contract that the parties are treating as the basis for determining Floating Amounts, provided the price is available from the Exchange when needed and applicable Market Disruption Events do not lead to the use of an alternative price). Under the NYMEX Light Sweet Crude Oil contract, various crude streams in addition to West Texas Intermediate are deliverable. For that reason, the NYMEX term is used, as illustrated.

Unit:	One barrel

> Annotation 4. Under the formulas included in Articles 5 and 6 of the *1993/2000 ISDA Commodity Derivatives Definitions*, the calculation of Fixed Amounts and Floating Amounts requires that the applicable Fixed Price and Floating Price be expressed as prices per unit of the relevant Commodity—as illustrated here, one barrel of crude oil, but in other transactions, one million British thermal units (MMBtu, or mmbtu) of natural gas, one megawatt hour (MWH, or mwh) of electricity, one ton of certain metals, etc. The term "Unit" is also used in the Commodity Reference Price Framework introduced by the *2000 Supplement* to those

definitions, as illustrated *supra* p. 561 and in the sample commodity floor confirmation, *infra* p. 590. In identifying the appropriate Unit for each transaction, the parties should be sure to adopt the unit used by the Price Source applicable for determining the relevant party's Floating Amounts (the Exchange on which a relevant futures contract is traded or the electronic or print publication that reports the relevant cash-market prices for the commodity). If the Unit used in the parties' transaction for some reason differs from that used by the Price Source in reporting prices, the confirmation must state an appropriate conversion rule.

Trade Date: April 16, 2002

Effective Date: April 16, 2002

Termination Date: April 16, 2005

Annotation 5. As is the case with Termination Dates under the *2000 ISDA Definitions* and *1991 ISDA Definitions*, under Section 3.5 of the *1993/2000 ISDA Commodity Derivatives Definitions*, if the specified Termination Date for a transaction falls on a day that is a Saturday or a Sunday or otherwise is not a good working day in any relevant city, the Termination Date will not be adjusted and the Term of the transaction will nonetheless end on the specified Termination Date, unless the parties affirmatively state otherwise. On the other hand, a Settlement Date or Payment Date scheduled to fall on the Termination Date will automatically be adjusted in accordance with the Following Business Day Convention unless otherwise specified by the parties (under Section 3.4 of the *1993/2000 ISDA Commodity Derivatives Definitions*).

Annotation 6. In most commodity swaps, the Calculation Periods are defined by reference to calendar periods (generally calendar months), and the parties do not want or need to adjust the ends of Calculation Periods, including the Termination Date.

Notional Quantity per
Calculation Period: 25,000 Units

Annotation 7. The Notional Quantity, or Notional Quantity per Calculation Period, in a commodity swap is the counterpart of the Notional Amount of an interest rate swap, within the ISDA framework. *See* Section 4.3 and Articles 5 and 6 of the *1993/2000 ISDA Commodity Derivatives Definitions* and Annotation 4 to the sample rate swap confirmation, *supra* p. 428.

Annotation 8. The ISDA form of confirmation for commodity swaps in Exhibit II-A to the *1993/2000 ISDA Commodity Derivatives Definitions* indicates in brackets that the parties may wish to specify the "Total Notional Quantity" for the transaction. That term may be useful in documenting credit support arrangements related to a commodity swap if the parties wish to fix the amount of collateral to be supplied by a party on a given date with respect to the transaction by reference to the transaction's Total Notional Quantity, and the reference may also be useful in connection with a firm's risk management audit and accounting procedures. The "Total Notional Quantity" for a transaction is also useful for what are sometimes referred to as "prepaid" or "reverse zero coupon" swaps—swaps in which the Fixed Price Payer's obligation is fully discharged at the outset of the transaction through a single payment calculated on the basis of the present value, discounted to that payment date, of the stream of Fixed Amounts that would have been payable periodically over the Term of the transaction in a conventional swap (possibly adjusted to take account of the greater credit risk for the Fixed Rate Payer in this kind of mismatched structure as compared with a structure in which the parties' payments are due on the same dates and can be netted).

Annotation 9. Another mismatched structure involves the use of differing schedules of Notional Quantity per Calculation Period for the two parties. Parties to transactions of this sort should carefully consider the tax ramifications of their proposed structure.

Calculation Periods: Each full or partial calendar month during the Term of the Transaction

Annotation 10. Since the Term of the transaction begins with its Effective Date, the first Calculation Period will be only a portion of April 2002. As noted in Annotation 8 to this sample confirmation, it is common for the Term of commodity swaps to consist of Calculation Periods determined by reference to calendar periods, at least where a commodity user or producer is a party to the transaction and is using the swap to manage price risk associated with customary budgeting, sales and invoicing practices for the underlying cash commodity. When this is the case, in a conventional commodity swap documented using ISDA definitions, it is simplest to specify the relevant calendar period as the Calculation Period, as illustrated here.

Annotation 11. Under the *1993/2000 ISDA Commodity Derivatives Definitions*, an alternative to specifying the calendar month as the Calculation Period is to specify the Period End Dates and rely on Section 4.4(b)(ii) of the definitions to indicate how the Calculation Periods will be measured. Under that provision (like Section 4.13 of the *2000 ISDA Definitions*) each Calculation Period extends "from, and including, one Period End Date to, but excluding, the next following applicable Period End Date during the Term of the Swap Transaction," but with the first Calculation Period beginning on and including the Effective Date and the last period ending on but excluding the Termination Date. This approach provides for overlapping Calculation Periods in which the last day of a period is not counted, for purposes of certain computations, as part of that period but is counted as the first day of the following period. The framework is conventional for interest rate-based derivatives and works especially well with transactions that involve LIBOR-based Floating Amounts, which are often entered into in connection with assets and liabilities that have terms or overlapping interest periods defined in a similar same way. *See* the introductory note on interest rate products, *supra* p. 408. However, the use of this kind of overlapping Calculation Period does not reflect sales practices in the cash commodity markets or in the commodity futures markets, and many participants in those markets who use OTC commodity derivatives find this approach confusing. If the parties to the sample transaction had used this approach but made the mistake of defining the Period End Dates as the last day in each relevant month, the result would have been to exclude the futures contract price for the last calendar day of each month (assuming it was a Commodity Business Day) from the Floating Price calculation for the Calculation Period ending on that day and, instead, to include that last day's price in the Floating Price for the Calculation Period relating to the following calendar month—a result not intended by the parties.

Annotation 12. Another alternative is to specify Period End Dates and rely on Section 4.4(b)(i) of the *1993/2000 ISDA Commodity Derivatives Definitions* to indicate how the Calculation Periods will be measured. This approach also results in overlapping Calculation Periods, but in such a way that the Period End Date with which a Calculation Period ends is considered included in that Calculation Period and excluded from the following Calculation Period. This is accomplished be specifying "(ERMA)" in stating the Period End Dates, *e.g.*, "Period End Dates (ERMA): the last day of each calendar month during the Term of the Transaction." The reference to ERMA is included because the ERMA form of master agreement, which was used to some extent in the late 1980s but increasingly less thereafter, defined Settlement Periods in a way that reaches the same result, although the ERMA Settlement Periods do not overlap: the first period begins on the Effective Date and ends on the first Period End Date, and the next Settlement Period begins on the day following the preceding Period End Date and ends on the next following Period End Date, and so forth.

Settlement Date: For each Calculation Period, the fifth Business Day after the end of the Calculation Period

Annotation 13. Under Section 3.4 of the *1993/2000 ISDA Commodity Derivatives Definitions*, "Settlement Date" and "Payment Date" are synonymous. Section 4.4 of the *1993/2000 ISDA Commodity Derivatives Definitions* (which, except for non-substantive drafting differences, is like Section 9.1 of the *2000 ISDA Definitions* and Section 10.1 of the *1991 ISDA Definitions*) provides that, if the parties do not otherwise specify, the Fixed Amount or Floating Amount associated with each Payment Date will be understood to be the Fixed Amount or Floating Amount calculated with respect to the Calculation Period ending on or closest in time to that Payment Date.

Annotation 14. Under Section 3.4 of the *1993/2000 ISDA Commodity Derivatives Definitions*, a Settlement Date scheduled to fall on a Saturday, a Sunday or a day that is otherwise not a good working day in a relevant city for payments will automatically be adjusted to fall on the following Business Day unless the parties specify otherwise. The Business Day Conventions and Commodity Business Day Conventions are defined in Section 1.5 of those definitions and are described *supra* p. 391.

Fixed Amount Details:

    Fixed Rate Payer: The Company

    Fixed Price: For each Calculation Period, USD 20 per barrel

Annotation 15. A Fixed Price must be stated as a price per Unit of the relevant commodity. *See* Annotation 4 to this sample confirmation, *supra* 533. A Fixed Price may also be stated as a price related to a Settlement Date or Payment Date. *See* Section 5.2 of the *1993/2000 ISDA Commodity Derivatives Definitions*. Section 5.1 of those definitions supplies the formula under which the Fixed Amount for each Payment Date or Settlement Date will be the product of the Notional Quantity for the related Calculation Period and the relevant Fixed Price unless the confirmation provides otherwise. Unlike the Fixed Amounts calculated for rate swap transactions (*see* Annotation 11 to the sample rate swap confirmation, *supra* p. 431), the Fixed Amounts calculated for commodity swaps are not calculated in respect of the number of days in a Calculation Period, so day count fractions are not relevant.

Floating Amount Details:

    Floating Price Payer: The Bank

    Commodity Reference Price: OIL—WTI—NYMEX

Annotation 16. This is one of the four Commodity Reference Prices listed in the *1993/2000 ISDA Commodity Derivatives Definitions* for West Texas Intermediate light sweet crude oil. To use this particular Commodity Reference Price, the parties must also indicate a related Specified Price and a Delivery Date, as illustrated below in the sample confirmation. Since the parties have completed that required information and specified that each Commodity Business Day in a Calculation Period will be a Pricing Date for purposes of determining the Bank's Floating Amount obligation in respect of that Calculation Period, under Section 6.1 of those definitions, the Floating Amount for a Calculation Period will be determined by multiplying the Notional Quantity for that Calculation Period by the Floating Price for that period. That Floating Price (under Section 6.2(a)(ii)(C) of those definitions) will be the arithmetic mean of the Relevant Prices for each of those Pricing Dates, and the Relevant Price for each of those Pricing Dates will be the closing price on the NYMEX (the "Specified Price" in ISDA parlance), stated as a price per barrel, for the futures contract for West Texas Intermediate light sweet crude oil listed for trading on the NYMEX on that Pricing Date as the futures contract for that commodity with the nearest following month of expiration (the "First Nearby Month," using ISDA's term). *See* Annotation 22 to this sample confirmation on how the First Nearby Month for a Pricing Date is determined.

Annotation 17. Day Count Fractions are not relevant for Floating Prices under the *1993/2000 ISDA Commodity Derivatives Definitions*. Therefore, if a commodity price derivative involves payments calculated on a rate base, such as LIBOR-based Floating Amounts, the parties should consider incorporating appropriate terms from the *2000 ISDA Definitions* to document that leg of the transaction.

Annotation 18. As discussed *supra* p. 562, although the *1993/2000 ISDA Commodity Derivatives Definitions* indicate that a listed Commodity Reference Price should be used to specify how Floating Amounts will be calculated when one of the listed Commodity Reference Prices captures the parties' business deal, those definitions also set forth an alternative approach in the guidelines of Section 7(d)(ii) for what are referred to as Commodity Reference Price Frameworks. One of the frameworks is designed for use when each Pricing Date's Relevant Price will be futures based, and the Price Source will be an exchange, and the second framework is designed for use when the Relevant Price will be determined by reference to cash-market prices reported in a print or electronic Price Source.

Annotation 19. Whether the Floating Amount is determined on the basis of a Commodity Reference Price created by the parties or one that is listed in Section 7.1(a) or Section 7.1(b) of the *1993/2000 ISDA Commodity Derivatives Definitions*, Section 7.3 supplies a rule relating to corrections of published or announced prices used by the parties for determining a Relevant Price for a Pricing Day. Under that rule, corrections published or announced within 30 days after their original publication or announcement by the person responsible for the publication or announcement will be taken into account, at the request of either party, for purposes of calculating an appropriate adjustment payment, so long as the party's request is made within 30 days after the correction is announced. The adjustment payment due as a result of using the corrected data must be paid not later than three Business Days after the notice requesting the payment, together with interest at an overnight offered rate for deposits in the London interbank market for each day from and including the day on which the incorrect payment was due, to but excluding the day the adjustment payment is made. If the parties wish to override that rule on correction, they may do so in their master agreement or in the appropriate confirmation.

Specified Price: The closing price

Annotation 20. Section 7.2(c)(xii) of the *1993/2000 ISDA Commodity Derivatives Definitions* lists standard ways of indicating the Specified Price for a Commodity to be used, as described in the preceding annotation, to determine the Relevant Price for a Pricing Day. The appropriate choice depends on the type of Price Source (publication or exchange); the Specified Price "must be a price reported or capable of being determined from information reported in or by the relevant Price Source." The alternatives are "(A) the high price, (B) the low price, (C) the average of the high price and the low price, (D) the closing price, (E) the opening price, (F) the bid price, (G) the asked price, (H) the average of the bid price and the asked price, (I) the settlement price, (J) the morning fixing, (K) the afternoon fixing or (L) any other price specified in the relevant confirmation."

    Delivery Date: First Nearby Month

Annotation 21. From commodity to commodity and exchange to exchange, the number of futures contracts listed for trading on any day can differ, and the last trading day varies from contract to contract and from month to month. For example, the NYMEX specifications for its Light, Sweet Crude Oil futures contracts provide that 30 consecutive months' contracts will be listed for trading on any given day, plus five long-dated futures, which are initially listed 36, 48, 60, 72 and 84 months prior to delivery. *See* http://www.nymex.com/markets/cont_all.cfm. On the Trade Date of the illustrated transaction, April 16, 2002, the relevant futures would be the contracts expiring in May through December of 2002, those expiring in each month in 2003 and 2004 and those expiring in January through April of 2005. Looking at April 16, 2002 as a Pricing Day for the swap contemplated in the sample confirmation, the futures contract for the First Nearby Month on that Pricing Day would be the May 2002 contract. However, the trading for each NYMEX Light, Sweet Crude Oil futures contract terminates at the close of business on the third business day prior to the 25th calendar day of the month preceding the delivery month of the contract (*id.*), so towards the end of April, the contract for the First Nearby Month for each Pricing Day will become the June contract, and the Relevant Price for each such Pricing Date will be determined on the basis of the closing price on the NYMEX for the June contract. As a result, and because the exchanges may change their method for determining the last trading day for a contract from time to time, the convention is to refer to the relevant futures contract in respect of any Pricing Date by the proximity to that date of the expiration month of the futures contract (*i.e.*, First Nearby Month, Second Nearby Month, etc., under Section 7.2(c)(vi) of the *1993/2000 ISDA Commodity Derivatives Definitions*).

Annotation 22. When transactions involve Floating Amounts determined by reference to futures contract prices and fewer than all the relevant Exchange trading days (Commodity Business Days, in ISDA parlance) in a Calculation Period are designated as Pricing Dates for that Calculation Period (or its related Payment Date or Settlement Date), the particular Pricing Date or Pricing Dates selected are generally named by reference to their relation to the end of trading of a Futures Contract as, say, the First Nearby Month's contract. The documentation of these transactions within the ISDA framework can often be simplified in a table showing the relationships between Calculation Periods or Payment Dates or Settlement Dates, Futures Contracts relevant for the related Pricing Dates and dates of publication of relevant print Price Sources. For example, in commodity swaps with Floating Amounts calculated by reference to NYMEX futures contract prices for natural gas, it is common for the Floating Amount for the Calculation Periods to correspond to calendar months and for the Floating Price for a Calculation Period (or the related Payment Date) to be determined by averaging the Specified Price (*e.g.*, the closing price) for the last three Exchange trading days for the natural gas futures contract that for most of that calendar month is, in ISDA parlance, the Futures Contract for the First Nearby Month. Because the First Nearby Month contract changes during a calendar month, it can be somewhat difficult to state this arrangement clearly by merely setting out a Specified Price, a Delivery Date and a prose definition of Pricing Dates. In these cases, a useful practice is to set forth in a table the information necessary to identify the relationship between a Settlement Date or Payment Date and a particular month's Futures Contract, and then the relationship between that contract and the relevant Pricing Dates. The approach might be implemented as follows:

Floating Price Payer: The Company
Commodity Reference Price: NATURAL GAS—HENRY HUB—NYMEX
Specified Price: The closing price
Delivery Date: See table below

Settlement Date (5th Business Day of:)	Futures Contract Delivery Date (Month)
May 2002	May 2002
June 2002	June 2002

Pricing Dates: For the Calculation Period preceding each Settlement Date, the last three Commodity Business Days on which the Futures Contract for the Delivery Date specified in the preceding table is listed on the NYMEX as the First Nearby Contract.

Tables can also be useful when the determination of a Floating Amount involves a print Price Source, as, say, in a basis swap involving a NYMEX futures contract-based Floating Amount (flat, or plus or minus a spread) against a cash-market price to be taken from *Inside F.E.R.C.'s Gas Market Report*. In natural gas transactions of the kind described above, in which the Pricing Date or Pricing Dates occur just before a particular futures contract ceases to be the First Nearby Contract, that pricing approach is generally dictated by the desire to obtain a futures-based Floating Price that is most likely to approximate cash-market prices during the "bid week" for natural gas for delivery in the delivery month of that futures contract. If a user or producer of natural gas has used futures-based derivatives (actual exchange-traded futures or OTC derivatives, like swaps, with a Floating Price leg calculated on the basis of futures) to "fix" its cost or income from cash-market transactions that will be priced during bid week, it may also seek to reduce the "basis risk" involved in using that futures-based derivatives transaction through a basis swap of the kind described above. In this event, a print Price Source commonly used on the cash-market price leg of the swap for purposes of the Floating Price applicable for a Settlement Date (or Calculation Period) is the first issue of *Inside F.E.R.C.* to be published in the relevant delivery month, since that is the issue in which bid week prices for natural gas deliveries in that month will appear, although the actual bid-week dates will be at the end of the preceding month. Some market participants use an additional column in a table like the one shown above to list the appropriate *In-*

side F.E.R.C. issue in an easily identifiable manner. Those who prefer to use the ISDA Commodity Reference Prices listed in the 2000 Supplement may simply use an *Inside FERC* or *Natural Gas Intelligence* Commodity Reference Price (*see* subsections (B) and (E) of Section 7.1(a)(xii) of that supplement) and identify as the Pricing Dates each Commodity Business Day in the relevant month's bid week.

    Pricing Dates: Each Commodity Business Day

Annotation 23. The parties must specify the Pricing Dates to be used to determine the Floating Price for each Calculation Period or Payment Date or Settlement Date. As noted earlier, under Section 6.2(a)(ii)(C) of the *1993/2000 ISDA Commodity Derivatives Definitions*, unless they have specified otherwise in their confirmation, when more than one Pricing Date is specified by them as applicable for a Calculation Period or a Payment Date or Settlement Date, the Floating Price for that period or date will be the arithmetic mean of the Relevant Prices for all those Pricing Dates. *See* Annotation 26 to this sample confirmation.

Annotation 24. In the illustrated transaction, it is not necessary to specify a rule for adjustment of a specified Pricing Date if it turns out not to fall on a Commodity Business Day, because the Pricing Dates for the transaction are defined as Commodity Business Days. As indicated in footnote 5 to the form of confirmation for commodity swaps in Exhibit II-A to the *1993/2000 ISDA Commodity Derivatives Definitions*, in other circumstances it may be necessary to state such a rule on adjustment. The various Commodity Business Day Conventions included in those definitions for the purpose are discussed *supra* p. 391. If a rule for adjustment is necessary and the parties do not specify one in their confirmation, a "default" rule will not be supplied by the *1993/2000 ISDA Commodity Derivatives Definitions*.

Annotation 25. Under Section 1.4 of the *1993/2000 ISDA Commodity Derivatives Definitions*, when a Commodity Reference Price is based on a price published by an Exchange, "Commodity Business Day" means a trading day on that Exchange. For other Commodity Reference Prices, "Commodity Business Day" means a day for which the relevant Price Source publishes a price or would publish a price but for the occurrence of a Market Disruption Event. In basis swaps, like the hypothetical refiner's crack-spread transaction described above (*supra* p. 548), the parties sometimes identify the Pricing Dates as each day that is a Commodity Business Day in respect of both, or all, relevant Price Sources, so as to exclude any day for which prices are reported for only one of the relevant commodities.

    Method of Averaging:

Annotation 26. If the parties do not specify a method of averaging, the Floating Price for a Calculation Period with multiple Pricing Days will be the unweighted arithmetic mean of the Relevant Prices for those Pricing Days, under Section 6.2(a)(ii)(C) of the *1993/2000 ISDA Commodity Derivatives Definitions*.

Rounding: If any of the Relevant Prices averaged to determine the Floating Price for a Calculation Period is reported by the applicable Price Source carried to a unit smaller than a cent (two decimal places), for purposes of averaging those Relevant Prices shall be rounded to the fourth decimal place.

Annotation 27. Article 9 of the *1993/2000 ISDA Commodity Derivatives Definitions* states rounding rules that will apply in calculating a Floating Amount unless the parties specify otherwise. The rules call for the rounding, if necessary, of all percentages to the nearest ten-thousandth of a percentage point, with five hundred-thousandths of a percentage point being rounded up, and for the rounding of all U.S. dollar amounts resulting from such calculations to the nearest cent and all such Sterling amounts to the nearest penny, with one-half cent or penny rounded up.

Annotation 28. If the ISDA default choice does not reflect the parties' intention, they should modify it in their confirmation. One way to do so is to provide for "Rounding of Payments Only," a means of indicating agreement to apply a stated rounding rule only to Fixed Amounts, Floating Amounts and Cash Settlement Amounts, and not to prices used to calculate those amounts.

Annotation 29. The sample illustrates another approach. For many swaps, the primary and fallback Price Sources chosen by the parties express the relevant commodity prices in the same manner. That will not, however, always be so. The difference between the ISDA rounding rule and the method preferred by the parties may be small but, in a transaction involving a substantial Notional Quantity, the difference may be significant. If the parties wish to modify the ISDA rule, in determining whether to do so in their master agreement or in confirming their transactions, they should consider whether the appropriate rounding convention will be the same for all the commodities that may be involved in their dealings.

Business Days: New York City

Annotation 30. The Introduction to this Part, *supra* p. 391, discusses ISDA conventions regarding Business Days.

Annotation 31. If the confirmation were silent on the specification of a place for purposes of the Business Day definition, the default choices, under Section 1.3 of the *1993/2000 ISDA Commodity Derivatives Definitions*, would be London for payments in Sterling and New York for payments in Dollars.

Market Disruption:

Market Disruption Events: Price Source Disruption
Disappearance of Commodity Reference Price
Material Change in Content
Trading Suspension, but only if the suspension is continuing at the time for determination of the Specified Price
Tax Disruption, but only if the parties' payment obligations in respect of the Transaction are not equally affected by the Tax Disruption Event

Annotation 32. Section 7.4 of the *1993/2000 ISDA Commodity Derivatives Definitions* deals with Market Disruption Events and Additional Market Disruption Events. These are events or circumstances in which the Relevant Price for a Pricing Date cannot be determined using the parties' chosen Commodity Reference Price or as to which the parties have agreed that, although it can be determined in that manner, the Relevant Price as so determined should not be used because it cannot be relied on to reflect the economics of the transaction bargained for by the parties. *See* the discussion of Section 7.4, *supra* p. 564. The ISDA definitions provide default choices that will automatically be deemed to be Market Disruption Events applicable to a transaction unless the parties have specified otherwise.

Annotation 33. If the parties had chosen to specify Price Materiality, then Price Source Disruption would also occur if the Specified Price as determined in accordance with the Commodity Reference Price differed by the specified "Price Materiality Percentage," or more, from what it would have been if it had been determined using dealer price quotations under the ISDA "COMMODITY-REFERENCE DEALERS" approach discussed above (*see supra* p. 560).

Annotation 34. When *De Minimis* Trading is specified as applicable, the parties should also specify the applicable number for Minimum Futures Contracts. *See supra* p. 569.

Disruption Fallbacks:	(A) In the case of a Tax Disruption Event:
	Negotiated Fallback, so that the event has equal impact on the parties' payment obligations in respect of the Transaction; and
	(B) In all other cases:
	(1) Fallback Reference Price (with alternate Commodity Reference Price specified below), (2) Negotiated Fallback, (3) Postponement, with 5 days in the same Calculation Period as the Maximum Days of Disruption, (4) Average Daily Price Disruption, with 5 days as the Maximum Days of Disruption, and (5) Calculation Agent Determination.
	Alternate Commodity Reference Prices are (in order of priority): (a) OIL-WTI-PLATT'S MARKETWIRE with the Delivery Date determined as if for the Futures Contract relevant for the Commodity Reference Price specified above and the average of the high and low prices for the relevant Pricing Date as the Specified Price and (b) COMMODITY-REFERENCE DEALERS, with the same Delivery Date and Specified Price.
	If the last of these alternates becomes applicable, it will be used to determine the Relevant Price so long as two dealer quotations are obtained.

> Annotation 35. Under Section 7.4(e) of the *1993/2000 ISDA Commodity Derivatives Definitions*, the Calculation Agent is supposed to use the first of the applicable Disruption Fallbacks that will provide the parties with a Relevant Price. On Disruption Fallbacks, *see supra* p. 569, where the rationale for the various customized changes illustrated above is explained. If the parties adopt the approach illustrated in the final sentence of the illustrated provision, they depart from the norm under ISDA's COMMODITY–REFERENCE DEALERS approach by agreeing that two, rather than three, quotations from Reference Dealers will suffice for purposes of determining a Pricing Date's Reference Price so that the second of the Disruption Fallbacks selected by the parties, negotiation, is averted.

Calculation Agent:	The Bank

3. Account Details

Payments to the Bank:

> Account for payments: Big Bank, N.A., New York, N.Y., ABA No. 000, CHIPS No. 000, Attention: Swaps Division

Payments to the Company:

> Account for payments: Account No. 00000 with Big Bank, N.A., New York, N.Y.

4. Offices. The Office of the Bank for the Transaction is its head office in New York. The Office of the Company for the Transaction is its office at the address specified for notices to it in the Schedule to the Agreement.

5. Other Terms.

> Annotation 36. *See* Chapter 3, *supra* p. 63, for examples of representations that the parties might include in this part of a confirmation for a commodity swap to deal with issues raised by U.S. and state laws dealing with gaming, the operation of bucket shops and restrictions on trading in commodity futures and options.

Please confirm that the foregoing correctly sets forth the terms of our agreement by executing the copy of this Confirmation enclosed for that purpose and returning it to us or by sending to us a letter or telex substantially similar to this letter, which letter or telex sets forth the material terms of the Transaction to which this Confirmation relates and indicates agreement to those terms. If you believe the foregoing does not correctly reflect the terms of our agreement, please give us notice as soon as possible of what you believe to be the necessary corrections.

Yours sincerely,

BIG BANK, N.A.

By: _____
   Name:
   Title: Vice President

Confirmed as of the date first
above written on   ,   :

OIL CONSUMER COMPANY

By: _____
   Name:
   Title:

> The Introduction to this Part, *supra* p. 369, and the annotations to the sample rate swap confirmation, *supra* p. 427, contain general commentary about the confirmation process and the use of ISDA's confirmation forms both before and after the parties have entered into a master agreement that is not repeated or expressly referred to in the annotations to the other sample confirmations in this book. *See also* the annotations to the commodity swap confirmation, *supra* p. 574. Generally speaking, the annotations to this sample confirmation will address only features of this floor confirmation that differ from features of the sample commodity swap confirmation.

[Letterhead of Big Bank, N.A.]

April 16, 2002

Commodity Price Floor—Cash-Settled

Copper Trading Company
West Street
New York, NY 00000-0000

Ladies and Gentlemen:

The purpose of this letter agreement is to confirm the terms and conditions of the transaction entered into between us on the Trade Date specified below (the "Transaction"). This letter agreement constitutes a "Confirmation" as referred to in the Master Agreement specified below.

> Annotation 1. This sample confirmation has been prepared using the forms supplied as Exhibits I and II-C to the *1993/2000 ISDA Commodity Derivatives Definitions*.

The definitions and provisions contained in the 1993 ISDA Commodity Derivatives Definitions (as supplemented by the 2000 Supplement), as published by the International Swaps and Derivatives Association, Inc., are incorporated into this Confirmation. In the event of any inconsistency between those definitions and provisions and this Confirmation, this Confirmation will govern.

1. This Confirmation supplements, forms part of, and is subject to, the Master Agreement dated as of April 16, 2002, as amended and supplemented from time to time (the "Agreement"), between Big Bank, N.A. (the "Bank") and Copper Trading Company (the "Company"). All provisions contained in the Agreement govern this Confirmation except as expressly modified below.

Sample Commodity Floor Confirmation

2. The terms of the particular Transaction to which this Confirmation relates—which is a cash-settled commodity price floor—are as follows:

Reference No.: 00000-00

> Annotation 2. At this spot in the sample commodity swap confirmation, *supra* p. 575, the parties specified the Commodity underlying the transaction and the relevant Unit in which prices are determined. Those details are set forth in this sample confirmation in connection with the Floating Amount specifications, as part of the Commodity Reference Price Framework approach discussed in the related annotations. *See infra* p. 590.

Trade Date: April 16, 2002

Effective Date: April 16, 2002

Termination Date: April 16, 2005

Notional Quantity per
Calculation Period: _____ Units

Calculation Periods: Each full or partial calendar month during the Term of the Transaction

> Annotation 3. Since the Term of the transaction begins with its Effective Date, the first Calculation Period will be only a portion of April 2002. *See* Annotation 10 to the sample commodity swap confirmation, *supra* p. 577.

Settlement Date: For each Calculation Period, the fifth Business Day after the end of the Calculation Period

Fixed Amount Details:

    Fixed Rate Payer: The Company

    Fixed Price: For each Calculation Period, [ ] U.S. cents per pound

> Annotation 4. *See* Annotation 15 to the sample commodity swap confirmation, *supra* p. 579, on the calculation of Fixed Amounts under the *1993/2000 ISDA Commodity Derivatives Definitions*. The Fixed Amounts provided for in the sample

confirmation are premium payable (usually up front but here in installments in arrears) for the floor protection.

Floating Amount Details:

    Floating Price Payer: The Bank

    Commodity: Copper, high grade

    Unit: One pound

    Exchange: COMEX

    Relevant Currency: USD

    Specified Price: Closing price

    Delivery Date: First Nearby Month

Annotation 5. The sample commodity swap confirmation (*supra* p. 575) illustrates the use of one of ISDA's Commodity Reference Price definitions listed in Section 7.1(a) in the *1993/2000 ISDA Commodity Derivatives Definitions* to indicate how the Floating Amount for each Calculation Period will be determined. That approach could have been used in this sample confirmation by specifying the Commodity Reference Price term "COPPER–COMEX" defined in Section 7.1(b) of those definitions, along with the Specified Price and the Delivery Date. Instead, this sample illustrates the use of one of the Commodity Reference Price Framework approaches provided for in Section 7(d)(ii) of those definitions, as discussed *supra* p. 562 and in Annotation 4 to the sample commodity swap confirmation, *supra* p. 575. Under either approach, once the parties specify terms that define the Calculation Periods for their transaction, and since they have indicated that each Commodity Business Day in each Calculation Period will be treated as a Pricing Date, the parties would have indicated that the Floating Amount for each Calculation Period will be determined, under Section 6.2(a)(i)(B) of those definitions, by multiplying the Notional Quantity for that Calculation Period by a price equal to the excess, if any, of the Floor Price specified below over the Floating Price for that period. That Floating Price (under Section 6.2(a)(ii)(C) of those definitions) will be the arithmetic mean of the Relevant Prices for each of those Pricing Dates, and the Relevant Price for each of those Pricing Dates will be the closing price (the Specified Price indicated above) on the COMEX division of the New York Mercantile Exchange, stated as a price per pound (the specified Unit), for the futures contract with the specified Delivery Date (the contract with the First Nearby Month as the delivery month) for copper meeting the COMEX grade and quality specifications for the futures contract.

Floor Price: USD [   ]

> Annotation 6. Since the Company bargained for floor protection against declining copper prices, as indicated in Annotation 10 to this sample confirmation, it will be owed a Floating Amount for each Calculation Period in which Floating Price (the average of the futures-based Relevant Prices) falls below the specified Floor Rate. If the parties had, instead, bargained for cap protection, the Floating Amount would be payable for each Calculation Period in which the Floating Price exceeded a specified Cap Rate. If the parties had entered into a collar transaction, each of them would have been identified as a Floating Price Payer, and the Floating Amount details for one would have specified a Cap Price, while the Floating Price details for the other would have specified a Floor Price. In addition, if the premium payable for the relevant cap protection exceeded that payable for the floor protection (given the levels at which the Cap Price and Floor Price were set), the party buying the cap protection would be required to pay a Fixed Amount. *See* the discussion on caps and floors *supra* p. 551.

Pricing Dates: Each Commodity Business Day

Method of Averaging:

Rounding: If any of the Relevant Prices averaged to determine the Floating Price for a Calculation Period is reported by the applicable Price Source carried to a unit smaller than a cent (two decimal places), for purposes of averaging those Relevant Prices shall be rounded to the fourth decimal place.

Business Days: New York City

Market Disruption:

    Market Disruption Events: Price Source Disruption
Disappearance of Commodity Reference Price
Material Change in Content
Trading Suspension, but only if the suspension is continuing at the time for determination of the Specified Price
Tax Disruption, but only if the parties' payment obligations in respect of the Transaction are not equally affected by the Tax Disruption event

    Disruption Fallbacks: (A) In the case of a Tax Disruption Event, Negotiated Fallback, so that the event has equal impact on the parties' payment obligations in respect of the Transaction; and

(B) In all other cases,

(1) Fallback Reference Price (as described below), (2) Negotiated Fallback, (3) Postponement, with 5 days in the same Calculation Period as the Maximum Days of Disruption, (4) Average Daily Price Disruption, with 5 days as the Maximum Days of Disruption, and (5) Calculation Agent Determination.

For this purpose, alternate Commodity Reference Prices is COMMODITY—REFERENCE DEALERS, with the Delivery Date and Specified Price to be determined as necessary to create a result consistent with the parties' intent in specifying their preferred Commodity Reference Price for the Transaction.

    Calculation Agent: The Bank

3. Account Details

Payments to the Bank:

    Account for payments: Big Bank, N.A., New York, N.Y., ABA No. 000, CHIPS No. 000, Attention: Swaps Division

Payments to the Company:

>Account for payments: Account No. 00000 with Big Bank, N.A., New York, N.Y.

4. Offices. The Office of the Bank for the Transaction is its head office in New York. The Office of the Company for the Transaction is its office at the address specified for notices to it in the Schedule to the Agreement.

5. Other Terms.

> Annotation 7. *See* Chapter 3, *supra* p. 63, for examples of the kinds of representations that the parties might include in this part of a confirmation for a commodity derivative to deal with issues raised by laws in the United States dealing with gaming, the operation of bucket-shops restrictions on trading in commodity futures and options.

Please confirm that the foregoing correctly sets forth the terms of our agreement by executing the copy of this Confirmation enclosed for that purpose and returning it to us or by sending to us a letter or telex substantially similar to this letter, which letter or telex sets forth the material terms of the Transaction to which this Confirmation relates and indicates agreement to those terms. If you believe the foregoing does not correctly reflect the terms of our agreement, please give us notice as soon as possible of what you believe to be the necessary corrections.

Yours sincerely,

BIG BANK, N.A.

By: _____
   Name:
   Title: Vice President

Confirmed as of the date first
above written on   , :

COPPER TRADING COMPANY

By: _____
   Name:
   Title:

> The Introduction to this Part, *supra* p. 369, and the annotations to the sample rate swap confirmation, *supra* p. 427, contain general commentary about the confirmation process and the use of ISDA's confirmation forms both before and after the parties have entered into a master agreement that is not repeated or expressly referred to in the annotations to the other sample confirmations in this book. Generally speaking, the annotations to this sample confirmation will address only features of this bullion swap confirmation that differ from features of the sample commodity swap confirmation.

[Letterhead of Big Bank, N.A.]

April 16, 2002

Bullion Swap Transaction—Cash-Settled

English Company PLC
Company House
Company Lane
London AB1C 2DE

Ladies and Gentlemen:

The purpose of this letter agreement is to confirm the terms and conditions of the transaction entered into between us on the Trade Date specified below (the "Transaction"). This letter agreement constitutes a "Confirmation" as referred to in the Master Agreement specified below.

> Annotation 1. This sample confirmation has been prepared using the forms supplied as Exhibits I and II-C to the *1997 ISDA Bullion Definitions*.

The definitions and provisions contained in the 1997 ISDA Bullion Definitions, as published by the International Swaps and Derivatives Association, Inc., are incorporated into this Confirmation. In the event of any inconsistency between those definitions and provisions and this Confirmation, this Confirmation will govern.

> Annotation 2. The *1997 ISDA Bullion Definitions* provide commodity price indexes (referred to as "Bullion Reference Prices") and price sources, for transactions involving gold, silver, platinum and palladium, as summarized *supra* p. 564. They also incorporate by reference certain terms defined in the *1991 ISDA Definitions* that are used in defining "GOFO," a loco London gold lending rate included for use by the parties in documenting their transactions, where applicable, and in "LGLR," an Implied Mid Market Gold Interest Rate compiled from USD–LIBOR–

> BBA less GOFO, adjusted by a factor to reflect current market spreads for gold lease transactions with a relevant term.

1. This Confirmation supplements, forms part of, and is subject to, the Master Agreement dated as of April 16, 2002, as amended and supplemented from time to time (the "Agreement"), between Big Bank, N.A. (the "Bank") and English Company PLC (the "Company"). All provisions contained in the Agreement govern this Confirmation except as expressly modified below.

2. The terms of the particular Transaction to which this Confirmation relates—which is a cash-settled commodity swap—are as follows:

Reference Number   000-00000

Notional Quantity per
Calculation Period: 15,000 Ounces

> Annotation 3. Article 1 of the *1997 ISDA Bullion Definitions* defines "Ounce" as meaning a fine troy ounce in the case of gold and a troy ounce in the case of silver, platinum and palladium.

Bullion: Gold

> Annotation 4. Article 1 of the *1997 ISDA Bullion Definitions* provides rules relating to good delivery and fineness for the covered bullion metals, by reference to the rules of the London Bullion Market Association (LBMA) for gold and silver and the London Platinum and Palladium Market (LPPM) for platinum and palladium. Those terms are particularly relevant for physically settled Bullion Trades (spot and forward sales) and Bullion Options documented under those definitions.

Trade Date: April 16, 2002

Effective Date: April 16, 2002

Termination Date: April 16, 2005

> Annotation 5. Under Section 6.9 of the *1997 ISDA Bullion Definitions* (like the corresponding provisions of the *2000 ISDA Definitions* and the *1993/2000 ISDA Commodity Derivatives Definitions*), if the specified Termination Date for a transaction falls on a day that is a Saturday or a Sunday or otherwise is not a good working day in any relevant city, the Termination Date will not be adjusted and the

> Term of the transaction will nonetheless end on the specified Termination Date, unless the parties affirmatively state otherwise. On the other hand, a Payment Date scheduled to fall on the Termination Date will automatically be adjusted in accordance with the Following Business Day Convention unless otherwise specified by the parties, under Section 6.8 of the *1997 ISDA Bullion Definitions*.

Calculation Periods:	Each full or partial calendar month during the Term of the Transaction
Payment Dates:	The fifth Bullion Business Day after the end of the Calculation Period

> Annotation 6. Section 7.4 of the *1997 ISDA Bullion Definitions* provides a rule relating to the relationship between Payment Dates and Calculation Periods that is slightly different from the rule set out in the corresponding provisions of the *1993/2000 ISDA Commodity Derivatives Definitions* and the *2000 ISDA Definitions*. Section 7.4 provides that, if the parties do not otherwise specify, the Fixed Amount or Floating Amount associated with each Payment Date will be understood to be the Fixed Amount or Floating Amount calculated with respect to the Calculation Period ending on or "closest in time prior to" that Payment Date. As discussed in Annotation 13 to the sample commodity swap confirmation, *supra* p. 578, the other sets of definitions look to the Calculation Period ending on or "closest in time to" that Payment Date, without the stipulation that its end be "prior" to the Payment Date if it does not end on the Payment Date. For conventional swaps settled in arrears, the difference should be academic.
>
> Annotation 7. Under Section 6.8 of the *1997 ISDA Bullion Definitions*, a Payment Date scheduled to fall on a Saturday, a Sunday or a day that is otherwise not a good working day in a relevant city for payments will automatically be adjusted to fall on the following Bullion Business Day unless the parties specify otherwise. The Business Day Conventions are defined in Section 6.2 of those definitions and are described *supra* p. 391. The rule is not stated to apply to Settlement Dates for Bullion Options documented under those definitions, as the term "Settlement Dates" is defined in such a way that those dates always fall on Bullion Business Days.

Fixed Amount Details:

Fixed Rate Payer:	The Bank
Fixed Price:	For each Calculation Period, USD [·] per Ounce

> Annotation 8. A Fixed Price must be stated as a price per Ounce of the relevant commodity. A Fixed Price must relate to a party and a Payment Date. *See* Section 8.2 of *1997 ISDA Bullion Definitions*. Section 8.1 of those definitions supplies the formula under which the Fixed Amount for each Payment Date (if not stated in a confirmation or otherwise determined in accordance with a confirmation) will be the product of the Notional Quantity for the related Calculation Period and the relevant Fixed Price.

Floating Amount Details:

    Floating Price Payer: The Company

    Commodity Reference Price: GOLD-COMEX

> Annotation 9. This is one of the three Bullion Reference Prices for Gold set out in the *1997 ISDA Bullion Definitions*. There is no need to supply a Price Source on a separate line, because the definitions indicate that the source for the relevant futures price information will be the COMEX. The parties could create a Bullion Reference Price different from those that are listed by specifying a Price Source and spelling out all relevant details. As indicated above, however, the *1997 ISDA Bullion Definitions* do not have express provisions on a Bullion Reference Price Framework like the Commodity Reference Price Framework contemplated in Section 7.1(d)(ii) of the *1993/2000 ISDA Commodity Derivatives Definitions*.
>
> Annotation 10. The parties could also specify that the Relevant Price for each Pricing Date in a Calculation Period will be determined applying the ISDA "BULLION–REFERENCE DEALERS" approach set out in Section 11.2 of the *1997 ISDA Bullion Definitions*, which is like the COMMODITY–REFERENCE DEALERS approach set out in Section 7.1(d)(ii) of the *1993/2000 ISDA Commodity Derivatives Definitions*. *See supra* p. 559. If they did so and did not identify the relevant Reference Dealers, the Calculation Agent would select four major dealers that are members of the LBMA as the Reference Dealers, pursuant to Section 11.2(b) of the *1997 ISDA Bullion Definitions*.
>
> Annotation 11. Day Count Fractions are not relevant for Floating Prices under the *1997 ISDA Bullion Definitions*. If a bullion derivative involves payments calculated on a rate base, such as LIBOR-based Floating Amounts, the parties should consider incorporating appropriate terms from the *2000 ISDA Definitions* to document that leg of the transaction.
>
> Annotation 12. The *1997 ISDA Bullion Definitions* do not supply a rule relating to corrections of prices erroneously reported by a price source. *See* Annotation 19 to the sample commodity swap confirmation, *supra* p. 580, on the rule applicable under the *1993/2000 ISDA Commodity Derivatives Definitions*.

Annotation 13. The *1997 ISDA Bullion Definitions* (unlike the *1993/2000 ISDA Commodity Derivatives Definitions*) do not rely on a concept of Specified Price (such as a high or low price or an opening or closing price). This is because each of the eleven Bullion Reference Prices listed in the definitions identifies precisely the price that is to be used, which might be a morning, afternoon or daily fixing price or, in the case of futures-based prices, the "Settlement Price" published by the relevant Exchange for the futures contract for the specified Delivery Date. The listed Commodity Reference Prices for gold, silver, platinum and palladium in the *1993/2000 ISDA Commodity Derivatives Definitions* do require the parties to indicate their agreement on the Specified Price for a futures contract.

Pricing Dates: Each Bullion Business Day

Annotation 14. The parties must specify the Pricing Dates to be used to determine the Floating Price for each Calculation Period or Payment Date.

Annotation 15. In the illustrated transaction, it is not, however, necessary to specify a rule for adjustment of a specified Pricing Date if it turns out not to fall on a Commodity Business Day, because the Pricing Dates for the transaction are defined as Bullion Business Days.

Annotation 16. Since the parties have not specified a method of averaging, the Floating Price for each Calculation Period will be the unweighted arithmetic mean of the Relevant Prices for the respective Pricing Days, as provided in Section 8.4(a)(ii)(C) of the *1997 ISDA Bullion Definitions*.

Market Disruption:

    Market Disruption Events: Price Source Disruption; Disappearance of Bullion Reference Price; Trading Suspension or Limitation; and Tax Disruption (as defined in the 1993 ISDA Commodity Derivatives Definitions (as supplemented by the 2000 Supplement), as published by the International Swaps and Derivatives Association, Inc.) if the parties' payment obligations in respect of the Transaction are not equally affected by the Tax Disruption event.

Annotation 17. Section 10.1 of the *1997 ISDA Bullion Definitions* deals with Market Disruption Events and Additional Market Disruption Events. *See supra* p. 566 for a discussion of the listed events and a comparison with the events listed in the *1993/2000 ISDA Commodity Derivatives Definitions*. Although the illustrated incorporation of Tax Disruption Event from the *1993/2000 ISDA Commodity Derivatives Definitions* might be appropriate in a cash-settled swap like that illustrated in the sample confirmation, for physically settled transactions documented under the *1997 ISDA Bullion Definitions*, the definitions supply their own rules, reflecting market practice, relating to value added taxes, as discussed *supra* p. 566.

Disruption Fallbacks: (A) In the case of a Tax Disruption Event, Negotiated Fallback, so that the event has equal impact on the parties' payment obligations in respect of the Transaction; and

(B) In all other cases, (1) Fallback Reference Price (use alternate Commodity Reference Price below), (2) Negotiated Fallback, (3) Postponement, with 5 days in the same Calculation Period as the Maximum Days of Disruption and (5) Calculation Agent Determination.

Alternate Commodity Reference Price: GOLD-REFERENCE DEALERS.

Annotation 18. Section 10.1(e) of the *1997 ISDA Bullion Definitions* provides that the Relevant Price for a Pricing Date will be determined in accordance with the first applicable Disruption Fallback. *See supra* p. 571 for a discussion of the events listed in those definitions and a comparison with the events listed in the *1993/2000 ISDA Commodity Derivatives Definitions*.

Annotation 19. There is no specification of Business Days to be applicable to the illustrated transaction. The *1997 ISDA Bullion Definitions* automatically define Bullion Business Day to be a working day in all of the following—London, New York, the location where payment is to be made and the delivery location. If this default rule is not appropriate for a particular transaction, the parties must override it in their confirmation. The *1993/2000 ISDA Commodity Derivatives Definitions* do not include "Bullion Business Day" as a defined term, although, as indicated, they include Commodity Reference Prices for gold, silver, platinum and palladium.

Rounding: Rounding of Payments Only

Annotation 20. Article 12 of the *1997 ISDA Bullion Definitions*, a somewhat expanded version of Article 9 of the *1993/2000 ISDA Commodity Derivatives Definitions*, provides rules on rounding that will apply for purposes of calculating a Floating Amount unless the parties specify otherwise. One way of modifying the default choice is to provide for "Rounding of Payments Only," a phrase which (under Article 12), will indicate the parties' agreement to apply the stated rounding rule

> only to In-the-Money Amounts and Floating Amounts, and not to prices used to calculate those amounts.

Calculation Agent: The Bank

3. Account Details

Payments to the Bank:

Account for payments: Big Bank, N.A., New York, N.Y., ABA No. 000, CHIPS No. 000, Attention: Swaps Division

Payments to the Company:

Account for payments: Account No. 00000 with Big Bank, N.A., New York, N.Y.

4. Offices. The Office of the Bank for the Transaction is its head office in New York. The Office of the Company for the Transaction is its office at the address specified for notices to it in the Schedule to the Agreement.

Please confirm that the foregoing correctly sets forth the terms of our agreement by executing the copy of this Confirmation enclosed for that purpose and returning it to us or by sending to us a letter or telex substantially similar to this letter, which letter or telex sets forth the material terms of the Transaction to which this Confirmation relates and indicates agreement to those terms. If you believe the foregoing does not correctly reflect the terms of our agreement, please give us notice as soon as possible of what you believe to be the necessary corrections.

Yours sincerely,

BIG BANK, N.A.

By: _____
   Name:
   Title: Vice President

Confirmed as of the date first
above written on   , :

ENGLISH COMPANY PLC

By: _____
   Name:
   Title:

> The Introduction to this Part, *supra* p. 369, and the annotations to the sample rate swap confirmation, *supra* p. 427, contain general commentary about the confirmation process and the use of ISDA's confirmation forms both before and after the parties have entered into a master agreement that is not repeated or expressly referred to in the annotations to the other sample confirmations in this book. Generally speaking, the annotations to this sample confirmation will address only features of this bullion swap confirmation that differ from features of the sample commodity swap confirmation.

[Letterhead of Big Bank, N.A.]

April 16, 2002

Bullion Trade—Physically Settled

English Company PLC
Company House
Company Lane
London AB1C 2DE

Ladies and Gentlemen:

The purpose of this letter agreement is to confirm the terms and conditions of the transaction entered into between us on the Trade Date specified below (the "Transaction"). This letter agreement constitutes a "Confirmation" as referred to in the Master Agreement specified below.

> Annotation 1. This sample confirmation has been prepared using the forms supplied as Exhibits I and II-A to the *1997 Short Form Bullion Definitions.*

The definitions and provisions contained in the 1997 ISDA Short Form Bullion Definitions, as published by the International Swaps and Derivatives Association, Inc., are incorporated into this Confirmation. In the event of any inconsistency between those definitions and provisions and this Confirmation, this Confirmation will govern.

> Annotation 2. Like the *1997 ISDA Bullion Definitions,* the *1997 Short Form Bullion Definitions* cover transactions in gold, silver, platinum and palladium. Only physically delivered spot and forward trades and options are, however, covered by the short-form definitions.

1. This Confirmation supplements, forms part of, and is subject to, the Master Agreement dated as of April 16, 2002, as amended and supplemented from time to time (the "Agreement"), between Big Bank, N.A. (the "Bank") and English Company PLC (the

"Company"). All provisions contained in the Agreement govern this Confirmation except as expressly modified below.

2. The terms of the particular Transaction to which this Confirmation relates—which is a cash-settled commodity swap—are as follows:

Reference No.:	00000-00
Trade Date:	April 16, 2002
Purchaser of Bullion:	The Company
Seller of Bullion:	The Bank
Bullion:	Platinum
Number of Ounces	[ ]

> Annotation 3. There is, of course, no need to provide for a Notional Quantity in a physically settled trade of this type. Nor is there any need to stipulate a Bullion Reference Price or a Price Source. As a result, the short-form definitions do not deal with these subjects. *See supra* note 1445 on the way they deal, as a result, with calculations that require the comparison of a strike price with a prevailing market price in connection with physically settled options that are treated as automatically exercised if they are in the money to a specified extent at the Expiration Time and have not been exercised by notice given by the Buyer.

Contract Price:	[ ]
Value Date:	May 16, 2002 or, if that day is not a Bullion Business Day, the first following day that is a Bullion Business Day.

> Annotation 4. Under the *1997 Short Form Bullion Definitions*, the Value Date must be a Bullion Business Day. These definitions, unlike ISDA's other booklets, do not contain definitions of Business Day Conventions and default choices as to conventions that are to apply if the parties fail to specify a choice. *See generally supra* p. 391. Accordingly, parties using the short-form definitions should consider what rule they wish to have apply in the event of an unexpected holiday and include a provision like the sample in their agreement.

PROVISIONS RELATING TO SETTLEMENT:

Delivery Location: London

> Annotation 5. The *1997 Short Form Bullion Definitions* contemplate that delivery will be in either London or Zurich, as indicated in Exhibit II-A of the form of confirmation attached to the definitions.

Consequences of Settlement Disruption Events: Negotiation
Cancellation and Payment

> Annotation 6. The approach of the *1997 Short Form Bullion Definitions* to Settlement Disruption Events is discussed *supra* p. 566.
>
> Annotation 7. There is no specification of Business Days to be applicable to the transaction. The short-form definitions approach the question of holidays by defining Bullion Business Day to be a working day in all of the following—London, New York, the location where payment is to be made and the delivery location—and then requiring all performance obligations to be performed on Bullion Business Days.

Calculation Agent: The Bank

3. Account Details

Payments to the Bank:

   Account for payments: Big Bank, N.A., New York, N.Y., ABA No. 000, CHIPS No. 000, Attention: Swaps Division

Delivery to the Company:

   Account for deliveries: [ ]

4. Offices. The Office of the Bank for the Transaction is its head office in New York. The Office of the Company for the Transaction is its office at the address specified for notices to it in the Schedule to the Agreement.

Please confirm that the foregoing correctly sets forth the terms of our agreement by executing the copy of this Confirmation enclosed for that purpose and returning it to us or by sending to us a letter or telex substantially similar to this letter, which letter or telex sets forth the material terms of the Transaction to which this Confirmation relates and indicates agreement to those terms. If you believe the foregoing does not correctly reflect the terms of our agreement, please give us notice as soon as possible of what you believe to be the necessary corrections.

Yours sincerely,

BIG BANK, N.A.

By: _____
    Name:
    Title: Vice President

Confirmed as of the date first above written on   , :

ENGLISH COMPANY PLC

By: _____
    Name:
    Title:

CREDIT, DEBT AND EQUITY DERIVATIVES

Introduction	605
Shared Issues in Credit, Debt and Equity Derivatives	608
Documentation Features Addressing Regulatory Issues	608
Documentation Features Addressing Market Conventions and Problems	610
Valuation and Settlement Conventions and Market Disruptions	611
The Standard ISDA Approaches	611
Issues Raised by the Standard Approaches	619
Events Affecting the Underlying Debt or Equity	627
Extraordinary Events Affecting a Reference Entity	630
Credit Derivatives	632
Equity Derivatives	630
Early Termination in Other Special Cases	636
Credit Default Swaps	639
Sample Credit Default Swap Confirmation	687
Equity Derivatives	717
Sample Equity Index Swap Confirmation	736

INTRODUCTION

The product descriptions and sample confirmations included in this section relate to derivatives linked to credit and market risks associated with debt, equity and other financial instruments or obligations. The product descriptions refer to the diverse ways in which these products are used. The sample confirmations illustrate how some of the products, in simple forms, may be documented when the parties choose to follow ISDA conventions. For many reasons, it would be a mistake to believe that the documents used in an actual transaction will look like these sample confirmations. Many major market professionals use their own, proprietary forms (especially for equity derivatives). Standard terms have been developed by trade associations for particular market segments and within market segments, for transactions in particular underlying assets. There is a high degree of tailoring of credit, debt and equity derivatives products to a customer's needs in light of the regulatory issues that arise in the circumstances.

Transactions involving emerging market instruments are often documented following EMTA's[1460] standard terms and recommended practices. Traditional OTC debt

---

[1460]EMTA published a Master Agreement for Options on Emerging Markets Instruments in 1994. The form assumes the transactions will adopt recognized practices that may differ from those in other markets and will be consistent with EMTA's Code of Conduct (which will, for example, be relevant as to delivery of assets). It provides Restructuring Alternatives to deal with restructurings of assets on which options have been written. (The alternative chosen specifies which party will be entitled to determine how to vote in the restructuring and make elections on, say, new assets for which the asset may be exchanged.) The form addresses options on When-Issued Bonds, that is, bonds that have not yet been issued when the parties enter into their transaction but the issuance of which, on specified terms, is to occur pursuant to a sovereign refinancing plan providing, for instance, that the obligations of the parties to settle an exercised option on a When-Issued Bond will expire if that instrument has not been issued before a specified Cut-Off Date. The form and accompanying confirmation forms are discussed in EMTA's *Market Practice Guide*. A list of EMTA's publications is available at www.emta.org. For discussion of emerging markets credit derivatives

and equity derivatives—physically settled stock and bond options and forward purchase and sale contracts—have largely been the province of regulated securities brokers and dealers in the U.S. market, and their documentation reflects this regulatory overlay.[1461] In many cases they are documented on proprietary forms developed by major security market professionals or, where bond options are concerned, standardized master agreements published by TBMA. One such agreement, the Master OTC Options Agreement,[1462] accommodates dealings in options on obligations of or guaranteed as to principal or interest by the U.S. Treasury or of a corporation in which the United States has a direct or indirect interest.[1463] The agreement is also designed to cover other securities identified by the parties in an Annex, including International Securities—securities which are denominated in a currency other than U.S. dollars, which may be cleared through a clearing facility outside the U.S. or which are issued by an issuer organized under the laws of a non-U.S. jurisdiction.[1464] In addition, there are reports that at least some market professionals that are very active in the credit derivatives markets will be using a standardized, pared down master agreement form specially prepared for use with credit default swaps in some of their dealings with each other.

Although they are used for diverse purposes, in distinct markets and following many different conventions, debt-, equity- and credit-linked derivatives present many common issues. This introductory note is an overview of some of these issues and how they are dealt with in three commonly used sets of standard terms for the product segments:

- the *1996 Equity Derivatives Definitions*,[1465]

---

transactions, See Jane Herring, *Credit Derivatives in emerging markets: a product analysis*, in CREDIT DERIVATIVES: APPLICATIONS FOR RISK MANAGEMENT 11.

[1461] *See supra* p. 156.

[1462] This form is available at www.bondmarkets.com. Those who use it agree (in Paragraph 6(b)) to comply with the market practice for the type of Underlying Securities involved, including the Uniform Practices applicable to transactions in certain securities between TBMA members, regardless of whether both parties are members, to the extent that practice does not conflict with the terms of the form or the confirmation for a particular option.

[1463] As indicated in Master OTC Options Agreement Guidance Notes, at 2, the basic coverage of the agreement tracks the language of Rule 3a12-7 under the Securities Exchange Act, providing an exemption from the provisions of the Act other than those that deal specifically with exempted securities, provided the related securities represent an obligation of $250,000 or more. The definition picks up GSE securities—agency and agency mortgage-backed securities. *See supra* note 521.

[1464] Terms addressing options on these International Securities and other "International Transactions" (options involving a non-U.S. party or a U.S. party acting from a non-U.S. branch or office) are set forth separately (in Annex IV to the Master OTC Options Agreement) to deal with matters relevant in transactions with cross-border elements, such as gross-up obligations and termination rights relating to the imposition of withholding taxes, indemnification for exchange loss incurred in connection with payment in a currency other than that agreed to by the parties and diverse local holidays in places or involving clearing systems (including Euroclear, Clearstream and TARGET) that are relevant to the parties' dealings.

[1465] This set of definitions expands on and includes (in somewhat modified form, in some cases) the provisions published in the *1994 ISDA Equity Option Definitions*. That set of definitions is not discussed here. The Introduction to the *1996 Equity Derivatives Definitions* (at ix) describes some of the more significant differences between those definitions and the *1994 ISDA Equity Option Definitions*.

- the *1997 Government Bond Option Definitions* and
- the *1999 Credit Derivatives Definitions.*

Each of these sets of definitions includes one or more exhibits showing how a transaction can be confirmed using the particular set of definitions. The following table lists the product types identified with these sets of ISDA definitions in their respective Introductions:

1996 Equity Derivatives Definitions	*1997 Government Bond Option Definitions*	*1999 Credit Derivatives Definitions*
Single index options Single share options (cash-settled and physically settled) Index basket options Share basket options (cash-settled and physically settled) Single index swaps Single share swaps Index basket swaps Share basket swaps	OTC options on specified European government bonds (cash-settled and physically settled)	Credit derivative transactions that reference loans or bonds

As indicated in their Introductions, these sets of ISDA definitions may also be a useful starting point for the documentation of other product types. A proposed revised version of the ISDA definitions for equity derivatives will also include terms for additional transaction types, including barrier options,[1466] conventional forward transactions on a single share and on baskets of shares, prepaid and variable forwards[1467] and physically settled variants of single share swaps.

In the course of the following discussion of shared features of credit, debt and equity derivatives documentation, practitioners are encouraged to examine in the context of the parties' dealings and objectives the standardized approaches illustrated by the various sets of ISDA definitions, which are similar to those found in other standardized terms used in the derivatives markets and in the proprietary forms of documents prepared by some market professionals. These comparisons of product-specific approaches can, we find, often contribute to a better understanding of the differences between the products themselves and the underlying market assumptions. In other cases the comparison may suggest that differences are at least in part merely conventions and can be ignored if they are inconsistent with the expectations of the parties and do not address a meaningful market need.

[1466] *See* infra note 1383.

[1467] These transaction types are described *infra* p. 723.

SHARED ISSUES IN CREDIT, DEBT AND EQUITY DERIVATIVES

Some of the issues common to credit, debt and equity derivatives arise because of concerns under securities laws and regulations. Other common issues arise because the parties to each transaction must generally consider the impact on their dealings of (1) conventions on valuation, settlement and disruptions and changes in the markets and clearing systems for the underlying debt, equity or other instrument or obligation; (2) potentially competing conventions in different segments of the OTC derivatives market; (3) the occurrence of extraordinary events affecting the underlying instrument or obligation, or its issuer or another obligor, and (4) other circumstances that the parties agree should lead to adjustments to the terms of their transaction or to its early termination.

DOCUMENTATION FEATURES ADDRESSING REGULATORY ISSUES

The documentation for credit, debt and equity derivatives often includes provisions drafted to take into account laws and regulations applicable to the purchase and sale of securities and other investment products and the markets for these instruments. This topic is discussed in Chapter 4,[1468] which also includes examples of provisions and structural features introduced into the documents in light of U.S. law involving, among other things, the registration of nonexempt securities offered to the public, registration and other requirements applicable to securities brokers and dealers and the prevention of fraud, market manipulation and insider trading. As discussed there, concerns of these and other kinds arise in connection with OTC derivatives that are characterized as securities for purposes of these laws or that provide for settlement through the transfer of securities, and in connection with security-based swap agreements, which are not regarded as securities for purposes of these laws but are nonetheless subject to many of their provisions dealing with fraud, market manipulation and trading by insiders or on insider information. These concerns may relate not only to the dealings between the parties but also to securities activities that a party may engage in to hedge its derivatives exposure or dispose of securities received in a credit, debt or equity derivative.

The master agreement forms published by ISDA include minimal representations and covenants relating to the contract under which two parties may engage in transactions. They do not include provisions on special regulatory issues of these kinds. Therefore, when market participants engage in derivatives linked to debt, equity and other financial instruments and obligations, they generally prepare their own provisions for master agreements and confirmations to address these issues, adapting models used in private placement documents, offering circulars and debt and equity trade confirmations. In connection with credit derivatives that may be settled through the transfer of interests in bank loans, the parties also turn to models—participation and assignment agreements and related documents—created for use in the secondary market for loans, where at least some market participants have firm policies on documentation that reflect standards published by bank supervisory agencies.[1469]

[1468] *Supra* p. 129.

[1469] *See* GOOCH & KLEIN, LOAN DOCUMENTATION 247, 305 for examples of bank loan assignment and participation agreements and discussion of elements included in these documents in response to regulatory standards or concerns relating to the U.S. securities laws.

Some special provisions of the kinds referred to above are drafted as illustrated in Chapter 4 and are widely used in documentation without much discussion. Questions relating to potentially applicable legal frameworks, or the appropriate characterization of a transaction for some purposes, are, however, often complex and debatable. When the parties disagree over issues of this kind,[1470] the introduction of special representations, acknowledgments, disclaimers, covenants, indemnities and other features into the transaction's documentation or structure to address these special concerns may lead to considerable negotiation. The sample confirmations for credit and equity derivatives set out below do not include special provisions of these types. The need for these provisions should be reviewed with counsel in all potentially relevant jurisdictions in light of such factors as:

- the nature of the transaction,
- the identities of the parties,
- the jurisdictions from which they are acting,
- regulatory or SRO rules applicable to the parties or their agents for purposes of entering into the transaction,
- the parties' objectives in entering into the transaction,
- any special relationships they may have with the issuer or with another person obligated in respect of the security or other obligation underlying the transaction, or another security for which it may be exchanged or into which it may be converted,
- the parties' other present and expected holdings and other dealings involving these securities (including hedging activities), and
- the rules of exchanges and other organized markets on which the securities, or options or futures involving the securities, are traded.

The parties to OTC derivatives linked to securities should also review with counsel whether their proposed dealings may give rise to concerns or reporting requirements under rules and regulations relating to margin requirements. In some cases, these requirements (for example, Regulations T, U and X of the Federal Reserve Board and margin rules imposed by SROs on their members) are plainly of concern because they expressly apply to a transaction of a particular kind, such as an option on a security. In others, the relevant issues arise less directly, because the requirements apply by their terms to credit extended or maintained for the purpose of purchasing or carrying securities (called "purpose credit")[1471] and some derivatives transactions on securities (such as options, pur-

---

[1470]These debates arise most frequently in the context of the possible tax or accounting treatment of OTC derivatives linked to securities, but they may also arise in other contexts, including those created by the securities laws and contractual restrictions to which a party is or may be subject in connection with the particular items of debt, equity or other obligations underlying a derivatives transaction or more generally.

[1471]Regulation T of the Board of Governors of the Federal Reserve System is generally applicable to credit extended or maintained for the purpose of buying or carrying securities, if extended by entities required to be registered as brokers or dealers under the Securities Exchange Act. Regulation U is applicable to credit extended by banks and certain "nonbank lenders" for the purpose of buying or carrying certain securities identified as "margin stock," if the credit is directly or indirectly secured by margin stock. Regulation X prohibits borrowers acting in the U.S. from willfully obtaining credit in violation of Regulation T or U. It

chases of deep-in-the-money options and forwards on securities) may be viewed as involving purpose credit. Where relevant, these complex requirements, and their exceptions, may be reflected in the parties' documentation in various ways not normally found in the documentation for other OTC derivatives.[1472]

DOCUMENTATION FEATURES ADDRESSING MARKET CONVENTIONS AND PROBLEMS

OTC credit, debt and equity derivatives must all be documented with attention to conventions as to payments, valuations and settlement that are applicable in relation to the underlying debt, equity or other obligation in the agreed markets and, if relevant, clearing systems. The documentation for these transactions must also deal with disruptions in these markets and clearing systems and other circumstances beyond the parties' control that may affect valuations under the particular derivatives transaction or, in a physically settled transaction, affect the ability of a party to make or take delivery. Finally, regardless of the product type, the documentation for these derivatives must correctly articulate the parties' understanding about cases in which the negotiated financial terms of their transaction may be modified, or the transaction may be terminated prematurely, because of extraordinary events affecting the underlying instrument, or its issuer or another relevant obligor, or because of other circumstances, such as market conditions that may affect the ability of one of the parties to maintain a hedge position, or to maintain it without incurring costs beyond those considered by the party in its pricing of the transaction.

---

also applies to U.S. persons (as well as any foreign person controlled by or acting on behalf of or in conjunction with a U.S. person) acting outside the U.S. and prohibits their obtaining credit outside the U.S. to purchase or carry "U.S. securities" unless the credit complies with the requirements of Regulation T or U (the former if the credit is obtained from a foreign branch of a broker-dealer, and the latter if it is obtained from another kind of lender). The impact of Regulation T on securities-linked OTC derivatives stems chiefly from its prohibition of purpose credit extended or maintained by a broker-dealer unless the credit is initially secured with sufficient qualifying collateral. The approach of Regulation U, by contrast, is to limit the amount of purpose credit that a bank or covered nonbank lender may extend.

[1472] For example, broker-dealers registered with the SEC provide in their documents that, when a transaction is subject to Regulation T, the customer will be required to post the higher of the amount of margin required by Regulation T and the amount required by the broker-dealer's own policies. The reference to the broker-dealer's own policies, rather than a more objective standard (like the widely used, exposure-driven approach discussed *infra* p. 1082) is generally explained by reference to the feature of Regulation T which, at least in some cases (such as a short position in a non-equity security or in a U.S. Treasury security), requires the broker-dealer to obtain initial margin with a value equal to 100% of the current market value of the underlying securities plus what is commonly referred to as "good faith margin"—the amount of margin that the creditor would require in exercising sound credit judgment. Reflecting Regulation T, the documents of these market participants also generally provide that, in a "covered option"—say, where the customer at the outset delivers as margin all the securities underlying an option it has written—additional collateral will not be required for the transaction. As a result, when these dealers use the standard 1994 ISDA New York law Credit Support Annex, they may modify the standard terms as illustrated *infra* p. 1272 to single out these transactions, treating the initially delivered securities as the Independent Amount of collateral required for the covered option and provide that the exposure represented by the option will not be considered in calculating mark-to-market collateral required under the parties' agreement.

Credit, Debt and Equity Derivatives

VALUATION AND SETTLEMENT CONVENTIONS AND MARKET DISRUPTIONS

THE STANDARD ISDA APPROACHES

The *1996 Equity Derivatives Definitions,* the *1997 Government Bond Option Definitions* and the *1999 Credit Derivatives Definitions* include provisions that address many of the documentation issues raised by the need to have the terms of a transaction reflect the valuation and settlement conventions, and the possible disruptions, in the related cash and exchange markets for an underlying debt or equity asset. In some cases, however, they do so in different ways.

Users of these definitions should be aware of the differences because, if a standard approach suggested by one set is not necessarily dictated by current market practice for a particular product, an approach available under a different set of definitions may be a useful starting point in drafting an alternative. More importantly, the ISDA definitions include presumed or "default" choices as to many matters that the parties will be treated as having made if they incorporate the definitions into the confirmation of a transaction and do not expressly override them. If their business agreement is inconsistent with the presumptions made in a set of definitions incorporated into a confirmation, a key function of the confirmation will be to set out the parties' agreement on the relevant matter in full, so as to override the presumption.

The following tables and related commentary point to examples of differences among these three sets of definitions. In each case, the table indicates the result that would obtain generally or in the specified kind of transaction if the parties' confirmation were silent on the specified point. Where relevant, the table references to the *1999 Credit Derivatives Definitions* include references to the following supplements: the *Restructuring Supplement* (May 11, 2001); the *Supplement Relating to Convertible, Exchangeable or Accreting Obligations* (November 9, 2001); and the *Supplement Relating to Successor and Credit Events* (November 28, 2001). In the notes at the ends of the tables, we indicate some cases in which changes or additions to the approaches described are being considered in connection with ISDA's projects to publish new sets of equity and credit derivatives definitions.

This first table summarizes important features of the ways in which the definitions address the valuation of underlying assets for purposes of cash settlement of a European style put option on a single share, a European style put option on a bond and a credit default swap. The valuation approach for share options reflected in the first column of this table is also applicable under the *1996 Equity Derivatives Definitions* for purposes of equity swaps in connection with each date identified by the parties as a Valuation Date, and the same approach would be taken for valuation in equity forward transactions under the proposed revision to ISDA's equity derivatives definitions. In the table, it is assumed that the ISDA "default" or fallback choices apply; the parties can, of course, make different choices in their documentation.

Table 1 — Cash Settlement Valuation Conventions		
1996 Equity Derivatives Definitions **Cash-settled European Share Put Option**	**1997 Government Bond Option Definitions** **Cash-settled European Bond Put Option**	**1999 Credit Derivatives Definitions** **Cash-settled Credit Default Swap**
Cash Settlement Amount: Excess of the Strike Price over the Settlement Price for the Share, but not less than zero. Sections 5.2 & 5.4.	*Cash Settlement Amount:* Excess of the Strike Price over the Spot Price for the Bond, but not less than zero. Section 7.2.	*Cash Settlement Amount:* Floating Rate Payer Calculation Amount *times* Excess of the Reference Price over the Final Price for a Reference Obligation, but not less than zero. Section 7.3. *See* Note 1.
Time of Valuation: As of the Valuation Time on the Expiration Date, unless a Market Disruption Event exists. Section 2.1(g). *See* Note 2. The fallback choice for the Valuation Time is the close of trading on the Exchange for the Share. Section 4.1. *See* Note 2.	*Time of Valuation:* As of the Valuation Time on the Exercise Date. Market disruptions are not treated as relevant, and the parties must specify the Valuation Time because no presumption applies. Section 7.2.	*Time of Valuation:* At the Valuation Time on the fifth Business Day after the Conditions to Payment are satisfied, unless fewer than two dealers of five selected by the Calculation Agent give firm bid Full Quotations for the Reference Obligation on the day. Section 7.5. *See* Note 3. The fallback choice for the Valuation Time is 11:00 a.m. in the Calculation Agent City. Section 7.14.
Weekends and Holidays: If the Expiration Date is not an Exchange Business Day, it will be moved to the following Exchange Business Day. Section 4.2. Exchange Business Days exclude days on which the Exchange is scheduled to close prior to its regular weekday closing time. Section 1.20. *See* Note 4.	*Weekends and Holidays:* If the Expiration Date is not an Exchange Business Day or a Seller Business Day, it will be moved to the following day that is both. Section 4.1(f). Same rule on Exchange Business Days as for Share option. Section 3.5.	*Weekends and Holidays:* The city relevant to determining Business Days will turn on the currency of denomination of the Floating Rate Payer Calculation Amount. Section 1.15.

Table 1 — Cash Settlement Valuation Conventions		
1996 Equity Derivatives Definitions **Cash-settled European Share Put Option**	*1997 Government Bond Option Definitions* **Cash-settled European Bond Put Option**	*1999 Credit Derivatives Definitions* **Cash-settled Credit Default Swap**
Market Disruptions: If there is a Market Disruption Event, valuation occurs on the first of the following five Exchange Business Days that is free of Market Disruption Events or on the last of those days if a Market Disruption Event exists on each of them. Section 4.2.	*Market Disruptions*: No provision to deal with valuations during market disruptions.	*Market Disruptions*: If two or more firm bid Full Quotations are not available on the Valuation Date, valuation moves to the first of the next three Business Days on which the Calculation Agent obtains at least two such Quotations. If they are still not available, further fallbacks apply over a period ending 15 Business Days after the Valuation Date. Section 7.8.
Valuation method: The official price—or if none, the mid-market price—per Share on the Exchange, unless there is a Market Disruption Event on the Valuation Date and each of the following five Exchange Business Days. Sections 1.15 and 4.2. Only in that case, use the Calculation Agent's "good faith estimate of the Exchange price for the Share that would have prevailed but for that Market Disruption Event as of the Valuation Time on that fifth Exchange Business Day." Section 4.2(a)(ii)(B). *See* Note 4.	*Valuation method*: In all cases, the price determined by the Calculation Agent in good faith. Sections 3.8 & 7.2(c).	*Valuation method*: The highest of the required Quotations obtained by the Calculation Agent from dealers polled, unless at least two are unavailable on or before the 15th Business Day after the Valuation Date. In that event, the Final Price for the Reference Obligation will be zero. Section 7.11.

Table 1 — Cash Settlement Valuation Conventions		
1996 Equity Derivatives Definitions Cash-settled European Share Put Option	**1997 Government Bond Option Definitions** Cash-settled European Bond Put Option	**1999 Credit Derivatives Definitions** Cash-settled Credit Default Swap
Dispute Resolution: No provision. The Calculation Agent is required to make all determinations in good faith and, in the absence of manifest error, its determinations and calculations are binding. Section 1.25. *See* Note 6.	*Dispute Resolution:* Disputes on spot price to be resolved by one or three independent third parties if the parties cannot agree. Section 5.3.	*Dispute Resolution:* Disinterested third party selected by the Calculation Agent in its reasonable discretion, after consultation with the parties, makes all determinations that are disputed or that the Calculation Agent has failed to make. Section 10.2.

Note 1. For purposes of this comparison with the way in which the share and bond options work, assume that the Conditions to Payment will be satisfied when the Buyer gives notice that an agreed Credit Event has occurred, the Floating Rate Payer Calculation Amount is the principal amount of Reference Obligations in respect of which the Buyer is obtaining credit protection, and the Reference Price is 100%.

Note 2. Market Disruption Event is defined as "the occurrence or existence on any Exchange Business Day during the one-half hour period that ends at the relevant Valuation Time of any suspension of or limitation imposed on trading (by reason of movements in price exceeding limits permitted by the relevant Exchange or otherwise)" in respect of the Share on the Exchange. Section 4.3. The proposed revised equity derivatives definitions would introduce various refinements to this approach. *See infra* p. 626.

Note 3. Full Quotation, presumed to apply, calls for firm quotations for an amount of the Reference Obligation with an outstanding principal equal to or greater than the Quotation Amount—the Floating Rate Payer Calculation Amount (assuming it and the Reference Obligation are denominated in the same currency). Under the fallback, whether the quotations are to include interest will depend on the practice in the market for the Reference Obligations, as determined by the Calculation Agent after consultation. Sections 7.8 & 7.9. Under a proposed revision, the presumed Valuation Date would be *on or earlier than* five Business Days, selected by the Calculation Agent.

Note 4. This approach would also apply in determining the Final Price of a Share for purposes of an equity swap documented under these definitions (Section 7.10) and, under the proposed revised definitions, for purposes of forward transactions on Shares, if the parties did not specify otherwise.

Note 5. The proposed revised equity derivatives definitions would expand this standard to include commercial reasonableness and to apply that standard to all exercises of judgment by the Calculation Agent.

Table 2 summarizes features of conventions relating to physical settlement of the same three kinds of transactions: a European style option on a single share, a European style bond option and a credit default swap, under the three sets of ISDA definitions.

Table 2–Physical Settlement Conventions		
1996 Equity Derivatives Definitions	*1997 Government Bond Option Definitions*	*1999 Credit Derivatives Definitions*
Settlement Date: In a Share option, the Settlement Date will be "the first day on which settlement of a sale of such Shares executed on [the] Exercise Date customarily would take place through the relevant Clearance System, unless a Settlement Disruption Event prevents delivery of such Shares on that day." Section 6.2.	**Settlement Date:** No "default choice" is supplied. The parties must specify the Settlement Date, or the method for determining it, for an option to be physically settled. However, that date will then be adjusted automatically if a Settlement Disruption Event occurs. Section 5.1(d).	**Settlement Date:** In a credit default swap, the Physical Settlement Date for the Buyer's delivery of a Portfolio of Deliverable Obligations (in exchange for the Seller's payment) is the end of a Physical Settlement Period starting when all applicable Conditions to Payment have been satisfied. The number of Business Days in that period is "the longest of the number of Business Days for settlement in accordance with then current market practice of any Deliverable Obligation being Delivered in the Portfolio, as determined by the Calculation Agent, after consultation with the parties." Sections 8.3 & 8.5.

Table 2–Physical Settlement Conventions		
1996 Equity Derivatives Definitions	**1997 Government Bond Option Definitions**	**1999 Credit Derivatives Definitions**
Settlement Disruptions: If a Settlement Disruption Event prevents delivery on the Settlement Date, that date is postponed to the first of the following 10 Clearance System Business Days on which a Settlement Disruption Event does not prevent settlement. Section 6.2. After that point, settlement is to occur on the first day thereafter on which settlement would customarily take place, through delivery of the Shares in any other commercially reasonable manner. Section 6.2. "Settlement Disruption Event" is defined as any event beyond the control of the parties as a result of which the relevant Clearance System cannot clear the transfer of the relevant Shares. Section 6.5.	***Settlement Disruptions:*** If a Settlement Disruption Event prevents delivery on the Settlement Date, that date is postponed to the first of the following 30 calendar days on which a Settlement Disruption Event does not prevent settlement. Section 6.2(b). After that point, the party required to deliver Bonds is required to use best efforts to deliver them in a commercially reasonable manner outside the Clearance System on a delivery versus payment basis. Section 6.2(b). "Settlement Disruption Event" is defined to be an event beyond the control of the parties as a result of which the relevant Clearance System cannot clear the transfer of the relevant Bonds. Section 6.2(a).	***Settlement Disruptions:*** Physical Settlement can be delayed or replaced by partial cash settlement if: (a) "due to an event beyond the control of Buyer, it is impossible or illegal for Buyer to Deliver, or due to an event beyond the control of Seller it is impossible or illegal for Seller to accept Delivery of, any portion of the Portfolio specified in the Notice of Intended Physical Settlement on the Physical Settlement Date" (*See* Note 1); or (b) the parties agreed partial cash settlement would apply to their transaction involving Assignable Loans or Consent Required loans and "due to the non-receipt of any requisite consents" on or before the 15th Business Day after the Physical Settlement Date, the relevant asset cannot be assigned or novated to Seller or its designee. Sections 9.4, 9.5 & 9.6. *See* Note 2.

Table 2–Physical Settlement Conventions		
1996 Equity Derivatives Definitions	*1997 Government Bond Option Definitions*	*1999 Credit Derivatives Definitions*
Dividend treatment: Following exercise, dividends on the Shares will be payable "to the party that would receive such dividends according to market practice for a sale of such Shares exercised on the Exercise Date to be settled through the relevant Clearance System." Section 6.7.	**Interest treatment:** The Bond Payment due to the party that is delivering the Bonds to be Delivered in physical settlement of an option will include accrued but unpaid interest, "computed in accordance with customary trade practices employed with respect to the Bonds." Section 6.3(b).	**Interest treatment:** Under the fallback choice, the size of the Portfolio of Deliverable Obligations to be delivered in physical settlement of a credit default swap will be determined excluding accrued but unpaid interest if the Deliverable Obligations are Borrowed Money obligations. Section 7.8(c)(iii). *See also infra* note 1531.

Note 1. These events include, "without limitation, failure of the relevant clearance system or due to any law, regulation or court order" but expressly exclude "market conditions or the failure to obtain any requisite consent with respect to the Delivery of Loans." In this case, any portion of the Portfolio that can be Delivered is settled as scheduled for the corresponding portion of the Physical Settlement Amount and the remaining portion is physically settled as soon as practicable thereafter, but if that settlement cannot occur on or before the 30th day after the Physical Settlement Date (which is the Latest Permissible Physical Settlement Date in this case) because of the illegality or impossibility, Partial Cash Settlement applies to that portion of the Portfolio. Section 9.4. *See infra* p. 618, for discussion of proposed changes to the partial cash settlement mechanisms, given the issues that partial cash settlement creates for intermediaries.

Note 2. In the second case, Partial Cash Settlement applies automatically, but, if the parties had agreed to fallback settlement through delivery of a loan participation (by selecting Direct Loan Participation or Indirect Loan Participation), only if the relevant participation is not effected on or before the 15th Business Day after the Physical Settlement Date (which is the Latest Permissible Physical Settlement Date in this case). Sections 9.5 & 9.6.

As summarized in Table 2, the *1999 Credit Derivatives Definitions* provide that, in certain cases, transactions originally intended to be physically settled will be settled in cash. There is concern in the market over the potential for abuse by a Buyer of these provisions, for example, in connection with assertions that the Buyer has been unable to obtain a consent necessary to permit it to transfer or novate a Deliverable Obligation to the Seller or its designee. Although a Buyer has a duty to take all reasonable steps to obtain these consents,[1473] concern remains that a less than scrupulous Buyer could select Assignable Loans or Consent Required Loans for which consent would be unlikely regardless of the use of reasonable efforts. There has also been concern about the Seller's position under the physical settlement mechanisms described above when a Buyer, for any reason, does not deliver a Deliverable Obligation identified by it in its Notice of Intended Physical Settlement given as a Condition to Payment.

Partial cash settlement can create special problems for financial intermediaries, regardless of whether it results from such "gaming" of the procedures. For example, if an intermediary expects to use Deliverable Obligations received under one transaction to settle another but learns, at the end of permitted period for Physical Settlement under the first transaction—the Latest Possible Physical Settlement Date—that the Buyer in that transaction will instead be expecting a cash settlement and retaining those obligations because it has not received a necessary consent, or that the Buyer simply will not be settling with the specified Deliverable Obligations, it may be too late for the intermediary to acquire substitute Deliverable Obligations to tender in the second transaction. There are related concerns over whether the intermediary, in such a case, would be entitled to require a mirror image cash settlement of the second transaction. If not, it could lose the benefit of the second transaction while having to make a payment on the first. Even if the intermediary were entitled to cash-settle both transactions, there may be concerns over its ability to time the related valuations in a way that will protect the intermediary against loss from a mismatch of valuation times. These potential problems arise as a structural matter within the *1999 Credit Derivatives Definitions*, because Section 8.1 requires the consummation of Physical Settlement with Deliverable Obligations identified in the Buyer's Notice of Intended Physical Settlement.

One approach aimed at addressing these concerns to some extent is to require that nonreceipt of a required consent will trigger, instead of Partial Cash Settlement, an obligation of the Buyer to enter into a participation agreement in respect of the relevant loan or deliver alternative obligations. However, to implement this approach, an exception to the rule of Section 8.1 would be necessary, as would a related deferral of the period for completion of the Physical Settlement, and the approach would, in any case, be unsatisfactory for an intermediary unless it could be certain that whatever it received in settlement from a Buyer as a participation interest could also be transferred by it, or subparticipated by it, in settlement of another transaction.

As a result, in its proposed revision to the *1999 Credit Derivatives Definitions*, ISDA is considering new approaches relating to Bonds and Loans that are not delivered. Where Bonds are concerned, if the Buyer fails to Deliver them within the five Business Days following the applicable Physical Settlement Date, unless the failure is caused by an illegality or impossibility of a kind described in the preceding tables, the Seller will have a right to close out all or a portion of the relevant Transaction by the purchase—referred to as a "buy-in"—of Bonds that have not been Delivered at any time, after giving the Buyer at least two Business Days' advance notice.[1474] The Seller's giving of this notice will sus-

---

[1473] See *infra* p. 709.

[1474] This notice would have to specify the Seller's intention, the anticipated buy-in date and the Bonds to be subject to the buy-in.

pend the Buyer's right to Deliver the relevant Bonds and, if the buy-in is consummated, on the Business Day following the settlement of the buy-in, the Buyer will be deemed to have Delivered the portion of the Portfolio covered by the buy-in and will be entitled to receive from the Seller—instead of the portion of the Physical Settlement Amount allocable to the Bonds subject to the buy-in, that amount less the amount paid by the Seller in the buy-in, including brokerage costs. This reduction in the amount payable cannot reduce it below zero (that is, the Buyer will not be responsible for a payment to the Seller) and the Seller will be required to conduct the buy-in using commercially reasonable procedures. If the buy-in is not consummated within five Business Days of the date specified by the Seller, the suspension of the Buyer's right to continue seeking to Deliver the relevant Bonds is lifted.

Under the proposed new approach for Loans that are not Delivered, the fifth Business Day after the Physical Settlement Date would be treated as an Alternative Procedure Start Date and the following procedures would apply to Loans that had not been Delivered by then, subject to exceptions for cases in which the parties have effectively agreed otherwise.[1475] First, at any time after the Alternative Procedure Start Date, the Buyer would be entitled to Deliver, in lieu of all or any part of the Loan, a Bond or Loan that satisfies specified criteria,[1476] and, second, if all the Loans not Delivered had not been replaced through this mechanism, or Delivery of the originally specified Loan, on or before the fifth Business Day following the Alternative Procedure Start Date, at any time thereafter the Seller would have the right to require the Buyer to settle through Delivery of Bonds or Loans selected by the Seller that satisfy specified criteria,[1477] so long as the Seller identifies a person ready, willing and able to Deliver the instruments to the Buyer at a price less than the Reference Price originally agreed upon by the parties when they struck their deal and the instrument may be further Delivered by the Buyer to the Seller without the need for consent of any other person.[1478]

ISSUES RAISED BY THE STANDARD APPROACHES

The parties are of course free to alter the results shown in the preceding tables. To avoid inadvertent choices, market participants often routinely spell out all the relevant choices in their confirmations. The parties also often create their own ways of dealing with circumstances that may affect scheduled valuation or settlement. This is perhaps

---

[1475] These are cases in which the parties have agreed that: (1) only the Reference Obligations for the Transaction will be Deliverable Obligations; (2) Consent Required Loans are Deliverable Obligations and partial cash settlement of these Loans is expressly permitted; (iii) Assignable Loans are Deliverable Obligations; (4) Direct Loan Participations are Deliverable Obligations and partial cash settlement is expressly permitted; or (5) the relevant failure to Deliver the Loans is due to illegality or impossibility as contemplated above in Table 2.

[1476] In addition to any other Deliverable Obligation Characteristics specified by the parties, the Bond would have to satisfy the Deliverable Obligation Characteristics known as Transferable and Not Bearer and the Loan would have to be Assignable and could not be a Consent Required Loan or a Direct Loan Participation. *See infra* p. 679 on these characteristics.

[1477] These criteria would be the same as those specified in the preceding note.

[1478] As a related matter, the proposed revisions would make clear that a Buyer may only physically settle a transaction with the Deliverable Obligations identified in the notice given by it as a Condition to Payment, except where the revised definitions expressly permit otherwise.

most often the case in "asset swaps" and similar transactions, in which an OTC swap, forward or option is designed to enable one of the parties to assume or transfer particular risks associated with a cash position in the underlying debt or equity. Tailored solutions take on particular importance if the debt or equity interests form part of the credit support for the transaction or another transaction between the parties, or a transaction between one of the parties and an affiliate of the other, or if one of the parties has agreed to hold the debt or equity interests as a hedge. In these cases, the documentation for the OTC derivatives transaction often includes valuation, settlement and related terms aimed at ensuring that the relevant payout under the transaction reflects the actual value received, or that could be obtained, in a private auction or market sale of the cash position at the time and otherwise on the terms agreed.

A common example of such a case is a total return swap between a financial intermediary and a customer in which the customer is required to make a payment if there is a decline in the value of the reference security over the term of the transaction and the intermediary is required to make a payment if the value increases over the term.[1479] In such transactions, the intermediary's hedge for its obligations will often be a cash position in the reference security, in an amount equal to the swap's notional amount, held by the intermediary itself or by one of its affiliates.[1480] Although the documentation for such a transaction may provide that the reference security will, in the first instance, be valued at the agreed time on the basis of the highest of the firm bid quotations for an identical cash position, obtained from a specified number of independent third parties, the customer will often seek the right to be a bidder, or to designate one, if the agreed minimum number of third-party bids is unavailable at the indicated time, or if the customer believes that the bids undervalue the cash position. The intermediary will often agree to the customer's request, so long as the intermediary, ultimately, is free to value the position otherwise for purposes of the swap if a sale is not actually consummated at the price bid by the customer or its designee, or if the customer is in default under the agreement at the specified valuation time.

Auction-like mechanisms of this kind are also common features of complex credit default swaps involving multiple reference entities, including those used in the structures referred to as synthetic CDOs, as discussed below.[1481] In these contexts, the parties may agree that, if an agreed Credit Event occurs with respect to an identified Reference Entity or Reference Obligation in the pool, and if all Conditions to Payment are satisfied in a timely manner, the party identified as the Seller of protection will be obligated to pay the Buyer a Cash Settlement Amount calculated to represent the discount from par (that is, from 100% of the outstanding principal) at which the market values of the Reference Obligation or any other obligation of the relevant Reference Entity that has the required characteristics on a Valuation Date after the Credit Event has occurred. In these cases, the Seller or its designee is often permitted to provide a bid in this market-based valuation

---

[1479] In addition to this total return "leg," the transaction would typically involve a second payment obligation on the part of the customer, reflecting the agreed compensation for the cost of carrying the reference security.

[1480] See Michael Haubenstock, Peter Crossey & Jonathan Davies, *Risk Management in a credit derivatives business*, in CREDIT DERIVATIVES: APPLICATIONS FOR RISK MANAGEMENT 35.

[1481] See infra p. 655.

approach and, if its bid is the highest, the cash settlement required under the swap will typically be calculated by reference to that bid.[1482]

These auction procedures are not provided for in ISDA's standardized terms for credit, debt or equity derivatives, but they have become a common method of addressing concerns related to standard valuation procedures. When the transaction involves the valuation of debt or equity on the basis of cash market quotations—or could involve this type of valuation if a relevant instrument ceased to be traded on an agreed exchange—the parties should look closely at each aspect of the valuation mechanism, and each step to be taken in its implementation, to determine what procedures are appropriate for their particular transaction and, if relevant, whether a specially designed solution, like these auction mechanisms, might be appropriate. Some of the central issues are:

- The nature of the quotations to be sought in the first instance, in terms of size and place on the bid/offer scale (*e.g.*, if a source will not give a firm quotation for a portfolio of the reference security with an aggregate principal amount, or number of shares, equal to the amount or number relevant to the parties' transaction (referred to as a "Full Quotation" in the *1999 Credit Derivatives Definitions*), should it be asked for the maximum amount or number for which it will give a firm quotation so that the weighted average of such smaller quotations—the Weighted Average Quotation method under that set of ISDA definitions[1483]—can be used as a fallback if the minimum number of full quotations is not available?)

- The criteria to be applied in selecting quotation sources and the process for selecting them (or, if the contract specifies sources, the qualifications for substitutes if a named source ceases to satisfy the criteria)[1484]

[1482] There would be a separate obligation to settle the cash purchase of the relevant Reference Obligations or other obligations for the price bid unless multiple sellers of protection involved in the structure bid the same price, in which case another of these bidders may, instead, be given preference in the cash purchase transaction. In these structures the sellers undertake obligations to make payments beginning at increasingly high levels—often referred to as risk "attachment" points—so that, in effect, the seller providing protection that begins at the highest level is not required to make a payment until the aggregate of the cash settlement amounts calculated after successive Credit Events exceeds that seller's attachment point. In these auction approaches, if multiple sellers of protection make the same highest bid, the seller at the lowest attachment point would normally be given preference over the sellers at higher attachment points in any determination of which should be entitled to consummate the cash purchase.

[1483] Weighted Average Quotation uses a weighted average of firm quotations for amounts of a Reference Obligation that are as large as available and at least equal to the minimum agreed by the parties or, if they have not specified a Minimum Quotation Amount, quotations of at least U.S.$ 1 million (or the equivalent in the relevant currency). Sections 7.10 & 7.13. *See infra* note 1532 regarding the inclusion or exclusion of accrued but unpaid interest in the quotations sought.

[1484] *See supra* p. 415 on the general subject of selecting rate and price sources. The sources initially selected may have been chosen because they are leading participants in the market for the relevant reference instrument and are not affiliated with either of the parties. The parties should consider including a contract provision regarding the choice of a substitute if, say, one of these sources withdraws from that market or becomes an affiliate of one of the parties, or if an additional source should be identified because two of the identified sources have merged or become affiliates.

- The window for seeking quotations

- The minimum and maximum number of quotations to be sought

- How the quotations obtained should be used, when only the minimum number is obtained and when more are obtained (*e.g.*, should the highest be used or should they be averaged, and if averaging is used, should all the quotations be included in the average?)

- Each party's role in the process, both in the first instance and if the agreed minimum number of quotations is not obtained from agreed sources (*e.g.*, if one of the parties will be obtaining the quotations, is it to do so in consultation with the other party (are both parties to be on the phone), and if one party is unable to obtain quotations, should the other party be entitled to try?)

- The turning point for use of an alternative approach—*i.e.*, is deferral of valuation the appropriate response if the agreed minimum number of quotations for the full agreed size or amount is unavailable at the specified time or should another type of quotation be used, if possible, before the parties postpone valuation (*e.g.*, do the parties prefer to postpone valuation or to value the reference portfolio using a weighted average of smaller firm quotations?)

- Are there circumstances in which a valuation of zero will be used, and when should they be avoided?[1485]

- If the transaction involves a basket of reference assets, how will the timing or method chosen for valuation change if only some of the assets can be valued as preferred, and at the same time?

The following tables describe how some of these issues are addressed in the *1999 Credit Derivatives Definitions*.[1486] They also point to some critical assumptions implicit in the cited valuation mechanisms. Although the approaches described in the tables were developed for use in respect of debt Obligations, the same issues and questions are relevant in valuations for equity derivatives when the relevant shares are not traded on an exchange or the parties wish to provide for valuation by dealers if the shares are delisted[1487]

[1485] One approach that is sometimes used provides that, if application of Article VII of the *1999 Credit Derivatives Definitions* would produce a Final Price of zero, those provisions, to that extent, will not apply and the Final Price will be based on an appraisal by an Independent Third Party. These provisions may call on the Calculation Agent to cause the Independent Third Party to make the appraisal on the basis of an expected recovery rate for the relevant Reference Obligation (expressed as a percentage of outstanding principal or face amount) that disregards any right of setoff or counterclaim that the Reference Entity or any other person might have and takes into account the terms of the Reference Obligation as in effect on the date the Independent Third Party undertakes the appraisal.

[1486] The tables are not intended to be comprehensive; they do not illustrate the ISDA approaches for transactions involving multiple valuation dates or multiple assets.

[1487] The delisting of the stock underlying an OTC derivatives transaction is often treated by the parties as a ground for cancellation of the transaction—with the consequences applicable, as described below (*see infra* p. 636), in connection with cancellation upon the occurrence of a Merger Event—unless the stock is listed, as of the same date, on another exchange in the same jurisdiction.

or if there are market disruptions. These definitions do not address these issues and leave it to the parties to do so.[1488]

[1488]Under Sections 2.1(g)(ii) and 7.10(b), the Settlement Price (Cash-settled Share Option) and Final Price (Share Swap Transaction) will be "determined by the Calculation Agent as provided in the related Confirmation at the Valuation Time on the Valuation Date" or, if none is specified, "the official price or, if there is no official price, the mid-market price per Share on the Exchange at the Valuation Time on the Valuation Date." However, the ISDA working group involved in preparing a revised version of the *1996 Equity Derivatives Definitions* has proposed adding delisting, understood in the sense described in the preceding note, to the events that may be handled through a negotiated close-out or the cancellation of the parties' transaction, in whole, if the transaction involves a single Share, or in part if the transaction involves a basket of Shares and some but not all are delisted. *See infra* p. 634 on the ISDA approach called "Cancellation and Payment."

Table 3 — Use of Quotations under *1999 Credit Derivatives Definitions* Regardless of Number of Valuation Dates & Assets Valued	
Quotation Types *By Bid/Offer Scale Position*	***Quotation Types*** *By Size of Quotation*
Under Sections 7.6 & 7.8: • Bid • Offer • Mid-market (arithmetic mean of bid and offer quotations provided by dealer that provides both) *Implicit assumptions:* If the Calculation Agent is a party, only involve the other party in seeking Quotations if the Calculation Agent's efforts are unavailing through the 10th Business Day after the scheduled Valuation Date. If necessary to determine size of acceptable Quotations, subdivide the period for seeking Quotations as shown in the next column. After the tenth Business Day following the Valuation Date, if the Calculation Agent's efforts have been unavailing, permit other party to seek Quotations for another five Business Days but then treat the asset as having a zero value if specified minimum number of Quotations is not obtained. A third-party Calculation Agent involves the parties only if its efforts are unavailing through the tenth Business Day after the scheduled Valuation Date. Then, if one or both of the parties obtains the minimum needed Quotations, those Quotations are used. Section 7.8(b).	Under Sections 7.7 & 7.8: • Full Quotations • Weighted Average Quotation *Implicit assumptions:* On the Valuation Date through third Business Day thereafter, use Full Quotations only if at least two are available. For up to four Business Days, moving the valuation is preferred over using Quotations for less than the full Quotation Amount of the Reference Obligation (or Floating Rate Payer Calculation Amount, if no Quotation Amount is specified). From the fourth through the tenth Business Day after the Valuation Date, use either Full Quotations or, if fewer than two are available, use a Weighted Average Quotation, but only move the valuation if neither approach works. Weighted Average Quotation is used for Reference Obligation amounts that are as large as available and at least equal to the Minimum Quotation Amount agreed by the parties or, if they have not specified a minimum, quotations of at least U.S.$ 1 million (or the equivalent in the relevant Obligation currency). Sections 7.10 & 7.13.

Under Section 7.9 of the *1999 Credit Derivatives Definitions*, the quotations called for as described in Table 3 are sought at the Valuation Time, to the extent reasonably practicable. Indicative quotations are used (under Section 9.9(l)) only if the relevant Obligation is not deliverable or assignable, when an event giving rise to an impossibility or illegality situation leads to the application of Partial Cash Settlement.

Table 4 — Valuation Methods for One Reference Obligation and One Reference Date under *1999 Credit Derivatives Definitions* Sections 7.7 & 7.11(a)	
"Highest"	**"Market"**
The Final Price (expressed as a percentage of principal) will be the highest of the Quotations obtained. *Implicit assumptions:* A single firm quotation of the agreed type should never be used. Section 7.11(b). The parties will always prefer a Weighted Average Quotation determined on the basis of quotations for amounts lower than the Quotation Amount to a single firm quotation that satisfies the Full Quotation test. The parties will also prefer to value the asset at zero if sufficient firm quotations to implement the Weighted Average Quotation approach are unavailable, even if a single firm quotation that satisfies the Full Quotation test is available.	The Final Price (expressed as a percentage of principal) will depend on whether the Quotations obtained are Full Quotations or a Weighted Average Quotation and will be: • the arithmetic mean of the Full Quotations after disregarding the highest and lowest, if more than three are obtained; • the Full Quotation remaining after disregarding the highest and lowest, if exactly three are obtained; • the arithmetic mean of the Full Quotations, if exactly two are obtained; • the Weighted Average Quotation, if fewer than two Full Quotations are obtained and the Weighted Average Quotation is determinable; • otherwise, zero. *Implicit assumptions:* Same as in the preceding column, and, in addition, when at least three Full Quotations are available, the high and low should always be disregarded as suspect, even though both should be used when exactly two Full Quotations are obtained.

As indicated in Tables 5 and 6, the standard valuation procedures in the *1999 Credit Derivatives Definitions* can result in the valuation of a Reference Obligation at zero on the 15th Business Day following a scheduled Valuation Date, notwithstanding the availability of a firm Full Quotation for the Obligation. Under a modified approach being considered for revised ISDA credit derivatives definitions in order to protect Sellers against the risk of zero valuations, at the point at which a Reference Obligation would be given a zero value under the *1999 Credit Derivatives Definitions*, the Quotation used to calculate the Final Price for the Reference Obligation (and, therefore, the amount payable by the Seller in cash settlement of a credit default swap) would be deemed to be any Full Quotation obtained from a Dealer at the Valuation Time on the 15th Business Day following the scheduled Valuation Date or, if none of the Dealers provided a Full Quotation on that day, the weighted average of any firm quotations for the Reference Obligation obtained from Dealers at the Valuation Time on that day. In calculating the Final Price, this weighted average would be applied to the aggregate portion of the Quotation Amount for which the Dealers provided those firm quotations were obtained, and a zero valuation would be assigned only to the balance of the Quotation Amount for which firm quotations were not obtained on that day at the Valuation Time.[1489]

Similarly, practice in the equity derivatives market involving valuations has evolved in various ways since the publication of the *1996 Equity Derivatives Definitions*, leading market participants to depart from some of the conventions summarized in Tables 1 through 4. The following are some of the ways in which the proposed revised version of the ISDA equity derivatives definitions would change and refine those conventions to reflect evolution in market practice and experience over the years with market disruptions:

- *After Hours Trading*

    For cases in which the parties have not specified otherwise, the Valuation Time relevant in connection with a Valuation Date will be the close of *the regular trading session*—including any extension of a regular trading session—on the relevant Exchange on that Valuation Date (in relation to the relevant Index or Share to be valued). It will be clarified that after-hours or other trading outside the hours of the regular trading session (as extended, if applicable) will be disregarded.

- *Unexpected Closings on Exchanges*

    Under a revised definition of "Valuation Time," if a relevant Exchange closes before its regularly scheduled closing time and the specified Valuation Time is after the early closing time, the Valuation Time will be moved forward to the close of the regular trading session on the Exchange on the relevant Valuation Date, in any case in which the early closing does not cause a Market Disruption Event.

    Similarly, a closing prior to the regular weekday closing time will not necessarily disqualify a day as an Exchange Business Day. A day may qualify as an Exchange Business Day if all relevant Exchanges and Related Exchanges are open for trading or if the Calculation Agent determines that the failure of any such Exchange or Related Exchange to open does not have a material effect on trading of the Relevant Shares, futures or options over the relevant Shares.

- *Market Disruption Events*

    The three principal proposed changes relating to Market Disruption Events involve the window for determining whether an event will be

---

[1489] A similar approach is also proposed for cases in which a third party is acting as Calculation Agent. As indicated *supra* p. 620, another approach used, at least in complex transactions, to avoid the harsh result of a zero valuation is to permit the Seller to bid, or designate another person to bid, for the relevant obligation.

treated as a Market Disruption Event, the handling of cases in which multiple Exchanges are relevant but not all are affected and distinctions among the events that may be treated as Market Disruption Events (in case the parties decide that the appropriate response may differ depending on the nature of the Market Disruption Event).

The Market Disruption Window. Instead of the half hour ending with the Valuation Time, the hour preceding the Valuation Time may be viewed as the appropriate window for determining whether a Market Disruption Event has occurred and, therefore, whether the Valuation Date should be postponed or the valuation procedure should otherwise be modified as described above.[1490]

Market Disruption Events and Multiple Exchanges. If more than one Exchange is specified by the parties to be relevant to their transaction and a Market Disruption Event does not involve all the relevant Exchanges, the Exchange or Exchanges on which the Market Disruption Event has occurred will be disregarded for purposes of valuations. That is, a Market Disruption Event will not be treated as having occurred unless all relevant Exchanges are affected.

Distinguishing among Market Disruption Events. The various kinds of circumstances that may be treated as Market Disruption Events may be viewed separately as Trading Disruptions and Exchange Disruptions.

A Trading Disruption would be any material suspension of or limitation imposed on trading by the relevant Exchange or a Related Exchange or otherwise, including a limit by reason of movements in price exceeding established limits, if it relates to the relevant Share or the level of the relevant Index or to options contracts or future contracts relating to the Share or Index on a Related Exchange. As in the current definitions, the determination of materiality would be left to the Calculation Agent.

An Exchange Disruption would include any event that materially disrupts or impairs the ability to effect transactions in the relevant Shares on the specified Exchange or, in cases involving an Index, transactions in securities that comprise 20% or more of the level of the Index, on any relevant Exchanges, or the ability to effect options or futures relating to the Shares or Index on any Related Exchanges. The determination of materiality, again, is left to the Calculation Agent. The proposal would clarify that an Exchange Disruption may include, among other events, the temporary closure and re-opening of an Exchange or Related Exchange, a material systems failure of the trading, communications or connectivity systems to an Exchange or Related Exchange and a relocation of trading of Shares from one Exchange to another.

EVENTS AFFECTING THE UNDERLYING DEBT OR EQUITY

The following table summarizes conventions generally applicable under the specified set of ISDA definitions in connection with changes to the assets underlying a transaction.

[1490] *See supra* p. 613.

Table 5 — Changes in the Underlying Assets		
1996 Equity Derivatives Definitions	**1997 Government Bond Option Definitions**	**1999 Credit Derivatives Definitions**
Under Section 9.1: The terms of a Share transaction will be adjusted to deal with Potential Adjustment Events (specific reclassifications, dividends, Share repurchases and other events that may have a diluting or concentrative effect on the theoretical value of the Shares). A "Merger Event" (*see* Table 7) is not a Potential Adjustment Event. The Calculation Agent determines the adjustments and their effective date to account for the diluting or concentrative effect and may but need not do so by reference to adjustments made on an exchange on which options on the relevant Shares are traded. A similar rule applies to equity index transactions if the relevant exchange changes the terms of the related futures contract.	Redemptions and other unscheduled reductions in principal are not addressed.	Under Section 2.27: Obligations relevant to Credit Events and to settlement can be replaced by Substitute Reference Obligations after (a) an Obligation Exchange (a mandatory transfer of the Obligation other than in accordance with its terms in effect as of the Trade Date or issuance date, if later) and (b) redemptions, loss of a guaranty from a Reference Entity and some Succession Events (*see infra* p. 631) and other events described in Table 6. The securities, obligations or other assets delivered in an Obligation Exchange replace the affected Obligation or the Calculation Agent selects a Substitute Reference Obligation after consulting with the parties. *See* Table 6 on the results if this does not occur by the Scheduled Termination Date or the Grace Period Extension Date.

Table 6 — Substitute Reference Obligations under *1999 Credit Derivatives Definitions* Section 2.27		
Event Affecting Reference Obligation	***Criteria for Substitute Reference Obligation***	***Result if Substitute Not Identified by Cut-off***
Any of the following happens to a Reference Obligation other than because of a Credit Event: (1) The Reference Obligation is redeemed in whole; or (2) in the opinion of the Calculation Agent: • the aggregate amounts due under the Reference Obligation have been materially reduced by redemption or otherwise (other than due to scheduled redemption, amortization or prepayments), • if the Reference Obligation is guaranteed by a Reference Entity, the guarantee ceases to be valid and binding on that Reference Entity in accordance with the guarantee's terms, or • for any other reason, a Reference Obligation is no longer an obligation of a Reference Entity.	• It must be an Obligation that ranks pari passu with the affected Reference Obligation in priority of payment immediately before the relevant change occurs, unless no such pari passu Obligation exists, in which case, the Substitute Reference Obligation, at Buyer's option, may be an Obligation that ranks senior in priority of payment to the affected Reference Obligation; and • it must preserve the economic equivalent of the delivery and payment obligations of the parties to the Credit Derivative Transaction and be issued or guaranteed (unconditionally as to payment of principal and interest but for any requirement for the beneficiary to give notice that a payment is due under such guarantee) by a Reference Entity.	Transaction with one Reference Obligation: the parties' obligations will cease. Transaction with multiple Reference Obligations: all those affected will cease to be Reference Obligations and, if all are affected, the parties' obligations will cease.

As with the conventions relating to valuations and market disruption events described in the preceding section, since the publication of the *1996 Equity Derivatives Definitions* and the *1999 Credit Derivatives Definitions* the experience of market participants has led to changes in practices regarding the identification of events that may potentially give rise to an adjustment to the Shares underlying equity derivatives and the identification of events that may give rise to the designation of a Substitute Reference Obligation for a credit default swap. The proposed revised versions of ISDA's equity and credit derivatives definitions will reflect some of these changes.

For example, in the project to revise the equity derivatives definitions, proposed changes to the treatment of Potential Adjustment Events include the addition of separate categories for tender offers of anywhere from 10% to 50% of the outstanding voting stock of the Issuer of the Shares underlying an equity derivatives transaction and the occurrence of events that trigger changes to an Issuer's capital structure under arrangements—often called poison pills—adopted to discourage takeovers. The presumed approach to be taken in light of these events, however, remains as described in Table 5—whether or not an adjustment should be made and, if one is made, when and how the adjustment should be made, are all questions left to the Calculation Agent, which may but need not make the adjustment by reference to adjustments made on an options exchange on which options on the relevant Shares are traded. The proposed revisions to the equity derivatives definitions would also add delisting to the events affecting the underlying Shares that may lead to close-out of equity derivatives

In the project to revise the ISDA credit derivatives definitions, one proposed change in this area would alter the approach summarized in Table 6 relating to the cases in which a Substitute Reference Obligation may be designated to add any case in which a Reference Obligation is subordinated.[1491] Other changes would reflect the broader proposal to modify the treatment of guaranties in the definitions, as discussed below.[1492] These changes too retain the general approach described in Table 6 regarding the threshold question of whether certain changes to the Reference Obligation are material (the Calculation Agent decides this question unilaterally) and, in all cases, the question of what the Substitute Reference Obligation should be (this the Calculation Agent decides after consultation with the parties).

EXTRAORDINARY EVENTS AFFECTING A REFERENCE ENTITY

In credit, debt and equity derivatives, the documentation should specify whether extraordinary events affecting the issuer or another entity should result in the early termination of the parties' transaction or in an adjustment to its terms.

CREDIT DERIVATIVES

The *1999 Credit Derivatives Definitions* assume that the Buyer in a credit derivative transaction may wish to terminate the transaction if the Seller and a Reference Entity merge, consolidate or amalgamate with each other, if one of them transfers all or substantially all its assets to the other, or if the Reference Entity and the Seller become "Affiliates," as defined in the 1992 ISDA master agreement forms, *i.e.*, if one directly or indirectly comes to control the other, or if they come under common control—with "control" understood in terms of ownership of a majority of voting power. The rationale is that, when the Buyer enters into the credit derivative transaction, it does so to reduce its credit exposure to the Reference Entity and, once the Seller and the Reference Entity become the same entity or become Affiliates, or if one of them transfers substantially all its assets to the other, the benefit of that bargain may be lost. As a result, if any of these events occurs,

---

[1491] Greater clarity on subordination was introduced into the *1999 Credit Derivatives Definitions* in 2001 in the refinements to the Restructuring Credit Event made through the *Restructuring Supplement*, as described *infra* note 1610.

[1492] See *infra* note 1599.

it is treated as an Additional Termination Event affecting the Seller as sole Affected Party for purposes of ISDA-based master agreements,[1493] so the Buyer has the right (but not the obligation) to terminate, and seek an early termination settlement for, all credit derivative transactions with the Seller involving the relevant Reference Entity.[1494]

In all other cases, the *1999 Credit Derivatives Definitions* (unlike the *1996 Equity Derivatives Definitions*) assume that the parties intend for their credit derivative transactions to continue on the agreed terms regardless of a change in the identity of the issuer of a Reference Obligation or any other Reference Entity. Accordingly, "Reference Entity" means each entity specified as such in the relevant confirmation and any "Successor," defined as:

> (a) in relation to a Reference Entity that is not a Sovereign, a direct or indirect successor to a Reference Entity that assumes all or substantially all of the obligations thereof by way of merger, consolidation, amalgamation, transfer or otherwise, whether by operation of law or pursuant to any agreement, as determined by the Calculation Agent (after consultation with the parties), and (b) in relation to a Sovereign Reference Entity, any direct or indirect successor to that Reference Entity irrespective of whether such successor assumes any of the obligations of such Reference Entity.[1495]

The assumption that the parties will wish their transaction to remain in place notwithstanding a Succession Event is retained in the *Supplement Relating to Successor and Credit Events,* which was adopted in 2001 (among other things) to deal more precisely with cases in which multiple entities assume obligations of a Reference Entity.[1496] The

---

[1493] *1999 Credit Derivatives Definitions*, § 2.28.

[1494] *See* Section 5(b)(v) of the annotated sample master agreement, *infra* p. 846, and *see* the annotations to Part 1(h) of the related schedule, *infra* p. 907, regarding Additional Termination Events.

[1495] *1999 Credit Derivatives Definitions*, §§ 2.1 & 2.2.

[1496] The term "Succession Event" was introduced by this supplement and means: "a merger, demerger (whether by voluntary exchange of obligations or otherwise), consolidation, amalgamation, transfer or other similar event affecting a Reference Entity, whether by operation of law or pursuant to any agreement." The supplement sets out numerical standards by reference to which the Calculation Agent is to determine, using the Best Available Information, whether there will be a single Successor or multiple Successors to a Reference Entity that is not a Sovereign. If none of the standards is met and the original Reference Entity continues to exist, it will continue as the Reference Entity. The determination is generally based on an allocation to the potential successors of liabilities consisting of Relevant Obligations, which are the original Reference Entity's Bonds and Loans outstanding (other than to Affiliates) immediately prior to the announcement of the Succession Event. If there are multiple Successors, the original credit derivative transaction is split into a number of New Credit Derivative Transactions equal to the number of Successors, with a pro rata allocation of the original transaction's notional bases for the calculation of potential payouts and Fixed Amounts (premium). The determination must be made as soon as reasonably practicable after the Calculation Agent becomes aware of the Succession Event, but not earlier than 14 days after the legally effective date of the Succession Event. For a Sovereign Reference Entity, "Successor" is defined to mean "any direct or indirect successor to that Reference Entity irrespective of whether such successor assumes any of the obligations of such Reference Entity." *Supplement Relating to Successor and Credit Events*, Section I(g). The supplement also provides, in Section I(c)(iii), that, if the transaction involves a specified Reference Obligation and "any one or more such Successors have not assumed the Reference Obligation," a Substitute Reference Obligation will be selected under Section 2.27. *See* Table 6, *supra* p. 629.

1999 Credit Derivatives Definitions assume, similarly, that the parties to a credit default swap will wish their transaction to remain in place on the agreed terms regardless of a possible takeover or nationalization of a relevant Reference Entity.

The basis for these assumptions is the belief of market professionals that the Seller in a credit default swap will always price the transaction taking into account these merger, demerger and other "Event" risks. Therefore, if the parties to a credit default swap use the *1999 Credit Derivatives Definitions* and wish to treat a Reference Entity's takeover, nationalization, merger, demerger, consolidation or similar event as a ground for early termination, or as a trigger for a payout, they will have to articulate their agreement on the subject in full in the confirmation. In the case of nationalization, although the question in many cases might not be relevant to the buyer of protection under the swap, it may be of consequence to complex transactions in which certain criteria must be met by every Reference Entity in the pool and others, relating to diversification targets, must be met by the pool as a whole. When any of these criteria may turn on whether a Reference Entity is a sovereign or sovereign-owned, the nationalization of a Reference Entity could result in noncompliance with the pool's diversification standards. Depending on the nature of the consequences in any particular transaction, buyers and sellers of protection in these credit default swaps may wish to consider whether nationalization should receive special treatment.

EQUITY DERIVATIVES

The *1996 Equity Derivatives Definitions* address three circumstances affecting the issuer of the specified Shares in which the parties may, it is assumed, wish to terminate their transaction prematurely or adjust its terms. These circumstances are Nationalization, Insolvency and Merger Event, understood as follows:

Table 7 — *1996 Equity Derivatives Definitions*		
Nationalization	**Insolvency**	**Merger Event**
"[A]ll the Shares or all the assets or substantially all the assets of an Issuer are nationalized, expropriated or are otherwise required to be transferred to any governmental agency, authority or entity." Section 9.6(a)(i).	"[B]y reason of the voluntary or involuntary liquidation, bankruptcy or insolvency of or any analogous proceeding affecting an Issuer, (A) all the Shares of that Issuer are required to be transferred to a trustee, liquidator or other similar official or (B) holders of the Shares of that Issuer become legally prohibited from transferring them." Section 9.6(a)(ii).	Any (i) reclassification or change of such Shares that results in a transfer of or an irrevocable commitment to transfer all of such Shares outstanding, (ii) consolidation, amalgamation or merger of the Issuer with or into another entity (other than . . . [one] in which such Issuer is the continuing entity and which does not result in any such reclassification or change of all of such Shares outstanding) or (iii) other takeover offer for such Shares that results in a transfer of or an irrevocable commitment to transfer all such Shares (other than such Shares owned or controlled by the offeror), in each case if the Merger Date is on or before, in the case of a Physically-settled Option Transaction, the Expiration Date or, in any other case, the final Valuation Date." Section 9.2(a).

Consistent with the modifications described in the preceding section under which certain tender offers would be treated as Potential Adjustment Events that could give rise to adjustment of the terms of an equity derivatives transaction, ISDA is considering an expansion of the definition of "Merger Event" to include tender offers for all the underlying Shares or for 50% or more of the outstanding voting shares of any class of the Issuer that results in a transfer of, or an irrevocable commitment to transfer, all such shares (other than those owned or controlled by the offeror).[1497] Merger Events would also in-

---

[1497] A related modification would modify the definition of "Merger Date" in relation to these tender offers to be the date of actual purchase of shares sufficient to result in treatment of the event as a tender offer, as determined by the Calculation Agent.

clude any of the kinds of events listed in Table 7 as such, or described in the preceding sentence, if the Issuer continued as a body corporate but the holders of the class of Shares underlying the derivatives transaction immediately before the event collectively own less than 50% of that class of Shares of the Issuer immediately after the event. The time for determining whether a Merger Event has occurred—the Merger Date—would be the Settlement Date for the relevant transaction, in the case of physically settled forwards or swaps, and would remain as described Table 7 for options and all other transactions documented under the revised definitions.

Under the *1996 Equity Derivatives Definitions,* the parties must state how they wish to deal with Nationalization, Insolvency and Merger Event; the definitions each of the circumstances do not supply a "default choice." Where Merger Events are concerned, the definitions offer three alternative approaches:[1498]

"Alternative Obligation": The transaction continues with its terms adjusted, if necessary, by the Calculation Agent, so that, in a scheduled physical settlement of the transaction or a required valuation for purposes of cash settlement, the consideration that a holder of the number of the relevant Shares transaction would have received in the Merger Event will be physically delivered or valued in lieu of the original Shares.[1499]

"Options Exchange Adjustment": The transaction continues with its terms adjusted by the Calculation Agent in the manner corresponding to that used for the adjustment of exchange-traded options on the relevant Shares.[1500]

"Cancellation and Payment": The transaction is cancelled or terminated as of the Merger Date, and a cancellation or termination payment is due. In an option, the payment is payable by the Seller. If the parties do not agree on the amount, it is determined by the Calculation Agent, if possible on the basis of quotations obtained from leading market dealers asked for their expert opinions as to the fair value of an option that would preserve

---

[1498] The complex provisions summarized here are set out in Article 9 of the *1996 Equity Derivatives Definitions*.

[1499] If stock of the surviving entity or offeror would be received and a holder of the Shares would not be entitled to have received it at the time for settlement under the derivative transaction, the Settlement Date is postponed to the first Clearance System Business Day on or after the first day on which the holder of the Shares, having received the New Shares, would be able to deliver them to the other party to the transaction. *1996 Equity Derivatives Definitions*, § 9.4(a). If other securities, cash or other consideration would be received in the Merger Event by a holder of the Shares, in a physically-settled option transaction, this Other Consideration is to be delivered without waiting for the settlement date for the transaction, as soon as reasonably practicable after the later of the Exercise Date for the option and the first day on which a holder of the relevant Shares, having received the Other Consideration, would be able to deliver it to the other party. *Id.*, § 9.4(b). In a cash-settled transaction, the Other Consideration is to be valued by the Valuation Agent on each Valuation Date in a commercially reasonable manner. *Id.*, § 9.4(c). There is no provision for the valuation to assume investment of, or interest on, Other Consideration consisting of cash.

[1500] If options on the Shares are traded on more than one exchange and no Options Exchange is specified by the parties, Section 9.1(d) of the *1996 Equity Derivatives Definitions* applies in determining which exchange is relevant for purposes of the adjustments. If options on the Shares cease to be traded on an exchange, the Calculation Agent will make all determinations relating to adjustments, and, in all cases, the Calculation Agent will determine when the relevant adjustments should become effective. *Id.*, § 9.1(b). The Calculation Agent is required to make all determinations in good faith and, in the absence of manifest error, its determinations and calculations are binding. *Id.*, § 1.25. These definitions do not include a dispute resolution mechanism.

for the Buyer the economic equivalent of any payment or delivery that would have been required after the Merger Date (assuming satisfaction of all applicable conditions).[1501] In a swap, the payment is calculated in the manner that would apply under ISDA's Market Quotation approach, treating the Merger Event as an Additional Termination Event and the transaction as the only Affected Transaction. If both parties are Equity Amount Payers, both are treated as Affected Parties for this purpose; if the affected Shares are the basis for calculating the Equity Amount for both parties, or if the affected Shares are relevant only to the Equity Amounts payable by one of the parties, the other party will be treated as the sole Affected Party. Otherwise, the party that is not the Equity Amount Payer is treated as the Affected Party.[1502] Loss would be substituted for Market Quotation under the proposed changes to this approach for the revised ISDA equity derivatives definitions.[1503]

Proposed changes to the ISDA equity derivatives definitions would add three further alternative approaches to the handling of Merger Events. Under the current proposals, they would be referred to as "Calculation Agent Adjustment," "Modified Alternative Obligation" and "Partial Cancellation and Payment." Like the other approaches, each would leave substantial discretion to the Calculation Agent.

Under Calculation Agent Adjustment, the Calculation Agent would first determine whether or not an adjustment or adjustments to the transaction's terms would produce a commercially reasonable result. If it determined that adjustments would be possible applying this standard, the Calculation Agent would also determine how and when to adjust the exercise, settlement, payment or other terms of the transaction as it determines appropriate to account for the Merger Event If the Calculation Agent determined that adjustments that it could make would not produce a commercially reasonable result, the transaction would be terminated, treating the Merger Event as an Additional Termination Event under the parties' master agreement, the transactions involving Shares subject to the Merger Event as the Affected Transaction and both parties as Affected Parties.

Under Modified Alternative Obligation, the transaction would continue, treating the consideration received in the Merger Event as the Shares underlying the transaction, as under the Alternative Obligation approach described above, but the definitions would give more definition to the steps to be followed by the Calculation Agent in making the related adjustments to the terms of the continuing transaction so as to preserve the economic equivalent of the transaction's value for the parties. As the first step, the Calcula-

---

[1501] The factors to be considered by the dealers are listed in Section 9.7(b) of the *1996 Equity Derivatives Definitions*. That provision supplies the rules for determining the amount of the payment using the quotations obtained (or, in some cases, an average, after disregarding the highest and lowest). If none are obtained, the Calculation Agent determines the amount of the payment. *Id.* There are proposals to modify this approach in the revised ISDA equity derivatives definitions, to provide for consideration of the information provided by the Calculation Agent and such other factors as the quoting dealer deems appropriate, including the volatility and information relating to dividends and borrowing costs associated with borrowings of the relevant Shares (referred to as the stock loan rebate rate), as well as the consideration, if any, paid to holders of those Shares as a result of the Extraordinary Event.

[1502] *See supra* p. 248 for discussion of Market Quotation and the consequences of treating one party as the sole Affected Party or both parties as Affected Parties in connection with early termination of transactions under the 1992 ISDA master agreement forms.

[1503] *See supra* p. 236 for discussion of Loss.

tion Agent would seek to measure the change in the transaction's value resulting from the announcement of the Merger Event.[1504] The second step would be taken on the Merger Date and would require the Calculation Agent to adjust the transaction's terms in light of that measurement of the transaction's change in value.

The third new alternative would refine the existing Cancellation and Payment approach for transactions involving baskets of Shares if only some were affected by Merger Events. Under this Partial Cancellation and Payment approach, the transaction would continue with respect to the Shares in the basket that were not involved in the Merger Event, there would be a payment, calculated as under the Cancellation and Payment approach, as compensation for close-out of the portion of the transaction involving the affected Shares and the Calculation Agent would adjust the terms of the continuing portion of the transaction as provided in Modified Alternative Obligation approach.

Where Nationalization and Insolvency are concerned, the choices available under the *1996 Equity Derivatives Definitions* are the Cancellation and Payment approach described above and an approach referred to as Negotiated Close-out, under which the parties may, but are not obligated to, terminate the transaction on mutually acceptable terms and, if they do not agree to terminate the transaction, it will continue on the terms then in effect. An exception to this rule applies to options subject to physical settlement—if the parties to such an option do not agree on close-out terms, either party may elect to have the Cash Settlement provisions of the *1996 Equity Derivatives Definitions* apply to the settlement of the option, except that the Calculation Agent will disregard Section 4.2 on Market Disruption Events with respect to any such event occurring on a Valuation Date and make the necessary valuation based on its own good faith estimate.

Under the current proposal for revised ISDA equity derivatives definitions, there would be a third choice for handling an Issuer's Insolvency or Nationalization in transactions involving a basket of Shares. It would be the Partial Cancellation and Payment approach that would also be made available in connection with Merger Events, as described above, and would permit the parties to choose to leave in place, and adjust, the terms of the transaction that did not involve the affected Issuer.

EARLY TERMINATION IN OTHER SPECIAL CASES

It is not unusual for the parties to credit, debt and equity derivatives to agree at the outset that one of them may be entitled to terminate the transaction early in other special circumstances. Some of these provisions are motivated by credit concerns; others, by a desire of one of the parties to protect its expected return on the transaction or to protect itself if it ceases to be able to maintain a hedge position.

A common example of a termination provision motivated by credit concerns is a right to terminate tied to a substantial decline in the market value of the debt or equity instrument involved in the derivative. These provisions are required when one of the parties

---

[1504] The ISDA working group is considering two alternatives for this measurement. One would involve reliance on expert opinions given by leading market dealers, and the other would involve modeling the value of the portion of the transaction's originally scheduled term after the Merger Date, both with the original Shares and with the new Shares to be received in the Merger Event, taking into account factors widely used in the market for the purpose.

believes that its exposure to loss on the transaction may increase disproportionately once the instrument's value declines below a particular level. For instance, in a total return swap between a financial intermediary and its counterparty, the financial intermediary may hold a position in the reference assets as its hedge. If the counterparty's obligations include—as is commonly the case in these swaps—both a floating amount calculated by reference to an interest rate and a floating amount calculated by reference to any decline in the value of the reference assets over the transaction's term, the intermediary's willingness to engage in the swap might be conditioned on a right to terminate the transaction if the value of the reference asset fell below a specified level, especially if there were a strong correlation between the value of the reference assets and the credit risk associated with the customer's obligations under the swap.[1505]

Perhaps even more common in equity derivatives are special termination provisions of the second kind—provisions aimed at protecting financial intermediaries against loss, or reduced return, if the cost of maintaining a hedge increases, or if it, or one of its affiliates, finds that it is unable to maintain a hedge at all. For the counterparties, these termination rights of course raise important concerns relating to the loss of a potentially valuable transaction, so they often seek very clear definition of the level of risk of increased hedging costs that the intermediary will bear and of the circumstances (such as lack of liquidity in the reference shares in the securities lending market) in which the inability to hedge will be grounds for terminating the transaction. A proposed provision on this subject is being considered for inclusion in the projected new ISDA equity derivatives definitions.[1506]

These termination provisions and others sometimes included in credit, debt and equity derivatives[1507] often provide that the parties will merely shorten the transaction's

---

[1505]These provisions are often found, *e.g.*, in total return swaps on obligations of emerging market issuers when the swap counterparty is from the same jurisdiction and in the same industry, or when the reference obligations are sovereign treasury instruments and there is a concern that any substantial decline in the value of those obligations may presage a local crisis in which exchange controls or a severe currency devaluation may prevent the swap counterparty from performing its obligations.

[1506]The contours of the provision are still being shaped. The main features involve treating as an Additional Termination Event with respect to a party a "Hedging Disruption Event," which would be triggered if it becomes impossible or impracticable for a party—the Hedging Party—to borrow, or maintain a borrowing, of underlying Shares, or to establish, reestablish, substitute or maintain any other transaction or transactions it deems necessary to hedge the equity price risk of the relevant transaction. Consideration is being given to including cases in which it merely becomes inadvisable for the Hedging Party to maintain or establish such a hedge transaction. Consideration is also being given to how the parties might identify a benchmark rate with which the Hedging Party's cost of a borrowing of Shares would be compared to determine whether such a borrowing had become impracticable. As nonexclusive examples of factors that might trigger a Hedging Disruption Event, the proposed definition includes (1) material illiquidity in the market for Shares that are the subject of the relevant Hedging Transactions, (2) certain changes in law or regulation after a transaction's Trade Date (*e.g.*, rendering it illegal for the Hedging Party to hold, acquire or dispose of the Shares or materially more costly for it to perform its obligations under the transaction, whether for tax or other reasons), (3) a material decline in the credit standing of the party providing any Hedging Transaction to the Hedging Party and (4) the general unavailability of market participants or lenders of Shares willing to deal on commercially reasonable terms, or of Hedging Transactions offered on such terms.

[1507]For example, the buyer of a credit derivative may seek the right to terminate the transaction in part or in whole when it is buying protection in respect of a callable bond or a loan that can be prepaid at the borrower's option. The proposed revised ISDA equity derivatives definitions would also include changes in law of the kind described in the preceding footnote and a party's failure to deliver Shares under a Transaction

term, accelerating the point at which final valuation and settlement will occur or, in the case of credit default swaps, ending the transaction's coverage in relation to Credit Events. These cases are substantively different from early termination under Section 6 of an ISDA-based master agreement and from Cancellation and Payment—the alternative, described above, available in connection with Merger Events, Nationalization and Insolvency. In these other special cases, the parties often do not value or make a settlement payment in respect of the unexpired portion of the transaction's original term. Since the ISDA definition sets discussed in this chapter do not provide for these special cases,[1508] the parties must be certain to spell out how they wish to deal with these early terminations. Among other things, they should consider how they wish to treat a fixed or floating amount payment obligation calculated at a reference interest rate.[1509] The confirmation will usually provide that accrual of that amount will end at the point of early termination. In some cases involving periodic floating amount payments, the parties may also intend that the payee receive a further payment, like the compensation for broken funding or protection against reinvestment risk conventionally given to lenders in LIBOR-based financings, if the reference interest rate prevailing at the time of early termination is lower than the rate for the period in which the early termination occurs. In this case, the parties should specify how that payment will be calculated and when it will be due.[1510]

---

when due as a result of illiquidity in the market for the Shares as Additional Termination Events in some cases.

[1508]This "flat settlement" approach to early termination, as it is sometimes called, is qualitatively different from a "walkaway" provision (*see supra* p. 229) in which a transaction's replacement value at the time of early termination is calculated but is not payable to a defaulting party.

[1509]Examples would be a fixed amount payable under a credit default swap by the buyer and a floating amount typically payable under a total return swap by the party entitled to payments calculated by reference to any increase in value in the reference debt or equity instrument.

[1510]On broken-funding clauses and make-whole clauses, *see* GOOCH & KLEIN, LOAN DOCUMENTATION 90–91 & 383–86. In total return swaps, these provisions are sometimes drafted so that the party entitled to the interest-rate based payment is protected against reinvestment risk by receiving a payment if the reference rate has declined since the last rate reset date preceding early termination and is obligated to make a payment if the reference rate has increased.

CREDIT DEFAULT SWAPS

Introduction..639
    Credit Default Products..640
    Credit Spread Products...640
    Total Return Products 641
Credit Default Swaps 642
    Conventional Credit Default Swaps...642
    Uses of OTC Credit Default Swaps and Other Credit Derivatives........................649
    The Cost of Credit Default Swap Protection...651
    Portfolio Credit Default Swaps in Synthetic Securitizations.................................654
Common Documentation Issues in Credit Default Swaps 660
    The Credit Default Swap within an ISDA-based Master Agreement.....................661
    Credit Event Definitions 662
    Defining the Protection Period and Related Issues 668
    Obligations and Deliverable Obligations 671
    Changed Circumstances...683
    The Parties' Relationship...684
    Dispute Resolution...684
    Other Special Concerns..686

INTRODUCTION

The credit default swap is the most common of the transactions generally identified as credit derivatives, a class often described as including:

- credit default products,
- credit spread products and
- total return, or total rate of return, swaps relating to debt.[1511]

Features of these product types are also commonly imbedded in credit-linked notes (CLNs) and similar securities and deposit instruments. As a result, they too are sometimes referred to as credit derivatives.[1512]

[1511] These categories are, for example, used in supervisory guidance for bank examiners issued by several U.S. bank regulatory agencies. *See, e.g.,* BOARD OF GOVERNORS OF THE FEDERAL RESERVE SYSTEM, DIVISION OF BANKING SUPERVISION AND REGULATION, SUPERVISORY GUIDANCE FOR CREDIT DERIVATIVES 1 (SR 96-17 (GEN), Aug. 12, 1996), *available at* http://www.federalreserve.gov//boarddocs/SRLetters/1996/sr9617.htm, which describes credit derivatives as "financial instruments used to assume or lay off credit risk on loans and other assets, sometimes to only a limited extent." *See also* FEDERAL DEPOSIT INSURANCE CORPORATION, DIVISION OF SUPERVISION, SUPERVISORY GUIDANCE FOR CREDIT DERIVATIVES 1 (Aug. 15, 1996), *available at* http://www.fdic.gov/news/news/financial/1996/fil9662a.html, which describes credit derivatives as "arrangements that allow one party (the 'beneficiary') to transfer the credit risk of a 'reference asset' to another party (the 'guarantor')." *See* Paul Varotsis, *Credit Derivatives: a revolution in the financial markets, in* CREDIT DERIVATIVES: APPLICATIONS FOR RISK MANAGEMENT 1. On the treatment of credit derivatives under the U.S. securities laws, *see supra* pp. 142 & 143.

[1512] OCC, ADMINISTRATOR OF NATIONAL BANKS, OCC Bulletin 96-43, *Credit Derivatives* 1, 2 (Aug. 12, 1996), includes credit-linked notes in its "initial guidance on supervisory issues related to [national] bank participation in the developing market for credit derivatives." Credit default protection is sometimes imbedded in other kinds of derivatives, as an alternative to what are sometimes called risk participations, or unfunded participations, in which one party agrees to make a payment to the other if a third party defaults in a

Credit derivatives are often highly tailored to the particular needs of the parties—the specific risks that each of them is seeking to transfer or assume and the motivation for the transfer. As a result, an individual transaction may mix features of the three product categories described above as well as other risk transfer features.[1513]

CREDIT DEFAULT PRODUCTS

Credit default products can be thought of as designed to manage or trade the risk of reduced or delayed payment on a financial asset, and therefore of decline in its value, if the issuer or another person obligated to make the payment (such as a guarantor) is the subject of a specified kind of default, moratorium on payments, bankruptcy, insolvency or similar proceeding, debt restructuring or repudiation or other "credit event." The protection afforded by these transactions will result in a payoff if, and only if, one of these credit events occurs.[1514]

CREDIT SPREAD PRODUCTS

Credit spread products are designed to permit the parties to manage or trade the risk of change in the price or yield of a financial asset relative to the price or yield of a benchmark. The benchmark generally is a "risk free" government obligation (in a derivative involving the "absolute spread"). The "credit spread" of a financial asset, as that term is commonly used, is in theory the market's assessment of the relative risk of default under that asset as compared with the hypothetically risk-free benchmark.[1515] The credit spread derivative can also be used to isolate and trade changes in the differential in the credit risks of two credit-sensitive instruments (in a derivative involving a "relative spread").[1516] Whether or not a payment will be due under a credit spread transaction will depend only on whether a change in the price or yield differential has occurred at the

---

payment due under a specified transaction—say a swap—but the parties also agree to share proportionately in payments received and other recoveries from that third party in relation to the swap. On CLNs, see David K. A. Mordecai, *Event risk management and arbitrage: synthetic credit structures, in* CREDIT DERIVATIVES: APPLICATIONS FOR RISK MANAGEMENT 71.

[1513] For example, as used in connection with emerging markets financial assets, credit derivatives often combine features designed to transfer both default and convertibility risk. *See, e.g.,* Satyajit Das, *Credit Derivatives—Instruments, in* CREDIT DERIVATIVES 28, 73–76.

[1514] The most commonly used credit default products, credit default swaps, do not, however, isolate credit risk from market risk in quantifying the payoff. *See infra* p. 665 and *see* Annotation 55 to the sample credit default swap, *infra* p. 707. For discussion of credit risk options (CROs) and options on credit spreads (OCSs), *see* Kayle, *supra* note 1044, at 226–27.

[1515] *See, e.g.,* John C. Hull & Alan White, *Valuing Credit Default Swaps I: No Counterparty Default Risk,* J. DERIVATIVES, FALL 2000, at 29, 30: "If we assume that the only reason a corporate bond sells for less than a similar Treasury bond is the possibility of default, it follows that: Value of Treasury Bond–Value of Corporate Bond = Present Value of Cost of Defaults."

[1516] *See* Satyajit Das, *supra* note 1513, at 28. This measurement of credit risk and the discussion above assume, among other things, risky and risk free assets denominated in the same currency and do not, of course, take into account, or seek to isolate, the effect that tax considerations may have on the difference between the prices or yields of two instruments when the return on one is subject to taxation and the return on the other is tax-exempt for the investor. In some cases credit spread transactions use as the benchmark the swap rate for an interest rate swap with a maturity comparable to that of the reference instrument. Hardy M. Hodges, *Credit Derivatives Pricing Dictionary, in* HANDBOOK OF CREDIT DERIVATIVES 139, 140–41 (1999).

agreed valuation time. Unlike credit default products, the payment on a credit spread product is not dependent on the happening of a specified credit event.[1517]

TOTAL RETURN PRODUCTS

Total return credit derivative products on debt can be thought of as designed to manage or trade both the credit risks and the market risks associated with the reference obligations over an agreed period. Like credit spread derivatives, they generally provide for payments without regard to whether any particular credit event occurs.[1518]

In a total return swap on a debt instrument, one of the parties pays over amounts calculated to reflect the appreciation in value (if any) of the reference obligations plus interest paid on them during each agreed period. This party—sometimes referred to as the "total return payer" or "protection buyer"—can be thought of as trading away the possible economic rewards, or positive performance, of a notional investment in the reference obligation over a specified period (that is, any increase in its value plus amounts equal to actual distributions on the obligation), in return for the stream of payments the other party agrees to pay.

The other party, the "total return recipient" or "protection seller," agrees to pay amounts equal to any decline in value of the reference obligations plus an amount calculated at LIBOR (plus or minus an agreed spread) on the notional amount. This party assumes the economic risk of negative performance of the same notional investment over the same period and, at the same time, agrees to compensate the protection buyer for an agreed hypothetical cost of funding that would be associated with carrying the investment for the period. This part of the transaction is sometimes called the "interest rate leg" of the swap.[1519]

In total return swaps on debt, the swap's term may be designed to end when the reference obligation matures, either at its scheduled maturity or when its principal amount becomes payable upon acceleration in connection with specified defaults. When this is done, the total return receiver's obligation on the total return leg may be the difference between the reference obligation's outstanding principal amount, plus accrued interest, and the actual amount of principal and accrued interest paid. When credit default features like these are included in total return swaps, the final payment due from the total return receiver may be due only against delivery of the reference obligations or a participation interest in them.

[1517]However, according to one observer, "[t]ypically the [credit spread] options are structured to knock-out (i.e., expire worthless) upon a default, so that the economics of the instruments separate spread risk and default risk." Hodges, *supra* note 1516, at 141-42.

[1518]As with some credit spread transactions, *see supra* note 1517, some total return swaps terminate if a default by the obligor on the reference obligation occurs, bringing forward the date of final valuation and subsequent settlement.

[1519]Because total return swaps have this structure, they have been described as "funding" trades, "whereby one party funds an underlying asset and passes the full economics of the asset to the counterparty in exchange for a floating rate index (usually LIBOR) plus a *spread*." Hodges, *supra* note 1516, at 154.

CREDIT DEFAULT SWAPS

CONVENTIONAL CREDIT DEFAULT SWAPS

The General Structure. A credit default swap[1520] can be described, using the standard terminology published in the *1999 Credit Derivatives Definitions,* as follows:

- The Buyer, as the Fixed Rate Payer, agrees to make periodic Fixed Amount payments to the Seller.[1521] The Seller, as the Floating Rate Payer, agrees in return to make a payment to the Buyer if any of the specified Credit Events relating to an agreed Reference Entity (a term that will include its Successors)[1522] or Obligation or class of Obligations occurs during the agreed period, provided that the specified Conditions to Payment are satisfied as required.[1523] The Fixed Amounts payable to the Seller are calculated on a Fixed Rate Payer Calculation Amount, which reflects the face or principal amount of the Reference Entity's obligations on which the Seller is providing protection.[1524]

- If the swap is cash-settled, the Seller's settlement payment, the Cash Settlement Amount, is due without further performance from the Buyer. It is generally calculated by reference to any decline in value of a specified Reference Obligation, stated as a percentage of par value and measured in an agreed manner, the Valuation Method. The valuation is performed on a single Valuation Date, or in an agreed manner in respect of multiple Valuation Dates,[1525] within a specified period

---

[1520] The *1999 Credit Derivatives Definitions* use the term "Credit Derivative Transaction" to refer generically to credit default swaps of the kinds described below and products sometimes referred to as "default put options" or "credit default options." *See, e.g.,* Hodges, *supra* note 1516, at 144–45, for discussion of default put options. In conventional transactions, the primary difference between the two products is often that the Buyer pays an upfront premium for the option product but makes periodic payments of fixed amounts, in arrears, under a swap, although the term "default put option" is also sometimes used to distinguish transactions in which the Buyer can require the Seller to take physical delivery of the reference obligation if a credit event occurs.

[1521] The Buyer is always referred to in the *1999 Credit Derivatives Definitions* as the Fixed Rate Payer. This reflects the prevailing practice of compensating the Seller through periodic payments calculated at a fixed rate or expressed as fixed amounts. A transaction could, however, be structured to compensate the Seller through floating-rate payments.

[1522] *See supra* p. 631.

[1523] The Conditions to Payment may differ from one transaction to the next, but they will, under the *1999 Credit Derivatives Definitions,* always include delivery of a Credit Event Notice that is effective during the Notice Delivery Period and, in any physically settled transaction, will always include effective delivery of a Notice of Intended Physical Settlement. These conditions are discussed in Annotations 41–46 to the sample credit default swap confirmation, *infra* p. 701, as is another commonly applicable Condition to Payment, effective delivery of a Notice of Publicly Available Information confirming facts relevant to the determination of the existence of the Credit Event.

[1524] *See infra* p. 651 for discussion of the pricing of these transactions.

[1525] There are several ISDA choices regarding valuations to be performed on multiple Valuation Dates, which differ depending on whether the transaction involves a single Reference Obligation or multiple Reference Obligations. The presumption in each case, if the parties are silent, is that the final valuation will be based on an unweighted average of the highest relevant values. *1999 Credit Derivatives Definitions,*

after the relevant Credit Event occurs and related Conditions to Payment are satisfied.[1526] In most cases, the decline will be calculated by subtracting a Final Price for the Reference Obligation determined using the agreed Valuation Method from a stated Reference Price reflecting the obligation's agreed market value at the time the parties enter into the swap. In a variant often referred to as a "binary" or "digital" credit default swap, the Cash Settlement Amount is a specified amount or percentage of par.[1527] Under either approach, the applicable percentage is multiplied by an agreed notional amount, the Floating Rate Payer Calculation Amount.[1528]

- If the swap is physically settled, the Seller's payment of the Physical Settlement Amount is due against Delivery by the Buyer of a specified amount, or Portfolio, of Deliverable Obligations of the Reference Entity.[1529] The Physical Settlement Amount will be determined by multi-

---

§§ 7.11(b) & (d). Multiple Valuation Dates may be chosen for various reasons, including a wish to avoid a payoff calculated by reference to quotations that may be skewed because of aberrant market conditions on a single day or because of the size of the position to be valued (that is, the position may be too large, in relation to normal liquidity in the market, for bids for the entire position to be an accurate reflection of the value of the Obligation).

[1526] *See* Tables 1, 3 and 4 in the introductory note on credit, debt and equity derivatives, *supra* pp. 612, 624 & 625, for discussion of ISDA's terminology and assumptions relating to the calculation, under Section 7.3 of the *1999 Credit Derivatives Definitions,* of the Cash Settlement Amount. *See* the timelines in this section, *infra* p. 646, and *see* Annotations 60 and 61 to the sample credit default swap confirmation, *infra* p. 709, for discussion of the timing for calculation of the Final Price.

[1527] *See* BOARD OF GOVERNORS OF THE FEDERAL RESERVE SYSTEM, *supra* note 21 § 4350.1, at 3 (Feb. 1998), explaining the use of the term "binary" for these swaps as reflecting the fact that "they either pay the prespecified amount or nothing, depending on whether default occurs," and observing that binary swaps "are often used when the reference asset is not liquid but when loss in the event of default is otherwise subject to estimation. For example, if the reference asset is a senior, unsecured commercial bank loan, and such loans have historically recovered 80 percent of face value in the event of default, a binary default with a 20 percent contingent payout may be appropriate." *See also* Hull, *supra* note 1515, at 30–31, 37, on the estimation of default probabilities using publicly traded bonds of another company when sufficient publicly traded bonds of the Reference Entity are not available, and on recovery rate assumptions and related issues.

[1528] In some cases the parties may agree that the difference between the Reference Price and the Final Price must meet a materiality requirement for a payout to be due. Because this practice is not widespread, ISDA has not actively pursued earlier plans to develop standard price materiality terms. The form of confirmation for credit default transactions published by ISDA in 1998, before development of the *1999 Credit Derivatives Definitions*, included price materiality terms. *See* Annotation 55 to the sample credit default swap, *infra* p. 707.

[1529] The rules summarized here are found in Sections 8.1, 8.3 and 8.6 of the *1999 Credit Derivatives Definitions. See also infra* note 1532 and Annotation 38 to the sample credit default swap confirmation, *infra* p. 700, on the size of the Portfolio of Deliverable Obligations to be delivered in physical settlement of transactions under these definitions. The term "Deliver" and related concepts are, under Section 8.2 of these definitions, broadly defined to include whatever is necessary, including "executing all necessary documentation and taking any other necessary actions . . . to convey all right, title and interest in" the relevant portion of the Portfolio of Deliverable Obligations," "in the manner customary for the settlement of the applicable Deliverable Obligations" at the time, whether by way of delivery, novation, transfer, assignment or sale, free and clear of liens, charges, claims or encumbrances and counterclaims and defenses other than Reference Entity assertions relating to the defenses listed in defining "Credit Event" in clauses (a) through (d) of Section 4.1 of the definitions, quoted *infra* p. 663. A Deliverable Obligation can, naturally, be tendered to the Seller

plying the initial Reference Price for the Reference Obligations by the Floating Rate Payer Calculation Amount. The Deliverable Obligations in the Portfolio will be required to have an outstanding principal balance or face amount equal to that Physical Settlement Amount (if the Deliverable Obligations are Borrowed Money obligations), or a Due and Payable Amount at the time of settlement equal to the Floating Rate Payer Calculation Amount (if they are not).[1530] If the size of the Portfolio actually Delivered by the Buyer is lower than the Physical Settlement Amount payable by the Seller, the amount payable to the Buyer by the Seller will be reduced to reflect the shortfall. The Seller will never be required to pay an amount greater than the Physical Settlement Amount, even if the size of the Portfolio Delivered by the Buyer (measured in those terms) is higher.[1531]

- In both cash-settled and physically settled credit default swaps the parties' decision on how to treat accrued and unpaid interest may have an impact on the preceding general descriptions of the valuation and settlement mechanisms.[1532]

---

subject to these defenses and counterclaims of the Reference Entity if the risk that they may be raised is being assumed by the Seller in entering into the relevant credit default transaction.

[1530] *See infra* p. 673 for further discussion of Borrowed Money obligations and other Obligation Categories.

[1531] This feature of the conventional Physical Settlement terms reflected in the *1999 Credit Derivatives Definitions* would be relevant if the Deliverable Obligations to be Delivered by the Buyer were obligations in respect of Borrowed Money, as is generally the case, and the parties had agreed that accrued and unpaid interest should be taken into account in measuring the size of the Portfolio due from the Buyer (by specifying "Include Accrued Interest"). In this case, the amount of accrued and unpaid interest may be such that Buyer cannot Deliver Deliverable Obligations with an outstanding principal amount precisely equal to the Physical Settlement Amount, given the standard sizes of the authorized denominations of the Deliverable Obligations. For example, if (1) the Physical Settlement Amount was U.S.$ 10 million, (2) the smallest authorized denomination of the bonds held by the Buyer as Deliverable Obligations was U.S.$ 1,000 and (3) the aggregate accrued and unpaid interest on the bonds was U.S.$ 200,000, the Buyer would Deliver Deliverable Obligations with an aggregate principal of U.S.$ 9,803,000 and a claim for accrued interest of $196,060, for a total of U.S.$ 9,999,060, against an equal amount payable by the Seller as a reduced Physical Settlement Amount. The Buyer would retain 197 bonds and the related claim for accrued and unpaid interest, because delivering any more bonds would increase the amount payable by the Seller above its cap of U.S.$ 10 million, the Physical Settlement Amount.

[1532] In a cash-settled transaction, the issue should be discussed in the context of the method to be used in valuing the Reference Obligations if they are interest-bearing. If the parties are silent on this subject in confirming their swap, Section 7.8(c)(iii) of the *1999 Credit Derivatives Definitions* provides that the Calculation Agent, after consultation with the parties, will determine whether valuation should be done using quotations that exclude or include accrued interest, on the basis of current market practice at the time of valuation in the market for the Reference Obligations. In a physically settled transaction, the subject of accrued and unpaid interest arises in the context of the Portfolio of Deliverable Obligations to be delivered by the Buyer to the Seller in exchange for the Physical Settlement Amount. If the Deliverable Obligations are interest-bearing, the parties should consider whether the size of the Portfolio should be determined including or excluding any accrued but unpaid interest on the Deliverable Obligations at the time of Delivery. As indicated in Table 2 in the introductory note on credit, debt and equity derivatives, *supra* p. 615, if the parties are silent on this subject, the size of the required Portfolio will be determined excluding that accrued and unpaid interest, so the Buyer will be delivering a Portfolio of Deliverable Obligations that carries with it a claim for that interest, but it will be receiving a Physical Settlement Amount calculated without regard to that interest.

Credit default swaps of this kind are sometimes referred to as "single-name" transactions. They are distinguished in this way from multi-name swaps, which are more than the mere unification of single-name swaps into one transaction. Multi-name swaps predicate payoff in connection with a Credit Event on the occurrence of additional specified contingencies unrelated to the Credit Event but related to circumstances involving other Reference Entities whose instruments are included in the underlying "pool" or "portfolio."[1533]

One variant is the first-to-default basket swap. In this product, the payout due from the Seller in respect of a basket of named Reference Entities is triggered by the first Credit Event affecting any of the Reference Entities. Other types of transactions adopt the same operative principle but involving subsequent Credit Events (second- or third-to-default swaps, etc.).[1534]

More prevalent in substantial transactions is a variant that triggers a loss payout from the Seller in connection with a Credit Event on the accumulation of a specified amount of prior losses for which the Seller is not responsible. These transactions with "subordination" and "retained risk"[1535] features are used in complex structures involving multiple "tiers," "layers" or "tranches" of risk defined by reference to the specific levels of accumulated losses that must occur before the Seller of protection for each tranche may incur liability. The ratings of the Reference Entities in the pool, the country, regional, industry and other indices of diversification of the risk associated with the pool and the cushions of subordination available (through swaps, CLNs or otherwise) to absorb losses before a Seller may be required to make a payment are among the factors considered by rating agencies when they assign ratings in these structures, which may be referred to as

---

[1533] They are, therefore, sometimes referred to as contingent credit default swaps: "In a *contingent credit default swap,* the payoff requires both a credit event and an additional trigger. The additional trigger might be a credit event with respect to another reference entity or a specified movement in some market variable." Hull, *supra* note 1515, at 30.

[1534] *See* FITCH IBCA, DUFF & PHELPS, SYNTHETIC CDOs: A GROWING MARKET FOR CREDIT DERIVATIVES 7 (2001), *available at* www.fitchratings.com/corporate/reports/report.cfm?rpt_id=120960: "In a typical portfolio CDS, the arranger seeks to transfer first loss or second loss exposure on a predetermined percentage of the reference portfolio in return for an annual premium. The seller of credit protection effectively is taking a levered position in the reference portfolio, with the leverage inversely related to the loss percentage. For example, a 5% first loss exposure is equivalent to a 20x levered position in the underlying reference portfolio. This has important analytical implications since a single default, however low the statistical probability, can result in a high loss severity depending on the size of the first loss position and the corresponding leverage."

[1535] Although the use of these terms is far from consistent, the retained risk, or retention, concept is often associated with the percentage of the total credit risk represented by the portfolio that the ultimate Buyer of protection does not pass on to others through credit default swaps, CLNs or otherwise so that the providers of default protection on the remaining, traded, risks will view the ultimate Buyer's interests as "aligned" with theirs. That is, in managing (administering and taking actions) as a creditor in respect of the underlying pool of loan or other assets, the ultimate protection buyer shares the sellers' goal of seeking to minimize loss from default at least so long as the accumulated losses have not exhausted the retained loss amount. "Subordination," on the other hand, is a term commonly used from the perspective of a particular seller of protection to refer to all of the losses that must be absorbed by others—both other protection sellers and the ultimate buyer—before that seller may be called upon to make a payment.

"synthetic securitizations."[1536] They are also referred to as "synthetic CLO" transactions because they are modeled on CLOs, or collateralized loan obligations, in which a portfolio of loan assets transferred to a special purpose vehicle (SPV) serves as collateral for obligations issued by the SPV to investors.[1537] A variant, referred to as a "synthetic CDO" (collateralized debt obligation), occurs when the risks in the portfolio being absorbed by the Sellers of protection in the credit default swaps (and the buyers of CLNs in the structure) may be various kinds of debt, including loans, bonds, asset backed securities (ABSs) and even securities issued in other CDOs.[1538]

The various dates at or before which specified events must have occurred or specified actions must have been taken in order for a payout to be due from the Seller to the Buyer in conventional credit default swaps are illustrated in the following timelines. The timelines apply the *1999 Credit Derivatives Definitions* and the fallback choices applicable under them if the parties do not agree to different terms.

The timelines assume transactions involving only a single settlement and, in the case of the cash-settled swap, a single Valuation Date. They also assume that nothing will interfere with the determination of a Final Price to be used in a Cash Settlement Amount or with the ability of Buyer or Seller to complete Physical Settlement. Tables 1 and 2 in the introductory note on credit, debt and equity derivatives refer to ISDA conventions regarding events and circumstances of these kinds (which may, in some cases, lead to deferral of a settlement date and, in others, to cash settlement of a transaction agreed with Physical Settlement terms) and to cases in which quotations obtained from dealers are insufficient to establish a Final Price.[1539]

The initial sequence of events is the same for the cash-settled and physically settled transactions, as follows:

[1536] *See*, MOODY'S INVESTORS SERVICE, UNDERSTANDING THE RISKS IN CREDIT DEFAULT SWAPS (2001).

[1537] *See infra* p. 654.

[1538] "[I]n its simplest form, a synthetic CDO may have three tranches, an 'equity' tranche, rated below BBB, a 'mezzanine' tranche, rated BBB, and a 'senior' tranche rated AAA. An increasingly common variation on this arrangement, however, is for the senior tranche to be divided up further to create what is commonly called a 'super senior' tranche, which benefits from the subordination of the senior tranche and thus has 'better-than-AAA' risk. In particular, for the super senior tranche to sustain a default-related loss, the magnitude of defaults in the underlying portfolio would have to be such as to engulf the entire AAA-rated senior tranche, which is very remote risk." Antulio N. Bomfim, *Understanding Credit Derivatives and their Potential to Synthetic Riskless Assets* 19 (July 11, 2001), *available at* http://www.federalreserve.gov/pubs/feds/2001/200150/200150abs.html. *See also* Laurie S. Goodman, *Synthetic CDOs: An Introduction*, J. OF DERIVATIVES, Spring 2002, at 60; Charles A. Stone & Anne Zissu, *Synthetic Collateralized Loan Obligations: Olan Enterprises, PLC*, J. OF DERIVATIVES, Spring 2002, at 73; David K. A. Mordecai, *Event risk management and arbitrage: synthetic credit structures, in* CREDIT DERIVATIVES: APPLICATIONS FOR RISK MANAGEMENT 71, 74, and the bibliography included therein at 99. These transactions are discussed further *infra* p. 654.

[1539] *See supra* pp. 612 & 615.

Credit Default Swaps

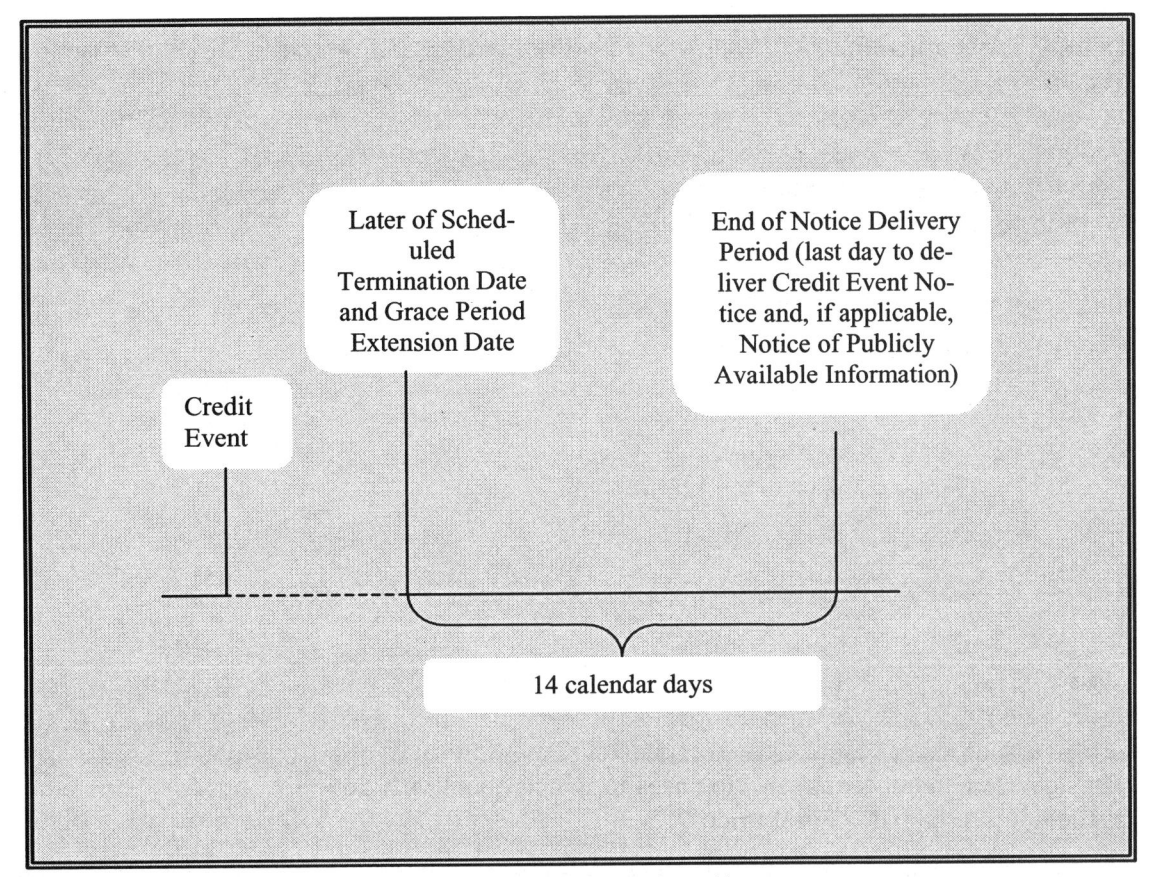

Figure 12. Post Credit Event Timetable

Under the *1999 Credit Derivatives Definitions,* the "credit triggers" are the agreed Credit Events but may also be a Potential Failure to Pay—a Reference Entity's payment failure that has not yet ripened into a Credit Event because a grace period has not lapsed or another applicable condition has not been satisfied. If the parties have specified that Grace Period Extension applies to their swap, a Potential Failure to Pay may give rise to a payout under the swap if it ripens into a Failure to Pay on or before the day referred to in the *1999 Credit Derivatives Definitions* as the Grace Period Extension Date. Clarity in defining the period of protection under the swap and its relation to the Fixed Amounts payable to the Seller are of paramount importance in structuring and documenting credit default swaps, as is the parties' understanding about the circumstances in which a Buyer may lose its right to a payout even if a credit trigger has occurred during the protection period, *e.g.,* if a Potential Failure to Pay does not become a Credit Event on or before the Grace Period Extension Date, or if any of the applicable Conditions to Payment is not satisfied by the required time.

The subsequent events for the cash-settled transaction may be illustrated as follows, given our assumptions that there will be a single Valuation Date and nothing will interfere with the determination on that date of a Final Price to be used in a Cash Settlement Amount:

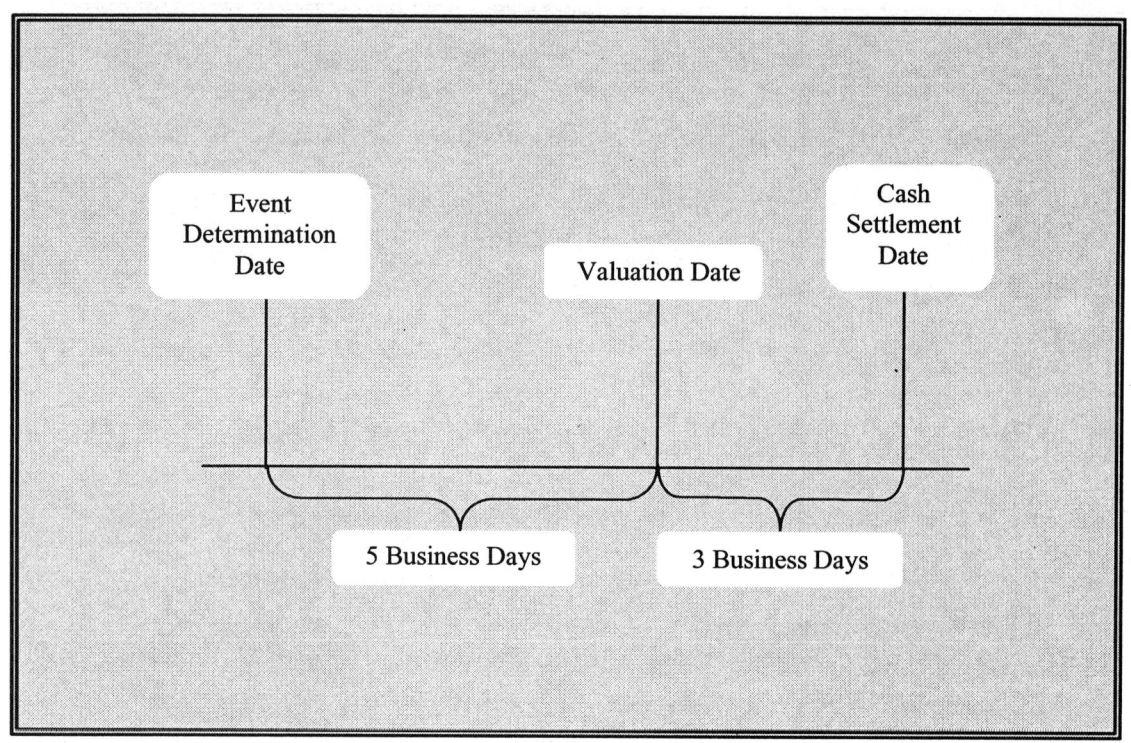

Figure 13. Cash Settlement Timetable (if Event Determination Date occurs within Notice Delivery Period)

Under ISDA's current proposal for revised credit derivatives definitions, this timeline would change somewhat because the Valuation Date, instead of necessarily being the fifth Business Day after the Event Determination Date (the date all Conditions to Payment have been satisfied), could be that fifth Business Day or any earlier day in the period of five Business Days following the Event Determination Date,[1540] presumably as selected by the Calculation Agent.

The subsequent events for the physically settled transaction may be illustrated as follows, again, given our assumption that there will be a single Valuation Date:

[1540] *See* Annotation 66 to the sample credit default swap confirmation, *infra* p. 712, for concerns that Sellers may have in connection with the proposed change.

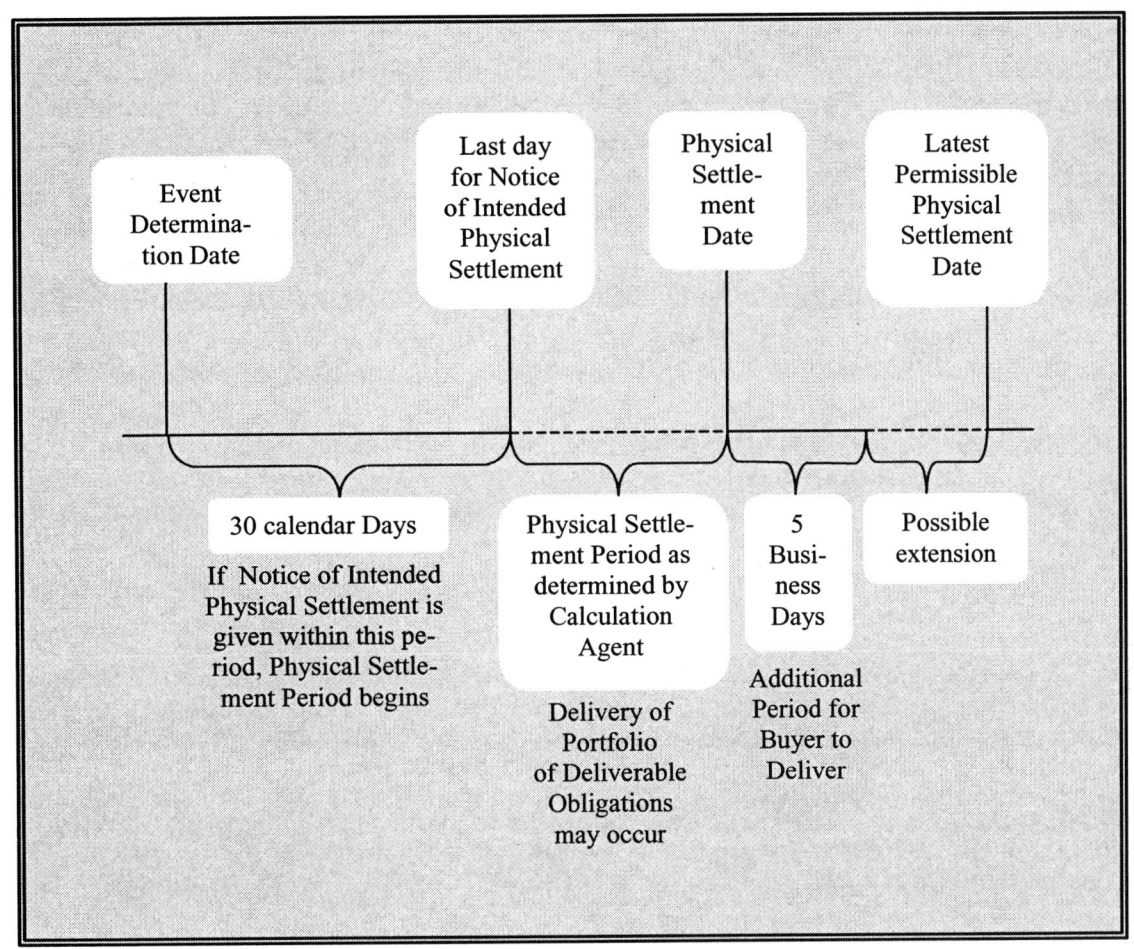

Figure 14. Physical Settlement Timetable (if Event Determination Date occurs within Notice Delivery Period)

USES OF OTC CREDIT DEFAULT SWAPS AND OTHER CREDIT DERIVATIVES

From a functional standpoint, credit derivatives may be used to hedge, to trade credit risks embodied in assets and to replicate credit risks viewed as attractive additions to investment portfolios but that either are not available, or are available only at higher transaction costs, through investments.[1541] Most reports indicate that the principal users of these products are banks and other financial institutions and asset managers.

As originators of loans, commercial banks are natural candidates to be buyers of credit default products. Internal and regulatory limits on the credit they may extend to a single "name" or to borrowers in the same industry or from the same region, and the de-

---

[1541] Bomfim, *supra* note 1538, contains an interesting discussion of strategies using credit derivatives to synthesize "an asset with a credit risk profile that, at least in principle, resembles that of Treasury securities" and states that "[o]nce the credit derivatives market reaches its full maturity, such strategies could potentially be appealing to buy-and-hold investors who are attracted to the safety of U.S. Treasury securities, but who are facing the prospect of a shrinking stock of federal government debt." *Id.* at 1.

sire to achieve greater efficiencies in the use of capital,[1542] all motivate banks to transfer credit default risk to willing counterparties, both in conventional securitizations and in synthetic CLOs or CDOs, as described below. The natural ultimate sellers of protection are insurance companies and other institutional investors and money managers that cannot or do not originate or administer loan and similar assets.[1543]

Institutional investors that include convertible bonds in their portfolios often buy credit default swap protection on the issuer of the bonds to create synthetic equity—that is, to keep the equity market risk of the stock for which the bonds may be exchanged while passing the default risk of the bonds along to the seller of the swap protection. Companies in other business sectors are also reported to use credit derivatives to manage selected kinds of credit risk in their businesses, such as sovereign risk associated with major projects abroad. Credit spread transactions on individual corporate bonds are used "for corporate liability management, to take customized views with respect to credit risk, and to execute capital structure arbitrage by exploiting relative mispricing of different liabilities of the same or related issuers."[1544] Corporates do not yet seem to be making substantial use of credit default products as alternatives to their traditional approaches to managing the credit risks to which they are exposed.[1545]

[1542] As discussed *supra* p. 13, banks in many jurisdictions are subject to capital adequacy regimes that require them to maintain capital in respect of on- and off-balance-sheet assets involving credit risk, as well as other risks. Much has been written about the use of credit default swaps by banks seeking to obtain what is often referred to as "capital relief" without actually disposing of a loan asset through an assignment, or disposing of the beneficial ownership of a loan asset through the sale of a participation. On this subject and on the impact of credit derivatives on supervisory assessment and rating of a bank's "asset quality" (prospects for payment or repayment), *see, e.g.,* Daniel C. Staehle, *The Supervision of Credit Derivative Activities of Banking Organizations, in* HANDBOOK OF CREDIT DERIVATIVES 293, 303–18. Banks are among the principal professional participants in the derivatives market and are also subject to capital adequacy requirements in respect of their derivatives activities. They are reported to be using credit default swaps to obtain capital relief in respect of this aspect of their business too. *See* Goodman, *supra* note 1538, at 62. For the situation under capital adequacy rules applicable to many U.S. bank users of credit default swaps, *see* BOARD OF GOVERNORS OF THE FEDERAL RESERVE SYSTEM, SUPERVISORY GUIDANCE FOR CREDIT DERIVATIVES, *supra* note 1511, and, in relation to credit default swaps used in synthetic CLOs and CDOs, the joint supervisory guidance issued by the OCC and the Board of Governors as CAPITAL TREATMENT FOR SYNTHETIC COLLATERALIZED LOAN OBLIGATION (SR 99-32 (SUP, Nov. 17, 1999), *available at* http://www.federalreserve.gov//boarddocs/srletters/1999/SR9932.HTM.

[1543] *See, e.g.,* Robert Reoch, *The Market for Credit Derivatives, in* CREDIT DERIVATIVES 387, 395; Hermann Watzinger, *The Market Participants: Applying Credit Derivatives, in* CREDIT DERIVATIVES: APPLICATIONS FOR RISK MANAGEMENT 23, 25.

[1544] Frank Iacono, *Credit Derivatives, in* HANDBOOK OF CREDIT DERIVATIVES 22, 30–32.

[1545] *See* Carola Schenk & Matthew Crabbe, *A Slow Burning Fuse,* RISK, June 2001, p. 30. *See also* Joyce A. Frost, *Credit Risk Management from a Corporate Perspective, in* HANDBOOK OF CREDIT DERIVATIVES 87, 87–88:

> Direct sources of credit risk [for this class of corporations] originate in investment portfolios, commercial contracts (*e.g.*, short-term trade receivables), or other contracts, usually longer term (*e.g.*, customer financing commitments, leases, long-term fixed price commodity, or take or pay contracts). The most common direct source of credit risk is through standard trade receivables. Depending on the size of the receivables relative to its capital or the general credit quality of its receivables, a company may take a more active role in managing the credit risk. When a particular credit starts to become problematic, a company traditionally has had several options to manage the risk. It can reduce

THE COST OF CREDIT DEFAULT SWAP PROTECTION

The cost of protection under a credit default swap—the Fixed Amounts payable to the Seller, as described above—will depend on numerous factors, which will typically include the following:

- a model's prediction of the probability that the selected credit triggers will occur during the agreed period of protection in relation to any of the specified Reference Entities and Obligations;

- historical recovery rates on the relevant Obligations after similar events have occurred;

- liquidity, or the effects of supply and demand, at the time in the market for similar credit derivatives and, at least in some cases, in the various markets for alternative protection through more traditional credit risk management tools, such as financial guaranty insurance;[1546]

- whether the transaction is to be cash-settled or physically settled;

- the credit quality of the provider of the protection and the degree of correlation between the risk it will default and the risk of default by the Reference Entity.[1547]

---

business to the customer which is not particularly appealing if the credit in question is one of the firm's best customers, or do nothing, maintaining the status quo. Although the latter is a cross-your-fingers approach, it is a route often taken. Other traditional ways of managing the risk [are] . . . through factoring, which tends to be relatively expensive; securitization, although the company typically retains a first loss position in the portfolio so it does little to reduce the risk; or accounts receivable insurance. Credit derivatives can be an efficient and effective solution . . . .

[1546] According to one commentator, "[t]he pricing of credit derivative products is still largely in a developmental phase . . . [as] evidenced by the increasing number of academic papers on this topic over the last few years, and the number of differing pricing methodologies." Hodges, *supra* note 1516, at 139. The author describes some of these methodologies, under "Pricing Models." *Id.* at 152. For additional discussion, *see* Wai-yan Cheng, *Recent Advances in Default Swap Valuation*, J. DERIVATIVES, Fall 2001, at 18; Sanjiv R. Das, *Pricing Credit Derivatives*, in HANDBOOK OF CREDIT DERIVATIVES 101; Andrea Fabbri, *Pricing Credit Default Swaps*, DERIVATIVES WEEK, Jan. 29, 2001, at 6 (Learning Curve column); Hull, *supra* note 1515, at 29; John C. Hull & Alan White, *Valuing Credit Default Swaps II: Modeling Default Correlations*, J. DERIVATIVES, Spring 2001, at 12; Andreas Petrie, Klaus-Peter Schommer & Ingo Schneider, *The Pricing Of Credit Derivatives*, in CREDIT DERIVATIVES: APPLICATIONS FOR RISK MANAGEMENT, at 53. *See also* an overview published early in the development of the credit derivatives market by James BeSaw, *Pricing Credit Derivatives*, DERIVATIVES WEEK, Sept. 8, 1997, at 6 (Learning Curve column). On the pricing differentials among credit derivatives and more traditional products used to manage credit risk, such as financial guaranty insurance, risk participations and conventional put options, *see* Tanya Styblo Beder & Frank Iacono, *The Good, the Bad–and the Ugly?*, in CREDIT RISK SUPPLEMENT, published with the July 1997 edition of RISK magazine.

[1547] "The issue of how to determine and charge for counterparty credit exposure is in large part an empirical one, since it depends on computing the joint likelihood of arriving in different credit states, which will in turn depend on an estimate of credit quality correlation between the protection seller and reference entity, which cannot be directly observed." Blythe Masters & Kelly Bryson, *Credit Derivatives and Loan Portfolio Management*, in HANDBOOK OF CREDIT DERIVATIVES 43, 49–50. The factors involved in the pricing exercise are most transparent in the criteria used by rating agencies in providing ratings for synthetic CDOs involving credit default swaps and CLNs. *See, e.g.,* STANDARD & POOR'S, GLOBAL CASH FLOW AND

Buyers may therefore find that considerable benefits may flow from structuring a transaction so as to take into account the sensitivity of pricing to their choices relating, for example, to Credit Events and to thresholds that may apply before the Seller will be required to make a payment.

For example, if a Buyer is considering a credit default swap as protection against loss on an investment in a single debt security, it might well initially consider treating all defaults on the broadest possible class of obligations of the issuer as Credit Events that could trigger a payment under the swap, on the theory that the issuer's default on any other obligation might foretell default on the security held by the Buyer or at least might have an adverse effect on the price of that security. In addition, if the security was guaranteed, the Buyer might want the credit default swap to name both the issuer and the guarantor as Reference Entities and to have the Credit Events apply to the broadest possible class of Obligations of both. However, if the Buyer found that the cost of this expansive protection was excessive, it might seek to reduce the cost in one or more ways, depending on its goals in entering into the transaction.

As discussed above, the Buyer might, for example, consider a "worst of" or "first to default" swap, in which case the swap's protection would end at the point of the first credit event affecting an obligation or issuer in a basket of reference entities thought to have positively correlated default risks, including the issuer of the Buyer's particular investment. In this case, the payout would be calculated by reference to the post-default decline in value of the first defaulted reference obligation, regardless of whether the Buyer needed subsequent default protection in respect of a security it held. A payout measured at the time would not necessarily compensate the Buyer for any actual loss it might incur in connection with a credit event relating to that security or its issuer. Nonetheless, depending on the degree of correlation with the obligation that proved to involve the worst credit default risk, the swap's protection might suffice for the Buyer's purposes.[1548]

Although the size of the credit derivatives market has grown considerably in recent years, the limited number of market participants willing to act as sellers of protection for some reference entities and classes of obligations, the lack of historical data regarding default and recovery rates and, in some cases, the variety of approaches to and difficulties

---

SYNTHETIC CDO CRITERIA (Mar. 21, 2002). In these cases, as described *supra* note 1538, the default risk represented by the assets or "names" (Reference Entities) in the underlying pool of debt obligations is tiered, ratings—ranging from "AAA," at the senior level, or even higher for a "super senior piece," through a "mezzanine" (of, say, "BBB") and down to "BBB-" or below)—are assigned to reflect the risk of loss associated with the different tiers, or tranches, and the amount payable—expressed in terms of CLN coupon or credit default swap premium—is progressively higher for providers of default protection as the tranche ratings are progressively lower. The potential reward is greatest for the so-called equity—usually retained by the sponsor of the structure—because it stands to receive all of the economic value (principal and interest, or market value) of the pool less the amounts paid as coupon or premium on the CLNs and credit default swaps in the rated tranches if no defaults occur, in exchange for effectively absorbing all of the risk of losses (the "first loss" position) in the bottom-most, unrated, tranche. That is, there is no reduction in the payments due to investors in CLNs in rated tranches, and no payout due from providers of credit default swaps in rated tranches, until the accumulated losses exceed the maximum that the equity tranche must absorb.

[1548]On the theory behind the lower pricing of these products, *see* Angelo Arvanitis, *'Worst of' Default Swaps*, DERIVATIVES WEEK, July 13, 1998, at 6 (Learning Curve column).

in the pricing of protection[1549] may result in wide bid/offer spreads for these transactions as well as substantial differences in the prices quoted by professional market participants for the same transaction. These facts are relevant not only in the context of the initial negotiation of the terms of a transaction but also in the context of a possible early termination, in the event of a default or otherwise.[1550]

It should be noted that the Buyer may find, at least in some segments of the credit derivatives market, that protection in respect of some Credit Events is priced differently from protection in respect of others or is not available at all. The prime example has been protection in respect of the Restructuring Credit Event. The Credit Events known in the *1999 Credit Derivatives Definitions* as Obligation Default and Obligation Acceleration—sometimes referred to as "soft" Credit Events—are no longer used in most conventional single-name credit default swap trading.[1551] The rating agencies involved in rating synthetic CDOs generally allow only specified Credit Events,[1552] and those permitted, both in conventional trading and in synthetic CDOs may differ depending on whether the issuer is a corporate credit or a sovereign. The Repudiation/Moratorium Credit Event will generally be allowed by a seller of protection only with respect to sovereign risk or in credit

---

[1549] According to Das, *supra* note 1546, at 104–105, writing in 1999, some of the difficulties were: use of products that were still not standardized; poor historical information on credit risks, and changing economic conditions, which make past data unreliable; prices evidencing slow adjustment to rating changes, and ratings not always adjusting concurrently with real credit quality changes; use of illiquid underlying securities, making replication of derivatives somewhat difficult; few useful indices for credit related instruments; for emerging markets transactions, poor credit information and insufficient research on the statistical properties of asset prices. Substantial improvements in many of these areas and growing liquidity in at least some segments of the market since then have been sufficient for rating agencies to consider the use of credit default swaps by "AAA"-rated structured investment vehicles (SIVs). *See Rating Agencies to Allow Triple A Funds to Use Credit Swaps,* DERIVATIVES WEEK, Feb. 18, 2002, at 1.

[1550] The parties should carefully analyze whether the approach they would normally use to calculate an early termination settlement payment is appropriate for credit default swaps, or whether some refinement is advisable. For example, the standard ISDA approach to the calculation of an early termination settlement payment using the Market Quotation measure (*see supra* p. 241), involves seeking quotations for the upfront cost of a Replacement Transaction that would preserve the economic effects of all payments scheduled to be made after the Early Termination Date. In credit default swaps, the credit rating of the Seller of protection is often more relevant to pricing than it is in other segments of the derivatives market. Normal criteria for the Reference Market-makers selected to provide these quotations may not, therefore, always, be appropriate. In addition, if a Credit Event has occurred before the Early Termination Date and the Buyer of protection has satisfied all related Conditions to Payment but the scheduled date for the valuation of the payout has not occurred, some question whether it is appropriate to use Market Quotation in substitution for the agreed method of valuing the relevant Reference Obligations. Those who believe it is not modify the standard ISDA approach by providing that the valuation of the Reference Obligations will proceed, either as scheduled or in some cases on a somewhat expedited basis, and the amount determined to be payable by the Seller will be treated as an Unpaid Amount (*see supra* p. 860) under the ISDA Master Agreement approach to early termination settlement payments.

[1551] *See* Mike Topping, *CDS Market Moves Toward Trans-Atlantic Standardisation,* FINANCIAL PRODUCTS, Apr. 17–23, 2002, at 1 (referring to the European market's dropping Repudiation/Moratorium and Obligation Acceleration as standard Credit Events for non-emerging market single Reference Entity swaps).

[1552] *See, e.g.,* STANDARD & POOR'S, *supra* note 1547.

derivatives involving emerging market risk, for example.[1553] For a Buyer seeking to obtain capital or other regulatory relief through a credit default swap, any related regulatory requirements regarding the inclusion of Credit Events necessary to achieve the Buyer's goal will, naturally, be critical.

PORTFOLIO CREDIT DEFAULT SWAPS IN SYNTHETIC SECURITIZATIONS

The preceding discussion of simple credit default swaps and the hypothetical transaction reflected in the following sample confirmation illustrate how the Buyer and Seller might use and document these swaps to transfer or assume risk relating to a single Reference Obligation. In those examples, as noted, although the Buyer may define the applicable Credit Events to include defaults under a broad group of Obligations of the same entity, the actual Cash Settlement Amount or Physical Settlement Amount payable to the Buyer is calculated by reference to a single Reference Obligation, and the swap involves a single potential payout. Although single-name credit default swaps appear to represent a very substantial part of the credit derivatives market, the most substantial of the reported credit default swaps are entered into in connection with portfolio structures. These transactions often present portfolios of many Reference Entities and the default risk of Obligations totaling hundreds of millions or, in some cases, more than a billion, in principal or face amount, with the potential for multiple settlements following Credit Events and, therefore, multiple Valuation Dates at which Cash Settlement Amounts will be calculated in respect of defaulted Obligations, or Obligations of Reference Entities that have been involved in Credit Events other than payment defaults, such as bankruptcy, insolvency or similar proceedings, debt moratoria, in the case of sovereigns, or debt restructurings.

The *Trading and Capital-Markets Activities Manual* published by the Board of Governors of the Federal Reserve System[1554] describes the synthetic CLO structure, in part, as follows:

> [T]he banking organization identifies a specific portfolio of credit exposures, which may include loan commitments, and then purchases default protection from a special-purpose vehicle. In this case, the credit risk on the identified reference portfolio is transferred to the SPV through the use of credit-default swaps. In exchange for the credit protection, the institution pays the SPV an annual fee.
>
> To support its guarantee, the SPV sells credit-linked notes (CLNs) to investors and uses the cash consideration to purchase Treasury notes

---

[1553] *See, e.g.,* Tom Bergin, *New contract creates 3-tier US default swaps mkt* (Reuters, London, May 5, 2001); Topping, *supra* note 1551.

[1554] The structure is illustrated in a diagram in BOARD OF GOVERNORS OF THE FEDERAL RESERVE SYSTEM, *supra* note 21, § 4353.1, at 3 (March 1999). Diagrams and discussions of some of these structures, including the "BISTRO"—Broad Index Secured Trust Offering—structure designed by J.P. Morgan, are also available from other published sources, such as Masters, *supra* note 1547, at 77–80, and Walter Gontarek & Peter Nowell, *Insurable risks,* FUTURES & OTC WORLD, March 2000, at 45, 48–49. Goodman, *supra* note 1538, at 62–65, and Stone & Zissu, *supra* note 1538, at 74–76, describe and diagram other examples and give mathematical examples of how the capital treatment differs depending on whether a transaction is synthetic or not, and on how synthetic structures are composed.

that are then pledged to the banking organization to cover any default losses. CLNs are obligations whose principal repayment is conditioned upon the default or nondefault of a referenced asset. The CLNs may consist of more than one tranche, for example, Aaa-rated senior notes and Ba2-rated subordinated notes, and are issued in an amount that is sufficient to cover some multiple of expected losses—typically, about 7 percent of the notional amount of the reference portfolio.

. . .

[D]efault swaps on each of the obligors in the reference portfolio are executed and structured to pay the average default losses on all senior, unsecured obligations of defaulted borrowers. . . .

If any obligor linked to a CLN in the SPV defaults, the institution will call the note and redeem it based either on the post-default market value of the reference security of the defaulted obligor or on a fixed percentage of par that reflects the historical recovery rate for senior unsecured debt. The fixed percentage method is used when the linked obligor has no publicly traded debt.[1555]

Thus, in the structure described, the CLN investors provide funds for the purchase of Treasury instruments that collateralize the credit protection sold by the SPV to the bank that originated the credit exposures in the portfolio, as well as the payments due to other participants in the structure, including these CLN investors. The principal amount of the underlying pool of loans covered by risks that these investors will absorb is, therefore, referred to as making up the funded portion of the structure. The principal amount of the pool covered by risks that the swap providers will absorb is, in contrast, referred to as unfunded, because the swap providers make no payment to the SPV with which collateral can be acquired. The principal amount of the pool of loans representing losses that the sponsor of the structure will absorb is, as noted earlier, referred to as the equity, or first-loss piece. Rating agencies may assign ratings to some or all of the tranches of risks associated with the different levels of losses to be absorbed by CLN investors and swap providers, to reflect extrapolated estimates of the comparable rating that would be assigned to the risk of loss on corporate bonds, and the equity tranche is unrated. The same general structural concepts apply in a synthetic CDO, in which the underlying default risks may include both loans and bonds, commitments to make loans, ABS and even risks associated with other CDOs.

In the simplest case involving cash settlement and a defined (or static) pool of Reference Obligations, at a specified time after a Credit Events occurs, the post-Credit Event value of the relevant Reference Obligation is determined—much as it would be in the simple, single-name credit default swap described above—and the difference between par and that value is treated as a loss. Once the accumulated losses exceed the notional size of the unrated equity tranche, the providers of protection on the rated tranches begin

---

[1555]BOARD OF GOVERNORS OF THE FEDERAL RESERVE SYSTEM, *supra* note 21, § 4353.1, at 3–4 (March 1999) (footnote omitted). The description in this manual of these structures and more traditional CLOs refers to some of the ways in which the originators of the loans may retain a portion of the credit risk being securitized. *Id.* at 1, 14–16.

to absorb losses, beginning with those lowest—most "junior"—in the structure. In their tranche order (with the lowest rated first), the CLNs are redeemed below par and the investors absorb losses, as the Treasury instruments are sold to generate the funds necessary for the SPV to make payments to the bank that purchased the credit default protection through the synthetic CLO or CDO. Once accumulated losses exceed the sum of the levels absorbed by the CLN investors, the providers of unfunded protection through the credit default swaps are called on to make payouts under their swaps.

The comparative attractions of the traditional CLO and the synthetic CLO to the loan originator are described in this manual as follows:

> CLOs offer banking institutions a means of achieving a broad range of financial objectives, including, but not limited to, the reduction of credit risk and regulatory capital requirements, access to an efficient funding source for lending or other activities, increased liquidity, and increased returns on assets and equity. Furthermore, institutions are able to realize these benefits without disrupting customer relationships [because they continue to service the transferred loans].
>
> . . .
>
> In most CLO structures, assets are actually transferred into the SPV. In the synthetic securitizations, the underlying exposures that make up the reference portfolio remain on the institution's balance sheet. The credit risk is transferred into the SPV through credit-default swaps or CLNs. In this way, the institution is able to avoid sensitive client relationship issues arising from loan-transfer notification requirements. Client confidentiality may also be maintained.[1556]

Regarding confidentiality concerns, Section 9.1(b)(iv) of the *1999 Credit Derivatives Definitions* includes the following as an agreement of each party, effective as of the date they enter into each Credit Derivative Transaction with each other, and applicable for so long as either of them has any obligation under the transaction:

> each party and its Affiliates and the Calculation Agent may, whether by virtue of the types of relationships described herein or otherwise, on the Trade Date or at any time thereafter, be in possession of information in relation to a Reference Entity or any Obligation Guarantor that is or may be material in the context of such Credit Derivative Transaction and that may or may not be publicly available or known to the other party, and such Credit Derivative Transaction does not create any obligation on the part of such party, its Affiliates or the Calculation Agent to disclose to the

---

[1556]*Id.* at 1, 4. There may also be important differences in the measure of capital relief that may be available under a conventional CLO and a synthetic CLO. *See, e.g.,* Goodman, *supra* note 1538, at 63–69, and Stone & Zissu, *supra* note 1538, at 77–80.

other party any such relationship or information (whether or not confidential).[1557]

Building on the structure described above, sometimes the originator of the underlying assets or other ultimate buyer of default protection eliminates the CLNs through the use of back-to-back credit default swaps. In these cases, a single professional participant in the credit derivatives market, performing the classic function of a financial intermediary, might act as the primary Seller in a portfolio credit default swap with the ultimate protection seller. To hedge its position in this swap, it would then act as Buyer in tiers of mirror image swaps with other Sellers. Through the mirror swaps, these other Sellers take the risks that would have been assumed by purchasers of credit-linked notes in the more traditional, partially funded synthetic securitization structure. As defaults and other Credit Events occur, the affected Reference Obligations or Reference Entities are removed from the portfolio and the aggregate payments due from the various other Sellers fund the payments due from the primary Seller to the ultimate buyer of protection. The settlement obligations of each of these other Sellers will reflect only the particular level of risk that it has assumed and, where multiple Sellers participate in the same risk level, only the percentage of that risk that is allocable to that particular Seller.[1558] As a general matter, the higher the level of the protection obtained in the structure from unfunded, rather than funded, sources, the lower the cost to the ultimate buyer of protection.

Regardless of whether a CDO is synthetic, those who participate by taking on default risk, through swaps or otherwise, may have varied motivations. They may not be banks or otherwise in the business of lending and, therefore, may not themselves be able to originate assets with the same credit exposure profiles. Even if they are loan originators, they may not be in a position to gain exposure to the same classes or mix of classes of credit risk as efficiently as they can through the CDO. The components of the portfolio in these transactions can have specified common characteristics but involve obligors from different regions and industries, grouped in ratings "buckets" that reflect historical performance data and recovery rates. The transactions enable the CLN purchasers, or the Sellers in credit default swaps, to select a specific layer of risk to such a diversified portfolio of obligations through a single transaction. For the Seller in a credit default swap, this tiered assumption of credit risk is possible without an initial investment of capital and generates a flow of periodic Fixed Amount payments like the periodic interest that would have been payable on a CLN. If the structure involves both funded and unfunded tranches of protection, naturally there will be return differentials that reflect both the differing levels of risk being absorbed and the fact that the CLN investor is providing leverage for the structure by furnishing the capital used to acquire collateral.

[1557] The courts have not yet had the occasion to consider the effectiveness of this provision in the light of the CFMA's amendment of the U.S. securities laws extending to security-based swap agreements the antifraud provisions. *See supra* p. 145.

[1558] *See* Fitch IBCA, Duff & Phelps, *supra* note 1534, at 5. Published references to CDOs also illustrate a disintermediated variant in which the Sellers that assume the various tranches of risk do so directly, through credit default swaps with the bank that originates the portfolio of loans. *See, e.g.,* Gontarek, *supra* note 1554, at 48, illustrating a synthetic securitization of a U.S. investment grade loan portfolio through four credit derivative tranches involving "super-AAA" and AAA rated tranches, described as attractive to reinsurers and monoline insurers, a mezzanine tranche of BBB rated risk, described as attractive to fund managers, and an unrated tranche, described as attractive to high yield investors.

In fact, the ultimate protection seller may not be the entity named as the Seller in the upstream credit default swap. These entities are often trusts and special purpose vehicles that have been created to enter into the swaps with the backing of a financial guaranty insurance policy.[1559] The risk underwritten in the policy may, in turn, be passed along in whole or in further fragmentation through reinsurance contracts,[1560] which share in the policy risk on a "quota" or "first loss" basis—that is, by reference to a specified proportion of each loss (or particular classes of loss) or only after a specified amount of accumulated losses have been absorbed. Insurance companies that participate in the market in these structures will often provide protection only in respect of losses directly attributable to settlement payoffs (Cash Settlement Amounts or Physical Settlement Amounts) due as a result of Credit Events, because for commercial and regulatory purposes they view themselves as providing coverage in respect of the credit risks associated with the Reference Entities and their relevant Obligations.[1561]

These varied portfolio structures enable the ultimate buyers of protection to achieve goals that, in addition to those described in the preceding quotation from the Federal Reserve,[1562] include improvement of risk adjusted return on capital (RAROC) by trading away credit risks that are priced differently in the bank loan and capital or insurance markets.[1563] In this regard, the distinction between a "balance sheet" synthetic CDO and an "arbitrage" synthetic CDO can have an important effect on the structure and the documentation.

[1559] These entities are often referred to as transformers, because their obligations as sellers of credit default swap protection can be guaranteed with financial guaranty insurance, thereby "transforming" the default risk of the pool underlying their credit default swaps into risk that can be absorbed through insurance and then, as described in the next note, reinsured.

[1560] On the role of insurance companies in CDOs, *see* FINANCIAL SERVICES AUTHORITY, CROSS-SECTOR RISK TRANSFERS (May 2002), a discussion paper *available at* http://www.fsa.gov.uk/pubs/ discussion/dp11.pdf. Here too the market operates using a variety of structures. If the ultimate risk is taken at least in part through a reinsurance contract, the reinsurer will generally need to be comfortable that its counterparty—the "cedant"—is passing along risk that constitutes insurance. Since the local law of the cedant may be determinative on this issue, the cedant's own undertaking up the chain may take the form of a traditional insurance policy written in favor of an insured but, if that local law views a credit default swap as insurance provided it has specified hallmarks of insurance, the cedant's undertaking may be set out in a document that in most respects looks like an ISDA-based credit default swap confirmation. The nature of insurance and precisely what distinguishes insurance from a credit default swap is a complex subject about which much has been written. *See, e.g.,* David Z. Nirenberg & Richard J. Hoffman, *Are Credit Default Swaps Insurance?*, DERIVATIVES REPORT, December 2001, at 7.

[1561] As a result, in some cases early termination settlement payments calculated pursuant to Section 6(e) of the ISDA master agreement forms will not be covered by these policies or reinsurance contracts. When this is the case, some or all of the links in the chain of transactions, between the ultimate buyer and seller of protection, may provide for "flat" early termination settlement in respect of premium, or Fixed Amounts, payable and accrued through the Early Termination Date and payoffs for Credit Events that have occurred on or before that date, if the Conditions to Payment have been satisfied on or before that date.

[1562] *Supra* note 1527. *See* Stone & Zissu, supra note 1538 at 78–79 for discussion of return on equity in synthetic CLOs.

[1563] *See, e.g.,* Rajeev Misra & John Tierney, *Managing a corporate risk portfolio: Convergence between corporate loans, bonds and default swaps,* 7 DERIVATIVES USE, TRADING & REGULATION 231, 236–37 (2001).

In the "balance sheet" synthetic CDO, the ultimate buyer is seeking protection—often substantially capital relief—in respect of risk-generating assets that it continues to hold throughout the term of the related credit default swaps, or at least as long as the assets remain in the swap's underlying pool. The pool of Reference Entities and Reference Obligations is, therefore, typically fully disclosed, and it is often largely static. That is, the pool assets are identified in a schedule attached to the confirmation of the credit default swap and may change only in narrowly defined cases or situations recognized as standard causes for change in the *1999 Credit Derivatives Definitions* or one of its supplements—the Obligation Exchanges, Succession Events and other circumstances identified in Table 5 of the introductory note on credit, debt and equity derivatives.[1564] The Reference Entities will be removed from the pool in connection with payouts after Credit Events, as described above, and in these narrowly defined cases.[1565]

The term "arbitrage" is used in connection with synthetic and other CDOs in various ways but, in a broad sense, has been described and compared with the balance sheet CDO as follows:

> Arbitrage CDOs are designed to capture the positive spread between relatively higher-yielding assets and lower-cost, more highly rated liabilities. The assets in arbitrage deals are typically acquired by the collateral manager in the open market, and traditionally have been high-yield assets with large spreads. The difference between the yield on the assets and the rated liabilities is used to compensate the equity investors that take the first-loss position.
>
> In contrast, balance sheet CDO issuance is motivated by the desire of the sponsoring institution to reduce regulatory capital requirements, increase

---

[1564]*Supra* p. 628. In transactions with largely static, identified pools of Reference Obligations, the following are typical cases in which the amount of credit default swap coverage (the Floating Rate Payer Calculation Amount) allocated to a Reference Entity may automatically decline or the ultimate Buyer of protection may have full or limited freedom to make adjustments to the pool: (1) if the Reference Obligation is a credit agreement, a reduction in the amount of the loan commitment; (2) a partial reduction in the principal of the Reference Obligation or its repayment in full at maturity; and (3) a sale by the Buyer of its interests in respect of the Reference Obligation. If the Buyer enters into the swap in order to reduce the amount of capital it must maintain in respect of exposure to the Reference Entity, the Buyer will often also seek the right to terminate the swap or to reduce its coverage if the applicable capital adequacy regime changes. From the perspective of the Seller, all unscheduled reductions in coverage reduce its rights to future premium unless the reduction is offset by replacement of the affected Reference Obligation. In some cases, the parties agree that the Seller will be entitled to a minimum guaranteed premium.

[1565]Again, not all structures of this kind are the same. Some may provide for substitutions or for replacement of a matured Reference Obligation with another, equally ranking Obligation of the same Reference Entity, either with the involvement of the Seller or subject to the satisfaction of specified criteria; the criteria might be reflected in a determination by rating agency. Misra, *supra* note 1563, at 237, describes an example in which the bank acting as ultimate buyer of protection designed a structure enabling it to "replenish the pool in consultation with the protection seller" as "the reference pool amortises or names drop out" and includes an interesting discussion of factors that motivate banks to use credit derivatives and other techniques to manage credit risk in their asset portfolios.

lending capacity, lower the cost of funding, manage risk, and/or diversify funding sources.[1566]

In these cases, the pool may be partially or totally "blind" to the seller of protection, at least at the outset,[1567] and it is often actively managed by the ultimate buyer of protection, at least in the normal course. The seller may not know the identities of the Reference Entities at the outset, but it will know that the pool satisfies specified guidelines. The guidelines will relate to diversification within the pool, by specifying concentration limits by Reference Entity, industry, country, region, obligor and obligation type. They will also relate to credit quality and set maximum and minimum standards for the principal of obligations at various points on the rating spectrum and rules on unrated obligations and implied ratings. The CDO manager will be permitted to make changes to the pool, so long as none of the changes moves the pool further away from compliance with the guidelines than it was before the change was made, at least as a general matter.[1568] The variety of approaches in this regard is significant. The occurrence of specified events may result in a permanent or temporary end to active management of the pool and disclosure of the composition of the pool to the protection sellers on a real-time basis.

COMMON DOCUMENTATION ISSUES IN CREDIT DEFAULT SWAPS

The following sample confirmation for a cash-settled credit default swap uses the short form of confirmation published as an exhibit to the *1999 Credit Derivatives Definitions*. The annotations to the sample refer to some of the issues raised by the use of that form with those definitions, both for the illustrated transaction and for cash-settled credit default swaps involving other kinds of Reference Entities, Reference Obligations and Obligations other possible Valuation Methods. The annotations also point to some of the differences that would be seen if the same hypothetical transaction were agreed on Physical Settlement terms, as well as some of the differences between use of the short-form confirmation with the *1999 Credit Derivatives Definitions* and use of the *ISDA Long-Form Credit Swap Confirmation* published in January 1998.[1569]

The following are more general observations about documentation concerns that arise in connection with credit default swaps. Although the observations relate to basic and generic questions, it is often critical to return to these basics in analyzing credit default swaps involved in complex structures, because they involve highly individualized documentation that departs from standard ISDA terms, which were drafted for use in con-

---

[1566]STANDARD & POOR'S, GLOBAL CASH FLOW AND SYNTHETIC CDO CRITERIA, *supra* note 1547 at [3].

[1567]An involved rating agency or auditor will have the appropriate disclosure, however, and the providers of default protection will generally receive pool information with a lag sufficient to enable the pool manager to feel it is protected against the risk of interference with its buying and selling strategies.

[1568]Compliance with these requirements is tested through rating agency models and verified through reports from independent third parties.

[1569]A more thorough description of issues raised by the *ISDA Long-Form Credit Swap Confirmation* and a sample confirmation prepared using that form are found in Anthony C. Gooch & Linda B. Klein, *Documentation Begins to Come Into Focus for OTC Credit Derivatives*, 3 DERIVATIVES, TAX, REGULATION, FINANCE 211 (1998).

Credit Default Swaps

nection with simple, single-name transactions and, as published, simply do not work with these portfolio transactions.

THE CREDIT DEFAULT SWAP WITHIN AN ISDA-BASED MASTER AGREEMENT

When a buyer and a seller of default protection first begin to engage in credit derivatives with each other, they should consider how the transactions they intend to enter into fit within the framework of an existing or proposed ISDA-based master agreement and any related credit support arrangements between them. Some important issues are as follows:

- Will the legal treatment of the credit derivative transactions for purposes of insolvency or similar laws that may be applicable to the counterparty be the same as the treatment of more conventional OTC derivatives and, if not, will the differences affect the enforceability of the rights to designate an early termination date and determine a single, net, settlement amount under Section 6 of the master agreement?[1570]

- Will those insolvency and similar laws permit a party to apply collateral posted as security in connection with the counterparty's obligations under credit derivatives to all its obligations under the master agreement, as is generally intended in these cases?[1571]

- If the credit default swap is being executed as part of a CDO or other structured transaction, should it be isolated from the parties' other dealings with each other—documented under a separate agreement—so as to reduce the risk to the ultimate Buyer and the ultimate Seller in the structure that extrinsic dealings will interfere with the intended operation of the swap?

- Even if the transaction is isolated from netting and setoff and grounds for early termination relating to other dealings between the parties, should the standard grounds for early termination be modified for the transaction?[1572]

- Will the parties' normal approach to the calculation of any payment that may be due in connection with early termination under Section 6 of their master agreement work well as applied to the intended credit derivatives?[1573]

[1570] *See supra* pp. 303, 312–316 & 324.

[1571] *See supra* pp. 307, 316 & 326.

[1572] *See supra* note 2101 on isolating derivatives entered into by special purpose vehicles in securitization transactions and *supra* p. 664 on defining Credit Events in such cases.

[1573] *See supra* note 1508 on issues relating to flat settlement of credit derivatives. Given the complexity of some structures in which credit default swaps are used, if the parties normally choose the Market Quotation approach to valuing an early termination settlement payment, should they retain the feature under which a fallback to Loss is mandatory if fewer than three quotations are obtained? What, if anything, should they do to clarify the assumptions that the Reference Market-maker should make in providing a quotation for

- If the parties have established in their master agreement that one of them will be the Calculation Agent for all transactions, is that rule sensible in connection with intended credit derivatives, in light of the role of the Calculation Agent in these transactions?[1574]

CREDIT EVENT DEFINITIONS

The ISDA Credit Event Definitions Generally. The standardized definitions of Credit Events in the *1999 Credit Derivatives Definitions* reflect the general consensus among market professionals at the time they were published regarding the kinds of events Buyers were most often seeking to cover through credit default transactions. Like all standardized definitions, however, they may not exactly suit the needs of the parties to any particular transaction, especially when the risk being transferred is unusual or complex. Market experience with the use of the standard terms for more transactions, and for novel ones, often leads to their modification.

For example, the Credit Event definitions in the *1999 Credit Derivatives Definitions* are different from those included in the earlier *ISDA Long-Form Credit Swap Confirmation*, reflecting market experience with that earlier form and its Credit Event definitions, as well as specially crafted definitions that individual market participants had developed in the interim. The changes are primarily of two kinds. First, as indicated in the Practice Notes in the Introduction to the *1999 Credit Derivatives Definitions,* two of the Credit Events included in the earlier form, Credit Event Upon Merger and Downgrade, are not included in the 1999 definitions because experience showed they were rarely used.[1575] Second, the definition of the "Restructuring" Credit Event as included in the earlier form had been found in practice, in some cases, to lead to disputes about whether a Credit Event had occurred. The revised definition of that Credit Event in the *1999 Credit Derivatives Definitions* represented a significant step toward averting similar disputes. Experience showed, however, that still further modification was warranted, which led to the publication of the *Restructuring Supplement* in 2001. Further changes to the Restructuring Credit Event are being considered in the project to develop a revised set of ISDA definitions for credit derivatives, largely because the approach adopted in the *Restructuring Supplement* has not proven acceptable in the European market. These developments and

---

a Replacement Transaction? *See supra* p. 263, discussing concerns that have been raised by an English court decision strictly interpreting what may and may not be taken into account in the calculation of a Settlement Amount in respect of post-termination scheduled cash flows. If the parties have adopted ISDA's Replacement Value approach discussed *supra* p. 243, many of these issues cease to exist. Others, particularly regarding the enforceability of an approach leaving a party to choose among many competing methods of calculating a settlement amount, may arise.

[1574]*See, e.g.,* Tables 1, 3 and 4 in the introductory note on credit, debt and equity derivatives, pp. 612, 624 & 625, on some of the important matters that may be determined by the Calculation Agent under the *1999 Credit Derivatives Definitions.* Section 1.13 of those definitions sets out a list of other determinations to be made by the Calculation Agent and specifies (at 3) that, "[w]henever the Calculation Agent is required to act or to exercise judgment, it will do so in good faith and in a commercially reasonable manner." As a general matter, the parties may use the confirmation of a credit default swap to overcome a master agreement provision identifying which of them will be the Calculation Agent, unless they have strictly precluded that possibility in their master agreement—something rarely, but sometimes, done.

[1575]*1999 Credit Derivatives Definitions,* at vi.

Credit Default Swaps 663

others, involving the Bankruptcy and Repudiation/ Moratorium Credit Events are discussed further below.[1576]

Testing Use of the Standard Definitions with Specific Obligations. As a prospective Buyer considers using the Credit Events published in the *1999 Credit Derivatives Definitions* to transfer specific credit-related risks to a Seller, the Buyer should carefully analyze the possible need for modification of the ISDA standard wording in light of the terms of the relevant Obligation or Obligation Category.[1577] Consider, by way of example, one of the most commonly used Credit Events, Failure to Pay, which is defined as follows in Section 4.5 of the *1999 Credit Derivatives Definitions:*

> "Failure to Pay" means, after the expiration of any applicable (or deemed) Grace Period (after the satisfaction of any conditions precedent to the commencement of such Grace Period), the failure by a Reference Entity to make, when and where due, any payments in an aggregate amount of not less than the Payment Requirement under one or more Obligations.

The assumption underlying this definition and its use in the market is that there will be no room for dispute about whether a payment failure has in fact occurred or whether a default has been cured during the applicable grace period, and the assumption works as expected with conventional debt obligations of the kinds that fall within the ISDA Obligation Categories most frequently used, which are the subsets of Borrowed Money referred to as "Bond," "Loan" and "Bond or Loan."

With conventional loan, bond and similar obligations, if an obligor is late with a payment or purports to discharge its payment obligations other than at the place where they are due or in a currency other than the currency in which they are due,[1578] creditors will view the obligor as in default regardless of whether the situation is attributable to a change in law in the obligor's jurisdiction, such as the imposition of exchange controls or force majeure. Similarly, Section 4.1 of the *1999 Credit Derivatives Definitions* states that a Failure to Pay—and all other Credit Events—will exist if the relevant circumstances exist "whether or not such occurrence arises directly or indirectly" from any of the following:

> (a) any lack or alleged lack of authority or capacity of a Reference Entity to enter into any Obligation, (b) any actual or alleged unenforceability, illegality, impossibility or invalidity with respect to any Obligation, however described, (c) any applicable law, order, regulation, decree or notice, however described, or the promulgation of, or any change in, the interpretation by any court, tribunal, regulatory authority or similar adminis-

---

[1576] *See infra* p. 666.

[1577] Other issues may arise because the particular Obligations have features not contemplated by the standard Obligation Categories and Obligation Characteristics published by ISDA. *See infra* p. 677.

[1578] The definition of "Failure to Pay" in the *ISDA Long-Form Credit Swap Confirmation* was revised in light of experience in late 1998 with Russia's purported discharge of debt obligations through payments into blocked accounts in Russia. The revised definition in the *1999 Credit Derivatives Definitions* is intended to make clear that a Credit Event may exist if a payment is not made *where* due, even if it is made when due.

trative or judicial body with competent or apparent jurisdiction of any applicable law, order, regulation, decree or notice, however described, or (d) the imposition of, or any change in, any exchange controls, capital restrictions or any other similar restrictions imposed by any monetary or other authority, however described.

However, if Buyers and Sellers are considering credit default swaps in relation to other types of Obligations, they should consider the possible need for modifications to the "Failure to Pay" definition if events of force majeure and supervening illegality, and payment failures caused by these kinds of events, are not treated as defaults in the relevant market. In the OTC derivatives markets, for example, payment failures caused by supervening illegality and events of force majeure are not generally treated as events of default or dealt with through grace periods, as that term is normally understood. Rather, the standard market documents merely provide for rights to cause the early termination or liquidation of the affected transactions, perhaps after a waiting period or efforts to avoid the problem, or both.[1579] If the parties intend in a particular case to capture within the Failure to Pay Credit Event a Reference Entity's payment delay caused solely by circumstances beyond its control in circumstances that do not directly or indirectly result from a deterioration in the financial condition or credit standing of the Reference Entity they should modify the "Failure to Pay" definition accordingly.[1580]

The use of credit default swaps to transfer risk in respect of asset backed securities is another case that highlights the importance of examining standard Credit Event definitions in the context of each transaction. Typically, in securitizations a special purpose vehicle will issue securities under which, absent extraordinary circumstances, the cash flow generated by the assets backing the securities will be channeled first to investors holding the most senior tranches and then, to the extent available, to holders of more junior tranches. In ABS structures, scheduled payments that are not made to the junior investors will be deferred, at least in some circumstances. Therefore, generally, where credit default swap protection is written in respect of an ABS, these extraordinary circumstances, and not the conventional Failure to Pay, should be treated as a Credit Event, unless the ABS belongs to a senior tranche providing that the failure to make a payment when scheduled will constitute a default and not result in deferral.

[1579] On the treatment of force majeure and supervening illegality in OTC derivatives, *see supra* p. 247. It should be noted that the terms of the parties' credit default swaps may override the standard ISDA Master Agreement provisions relating to the treatment of supervening illegality. As mentioned in Table 2, *supra* p. 616, and *infra* p. 708, Section 9.4 of the *1999 Credit Derivatives Definitions* provides a rule pursuant to which a swap entered into with Physical Settlement terms may either have Physical Settlement deferred or be settled through Partial Cash Settlement if, due to an event beyond the control of the Buyer, it is impossible or illegal for it to make the Delivery or if, due to an event beyond the control of the Seller, it is impossible or illegal for it to accept Delivery.

[1580] For example, the Buyer and Seller might agree to exclude payment delays caused solely by specified events identifiable as force majeure. They could provide that the standard Failure to Pay definition will not apply to a payment failure caused solely by listed types of circumstances beyond a Reference Entity's control in circumstances that do not directly or indirectly result from a deterioration in the financial condition or credit standing of the Reference Entity. If such a modification is made, the buyer of protection under the credit default swap would likely want to make clear that payment failures caused by changes in law are understood to remain within the definition of Failure to Pay.

Testing the Credit Events against Standards of Objectivity. Disputes about whether a Credit Event has occurred tend to arise whenever one of the parties (or a Calculation Agent) is empowered to make a subjective determination that is critical to the existence or nonexistence of a Credit Event. The protection sought by the Buyer in a credit default swap may be lost if it cannot establish that a Credit Event has occurred. On the other hand, the definition of Credit Event may in fact give rise to a demand for a payout in circumstances beyond those expected by the Seller—that is, where the Buyer's claim appears to a considerable extent to be attributable to factors other than the related deterioration of the Reference Entity's credit standing. The parties generally aim to define Credit Event objectively, so as to avoid the potential for disputes about whether or not a such an event has occurred.

By way of example, the definition of the Credit Event known as "Restructuring" in the *ISDA Long-Form Credit Swap Confirmation* was, as indicated earlier, refined in the version included in the *1999 Credit Derivatives Definitions*, precisely to eliminate some elements of subjective determination. Under the earlier form, whether or not a Restructuring had occurred depended in part on a determination of whether specified events had produced a material impact on the terms of an Obligation of a Reference Entity. The *1999 Credit Derivatives Definitions* seek to eliminate this subjective element as a potential source for dispute between Buyers and Sellers by listing changes to the terms of an Obligation, or its ranking, that typify Restructurings of obligors in financial distress.[1581] Further, they provide that a change in the terms of an Obligation will not be treated as a Restructuring if the change, agreement to the change or its announcement occurs in circumstances "where such event does not directly or indirectly result from a deterioration in the creditworthiness or financial condition of the Reference Entity."[1582] It appears that even this formulation may give rise to questions, because Buyers and Sellers of credit default protection may not see eye to eye on how far back in time one should have to look in determining whether, say, an extension of the maturity of a loan in connection with a Reference Entity's replacement of an existing credit facility directly or indirectly results from a deterioration in the entity's financial condition.[1583]

Where the "Restructuring" Credit Event is concerned, there are other, more intractable, tensions between the goals of ultimate Buyers and Sellers of default protection. For example, there are cases in which the Buyer itself may play a decisive role in triggering the occurrence of the Credit Event, in its role as a creditor entitled to vote on whether a Reference Entity's Restructuring will go forward. The Buyer in such a case may make choices about settlement under a credit default swap based on the Restructuring so as to reap arbitrage profits, rather than merely to recoup losses resulting from the Reference

---

[1581] Subject to specified exceptions, the listed changes are "(i) a reduction in the rate or amount of interest payable or the amount of scheduled interest accruals; (ii) a reduction in the amount of principal or premium payable at maturity or at scheduled redemption dates; (iii) a postponement or other deferral of a date or dates for either (A) the payment or accrual of interest or (B) the payment of principal or premium; (iv) a change in the ranking or priority of payment of any Obligation, causing the subordination of such Obligation; or (v) any change in the currency or composition of any payment of interest or principal." *1999 Credit Derivatives Definitions,* § 4.7(a).

[1582] *Id.* § 4.7(b)(iii).

[1583] Questions of this kind have, it appears, arisen in connection with the replacement by Xerox Corporation of a credit facility in the Spring of 2002.

Entity's decline. This can occur if obligations of the Reference Entity that were not involved in the Restructuring will qualify as Deliverable Obligations for purposes of settlement of the credit default swap. It may be that, after the Restructuring, those other Deliverable Obligations trade at a discount to the restructured obligations held by the creditor-Buyer, say, because their maturity is considerably longer than that of the restructured obligations, or because the creditors holding the restructured obligations, including the Buyer, have obtained through the Restructuring valuable rights or security that were not made available to the obligations outside the Restructuring. If permitted by the documents to do so, the Buyer may tender the "cheapest-to-deliver" obligations in settlement of the swap, holding on to the restructured obligation that motivated its execution of the swap in the first place and other obligations of the Reference Entity with higher recovery values, given their maturities and other factors affecting liquidity.[1584]

The *Restructuring Supplement* was published by ISDA in 2001 primarily to deal with these issues in a way that would not reintroduce subjectivity into the definition of "Restructuring" or disturb the general principle (stated in Section 9.1(b)(iii) of the *1999 Credit Derivatives Definitions*) that each party to the credit default swap (and its affiliates) should be permitted to conduct its dealings with Reference Entities without responsibility to the other party for the consequences. To this end, the *Restructuring Supplement* made two key changes.

First, it narrowed the "Restructuring" Credit Event so that it applies only to a Multiple Holder Obligation—an Obligation that

> (i) at the time the Credit Event Notice is delivered, is held by more than three holders that are not Affiliates of each other and (ii) with respect to which a percentage of holders (determined pursuant to the terms of the Obligation) at least equal to sixty-six-and-two-thirds is required to consent to the event which would otherwise constitute a Restructuring Credit Event.[1585]

One effect of this change is that, if an Obligation is held by three or fewer parties at the time the Credit Event Notice is given, it cannot be the subject of a "Restructuring" Credit Event.[1586] Even if it has the required number of holders that are not related parties at that time, it still cannot be the subject of such an event if, by its terms, fewer than two thirds of the holders can bind the creditors to an amendment implementing a restructuring event of the relevant kind.

Second, in connection with transactions subject to Physical Settlement, the *Restructuring Supplement* permits the parties to elect to narrow the Buyer's choices among Deliverable Obligations that can be tendered in a settlement based on Restructuring as the

---

[1584] This is in fact what happened after the rescheduling of debt owed by Conseco to bank lenders in 2000, leading market participants to question how the Restructuring Credit Event might be changed. *See A Non-Event? Conseco Loan Restructuring Confounds Credit Players,* DERIVATIVES WEEK, Oct. 9, 2000, at 1 (referring to disputes over a corporate syndicated bank loan rescheduling).

[1585] The limitation and the definition of "Multiple Holder Obligation" were added to the *1999 Credit Derivatives Definitions* in Section 4.10, introduced by the *Restructuring Supplement*.

[1586] Some market participants believe this test should have to be satisfied at the time holders are asked to vote, and vote, on the restructuring, and not only when the Credit Event Notice is given.

only Credit Event, by specifying in their documentation that "Restructuring Maturity Limitation" will be applicable. The first of the narrowing features of Restructuring Maturity Limitation excludes from a Buyer's Portfolio of Deliverable Obligations any item with a final maturity later than the Restructuring Maturity Limitation Date. That date is the earlier of (1) 30 months following the date on which the Restructuring is legally effective in accordance with the terms of the documentation governing the Restructuring (defined as the "Restructuring Date") and (2) the latest final maturity date of any Restructured Bond or Loan—those included in the Restructuring—but in any event not earlier than the Scheduled Termination Date of the transaction or later than 30 months following the Scheduled Termination Date.

The second narrowing feature of Restructuring Maturity Limitation excludes illiquid obligations in certain cases. A Deliverable Obligation cannot be included in the Portfolio of Deliverable Obligations, in a Physical Settlement triggered by delivery by the Buyer of a Credit Event Notice in which Restructuring is the only Credit Event specified, unless it is a Fully Transferable Obligation. As noted in ISDA's commentary on the form, "if the Seller triggers a Restructuring Credit Event, the Buyer may deliver any Deliverable Obligation."[1587]

"Fully Transferable Obligation" is defined to include all Transferable Bonds, but any other Deliverable Obligation (*e.g.*, a Loan) will not be included unless, on the relevant Physical Settlement Date it can, without need for the consent of any person,[1588] be assigned or novated to all Eligible Transferees. "Eligible Transferees" includes (1) banks and other financial institutions, (2) insurance and reinsurance companies, (3) mutual funds and similar collective investment vehicles and (4) registered or licensed brokers and dealers that are legal entities, so long as, in all cases, they have total assets of at least U.S.$ 500 million. Affiliates of all of these classes of investors are Eligible Transferees. Other legal entities and trusts are Eligible Transferees if they meet specified asset tests either alone, as part of a group or through credit support. Sovereigns, Sovereign Agencies and Supranational Organizations are Eligible Transferees.

In light of the addition of these limitations, the *Restructuring Supplement* also added to the *1999 Credit Definitions* a provision (Section 3.10) under which, if a Restructuring occurs, a Notifying Party will be permitted to give multiple Credit Event Notices, specifying the portion of the transaction's coverage (the Floating Amount Payer Calculation Amount) to which the notice applies (the "Exercise Amount"),[1589] so that, for

---

[1587] ISDA, *Commentary on Restructuring Supplement* 1 (2001).

[1588] The issue of consent is determined taking into account only the terms of the Deliverable Obligation and any related transfer or consent documents which have been obtained by the Buyer. *See* Allen & Overy, Memorandum for ISDA Members, November 27, 2001, *available at* www.isda.org. A requirement that notification of transfer of a Deliverable Obligation be provided to a trustee, fiscal agent, administrative agent, clearing agent or paying agent for a Deliverable Obligation is not treated as a requirement for consent. *1999 Credit Derivatives Definitions* § 2.29, as added by the *Restructuring Supplement.*

[1589] Each Credit Event Notice operates so that the transaction is treated as if it were split in two. Settlement takes place only in respect of the Exercise Amount, and that portion of the transaction terminates, while the other part of the transaction continues with a Floating Rate Payer Calculation Amount equal to the balance. The Exercise Amount must be at least 1 million units of the currency in which the Floating Rate Payer Calculation Amount is denominated and must be an integral multiple of 1 million units of that currency.

example, a protection Buyer is not completely foreclosed from obtaining the benefit of its bargain if it cannot put together a Portfolio of Deliverable Obligations that satisfy the limitations. Since the limitations apply only when a Credit Event Notice identifies Restructuring as the only Credit Event, the Notifying Party could obtain successive partial settlements as it obtained qualifying obligations or, if another Credit Event occurred—say Bankruptcy of the Reference Entity—the Notifying Party could give a subsequent Credit Event Notice enabling it to deliver any Obligation that satisfied the normally applicable Deliverable Obligation Characteristics, without regard to the limitations imposed when only a Restructuring has occurred.[1590]

Although the *Restructuring Supplement* approach—often referred to as modified Restructuring—was widely adopted in the U.S. credit derivatives market quite quickly, the European market found it too restrictive in its limitations on a lender that wishes to buy credit default swap protection for a loan with assurance that, in the event of a Restructuring, the loan or anything obtained in the Restructuring will be deliverable in settlement of the swap. The restrictions in the modified approach have also led to the continuing use of the original formulation in connection with sovereign Reference Entities. As a result, there are proposals for further revisions to the requirements relating to delivery of a Fully Transferable Obligation and the Restructuring Maturity Limitation in new ISDA definitions for credit derivatives.

Since the publication of the *Restructuring Supplement,* market participants have also continued to consider other potential sources for disagreement over Restructurings. For example, an ISDA committee that considers market concerns over issues of these kinds recommended modification of the way in which the *1999 Credit Derivatives Definitions* treat a change in the currency of an Obligation as a Restructuring. Pursuant to the recommendation, as implemented in the *Supplement Relating to Successor and Credit Events,* the definition of "Restructuring" will, for parties who adopt that supplement, be modified so that a change in the currency of an Obligation will not be treated as a Restructuring if the new currency is that of an OECD member country with the highest possible local currency long-term debt rating (AAA or the equivalent) from a specified rating agency (S&P, Moody's and Fitch).

DEFINING THE PROTECTION PERIOD AND RELATED ISSUES

Particularly critical in the documentation for credit default swaps is that it correctly reflect the parties' expectations and assumptions about the swap's period of protection and how it relates to the accrual of Fixed Amounts payable to the Seller for the risk it assumes over that period. Also key is the specification of the point by which the agreed Conditions to Payment must be satisfied. Some of the most important aspects of these issues as they arise under the *1999 Credit Derivatives Definitions,* are:

- Under the *1999 Credit Derivatives Definitions,* the swap's Effective Date is the first day of the period of protection conferred by the swap,

---

[1590] The *Restructuring Supplement* states that only an agreement of the requisite holders of a Reference Obligation to have their claims satisfied after those of holders of other Obligations in the Reference Entity's liquidation, dissolution, reorganization or winding up will be a subordination sufficient to constitute a Restructuring. *See* Annotation 53 to the following sample confirmation on use of these *Restructuring Supplement* limitations in some cash-settled transactions.

because a Credit Event that occurs on that day may ultimately lead to a payout to the Buyer.[1591] The Fixed Amounts payable to the Seller for the swap's protection begin to accrue on the Effective Date.[1592]

- If the parties agree on an Effective Date after the Trade Date and intend the swap's coverage to include Credit Events that occur in the intervening period, the parties will have to modify the ISDA approach and, if they do, the Seller will expect the Fixed Amounts payable to it to begin to accrue on the Trade Date.[1593]

- The Fixed Amounts payable to the Seller are calculated in respect of Fixed Rate Payer Calculation Periods. Each Fixed Amount is usually payable at the end of the corresponding period, although transactions are sometimes structured to provide for payments of Fixed Amounts in advance. As a general matter, the end of Fixed Amount accrual, at the end of the last of these periods, should coincide with the time at which a further event relating to a Reference Entity or one of its agreed Obligations can no longer give rise to a payout to the Buyer.[1594] Identification of this end point is of course of paramount importance.

- The Scheduled Termination Date identified by the parties is generally the end point for the accrual of Fixed Amounts and for the period during which a payout obligation of the Seller can be triggered, subject to events that may lead to earlier termination of the swap's protection. Accordingly, any Credit Event that occurs after the Scheduled Termination Date should never lead to a payout by the Seller to the Buyer, unless the parties have adopted Grace Period Extension as applicable to their swap. If the parties have agreed to Grace Period Extension, and a Potential Failure to Pay (a payment failure that may subsequently ripen into a Credit Event, with the lapse of a grace period or satisfaction of another condition) occurs on or before the Scheduled

---

[1591] The concept of the period of protection is embodied in the definition of the "Credit Event Notice" that must be given in such a way that it is effective during the Notice Delivery Period in order for a payoff to be required. A Credit Event Notice (as defined in Section 3.3 of the *1999 Credit Derivatives Definitions*) must describe a Credit Event "that occurred on or after the Effective Date."

[1592] *1999 Credit Derivatives Definitions* § 2.9.

[1593] In fact, ISDA is considering a revision to the current approach under which Credit Events occurring between the Trade Date and the Effective Date could be treated as subject to protection.

[1594] Because the Seller is providing coverage for events occurring on the last day of the final Fixed Rate Payer Calculation Period, that day is included in the accrual of the final Fixed Amount. This accrual convention differs from that applied in calculating Fixed Amounts in interest rate and currency swaps, where the last day of a Calculation Period is generally excluded, reflecting conventions in the calculation of interest on debt obligations. *See supra* p. 401 for discussion of the calculation of Fixed Amounts in interest rate swaps. The related provisions in the *1999 Credit Derivatives Definitions* appear in Article V, using terms defined in Articles I and II, such as Fixed Amount, Fixed Rate Payer, Fixed Rate Payer Calculation Amount, Fixed Rate Payer Period End Date, Fixed Rate Payer Calculation Period and Fixed Rate Payer Payment Date, as well as Business Day Conventions like the ones used in rate swaps (*e.g.,* Following, Modified Following and Preceding).

Termination Date, the Fixed Amounts payable to the Seller will cease to accrue on the Scheduled Termination Date regardless of whether the Potential Failure to Pay ripens into a Credit Event that entitles the Buyer to a payout.[1595]

If a Credit Event occurs, the protection afforded by the swap will end (even though the Scheduled Termination Date has not yet occurred) on the later of (1) the date the related Credit Event Notice becomes effective and (2) if the parties have specified that Notice of Publicly Available Information is applicable, the date that notice becomes effective, at least insofar as the swap's protection relates to the Reference Entity involved in the relevant Credit Event or to Obligations of that Reference Entity. The *1999 Credit Derivatives Definitions* provide that a transaction's final Fixed Rate Payer Calculation Period will end on that date, thereby ending accrual of the Fixed Amounts payable to the Seller.[1596] Since the fundamental assumption of these transactions is that Fixed Amounts will accrue so long as an event relating to a Reference Entity or its agreed Obligations may give rise to a payout from the Seller, this cut-off of the Fixed Amounts assumes a swap with a single payout and only one Reference Entity. If this is not the case, the parties must stipulate their intent in this regard.[1597] This approach also assumes that, for purposes of a transaction involving multiple Reference Entities and potential payouts, the parties will make clear that, when the Event Determination Date occurs in relation to a Credit Event involving one of those Reference Entities, the Fixed Amounts will only cease to accrue on that portion of the Fixed Rate Payer Calculation Amount which reflects the Seller's exposure to the credit risk of that Reference Entity.[1598]

[1595] This extension does not lengthen the Protection Period for other kinds of Credit Events under the same transaction. So, for example, if the parties have agreed that Obligation Acceleration is another applicable Credit Event and it occurs after the Scheduled Termination Date but on or before the Grace Period Extension Date but the sole Obligation payment failure that occurred on or before the Scheduled Termination Date is cured and never ripens into a Credit Event, the Obligation Acceleration cannot give rise to a payout under the swap.

[1596] *See* Sections 2.9 and 5.4 of the *1999 Credit Derivatives Definitions*. *See supra* p. 646 for discussion of timing issues involving the satisfaction of Conditions to Payment and their relation to the Seller's entitlement to Fixed Amounts and the Buyer's entitlement to a Cash Settlement Amount or a Physical Settlement Amount.

[1597] *See* Annotation 30 to the sample credit swap confirmation, *infra* p. 697, regarding one approach.

[1598] The parties may, for example, both (1) indicate that the relevant Reference Entity will cease to be treated as such and (2) state a rule on automatic reduction of the Fixed Rate Payer Calculation Amount. Another approach is to provide that the aggregate settlement amounts payable by the Seller will not exceed the Fixed Rate Payer Calculation Amount and provide for automatic reduction of that amount. The reduction should not, of course, be effective before the time at which the Seller's exposure to the Reference Entity is correspondingly reduced. In complex portfolio structures involving multiple layers of protection, there may be a substantial period between the Event Determination Date relating to a Credit Event and the date of determination of the amount payable in connection with the event, and steps leading towards settlement may be going on simultaneously in relation to multiple Credit Events or obligations. During that period, it may not be clear which layer or layers of protection may be charged with all or part of the payment attributable to any particular Credit Event or obligation. In these cases, it is common to provide that the Fixed Rate Payer Calculation and Floating Rate Payer Calculation Amounts relating to a Seller's layer of risk will be reduced simultaneously in relation to each payoff on the date the payoff is due. If this process is ongoing on the payment date for the final Fixed Amount, Buyers sometimes propose deferral (with interest) of that payment so that, once the allocation of the payoffs among the Sellers is known, the amount of the final payment to each

Credit Default Swaps

OBLIGATIONS AND DELIVERABLE OBLIGATIONS

While the "Bankruptcy" Credit Event relates to the Reference Entity or Reference Entities specified by the parties, the other Credit Events available in the ISDA standard documentation relate to Obligations. In some transactions they relate to a single financial asset identified as the Reference Obligation. In others, they relate to all Obligations of a Reference Entity that fall within a specified Obligation Category, often subject to exclusions that the parties indicate by identifying Excluded Obligations or by identifying Obligation Characteristics that must be satisfied.

For Buyers seeking protection against loss on specific obligations, the decision whether to include other obligations of the same issuer or obligations of another Reference Entity will, as noted, generally reflect a balancing of the increased cost of protection against the Buyer's concern that defaults under those other obligations might presage, or result in, losses on the obligations the Buyer holds. When the credit of a guarantor of the obligations is critical, the Buyer would normally identify the guarantor as a Reference Entity.[1599] When the Reference Entity is a sovereign, it is common to add various agencies, instrumentalities, ministries, departments and other authorities of the sovereign, including the central bank, as Reference Entities, because many sovereigns borrow and issue debt through these arms of government. The *1999 Credit Derivatives Definitions* facilitate this process with broad definitions of "Sovereign" and "Sovereign Agency."[1600]

The Seller, too, may have concerns about the breadth of the Obligation Category chosen by the Buyer for various reasons and, therefore, may condition its willingness to enter into a transaction on a narrowing of the category through the specification of applicable Obligation Characteristics. In some cases these concerns arise because of the Seller's doubts about the correlations between the instruments chosen by the Buyer and those that are reflected in the data available to the Seller for use in pricing the transaction.

---

of them can be limited by reference to accrual on the Event Determination Date for the final Credit Event generating losses allocated to that Seller. These proposals are, naturally, not popular with Sellers. U.S. bank supervisory agencies have, however, advised that they expect the banks subject to their supervision to make appropriate adjustments in their regulatory reports to reflect the estimated loss to them relating to the time value of money which is not taken into account when there is a gap between a Reference Entity's default and the date the bank is entitled to receive a swap payout. *See* OCC & BOARD OF GOVERNORS OF THE FEDERAL RESERVE SYSTEM, *supra* note 1542, at 6.

[1599] ISDA is considering substantial changes to the treatment of guaranties under credit derivatives. Some would exclude certain kinds of guaranty instruments, or instruments of guarantors with certain kinds of relationships to the entity whose obligations are guaranteed, because of concerns over possible defenses that might be raised by the guarantors. Another would clarify that a guaranty must be in a written instrument, thereby excluding guaranties provided for by law—such as sovereign pledges of the sovereign's full faith and credit for certain obligations of public-sector entities. Still other changes in this area would provide clarifications regarding how certain Obligation Characteristics should be satisfied, how some Credit Events should be interpreted and how a transaction should be settled when a guarantor is a Reference Entity. For example, it will be made clear that a Restructuring need occur only with respect to the underlying obligation guaranteed, that only that obligation must satisfy the Pari Passu Ranking characteristic (*see infra* p. 674), when it applies, and that Delivery of a guaranteed obligation in a transaction involving Physical Settlement requires delivery of both the guaranteed obligation and the guaranty.

[1600] *1999 Credit Derivatives Definitions*, §§ 2.23 & 2.24.

Pricing can, as discussed earlier, involve complex assumptions, some of which are based on default statistics and probabilities and recovery rates.[1601]

If an Obligation chosen by the Buyer is atypical, the Seller is likely to seek to have it excluded from those that may give rise to a Credit Event. Three examples of such atypical instruments would be subordinated debt, sovereign debt owed to official creditors and debt with payouts indexed to changes in the performance of something other than interest rates, such as the price of a commodity or basket of commodities or the level of a securities index.

The inclusion of subordinated debt is problematic because the creditor will be entitled to payments only after all payments due and owing to senior creditors have been made. In the case of sovereign debt to official creditors, the Seller may be concerned that matters other than the general financial condition of the obligor may influence the obligor's decision on whether to go into default on the Reference Obligation. This is so because a sovereign may seek to reschedule its debt under loans made by other sovereigns even though it is current, at the time, on its obligations to investors and lenders generally. The case of indexed debt is somewhat more complex. First, adverse changes in the commodity or securities markets might lead a debtor to seek to reschedule, or even to delay paying, its indexed debt while remaining current on other debt. Second—and this is usually the greater concern—the market price for the underlying commodity or securities may be an important factor in valuing the indexed debt, and perhaps more important than the issuer's credit standing. These concerns lead Sellers to limit the credit default swap protection they write to cases in which the parties have, through selection of the appropriate Obligation Characteristics, excluded debt of these kinds from those that may give rise to a Credit Event.[1602]

Looking at the issue in another way, Sellers will most readily provide protection for obligations that, in the context of a Credit Event, will represent claims for their full principal or face amount (or would if acceleration occurred). If not—say, because the obligation is subordinated or because return may be reduced as a result of indexation of principal to commodity or other prices or yields—the credit default transaction will not work well as a mechanism for the pricing and transfer of pure default risk. The price quoted for the obligation in its valuation for a cash settlement transaction could involve a sizable discount, attributable to the subordination or indexation features, as compared with a conventional debt obligation of the same Reference Entity reflecting a full claim for the face amount.

The *1999 Credit Derivatives Definitions* list six Obligation Categories[1603] and eight Obligation Characteristics,[1604] all of which are identified in a matrix set out in the short form of confirmation included as an exhibit to those definitions, as illustrated in the

---

[1601] *See supra* p. 651.

[1602] The applicable Obligation Characteristics would be Pari Passu Ranking, Not Sovereign Lender and Not Contingent. *See* the discussion *infra* pp. 674, 675 & 676. For reasons like those that lead to exclusion of indexed debt, Sellers may also be reluctant to provide protection with respect to Obligations with volatile markets because of their interest or yield structure.

[1603] *1999 Credit Derivatives Definitions*, § 2.18(a).

[1604] *1999 Credit Derivatives Definitions*, § 2.18(b).

Credit Default Swaps 673

following sample credit default swap confirmation.[1605] The Obligation categories are as shown in the following table:

Obligation Categories	
"Payment" Includes any obligation (present or future, contingent or not) for the payment or repayment of money, including the next category, Borrowed Money	**"Reference Obligations Only"** Includes only the particular obligations identified as such by the parties
"Borrowed Money" Includes deposits and reimbursement obligations arising from drawings under letters of credit as well as the obligations "in respect of borrowed money" that fall within the Bond and Loan categories	**"Loan"** Includes a Borrowed Money obligation if it arises under a term loan agreement, revolving loan agreement or other similar credit agreement but excludes Bonds and other types of Borrowed Money obligations
"Bond" Includes a Borrowed Money obligation other than a Loan if the obligation is "in the form of, or represented by, a bond, note (other than notes delivered pursuant to Loans), certificated debt security or other debt security," but excludes other Borrowed Money obligations	**"Bond or Loan"** Includes any obligation within either of those two separate categories

The Obligation Categories are designed so that parties need select only one of them. Any obligation for a payment that would be picked up by the other categories would be included in the broadest of the categories, Payment, along with any other kind of payment obligation (as a result of which Payment is rarely used in credit derivatives). Borrowed Money is somewhat narrower and often used. Loan and Bond are subsets of Borrowed Money. Reference Obligations Only is the narrowest, including nothing but the specific obligation identified as such by the parties and, in limited cases,[1606] a Substitute Reference Obligation.[1607]

When the parties select any category other than Reference Obligation Only, Section 2.14 of the *1999 Credit Derivatives Definitions* specifies that the category will include the indicated kinds of obligations, regardless of whether they are incurred by the Reference Entity as principal or surety or otherwise, regardless of whether the obligation

---

[1605] *See infra* p. 708.

[1606] *See* the table in the introductory note on credit, debt and equity derivatives, *supra* p. 629.

[1607] *See 1999 Credit Derivatives Definitions*, § 2.27.

exists at the time the parties execute their transaction or arises later, and regardless of whether it is contingent or has other special characteristics.

Except when the parties have chosen Reference Obligations Only as the Obligation Category, they may then narrow the scope of the category through their selection among the eight Obligation Characteristics, which are as follows:[1608]

- **Pari Passu Ranking**

An obligation has this Obligation Characteristic only if it ranks at least pari passu in priority of payment with the most senior Reference Obligation or, if no Reference Obligation is specified (which would be possible in a physically settled transaction), with the obligations of the relevant Reference Entity that are neither subordinated by their terms (or otherwise) nor secured.

The *Restructuring Supplement* adds that, in determining whether an Obligation qualifies under these tests, ranking in priority of payment of a Reference Obligation is determined as of the later of (1) the Trade Date of the relevant transaction and (2) the date on which the obligation was issued or incurred. Changes in ranking after the relevant date are disregarded.[1609] Otherwise, in a swap with a single Reference Obligation as the only Deliverable Obligation, the Buyer would not be permitted to tender the Reference Obligation to obtain the Physical Settlement Amount if the obligation had been subordinated through a Restructuring.[1610]

- **Specified Currency**

An obligation has this Obligation Characteristic only if it is payable (1) in the Specified Currency identified in the Confirmation or (2) in one of the Standard Specified Currencies—the euro and the lawful currencies of Canada, France, Germany, Italy, Japan, the United Kingdom and the United States—if "Specified Currency" is checked but no particular currency is identified.

[1608] The Obligation Characteristics are spelled out in *1999 Credit Derivatives Definitions* § 2.18(b).

[1609] *1999 Credit Derivatives Definitions*, § 2.30(a), as added by the *Restructuring Supplement*.

[1610] Under the definition of "Restructuring" in Section 4.7(a)(iv) of the *1999 Credit Derivatives Definitions,* subject to the conditions discussed *supra* p. 665, "a change in the ranking in priority of payment of any Obligation, causing the subordination of such Obligation" will constitute a Restructuring. However, Section 2.30(b), as added by the *Restructuring Supplement,* clarifies that "subordination" for this purpose means only "an amendment to the terms of such Obligation or other contractual arrangement pursuant to which the requisite percentage of holders of such Obligations ('Subordinated Holders') agree that, upon the liquidation, dissolution, reorganization or winding up of the Reference Entity, claims of holders of any other Obligations will be satisfied prior to the claims of Subordinated Holders." The provision goes on to say that "the provision of collateral, credit support or credit enhancement with respect to any obligation will not, of itself, constitute a change in the ranking in priority of payment of any Obligation causing the subordination of such Obligation."

- **Listed**

  To have this Obligation Characteristic, an obligation must be quoted, listed or ordinarily purchased and sold on an exchange. This characteristic applies only to Bonds. For example, if the parties selected "Bond or Loan" as an Obligation Category, only Bonds within the category would be subject to the "Listed" Obligation Characteristic.

- **Not Domestic Law**

  An obligation has this Obligation Characteristic only if it is not governed by the laws of the relevant Reference Entity, if it is a Sovereign, or the jurisdiction of organization of the relevant Reference Entity, if it is not a Sovereign.[1611]

- **Not Sovereign Lender**

  An obligation has this Obligation Characteristic only if it is not primarily owed to a Sovereign or a Supranational Organization.[1612] The definition expressly includes so-called Paris Club Debt, which typically arises from bilateral lending transactions involving a developing country, as borrower, and an OECD country lender.[1613]

- **Not Domestic Issuance**

  An obligation has this Obligation Characteristic only if, when issued or reissued or incurred, it was not intended to be offered for sale primarily in the domestic market of the relevant Reference Entity.[1614]

- **Not Domestic Currency**

  To have this Obligation Characteristic, an obligation must be payable in a currency other than the Domestic Currency of the relevant Reference Entity.[1615]

[1611] The common understanding is that the jurisdiction of organization of an entity, in this context, would be determined as it ordinarily would—by reference to the laws under which it is organized, not the laws of the place where one of its offices is located, if that is different. *See infra* p. 678 for discussion of issues that may arise in connection with obligations of branches.

[1612] "Primarily" for this purpose appears to be understood to exclude obligations only if a majority of the class of obligations is held by a Sovereign or Supranational Organization, and not, say, if a Sovereign or the World Bank simply happens to be among the holders.

[1613] The membership of the Paris Club is not fixed. In addition to the 30 OECD countries, other official creditors that are willing to accept the Club's practices and procedures participate if they are relevant to a particular debtor country. Russia became a member of the Paris Club in 1997.

[1614] The Buyer may wish to be precise in defining whether an obligation is or is not to be characterized as of domestic issuance if this is relevant to the protection it is seeking, because of the potential for disputes over the meaning of "primarily" in this context.

[1615] "Domestic Currency" means the currency specified as such by the parties and any successor currency, except that the successor currency will be disregarded if it is the euro or the lawful currency of Canada, France, Germany, Italy, Japan, the United Kingdom or the United States. If the parties do not specify a Domestic Currency, it will be the lawful currency or successor currency of (1) the Reference Entity, if it is a

- **Not Contingent**

  An obligation has this Obligation Characteristic only if the payment or repayment of principal is not determined by reference to any formula or index and is not subject to any contingency, and it bears interest at a fixed or floating rate that is paid on a periodic basis and computed on a benchmark interest rate plus or minus any applicable spread.

  Considerable uncertainty about the scope of this Obligation Characteristic led to publication of the *Supplement Relating to Convertible, Exchangeable or Accreting Obligations*, which:

  1. defines the classes of Accreting Obligations,[1616] Convertible Obligations[1617] and Exchangeable Obligations[1618]

  2. clarifies that the parties may identify them as Excluded Deliverable Obligations, and

  3. provides that if the parties do not do so, these obligations will not be disqualified from being Deliverable Obligations solely because they are Accreting Obligations, Convertible Obligations or Exchangeable Obligations, provided in the last two cases that the related right to convert or exchange the obligation, or to require the issuer to purchase or redeem the obligation,[1619] has not been exercised on or before the date of Deliv-

---

Sovereign, or (2) in other cases, of the jurisdiction in which the Reference Entity is organized. *See infra* p. 678 on issues raised by the reference to the jurisdiction in which a Reference Entity is organized.

[1616] "Accreting Obligation" means any obligation (including a Convertible Obligation or an Exchangeable Obligation) with terms that expressly provide for payment on acceleration of an amount equal to the obligation's original issue price (whether or not that was equal to the obligation's face amount) plus an additional amount or amounts—which may be on account of original issue discount or other interest accruals not payable on a periodic basis—that will or may accrete. If these characteristics are present, the obligation is not disqualified as an Accreting Obligation merely because (a) payment of these additional amounts is subject to a contingency or determined by reference to a formula or index or (b) the obligation also provides for periodic payment of cash interest.

[1617] "'Convertible Obligation' means any obligation that is convertible, in whole or in part, into Equity Securities solely at the option of holders of such obligation or a trustee or similar agent acting for the benefit only of holders of such obligation."

[1618] "'Exchangeable Obligation' means any obligation that is exchangeable, in whole or in part, for Equity Securities solely at the option of holders of such obligation or a trustee or similar agent acting for the benefit only of holders of such obligation."

[1619] This requirement applies only if the issuer has exercised the right to pay the purchase or redemption price, in whole or in part, in Equity Securities, which are defined in Section 4 of the *Supplement* to mean:

(a) in the case of a Convertible Obligation, equity securities of the issuer of such obligation or depositary receipts representing equity securities of the issuer of such obligation; and

(b) in the case of an Exchangeable Obligation, equity securities of a person other than the issuer of such obligation or depositary receipts representing equity securities of a person other than the issuer of such obligation.

Credit Default Swaps 677

ery (or, if it has been exercised, provided the exercise has been effectively rescinded).[1620]

Notwithstanding the apparent intent that the Obligation Categories be viewed as comprehensive except where specific kinds of obligations are identified as excluded, questions have arisen about whether specific types of obligations fall within some of the them, either generally or as narrowed through specification of an Obligation Characteristic. Other questions have arisen about the intended scope of some of the Obligation Characteristics. If the Buyer believes the scope of a category or characteristic may be ambiguous, its interests will usually be best served through modification of the definition. The following are some examples of areas of possible ambiguity:

- **Borrowed Money**

    Obligations fall in the category only if they are "in respect of borrowed money." Questions arise with respect to obligations issued in connection with a restructuring that modify or represent a settlement in respect of earlier obligations, some of which were originally incurred as borrowings and some of which were not. In the past the question whether such obligations are borrowed-money obligations has been raised in connection with so-called Brady bonds issued by foreign sovereigns.

- **Guaranties**

    Although Section 2.14 of the *1999 Credit Derivatives Definitions* indicates that obligations are included within a category regardless of whether the Reference Entity is acting as principal, surety or otherwise, questions arise if the relevant category lists particular forms of instruments or agreements treated as acceptable evidence of obligations within the category and the Reference Entity's guaranty does not take one of these forms. This question has been raised in connection with guaranties of obligations in the Bond and Loan categories.

    When the parties specify that an Obligation must be Not Contingent, a commonly heard question is whether all guaranties are excluded because guaranties are, by their nature, contingent on a failure of performance by the principal obligor. The common understanding, however, is that this characteristic was intended to apply to financial obligations under which the occurrence of a contingency may give rise to a claim for less than par, such as obligations commonly referred to as hybrid instruments or securities—cases in which the amount payable may depend, *e.g.*, on a specified price or index, or a change in a price or index—as well as instruments or securities under which an obliga-

---

[1620]Market participants also adapt this rule to apply to Obligations used to determine Cash Settlement Amounts in cash-settled transactions when the Buyer is permitted to choose these obligations during the term of the transaction.

tion may cease to exist, or its nature may change, if a specified event occurs, or does not occur, and not to guaranties generally.[1621]

- **Listed**

    Although "Listed" is defined to mean "an obligation that *is* quoted, listed or ordinarily purchased or sold on an exchange," the *1999 Credit Derivatives Definitions* do not indicate whether this test must be satisfied only when the obligation is first issued or also when the parties are determining whether a Credit Event has occurred.[1622]

- **Not Contingent**

    As noted under "Guaranties," doubts have arisen as to whether the category excludes normal guaranty obligations. The many questions raised about convertible and exchangeable obligations and discount or zero coupon obligations led to the publication of the *Supplement Relating to Convertible, Exchangeable or Accreting Obligations*.[1623]

- **Branch Obligations**

    Three Obligation Characteristics define obligations that are included or excluded in terms of a relevant Reference Entity's jurisdiction of organization: Not Domestic Currency, Not Domestic Law and Not Domestic Issuance. Questions arise as to their application to obligations of branches outside the entity's jurisdiction of organization. Regarding Not Domestic Law, it is not clear whether the intent was to disregard the jurisdiction in which the specific branch is situated when an obligation is identified as incurred by that branch, on the theory that the branch's obligations are also obligations of the entire entity. The question can be important, for example, in transactions involving pools, where the pool guidelines limit permitted concentrations of obligations involving, say, emerging market "country risk." The parties should consider clarifying this point in their documentation.

In physically settled transactions, both parties must be cautious not only about their choices of Obligations and Obligation Characteristics but also in analyzing the implications of their choices of Deliverable Obligations and Deliverable Obligation Characteristics. As Obligation Characteristics narrow the types of Obligations that can give rise to a Credit Event, Deliverable Obligation Characteristics define the types of Obligations

---

[1621] *See supra* p. 672 for discussion of the reason why obligations that do not satisfy the Not Contingent characteristic are often excluded from credit derivatives. *See also supra* note 1599 for discussion of proposed changes to the current treatment of guaranties under the ISDA definitions.

[1622] In contrast, Not Domestic Issuance clearly indicates that only facts at the time of issuance or reissuance are relevant. Parties making use of the "Listed" Obligation Characteristic should consider clarifying this point in their documentation.

[1623] *See supra* p. 676.

Credit Default Swaps

that the Buyer may Deliver in exchange for a Physical Settlement Amount, once a Credit Event has occurred and all applicable Conditions to Payment have been satisfied.[1624]

Section 2.19 of the *1999 Credit Derivatives Definitions* identifies the following eight Deliverable Obligations Characteristics.[1625]

Deliverable Obligation Characteristics
"Assignable Loan"   As of the Physical Settlement Date, assignment or novation of the Loan to (1) any third party or (2) "at a minimum, to commercial banks and financial institutions" (wherever organized) that are not then lenders or members of the lending syndicate asset is permitted without consent of an agent, the Reference Entity or any guarantor of the Loan (and without consent of the borrower, if the Reference Entity is a guarantor).
"Consent Required Loan"   As of the Physical Settlement Date, assignment or novation of the Loan requires the consent of an agent, the Reference Entity or a guarantor of the Loan (or with consent of the applicable borrower, if the Reference Entity is a guarantor)
"Direct Loan Participation"   On the Physical Settlement Date, the Buyer can create or procure the creation of a direct Loan participation agreement between the Seller, as participant, and either the Buyer or a Qualifying Participation Seller, as participation seller, but only if the seller is then a lender or a member of the lending syndicate and the participation agreement gives the Seller recourse to the participation seller for a specified share in any payments under the relevant Loan received by the participation seller.   Unless the parties to the Credit Derivative Transaction specify the characteristics of Qualifying Participation Sellers, there will be no Qualifying Participation Sellers.

[1624]If the parties choose Reference Obligations Only, no Deliverable Obligation Characteristics need be specified. Any that are specified will be ignored. In this case, the Buyer will only be permitted to Deliver the Reference Obligations or a Substitute Reference Obligation selected in accordance with Section 2.27. *See supra* p. 673.

[1625]Section 2.20 of the *1999 Credit Derivatives Definitions* provides that (1) Deliverable Obligation Characteristics that are inappropriate for the relevant Deliverable Obligation Category will be disregarded, and (2) the Buyer is entitled to Deliver Loan obligations that satisfy any of multiple specified Deliverable Obligation Characteristics if they are mutually inconsistent.

> **"Indirect Loan Participation"**
>
> The requirements are the same as under Direct Loan Participation except that the participation seller (the Buyer or a Qualifying Participation Seller) need not be a lender or a member of the lending syndicate on the Physical Settlement Date. Thus, the participation seller need not have a direct contractual relationship with the Reference Entity in respect of the Loan. In the U.S. secondary market for loan assets, these would be referred to as subparticipations. The ISDA terms make no presumptions about features that might disqualify an indirect loan participation, so the parties must specify their own.[1626]
>
> ---
>
> **"Transferable"**
>
> The Obligation must be transferable to institutional investors without any contractual, statutory or regulatory restriction, except that the following restrictions do not disqualify the Obligation:
>
> (1) contractual, statutory or regulatory restrictions that exist as conditions to eligibility for resale pursuant to Rule 144A or Regulation S under the Securities Act (*see supra* pp. 161 & 162) or similar resale eligibility requirements under other legal frameworks, and
>
> (2) restrictions on permitted investments such as statutory or regulatory investment restrictions on insurance companies and pension funds.
>
> ---
>
> **"Maximum Maturity"**
>
> The Obligation's remaining maturity from the Physical Settlement Date cannot exceed the period specified in the Credit Derivative Transaction Confirmation. There is no ISDA presumption as to the period of maximum maturity (except under the separate requirements of the *Restructuring Supplement* discussed *supra* p. 666).
>
> ---
>
> **"Accelerated or Matured"**
>
> On or prior to the Physical Settlement Date the total amount (other than default interest, indemnities, tax gross-up and other similar amounts) owed under the Obligation (whether by reason of acceleration or otherwise) is due and payable in full (or would be but for any limitation imposed by applicable insolvency laws).
>
> ---
>
> **"Not Bearer"**
>
> The Obligation is not a bearer instrument, unless interests with respect to it are cleared via the Euroclear system, Clearstream (the ISDA definitions use the former name, Cedel Bank) or another internationally recognized clearing system.

When the parties make the *Restructuring Supplement* applicable to their transaction and specify Restructuring Maturity Limitation Applicable, in addition to satisfying any char-

---

[1626] On participations and concerns to which they may give rise, *see* Gooch & Klein, *Loan Documentation* 247.

acteristics selected from those listed in the table, a Deliverable Obligation will have to satisfy further limitations on final maturity and transferability if the Physical Settlement is brought about by a Credit Event Notice delivered by the Buyer identifying Restructuring as the only Credit Event.[1627]

In a transaction providing for Physical Settlement, in addition to the Deliverable Obligation Characteristics selected by the parties and any additional limitations under the *Restructuring Supplement* that are applicable in the circumstances, the Deliverable Obligations tendered by the Buyer (other than Direct Loan Participations and Indirect Loan Participations) are limited to those in respect of which it can represent as follows as of the Physical Settlement Date and any subsequent date on which it delivers any portion of the Portfolio:

> [I]t has conveyed (or, if applicable, caused to be conveyed) to Seller (or, if applicable, its designee) all right, title and interest in the portion of the Portfolio Delivered on such date free and clear of all claims, charges, liens and encumbrances (including, without limitation, any counterclaim, defense (other than a counterclaim or defense based on the factors set forth in Section 4.1(a)–(d))[1628] or right of setoff by or of the Reference Entity.[1629]

The Buyer is also required, "subject to reasonable verification," to "indemnify and hold harmless Seller for any loss, liability, claim, damage and expense whatsoever incurred arising out of Buyer's breach" of these representations.[1630]

The following is a summary of how the various categories and characteristics would operate together in a case in which the parties made the choices that are illustrated in the sample credit default swap confirmation, as follows:

- the named entity will be the sole Reference Entity[1631]

- the applicable Obligation Category will be Bond

- Bankruptcy, Failure to Pay, Obligation Acceleration, and Restructuring will be the applicable Credit Events

- the Default Requirement will be U.S.$ 10 million

[1627] *See supra* p. 666.

[1628] These exceptions are described *supra* note 1529.

[1629] The Buyer is deemed to make this representation under Section 9.3(a) of the *1999 Credit Derivatives Definitions*.

[1630] *Id.* Naturally, if the parties enter into cash-settled transactions that leave the Buyer free to choose the Obligations that will be valued for purposes of determining a Cash Settlement Amount, the parties should provide in their confirmation that the agreed selection among the Deliverable Obligation Characteristics will apply to narrow the Borrower's permitted freedom of selection. Depending on the structure of the transaction, the Seller may want to ensure that the deemed representation of the Buyer quoted above and the related indemnity are, subject to appropriate modifications, treated as applicable in connection with the Obligations valued in the calculation of a Cash Settlement Amount.

[1631] *See supra* p. 631 on the automatic inclusion of Successors within the definition of the term "Reference Entity" under the *1999 Credit Derivatives Definitions*.

- the *Restructuring Supplement*, the *Supplement Relating to Successor and Credit Events* and the *Supplement Relating to Convertible, Exchangeable or Accreting Obligations* will apply

Given these choices, if the parties had not chosen any Obligation Characteristics, any of the events or circumstances listed below could lead to an obligation of the Seller to make a payment to Buyer, if it occurred or existed during the period of protection and, in each case other than the first (Bankruptcy), if the relevant event related to a qualifying Bond—that is, any obligation for Borrowed Money of the Reference Entity that was represented by bonds, notes or other debt securities other than loans.

This list is a summary of the salient Obligation Characteristics for the chosen Credit Events that are more fully set out in Article IV of the *1999 Credit Derivatives Definitions*, as amended by the specified supplements to those definitions. Article IV also includes two other Credit Event types that the hypothetical parties have not selected: Obligation Default and Repudiation/Moratorium. Obligation Default is rarely used. It covers cases in which the agreed types of Obligations in an aggregate amount at least equal to the Default Requirement may be declared due and payable before they are scheduled to mature as a result of an event of default or similar condition or event. Repudiation/Moratorium is used more in the markets for credit derivatives involving sovereign and emerging markets Reference Entities than in the market for credit default swaps on private-sector corporate "names." It covers cases in which the Reference Entity or any Governmental Authority charged with the regulation of the financial markets where the Reference Entity is organized disaffirms, disclaims, repudiates or rejects, or challenges the validity of, the Reference Entity's Obligations in the selected category, in an aggregate amount not less than the Payment Requirement, or declares or imposes a moratorium, standstill or deferral with respect to one or more of those Obligations in such an aggregate amount.

- "Bankruptcy": the Reference Entity becomes insolvent, fails generally to pay its debts as they become due, admits its inability to do so in a writing submitted in a judicial, regulatory or administrative proceeding or filing (the description of the necessary kind of writing was added by the *Supplement Relating to Successor and Credit Events*), or becomes the subject of certain bankruptcy or similar proceedings and related events

- "Failure to Pay": the Reference Entity fails to make a payment when and where due under any Bond Obligation and does not cure the failure during any applicable Grace Period, if the aggregate amount of the payment failures is not less than the Payment Requirement (U.S.$10 million in this case)

- "Obligation Acceleration": any of the Reference Entity's repayment obligations in respect of Bond Obligations are accelerated (*i.e.*, principal amounts payable under the Bonds are declared to be due before their scheduled final maturity as a result or on the basis of a default or similar event), if the aggregate amount accelerated is not less than the Payment Requirement

Credit Default Swaps 683

- "Restructuring": the Reference Entity or a Governmental Authority announces or decrees a restructuring of the Reference Entity's Bond Obligations in an aggregate amount not less than the Default Requirement in a form that is binding on the Reference Entity, or the Reference Entity or such a Governmental Authority agrees to a restructuring of at least that amount of the Reference Entity's Bond Obligations with the holder or holders of those Obligations and (1) the restructuring meets any of a series of specified characteristics that evidence financial distress—as described in the earlier discussion of this Credit Event[1632]—and (2) in light of the parties' adoption of the *Restructuring Supplement*, the relevant Obligation is a Multiple Holder Obligation—one which, at the time the Credit Event Notice is given, has at least three holders that are not Affiliates of each other and which requires the consent of at least 66-2/3% of the holders to the event.[1633]

In the sample confirmation, the parties have narrowed the application of these selected Credit Events by specifying the following as the applicable Obligation Characteristics: Pari Passu Ranking, Listed and Not Contingent. As a result, none of the agreed Credit Events can lead to a payment obligation on the part of the Seller if the Credit Event affects only Bond obligations of the Reference Entity that, on the swap's Trade Date or any later date of issuance of the Bonds, are subordinate in priority of payment to its obligations under the identified Reference Obligation. This is so because those subordinated Bond obligations would not satisfy the Obligation Characteristic known as "Pari Passu Ranking." In addition, if the Credit Event affects only privately placed notes of the Reference Entity that are not quoted, listed or ordinarily purchased and sold on an exchange, it will not give rise to a payment obligation of the Seller, because they will not be Listed. Finally, if the Reference Entity has issued commodity index-linked bonds with principal obligations that vary with changes in, say, the price of oil, and if the agreed Credit Events have affected only those bonds, the Credit Event will not give rise to a payment obligation of the Seller under the swap because those bonds will not qualify as Not Contingent.

CHANGED CIRCUMSTANCES

The parties to credit derivatives should consider whether extraordinary events affecting the underlying Reference Obligations or Reference Entities or the regulatory treatment of their transaction deserve special attention. The particular events and circumstances that may warrant special treatment and the appropriate handling of a particular event or circumstance will very much depend on the objectives of the party seeking protection under the credit derivative transaction. Some examples are discussed in the preceding introductory note on credit, debt and equity derivatives.[1634]

[1632] *See supra* note 1581 and accompanying text.

[1633] *See supra* p. 666.

[1634] *See supra* p. 624.

THE PARTIES' RELATIONSHIP

Disputes relating to OTC derivatives have highlighted the desirability of clarity regarding the parties' relationship and their expectations about related subjects, such as whether one party may rely on the other party for advice or to ensure that the transaction will operate in a particular way.[1635] Concerns about misunderstandings on these and similar subjects can exist to a heightened degree in credit derivatives, in part because one of the parties often has a hedging position in a Reference Obligation and a relationship with the Reference Entity. That may give it privileged access to information that the other party does not have access to, or that may become available to it only at some later time. The representations and agreements of the parties in Article IX of the *1999 Credit Derivatives Definitions* deal with many of these concerns.[1636] The parties should consider whether their particular dealings warrant the use of additional provisions in this area.

In complex pool credit derivatives structures, where the ultimate buyer of protection has a contractual relationship only with its counterparty and the counterparty is not the ultimate seller of the protection, these subjects can be particularly important and particularly difficult. To monitor the performance of the underlying pool, compliance with pool guidelines and, more generally, compliance by the ultimate buyer with the requirements of the swap, the ultimate seller of protection will expect the documentation to require the ultimate buyer to provide the relevant information and will expect to receive all information that the ultimate buyer does provide. If the documents do not give it the right to obtain this information directly, some indirect means of enabling the ultimate protection seller to safeguard its interests will generally have to be found. These solutions are often reached only through considerable compromise, taking into account the degree to which the various parties along the chain leading from the ultimate protection buyer to the ultimate protection seller have interests aligned with those of the ultimate seller and their ability to influence whether it ultimate receives what it requires.

DISPUTE RESOLUTION

In credit derivatives transactions, the Calculation Agent makes critical determinations. These include determinations of amounts that Sellers may be required to pay to Buyers and as to important matters such as whether Substitute Reference Obligations are necessary and whether entities qualify as Successors to Reference Entities.[1637] Even though the *1999 Credit Derivatives Definitions* provide as the default choice that the Seller will act as the Calculation Agent if no express choice is made, the choice of market participants is often for the Buyer to do so. The Calculation Agent is required to make all determinations in good faith and in a commercially reasonable manner, but the parties acknowledge that it is not acting as a fiduciary in making its determinations.[1638]

[1635]*See* Chapter 5, *supra* p. 177. *See also supra* p. 145 on the extension to security-based derivatives, including some credit derivatives, of the antifraud provisions of the U.S. securities laws.

[1636]*See supra* p. 656 and *see* Annotation 46 to the following sample credit default swap confirmation, *infra* p. 703.

[1637]*See 1999 Credit Derivatives Definitions*, § 1.13; and *see* Annotation 14 to the following sample credit default swap confirmation, *infra* p. 691.

[1638]*1999 Credit Derivatives Definitions*, § 1.13.

The parties may elect to resolve disputes over determinations made by the Calculation Agent in accordance with Section 10.2 of the *1999 Credit Derivatives Definitions.* Under that provision, the Disputing Party has a right to require that the Calculation Agent have the disputed determination made by a disinterested third party selected by the Calculation Agent after consultation with the parties. Although the provision initially also refers to disputes that may arise because the Calculation Agent fails to make a required determination, the remainder of the provision does not actually deal with that possibility. The costs of the disinterested third party are to be borne by the Disputing Party if the disinterested third party substantially agrees with the Calculation Agent and by the Calculation Agent if the third party does not.

Given the importance of the determinations to be made by the Calculation Agent, the parties sometimes modify this standard provision, particularly in substantial transactions.[1639] Examples are modifications that:

- deal in more detail with failures of the Calculation Agent to make required determinations;

- provide for resolution of disputes by majority vote of three independent parties (one selected by each party and a third selected by those two independent parties);

- deal in more detail with the allocation of the costs of the process;

- deal in more detail with rights to withhold payment pending resolution of the dispute and the duty to pay interest on amounts withheld; and

- provide for restrictions on communications between the parties and the independent third party or parties while the dispute resolution process is in progress.

In some cases—usually with credit default swaps involved in synthetic CDOs—the Seller also seeks to make clear that whether or not a Credit Event has actually occurred is not a matter that must necessarily be determined through the dispute resolution mechanism in Section 10.2 of the definitions. That is, whether the Buyer has a right to receive a payment is a matter of fact and not something that the Seller must challenge through that process.

The introduction to the *1999 Credit Derivatives Definitions*[1640] refers to an ISDA project to develop a dispute resolution mechanism for credit derivatives, which would be known as the ISDA Dispute Resolution Guidelines and would replace the mechanism of Section 10.2 of those definitions.[1641] ISDA has since given priority to refinement to the definitions themselves.

[1639]*See, e.g.*, the provision on "Replacement of Calculation Agent" in the sample confirmation for an HDD weather swap transaction, *infra* p. 777.

[1640]At ix.

[1641]*See* Annotation 70 to the following sample credit default swap confirmation, *infra* p. 715.

OTHER SPECIAL CONCERNS

Like other OTC derivatives, credit derivatives and the transactions through which they are settled or hedged may raise important legal, tax and accounting issues.[1642] However, because these transactions are more recent creations than interest rate, currency, commodity-priced and even equity-linked OTC derivatives, some of these issues have not yet been addressed or are still being considered by legislators, regulators, accounting professionals and others. Market participants who are new to these transactions and those involved in novel structures, regardless of their prior experience, should review their objectives and plans with their legal and other advisors.

[1642] Some of these issues are discussed in Chapters 3, 4 and 8, *supra* pp. 63, 129 & 350, and in the introductory note on credit, debt and equity derivatives, *supra* p. 605.

> The Introduction to this Part, *supra* p. 369, and the annotations to the sample rate swap confirmation, *supra* p. 427, contain general commentary about the confirmation process and the use of ISDA's confirmation forms both before and after the parties have entered into a master agreement that is not repeated or expressly referred to in the annotations to the other sample confirmations in this book.

[Letterhead of Big Bank, N.A.]

April 16, 2002

Credit Derivative Transaction

Institutional Investor Inc.
One Investment Plaza
New York, NY 10000-1000

Ladies and Gentlemen:

The purpose of this letter agreement (this "Confirmation") is to confirm the terms and conditions of the Credit Derivative Transaction entered into between us on the Trade Date specified below (the "Transaction"). This Confirmation constitutes a "Confirmation" as referred to in the Master Agreement specified below.

> Annotation 1. This sample confirmation uses the form supplied as an exhibit to the *1999 Credit Derivatives Definitions* (the "*ISDA CDS Confirmation Form*"), with some modifications. In the first of the modifications, the sample retains the widespread derivatives market practice of having the initial reference to the confirmation identify it as a "letter agreement." Although this practice was used in the exhibits to the *1991 ISDA Definitions* and several subsequent sets of definitions, more recently published sets of definitions, including the *1999 Credit Derivatives Definitions*, simply begin by referring to the confirmation as a "letter" or "facsimile."
>
> Annotation 2. The *1999 Credit Derivatives Definitions* were prepared primarily with credit default transactions in mind but do not use that term. Instead, they apply to "Credit Derivative Transactions," and (under Section 1.1) will treat as a Credit Derivative Transaction any transaction identified as such in the related Confirmation and "any transaction that incorporates these Definitions."

The definitions and provisions contained in the 1999 ISDA Credit Derivatives Definitions, as amended and supplemented by each of the supplements listed below (as so modified and supplemented, the "Credit Derivatives Definitions"), are incorporated into this Confirmation, each as published by the International Swaps and Derivatives Association, Inc., subject to the modifications expressly provided below: the Restructuring Supplement (dated May 11, 2001); the Supplement Relating to Convertible, Exchangeable or Accreting Obligations (dated November 9, 2001); and the Supplement Relating to Successor and Credit Events (dated November 28, 2001). In the event of any inconsistency between the Credit Derivatives Definitions and this Confirmation, this Confirmation will govern.

> Annotation 3. Under this standard ISDA approach to the incorporation by reference of a set of definitions, supplements and revisions to the *1999 Credit Derivatives Definitions* will not apply to the parties' transaction unless they affirmatively modify their documentation to that effect. In the illustrated case, the parties have elected to adopt the three supplements to the *1999 Credit Derivatives Definitions* discussed above (*see supra* pp. 631, 666 & 676). Modifications to the *ISDA CDS Confirmation Form* related to these supplements are identified in these annotations.
>
> Annotation 4. The illustrated swap is a simple transaction involving a single Reference Entity and a single Reference Obligation. As is contemplated in the *1999 Credit Derivatives Definitions*, Sections 1.3 & 1.7, the Transaction's "Term" will end if a settlement date occurs, cutting off the possibility of further settlements in the ordinary course, except in connection with a Restructuring Credit Event. *See also* the following: Annotation 9 to this sample confirmation for discussion of the end of a transaction's Term; *supra* p. 631 for discussion of Succession Events that can lead to the splitting of a swap into multiple transactions (with related possible multiple settlements); *supra* p. 667 for discussion of possible multiple settlements in connection with a Restructuring; and *supra* p. 616 for discussion of split settlements in other extraordinary cases.
>
> Annotation 5. When transactions involve reference pools or otherwise provide for multiple settlements, the confirmation (often at this spot) overrides the presumption that the transaction's Term will end with the first settlement. For example, a confirmation might, depending on the terms of the transaction, state something along the following lines (using the confirmation's special defined term, "Credit Derivatives Definitions"):
>
> "There may be multiple Settlement Dates and related settlements under the Transaction in circumstances beyond those contemplated in the Credit Derivatives Definitions. To implement the parties' intent in this regard, the Credit Derivatives Definitions will be construed as separately applicable to each Reference Entity and its Obligations specified herein so that each of the parties has the rights and obligations it would have if there were a separate Credit Derivative Transaction hereunder in respect of each Reference Entity and its Obligations, subject to the limitations expressed in this Confirmation. All provisions of the Credit Derivatives Definitions relating to the Termination Date of a Credit Derivative Transaction (and its direct or indirect effects on the rights and obligations of the parties) in connection with the first settlement and Event Determination Date will be treated as applicable to these assumed separate Credit Derivatives Transactions, so that only a single settlement and Event Determination Date may occur with respect to each of them, but multiple

> settlements and Event Determination Dates may occur with respect to the Transaction hereunder. The foregoing may not be construed to imply that the rights and obligations of the parties under the Transaction are severable or transferable separately in any circumstances other than those expressly provided for in the Credit Derivatives Definitions or the Agreement."
>
> This example uses the defined term "Credit Derivatives Definitions" in relation to multiple settlements because they may occur under the *Restructuring Supplement, supra* p. 667, or the *Supplement Rating to Successor and Credit Events, supra* p. 631, or in connection with partial cash settlements pursuant to Sections 9.4 through 9.6 of the *1999 Credit Derivatives Definitions, supra* p. 616.

This Confirmation supplements, forms a part of, and is subject to, the Master Agreement dated as of April 16, 2002, as amended and supplemented from time to time (the "Agreement"), between Big Bank, N.A. (the "Bank") and Institutional Investor Inc. (the "Counterparty"). All provisions contained in the Agreement govern this Confirmation except as expressly modified below.

> Annotation 6. *See* the Introduction to Part 2, *supra* p. 369, on the basic approach of the ISDA forms that makes the confirmation of each transaction a part of, and subject to, the terms of the master agreement between the parties. Footnote 1 to the form of confirmation in the *1999 Credit Derivatives Definitions* supplies text that the parties may use to treat transactions as subject to a master agreement with the terms set forth in an ISDA master agreement form if they have not yet entered into a master agreement. The use of a provision of that kind and common modifications are discussed *supra* p. 378. The product description preceding this sample confirmation (*supra* p. 619) identifies features of ISDA master agreement forms that the parties sometimes modify in connection with credit default swaps.

The terms of the Transaction to which this Confirmation relates are as follows:

1. General Terms:

   Trade Date: April 16, 2002

> Annotation 7. As discussed *supra* p. 669, if the specified Effective Date is after the Trade Date on which the parties reach agreement on a transaction, they should be sure they have reached an understanding about whether the transaction's protection is intended to cover Credit Events that occur before the Effective Date. If they are silent on this subject, protection will not begin until the Effective Date.
>
> Annotation 8. In determining whether some Credit Events exist, and for some other purposes, the *1999 Credit Derivatives Definitions* provide that the parties must look at the terms of a relevant Obligation as in effect on the Trade Date or, if the Obligation is issued after that date, on its issue date. This is necessary because, even though some credit default transactions define possible Credit Events only by

reference to a single Reference Obligation (and its related issuer or other Reference Entity), credit default transactions more commonly identify the Obligations relevant for identifying Credit Events—and in physically settled transactions, the Deliverable Obligations that may tendered in a settlement—as including a broad category of Obligations of a Reference Entity that have the requisite Obligation Characteristics or Deliverable Obligation Characteristics (*see supra* p. 673), regardless of whether they are outstanding on the Trade Date. In addition, in some circumstances, a Reference Obligation outstanding on the Trade Date and selected as the only relevant Obligation for purposes of their transaction may be replaced by a Substitute Obligation issued later. *See supra* p. 624.

Effective Date: April 16, 2002

Scheduled Termination Date: April 17, 2006

Annotation 9. Under the *1999 Credit Derivatives Definitions,* Sections 1.3 & 1.7, the Effective Date and the Termination Date mark the beginning and end of a transaction's Term. The Termination Date will be the Scheduled Termination Date identified by the parties except in the following cases:

• If Grace Period Extension applies (*see infra* p. 647) and a Potential Failure to Pay occurs on or before the Scheduled Termination Date, the Termination Date will be the Grace Period Extension Date (Section 1.10).

• If Notice of Intended Physical Settlement is not effective within the prescribed 30-day period after the Event Determination Date, the Termination Date will be the last day of that period (Section 3.4).

• If a Credit Event that may lead to a payout occurs, the Cash Settlement Date, the Physical Settlement Date or, if the Buyer cannot effect Delivery on the Physical Settlement Date and wishes to continue trying, the fifth Business Day after the Physical Settlement Date, will be the Termination Date (Sections 7.2, 8.3, 9.3(c)(ii) & 9.9).

The definitions do not expressly set forth the consequences of the adjustments of the Termination Date and the end of the Term. In appropriate cases, the parties may wish to make their confirmations explicit on the results they intend to have flow from such adjustments.

Annotation 10. The Scheduled Termination Date is the last day of the period of protection—the cutoff for credit triggers that may ultimately give rise to a payout to the Buyer from the Seller. *See supra* p. 669 for discussion of this subject and *see* Annotation 41 to this sample confirmation, *infra* p. 701, regarding the ability of the Notifying Party to keep the period of protection open through that date, and satisfy Conditions to Payment even after that date, even though a Credit Event occurs much earlier in a transaction's Term.

Annotation 11. Under Section 2.9 of the *1999 Credit Derivatives Definitions,* the first Fixed Rate Payer Calculation Period will always begin on, and include, the Effective Date, and the final Fixed Rate Payer Calculation Period will always end on, and include, either the Scheduled Termination Date or, if earlier, the Event Determination Date relating to the relevant Credit Event, that is, when the Credit Event Notice becomes effective and, if applicable, Notice of Publicly Available Information is also effective. The inclusion of the Scheduled Termination Date or Event Determination Date is a departure from practice in the calculation of fixed amounts payable in some other kinds of derivatives, such as interest rate and currency swaps. *See, e.g., supra* p. 384. This is purposely so because, under the *1999 Credit Derivatives Definitions,* the Seller may be required to make a payment on account of a Credit Event or Potential Failure to Pay that occurs on the Scheduled Termination Date or Event Determination Date.

Annotation 12. Since the end of the Term of a Credit Derivative Transaction documented under these ISDA definitions will not necessarily mark the end of all the parties' related obligations, users of these definitions should analyze whether any important terms of their master agreements or related credit support arrangements operate by reference to a transaction's Term and, if so, whether any modification is appropriate in connection with transactions documented using the *1999 Credit Derivatives Definitions.*

Floating Rate Payer:	The Counterparty (the *"Seller"*)
Fixed Rate Payer:	The Bank (the *"Buyer"*)
Calculation Agent:	The Buyer

Annotation 13. Although third parties are sometimes used as Calculation Agents, it is more usual to find one of the parties to a credit default swap named to fill that role. If the parties are silent on this subject, they will be deemed to have selected the Seller as the Calculation Agent, under Section 1.13 of the *1999 Credit Derivatives Definitions*. In practice, however, Buyers often act as Calculation Agent. As indicated in a footnote to the *ISDA CDS Confirmation Form*, if the parties use a third-party Calculation Agent, they should consider what documentation is desirable to set out its undertaking to act as such.

Annotation 14. In many kinds of derivatives, there is little of consequence that the Calculation Agent may be called upon to do; its main function is to calculate obligations on the basis of published sources of rates and prices and to select Reference Dealers and similar entities to provide relevant rate and price quotations in the absence of data from the selected published rate or price source. Under the *1999 Credit Derivatives Definitions*, although the Calculation Agent's role is largely administrative, it may be called on, among other things, to:

- select (after consultation with the parties) the Dealers to be polled for Quotations used in determining the Final Price in a cash-settled transaction;

- determine (after consultation with the parties) whether accrued but unpaid interest should be included or excluded in the valuation of an Obligation;

- select the exchange rate (the "Currency Rate") to be used in translating the face or principal amount of an Obligation, if it is denominated in a currency other than the one selected by the parties for purposes of valuation and measurement of a Portfolio of Deliverable Obligations;

- determine (after consultation with the parties) the number of days in the Physical Settlement Period, which should be "the longest of the number of Business Days for settlement in accordance with then current market practice of any Deliverable Obligation being Delivered in the Portfolio";

- determine whether in its opinion a Substitute Reference Obligation should be used in a transaction, in the cases shown in Table 6 in the introductory note on credit, debt and equity derivatives, *supra* p. 629, and select the Substitute Reference Obligation;

- determine whether an entity is a Successor to a Reference Entity; and

- select a disinterested third party to make a determination, if the Calculation Agent has failed to make the determination or the other party has disputed the Calculation Agent's determination.

Although some of these tasks are to be performed by the Calculation Agent after consultation with the parties and in all cases there is a general rule, in Section 1.13 of the *ISDA Credit Derivatives Definitions,* where these tasks are listed, that whenever "required to act or to exercise judgment," the Calculation Agent must do so "in good faith and in a commercially reasonable manner," some market participants are uncomfortable with leaving at least some of these matters to the Calculation Agent (such as the choice of Dealers and of a disinterested third party to be involved in resolving disputes).

Calculation Agent City: New York City

Annotation 15. This term is used to determine the effective day of notices required to satisfy Conditions to Payment (a Credit Event Notice, a Notice of Publicly Available Information and a Notice of Intended Physical Settlement). If delivered at or before 4:00 p.m. in the Calculation Agent City on a Calculation Agent City Business Day, the notice will be effective on that day. Otherwise it will be effective on the following Calculation Agent City Business Day.

Business Day: New York City

Annotation 16. Business Days are relevant, among other things, in defining the periods within which obligations must be performed and notices given. As is the case with other kinds of derivatives under other sets of ISDA definitions, if a payment or delivery is to be made or another action taken on a day that turns out not to be a Business Day, under the *1999 Credit Derivatives Definitions*, Section 2.11, the parties may, as illustrated below, specify a Business Day Convention pursuant to which the relevant day will be moved. The parties generally specify the city or cities relevant to the identification of Business Days in a confirmation. Business Days are also relevant in determining the Valuation Dates used in the calculation of Cash Settlement Amounts in cash-settled transactions.

Annotation 17. This specification of New York City assumes that both parties will be acting from New York City and that no other city will be relevant to the timing of payments, the length of periods relevant for calculating payments or other matters, because the Reference Obligation is a U.S. dollar denominated fixed-rate obligation and the Buyer's payment obligations are calculated at a fixed rate. Different circumstances in these or other aspects of the transaction (such as the listing of the Reference Obligation on an exchange or its trading through a settlement system) might warrant naming additional cities for purposes of determining whether a given day will be treated as a Business Day for some or all purposes of the transaction. Although Section 1.15 of the *1999 Credit Derivatives Definitions* supplies a definition of "Business Day" if the parties do not identify a city or cities, the lack of specificity of Section 1.15 could lead to an undesirable result in some cases.

Annotation 18. For example, as discussed *supra* p. 620, Sellers sometimes negotiate for the right to participate (or appoint an agent to participate) in the Dealer poll used to value Obligations in connection with cash settlement and in a separate cash-market auction of the Obligations, so the Seller can protect itself against what it believes to be an undervaluation of the Obligations or, in the absence of the required Dealer bids, a zero valuation. In these cases, it is, naturally, critical that the process be scheduled to occur so that the Seller (or its designee) can participate. Since Valuation Dates must be Business Days, these Sellers should consider whether the city from which the Seller or its designee will be acting should be taken into account in defining "Business Day" and whether the time set for the valuation process is such that the Seller or its designee will be open for business.

Business Day Convention:	Modified Following (which shall apply to any date referred to in this Confirmation that falls on a day that is not a Business Day).

Annotation 19. The Business Day Convention choices under the *1999 Credit Derivatives Definitions* follow those available under the *2000 ISDA Definitions*. See *supra* p. 391 for discussion of those conventions. The choice in the sample provision is the same as the fallback choice under the *1999 Credit Derivatives Defini-*

tions (Section 2.11(b)). Under those definitions, many actions to be taken in connection with the timetable leading to settlement after a Credit Event are scheduled to occur by reference to periods measured in Business Days (*see supra* p. 646) and, so, will adjust automatically for holidays. Those ISDA practices are, however, often modified in complex transactions involving multiple settlements after potentially lengthy periods. In those cases, the parties should consider whether the illustrated Business Day Convention, which is commonly used, makes sense in the context of the relevant valuation or settlement process. Other areas in which the Business Day Convention normally comes into play are a transaction's Term and Fixed Rate Payer Calculation Periods, because the Scheduled Termination Date and Fixed Rate Payer Payments Dates are usually identified as calendar dates, as illustrated in this sample, and the maximum Grace Period applicable in determining whether a Reference Entity's late payments under Obligations constitutes a Credit Event as a Failure to Pay (*see* Annotation 49 to this sample confirmation, *infra* p. 705), is usually expressed in terms of calendar days.

Reference Entity: ABC Co.

Annotation 20. A Successor to the identified Reference Entity will automatically become a Reference Entity, under Section 2.1 of the *1999 Credit Derivatives Definitions*. The definitions as originally published contemplate a single Successor, but the *Supplement Relating to Successor and Credit Events* recognizes the possibility of multiple Successors and, for non-Sovereigns, provides for their identification by reference to numerical standards referring to their assumption of obligations of the Reference Entity outstanding immediately before the relevant Succession Event. If the Reference Entity is a Sovereign, there is no provision for multiple Successors nor a requirement that the successor assume any of the predecessor's obligations, given the problems that an assumption requirement could create in, say, a case like the dissolution of the former Soviet Union. The identification of a Successor under the *1999 Credit Derivatives Definitions* without this supplement, or for a Sovereign, is left to the Calculation Agent, without the benefit of numerical standards like those used in the supplement. *See supra* p. 632 regarding the underlying presumption of the *1999 Credit Derivatives Definitions* that the Seller of protection under a credit derivative is assuming (and pricing for) the risks associated with mergers, demergers, consolidations, amalgamations and transfers of obligations of Reference Entities. It is, naturally, critical to ensure that the intended Reference Entity and Reference Obligation are correctly identified. *See supra* note 11 on disputes over these questions.

Reference Obligation(s): The obligation identified as follows:

Primary Obligor:	Reference Entity
Guarantor:	None
Maturity:	12/22/2010
Coupon:	6.15%
CUSIP/ISIN:	CUSIP 00000XX0
Original Issue Amount:	USD 75,000,000

> Annotation 21. These six characteristics for the Reference Obligation are listed in the *ISDA CDS Confirmation Form*. If others are relevant for identifying a particular Reference Obligation, they should be added. If a Reference Obligation has a guarantor or other provider of credit support, the standard Credit Event definitions should be closely examined, to ascertain whether changes are appropriate. If the Buyer of the protection is concerned about credit risk in relation to the guarantor, and not the issuer, of the Reference Obligation, the guarantor could be named as the Reference Entity. *See supra* pp. 673 & 677 on the definition of "Obligation" to include guaranty obligations and on related concerns involving the "Not Contingent" Obligation Characteristic.
>
> Annotation 22. In transactions subject to physical settlement, the parties need not identify a Reference Obligation; only Obligations and Deliverable Obligations must be specified. On the other hand, the cash settlement provisions in Article VII of the *1999 Credit Derivatives Definitions* assume that a Reference Obligation will generally be specified for a transaction subject to cash settlement. For example, the Final Price used to determine the Cash Settlement Amount is defined by reference to the "price of the Reference Obligation . . . determined in accordance with the specified Valuation Method." If the parties agree in advance on a stated Cash Settlement Amount or, say, that the Cash Settlement Amount will be a stated percentage of the Floating Rate Payer Calculation Amount, they will not need to identify a Reference Obligation. In complex pool transactions that do not involve Reference Obligations and, instead, permit Buyers to choose the qualifying Obligations to be valued for purposes of cash settlement—often called "Valuation Obligations"—the parties may specify how the Final Price will be determined without relying on the provisions of the *1999 Credit Derivatives Definitions* or may state that specified provisions of those definitions relating to Reference Obligations will be treated as applying to the Valuation Obligations selected by the Buyer.

Reference Price: 100%

> Annotation 23. The Reference Price is used to determine the Cash Settlement Amount or Physical Settlement Amount that the Seller may be required to pay. *See supra* pp. 642 & 643. The *1999 Credit Derivatives Definitions* assume the parties will express the Reference Price as a percentage of the face or principal amount of

the Reference Obligation, in the case of a cash-settled transaction, or the face or principal amount of the Deliverable Obligations, in the case of a physically settled transaction. For example, the parties might choose to specify a Reference Price of 75% if (say, because of the discount at which the Reference Obligation was then trading) the parties agreed that in a cash settlement of their transaction after a Credit Event, the Buyer should be entitled to no more than 75% of the Reference Obligation's then outstanding principal amount. The formulation that would produce this result (in Section 7.3 of the *1999 Credit Derivatives Definitions*) provides that (absent the parties' specification to the contrary) the Cash Settlement Amount will be the greater of (1) zero and (2) the Floating Rate Payer Calculation Amount (in our example, the outstanding principal of the Reference Obligation at the Trade Date) multiplied by the difference between the Reference Price and the Final Price (determined so as to reflect the Reference Obligation's post-Credit Event market value). *See* Dominic O'Kane & Robert McAdie, *Trading the Default Swap Basis,* DERIVATIVES WEEK, Mar. 11, 2002, at 7 (Learning Curve column) on various approaches to hedging with credit default swaps that relate to the relationship between the swap's notional coverage and the Reference Obligation's market value or face or principal amount.

2. Fixed Payments:

Annotation 24. The various items in this part of the sample confirmation operate to define the Buyer's basic payment obligation in much the same way Fixed Amount obligations would be defined in a simple interest rate swap transaction, except that, under the *1999 Credit Derivatives Definitions*, the Fixed Amount payable in respect of the final Fixed Rate Payer Calculation Period should include the last day of that period, because an event or circumstance that occurs on that day may ultimately give rise to a payout by the Seller. *See* Annotation 11 to this sample confirmation, *supra* p. 691, and *see supra* p. 384 on the calculation of Fixed Amounts under interest rate swaps.

Fixed Rate Payer Calculation
Amount: USD 25,000,000

Annotation 25. This is the base for calculating the Fixed Amounts payable to the Seller for the protection it is selling. If no Fixed Rate Payer Calculation Amount is specified, it will (under *1999 Credit Derivatives Definitions*, § 2.7) be the Floating Rate Payer Calculation Amount used to calculate any payout to which the Buyer may become entitled, on the logical assumption that the Fixed Amounts payable to the Seller should be calculated on the basis of the same amount that may ultimately serve as the basis for calculating a payout to the Buyer.

Annotation 26. If the Buyer's goal is to obtain protection in respect of a single obligation of the Reference Entity and the principal of that obligation amortizes, the

Fixed Rate Payer Calculation Amount and Floating Rate Payer Calculation Amount under the credit default swap will normally amortize as the Reference Obligation is paid down. The Fixed Rate Payer Calculation Amount should not, however, automatically decline on the scheduled amortization dates because, if the Reference Entity fails to pay an installment of principal due on a scheduled amortization date, the Seller may remain at risk of having to make a payout based on the Reference Obligation's actual outstanding principal.

Annotation 27. In many cases, however, the Buyer is not seeking protection against loss on a particular Reference Obligation but, rather, a percentage of its total exposure to that Reference Entity. In these cases (including the synthetic arbitrage CDOs discussed *supra* p. 659), the confirmation will identify the same amount as the Fixed Rate Payer Calculation Amount and the Floating Rate Payer Calculation Amount and that amount will remain unchanged until it is reduced in connection with a Credit Event that serves as the basis for a claim by the Buyer, or until the Reference Entity is removed from the pool of Reference Entities.

Annotation 28. Regardless of the nature of the transaction, reductions to the Fixed Rate Payer Amount and Floating Rate Payer Calculation Amount should generally be simultaneous, so that the Fixed Amount payable to the Seller is always calculated on the same base as is used to determine potential claims against it for future Credit Events. In multiple payout transactions, if the Seller is late with a payment in respect of a Credit Event, the Buyer's remedies will consist of a claim for interest on the overdue amount and, when applicable, the right to cause the early termination of the transaction, in a settlement in which the Seller's overdue payment will constitute an Unpaid Amount (*see supra* p. 860). To seek, instead, or in addition, to provide that the Floating Rate Payer Calculation Amount used to calculate the Seller's exposure to future Credit Events will not be reduced until the overdue payout is made distorts the economic symmetry of the parties' bargain.

Annotation 29. In many cases these reductions relating to a Credit Event will occur with effect on the related Event Determination Date, when the Credit Event Notice becomes effective and, if applicable, Notice of Publicly Available Information is also effective. This approach is consistent with the reasoning underlying Section 2.9 of the *1999 Credit Derivatives Definitions,* pursuant to which, in a transaction with a single payout, the final Fixed Rate Payer Calculation Period (and with it accrual of Fixed Amounts) ends on the earlier of the Scheduled Termination Date and the Event Determination Date. *See supra* note 1598 for cases in which the Fixed Rate Payer Calculation Amount and the Floating Rate Payer Calculation Amount may be reduced at a later time.

Annotation 30. Article V of the *1999 Credit Derivatives Definitions,* with its formula for the calculation of Fixed Amounts, does not contemplate the possibility that the Fixed Rate Payer Calculation Amount will change during the course of a Fixed Rate Payer Calculation Period, reflecting the underlying assumption mentioned above that Fixed Amounts will cease to accrue on the first Event Determination Date, although an actual payout may occur later. As a result, whenever these ISDA definitions contemplate the possibility of multiple payouts in extraordinary circumstances, they take the approach of providing that the transaction will be subdivided or treated as if it had been. Examples are Section 2.2(d) of the definitions, as amended by the *Supplement Relating to Successor and Credit Events* (*see supra* note 1496), and Section 3.10, as added by the *Restructuring Supplement* (*see supra* p. 667).

Annotation 31. In other cases, if the Fixed Rate Payer Calculation Amount for a transaction may change during the course of a Fixed Rate Payer Calculation Period, a common approach is to treat the Fixed Rate Payer Calculation Amount for the relevant period as the weighted average of separately determined Fixed Rate Payer notional amounts for each day in that period. This separate notional amount for each day generally (for the reasons indicated in Annotation 28 to this sample confirmation) ought to be the Floating Rate Payer Calculation Amount, as reduced to reflect reductions effective at or before midnight on the preceding Calculation Agent Business Day.

Fixed Rate Payer Payment Date(s):	The 15th day of each January, April, July and October in each year, commencing with July 15, 2002 and ending with the Scheduled Termination Date, subject to Section 2.10 of the ISDA Derivatives Definitions

Annotation 32. As an alternative to the illustrated approach, the parties could identify the last day of each Fixed Rate Payer Calculation Period (Fixed Rate Payer Period End Dates) and indicate that the payment date for each of the periods will be a specified number of days, or Business Days, after the end of the period. The *ISDA CDS Confirmation Form* illustrates how this may be done. In the sample confirmation the parties have indirectly specified the Fixed Rate Payer Calculation Periods by identifying the Fixed Rate Payer Payment Dates. Each of those periods will end on one of the specified dates, subject to one possible exception, which will apply if the Conditions to Payment relating to a Credit Event are satisfied before the Scheduled Termination Date. If this occurs, both the final Fixed Rate Payer Calculation Period and its related Fixed Rate Payer Payment Date will change: the period will end on the Event Determination Date (under Section 2.9 of the ISDA definitions) and the related payment date will occur on the earlier of the Scheduled Termination Date and the Settlement Date relating to the Credit Event (under Section 2.10 of the definitions). Thus, if the Scheduled Termination Date occurs first, the Seller is not required to wait until the Settlement Date for its payment.

Fixed Rate:	x% per annum.
Fixed Rate Day Count Fraction:	Actual/360

> Annotation 33. The Actual/360 day count fraction appears to be the most commonly used in calculating Fixed Amounts payable in credit default swaps involving U.S. dollar payments, which seems logical, since the Fixed Amounts are meant as compensation for the Seller's assumption of Credit Event risk in respect of the precise number of days in the period of protection under the swap. *See supra* p. 405 on day count fraction conventions and their use in the derivatives market.

3. Floating Payment:

    Floating Rate Payer Calculation Amount: USD 25,000,000

> Annotation 34. The Floating Rate Payer Calculation Amount is the base for calculating any Cash Settlement Amount or Physical Settlement Amount to which a Buyer may be entitled. The Floating Rate Payer Calculation Amount and the Fixed Rate Payer Calculation Amount will normally be the same and, in transactions involving protection linked to a particular Reference Obligation, will decline as the principal of the obligation is repaid. *See* Annotations 26–30 to this sample confirmation, *supra* p. 696, on changes in the Floating Rate Payer Calculation Amount and its linkage to changes in the Fixed Rate Payer Calculation Amount.
>
> Annotation 35. In a credit default swap structured and documented following the conventions reflected in the *1999 Credit Derivatives Definitions,* the Floating Rate Payer Calculation Amount is the maximum the Seller can be required to pay as a Cash Settlement Amount or a Physical Settlement Amount unless the parties have built leverage into the transaction by specifying a Reference Price greater than 100% (*see* Annotation 23 to this sample confirmation, *supra* p. 695). This is because the Cash Settlement Amount or Physical Settlement Amount is determined by multiplying the Floating Rate Payer Calculation Amount by the excess of the Reference Price (a percentage) over the Final Price (also a percentage). In a swap involving Cash Settlement, the maximum excess would be 100%, if the Reference Obligation had a Final Price of zero. *See supra* p. 612. In a swap involving Physical Settlement, the percentage will always be 100% unless the Reference Price is lower (because the Physical Settlement Amount is stated in Section 8.4 to be the Floating Rate Payer Calculation Amount multiplied by the Reference Price). The Cash Settlement Amount and the Physical Settlement Amount are payable in the currency in which the Floating Rate Payer Calculation Amount is denominated, unless the parties expressly choose a different Settlement Currency. *See* Section 6.3 of those definitions.
>
> Annotation 36. A Buyer may seek protection against loss in respect of a Reference Obligation denominated in one currency (the "Obligation Currency," under the *1999 Credit Derivatives Definitions*, § 4.8(c)) using a credit default swap with a Floating Rate Payer Calculation Amount denominated in a second currency. In such a case, the Floating Rate Payer Calculation Amount will normally be the equivalent in that second currency of the outstanding principal of the Reference Obligation at

the time the trade is done, using a spot exchange rate. If the parties have not selected a Settlement Currency other than the currency of the Floating Rate Payer Calculation Amount, a subsequent change in the exchange rate will not affect the Cash Settlement Amount or Physical Settlement Amount to which the Buyer may be entitled. In a Physical Settlement, however, as shown in the next two annotations, the size of the Portfolio of Deliverable Obligations due from the Buyer if it wants to receive the entire Physical Settlement Amount will increase or decline if the Obligation Currency weakens or strengthens against the currency of the Floating Rate Payer Calculation Amount.

Annotation 37. In a swap of the kind referred to in the preceding annotation, if only one Cash Settlement will be involved, exchange rates should (given the stated assumption about the Settlement Currency) come into play only when the Calculation Agent must seek price (Bid, Offer or Mid-market) Quotations (*see supra* p. 624) for a Quotation Amount of the Reference Obligation in order to determine the Cash Settlement Amount. If the Quotation Amount is not specified, it would be the equivalent in the relevant Obligation Currency of the Floating Rate Payer Calculation Amount, determined by the Calculation Agent "in a commercially reasonable manner by reference to exchange rates in effect at the time the relevant Quotation is being obtained." *1999 Credit Derivatives Definitions*, § 7.12.

Annotation 38. If the same swap, with a single settlement, provided for Physical Settlement and the parties had not selected a Settlement Currency different from the currency of the Floating Rate Payer Calculation Amount, exchange rates come into play (under *1999 Credit Derivatives Definitions*, § 8.6) in determining the required size of the Portfolio of Deliverable Obligations that the Seller must tender to receive the Physical Settlement Amount and the Physical Settlement Amount that the Seller must pay for the Portfolio. This is so because the Deliverable Obligations in the Portfolio must (subject to any appropriate adjustments for accrued interest (*see supra* note 1531) represent obligations to pay principal or Due and Payable Amounts equal to the Physical Settlement Amount—which, as noted above, will be a percentage of the Floating Rate Payer Calculation Amount. If the Obligation Currency of the Deliverable Obligations is different from the currency of the Floating Rate Payer Calculation Amount, the equivalent Currency Amount, as it is called, is determined by the Calculation Agent using spot rates published by sources specified in Section 8.9 of the ISDA definitions (a mid-point rate from the Reuters screen page FEDSPOT displaying data from the Federal Reserve Bank of New York, if the Settlement Currency is U.S. dollars, a MEAN price from Reuters screen page EUROFX/1, if the Settlement Currency is euros) or in another commercially reasonable manner chosen by the Calculation Agent after consultation with the parties. If the final spot exchange rate is different from the spot rate used to set the Floating Rate Payer Calculation Amount at the outset of the swap's term and the Buyer wishes to receive the full Physical Settlement Amount, the Buyer must assemble a Portfolio that adjusts for the weakening or strengthening of the Obligation Currency against the Settlement Currency over the period, because the Seller is required (under *1999 Credit Derivatives Definitions*, §8.1) to pay only the portion of the Physical Settlement Amount that corresponds to the portion of the Portfolio that the Buyer has Delivered.

Annotation 39. When credit default swaps depart from the standard conventions summarized above, the parties should closely examine the formula used to calculate settlement amounts to ensure that those departures have indeed been bargained for and consciously taken into account in the pricing of the transaction. This issue commonly arises in portfolio transactions providing for multiple settlements in connection with valuations of Obligations denominated in multiple currencies. It could, however, arise in a simpler, single-name transaction. Say, for example, that after a Credit Event the Buyer would like to receive a stated U.S. dollar amount against delivery of its holdings at the Trade Date of the swap of a single, nonamortizing Reference Obligation denominated in another currency. In this case, the parties would have to state the agreed Physical Settlement Amount and override the conventional rules (in Section 8.6 of the *1999 Credit Derivatives Definitions*) regarding the composition of the Portfolio by identifying the specific obligations that would constitute the Portfolio, subject to changes required by operation of the *Restructuring Supplement,* the *Supplement Relating to Successor and Credit Events* and the provisions of Article IX of those definitions dealing with the cases in which Partial Cash Settlement may occur. *See* Table 2 in the introductory note on credit, debt and equity swaps, *supra* p. 615. Because this special arrangement effectively imbeds a currency option in the credit default swap, the Buyer would probably want to compare the price (in terms of the Fixed Rate payable by it) quoted to it for the special arrangement with the separate costs of a standard credit default swap and currency option.

Conditions to Payment:

Annotation 40. The Conditions to Payment work with other provisions of the *1999 Credit Derivatives Definitions*, as discussed *supra* p. 668, as requirements that must be satisfied within specified periods to determine whether and when a Cash Settlement Amount or Physical Settlement Amount may be payable to the Buyer (*see* the timelines *supra* pp. 646–648). In connection with Physical Settlement, Payment is (generally speaking) to be made against delivery of the Deliverable Obligations identified in the Condition to Payment referred to as Notice of Intended Physical Settlement, which is not reflected in the sample above because the illustrated swap provides for Cash Settlement. Under the *1999 Credit Derivatives Definitions*, §§ 3.4 & 3.9, the required notices may be given orally, with hard copy to follow, although some market participants modify this rule.

Credit Event Notice

Notifying Party: Buyer or Seller

Annotation 41. After a Credit Event occurs, the Notifying Party determines when the process leading towards settlement will start by delivering the required

Credit Event Notice and the Specified Number of items of Publicly Available Information supporting the existence of the Credit Event if, as is customary and shown here, the parties have stated that Notice of Publicly Available Information is Applicable. The Buyers are usually the Notifying Parties. However, when a Seller prices the protection, it will do so on the basis of assumptions regarding recovery probabilities within customary periods following default (like the ones assumed by rating agencies in rating obligations or tranches of risk in a CDO or similar structure). *See, e.g.,* STANDARD & POOR'S, GLOBAL CASH FLOW AND SYNTHETIC CDO CRITERIA, *supra* note 1547, pp. 72–73, on Standard & Poor's general assumptions on the timing of recoveries on defaulted assets, its general requirement for the timing of valuations in synthetic CDOs: "no sooner than 45 business days (or 60 calendar days) from the calculation agent's declaration of a credit event") and its view, subject to exceptions, that "the further out from the event the valuation date is . . . the better the recovery prospects." The stated 45 business day, or 60 calendar day, period requirement, as stated, would not necessarily be counted from the actual occurrence of the Credit Event because under the ISDA *1999 Credit Derivatives Definitions* (Section 1.9) the period for satisfaction of Conditions to Payment (the Notice Delivery Period) is tied to the last day of the transaction's period of protection (the Scheduled Termination Date or Grace Period Extension Date, if applicable), and not the date a Credit Event occurs. The Seller will often seek to be named as a Notifying Party, or it may seek to place an outside limit, measured from the occurrence or public announcement of a Credit Event, on the period (the Notice Delivery Period) within which the Conditions to Payment relating to the Credit Event may be satisfied. (For example, "Notice Delivery Period" could be defined to mean the shorter of the period provided for in those definitions and the period ending a specified number of days after the Seller delivers to the Buyer Notice of Publicly Available Information relating to the Credit Event.) When a Buyer's goal in entering into a transaction includes achieving capital relief, regulatory requirements regarding the Buyer's ability to be a Notifying Party will be critical.

Notice of Publicly Available
Information: Applicable

Public Sources: Standard Public Sources

Specified Number: Two

Annotation 42. Publicly Available Information must "reasonably confirm" any of the facts relevant to determining that a Credit Event described in a Credit Event Notice has occurred (*1999 Credit Derivatives Definitions*, § 3.5(a)), but it need not state that the occurrence has met any applicable Payment Requirement or Default Requirement, that an applicable Grace Period has lapsed or that the relevant event satisfies any subjective requirements. *Id.* § 3.5(c).

Annotation 43. The Specified Number and Public Sources selections shown in the sample are the same as the choices that apply if the parties are silent on the subject. The Standard Public Sources consist of the Bloomberg, Dow Jones Telerate and Reuter Monitor Money Rates services and the Dow Jones New Wire, *The Wall Street Journal, The New York Times*, the *Financial Times*, and *Nihon Keizai Shinbun* and their successors. *1999 Credit Derivatives Definitions*, § 3.7. Not all information published in a Standard Public Source will automatically qualify as Publicly Available Information. Section 3.5(b) of those definitions disqualifies information if either of the parties or any of their respective Affiliates is cited as the sole source of the information, unless the party or Affiliate is acting in its capacity as trustee, fiscal agent, administrative agent, clearing agent or paying agent for an Obligation. This exclusion can be important to Buyers seeking protection in respect of loans and other privately placed obligations. The *Supplement Relating to Successor and Credit Events* modifies Section 3.5(a) of those definitions so that an "Officer's Certification"—a certificate signed by a Managing Director (or other substantively equivalent title) of the Buyer certifying the occurrence of a Credit Event)—is required to satisfy the condition on Publicly Available Information in a case in which the Buyer, in such a capacity, is the sole source of information and is also a holder of the Obligations with respect to which a Credit Event has occurred.

Annotation 44. Not all Publicly Available Information must be published in a Standard Public Source. The *1999 Credit Derivatives Definitions* provide (in Section 3.5(a)(ii)) that Publicly Available Information includes information received from a Reference Entity that is not a party to the relevant Credit Derivative Transaction or a Sovereign Agency in respect of a Reference Entity that is a Sovereign (that is, an agency, instrumentality, ministry, department or other authority of the Sovereign, including the central bank) or a trustee, fiscal agent, administrative agent, clearing agent or paying agent for an Obligation. Under Section 3.5(a)(iii), it can also include information in a petition or filing that institutes insolvency or similar proceedings for the Reference Entity (whether or not the filing is made by the Reference Entity) and information contained in an order, decree or notice of a court, tribunal, regulatory authority or similar administrative or judicial body.

Annotation 45. There is, however, a widespread practice of treating information of these kinds as acceptable only if it is delivered with an appropriate certification as to its genuineness and completeness and, sometimes, other matters. For example, if the recipient of such a certificate and information is not the ultimate seller of protection and will, therefore, have to pass it along to a third party in settlement of a hedging transaction, the recipient would want to be sure that it was free to do so without violating any duty of confidentiality. Recipients of nonpublic information may also have securities law concerns. *See supra* pp. 147 & 168.

Annotation 46. With respect to confidentiality, each of the parties to a Credit Derivative Transaction governed by the *1999 Credit Derivatives Definitions* represents to the other (under Section 9.1(b)(v)) that, "unless it is otherwise bound by or subject to a confidentiality obligation or agreement, a party receiving any information from the other party with respect to such Credit Derivative Transaction shall not become subject to any obligation of confidentiality in respect of that information and the transferor of such information shall indemnify and hold harmless the transferee for any loss, liability, claim, damage and expense whatsoever incurred by the transferee arising out of the breach of any law or understanding or agreement with respect to the confidentiality of that information to which the transferor may be party." Section 3.5(b) of the definitions also provides that, if a party receives potentially nonpublic information from one of the sources specified in Section 3.5(a)(ii) (*see* Annotation 44 to this sample confirmation), that party "may assume that such information has been disclosed to it without violating any law, agreement or understanding regarding the confidentiality of such information and that the party delivering such information has not taken any action or entered into any agreement or understanding with the Reference Entity or any Affiliate of the Reference Entity that would be breached by, or would prevent, the disclosure of such information to third parties." Potential recipients of nonpublic information delivered to satisfy Conditions to Payments under credit default swaps should nonetheless consider whether these provisions, including the quoted indemnity, are sufficient in the particular circumstances of their transactions.

Credit Events: The following Credit Events shall apply to the Transaction:

Annotation 47. Credit Event definitions are discussed beginning *supra* p. 662. Other choices under the *1999 Credit Derivatives Definitions*, in addition to the four chosen for the illustrated transaction, are Repudiation/Moratorium and Obligation Default. *See supra* p. 682. The *ISDA Long-form CDS Confirmation* permitted the parties to treat "Downgrade" as a Credit Event. That choice was eliminated as inconsistent with the market's evolution towards credit default products that would only provide for payouts in cases clearly indicating Reference Entity financial distress, such as payment failures that have not been cured and other conditions pointing to imminent inability to make payments to creditors. Because of concerns over possible disputes regarding what should properly be treated as triggering Repudiation/Moratorium, ISDA proposes to modify that Credit Event so that, among other things, the relevant statement treated as a repudiation, disaffirmation, disclaimer or rejection of obligations on behalf of a Reference Entity must, within a specified period, be followed by an actual payment failure or restructuring that would qualify as a Credit Event but for their involvement of amounts of obligations that fall short of the agreed Payment Requirement or Default Requirement.

Bankruptcy

Annotation 48. Section 4.2(i) of the definition of "Bankruptcy" in the *1999 Credit Derivatives Definitions* is modeled on the definition in Section 5(a)(vii) of the ISDA master agreement forms and applies if a Reference Entity takes any action in furtherance of, or indicating its consent to, approval of, or acquiescence in, any of the other events or circumstances identified in that definition as a Bankruptcy trigger. The newer thinking is that a credit default payout should not be required merely because a Reference Entity's directors take some sort of action to prepare for a financial crisis that is in fact averted, say if a temporary liquidity problem is overcome with funding from a source that had not been identified when the board acted. These concerns were raised by the rating agencies (*see, e.g.,* Moody's, *supra* note 1536, at 6). As a result, this Credit Event was modified in the *Supplement Relating to Successor and Credit Events* to narrow the cases in which admissions of inability to pay may be treated as Credit Events (they must be made in a judicial, regulatory or administrative proceeding or filing) and so that "any action taken in furtherance of, or indicating . . . consent to, approval of, or acquiescence in" in any of the other Bankruptcy triggering events do not form part of the Bankruptcy Credit Event.

Failure to Pay

Grace Period Extension Applicable
Grace Period: 30 days

Payment Requirement: USD 1,000,000 or its equivalent in the relevant Obligation Currency as of the occurrence of the relevant Potential Failure to Pay or Failure to Pay, as applicable

Annotation 49. The parties' agreement that Grace Period Extension applies means (*see supra* p. 647) that a Credit Event may be treated as having occurred if the Reference Entity fails to make a payment due under an Obligation on or before the Scheduled Termination Date, even if the payment failure does not ripen into an event of default until after the Scheduled Termination Date. Whether it does ripen into a Payment Failure for this purpose is determined by reference to the Grace Period. The determination of the length of this period can be somewhat complex.

Annotation 50. The Grace Period specified in the sample is the maximum period the parties have agreed will apply unless the relevant Obligation provides for a shorter grace period, in which case either that shorter period will apply or a period of three Grace Period Business Days will apply, if the Obligation provides for a lesser grace period. Grace Period Business Days are determined in light of working days for banks and foreign exchange markets in the place or places specified in the relevant Obligation or, if none are specified, in the jurisdiction of the currency in which the Obligation is denominated. The 30 days specified in the sample as the maximum Grace Period is also the maximum provided for in the *1999 Credit Derivatives Definitions* (Section 1.11(ii)) if the parties are silent on the matter but have said that Grace Period Extension is applicable to their transaction. If the parties specify that Grace Period Extension will not apply—which is common—or are silent about its application and the relevant Obligation has no provision for grace periods, the ISDA definitions operate to prevent the Buyer from treating a Reference Entity's failure to make a payment when due under an Obligation as a Credit Event until the earlier of the Scheduled Termination Date for the transaction and the third Grace Period Business Day after the due date for the missed payment. In these determinations as to grace periods under Obligations, the ISDA definitions specify that the parties should look at the Obligation's terms as in effect on the later of the Trade Date of their transaction and the date of issuance of the Obligation.

Annotation 51. Payment Requirement is a *de minimis* threshold. If a Reference Entity fails to make payments when due under Obligations but the aggregate amount of the late payments is less than the Payment Requirement, a Credit Event will not have occurred. The amount specified in the sample is the same as the one that would apply if the parties had been silent. In the example, if an Obligation Currency is not U.S. dollars and the Reference Entity's relevant missed payment occurs toward the end of a transaction's term, this standard ISDA approach may require satisfaction of the Payment Requirement twice: once on the payment's due date, to determine whether a Potential Failure to Pay has occurred and, so, to determine whether the Grace Period Extension terms dictate that the parties wait to see whether the nonpayment ripens into a Failure to Pay after the Scheduled Termination Date, and, if that test is passed, a second time, at the end of the Grace Period, to determine whether a Credit Event has occurred. If the parties believe that changes in exchange rates during this period should be irrelevant to whether a payout should occur in such a case, they should consider stating something like the following: "USD 1,000,000 or its equivalent in the relevant Obligation Currency as of the occurrence of the Credit Event or, for purposes of determining whether a Credit Event may occur after the Scheduled Termination Date under the Grace Period Extension terms, only as of the occurrence of the relevant Potential Failure to Pay." In addition, if the parties are concerned about problems that may arise because the standard ISDA language refers to the determination of currency equivalents "as of the occurrence" of a particular event and exchange rates normally change throughout the day, the parties may wish to consider reducing the potential for disputes by specifying an objective method for determining these equivalents (for example, "determined in the manner specified in Section 8.9 of the Credit Derivatives Definitions for determining Currency Amount equivalents"). *See* Annotation 38 to this sample confirmation, *supra* p. 700.

	Obligation Acceleration
	Restructuring
Default Requirement:	USD 10,000,000 or its equivalent in the relevant Obligation Currency as of the occurrence of the Obligation Acceleration or Restructuring

Annotation 52. The Default Requirement applicable to Obligation Acceleration and Restructuring is another *de minimis* threshold like the Payment Requirement referred to in the preceding annotation. Here too, the illustrated choice is the same as the choice the parties would be treated as having specified if they had been silent. It is expressed using the ISDA standard reference to equivalence determina-

tions' being made "as of" a particular time, raising the potential issue discussed in the preceding annotation as well as a question of how the parties will determine the precise time of day when the underlying events will have become Credit Events.

Annotation 53. The Restructuring Credit Event and the important changes to it made by the *Restructuring Supplement* are discussed *supra* p. 666. For the reasons discussed there, some of the changes limit the kinds of Obligations that can trigger a Restructuring Credit Event and others limit the Deliverable Obligations that a Buyer will be permitted to tender in a Physical Settlement if the only Credit Event identified in the related Credit Event Notice is Restructuring and the confirmation specifies "Restructuring Maturity Limitation Applicable." The sample confirmation does not include that specification because the illustrated swap provides for Cash Settlement. When the parties to cash-settled swaps structure their dealings so that the Buyer is free to choose the Obligations that will determine whether a Credit Event has occurred, however, the parties often make appropriate adaptations of the language in the *Restructuring Supplement* so that these limitations on Deliverable Obligations will apply to the Obligations that may be chosen for valuation leading to a Cash Settlement under their transactions.

Annotation 54. These limitations introduced by the *Restructuring Supplement* in part reflect an attempt to protect a Seller against having to make a payout apparently attributable less to the Reference Entity's condition than to the features of the Deliverable Obligations—such as limitations on their transferability and their tenor. Other approaches to these concerns in connection with any Credit Event, and not just Restructuring, take a somewhat different tack, in seeking to provide a method that the parties can use to identify a portion of the decline in value of an Obligation attributable to changes in the interest rate environment and then deduct that portion from the payout due to the Buyer in a Cash Settlement transaction.

Annotation 55. One such approach was contemplated in the *ISDA Long-Form Credit Swap Confirmation* (*see supra* note 1569). At the time it published the *1999 Credit Derivatives Definitions,* ISDA considered publishing a variant of that approach in a Materiality Annex that would be available on the ISDA Web site and in the *User's Guide* to those definitions, but the project was not pursued for lack of market interest. Insofar as it related to fixed-rate Reference Obligations, the approach basically involved stating an agreed Initial Price for the Reference Obligation and providing for a payout after a Credit Event only if (1) the Initial Price exceeded the Final Price and (2) the difference exceeded an Interest Rate Adjustment Amount by a measure of materiality referred to as the Price Decline Requirement. The Interest Rate Adjustment Amount was the feature intended to isolate price decline attributable to interest rate risk from price decline attributable to credit risk. *See* Anthony C. Gooch & Linda B. Klein, *Documentation Begins to Come Into Focus for OTC Credit Derivatives,* 3 DERIVATIVES, TAX, REGULATION, FINANCE 211, 225 (1998).

Obligation(s):

Obligation Category (Select only one):	Obligation Characteristics (Select all that apply):
[ ] Payment [x] Borrowed Money [ ] Reference Obligations Only [ ] Bond [ ] Loan [ ] Bond or Loan	[x] Pari Passu Ranking [x] Specified Currency: _____ [x] Not Sovereign Lender [ ] Not Domestic Currency [ ] Not Domestic Law [x] Listed [x] Not Contingent [ ] Not Domestic Issuance

Annotation 56. The parties often list only the choices they have made, rather than setting out the entire matrix of possible choices. The various Obligation Categories and Obligation Characteristics and, for Physical Settlement transactions, the Deliverable Obligation Characteristics, and how they operate, are discussed *supra* p. 671. As is illustrated in the *ISDA CDS Confirmation Form*, the parties may also specify that Obligations with certain characteristics, or certain Obligations, are Excluded Obligations that will not be taken into account in determining whether a Credit Event has occurred and may, similarly, identify as Excluded Deliverable Obligations specific kinds of Obligations or Obligations that may not be included in the Portfolio that the Buyer must tender to receive the appropriate portion of the Physical Settlement Amount. Because the parties have chosen Specified Currency as an Obligation Characteristic but have not specified the relevant currencies, the ISDA "default" choices will apply, as indicated *supra* p. 674.

4. Settlement Terms:

    Settlement Method: Cash Settlement

Annotation 57. The Settlement Method—Cash Settlement or Physical Settlement—is a critical term in the pricing and hedging of credit default swaps. There is, therefore, no initial presumption on this matter supplied by the *1999 Credit Derivatives Definitions*. The definitions do, however, provide that an agreed Physical Settlement transaction will be subject to Partial Cash Settlement in two cases (*see supra* p. 616): Physical Settlement by one party or the other has, as a result of circumstances beyond its control, become illegal or impossible and the problem has not been resolved before the Latest Possible Physical Settlement Date; or, in a transaction involving Direct Loan Participations, Indirect Loan Participations, Assignable Loans or Consent Required Loans as Deliverable Obligations, the parties have agreed in the confirmation (Sections 9.5 through 9.7 of those definitions indicate how) to a fallback to Partial Cash Settlement if the relevant participation has not been effected by the Latest Possible Physical Settlement Date or a consent required for transfer of a relevant loan has not been received by that date and, in a case where participation delivery is an initial agreed fallback relating to the nondelivery of the loan, the participation has not been effected by that date.

Annotation 58. On reasons why the Partial Cash Settlement provisions may be viewed as problematic and proposed changes to the definitions to deal with these problems, at least in part, *see supra* p. 617. The Partial Cash Settlement provisions must be read in the context of the Buyer's representations, indemnities and agreements in Section 9.3 of those definitions, including its obligation to take any action necessary or customary or desirable and reasonably requested by the Seller in connection with Delivery of the Portfolio of Deliverable Obligations. That provision expressly requires a Buyer to demonstrate to the reasonable satisfaction of a Seller that the Buyer "has taken all reasonable steps to obtain any requisite consents" and to keep the Seller "apprised of any occurrence of which Buyer is (or reasonably should be) aware that may affect Buyer's ability to Deliver to Seller the portion of the Portfolio specified in the Notice of Intended Physical Settlement." A Seller, for its part, agrees in the same provision to cooperate reasonably with the Buyer in these endeavors.

Terms Relating to Cash Settlement:

Annotation 59. In a transaction providing for Physical Settlement, this line would refer to Terms Relating to Physical Settlement, the items listed below through the Valuation Method would not be included and, instead, if it made sense to do so in the context of their particular transaction, the parties might specify the length of a Physical Settlement Period rather than leaving it to be determined by the Calculation Agent as the longest number of Business Days for settlement at the time in accordance with then current market practice in relation to any of the Deliverable Obligations included in the Portfolio identified by the Buyer in the required Notice of Intended Physical Settlement. *See supra* p. 648 for a timeline illustration of when this period begins. *See supra* p. 618 for discussion of proposed changes to protect Sellers in cases in which the Buyer does not deliver items identified in a Notice of Intended Physical Settlement.

Valuation Date: Single Valuation Date:
                   5 Business Days

Annotation 60. The sample provision indicates when the valuation of a Reference Obligation for purposes of settlement should occur, by reference to the length of a selected period beginning on the Event Determination Date—the date when the Credit Event Notice becomes effective and, if applicable, Notice of Publicly Available Information is also effective. *See* Annotations 40 & 41 to this sample confirmation, *supra* p. 701, and *see supra* p. 646 for a related timeline and discussion of issues that can be raised for a Seller when the Buyer completely controls this timing. When the parties specify "Multiple Valuation Dates" in this spot, the completion specifies three things: the Number of Valuation Dates, the length of the period beginning on the Event Determination Date after which the first Valuation Date will occur and the length of the period or periods between Valuation Dates. *See supra* 642 on the use of Multiple Valuation Dates.

Annotation 61. The illustrated choice is the one the parties would be treated as having made if they had been silent. In complex transactions, the use of substantially longer periods is common, and in some cases the parties may find it useful to define Valuation Dates by reference to Valuation Business Days determined to take into account holidays in cities, or in markets, that are not included among the cities identified for purposes of determining Business Days. For example, if a Reference Obligation or other Obligation to be valued is a bond listed on a particular exchange, the parties may wish to say something like "The day falling three Business Days after the Event Determination Date or, if that day is not a Valuation Business Day, the first Valuation Business Day thereafter. For this purpose, 'Valuation Business Day' means a [Business Day] [Calculation Agent Business Day] on which each Relevant Exchange is scheduled to be open for trading [during the general trading session]; and 'Relevant Exchange' means each securities exchange [or [other possibly relevant types of organized markets, say, for foreign government treasury securities]] on which any [Reference] Obligation to be valued is admitted for trading." *See* Table 1 in the introductory note on credit, default and equity derivatives, *supra* p. 612, on the succession of events that will occur under the standard ISDA approach if a valuation cannot be completed as agreed on a scheduled Valuation Date and *see supra* p. 620 for related concerns, including the possibility that a Reference Obligation may ultimately be valued at zero.

    Valuation Time: Approximately 11:00 a.m., in the Calculation Agent City

Annotation 62. Cash-settled credit default swaps sometimes specify the actual amount payable to the Buyer as the Cash Settlement Amount. In such cases, if the parties also specify the Cash Settlement Date by reference to a number of days following satisfaction of all Conditions to Payment, they need not normally specify a Valuation Date or a Valuation Time. The presumed Valuation Time, if the parties are silent on this matter, is 11:00 a.m., in the Calculation Agent City, under the *1999 Credit Derivatives Definitions* (Section 7.14). The use of other times is, however, common. *See* Annotation 32 to the sample equity index swap confirmation, *supra* p. 746, for further discussion of related issues.

    Quotation Method: Bid

Sample Credit Default Swap Confirmation

> Annotation 63. *See* Table 3 in the introductory note on credit, debt and equity derivatives, *supra* p. 624, regarding the ISDA conventions relating to the various possible Quotation Methods to be used in the determining the Final Price of a relevant Obligation—and, therefore, the Cash Settlement Amount—how these methods are applied and related presumptions and issues.

Quotation Amount: USD 25,000,000

> Annotation 64. The Quotations relevant in determining the Final Price of the Reference Obligation are sought in respect of the Quotation Amount, which would generally be the Floating Rate Payer Calculation Amount, is the approach illustrated here and is presumed to apply under Section 7.12 of the *1999 Credit Derivatives Definitions* if the parties are silent on the matter. An alternative offered in those definitions (in Section 7.16) is "Representative Amount," a term defined to mean "an amount that is representative for a single transaction in the relevant market and at the relevant time, such amount to be determined by the Calculation Agent in consultation with the parties." Sometimes the parties find that term useful in identifying the Minimum Quotation Amount that will be applicable if the Final Price cannot be determined on the basis of firm Quotations for the full Quotation Amount and, following the ISDA valuation conventions described *supra* p.624, the Final Price is ultimately to be determined on the basis of a weighted average of Quotations for the Minimum Quotation Amount. If the parties are silent as to the Minimum Quotation Amount—as is illustrated here—the ISDA definitions (in Section 7.13) provide for use of the lower of U.S.$ 1 million and the Quotation Amount, or the relevant equivalent in the Obligation Currency. (*See* Annotations 36, 37 & 39 to this sample confirmation, *supra* pp. 699, 700 & 701 on currency translations in the determination of a Quotation Amount and related issues involving the calculation of the Cash Settlement Amount.) Some of the implications of the two approaches are brought into focus by positing a credit default swap that is, as described *supra* note 631, split into separate swaps because of a Succession Event affecting the original Reference Entity. If the resulting equal parts of the original swap's Floating Rate Payer Calculation Amount were smaller than the standard size for a single transaction in the market for the relevant Reference Obligation and, as a result, the Calculation Agent could not obtain firm Quotations, the Representative Amount approach would dictate seeking Quotations for a standard sized transaction, whereas the approach prescribed by Section 7.13 of the ISDA definitions would dictate seeking Quotations in an amount equal to the lower of U.S.$ 1 million (or the equivalent) or the relevant percentage share of the original swap's Floating Rate Payer Calculation Amount.

Dealer(s):   Dealer A, Dealer B and Dealer C

Annotation 65. The specified Dealers are the agreed sources for Quotations to be used in determining the Market Value of the Reference Obligation and, according to Section 7.15 of the *1999 Credit Derivatives Definitions*, should not include either of the parties or any their Affiliates but otherwise will qualify if they are dealers in obligations of the types for which Quotations are being obtained. Therefore, as a technical matter the selected entities should be licensed, registered or otherwise qualified or permitted to be dealers in the Obligations being valued. If the parties do not designate Dealers, or if any that they designate cease to be active dealers in the relevant Obligations, the same provision of the ISDA definitions permits the Calculation Agent to select substitute Dealers after consultation with the parties. In some cases this standard is tightened to require the prior consent of the party that is not the Calculation Agent and, at least in some circumstances, to permit that party to be or designate a Dealer or to require the replacement of a Dealer. *See* Annotation 33 to the sample HDD swap confirmation, *infra* pp. 778, and the annotations to the specification of the Calculation Agent in the sample schedule in Part 3, *infra* p. 922 for further discussion of this subject. *See supra* note 1484 on other kinds of limitations on Dealers in credit derivatives.

Settlement Currency:	USD
Cash Settlement Date:	3 Business Days after effective notice to the Seller of the Final Price, the Cash Settlement Amount and each other related matter that the Calculation Agent is required to specify by notice to the parties pursuant to Section 1.13 of the Credit Derivatives Definitions

Annotation 66. The sample provision departs from the standard completion contemplated in the *ISDA CDS Confirmation Form*. If the parties merely state a number of Business Days here, under Section 7.2 of the *1999 Credit Derivatives Definitions*, the parties would be understood to be agreeing to settlement that number of Business Days after the calculation of the Final Price. Section 1.13 of the definitions provides that the Calculation Agent must, "as soon as practicable after obtaining any Quotation, notify the parties in writing of each such Quotation that it receives in connection with the calculation of the Final Price" and, further, "provide to the parties a written computation showing its calculation of the Final Price." The sample provision links these two requirements. An alternative sometimes used is to define a term such as "Final Valuation Notice" or "Cash Settlement Notice" to refer to all information that the Seller is entitled to receive, and the Calculation Agent is required to give, in connection with a Cash Settlement, provide the latest date after the relevant Valuation Date on which that notice must be given and link the Cash Settlement Date to delivery of that notice. In all cases the Seller will want the period before settlement is due to be sufficient to enable it to consider the information and,

if appropriate, commence a dispute resolution process. Other relevant factors may be the standard settlement cycle for the relevant kind of Reference Obligation and for spot FX transactions. The former would, for example, be relevant if in connection with cash settlement the Buyer was intending an actual sale of the Reference Obligation (*see supra* p. 620 on cases in which a cash auction of the Reference Obligation is run in tandem with settlement of the swap). The cycle for settlement of foreign exchange trades would be relevant if such a cash sale transaction involved parties from jurisdictions with different home currencies or if the Seller's functional currency were different from the Settlement Currency.

Cash Settlement Amount:

Annotation 67. This line item is included for use if the parties wish to depart from the standard approach, in Section 7.3 of the *1999 Credit Derivatives Definition,* which defines the Cash Settlement Amount to be the greater of (a) the Floating Rate Payer Calculation Amount multiplied by the difference between the Reference Price and the Final Price and (b) zero. *See* Table 1 in the introductory note on credit, debt and equity derivatives, *supra* p. 612.

Quotations:

Annotation 68. Section 7.8 of the *1999 Credit Derivatives Definitions* provides how the Calculation Agent should go about attempting to obtain Quotations, as summarized in Table 3 in the introductory note on credit, debt and equity derivatives, *supra* p. 624. The parties may expressly indicate in their confirmation that the Calculation Agent should seek Quotations for the Reference Obligation that include or that exclude accrued but unpaid interest, or the parties may remain silent on the subject. If they remain silent, as they do in this sample, the Calculation Agent should determine, after consultation with the parties, based on then current market practice in the market of the Reference Obligation, whether the Quotations should include or exclude accrued but unpaid interest. *See supra* note 1531 on the effect of this choice in a transaction involving Physical Settlement.

Valuation Method: Highest

Annotation 69. When a swap involves only one Reference Obligation and one Valuation Date, the *1999 Credit Derivatives Definitions* contemplate two possible Valuation Methods from which to choose: "Market," which involves taking the Market Value determined for the Valuation Date, and "Highest," which involves taking the highest Quotation received by the Calculation Agent in the valuation process. *See* Table 4 in the introductory note on credit, debt and equity derivatives, *supra* p. 625. Where there is one Reference Obligation but there are multiple Valuation Dates, the parties are given a choice among "Average Market," which means the unweighted arithmetic mean of the Market Values for each of the Valuation Dates (each of which, in turn, will generally be an average, if sufficient Quotations are obtained), "Highest," which involves taking the highest Quotation received on any Valuation Date, and "Average Highest," which means the unweighted arithmetic mean of the highest Quotations received with respect to each of the Valuation Dates. For transactions with multiple Reference Obligations, there are also permutations referred to as "Blended Market" and "Blended Highest," for use on the basis of the unweighted arithmetic mean of the Market Values for the Reference Obligations or the unweighted arithmetic mean of the highest Quotations for each of the Reference Obligations, for the relevant Valuation Date.

5. Dispute Resolution: The following will apply in lieu of Section 10.2 of the Credit Derivatives Definitions:

If the Calculation Agent fails to make a determination required by the Credit Derivatives Definitions in a timely manner, or if the other party (the "Disputing Party") disputes a calculation or determination made by the Calculation Agent, it may give the Calculation Agent notice to that effect, specifying the nature of the dispute. If, 24 hours after notice of the dispute is effective, the parties have neither resolved the dispute to their mutual satisfaction nor agreed on an independent third party to resolve the dispute, each of them will, within 36 hours after that notice of the dispute is effective, appoint an independent third party to participate in a dispute resolution panel, and these two panelists will be instructed by the parties to appoint a third panelist, to resolve the dispute as promptly as possible by way of majority vote and, during their deliberations on the disputed matter, to have no communications with either party to the Transaction unless the other party and each of the other members of the panel are involved. The decision of the single third party selected jointly by the parties, or of a majority vote of the panelists (in the event a single third party is not jointly selected within the specified period), will be binding on the parties in the absence of manifest error. Each of the parties will pay one half of the aggregate charges, costs and expenses of the single third party or panel members.

Pending resolution of a dispute pursuant to this provision, if the dispute has a bearing on the amount of a payment claimed by the Buyer, the disputed portion of the relevant amount will not be payable by the Seller except to the extent it is determined to be payable by it through this mechanism. To the extent it is payable, the Seller will pay the amount on the Business Day following the date the single third party, or the panel members, give the Seller notice of the amount. The Seller will, on the Business Day after demand from the Buyer, also pay interest on that amount determined to be payable by it, calculated for each day during the period beginning on and including the day the disputed amount was originally scheduled to have been paid and ending on but excluding the date the payment is due, on an Actual/360 basis, at a rate per annum for each such day equal to the overnight rate for deposits in the Settlement Currency offered by major banks in the London interbank market at approximately 11:00 a.m., London time, on that day, as announced by any electronic or print source of data on such deposit rates as the Buyer may select from among those widely used at the time in the derivatives market. The demand will set forth in reasonable detail how the interest claimed was calculated.

This dispute resolution mechanism will in no way preclude the resolution of any dispute relating to the Transaction through Proceedings as contemplated in the Agreement.

> Annotation 70. *See supra* p. 685 on Section 10.2 of the standard provision on dispute resolution in Section 10.2 of the *1999 Credit Derivatives Definitions* and on ISDA's project to develop other Dispute Resolution Guidelines.

6. Notice and Account Details:

    Telephone, Telex and/or Facsimile Number and Contact Details for Notices:

    Buyer:

Address:	One Financial Center New York, NY 00000 Attention: Swaps Group Leader
Telex No.:	00000 Answerback: BB
Facsimile No.:	(212) 000-0000
Telephone No.:	(212) 000-0000

    Seller:

Address:	One Investment Plaza New York, NY 10000-1000 Attention: Financial Director
Telex No.:	000000 Answerback: IICO
Facsimile No.:	(212) 000-0000
Telephone No.:	(212) 000-0000

    Account Details

Account Details of Buyer:	Big Bank, N.A., New York, N.Y., ABA No. 000, CHIPS No. 000, Attention: Swaps Division
Account Details of Seller:	Account No. 00000 with Big Bank, N.A., New York, N.Y.

7. Offices:

Seller: The Office of the Seller for the Transaction is its office at the address specified for notices to it in the Schedule to the Agreement.

Buyer: The Office of the Buyer for the Transaction is its head office in New York.

Please confirm that the foregoing correctly sets forth the terms of our agreement by executing a copy of this Confirmation and returning it to us by or by sending to us a letter substantially similar to this letter, which letter sets forth the material terms of the Credit Derivative Transaction to which this Confirmation relates and indicates your agreement to those terms. If you believe the foregoing does not correctly reflect the terms of our agreement, please give us notice as soon as possible of what you believe to be the necessary corrections.

> Annotation 71. The sample is different from the standard closing in the *ISDA CDS Confirmation Form* in that the latter asks the recipient to confirm its agreement to be bound by the terms of the preceding text. Since the ISDA master agreement forms provide that the parties are bound by their agreement on the terms of a Transaction from the moment that agreement is reached, and the agreement may be reached before the Confirmation is executed, this sample preserves a more traditional approach, using language taken from the form of closing set out in an exhibit to the *2000 ISDA Definitions*.

Yours sincerely,

BIG BANK, N.A.

By: _____
    Name:
    Title: Vice President

Confirmed as of the date first
above written on   , 20 :

INSTITUTIONAL INVESTOR INC.

By: _____
Name:
Title:

EQUITY DERIVATIVES

INTRODUCTION

In the most common form of equity swap, one party agrees to pay an amount equal to the appreciation (if any) of a hypothetical equity investment over a specified period, plus an amount equal to any dividends on the hypothetical investment during the period. The notional investment might be in a particular stock, in a basket of stocks or in all the stocks that make up a particular equity index. This part of the transaction is referred to as the "equity leg," and this party is called the "equity return payer. The other party agrees to pay an amount equal to any decline in the value of the same hypothetical investment over the same period plus payments calculated at an annual rate—usually LIBOR (flat or plus or minus a spread)—on the notional amount of the investment.[1643] This second part of the transaction is referred to as the "interest rate leg," and this party is called the "equity return receiver."[1644] The equity swap is analogous to the total return swap on a debt instrument.[1645]

It is sometimes useful to think of the equity swap as replicating the cash flows that the equity return receiver would have experienced if it could have borrowed an amount equal to the notional amount in the debt market and invested it in the equity. The equity return payer is in the position it would have been in if it had shorted the equity and invested the proceeds in floating-rate debt.

Figure 15 illustrates an equity swap between an investor holding a position in the equity underlying the swap and a counterparty holding an FRN (a floating rate note) or other asset with a LIBOR-based coupon. The top pair of arrows reflects the payment that will be made by one party or the other on account of a change in the price of the equity, determined by reference to what are referred to as the Initial Price and the Final Price for the relevant period.[1646] These equity price return payments are calculated on a notional

---

[1643] *See supra* p. 408 on LIBOR—the London interbank offered rate, particularly as it relates to interest rate products in the derivatives market.

[1644] On equity swaps generally, *see* John F. Marshall, Eric H. Sorensen & Alan L. Tucker, *Equity Derivatives: The Plain Vanilla Equity Swap and Its Variants*, 1 J. FIN. ENGINEERING 219 (1992). *See also* Jeremy Carter, *Repos Versus Total Return Swaps*, DERIVATIVES WEEK, Oct. 15, 2001, at 8, on the increasing use by hedge funds of total return swaps as an alternative to repos for taking on short-term exposure to stocks and reporting a market professional's statement, by way of example, that his firm would charge LIBOR plus 18 basis points to a "quoted regulated investment fund—rated single A by Standard & Poor's" for a one-month total rate of return swap on DaimlerChrysler shares at the time. *See also, e.g.,* Francis E. Laatsch, *Tax Clienteles, Arbitrage, and the Pricing of Total Return Equity Swaps*, J. DERIVATIVES, Winter 2000, at 37, discussing ways in which tax rates may affect equity swap spreads and suggesting various strategies to take tax considerations into account.

[1645] *See supra* p. 641—as noted, the total return swap on debt may be structured so that the transaction terminates when the underlying obligation matures, at scheduled maturity or upon acceleration.

[1646] The introductory note on credit, debt and equity derivatives, *supra* p. 605, summarizes some of the ISDA conventions applicable in determining the Final Price. In a swap with a single period, the Initial

amount equal to the agreed value of the underlying equity position at the outset of the period The LIBOR-based payment in the swap's interest-rate leg is calculated on an equal notional amount. If the Final Price is the same as the Initial Price, neither party makes a payment reflecting price return for the period. The third arrow reflects the equity return payer's obligation to make payments calculated by reference to dividends on the underlying equity,[1647] and the fourth represents the other party's obligation to make LIBOR-based payments.[1648]

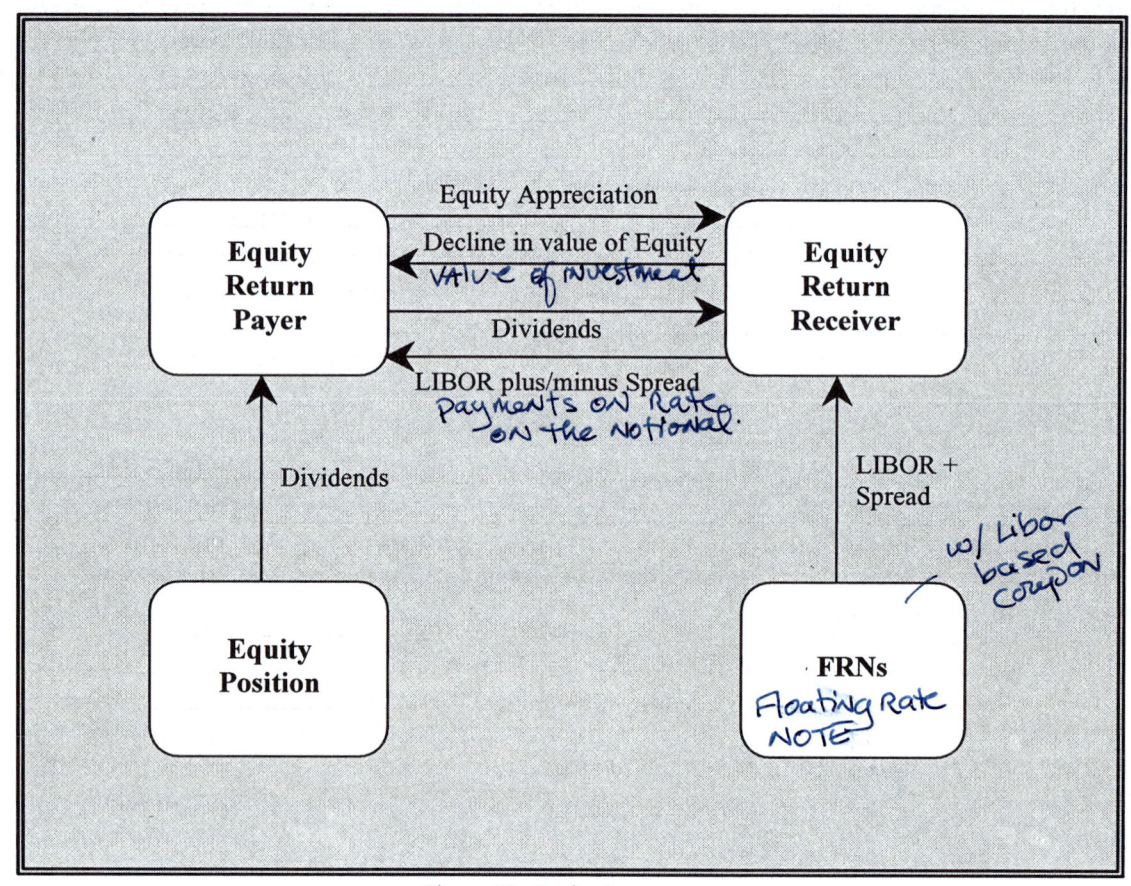

Figure 15. Equity Swap

Like other equity derivatives, a swap of this kind may, as indicated, be entered into in respect of a single stock, a basket of stocks, a stock index (such as the S&P 500,

---

Price, or the method for determining it, will be stated by the parties in the confirmation. In a multiple-period swap, the Final Price for each period will be the Initial Price for the following period. See infra p. 734 and see Annotation 20 to the sample equity index swap confirmation, infra p. 742, for discussion of some of issues that arise in connection with swaps with multiple periods when the parties seek to have the swap's notional amount adjust from time to time to reflect how principal invested in a hypothetical portfolio consisting of the swap's underlying equity would have performed over the swap's entire term.

[1647] See infra p. 731 on the treatment of dividends in these swaps.

[1648] If the swap were documented under an ISDA-based master agreement, all payments due on the same day in the same currency under the same transaction would be netted. See infra p. 807. See Annotation 49 to the sample equity swap confirmation, infra p. 752, on issues that arise in connection with potential mismatches of payment dates on the two legs of a swap like the one illustrated.

the FT-SE 100 or the Nikkei 225), and even baskets of indices.[1649] Instead of swapping an equity return for an interest rate return, the parties might agree to swap one set of equity returns—the total return on one stock, a basket of stocks an equity index or a basket of indices—for another.[1650]

The equity swap, with its varied manifestations, is a creature of the OTC derivatives market, which also trades in many other products designed to enable the parties to transfer or assume exposure to equity market risk. These OTC products include options, synthetic options, forward purchase and sale contracts, swaps like those described above and highly tailored transactions of varying degrees of complexity that may have multiple option-like features or combine features of swaps or forwards with those of options. These privately negotiated transactions complement exchange-traded equity derivatives, which include equity and equity-index options, warrants and, in some cases, futures and options on futures. Equity derivative features are also often imbedded in instruments under which the principal or interest, or both, ultimately payable to an investor may depend on the performance of stocks or indices as well as other contingencies.[1651] As a result of these imbedded features, these instruments are sometimes referred to as derivatives, but for many legal and regulatory purposes they are known as hybrid instruments or hybrid securities.[1652]

The traditional OTC equity derivatives, such as conventional equity forwards and stock options, are physical settlement contracts.[1653] Under the former, the parties agree at the outset on a price and time at which the seller will be obligated to deliver a specified number of shares against payment by the buyer of the agreed price per share,[1654] regard-

---

[1649] Parties to derivative transactions involving indices that are the subject of a third party's proprietary trademark or service mark should consider with counsel in each case whether a license agreement from the owner of the mark will be required in order to use it in the derivatives transaction. It is not unusual in these cases to find in the documentation acknowledgments of each of the parties that the sponsor of the relevant index has no role in connection with the parties' transaction, and that neither party has any responsibility for, *e.g.*, failure of the sponsor to maintain the index or, except as the transaction's terms expressly provide, for any adjustment or lack of adjustment to the index.

[1650] For example, *Hedge Funds Expected To Act on Japan Index Rebalancing*, DERIVATIVES WEEK, Oct. 29, 2001, at 5, describes an anticipated use of a total return structure motivated by a scheduled rebalancing of the stocks in a Japanese equity index. Hedge funds were expected to enter into swaps in which, on one leg, they would pay the return on stocks that were being removed from the index and, on the other, they would receive the return on stocks being added.

[1651] *See generally* DAS, *supra* note 1402. *See also* DICTIONARY OF RISK MANAGEMENT 111–12, defining "Equity-Linked Notes (ELN)" and "Equity Range Notes," for descriptions of the ways in which some of these products are designed and diagrams of variants under which the investor's exposure to equity risk and potential for benefit from, or participation in, equity upside, is unlimited, capped or limited to performance within a specified range of prices. The first of those entries also lists some of the many proprietary names used to identify these products.

[1652] *See supra* note 368.

[1653] Where equity derivatives are concerned, traditional physical settlement provisions are sometimes referred to as terms for "gross physical settlement," to distinguish them from "net share settlement," which is discussed *infra* p. 721. *See, e.g.*, BOARD OF GOVERNORS OF THE FEDERAL RESERVE SYSTEM, *supra* note 373.

[1654] Forward prices reflect the future value of a current spot price, calculated using an assumed interest rate that mimics the cost of carrying the underlying asset over the transaction's term. The forward price

less of whether the market price of the stock at the time is higher or lower. As with other conventional forward contracts, the seller obtains protection against declining stock prices by being assured (assuming the buyer performs) of receiving the agreed forward price even if the market price is lower but, in exchange, the seller also assumes the risk that it will receive a below-market price if the price of the stock at the valuation time is above the forward price. The buyer, for its part, obtains protection against rising stock prices by being assured (assuming the seller performs) that it will acquire the underlying shares at the forward price but, in exchange, assumes the risk that it will have to pay an above-market price if the price of the stock at the valuation time is below the forward price.[1655]

The seller (writer) of a conventional equity option receives a one-time, upfront premium[1656] for extending to the purchaser the right, but not the obligation, to purchase (a call option) or sell (a put option) a specified number of shares at an agreed exercise, or strike, price if the stock's market price at the agreed time is higher than the strike (the call) or lower than the strike (the put).[1657] As with other kinds of options, the period within which this contractual right may be exercised is identified with the conventional names "European style" (exercisable only on the option's expiry date, at or before the expiry time) and "American style" (exercisable on any day during the option's term, at or before the expiry time on the expiry date), although more complex option styles also exist.[1658] Like a party to a stock forward, the option buyer obtains protection against rising stock prices (in a call) or falling stock prices (in a put) but, unlike the buyer or seller in the forward, the buyer of a conventional option provides no protection against price change to the seller.

Many OTC equity derivatives, including equity swaps, are cash-settled. Cash settlement involves a comparison of the market price of the underlying equity or the level of the underlying equity index at an agreed valuation time with a specified price or level. For example, in the case of an option, the market price or level will be compared with the strike (exercise) price.[1659] In a conventional equity swap for a single period, relating to a single stock, the stock's price at the outset of the swap's term will be compared with its price on the agreed valuation date at the end of the swap's term, in order to determine whether a payment is due on account of appreciation or decline in value of the underlying stock and, if so, which of the parties will be required to make the payment.

---

can be arbitraged by borrowing and buying the underlying security, on one hand, or by selling it short and investing the proceeds in a debt instrument, on the other. HULL, *supra* note 646, at 55.

[1655] *See supra* pp. 76 & 515 for discussion of commodity and currency forward contracts.

[1656] The option is said to be "at-the-money" if the strike price is set at the price that the market expects to prevail for the option at the time it is written. The premium will be reduced if the buyer is willing to accept the additional exposure implied by an "out-of-the-money" option. *See supra* note 1386 and the sources cited there.

[1657] The terms of exchange-traded and OTC options are usually adjusted for stock splits, stock dividends and rights offerings, but not for cash dividends. Hull, *supra* note 646, at 155.

[1658] *See supra* pp. 457 & 525 for discussion of option styles in the contexts of swaptions and currency options.

[1659] Exercise would be automatic if the market price were, in a call, at least 101% of the strike and, in a put, less than or equal to 99% of the strike, under the *1996 Equity Derivatives Definitions*.

This aspect of an equity swap is similar to what one would find in a cash-settled stock forward contract, where the stock's market price on the agreed date just before the settlement date would be compared with the forward price stated in the contract.[1660] The cash settlement amount, reflecting the difference between the two prices (multiplied by the number of shares underlying the forward) would be payable by the seller to the buyer if the forward price were lower than the final market price or by the buyer to the seller if it were higher. A conventional cash-settled equity forward contract involves only this one payment, because it is designed only to provide protection against rising equity prices, for the buyer, and against declining equity prices, for the seller. In the common equity swap, however, as described above, the equity return payer and equity return receiver are also trading the cost of carrying the underlying equity position, so there will always be a payment on the interest rate leg, regardless of whether the value of the underlying stock appreciates or declines over the swap's term.

Some OTC equity derivatives provide for a third settlement approach, in addition to cash and physical settlement, which is commonly referred to as "net share settlement." Reduced to its simplest terms, in a net share settlement a party that would have been entitled to receive a cash payment will instead be entitled to receive a number of shares sufficient to generate sale proceeds equal, as nearly as possible, to that cash settlement, and if the exact amount cannot be reached through delivery of whole shares, cash settlement is used in respect of fractions of a share.[1661] A party is sometimes given the right to elect between various physical, cash and net share settlement alternatives. However, as a result of concerns under applicable securities laws, there may be conditions attached to that party's right to elect to settle in a particular manner. These conditions, typically, relate to the other party's ability to engage in market activities associated with the settlement without risk of violating applicable law.[1662]

Like other OTC derivatives, equity swaps often graft onto the paradigm customized features of various kinds. Some are aimed at addressing goals beyond the manage-

---

[1660] The gap between the valuation date and the settlement date usually reflects the standard settlement cycle for a cash transaction in the relevant market.

[1661] For example, BOARD OF GOVERNORS OF THE FEDERAL RESERVE SYSTEM, *supra* note 373, at 2, describes net share settlement in the context of forward purchases by banking organizations of their own stock as follows:

> [T]he difference between the prevailing market price and the forward price is settled in common shares. If, at settlement date, the prevailing stock price is higher than the forward price, the counterparty sells to third parties the number of shares necessary to cover its costs and remits the remaining shares to the banking organization to be retired as treasury stock. If the prevailing stock price is lower than the forward price, the banking organization must issue additional shares to cover the counterparty's costs and the decline in stock price. (footnote omitted)

[1662] Conditions of this kind are often imposed when equity derivatives are entered into by issuers, their affiliates or "insiders" in respect of the issuer's stock, if the counterparty could be expected to dispose of or acquire the underlying shares in connection with cash settlement or net share settlement. The securities law issues include those that arise if, at the time for the scheduled settlement, the counterparty would be unable to dispose of the stock freely in the public market (say, because the stock has not been registered as required for public offerings) or would be restricted in its market activities, or might be prohibited from engaging in market activities in the stock, because of an ongoing public offering or tender offer or because of concerns regarding material nonpublic information. *See supra* pp. 159 & 166.

ment of equity price risk, such as protecting the equity return receiver against currency exchange rate risk.[1663] Other common variants are aimed at reducing the cost of the transaction to one of the parties. For example, the buyer of an option might find the premium unattractively high,[1664] or a party considering a swap might not be willing to surrender all the potential upside benefits in order to obtain protection on the down side. In such cases, that party may decide to enter into a contract providing for reduced protection, or a smaller potential gain, in order to reduce the related cost or preserve some of the potential benefit it would give up in a conventional transaction.

In addition, tailored transactions of these kinds are sometimes chosen to avoid adverse tax or other consequences that might flow from a more conventional transaction providing full protection against adverse movements in equity price. Realization-based tax regimes may, for instance, include constructive sale rules, which for some purposes—notably the recognition of gain—and subject to exceptions treat taxpayers as having disposed of appreciated property if the taxpayer has virtually insulated itself against market risk in respect of the property.[1665] When these rules apply, an investor seeking protection against loss from declining prices on stock holdings over a particular period might choose less than full protection through an OTC derivatives contract so as to avoid being treated as having constructively sold the stock upon entering into the transaction.

The techniques used to create these highly tailored transactions were in many cases first developed to achieve cost reductions in the interest rate derivatives market. This was the case, for example, with caps and floors and participating swaps.[1666] As applied to equity swaps, the equity return payer might agree to a reduction in the payment it will be entitled to receive on the equity leg if the price of the stock declines in order to achieve a desired spread over LIBOR on the interest rate leg. Conversely, the equity return receiver might agree to a reduction in the payment it will be entitled to receive on the equity leg if the price of the stock rises in order to reduce the cost to it of the payments on the swap's interest rate leg, or the equity return payer might be willing to forgo a degree of protection against decline in the stock's value in order to retain some of the potential benefits of appreciation of the stock. The reduction in the level of protection might take the form of a participation, so that the relevant party would pay less than 100% of the

---

[1663] *See* DICTIONARY OF RISK MANAGEMENT 229, defining "Quanto Swap" as "[m]ost frequently, an equity swap providing for translation of the percentage equity return in a non-domestic equity or index into the base currency of the equity return receiver to provide currency protection."

[1664] *See, e.g.,* Don M. Chance & Don Rich, *The Pricing of Equity Swaps and Swaptions,* J. DERIVATIVES, Summer 1998, at 19, and Masaaki Kijima & Yukio Muromachi, *Pricing Equity Swaps in a Stochastic Interest Rate Economy,* J. DERIVATIVES, Summer 2001, at 19. *See supra* notes 1381 & 1379 on the pricing of options.

[1665] *See* Edward D. Kleinbard & Erika W. Nijenhuis, *Everything I Know About New Financial Products I Learned from DECs, in* 14 TAX STRATEGIES FOR CORPORATE ACQUISITIONS, DISPOSITIONS, SPIN-OFFS, JOINT VENTURES, FINANCINGS, REORGANIZATIONS & RESTRUCTURINGS 1183, 1198 (PLI Tax L. & Estate Planning Series, Tax L. & Practice Course Handbook Series No. J-517, 2001), describing the constructive sale rules in Section 1259 of the IRC.

[1666] *See supra* pp. 439 & 554.

stock price appreciation or decline.[1667] An alternative format places caps on what each party would be required to pay.

Another common approach grafts an equity price collar onto the basic swap model. Collars, originally developed to provide limited protection against interest rate risk,[1668] go by many different names, such as "range forward contracts," in the equity derivatives market.[1669] In a collar on stock held by an investor, the first part of the transaction would operate like a put, entitling the investor to require its counterparty to purchase the underlying stock if the market price at the agreed time were below a specified strike or exercise price (or to cash or net share settle in this case). The second part of the transaction would operate like a call, entitling the counterparty to purchase the stock from the investor at a second agreed strike exercise price (or to cash or net share settle), if the market price were higher at the specified valuation time. If the price of the stock at the valuation time were within the "collar" formed by the two strike or exercise prices, no settlement would occur. In a transaction variously referred to as a "cashless," "costless" or "zero-cost" collar, the strike or exercise prices are set at levels such that the premiums that would otherwise be payable for the put and call protection are equal and cancel each other out. In an equity swap with a collar feature, the equity return payer retains the benefit of appreciation of the underlying stock up to the higher band of the collar and the risk of decline in the stock's value down to the lower band of the collar.

Equity derivatives products combine conventional derivatives types in many other ways so as to balance protection and cost objectives. Some of the variants are commonly identified as having "knock-in," "knock-out," and "variable" features. In a transaction with a knock-in feature, protection against the risk of higher or lower stock prices or index levels applies only if the price or level reaches an identified knock-in barrier or level within an identified period. In a transaction with a knock-out feature, on the other hand, the protection automatically ceases to apply if the price or level reaches an identified knock-out barrier or level at any time, or within a specified period.[1670]

The "variable" feature of an equity derivatives transaction typically signals that the number of underlying shares to be used for purposes of settlement will be determined at the end of the transaction's term, or at another specified time after its trade date, by applying a formula to the equity's then current market price. For example, in a prepaid variable stock forward, the parties could agree that, on a forward settlement date, the number of shares to be sold and purchased will be determined by reference to one agreed settlement price if the stock's market price is anywhere up to and including a specified level

---

[1667]Participating transactions of this kind, at one time more frequently referred to as "percentage swaps," have been used in the OTC equity derivatives markets for quite some time, not only to reduce cost through participation in equity exposure in this way but also to gain leveraged exposure to equity through a participation in excess of 100%. *See, e.g.,* Tanya Styblo Beder, *Equity Derivatives for Investors*, 1 J. FIN. ENGINEERING 174, 191 (1992), referring to an "index percentage swap" as a transaction in which "one of the swap flows is calculated based upon a percentage of the performance of a stock market index. The percentage may be less than 100 percent or greater than 100 percent to provide a leveraged or deleveraged rate of equity return."

[1668]*See supra* p. 448.

[1669]For other names, *see* DICTIONARY OF RISK MANAGEMENT 113, defining "Equity Risk Reversal."

[1670]On these barrier options, as they are often called, *see supra* note 1383.

but will be determined by reference to a different settlement price if the stock's price is above the specified level. These variable features are sometimes the basis for complex financing structures used by issuers in respect of their own stock when access to new equity is critical for the issuer. In these cases, the variable transaction can operate to provide the issuer with assurance that the issuer will be able to raise equity financing at some price (assuming the counterparty performs).[1671]

USES OF OTC EQUITY DERIVATIVES

Investors and issuers both use physically settled OTC equity derivatives products to lock in the price at which they may (in the case of options) or will (in the case of forwards) purchase or sell the underlying equity securities. They also use OTC equity derivatives with physical, cash and net share settlement features to achieve goals that they might not otherwise be able to achieve, or achieve as efficiently, with exchange-traded derivatives or through direct investments or other cash-market transactions in equity.[1672] Like OTC rate and commodity swaps and similar derivatives, privately negotiated equity derivatives are used by investors as alternatives to standardized exchange-traded futures

---

[1671] On these "forward equity sales," *see* Philip L. Baird & Thomas E. McCue, *Forward Equity Sales: An Alternative Method of Raising Capital, in* DERIVATIVES RISK MANAGEMENT SERVICE 7H-1. The authors describe, by way of example, a transaction between Merrill Lynch International and Meditrust, in which Meditrust sold shares to Merrill, received payment and agreed that one year later the parties would adjust the number of shares sold (and thus the purchase price) by reference to the shares' market price—Meditrust would deliver additional shares if the share price had declined and Merrill would return shares if the price had risen. According to the authors, the transactions were designed for use by real estate investment trusts—REITs—because their very structure dictates a need to have assured access to new equity if they are to grow. The REIT is established to invest in real estate that generates income which can be passed through to investors without taxation at the trust level (that is, only the investor, and not the trust, is taxed on income from the trust's assets). To achieve this goal, various requirements must be met, one of which is that the trust distribute at least 95% of its taxable income as dividends. Hence the need for the trust to continually issue new equity in order to grow. *Id.* at 7H.02–7H.05. *See also* JAMES M. PEASLEE & DAVID Z. NIRENBERG, FEDERAL INCOME TAXATION OF SECURITIZATION TRANSACTIONS 12–13 n.2, 658 (2001).

[1672] Although in most cases the reasons for using derivatives relate to cost or the lack in the public markets of a sufficiently flexible risk management tool, the obstacles to the use of the exchanges or the public securities markets are sometimes of a regulatory nature. *Hedge Fund To Expand OTC Options Purchases,* DERIVATIVES WEEK, Jan. 28, 2002, at 7, quotes an analyst for a hedge fund in Hong Kong as explaining that his firm would be increasing its use of OTC options on the stock of Indian companies because the efficient use of direct investments would require the firm to obtain a securities license in India. *See also* Peter J. Chepucavage, *Short Sales and Security Futures: The Need for Comprehensive Short Sale Regulation,* FUTURES & DERIVATIVES L. REP., Sept. 2001, at 12, for discussion of the use of OTC equity derivatives in the U.S. market in light of regulatory and SRO restrictions on short sales of securities. These rules, such as Rule 10a-1(a)(1) under the Securities Exchange Act and NASD Rule 3350, are aimed primarily at preventing short sellers from driving the market for securities down, or accelerating a declining market, through continuing sales at ever lower prices or at times when their short sales would exhaust available bids and, thus, result in sales by long sellers (those who own the securities) at lower prices. When applicable, Rule 10a-1(a)(1) prohibits short sales on minus ticks or zero-minus ticks, that is, at a price below the one at which the immediately preceding sale was effected, or at the last sale price if it is lower than the last different price, subject to minor exceptions. The NASD rule operates somewhat differently and by reference to bids rather than transactions. Although "security-based swap agreements" are subject to specified antifraud and anti-manipulation provisions of the U.S. securities laws and related rules (*see supra* p. 145), these short-sale restrictions do not apply to them.

and options or cash market transactions in securities.[1673] In addition to having more flexible terms,[1674] the OTC derivatives may be available on margin or other credit support terms that are less burdensome than those applicable to exchange-traded equity derivatives.[1675] It may also be that standardized futures or options relating to the relevant equity interests simply are not available[1676] or are not directly useful to the investor because of position or similar restrictions.[1677] In certain cases, the OTC derivatives may afford particular tax advantages.[1678]

[1673] *See supra* p. 84 on changes to U.S. law under the CFMA relating to security futures and other equity-linked derivatives under U.S. law.

[1674] For example, OTC equity options may have premium payment and valuation and payout terms that are not available in standardized products. Examples are contingent premium or deferred premium options, under which the premium is higher than that payable for an ordinary option but is payable only if the option is in the money at expiration, and lookback options, in which the buyer obtains (again at a premium higher than that applicable in an ordinary option) the right to buy the underlying asset at its highest price, or sell the underlying asset at its lowest price, registered during a specified period prior to the expiry date. *See* DICTIONARY OF RISK MANAGEMENT 68, 88 & 175. On strategies using lookback call equity options, *see HSBC to Buy Equity Call Options,* DERIVATIVES WEEK, Jan. 21, 2002, at 8. *See also* Karen Xuan Fang, *Lookback Options - The Advantages,* DERIVATIVES WEEK, Dec. 10, 2001, at 5 (Learning Curve column), describing investor use of lookback structures involving equity indices as "common practice in the over-the-counter derivatives market" by investors seeking to re-enter the market at its bottom after periods of decline following major shocks.

[1675] *See supra* p. 609 on the margin regulations adopted by the Federal Reserve Board, which in many cases may limit the amount of credit that may be extended for the purpose of buying or carrying equity (and other security) positions, impose specific margin and related requirements and apply to some OTC derivatives. Where applicable, these margin regulations—for example those applicable to security brokers and dealers under Regulation T—may prescribe not only the amounts and kinds of initial margin that may be required from a customer but also the "payment period" within which the customer must satisfy a deficiency in a margin account that is created or increased by a new transaction to avoid the sales of securities in the customer's margin account that the broker or dealer may be required to effect to cure the deficiency. *See also* 1 SECURITIES & DERIVATIVES REGULATION ¶ 9.07[4][a]. Additional margin requirements may apply under the rules of an SRO. *See id.* ¶ 9.07[4][b].

[1676] *See supra* p. 74 on U.S. law restrictions that banned single stock futures and futures on narrow equity indices and hampered the development of futures on broad-based equity indices until the enactment of the CFMA in December 2000.

[1677] OTC equity derivatives may be chosen as an alternative or a supplement to a direct equity investment or an investment in exchange-traded equity derivatives when the size of the investment the end-user would otherwise make is so large that a direct investment for the full amount might have an undesirable effect on the market for the securities or when position limits on exchange-traded futures contracts might be an obstacle to using those instruments as a complete hedge. *See* the discussion of *Caiola v. Citibank, N.A., supra* p. 138. On position limits, *see* Johnson, *supra* note 230, at § 2.04(9). *See also* Ronald Filler, *Futures Block Trading Facilities—A Fresh New Idea,* FUTURES & DERIVATIVES L. REP., July-Aug. 2001, at 12, on increased use of OTC equity derivatives as a result of restrictions on negotiated block trades involving equity-linked futures.

[1678] *See, e.g.,* Francis E. Laatsch, *Tax Clienteles, Arbitrage and the Pricing of Total Return Equity Swaps,* J. DERIVATIVES, Winter 2000, at 37–38.

> Total return swaps . . . imply a clientele effect because of differential tax treatment of capital gains and ordinary income. . . . If the tax rate on the income portion of the underlying asset differs from the tax rate on the capital gains portion, the effective tax rates on an investor will in large measure determine which side of the swap a party enters. . . . If some investors are subject to taxes, while others are not, then, holding all else constant, the taxable entity should structure the swap contract to obtain a tax-advantaged position.

Investors often use OTC equity derivatives to eliminate or reduce exposure. They may also use them for diversification purposes—to take on exposure to an equity position for a limited period at lower transaction and tax costs than those they would incur if they sold the underlying stock and later reacquired it or purchased the stock and later sold it. In these cases, which are sometimes referred to, respectively, as using derivatives to "monetize"[1679] and "replicate" equity positions,[1680] the investor would incur transaction costs (such as brokerage commissions) twice. For investors seeking temporarily to assume or trade away exposure on a basket of equities, or on all the equities underlying an equity index, the use of OTC derivatives as an alternative to cash-market transactions can present substantial savings in transaction costs.[1681] The OTC equity swap is one of the principal tools used for these purposes.

The issue of tax savings typically arises for investors who are subject to realization-based tax regimes, which assess tax on investment gains upon the occurrence of realization events such as sales,[1682] as opposed to investors subject to mark-to-market tax regimes, which impose tax on gains measured at specified intervals regardless of whether any realization event has occurred.[1683]

OTC equity derivatives are sometimes used by investors to gain exposure to foreign stock so as to obtain the economic effects of a cash investment but without exposure

---

[1679] *See, e.g.*, Julius Leiman-Carbia, *Hedging & Monetization Product Overview*, in collected materials from the Goldman Sachs Single Stock Risk Management Conference, Mar. 6, 2002; SALOMONSMITHBARNEY, HEDGING AND MONETIZING CONCENTRATED EQUITY POSITIONS FOR PRIVATE CLIENTS 5, 14–16 & 27 (1999), discussing strategies to "[g]enerate liquidity or 'monetize' the value of a stock position by providing investors with a means to receive cash for a significant portion of the value of the equity position" and giving as examples of monetization strategies combinations of loans with an investor's purchase of a put option, a collar or an equity swap with respect to a security. The amount of the loan (as a percentage of the market value of the equity position) depends, in the examples, on whether or not the investor uses the proceeds to acquire or carry a position in securities, because of the impact on the loans of the margin regulations discussed *supra* p. 609.

[1680] "Replication" and "synthetic asset" are terms commonly used in this context for derivatives and related transactions when used by insurance companies for purposes of portfolio diversification in lieu of a direct cash market investment. As incorporated since December 2000 in the Purposes and Procedures Manual of the NAIC Securities Valuation Office, the term "RSAT" is used to stand for a "Replication (Synthetic Asset) Transaction" and means "a derivative transaction entered into in conjunction with other investments in order to reproduce the investment characteristics of otherwise permissible investments" for an insurer. See Kevin Driscoll, *Replication (Synthetic Asset) Transactions,* J. DERIVATIVES, Fall 2001, at 62, 64. The NAIC is the National Association of Insurance Commissioners in the United States. Whether or not an insurer is permitted to use RSATs depends on state law, but the states usually model their laws on the NAIC standards. New York state regulations have permitted the use of derivatives for purposes of replication since January 2001. *Id.* at 68. Prior to that date, under New York law insurers were permitted to use derivatives only in hedging and income generation transactions.

[1681] *See generally* Julie A. Allen & Janet L. Showers, *Equity-Index-Linked* Derivatives: An *Investor's Guide* (Salomon Brothers, April 1991); Tanya Styblo Beder, *supra* note 1667.

[1682] As noted *supra* p. 722, realization-based tax regimes may provide for taxation of gains in connection with constructive sales—transactions that eliminate substantially all of the opportunity for gain and risk of loss from an appreciated asset. As a result, when investors use derivatives to seek to reduce exposure to equity, they should consult with their tax advisers about the potential tax consequences of their proposed transactions.

[1683] *See, e.g.,* Kleinbard, *supra* note 1665.

to currency exchange risk or foreign withholding taxes.[1684] There are sometimes other obstacles or drawbacks to direct investments in foreign equities that investors avoid by using equity derivatives.[1685] Finally, as suggested earlier, OTC equity derivatives may be used by investors in complex, highly tailored transactions to obtain, or to transfer to a counterparty, only selected economic effects of a transaction in, or ownership of, the underlying equity securities.[1686]

Issuers often use OTC derivatives on their own stock to manage risks associated with stock repurchase, or buyback, programs maintained in connection with employee stock option plans. If, as will generally be the case, the issuer must deliver shares into the plan regardless of whether the employees have exercised their options, the issuer may use derivatives to manage the risk of increasing costs of complying with plan requirements as the stock's market price rises. Issuers have used a wide variety of OTC derivatives—including put and call options and equity collars or single-pay contracts and forward purchase contracts in this context,[1687] and complex tax and accounting issues[1688] and regulatory restrictions[1689] often affect their choices. As noted above, issuers for which access to new equity is critical are also reported to use forward equity sales to obtain capital more quickly and cheaply (but perhaps with more risk) than would otherwise be available to them.[1690] Similar structures are used by investors as means of generating liquidity from stock positions while retaining the ability to participate in future price appreciation.[1691]

[1684] *See generally* Allen & Showers, *supra* note 1681. *See also* Thomas A. Russo, *Regulation of Equity Derivatives*, in PLI 1993, at 335, 343–44, on these advantages and possible comparative withholding tax advantages of an OTC derivative as compared with an actual equity investment. The term "quanto" is often used to refer to equity derivatives used to take on or transfer equity exposure without exchange rate exposure. *See supra* note 1663.

[1685] Collective investment vehicles, pension plans and other institutional investors may, for example, be permitted to use equity derivatives to gain exposure to foreign equity but may be restricted in their ability to make direct investments where custody of the assets cannot, or cannot practicably, be maintained in a place or manner prescribed by law or contract.

[1686] *See* John F. Marshall, Eric H. Sorensen & Alan L. Tucker, *supra* note 1644.

[1687] For examples of strategies involving put and call options, forward contracts and equity collar transactions, *see, e.g.,* Philip L. Baird, III & Thomas E. McCue, *Should Firms Purchase Call Options on Their Own Stock: The Case of Cephalon,* in DERIVATIVES RISK MANAGEMENT SERVICE 7E-1; Philip L. Baird, III & Thomas E. McCue, *Hedging Share Repurchases With Cashless Collars,* in DERIVATIVES RISK MANAGEMENT SERVICE 7F-1.

[1688] *See, e.g.,* FASB, *supra* note 374. *See also* Glen A. Rae, *Issuer Derivatives,* in PLI 2001, at 331, 345–46; Richard G. Spears, *Tax Aspects of Equity Derivatives Used in Corporate Finance,* in DERIVATIVES RISK MANAGEMENT SERVICE 8B-1.

[1689] For example, under U.S. capital adequacy regulations, banks may not be permitted to treat as Tier 1 capital stock that is subject to forward equity purchase agreements. *See* BOARD OF GOVERNORS OF THE FEDERAL RESERVE SYSTEM, *supra* note 373, at ¶ 47–673.

[1690] *See supra* note 1671.

[1691] *See, e.g.,* SALOMONSMITHBARNEY, *supra* note 1679, at 16–18, discussing a product referred to as Enhanced Equity Monetization Securities, or EMS, and giving as an example a transaction involving 100,000 shares of a stock with a current market price of $50.00, which the investor pledges at the outset of the transaction. In the example, the investor agrees to a Downside Protection Price ("DPP") of $47.50 (95% of the market price at the time of the trade) and a Capped Upside Participation Price ("CUPP") of $62.50 (125% of that price):

Special Legal Issues

The parties to OTC equity derivatives transactions may encounter difficult accounting, tax and other legal and regulatory issues in connection with their activities. Some of the securities and commodity law issues are discussed elsewhere in this book.[1692] Whether a proposed use of equity derivatives may give rise to these or other concerns should be considered with counsel and other professional advisers. The answers to these questions may turn on numerous variables, such as:

- the identities and circumstances of the particular parties,
- whether a party holds the underlying securities,
- how a party may hedge its exposure under the transaction or put itself in a position to perform its obligations under the transaction through activities in the securities markets,
- the extent to which the economic benefits and burdens of the underlying securities are transferred through the derivatives transaction, and for how long,
- the way in which the transaction allocates other indicia of ownership of the underlying securities (such as voting rights) as between the parties and,
- in the case of transactions by issuers in respect of their own stock, additional factors that may depend on the accounting result that the issuer is seeking to achieve.

Documentation Conventions and Related Issues

The introductory note on credit, debt and equity derivatives[1693] discusses documentation and structuring issues that the parties to OTC equity derivatives generally, in-

---

After settlement, the investor receives, indicatively, $42.22 per share or 84.43% of current market value. . . . At maturity, the investor will deliver a certain number of shares, or the cash value of the shares, based on the stock price at maturity. If the stock price is at or below the DPP, the investor will deliver 100,000 shares. . . . If the stock price is between the DPP and the CUPP, a ratio of shares with a value equal to DPP is delivered [by the investor]. . . . The remaining shares are returned to the investor. If the stock price is at or above the CUPP, a ratio of shares with value equal to the DPP plus the appreciation above the CUPP is delivered to Salomon Smith Barney. The remaining shares are returned to the investor. *Id.* at 18.

The advantages of the EMS for the investor are described as follows:

The investor monetizes a greater percentage of an equity holding than with a collar and loan structure without realizing a taxable event. Unlike a collar and a loan, **all** proceeds can be reinvested into marketable securities [that is, without limitations under the margin regulations described *supra* p. 609]. The investor also protects the value of the equity holding while maintaining some upside price exposure. The investor retains ownership, voting rights, and dividends. *Id.*

[1692]*See supra* pp. 63 (commodities laws), 129 (securities laws) & 177 (counterparty relationships and duties).

[1693]*Supra* p. 605.

cluding equity swaps, should consider in connection with their transactions. That discussion is framed in the context of the *1996 Equity Derivatives Definitions* and describes many of the important conventions that apply under those definitions. The discussion also refers to some of the proposed changes to the conventions stated in those definitions. The following discussion and the annotations to the sample equity swap confirmation[1694] provide further background on the ISDA terminology and conventions applicable to equity swaps and explore some related issues in more detail.

An equity swap of the kind referred to at the opening of this product description, involving an equity leg and an interest rate leg, cannot be fully documented using only the *1996 Equity Derivatives Definitions*. Article 7 of those definitions, on equity swaps, deals only with the equity leg. To pick up the ISDA conventions applicable to the interest rate leg, the parties typically also incorporate relevant provisions from one of the sets of ISDA definitions used for interest rate derivatives—the *2000 ISDA Definitions* or, for those who have not yet adopted them, the *1991 ISDA Definitions*, with or without the *1998 Supplement to the 1991 ISDA Definitions*.[1695]

The conventions applicable under those sets of definitions to document the interest rate leg are discussed elsewhere in this book.[1696] The *1996 Equity Derivatives Definitions* provide terminology and conventions for the calculation of an equity leg of four different types of swaps, which are named to indicate whether the swap's Equity Amount for each relevant period—reflecting price or value appreciation or decline—will be calculated by reference to (1) a single stock, identified as the Share, of a specified Issuer,[1697] (2) a Basket composed of Shares of specified Issuers in the proportions and numbers of Shares indicated in the Confirmation,[1698] (3) a single equity Index or (4) a Basket of equity indices.[1699]

The distinctions among the four types—Share Swap Transaction, Share Basket Swap Transaction, Index Swap Transaction and Index Basket Swap Transaction—are relevant under these ISDA definitions in various ways. These include the treatment in

---

[1694] *Infra* p. 736.

[1695] *See* Annotation 3 to the sample equity swap confirmation, *infra* p. 737. The *1991 ISDA Definitions* included terminology that could be used in confirming OTC equity derivatives relating to six equity indices, the S&P 500, FT-SE 100, NIKKEI 225, TOPIX, CAC-40 and DAX indices. Those provisions are not included in the *2000 ISDA Definitions*, which provide terminology and conventions designed for use only with interest rate and currency derivatives.

[1696] *See supra* pp. 408 & 427 for general discussion of interest rate products and a sample interest rate swap confirmation.

[1697] "Share" and "Issuer" are defined in Sections 1.11 and 1.13 of the *1996 Equity Definitions*. *See supra* p. 631 on the various choices offered in connection with succession problems arising out of certain consolidations, amalgamations and mergers.

[1698] "Basket" is defined in Section 1.12 of the *1996 Equity Definitions* and is used in connection with baskets of stocks and baskets of equity indices. Exhibits II-I and II-J to those definitions set out special terms that the parties can use in swaps involving Baskets, including formats for tables with relevant information relating to each item in the Basket and its weighting in the Basket.

[1699] Similar distinctions are drawn (in Section 1.2 of the *1996 Equity Derivatives Definitions*) among Index Option Transactions, Share Option Transactions, Index Basket Option Transactions and Share Basket Option Transactions.

Article 4 of Market Disruption Events affecting the determination of an Equity Amount at a scheduled time and the treatment in Article 9 of modifications to a swap's terms or to the underlying equity or even the cancellation of a swap in connection with Potential Adjustment Events, Merger Events, Nationalization and Insolvency events.[1700] Article 8 of these ISDA definitions deals with issues relevant only to Index Transactions and Index Basket Transactions.[1701] As a result, in confirming their transactions, the parties should identify the relevant type of swap, as is illustrated in the sample confirmation.[1702]

In the *1996 Equity Derivatives Definitions*, the party required to pay an Equity Amount reflecting price or index appreciation is called the Equity Amount Payer, and the party required to pay an Equity Amount reflecting price or index decline is referred to simply as the "other party." If the swap has an interest-rate leg, this other party is also referred to as the Floating Amount Payer in the part of a swap's confirmation relating to that leg, in the format suggested in Exhibit II-G to those definitions.

In any case, the Equity Amount payable for each period in the swap's Term is determined by multiplying the agreed Equity Notional Amount by the relevant Rate of Return. The Rate of Return is determined in accordance with the following formula:

$$\frac{\text{Final Price - Initial Price}}{\text{Initial Price}} \times \text{Multiplier}$$

If the Equity Amount is positive, it is due from the Equity Amount Payer to the other party. If it is negative, the other party is obligated to pay the absolute amount of the Equity Amount to the Equity Amount Payer.[1703]

The Equity Amounts are payable in respect of periods defined by reference to Valuation Dates, and the parties must specify the Valuation Dates or the manner in which they will be determined. The Valuation Dates are subject to adjustment if they fall on days that are not "Exchange Business Days," a term defined by reference to days that are scheduled to be full, normal trading days on each exchange or quotation system identified by the parties as an "Exchange" or a "Related Exchange" or any successor to such an Exchange.[1704] Since the adoption of that convention, many participants in the market have moved away from its use and, instead, agree that a day may be treated as an Exchange

---

[1700] *See* Tables 1, 5 and 7 in the introductory note to credit, debt and equity derivatives, *supra* pp. 612, 628 & 633, on some aspects of the handling of these events.

[1701] In each case, the provisions are applicable to both swaps and options. They provide rules for dealing with adjustments and corrections to an Index (*see* Annotation 8 and Annotation 34 to the sample equity swap confirmation, *infra* pp. 738 & 746).

[1702] *See* Annotation 5 to the sample equity swap confirmation, *infra* p. 737.

[1703] *See* Section 7.1 of the *1996 Equity Derivatives Definitions*.

[1704] Section 1.20 of the *1996 Equity Derivatives Definitions* defines "Exchange Business Day" to exclude any day on which trading on an Exchange or Related Exchange is scheduled to close prior to its regular weekday closing time. Sections 1.16 and 1.17 define "Exchange" and "Related Exchange," both terms relevant in connection with Market Disruption Events and Settlement Disruption Events, as described in Tables 1 and 2 in the introductory note on credit, debt and equity derivatives, *supra* pp. 612 & 615.

Business Day even if the relevant Exchanges and Related Exchanges are scheduled to be open for only part of the day.[1705]

In most cases, the Valuation Dates are also subject to postponement in connection with Market Disruption Events in respect of the relevant share or index on the specified day.[1706] The *1996 Equity Derivatives Definitions* also provide a framework within which the parties may determine Equity Amounts by comparing a relevant period's Initial Price with a Relevant Price for multiple Averaging Dates, rather than the Final Price for a single Valuation Date.[1707]

Adjustments to Valuation Dates and Settlements Dates for cash-settled and physically settled transactions are described in Tables 1 and 2 in the introductory note on credit, debt and equity derivatives.[1708] Like the definition of "Exchange Business Day," they operate on the assumption that the underlying equity or index, or a related option,[1709] is traded on an exchange or quotation system.[1710] If this is not the case, the parties must address how they intend to deal with holidays and events that could disrupt off-exchange dealings in the underlying equity or equities. If an exchange or quotation system identified as an Exchange in respect of a Share or Index ceases to list or otherwise include it, the *1996 Equity Derivatives Definitions* provide that the parties will negotiate in good faith to agree on another exchange or quotation system to be taken into account for purposes of their transaction, but market participants often treat delisting or loss of traded status as grounds for the early termination of their transactions.[1711]

To indicate how the parties intend to deal with dividends, the parties must choose whether their swap will provide for payments on a Price Return or Total Return basis. The choice will not alter the formula used to calculate Equity Amounts for the swap in respect of price or value appreciation or decline. It will merely indicate whether Dividend Amounts will also figure in the swap.

If Price Return is specified, the Equity Amount (a payment on account of appreciation or decline in value of the underlying Share, Index or Basket) is the only amount

---

[1705]*Supra* p. 626 discusses this change in convention, as well as other changes relating to unscheduled closings, which ISDA proposes to take into account in a revised version of its equity derivatives definitions.

[1706]*See* Section 4.2 of the *1996 Equity Derivatives Definitions*. An exception to this rule applies if the parties adopt the ISDA convention referred to in Section 4.5 of those definitions as "Futures Price Valuation." *See* Annotations 40 and 41 to the sample confirmation, *infra* p. 748, on the way in which Equity Amounts are determined if Futures Price Valuation is specified.

[1707]*See* Annotations 38 & 39 to the sample equity swap confirmation, *infra* p. 748.

[1708]*Supra* pp. 612 & 615.

[1709]These definitions do not refer to equity futures in the valuation mechanisms, so appropriate modifications must be made by the parties if these instruments are relevant to their transactions or to hedges for their transactions.

[1710]*See* Section 1.16 of the *1996 Equity Derivatives Definitions*, defining "Exchange," and Section 1.17, defining "Related Exchange," a term relevant in connection with Market Disruptions, as described in Tables 1 and 2 in the introductory note on credit, debt and equity derivatives, *supra* pp. 612 & 615.

[1711]This practice will be recognized in ISDA's proposed revised equity derivatives definitions. *See supra* p. 630.

paid on the equity leg of the transaction. No account is taken or payment made in connection with dividends.[1712] Price Return, therefore, might be selected by an equity return payer that held an investment in the underlying stock position and wished to retain dividend income it received on the stock but temporarily give up the potential for gain from price appreciation on the stock in order to receive protection against the risk of price decline; the investor would also receive a stream of cash payments on the interest-rate leg of the swap, roughly representing the cost of carrying the asset. Price Return would also be the appropriate selection in a swap involving an Index or Index Basket where the equity return payer on the component stocks, as reflected in the level of the index, expected to hedge its position through exchange-traded or other derivatives that would not generate the relevant dividend cash flow. Finally, Price Return would also be the appropriate choice for an Index Swap Transaction if the level or value of the underlying index were adjusted to reflect all dividends.[1713]

If Total Return is specified, the Equity Amount payable by one party to the other in respect of appreciation or decline in price or value of the underlying Share, Index or Basket will be calculated just as if the parties had specified that Price Return would apply[1714] but, by choosing Total Return, the parties will have indicated an intention to provide somehow for the transfer of the economic benefit of dividends from the Equity Amount Payer to the other party.

If the parties choose Total Return but are otherwise silent on their intent relating to dividends, they will in effect be agreeing that the Equity Amount Payer will be required to pay to the other party a Dividend Amount in respect of dividends on the underlying stock to be calculated as provided in the swap's confirmation.[1715] By providing this choice, the *1996 Equity Derivatives Definitions* implicitly assume that the parties will state that the Dividend Amount will include only dividends actually paid on the underlying stock during the relevant Dividend Period, rather than dividends for which the ex-dividend date has occurred but payment has not. Although the market price for the stock will normally adjust for trading purposes on the ex-dividend date and is, therefore, the date used in the calculation of the total return on the major equity indices,[1716] when a party to an equity swap obligates itself to pay Dividend Amounts to its counterparty, it will generally do so only if it is scheduled to have received the relevant amounts by the date for payment, unless the swap's terms are adjusted to compensate the party making the Dividend Amount payments for the cost of funding the payment.

The Dividend Amount payment must be made on the Dividend Payment Date corresponding to the relevant Dividend Period. The *1996 Equity Derivatives Definitions* do

---

[1712] *See* Section 7.1(a) of the *1996 Equity Derivatives Definitions*.

[1713] Ordinary cash dividends are disregarded in calculating the level of many of the indices used in equity swaps and other OTC derivatives—including the S&P 500, which is used as the Index in the sample equity swap confirmation—but some equity indices are calculated taking into account all dividends.

[1714] *See* Sections 7.1(b) & 7.1(c) of the *1996 Equity Derivatives Definitions*.

[1715] *See* Section 7.1(b) of the *1996 Equity Derivatives Definitions*.

[1716] *See* STANDARD & POOR'S, 1999/2000 S&P 500 DIRECTORY 24 (1999)(explaining that the total-return calculation of the S&P 500 Index uses the ex-dividend date rather than the payment date "because the marketplace price adjustment for the dividend occurs on the ex-dividend date").

not concern themselves with whether the Dividend Payment Dates stated by the parties, or determined in the manner specified by the parties, actually correspond to the dates on which dividends are paid by the issuer of the underlying stock,[1717] nor do they provide for any adjustment to the amount due from the Equity Amount Payer if the Equity Payment Dates and actual dividend payment dates are not in fact the same. As a result, if the parties intend to replicate dividend cash flows through their swap in all respects—including amount and date of payment—unless they can be sure that their specified Equity Payment Dates and the relevant dividend payment dates will always be the same, the parties must make their own provisions for interest adjustments.[1718]

If the parties choose Total Return for their transaction and also specify that Re-investment of Dividends will apply, the Equity Amount Payer will not make cash Dividend Amount payments. Instead, the Equity Notional Amount will be adjusted on each Dividend Payment Date by an amount equal to the dividends attributable to the related Dividend Period. Here too, the *1996 Equity Derivatives Definitions* do not concern themselves with whether the parties have set the Dividend Payment Dates to correspond to the dates on which the dividends are actually paid by the issuer of the underlying stock. Therefore, if the parties intend a swap's Equity Notional Amount to grow just as invested principal would grow in a cash investment in the underlying stock through automatic re-investment of dividends, the parties must make provision for cases in which swap Equity Payment Dates do not match actual dividend reinvestment dates on the underlying Shares.

Suppose, for example, that the parties entered into a Price Return swap on an Equity Notional Amount of U.S.$ 100,000,000, equal to the market value of 5 million shares of common stock of X Corporation at the time of the trade. Suppose, further, that, between the Effective Date and the first Valuation Date, X Corporation paid a dividend of 15 cents a share, and that the stock appreciated 3% during the period. On the first Equity Payment Date, regardless of whether the parties specified Price Return or Equity Return, the Equity Amount Payer would owe U.S.$ 3,000,000 (which would be netted against the amount due from the counterparty on the interest rate leg of the swap). If the parties had chosen Price Return, that would be the only payment due on that date on the equity leg of the swap. If they had chosen the Total Return without Re-investment of Dividends, the Equity Amount Payer would owe U.S.$ 3,750,000 (the appreciation plus 15 cents a share on 5 million shares). If the parties had chosen Total Return with Re-investment of Divi-

---

[1717] Under Section 7.12, subject to any adjustment for holidays provided for by the parties, the first Dividend Period begins on the day the Initial Price is determined and ends on the first Valuation Date during the swap's Term. Subsequent Dividend Periods run from Valuation Date to Valuation Date. If the parties fail to specify Dividend Payment Dates, the Equity Payment Dates specified by them will be treated as the Dividend Payment Dates. If the parties fail to specify when the Initial Price for the first period in a swap is determined, the first Dividend Period will automatically be treated as beginning on the swap's Trade Date. If this is not the parties' intent, they should specify the date at which the Initial Price is determined, even if they actually state the Initial Price.

[1718] If the Equity Amount Payer intends to reduce the amounts it will pay in respect of dividends to take account of taxes withheld by the issuer or other costs (such as the cost of converting the dividends actually received by the Equity Amount Payer to the currency in which the swap payments must be made), the parties' documentation must deal with these matters, as they are not covered in the *1996 Equity Derivatives Definitions*.

dends, the Equity Amount Payer would owe U.S.$3,000,000 and the Equity Notional Amount for the following calculation period would increase to U.S.$ 100,750,000.

If the parties intend to use an equity swap to replicate the performance of an investment in an equity portfolio, applying the conventions provided in the *1996 Equity Derivatives Definitions*, the parties will specify Equity Notional Reset as applicable to their transaction. When this choice is made, the result is that the initially stated Equity Notional Amount applies for the first Equity Payment Date to determine the Equity Amount (if any) payable on that date, and the Equity Notional Amount for the next Equity Payment Date will be the sum of that Equity Amount (positive or negative) and the prior Equity Payment Date's Equity Notional Amount, and so on.

The parties might, on the other hand, use an equity swap to simulate the total return on a direct equity investment of a constant amount of money, that is an investment in which the investor periodically sold stock as the value of the investment rose and invested more money as the value of the investment declined, perhaps as part of a constant-asset-allocation strategy.[1719] Given this objective, the parties would not select Equity Notional Reset.

Although the *1996 Equity Derivatives Definitions* do not provide terminology for the calculation of cash flows on an interest rate leg of an equity swap, they do provide that the Notional Amount specified by the parties for the calculation of payments on the interest rate leg will increase or decrease in tandem with changes to the Equity Notional Amount that occur as a result of their agreement that a transaction will involve Equity Notional Reset.[1720] There is, however, no such provision for automatic adjustment to the Notional Amount for the interest-rate leg of a swap to take account of increases in the Equity Notional Amount that result from Re-investment of Dividends.

Tables 5 and 7 in the introductory note on credit, debt and equity derivatives[1721] and the related text summarize some of the ways in which the *1996 Equity Derivatives Definitions* contemplate modifications to the terms of a transaction in connection with events affecting the underlying equity or index or the issuer of relevant equity instruments. In some cases, the definitions provide that a transaction will be cancelled or the underlying equity will change. As indicated, these events are identified as Potential Adjustment Events, Merger Events, Nationalization and Insolvency. Those who adopt these ISDA definitions should, as discussed in that introductory note, closely examine in the context of their particular dealings whether they wish to make changes to the definitions of the various triggering events and to the related ISDA presumptions on how the events will be treated, including the latitude given to the Calculation Agent in connection with the relevant adjustments and, where applicable, the calculation of the amount that will be payable in connection with cancellation of a transaction.[1722]

[1719] *See* Allen & Showers, *supra* note 1681, at 22–24 for discussion of this kind of swap.

[1720] *See* Section 7.11(c) of the *1996 Equity Derivatives Definitions*.

[1721] *Supra* pp. 628 & 633.

[1722] If the parties adopt Futures Price Valuation (described in Annotations 40 and 41 to the sample equity swap confirmation, *infra* p. 748), they should consider how they would deal with a case in which the relevant exchange-traded contract is permanently discontinued. The ISDA rules on this subject (in Section 4.5 of the *1996 Equity Derivatives Definitions*) may not provide a complete and satisfactory answer.

These issues are commonly subjects of negotiations, and the negotiations often lead to departures from the standard ISDA provisions. As a result, ISDA is considering a new edition of the *Equity Derivatives Definitions* which, among other things, is expected to include modified approaches to Merger Events and the provisions relating to the cancellation of transactions in connection with these events, as well as provisions for additional approaches to handling extraordinary events, such as Nationalization and Insolvency of an issuer of a transaction's underlying equity, Potential Adjustment Events, delisting of underlying shares and certain changes in law and market conditions that adversely affect a party's ability to hedge its position in a derivatives transaction.[1723] To deal with disputes that may arise over important determinations made by the Calculation Agent, an approach being considered would involve the parties' sharing the cost of resolving these disputes by recourse to a mutually acceptable third party or a panel of three independent dealers in the underlying equity or in derivatives relating to the equity in question, one appointed by each of the parties and the third appointed by the other two.

SAMPLE CONFIRMATION

The following sample confirmation involves Equity Amounts calculated by reference to changes in the level of an equity index. By entering into such a transaction, the Company (which might or might not have the power, authority or regulatory authorization to invest directly in the component securities underlying the index used in the swap) might achieve the same economic results it could have obtained by borrowing $50,000,000 at LIBOR and investing the proceeds of the loan in those securities. The Company might wish to enter into the swap transaction for various reasons, including possible savings on transaction costs and withholding taxes involved in a loan and a direct equity investment. The Company might select the swap mechanism rather than using exchange-traded derivatives on the index because the swap would not involve a need for active management by the Company of a futures portfolio;[1724] by using the swap, the Company might also be able to obtain credit support requirements more flexible than the margin requirements for the available futures contracts.[1725] By choosing to enter into the swap to achieve those results, however, the Company will also have taken on the credit risk of its swap counterparty, subject to mitigation through credit-support arrangements negotiated by the Company and the swap provider.

[1723] *See supra* p. 635.

[1724] Under the contract specifications for the S&P 500 futures contract traded on the Chicago Mercantile Exchange (CME), there are futures contracts for four contract months (March, June, September and December). STANDARD & POOR'S, *supra* note 1716, at 71. The CME also trades an E-Mini S&P 500 futures contract (one-fifth the size of the full-size contract), as well as options on S&P 500 futures. The Chicago Board Options Exchange trades options on various S&P indices. *Id.* at 77. There are numerous S&P Index mutual funds that establish equity portfolios to track the performance of the index, *see id.* at 87, as well as insurance products that are linked to or based upon the S&P 500. *Id.* at 98.

[1725] In addition, the margin regulations discussed *supra* p. 609 could have an impact on the amount of a borrowing by the Company to make direct investment in a portfolio of stock designed to mimic the S&P 500.

> The Introduction to this Part, *supra* p. 369, and the annotations to the sample rate swap confirmation, *supra* p. 427, contain general commentary about the confirmation process and the use of ISDA's confirmation forms both before and after the parties have entered into a master agreement that is not repeated or expressly referred to in the annotations to the other sample confirmations in this book.

[Letterhead of Big Bank, N.A.]

April 16, 2002

Equity Index Swap Transaction

> Annotation 1. This sample confirmation was prepared using the forms supplied as Exhibits I and II-G to the *1996 Equity Derivatives Definitions,* with some modification.
>
> Annotation 2. *See supra* p. 149 on special provisions reflecting concerns under the U.S. securities laws that are often included in confirmations for debt and equity derivatives. The GLBA imposes certain restrictions on the counterparties with which banks organized in the United States, like the hypothetical provider of this swap, may engage in equity derivatives. *See supra* p. 159.

English Company PLC
Company House
Company Lane
London AB1C 2DE

Ladies and Gentlemen:

The purpose of this letter agreement is to confirm the terms and conditions of the transaction entered into between us on the Trade Date specified below (the "Transaction"). This letter agreement constitutes a "Confirmation" as referred to in the Master Agreement specified below.

The definitions and provisions contained in the 1996 ISDA Equity Derivatives Definitions and Articles 1 through 9 of the 2000 ISDA Definitions and related provisions of Annex A to those definitions (all as published by the International Swaps and Derivatives Association, Inc.) are incorporated into this Confirmation. In the event of any inconsistency between the definitions and provisions contained in the 1996 ISDA Equity Derivatives Definitions and those contained in the 2000 ISDA Definitions incorporated into this Confirmation, the former will govern. In the event of any inconsistency between those definitions and provisions and this Confirmation, this Confirmation will govern.

Sample Equity Index Swap Confirmation

> Annotation 3. As discussed *supra* p. 729, the *1996 Equity Derivatives Definitions* do not supply some basic provisions used in documenting a swap that has both an equity leg and an interest rate leg. For this reason, even though those definitions are used in this sample confirmation to document the equity leg, the relevant parts of the *2000 ISDA Definitions* are incorporated to document the interest rate leg, as reflected in the provisions on Floating Amounts, *infra* pp. 750–753.
>
> Annotation 4. Before incorporating all or part of two different sets of ISDA definitions into the same master agreement or confirmation, the parties should consider the potential for inconsistency and state a rule about which set will prevail with respect to the transaction or with respect to the obligations of a particular party, as appropriate. In this case the parties have specified that the *1996 Equity Derivatives Definitions* will govern in the case of inconsistencies, to take advantage of a rule (*see* Annotation 48 to this sample confirmation, *infra* p. 751) that will result in adjustments to the Notional Amount for the swap's LIBOR-based payments that are not provided for in the *2000 ISDA Definitions*.

1. This Confirmation supplements, forms part of, and is subject to, the Master Agreement dated as of April 16, 2002, as amended and supplemented from time to time (the "Agreement"), between Big Bank, N.A. (the "Bank") and English Company PLC (the "Company"). All provisions contained in the Agreement govern this Confirmation except as expressly modified below.

2. The terms of the particular Transaction to which this Confirmation relates—which is an Index Swap Transaction—are as follows:

> Annotation 5. Various provisions of the *1996 Equity Derivatives Definitions* supply rules that apply differently to the four classes of transactions covered by the definitions—Share Swap Transactions, Index Swap Transactions, Share Basket Swap Transactions and Index Basket Swap Transactions—hence the identification of the transaction as an Index Swap Transaction. These rules include those applicable under Article 4, in connection with Market Disruptions (*see* Table 1 in the introductory note on credit, debt and equity derivatives, *supra* p. 612) and Article 9 in connection with Adjustment Events and Merger Events (*see* Tables 5 and 7, *supra* pp. 628 & 633).

General Terms:

    Reference No.:   00000-00

    Trade Date: April 16, 2002

    Effective Date: April 18, 2002

Annotation 6. *See* Annotations 5 and 6 to the sample rate swap confirmation, *supra* p. 429, with respect to the Trade Date and Effective Date of swaps generally. In security-linked derivatives the time lapse between the Trade Date and the Effective Date often reflects the length of a standard settlement period for a transaction in an underlying cash market, because one of the parties may be hedging its obligations through a purchase or sale of the underlying securities. In transactions such as the sample swap, which involve payments calculated by reference to LIBOR, a time lapse between the Trade Date and the Effective Date is also useful to accommodate the convention for LIBOR settings in the London interbank deposit market. As described *supra* p. 408, the convention in that market is to quote offered rates for U.S. dollar deposits two London banking days before the "value date" for the deposit. As a result, in swaps and other OTC derivatives with LIBOR-based payments, the Trade Date may predate the Effective Date so that LIBOR for the first Calculation Period can be set before the Effective Date.

Termination Date: October 18, 2005, subject to adjustment as provided below for all Payment Dates

Annotation 7. This term is defined in the *2000 ISDA Definitions*. As described in Annotation 7 to the sample rate swap confirmation, *supra* p. 429, under those definitions the accrual of the Floating Amount payable in respect of the final Calculation Period will end on, and exclude, the date identified as the Termination Date unless the parties expressly provide that the Termination Date is subject to adjustment should it fall on a day that is not a Business Day. In this case the parties have agreed to extend the LIBOR accrual for the final Calculation Period past the scheduled Termination Date, just as they are agreeing below to adjust all the Calculation Periods, if the periods happen to be scheduled to end on days that are not Business Days. In addition, they agree below to adjust scheduled payments on all LIBOR-based Floating Amounts so that each quarterly payment due on the swap's interest-rate leg will be due on the Equity Payment Date relating to the same three-month period. *See* Annotation 49 to this sample confirmation, *infra* p. 752.

Index: "S&P 500," which means the Standard & Poor's 500 Composite Stock Price Index, which on the Trade Date is calculated and published by Standard & Poor's, a division of The McGraw-Hill Companies

Annotation 8. The *1996 Equity Derivatives Definitions* provide a framework for calculating Equity Amounts in an Index Swap Transaction by reference to changes in the levels of an Index (*see supra* p. 730) but leave it to the parties to supply a definition of the relevant Index. The illustrated definition names the sponsor of the specified Index on the Trade Date only for purposes of identification.

Section 8.1(a) of the ISDA definitions provides a rule relating to Index sponsor succession as well as rules relating to changes in the formula or method used to calculate an Index.

Annotation 9. Under the ISDA rule relating to Index sponsor succession, if an Index level relevant to a transaction is not calculated and announced by the sponsor but is calculated and announced "by a successor sponsor acceptable to the Calculation Agent," the change in sponsor will not affect the parties' ongoing use of the announced Index levels. Under the second rule, if the Index is "replaced by a successor index using, in the determination of the Calculation Agent, the same or a substantially similar formula for and method of calculation as used in the calculation of that Index," again, the parties' dealings continue using the successor index.

Annotation 10. There is no rule about how the parties should proceed if a successor sponsor is not acceptable to the Calculation Agent or if the identified Index is replaced by an index that, in the determination of the Calculation Agent, is not "the same" or "substantially similar." There is, however, a rule in Section 8.1(b) stated to apply if a sponsor fails to calculate and announce a relevant index on a Valuation Date or if there is "a material change in the formula for or the method of calculating" an Index or a sponsor "in any other way materially modifies" an Index "other than a modification prescribed in that formula or method to maintain that Index in the event of changes in constituent stock and capitalization and other routine events." In these cases, the Calculation Agent itself is to calculate the relevant Final Price for a swap in accordance with the formula and method last in effect prior to the change or failure, "but using only those securities that comprised the Index immediately prior to that change or failure (other than those securities that have since ceased to be listed on any relevant Exchange)."

Annotation 11. The *1996 Equity Derivatives Definitions* do not provide guidance on how the Calculation Agent should make these determinations regarding successor sponsors or successor indices or regarding material changes affecting an Index. Other sets of ISDA definitions provide that all determinations and calculations to be made by the Calculation Agent must be made in good faith, and some go on to require that the determinations and calculations be made in a commercially reasonable manner and, sometimes, after consultation with the parties. When the parties use the *1996 Equity Derivatives Definitions*, they may wish to adopt general standards of these kinds (as illustrated *infra* p. 753) and provide a mechanism for the resolution of disputes regarding a Calculation Agent's calculations and determinations and its failure to make calculations and determinations. In its projected revision to those definitions, ISDA proposes to add a statement of the standard to which the Calculation Agent will be held in acting and exercising its judgment.

Annotation 12. During trading hours, the value of the S&P 500 is calculated by both Automatic Data Processing ("ADP") and Bridge Data, under contracts with Standard & Poor's. ADP, the "primary calculator," calculates the Index every 15 seconds and disseminates it to its subscribers and to the Chicago Mercantile Exchange, the Chicago Board Options Exchange ands the American Stock Exchange, which trade products based on the S&P 500. ADP revalues the S&P 500 every 15 seconds during the hours that stocks in the index trade on the exchanges on which they are listed. Bridge Data serves as a backup source of price quotes. Intraday quotes from the two sources may differ slightly because of timing differences in when they receive the underlying data. Standard & Poor's reports the S&P 500 to major newswire services and through its own service. The closing index value for each day is verified and disseminated by Standard & Poor's. Information about the "Distribution of S&P 500 Index Values" can be found in *Standard & Poor's, supra* note 1716, at 10. In specifying the Initial Price and Final Price—the terms used in the calculation of Equity Amounts on the basis of S&P 500 levels—the confirmation provides for using the S&P 500 value as reported by the index sponsor, regardless of whether it was calculated by the primary or the secondary calculator.

Exchanges:	New York Stock Exchange, American Stock Exchange and NASDAQ
Related Exchanges:	Chicago Mercantile Exchange

Annotation 13. "Exchange" in an equity derivative documented using the *1996 Equity Derivatives Definitions* is primarily intended to mean the exchange or quotation system on which the underlying equity or equities trade. "Related Exchange" is intended to mean futures and options exchanges where exchange-traded derivatives on the underlying equity or equities, or the relevant index, trade. These ISDA definitions do not supply fallback choices if the parties fail to specify Exchanges or Related Exchanges, although they do provide (in Section 1.16) for treating as an Exchange any successor to an identified Exchange. When equity swaps involve stock that is both traded on an exchange in the issuer's jurisdiction and the subject of American depositary receipts or global depositary receipts traded elsewhere, the parties will generally consider whether the relevant exchanges in both jurisdictions should be identified as Exchanges for purposes of their transaction.

Annotation 14. In the *1996 Equity Derivatives Definitions,* "Exchange" and "Related Exchange" are used (in Section 1.20) in defining the term "Exchange Business Day," which, in turn, is used in determining whether a particular day is to be used as a Valuation Date on which the Index level is to be determined for purposes of calculating an Equity Amount that may be payable under a swap (in the sample transaction, the Initial Price for the first period and the Final Price for each period). For these purposes, even if a day would not qualify as a Business Day for other purposes of a transaction—such as for the purpose of determining whether the designated day is an Equity Payment Date—that day will nonetheless continue to qualify as a Valuation Date, and not need be adjusted, so long as the designated day is scheduled to be a full trading day on each Exchange and Related Exchange in respect of the Index component securities and options and futures on the Index. (Section 4.2 of the *1996 Equity Derivatives Definitions*.) *See supra* p. 626 regarding changes in market practice involving the treatment of a day as an Exchange Business Day even if an Exchange or Related Exchange is scheduled on that day to be open for only part of the day, as well as other changes relating to early closings.

Sample Equity Index Swap Confirmation

> Annotation 15. Suspensions of or limitations on trading in the relevant stocks or exchange-traded index derivatives on the identified Exchanges and Related Exchanges are relevant in determining whether a Market Disruption Event will be treated as having occurred on a Valuation Date. *See* Note 2 to Table 1 in the introductory note on credit, debt and equity derivatives, *supra* p. 614, on the postponements of valuations and other consequences that follow from the occurrence of a Market Disruption Event on a Valuation Date. Where an Index is concerned, the kind of suspension or limitation that triggers a Market Disruption Event is one that occurs "by reason of movements in price exceeding limits permitted by the relevant exchange or otherwise," if the suspension or limitation affects trading "on any Exchange in securities that comprise at least 20% of the level of the relevant Index" or trading on any Related Exchange in any option contract or future contract on the relevant Index. Although a party to an Index swap will, naturally, wish to identify as an Exchange each exchange or quotation system that is critical to its hedging positions, the parties may find it appropriate to identify only the principal exchanges and quotation systems for trading in the relevant stocks and futures or options, so that disruptions on other exchanges or quotation systems do not trigger valuation postponements and payments under their transaction. Proposed revisions to the *1999 ISDA Equity Derivatives Definitions* would, as discussed *supra* p. 626, modify in various ways the handling and definition of Market Disruption Events.

Equity Amounts:

> Annotation 16. In the ISDA format for this line of an equity swap confirmation, there are bracketed indications that the parties may wish to identify the relevant party (by including "payable by [Party A][Party B]"). The sample does not do so because, in the illustrated swap, the Equity Amount may be payable by either party, as discussed *supra* p. 730. If the Equity Amount is a positive number, reflecting a rise in the level of the Index between any two relevant measurement points, the Equity Amount will be payable by the Equity Amount Payer. If it is negative, reflecting a decline, the absolute value of the negative number will be payable by the other party. There are also transactions in which the parties swap equity exposures. That is, Party A agrees to be the Equity Amount Payer in respect of one stock, basket, index or index basket and Party B agrees to be the Equity Amount Payer in respect of another. In these cases, one set of relevant terms would be set out under "Equity Amounts payable by Party A" and the other under "Equity Amounts payable by Party B."

Equity Amount Payer: The Bank

> Annotation 17. The ISDA template for this part of a swap confirmation calls only for the identification of the Equity Amount Payer. Once the identity of that party is known, the provisions of the *1996 Equity Derivatives Definitions* relating to

equity swaps automatically operate to indicate the payment obligations of both the identified Equity Amount Payer and the "other party." *See supra* p. 730.

Equity Notional Amount: USD 50,000,000

Annotation 18. As illustrated, the *1996 Equity Derivatives Definitions* use a concept of Equity Notional Amount rather than the Notional Quantity of "relevant units" used in the Price Option mechanics of the *1991 ISDA Definitions* to document equity swaps. The Equity Notional Amount concept works better for equity-index derivatives, since identifiable units of composite equity indices do not exist.

Annotation 19. The *1996 Equity Derivatives Definitions* contemplate various cases in which the specified Equity Notional Amount will be adjusted. The following annotation describes one, which applies because the parties have specified that Equity Notional Reset is applicable to their transaction. The Equity Notional Amount is also adjusted if the parties specify (as they do below in this sample) that they are transacting on a Total Return basis with Re-investment of Dividends. *See* Annotation 45 to this sample confirmation, *infra* p. 750. Finally, in an equity swap relating to a single Share or a Basket of Shares, the Equity Notional Amount (as well as other terms) will be subject to adjustment in connection with Potential Adjustment Events, which include extraordinary dividends, subdivisions, consolidations or reclassifications of Shares, distributions of dividends in the form of Shares or other share capital or securities, rights, warrants or other assets, an Issuer's call in respect of Shares that are not fully paid or an Issuer's repurchase of Shares and other similar events that may have a diluting or concentrative effect on the theoretical value of the relevant Shares. *See* Table 5 in the introductory note on credit, debt and equity derivatives, *supra* p. 628. The Equity Notional Amount of a swap linked to an equity index is not subject to adjustment in connection with these Potential Adjustment Events, reflecting an assumption that adjustments to the index will adequately address events that may give rise to dilution or concentration. *But see* Annotation 10 to this sample confirmation, *supra* p. 739, on the way in which these ISDA definitions deal with modifications to an Index or the formula or method of calculating the Index "(other than a modification prescribed in that formula or method to maintain the Index in the event of changes in constituent stock and capitalization and other routine events)" if they are viewed by the Calculation Agent as material.

Equity Notional Reset: Applicable

Annotation 20. In the illustrated transaction, the parties have chosen to make Equity Notional Reset applicable, so the Equity Notional Amount declines or increases with the determination of Equity Amounts reflecting changes in the level of the S&P 500. *See supra* p. 734. In this way, the parties reflect their decision to have the swap simulate an initial direct equity investment in a portfolio of stocks that replicates the index's weighting scheme and that is held for the full term of the swap, without any additional investment or disinvestment as the index value rises or falls, except for reinvestment of dividends, which the parties have separately provided for below. *See* Annotation 45 to this sample confirmation, *infra* p. 750.

Annotation 21. If the parties had specified that Equity Notional Reset would not be applicable, the Equity Notional Amount would have remained fixed throughout the term of the transaction. This would be appropriate if the parties had intended a swap that would simulate a direct equity investment of a constant amount of money in a portfolio of stock designed to mimic the composition of the index, regardless of how the index performed from time to time over the life of the swap—that is, a direct investment in which the investor (1) sells stock on a Valuation Date if the level of the index on the Valuation Date is higher than it was on the preceding Valuation Date (or at the outset of the swap's term, in the case of the first Valuation Date), (2) makes an additional investment on a Valuation Date if the level of the index on the Valuation Date is lower and (3) does not reinvest dividends.

Annotation 22. Under Section 7.11(c) of the *1996 Equity Derivatives Definitions,* the Notional Amount used to calculate the LIBOR-based Floating Amounts payable on the illustrated swap's interest-rate leg will automatically reset in tandem with each adjustment of the Equity Notional Amount made to implement the Equity Notional Reset feature of the transaction (but not those made to implement dividend reinvestment).

Equity Payment Dates:	The third Currency Business Day after each Valuation Date

Annotation 23. These are the dates on which Equity Amounts are payable. *See supra* p. 730. By defining these payment dates by reference to days that will qualify as Currency Business Days, the parties have already taken weekends and holidays into account. Under Section 1.21 of the *1996 Equity Derivatives Definitions* a Currency Business Day will be "any day on which commercial banks are open for business (including dealings in foreign exchange and foreign currency deposits) in the principal financial center for the relevant currency"—which, in this transaction is the U.S. dollar. In identifying Equity Payment Dates the parties often introduce their own terminology (sometimes using a term such as Settlement Business Day) when they wish to avoid any possible ambiguity over which city should be treated as the principal financial center for a relevant currency, to introduce an appropriate rule relating to TARGET business days (*see infra* p. 1312) for equity swaps with payments denominated in euros, or to take into account, in addition to commercial bank business days, scheduled trading or workings days on a relevant exchange or clearance system.

Type of Return:	Total Return

Annotation 24. By specifying "Total Return," the parties have indicated that the equity leg of their swap will take into account both price appreciation or decline (rise and fall in the level of the S&P 500) and dividends on the stocks in the index. If they did not want dividends to figure in their swap at all, in a transaction using the conventions in the *1996 Equity Derivatives Definitions*, the parties would have chosen "Price Return." *See supra* p. 731 for discussion of these conventions. Some equity indices are automatically adjusted to reflect all dividends on the component stocks. Where that is the case, Price Return would be the appropriate choice. The level of the S&P 500, chosen as the Index in the illustrated swap, is not calculated taking ordinary cash dividends into account.

Multiplier: None

Annotation 25. If the parties wished to introduce an element of leverage in the equity leg of the swap, they could do so by specifying a Multiplier, which would have the effect of varying the Rate of Return and, thus, the Equity Amount for each Equity Payment Date.

Initial Price: The level of the Index at the Valuation Time on the Trade Date, as published by the Index sponsor

Annotation 26. To determine the Equity Amount for each Valuation Date during the Term of the illustrated transaction, the parties compare an Initial Price with a Final Price in relation to the Valuation Date. The Initial Price for the first Valuation Date is the one specified by the parties in the confirmation, or determined in the manner they specify. The Initial Price for each subsequent Valuation Date is the Final Price for the preceding Valuation Date. *See* Section 7.9 of the *1996 Equity Derivatives Definitions*. When the parties agree to Total Return transactions, which (as discussed below) involve Dividend Amounts calculated by reference to the dividends on the underlying equity or equities as well as price or value appreciation or decline, the date on which the Initial Price is determined is the beginning of the swap's first Dividend Period (under Section 7.12(b) of these ISDA definitions). Therefore, even if the parties state the Initial Price rather than a method for its calculation in their confirmation, they should consider specifying the date on which the Initial Price was determined.

Annotation 27. In the illustrated transaction, the parties have indicated that the Initial Price for the first Valuation Date will be the level of the S&P 500 at the Valuation Time on the Effective Date, which is also the Reset Date used for the first LIBOR setting on the transaction's interest-rate leg. Under ISDA terminology, the "Reset Date" is the day on which the new rate takes effect, not the day the new rate is set. Rather, as discussed *supra* p. 413, the rate is set on the second London Banking Day before the Reset Date. The subsequent LIBOR settings will take effect on the Equity Payment Dates for the equity leg, so that LIBOR in each case will be set on the second London Banking Day before the relevant Equity Payment Date.

Annotation 28. When the conventions in the underlying markets for the two sides of an equity swap are different, the parties should examine the importance to each of them of adhering to the underlying market conventions, rather than automatically taking readings of, say, two equity indices or an index and an interest rate, on the same day. Taking readings on different days for the two sides of the swap need not affect when payments are made, so mere differences in rate- or price-setting dates should not affect the parties' ability to have their Payment Dates match and their respective payments made on a net basis, if that is what they choose to do. *See* the specification of Company Payment Dates in this sample confirmation and the related annotations, *infra* p. 751.

Final Price:	The level of the Index at the Valuation Time on the relevant Valuation Date, as published by the Index sponsor

Annotation 29. Under Section 7.10 of the *1996 Equity Derivatives Definitions* the Final Price for each Valuation Date in a swap like the one illustrated will be the level of the Index at the Valuation Time on the relevant Valuation Date, determined as provided in the confirmation. However, rather than having the Equity Amount for each Valuation Date calculated on the basis of the Index level at a single time on a single day, as in this swap, the parties may choose to take an average of the closing Index levels on multiple days, say each Valuation Date and the preceding three, five or ten Exchange Business Days, or at several different times on a stated day, to reduce the possibility that the cash flows of the equity leg of the transaction might be affected by a price aberration on a single day or a Market Disruption Event during the period preceding only a single time. *See* Annotation 38 to this sample confirmation, *infra* p. 748, on the Averaging Date framework provided for in these ISDA definitions. *See also* Stephen R. Greene, *Multiple Valuation Dates and Multiple Valuation Times in OTC Equity Index Options*, transcript of paper prepared for the Equity Derivatives Workshop at ISDA's Conference at The Dorchester Hotel, London, on Mastering the 1992 ISDA Master Agreements (November 20, 1992).

Annotation 30. The ISDA definitions also provide an alternative valuation framework, referred to as Futures Price Valuation, under which the price return component of the relevant equity leg of a swap will automatically be the official settlement price of a specified exchange-traded derivatives contract. *See* Annotations 40 and 41 to this sample confirmation, *infra* p. 748.

Valuation Time:	11:00 a.m., New York City time

Annotation 31. *See* Annotation 12, *supra* p. 739, on the frequency with which the S&P 500 is calculated and disseminated. The frequency with which an index is calculated and the times at which there is customarily the greatest liquidity in trading in index futures and options are among the factors that the parties consider in choosing the Valuation Time. A common choice is the closing time on an Exchange specified by the parties. Section 7.2 of the *1991 ISDA Definitions*, which included definitions for six equity index price options commonly used in equity derivatives at the time (S&P 500, FT-SE 100, NIKKEI 225, TOPIX, DAX and CAC-40), defined the relevant index values as those existing at the close of business in the city that is home to the principal exchange for trading in the stocks that make up the indices (New York, London, Tokyo, Frankfurt and Paris). In the sample confirmation, the parties have chosen a Valuation Time that is relatively early in the day in New York but (depending on the time of the year) close to or at the end of the business day in London, where one of the hypothetical parties is located.

Annotation 32. Under the *1996 Equity Derivatives Definitions* (Section 4.3), unless the parties agree otherwise, they will look at market conditions during the half hour preceding the Valuation Time to determine whether the valuation scheduled for that day should be postponed because of a Market Disruption Event. If the transaction relates to an Index with component stocks traded on multiple exchanges, or an Index in respect of which futures or options are traded on multiple exchanges, the parties should consider whether the closing time on a single exchange is an appropriate choice. It would, for example, be possible to agree that Equity Amounts will be determined by reference to the Index level announced by the Index sponsor as the closing level for the relevant Valuation Date. The Index sponsor will only determine this closing level after the close of the principal trading session on all exchanges on which the component stocks are traded. The parties could also specify that, for purposes of provisions relating to Market Disruption Events, the parties will determine whether a day will be treated as a Valuation Date by reference to conditions existing at a specified time of day in a particular city on specified Exchanges and Related Exchanges scheduled to be open at the time for trading (or trading in their principal trading session) in respect of the relevant stocks or derivatives contracts. *See* Annotations 40 and 41 to this sample confirmation, *infra* p. 748, on the special valuation conventions that apply if the parties to an equity index transaction choose to make the transaction subject to "Futures Price Valuation."

Annotation 33. Section 1.15 of the *1996 Equity Derivatives Definitions* supplies fallback choices that will be applied in certain cases in connection with valuations if the parties are silent about the Valuation Time or a Relevant Price. For example, in an equity swap based on a single Share, the presumed choice if the parties are silent is the official price or, if there is no official price, the mid-market price per Share on the Exchange at the Valuation Time on the relevant Valuation Date or Averaging Date.

Annotation 34. Section 8.2 of the *1996 Equity Derivatives Definitions* supplies a rule relating to corrections of published or announced Index levels in Index Transactions and Index Basket Transactions. Under that rule, corrections published or announced within 30 days after their original publication or announcement by the person responsible for the publication or announcement will be taken into account, at the request of either party made within 30 days after publication of the correction, for purposes of calculating an appropriate adjustment payment. The payment is stated to be due not later than three Currency Business Days after the effectiveness of the notice requesting the adjustment payment, together with interest at the recipient's certified cost of funding the amount due from (and including) to (but excluding) the date the adjustment payment is made. If the parties wish to modify or override that rule on correction, they may do so in their master agreement or in the appropriate confirmation.

Valuation Dates:	January 18, April 18, July 18 and October 18 in each year, commencing with July 18, 2002 and ending with the Termination Date

Annotation 35. As used in the *1996 Equity Derivatives Definitions*, "Valuation Date" serves much the same purpose as did the term "Reset Date" for purposes of valuations in equity swaps documented under the *1991 ISDA Definitions*. *See supra* p. 403. As described in Annotation 29 to this sample confirmation, the Final Price for the first Equity Amount that might be payable under the illustrated swap will be set on the first Valuation Date and that Equity Amount will be calculated by comparing that Final Price with the Initial Price for the period beginning with the Trade Date. That Valuation Date's Final Price will also be the Initial Price for the next measurement period for the swap's equity leg, and the Final Price for that period will be determined on the next Valuation Date, and so on.

Annotation 36. The parties have not specified a rule to address a case in which the 18th of the relevant month falls on a weekend or a holiday, because Section 4.2 of the *1996 Equity Derivatives Definitions* automatically results in treating the following Exchange Business Day as the Valuation Date if a day identified as a Valuation Date is not an Exchange Business Day. (*See supra* p. 730 on the definition of "Exchange Business Day," which excludes scheduled trading days if the scheduled session is shorter than the normal full trading session on the relevant exchange or quotation system.) A similar rule (in Section 4.4(a) of those definitions) automatically applies to the specified Averaging Dates (*see* Annotation 38 to this sample confirmation) if those days turn out not to be Exchange Business Days.

Annotation 37. When the parties seek to achieve symmetry of the equity leg and the interest-rate leg of a swap and the swap provides that the payout on the equity leg will be calculated on the basis of a single day's stock price or index level, they sometimes specify that Valuation Dates for the equity leg will be a designated Exchange Business Day before the date that marks the end of the relevant Calculation Period on the interest-rate leg. So, for example, in a swap with a single period, the Final Price used in determining the Equity Amount could be set on a Valuation Date defined as the Exchange Business Day before the Termination Date.

Averaging Dates: Inapplicable

> Annotation 38. The parties to equity swaps sometimes structure their transactions so that each Equity Amount is calculated by reference to multiple dates, so as to avoid payouts that are affected by aberrations in a single day's stock price or index level. If the parties had adopted that approach, under the *1996 Equity Derivatives Definitions*, they would have identified here the days to be treated as Averaging Dates in respect of each Valuation Date. For example, the parties could have specified as the Averaging Dates "each Valuation Date and the immediately preceding three Exchange Business Days." Under Section 4.4(c) of the definitions, the Final Price for each Valuation Date would then automatically be the arithmetic mean of the Relevant Prices (that is, levels) of the Index on those Averaging Dates.
>
> Annotation 39. As indicated in the template in Exhibit II-G to these ISDA definitions, when parties choose this averaging approach, they also specify one of three choices for dealing with Market Disruption Events that occur on an Averaging Date. The choices are "Omission," "Postponement" and "Modified Postponement." As the name suggests, Omission simply means that the affected index determination is dropped in computing the average. If all the Averaging Dates are affected, the index level is calculated as if the final Averaging Date were the Valuation Date. If Postponement is specified, the index level is determined for each Averaging Date as if it were a Valuation Date, which could result in a single day's reading being counted more than once. Modified Postponement contains mechanics for eliminating double-counting.

Futures Price Valuation: Not applicable

Exchange-traded Contract: Not applicable

> Annotation 40. As indicated above, the *1996 Equity Derivatives Definitions* provide (in Section 4.5) an alternative method—Futures Price Valuation—for valuing an Index, under which the Equity Amount for each Equity Payment Date is calculated by reference to the Official Settlement Price of an exchange-traded futures contract or option on the Index identified by the parties as the Exchange-traded Contract. This Official Settlement Price is defined (in Section 4.5(b)(ii)) as the "official settlement price (however described under the rules of the relevant exchange or its clearing house) on maturity of any of the relevant Exchange-traded Contracts published by the exchange or its clearing house." The alternative automatically treats as a Valuation Date each day on which the Official Settlement Price for the Exchange-traded Contract is published, irrespective of whether there is a Market Disruption Event on that day, unless trading in the relevant contract never commences or ceases permanently.
>
> Annotation 41. Choice of this alternative will affect certain other features of the transaction. For example, if the terms of the Exchange-traded Contract are

changed by the relevant exchange, the Calculation Agent is required, if necessary, to adjust the Equity Notional Amount, the Initial Price and/or any other variable relevant to a swap's settlement terms "to preserve for each party the economic equivalent of any payment or payments (assuming satisfaction of each applicable condition precedent) by the parties in respect of the Transaction that would have been required after the date of such change" but is also required to ignore other changes to the method of calculation of the Official Settlement Price (Sections 4.5(e) & 4.5(f) of the *1996 Equity Derivatives Definitions*). Corrections to the Official Settlement Price are (under Section 4.5(h)) taken into account within a framework like that described in Annotation 34 to this sample confirmation for other kinds of reported price or value corrections.

Dividend Payment Dates: For each Dividend Period, the Equity Payment Date relating to the Valuation Date on which the Dividend Period ends

Annotation 42. Under Section 7.12(b) of the *1996 Equity Derivatives Definitions*, the Equity Payment Dates would automatically have been the Dividend Payment Dates even if the parties had remained silent on the subject. If the parties had agreed that Dividend Amounts (reflecting dividends on the component stocks in the Index) would be payable, they would be payable by the Equity Amount Payer to the other party on the Dividend Payment Dates. The parties have, instead, agreed that Dividend Amounts will be treated as if reinvested on Valuation Dates, as discussed in Annotation 45 to this sample confirmation.

Annotation 43. The Dividend Payment Dates in an equity swap documented under these ISDA definitions correspond to Dividend Periods that run from one Valuation Date to the next, except for the first Dividend Period, which begins on the date the Initial Price is determined or, if that date is not specified, the Trade Date of the swap. *See* Annotation 42 to this sample confirmation. The Valuation Date at the end of each Dividend Period is included in the calculation of the Dividend Amount relating to that period. If the parties had transacted on the basis of Price Return, dividends on the underlying stock would not have figured in their swap in any way so they would not have specified Dividend Payment Dates here or any other matter relating to dividends below.

Dividend Amount: For each Dividend Payment Date, an amount equal to all cash dividends paid in respect of equities comprising the Index during the relevant Dividend Period

Annotation 44. *See supra* p. 731 on the calculation of Dividend Amounts. When the parties enter into equity swaps that provide for payments calculated by reference to dividends on the underlying equity or equities (or for price return payments calculated assuming the reinvestment of the dividends) they should consult with counsel about issues that may arise under applicable tax laws.

    Re-investment of Dividends: Applicable

> Annotation 45. By making this choice, the parties have agreed that Dividend Amounts reflecting dividends on the stocks comprising the Index will not be paid but will automatically be added to the Equity Notional Amount. For example, if there has been a Dividend Amount of $750,000 for the Dividend Period ending on the first Valuation Date, the Equity Notional Amount used to calculate any Equity Amount payable on the following Equity Payment Date (reflecting a rise or fall in the level of the Index as measured at the related Valuation Date) will be $750,000 higher than the initial Equity Notional Amount agreed by the parties. In a case in which the parties select the Total Return provisions of the *1996 Equity Derivatives Definitions* and specify that Re-investment of Dividends is inapplicable, or remain silent on the subject, the Equity Amount Payer would be required to pay Dividend Amounts to the other party. *See supra* p. 731.
>
> Annotation 46. When the parties choose to make Re-investment of Dividends applicable to their swaps, the increases to the Equity Notional Amount described in the preceding annotation will be made even though an actual reinvestment of dividend income in a direct equity investment in the underlying stock might not be possible at the time. On the calculation of the S&P 500, its treatment of dividends and tracking error resulting from the investor's inability to reinvest dividends at the time the Index treats them as reinvested, *see* Standard & Poor's, *S&P 500 2001 Directory* 15–17 & 56.

    Floating Amounts payable by the Company:

> Annotation 47. The Company Floating Amount for each Calculation Period represents a payment to be made by the Company in the transaction, irrespective of whether an Equity Amount is payable by or to it under the swap's equity leg. If an Equity Amount is payable to it and the payment dates match (*see* Annotation 48 to this sample confirmation), only the net of the two amounts would be payable under the payment netting rule in Section 2(c) of an ISDA-based master agreement. *See infra* p. 807. Under Section 7.1(a)(ii) of the *1996 Equity Derivatives Definitions*, the Company will also be required to make payments to the Bank whenever the Final Price of the S&P 500 for a Valuation Date is lower than the Initial Price, since the transaction involves the Company's taking on this down-side risk, as if it held a basket of stocks with the same composition as the index. *See supra* p. 730.

    Floating Amount Payer: The Company

Notional Amount: For each Calculation Period, the amount that constitutes the Equity Notional Amount for the Valuation Date scheduled to fall on the last day of that Calculation Period

> Annotation 48. As indicated in Annotation 20 to this sample confirmation, *supra* p. 742, when the parties elect Equity Notional Reset, the *1996 Equity Derivatives Definitions* automatically provide (in Section 7.11(c)) for adjustments to the Notional Amount used in the interest-rate leg, so that it changes in tandem with the Equity Notional Amount as each successive Equity Amount payable in respect of price or value appreciation or decline results in an increase or decrease of the Equity Notional Amount for the following Equity Payment Date. The parties here have stated a broader rule, so that the Notional Amount for the swap's interest-rate leg will also adjust on account of Dividend Amounts added to the Equity Notional Amount, given the parties' election of Re-investment of Dividends.

Company Payment Dates: January 18, April 18, July 18 and October 18 in each year, commencing with July 18, 2002 and ending with the Termination Date, subject to the Modified Following Business Day Convention, and subject to the following.

If the Company Payment Date for a Calculation Period does not coincide with the Equity Payment Date for that Calculation Period (as a result of application of the Business Day Convention specified above, because of differences between Business Days and Exchange Business Days or because of postponement of the Valuation Date on which that Calculation Period is scheduled to end), the Floating Amount for the Calculation Period will not be due until that Equity Payment Date.

The deferral will not affect the calculation of the Floating Amount, but that amount will be payable with interest thereon (a) accruing for each day beginning on (and including) the last day of the Calculation Period and ending on (but excluding) the Equity Payment Date, at the Relevant Rate for that day, (b) calculated on an

Actual/360 basis (treating the period as if it were a Calculation Period) and (c) compounded daily.

The Relevant Rate for each day will be determined on the basis of the overnight offered rates for deposits in U.S. dollars for value on that day that appear on the Reuters Screen ISDA Page as of 11:00 a.m., London time, or, if that day is not a Business Day, the preceding Business Day (or, if such rate does not appear there, the overnight LIBOR rate for such day determined by the Calculation Agent in a commercially reasonable manner).

Annotation 49. *See* Annotation 8 to the sample rate swap confirmation, *supra* p. 430, on Business Day Conventions. The Modified Following Business Day Convention was chosen for this swap because the Company's Floating Amounts are computed on the basis of LIBOR and it is the standard convention for dealing with holidays in the London interbank market. *See supra* p. 408. For the same reason, both London and New York are taken into account in determining whether each Company Payment Date will be treated as a Business Day. London is not, however, taken into account for purposes of determining whether a scheduled Equity Payment Date will be postponed. Only Currency Business Days are considered for that purpose under the *1996 Equity Derivatives Definitions*, as discussed in Annotation 23 to this sample confirmation, *supra* p. 743. As a result, there can be mismatches between the payment dates for the equity leg and the interest-rate leg of the swap. In addition, the Equity Payment Dates will always be a stated number of Currency Business Days after the related Valuation Date, and scheduled Valuation Dates can be postponed if they do not fall on Exchange Business Days and if Market Disruption Events occur. In the second case, given a continuing disruption, the postponement could extend for up to five Exchange Business Days under Section 4.2 of the definitions. The sample provision addresses these mismatches.

Annotation 50. The illustrated approach to these potential mismatch problems differs in one respect from both of the alternatives suggested in Exhibit II-G to the *1996 Equity Derivatives Definitions*. Each of the alternatives offered by the ISDA template applies only if a Payment Date for the interest-rate leg will occur before the related Equity Payment Date. That is, those approaches do not take into account the possibility that a holiday in London (or in another city identified by the parties as relevant to the transaction's interest-rate leg) could cause the Payment Date for the interest-rate leg to fall after the related Equity Payment Date. Except for that difference, one of the two ISDA approaches is substantively the same as that offered in the sample provision above, although the drafting is different. The other approach involves extending the Payment Date for the interest-rate leg so that it coincides with a postponed Equity Payment Date. Under that approach, LIBOR for the ex-

> tended Calculation Period would continue to be the same during the deferral, LIBOR for the next Calculation Period would not be set until the second London banking day before the first day of the new Calculation Period, and that new period would be shorter than it otherwise would have been. This second approach can be unattractive for various reasons. For example, if an Equity Payment Date is postponed because of a market disruption, the parties will not necessarily know when the LIBOR reset should occur, because they may not be able to tell how long the market disruption will continue. In addition, the party obligated to make the LIBOR-based payments could lose (or gain) from a mismatch between its swap obligation and a related hedge, for which the LIBOR reset could occur as normally scheduled.

Floating Rate Option:	USD-LIBOR-LIBO
Designated Maturity:	3 months
Spread:	None
Floating Rate for initial Calculation Period:	2.50% per annum
Floating Rate Day Count Fraction:	Actual/360
Reset Dates:	First day of each Calculation Period

> Annotation 51. As noted earlier, the first day of each Calculation Period will correspond to an Equity Payment Date, barring (1) a postponement of an Equity Payment Date and (2) a mismatch produced because Business Days for purposes of the interest-rate leg of the swap are determined by reference to holidays in a city that is not relevant in the determination of Exchange Business Days—the days taken into account for purposes of adjustments to the scheduled Equity Payment Dates.

Business Days:	London and New York City
Compounding:	Inapplicable

3. Calculation Agent: The Calculation Agent will be the Bank or, if an Event of Default with respect to the Bank is continuing or an Early Termination Date has been designated in connection with such an Event of Default, the Company or the agent designated by it for the purpose. The Calculation Agent will make all calculations and determinations to be made by it in connection with the Transaction in good faith and in a commercially reasonable manner, after consultation with the parties.

Annotation 52. The sample provision includes language aimed at addressing the fact that the *1996 Equity Derivatives Definitions* do not include a general rule on how a Calculation Agent will make determinations, although there are rules specifically applicable to cases involving Potential Adjustment Events and similar circumstances. The sample provision also deals at least partially with a case in which a Calculation Agent might not make a necessary determination in a timely manner because of financial or other difficulties, if those difficulties also involved the occurrence of an Event of Default with respect to the Calculation Agent. An alternative is to deal more fully with a Calculation Agent's failure to make a determination or calculation and with disagreements over a calculation or determination that it has made. The parties could, for example, provide as follows:

"If the Calculation Agent fails to make a required determination in a timely manner, or if the other party (the 'Disputing Party') disputes a calculation or determination made by the Calculation Agent, it may give the Calculation Agent notice to that effect, specifying the nature of the dispute. If, 24 hours after notice of the dispute is effective, the parties have neither resolved the dispute to their mutual satisfaction nor agreed on an independent third party to resolve the dispute, each of them will, within 36 hours after that notice of the dispute is effective, appoint an independent third party to participate in a dispute resolution panel, and these two panelists will be instructed by the parties to appoint a third panelist, to resolve the dispute as promptly as possible by way of majority vote and, during their deliberations on the disputed matter, to have no communications with either party to the Transaction unless the other party and each of the other members of the panel are involved. The decision of the single third party selected jointly by the parties, or of a majority vote of the panelists, will be binding on the parties in the absence of manifest error. Each of the parties will pay one half of the aggregate charges, costs and expenses of the single third party or panel members."

4. Account Details

Account for Payments to the Bank:

    Big Bank, N.A., New York, N.Y., ABA No. 000, CHIPS No. 000, Attention: Swaps Division

Account for Payments to the Company:

    Account No. 00000 with Big Bank, N.A., New York, N.Y.

5. Offices. The Office of the Bank for the Transaction is its head office in New York. The Office of the Company for the Transaction is its office at the address specified for notices to it in the Schedule to the Agreement.

Please confirm that the foregoing correctly sets forth the terms of our agreement by executing a copy of this Confirmation and sending it to us, or by sending to us a substantially similar document which sets forth the material terms of the Transaction to which this Confirmation relates and indicates the Company's agreement to those terms.

> Annotation 53. The closing language, taken from Exhibit I to the *1996 Equity Derivatives Definitions*, omits the following phrase found in ISDA's other sets of definitions (except the *1998 FX and Currency Option Definitions*, as to which, *see* Annotation 10 to the sample FX forward confirmation, *supra* p. 523): "If you believe the foregoing does not correctly reflect the terms of our agreement, please give us notice as soon as possible of what you believe to be the necessary corrections." *See* the text preceding Annotation 30 to the sample rate swap confirmation, *supra* p. 437.

Yours sincerely,

BIG BANK, N.A.

By: _____
    Name:
    Title: Vice President

Confirmed as of the date first
above written on   , 20 :

ENGLISH COMPANY PLC

By: _____
    Name:
    Title:

WEATHER DERIVATIVES

In the OTC market, weather derivatives take forms very similar to those of interest rate and commodity swaps, caps, floors, collars and options.[1726] In weather derivatives, one or both of the parties will be required to make a payment or payments calculated by reference to weather phenomena, such as temperature or precipitation levels, storms, and even wind speed and sea wave size.[1727] The most common types are used for the management and trading of risks associated with the number of "heating degree days" ("HDDs") in the winter and "cooling degree days" ("CDDs") in the summer—standard proxies for energy demand for the heating and cooling of buildings.[1728]

The use of derivatives to address risks associated with weather phenomena began in the late 1990s.[1729] The insurance industry has written policies designed to protect against loss from adverse weather conditions for far longer. Its focus, however, has traditionally been on catastrophic weather events. Whereas "reinsurers typically write protection for events over two or three standard deviations from the mean – with a less than 1% chance of the insured loss occurring,"[1730] dealers in weather derivatives, in contrast, have tended to "aim to smooth out small and frequent peaks and troughs"[1731] for their customers. Until recently, another distinguishing feature has been that, while insurers and reinsurers have traditionally managed the risk of loss on weather insurance policies through diversification of the risks they have underwritten or reinsured, weather derivatives pro-

---

[1726] *See* Michael Corbally & Phuoc Dang, *Risk Products*, in WEATHER DERIVATIVES 105.

[1727] David Turner, *At last – an excuse to talk about the weather*, EURO, May 1999, at 20. *See generally* INSURANCE AND WEATHER DERIVATIVES; Erik Banks, *Weather Fundamentals*, in WEATHER DERIVATIVES 14; Lynda Clemmons & David Radulski, *The Economics of Weather*, in WEATHER RISK MANAGEMENT 44. On legal and documentation issues, *see* Adele Raspé, Legal and Regulatory Issues, in WEATHER DERIVATIVES 224.

[1728] Some transactions relate to "energy degree days" ("EDDs"), a term used for the aggregate of the number of HDDs and CDDs in a period. *See Introduction to Weather Risk Management*, paper available from http://www.ektweather.com. For glossaries of terms used in weather derivatives, *see id.* at 4, WEATHER DERIVATIVES 351; http://www.weatherderivs.com/Glossary.htm.

[1729] "The first weather derivative, a temperature-related power swap between Enron and Florida Power and Light, was transacted in August 1996." Lynda Clemmons, Vincent Kaminski & Joseph H. Hrgovcic, *Weather Derivatives: Hedging Mother Nature*, in INSURANCE AND WEATHER DERIVATIVES 179. Since then, market professionals who work in the area have formed the Weather Risk Management Association. The URL of the association's Web site is www.wmra.com. *See also Banks Enter Weather Derivatives Market*, DERIVATIVES WEEK, January 7, 2002, at 7 ("Investment banks entering the weather derivatives market gave the nascent industry a seal of approval just before Enron, one of its pioneers, filed for bankruptcy"); *Bank One To Enter U.S. Weather Derivatives Mart*, DERIVATIVES WEEK, January 28, 2002, at 2. On the origins of the market for weather derivatives, *see* Lynda Clemmons, *Introduction to Weather Risk Management*, in WEATHER DERIVATIVES 3. On various categories of market professionals, *see* Michael Corbally & Phuoc Dang, *Providers*, in WEATHER DERIVATIVES 55.

[1730] Mark Nicholls, *Winter Warms Weather Traders*, ENVIRONMENTAL FINANCE, Oct. 1999, at 1, citing Frank Caifa, associate director, new markets, at Swiss Re in New York.

[1731] *Id.* at 2.

fessionals have sought to manage the exposure of the transactions they execute with hedging techniques like those used by financial intermediaries in other derivatives businesses.[1732]

Convergence of the weather insurance and weather derivatives markets is, however, manifesting itself in various ways, including the availability in the two markets of products designed to manage the same kinds of risks[1733] and the emergence of market professionals that may offer both weather insurance and weather derivatives and use weather derivatives to hedge weather insurance exposure and vice versa.[1734] The relative ease with which derivatives and insurance products may be transformed into each other and the imbalance in supply and demand that has to date been an obstacle to the growth of the weather derivatives market[1735] have contributed to this convergence. In at least one fundamental way, however, the approach of insurers will remain different from that of de-

---

[1732] At least some weather derivatives exposure may be managed through positions in exchange-traded futures and options. *See infra* note 1744 regarding degree-day futures and options. Like some providers of OTC credit derivatives, major providers of weather derivatives are also reported to be hedging substantial portfolios of weather derivatives through offerings of structured obligations to institutional investors in the capital markets. *See* Victor Kremer, *Koch Gains on Enron in Weather-Backed Bond Race*, DERIVATIVES WEEK, Oct. 25, 1999, at 1, describing a securitization transaction in which investors were offered obligations of a special purpose vehicle with the understanding that the return on those obligations would be reduced (within specified limits) to reflect payoffs that the sponsor is required to make on the derivatives in the portfolio above certain levels. The proceeds of sale of these SPV obligations are typically used to make investments (in U.S. government or government-insured obligations and highly rated commercial paper and other obligations) that secure the SPV's obligations. The proceeds of sale may also be used in part to acquire other credit enhancements.

[1733] *See* Erik Banks & Jeff Bortniker, *Product and Market Convergence, in* WEATHER DERIVATIVES 150. *See also* Liz Bossley, *Exposed to the Weather?*, CORPORATE FINANCE, June 1999, at 42 ("[T]here is little to distinguish the American Insurance Group's Snow, Temperature or Rain Management (Storm) product from those of derivatives providers such as Enron or Koch"); and Paul Karis, *Come Rain or Shine*, CORPORATE INSURANCE & RISK, May 1999, at 44 ("Brockbank has a special weather product, Weather Stabilisation Insurance, which responds to temperature changes which affect revenue"). Insurers are reported to be using weather derivatives to manage some of their claims exposure. Weather derivatives with payoffs linked to rainfall levels, for example, may be used to supplement funding for flooding claims. *See* the product descriptions at http://www.wrma.org/who.html. *See also SG Creates Weather Derivatives, Cat Bond Fund*, DERIVATIVES WEEK, Apr. 17, 2000, at 3: "The fund was set up on behalf of an unnamed European insurance group, which wished to diversify its usual insurance exposure." For discussions of "Cat" or "catastrophe" bonds, *see* the following articles in INSURANCE AND WEATHER DERIVATIVES: Gail Belonsky, David Laster & David Durbin, *Insurance-Linked Securities*, at 155; Michael S. Canter, Joseph B. Cole & Richard L. Sandor, *Insurance Derivatives: A New Asset Class for the Capital Markets and a New Hedging Tool for the Insurance Industry*, at 107; R. McFall Lamm Jr, *The Catastrophe Reinsurance Market*, at 71, 80; and Robert H. Litzenberger, David R. Beaglehole & Craig E. Reynolds, *Assessing Catastrophe Reinsurance-Linked Securities as a New Asset Class*, at 121.

[1734] *See* Mark Nicholls, *Element Re hooks up with XL*, ENVIRONMENTAL FINANCE 4 (Oct. 2000).

[1735] "The growth of weather derivatives markets ... [has] been hobbled by the pattern of demand for weather protection. Most hedgers are involved in the sale or distribution of energy products. They tend to be exposed to the risk of a mild winter, or cool summer, when demand for energy drops. Weather dealers are keen to encourage end-users with opposite exposures to enter the market. This would allow dealers to offset their positions, and thus offer cheaper hedges to their clients." Mark Nicholls, *Energy consumers eye weather hedges*, ENVIRONMENTAL FINANCE, Oct. 2000, at 7, discussing efforts to bring together as participants in "aggregated weather contracts" energy consumers whose individual needs are insufficient to make weather derivatives economic as hedges.

rivatives providers: "[T]he purchaser must demonstrate a loss with an insurance claim; but pay-out on a derivative is automatic if weather data during the period being covered exceeds set boundaries."[1736] One commentator has noted that "a benefit of using a derivative rather than an insurance contract is the ability to trade out if the market moves and the profit outweighs the remaining risk."[1737]

The main classes of end-users in reported weather derivatives have been electric utilities,[1738] electricity distributors and marketers and large users of oil and gas products and agricultural commodities,[1739] but the product has theoretical applications for virtually any business that can be adversely affected by weather conditions that are abnormal or extreme. Commonly cited examples include the following:[1740]

- producers and sellers of seasonal foods and beverages, such as soft drinks and ice cream, and operators of theme parks, whose sales revenues may be adversely affected by abnormally cool weather during the summer;

[1736]*Now you can buy the weather you want*, INSURANCE DAY, Sept. 1999, at 6, 7. This fundamental difference is generally cited to distinguish other kinds of derivatives (such as credit derivatives) from insurance products that afford similar protections. It is referred to as follows in an informal opinion issued on February 15, 2000, by the Office of General Counsel of the Insurance Department of the State of New York (*available at* www.ins.state.ny.us) answering the question "Do weather derivatives constitute insurance under the New York Insurance Law?":

> Weather derivatives do not constitute insurance contracts under Section 1101(a) of the New York Insurance Law because the terms of the instrument do not provide that, in addition to or as part of the triggering event, payment to the purchaser is dependent upon that party suffering a loss. Under such instruments, the issuer is obligated to pay the purchaser whether or not that purchaser suffers a loss. Neither the amount of the payment nor the trigger itself in the weather derivative bears a relationship to the purchaser's loss. Absent such obligations, the instrument is not an insurance contract. However, it should be noted that there may be unique circumstances, not mentioned here, where the character of the specific financial instrument/and or the interest and obligations of the parties are such that the transaction would be an insurance contract.

[1737]Claire Smith, *Weather Derivatives: An enormous potential*, www.ft.com (July 15, 2000) 2.

[1738]*See* Nicholls, *supra* note 1730, at 1. The first two reported weather derivatives transactions in Europe involved Scottish Power, which "bought Europe's first weather swap to cover this [the 1999–2000] winter." Paul Karis, *supra* note 1733, at 44. *German Utility Enters Precipitation Swap,* DERIVATIVES WEEK, May 28, 2001, at 4, refers to an electric utility's use of a swap to hedge against a decline in revenue during the summer months if precipitation levels proved high, a risk because many of the utility's customers are farmers who use electric power for irrigation during periods of low rainfall. *See also Japanese Utilities Expected to Enter Weather Mart,* DERIVATIVES WEEK, Mar. 18, 2002, at 2.

[1739]On the use of growing degree days (GDDs) in the agricultural sector, *see* Michael Corbally & Phuoc Dang, *Underlying Markets and Indexes*, in WEATHER DERIVATIVES 87. For discussion of the correlation between GDDs and CDDs in some parts of the United States and the potential use of weather derivatives to hedge agricultural commodity price risk, *see* Geoffrey Considine, *Introduction to Weather Derivatives* 2, 7, www.cme.com/weather; *Introduction to Weather Risk Management, supra* note 1728, at 1.

[1740]*See generally* Martin Malinow, *End-users*, in WEATHER DERIVATIVES 66 & *Weather Risk Case Studies*, in WEATHER DERIVATIVES 291. *See also* case studies *available at* http://www.wrma.org/who.html and examples *available at* http://www.weatherderivs.com/WDExamples.htm.

- construction and offshore drilling companies and film producers, whose production costs may rise as a result of days of work lost to inclement weather;

- operators of winter or summer sports facilities, whose operating revenues may be adversely affected by levels of snow or rainfall as well as unseasonable temperatures; and

- manufacturers of seasonal clothing and sports equipment, whose sales revenues can be affected in a similar way.

In addition, manufacturers, retailers and others are reported to have entered into weather derivatives to fund sales promotions to customers.[1741]

Weather derivatives using HDDs and CDDs are, as noted, generally used to hedge business risks closely related to the volume of energy used in heating and cooling. The number of HDDs during a given winter period at a particular location reflects, in an approximate way, the volume of energy to be consumed in the heating of buildings at that location. In the U.S. market, the convention is generally to count one HDD for each degree by which the average temperature on a day is below 65°F.[1742] Similarly, transactions relating to summer temperatures are structured in terms of CDDs, as the number of CDDs during a summer period loosely reflects the volume of energy used in cooling. There is one CDD for each degree by which the average temperature on each day is above 65°F.[1743]

In a loose sense, the HDD convention assumes that consumers at a given location will have their heating thermostats switched off when the temperature is above 65°F and switched on when the temperature is below 65°F. Therefore:

- if the average temperature is 65°F or higher at the location on a given day, there would be zero HDDs for the day, since the convention is that HDDs can never be negative; and

- if the average temperature is below 65°F at the location for the day, there would be one HDD for each degree below 65°F (so, for example, there would be 5 HDDs if the average temperature for the day were 60°F).

Conversely, the CDD convention builds in an assumption that consumers at a given location will tend to have their cooling thermostats switched off when the temperature is 65°F or below but tend to switch them on when the temperature goes above 65°F. Therefore:

[1741]Bombardier, a manufacturer of snowmobiles, is reported to have offered customers a cash rebate, to be paid if snowfall in the customer's area in the next winter was 50% or more below average. Bossley, *supra* note 1733, at 42; Clemmons, *supra* note 1729, at 179.

[1742]"Degree days are a popular proxy for energy use because they closely track the extent to which consumers use their heating systems or air conditioners. Studies have shown that the correlation between gas and power use and heating degree days can be as high as 97%." Clemmons, *supra* note 1729, at 181.

[1743]In Europe, the baseline is generally 18°C. *See* Lynda Clemmons & Nick Mooney, *How weather hedging can keep you cool*, THE TREASURER, Mar. 1999, at 29.

- if the average temperature is 65°F or lower at the location on a given day, there would be zero CDDs for the day, since the convention is that CDDs can never be negative; and

- if the average temperature is above 65°F at the location for the day, there would be one CDD for each degree above 65°F (so, for example, there would be 5 CDDs if the average temperature for the day were 70°F).[1744]

The sum of daily HDDs over all or an agreed part of the winter season is seen as a proxy for energy demand for heating, and the sum of the daily CDDs over all or a part of the summer season is seen as a proxy for energy demand for cooling.[1745] In the U.S. OTC market, October through March is the traditional HDD season, and May through August is the period to be covered in whole or in part by CDD derivatives.[1746]

Temperature-related derivatives are also tailored to address business risks that are not directly associated with heating or cooling. In such transactions, the baseline, often referred to as the "average temperature degree day"("ATDD") or "variable degree day" ("VDD") strike level, may be set so that variances will reflect extremes in weather phenomena at the chosen location, for example, at 32°F for cold winter protection or 80°F for hot summer protection. In these cases, the derivative's payout in respect of a period will be calculated by reference to the difference between the actual average daily temperatures during the period in the specified location and the agreed ATDD strike level.

The first of the following sample confirmations illustrates a warm winter swap. This kind of transaction might, for example, be used by a heating oil producer or distributor if it were concerned about the effects of unusually warm winter weather on its sales volumes for the season. Under the sample confirmation, the hypothetical distributor has agreed with the counterparty on a strike level of HDDs, a dollar amount per HDD and a payout limit (the "Maximum Amount"). The counterparty has agreed to make a payment to the distributor if the number of HDDs during the period covered by the transaction (its "Term") falls below the agreed HDD strike level (which will occur if average daily winter temperatures are higher than the average reflected in the strike level, in which case the

---

[1744] Standardized HDD and CDD futures and options covering selected locations trade on the Chicago Mercantile Exchange. At any time HDD and CDD futures and options are listed for 12 consecutive contract months for each location. *See Weather Futures & Options*, www.cme.com/weather, which includes as an appendix an example of the use of the HDD futures contract by an electric utility to hedge risks of changes in winter weather. *Id.* at 7. "[A]t this point contracts exist for eight cities in the U.S.: Atlanta, Chicago, Cincinnati, Dallas, New York, Philadelphia, Portland and Tucson." Hélyette Geman, *The Bermuda Triangle: Weather, Electricity and Insurance Derivatives, in* INSURANCE AND WEATHER DERIVATIVES 197, 198.

[1745] As alternatives to transactions structured in terms of the sum of HDDs or CDDs in a period (sometimes referred to as a "cumulative" or "cum" structure), transactions can relate to average, minimum or maximum levels. *See* Introduction to Weather Derivatives, supra note 1728, at 2. *See* also H. Joseph Hrgovèiæ & Claudio Ribeiro, Power Demand Swaps, 2 Derivatives Use, Trading & Reg. 179 (2001), on the concept of management of weather risk as it translates to risk associated with power demand through derivatives with terms based on a volumetric index of average on-peak hourly demand for a power region, rather than degree days.

[1746] *Id.* at 4.

distributor's sales volume will tend to be less than expected), in return for which the distributor has promised to make a payment to the counterparty if the number of HDDs during the period is greater than the agreed strike level. As is usual in these transactions, the payment amount is calculated at the agreed dollar amount per HDD (that is, per degree Fahrenheit above or below the strike level on each day in the covered period), and the possible payout in either direction is subject to the agreed limit.[1747] Subject to that limit, the actual payment will be calculated by multiplying the agreed amount per HDD by any difference between the actual number of HDDs during the period and the agreed strike level of HDDs. Neither party pays the other a premium; the "cost" of the swap to the distributor is its contingent obligation to make payments under the transaction.

In setting the strike level and the agreed dollar amount per HDD, an end-user like the hypothetical distributor in the sample swap will typically consider its target minimum revenues for the winter months covered by the transaction in terms of sales volumes and projected sales prices.[1748] The swap will not affect its rights or obligations under its contracts with purchasers of heating oil but, if volumes decline because the winter is unusually warm, it will know that, so long as the counterparty performs its obligations under the swap, the payments received under the swap will supplement its sales revenues, enabling it to meet debt service and profit objectives (assuming, of course, that its projections of such factors as sales prices and customer loyalty are correct). If, however, average daily temperatures during the swap's term fall below those implied in the strike HDD level, the distributor will itself have to make payments, and that is its cost of managing the HDD risk. The terms of the swap, including in particular the number of HDDs set as the agreed strike, will reflect numerous factors, such as the term of the transaction, the availability of reliable sources of weather data for the relevant location[1749] and supply and demand levels in the market.[1750]

[1747] Some attribute the prevalence of such limits to the newness of the market and the related uncertainties: "Finally, given the immaturity of the market and the difficulty of arriving at a reasonable valuation methodology, it is a feature of almost all OTC instruments that they have dollar payout caps." Sailesh Ramamurtie, *Weather Derivatives and Hedging Weather Risks*, in INSURANCE AND WEATHER DERIVATIVES 174, 176.

[1748] The typical degree-day derivative would not directly address the distributor's price risk, as would a commodity price swap. *See* the introduction to weather risk products at http://www.ektweather.com/html/intro.html: ("The combination of a weather contract and a commodity price risk contract should improve the overall performance of a corporation's risk management program"). Commodity price derivatives are discussed *supra* p. 543. Degree-day derivatives may, however, be useful in some contexts in the management of agricultural commodity price risk. *See Introduction to Weather Risk Management*, *supra* note 1728, at 1; Considine, *supra* note 1739, at 2, 7.

[1749] The importance of reliable and secure sources of data is discussed further *infra* p. 762. For an interesting discussion of the use of historical data in weather derivatives pricing and of the differing costs of purchasing a weather derivative covering, say, the winter, on one hand, and a strip of derivatives for each of the months in the winter, on the other, *see* Considine, *supra* note 1739, at 3–6. On weather derivatives data and pricing generally, *see* Robert Henderson, *Pricing Weather Risk*, in WEATHER DERIVATIVES 167; Robert Henderson, Yu Li & Niraj Sinha, Data, in WEATHER DERIVATIVES 200.

[1750] On factors that affect weather derivatives pricing in some cases in ways that distinguish these transactions from other kinds of financial derivatives, *see* Mark Garman, Carlos Blanco, & Robert Erickson, *And Now the Weather . . .* , Part III of *An Introduction to Weather Derivatives*, DERIVATIVES WEEK, Nov. 29, 1999, at 6. Among other things, pricing is a function of liquidity in the market. Toward the end of 1999, potential end-users of weather derivatives were reported to be holding back from using these products given

The second of the sample confirmations included below illustrates how a hypothetical end-user (a major retailer, for example) could protect itself against the possibility of an extremely cold winter (with attendant diminished sales volumes) by purchasing an ATDD cap. Unlike swaps, caps or floors purchased for protection against adverse weather conditions do not require the purchaser to surrender the upside potential represented by the opposite, or "better," weather conditions. So, whereas the hypothetical distributor in the sample swap transaction described above gives up some benefits of high sales volumes if the winter is cold by agreeing to make swap payments (up to the agreed limit) in order to obtain protection under the swap if the winter is warm, the purchaser's cost of protection in the sample cap is limited to the option premium it pays.[1751]

Buyers of degree-day caps or floors can reduce premium cost by agreeing to relatively low payout limits or, like buyers of interest rate and other caps, by buying the desired option protection as part of a structure, such as a collar or a corridor, that combines derivatives of the same or different kinds. A customer could, for example, buy a degree-day cap as one leg of a collar and, in the other leg, sell the counterparty a degree-day floor at a different strike level. The premium payable by the counterparty for the second leg would operate to reduce, and potentially offset completely, the premium payable by the customer on the first leg but, of course, the customer would be exposed to the risk that it might be required to make payments under the second leg.[1752]

As noted above, the ability of weather market professionals to price their products effectively depends on the availability of weather data from dependable sources.[1753] The existence of these sources for any particular location is of course critical to the development of products that will serve as satisfactory tools to manage business risks associated with weather phenomena at that location. When the available data are not closely correlated to the risk against which an end-user is seeking protection, it must consider the exposure created by the resulting "basis risk."[1754] For all these reasons, as illustrated in the following sample confirmations, the identification of the data sources to be used in determining the parties' payment obligations is a primary function of the documentation. The key terms in this regard include the primary data source and the fallbacks to be used when

---

then-prevailing levels of liquidity as reflected in wide bid-offer spreads. *See* Nicholls, *supra* note 1730, at 3, quoting Mark Williams of Citizen's Power: "'As liquidity improves in these products, I expect to see a huge market.' . . . 'With bid-offer spreads at 20-25%, you're taking a 20-25% loss on a mark-to-market basis on day one.'" As discussed in Nicholls, *Energy consumers eye weather hedges*, *supra* note 1735, at 7, the imbalance among end-users with opposite exposures to temperature-related weather phenomena continues to be an obstacle to liquidity in the market.

[1751]On the pricing of weather derivatives, *see generally* Eric Briys, Pricing Mother Nature, *in* INSURANCE AND WEATHER DERIVATIVES 168; Clemmons, *supra* note 1729; INSURANCE AND WEATHER DERIVATIVES 199–203.

[1752]*See* Mark Garman, Carlos Blanco & Robert Erickson, *And Now the Weather ...*, Part II of *An Introduction to Weather Derivatives*, DERIVATIVES WEEK, Nov. 22, 1999, at 6. Data are also becoming available on the Internet from private sources. *See* www.air-worldwide.com; www.climetrix.com.

[1753]*See* Garman, *supra* note 1750, at 6.

[1754]*See* Robert Dischel, *A Weather Risk Management Choice: Hedging with Degree-day Derivatives*, *in* INSURANCE AND WEATHER DERIVATIVES 184, 188–89 (comparing average minimum and maximum daily temperatures during 50 cooling seasons in Tucson, Arizona).

data from the primary source are unavailable, as well as the parties' agreement on how they will handle corrections and supplements to the data as initially published.

Data for some locations outside the United States are said either to be expensive or difficult to obtain.[1755] In the United States, ample and relatively reliable weather data are available without charge or at reasonable prices from federal government sources. The National Weather Service (NWS) and the National Climatic Data Center (NCDC) are agencies within the National Oceanic and Atmospheric Administration (NOAA). The NWS and the NCDC are responsible for providing weather and flood warnings, public forecasts and advisories for the United States, its territories and adjacent waters and ocean areas.

In the United States, several hundred weather stations are widely considered to be data sources of the "first order," taking into account their professional staffing and their satisfaction of standards for instrumentation and operations, as well as the frequency with which the instrumentation is calibrated. The stations operated at airports by the Federal Aviation Authority (FAA) are among those generally identified as recording temperature measurements with the greatest level of reliability and security. Data recorded using a standardized instrument package called the Automated Surface Observing Systems (ASOS)—which includes electronic temperature sensors and automated data collection and reporting procedures—are available on the NCDC Web site[1756] and used in weather derivatives as the sources of choice. Data are also available for Regional Climate Centers, which oversee field offices within their respective regions, on the NWS Web site.[1757] These regional center sources are also used in documenting weather derivatives in the U.S. market, as illustrated in the following sample confirmations.

The sample confirmations illustrate a customary market approach in degree-day derivatives to the use of data from a fallback source, if necessary data cannot be obtained from the primary source designated by the parties, and to the use of data for a fallback location (subject to adjustment), if acceptable data cannot be obtained for the agreed weather station. Also, reflecting delays in the publication of missing data and corrections to data previously published in the U.S.,[1758] the sample confirmations also reflect the market's practice of providing for adjustments to initial payment calculations so as to take account of subsequently published missing data, data corrections and the use of data for

---

[1755] *See Now you can buy the weather you want*, INSURANCE DAY, Sept. 1999; at 6, 7; Bossley, *supra* note 1733, at 42–43; Nicholls, *supra* note 1730, at 3, quoting Manos Cito of Prebon Yamane: ("'Temperature data is very accessible.' . . . 'But once you get into precipitation, wind, or snowfall, the lack of accurate data makes it harder to model weather derivatives.'"). *See* Dischel, *supra* note 1754, at 186–91 & 196, on the use of historical data and forecasts in pricing weather derivatives.

[1756] www.ncdc.noaa.gov.

[1757] www.nws.noaa.gov/regions.

[1758] *See* Kevin Marcus, *Weather Derivatives Play Vital Role in Hedging Risk*, ENERGY MARKETING, Sept./Oct. 1998, at 18, *available at* www.earthsat.com: "With such a large volume of reports coming from remote reporting stations, there are a significant number of daily errors that occur due to equipment malfunctions or communication problems. Currently the NWS does not issue certified (quality controlled) temperature and precipitation reports until about four months after the fact." *See also* Clemmons, *supra* note 1729, at 181: "In most cases, however, the discrepancies between the provisional and final data are very small in number and magnitude. Initial transfers of payments are typically made five days after the end of the accumulation period, and there is an adjustment, if necessary, three months later."

the intended primary weather station if it was not initially available, leading to an initial calculation that took into account data for the designated fallback location.

Many of the participants in the market for weather derivatives use documentation based on forms published by the Weather Risk Management Association (WRMA), customized, as in other segments of the derivatives market, to reflect the particular preferences of the market participant, as well as the preferences and needs of regional markets. There is substantial industry interest in the development of greater standardization, and an ISDA committee has been formed to work towards that end, with the aim at first of producing forms of confirmations for various common product types, weather derivatives definitions and provisions that might be used to adapt the standard credit support terms illustrated in Part 5 of this book to accommodate measurements of exposure more tailored to weather derivatives.

> The Introduction to this Part, *supra* p. 369, and the annotations to the sample rate swap confirmation, *supra* p. 427, contain general commentary about the confirmation process and the use of confirmation forms both before and after the parties have entered into a master agreement. That commentary is not repeated or expressly referred to in the annotations to the other sample confirmations in this book.

[Letterhead of Weather Derivatives Provider, Inc.]

April 16, 2002

Weather Index Derivative

Local Distributor Co.
100 Energy Center
New York, NY 00000-0000

Ladies and Gentlemen:

The purpose of this letter agreement is to confirm the terms and conditions of the transaction entered into between us on the Trade Date specified below (the "Transaction"). This letter agreement constitutes a "Confirmation" as referred to in the Master Agreement specified below.

The definitions and provisions contained in the 2000 ISDA Definitions, as published by the International Swaps and Derivatives Association, Inc., are incorporated into this Confirmation. For these purposes, all references in those Definitions to a "Swap Transaction" shall be deemed to apply to the Transaction. In the event of any inconsistency between those definitions and provisions and this Confirmation, this Confirmation will govern.

> Annotation 1. ISDA has not yet published product-specific definitions covering weather derivatives. In documenting these transactions it is, therefore, necessary to state in full most details relevant to the calculation and expression of the parties' payment obligations. WRMA has published forms of confirmation for weather derivatives of various types, which are available at http://www.wrma.org/ and appear in WEATHER DERIVATIVES 302 as Appendix 3. Although most of the conventions for interest rate and currency derivatives reflected in the *2000 ISDA Definitions* are not relevant in documenting the kinds of weather derivatives illustrated here, it is nonetheless possible to achieve some economy of expression by incorporating those definitions. For example, as illustrated here, incorporation of the *2000 ISDA Definitions* facilitates identification of the currency in which, and the days on which, payments will be due and reduces somewhat the task of defining the role of the Calculation Agent, through adoption of Section 4.14 of those definitions. Some of the terminology and rules of the *2000 ISDA Definitions*, however, are inconsistent with

> practices in the weather derivatives market, as is indicated in the following annotations, so the rule on inconsistencies stated above in this sample confirmation is important. We have used the term "index" in identifying the product to indicate that it should be characterized as a qualified financial contract for purposes of the New York statutes of frauds discussed *supra* p. 45.

1. This Confirmation supplements, forms part of, and is subject to, the Master Agreement dated as of April 16, 2002, as amended and supplemented from time to time (the "Agreement"), between Weather Derivatives Provider, Inc. ("WD Pro") and Local Distributor Co. (the "Company"). All provisions contained in the Agreement govern this Confirmation except as expressly modified below.

2. The terms of the particular Transaction to which this Confirmation relates—which is a Weather Index (HDD) Swap—are as follows:

Reference No.:	00000-00
Trade Date:	April 16, 2002
Effective Date:	November 1, 2002
Termination Date:	March 31, 2003
Calculation Period:	The Term of the Transaction, including the first and last day of the Term

> Annotation 2. This sample confirmation uses "Term" to describe the period during which risk coverage is available. Payment is due after the end of the Term, as discussed in Annotation 5 to this sample confirmation. Under Section 3.1 of the *2000 ISDA Definitions*, the Term of the illustrated transaction will begin on the Effective Date and end on the Termination Date. Under Section 3.3 of those definitions, if the specified Termination Date falls on a day that is a Saturday or a Sunday or otherwise is not a working day in any relevant city, the Termination Date will not be adjusted and the Term of the transaction will nonetheless end. In most weather derivatives linked to temperature phenomena, Calculation Periods are defined by reference to calendar periods (generally one or more calendar months), and the parties do not want or need to adjust the Termination Date or the ends of Calculation Periods.
>
> Annotation 3. As in other kinds of derivatives, the term "Calculation Period" is useful in weather derivatives for defining the period or periods in respect of which one party or the other may be required to make a payment. In the sample transaction, there is a single Calculation Period that is coextensive with the transaction's Term. Any payment due in respect of the HDDs in the Calculation Period will be due on a Payment Date a specified number of days after the end of that period, subject to subsequent adjustment. Because the confirmation incorporates the *2000*

ISDA Definitions, which reflect the interest rate and currency derivatives market convention of excluding the last day of each Calculation Period in making calculations (*see* Section 4.13 of those definitions), the sample provision must expressly override that convention by specifying that the last day of the Term will be included.

Annotation 4. Because there is only one Calculation Period, this sample confirmation does not need to state specifically the parties' intent not to adjust the length of the Calculation Period if it ends on a day that is not a Business Day, since the *2000 ISDA Definitions* establish a presumption that the Termination Date will not be adjusted. If the illustrated transaction had several monthly Calculation Periods, it would be necessary to deal with the subject specifically, which could be accomplished by defining "Calculation Periods" as "Each calendar month during the Term of the Transaction (including the first and last day of the month), subject to No Adjustment." Under Section 4.10 of the *2000 ISDA Definitions*, if the parties were silent as to this matter, the Period End Dates for Calculation Periods other than the last would automatically be treated as subject to adjustment in accordance with the Modified Following Business Day convention. *See* the chart *supra* p. 398 for a summary of the default choices on Business Day Conventions in the *2000 ISDA Definitions*.

Annotation 5. For those who incorporate the *2000 ISDA Definitions* in the confirmation for a transaction involving multiple Calculation Periods, an alternative approach would be to identify the "Period End Date" for each Calculation Period and then to add, either in the same entry or in the entry specifying how payments will be calculated: "Period End Dates will be included in calculating Floating Amounts."

Annotation 6. If the parties had chosen to have monthly Calculation Periods and settlements, they would have related the Strike Level and the Maximum Amount to each of the months. The Amount per HDD would usually remain constant throughout the Term of the transaction, but it could differ from month to month, say if the party seeking the HDD protection believed varying the coverage would better suit its needs during different periods, perhaps because of the schedule of its debt service obligations.

Annotation 7. End-users seeking degree-day protection for a period longer than one month should compare the cost of swap protection for the entire period at a single strike level with the cost of the desired protection through a swap in which the strike level is placed by reference to weather statistics for each separate month. *See* G. Considine, *Introduction to Weather Derivatives*, https://www.cme.com/weather/ at 5–6 ("One obvious question . . . is how to relate the value of a strip of monthly options to the value of a single option for a multi-month period . . . . The relationship between pricing at different timing scales can discover fundamental pricing disparities in weather contracts. A major utility recently found that it was cheaper to cover their winter season by buying a series of monthly contracts rather than buying a single contract for the whole season. In this situation, the market had not efficiently priced the risk associated with these options").

Payment Date:	The fifth Business Day after the end of the Calculation Period

> Annotation 8. An alternative approach using the *2000 ISDA Definitions* would be to specify "Payment Date: Delayed Payment, 5 Business Days." *See supra* p. 401, on ISDA's "Delayed Payment" convention. The illustrated approach is simpler to understand. Under either approach, if the transaction is documented using the *2000 ISDA Definitions*, there is no need to specify the relationship between a Payment Date and a Calculation Period because Article 9 of those definitions provides that, unless the parties have specified otherwise, if a Floating Amount is to be calculated by reference to a Calculation Period, it will be understood to be associated with the Calculation Period ending on or most recently before that Payment Date.

Business Days:	New York City

> Annotation 9. *See supra* p. 391 on ISDA conventions regarding Business Days. *See* Annotation 21 to this sample confirmation on the different uses in this sample confirmation of Business Days, on one hand, and Business Days in the Calculation Agent City, on the other.

Amount per HDD:	USD 40,000

> Annotation 10. The term referred to here as "Amount per HDD" is sometimes referred to as the "Notional Amount per HDD" or the "Ticket Value." It is the amount used to calculate any payment that will be due to or from the hypothetical end-user in this heating degree-day swap. As illustrated *infra* p. 769, if the number of HDDs during the transaction's Term is below the stated Strike Level, WD Pro will be obligated to make a payment, known as the "Floating Amount," calculated by multiplying the difference, expressed in terms of HDDs, by the Amount per HDD, subject to the applicable Maximum Amount, or payout limit. On the other hand, if the number of HDDs during the transaction's Term is above the Strike Level, the Company will be obligated to make a Floating Amount payment calculated by multiplying the difference, expressed in terms of HDDs, by the Amount per HDD, again subject to the stated Maximum Amount. As discussed in Annotation 8 to this sample confirmation, tailoring of this kind may also be achieved by varying the Strike Level of HDDs that will be applicable during different months in the Term of the transaction.

Maximum Amount: USD 25,000,000

> Annotation 11. As indicated in the preceding annotation, this is the limit on the Floating Amount that either party may be obligated to pay under the transaction. Some market participants use the term "Payout Limit" for this term.

Strike Level: 4,000 HDDs

> Annotation 12. The Strike Level, which some market participants refer to as the "Index Strike," is the baseline number of HDDs used to calculate the parties' Floating Amount obligations in the manner indicated in the next sample provision. In the illustrated swap, the Strike Level remains the same throughout the four-month Term of the transaction.

Floating Amounts:

If the Degree Day Total and the Strike Level differ, on the Payment Date the party identified in the following table as the Payer will pay the other an amount (the "Floating Amount") equal to the lower of (1) the applicable amount calculated as specified in the table and (2) the Maximum Amount:

Case:	Payer:	Floating Amount:
Degree Day Total higher than the Strike Level	Company	(Degree Day Total minus Strike Level) x Amount per HDD
Strike Level higher than the Degree Day Total	WD Pro	(Strike Level minus Degree Day Total) x Amount per HDD

If the Degree Day Total and the Strike Level are the same, neither party will be required to pay a Floating Amount.

> Annotation 13. This provision states the parties' Floating Amount payment obligations in terms of a comparison of the Strike Level with the actual number of HDDs for the Calculation Period, referred to in the sample as the "Degree Day Total." Some market participants prefer the term "Weather Index." As illustrated, if the Degree Day Total and the Strike Level are equal, neither party will be obligated to pay a Floating Amount. In all other cases, the relationship between the Degree Day Total and the Strike Level will determine which of the parties has a Floating Amount payment obligation and the amount to be paid. *See* Annotation 12 to this sample confirmation.
>
> Annotation 14. In the approach shown, only one party will have a positive Floating Amount. There will be a Floating Amount for WD Pro if the Strike Level

is greater than the Degree Day Total, and there will be a Floating Amount for the Company only if the Strike Level is lower than the Degree Day Total.

Annotation 15. An alternative approach sometimes used would, in a swap like that illustrated here, define "Floating Amount" so that it could be a positive amount or a negative amount determined by subtracting the agreed strike level of HDDs from the actual number of HDDs during the Calculation Period and then multiplying the result by the amount per HDD. This approach would then state that, if the Floating Amount is a positive number, the party in the position of the Company in this sample confirmation will pay the Floating Amount, and if the Floating Amount is a negative number, the other party will pay the absolute amount of that negative number, in each case subject to the payout limit. Another formulation sometimes used calls for determining the "difference between" the actual number of HDDs and the strike level, without specifying which is subtracted from which. We believe the approach illustrated in this sample confirmation is clearer than either of these alternatives.

Annotation 16. As a drafting matter, it is desirable to state the parties' Floating Amount payment obligation in objective terms, as is illustrated in the text preceding Annotation 13 to this sample confirmation, so that the obligation to make a payment in respect of a Floating Amount on the Payment Date will exist regardless of whether the Calculation Agent has made the necessary calculations. Section 4.14 of the *2000 ISDA Definitions*, which is incorporated into this sample confirmation, provides that the Calculation Agent will be responsible for calculating the Floating Amount payable on a Payment Date. Since the practice in weather derivatives is, however, to recalculate that amount in the circumstances described in Part 5(d) of this sample, it is necessary to impose the duty of recalculation on the Calculation Agent, as illustrated there. The provisions of Part 5 also deal with alleged mistakes in the Calculation Agent's determinations and the Calculation Agent's failure to make a necessary determination in a timely manner. In addition, the Calculation Agent is required below in this sample confirmation to make relevant temperature data available as they are released, if a party so requests. A party's exercise of its right to request the data periodically may facilitate prompt resolution of any potential disputes. *See* the sample provision preceding Annotation 34 to this sample confirmation.

Degree Day Total: The aggregate of the HDDs for each of the days in the Calculation Period

Annotation 17. *See* Annotation 15 to this sample confirmation on comparing the Degree Day Total with the Strike Level to determine whether a Floating Amount payment obligation exists.

HDD:	For each day, the number of degrees Fahrenheit, if any, by which the applicable Daily Average Temperature is below 65°F

> Annotation 18. If the Daily Average Temperature for the day is 65°F or above, the number of HDDs for that day will be zero. Some market participants prefer to define the number of HDDs in a day as "the higher of (a) zero and (b) 65°F minus the Daily Average Temperature for the day." As noted *supra* p. 759, 65°F is the baseline generally used in the U.S. market, whereas 18°C is the baseline generally used in Europe.

Daily Average Temperature:	The average of the maximum and minimum temperatures in degrees Fahrenheit at the Location for the relevant day, as reported by the Data Source, treating the day as beginning immediately after midnight on the preceding day and ending at and including midnight on the day, local time at the Location

> Annotation 19. Some market participants prefer to set out the rules for defining the beginning and end of each day in the provision stating how the number of HDDs for each day is to be determined.

Rounding:	The Daily Average Temperature shall not be rounded. Daily maximum and minimum temperatures shall be rounded to the nearest whole degree Fahrenheit, with .5 rounded up.

> Annotation 20. As illustrated, the maximum and minimum temperatures used to calculate the daily average are rounded to the nearest whole degree. The average of the two, which is used to determine the number of HDDs for any day, is not rounded. The decimal in the Daily Average Temperature (and, therefore, in the Degree Day Total) will always be zero or .5. This approach to rounding used in the U.S. weather derivatives market differs from the approach used by the National Weather Service and the National Atmospheric Administration, which round the daily average temperatures that they report to the nearest whole degree. Therefore, the reported data used in the weather derivatives market should be the maximum and minimum temperatures as reported, and not the average reported, for the day.

Calculation Date: The second Business Day in the Calculation Agent City before the Payment Date

> Annotation 21. Payments are to be made on Business Days, which take into account holidays in New York City, as the principal financial center for U.S. dollar payments, but calculations are to be done, and matters relating to calculations refer to, Business Days that take into account holidays in the Calculation Agent City (which happens to be the same as the place of payment in the example), because the Calculation Agent will be making the calculations and collecting the data to be used for the purpose.

Calculation Agent: WD Pro

Calculation Agent City: New York City

Data Source: The Primary Source, if it provides Sufficient Data at the specified time; otherwise the Secondary Source

Primary Source: The Web site of the NCDC, located at www.ncdc.noaa.gov (or any successor)

Secondary Source: The Web site for the regional center of the NWS that oversees the NWS field offices within the Location's field, located at www.nws.noaa.gov (or any successor)

Locations: For each day, the Weather Station or, to the extent Sufficient Data for the Weather Station are not available for that day from the Data Source (*see* Part 5(a)), the Fallback Weather Station

Weather Station: New York (La Guardia)
WBAN 14732

Fallback Weather Station: New York (Central Park)
WBAN 94728
or any substitute Fallback Weather station selected in accordance with Part 5(a) of this Confirmation

> Annotation 22. Information about weather stations (including the applicable WBAN number, if there is one) can be found at http://lwf.ncdc.noaa.gov/oa/ncdc.html. A provision in Part 5 of this sample confirmation, *infra* p. 775, establishes the

procedure for the use and adjustment of temperature data from the Primary Source and the Secondary Source for the Weather Station and the Fallback Weather Station, in that order of preference, to calculate a "Daily Average Temperature" for each day in the Calculation Period. The Degree Day Total for the period is then determined on the basis of the Daily Average Temperatures, as so calculated. Ultimately, if necessary maximum or minimum temperature data for both the Weather Station and the specified Fallback Weather Station are unavailable, a substitute fallback is identified, by looking to the nearest location for which satisfactory current and historical data are available. Whether data will be satisfactory, in this context, will depend on the parties' agreement regarding the adjustment of data for a fallback location.

Annotation 23. Generally, temperature data for a Fallback Weather Station are used after adjustment to reflect historical differences from temperatures recorded for the Weather Station. The choice of the Weather Station may affect both the period over which the historical comparison is to be done and the factors to be considered in making the adjustment. A lookback period of 30 years from the date of the missing data is commonly used, but in some cases a different period may be more appropriate. *See* Dischel, *supra* note 1754, on the choice of a period of historical data to use in pricing analysis and the possibility of molding the record "with good judgment into a better statement of the historical record than the untouched record." *Id.* at 186.

Annotation 24. In theory, at least some of the factors considered in predicting weather, and therefore in the pricing of the relevant transaction, should be considered, if the parties agree that risk of having to use data for a fallback location is significant. *See* G. Considine, *Introduction to Weather Derivatives*, www.cme.com/weather at 3–4, for discussion of some factors that may be considered in the context of pricing models: "[A] site at the end of an airport runway [where many weather stations are located] may exhibit different long-term trends from the region surrounding it . . . . [T]here is a need to carefully analyze the history of the specific station in question. The station data may be poor, the tower may have been moved, or the instrumentation may have changed . . . . Do we use the last 10 years? The last 20 years? How about 50 years? The problem is that climate is non-stationary. . . . The National Center for Environmental Prediction (NCEP) runs an operational tool that . . . examines whether the previous 10 years are a better climate predictor than the defined 'climate normal period' of 1961–1990. . . . Any city that has a strong warming trend will be better approximated using the most recent 10 years than using NCEP's 30-year normal."

3. Accounts for Payments

Payments to WD Pro:

>Account for payments: Big Bank, N.A., New York, N.Y., ABA No. 000, CHIPS No. 000, Attention: WD Pro Weather Derivatives Division

Payments to the Company:

    Account for payments: Account No. 00000 with Big Bank, N.A., New York, N.Y., Attention: Treasurer

4. Offices. The Office of WD Pro for the Transaction is its head office in New York. The Office of the Company for the Transaction is its office at the address specified for notices to it in the Schedule to the Agreement.

5. Other Matters.

(a) <u>Location</u>. The Location will be the Weather Station, if the Data Source has released maximum and minimum temperatures for the day for the Weather Station ("Sufficient Data"). If the Data Source has not released Sufficient Data for the Weather Station for the day but has released Sufficient Data for the listed Fallback Weather Station, and if Adjustment Comparison Data are available for the listed Fallback Weather Station, that weather station will be the Location. If the Location cannot be determined applying the preceding rules, the Location will be the weather station that is geographically nearest to the Weather Station for which each of the following requirements is satisfied: (i) the weather station records data using the Automated Surface Observing Systems (ASOS) and is included in the United States Historical Climatology Network (or any successor); (ii) the Data Source has released Sufficient Data for the weather station; and (iii) Adjustment Comparison Data are available for the weather station.

> Annotation 25. Under these procedures, if the maximum temperature and minimum temperature for a day for the chosen Weather Station have been released by either the Primary Source (the NCDC's Web site) or the Secondary Source (the Web site for the regional climate center where the Weather Station is located), "Sufficient Data" are treated as available for the Weather Station and no data for that day are collected for the Fallback Weather Station. Preference is given to temperatures released by the NCDC Web site. If the maximum and minimum temperatures for a day are not, however, available for the Weather Station from either the Primary Source or the Secondary Source at the cutoff time for collection of the data, the sample procedures call for use of the day's missing maximum or minimum temperature for the first possible Fallback Weather Station.
>
> Annotation 26. As illustrated *infra* p.784, market participants often formulate the first of the stated requirements for an ultimate fallback as the station's being recognized by the NWS as a "first order station." Although this expression is commonly used in the market, it does not appear to have a uniformly accepted meaning, and there is no official list of first order stations, or of criteria for resolving a dispute over whether a given station is of "first order."
>
> Annotation 27. In identifying the ultimate fallback, some market participants provide in their confirmations that a station identified by the Weather Risk Management Association as a successor station for the particular Fallback Weather Station chosen by the parties will be used.

(b) <u>Data Source</u>. The Data Source will be determined separately in collecting the maximum and minimum temperatures for each day at the Location. Whenever data are available from the Primary Source, it will be the Data Source for those data. If data that are not available from the Primary Source are available from the Secondary Source, the Secondary Source will be the Data Source for those data. Sufficient Data will be treated as available for a day and a Location if the maximum and minimum temperatures for the day are available from the Primary Source or the Secondary Source.

> Annotation 28. *See* Annotation 22 to this sample confirmation on how the rules for identifying the applicable Data Source are used with the procedures for identifying the applicable weather station Location in determining the Daily Average Temperature. These rules on the use of data from the Secondary Source may make it possible, as described above, to avoid the use of temperature data for a Fallback Weather Station (and, thus, the need for adjustments in calculating the Daily Average Temperature for a day). Similarly, if data for a Fallback Weather Station must be used, these rules may make it possible to consider only data for the Fallback Weather Station agreed on by the parties, enabling them to avoid identifying another, possibly less desirable, substitute as a proxy for temperatures at the Weather Station. However, if any data from the Secondary Source are used in determining the number of HDDs for a day, and therefore the Degree Day Total and the Floating Amount on the Calculation Date, a recalculation and an adjustment payment may be required. *See supra* p. 772.

(c) <u>Adjustments to Fallback Weather Station Data</u>. If a maximum or minimum temperature relating to a Fallback Weather Station (the "Fallback Base Temperature") is to be used in determining the Daily Average Temperature for any day, an adjustment to the Fallback Base Temperature will be made on the basis of the average maximum or minimum temperature (as applicable) in degrees Fahrenheit for the same day in each of the preceding 30 years, rounded to the nearest fourth decimal place, with .5 rounded up, as reported by the Data Source for each of the Weather Station and the relevant fallback weather station (the "Adjustment Comparison Data"). The 30-year average so calculated for the relevant fallback weather station and day will be subtracted from the 30-year average so calculated for the Weather Station, and the difference, whether a positive number or a negative number, will be the "Temperature Differential." If the Temperature Differential is a positive number, it will be added to the Fallback Base Temperature. If the Temperature Differential is a negative number, it will be subtracted from the Fallback Base Temperature. In either case, the maximum temperature or minimum temperature for the day resulting from the addition or subtraction will then be rounded to the nearest whole degree, with .5 rounded up.

> Annotation 29. *See* Annotation 24 to this sample confirmation for discussion of factors that may be relevant in setting the lookback period for comparing Weather Station data with Fallback Weather Station data for purposes of making the adjustment contemplated in the sample provision.

(d) <u>Recalculations and Related Payments</u>. The Floating Amount will be recalculated by the Calculation Agent on the second Business Day in the Calculation Agent City after the last day of the Adjustment Period:

> if the Data Source releases a correction to any of the data used in calculating the Floating Amount within 95 days after the end of the Calculation Period (the "Adjustment Period"), or
>
> if any data from a Secondary Source or relating to the Fallback Weather Station are used in calculating the Floating Amount and the relevant missing data from the Primary Source or for the Weather Station become available during the Adjustment Period.

If a party's Floating Amount as recalculated (the "Revised Floating Amount Obligation") exceeds its Floating Amount as originally calculated (its "Initial Floating Amount Obligation"), that party will make a payment equal to the difference to the other party. If a party's Revised Floating Amount Obligation is less than its Initial Floating Amount Obligation, the other party will make a payment equal to the difference to that party. Each adjustment amount payable pursuant to this paragraph shall be paid on the second Business Day following the end of the Adjustment Period together with interest calculated on the adjustment amount on an Actual/360 basis for each day from and including the Payment Date to but excluding the day the adjustment amount is paid at the rate determined using the USD-Federal Funds-H.15 Floating Rate Option for that day.

> Annotation 30. As indicated in the introductory material, corrections of previously released weather data are not unusual. *See supra* note 1758. As a result, it is customary in OTC weather derivatives to provide that the parties' payment obligations for a specified period will initially be settled shortly after the end of the period on the basis of information available a few days before but that subsequently released information will be taken into account in determining whether an adjustment payment will be required. Accordingly, in the sample transaction the Daily Average Temperature for each day in the Calculation Period is calculated first on the basis of data available on the Calculation Date. It will be recalculated if any of the maximum or minimum temperature data collected for the initial calculation relate to a Location other than the parties' first choice of Weather Station or are taken from the Secondary Source, and if better data become available during an agreed period. Therefore, the procedures on Location operate together with the provisions set out below relating to the Data Source so that the Daily Average Temperature for each day will be determined by reference to data for the chosen Weather Station whenever possible. Since weather conditions at a Fallback Weather Station may differ from those observed at the parties' chosen Weather Station, even when the two are not far distant, the objective is to avoid consideration of data for a Fallback Station, if possible. *See* Annotation 26 to this sample confirmation.
>
> Annotation 31. Under the approach illustrated in the sample provision, if a party is required to make an adjustment payment to take account of temperature data released after the Calculation Date, that payment will be made with interest for the period from the Payment Date to the date the adjustment payment is due. Some

> market participants do not provide as a matter of course for interest on the adjustment payments. The sample provision reflects an approach generally consistent with that of Section 7.6(c) of the *2000 ISDA Definitions*, but using the Fed Funds rate rather than a rate tied to the payee's cost of funds. Use of an objective rate such as Fed Funds or overnight LIBOR may prove more acceptable in some cases, particularly if there is a substantial disparity in the parties' costs of funds.

(e) <u>Notices from the Calculation Agent</u>. For purposes of Section 4.14(e)((iv) of the *2000 ISDA Definitions*, "reasonable details" with respect to any calculation or recalculation by the Calculation Agent shall include all data underlying the Calculation Agent's determination, including for each relevant day the underlying maximum and minimum temperatures (before and after rounding) and identification of the Location and Data Source for each temperature.

(f) <u>Data Available from the Calculation Agent</u>. If a party so requests by notice given at any time before the Calculation Date, the Calculation Agent will, as soon as practicable but in any event not later than the Business Day in the Calculation Agent City after the request notice is given, inform that party by notice of the number of HDDs accumulated through 5:00 p.m., local time in the Calculation Agent City, on the date the request notice is given, as determined by the Calculation Agent on the basis of the data then available. Each such notice will set out the underlying maximum and minimum temperatures.

> Annotation 32. Under the sample provision, the party that is not acting as Calculation Agent will, if it so requests, have regular access to temperature data being accumulated by the Calculation Agent, so that the party will be in a position to object to a determination made by the Calculation Agent, if it appears to be wrong. *See* Section 12 of the sample master agreement in Part 3 and related annotations, *infra* p. 876, on the standard ISDA provisions relating to the date on which a notice will be deemed effective.

(g) <u>Replacement of Calculation Agent</u>. If the Calculation Agent fails to fulfill its duty to make or give a party notice of any of the determinations or temperature data specified in this Confirmation and does not cure the failure within one Business Day in the Calculation Agent City after notice from that party, the failure will not constitute an Event of Default for purposes of the Agreement, but the party giving that notice may itself make the determination or appoint an independent third party thereafter to make the determinations, to supply the relevant data or to do both. If a party exercises either of these rights, it will as soon as practicable give notice to that effect to the Calculation Agent, which will thereafter cease to be the Calculation Agent. Thereafter, all references in this Confirmation to the Calculation Agent will be deemed references to the other party or the third party selected by it, and all references to the Calculation Agent City will be deemed references to the city from which that other party or third party is acting for the relevant purpose or purposes. If the functions previously performed by the Calculation Agent are split between a party and a third party, references to the Calculation Agent and the Calculation Agent City will be deemed references to the relevant party to the

Transaction and the city from which it is acting. If a third party is appointed as provided above, each of the parties will pay one half of the fees, costs and expenses payable to that third party for its services.

> Annotation 33. Because one of the parties is initially acting as Calculation Agent in the transaction illustrated in this sample confirmation, this paragraph provides that, if Calculation Agent has failed to fulfill its duties to make determinations or supply temperature data in a timely manner, the other party may itself make the determination or appoint an independent third party to make the determinations and supply the relevant data. Section 10.2 of the *1999 Credit Derivatives Definitions* provides for a somewhat different approach, under which a disinterested third party will always be used to resolve disputes. *See* Annotation 14 to the sample credit default swap confirmation, *supra* p. 691.

Please confirm that the foregoing correctly sets forth the terms of our agreement by executing the copy of this Confirmation enclosed for that purpose and returning it to us or by sending to us a letter or telex substantially similar to this letter, which letter or telex sets forth the material terms of the Transaction to which this Confirmation relates and indicates agreement to those terms. If you believe the foregoing does not correctly reflect the terms of our agreement, please give us notice as soon as possible of what you believe to be the necessary corrections.

Yours sincerely,

WEATHER DERIVATIVES
PROVIDER, INC.

By: _____

   Name:
   Title:

Confirmed as of the date first
above written on   , 20   :

LOCAL DISTRIBUTOR CO.

By: _____

   Name:
   Title:

> The Introduction to this Part, *supra* p. 369, and the annotations to the sample rate swap confirmation, *supra* p. 427, contain general commentary about the confirmation process and the use of ISDA's confirmation forms both before and after the parties have entered into a master agreement that is not repeated or expressly referred to in the annotations to the other sample confirmations in this book. The following annotations will address only features of this ATDD cap confirmation that differ from features of the preceding sample HDD swap confirmation.

[Letterhead of Weather Derivatives Provider, Inc.]

April 16, 2002

Weather Index Derivative

Local Retailer Inc.
Retail Mall
Indianapolis, IN 00000-0000

Ladies and Gentlemen:

The purpose of this letter agreement is to confirm the terms and conditions of the transaction entered into between us on the Trade Date specified below (the "Transaction"). This letter agreement constitutes a "Confirmation" as referred to in the Master Agreement specified below.

The definitions and provisions contained in the 2000 ISDA Definitions, as published by the International Swaps and Derivatives Association, Inc., are incorporated into this Confirmation. For these purposes, all references in those Definitions to a "Swap Transaction" shall be deemed to apply to the Transaction. In the event of any inconsistency between those definitions and provisions and this Confirmation, this Confirmation will govern.

1. This Confirmation supplements, forms part of, and is subject to, the Master Agreement dated as of April 16, 2002, as amended and supplemented from time to time (the "Agreement"), between Weather Derivatives Provider, Inc. ("WD Pro") and Local Retailer Inc. (the "Company"). All provisions contained in the Agreement govern this Confirmation except as expressly modified below.

2. The terms of the particular Transaction to which this Confirmation relates—which is a Weather Index (ATDD) Cap—are as follows:

> Annotation 1. As described *supra* p. 439, "cap" is the term generally used in the financial derivatives market for a transaction in which one party agrees to make a payment to the other if a specified interest rate, commodity price or other index

exceeds an agreed level. The baseline is referred to as the "cap rate" in the interest rate derivatives market but often as the "strike level" of degree days (HDDs, CDDs or ATDDs) in the weather derivatives market. Thus, the illustrated transaction is an ATDD cap because the cap protection seller, WD Pro, will be required to make a payment to the cap buyer if the number of ATDDs during the transaction's term is above the number of ATDDs agreed on as the strike level. In the illustrated transaction, the number of ATDDs is calculated by reference to daily average temperatures lower than 32°F.

Annotation 2. Conversely, in a "floor" transaction one party agrees to make a payment to the other if a specified interest rate, commodity price or other index is below an agreed level. So just as the hypothetical retailer has bought the ATDD cap protection illustrated here out of concern that its winter sales volume will suffer if unusual cold discourages shoppers, a distributor of snow ski apparel might buy an ATDD floor (using 32°F as the ATDD baseline, as illustrated here) out of concern that sales will suffer if the winter is unusually warm.

Annotation 3. The ATDD cap buyer could reduce or eliminate the premium payable by it for the illustrated cap protection by entering into a collar—selling its counterparty ATDD floor protection in the same transaction. In that case, the premium calculated for the floor protection would reduce or completely offset the premium payable for the cap, and the resulting transaction would be referred to as a "collar." In such a collar, the cap buyer would, of course, have a contingent obligation to make a payment to the floor buyer. *See supra* p. 448.

Reference No.:	00000-00
Trade Date:	April 16, 2002
Effective Date:	November 1, 2002
Termination Date:	March 31, 2003
Fixed Amount Payer:	The Company
Fixed Amount Payer Payment Date:	November 1, 2002, subject to adjustment in accordance with the Following Business Day Convention
Fixed Amount:	USD 1,500,000

Annotation 4. This part of the sample confirmation illustrates the use of terminology commonly found in the documentation for interest rate caps to state the Fixed Amount payment, or premium, due up front from the hypothetical retailer as buyer of the ATTD cap protection. *See* Annotation 2 to the sample rate cap confirmation, *supra* p. 445. The premium will reflect the illustrated structure in which a

Sample Weather Index (ATDD) Cap Confirmation

> single strike is compared with average daily temperatures over the entire winter season. The premium might be priced differently if the transaction's term were divided into separate Calculation Periods for each month during the winter season, with the possible payout for each month calculated by reference to a different strike level of ATDDs or a different Amount per ATDD. *See* Annotation 9 to the sample HDD swap confirmation, *supra* p. 767.

Floating Amount:

Floating Amount Payer:	WD Pro
Calculation Period:	The period from and including the Effective Date to and including the Termination Date
Floating Amount Payer Payment Date:	The fifth Business Day after the end of the Calculation Period, subject to adjustment in accordance with the Following Business Day Convention
Amount per ATDD:	USD 25,000
Maximum Amount:	USD 10,000,000
Strike Level:	500 ATDDs
Floating Amount:	If the Degree Day Total is higher than the Strike Level, the Floating Amount will be the lower of (1) (Degree Day Total minus Strike Level) x Amount per ATDD and (2) the Maximum Amount.
	If the Degree Day Total is equal to or lower than the Strike Level, the Floating Amount will be zero.

> Annotation 5. In a conventional degree day cap, there is a ceiling (here, the Maximum Amount) on the amount that the cap seller may be required to pay. Also, the cap seller will only be required to make a payment if the actual number of degree days (HDDs, CDDs, or ATDDs) in the covered period exceeds the strike level. ISDA's approach to the documentation of interest rate caps reaches this result by building the necessary comparison of the cap rate with the applicable floating rate base into the definition of the "Floating Rate" for the period covered, so that the Floating Rate for a Calculation Period is always the excess, if any, of that floating rate base over the specified cap rate. *See* Section 6.2(a)(i)(A) of the *2000 ISDA Definitions* and the *1991 ISDA Definitions*. This sample confirmation takes an analogous approach in specifying below how the Degree Day Total will be deter-

> mined. Under this approach, there is no need to address negative numbers, because the Degree Day Total can never be negative. *See supra* p. 417, discussing the negative interest rate provisions of Section 6.4 of the *2000 ISDA Definitions* and Section 8 of the *1998 Supplement to the 1991 ISDA Definitions*.

Degree Day Total: The aggregate of the ATDDs for each of the days in the Calculation Period

ATDD: For each day, the number of degrees Fahrenheit, if any, by which the applicable Daily Average Temperature is below 32°F

> Annotation 6. Some market participants prefer to define the number of ATDDs in a day as "the higher of (a) zero and (b) 32°F minus the Daily Average Temperature for the day." The definition of "Daily Average Temperature" makes clear that ATDDs are to be determined in relation to the Weather Station chosen by the parties, when possible. The definition also points to the use of adjusted temperature data for the Fallback Weather Station, when necessary. *See* Annotations 22–24 to the sample HDD swap confirmation, *supra* p. 772, for discussion of the use of fallback weather station data.

Daily Average Temperature: The average of the maximum and minimum temperatures in degrees Fahrenheit at the Location for the relevant day, as reported by the Data Source, treating the day as beginning immediately after midnight on the preceding day and ending at and including midnight on the day, local time at the Location

Rounding: The Daily Average Temperature shall not be rounded. Daily maximum and minimum temperatures shall be rounded to the nearest whole degree Fahrenheit, with .5 rounded up.

Calculation Date: The second Business Day in the Calculation Agent City before the Payment Date

Business Days: New York City

Calculation Agent: WD Pro

Calculation Agent City:	New York City
Data Source:	The Primary Source, if it gives the relevant data at the specified time; otherwise the Secondary Source
Primary Source:	The Web site of the NCDC, located at www.ncdc.noaa.gov (or any successor)
Secondary Source:	The Web site for the regional center of the NWS that oversees the NWS field offices within the relevant Location's field, located at www.nws.noaa.gov (or any successor)
Locations:	For each day, the Weather Station or, to the extent Sufficient Data for the Weather Station are not available for that day from the Data Source (*see* Part 5(a)), the Fallback Weather Station
Weather Station:	Indianapolis, IN WBAN 93819
Fallback Weather Station:	Indianapolis, IN WBAN 93821 or any substitute Fallback Weather station selected in accordance with Part 5(a) of this Confirmation

3. Accounts for Payments

Payments to WD Pro:

> Account for payments: Big Bank, N.A., New York, N.Y., ABA No. 000, CHIPS No. 000, Attention: WD Pro, Weather Derivatives Division

Payments to the Company:

> Account for payments: Account No. 00000 with Big Bank, N.A., New York, N.Y., Attention: Treasurer

4. Offices. The Office of WD Pro for the Transaction is its head office in New York. The Office of the Company for the Transaction is its office at the address specified for notices to it in the Schedule to the Agreement.

5. Other Matters.

(a) <u>Location</u>. The Location will be the Weather Station, if the Data Source has released maximum and minimum temperatures for the day for the Weather Station ("Sufficient Data"). If the Data Source has not released Sufficient Data for the Weather Station for the day but has released Sufficient Data for the listed Fallback Weather Station, and if Adjustment Comparison Data are available for the listed Fallback Weather Station, that weather station will be the Location. If the Location cannot be determined applying the preceding rules, the Location will be the weather station that is geographically nearest to the Weather Station for which each of the following requirements is satisfied: (i) the weather station is designated by the NWS as a first order station or is included in the United States Historical Climatology Network (or any successor); (ii) the Data Source has released Sufficient Data for the weather station; and (iii) Adjustment Comparison Data are available for the weather station.

(b) Data Source. The Data Source will be determined separately in collecting the maximum and minimum temperatures for each day at the Location. Whenever data are available from the Primary Source, it will be the Data Source for those data. If data that are not available from the Primary Source are available from the Secondary Source, the Secondary Source will be the Data Source for those data. Sufficient Data will be treated as available for a day and a Location if the maximum and minimum temperatures for the day are available from the Primary Source or the Secondary Source.

(c) Adjustments to Fallback Weather Station Data. If a maximum or minimum temperature relating to a Fallback Weather Station (the "Fallback Base Temperature") is to be used in determining the Daily Average Temperature for any day, an adjustment to the Fallback Base Temperature will be made on the basis of the average maximum or minimum temperature (as applicable) in degrees Fahrenheit for the same day in each of the preceding 30 years, rounded to the nearest fourth decimal place, with .5 rounded up, as reported by the Data Source for each of the Weather Station and the relevant fallback weather station (the "Adjustment Comparison Data"). The 30-year average so calculated for the relevant fallback weather station and day will be subtracted from the 30-year average so calculated for the Weather Station, and the difference, whether a positive number or a negative number, will be the "Temperature Differential." If the Temperature Differential is a positive number, it will be added to the Fallback Base Temperature. If the Temperature Differential is a negative number, it will be subtracted from the Fallback Base Temperature. In either case, the maximum temperature or minimum temperature for the day resulting from the addition or subtraction will then be rounded to the nearest whole degree, with .5 rounded up.

(d) Recalculations and Related Payments. The Floating Amount will be recalculated by the Calculation Agent on the second Business Day in the Calculation Agent City after the last day of the Adjustment Period:

> if the Data Source releases a correction to any of the data used in calculating the Floating Amount within 95 days after the end of the Calculation Period (the "Adjustment Period"), or

> if any data from a Secondary Source or relating to the Fallback Weather Station are used in calculating the Floating Amount and the relevant missing data from the Primary Source or for the Weather Station become available during the Adjustment Period.

If the Floating Amount as recalculated (the "Revised Floating Amount Obligation") exceeds the Floating Amount as originally calculated (the "Initial Floating Amount Obligation"), the Floating Rate Payer will make a payment equal to the difference to the other party. If the Revised Floating Amount Obligation is less than the Initial Floating Amount Obligation, the Fixed Rate Payer will make a payment equal to the difference to the Floating Rate Payer. Each adjustment amount payable pursuant to this paragraph shall be paid on the second Business Day following the end of the Adjustment Period together with interest calculated on the adjustment amount on an Actual/360 basis for each day from and including the Payment Date to but excluding the day the adjustment amount is paid at the rate determined using the USD-Federal Funds-H.15 Floating Rate Option for that day.

(e) <u>Notices from the Calculation Agent</u>. For purposes of Section 4.14(e)((iv) of the *2000 ISDA Definitions*, "reasonable details" with respect to any calculation or recalculation by the Calculation Agent shall include all data underlying the Calculation Agent's determination, including for each relevant day the underlying maximum and minimum temperatures (before and after rounding) and identification of the Location and Data Source for each temperature.

(f) <u>Data Available from the Calculation Agent</u>. If a party so requests by notice given at any time before the Calculation Date, the Calculation Agent will, as soon as practicable but in any event not later than the Business Day in the Calculation Agent City after the request notice is given, inform that party by notice of the number of ATDDs accumulated through 5:00 p.m., local time in the Calculation Agent City, on the date the request notice is given, as determined by the Calculation Agent on the basis of the data then available. Each such notice will set out the underlying maximum and minimum temperatures.

(g) <u>Replacement of Calculation Agent</u>. If the Calculation Agent fails to fulfill its duty to make or give a party notice of any of the determinations or temperature data specified in this Confirmation and does not cure the failure within one Business Day in the Calculation Agent City after notice from that party, the failure will not constitute an Event of Default for purposes of the Agreement, but the party giving that notice may itself make the determination or appoint an independent third party thereafter to make the determinations, to supply the relevant data or to do both. If a party exercises either of these rights, it will as soon as practicable give notice to that effect to the Calculation Agent, which will thereafter cease to be the Calculation Agent. Thereafter, all references in this Confirmation to the Calculation Agent will be deemed references to the other party or the third party selected by it, and all references to the Calculation Agent City will be deemed references to the city from which that other party or third party is acting for the relevant purpose or purposes. If the functions previously performed by the Calculation Agent are split between a party and a third party, references to the Calculation Agent and the Calculation Agent City will be deemed references to the relevant party to the Transaction and the city from which it is acting. If a third party is appointed as provided above, each of the parties will pay one half of the fees, costs and expenses payable to that third party for its services.

Please confirm that the foregoing correctly sets forth the terms of our agreement by executing the copy of this Confirmation enclosed for that purpose and returning it to us or by sending to us a letter or telex substantially similar to this letter, which letter or telex sets forth the material terms of the Transaction to which this Confirmation relates and indicates agreement to those terms. If you believe the foregoing does not correctly reflect the terms of our agreement, please give us notice as soon as possible of what you believe to be the necessary corrections.

Yours sincerely,

WEATHER DERIVATIVES
PROVIDER, INC.

By: _____

 Name:
 Title:

Confirmed as of the date first
above written on   , 20 :

LOCAL RETAILER INC.

By: _____
 Name:
 Title: